Lecture Notes in Computer Science 12006

More information about this series at http://www.springer.com/series/7410

Stanislaw Jarecki (Ed.)

Topics in Cryptology – CT-RSA 2020

The Cryptographers' Track at the RSA Conference 2020
San Francisco, CA, USA, February 24–28, 2020
Proceedings

 Springer

Editor
Stanislaw Jarecki
University of California
Irvine, CA, USA

ISSN 0302-9743   ISSN 1611-3349 (electronic)
Lecture Notes in Computer Science
ISBN 978-3-030-40185-6   ISBN 978-3-030-40186-3 (eBook)
https://doi.org/10.1007/978-3-030-40186-3

LNCS Sublibrary: SL4 – Security and Cryptology

This Springer imprint is published by the registered company Springer Nature Switzerland AG
The registered company address is: Gewerbestrasse 11, 6330 Cham, Switzerland

Preface

The RSA conference has been a major international event for information security experts since its inception in 1991. It is an annual event that attracts several hundred vendors and over 40,000 participants from industry, government, and academia. Since 2001, the RSA conference has included the Cryptographer's Track (CT-RSA), which provides a forum for current research in cryptography.

This volume represents the proceedings of the 2020 convening of the RSA Conference Cryptographer's Track, which was held at Moscone Center, San Francisco, California, during February 24–28, 2020.

As chair of the Program Committee, I would like to thank all the authors who contributed the results of their innovative research. My appreciation also goes to all the members of the Program Committee and their designated external reviewers, who carefully read and reviewed all of the submissions.

A total of 95 submissions were received for review, of which 28 papers were selected for presentation and publication. The selection process was a difficult task since there were many more high quality submissions than we could accept. The submissions were anonymous, and each submission was assigned to at least three reviewers (four if the paper included a Program Committee member as an author). The review and selection process was carried out with great care and transparency, and I am thankful to all Program Committee members for participating in discussions and giving valuable feedback to the authors of the submitted papers. I am also grateful to the Program Committee members who put in their time to shepherd some of the submissions.

The submission and review process, as well as the editing of the final proceedings, were greatly simplified by the webreview software written by Shai Halevi, which we used by the permission of the International Association for Cryptologic Research (IACR). Shai assisted us whenever we had any question about this software, and I would like to thank him for his generous support throughout the entire process. My sincere thanks go also to Ms. Christine Reiss from Springer Verlag and everyone on her team for their assistance in preparing and producing these proceedings.

Last but not least, on behalf of all CT-RSA participants I would like to thank Ms. Ashley Sutton who served as an RSA Conference liaison to the Cryptographer's Track. In this capacity, Ashley essentially played the role of a General Chair for the CT-RSA conference, and we are very grateful to her for all the work she did in organizing this conference and making it run smoothly.

February 2020   Stanislaw Jarecki

Organization

Program Chair

Stanisław Jarecki   University of California, Irvine, USA

Program Commitee

Masayuki Abe	NTT Secure Platform Laboratories, Japan
Shi Bai	Florida Atlantic University, USA
Paulo Barreto	University of Washington, USA
Josh Benaloh	Microsoft Research, USA
Olivier Blazy	Université de Limoges, France
Jeremiah Blocki	Purdue University, USA
Chris Brzuska	Aalto University, Finland
David Cash	University of Chicago, USA
Dario Catalano	University of Catania, Italy
Jung Hee Cheon	Seoul National University, South Korea
Céline Chevalier	Université Panthéon-Assas Paris 2, France
Sherman S. M. Chow	Chinese University of Hong Kong, Hong Kong, China
Pooya Farshim	University of York, UK
Rosario Gennaro	The City University of New York, USA
Goichiro Hanaoka	AIST, Japan
Helena Handschuh	Rambus Cryptography Research, USA
Marc Joye	OneSpan, Belgium
Vlad Kolesnikov	Georgia Tech, USA
Tancrède Lepoint	Google, USA
Anna Lysyanskaya	Brown University, USA
Mitsuru Matsui	Mitsubishi Electric, Japan
David Naccache	ENS/PSL, France
Svetla Nikova	KU Leuven, Belgium
Jiaxin Pan	Norwegian University of Science and Technology (NTNU), Norway
Kenneth Paterson	ETH Zurich, Switzerland
Ludovic Perret	CryptoNext Security, France
Bertram Poettering	IBM Research, Switzerland
David Pointcheval	CNRS and ENS/PSL, France
Bart Preneel	KU Leuven, Belgium
Alexander Russell	University of Connecticut, USA
Rei Safavi-Naini	University of Calgary, Canada
Victor Shoup	New York University, USA
Nigel Smart	KU Leuven, Belgium
Martijn Stam	Simula UiB, Norway

Michael Walter   IST Austria, Austria
Hong-Sheng Zhou   Virginia Commonwealth University, USA

External Reviewers

Thomas Agrikola
Yusuke Aikawa
Younes Talibi Alaoui
Tomer Ashur
Matilda Backendal
Josep Balasch
Carsten Baum
Arthur Beckers
Olivier Blazy
Estuardo Alpirez Bock
Carl Bootland
Cecilia Boschini
Hervé Chabanne
Yilei Chen
Wonhee Cho
Jérémy Chotard
Jean Paul Degabriele
Siemen Dhooghe
Jesus Diaz
Benjamin Dowling
Francois Dupressoir
Sabyasachi Dutta
Keita Emura
Mia Filic
Georg Fuchsbauer
Irene Giacomelli
Kristian Gjøsteen
Lorenzo Grassi
Vincent Grosso
Johann Großschädl
Aurore Guillevic
Thomas Haines
Mike Hamburg
Ben Harsha
Kenichiro Hayasama
Annelie Heuser
Seungwan Hong
Chloé Hébant
Ilia Iliashenko

Yanxue Jia
Dongwoo Kim
Jaeyoon Kim
Jaeyun Kim
Jiseung Kim
Sumin Kim
Lisa Kohl
Jooyoung Lee
Keewoo Lee
Seungbeom Lee
Seunghoon Lee
Shuai Li
Lin Lyu
Jack P. K. Ma
Varun Maram
Giorgia Azzurra Marson
Mark Marson
Takahiro Matsuda
Bart Mennink
Nele Mentens
Lauren De Meyer
Michael Meyer
Brice Minaud
Hiraku Morita
Elke De Mulder
Yusuke Naito
Tran Ngo
Ngoc Khanh Nguyen
Miyako Ohkubo
Michele Orrù
Rafail Ostrovsky
Clara Paglialonga
Duong Hieu Phan
Thomas Prest
Emmanuel Prouff
Chen Qian
Yuan Quan
Mario Di Raimondo
Adrian Ranea

Mélissa Rossi
Paul Rösler
Yusuke Sakai
Simona Samardjiska
Paolo Santini
Jacob C. N. Schuldt
Gregor Seiler
Jae Hong Seo
Setareh Sharifian
Kyung-Ah Shim
Tjerand Silde
Azam Soleimanian
Yongha Son
Daisuke Suzuki
Katsuyuki Takashima
Phuc Thai
Elmar Tischhauser

Mike Tunstall
Furkan Turan
Muni Venkateswarlu
Fre Vercauteren
Benedikt Wagner
Xiuhua Wang
Yuyu Wang
Lennert Wouters
Yanhong Xu
Shota Yamada
Kyosuke Yamashita
Michal Zajac
Wuwei Zhang
Yongjun Zhao
Ko Stoffelen
Khoa Nguyen

Contents

Generic Attack on Iterated Tweakable FX Constructions

Ferdinand Sibleyras[(✉)]

Inria, Paris, France
ferdinand.sibleyras@inria.fr

Abstract. Tweakable block ciphers are increasingly becoming a common primitive to build new resilient modes as well as a concept for multiple dedicated designs. While regular block ciphers define a family of permutations indexed by a secret key, tweakable ones define a family of permutations indexed by both a secret key and a public tweak. In this work we formalize and study a generic framework for building such a tweakable block cipher based on regular block ciphers, the iterated tweakable FX construction, which includes many such previous constructions of tweakable block ciphers. Then we describe a cryptanalysis from which we can derive a provable security upper-bound for all constructions following this tweakable iterated FX strategy. Concretely, the cryptanalysis of r rounds of our generic construction based on n-bit block ciphers with κ-bit keys requires $\mathcal{O}(2^{\frac{r}{r+1}(n+\kappa)})$ online and offline queries. For $r = 2$ rounds this interestingly matches the proof of the particular case of XHX2 by Lee and Lee (ASIACRYPT 2018) thus proving for the first time its tightness. In turn, the XHX and XHX2 proofs show that our generic cryptanalysis is information theoretically optimal for 1 and 2 rounds.

Keywords: Tweakable · Block cipher · Provable security · FX · Cryptanalysis · Optimality · XHX2

1 Introduction

Tweakable block ciphers have been the focus of many recent works in the field of symmetric cryptography as it provides a very interesting flexibility compared to regular block ciphers. Formally, a block cipher is defined as a family of permutations indexed by a secret key, thus an n-bit block cipher E indexed by a κ-bit key is an application $E : \{0,1\}^\kappa \times \{0,1\}^n \to \{0,1\}^n$. Whereas a tweakable block cipher is a family of permutations indexed by both a secret key and a public tweak, thus an n-bit tweakable block cipher $\tilde{E}$ indexed by a $\tilde{\kappa}$-bit secret key and a τ-bit public tweak is an application $\tilde{E} : \{0,1\}^{\tilde{\kappa}} \times \{0,1\}^\tau \times \{0,1\}^n \to \{0,1\}^n$. They have been formalized by Liskov, Rivest and Wagner [LRW11].

On the other hand, regular block ciphers benefit from a longer history of research which gave birth to many designs and implementations notably including the DES [DES77] and the AES [AES01]. Therefore a natural question is:

© Springer Nature Switzerland AG 2020
S. Jarecki (Ed.): CT-RSA 2020, LNCS 12006, pp. 1–14, 2020.
https://doi.org/10.1007/978-3-030-40186-3_1

how can we build a tweakable block cipher out of regular block ciphers? In fact this line of study inspired new modes of operations like OCB [RBBK01] and PMAC [BR02] that benefits from a relatively easy two-step proof: first we show that the main construction is secure when used along with a tweakable block cipher then we construct such tweakable block cipher with a regular block cipher to fully describe the mode. A first approach can be to append a tweak with the secret key such that the concatenation becomes the effective key to the regular block cipher. Given security under related key attacks this can work but at the cost of security: the size of the secret key will have to be reduced to make space for the tweak.

To go around this limitation Liskov et al. described two constructions LRW1 and LRW2 [LRW11]. In particular LRW2 is somehow remindful of the FX construction that adds an n-bit key before the input and another after the output of the underlying block cipher. The FX construction has been proposed by Killian and Rogaway [KR96] in a different context: they investigated DESX, an easy solution to protect DES against an exhaustive key search. FX consists in adding one n-bit subkey before and another one after the block cipher. With such strategy they proved that the time complexity of the best generic cryptanalysis goes from $\mathcal{O}(2^{\kappa})$ to $\mathcal{O}(2^{\kappa+n}/D)$ where D is the data or online query complexity. The FX construction has since been notably used in PRINCE [BCG+12] and PRIDE [ADK+14]. We can naturally iterate r rounds of the FX construction which requires to have r κ-bit subkeys along with $(r+1)$ n-bit subkeys. Then the idea to build a tweakable block cipher is to blend the tweak and the master key together in a predefined key schedule to obtain all the required subkeys for the computation.

1.1   Notations

First we formally describe the r-round tweakable iterated FX construction (Fig. 2) on which our results apply. Let $E_{1,2,\ldots,r}(u,\cdot)$ be r block ciphers with κ-bit key u and n-bit input and output. Let k be the $\tilde{\kappa}$-bit master key of the tweakable block cipher construction. Let t be a tweak of arbitrary length. Let $\gamma_i(k,t)$ be the subkey for the ith block cipher of length κ-bit for $1 \leq i \leq r$ and $\lambda_i(k,t)$ the n-bit subkeys to XOR in the state for $0 \leq i \leq r$. For example the $r = 2$-round tweakable FX construction (Fig. 1) $\tilde{E}_k(t,m)$ is described as:

$$\tilde{E}_k(t,m) = E_2\big(\gamma_2(k,t), E_1\big(\gamma_1(k,t), m \oplus \lambda_0(k,t)\big) \oplus \lambda_1(k,t)\big) \oplus \lambda_2(k,t)$$

We will focus on generic key recovery attacks. The goal of the cryptanalysis of $\tilde{E}_k(t,m)$ is to recover k by doing offline queries to $E_{1,2,\ldots,r}(\cdot,\cdot)$ and online queries to $\tilde{E}_k(\cdot,\cdot)$. We don't count the number of calls to the γ and λ functions generating the subkeys as queries because we don't assume any security property for them. In fact it is common for the subkeys to assume some almost uniformity, almost universality or almost XOR-universality property with respect to the tweak (See Definition 1). This makes the analysis proper for most of the constructions we cite except for $\tilde{F}[2]$ by Mennink [Men15] which can be seen as a 1-round tweakable FX where the subkey functions reuse the block cipher itself.

Definition 1. *Let $\delta > 0$ and a function $\lambda : \mathcal{K} \times \mathcal{T} \to \mathcal{Y}$ for non-empty sets $\mathcal{K}, \mathcal{T}, \mathcal{Y}$.*

- *$\lambda(k,t)$ is said to be δ-almost uniform if for any $t \in \mathcal{T}$ and any $y \in \mathcal{Y}$,*

$$\Pr\left(k \leftarrow_\$ \mathcal{K} : \lambda(k,t) = y\right) \leq \delta .$$

- *$\lambda(k,t)$ is said to be δ-almost universal (AU) if for any distinct t and $t' \in \mathcal{T}$,*

$$\Pr\left(k \leftarrow_\$ \mathcal{K} : \lambda(k,t) = \lambda(k,t')\right) \leq \delta .$$

- *$\lambda(k,t)$ is said to be δ-almost XOR-universal (AXU) if for any distinct t and $t' \in \mathcal{T}$ and any $y \in \mathcal{Y}$,*

$$\Pr\left(k \leftarrow_\$ \mathcal{K} : \lambda(k,t) \oplus \lambda(k,t') = y\right) \leq \delta .$$

While our results do not depend on the repartition of the tweak space, having arbitrary long tweaks is justified by the XTX transformation of Minematsu and Iwata [MI15]. Indeed XTX transforms a tweakable block cipher with a tweak of limited length to one with a tweak of arbitrary length without, in our case, affecting the general iterated tweakable FX structure as it simply affects the subkey functions.

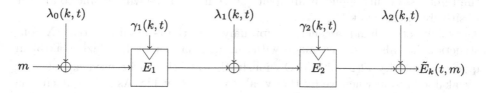

Fig. 1. 2-Round tweakable FX.

1.2 Previous Works

In the same paper where they formalize the concept of tweakable block ciphers, Liskov, Rivest and Wagner proposed two constructions often known as LRW1 and LRW2 [LRW11]. LRW1 consists in adding the tweak between two calls of the block cipher while LRW2 evaluates a keyed universal hash function on the tweak and adds it twice: before the input and after the output of the block cipher. These modes are described as $\tilde{E}_k(t,m) = E_k(t \oplus E_k(m))$ and $\tilde{E}_k(t,m) = E_k(m \oplus h(t)) \oplus h(t)$ respectively with the requirement that h be an almost XOR-universal function. They also provide security proofs roughly up to $2^{n/2}$ for both schemes. Matching attacks on LRW1 and LRW2 are trivial as they both allow for an easy distinguisher after the first collision at the birthday bound. Other constructions of tweakable block cipher related to LRW2 include XE and XEX by Rogaway [Rog04] and used in the OCB mode of operation.

In the quest for optimal security Mennink proposed the constructions $\tilde{F}[1]$ and $\tilde{F}[2]$ [Men15]. The latter reaches a provable security of 2^n queries which is the optimal security in the standard model for regular block ciphers. Other works tried to build a tweakable block cipher based solely on public permutations in the style of Even-Mansour [EM93]. Such tweakable block ciphers includes TEM [CLS15] and XPX [Men16] that are also subject to a tight birthday bound security of $\mathcal{O}(2^{n/2})$. Then Jha, List, Minematsu, Mishra and Nandi described a framework called XHX [JLM+17] and proved its security up to $2^{(n+\kappa)/2}$. They also describe generalised XHX, GXHX. In particular this means that a provable security beyond 2^n is reachable but in the ideal cipher model where rekeying is possible. This framework uses a single-round FX framework where all 3 subkeys are derived from a universal hash function on the secret master key and an arbitrarily long tweak.

So far, with the exception of GXHX, the proofs of all schemes cited can be shown to be tight. However, things become more involved when trying to iterate those constructions. Landecker et al. [LST12] proposed to iterate two independent evaluations of LRW2 and proved a security up to $2^{2n/3}$ queries. An attack on cascaded LRW2 (or CLRW2) has been later proposed by Mennink [Men18] in query complexity $\mathcal{O}(2^{3n/4})$ not completely closing the gap. Then, recently, Lee and Lee proposed XHX2 [LL18] by iterating two independent rounds of XHX. They managed to prove a query security lower bound of $\min\{2^{\frac{2}{3}(n+\kappa)}, 2^{n+\kappa/2}\}$ and left the tightness of this bound as an open question which we will be able to answer positively in this work.

On the other hand, a generic cryptanalysis of the r-round iterated FX construction has already been made with the original attack by Gaži [Gaž13] in query complexity $\mathcal{O}(2^{\frac{r-1}{r}n+\kappa})$. Obviously this attack can be used against our tweakable version when we fix the tweak to a single value. As it is written, the attack starts by querying all the code books of the secret cipher that makes the maximum possible 2^n calls. However this natural limitation of regular block ciphers has no ground in the presence of tweaks. Much like one can have security proofs beyond 2^n calls, one could attack a tweakable cipher using more than 2^n tweak/plaintext/ciphertext triples.

1.3   Results

Our generic iterated tweakable FX framework is pertinent to all cited constructions as shown in Table 1. Using a single-round FX to blend in the tweak is the most common approach and may be considered as well understood. However there seem to be additional security to be gained in iterating those constructions. Some works [LST12, LL18] tend to do and prove just that. The focus on 2 rounds is justified by the fact that we don't know of any constructions based on

Table 1. Some previously proposed schemes and description of how it fits in our iterated tweakable FX generic framework. Multiplications ($\times$) are over the finite field $GF(2^n)$.

Ref.	Scheme	r	Subkey functions
[LRW11]	LRW2	1	$\lambda_0(k,t) = \lambda_1(k,t)$ a uniform and AXU function.
			$\gamma_1(k,t) = k$
[Men15]	$\tilde{F}[1]$	1	$\lambda_0(k,t) = \lambda_1(k,t) = t \times k \qquad \gamma_1(k,t) = t \oplus k$
[Men15]	$\tilde{F}[2]$	1	$\lambda_0(k,t) = \lambda_1(k,t) = E_1(2 \times k, t) \ \ \gamma_1(k,t) = t \oplus k$
[Men16]	XPX	1	$\kappa = 0$ so $E_1(\cdot, m) = P(m) \qquad t = t_{11} \parallel t_{12} \parallel t_{21} \parallel t_{22}$
			$\lambda_0(k,t) = t_{11}k \oplus t_{12}P(k) \qquad \lambda_1(k,t) = t_{21}k \oplus t_{22}P(k)$
[JLM+17]	XHX	1	$\gamma_1(k,t)$ a uniform and AU function.
			$\lambda_0(k,t) = \lambda_1(k,t)$ a uniform and AXU function.
[LRW11]	LRW1	2	$\lambda_0(k,t) = \lambda_2(k,t) = 0 \qquad \lambda_1(k,t) = t$
			$\gamma_1(k,t) = \gamma_2(k,t) = k$
[LST12]	CLRW2	2	$\lambda_0(k,t)$ and $\lambda_2(k,t)$ two uniform and AXU functions.
			$\lambda_1(k,t) = \lambda_0(k,t) \oplus \lambda_2(k,t) \qquad \gamma_1(k,t) = \gamma_2(k,t) = k$
[LL18]	XHX2	2	$\gamma_1(k,t)$ and $\gamma_2(k,t)$ two uniform and AU functions.
			$\lambda_0(k,t)$ and $\lambda_2(k,t)$ two uniform and AXU functions.
			$\lambda_1(k,t) = \lambda_0(k,t) \oplus \lambda_2(k,t)$

block ciphers using more than 2 rounds and the single-round ones mostly have already well understood matching attacks (Table 2). However we believe it is also interesting to know what kind of security bounds we might hope to achieve by iterating even further.

So in this paper we ask ourselves what is the best security bound attainable when using the iterated FX paradigm for building tweakable block ciphers from regular block ciphers. To do this we improve on the attack described by Gaži [Gaž13] to apply it in the tweakable block cipher setting.

First we show an information theoretic attack for $r = 2$ rounds when $\kappa \leq 2n$ with offline and online query complexity of:

$$Q = \mathcal{O}(2^{\frac{2}{3}(n+\kappa)} \cdot \sqrt[3]{\tilde{\kappa}/n}) \, .$$

Note that $Q = \mathcal{O}(2^{\frac{2}{3}(n+\kappa)})$ under the reasonable assumption that the size of the master secret key is linear with respect to the state size, that is, $\tilde{\kappa} = \mathcal{O}(n)$.

The recent construction XHX2 by Lee and Lee [LL18] is a particular case of our setting where $\lambda_1(k,t) = \lambda_0(k,t) \oplus \lambda_2(k,t)$. Their provable security bound is $2^{\frac{2}{3}(n+\kappa)}$ whenever $\kappa \leq 2n$ and therefore matches our attack. Thus our results prove the tightness of their bound and their bound proves the optimality of the attack.

We then extend the attack to multiple rounds of the same construction. This gives an attack on r rounds when $\kappa \leq rn$ with query complexity:

$$Q = \mathcal{O}(2^{\frac{r}{r+1}(n+\kappa)} \cdot \sqrt[r+1]{\tilde{\kappa}/n}) .$$

Again note that $Q = \mathcal{O}(2^{\frac{r}{r+1}(n+\kappa)})$ under the assumption that $\tilde{\kappa} = \mathcal{O}(n)$.

Table 2. Some previously proposed schemes with their known asymptotic bounds.

Ref.	Scheme	r	Proof	Known attack	Our generic attack
[LRW11]	LRW2	1	$2^{n/2}$	$2^{n/2}$	$2^{\frac{1}{2}(n+\kappa)}$
[Men15]	$\tilde{F}[1]$	1	$2^{\frac{2}{3}n}$	2^n	2^n (as $\kappa = n$)
[Men16]	XPX	1	$2^{n/2}$	$2^{n/2}$	$2^{n/2}$ (as $\kappa = 0$)
[JLM+17]	XHX	1	$2^{\frac{1}{2}(n+\kappa)}$	$2^{\frac{1}{2}(n+\kappa)}$	$2^{\frac{1}{2}(n+\kappa)}$
[JLM+17]	GXHX	1	$2^{\frac{1}{2}(n+\kappa)}$	none	$2^{\frac{1}{2}(n+\kappa)}$
[Men15]	$\tilde{F}[2]$	1	2^n	2^n	N.A.
[LRW11]	LRW1	2	$2^{n/2}$	$2^{n/2}$	$2^{\frac{2}{3}(n+\kappa)}$
[LST12]	CLRW2	2	$2^{2n/3}$	$2^{3n/4}$	$2^{\frac{2}{3}(n+\kappa)}$
[LL18]	XHX2	2	$2^{\frac{2}{3}(n+\kappa)}$	none	$2^{\frac{2}{3}(n+\kappa)}$

2   Cryptanalysis of 2-Round Tweakable FX

In this section we give an algorithm to extract the master key of a 2-round tweakable FX construction, Algorithm 1, then we show how it works by deriving the constants used and thus deriving the total query complexity.

2.1   The Algorithm

This cryptanalysis of Algorithm 1 is a key recovery attack and follows the idea of the original cryptanalysis by Gaži [Gaž13]: we want just enough data to construct contradictory paths for each wrong key. First we do all the required offline computations under all possible κ-bit key. Input values are the sets S_1 and S_2 which can be chosen randomly and the input/output pairs under the key j are stored in $\mathcal{L}_{j,1}$ and $\mathcal{L}_{j,2}$ for E_1 and E_2 respectively. Then we store all observable tweak/plaintext/ciphertext triples in $\mathcal{L}_0$. We don't need to choose the set S_0 of inputs to the tweakable block cipher as the attack works in the known plaintext setting. At last we can test all the κ-bit keys; potential master keys k only using the stored values by reconstructing the paths round by round.

Indeed sets $\mathcal{A}$ and $\mathcal{B}$ reconstruct the paths under the current key guess and the condition $\forall (t, m, b) \in \mathcal{B} : (t, m, b \oplus \gamma_5(k, t)) \in \mathcal{L}_0$ is checking whether there is a contradictory path (if not satisfied) or not (if satisfied). The additional condition $|\mathcal{B}| \geq \nu$ is simply here to ensure a good reduction.

For completeness we provide Algorithm 2 to show how to construct the sets $\mathcal{A}$ and $\mathcal{B}$. To construct $\mathcal{A}$ is to apply Algorithm 2 with inputs $S_0, \mathcal{L}_{\gamma_1(k,t),1}, \lambda_0(k,t)$. It is basically looking over all elements of the first set and checking if a shifted version of a value exists somewhere in the second set then, if found, it records the starting and ending values.

The constants ν and Q are derived in Sect. 2.2 and the algorithm already ensures that the total query complexity is of magnitude Q. Indeed once we construct the sets $\mathcal{L}_{j,i}$ and $\mathcal{L}_0$ we will have all the necessary queries to perform the attack. Since $|\mathcal{L}_{j,i}| = |S_i| = Q/2^\kappa$ and there are 2^κ different possible subkeys then the total number of queries to E_1 and E_2 is Q. Then we also construct $\mathcal{L}_0$ so the number of online queries will also be $|\mathcal{L}_0| = |S_0| = Q$.

Algorithm 1. Cryptanalysis of 2-round tweakable FX construction.

Input: $\tilde{\kappa}, n, \kappa \leq 2n, \tilde{E}, E_1, E_2, \gamma_1, \gamma_2, \lambda_0, \lambda_1, \lambda_2$
Output: k : the master key of $\tilde{E}$
$\nu \leftarrow \tilde{\kappa}/n$
$Q \leftarrow 2^{\frac{2}{3}(n+\kappa)} \cdot \sqrt[3]{\nu}$ $\triangleright$ Constants derived in Section 2.2

Randomly sample $S_1 \subset \{0,1\}^n$ with $|S_1| = Q/2^\kappa = 2^{\frac{2n-\kappa}{3}} \sqrt[3]{\nu}$.
Randomly sample $S_2 \subset \{0,1\}^n$ with $|S_2| = Q/2^\kappa = 2^{\frac{2n-\kappa}{3}} \sqrt[3]{\nu}$.
for all $j \in \{0,1\}^\kappa$ **do**
  $\mathcal{L}_{j,1} \leftarrow \{(m, E_1(j,m)) : m \in S_1\}$
  $\mathcal{L}_{j,2} \leftarrow \{(m, E_2(j,m)) : m \in S_2\}$ $\triangleright$ Offline Queries Sets
end for

Let $S_0 \subset \{0,1\}^* \times \{0,1\}^n$ with $|S_0| = Q$ be an observable tweak/message set.
$\mathcal{L}_0 \leftarrow \{(t, m, \tilde{E}(t,m)) : (t,m) \in S_0\}$ $\triangleright$ Online Queries Set

for all $k \in \{0,1\}^{\tilde{\kappa}}$ **do**
  $\mathcal{A} \leftarrow \{(t,m,a) : (t,m) \in S_0, (m \oplus \lambda_0(k,t), a) \in \mathcal{L}_{\gamma_1(k,t),1}\}$
  $\mathcal{B} \leftarrow \{(t,m,b) : (t,m,a) \in \mathcal{A}, (a \oplus \lambda_1(k,t), b) \in \mathcal{L}_{\gamma_2(k,t),2}\}$ $\triangleright$ by Algorithm 2
  if $|\mathcal{B}| \geq \nu$ **and** $\forall (t,m,b) \in \mathcal{B} : (t,m,b \oplus \lambda_2(k,t)) \in \mathcal{L}_0$ **then**
    return k
  end if
end for
return $\emptyset$ $\triangleright$ No proper key in the set

2.2 Deriving the Constants

The Query Complexity. To derive the constant Q used in Algorithm 1 we first focus on what happens when we guess the correct master key k. In that case we want to make sure that $|\mathcal{B}| \geq \nu$ happens with good probability as the other constraint is always true by construction of the scheme.

First let's look at the set $\mathcal{A}$:

$$\mathcal{A} \leftarrow \{(t,m,a) : (t,m) \in S_0, (m \oplus \lambda_0(k,t), a) \in \mathcal{L}_{\gamma_1(k,t),1}\}$$

By construction there are Q values $(t, m) \in S_0$ and, as S_1 is chosen randomly and independently, there is a $|S_1|/2^n$ probability that $(m \oplus \lambda_0(k,t)) \in S_1$ for each (t, m) observed and thus that there exists an a such that $(m \oplus \lambda_0(k,t), a) \in \mathcal{L}_{\gamma_1(k,t),1}$. Therefore in expectation we have $|\mathcal{A}| = Q^2/2^{n+\kappa}$.

We do the same reasoning for $\mathcal{B}$:

$$\mathcal{B} \leftarrow \left\{ (t, m, b) : (t, m, a) \in \mathcal{A}, (a \oplus \lambda_1(k,t), b) \in \mathcal{L}_{\gamma_2(k,t),2} \right\}$$

to find that in expectation $|\mathcal{B}| = Q^3/2^{2n+2\kappa}$.

Algorithm 2. Set construction.

Input: $\mathcal{S}_1, \mathcal{S}_2, \ell$
Output: $\mathcal{S}_3 \leftarrow \left\{ (e, s_3) : (e, s_1) \in \mathcal{S}_1, (s_1 \oplus \ell, s_3) \in \mathcal{S}_2 \right\}$
  $\mathcal{S}_3 \leftarrow \emptyset$
  for all $(e, s_1) \in \mathcal{S}_1$ **do**
    if $\exists s_3 : (s_1 \oplus \ell, s_3) \in \mathcal{S}_2$ **then**
      $\mathcal{S}_3 \leftarrow \mathcal{S}_3 \cup \{(e, s_3)\}$
    end if
  end for
  return $\mathcal{S}_3$

With some regularity assumptions, if $|\mathcal{B}| = \nu$ in expectation then $|\mathcal{B}| \geq \nu$ with constant probability. Therefore we put:

$$Q^3/2^{2n+2\kappa} = \nu \implies Q = 2^{\frac{2}{3}(n+\kappa)} \cdot \sqrt[3]{\nu}$$

The Number of Paths. The constant Q was derived so that we don't have false negatives, that is, we succeed with good probability when we guess the good key k. Now we derive the constant ν so that we don't have any false positive that means the test fails with good probability for all the wrong guesses of k.

First notice that the fact that $|\mathcal{B}| = \nu$ in expectation is true for all guesses of k, good or wrong. If $|\mathcal{B}| < \nu$ then the test fails as it should. If $|\mathcal{B}| \geq \nu$ then we need to look at the second condition that is $\forall (t, m, b) \in \mathcal{B} : (t, m, b \oplus \lambda_3(k,t)) \in \mathcal{L}_0$. If the guess is wrong then for a given $(t, m, b) \in \mathcal{B}$ we have $(b \oplus \lambda_3(k,t)) = \tilde{E}(t, m)$ with a 2^{-n} probability. Since $|\mathcal{B}| \geq \nu$ then the second condition is satisfied with probability $(2^{-n})^\nu = 2^{-\nu \cdot n}$. The test must fail for all the wrong guesses and there are $2^{\tilde{\kappa}} - 1$ such wrong guesses so all the tests should fail at least with constant probability when:

$$2^{\tilde{\kappa}} \cdot 2^{-\nu \cdot n} \leq 1 \implies \tilde{\kappa} - \nu \cdot n \leq 0 \implies \nu \geq \tilde{\kappa}/n$$

thus we take $\nu = \tilde{\kappa}/n$.

2.3   Constraints

For all of this to work there are some constraints that need to be spelled out. First we require that:

$$1 \le |S_i|$$
$$\Longleftrightarrow 1 \le 2^{\frac{2}{3}n - \frac{1}{3}\kappa} \cdot \sqrt[3]{\nu}$$
$$\Longleftrightarrow \kappa \le 2n + \log(\nu)$$

which limits to possible size of κ to a multiple of the state size n. Very few block ciphers admit a key larger than $2n$ so this is not a strong limitation in practice.

We also need to have diverse tweakable subkeys. Indeed so far we did not require that the functions $\gamma_i(k,t)$ depends on t which means that the tweak can be put, or not, at any stage of the construction but we still require that the tweak changes something. Therefore we can deduce such requirement:

$$\forall k \in \{0,1\}^{\tilde{\kappa}} \ \forall (t,m) \in S_0 \ \forall (t',m') \in S_0 \ :$$
$$t \ne t' \implies \exists i : \gamma_i(k,t) \ne \gamma_i(k,t') \text{ OR } \lambda_i(k,t) \ne \lambda_i(k,t')$$

which means that for every pairs of two different observed tweaks at least one of the respective implied subkeys must be different. This condition mostly ensure that this is a reasonable tweakable block cipher construction. Indeed in the case where two tweaks imply the exact same subkeys then one can quickly realise that it gets the same permutation for two different tweaks which is a near zero probability event for a perfect tweakable block cipher and hence it's a distinguisher.

3   Cryptanalysis of r-Round Tweakable FX

Starting from the attack of Sect. 2 we show how to generalise it to attack $r \ge 1$ rounds of the same construction in $Q = \mathcal{O}(2^{\frac{r}{r+1}(n+\kappa)} \cdot \sqrt[r+1]{\tilde{\kappa}/n})$ query complexity. The strategy is the same, we begin by doing all the necessary queries before reconstructing paths round by round to finally check whether there is a contradictory path or not. This is Algorithm 3.

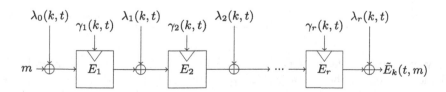

Fig. 2. r-Round tweakable FX.

3.1   Constants and Complexity

The Query Complexity. We derive the constant Q used in Algorithm 3 in the same way as we did for the 2-round version. First we focus on what happens when we guess the correct master key k. In that case we want to make sure that $|\mathcal{B}| \geq \nu$ happens with good probability as contradictory paths cannot exist under the correct key.

Let's look at the set $\mathcal{A}_1$:

$$\mathcal{A}_1 \leftarrow \big\{ (t, m, a) : (t, m) \in S_0, (m \oplus \lambda_0(k, t), a) \in \mathcal{L}_{\gamma_1(k,t),1} \big\}$$

Algorithm 3. Cryptanalysis of r-round tweakable FX construction.

Input: $\tilde{\kappa}, n, \kappa \leq rn, \tilde{E}, E_1, E_2, ..., E_r, \gamma_1, \gamma_2, ..., \gamma_r, \lambda_0, \lambda_1, \lambda_2, ..., \lambda_r$
Output: k : the master key of $\tilde{E}$
1: $\nu \leftarrow \tilde{\kappa}/n$
2: $Q \leftarrow 2^{\frac{r}{r+1}(n+\kappa)} \cdot \sqrt[r+1]{\nu}$

3: **for all** $i \in \{1, ..., r\}$ **do**
4:     Randomly sample $S_i \subset \{0,1\}^n$ with $|S_i| = Q/2^\kappa = 2^{\frac{rn-\kappa}{r+1}} \sqrt[r+1]{\nu}$.
5: **end for**
6: **for all** $j \in \{0,1\}^\kappa$ **do**
7:     **for all** $i \in \{1, ..., r\}$ **do**
8:         $\mathcal{L}_{j,i} \leftarrow \big\{ (m, E_i(j, m)) : m \in S_i \big\}$ ▷ Offline Queries Sets
9:     **end for**
10: **end for**

11: Let $S_0 \subset \{0,1\}^* \times \{0,1\}^n$ with $|S_0| = Q$ be an observable tweak/message set.
12: $\mathcal{L}_0 \leftarrow \big\{ (t, m, \tilde{E}(t, m)) : (t, m) \in S_0 \big\}$ ▷ Online Queries Set

13: **for all** $k \in \{0,1\}^{\tilde{\kappa}}$ **do**
14:     $\mathcal{A}_1 \leftarrow \big\{ (t, m, a) : (t, m) \in S_0, (m \oplus \lambda_0(k, t), a) \in \mathcal{L}_{\gamma_1(k,t),1} \big\}$
15:     **for all** $i \in \{2, ..., r\}$ **do**
16:         $\mathcal{A}_i \leftarrow \big\{ (t, m, a) : (t, m, \bar{a}) \in \mathcal{A}_{i-1}, (\bar{a} \oplus \lambda_{i-1}(k, t), a) \in \mathcal{L}_{\gamma_i(k,t),i} \big\}$
17:     **end for**   ▷ by Algorithm 2
18:     **if** $|\mathcal{A}_r| \geq \nu$ **and** $\forall (t, m, a) \in \mathcal{A}_r : (t, m, a \oplus \lambda_r(k, t)) \in \mathcal{L}_0$ **then**
19:         **return** k
20:     **end if**
21: **end for**
22: **return** $\emptyset$ ▷ No proper key in the set

By construction there are Q values $(t, m) \in S_0$ and, as S_1 is chosen randomly and independently, there is a $|S_1|/2^n$ probability that $\exists a : (m \oplus \lambda_0(k, t), a) \in \mathcal{L}_{\gamma_1(k,t),1}$ for all observed tweak/message pairs (t, m). Therefore, in expectation, we have $|\mathcal{A}_1| = Q^2/2^{n+\kappa}$.

Then we can easily prove by induction that $|\mathcal{A}_i| = Q^{i+1}/2^{i(n+\kappa)}$ as it is true for $|\mathcal{A}_1|$ and $|\mathcal{A}_{i+1}| = |\mathcal{A}_i| \cdot |S_{i+1}|/2^n$. Thus we get $|\mathcal{A}_r| = Q^{r+1}/2^{r(n+\kappa)}$.

With some regularity assumptions, if in expectation $|\mathcal{A}_r| = \nu$ then $|\mathcal{A}_r| \geq \nu$ with constant probability. Therefore we put:

$$Q^{r+1}/2^{r(n+\kappa)} = \nu \implies Q = 2^{\frac{r}{r+1}(n+\kappa)} \cdot \sqrt[r+1]{\nu}$$

The Number of Paths. The constant Q was derived so that we avoid false negative when we guess the good key k. Now we derive the constant ν to avoid false positives.

If $|\mathcal{A}_r| < \nu$ then the test fails as it should. If $|\mathcal{A}_r| \geq \nu$ then the second condition is satisfied with probability $(2^{-n})^{\nu} = 2^{-\nu \cdot n}$. The test must fail for all the $2^{\tilde{\kappa}} - 1$ wrong guesses so all the tests should fail at least with constant probability when:

$$2^{\tilde{\kappa}} \cdot 2^{-\nu \cdot n} \leq 1 \implies \tilde{\kappa} - \nu \cdot n \leq 0 \implies \nu \geq \tilde{\kappa}/n$$

thus we take $\nu = \tilde{\kappa}/n$.

For all of this to work there are again some constraints. First we require that:

$$1 \leq |S_i|$$
$$\iff \kappa \leq rn + \log(\nu)$$

which limits to possible size of κ to a multiple of the state size n.

Then we have the condition that the tweak changes something:

$$\forall k \in \{0,1\}^{\tilde{\kappa}} \ \forall (t,m) \in S_0 \ \forall (t',m') \in S_0 \ :$$
$$t \neq t' \implies \exists i : \gamma_i(k,t) \neq \gamma_i(k,t') \text{ OR } \lambda_i(k,t) \neq \lambda_i(k,t')$$

Notice that this condition prevents the known matching attack on XHX. Indeed, as for XHX $r = 1$ and $\lambda_0 = \lambda_1$, a collision on the full subkeys is expected after trying $\mathcal{O}(2^{(n+\kappa)/2})$ different tweaks. Our attack has the same complexity and also work on the generalised setting GXHX that doesn't enforce $\lambda_0 = \lambda_1$. This shows that the security cannot improve even if a collision on the full subkeys is made hard by, for example, choosing many different subkey functions or by using a mode of operation that limits the amount of different observable tweaks.

3.2   Discussion

Using Tweakable Block Ciphers. If instead of regular block ciphers we use tweakable block ciphers then it is not trivial to adapt this attack. Indeed we use the fact that the master key and the tweak must be blended before computation and not separately plugged in a tweakable block cipher. Such construction of a tweakable block cipher based on another tweakable block cipher could be used to increase security and/or the size of the tweak in a way that the original FX construction builds a stronger block cipher from another block cipher. However on the cryptanalysis side what can always be done is to fix a single tweak and apply the original attack by Gaži [Gaž13] in query complexity $\mathcal{O}(2^{\frac{r-1}{r}n+\kappa})$ or $\mathcal{O}(2^{\frac{r}{r+1}(n+\kappa)})$ when $\kappa \leq \frac{n}{r}$.

Weaker Constructions. This attack is generic given any reasonable key schedule represented by the λ and γ functions. However they are particular cases where better attacks are possible. In particular the cascaded LRW2 construction is a 2-round tweakable FX construction where the key in the block cipher does not vary with the tweaks (γ_1 and γ_2 don't depend on t). This construction permits an attack in $\mathcal{O}(2^{\frac{3n}{4}})$ by Mennink [Men18] using only two different tweaks which beats our generic attack as soon as $\kappa > \frac{n}{8}$.

Tweak-Rekeying. In fact our generic attack being a key recovery attack it will require at least 2^κ calls to the underlying block cipher. As soon as $k \geq n$ this implies a complexity above 2^n. Mennink [Men17] showed that provable 2^n security is unattainable in the standard block cipher model used for the proofs of schemes without tweak-rekeying. Therefore our generic attack can only hope to be tight for schemes that use tweak-rekeying and thus that are proved in the ideal block cipher model.

Key Recovery and Distinguisher. The fact that the complexity of this cryptanalysis depends on the size of the master key, even if a little, makes it hardly comparable to distinguishers that are independent of the master key size. Instead of waiting for some bad event to occur we collect just enough information to completely determine the master key. In the case of XHX the known distinguisher has the same asymptotic complexity but the widely different approaches make them hard to combine: a bad event for the known distinguisher gives no information on the master key. However for XHX2, and generally for $r \geq 2$ rounds of the tweakable FX construction proved in the ideal cipher model, it may well be the case that a key recovery approach is more relevant than looking for a suitable bad event for a distinguisher.

Towards Simplicity. The attack on generic 2-round tweakable FX is also tight since Lee and Lee could prove with XHX2 [LL18] that we can reach this level of security even when $\lambda_1(k,t) = \lambda_0(k,t) \oplus \lambda_2(k,t)$ with some conditions on those functions. Moreover the previously known matching attack on XHX [JLM+17] exploited the fact that $\lambda_0(k,t) = \lambda_1(k,t)$ but our generic attack shows that it cannot be made more secure without this simplification. Another way to say it is that enforcing $\lambda_0(k,t) = \lambda_1(k,t)$ does not affect the provable security bound.

Using this iterated tweakable FX paradigm, one can therefore wonder how much it is possible to simplify the subkey functions while maintaining an optimal provable security with respect to the generic security upper bound shown in this work.

Acknowledgement. The author would like to thank the 2018 Asian Symmetric Key Workshop and Gaëtan Leurent for useful discussions. This work was partially supported by the French DGA.

References

[ADK+14] Albrecht, M.R., Driessen, B., Kavun, E.B., Leander, G., Paar, C., Yalçın, T.: Block ciphers – focus on the linear layer (feat. PRIDE). In: Garay, J.A., Gennaro, R. (eds.) CRYPTO 2014. LNCS, vol. 8616, pp. 57–76. Springer, Heidelberg (2014). https://doi.org/10.1007/978-3-662-44371-2_4

[AES01] Advanced Encryption Standard (AES). National Institute of Standards and Technology (NIST), FIPS PUB 197, U.S. Department of Commerce, November 2001

[BCG+12] Borghoff, J., et al.: PRINCE – a low-latency block cipher for pervasive computing applications. In: Wang, X., Sako, K. (eds.) ASIACRYPT 2012. LNCS, vol. 7658, pp. 208–225. Springer, Heidelberg (2012). https://doi.org/10.1007/978-3-642-34961-4_14

[BR02] Black, J., Rogaway, P.: A block-cipher mode of operation for parallelizable message authentication. In: Knudsen, L.R. (ed.) EUROCRYPT 2002. LNCS, vol. 2332, pp. 384–397. Springer, Heidelberg (2002). https://doi.org/10.1007/3-540-46035-7_25

[CLS15] Cogliati, B., Lampe, R., Seurin, Y.: Tweaking even-mansour ciphers. In: Gennaro, R., Robshaw, M. (eds.) CRYPTO 2015. LNCS, vol. 9215, pp. 189–208. Springer, Heidelberg (2015). https://doi.org/10.1007/978-3-662-47989-6_9

[DES77] Data encryption standard. National Bureau of Standards, NBS FIPS PUB 46, U.S. Department of Commerce, January 1977

[EM93] Even, S., Mansour, Y.: A construction of a cipher from a single pseudorandom permutation. In: Imai, H., Rivest, R.L., Matsumoto, T. (eds.) ASIACRYPT 1991. LNCS, vol. 739, pp. 210–224. Springer, Heidelberg (1993). https://doi.org/10.1007/3-540-57332-1_17

[Gaži13] Gaži, P.: Plain versus randomized cascading-based key-length extension for block ciphers. In: Canetti, R., Garay, J.A. (eds.) CRYPTO 2013. LNCS, vol. 8042, pp. 551–570. Springer, Heidelberg (2013). https://doi.org/10.1007/978-3-642-40041-4_30

[JLM+17] Jha, A., List, E., Minematsu, K., Mishra, S., Nandi, M.: XHX - a framework for optimally secure tweakable block ciphers from classical block ciphers and universal hashing. Cryptology ePrint Archive, Report 2017/1075 (2017). https://eprint.iacr.org/2017/1075

[KR96] Kilian, J., Rogaway, P.: How to protect DES against exhaustive key search. In: Koblitz, N. (ed.) CRYPTO 1996. LNCS, vol. 1109, pp. 252–267. Springer, Heidelberg (1996). https://doi.org/10.1007/3-540-68697-5_20

[LL18] Lee, B.H., Lee, J.: Tweakable block ciphers secure beyond the birthday bound in the ideal cipher model. In: Peyrin, T., Galbraith, S. (eds.) ASIACRYPT 2018. LNCS, vol. 11272, pp. 305–335. Springer, Cham (2018). https://doi.org/10.1007/978-3-030-03326-2_11

[LRW11] Liskov, M., Rivest, R.L., Wagner, D.: Tweakable block ciphers. J. Cryptol. 24(3), 588–613 (2011)

[LST12] Landecker, W., Shrimpton, T., Terashima, R.S.: Tweakable blockciphers with beyond birthday-bound security. In: Safavi-Naini, R., Canetti, R. (eds.) CRYPTO 2012. LNCS, vol. 7417, pp. 14–30. Springer, Heidelberg (2012). https://doi.org/10.1007/978-3-642-32009-5_2

[Men15] Mennink, B.: Optimally secure tweakable blockciphers. In: Leander, G. (ed.) FSE 2015. LNCS, vol. 9054, pp. 428–448. Springer, Heidelberg (2015). https://doi.org/10.1007/978-3-662-48116-5_21

[Men16] Mennink, B.: XPX: generalized tweakable even-mansour with improved security guarantees. In: Robshaw, M., Katz, J. (eds.) CRYPTO 2016. LNCS, vol. 9814, pp. 64–94. Springer, Heidelberg (2016). https://doi.org/10.1007/978-3-662-53018-4_3

[Men17] Mennink, B.: Insuperability of the standard versus ideal model gap for tweakable blockcipher security. In: Katz, J., Shacham, H. (eds.) CRYPTO 2017. LNCS, vol. 10402, pp. 708–732. Springer, Cham (2017). https://doi.org/10.1007/978-3-319-63715-0_24

[Men18] Mennink, B.: Towards tight security of cascaded LRW2. In: Beimel, A., Dziembowski, S. (eds.) TCC 2018. LNCS, vol. 11240, pp. 192–222. Springer, Cham (2018). https://doi.org/10.1007/978-3-030-03810-6_8

[MI15] Minematsu, K., Iwata, T.: Tweak-length extension for tweakable blockciphers. In: Groth, J. (ed.) IMACC 2015. LNCS, vol. 9496, pp. 77–93. Springer, Cham (2015). https://doi.org/10.1007/978-3-319-27239-9_5

[RBBK01] Rogaway, P., Bellare, M., Black, J., Krovetz, T.: OCB: a block-cipher mode of operation for efficient authenticated encryption. In: Reiter, M.K., Samarati, P. (eds.) ACM CCS 2001, pp. 196–205. ACM Press, November 2001

[Rog04] Rogaway, P.: Efficient instantiations of tweakable blockciphers and refinements to modes OCB and PMAC. In: Lee, P.J. (ed.) ASIACRYPT 2004. LNCS, vol. 3329, pp. 16–31. Springer, Heidelberg (2004). https://doi.org/10.1007/978-3-540-30539-2_2

Universal Forgery Attack Against GCM-RUP

Yanbin Li[1,2], Gaëtan Leurent[3], Meiqin Wang[1,2(✉)], Wei Wang[1,2],
Guoyan Zhang[1,2], and Yu Liu[1,2]

[1] School of Cyber Science and Technology, Shandong University, Jinan, China
mqwang@sdu.edu.cn
[2] Key Laboratory of Cryptologic Technology and Information Security
(Shandong University), Ministry of Education, Jinan, China
[3] Inria, Paris, France

Abstract. Authenticated encryption (AE) schemes are widely used to
secure communications because they can guarantee both confidentiality
and authenticity of a message. In addition to the standard AE security
notion, some recent schemes offer extra robustness, i.e. they maintain
security in some misuse scenarios. In particular, Ashur, Dunkelman and
Luykx proposed a generic AE construction at CRYPTO'17 that is secure
even when releasing unverified plaintext (the RUP setting), and a concrete instantiation, GCM-RUP. The designers proved that GCM-RUP is
secure up to the birthday bound in the nonce-respecting model.

In this paper, we perform a birthday-bound universal forgery attack
against GCM-RUP, matching the bound of the proof. While there are
simple *distinguishing* attacks with birthday complexity on GCM-RUP,
our attack is much stronger: we have a partial *key recovery* leading to
universal forgeries. For reference, the best known universal forgery attack
against GCM requires $2^{2n/3}$ operations, and many schemes do not have
any known universal forgery attacks faster than 2^n. This suggests that
GCM-RUP offers a different security trade-off than GCM: stronger protection in the RUP setting, but more fragile when the data complexity
reaches the birthday bound. In order to avoid this attack, we suggest a
minor modification of GCM-RUP that seems to offer better robustness
at the birthday bound.

Keywords: GCM-RUP · Partial key recovery · Universal forgery ·
Birthday bound

1 Introduction

Authenticated encryption (AE) schemes aim to achieve both confidentiality and
authentication of the encapsulated data. The first AE schemes were designed
by combining a symmetric encryption scheme with a message authentication
code (MAC). The encryption scheme provides confidentiality while the message
authentication code ensures authenticity. Several generic composition schemes

© Springer Nature Switzerland AG 2020
S. Jarecki (Ed.): CT-RSA 2020, LNCS 12006, pp. 15–34, 2020.
https://doi.org/10.1007/978-3-030-40186-3_2

have been formalized and analyzed by Bellare and Namprempre [3]: Encrypt-and-MAC, MAC-then-Encrypt, and Encrypt-then-MAC. Their analysis considers black-box composition, without specific details of the underlying symmetric encryption scheme and MAC, in order to only focus on the security of the generic composition at a high level. Their analysis shows that only the Encrypt-then-MAC composition is generically secure.

Later, new AE modes have been proposed [11,18,30] to provide confidentiality and authentication in a single scheme, which is more efficient than the generic composition of conventional mechanisms. AE schemes are now widely used in Internet protocols, and there is an ongoing effort to design and standardize new AE schemes with the recent CAESAR competition [35], and the NIST lightweight standardisation effort [38] currently running. The design and cryptanalysis of AE schemes is a very active topic in the cryptographic community today.

One of the most widely used AE schemes today is the Galois/Counter mode (GCM) [8,23], an AE scheme following the Encrypt-then-MAC paradigm. GCM has been widely deployed thanks to its excellent software performance and hardware support, and because there are no intellectual property restrictions to its use. It has been standardized in TLS [7], ISO/IEC [37], NSA Suite B [39] and IEEE 802.1 [36]. GCM encrypts data using a variation of the counter mode of operation (CTR) which requires a single block cipher encryption per message block, and does not need to perform block cipher decryption, even when decrypting the message. The ciphertext and associated data are authenticated with a Wegman-Carter-Shoup authenticator, where the keyed universal hash function is a polynomial evaluation over a binary Galois field. However, GCM is not robust against implementation errors or misuse. In particular, if a nonce is used just two times, the confidentiality and authentication for GCM are compromised with Joux's "forbidden attack" [17]. GCM also loses its security if a device releases the plaintext corresponding to invalid ciphertext before verifying the tag. Therefore, variants of GCM have been proposed to achieve some more robust security notions.

In 2015, Gueron et al. presented GCM-SIV [12] combining GCM's underlying components with the SIV paradigm designed by Rogaway and Shrimpton [31], to provide nonce-misuse resistance. Later, at CRYPTO'17, Ashur et al. introduced a generic construction of AE scheme using a tweakable block cipher (TBC), which resists attacks in the RUP setting [2] (with Release of Unverified Plaintext). Based on the generic AE scheme, an instantiation GCM-RUP with high-efficiency is put forward using AES-GCM's components. The designers proved that GCM-RUP is secure up to the birthday bound in the nonce-respecting model and RUP setting. On the other hand, no attacks are known so far against the authentication part of GCM-RUP. Therefore we do not know whether the proof is tight, and we do not know what kind of security degradation to expect after the birthday bound.

1.1   Contributions

In this paper we describe a universal forgery attack against GCM-RUP with time and data complexity close to $2^{n/2}$, where n denotes the block size of the underlying block cipher. This attack matches the security proof given in [2], showing that it is tight. However, our main result is not only about tightness of the (birthday) security bound, but rather about how badly the construction of GCM-RUP breaks when the bound is reached: a universal forgery attack is much stronger than a distinguishing attack.

This is significant because no similar attack is known against GCM: on the one hand there are attacks with roughly $\sqrt{n} \times 2^{n/2}$ queries and time 2^n [20,22,26], and on the other hand attacks with $\sqrt{n} \times 2^{2n/3}$ queries and time $n \times 2^{2n/3}$ [20]. Our results show that universal forgery attacks against GCM-RUP are easier than against GCM, even though the security bounds from the proofs are similar, and both proofs are known to be tight (with simple distinguishing attacks).

Our attack is based on the following techniques:

- We show that inner collisions in the authentication part of GCM-RUP can be detected efficiently, and give out the output difference of the universal hash function GHASH_{K_2};
- Due to the structure of GHASH, we build a polynomial equation in K_2, which can be solved efficiently;
- Finally, when K_2 is known, we can sign arbitrary messages. This defines a universal forgery attack with complexity $2^{n/2}$ (time and data).

Since our attack points out a weakness in the structure of GCM-RUP, we also suggest a minor modification to GCM-RUP to prevent the leakage of the output of GHASH_{K_2} by using an extra block cipher call E_{K_4} to encrypt the output of GHASH_{K_2}. The objective of our variant is to achieve better security in the RUP setting and in the classical setting.

Many designs use GHASH because of its high performances. However, the output of GHASH may leak information about the key, as exploited in our attack. Therefore, the stronger GHASH variant we proposed could be applied to not only GCM like scheme but also future GHASH-based designs.

1.2   Related Works

Modes of operation are usually studied with security proofs, but there is a growing interest in generic attacks, showing how the security degrades when the proof doesn't hold. In particular, many attacks focus on (partial) key-recovery: most modes of operations have distinguishing attacks with birthday complexity $2^{n/2}$, but key-recovery and universal forgery attacks with the same complexity show that some schemes are more fragile than others when approaching the birthday bound.

For instance, in 1996, Preneel and Van Oorshot gave a full key recovery attack against the Envelope MAC with complexity $2^{n/2}$ [29]. In 2003, Mitchell studied several variants of CBC-MAC and compared their security against key-recovery attacks [25]; for some schemes the best attack reported requires an exhaustive search over an n-bit key, but attacks with birthday complexity can recover a partial key for TMAC and OMAC [33], leading to stronger forgery attacks. More recently, a series of works has shown birthday attacks against HMAC, with full key recovery when the hash function uses an internal checksum [19] and universal forgeries [27] in general. During the CAESAR competition, it was pointed out that the security of AEZ [14] collapses at the birthday bound, with a full key recovery [10]. The scheme was modified to avoid the attack, but a variant is still applicable [6].

Besides MAC algorithms, there has also been work on message-recovery attacks on encryption modes, with a stronger impact than distinguishers. The well-known collision attack against CBC has been shown to be usable in practice with 64-bit block ciphers [4], and message-recovery attacks have also been shown against the CTR mode [20], even though the well-known distinguisher is much weaker.

All these results clearly show the importance of cryptanalysis work against modes of operation, even when the attacks do not contradict the proofs. In addition, this type of work sometimes detects mistakes in the proofs, as shown with GCM [16] and OCB2 [15].

1.3   Organization

The remainder of this paper is organized as follows. Section 2 gives the preliminaries. Section 3 briefly describes the generic construction and its instantiation GCM-RUP. We recover the authentication key in Sect. 4, and a universal forgery is provided in Sect. 5. Section 6 recommends a minor modification to GCM-RUP to resist our forgery attack. Finally, Sect. 7 concludes this paper.

2   Preliminaries

This section will show notations, operations, some cryptographic schemes and security definitions used in this paper.

2.1   Notations and Operations

- n: The block size of the block cipher (for GCM-RUP, $n = 128$).
- $\{0,1\}^{\leq x}$: The set of strings with length no greater than x bits.
- $\{0,1\}^*$: The set of strings with arbitrary length.
- $|X|$: Length of X, if $X \in \{0,1\}^*$.
- $X \oplus Y$: Bit-wise exclusive OR of X and Y, if $X, Y \in \{0,1\}^*$.
- $X \cdot Y$: Galois field multiplication of X and Y, if $X, Y \in \{0,1\}^n$.
- $X\|Y$ or XY: Concatenation of X and Y, if $X, Y \in \{0,1\}^*$.
- ε: The empty string.
- 0^n: n-bit string consisting of only zeros.
- $len_n(X)$: Length of X modulo 2^n as an n-bit string.

- $X0^{*n}$: X padded on the right with 0-bits to get a string of length a multiple of n.
- $|X|_n$: X's length in n-bit blocks $|X|_n = \lceil |X|/n \rceil$.
- $X[1]X[2]\ldots X[x] \overset{n}{\leftarrow} X$: Split X into substrings such that $|X[i]| = n$ for $i = 1,\ldots,x-1$, $0 < |X[x]| \leq n$, and $X[1]\|\ldots\|X[x] = X$.
- $int(Y)$: Map the j bits string $Y = a_{j-1}\ldots a_1 a_0$ to the integer $i = a_{j-1}2^{j-1} + \cdots + a_1 2 + a_0$.
- $str_j(i)$: Map the integer $i = a_{j-1}2^{j-1} + \cdots + a_1 2 + a_0 < 2^j$ to the j-bit string $a_{j-1}\ldots a_1 a_0$.
- $inc_m(X)$: The function which adds one modulo 2^m to X when viewed as an integer: $inc_m(X) := str_m(int(X) + 1 \; mod \; 2^m)$.
- $msb_j(X)$: j most significant bits of X: $msb_j(a_{i-1}\ldots a_1 a_0) := a_{i-1}\ldots a_{a-j}$.
- $lsb_j(X)$: j least significant bits of X: $lsb_j(a_{i-1}\ldots a_1 a_0) := a_{j-1}\ldots a_0$.
- $F \leftarrow E(C\|\cdot)$: Define $F(X) = E(C\|X)$ where C is fixed as constant.
- $a \overset{?}{=} b$: Evaluate to $\top$ if a equals b, and $\bot$ otherwise.

2.2 AE, Separated AE and TBC

An authenticated encryption scheme is a symmetric key algorithm that provides both confidentiality and authenticity. Bellare and Namprempre [3] defined the formal notion of authenticated encryption as follows:

Definition 1 (AE [3]). *An AE scheme consists of a pair of functions, the encryption function* Enc *and the decryption function* Dec,

$$\mathsf{Enc} : \mathcal{K} \times \mathcal{N} \times \mathcal{A} \times \mathcal{M} \to \mathcal{C},$$
$$\mathsf{Dec} : \mathcal{K} \times \mathcal{N} \times \mathcal{A} \times \mathcal{C} \to \mathcal{M} \cup \{\bot\},$$

with $\mathcal{K}$ the key space, $\mathcal{N}$ the nonce space, $\mathcal{A}$ the associated data space, $\mathcal{M}$ the message space, $\mathcal{C}$ the ciphertext space, and $\bot$ an error symbol not contained in $\mathcal{M}$, which represents verification failure. It must be the case that for all $K \in \mathcal{K}$, $N \in \mathcal{N}$, $A \in \mathcal{A}$ and $M \in \mathcal{M}$,

$$\mathsf{Dec}_K^N(A, \mathsf{Enc}_K^N(A, M)) = M.$$

The decryption process typically has two phases: plaintext computation and verification; the plaintext obtained from decryption is only given out after successful verification. However, keeping the full plaintext in memory can be an issue for constrained devices, and side-channel attacks can potentially recover information about the plaintext while it is decrypted. Therefore, new models have been introduced to take into account the effect of releasing unverified plaintext. In particular, Andreeva *et al.* [1] defined *separated* AE schemes where the plaintext computation is disconnected from verification; in this model the decryption function always releases the plaintext, without verifying it. Formally, a separated AE scheme is defined as:

Definition 2 (separated AE [1]). *A separated AE scheme consists of a triplet of functions, the encryption function* SEnc, *the decryption function* SDec, *and the verification function* SVer, *where*

$$SEnc : \mathcal{K} \times \mathcal{N} \times \mathcal{A} \times \mathcal{M} \to \mathcal{C},$$
$$SDec : \mathcal{K} \times \mathcal{N} \times \mathcal{A} \times \mathcal{C} \to \mathcal{M},$$
$$SVer : \mathcal{K} \times \mathcal{N} \times \mathcal{A} \times \mathcal{C} \to \{\top, \bot\},$$

with $\mathcal{K}$ *the key space,* $\mathcal{N}$ *the nonce space,* $\mathcal{A}$ *the associated data space,* $\mathcal{M}$ *the message space,* $\mathcal{C}$ *the ciphertext space. The special symbols* $\top$ *and* $\bot$ *indicate the success and failure of the verification, respectively. It must be the case that for all* $K \in \mathcal{K}$, $N \in \mathcal{N}$, $A \in \mathcal{A}$ *and* $M \in \mathcal{M}$,

$$SDec_K^N(A, SEnc_K^N(A, M)) = M \quad and \quad SVer_K^N(A, SEnc_K^N(A, M)) = \top.$$

Finally, we need to introduce the notion of tweakable block cipher (TBC), which is used in GCM-RUP. A tweakable block cipher is a generalization of a block cipher with an additional tweak input, generating a family of independent block ciphers [21]:

Definition 3 (TBC [21]). *A TBC could be regarded as a pair of functions* (E,D), *with*

$$E : \mathcal{K} \times \mathcal{T} \times \mathcal{X} \to \mathcal{X},$$
$$D : \mathcal{K} \times \mathcal{T} \times \mathcal{X} \to \mathcal{X},$$

where $\mathcal{K}$ *is the key space,* $\mathcal{T}$ *is the tweak space, and* $\mathcal{X}$ *is the domain. For all* $K \in \mathcal{K}$, $T \in \mathcal{T}$ *and* $X \in \mathcal{X}$, E_K^T *is a permutation of* $\mathcal{X}$ *with* D_K^T *as inverse and*

$$D_K^T(E_K^T(X)) = X.$$

3   Brief Description of GCM-RUP [2]

Ashur, Dunkelman and Luykx proposed a generic construction of an efficient separated AE scheme at CRYPTO'17 [2]. Their construction uses an encryption scheme and a TBC, and achieves security in the RUP setting, assuming that the encryption scheme is strongly indistinguishable-from-random-bits (SRND) [13, 32], and the TBC is a strong pseudorandom permutation (SPRP) [32]. Based on the generic construction, a dedicated instantiation GCM-RUP is built using AES-GCM's primitives. This section will describe this construction and GCM-RUP.

3.1   Generic Construction with RUP Security [2]

Let (Enc,Dec) be an encryption scheme (without authentication), with $\mathcal{K}$ the key space, $\mathcal{N}$ the nonce space, $\mathcal{M}$ the message space, and $\mathcal{C}$ the ciphertext space. Let

(E,D) denote a TBC with key space $\mathcal{L}$, tweak space $\mathcal{T} = \mathcal{C}$, and domain $\mathcal{X} = \mathcal{N}$. Then define the separated AE scheme (SEnc,SDec,SVer) as follows,

$$\mathsf{SEnc}_{K,L}^{N}(A, M) := \big(S = \mathsf{E}_{L}^{A,C}(N), C = \mathsf{Enc}_{K}^{N}(\alpha \| M)\big),$$

$$\mathsf{SDec}_{K,L}(A, S, C) := \mathsf{lsb}_{|C|-\tau}(\mathsf{Dec}_{K}^{\mathsf{D}_{L}^{A,C}(S)}(C)),$$

$$\mathsf{SVer}_{K,L}(A, S, C) := \mathsf{msb}_{\tau}(\mathsf{Dec}_{K}^{\mathsf{D}_{L}^{A,C}(S)}(C)) \overset{?}{=} \alpha,$$

where $(K, L) \in \mathcal{K} \times \mathcal{L}$ is the key, $\mathcal{N}$ is the nonce space, $\mathcal{A}$ is the associated data space, $\mathcal{M}$ is the message space, $\mathcal{N} \times \mathcal{C}$ is the ciphertext space, and $\alpha \in \{0,1\}^{\tau}$ is some pre-defined constant. The construction is depicted in Fig. 1. The procedures of encryption, decryption and verification are illustrated in Fig. 1(a), (b) and (c), respectively.

The novelty of the generic construction is that the nonce is encrypted using the ciphertext as a tweak. This provides security in the RUP setting, because if an attacker modifies the ciphertext or the encrypted nonce, the decryption oracle will output a random plaintext. The authentication security comes from the redundancy in the plaintext, with the pre-defined constant α (known by both sides); the length of α determines the security level. In order to maintain security up to the birthday bound on the block size, the size of α and the nonce size are fixed to be the same as the block size n.

3.2   GCM-RUP [2]

GCM-RUP is an instantiation of the generic construction using the counter mode (CTR) for encryption and the XTX construction [24] with GHASH for the tweakable block cipher. It reuses the component of GCM in order to benefit from the efficient implementations available, while offering more robustness with security in the RUP setting. Before describing GCM-RUP itself, we first define the primitives borrowed from GCM. Let n denote the block length of the available block cipher, in this case $n = 128$.

The first one is the universal hash function GHASH, which takes a key H and two strings M and M' as input (in GCM, GHASH is used in the Wegman-Carter construction to build a MAC [34]). The core of GHASH is defined with a single string M constituted of full blocks, and evaluates a polynomial defined from M at H as follows,

$$\mathsf{GHASHcore}_{H}(M) = \bigoplus_{i=0}^{|M|_n-1} M[i] \cdot H^{|M|_n - i}. \tag{1}$$

The symbol "$\cdot$" represents multiplication in the Galois field $GF(2^n)$. All the computations are performed by the rule of operations defined in finite field. GHASH is defined from GHASHcore; it takes two strings M and M' as input, zero-pads and concatenates them, and adds the binary representation of the lengths of M and M' before processing the result through GHASHcore,

$$\mathsf{GHASH}_{H}(M, M') = \mathsf{GHASHcore}_{H}(M0^{*n} \| M'0^{*n} \| str_{n/2}(|M|) \| str_{n/2}(|M'|)),$$

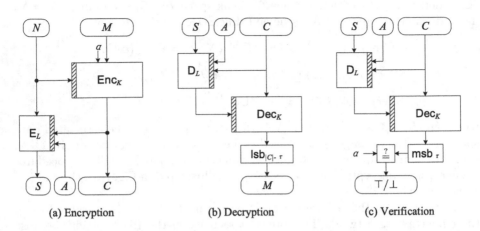

Fig. 1. Generic construction with RUP security

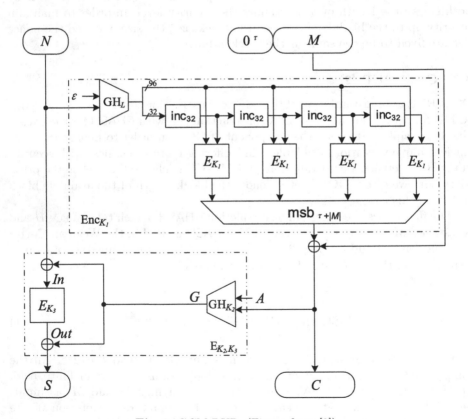

Fig. 2. GCM-RUP (Figure from [2])

where the function $str_j(i)$ maps the integer $i = a_{j-1}2^{j-1} + \cdots + a_1 2 + a_0 < 2^j$ to the j-bit string $a_{j-1} \ldots a_1 a_0$. Algorithm 1 describes the procedure of the function.

Algorithm 1. GHASH$_H(M, M')$

Input: $H \in \{0,1\}^n$, $M \in \{0,1\}^{\leq n(2^{n/2}-1)}$, $M' \in \{0,1\}^{\leq n(2^{n/2}-1)}$
Output: $Y \in \{0,1\}^n$
1: $X \leftarrow M0^{*n} \| M'0^{*n} \| str_{n/2}(|M|) \| str_{n/2}(|M'|)$
2: $X[1]X[2] \ldots X[x] \overset{n}{\leftarrow} X$
3: $Y \leftarrow 0^n$
4: **for** $1 \leq j \leq x$ **do**
5:     $Y \leftarrow H \cdot (Y \oplus X[j])$
6: **end for**
7: **return** Y

The second important auxiliary function is the CTR mode. Given a counter value X, a positive integer m and a predefined keyed function F as input, this function CTR$[F](X, m)$ outputs a string S with m blocks. Each block of S is computed by $S[i] = F(inc_x^i(X))$, where inc_x represents counter incrementation, adding one modulo 2^x to X, with the convention that inc_x^i represents i successive implementations. The CTR mode is defined in Algorithm 2.

Algorithm 2. CTR$[F](X, m)$

Input: $F : \{0,1\}^x \to \{0,1\}^n$, $X \in \{0,1\}^x$, $m \in \mathbb{N}$
Output: $S \in \{0,1\}^{mn}$
1: $I \leftarrow X$
2: **for** $1 \leq j \leq m$ **do**
3:     $S[j] \leftarrow F(I)$
4:     $I \leftarrow inc_x(I)$
5: **end for**
6: $S \leftarrow S[1]S[2] \ldots S[m]$
7: **return** S

Finally, GCM-RUP uses three keys: K_1 is used for the CTR encryption, and K_2 and K_3 are used for the TBC following the XTX construction (K_2 is used for GHASH, and K_3 is used for the underlying block cipher call). GCM-RUP encrypts a message M together with its associated data A and a nonce N, into a ciphertext C and an encrypted nonce S. The associated data, the message and the ciphertext are all seen as sequences of blocks of length n. GCM-RUP follows the generic construction given above, and is described in Fig. 2, with pseudocode in Algorithm 3 (with ε an empty string). In the figure, Enc$_{K_1}$ corresponds to CTR mode encryption, and E_{K_2, K_3} to the TBC.

Algorithm 3. GCM-RUP$_{K_1,K_2,K_3}(N, A, M)$

Input: $K_1 K_2 K_3 \in \{0,1\}^{3n}$, $A \in \{0,1\}^{n2^{32}}$, $M \in \{0,1\}^{n2^{32}}$
Output: $(S, C) \in \{0,1\}^n \times \{0,1\}^{\tau + |M|}$
1: $M \leftarrow 0^\tau \| M$
2: $L \leftarrow E_{K_1}(0^n)$
3: $I \leftarrow \mathsf{GHASH}_L(\varepsilon, N)$
4: $m \leftarrow |M|_n$
5: $F \leftarrow E_{K_1}(\mathrm{msb}_{96}(I)\|\cdot)$
6: $S \leftarrow \mathsf{CTR}[F](inc_{32}(\mathrm{lsb}_{32}(I)), m)$
7: $C \leftarrow M \oplus \mathrm{msb}_{|M|}(S)$
8: $G \leftarrow \mathsf{GHASH}_{K_2}(A, C)$
9: $S \leftarrow E_{K_3}(N \oplus G) \oplus G$
10: **return** (S, C)

As an instantiation of the generic construction with RUP security, GCM-RUP is secure under RUP setting. More precisely, GCM-RUP can provide security up to the birthday bound on the block size (because this is the security of the underlying AE scheme and TBC).

4 Partial Authentication Key Recovery for GCM-RUP

Our analysis focuses on the GHASH_{K_2} function, which can be written as a polynomial in K_2. In this section, we analyze properties of GHASH_{K_2} which are then used to recover K_2. After recovering K_2, it is possible to perform a forgery attack for GCM-RUP.

The main property used in our attacks is that G, the output of GHASH_{K_2} as defined in Fig. 2, is linearly dependent on the input (A, C) for fixed K_2. Therefore, the output difference ΔG of values G emerging in encryption operations of two input tuples (N_1, A, M) and (N_2, A, M) is independent of the value of (A, M), and is only a function of N_1 and N_2.

Based on this property, we retrieve K_2 with the following two steps.

- For a fixed associated data and message, we search for a pair of nonces (N_1, N_2) which produce a collision for the input of E_{K_3} using a birthday attack. For such pair of nonces (N_1, N_2), $\Delta G = N_1 \oplus N_2 = S_1 \oplus S_2$.
- With a known ΔG, a polynomial equation in K_2 is derived from the GHASH_{K_2} definition. Then K_2 can be retrieved by solving this equation.

In this section, we will give the detailed description of the recovery of K_2.

4.1 Properties of GHASH

Let $\varPi = (\mathsf{SEnc}, \mathsf{SDec}, \mathsf{SVer})$ denote the scheme GCM-RUP. We focus on the component GHASH_{K_2} with inputs the associated data A and the ciphertext C. In order to clearly describe the attack, we rewrite GHASH_{K_2} as

$$G = \mathsf{GHASH}_{K_2}(A, C) = \mathsf{GHASHcore}_{K_2}(A\|C\|str_{n/2}(|A|)\|str_{n/2}(|C|)).$$

According to the definition of GHASHcore given by Eq. (1), G is linear in the GHASHcore input $(A\|C\|str_{n/2}(|A|)\|str_{n/2}(|C|))$ for a fixed K_2. Therefore, we consider the difference ΔG in the output of GHASH_{K_2} for a pair of inputs.

Property 1. *When processing a fixed associated data A and message M under two distinct nonces (N_1, N_2) with GCM-RUP, the output difference ΔG of GHASH_{K_2} is only dependent on N_1 and N_2, but independent on A and M. This also holds for the input difference of E_{K_3}.*

Proof. For two tuples (N_1, A, M) and (N_2, A, M), query SEnc and get

$$(S_1, C_1) \leftarrow \mathsf{GCM\text{-}RUP}(N_1, A, M),$$
$$(S_2, C_2) \leftarrow \mathsf{GCM\text{-}RUP}(N_2, A, M).$$

Let G_1 and G_2 represent the corresponding outputs of the function GHASH_{K_2} in the encryptions under nonces N_1 and N_2, respectively,

$$G_1 = \mathsf{GHASH}_{K_2}(A, C_1),$$
$$G_2 = \mathsf{GHASH}_{K_2}(A, C_2),$$

where

$$C_1 = (0^\tau\|M) \oplus \mathsf{Enc}_{K_1}(N_1),$$
$$C_2 = (0^\tau\|M) \oplus \mathsf{Enc}_{K_1}(N_2),$$

the function Enc_{K_1} is defined in the upper dotted box in Fig. 2. Hence,

$$\begin{aligned}\Delta G &= G_1 \oplus G_2 \\ &= \mathsf{GHASH}_{K_2}(A, C_1) \oplus \mathsf{GHASH}_{K_2}(A, C_2).\end{aligned} \tag{2}$$

From the definition of GHASH, we have

$$\begin{aligned}\Delta G &= \mathsf{GHASHcore}_{K_2}\big(A \oplus A\|C_1 \oplus C_2\| \\ &\quad (str_{n/2}(|A|)\|str_{n/2}(|C_1|)) \oplus (str_{n/2}(|A|)\|str_{n/2}(|C_2|))\big) \\ &= \mathsf{GHASHcore}_{K_2}(0^{|A|}\|\Delta C\|0^n) \\ &= \mathsf{GHASHcore}_{K_2}(0^{|A|}\|\mathsf{Enc}_{K_1}(N_1) \oplus \mathsf{Enc}_{K_1}(N_2)\|0^n),\end{aligned} \tag{3}$$

which shows that the output difference of the function GHASH_{K_2} depend only on N_1 and N_2 for two tuples (N_1, A, M) and (N_2, A, M). The input difference of E_{K_3} can be computed as

$$\begin{aligned}\Delta In &= N_1 \oplus N_2 \oplus \Delta G \\ &= N_1 \oplus N_2 \oplus \mathsf{GHASHcore}_{K_2}(0^{|A|}\|\Delta C\|0^n),\end{aligned} \tag{4}$$

so it is also independent of A and M. $\square$

In particular, if we can recover a value ΔG, we can then extract K_2 by solving a polynomial equation, given the ciphertext difference ΔC and the output difference ΔG:

$$\Delta G = \mathsf{GHASHcore}_{K_2}(0^{|A|}\|\Delta C\|0^n).$$

For simplicity, we assume that $|M| = n$ and $\tau = n$, this implies $|C_1| = |C_2| = 2n$:

$$\Delta G = \Delta C[0] \cdot K_2^3 \oplus \Delta C[1] \cdot K_2^2.$$

This a polynomial equation in K_2 in the Galois field with 2^{128} elements. Luckily, there are efficient algorithm to factor polynomials over finite fields. For instance, the Cantor-Zassenhaus algorithm [5] requires $\mathcal{O}(n^2(\log(r)\log(q)+n))$ field operations to factor a degree-n polynomial with r irreducible factors over a field with q elements. In practice, with the parameters used here, this takes negligible time using the implementation of SageMath [40].

4.2 Recovering K_2 from Inner Collisions

As explained earlier, the first step of the attack is to identify collisions in the input of E_{K_3}, defined as $In = N \oplus G$. Following the analysis above, we start with a fixed associated data A and message M, and query SEnc for q different nonces, to receive the corresponding encrypted nonces S and ciphertexts C.

In order to simplify the description, we focus on the value In, and we consider the function mapping N, A, M to In, denoted as PEnc, and represented by Fig. 3. The output values of PEnc can not be accessed by the attacker, but collisions in PEnc can be detected. As for In and the output Out of E_{K_3},

$$In = N \oplus G,$$
$$Out = S \oplus G.$$

When the collisions happen, $\Delta In = \Delta Out = 0$, which means

$$N_1 \oplus N_2 \oplus G_1 \oplus G_2 = 0,$$
$$S_1 \oplus S_2 \oplus G_1 \oplus G_2 = 0.$$

Thus, $N_1 \oplus N_2 = S_1 \oplus S_2 = \Delta G$. If the collisions $\Delta N = \Delta S$ can be detected, the collisions in PEnc can be detected. Meanwhile, this type of collisions give out the value of ΔG, which can be used to recover K_2. Moreover, the corresponding pairs can be identified efficiently. We just build a list of all nonces indexed by $N_i \oplus S_i$, sort the list and look for collisions: each collision corresponds to a pair with $N_1 \oplus S_1 = N_2 \oplus S_2$ i.e. $N_1 \oplus N_2 = S_1 \oplus S_2$. We now consider the converse, and evaluate the probability of a collision in PEnc when $N_1 \oplus N_2 = S_1 \oplus S_2$.

We formally define the two events as X and Y:

- X ($N_1 \oplus N_2 = S_1 \oplus S_2$): the event identifying pairs of nonces (N_1, N_2) with the input difference equal to the output difference of E_{K_3}, which is called *outer collision* (equivalently, it can be defined as $\Delta In = \Delta Out$).
- Y ($\Delta In = 0$): the event identifying pairs of nonces with collision in PEnc, i.e. zero input difference for E_{K_3}, which is called *inner collision*.

First, we observe that $Y \subseteq X$, because if $\Delta In = 0$, then $\Delta Out = 0$ and $N_1 \oplus N_2 = S_1 \oplus S_2 = \Delta G$. Therefore, we have

$$\Pr[Y|X] = \frac{\Pr[Y]}{\Pr[X]}.$$

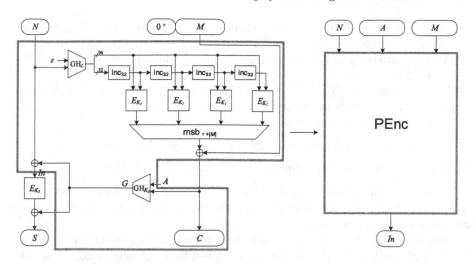

Fig. 3. Representation of the function PEnc

Moreover, we have $\Pr[Y] = 2^{-n}$ because the output of PEnc with a fresh nonce is random, assuming that E is a PRF. In order to compute $\Pr[X]$, we consider two cases, depending on event Y:

1. $\Delta In = 0$. Then we have necessarily $\Delta Out = 0$, i.e. $Pr[X|\Delta In = 0] = 1$.
2. $\Delta In \neq 0$. A pair with non-zero input difference must produce a non-zero output difference. Assuming that E is a PRF, we have $Pr[X|\Delta In \neq 0] = \frac{1}{2^n-1}$.

Therefore,

$$
\begin{aligned}
Pr(X) &= Pr[\Delta In = \Delta Out] \\
&= Pr[\Delta In = \Delta Out|\Delta In = 0] \times Pr[\Delta In = 0] \\
&\quad + Pr[\Delta In = \Delta Out|\Delta In \neq 0] \times Pr[\Delta In \neq 0] \\
&= 1 \times \frac{1}{2^n} + \frac{1}{2^n-1} \times \frac{2^n-1}{2^n} \\
&= \frac{1}{2^{n-1}}.
\end{aligned}
\tag{5}
$$

Finally, we can conclude

$$
\Pr[\Delta In = 0 | N_1 \oplus N_2 = S_1 \oplus S_2] = \frac{2^{-n}}{2^{-n+1}} = \frac{1}{2}.
\tag{6}
$$

Attack Procedure. We can now give the detailed procedure to recover K_2:

1. Choose an arbitrary associated data A and a single-block message M, then query SEnc for q different nonces N and receive the corresponding encrypted

nonces S and ciphertexts C; save them in a table indexed by $N \oplus S$. With a suitable value of q (in the order of $2^{n/2}$), there are two pairs of nonces (N_1, N_2) satisfying $N_1 \oplus N_2 = S_1 \oplus S_2$, one of which is expected to further satisfy $\Delta In = 0$.

2. For each pair with $N_1 \oplus N_2 = S_1 \oplus S_2$, assuming that $\Delta In = 0$, we have $\Delta G = \Delta S$ and we obtain a cubic polynomial equation with unknown variable K_2, which can be solved with factoring tools:

$$\Delta S = \mathsf{GHASHcore}_{K_2}(0^{|A|} \| \Delta C \| 0^n) = \Delta C[0] \cdot K_2^3 \oplus \Delta C[1] \cdot K_2^2.$$

3. Identify the correct candidate for K_2 with forgery attempts.

Using two pairs of nonces, this attack suggests a small set of six key candidates. The correct key can be identified with forgery attempts, or by using more pairs and looking for a repeated key candidate.

More precisely, we will describe how to construct a forgery with known candidate of K_2 for GCM-RUP in Sect. 5 for a given message, which can be used to filter the correct K_2. There would be two cases:

- If the forgery is constructed under the correct candidate for K_2, it can pass the verification algorithm of GCM-RUP.
- If the forgery is constructed under the wrong candidate for K_2, it will receive a failure of the verification of GCM-RUP.

We only need to query the verification oracle SVer six times to identify the correct K_2. The cost for this step is negligible.

Complexity Estimation. As already mentioned, the probability of two random nonces N_1 and N_2 satisfying $\Delta In = 0$ is 2^{-128}. Starting from a set of q queries, we can evaluate the probability p of finding an inner collision following the analysis of the birthday paradox:

$$p \simeq 1 - e^{-q^2/(2 \times 2^{128})}.$$

Thus,

$$q \simeq \sqrt{2 \times 2^{128} \ln \frac{1}{1-p}}.$$

Table 1 shows number of nonces needed to achieve the given probability of success.

4.3   Experimental Verification with Mini-GCM-RUP

In order to verify our attack theory, we use a mini version of GCM-RUP constructed with the 16-bit block cipher 4-round Mini-AES [28] to experimentally recover K_2. This experiment identifies pairs of nonces in event X and Y from 2^9 random nonces, and recover K_2 with SageMath. We execute this experiment several times to give some results to show the validity of probabilities of event X and Y in our paper, the detail is listed in Table 2.

In this table, we see that probabilities of event X and Y conform to Eqs. 5 and 6, respectively. The complexity of this experiment is dominated by 2^9.

Table 1. Number of nonces needed to achieve the given success probability

Number of nonces to identify inner collision	Probability of finding inner collision
2^{63}	11%
2^{64}	39%
2^{65}	86%
2^{66}	99.9%

Table 2. Experimental verification with Mini-GCM-RUP

(K_1, K_2, K_3)	Pair of nonces in X	ΔIn	$Pr(X)$	$Pr(Y\|X)$
(0x3d0e,0x2afc,0x2e91)	(0x2704,0x0889)	0	$\frac{1}{2^8}$	1
	(0x7649,0x7b0d)	0		
(0x4ef3,0x454b,0x1e9a)	(0x2323,0x602d)	0	$\frac{7}{2^9}$	$\frac{3}{7}$
	(0x11b7,0x2b2e)	0x0af7		
	(0x7bab,0x3a72)	0		
	(0x1215,0x1e05)	0xa3b5		
	(0x6593,0x093d)	0xbce8		
	(0x09bd,0x2db2)	0x03cf		
	(0x7d35,0x5e97)	0		
(0x5388,0x2641,0x7a4f)	(0x0ba9,0x46f5)	0x5393	$\frac{3}{2^8}$	$\frac{1}{2}$
	(0x684d,0x5786)	0		
	(0x334c,0x22e1)	0x0636		
	(0x4487,0x13f0)	0		
	(0x5413,0x03d8)	0		
	(0x5a91,0x179f)	0x0c06		
(0x5691,0x2ee9,0x5a68)	(0x3874,0x7546)	0x3fcb	$\frac{1}{2^8}$	$\frac{1}{2}$
	(0x44b0,0x4323)	0		

5   Universal Forgery Attack of GCM-RUP

In this section, we will construct forgeries for GCM-RUP given a candidate for K_2. We consider a challenge message M^* (and possibly a challenge associated data A^*), and our goal is to construct a valid ciphertext for M^*.

5.1   Almost Universal Forgery Attack

The first forgery attack makes only one query to the encryption oracle SEnc and then constructs a forgery by solving an equation over $GF(2^{128})$.

For an arbitrary nonce N, associated data A and message M (with $|M| = |M^*|$), query (N, A, M), and receive the corresponding ciphertext (S, C). Let $G = \mathsf{GHASH}_{K_2}(A, C)$, and the keystream used to XOR message is computed by

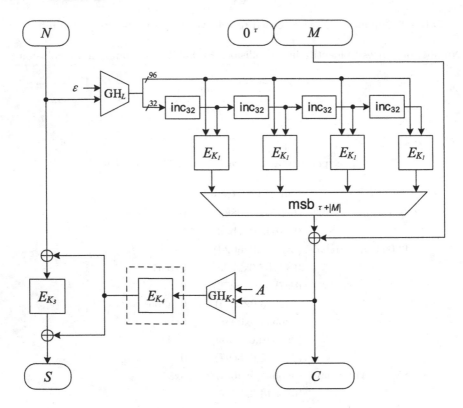

Fig. 4. A variant for GCM-RUP

$$\mathsf{Enc}_{K_1}(N) = C \oplus (0^\tau \| M).$$

We create a valid encryption of M^* by reusing the same nonce N and the values G and S.

First, we compute C^* corresponding to M^*:

$$\begin{aligned} C^* &= 0^\tau \| M^* \oplus \mathsf{Enc}_{K_1}(N) \\ &= 0^\tau \| M^* \oplus (C \oplus 0^\tau \| M). \end{aligned} \tag{7}$$

Then we construct A' such that

$$\mathsf{GHASH}_{K_2}(A', C^*) = \mathsf{GHASH}_{K_2}(A, C),$$

where A, C, C^* and K_2 are known. This gives a linear equation over $GF(2^{128})$ which can easily be solved assuming that $|A'| \geq 128$ and $K_2 \neq 0$.

To summarize, for any chosen message M^*, we can give a successful forgery (A', M^*, S', C') satisfying $(S' = S, C' = 0^\tau \| M^* \oplus (C \oplus 0^\tau \| M))$. This is an almost universal forgery, because we can choose M^* freely but not A'.

5.2   Universal Forgery Attack

Alternatively, we can design an attack where we choose both A^* and M^*, using $2^{n/2}$ queries. First, we make $2^{n/2}$ queries (N_i, A, M), for fixed A and M with $|M| = |M^*|$, and receive the corresponding (S_i, C_i). Since K_2 is known, we can compute $G_i = \mathsf{GHASH}(A, C_i)$, and recover the corresponding inputs and outputs to E_{K_3}: $E_{K_3}(N_i \oplus G_i) = S_i \oplus G_i$.

Then, we can use the same nonces N_i to build a forgery. For each N_i, we build the corresponding C_i' from M^* and C_i as above, and we check whether $N_i \oplus \mathsf{GHASH}(A^*, C_i')$ is in the set of known inputs to E_{K_3}. With high probability, one of the nonces will result in a match $N_i \oplus \mathsf{GHASH}(A^*, C_i') = N_j \oplus G_j$, and we deduce a forgery using $S' = S_j \oplus G_j \oplus \mathsf{GHASH}(A^*, C_i')$.

6   Variant of GCM-RUP

Our forgery attack against GCM-RUP highlights a potential weakness on the structure of GCM-RUP: the output difference of the function GHASH_{K_2} can be recovered with birthday complexity and this leads to a recovery of K_2. In order to prevent this attack, we suggest to add a block cipher call in the TBC construction used in GCM-RUP, as shown in Fig. 4, to avoid leakage of the output difference of the function GHASH_{K_2}.

This modified TBC still follows the XTX construction of Iwata and Minematsu [24], using universal hash function $E_{K_4}(\mathsf{GHASH}_{K_2}(A, C))$ instead of the original $\mathsf{GHASH}_{K_2}(A, C)$. The new universal hash function has the same security bounds, but does not leak the key from an output difference. Thus, the security proof of GCM-RUP is still applicable to this variant. But we do not provide a formal security proof. The extra block cipher has a limited impact on efficiency, and might offer better security by avoiding our attack.

More generally, the modified GHASH could replace GHASH in other designs. In particular, the corresponding modification of GCM would prevent the universal forgery attack with complexity $2^{2n/3}$ given in [20]. We believe that this construction is worth further study. Further work will be needed to determine whether this modification actually provides extra security and how much.

7   Conclusion

This paper shows a birthday-bound attack against GCM-RUP [2] using inner collisions to recover the output difference of the function GHASH_{K_2}. Hence, K_2 can be retrieved by solving a polynomial equation, and this directly leads to a universal forgery attack against GCM-RUP. This forgery attack shows that the construction of GCM-RUP breaks drastically when the security bound is reached. This is surprising because no such attack is known on GCM: the best known universal forgery attack requires $2^{2n/3}$ operations.

Finally, a minor modification of GCM-RUP is suggested to prevent this kind of attack, using an additional block cipher to protect the output of GHASH.

With little performance loss, this design focusing on GHASH can be applied to all GHASH-based designs.

In a more general setting, our attack technique can be applied to the LRW construction [21] with a polynomial universal hash function, as used in OCB, for instance. Actually, the corresponding attack on OCB would match the previous attack by Ferguson [9].

Acknowledgement. This work was supported by the National Natural Science Foundation of China under Grant Nos. 61572293 and 61602276, National Cryptography Development Foundation of China under Grant No. MMJJ20170102, Major Scientific and Technological Innovation Projects of Shandong Province, China under Grant No. 2017CXGC0704, Natural Science Foundation of Shandong Province, China under Grant No. ZR2016FM22.

References

1. Andreeva, E., Bogdanov, A., Luykx, A., Mennink, B., Mouha, N., Yasuda, K.: How to securely release unverified plaintext in authenticated encryption. In: Sarkar, P., Iwata, T. (eds.) ASIACRYPT 2014. LNCS, vol. 8873, pp. 105–125. Springer, Heidelberg (2014). https://doi.org/10.1007/978-3-662-45611-8_6
2. Ashur, T., Dunkelman, O., Luykx, A.: Boosting authenticated encryption robustness with minimal modifications. In: Katz, J., Shacham, H. (eds.) CRYPTO 2017. LNCS, vol. 10403, pp. 3–33. Springer, Cham (2017). https://doi.org/10.1007/978-3-319-63697-9_1
3. Bellare, M., Namprempre, C.: Authenticated encryption: relations among notions and analysis of the generic composition paradigm. In: Okamoto, T. (ed.) ASIACRYPT 2000. LNCS, vol. 1976, pp. 531–545. Springer, Heidelberg (2000). https://doi.org/10.1007/3-540-44448-3_41
4. Bhargavan, K., Leurent, G.: On the practical (in-)security of 64-bit block ciphers: collision attacks on HTTP over TLS and OpenVPN. In: Weippl, E.R., Katzenbeisser, S., Kruegel, C., Myers, A.C., Halevi, S. (eds.) ACM CCS 2016, pp. 456–467. ACM Press, October 2016
5. Cantor, D.G., Zassenhaus, H.: A new algorithm for factoring polynomials over finite fields. Math. Comput. **36**, 587–592 (1981)
6. Chaigneau, C., Gilbert, H.: Is AEZ v4.1 sufficiently resilient against key-recovery attacks? IACR Trans. Symm. Cryptol. **2016**(1), 114–133 (2016). http://tosc.iacr.org/index.php/ToSC/article/view/538
7. Dierks, T., Allen, C.: RFC 2246 - The TLS Protocol Version 1.0. Internet Activities Board, January 1999
8. Dworkin, M.: Recommendation for Block Cipher Modes of Operation: Galois/Counter Mode (GCM) and GMAC. National Institute of Standards and Technology. SP 800–38D, November 2007
9. Ferguson, N.: Collision attacks on OCB. Comment to NIST, February 2002
10. Fuhr, T., Leurent, G., Suder, V.: Collision attacks against CAESAR candidates - forgery and key-recovery against AEZ and marble. In: Iwata, T., Cheon, J.H. (eds.) ASIACRYPT 2015. LNCS, vol. 9453, pp. 510–532. Springer, Heidelberg (2015). https://doi.org/10.1007/978-3-662-48800-3_21

11. Gligor, V.D., Donescu, P.: Fast encryption and authentication: XCBC encryption and XECB authentication modes. In: Matsui, M. (ed.) FSE 2001. LNCS, vol. 2355, pp. 92–108. Springer, Heidelberg (2002). https://doi.org/10.1007/3-540-45473-X_8

12. Gueron, S., Lindell, Y.: GCM-SIV: full nonce misuse-resistant authenticated encryption at under one cycle per byte. In: Ray, I., Li, N., Kruegel, C. (eds.) Proceedings of the 22nd ACM SIGSAC Conference on Computer and Communications Security, Denver, CO, USA, 12–16 October 2015, pp. 109–119. ACM (2015)

13. Halevi, S., Rogaway, P.: A parallelizable enciphering mode. In: Okamoto, T. (ed.) CT-RSA 2004. LNCS, vol. 2964, pp. 292–304. Springer, Heidelberg (2004). https://doi.org/10.1007/978-3-540-24660-2_23

14. Hoang, V.T., Krovetz, T., Rogaway, P.: Robust authenticated-encryption AEZ and the problem that it solves. In: Oswald, E., Fischlin, M. (eds.) EUROCRYPT 2015. LNCS, vol. 9056, pp. 15–44. Springer, Heidelberg (2015). https://doi.org/10.1007/978-3-662-46800-5_2

15. Inoue, A., Iwata, T., Minematsu, K., Poettering, B.: Cryptanalysis of OCB2: attacks on authenticity and confidentiality. In: Boldyreva, A., Micciancio, D. (eds.) CRYPTO 2019. LNCS, vol. 11692, pp. 3–31. Springer, Cham (2019). https://doi.org/10.1007/978-3-030-26948-7_1

16. Iwata, T., Ohashi, K., Minematsu, K.: Breaking and repairing GCM security proofs. In: Safavi-Naini, R., Canetti, R. (eds.) CRYPTO 2012. LNCS, vol. 7417, pp. 31–49. Springer, Heidelberg (2012). https://doi.org/10.1007/978-3-642-32009-5_3

17. Joux, A.: Comments on the Draft GCM Specification - Authentication Failures in NIST Version of GCM. http://csrc.nist.gov/groups/ST/toolkit/BCM/documents/comments/800-38Series-Drafts/GCM/Jouxcomments.pdf

18. Jutla, C.S.: Encryption modes with almost free message integrity. In: Pfitzmann, B. (ed.) EUROCRYPT 2001. LNCS, vol. 2045, pp. 529–544. Springer, Heidelberg (2001). https://doi.org/10.1007/3-540-44987-6_32

19. Leurent, G., Peyrin, T., Wang, L.: New generic attacks against hash-based MACs. In: Sako, K., Sarkar, P. (eds.) ASIACRYPT 2013. LNCS, vol. 8270, pp. 1–20. Springer, Heidelberg (2013). https://doi.org/10.1007/978-3-642-42045-0_1

20. Leurent, G., Sibleyras, F.: The missing difference problem, and its applications to counter mode encryption. In: Nielsen, J.B., Rijmen, V. (eds.) EUROCRYPT 2018. LNCS, vol. 10821, pp. 745–770. Springer, Cham (2018). https://doi.org/10.1007/978-3-319-78375-8_24

21. Liskov, M., Rivest, R.L., Wagner, D.: Tweakable block ciphers. In: Yung, M. (ed.) CRYPTO 2002. LNCS, vol. 2442, pp. 31–46. Springer, Heidelberg (2002). https://doi.org/10.1007/3-540-45708-9_3

22. Luykx, A., Preneel, B.: Optimal forgeries against polynomial-based MACs and GCM. In: Nielsen, J.B., Rijmen, V. (eds.) EUROCRYPT 2018. LNCS, vol. 10820, pp. 445–467. Springer, Cham (2018). https://doi.org/10.1007/978-3-319-78381-9_17

23. McGrew, D.A., Viega, J.: The security and performance of the Galois/Counter Mode (GCM) of operation. In: Canteaut, A., Viswanathan, K. (eds.) INDOCRYPT 2004. LNCS, vol. 3348, pp. 343–355. Springer, Heidelberg (2004). https://doi.org/10.1007/978-3-540-30556-9_27

24. Minematsu, K., Iwata, T.: Tweak-length extension for tweakable blockciphers. In: Groth, J. (ed.) IMACC 2015. LNCS, vol. 9496, pp. 77–93. Springer, Cham (2015). https://doi.org/10.1007/978-3-319-27239-9_5

25. Mitchell, C.J.: On the security of XCBC, TMAC and OMAC. Technical Report RHUL-MA-2003-4, 19 August 2003. http://www.rhul.ac.uk/mathematics/techreports. Also available from NIST's web page at http://csrc.nist.gov/CryptoToolkit/modes/comments/

26. Nandi, M.: Bernstein bound on WCS is tight - repairing Luykx-Preneel optimal. In: Shacham, H., Boldyreva, A. (eds.) CRYPTO 2018. LNCS, vol. 10992, pp. 213–238. Springer, Cham (2018). https://doi.org/10.1007/978-3-319-96881-0_8

27. Peyrin, T., Wang, L.: Generic universal forgery attack on iterative hash-based MACs. In: Nguyen, P.Q., Oswald, E. (eds.) EUROCRYPT 2014. LNCS, vol. 8441, pp. 147–164. Springer, Heidelberg (2014). https://doi.org/10.1007/978-3-642-55220-5_9

28. Phan, R.C.W.: Mini advanced encryption standard (mini-AES): a testbed for cryptanalysis students. Cryptologia **XXVI**(4), 283–306 (2002). https://staff.guilan.ac.ir/staff/users/rebrahimi/fckeditorrepo/file/mini-aes-spec.pdf

29. Preneel, B., van Oorschot, P.C.: On the security of two MAC algorithms. In: Maurer, U. (ed.) EUROCRYPT 1996. LNCS, vol. 1070, pp. 19–32. Springer, Heidelberg (1996). https://doi.org/10.1007/3-540-68339-9_3

30. Rogaway, P., Bellare, M., Black, J.: OCB: a block-cipher mode of operation for efficient authenticated encryption. Trans. Inf. Syst. Secur. **6**(3), 365–403 (2003)

31. Rogaway, P., Shrimpton, T.: A provable-security treatment of the key-wrap problem. In: Vaudenay, S. (ed.) EUROCRYPT 2006. LNCS, vol. 4004, pp. 373–390. Springer, Heidelberg (2006). https://doi.org/10.1007/11761679_23

32. Shrimpton, T., Terashima, R.S.: A modular framework for building variable-input-length tweakable ciphers. In: Sako, K., Sarkar, P. (eds.) ASIACRYPT 2013. LNCS, vol. 8269, pp. 405–423. Springer, Heidelberg (2013). https://doi.org/10.1007/978-3-642-42033-7_21

33. Sung, J., Hong, D., Lee, S.: Key Recovery attacks on the RMAC, TMAC, and IACBC. In: Safavi-Naini, R., Seberry, J. (eds.) ACISP 2003. LNCS, vol. 2727, pp. 265–273. Springer, Heidelberg (2003). https://doi.org/10.1007/3-540-45067-X_23

34. Wegman, M.N., Carter, L.: New hash functions and their use in authentication and set equality. J. Comput. Syst. Sci. **22**, 265–279 (1981)

35. The CAESAR committee: CAESAR: Competition for Authenticated Encryption: Security, Applicability, and Robustness. http://competitions.cr.yp.to/caesar.html

36. IEEE Standard for Local and Metropolitan Area Networks Media Access Control (MAC) Security. IEEE Std 802.1AE-2006 (2006)

37. Information Technology - Security Techniques - Authenticated Encryption, ISO/IEC 19772:2009. International Standard ISO/IEC 19772 (2009)

38. NIST: Lightweight Cryptography. https://csrc.nist.gov/Projects/Lightweight-Cryptography

39. National Security Agency, Internet Protocol Security (IPsec) Minimum Essential Interoperability Requirements, IPMEIR Version 1.0.0 Core (2010). http://www.nsa.gov/ia/programs/suitebcryptography/index.shtml

40. Sage Documentation. SageMath Help. http://www.sagemath.org/

My Gadget Just Cares for Me - How NINA Can Prove Security Against Combined Attacks

Siemen Dhooghe[✉] and Svetla Nikova[✉]

imec-COSIC, KU Leuven, Leuven, Belgium
{siemen.dhooghe,svetla.nikova}@esat.kuleuven.be

Abstract. Differential Power Analysis and Differential Fault Analysis threaten the security of even the most trustworthy cryptographic primitives. It is important we protect their implementation such that no sensitive information is leaked using side channels and it withstands injected faults or combined physical attacks.

In this work, we propose security notions tailored against advanced physical attacks consisting of both faults and probes on circuit wires. We then transform the security notions to composable security notions. The motivation for this research includes the ease of verification time; the creation of secure components; and the isolation of primitives in larger protocols such as modes of operations. We dub our notion *NINA*, which forms the link between the established *Non-Interference (NI)* property and our composable active security property, *Non-Accumulation (NA)*.

To illustrate the NINA property, we use it to prove the security of two multiplication gadgets: an error checking duplication gadget and an error correcting duplication gadget. The NINA proofs for error detecting gadgets capture the effect of Statistical Ineffective Fault Analysis (SIFA), an attack vector which threatens most current masked implementations. Additionally, we study error correcting techniques. We show that error correcting gadgets can attain the *Independent NINA* property. A stronger property which captures a clear separation between the effect of faults and probes. Thus, we show that clever error correcting gadgets improve on error detecting ones by achieving significant higher levels of combined security along with guaranteed output delivery.

Keywords: Combined security · DFA · DPA · Masking · SIFA

1 Introduction

Differential Fault Analysis (DFA), proposed by Biham and Shamir in 1997 [8], is an attack on a physical device which effectively reveals the secret key of a cipher using well-placed faults in the encryption procedure. Differential Power Analysis (DPA) is an attack which uses a cryptographic device's power consumption to launch a divide-and-conquer attack on the private key as first described by

© Springer Nature Switzerland AG 2020
S. Jarecki (Ed.): CT-RSA 2020, LNCS 12006, pp. 35–55, 2020.
https://doi.org/10.1007/978-3-030-40186-3_3

Kocher et al. in 1999 [26]. To facilitate key-extraction, several physical attacks can be used against the implementation, we differentiate passive, active, and combined attacks. Passive attacks observe the behaviour of a device during its process, such as observing the process time or the device's power consumption. Active attacks tamper with the device's functioning, such as inducing computational errors by fault injections. Using passive and/or active attacks for either enhanced tampering or observation of the device's reaction to tampering are called combined attacks.

In order to defend against physical attacks without using expensive custom hardware such as shields and detectors it is the algorithm that needs to counteract passive, active, and combined attacks by securing it in a formal security model. Passive adversary models and their corresponding security notions have improved significantly over the last fifteen years, largely due to the introduction of the probing adversary by Ishai et al. [25]. This adversary is capable of reading the exact values on a number of circuit wires. The minimal number of wires the adversary observes to learn a sensitive variable is defined as the order of probing security. Duc et al. showed that the noisy leakage model [10,30] reduces to the probing model assuming the presence of sufficient noise and independent wire leakage, and more specifically that an implementation's signal to noise ratio is exponentially related to its probing security order [18]. While the probing model helps to verify implementations, the time complexity is exponential in the security order which is therefore not cost effective for larger implementations such as symmetric ciphers. To streamline this verification procedure, Barthe et al. proposed a composable security definition called Strong Non-Interference (SNI) [3]. This approach views circuits as the composition of several components and forms a sufficient security condition, such that when multiple components are linked together the total circuit is probing secure. Composable security definitions allow designers to verify and optimise separate circuit components which are small enough for a brute force verification technique. This technique has been adopted in several tools to quickly verify implementations based on modular designs [4,7,13]. The importance of a formal security notion, such as the probing model, includes the need of assurance in high-end secure devices. To guarantee such assurance, the Common Criteria was proposed as an international standard. These criteria specify the security and assurance users can have in their sensitive devices where the strongest criterion requires a target of evaluation to have a verified design which is only possible with formal security notions [20].

Apart from security models, the current literature provides countermeasures against passive attacks. One example is the methodology of Ishai, Sahai and Wagner (ISW) which guarantees protection of arbitrary circuits against passive attacks using the previous discussed probing model [25]. This countermeasure led to further study to increase its security and efficiency [5–7,9,12,19,22,34]. Another methodology to secure implementations is described in Threshold Implementations by Nikova et al. [28]. By extensively using the masking scheme's and the cipher's properties, they minimise the countermeasure's latency and randomness costs and, as a result, the method has been used to defend various symmetric primitives [2, 15, 23, 27, 29].

Despite having formal security notions and countermeasures against passive attacks, there are only few works which consider active and combined attacks. The first is Private Circuits II [24] which provides a countermeasure where the active adversary is modelled as one who faults a bounded number of wires per clock cycle. By viewing faults as probes, the work naturally offers protection against a combined adversary. However, the implementation of the countermeasure and its efficiency is currently still a challenge [14]. Later on, the work of ParTI [33] proposes to encode intermediate variables with error correcting codes to detect errors. To protect against passive attacks, they apply threshold implementations on top of the encoding. The results are promising as they succeed in protecting the LED cipher on FPGA. However, they only provide argumentation for active security leaving out combined security and a formal adversary model. As efficiency is a major concern for practical applications, the work of Impeccable Circuits [1] only focuses on active attacks to find very efficient countermeasures. They consider an adversary who faults up to a given number of gates and consider compositional security, i.e., they look at the propagation of faults in their components. Previous works looked at adversaries faulting and reading separate wires, the work of CAPA [31] considers stronger adversaries. They use multiparty computation to provide provable security against combined attacks by proposing a new adversary model, the tile probe-and-fault model. This model considers an adversary who is capable of reading and faulting whole areas in the implementation thus ensuring hardware protection against combined attacks. However, due to their security model the countermeasures are heavy.

The adversaries considered in Private Circuits II and Impeccable Circuits are a good start towards formalising active and combined security but they do not yet allow for composable combined security definitions which are needed by designers. In this work, we combine the wire faulting adversary with the usual probing adversary to consider an attacker who can read and fault a given number of wires in a circuit. Similar to the proposition of Non-Interference by Barthe et al. [3], we build further on our adversary model by considering a modularised circuit and proposing sufficient security conditions (Strong Non-Accumulation and Strong NINA) such that modular compositions remain secure.

1.1 Contributions

The focus of our work is to propose compositional security notions which capture active and combined attacks. We propose the following three security models which provide either composable active or combined security.

- **Non-Accumulation.** With the Non-Accumulation (NA) model, we require that an injected fault only affects one output share of the gadget. Thus, an injected fault does not spread (accumulate) to more shares allowing the use of error detection mechanisms to identify whether faults have occurred in the design. As a result, the NA model effectively moves the verification process from large circuits to smaller subcomponents.

- **NINA.** The models of Non-Interference (NI) and Non-Accumulation (NA) are combined to form the NINA model capturing combined security. The model requires that a probed and faulted gadget returns an output where only a few output shares are faulted and where the adversary learns only a subset of the input shares. Due to NINA simulating the correctness of the unmasked output, it captures attackers using ineffective faults [11].
- **Independent NINA.** As the NINA notion requires the provision of shares to the simulator for every fault or probe injected in the gadget, its provided combined security is limited. We propose a stronger notion, dubbed Independent NINA, which separates the effect of faults and probes, and relaxes the requirement of giving shares to the simulator for each injected fault. The ININA notion can be attained by a gadget using error correction techniques and clever use of injected randomness.

To show our security notions in action, we propose two Strong NINA (SNINA) secure multiplication gadgets.

- **Error Detection:** We propose a multiplication gadget using duplicated Boolean shares with an error detecting mechanism. We show that the gadget is vulnerable to a Statistical Ineffective Fault Attack (see [17]) but the probability for the attack to succeed can be made arbitrarily small by increasing the number of shares. Thus, we prove that the gadget still attains SNINA security. Last, we provide an abort mechanism to show the gadget does not rely on an ideal abort command.
- **Error Correction:** For the second construction, we adapt the error detecting gadget and add error correction methods. The result is a gadget which is impervious to ineffective faults and, moreover, we show the gadget achieves the stronger notion of Strong ININA. This notion proves that the level of combined security is higher than the error detection variant, i.e., the adversary does not gain any advantage by using faults in addition to probes. This shows that, although error correction techniques are more expensive, they give a significant increase in protection against combined attacks as well as guaranteed output delivery.

For the proofs of the composability of the NINA notion and the security of our proposed gadgets, we refer to the full version of the work [16].

2   The Circuit Model and Secret Sharing

We introduce gadgets, private circuits, and the notion of simulatability. Similar to [25], we represent computations in arithmetic circuit form, a directed acyclic graph whose nodes are operations over a finite field $\mathbb{F}$ and whose edges are wires. Additionally, we consider probabilistic arithmetic circuits, meaning circuits with nodes having no input and uniform random elements over $\mathbb{F}$ as output; this randomness is independent and identically distributed, and the correctness of the circuit is not dependent on it. In order to resist fault attacks, we consider nodes with no output and which can abort the computation. This abort signal works as a broadcast making all wires in the circuit read $\perp$ when the signal is sent out.[1] The adversary also receives this abort signal as it can view from the state of the output whether the circuit aborted or not.

In order to defend algorithms against side-channel attacks a sound and widely deployed approach is the masking countermeasure which was introduced at the same time by Chari et al. [10] and by Goubin and Patarin [21]. The technique splits each key-dependent variable x in the algorithm into shares x_i such that $x = \sum_i x_i$ over a finite field $\mathbb{F}$. In case this field is binary, this masking method is referred to as Boolean masking. If no d shares give information on the secret we say that the masking scheme has a passive threshold d. We also work with independent share vectors x and y as those where the shares of x are independent from the shares of y.

To defend an algorithm against fault attacks the core idea is to utilise redundancy to enable detection of the injected faults. This redundancy is found in encoding intermediate variables using error detecting codes. A popular encoding method is to duplicate intermediate variables, such that, by checking whether all duplicates are equal, an algorithm can detect injected faults. If all sets of k faulty shares in a share vector are detectable, we say that the encoding scheme has an active threshold k.

Using masking and encoding of variables as the core idea to protect secrets against passive and active attacks, we introduce terminology to protect algorithms. A probabilistic circuit with shared inputs/outputs and, if needed, the capability to abort the computation is dubbed a gadget.

Definition 1 (Gadget). *A gadget G is a probabilistic circuit with input in $\mathbb{F}^{nm}$ (m inputs where each input is divided into n shares), uniform randomness $r \in \mathbb{F}^{\alpha}$, and a shared output in $\mathbb{F}^{nm'}$ or abort $\perp$.*

Concerning symmetric primitives, the secrets are each potential intermediate variable of the primitive. In other words, to protect the primitive against passive or active attacks, it works solely over shared variables.

Additionally, we define private circuits as probabilistic circuits consisting of a gadget, where its inputs are first shared and the shared outputs are reconstructed.

Definition 2 (Private Circuit [25]). *A private circuit implementing the function $f : \mathbb{F}^m \to \mathbb{F}^{m'}$ is defined by a triple $(\mathcal{I}, \mathcal{C}, \mathcal{O})$, where*

- $\mathcal{I} : \mathbb{F}^m \to \mathbb{F}^{nm}$ *is a probabilistic circuit with uniform randomness, called input encoder;*
- $\mathcal{C} : \mathbb{F}^{nm} \to \mathbb{F}^{nm'}$ *is a gadget with uniform randomness and the ability to abort;*
- $\mathcal{O} : \mathbb{F}^{nm'} \to \mathbb{F}^{m'}$ *is a circuit with the ability to abort, called output decoder.*

Since we will be working with composable security definitions, we typically consider that private circuits are composed of several gadgets, i.e., the output of one gadget forms the input of another.

---

[1] On hardware this functionality is replaced a specialised mechanism such as a cascading gadget from [24].

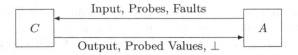

Fig. 1. Interaction between a circuit C and an adversary A.

We aim to protect against passive, active or combined adversaries as those who interact with a circuit by placing probes, faults, or both respectively. As shown in Fig. 1, the circuit responds to this adversary by setting or toggling the values on the faulted wires and returning the values on the probed wires. The state of the abort signal (true or false) is returned as well.

In order to make simulation based proofs for the secrecy of shared variables in gadgets, we define simulatability similar to the definitions proposed in [5,9]. However, we additionally consider that up to k wires in that gadget have been faulted and that the gadget can abort. Here the adversary (distinguisher) is either interacting with the actual gadget or with a simulator. This simulator is given only a part of the input and does not know the secrets of the gadget. The distinguisher's goal is to determine whether it is interacting with the simulator or with the actual gadget. A failure to do so implies that the adversary can know at most the shares given to the simulator and as a result only some inputs of the gadget.

Definition 3 (Simulatability). *Let $P = \{p_1, ..., p_d\}$ be a set of d probes of a gadget C with m inputs where each input is divided into n shares. Let the set of q shares of each input given to the simulator be denoted by $I = \{(i_1, j_1), ..., (i_m, j_q)\} \subset \{1, ..., m\} \times \{1, ..., n\}$. Let $F = \{(f_1, e_1), ..., (f_k, e_k)\}$ be a set of k injected faults e_i (either set or add) on the wire f_i in C. Denote $C_{P,F}$ as the circuit C with probed wires as per P and injected faults as per F. Finally, let $\perp \in \{0, 1\}$ denote the state of the abort signal in the circuit.*

We define the simulator S and distinguisher D as the following probabilistic functions.

$$S : \mathbb{F}^q \times \mathbb{F}^m \times \mathbb{F}^k \to \mathbb{F}^d \times \{0, 1\}$$

$$D : \mathbb{F}^d \times \{0, 1\} \times \mathbb{F}^k \times \mathbb{F}^{nm} \to \{0, 1\}$$

We say that the set of probes P and the state of the abort signal $\perp$ of the faulted circuit C_F can be simulated with the set of values on the input wires I if there exists a simulator S, such that for any distinguisher D and any inputs $a_{*,*}$, we have that

$$\left| \Pr[D(C_{P,F}(a_{*,*}), F, a_{*,*}) = 1] - \Pr[D(S(I, F), F, a_{*,*}) = 1] \right|$$

is negligible in the passive threshold of the sharing scheme, where the probability is taken over the random coins in C, S and D.

We note that for composable security, as we will see later on, we require that the probability for the distinguisher to view the difference between the circuit and the simulator is negligible and we should take care composing gadgets when it is not.

3 Security Definitions

In this section we specify orders of passive, active, and combined security and expand them to composable security notions which is the focus of our work.

3.1 Orders of Security

Passive Security. To model passive security we consider the known probing adversary who can read the exact values of up to a threshold number of wires in a gadget. The order of passive security is the well-known order of probing security.

Definition 4 (Order of passive security [25,32]). *A private circuit is d^{th}-order passive secure (d^{th}-order probing secure) if every d-tuple of the gadget's intermediate variables is independent of any sensitive variable.*

Active Security. We ensure protection against an adversary who is capable of faulting a given number of wires in the circuit. We note that similar adversaries have been proposed in Private Circuits II [24] and Impeccable Circuits [1]. The order of active security is determined by the number of wires in the circuit the adversary needs to fault in order to create an incorrect output. Such incorrect outputs are important as they can activate DFA attacks, thus to secure implementations we require that the private circuit either gives back a correct output or the process is aborted.

Definition 5 (Order of active security). *A private circuit is k^{th}-order active secure if any set of k faults on the gadget's intermediate variables results in either abort $\perp$ or a correct output (reconstructed output of the unfaulted circuit).*

Note that active security guarantees output correctness and does not consider fault attacks which target the privacy of a scheme such as ineffective faults.

Combined Security. We protect against a combined adversary who both faults and probes wires and consider a private circuit secure if it retains both its privacy and correctness against the combined adversary. This gives us the following combined security definition.

Definition 6 (Order of combined security). *A private circuit is (d, k)-order combined secure if for any set of k faults and d probes on the gadget's intermediate variables, the following holds.*

(a) Privacy: The probed d-tuple with the state of the abort signal is independent of any sensitive variable.

(b) Correctness: The circuit either aborts $\perp$ or gives a correct output.

The combined security model with $d = 0$ still differs from the active security model as the combined security model considers that an adversary can use the knowledge on the state of the abort signal to derive the private circuit's internal variables. The difference between the two models thus lies in the combined security model looking at both the privacy and correctness of a circuit while active security only considers its correctness.

3.2   Composable Notions of Security

We note that the previously discussed security conditions are not composable, i.e., the composition of multiple secure gadgets can be insecure. Thus, the previous security conditions should be applied to the entire implementation, instead we look at composable security notions.

Passive Security. The security notion for composable passive security has been studied by Barthe et al. [3] who defined the notion of Non-Interference (NI) using simulation based security (see Definition 3).

Definition 7 (d Non-Interferent (d-NI) [3]). *A gadget G is d-NI if any set of at most $d' \leq d$ probes can be simulated with at most d' shares of each input.*

Intuitively, the above model grants composable security since a probed value in a gadget can be simulated with an input share, which on its turn is the output share of a previous gadget. In case the latter gadget is also non-interferent, this output value can again be simulated with an input share. This chains until we reach the encoding function in a private circuit (Definition 2). Since the adversary can only probe d values we only need to use a secret sharing scheme of passive threshold at least d to protect against our probing adversary. While the notion of non-interference is a good start and captures a composable security notion over the serial composition of gadgets, the notion is not sufficient to provide protection when gadgets are composed in parallel (e.g., when two gadgets share the same input). To this end Barthe et al. introduced the notion of Strong Non-Interference (SNI).

Definition 8 (d-Strong Non-Interferent (d-SNI) [3]). *A gadget G is d-SNI if any set of d_1 probes on its intermediate variables and every set of d_2 probes on its output shares such that $d_1 + d_2 \leq d$, the totality of the probes can be simulated by only d_1 shares of each input.*

We note that intermediate variables can also be the input or output variables of the gadget.

When the above notion of non-interference is combined with a sharing scheme with a high enough passive threshold, the composable notion provides for probing security.

Active Security. Recall that we defined the order of active security as the maximal number of faulty wires such that the circuit still returns a correct output. We now make this into a composable notion, thus we look at the effect of a fault in a gadget which is part of a larger whole. Ideally an injected fault in the gadget is not propagated, i.e., the fault does not affect the output of that gadget. However, the adversary can always fault its output directly, meaning that we can never guarantee that all outputs of a faulted gadget are correct. Instead, we are interested in gadgets which do not accumulate faults. In other words, we need a fault on a single input or intermediate wire to affect only a single output of the gadget. We relax this requirement by allowing countermeasures to abort the computation (e.g., by using error detecting methods). We thus find composable active security notions which are similar in nature to the definitions of NI and SNI discussed earlier. Our first notion is Non-Accumulation (NA).

Definition 9 (k-Non-Accumulative (k-NA)). *A gadget G is k-NA if for any set of $k' \leq k$ errors, the gadget either aborts or gives an output with at most k' errors.*

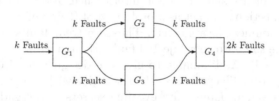

Fig. 2. An example of the propagation of faults over several k-NA gadgets for which a stronger composability notion is needed.

For a gadget which is k-NA, k faults on its intermediate variables result in the gadget giving an output with at most k faults. When composing gadgets, a stronger notion of non-accumulation is needed to guarantee the security of the composition. For example, consider the case given in Fig. 2 where each gadget G_i is k-NA. If an adversary injects k faults in the input of G_1, the gadget will give an output with at most k faulty shares. These faults propagate to the inputs of G_2 and G_3 which, because both gadgets are k-NA, results in a worst case scenario where G_4 gets an input with a total of $2k$ faulty shares. The end result is a sharing with $2k$ faulty shares even though only k faults were injected. To avoid such an accumulation of faults, one needs gadgets which are capable of erasing the errors from their input. The following definition of Strong Non-Accumulation (SNA) is sufficient to arbitrarily compose gadgets and be assured of their active security.

Definition 10 (k-Strong Non-Accumulative (k-SNA)). *A gadget G is k-SNA if for any set of k_1 errors on each input and every set of k_2 errors on the intermediate variables, with $k_1 + k_2 \leq k$, the gadget either aborts or gives an output with at most k_2 errors.*

When the non-accumulation notions are combined with a sharing scheme with a high enough active threshold, the composable notions provide active security.

Combined Security. We now look at composable security notions considering circuits which are both probed and faulted. First, we need to guarantee the correctness of the output of each gadget. To capture the effect of faults in compositions of gadgets, we use an argument similar to the one on active security. Thus, we need that an injected fault in a gadget propagates to at most one output share. However, the adversary can now place probes and thus learn part of the computation made in the gadgets. As a result, the combined security notion needs to capture the probability of an adversary breaking the correctness of a gadget given several faults and probes. In this work we only propose countermeasures where the correctness can not be broken, to give an example of a countermeasure for which this probability is non-trivial we refer the reader to the CAPA countermeasure [31]. Apart from guaranteeing the correctness of a gadget, we also guarantee its sensitive variable privacy for which we use simulation based arguments similar to non-interference. As mentioned by Clavier et al. [11], fault injections can act as a probing tool (think of an adversary faulting away the randomness in a gadget). Thus, we treat faults as probes giving extra shares to the simulator per injected fault (though we see later on that this is not always needed). Additionally, to give the designer the freedom to make countermeasures more efficient we consider security with abort. To capture the effect of the abort signal potentially revealing secrets in the gadget, we require the simulator to reproduce this signal given the injected errors and some input shares. As a result, we design a composable security notion of order (d, k) such that the gadget is (d', k')-order combined security for all sets of $d' + k' \leq d$ probes and $k' \leq k$ faults. We dub our notion NINA derived from the concatenation of the names Non-Interference (NI) and Non-Accumulation (NA).

Definition 11 ((d, k)-NINA). *A gadget G is (d, k)-NINA if for any set of $k' \leq k$ errors and any set of d' probes, such that $d' + k' \leq d$, the following holds.*

(a) *Privacy: The probes and the abort signal can be simulated with $d' + k'$ shares of each input and the injected errors.*

(b) *Correctness: The gadget either aborts or gives an output with at most k' errors.*

The NINA notion, combined with a sharing scheme having a sufficient passive and active threshold, implies the notion of combined security (see Definition 6). This follows from the simulation based security stating that the adversary can learn up to a threshold number of the gadget's inputs which, if lower than the passive threshold of the sharing scheme, gives no information on the gadget's secrets. Similarly, since the adversary can only fault up to a threshold number of outputs, a decoding gadget can detect or correct those errors given that the sharing scheme has enough redundancy in it. A formal proof of this implication is found in the full version of the paper.

Theorem 1 *A (d, k)-NINA gadget G with input encoding $\mathcal{I}$ and output decoding $\mathcal{O}$ using a secret sharing scheme with passive threshold at least d and active threshold at least k is (d', k')-order combined secure for any $d' + k' \leq d$ and $k' \leq k$.*

As a result, if we prove a gadget is NINA, we know it is combined secure. However, just as with non-interference, the NINA notion is not sufficient for composability. To this end we introduce "Strong NINA" (SNINA).

Definition 12 ((d, k)-SNINA). *A gadget G is (d, k)-SNINA if for any set of k_1 errors on each input and k_2 intermediate errors, any set of d_1 intermediate probes, any set of d_2 probes on the output, such that $d_1 + d_2 + k_1 + k_2 \leq d$ and $k_1 + k_2 \leq k$, the following holds.*

(a) Privacy: The probes and the abort signal can be simulated with $d_1 + k_1 + k_2$ shares of each input and the injected errors.

(b) Correctness: The gadget either aborts or gives an output with at most k_2 errors.

The notion of SNINA is sufficient for composability. In other words the composition of two SNINA gadgets is again SNINA (a proof is given in the full version).

Theorem 2. *The composition of two (d, k)-SNINA gadgets is (d, k)-SNINA.*

The above theorem together with Theorem 1 implies that the notion of SNINA is a sufficient condition to achieve composable combined security. The relations between the SNINA notion and other security models is shown in Fig. 3.

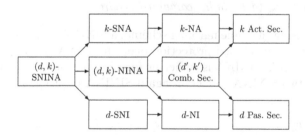

Fig. 3. A short overview of security models and relations between them.

Nevertheless, we find that there is a stronger property than NINA which gives improved protection. In case we use error correcting techniques instead of error detecting ones, specialised gadgets can attain a stronger security condition where faults are no longer modelled as probes. Thus, we propose a security notion where we claim an adversary can not learn anything by faulting a gadget which manifests itself in the security definition as the simulator not getting an extra input share for an injected fault. The result of this change is captured in the following definition which we dub "Independent NINA" or ININA.

Definition 13 ((d,k)-ININA). *A gadget G is (d,k)-ININA if for any set of $k' \leq k$ errors and any set of d' probes, such that $d' \leq d$, the following holds.*

(a) Privacy: The probes can be simulated with d' shares of each input and the injected errors.

(b) Correctness: The gadget gives an output with at most k' errors.

The above definition can again be made into a property which is sufficient for arbitrary compositions. This gives us the notion of "Strong Independent NINA" or SININA for short.

Definition 14 ((d,k)-SININA). *A gadget G is (d,k)-SININA if for any set of k_1 errors on each input and k_2 intermediate errors, any set of d_1 intermediate probes, any set of d_2 probes on the output, such that $d_1 + d_2 \leq d$ and $k_1 + k_2 \leq k$, the following holds.*

(a) Privacy: The probes can be simulated with d_1 shares of each input and the injected errors.

(b) Correctness: The gadget gives an output with at most k_2 errors.

It is evident that the ININA notions are stronger than the NINA notions, thus the above notions also provide combined security. However, the notion provides directly (d, k)-combined security instead of (d', k')-order combined secure for any $d' + k' \leq d$ and $k' \leq k$. The proof of the following theorem is given in the full version of the paper.

Theorem 3. *A (d,k)-ININA gadget G with input encoding $\mathcal{I}$ and output decoding $\mathcal{O}$ using a secret sharing scheme with passive threshold at least d and active threshold at least k is (d, k)-order combined secure.*

As a result, using the same masking scheme, a SININA secure gadget provides significant improved combined protection over an SNINA secure gadget.

Similar to SNINA, SININA is sufficient for composability. In other words the composition of two SININA gadgets is again SININA (a proof is given in the full version of the paper).

Theorem 4. *The composition of two (d,k)-SININA gadgets is (d,k)-SININA.*

4 Combined Secure Duplicated Boolean Masking

In this section we introduce a combined secure methodology for an arbitrary security order. We work over bits $\mathbb{F}_2$, share values using Boolean secret sharing and encode using duplication. We first quickly introduce the secret sharing scheme and then move on to show our methodology. The security of the gadgets is proven in the full version of the paper.

4.1 Duplicated Boolean Masking

For the proposed countermeasures, we make use of a duplicated Boolean masking approach which shares a secret x as a vector

$$(x_{1,1}, ..., x_{1,k+1}, x_{2,1}, ..., x_{d+1,k+1}),$$

such that $\sum_{i=1}^{d+1} x_{i,\ell} = x$ for all $\ell \in [k+1]$ and $x_{i,1} = ... = x_{i,k+1}$ for all $i \in [d+1]$. This method has a passive threshold d meaning that no d shares give information on the secret x and an active threshold k meaning that any faults on at most k shares could be detected in the share vector.

4.2 Duplicated Boolean Methodology

We recall that our secret sharing scheme has a passive threshold d, meaning that an adversary needs to view at least $d + 1$ shares to recover the secret, and an active threshold k, thus an adversary needs to inject at least $k + 1$ errors for the fault to be undetectable. We note that our methodology is similar to the one from Private Circuits II [24]. The pseudo-code to secret share a value is given in Algorithm 1.

Algorithm 1. Duplicated Boolean sharing a secret a

Input: Secret a and uniform random values r_i
Output: Duplicated Boolean shares of a

> **for** $\ell \leftarrow 1$ **to** $k + 1$ **do**
> > **for** $i \leftarrow 1$ **to** d **do**
> > > $a_{i,\ell} \leftarrow r_i$;
> >
> > **end**
> > $a_{d+1,\ell} \leftarrow a + \sum_{i=1}^{d} a_{i,\ell}$;
>
> **end**

The addition between independent shared variables is quite simple and needs only component-wise addition between the shares. Thus, the addition between the sharing of a and b, giving a sharing of $c = a + b$, is made by $c_{i,\ell} = a_{i,\ell} + b_{i,\ell}$. To secure operations between shares and constants we ensure that the constant is not a single point of failure, as such it also needs to be duplicated, namely each constant is replicated $(k + 1)$ times to form a $(k + 1)$ tuple which is the encoded value of the constant. The addition of a shared value a with a constant c is done by adding the duplicated constant to the duplicated first Boolean share of the variable.

$$\forall \ell \in [k + 1] : \quad a_{1,\ell} \leftarrow a_{1,\ell} + c_\ell$$

A multiplication with a constant is done by multiplying the duplicated constant to each share.

$$\forall i \in [d + 1], \forall \ell \in [k + 1] : \quad a_{i,\ell} \leftarrow a_{i,\ell} \cdot c_\ell$$

Since the above operations are all local, they are evidently (d, k)-NINA.

While linear operations are easily implemented, the multiplication between shared and encoded variables is more difficult. We give pseudo-code of our multiplication gadget in Algorithm 2. The gadget starts by multiplying two independent share vectors of a and b to create all cross products of the form $a_i b_j$. These cross products are then remasked by adding unique randomness $r_{i,j}$ created by an RNG (which is important for the SNI property). Since we add the same randomness over all duplicated cross products ($u_{i,j,\ell}$ for $\ell \in [k+1]$) all these cross products should equal each other if no fault was injected. As a result, we can error check them (which is important for the SNA property).[2] To detect errors in the cross products it is sufficient to compare a share to all its duplicated versions, in symbols:

$$\forall i, j \in [d+1], \forall \ell \in [k+1] : \ u_{i,j,1} = u_{i,j,\ell} \,.$$

Since we are working over bits, this translates to aborting the computation in case one of the $u_{i,j,1} + u_{i,j,\ell}$ is equal to 1. This abort operation is considered as a command causing all variables in the implementation to read $\bot$ as explained in Sect. 2 (in Sect. 4.3, we describe a cascading gadget in case an abort operation is not available). In case no error is detected, the gadget sums up all the cross products for different indices j and returns a duplicated Boolean sharing of ab. The proof that this multiplication procedure is SNINA is given in the full version of the paper. From this proof we see that there is a statistical ineffective fault attack (see [17]) which breaks the privacy of the algorithm. This attack works as follows, the adversary adds a non-zero fault to one of the $a_{i,\ell}$ shares (similarly $b_{i,\ell}$ shares). In case the operation does not abort, the adversary learns that all $b_{i,\ell} = 0$ (similarly all $a_{i,\ell} = 0$), which means the adversary learns an input secret and breaks the privacy of the gadget. The probability for this attack to succeed is equal to $1/|\mathbb{F}_2|^{d+1}$. Due to the attack aborting the computation when it fails, this attack does not threaten the composability of the gadget.[3] To increase the protection against the ineffective fault, the probability for the attack to succeed needs to be made sufficiently small which is done by increasing the number of shares or by increasing the field size $|\mathbb{F}|$. In Sect. 5 we look at an error correcting variant of the multiplication gadget which is not vulnerable to an ineffective fault.

In Algorithm 3 we provide a method to refresh the randomness of a shared variable and check whether there are errors present on its shares. A proof of the SNINA condition of Algorithm 3 is given in the full version of the work. We note that this gadget can be used to transform a NINA secure operation into its SNINA variant by serially composing the NINA gadget with Algorithm 3.

---

[2] Note that if an adversary injects a fault directly in one of the random values $r_{i,j}$, it would not be detected. Nevertheless, the gadget still outputs a valid duplicated Boolean sharing so it does not affect the correctness of the gadget. This fault should be carefully investigated for its effects on the gadget's privacy.

[3] To clarify, the passive threshold of the sharing does not need to increase to assure composability due to the only attack, causing simulator failure, aborting the computation on success.

Algorithm 2. Multiplying duplicated Boolean shared values

Input: Independent shares of a and b, and uniform random $r_{i,j}$
Output: Shares of ab or $\perp$

    for $\ell \leftarrow 1$ **to** $k+1$ **do**
        for $i \leftarrow 1$ **to** $d+1$ **do**
            $u_{i,i,\ell} \leftarrow a_{i,\ell}b_{i,\ell}$;
            for $j \leftarrow i+1$ **to** $d+1$ **do**
                $u_{i,j,\ell} \leftarrow a_{i,\ell}b_{j,\ell} + r_{i,j}$;
                $u_{j,i,\ell} \leftarrow a_{j,\ell}b_{i,\ell} + r_{i,j}$;
            end
        end
    end
    for $\ell \leftarrow 2$ **to** $k+1$ **do**
        for $i \leftarrow 1$ **to** $d+1$ **do**
            for $j \leftarrow 1$ **to** $d+1$ **do**
                $t_{i,j,\ell} \leftarrow u_{i,j,1} + u_{i,j,\ell}$;
                if $t_{i,j,\ell} = 1$ **then return** $\perp$;
            end
        end
    end
    for $\ell \leftarrow 1$ **to** $k+1$ **do**
        for $i \leftarrow 1$ **to** $d+1$ **do**
            $c_{i,\ell} \leftarrow \sum_{j=1}^{d+1} u_{i,j,\ell}$;
        end
    end

This follows from Theorem 5 which states that the serial composition between a NINA gadget and an SNINA gadget is again SNINA. The proof of this theorem is found in the full version of the paper.

Theorem 5. *The serial composition of a single input, output (d,k)-NINA gadget with a (d,k)-SNINA gadget is again (d,k)-SNINA.*

Thus, sometimes one can substitute SNINA gadgets with NINA ones without sacrificing security. This reduces costs as NINA secure gadgets are generally more efficient than their SNINA variants.

Together, all gadgets described in this section form a methodology to secure arbitrary circuits as each algorithm over a finite field can be described in terms of additions and multiplications.

4.3 A Cascading Gadget

In case an abort mechanism is not available, we provide a circuit which erases all data when a fault is detected. This method is similar to the cascading gadget described in [24] and thus we lend its name. We first make variables for the abort

---

Algorithm 3. Refreshing and checking a duplicated Boolean sharing

---

Input: Duplicated Boolean shares of a and uniform random values $r_{i,j}$
Output: Refreshed and checked shares of a or $\perp$

> **for** $\ell \leftarrow 2$ **to** $k+1$ **do**
>> **for** $i \leftarrow 1$ **to** $d+1$ **do**
>>> $t_{i,\ell} \leftarrow a_{i,1} + a_{i,\ell}$;
>>> **if** $t_{i,\ell} = 1$ **then return** $\perp$;
>> **end**
> **end**
> **for** $\ell \leftarrow 1$ **to** $k+1$ **do**
>> **for** $i \leftarrow 1$ **to** $d+1$ **do**
>>> **for** $j \leftarrow i+1$ **to** $d+1$ **do**
>>>> $a_{i,\ell} \leftarrow a_{i,\ell} + r_{i,j}$;
>>>> $a_{j,\ell} \leftarrow a_{j,\ell} + r_{i,j}$;
>>> **end**
>> **end**
> **end**

---

flag, we consider $\perp_\ell$ for $\ell \in [k]$. A priori, all $\perp_\ell$ are equal to zero, however, when a fault is injected we require that each $\perp_\ell$ is set to one. In case the abort flag equals all one, no $k-1$ faults can change each $\perp_\ell$ back to zero. The above described functionality is implemented by duplicating the error checks in Algorithms 2 and 3. For example, the error checking component (the first lines) of Algorithm 3 would be changed to the following.

> **for** $m \leftarrow 1$ **to** k **do**
>> **for** $\ell \leftarrow 2$ **to** $k+1$ **do**
>>> **for** $i \leftarrow 1$ **to** $d+1$ **do**
>>>> $\perp_m \leftarrow (a_{i,1} + a_{i,\ell}) \vee \perp_m$;
>>> **end**
>> **end**
> **end**

From the above algorithm it is clear that in case one of the $a_{i,1}$ does not equal $a_{i,\ell}$, all $\perp_m$ are set to one and no $k-1$ faults can set them all back to zero.

With the above abort flag as a global variable and its functionality as described above, we can easily describe a gadget which erases its input in case a $\perp_m$ is equal to one. We give the pseudo-code of this gadget in Algorithm 4.

In case Algorithm 4 is serially composed with each Algorithm 2 or Algorithm 3, our duplicated Boolean masking methodology is secure against combined attacks without the need of an ideal abort command.

Algorithm 4. Cascading a duplicated Boolean sharing

Input: Shares of a and the abort state $\perp_m$ for $m \in [k]$
Output: The shares of a or all 0

    for $\ell \leftarrow 1$ to $k+1$ do
        for $i \leftarrow 1$ to $d+1$ do
            $a_{i,\ell} \leftarrow a_{i,\ell} \prod_{m=1}^{k}(1 + \perp_m)$;
        end
    end

---

5   A Correcting Multiplication

In the previous section we gave a combined secure methodology based on detecting errors using duplicated Boolean shares. However, Algorithm 2 is vulnerable against a statistical ineffective fault. To avoid this vulnerability one can use an error correction method instead of an error detection one. As there is no longer an abort signal, a fault does not change the state of the output and as a result ineffective faults are now actually ineffective. Note that this comes at the increased cost of using extra shares and operations to enable error correction.

Instead of just replacing the error detection mechanisms with error correction ones, we go one step further and create an error correcting variant of Algorithm 2 which attains Strong Independent NINA security (Definition 14). Whereas Algorithm 2 was secure against d probes and k faults where the combined number of probes and faults do not exceed d, our new algorithm does not require this restriction thus it is secure against up to d probes and k faults at the same time. In other words, a k-active adversary faulting the new multiplication gadget does not harm the privacy of the gadget.

We introduce the error correcting multiplication gadget. We again work over bits $\mathbb{F}_2$, share values using d Boolean secret shares, but now encode using $2k+1$ duplicated shares (instead of $k+1$ shares). As such, the secret sharing scheme has a passive threshold d, meaning that an adversary needs to view at least $d+1$ shares to recover the secret, and an active threshold $2k$, thus an adversary needs to inject at least $k+1$ errors for the fault to be uncorrectable (note the difference with the undetectability of faults). We give the pseudo-code of the multiplication gadget in Algorithm 5. The error correcting gadget works similar to the error detecting one. It starts by multiplying two independent share vectors of a and b to create all cross products. These cross products are then remasked by adding $k+1$ random elements $r_{i,j,\ell}$ to each of them. As a result, since each cross product is masked by $k+1$ random values, no set of k faults can remove all random values on a cross product. Since we add the same randomness over all duplicated cross products ($u_{i,j,\ell}$ for $\ell \in [2k+1]$) all these cross products still equal each other if no fault was injected. As a result, we can error correct them. An error correction on duplicated shares is done by majority voting the shares. If at least $k+1$ out of $2k+1$ cross products were equal to zero, the result of this majority vote is zero otherwise it is equal to one. For brevity, we denote this

---

Algorithm 5. Multiplying shares with error correction

Input: Independent shares of a and b, and uniform random $r_{i,j,\ell}$
Output: Shares of ab

> **for** $\ell \leftarrow 1$ **to** $2k+1$ **do**
>> **for** $i \leftarrow 1$ **to** $d+1$ **do**
>>> $u_{i,i,\ell} \leftarrow a_{i,\ell}b_{i,\ell}$;
>>> **for** $j \leftarrow i+1$ **to** $d+1$ **do**
>>>> $u_{i,j,\ell} \leftarrow a_{i,\ell}b_{j,\ell}$;
>>>> $u_{j,i,\ell} \leftarrow a_{j,\ell}b_{i,\ell}$;
>>>> **for** $m \leftarrow 1$ **to** $k+1$ **do**
>>>>> $u_{i,j,\ell} \leftarrow u_{i,j,\ell} + r_{i,j,m}$;
>>>>> $u_{j,i,\ell} \leftarrow u_{j,i,\ell} + r_{i,j,m}$;
>>>> **end**
>>> **end**
>> **end**
> **end**
> **for** $\ell \leftarrow 1$ **to** $2k+1$ **do**
>> **for** $i \leftarrow 1$ **to** $d+1$ **do**
>>> **for** $j \leftarrow 1$ **to** $d+1$ **do**
>>>> $v_{i,j,\ell} \leftarrow \mathrm{Maj}(u_{i,j,1}, ..., u_{i,j,2k+1})$;
>>> **end**
>> **end**
> **end**
> **for** $\ell \leftarrow 1$ **to** $2k+1$ **do**
>> **for** $i \leftarrow 1$ **to** $d+1$ **do**
>>> $c_{i,\ell} \leftarrow \sum_{j=1}^{d+1} v_{i,j,\ell}$;
>> **end**
> **end**

---

operation "Maj", where we assume for simplicity that a probing adversary can view all arguments given to the Maj function with one probe. We stress that this error correction procedure is independently applied to each cross product, such that a single fault can only affect one cross product. Our multiplication gadget again ends by summing up all the cross products for different indices j and returns a duplicated Boolean sharing of ab. The proof that this multiplication procedure is SININA is given in the full version of the work.

6   Conclusion

We provided security notions considering circuits with probed and/or faulted wires. We then extended them to active and combined composable notions similar to the extension from the probing model to Non-Interference (NI). The first notion of Non-Accumulation (NA) addresses composable active security which states that a gadget is secure if injected faults affect only one output each.

The second is the notion of composable combined security (NINA). A gadget is considered NINA if an injected fault only affects one output and a fault or probe can be simulated using only one input. We discussed both error detection and error correcting gadgets and showed that the error detection mechanism is prone to ineffective faults whereas error correction comes at an increased cost but gives significantly improved protection (Independent NINA).

The notions for composable security offer the ability to efficiently verify building blocks of larger implementations and allow for the search of efficient functions which achieve security in the corresponding model. Moreover, these composable notions enable us to use secured primitives in a larger whole such as modes of operations.

Acknowledgements. The authors would like to thank Thomas De Cnudde, Adrián Ranea, Vincent Rijmen, and Nigel Smart for their useful comments and ideas.

This work was supported in part by the Research Council KU Leuven: C16/18/004, by the NIST Research Grant 60NANB15D346, and by the EU H2020 project FENTEC. Siemen Dhooghe is supported by a Ph.D. Fellowship from the Research Foundation - Flanders (FWO). Svetla Nikova was partially supported by the Bulgarian National Science Fund, Contract No. 12/8.

References

1. Aghaie, A., Moradi, A., Rasoolzadeh, S., Schellenberg, F., Schneider, T.: Impeccable circuits. Cryptology ePrint Archive, Report 2018/203 (2018)
2. Arribas, V., Bilgin, B., Petrides, G., Nikova, S., Rijmen, V.: Rhythmic Keccak: SCA security and low latency in HW. IACR Trans. Cryptogr. Hardw. Embed. Syst. **2018**(1), 269–290 (2018). https://doi.org/10:13154/tches.v2018.i1.269-290
3. Barthe, G., et al.: Strong non-interference and type-directed higher-order masking. In: Weippl, E.R., Katzenbeisser, S., Kruegel, C., Myers, A.C., Halevi, S. (eds.) Proceedings of the 2016 ACM SIGSAC Conference on Computer and Communications Security, Vienna, Austria, 24–28 October 2016, pp. 116–129. ACM (2016). https://doi.org/10.1145/2976749.2978427
4. Barthe, G., Belaïd, S., Fouque, P., Grégoire, B.: maskVerif: a formal tool for analyzing software and hardware masked implementations. IACR Cryptology ePrint Archive 2018, 562 (2018). https://eprint.iacr.org/2018/562
5. Belaïd, S., Benhamouda, F., Passelègue, A., Prouff, E., Thillard, A., Vergnaud, D.: Randomness complexity of private circuits for multiplication. In: Fischlin, M., Coron, J.-S. (eds.) EUROCRYPT 2016. LNCS, vol. 9666, pp. 616–648. Springer, Heidelberg (2016). https://doi.org/10.1007/978-3-662-49896-5_22
6. Belaïd, S., Benhamouda, F., Passelègue, A., Prouff, E., Thillard, A., Vergnaud, D.: Private multiplication over finite fields. In: Katz, J., Shacham, H. (eds.) CRYPTO 2017. LNCS, vol. 10403, pp. 397–426. Springer, Cham (2017). https://doi.org/10.1007/978-3-319-63697-9_14
7. Belaïd, S., Goudarzi, D., Rivain, M.: Tight private circuits: achieving probing security with the least refreshing. In: Peyrin, T., Galbraith, S. (eds.) ASIACRYPT 2018. LNCS, vol. 11273, pp. 343–372. Springer, Cham (2018). https://doi.org/10.1007/978-3-030-03329-3_12

8. Biham, E., Shamir, A.: Differential fault analysis of secret key cryptosystems. In: Kaliski, B.S. (ed.) CRYPTO 1997. LNCS, vol. 1294, pp. 513–525. Springer, Heidelberg (1997). https://doi.org/10.1007/BFb0052259

9. Cassiers, G., Standaert, F.: Improved bitslice masking: from optimized non-interference to probe isolation. IACR Cryptology ePrint Archive 2018, 438 (2018). https://eprint.iacr.org/2018/438

10. Chari, S., Jutla, C.S., Rao, J.R., Rohatgi, P.: Towards sound approaches to counteract power-analysis attacks. In: Wiener, M. (ed.) CRYPTO 1999. LNCS, vol. 1666, pp. 398–412. Springer, Heidelberg (1999). https://doi.org/10.1007/3-540-48405-1_26

11. Clavier, C.: Secret external encodings do not prevent transient fault analysis. In: Paillier, P., Verbauwhede, I. (eds.) CHES 2007. LNCS, vol. 4727, pp. 181–194. Springer, Heidelberg (2007). https://doi.org/10.1007/978-3-540-74735-2_13

12. Coron, J.-S.: High-order conversion from Boolean to arithmetic masking. In: Fischer, W., Homma, N. (eds.) CHES 2017. LNCS, vol. 10529, pp. 93–114. Springer, Cham (2017). https://doi.org/10.1007/978-3-319-66787-4_5

13. Coron, J.-S.: Formal verification of side-channel countermeasures via elementary circuit transformations. In: Preneel, B., Vercauteren, F. (eds.) ACNS 2018. LNCS, vol. 10892, pp. 65–82. Springer, Cham (2018). https://doi.org/10.1007/978-3-319-93387-0_4

14. De Cnudde, T., Nikova, S.: More efficient private circuits II through threshold implementations. In: 2016 Workshop on Fault Diagnosis and Tolerance in Cryptography, FDTC 2016, Santa Barbara, CA, USA, 16 August 2016, pp. 114–124. IEEE Computer Society (2016). https://doi.org/10.1109/FDTC.2016.15

15. De Cnudde, T., Reparaz, O., Bilgin, B., Nikova, S., Nikov, V., Rijmen, V.: Masking AES with $d+1$ shares in hardware. In: Gierlichs, B., Poschmann, A.Y. (eds.) CHES 2016. LNCS, vol. 9813, pp. 194–212. Springer, Heidelberg (2016). https://doi.org/10.1007/978-3-662-53140-2_10

16. Dhooghe, S., Nikova, S.: My gadget just cares for me - how NINA can prove security against combined attacks. IACR Cryptology ePrint Archive 2019, 615 (2019). https://eprint.iacr.org/2019/615

17. Dobraunig, C., Eichlseder, M., Korak, T., Mangard, S., Mendel, F., Primas, R.: SIFA: exploiting ineffective fault inductions on symmetric cryptography. IACR Trans. Cryptogr. Hardw. Embed. Syst. **2018**(3), 547–572 (2018)

18. Duc, A., Dziembowski, S., Faust, S.: Unifying leakage models: from probing attacks to noisy leakage. In: Nguyen, P.Q., Oswald, E. (eds.) EUROCRYPT 2014. LNCS, vol. 8441, pp. 423–440. Springer, Heidelberg (2014). https://doi.org/10.1007/978-3-642-55220-5_24

19. Faust, S., Grosso, V., Pozo, S.M.D., Paglialonga, C., Standaert, F.: Composable masking schemes in the presence of physical defaults & the robust probing model. IACR Trans. Cryptogr. Hardw. Embed. Syst. **2018**(3), 89–120 (2018). https://doi.org/10.13154/tches.v2018.i3.89-120

20. Gollmann, D.: Computer Security, 3 edn. Wiley (2011). http://eu.wiley.com/WileyCDA/WileyTitle/productCd-1118801326.html

21. Goubin, L., Patarin, J.: DES and differential power analysis the "Duplication" method. In: Koç, Ç.K., Paar, C. (eds.) CHES 1999. LNCS, vol. 1717, pp. 158–172. Springer, Heidelberg (1999). https://doi.org/10.1007/3-540-48059-5_15

22. Groß, H., Mangard, S., Korak, T.: Domain-oriented masking: compact masked hardware implementations with arbitrary protection order. In: Bilgin, B., Nikova, S., Rijmen, V. (eds.) Proceedings of the ACM Workshop on Theory of Implementation Security, TIS@CCS 2016 Vienna, Austria, October 2016, p. 3. ACM (2016). https://doi.org/10.1145/2996366.2996426

23. Groß, H., Schaffenrath, D., Mangard, S.: Higher-order side-channel protected implementations of KECCAK. In: Kubátová, H., Novotný, M., Skavhaug, A. (eds.) Euromicro Conference on Digital System Design, DSD 2017, Vienna, Austria, 30 August–1 September 2017, pp. 205–212. IEEE Computer Society (2017). https://doi.org/10.1109/DSD.2017.21

24. Ishai, Y., Prabhakaran, M., Sahai, A., Wagner, D.: Private circuits II: keeping secrets in tamperable circuits. In: Vaudenay, S. (ed.) EUROCRYPT 2006. LNCS, vol. 4004, pp. 308–327. Springer, Heidelberg (2006). https://doi.org/10.1007/11761679_19

25. Ishai, Y., Sahai, A., Wagner, D.: Private circuits: securing hardware against probing attacks. In: Boneh, D. (ed.) CRYPTO 2003. LNCS, vol. 2729, pp. 463–481. Springer, Heidelberg (2003). https://doi.org/10.1007/978-3-540-45146-4_27

26. Kocher, P., Jaffe, J., Jun, B.: Differential power analysis. In: Wiener, M. (ed.) CRYPTO 1999. LNCS, vol. 1666, pp. 388–397. Springer, Heidelberg (1999). https://doi.org/10.1007/3-540-48405-1_25

27. Moradi, A., Poschmann, A., Ling, S., Paar, C., Wang, H.: Pushing the limits: a very compact and a threshold implementation of AES. In: Paterson, K.G. (ed.) EUROCRYPT 2011. LNCS, vol. 6632, pp. 69–88. Springer, Heidelberg (2011). https://doi.org/10.1007/978-3-642-20465-4_6

28. Nikova, S., Rechberger, C., Rijmen, V.: Threshold implementations against side-channel attacks and glitches. In: Ning, P., Qing, S., Li, N. (eds.) ICICS 2006. LNCS, vol. 4307, pp. 529–545. Springer, Heidelberg (2006). https://doi.org/10.1007/11935308_38

29. Poschmann, A., Moradi, A., Khoo, K., Lim, C., Wang, H., Ling, S.: Side-channel resistant crypto for less than 2, 300 GE. J. Cryptol. 24(2), 322–345 (2011). https://doi.org/10.1007/s00145-010-9086-6

30. Prouff, E., Rivain, M.: Masking against side-channel attacks: a formal security proof. In: Johansson, T., Nguyen, P.Q. (eds.) EUROCRYPT 2013. LNCS, vol. 7881, pp. 142–159. Springer, Heidelberg (2013). https://doi.org/10.1007/978-3-642-38348-9_9

31. Reparaz, O., et al.: CAPA: the spirit of beaver against physical attacks. In: Shacham, H., Boldyreva, A. (eds.) CRYPTO 2018. LNCS, vol. 10991, pp. 121–151. Springer, Cham (2018). https://doi.org/10.1007/978-3-319-96884-1_5

32. Rivain, M., Prouff, E.: Provably secure higher-order masking of AES. In: Mangard, S., Standaert, F.-X. (eds.) CHES 2010. LNCS, vol. 6225, pp. 413–427. Springer, Heidelberg (2010). https://doi.org/10.1007/978-3-642-15031-9_28

33. Schneider, T., Moradi, A., Güneysu, T.: ParTI – towards combined hardware countermeasures against side-channel and fault-injection attacks. In: Robshaw, M., Katz, J. (eds.) CRYPTO 2016. LNCS, vol. 9815, pp. 302–332. Springer, Heidelberg (2016). https://doi.org/10.1007/978-3-662-53008-5_11

34. Ueno, R., Homma, N., Sugawara, Y., Nogami, Y., Aoki, T.: Highly efficient $GF(2^8)$ inversion circuit based on redundant GF arithmetic and its application to AES design. In: Güneysu, T., Handschuh, H. (eds.) CHES 2015. LNCS, vol. 9293, pp. 63–80. Springer, Heidelberg (2015). https://doi.org/10.1007/978-3-662-48324-4_4

Modeling Memory Faults in Signature and Authenticated Encryption Schemes

Marc Fischlin[1] and Felix Günther[2(✉)]

[1] Cryptoplexity, Technische Universität Darmstadt, Darmstadt, Germany
`marc.fischlin@cryptoplexity.de`
[2] Department of Computer Science, ETH Zürich, Zürich, Switzerland
`mail@felixguenther.info`

Abstract. Memory fault attacks, inducing errors in computations, have been an ever-evolving threat to cryptographic schemes since their discovery for cryptography by Boneh et al. (Eurocrypt 1997). Initially requiring physical tampering with hardware, the software-based rowhammer attack put forward by Kim et al. (ISCA 2014) enabled fault attacks also through malicious software running on the same host machine. This led to concerning novel attack vectors, for example on deterministic signature schemes, whose approach to avoid dependency on (good) randomness renders them vulnerable to fault attacks. This has been demonstrated in realistic adversarial settings in a series of recent works. However, a unified formalism of different memory fault attacks, enabling also to argue the security of countermeasures, is missing yet.

In this work, we suggest a generic extension for existing security models that enables a game-based treatment of cryptographic fault resilience. Our modeling specifies exemplary memory fault attack types of different strength, ranging from random bit-flip faults to differential (rowhammer-style) faults to full adversarial control on indicated memory variables. We apply our model first to deterministic signatures to revisit known fault attacks as well as to establish provable guarantees of fault resilience for proposed fault-attack countermeasures. In a second application to nonce-misuse resistant authenticated encryption, we provide the first fault-attack treatment of the SIV mode of operation and give a provably secure fault-resilient variant.

Keywords: Fault attacks · Security model · Fault resilience · Deterministic signatures · Nonce-misuse resistant authenticated encryption

1 Introduction

Since their first treatment in the cryptographic realm by Boneh, DeMillo, and Lipton [20] in 1997, fault attacks (i.e., attacks that induce unexpected disturbances during computations) have evolved as an important class of attacks to

© Springer Nature Switzerland AG 2020
S. Jarecki (Ed.): CT-RSA 2020, LNCS 12006, pp. 56–84, 2020.
https://doi.org/10.1007/978-3-030-40186-3_4

assess the strength of cryptographic systems. While the possibility of faults accidentally occurring in hardware chips was already known in the 1970s [42], the work by Boneh et al. as well as others [20,39] demonstrated that faults can have devastating effects on the security of cryptographic systems, more specifically RSA and other signatures making use of the Chinese Remainder Theorem. The attack by Boneh, DeMillo, and Lipton inspired—beginning with Biham and Shamir introducing differential fault analysis [18]—a long line of research on different types of fault attacks challenging the security of cryptographic systems. These in particular encompass a wealth of different hardware tampering attacks, ranging from manipulation of the system's voltage, clock, or temperature to electromagnetic disturbances or laser irradiation (see, e.g., [3,4] for an overview).

For a long time, countermeasures against fault attacks focused on making the cryptographic hardware tamper-resilient (or tamper-proof). In 2014 however, a break-through research result by Kim et al. [40] demonstrated that faults can be remotely injected in modern hardware through software access only. More specifically, their attack leveraged that high-frequency repeated read/write operations to some memory address ("hammering") in DRAM memory may induce disturbance errors in other nearby addresses. Kim et al. described how in a so-called *rowhammer attack* a malicious process can induce controlled disturbances (i.e., bit flips as differential faults) in the memory of another process, circumventing the memory isolation security mechanisms of the computing system. In follow-up work, the rowhammer attack was refined further. Specifically, Razavi et al. [50] improved the attack in a way that enabled flipping individual bits in nearby memory in a fine-grained manner, even across the boundaries of virtual machines hosted on the same hardware.

It does not come as a surprise that software fault attacks like rowhammer can have critical security implications for cryptographic systems. Razavi et al. [50] already demonstrated how bit-flipping attacks in RSA public-keys stored by the SSH protocol for authentication [61] enable easy factorization and thereby break the authentication system. More recently, Poddebniak et al. [48] formalized rowhammer-style attacks that specifically target the setting of deterministic signature schemes, opening up a new type of attack vector in this area.

Deterministic signature schemes emerged from the insight that good randomness might not always be available in the signing process due to failures in the random number generation. This may be due to restricted hardware settings where no good randomness source is available or a result of badly implemented or flawed random number generators [24,28,34,36]. In such cases, signature schemes like DSA or ECDSA [46] that crucially rely on good per-message randomness in the signing process will fail catastrophically. Prominent incident examples include the compromise of the ECDSA signature keys for Sony's Playstation 3 [30] or key leaks in cryptocurrencies [21,22].

To obviate the dependency on good randomness in the signing process, M'Raïhi et al. [44] put forward the concept of making signature schemes deterministic through what we call *de-randomization*. The idea is to replace the ephemeral randomness sampled in the signing process by the output of a random oracle [14] evaluated on the secret signing key and the message to be signed. This way, no genuine randomness source is required for signing while the used input remains uniformly random from the perspective of an adversary without knowledge of the secret signing key. The de-randomizing approach has been widely adopted, e.g., in the specification of deterministic versions of DSA and ECDSA through RFC 6979 [49] or upfront in the design of the EdDSA signature algorithm proposed by Bernstein et al. [16].

Poddebniak et al. [48] now show that the introduced determinism in such schemes enables new kinds of fault attacks. More specifically, they formalize how rowhammer-style attacks can be deployed to recover signing keys by injecting faults in the deterministic computation of ECDSA and EdDSA signatures. This is done in such a way that two signatures on two different messages are computed (one original, and one resulting from the memory fault attack), but with the signing algorithm (re-)using the same per-message random nonce. They then demonstrate the practical feasibility of their attacks on an EdDSA implementation in a realistic setting across virtual machines.

In their work, Poddebniak et al. [48, Section 9] touch upon a number of countermeasures. Notably, they specifically highlight that the commonly suggested countermeasure to verify the signature before releasing it in order to check correctness of the computation [20,41] turns out to be ineffective in protecting against their attack: the resulting signature is actually valid for the message modified through the fault attack. They conclude that the only cryptographic mechanism that would render their attack infeasible is to re-integrate randomness in the signing process *in addition* to the deterministically derived per-message nonce. This supports the design of the XEdDSA signature scheme by Perrin [47] deployed in the Signal secure messaging protocol [58], which augments the EdDSA nonce derivation with an additional random value in order to protect against glitches in the computation, referring to an observation by Schmidt [57].

In several works concurrent and closely related to that by Poddebniak et al. [48], Romailler and Pelissier [54], Ambrose et al. [1], as well as Samwel et al. [55,56] studied differential fault and side-channel attacks on deterministic signatures in general and the ECDSA and EdDSA schemes specifically, also revisiting a previous result by Barenghi and Pelosi [5]. Notably, all works agree that adding randomness back into the signing process is necessary in order to prevent the described fault attacks. Indeed, the lattice-based signature proposals qTesla[1] and Dilithium[2] for NIST's post-quantum standardization process both include now a randomized version in the second round update because of the attacks.

Contributions. At this point, the current state of understanding of memory fault attacks (on deterministic signatures and more generally) leaves us with

---

[1] https://qtesla.org/.

[2] https://pq-crystals.org/.

the questions of how to formally capture different types of memory faults and relate their strength, and how to assess whether proposed attack countermeasures indeed provide security against certain classes of fault attacks. In this work, we approach an answer to these questions through establishing a generalized game-based security model capturing cryptographic fault resilience. We then apply this model to recapitulate the fault attacks discussed, establish provable security results for proposed countermeasures, and derive novel measures for the setting of nonce-based authenticated encryption.

Security Model Extension for Fault Resilience. We introduce, in Sect. 2, a game-based framework for extending existing security models in order to capture memory fault attacks resp. resilience against such attacks. Our approach generalizes fault attacks of different strength on memory variables through a modeling technique akin to callback functions in programming languages. The specific types we define range from full adversarial control to controlled (rowhammer-style) bit flips to random faults, both transient and persistent; further types of memory fault attacks can be easily captured in our formalism.

As a result, our security model on the one hand allows us to formalize weaknesses in a cryptographic scheme through describing memory fault attacks as an abstract set of adversarial interactions with the scheme. On the other hand, the model enables us to positively establish provable security results for the fault resilience of a scheme against well-defined classes of fault attacks. We will use our model in the former way to demonstrate how known memory fault attacks are reflected in the model. In the latter way, we employ it to evaluate the provable security guarantees of potential countermeasures reconciling weak-randomness and fault-attack protection.

Fault Resilience of Signatures. We then apply our model (in Sect. 3) to assess the fault resilience of digital signature schemes. To this end, we first augment the classical notion of unforgeability with our security model extension to capture memory fault attacks. A key point in the augmented model is to attribute the signature to a message, because the adversary may alter the message content during the signing process. The extension enables us to formally restate the concept of above fault attacks on deterministic signatures [1,48,54,56] in terms of our security model, as a sanity check for our modeling so to speak.

More importantly, we then formalize the proposed countermeasure to include additional randomness in the signature generation process along with potential fault-attack vectors. One countermeasure, used in XEdDSA, is to derive the necessary randomness for signing by applying a pseudorandom function to the message, but also mixing in a random value in this pseudorandom function evaluation. An alternative countermeasure is to compute the exclusive-or of the pseudorandom value with the random string. We are able to formally establish that both approaches indeed achieve the desired goal of providing combined security: achieving fault resilience when good randomness is present while upholding regular security of a de-randomized scheme under arbitrarily weak randomness.

Fault Resilience of Authenticated Encryption. Finally, we demonstrate the generality of our security model extension by applying it to another setting (in Sect. 4), namely that of nonce-based and nonce-misuse resistant authenticated encryption [51–53]. Somewhat similar to the setting of deterministic signatures, nonces were introduced to authenticated encryption schemes in order to obviate the need for randomness in the encryption process, again for (good) randomness not always being available.

There has been some preliminary work on fault attacks on nonce-based authenticated encryption (e.g., [26,27]). To the best of our knowledge, we however provide the first fault-attack treatment of the SIV mode of operation proposed by Rogaway and Shrimpton [53], aiming also at nonce-misuse resistance. Unfortunately, the SIV mode does not provide any fault resilience even under the weakest types of (random single-bit flip) fault attacks in our model. However, we can show that translating concepts similar to the additional-randomness countermeasure for deterministic signatures allows us to derive a randomness-augmented mode SIV$ which provides strong misuse-resistant authenticated encryption security while protecting against differential fault attacks.

Further Related Work. Faults in cryptographic schemes and formal ways of establishing fault resilience have been studied in different settings before. Ishai et al. [37] model faults in gate-wise computations in (conducting) circuits, focusing rather on hardware than on memory-based faults like rowhammer. Their approach ensures security through "self-destructing circuits," whereas our model aims at upholding functionality *and* security under a defined class of faults. Faults in (memory) variables of cryptographic schemes have been considered by Coron and Mandal [25] in their provable-security model tailored to random faults in RSA signatures. Barthe et al. [6] treated non-random fault attacks on RSA in a model generalizing attacks from [32]. Extending the principle idea of provable-security treatment of memory-variable faults, we provide a generic security model capturing general memory faults in arbitrary cryptographic primitives.

Memory-based fault attacks like rowhammer can also be used to modify the *control flow* of programs (through return addresses and the like). Similar tampering with program control flow is possible through a range of hardware tampering, in cases enabling fine-grained instruction skipping [3,4]. This naturally also effects cryptographic implementations (see, e.g., attacks on elliptic curve cryptography [17,19,59]) and could potentially be seen as an extreme, transient form of algorithm substitution attacks [13]. It remains unclear how cryptographic schemes themselves can counter control-flow faults, and thus in this work we focus on faults modifying their *data* residing in memory.

Related-key attack (RKA) security [12,33] studies fault attacks in a setting where faults are restricted to the key material of cryptographic primitives, bound to a class of related-key deriving functions. While RKA security can be a building block for achieving strong fault resilience, our model more generally considers memory faults of various types that affect arbitrary memory variables. We leave studying the detailed relationship between RKA security notions and memory fault resilience as a possible avenue for future work.

As remarked above, one of the challenges for signature schemes is to link the signature to a message, because the message may change during the signing process. The notion of incremental cryptography [10] faces a similar problem of attributing signature creations to messages in a setting where the adversary may tamper with the input. The idea of incremental signature schemes is to sign a message from scratch, and when the message is later slightly edited, one is able to update the signature fast by accessing only a few message blocks. In a strong notion for virus protection [11], Bellare et al. consider the possibility that the adversary may alter the message before making an update call to create a new signature. Since the update algorithm can only access a bounded number of message blocks it cannot check validity of the entire message and potentially works on a substituted message. From a security viewpoint this too raises the question which message one assigns to the derived signature. Bellare et al. [11] correlate the unaltered message which the signer would have expected to the signature.

Note that incremental signatures on the one hand touch a simpler problem than in our case. This is so because, there, the adversary can change the message only once, before calling the signature creation. In contrast, our adversary may continuously provide different values during the signing process, every time the data is accessed. At the same time our case does not deal with fast updates and may read the entire message. When adapting our fault-resilience model to the setting of signatures in Sect. 3.1, we will see that with introduced faults, the challenge message-signature pair to record turns out to be the (at most) one valid combination seen among all faulted variables.

In the setting of hedged public-key encryption as introduced by Bellare et al. [7], similar combiner techniques are employed as in the countermeasures reconciling weak-randomness and fault-attack protection for deterministic signatures and authenticated encryption we discuss in Sects. 3.3 and 4.3. We leave it as an open question for future work to study whether such techniques enable fault-resilient security for hedged public-key encryption, too.

Concurrent Work. In concurrent and independent work, Aranha et al. [2] studied the security of hedged randomness derivation in Fiat-Shamir–type signatures under fault attacks. Focusing on the Fiat-Shamir transform, they treat tailored (memory) fault types occurring in such design and particularly study Schnorr signatures as well as the NIST post-quantum signature candidate Picnic2[3]. Their model considers a limited adversary capable of injecting (only) a single fault as setting or flipping a single bit in a function input or output. Our approach is more generic, introducing a generic extension to capture arbitrary and strong memory fault attacks in any cryptographic scheme. Beyond also studying signatures and their de-randomization and hedging as prime practical

---

[3] https://microsoft.github.io/Picnic/.

example, we exemplify this generality by furthermore treating nonce-misuse–resistant authenticated encryption in our framework.

2 Modeling Fault Resilience

We begin with developing our generic security model extension for capturing memory fault attacks on cryptographic primitives. Such attacks arise through various means in practice and may range from single or few random bit-flips over rowhammer-style controlled flips of one or several bits to full control over the memory enabling injection of arbitrary values. Their effects may be transient and vanish after some subsequent memory access, or a persistent change to the affected bits in memory. In the security model extension we propose in the following, we capture all these different types of faults in a generic manner and formally relate their strength.

At the heart of our model is the observation that while memory fault attacks may be executed at arbitrary points during an execution, they come into effect only when variables are *read* from memory. We therefore capture the adversary's capability to induce faults (of various types) into memory by providing it with means to influence variable values when an algorithm reads them from memory (i.e., uses them). Technically, we model such influence by introducing *callbacks* to the adversary whenever a variable x is used within an algorithm. Resembling callback functions in programming languages, an adversary is then given the option to *alter* (i.e., fault) the value read/used for this variable.

The ways the adversary is allowed to alter the variable reflects the type of fault attack in consideration: In a *full fault* attack the adversary can provide an arbitrary value to be used. In a *differential fault* attack (flipping bits in a controlled way, as in the rowhammer attack [40,50]), the adversary instead provides a bitstring to be XORed to the variable it is used (while not learning the resulting value itself). In a fault attack introducing *random faults*, the adversary finally can merely choose how many bits to be flipped (with neither control over the position nor obtaining the resulting value). In all cases, the introduced fault can be either *transient*, applying only to the one read operation faulted, or *persistent*, in which case the variable is overwritten with the faulted value.

Our model does not fix one type of fault attack, but flexibly allows to consider different attack types for each individual memory variables in a scheme. This captures that some memory variables may be harder to fault than others, e.g., for being shorter (and thus more difficult to target with rowhammer-style bit flips) or residing in specially-protected memory. To enable this flexibility, we first of all explicitly indicate in syntax that some memory variable x is considered to be faultable by writing it as $\lfloor x \rfloor$ with corner brackets when assigned. We then indicate positions where a variable x can be faulted, modeled through an adversarial callback, by writing its usage as $\langle x \rangle$ within angle brackets. This finally enables security statements that formalize individual fault attacks on each annotated variable. For example, we can that way capture an attacker injecting (in the same attack) differential fault attacks into some variable x and random fault attacks into some other variable y.

Applying our security model extension to existing game-based security definitions yields notions that capture the original type of security under the considered fault attacks. To this end, the cryptographic scheme under consideration is augmented by adding indications for faultable memory variables (e.g., $\llcorner x \lrcorner$) and callbacks (e.g., $\langle x \rangle$) in its algorithm descriptions. The actual security experiments remain syntactically largely unchanged, but now incorporate adversarial faulting access to memory variables as indicated by the scheme.

Observe that while the extended security model's dependency on the particular implementation and memory variable layout of a scheme might, at first glance, seem to yield a somewhat dedicated security result, such dependency is ultimately not surprising: the (non-)vulnerability of a scheme to memory fault attacks inevitably depends on the handling of memory variables. At the same time, abstract cryptographic algorithm representations are still reasonably close to their implementation in terms of memory variables, and our model captures strong and fine-grained adversarial faults on those variables.

A noteworthy change in the augmented security experiment however may regularly be required in the evaluation of winning conditions and permissible queries. As the latter may rely on faultable variables, we need to define which of possibly several values of the now changing variable to use when evaluating such conditions. For this purpose, our extension further provides access to the list of values that each faultable variable took within some algorithm: we write x_{Alg} for the sequential list of values that variable x took within some previously invoked algorithm Alg. The unforgeability experiment for signatures detailed in Sect. 3 is an example for such a modified winning condition. There, we will make use of the list m_{Sign} containing all values of the message variable m used within the signing algorithm to define the list of original signatures the adversary obtained through the signing oracle.

2.1   Fault Types

For our security model extension, we explicitly specify four different types of faults that an adversary may inject, and further distinguish between transient and persistent faults. We however stress that the model itself is generic and can be extended to encompass further fault types if desired.

On any read of a faultable variable x indicated by a callback $\langle x \rangle$, the adversary $\mathcal{A}$ is invoked with an identifier for the read variable, indicated by $\mathcal{A}(\langle x \rangle)$. ($\mathcal{A}$ implicitly keeps state between callbacks.) Note that this identifier is merely a handle in order for $\mathcal{A}$ to know *which variable* the callback is for, but without learning the *variable value* itself. Of course, the adversary knows the scheme's code itself; we furthermore let the handle for a variable also disclose the variable's bit-length to $\mathcal{A}$. In case of *transient* faults, the callback only temporarily modifies the value read for this variable for this specific read operation, but does not alter the variable itself beyond that. I.e., several transient-fault callbacks $\langle x \rangle$ on some variable x are always with respect to the original, non-faulted variable value of x. In contrast, for *persistent* faults, the callback modifies the variable in memory, which then also is used for the actual read operation.

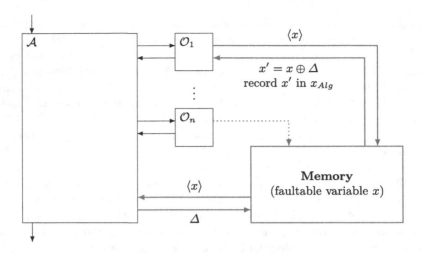

Fig. 1. Illustration of how our proposed extension for fault resilience (on the right in blue) integrates through callbacks with the interaction of an adversary $\mathcal{A}$ and oracles $\mathcal{O}_1, \ldots, \mathcal{O}_n$ within some classical security experiment (on the left in black). As an example, we depict the callback query $\langle x \rangle$ and response for a transient differential fault on some variable x. (Color figure online)

Beyond the distinction between transient and persistent faults, the fault-injection callback $\langle x \rangle$ for some variable x behaves differently for each fault type as described in the following and formalized in Fig. 2. We further illustrate the integration of our callback-based model with an existing security experiment at the example of a transient differential fault attack in Fig. 1.

Full faults: In a full fault attack, the adversary is allowed to arbitrarily modify the faulted memory variable x.[4] This is modeled by giving the adversary full control over the variable whenever it is read.

Differential faults: In a differential-fault attack, the adversary can flip (up to) a certain number $w \in \mathbb{N}$ of bits in the faulted memory variable x in a controlled way. This is modeled by having the adversary supply a difference value Δ which is then XORed to the variable value whenever read, where the Hamming weight $\mathsf{hw}(\Delta)$ of the difference value must not exceed w. As a shorthand, whenever $w \geq |x|$, we omit w.

Random faults: In a random-fault attack, the adversary can flip (up to) a certain number $N \in \mathbb{N}$ of random bits in the faulted memory variable, without controlling which bits are flipped. This is modeled by letting the adversary specify a number $n \leq N$ whenever the variable is read and then flip n randomly positioned bits of the variable value in the callback response. As a shorthand, whenever $N \geq |x|$, we omit N.

No faults: For completeness, we also specify a "no-fault" behavior of the variable callback (directly returning x), which enables formal comparisons of

---

[4] The adversary can opt to not modify the variable by returning a special symbol $\bot$.

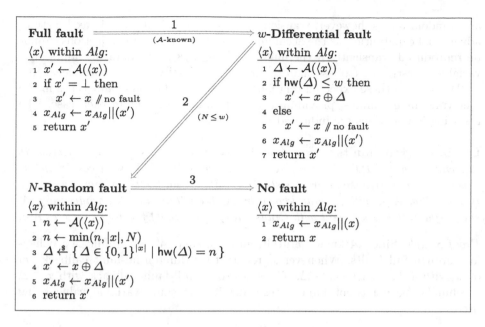

Fig. 2. Specification of and implications between the four fault types: full faults, (w-)differential faults, (N-)random faults, and no faults. In case of a persistent fault, the returned value also overwrites the variable value. Implication arrows are annotated with the respective lemma (above) and conditions (below).

classical security notions within the same notational framework. In general, we omit annotating callbacks for non-faulted variables, though.

2.2 Relations

It is not surprising that full faults represent the strongest fault attacks in our model on memory variables known by the adversary at the time of the callback, e.g., some public parameter or a message input provided to a signing algorithm by $\mathcal{A}$. An adversary can capture any other fault behavior on such variables (which we call "$\mathcal{A}$-known") by providing the resulting faulted variable value directly. Note that this is not true for memory variables unknown to the adversary (e.g., the secret-key input to a signing algorithm): for such variables, the capability to flip bits is incomparable in power to overwriting the value with an adversarially-chosen one.

Furthermore, differential faults imply random faults for $N \leq w$, as the adversary can sample a difference value Δ encoding $n \leq N$ random bit flips on its own, which has permissible Hamming weight $\mathsf{hw}(\Delta) = n \leq N \leq w$. Finally, all fault types imply no faulting, as each allow the choice to leave the variable value unchanged.

Regarding the relations between transient and persistent faults, both variants are trivially equivalent for the full and no-fault types. In the case of differential and random faults, however, transient and persistent faults are indeed distinct adversarial capabilities, as the accumulation of persistent fault injections cannot be reproduced transiently if the number of bit flips or random bit faults on a variable is restricted (to less than $|x|$ for a differentially-faulted variable x).

We capture these expected relations between the different fault types in the following three lemmas, providing a brief formal argument in each case. The resulting implications are indicated by arrows in Fig. 2.[5]

Lemma 1 (Full faults $\overset{(\mathcal{A}\text{-known})}{\Longrightarrow}$ w-differential faults). *For any security experiment, any PPT adversary $\mathcal{A}$, and any $w \in \mathbb{N}$, if $\mathcal{A}$ is successful in the experiment with (transient or persistent) w-differential faults on some variable x in algorithm Alg, with x being known by $\mathcal{A}$, then there exists an adversary $\mathcal{A}'$ successful in the experiment with (transient or persistent) full faults on x in Alg.*

Proof Sketch. Since $\mathcal{A}$ knows x itself, an adversary $\mathcal{A}'$ can mimic $\mathcal{A}$'s behavior through full faults. Whenever $\mathcal{A}$ replies to a differential-fault callback $\langle x \rangle$ on x with a difference value Δ, $\mathcal{A}'$ replies to its full-fault callback with $x \oplus \Delta$ (accumulating persistent faults), resulting in the same variable value being used. □

Lemma 2 (w-differential faults $\overset{(N \leq w)}{\Longrightarrow}$ N-random faults). *For any security experiment, any PPT adversary $\mathcal{A}$, and any $w, N \in \mathbb{N}$ with $N \leq w$, if $\mathcal{A}$ is successful in the experiment with transient (resp. persistent) N-random faults on some variable x in algorithm Alg, then there exists an adversary $\mathcal{A}'$ successful in the experiment with transient (resp. persistent) w-differential faults on x in Alg.*

Proof Sketch. Observe that $\mathcal{A}'$ can mimic $\mathcal{A}$'s behavior as follows: whenever $\mathcal{A}$ replies with some value $n \leq N$ to a random-fault callback $\langle x \rangle$ on x, $\mathcal{A}'$ instead samples n distinct random positions $p_1, \ldots, p_n \overset{\$}{\leftarrow} \{1, \ldots, |x|\}$ and replies with a difference value $\Delta \in \{0,1\}^{|x|}$ which is the all-zero string except for bit positions $p_1, \ldots, p_n$. Such response results in the same variable value and is permissible as $\mathsf{hw}(\Delta) = n \leq N \leq w$. This strategy works both in the transient and in the persistent fault setting. In the persistent case, the differential faults of $\mathcal{A}'$ accumulate, correctly mimicking the accumulating random faults of $\mathcal{A}$. □

Lemma 3 (Full/w-differential/N-random faults $\Longrightarrow$ no faults). *For any security experiment, any PPT adversary $\mathcal{A}$, and any $w, N \in \mathbb{N}$, if $\mathcal{A}$ is successful in the experiment without faults on some variable x in algorithm Alg, then there exist adversaries $\mathcal{A}'$, $\mathcal{A}''$, and $\mathcal{A}'''$ successful in the experiment with (transient or persistent) full faults, w-differential faults, resp. N-random faults on x in Alg.*

---

[5] One can also argue that the notions form a strict hierarchy (i.e., that the reverse implications do not hold), if used to attack cryptographic schemes. E.g., bending an $\mathcal{A}$-known λ-bit string x to some random string r (say, to trigger randomness reuse in a scheme) is easily achieved via full faults, but only with probability $2^{-\lambda/2}$ for differential faults with $w = \lambda/2$. Similarly, flipping $w = \lambda/2$ bits in x to 0 is easy with w-differential faults, but hard with random faults.

Proof Sketch. In the case of full faults, $\mathcal{A}'$ can mimic $\mathcal{A}$'s behavior by always returning the special symbol $\bot$ on a callback $\langle x \rangle$. In the case of differential faults, $\mathcal{A}'$ mimics the behavior by always replying with the zero-string $\Delta = 0^{|x|}$ to $\langle x \rangle$. In the case of random faults, $\mathcal{A}'$ does so by always replying 0 to $\langle x \rangle$. $\square$

3   Fault-Resilient Signatures

As the first application of our security model extension, we consider fault attacks against signature schemes and study the resilience of different designs against such attacks. We begin by augmenting the classical security notions for existential and strong unforgeability under chosen-message attacks for signatures with our extension to capture fault resilience, as described in Sect. 2. We then study the effects of faults specifically on a de-randomized (deterministic) signature schemes and analyze to which extent the proposed countermeasure to include additional randomness [1,48,54,56] provably provides fault resilience.

3.1   Fault-Resilient Signature Unforgeability

When augmenting the security notion for classical signature unforgeability, the essential question to answer is: which message–signature pairs did the adversary trivially learn through its signing oracle $\mathcal{O}_{\mathsf{Sign}}$ while tampering the message input *during* the signing process?

In the classical EUF-CMA security experiment without faults, the adversary $\mathcal{A}$ obtains a signature σ on message m under secret key sk, and the oracle $\mathcal{O}_{\mathsf{Sign}}$ records (m, σ) in the set of oracle signatures Q. In the fault-resilience setting, the adversary however is now able to modify the message while the signing process is going on. As the simplest case, imagine $\mathcal{A}$ submitting some message m to the signing oracle, but then introducing a single-bit fault when the message is read once within the scheme's Sign algorithm, leading to the signature being produced on some $m' \neq m$. If the fault-resilient unforgeability experiment simply recorded (m, σ) in the oracle signature list Q, then $\mathcal{A}$ could trivially win against any signature scheme by outputting (m', σ) as its forgery.

The key observation for lifting the classical signature unforgeability experiment to the fault-resilience setting is hence that the list Q should record the signature σ together with the *actual* message it was generated on by the signing algorithm. With the adversary being able to potentially fault the message several times during the signing process (depending on the structure of the latter), it at first sight may seem unclear which of the messages in the set m_{Sign} of messages accessed during the signing process to record in Q. Our definition is based on the idea to include the messages which the signer "assumes to have signed correctly" during the attack, i.e., we restrict ourselves to the subset $m_{\mathsf{Sign}}^{\mathsf{valid}}$ of messages for which the output signature σ actually verifies under the challenge public key pk and which are not already included in Q. In other words, these are the new messages which the signer may have authenticated in the signing step. If there are two or more such valid messages in $m_{\mathsf{Sign}}^{\mathsf{valid}}$ then the signer cannot

$$
\begin{array}{ll}
\hline
\mathsf{Expt}_{\mathcal{S},\mathcal{A}}^{\mathsf{frEUF\text{-}CMA}}(1^\lambda): & \mathcal{O}_{\mathsf{Sign}}(m): \\
\hline
\end{array}
$$

$\mathsf{Expt}_{\mathcal{S},\mathcal{A}}^{\mathsf{frEUF\text{-}CMA}}(1^\lambda):$	$\mathcal{O}_{\mathsf{Sign}}(m):$
1 $(sk, pk) \xleftarrow{\$} \mathsf{KGen}(1^\lambda)$	1 $\sigma \xleftarrow{\$} \mathsf{Sign}(sk, m)$
2 $Q \leftarrow \emptyset$	2 $m_{\mathsf{Sign}}^{\mathsf{valid}} \leftarrow \{m' \in m_{\mathsf{Sign}} \mid \mathsf{Verify}(pk, m', \sigma) = 1$
3 clash $\leftarrow$ false	$\qquad$ and $(m', *) \notin Q\}$
4 $(m^*, \sigma^*) \xleftarrow{\$} \mathcal{A}^{\mathcal{O}_{\mathsf{Sign}}}(1^\lambda, pk)$	3 if $\lvert m_{\mathsf{Sign}}^{\mathsf{valid}} \rvert \geq 2$ then clash $\leftarrow$ true
5 return 1 iff clash or	4 $Q \leftarrow Q \cup \left\{ (m, \sigma) \mid m \in m_{\mathsf{Sign}}^{\mathsf{valid}} \right\}$
$\qquad [(m^*, *) \notin Q$	5 return σ
$\qquad$ and $\mathsf{Verify}(pk, m^*, \sigma^*) = 1]$	

Fig. 3. Security experiment for *fault-resilient existential unforgeability under chosen-message attacks* (frEUF-CMA) for signature schemes. We write $(a, *) \notin Q$ if $\nexists b$ s.t. $(a, b) \in Q$. The lines 2–4 in $\mathcal{O}_{\mathsf{Sign}}$ are changed compared to the classical EUF-CMA notion. Recall that m_{Sign} is the set of values the message variable m took during the signing process in line 1 due to fault callbacks.

reliably identify the intended message. In this case we declare the adversary to win, captured via a flag clash which is set to true if there are multiple messages in $m_{\mathsf{Sign}}^{\mathsf{valid}}$ for any request.

The above definition in particular complies with the case that the adversary mounts a regular attack and does not tamper with the messages at all. In this case we would collect all signed messages in Q—one for each $\mathcal{O}_{\mathsf{Sign}}$ query (unless a message repeats and we do not extend Q)—as in the regular case, but clash would never become true. The fact that we declare the adversary to win if there are two messages in $m_{\mathsf{Sign}}^{\mathsf{valid}}$ immediately, without requiring the adversary to output the other (faulted) message as a forgery, releases the adversary from having to know the other message. This gives a stronger security guarantee, especially for random faults where bit flips may happen at unknown positions.

Put together, our signature unforgeability experiment adapted to the fault resilience setting allows the adversary to inject faults within the signature generation (as specified by the signature scheme in question). In its list of obtained signatures Q, it records the *first* value of the messages m used within the signing algorithm for which the generated signature σ verifies under the challenge public key. The augmented security definition for fault-resilient signature unforgeability is as follows; the according security experiment in Fig. 3 highlights the changes from the classical experiment.

Definition 1 (Fault-resilient existential unforgeability of signatures).
Let $\mathcal{S} = (\mathsf{KGen}, \mathsf{Sign}, \mathsf{Verify})$ be a signature scheme and experiment $\mathsf{Expt}_{\mathcal{S},\mathcal{A}}^{\mathsf{frEUF\text{-}CMA}}$ for an adversary $\mathcal{A}$ be defined as in Fig. 3.

We say that $\mathcal{S}$ provides fault-resilient existential unforgeability under chosen-message attacks *(frEUF-CMA) if for all PPT adversaries the following advantage function is negligible in the security parameter:*

$$
\mathsf{Adv}_{\mathcal{S},\mathcal{A}}^{\mathsf{frEUF\text{-}CMA}}(\lambda) := \Pr\left[\mathsf{Expt}_{\mathcal{S},\mathcal{A}}^{\mathsf{frEUF\text{-}CMA}}(1^\lambda) = 1 \right].
$$

3.2 De-randomized Signatures Are Not Fault-Resilient

We now exercise our fault-resilient unforgeability notion to establish that de-randomized schemes are vulnerable to the weakest fault injection attack of random one-bit flips. This in particular confirms the corresponding observations by Poddebniak et al. and others [1,48,54,56] in our formalism. To recap, de-randomization here refers to the approach to deterministically extract a per-message random value from the secret signing key and message input, replacing an otherwise needed true random sampling of a per-message nonce. This approach is employed, e.g., in the deterministic variants of the DSA and ECDSA signature schemes [49] and similarly in a more direct manner in the EdDSA signature scheme [16]. The latter scheme actually uses two pseudorandomly derived sub keys for signing and for nonce generation but this does not invalidate the attack.

We establish our result through the following abstractly de-randomized signature scheme $\mathcal{S}_{dr}$ generalizing the above approach. The scheme $\mathcal{S}_{dr} = (\mathsf{KGen}_{dr}, \mathsf{Sign}_{dr}, \mathsf{Verify}_{dr})$ de-randomizes a randomized signature scheme $\mathcal{S} = (\mathsf{KGen}, \mathsf{Sign}, \mathsf{Verify})$. In order to generate necessary randomness for $\mathcal{S}$'s signing algorithm, Sign_{dr} invokes a cryptographic hash function $\mathsf{H} \colon \{0,1\}^* \to \{0,1\}^{\geq \lambda}$ (modeled as a random oracle [14]) on the scheme's secret signing key and the message to be signed. The key generation and verification algorithms KGen_{dr} and Verify_{dr} are as for the randomized scheme, the modified signing algorithm Sign_{dr} is defined as follows:

$\underline{\mathsf{Sign}_{dr}(sk, \llcorner m \lrcorner)\colon}$
1 $r \leftarrow \mathsf{H}(sk, \langle m \rangle)$
2 $\sigma \leftarrow \mathsf{Sign}(sk, \langle m \rangle; r)$
3 return σ

In order to capture fault attacks, the definition of Sign_{dr} defines the message m to be faultable (indicated through corner brackets $\llcorner m \lrcorner$ on definition and angle brackets $\langle m \rangle$ on reads).[6]

As required by the DSA and ECDSA standards [46], the per-message random number (or *nonce*) r must be freshly generated for each message to be signed. If not, two signatures σ_0, σ_1 generated on distinct messages $m_0 \neq m_1$ using the *same* nonce r enable recovery of the secret signing key sk from the two signature equations [60]. In the de-randomized versions of DSA and ECDSA, and likewise in the deterministic EdDSA scheme, this requirement is aimed to be satisfied through deterministically deriving the random nonce via a hash function from the secret signing key and input message.

However, as observed before [1,48,54,56], a fault introduced within the message memory variable m between reading m for deriving the nonce r and reading m again for computing the signature (with nonce r), recovers the nonce reuse

---

[6] For completeness, observe that the fault attack described in the following applies also when introducing faults into r instead of m. Due to the usually larger size of m, facilitating bit flips in m through row-hammer attacks, we focus on faulting m, but note that similar results apply for faulting r.

scenario and, with it, a signing key extraction attack. In the following theorem, we formalize this observation in our generalized fault resilience setting. Let us call the underlying randomized signature scheme S *forgeable under nonce repetition* when given two distinct messages $m_0 \neq m_1$ and two valid corresponding signatures σ_0, σ_1 generated with the same random nonce r it is easy to produce an EUF-CMA forgery signature σ^* for some fresh message $m^* \notin (m_0, m_1)$. In particular, DSA, ECDSA, and the signing process underlying EdDSA are forgeable under nonce repetition.

Theorem 1. *Let S be a signature scheme forgeable under nonce repetition. Then the de-randomized signature scheme $S_{dr} = (\mathsf{KGen}_{dr}, \mathsf{Sign}_{dr}, \mathsf{Verify}_{dr})$ derived as described above is not frEUF-CMA-secure for any type of fault resilience.*

Proof. We show that S_{dr} is not frEUF-CMA-secure under the weakest form of fault attacks, namely (transient or persistent) 1-random faults (i.e., $N = 1$). This immediately also establishes the result under N-random faults with $N > 1$ and, through Lemmas 1 and 2, under differential and full faults.

The adversary A begins by calling the $\mathcal{O}_{\mathsf{Sign}}$ oracle on message $m_0 = 0^\lambda$. For the resulting two callbacks $\langle m \rangle$ on m (in lines 1, resp. 2, of the Sign_{dr} algorithm) the adversary returns 0, i.e., introduces no faults. It obtains the resulting signature σ_0 (generated using some nonce r) which is valid for m_0.

The adversary then calls $\mathcal{O}_{\mathsf{Sign}}$ on message $m_0 = 0^\lambda$ again, this time returning 0 on the first callback to leave the message unchanged, but 1 on the second callback (line 2 of Sign_{dr}) to flip a message bit at a random position. This call results in a signature σ_1 generated using the same nonce r as in the first call which is valid on m_1, where by m_1 we denote the message value resulting from the single-bit random fault introduced through the second callback.

The adversary finally iterates over $i \in \{1, \ldots, \lambda\}$ to find the flipped bit position in m_1 (i.e., the single 1-entry in m_1) by invoking the Verify_{dr} algorithm on an λ-bit message with the i-th bit set to 1, together with σ_1. As the underlying signature scheme S is forgeable under nonce repetition and $m_0 \neq m_1$, A can now use (m_0, σ_0) and (m_1, σ_1) to produce a valid EUF-CMA signature and win in the frEUF-CMA experiment. □

We note that similar attacks apply to other deterministic signature schemes such as RSA-FDH [15], showing that the additional property of uniqueness may not help to overcome fault attacks. If we describe the FDH scheme as a two-stage process $\lfloor h \rfloor \leftarrow \mathsf{H}(\langle m \rangle)$, $\sigma \leftarrow \mathsf{Sign}(sk, \langle h \rangle)$, then the adversary can compute a hash value h^* of some message m^*, then call the signing oracle about some other message m, overwriting $\langle h \rangle$ with h^* in the signing process to get a signature for m^*. Even in case of a hash collision $h = h^*$ only m would be considered as used up, such that A would win the fault-resistance game. This works for full and differential faults but is unknown to work for random faults.

3.3 Combining Randomization and De-randomization

In seeking to overcome security failures due to weak randomness sources, de-randomized signature schemes forgo using any ephemeral randomness in the signing process. As discussed before, fault attacks can however revive these security failures by introducing nonce repetitions in the signing process. To insulate a signature scheme against both weak randomness and fault attacks—or, viewed differently, the de-randomization of a randomized signature scheme against fault attacks—, it is hence advisable to follow an approach that combines ephemeral randomness and de-randomization techniques. The agreed-upon only countermeasure effective against the previously described fault attacks [1,48,54,56] is to use an additional randomness value in the per-message nonce derivation. This is in support of the XEdDSA signature scheme design [47] deployed in the Signal protocol [58] for secure messaging, which combines deterministically generating a per-message nonce with an additional random value in order to derive the randomness used in the signing process.

We capture this combiner approach again through a generalized, abstract signature scheme S_c. The scheme $S_c = (\mathsf{KGen_c}, \mathsf{Sign_c}, \mathsf{Verify_c})$ is based on a randomized signature scheme $S = (\mathsf{KGen}, \mathsf{Sign}, \mathsf{Verify})$ for which it generates the randomness needed in S's signing algorithm in two steps: First, it samples an ephemeral random value r' (e.g., in the case of XEdDSA, r' is sampled as a random 512-bit string). Then, r' together with the signing key and input message enters a cryptographic hash function $\mathsf{H} \colon \{0,1\}^* \to \{0,1\}^{\geq\lambda}$ (again modeled as a random oracle) in order to derive the signing randomness r.[7] Key generation and verification are as for the randomized scheme, the modified signing algorithm $\mathsf{Sign_c}$ is defined as follows:

$\mathsf{Sign_c}(sk, \llcorner m \lrcorner)$:
1 $\llcorner r' \lrcorner \stackrel{\$}{\leftarrow} \{0,1\}^\lambda$
2 $\llcorner r \lrcorner \leftarrow \mathsf{H}(sk, \langle m \rangle, \langle r' \rangle)$
3 $\sigma \leftarrow \mathsf{Sign}(sk, \langle m \rangle; \langle r \rangle)$
4 return σ

The definition of $\mathsf{Sign_c}$ is accordingly annotated to capture fault attacks. This time, we consider faults not only for message m but also in the randomness variables r' and r. Note that the $\mathsf{Sign_c}$ algorithm can furthermore be seen to tolerate (transient) faults in the secret signing key sk when used in the derivation of randomness through H; yet considering fault attacks on sk also in the signing process will require signature schemes secure against related-key attacks [9, 12, 33], whose fault-resilience treatment we leave as an avenue for future work.

We now establish that the combiner countermeasure captured in S_c indeed provides security against either weak randomness sources or (differential) fault attacks. We do so by showing that the approach lifts EUF-CMA security of the underlying signature scheme to fault-resilient unforgeability frEUF-CMA for S_c, when H is modeled as a random oracle. Note that the security statement is

---

[7] Note that we treat the underlying (randomized) signature scheme S as well as the hash function H in a black-box manner both for the positive fault resilience results here, as well as for the generic fault attacks on S_{dr} before. Of course, studying the fault resilience of specific such constructions is a valuable target on its own, which we leave for future work.

closely linked to the description of the scheme: We move from a purely functional description of the signature scheme to a high-level procedural representation in which the adversary can now interfere with sub steps. Such an *algorithmic implementation* still treats some steps as atomic (or, monolithic) procedures in which the adversary can only tamper with the input, but not interact with intermediate steps. Examples of such atomic steps are basic operations like assignments but may also refer to cryptographic procedures. For instance, $\mathsf{Sign}_c(sk, \llcorner m \lrcorner)$ treats the hashing with H and signing with the original signing algorithm Sign as atomic operations. One can thus view the algorithmic implementation as determining points in executions in which attacks can modify variables.

We make use of our strongest full fault attack type in order to capture that weak randomness samples r' may be fully controlled by the adversary. Let us stress that this first part of the result—full fault resilience in r'—is not meant as establishing resilience against strong faults targeted (only) at r', but really constitutes a baseline result showing that the combiner construction $\mathcal{S}_c$ provides *at least* the security of $\mathcal{S}$ even if the added randomness r' is completely flawed. The second part then establishes differential-fault resilience—for any number w of faulted bits—if r' is indeed random.

A noteworthy fact in the proof is that it shows we can use the same secret key sk for the signing step and the hash evaluation, when assuming H behaves like a random oracle. Usually, the secret key consists of two (possibly pseudorandomly derived) portions, one used for signing and one in the hash evaluation. An example where the key splitting is done is the EdDSA signature algorithm [16]. Our proof, of course, could be adapted to capture this case as well.

Theorem 2. *Let $\mathcal{S}$ be a randomized EUF-CMA-secure signature scheme. Then, in the random oracle model, the algorithmic implementation of the combined signature scheme $\mathcal{S}_c = (\mathsf{KGen}_c, \mathsf{Sign}_c, \mathsf{Verify}_c)$ given above is*

(a) frEUF-CMA-secure under full faults on variable r', with

$$\mathsf{Adv}^{\mathsf{frEUF\text{-}CMA}}_{\mathcal{S}_c, \mathcal{A}}(\lambda) \leq \mathsf{Adv}^{\mathsf{EUF\text{-}CMA}}_{\mathcal{S}, \mathcal{A}'}(\lambda), \quad and$$

(b) frEUF-CMA-secure under differential faults on variables m, r', and r, with

$$\mathsf{Adv}^{\mathsf{frEUF\text{-}CMA}}_{\mathcal{S}_c, \mathcal{A}}(\lambda) \leq q_H \cdot q_S \cdot 2^{-\lambda} + \mathsf{Adv}^{\mathsf{EUF\text{-}CMA}}_{\mathcal{S}, \mathcal{A}'}(\lambda),$$

for $\mathcal{A}'$ given in the proofs and q_H, q_S denoting the number of queries made to the random oracle and the signing oracle, respectively, by $\mathcal{A}$.

Let us stress again that the theorem refers to the actual algorithmic implementation of Sign_c, treating the underlying signature procedure Sign as atomic. There might still be fault attacks on this step if one fleshed out the algorithmic implementation of that signing procedure. But this would depend on the actual scheme and is not captured by our general theorem. Note that the de-randomized solution Sign_{dr} in the previous section is indeed insecure even if the underlying scheme is atomic, as long as it breaks under nonce repetitions. In this sense the theorem here confirms that putting the randomness in the hashing helps.

Proof. We separately prove the two sub-cases.

Ad (a). The first case models that r' is drawn from a weak randomness source. Here, the full-fault capabilities allow $\mathcal{A}$ to arbitrarily chose any value for r' through the callback in line 1 of the Sign_c algorithm, including repeating r' across different signatures. We will rely on the non-faultable secret key sk input to the hash function, unknown to the adversary, to establish that the derived value r (per message m) is indeed uniformly random as required. Since the message cannot be faulted in the case here, the adversary cannot win due to clash and we do not need to consider this attack option here.

To see the security in this case, we first exclude (by aborting the security experiment) the case that the adversary $\mathcal{A}$ ever queries the random oracle H on an input $(sk, \cdot, \cdot)$ including the scheme's secret key sk as the first component. This can reduce $\mathcal{A}$'s advantage $\mathsf{Adv}^{\mathsf{frEUF\text{-}CMA}}_{\mathcal{S}_\mathsf{c}, \mathcal{A}}$ by at most the advantage of the following adversary $\mathcal{A}'$ against the EUF-CMA security of $\mathcal{S}$, which by assumption is negligible.

Adversary $\mathcal{A}'$ simulates $\mathsf{Expt}^{\mathsf{frEUF\text{-}CMA}}_{\mathcal{S}_\mathsf{c}, \mathcal{A}}$ for $\mathcal{A}$, using its own signing oracle for computing the signature in line 3 of Sign_c as follows. At the outset of the experiment, $\mathcal{A}'$ initializes an empty list $\mathcal{L}$. Whenever Sign is to be invoked on some message m and randomness r in the simulation, $\mathcal{A}'$ first checks if $(m, r, \sigma) \in \mathcal{L}$ for some σ. If so, $\mathcal{A}'$ returns σ. Otherwise, $\mathcal{A}'$ invokes its signing oracle on m to obtain a signature σ, stores (m, r, σ) in a list $\mathcal{L}$, and returns σ. Furthermore, whenever $\mathcal{A}$ queries the random oracle H on some value $(x, \cdot, \cdot)$, adversary $\mathcal{A}'$ checks whether x equals the challenge secret key sk by computing $\sigma \leftarrow \mathsf{Sign}(x, m^*; r^*)$ for a fresh message and randomness m^*, r^* and checking whether $\mathsf{Verify}(pk, m^*, \sigma^*) = 1$. If so, $\mathcal{A}'$ outputs (m^*, σ^*) as its forgery and stops. Otherwise, $\mathcal{A}'$ returns a random value as the answer for the hash query (but obeying consistency across queries). Eventually, $\mathcal{A}'$ outputs the forgery of $\mathcal{A}$ as its own forgery when $\mathcal{A}$ stops.

Whenever $\mathsf{Expt}^{\mathsf{frEUF\text{-}CMA}}_{\mathcal{S}_\mathsf{c}, \mathcal{A}}$ would abort due to $\mathcal{A}$ querying sk to the random oracle, $\mathcal{A}'$ wins in the $\mathsf{Expt}^{\mathsf{EUF\text{-}CMA}}_{\mathcal{S}, \mathcal{A}'}$ experiment through its valid forgery (m^*, σ^*). The probability of the first event occurring is hence bounded by the (negligible) advantage of $\mathcal{A}'$ in the latter experiment.

Otherwise, whenever $\mathcal{A}$ does not query sk to the random oracle, r is derived as a uniformly random value per message m which is secret to $\mathcal{A}$ in each of its $\mathcal{O}_\mathsf{Sign}$ queries. Observe that, by construction, Sign_c is deterministic when fixing r' (and thus r), which is taken into account in the reduction through $\mathcal{A}'$ keeping the list $\mathcal{L}$ of signatures for each (m, r) pair seen. Adversary $\mathcal{A}'$ hence provides a sound simulation of the non-aborting $\mathsf{Expt}^{\mathsf{frEUF\text{-}CMA}}_{\mathcal{S}_\mathsf{c}, \mathcal{A}}$ when implicitly setting r to the internal randomness choice of its signature oracle. As the trial signature computation under candidate secret keys x do not involve the signing oracle of $\mathcal{A}'$, a valid forgery by $\mathcal{A}$ in $\mathsf{Expt}^{\mathsf{frEUF\text{-}CMA}}_{\mathcal{S}_\mathsf{c}, \mathcal{A}}$ also constitutes a valid forgery by $\mathcal{A}'$ in $\mathsf{Expt}^{\mathsf{EUF\text{-}CMA}}_{\mathcal{S}, \mathcal{A}'}$. This again is bounding the advantage of $\mathcal{A}$ in the former by the (negligible) advantage of $\mathcal{A}'$ in the latter.

Ad (b). The second case models strong differential fault attacks (like rowhammer). This time, the adversary is allowed to inject arbitrary bit flips in the message variable m as well as the internal randomness variables r' and r. We will rely on the randomness of r' persisting through bit flips in r', the random oracle derivation, and the resulting r to establish that the derived value r is still uniformly random.

Consider the reduction $\mathcal{A}'$ of a successful $\mathcal{A}$ in $\mathsf{Expt}_{\mathcal{S}_c,\mathcal{A}}^{\mathsf{frEUF\text{-}CMA}}$ to the EUF-CMA security of $\mathcal{S}$, which simulates $\mathsf{Expt}_{\mathcal{S}_c,\mathcal{A}}^{\mathsf{frEUF\text{-}CMA}}$ by simply invoking its own $\mathcal{O}_{\mathsf{Sign}}$ oracle to compute the signature in line 3 of Sign_c. When $\mathcal{A}$ outputs its forgery, $\mathcal{A}'$ outputs the same forgery in its experiment $\mathsf{Expt}_{\mathcal{S},\mathcal{A}'}^{\mathsf{EUF\text{-}CMA}}$.

We need to argue that the simulation provided to $\mathcal{A}$ is sound. In particular, this requires that the potentially faulted values r used to invoke the signing oracle $\mathcal{O}_{\mathsf{Sign}}$ are indeed uniformly random and secret to the adversary for each call as required for the EUF-CMA security of $\mathcal{S}$. To this end, let us trace the randomness used by $\mathcal{A}'$ in any invocation of Sign_c, originating from sampling r' to submitting (faulted) value r to the $\mathcal{O}_{\mathsf{Sign}}$ oracle.

- In line 1 of Sign_c, the value r' is sampled uniformly at random (and hidden from $\mathcal{A}$).
- In line 2, $\mathcal{A}$ is first invoked through the callback $\langle r' \rangle$ on r' and returns some difference value Δ_0. The callback returns the value $r'_{\Delta_0} = r' \oplus \Delta_0$ to be used in the hash function computation, which is still uniformly random distributed and unknown to $\mathcal{A}$ as r' was.
  Since H is a random oracle, the resulting value r is again uniformly random. Furthermore, the probability that $\mathcal{A}$ guesses r'_{Δ_0} in a query to the random oracle H is at most $2^{-\lambda}$, so r remains unknown to $\mathcal{A}$ with all but negligible probability over all random oracle queries. Note that we do not rely on the secrecy (nor integrity) of sk in this step since the unknown r'_{Δ_0} acts as an ephemeral key here.
- In line 3, $\mathcal{A}$ may again inject a differential fault Δ_1, this time on r. For the same reason as above, the resulting value $r_{\Delta_1} = r \oplus \Delta_1$ stays uniformly distributed and unknown to $\mathcal{A}$.

Using the faulted value r_{Δ_1} of r as the input to the $\mathcal{O}_{\mathsf{Sign}}$ oracle by $\mathcal{A}'$ is hence sound. Thus, if $\mathcal{A}$ wins in the original attack, either via a forgery or via a clash, then this also holds in the simulated attack with the (randomized) signing algorithm. For forgeries of fresh messages, the (negligible) advantage of $\mathcal{A}'$ against the EUF-CMA of $\mathcal{S}$ bounds the frEUF-CMA advantage of $\mathcal{A}$ against $\mathcal{S}_c$, as desired.

Finally, we have to account for $\mathcal{A}$ winning through a potential clash during the (now probabilistic) signing step. In each query there are at most two messages appearing during the signing process, the first one $m^{(1)}$ in the computation of $\lfloor r \rfloor \leftarrow \mathsf{H}(sk, \langle m \rangle, \langle r' \rangle)$ in Line 2, the second one $m^{(2)}$ in the computation of $\sigma \leftarrow \mathsf{Sign}(sk, \langle m \rangle; \langle r \rangle)$ in Line 3. The second one certainly verifies with σ under the public key. Now, if $\mathcal{A}$ triggers a clash, both messages must be included in the set $m_{\mathsf{Sign}}^{\mathsf{valid}}$. This means that the first message $m^{(1)}$, too, needs to verify, be different from the second one, and must not have been included in Q by any prior $\mathcal{O}_{\mathsf{Sign}}$

query. Hence, when detecting a clash, $\mathcal{A}'$ can immediately output $m^{(1)}$ together with σ as its own forgery. That forgery is valid, as $m^{(1)}$ was never asked to the signing oracle of $\mathcal{A}'$ before. Hence, the probability for this attack option of $\mathcal{A}$ to succeed can also be bounded by the EUF-CMA security of $\mathcal{S}$. $\qquad\qquad\square$

An XOR Variant. For completeness, let us note that a variant of the combiner scheme $\mathcal{S}_c$ above that merges the additional randomness via an XOR instead of including it under the hash function evaluation achieves similar security results; see the full version [31] for a technical description and security argument.

4   Fault-Resilient Authenticated Encryption

We now turn to studying the effects of fault attacks on authenticated encryption schemes and how to enable fault resilience in this setting. In an effort to obviate the need for strong randomness in the encryption process, the understanding of modern authenticated encryption switched to a nonce-based syntax, in which a non-repeating nonce value enters encryption in replacement of fresh per-message randomness. Regularly, authenticated encryption schemes then indeed rely on the nonce not to repeat and generally do not uphold any security guarantees if this condition is violated. A prominent example is the widely adopted Galois/Counter mode (GCM) [29], combined, e.g., with the AES block cipher. While being secure as an authenticated encryption scheme [43], authentication guarantees are immediately lost in case of nonce repetitions [38].

A strengthened security notion introduced by Rogaway and Shrimpton [53] augments authenticated-encryption security with resistance against *nonce misuse*: it demands that security is upheld even if nonces repeat, such that an adversary may only learn when a full triple (N, A, m) of nonce, associated data, and message is repeated, but ciphertexts otherwise look random. Since its introduction, nonce-misuse resistance has become a design target for authenticated encryption schemes, put forth, e.g., in the CAESAR competition for authenticated encryption ciphers [23].

4.1   Fault-Resilient Security of Authenticated Encryption

In order to study the effects of fault attacks on authenticated encryption schemes based on our generic model, we first lift the security notions for authenticated encryption to the fault resilience setting. Our notion liberally allows probabilistic encryption to accommodate fault-resilient constructions combining nonces and randomness under the same syntax. We focus on faults in the encryption process here, as it is encryption where different variants for avoiding ephemeral randomness and nonce glitches are implemented. Our notions can however be extended to also consider faults attacks on the decryption process.

As the major change from regular security definitions, we need to define how to rule out trivial queries decrypting the response of an encryption query. We

$\text{Expt}_{\mathcal{AE},\mathcal{A}}^{\text{frAE-\$},b}(1^\lambda)$:

1 $K \xleftarrow{\$} \text{KGen}(1^\lambda)$
2 $Q \leftarrow \emptyset$
3 clash $\leftarrow$ false
4 $b' \xleftarrow{\$} \mathcal{A}^{\mathcal{O}_{\text{Enc}}, \mathcal{O}_{\text{Dec}}}(1^\lambda)$
5 if clash then $b' \leftarrow b$
6 return b'

$\mathcal{O}_{\text{Enc}}(N, A, m)$:

7 $c_1 \xleftarrow{\$} \{0,1\}^{|c_0|}$
8 $c_0 \xleftarrow{\$} \text{Enc}(K, N, A, m)$
9 $NA_{\text{Enc}}^{\text{valid}} \leftarrow \{(N', A') \in N_{\text{Enc}} \times A_{\text{Enc}} \mid$
     $\text{Dec}(K, N', A', c_b) \neq \bot$
     and $(N', A', c_b) \notin Q\}$
10 if $|NA_{\text{Enc}}^{\text{valid}}| \geq 2$ then
11   clash $\leftarrow$ true
12 $Q \leftarrow Q \cup \{(N', A', c_b) \mid$
     $(N', A') \in NA_{\text{Enc}}^{\text{valid}}\}$
13 return c_b

$\mathcal{O}_{\text{Dec}}(N, A, c)$:

14 if $b = 1$ or $(N, A, c) \in Q$ then
15   return $\bot$
16 else
17    $m \leftarrow \text{Dec}(K, N, A, c)$
18   return m

$\text{Expt}_{\mathcal{AE},\mathcal{A}}^{\text{frAE-ror},b}(1^\lambda)$:

1 $K \xleftarrow{\$} \text{KGen}(1^\lambda)$
2 $Q \leftarrow \emptyset$
3 clash $\leftarrow$ false
4 $b' \xleftarrow{\$} \mathcal{A}^{\mathcal{O}_{\text{Enc}}, \mathcal{O}_{\text{Dec}}}(1^\lambda)$
5 if clash then $b' \leftarrow b$
6 return b'

$\mathcal{O}_{\text{Enc}}(N, A, m)$:

7 if $b = 1$ then $m \xleftarrow{\$} \{0,1\}^{|m|}$
8 $c \xleftarrow{\$} \text{Enc}(K, N, A, m)$
9 $NA_{\text{Enc}}^{\text{valid}} \leftarrow \{(N', A') \in N_{\text{Enc}} \times A_{\text{Enc}} \mid$
     $\text{Dec}(K, N', A', c) \neq \bot$
     and $(N', A', c) \notin Q\}$
10 if $|NA_{\text{Enc}}^{\text{valid}}| \geq 2$ then
11   clash $\leftarrow$ true
12 $Q \leftarrow Q \cup \{(N', A', c) \mid$
     $(N', A') \in NA_{\text{Enc}}^{\text{valid}}\}$
13 return c

$\mathcal{O}_{\text{Dec}}(N, A, c)$:

14 if $b = 1$ or $(N, A, c) \in Q$ then
15   return $\bot$
16 else
17    $m \leftarrow \text{Dec}(K, N, A, c)$
18   return m

Fig. 4. Security experiments for *fault-resilient* authenticated encryption schemes. Lines 9–12 in $\mathcal{O}_{\text{Enc}}$ are changed compared to the classical notions. Recall that N_{Enc} and A_{Enc} are the set of values the nonce, resp. AD, variable N, resp. A, took during the encryption process in line 8 due to fault callbacks.

do so analogously to the signature setting described in Sect. 3.1, namely by considering, through a list $NA_{\text{Enc}}^{\text{valid}}$, the new combinations of (N, A, c) which decrypt successfully, taking candidate values for N and A from N_{Enc}, resp. A_{Enc}, the lists of values taken by N, resp. A, within Enc. Intuitively, these are the new tuples which the encryption algorithm can be considered to have produced. If there is just one such combination this gets added to Q as the single resulting challenge ciphertext to be prohibited for the decryption oracle. If there are however multiple combinations, we declare the adversary to win by setting the clash flag. One can think of this saying that the adversary has managed to produce multiple (valid) encryption tuples from a single, faulted encryption call. We again then declare the adversary to win immediately.

We again consider both randomness and real-or-random indistinguishability under fault attacks, with the latter being weaker than the former.

$$
\begin{array}{ll}
\underline{\mathsf{KGen_{SIV}}(1^\lambda):} & \underline{\mathsf{Dec_{SIV}}(K, N, A, c):} \\
\quad 1 \quad K_1, K_2 \xleftarrow{\$} \{0,1\}^\lambda & \quad 1 \quad (K_1, K_2) \leftarrow K \\
\quad 2 \quad \text{return } K = (K_1, K_2) & \quad 2 \quad (IV, c') \leftarrow c \\
 & \quad 3 \quad m \leftarrow \mathsf{Dec}(K_2, c'; IV) \\
\underline{\mathsf{Enc_{SIV}}(K, \llcorner N \lrcorner, \llcorner A \lrcorner, \llcorner m \lrcorner):} & \quad 4 \quad IV' \leftarrow \mathsf{PRF}(K_1, (N, A, m)) \\
\quad 1 \quad (K_1, K_2) \leftarrow K & \quad 5 \quad \text{if } IV = IV' \text{ then} \\
\quad 2 \quad \llcorner IV \lrcorner \leftarrow \mathsf{PRF}(K_1, (\langle N \rangle, \langle A \rangle, \langle m \rangle)) & \quad 6 \quad\quad \text{return } m \\
\quad 3 \quad c' \leftarrow \mathsf{Enc}(K_2, \langle m \rangle; \langle IV \rangle) & \quad 7 \quad \text{else} \\
\quad 4 \quad \text{return } c = (IV, c') & \quad 8 \quad\quad \text{return } \bot
\end{array}
$$

Fig. 5. The synthetic initialization vector (SIV) mode of operation based on a pseudo-random function PRF and an IV-based encryption scheme $\mathcal{E}$.

Definition 2 (Fault-resilient security of authenticated encryption). *Let $\mathcal{AE} = (\mathsf{KGen}, \mathsf{Enc}, \mathsf{Dec})$ be an authenticated encryption scheme and experiments $\mathsf{Expt}_{\mathcal{AE},\mathcal{A}}^{\mathrm{frAE\text{-}\$},b}$ and $\mathsf{Expt}_{\mathcal{AE},\mathcal{A}}^{\mathrm{frAE\text{-}ror},b}$ for an adversary $\mathcal{A}$ and a bit b be defined as in Fig. 4. We restrict $\mathcal{A}$ to ask any query (N, A, m) to $\mathcal{O}_{\mathsf{Enc}}$ at most once.*

We say that $\mathcal{AE}$ is AE-\$-secure with fault resilience, *resp.* AE-ror-secure with fault resilience, *if for all PPT adversaries and* AE-SEC = AE-\$, *resp.* AE-SEC = AE-ror, *the following advantage function is negligible in the security parameter:*

$$
\mathsf{Adv}_{\mathcal{AE},\mathcal{A}}^{\mathrm{frAE\text{-}SEC}} := \left| \Pr\left[\mathsf{Expt}_{\mathcal{AE},\mathcal{A}}^{\mathrm{frAE\text{-}SEC},0}(1^\lambda) = 1 \right] - \Pr\left[\mathsf{Expt}_{\mathcal{AE},\mathcal{A}}^{\mathrm{frAE\text{-}SEC},1}(1^\lambda) = 1 \right] \right|.
$$

When $\mathcal{A}$ never repeats the nonce value N between any two $\mathcal{O}_{\mathsf{Enc}}$ calls, we call it nonce-respecting; *otherwise we say the scheme is* nonce-misuse resistant.

4.2 SIV Is Not Fault-Resilient

As an example for a nonce-misuse resistant authenticated encryption scheme, we will study the SIV (for "synthetic initialization vector") mode of operation introduced by Rogaway and Shrimpton [53]. It achieves classical, misuse-resistant randomness indistinguishability AE-\$ by combining a pseudorandom function and an IND\$-CPA-secure IV-based encryption scheme [53]. SIV was also considered for generic composition in a work together with Namprempre [45] and optimized through combination with GCM by Gueron and Lindell [35].

SIV is defined as in Fig. 5 based on a pseudorandom function PRF: $\{0,1\}^\lambda \times \{0,1\}^* \to \{0,1\}^\lambda$ and a conventional IV-based encryption scheme $\mathcal{E} = (\mathsf{KGen}, \mathsf{Enc}, \mathsf{Dec})$ with initialization vectors from $\{0,1\}^\lambda$. We write the IV-based encryption algorithm Enc as $c \leftarrow \mathsf{Enc}(K, m; IV)$ for encrypting a message m under key K and initialization vector IV into a ciphertext c. Analogously, we write IV-based decryption as $m \leftarrow \mathsf{Dec}(K, c; IV)$ for decrypting a ciphertext c under key K and initialization vector IV into a message m.

In our definition of SIV, we consider potential fault attacks on the nonce N, associated data A, message m, and synthetic initialization vector IV within

$\underline{\mathsf{KGen}_{\mathsf{SIV\$}}(1^\lambda):}$
1 $K_1, K_2 \xleftarrow{\$} \{0,1\}^\lambda$
2 return $K = (K_1, K_2)$

$\underline{\mathsf{Enc}_{\mathsf{SIV\$}}(K, \llcorner N \lrcorner, \llcorner A \lrcorner, \llcorner m \lrcorner):}$
1 $(K_1, K_2) \leftarrow K$
2 $\llcorner r \lrcorner \xleftarrow{\$} \{0,1\}^\lambda$
3 $\llcorner IV \lrcorner \leftarrow \mathsf{PRF}(K_1, (\langle N \rangle, \langle A \rangle, \langle m \rangle, \langle r \rangle))$
4 $c' \leftarrow \mathsf{Enc}(K_2, \langle r \rangle \| \langle m \rangle; \langle IV \rangle)$
5 return $c = (IV, c')$

$\underline{\mathsf{Dec}_{\mathsf{SIV\$}}(K, N, A, c):}$
1 $(K_1, K_2) \leftarrow K$
2 $(IV, c') \leftarrow c$
3 $r \| m \leftarrow \mathsf{Dec}(K_2, c'; IV)$
4 $IV' \leftarrow \mathsf{PRF}(K_1, (N, A, m, r))$
5 if $IV = IV'$ then
6   return m
7 else
8   return $\perp$

Fig. 6. The randomness-augmented synthetic initialization vector mode SIV\$ based on a pseudorandom function PRF and an IV-based encryption scheme $\mathcal{E}$.

the encryption algorithm (cf. the according annotation in Fig. 5). Our following result shows that SIV does not achieve fault-resilient security, even in the weaker AE-ror sense. More specifically, assuming pseudorandomness of the deployed PRF, AE-ror security of SIV breaks under (transient or persistent) single-bit random faults (i.e., the weakest form of fault attacks in our model) on either of the adversarially-provided values N, A, or m for encryption. As for AE-\$ security, it is easy to see that faults can induce collisions in the IV computation, which then are easy to distinguish from randomly sampled values. Due to space restrictions, we defer the proof to the full version [31].

Theorem 3. *Let* PRF *be a pseudorandom function. Then the SIV authenticated encryption mode* $\mathcal{AE}_{\mathsf{SIV}} = (\mathsf{KGen}_{\mathsf{SIV}}, \mathsf{Enc}_{\mathsf{SIV}}, \mathsf{Dec}_{\mathsf{SIV}})$ *from Fig. 5 is not* frAE-ror-*secure against any type of faults on the encryption inputs* N, A, *and* m.

4.3 SIV\$: Randomness-Augmented SIV

In order to overcome SIV's vulnerability to fault attacks in the encryption inputs, we propose and discuss an approach of augmenting the encryption process with ephemeral randomness in order to protect against faults. This approach translates concepts employed in the setting of signature schemes (e.g., in the XEdDSA scheme [47], cf. Section 3.3) to the realm of authenticated encryption which, to the best of our knowledge, have not been previously considered in this setting before.

Observe that the reason for SIV falling short of protecting against fault attacks is that such attacks can force the synthetic IV value to collide for different inputs (N, A, m) of nonce, associated data, and message. This resembles the setting for de-randomized deterministic signatures, where fault attacks may lead to the random per-message nonce being repeated. We show that an analogous combiner approach to derive the synthetic IV from both the values N, A, and m as well as an *additional ephemeral random* input provides strong combined security against either weak randomness sources or fault attacks.

We denote the randomness-augmented synthetic initialization vector mode as SIV\$, described in Fig. 6. Like SIV, the scheme $\mathsf{SIV\$} = (\mathsf{KGen_{SIV\$}}, \mathsf{Enc_{SIV\$}}, \mathsf{Dec_{SIV\$}})$ is based on a pseudorandom function $\mathsf{PRF} \colon \{0,1\}^\lambda \times \{0,1\}^* \to \{0,1\}^\lambda$ and an IV-based encryption scheme $\mathcal{E} = (\mathsf{KGen}, \mathsf{Enc}, \mathsf{Dec})$. In contrast to SIV, the encryption operation of SIV\$ is now randomized. Prudently including the ephemeral randomness value r as a λ-bit prefix to the encrypted message, we ensure that SIV\$ maintains the same outer ciphertext format as SIV, including its strong randomness indistinguishability.[8] The ciphertext size increases by one block.

As we show next, SIV\$ indeed protects against (either) weak randomness sources (modeled as full-fault attacks on the ephemeral randomness r)[9] or strong differential fault attacks (for any number w of faulted bits) on all adversarial encryption inputs N, A, and m as well as the internal randomness r and synthetic initialization vector IV. Under the same assumptions needed to establish regular security for SIV [53], namely PRF being a pseudorandom function and $\mathcal{E}$ being IND\$-CPA-secure, we show that SIV\$ upholds strong randomness indistinguishability (frAE-\$) under such faults. Again, considering fault attacks also on the PRF and encryption keys requires schemes secure against related-key attacks [8,12,33] and is left for future work. Due to space restrictions, we defer the proof to the full version [31].

Theorem 4. *Let* PRF *be a pseudorandom function and* $\mathcal{E}$ *an* IND\$-CPA-*secure IV-based encryption scheme. Then the algorithmic implementation of the randomness-augmented SIV mode* $\mathsf{SIV\$} = (\mathsf{KGen_{SIV\$}}, \mathsf{Enc_{SIV\$}}, \mathsf{Dec_{SIV\$}})$ *from Fig. 6 is, in a nonce-misuse resistant manner,*

(a) frAE-\$-*secure under full faults on variable* r, *with*

$$\mathsf{Adv}^{\mathsf{frAE}\text{-}\$}_{\mathsf{SIV\$},\mathcal{A}}(\lambda) \leq 2 \cdot \left(\mathsf{Adv}^{\mathsf{PRF}\text{-}\mathsf{sec}}_{\mathsf{PRF},\mathcal{A}'}(\lambda) + q_D \cdot 2^{-\lambda} + \mathsf{Adv}^{\mathsf{IND\$}\text{-}\mathsf{CPA}}_{\mathcal{E},\mathcal{A}''}(\lambda) \right), \quad and$$

(b) frAE-\$-*secure under differential faults on all of the variables* N, A, m, r, *and* IV, *with*

$$\mathsf{Adv}^{\mathsf{frAE}\text{-}\$}_{\mathsf{SIV\$},\mathcal{A}}(\lambda) \leq \mathsf{Adv}^{\mathsf{PRF}\text{-}\mathsf{sec}}_{\mathsf{PRF},\mathcal{A}'}(\lambda) + \mathsf{Adv}^{\mathsf{IND\$}\text{-}\mathsf{CPA}}_{\mathcal{E},\mathcal{A}''}(\lambda),$$

for $\mathcal{A}'$, $\mathcal{A}''$ *given in the proofs and* q_D *denoting the number of queries made to the decryption oracle by* $\mathcal{A}$.

---

[8] Alternatively, one may include r as additional component in the ciphertext. This however degrades security to real-or-random indistinguishability in case of weak randomness values r.

[9] Analogous to the signature case in Theorem 2, the first part of the statement again only serves as a baseline result. It shows that SIV\$ provides at least the security of SIV even if the added randomness r' is completely flawed.

5   Conclusion

We introduced a game-based treatment of cryptographic fault resilience which enables generic extensions of existing security notions to capture memory fault attacks. Our model exemplifies how different attack types can be captured through a hierarchy of callback-style adversarial interactions within accordingly augmented security notion. Applying our modeling technique to deterministic signature schemes, we revisit known fault attacks on deterministic signature schemes. Moreover, we can, for the first time, give provable security guarantees for proposed countermeasures in the realm of signatures and translate both attacks and provably-secure countermeasures to the setting of nonce-misuse resistant authenticated encryption.

Potential future research questions arise both in modeling and applications. Applying the modeling of fault resilience to other security notions possibly yields new insights into fault attacks and protection for other cryptographic primitives. Security against related-key attacks targeting partial effects of memory faults lends itself to be a viable building block here. Another worthwhile effort is to look beyond our strict monolithic treatment of the cryptographic primitives and investigate in how far the structure of the primitive, say, iterative hashing as in SHA-2 or SHA-3, affects memory fault attacks. Of course, such a treatment could be performed all the way down to the lower implementation level. Finally, while our modeling provides a general way to capture memory faults, capturing control-flow fault attacks in a meaningful way for game-based, cryptographic security notions remains a challenging open problem.

Acknowledgments. Felix Günther is supported in part by Research Fellowship grant GU 1859/1-1 of the German Research Foundation (DFG) and National Science Foundation (NSF) grants CNS-1526801 and CNS-1717640. This work has been co-funded by the DFG as part of project P2 within the CRC 1119 CROSSING. Most of the work on this paper was done while Felix Günther was at UC San Diego.

References

1. Ambrose, C., Bos, J.W., Fay, B., Joye, M., Lochter, M., Murray, B.: Differential attacks on deterministic signatures. In: Smart, N.P. (ed.) CT-RSA 2018. LNCS, vol. 10808, pp. 339–353. Springer, Cham (2018). https://doi.org/10.1007/978-3-319-76953-0_18
2. Aranha, D.F., Orlandi, C., Takahashi, A., Zaverucha, G.: Security of hedged Fiat-Shamir signatures under fault attacks. Cryptology ePrint Archive, Report 2019/956 (2019). https://eprint.iacr.org/2019/956
3. Bar-El, H., Choukri, H., Naccache, D., Tunstall, M., Whelan, C.: The sorcerer's apprentice guide to fault attacks. Proc. IEEE **94**(2), 370–382 (2006)
4. Barenghi, A., Breveglieri, L., Koren, I., Naccache, D.: Fault injection attacks on cryptographic devices: theory, practice, and countermeasures. Proc. IEEE **100**(11), 3056–3076 (2012)
5. Barenghi, A., Pelosi, G.: A note on fault attacks against deterministic signature schemes. In: Ogawa, K., Yoshioka, K. (eds.) IWSEC 2016. LNCS, vol. 9836, pp. 182–192. Springer, Cham (2016). https://doi.org/10.1007/978-3-319-44524-3_11

6. Barthe, G., Dupressoir, F., Fouque, P.-A., Grégoire, B., Tibouchi, M., Zapalowicz, J.-C.: Making RSA–PSS provably secure against non-random faults. In: Batina, L., Robshaw, M. (eds.) CHES 2014. LNCS, vol. 8731, pp. 206–222. Springer, Heidelberg (2014). https://doi.org/10.1007/978-3-662-44709-3_12
7. Bellare, M., et al.: Hedged public-key encryption: how to protect against bad randomness. In: Matsui, M. (ed.) ASIACRYPT 2009. LNCS, vol. 5912, pp. 232–249. Springer, Heidelberg (2009). https://doi.org/10.1007/978-3-642-10366-7_14
8. Bellare, M., Cash, D.: Pseudorandom functions and permutations provably secure against related-key attacks. In: Rabin, T. (ed.) CRYPTO 2010. LNCS, vol. 6223, pp. 666–684. Springer, Heidelberg (2010). https://doi.org/10.1007/978-3-642-14623-7_36
9. Bellare, M., Cash, D., Miller, R.: Cryptography secure against related-key attacks and tampering. In: Lee, D.H., Wang, X. (eds.) ASIACRYPT 2011. LNCS, vol. 7073, pp. 486–503. Springer, Heidelberg (2011). https://doi.org/10.1007/978-3-642-25385-0_26
10. Bellare, M., Goldreich, O., Goldwasser, S.: Incremental cryptography: the case of hashing and signing. In: Desmedt, Y.G. (ed.) CRYPTO 1994. LNCS, vol. 839, pp. 216–233. Springer, Heidelberg (1994). https://doi.org/10.1007/3-540-48658-5_22
11. Bellare, M., Goldreich, O., Goldwasser, S.: Incremental cryptography and application to virus protection. In: 27th ACM STOC, pp. 45–56. ACM Press, May/Jun 1995
12. Bellare, M., Kohno, T.: Hash function balance and its impact on birthday attacks. In: Cachin, C., Camenisch, J.L. (eds.) EUROCRYPT 2004. LNCS, vol. 3027, pp. 401–418. Springer, Heidelberg (2004). https://doi.org/10.1007/978-3-540-24676-3_24
13. Bellare, M., Paterson, K.G., Rogaway, P.: Security of symmetric encryption against mass surveillance. In: Garay, J.A., Gennaro, R. (eds.) CRYPTO 2014, Part I. LNCS, vol. 8616, pp. 1–19. Springer, Heidelberg (2014). https://doi.org/10.1007/978-3-662-44371-2_1
14. Bellare, M., Rogaway, P.: Random oracles are practical: a paradigm for designing efficient protocols. In: Denning, D.E., Pyle, R., Ganesan, R., Sandhu, R.S., Ashby, V. (eds.) ACM CCS 93, pp. 62–73. ACM Press, November 1993
15. Bellare, M., Rogaway, P.: The exact security of digital signatures-how to sign with RSA and Rabin. In: Maurer, U. (ed.) EUROCRYPT 1996. LNCS, vol. 1070, pp. 399–416. Springer, Heidelberg (1996). https://doi.org/10.1007/3-540-68339-9_34
16. Bernstein, D.J., Duif, N., Lange, T., Schwabe, P., Yang, B.-Y.: High-speed high-security signatures. In: Preneel, B., Takagi, T. (eds.) CHES 2011. LNCS, vol. 6917, pp. 124–142. Springer, Heidelberg (2011). https://doi.org/10.1007/978-3-642-23951-9_9
17. Biehl, I., Meyer, B., Müller, V.: Differential fault attacks on elliptic curve cryptosystems. In: Bellare, M. (ed.) CRYPTO 2000. LNCS, vol. 1880, pp. 131–146. Springer, Heidelberg (2000). https://doi.org/10.1007/3-540-44598-6_8
18. Biham, E., Shamir, A.: Differential fault analysis of secret key cryptosystems. In: Kaliski, B.S. (ed.) CRYPTO 1997. LNCS, vol. 1294, pp. 513–525. Springer, Heidelberg (1997). https://doi.org/10.1007/BFb0052259
19. Blömer, J., Günther, P.: Singular curve point decompression attack. In: 2015 Workshop on Fault Diagnosis and Tolerance in Cryptography (FDTC), pp. 71–84 (2015)
20. Boneh, D., DeMillo, R.A., Lipton, R.J.: On the importance of checking cryptographic protocols for faults (extended abstract). In: Fumy, W. (ed.) EUROCRYPT 1997. LNCS, vol. 1233, pp. 37–51. Springer, Heidelberg (1997). https://doi.org/10.1007/3-540-69053-0_4

21. Breitner, J., Heninger, N.: Biased nonce sense: lattice attacks against weak ECDSA signatures in cryptocurrencies. In: Goldberg, I., Moore, T. (eds.) FC 2019. LNCS, vol. 11598, pp. 3–20. Springer, Cham (2019). https://doi.org/10.1007/978-3-030-32101-7_1

22. Brengel, M., Rossow, C.: Identifying key leakage of bitcoin users. In: Bailey, M., Holz, T., Stamatogiannakis, M., Ioannidis, S. (eds.) RAID 2018. LNCS, vol. 11050, pp. 623–643. Springer, Cham (2018). https://doi.org/10.1007/978-3-030-00470-5_29

23. CAESAR: Competition for authenticated encryption: Security, applicability, and robustness. https://competitions.cr.yp.to/caesar.html

24. CERT Vulnerability Notes Database: Vulnerability note VU#925211: Debian and Ubuntu OpenSSL packages contain a predictable random number generator (2008). https://www.kb.cert.org/vuls/id/925211

25. Coron, J.-S., Mandal, A.: PSS is secure against random fault attacks. In: Matsui, M. (ed.) ASIACRYPT 2009. LNCS, vol. 5912, pp. 653–666. Springer, Heidelberg (2009). https://doi.org/10.1007/978-3-642-10366-7_38

26. Dobraunig, C., Eichlseder, M., Korak, T., Lomné, V., Mendel, F.: Statistical fault attacks on nonce-based authenticated encryption schemes. In: Cheon, J.H., Takagi, T. (eds.) ASIACRYPT 2016, Part I. LNCS, vol. 10031, pp. 369–395. Springer, Heidelberg (2016). https://doi.org/10.1007/978-3-662-53887-6_14

27. Dobraunig, C., Mangard, S., Mendel, F., Primas, R.: Fault attacks on nonce-based authenticated encryption: application to keyak and ketje. In: Cid, C., Jacobson, M.J. (eds.) SAC 2018. LNCS, vol. 11349, pp. 257–277. Springer, Heidelberg (2019). https://doi.org/10.1007/978-3-030-10970-7_12

28. Dorrendorf, L., Gutterman, Z., Pinkas, B.: Cryptanalysis of the windows random number generator. In: Ning, P., De Capitani di Vimercati, S., Syverson, P.F. (eds.) ACM CCS 2007, pp. 476–485. ACM Press, October 2007

29. Dworkin, M.: Recommendation for block cipher modes of operation: Galois/Counter Mode (GCM) and GMAC, November 2007. nIST Special Publication 800–38D

30. fail0verflow: Console hacking 2010: PS3 epic fail. In: 27th Chaos Communication Congress. Chaos Computer Club (2010)

31. Fischlin, M., Günther, F.: Modeling memory faults in signature and authenticated encryption schemes. Cryptology ePrint Archive, Report 2019/1053 (2019). https://eprint.iacr.org/2019/1053

32. Fouque, P.-A., Guillermin, N., Leresteux, D., Tibouchi, M., Zapalowicz, J.-C.: Attacking RSA–CRT signatures with faults on montgomery multiplication. In: Prouff, E., Schaumont, P. (eds.) CHES 2012. LNCS, vol. 7428, pp. 447–462. Springer, Heidelberg (2012). https://doi.org/10.1007/978-3-642-33027-8_26

33. Gennaro, R., Lysyanskaya, A., Malkin, T., Micali, S., Rabin, T.: Algorithmic tamper-proof (ATP) security: theoretical foundations for security against hardware tampering. In: Naor, M. (ed.) TCC 2004. LNCS, vol. 2951, pp. 258–277. Springer, Heidelberg (2004). https://doi.org/10.1007/978-3-540-24638-1_15

34. Goldberg, I., Wagner, D.: Randomness and the Netscape browser. Dr. Dobb's J. **21**, 66–71 (1996)

35. Gueron, S., Lindell, Y.: GCM-SIV: full nonce misuse-resistant authenticated encryption at under one cycle per byte. In: Ray, I., Li, N., Kruegel, C. (eds.) ACM CCS 2015, pp. 109–119. ACM Press, October 2015

36. Gutterman, Z., Pinkas, B., Reinman, T.: Analysis of the linux random number generator. In: 2006 IEEE Symposium on Security and Privacy, pp. 371–385. IEEE Computer Society Press, May 2006

37. Ishai, Y., Prabhakaran, M., Sahai, A., Wagner, D.: Private circuits II: keeping secrets in tamperable circuits. In: Vaudenay, S. (ed.) EUROCRYPT 2006. LNCS, vol. 4004, pp. 308–327. Springer, Heidelberg (2006). https://doi.org/10. 1007/11761679_19

38. Joux, A.: Authentication failures in NIST version of GCM (2006). http://csrc.nist. gov/groups/ST/toolkit/BCM/documents/Joux_comments.pdf

39. Joye, M., Lenstra, A.K., Quisquater, J.J.: Chinese remaindering based cryptosystems in the presence of faults. J. Cryptol. **12**(4), 241–245 (1999)

40. Kim, Y., et al.: Flipping bits in memory without accessing them: an experimental study of DRAM disturbance errors. In: Proceeding of the 41st Annual International Symposium on Computer Architecuture, ISCA 2014, pp. 361–372. IEEE Press, Piscataway, NJ, USA (2014)

41. Lenstra, A.K.: Memo on RSA signature generation in the presence of faults (1996)

42. May, T.C., Woods, M.H.: A new physical mechanism for soft errors in dynamic memories. In: 16th International Reliability Physics Symposium, pp. 33–40, April 1978

43. McGrew, D.A., Viega, J.: The security and performance of the Galois/Counter Mode (GCM) of operation. In: Canteaut, A., Viswanathan, K. (eds.) INDOCRYPT 2004. LNCS, vol. 3348, pp. 343–355. Springer, Heidelberg (2004). https://doi.org/ 10.1007/978-3-540-30556-9_27

44. M'Raïhi, D., Naccache, D., Pointcheval, D., Vaudenay, S.: Computational alternatives to random number generators. In: Tavares, S., Meijer, H. (eds.) SAC 1998. LNCS, vol. 1556, pp. 72–80. Springer, Heidelberg (1999). https://doi.org/10.1007/ 3-540-48892-8_6

45. Namprempre, C., Rogaway, P., Shrimpton, T.: Reconsidering generic composition. In: Nguyen, P.Q., Oswald, E. (eds.) EUROCRYPT 2014. LNCS, vol. 8441, pp. 257–274. Springer, Heidelberg (2014). https://doi.org/10.1007/978-3-642-55220-5_15

46. National Institute of Standards and Technology: Digital Signature Standard (DSS) (FIPS PUB 186–4), July 2013

47. Perrin, T.: The XEdDSA and VXEdDSA signature schemes (2016). https://signal. org/docs/specifications/xeddsa/

48. Poddebniak, D., Somorovsky, J., Schinzel, S., Lochter, M., Rösler, P.: Attacking deterministic signature schemes using fault attacks. In: 2018 IEEE European Symposium on Security and Privacy, EuroS&P 2018, pp. 338–352. IEEE, April 2018

49. Pornin, T.: Deterministic Usage of the Digital Signature Algorithm (DSA) and Elliptic Curve Digital Signature Algorithm (ECDSA). RFC 6979 (Informational), August 2013. https://www.rfc-editor.org/rfc/rfc6979.txt

50. Razavi, K., Gras, B., Bosman, E., Preneel, B., Giuffrida, C., Bos, H.: Flip Feng Shui: hammering a needle in the software stack. In: Holz, T., Savage, S. (eds.) USENIX Security 2016, pp. 1–18. USENIX Association, August 2016

51. Rogaway, P.: Authenticated-encryption with associated-data. In: Atluri, V. (ed.) ACM CCS 2002, pp. 98–107. ACM Press, November 2002

52. Rogaway, P.: Nonce-based symmetric encryption. In: Roy, B., Meier, W. (eds.) FSE 2004. LNCS, vol. 3017, pp. 348–358. Springer, Heidelberg (2004). https://doi.org/ 10.1007/978-3-540-25937-4_22

53. Rogaway, P., Shrimpton, T.: A provable-security treatment of the key-wrap problem. In: Vaudenay, S. (ed.) EUROCRYPT 2006. LNCS, vol. 4004, pp. 373–390. Springer, Heidelberg (2006). https://doi.org/10.1007/11761679_23

54. Romailler, Y., Pelissier, S.: Practical fault attack against the Ed25519 and EdDSA signature schemes. In: 2017 Workshop on Fault Diagnosis and Tolerance in Cryptography (FDTC), pp. 17–24 (2017)
55. Samwel, N., Batina, L.: Practical fault injection on deterministic signatures: the case of EdDSA. In: Joux, A., Nitaj, A., Rachidi, T. (eds.) AFRICACRYPT 2018. LNCS, vol. 10831, pp. 306–321. Springer, Cham (2018). https://doi.org/10.1007/978-3-319-89339-6_17
56. Samwel, N., Batina, L., Bertoni, G., Daemen, J., Susella, R.: Breaking Ed25519 in WolfSSL. In: Smart, N.P. (ed.) CT-RSA 2018. LNCS, vol. 10808, pp. 1–20. Springer, Cham (2018). https://doi.org/10.1007/978-3-319-76953-0_1
57. Schmidt, B.: [curves] EdDSA specification (2016). https://moderncrypto.org/mail-archive/curves/2016/000768.html
58. Signal: Technical documentation. https://whispersystems.org/docs/
59. Takahashi, A., Tibouchi, M.: Degenerate fault attacks on elliptic curve parameters in OpenSSL. In: 2019 IEEE European Symposium on Security and Privacy, EuroS&P 2019. IEEE, June 2019, to appear
60. Vaudenay, S.: The security of DSA and ECDSA. In: Desmedt, Y.G. (ed.) PKC 2003. LNCS, vol. 2567, pp. 309–323. Springer, Heidelberg (2003). https://doi.org/10.1007/3-540-36288-6_23
61. Ylonen, T., Lonvick, C. (ed.) The Secure Shell (SSH) Authentication Protocol. RFC 4252 (Proposed Standard), January 2006. https://www.rfc-editor.org/rfc/rfc4252.txt, updated by RFCs 8308, 8332

Cryptanalysis of the Multivariate Encryption Scheme EFLASH

Morten Øygarden[1](✉), Patrick Felke[2], Håvard Raddum[1], and Carlos Cid[1,3]

[1] Simula UiB, Bergen, Norway
{morten.oygarden,haavardr}@simula.no
[2] University of Applied Sciences Emden-Leer, Emden, Germany
patrick.felke@hs-emden-leer.de
[3] Royal Holloway University of London, Egham, UK
carlos.cid@rhul.ac.uk

Abstract. EFLASH is a multivariate public-key encryption scheme proposed by Cartor and Smith-Tone at SAC 2018. In this paper we investigate the hardness of solving the particular equation systems arising from EFLASH, and show that the solving degree for these types of systems is much lower than estimated by the authors. We show that a Gröbner basis algorithm will produce *degree fall polynomials* at a low degree for EFLASH systems. In particular we are able to accurately predict the number of these polynomials occurring at step degrees 3 and 4 in our attacks. We performed several experiments using the computer algebra system MAGMA, which indicate that the solving degree is at most one higher than the one where degree fall polynomials occur; moreover, our experiments show that whenever the predicted number of degree fall polynomials is positive, it is exact. Our conclusion is that EFLASH does not offer the level of security claimed by the designers. In particular, we estimate that the EFLASH version with 80-bit security parameters offers at most 69 bits of security.

1 Introduction

Public-key cryptosystems whose security is based on the hardness of solving multivariate polynomial systems over finite fields have been studied for several decades. This problem is believed to be hard to solve even for full–scale quantum computers, and so multivariate cryptography has received increasing attention the past years as post–quantum cryptography has become ever more important. A noteworthy initiative in this area is the ongoing post–quantum standardization process by the National Institute of Standards and Technology (NIST).

One of the earliest and most notable examples of multivariate cryptosystems is the encryption scheme C^* proposed by Matsumoto and Imai in 1988 [22]. Their idea was to let the public polynomial system defined over a small base field have a secret, but simple description over a larger extension field, where decryption can be done efficiently. While C^* was broken by Patarin in 1995 [23], several schemes were later proposed based on the same underlying idea; these are often

© Springer Nature Switzerland AG 2020
S. Jarecki (Ed.): CT-RSA 2020, LNCS 12006, pp. 85–105, 2020.
https://doi.org/10.1007/978-3-030-40186-3_5

referred to as *big field schemes*. One generalisation is to make the central map over the extension field more complex. Examples include HFE and its variants [24], as well as k–ary C^* [18]. Another idea is to keep the simple description over the extension field, but alter the resulting public key with modifiers that enhance the security against known attacks, as for example done in SFLASH [25] and PFLASH [7].

While there are presently several multivariate *signature* schemes that have resisted years of cryptanalysis, designing multivariate *encryption* schemes seems to be much more challenging. Examples of multivariate encryption schemes that have been successfully cryptanalysed include not only the original C^* [22,23], but also HFE [3,24], ABC [21,28], ZFHE [5,27] and SRP [26,29]. This observation is further echoed by the fact that all four multivariate cryptosystems that have made it to the second round of the NIST standardization process are signature schemes. EFLASH [6], proposed by Cartor and Smith-Tone at SAC 2018, is yet another attempt to design a secure and efficient multivariate encryption scheme. At its core, EFLASH is a modified C^* scheme with a new decryption strategy to maintain effectiveness.

1.1   Our Contribution

We present a direct algebraic cryptanalysis of EFLASH, based on the notion of *first fall degree*. We do so by developing a method to estimate this degree for the equation systems arising from EFLASH – an original approach which is different from the rank–based analysis that has been used against somewhat similar HFE variants. We are not only able to predict the first fall degree itself, but also the exact number of first fall polynomials occurring at step degrees 3 and 4. Our analysis indicates that EFLASH does not offer the level of security claimed by the designers; in particular, we are able to successfully cryptanalyse the EFLASH version with 80-bit security parameters. Ultimately, we hope that our approach can lead to a deeper understanding of the impact similar modifiers have on big field schemes.

1.2   Organisation

The paper is organised as follows. In Sect. 2 we go through the required preliminaries for our analysis. This includes a description of EFLASH, a brief discussion on the complexity of Gröbner basis algorithms, along with the notions of first fall and solving degrees, as well as some results on univariate and multivariate representation of polynomials. In Sect. 3 we present and discuss the previously suggested bound on the first fall degree of EFLASH. In Sect. 4 we develop the theory behind our new approach for estimating this degree for EFLASH, and put it to the test by experiments in Sect. 5. We discuss the implications that our analysis and experiments have on the security of EFLASH in Sect. 6. Potential follow-up work is discussed in Sect. 7, with our conclusions in Sect. 8.

2   Preliminaries

2.1   Description of EFLASH

EFLASH is a public-key encryption scheme proposed at SAC 2018 [6]. The system is built around the C^* encryption scheme by Matsumoto and Imai [22], using both the minus-modifier that removes some polynomials from the public key, and the embedding of the plaintext space $\mathbb{F}_q^n$ into a larger space $\mathbb{F}_q^d$. The signature scheme PFLASH [7,13] is built in the same way, and EFLASH can be seen as the encryption variant of PFLASH.

The C^* scheme has operations taking place in $\mathbb{F}_q^d$ and $\mathbb{F}_{q^d}$. The encryption for C^* can be explained as follows: the plaintext and ciphertext spaces are both $\mathbb{F}_q^d$. Let S and T be two invertible $d \times d$-matrices over $\mathbb{F}_q$, defining linear transformations of $\mathbb{F}_q^d$. Fix an isomorphism between $\mathbb{F}_q^d$ and $\mathbb{F}_{q^d}$, denoted by ϕ, where $\phi : \mathbb{F}_q^d \longrightarrow \mathbb{F}_{q^d}$. Finally, we have the central mapping $X \mapsto X^{1+q^\Theta}$ over $\mathbb{F}_{q^d}$. These mappings are combined together into P' as follows

$$P' = T \circ \phi^{-1} \circ X^{1+q^\Theta} \circ \phi \circ S. \tag{1}$$

Since the exponent of X has q-weight 2 and all other operations are linear, P' can be expressed as d quadratic polynomials in d variables over $\mathbb{F}_q$. The secret key of the C^* scheme are the two matrices S, T, and the public key consists of the polynomials P'. Encryption of a plaintext x into the ciphertext y is done by computing $y = P'(x)$. Decryption by someone knowing S and T can be done efficiently by inverting all operations in (1).

In [23] the basic C^* scheme was broken, by finding bilinear polynomials $f_i(x, y) = 0$ that relate the plaintext x with the ciphertext y. Computing the polynomials f_i's turns out to be easy, more so when knowing S and T. In fact, the most efficient decryption is actually done by inserting the values of y in the f_i's, and solving the resulting linear system of equations to recover the plaintext.

EFLASH expands the C^* scheme by adding an embedding π at the beginning and a projection τ in the end. More specifically, for $n < m < d$, the operations π and τ are defined as

$$\pi : \quad \begin{array}{c} \mathbb{F}_q^n \longrightarrow \mathbb{F}_q^d \\ (x_1, \ldots, x_n) \longmapsto (x_1, \ldots, x_n, 0, \ldots, 0) \end{array}$$

and

$$\tau : \quad \begin{array}{c} \mathbb{F}_q^d \longrightarrow \mathbb{F}_q^m \\ (y_1, \ldots, y_d) \longmapsto (y_1, \ldots, y_m). \end{array}$$

The plaintext space of EFLASH is then $\mathbb{F}_q^n$ and the ciphertext space is $\mathbb{F}_q^m$. The mappings π and τ are added as wrappers around the C^* scheme, so the complete EFLASH mapping P becomes

$$P = \tau \circ P' \circ \pi.$$

The complete diagram of mappings is shown in Fig. 1.

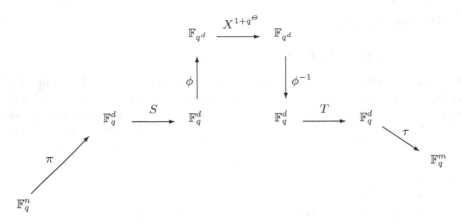

Fig. 1. Diagram of EFLASH mappings.

The extra mappings π and τ just add and remove some coordinates, so P can still be expressed as m quadratic polynomials over $\mathbb{F}_q$ in n variables. The size of the projection τ is an important parameter, so for convenience we define $a = d - m$ to be the number of polynomials removed from P'. The public key of EFLASH consists of the m polynomials in P, and the secret key is still the two matrices S, T (we assume the exponent Θ is publicly known).

Encryption in EFLASH is done the same way as for C^*: the plaintext x is transformed into ciphertext y by computing $y = P(x)$. On the other hand decryption is not as completely straightforward as for C^*. For a given ciphertext $y = (y_1, \ldots, y_m)$, the decryptor will exhaustively try all possible values for the missing coordinates $y_{m+1}, \ldots, y_d$, and decrypt every choice using the bilinear polynomials $f_i(x, y)$ from the C^* scheme. This results in up to q^a possible plaintexts embedded in $\mathbb{F}_q^d$, and the one whose last $d - n$ coordinates are all zero is chosen as the correct one. As $n < m$ we can expect there will be only one possible plaintext fulfilling the restriction given by π. In [6] the authors analyse the probability of there being two or more possible plaintexts matching a given ciphertext, which would lead to a decryption failure. For the suggested choices of n, m, d the probability is approximately 2^{-17}, which is still non-negligible.

Table 1 shows the parameters suggested in [6] for 80- and 128-bit security levels against an attacker with either a classical or quantum computer available.

In the remainder of the paper we will fix $q = 2$. Although most of the theory presented in later sections can be generalised to other fields, this is what is often used in practice and in particular what is suggested in EFLASH (Table 1).

Table 1. Suggested parameters (q, n, m, d) for EFLASH.

	80-bit security	128-bit security
Classical adversary	$(2, 80, 96, 101)$	$(2, 134, 150, 159)$
Quantum adversary	$(2, 160, 176, 181)$	$(2, 256, 272, 279)$

2.2   Gröbner Basis Algorithms

As is the case for all multivariate encryption schemes, the plaintext $(a_1, ..., a_n)$ associated to the ciphertext $(y_1, ..., y_m)$ can be found through direct attacks, that is, by solving the polynomial system

$$p_1(x_1, ..., x_n) + y_1 = \ldots = p_m(x_1, ..., x_n) + y_m = 0,$$

where $p_i(x_1, ..., x_n)$, $1 \leq i \leq m$, are the quadratic polynomials that make up the public key P. The usual strategy for solving such a system is to compute a Gröbner basis (see [8] for further details) for the ideal $\langle p_i + y_i \rangle_{1 \leq i \leq m}$ in the grevlex monomial order, using a state–of–the–art algorithm such as F_4 [14] or F_5 [15]. Since we implicitly include the field equations, the system generates a radical ideal. The solution of this system can by design be assumed to be unique and thus we are able to solve it directly from the Gröbner basis, which is by the above remark $x_1 + a_1, \ldots, x_n + a_n$ for any term ordering.

In our setting the F_4 algorithm will proceed step–wise, and to each step there is an associated *step degree D*, which is the maximal degree of the polynomials involved in this step. The complexity of each step is dominated by reduction of a Macaulay matrix associated with these polynomials. If we define the *solving degree*, D_{solv}, to be the step degree associated with the largest such matrix (this notation was introduced in [12]), then the complexity of the algorithm (in the Boolean case) can be estimated by:

$$\text{Complexity}_{\text{GB}} = \mathcal{O}\left(\left(\sum_{i=0}^{D_{solv}} \binom{n}{i} \right)^\omega \right), \tag{2}$$

where n is the number of variables and $2 \leq \omega \leq 3$ is the linear algebra constant. This makes D_{solv} crucial for estimating the complexity of a direct attack, but in general this value is difficult to determine. It is also worth noting that D_{solv} is not necessarily the highest degree encountered in the algorithm; indeed [12] shows examples of this for HFE–systems, while we will also see examples where this is the case for EFLASH in Sect. 5.

An important class of polynomial systems where D_{solv} can be determined is the class of *semi–regular sequences* [1]. In this case D_{solv} will coincide with the degree of regularity D_{reg}, which for quadratic polynomial systems over $\mathbb{F}_2$ can be calculated as the degree of the first non–positive term in the series [2]:

$$T_{m,n}(z) = \frac{(1+z)^n}{(1+z^2)^m}. \tag{3}$$

From experiments it seems to be the case that randomly generated polynomial systems will behave as semi–regular sequences [1], and the degree of regularity is in many instances sensible to use for complexity estimation. However, it is well known that polynomial systems associated with big field multivariate cryptography tend to have a lower solving degree than what is predicted by the degree of regularity; see for example [16]. For these schemes the notion of *first fall degree*

(Definition 1), which in general provides a lower bound for the solving degree, has often been used to estimate the complexity of solving such systems [10,11]. The authors of EFLASH have also chosen this path, and in [6] a bound for the first fall degree was derived and used to estimate the resistance of this scheme against algebraic attacks. We will later argue that this derived bound for the first fall degree is not tight, but the idea of using this invariant as an approximation for the solving degree seems justified for EFLASH. Indeed, in all our experiments we find the solving degree to be either the same or one greater than the first fall degree (see Sect. 5). We end this subsection by recalling the definition of first fall degree.

Consider the graded quotient ring $B = \mathbb{F}_2[x_1, ..., x_n]/\langle x_1^2, ..., x_n^2 \rangle$, where $B_\nu \subset B$ is the set of homogeneous polynomials of degree ν in B. Let $p_1^h, ..., p_m^h \in B_2$ be the homogeneous quadratic part of the polynomials in the public-key P, and $p_i^l, 1 \leq i \leq m$ be the corresponding linear, or lower-degree, terms, so that $p_i = p_i^h + p_i^l$. We can then define the map

$$\psi_{\nu-2} : \quad B_{\nu-2}^m \quad \longrightarrow \quad B_\nu$$
$$(f_1, ..., f_m) \longmapsto \sum_{i=1}^m f_i p_i^h$$

Any element of $ker(\psi_{\nu-2})$ is called a *syzygy*. Now let $\nu = 4$. Then particular syzygies are the *Kozul syzygies*, generated by $(0, ..., 0, p_j^h, 0, ..., 0, p_i^h, 0, ..., 0)$ where p_j^h is in position i and p_i^h is in position j, and the *field syzygies* generated by $(0, ..., 0, p_i^h, 0, ..., 0)$ (p_i^h in position i). These syzygies will boil down to the relations $p_j^h p_i^h + p_i^h p_j^h = 0$ and $(p_i^h)^2 = 0$. Since they are always present, and not depending on the polynomials p_i^h themselves, these syzygies generate the *trivial syzygies*, $T(\psi_{\nu-2}) \subseteq ker(\psi_{\nu-2})$.

Definition 1. *The* first fall degree *associated with the quadratic polynomial system $p_1, ..., p_m$ is the natural number*

$$D_{ff} = min\{ d \geq 2 \mid ker(\psi_{d-2})/T(\psi_{d-2}) \neq 0 \}.$$

Remark 1. *The elements* $(0, ..., 0, p_j^h, 0, ..., 0, p_i^h, 0, ..., 0)$ *and* $(0, ..., 0, p_i^h, 0, ..., 0)$ *will, strictly speaking, not be syzygies themselves when solving for $p_1, ..., p_m$ in $\mathbb{F}_2[x_1, ..., x_n]$. For example, $p_j^h p_i + p_i^h p_j \neq 0$ will in general be of degree 3. We still call these degree falls trivial, as they do not give any new or useful information in an actual attack. This fact can be seen as follows.*

When trying to solve a system by multiplying equations with all monomials up to some degree, the multiplications are done by increasing degrees. That is, all monomials of degree $\leq D - 1$ are used before multiplying with monomials of degree D. The Kozul syzygies will give the degree fall polynomial

$$p_j^h p_i + p_i^h p_j = p_j^h (p_i^h + p_i^l) + p_i^h (p_j^h + p_j^l) = p_j^h p_i^l + p_i^h p_j^l.$$

However, the very same polynomial can be expressed using only multiplication with the lower-degree monomials in p_j^l and p_i^l:

$$p_i^l p_j + p_j^l p_i = p_i^l (p_j^h + p_j^l) + p_j^l (p_i^h + p_i^l) = p_i^l p_j^h + p_j^l p_i^h.$$

Hence the degree fall generated by p_i^h and p_j^h does not give us anything new when we already have multiplied with all lower-degree terms. Moreover it is a priori clear that these polynomials reduce to zero modulo p_j, p_i and therefore give no new information when computing a Gröbner basis, except slowing the computation down.

The same holds for the field syzygies, where it is easy to see that the polynomial $p_i p_i = p_i$ can be "generated" by the (lower-degree) constant 1 as $1 \cdot p_i$.

2.3   Univariate and Multivariate Representation of Polynomials

Our analysis will heavily rely on the easy description the central map of EFLASH has as univariate polynomial over the extension field. The idea of exploiting this simple description in cryptanalysis was also used in the Kipnis–Shamir attack on HFE in [20], and we refer to their work for further details on the following result. We will write $w(t)$ to denote the *binary weight* of an integer t. Recall that this is defined as $\sum z_i$, where $t = \sum z_i 2^i$ is the 2–adic representation of t.

Theorem 1. *Let $P(X) \in \mathbb{F}_{2^d}[X]/\langle X^{2^d} + X \rangle$ and fix an isomorphism ϕ between $\mathbb{F}_{2^d}$ and $(\mathbb{F}_2)^d$. With this isomorphism, $P(X)$ admits d unique polynomials $p_1, ..., p_d \in \mathbb{F}_2[x_1, ..., x_d]/\langle x_1^2 + x_1, ..., x_d^2 + x_d \rangle$. Furthermore, the degree of the polynomials $p_1, ..., p_d$ is given by $max\{w(t) \mid X^t \in \mathcal{M}_P\}$, where $\mathcal{M}_P$ is the set of monomials in $P(X)$ with non-zero coefficients.*

Based on this result we will define the *2–weight* associated with a polynomial $P(X) \in \mathbb{F}_{2^d}[X]/\langle X^{2^d} + X \rangle$ to be $w(P) = max\{w(t) \mid X^t \in \mathcal{M}_P\}$. There are two particular actions over the extension field, and their corresponding actions over the base field, that are worth pointing out. First, we note that raising $P(X)$ to a power of 2, i.e. $(P(X))^{2^i}$, will correspond to applying an invertible linear transformation on the associated multivariate polynomials $p_1, ..., p_d$.

The second action is that the multivariate polynomials associated with the product $H(X)P(X)$ will be d sums of the form $\sum h_j p_i$, where h_i is a multivariate polynomial of maximum degree equal to $w(H)$. These actions (on the multivariate polynomials) are exactly the ones performed by Gröbner basis algorithms. Linear maps do not affect the degree of the polynomials, so if $T \circ \phi^{-1} \circ P(X) \circ \phi \circ S$ is the central map of an unmodified big field scheme (e.g. original C^* or HFE), then the degree fall polynomials encountered when computing a Gröbner basis can be described by the two aforementioned actions on the univariate polynomial $P(X)$. More specifically, we will call any combination

$$F(X) = \sum_{i,j} [C_{i,j} H_i(X) P(X)]^{2^j} \in \mathbb{F}_{2^d}[X]/\langle X^{2^d} + X \rangle,$$

where

$$w(F) < w(P) + max\{w(H_i)\},$$

a *2–weight fall polynomial*. This will in turn admit d multivariate degree fall polynomials.

We note that in the Faugère–Joux attack on HFE [16] these 2–weight fall polynomials are the reason for the effectiveness of algebraic attacks on this cryptosystem. Likewise, in [18] specific q–weight fall polynomials (i.e. the natural generalisation to other fields of size q) were constructed in order to show the first fall degree of k–ary C^*, another generalisation of C^*. Things get more complicated as modifiers are added to the public key, particularly in the case for the minus modifier. However we will describe how to deal with this in Sect. 4.

3   Suggested First Fall Degree Bound

In this section we discuss an upper bound for the first fall degree that was suggested for EFLASH in [6][1]. Since EFLASH can be seen as a special case of HFE-, the bound is derived following a similar line of reasoning as was used for this latter scheme in [11]. The idea is to first examine how the minus modifier affects the Q–rank of the quadratic form associated with the central map, and then apply this to the upper bound derived in Theorem 4.1 of [10]. The arguments made in Section 5.1 of [6] is that the minus modifier is even more effective at increasing the Q–rank when applied to EFLASH than it is for HFE-, due to the extreme sparseness of the central map of the former. This led to the following upper bound for EFLASH [6]:

$$D_{ff,EFLASH} \leq a + 3. \tag{4}$$

However we argue that focusing on Q–rank alone does not reveal the entire picture when the (unmodified) central map is as simple as it is in EFLASH. To this end we introduce the following notation, which will also be important for our own estimates of first fall degree:

Definition 2. *Consider the quotient ring* $\mathbb{F}_{2^d}[X]/\langle X^{2^d} + X \rangle$, *and an instance of* C^*. *Let* $y \in \mathbb{F}_2^d$ *represent a given ciphertext, and* $V = \phi \circ T^{-1}(y)$. *We then define*

$$Q = X^{1+2^\Theta} + V \tag{5}$$

to represent the central map associated to C^* *over* $\mathbb{F}_{2^d}[X]/\langle X^{2^d} + X \rangle$. *We also define the following 2–weight fall equations:*

$$\alpha = X^{2^{d-\Theta}}Q + X^{2^\Theta}Q^{2^{d-\Theta}} = X^{2^{d-\Theta}}V + X^{2^\Theta}V^{2^{d-\Theta}}, \tag{6}$$

$$\beta_1 = XQ = X^{2+2^\Theta} + XV \text{ and} \tag{7}$$

$$\beta_2 = X^{2^\Theta}Q = X^{1+2^{\Theta+1}} + X^{2^\Theta}V. \tag{8}$$

---

[1] The authors call this the degree of regularity, but are in fact describing the first fall degree.

Since we are not removing any polynomials (i.e. a $= 0$), Eq. (4) predicts that the polynomial Q defined above has first fall degree 3 (this is also pointed out in Example 4.3 in [10]). Here Q is treated as any polynomial with Q–rank 2, and following the proof of Theorem 4.1 in [10], we find that the predicted first fall degree is due to the existence of the univariate polynomials β_1 and β_2, which would correspond to quadratic multivariate polynomials. However, in the definition above there is also a third 2–weight fall polynomial, α, which will correspond to linear multivariate polynomials (these are the same that Patarin found in his original attack on C^* [23]). Thus there seems to be more information in the system than what is captured by methods based on the Q–rank alone. It is indeed the case that removing public polynomials makes it more difficult for an attacker, but we will see in the next section that there may still be combinations of multivariate degree fall polynomials, generated by the relations α, β_1 and β_2 present in the polynomial system. Again, methods based on the Q–rank alone do not seem to fully capture this.

Another notable difference between EFLASH and HFE- is the large dimension of the embedding ($n < d$) present in the former. We will see that this modifier also plays a role in determining the number of degree fall polynomials in a system. While it does not have the same impact as the minus modifier, there are parameters for which this affects the first fall degree of a system; see Sect. 5 for examples.

4   The First Fall Degree of EFLASH

This section starts off with a brief discussion on the impact the choice of Θ may have on the security of EFLASH. The condition that $\gcd(2^d - 1, 2^\Theta + 1) = 1$ is needed for the map X^{1+2^Θ} to be a bijection, and has been a requirement for this family of cryptosystems ever since the original paper of Matsumoto and Imai [22]. While not explicitly stated in [6], it seems reasonable to assume that this is also the case for EFLASH. We will later see that the total number of degree fall polynomials in the original C^*–scheme will have a big impact on the complexity of algebraic attacks towards EFLASH.

The question of how different choices of Θ affect the number of degree fall polynomials has partly been studied in [9]. In that work the authors consider the effect Θ has on the number of linearisation equations, which can be seen as a special subset of degree fall polynomials of degree 1. Examples of special values for Θ from this work are $\Theta = d/3$ and $\Theta = 2d/3$. In these cases it is shown that there are only $2d/3$ linearisation equations, and so it is unlikely that these choices for Θ can be used in an efficient instantiation of EFLASH (as d linear equations are used for decryption). On the other hand, there are also cases found in [9] that renders more than d linear equations, which could benefit an attacker. What would amount to special cases in our analysis will ultimately go beyond linear equations: for $D = 3$, degree falls polynomials will also include quadratic polynomials, and cubic polynomials when $D = 4$. It is beyond the scope of this paper to identify every such special case. Therefore for the rest of this paper, all equations and formulas are assumed to hold for *general* choices of Θ. *General* is here used in a non–technical sense by which we mean that we expect the result in question to hold for all values $\Theta = 0, 1, \ldots, d - 1$, save for a few exceptions.

4.1   The Effect of Removing Polynomials

We wish to obtain a representation of the central map of EFLASH that in some sense not only preserves the easy description given over the univariate polynomial ring, but also keeps track of what is lost due to the minus modifier, τ. Consider the cryptosystem in a state before τ has been applied (but after the linear transformation T, see Fig. 1). Finding a plaintext associated with a fixed ciphertext would amount to solving the system of quadratic polynomials $p_i(x_1, \ldots, x_n) = 0$, for $1 \le i \le d$ (for ease of notation we are assuming the fixed ciphertext to be part of the p_i–polynomials). Let

$$\begin{bmatrix} q_1 \\ q_2 \\ \vdots \\ q_d \end{bmatrix} = T^{-1} \begin{bmatrix} p_1 \\ p_2 \\ \vdots \\ p_d \end{bmatrix}, \tag{9}$$

in other words, each q_i is a linear combination of the polynomials $p_1, \ldots, p_d$.

Even though the polynomials p_j are depending on the x–variables, we will at an intermediate step want to consider them as formal variables. In an effort to keep the notation precise, we will write $\hat{p}_1, \ldots, \hat{p}_a$ to denote the polynomials as formal variables that will be removed by τ. On the other hand, $\bar{p}_{a+1}, \ldots, \bar{p}_d$ will denote the formal variables associated with the polynomials unaffected by τ (i.e. the public polynomials). We will also write q_i^* to denote the linear combinations defined in Eq. (9), but now depending on the formal variables $\hat{p}_j$ and $\bar{p}_k$.

In the previous section we have considered sums of the form $\sum X^{2^{i_1} + \ldots + 2^{i_k}} Q^{2^j}$ in the univariate polynomial ring $\mathbb{F}_{2^d}[X]/\langle X^{2^d} + X \rangle$. We will now inspect the same sums, but treat Q as a formal variable in the bivariate polynomial ring $\mathcal{A}_{XQ} := \mathbb{F}_{2^d}[X, Q]/\langle X^{2^d} + X, Q^{2^d} + Q \rangle$. We will furthermore write Q as $Q = (q_1^* + q_2^* \gamma + \ldots + q_d^* \gamma^{d-1})$, where γ is a primitive element associated with the isomorphism ϕ. We then consider the following composition of maps:

$$\mathcal{A}_{XQ} \xrightarrow{\phi^{-1}} (\mathbb{F}_2[x_1, \ldots, x_n, \hat{p}_1, \ldots, \hat{p}_a, \bar{p}_{a+1}, \ldots, \bar{p}_d])^d \xrightarrow{ev_{P,a}} (\mathbb{F}_2[x_1, \ldots, x_n])^d$$

where $ev_{P,a}$ acts entry–wise in the d–vector space by "evaluating" the formal variables $\hat{p}$ to 0, and regarding $\bar{p}$ as polynomials in x–variables. To be more precise, $ev_{P,a} : (z_1, \ldots, z_d) \mapsto (ev_{P,a}^*(z_1), \ldots, ev_{P,a}^*(z_d))$, where:

$$ev_{P,a}^* : \mathbb{F}_2[x_1, \ldots, x_n, \hat{p}_1, \ldots, \bar{p}_d] \longrightarrow \mathbb{F}_2[x_1, \ldots, x_n]$$

$$x_i \longmapsto x_i \text{ for } 1 \le i \le n$$

$$\hat{p}_j \longmapsto 0 \text{ for } 1 \le j \le a$$

$$\bar{p}_k \longmapsto p_k(x_1, \ldots, x_n) \text{ for } a + 1 \le k \le d.$$

It is straightforward to check that if t is an integer with 2-weight $D - 2$, then $ev_{P,a} \circ \phi^{-1}(X^t Q)$ will result in d polynomials of degree at most D, which are generated by the public polynomials $p_{a+1}, ..., p_d$. We will use this new notation to show the following lemma, which will be key in our ensuing analysis. An interpretation is that the minus modifier τ only obscures the degree fall polynomials by adding polynomials generated from a small set, namely the removed polynomials $p_1, ..., p_a$.

Lemma 1. *Let $ev_{P,0} \circ \phi^{-1}(\sum X^{k_1} Q^{k_2})$ give d polynomials over $\mathbb{F}_2[x_1, ..., x_n]$ that are degree fall polynomials of degree $< D = w(k_1) + 2w(k_2)$. Then, for $a > 0$ the degree D-parts of the d polynomials $ev_{P,a} \circ \phi^{-1}(\sum X^{k_1} Q^{k_2})$ are generated by $p_1, ..., p_a$.*

Proof. Let g be any of the d polynomials in $\mathbb{F}_2[x_1, ..., x_n, \hat{p}_1, ..., \bar{p}_d]$, that are in the image of $\phi^{-1}(\sum X^{k_1} Q^{k_2})$. Fix polynomials $h_1, h_2, ..., h_{a+1}$ such that we can write g on the triangular form:

$$g = h_1(x_1, ..., x_n, \hat{p}_2, ..., \hat{p}_a, \bar{p}_{a+1}, ..., \bar{p}_d)\hat{p}_1$$
$$+ h_2(x_1, ..., x_n, \hat{p}_3, ..., \hat{p}_a, \bar{p}_{a+1}, ..., \bar{p}_d)\hat{p}_2$$
$$\vdots$$
$$+ h_a(x_1, ..., x_n, \bar{p}_{a+1}, ..., \bar{p}_d)\hat{p}_a$$
$$+ h_{a+1}(x_1, ..., x_n, \bar{p}_{a+1}, ..., \bar{p}_d)$$

Recall that when $a > 0$ then $ev_{P,a}^*(\hat{p}_j) = 0$ for $1 \leq j \leq a$. Since we are working over a field of characteristic 2, we can equivalently think of this as addition with all terms containing the $\hat{p}_j$-variables and then evaluating everything using $ev_{P,0}^*$. Note that all $\hat{p}_i$ change to $\bar{p}_i$ when evaluated with $ev_{P,0}^*$ instead of $ev_{P,a}^*$. This can then be written out as follows:

$$ev_{P,a}^*(g) = ev_{P,0}^*(g + \sum_{1 \leq i \leq a} h_i \bar{p}_i)$$
$$= ev_{P,0}^*(g) + ev_{P,0}^*\left(\sum_{1 \leq i \leq a} h_i \bar{p}_i\right)$$
$$= ev_{P,0}^*(g) + \sum_{1 \leq i \leq a} h_i p_i.$$

By assumption $ev_{P,0}^*(g)$ has degree $< D$ so any term of degree D must come from $\sum_{1 \leq i \leq a} h_i p_i$, which proves the statement. $\square$

One observation that can be drawn from this lemma is that if the number of degree fall polynomials that would be generated by a similar polynomial system with $a = 0$ exceed the number of highest degree combinations generated by the removed polynomials (i.e. the possible combinations of $x_{i_1}...x_{i_{D-2}}\hat{p}_j$), then there will be linear combinations of the degree fall polynomials that can be written without the use of $\hat{p}_j$-elements. These can in turn be found by an attacker through the use of Gröbner basis algorithms. This is the intuition that will be further explored in the following subsections, but first we illustrate the point for the bilinear equations in the following example:

Example 1. *Consider an EFLASH instance with $a = 1$. Recall from Eq. (6) in Definition 2 that the bilinear relations come from $\alpha = X^{2^{d-\Theta}} Q + X^{2^{\Theta}} Q^{2^{d-\Theta}}$. By Lemma 1 we can write $ev_{P,1} \circ \phi^{-1}(\alpha)$ as d polynomials in the ring $\mathbb{F}_2[x_1, ..., x_n]$, whose degree 3–part are linear combinations of $x_i \hat{p}_1$ for $1 \leq i \leq n$. This means that the homogeneous degree 3–part has at most dimension n, whereas the image of $ev_{P,1} \circ \phi^{-1}(\alpha)$ has dimension d (under the assumption that the resulting d polynomials are linearly independent). Since $d > n$ for EFLASH, this means that there will be $d - n$ different independent linear combinations of these polynomials that can be written without using $\hat{p}_1$. As a result a Gröbner basis algorithm will find $d - n$ linear relations at $D = 3$.*

It is worth pointing out that the embedding modifier π, while needed to protect against differential attacks and more sophisticated attacks, as e.g. in [4], actually weakens the effect of the minus modifier τ. Indeed, had there been no embedding, i.e. $d = n$, we would not expect to find any linear relations at $D = 3$ in the example above. Thus in this special case we see there is a trade-off between π and τ. Without the embedding one would have to deal with the above mentioned attacks while the classic attack by Patarin would be prevented. On the other hand, by applying the embedding you would get back parts of the linear relations from Patarin's classical attacks while preventing the above attacks. This shows that more research is required to better understand how to securely combine the two kinds of modifiers.

In the next two subsections we will focus on how things evolve when increasing the step degree D. We start by generalising Example 1 to include more degree falls at $D = 3$.

4.2   First Fall Polynomials at $D = 3$

In Definition 2 we saw that with $a = 0$, we will in addition to the linear polynomials given by α (Eq. (6)) also have two more quadratic degree falls given by β_1 and β_2 (Eqs. (7) and (8)). The $3d$ multivariate polynomials associated to these will in general account for all the degree fall polynomials that show up at step degree $D = 3$. Lemma 1 implies that when $a > 0$ these polynomials will generally be of degree 3, where the degree 3–part is further generated by the polynomials $x_i p_j$, for $1 \leq i \leq n$ and $1 \leq j \leq a$. Hence there are $3d$ resulting polynomials where the top degree is generated by na elements, and so an estimate of the number of degree fall polynomials at $D = 3$ can be found by merely subtracting the two. To be more precise, recall from Sect. 2.2 that $ker(\psi_{D-2})/T(\psi_{D-2})$ denotes the vector space of non–trivial degree fall polynomials at degree D. We write $\{\#P_{df}\}_D = dim(ker(\psi_{D-2})/T(\psi_{D-2}))$ for its dimension, and derive the following estimate for $\{\#P_{df}\}_3$:

$$N_3(n, d, a) = 3d - na. \tag{10}$$

When N_3 is negative, we do not expect to find any degree fall polynomials. In this case we take $\max\{N_3, 0\}$ as the estimate for $\{\#P_{df}\}_3$. The accuracy of this estimate will be tested in Sect. 5

4.3   First Fall Polynomials at $D = 4$

The analysis gets more complicated at step degree 4, mainly due to the syzygies appearing in the polynomial system at this degree. More specifically we wish to find out what polynomials in $\mathcal{A}_{XQ}$ that will correspond to multivariate degree falls that are considered trivial, in the sense of Remark 1, by Gröbner basis algorithms. The following lemma classifies these polynomials.

Lemma 2. *The polynomials associated with*

$$ev_{P,a} \circ \phi^{-1}\big[(X^{1+2^{\Theta}})^{2^{k_1}} Q^{2^{k_2}}\big], \text{ for } 0 \leq k_1, k_2 \leq d-1.$$

can be written on the form:

$$\sum_{\substack{1 \leq i \leq d \\ a+1 \leq j_1 \leq d \\ i \neq j_1}} b_{i,j_1} p_i p_{j_1} + \sum_{a+1 \leq j_2 \leq d} c_{j_2} p_{j_2}, \text{ for } b_{i,j_1}, c_{j_2} \in \mathbb{F}_2. \tag{11}$$

Proof. We prove the statement for the case $k_2 = 0$ (other values of k_2 can be written as a power of 2 of this case). For the ciphertext $(y_1, ..., y_d)$, write:

$$\begin{bmatrix} y_1' \\ y_2' \\ \vdots \\ y_d' \end{bmatrix} = T^{-1} \begin{bmatrix} y_1 \\ y_2 \\ \vdots \\ y_d \end{bmatrix}.$$

Recall that we included the ciphertext in the definition of the p_i–polynomials, so this must be accounted for when considering $X^{1+2^{\Theta}}$ (which will contain no constant terms). We then have:

$$(X^{1+2^{\Theta}})^{2^{k_1}} Q = \left[\sum_{i=1}^{d} (q_i + y_i')\gamma^{(i-1)2^{k_1}} \right] \cdot \left[\sum_{j=1}^{d} q_j^* \gamma^{j-1} \right],$$

and so if g is any of the d polynomials in $\phi^{-1}((X^{1+2^{\Theta}})^{2^{k_1}} Q)$, we can write:

$$g = q_1^* \left[\sum_{i=1}^{d} g_{1i}(q_i + y_i') \right] + ... + q_d^* \left[\sum_{i=1}^{d} g_{di}(q_i + y_i') \right]$$

for some $g_{ji} \in \mathbb{F}_2$. Recall that the q_i's are linear combinations of $p_1, ...p_d$ (written out in $\mathbb{F}_2[x_1, ..., x_n]$) and will be unaffected by $ev_{p,a}^*$. The q_i^*'s are linear combinations of the formal variables $\hat{p}_1, ..., \bar{p}_d$. Since the evaluation map sends all the variables $\hat{p}_1, ...\hat{p}_a$ to zero, the statement (11) in the lemma now follows from $ev_{p,a}^*(g)$. $\qquad\square$

We note that a system of quadratic polynomials $p_1, ..., p_d$ with the property that a sum of the form $\sum_{i \neq j} b_{i,j} p_i p_j$, with $b_{i,j} \in \mathbb{F}_2$, results in a non–trivial degree fall (i.e. one not generated by Kozul Syzygies) would be a very degenerate system, not suitable for multivariate cryptography. We may assume therefore that a polynomial system associated with C^* is very unlikely to have this property. Thus, under the assumption that no such non–trivial relation exists, Lemma 2 implies that any degree fall polynomial that originates from a sum of the form $\sum_{k_1, k_2} c_{k_1, k_2} (X^{1+2^\Theta})^{2^{k_1}} Q^{2^{k_2}}$ is simply a linear combination of the public polynomials $p_{a+1}, ..., p_d$. As this gives no new information to an attacker, it should be regarded as trivial (similar to what was discussed in Remark 1).

We may now return to the question of what degree fall combinations that should be counted. The polynomials α, β_1 and β_2 discussed earlier, when multiplied with X^{2^i} will also generate degree fall polynomials for $D = 4$. Indeed, our experiments suggest that all of degree fall polynomials at this step degree are generated by these elements.

At first glance there will be $3dn$ multivariate polynomials associated with the elements $X^{2^i} \alpha$, $X^{2^i} \beta_1$ and $X^{2^i} \beta_2$ for $1 \leq i \leq d$. Note that here we are using the fact that the variable X may be written using linear combinations of the n variables $x_1, ..., x_n$. Hence, multiplying by all $X, X^2, ..., X^{2^{d-1}}$ will effectively only give n different combinations, as opposed to d. However, not all of these should be counted, for various reasons. We list the exceptions below:

- $X\beta_1 = X^2 Q$ and $X^{2^\Theta} \beta_2 = X^{2^{\Theta+1}} Q$ are both generated at step degree $D = 3$, and not step degree $D = 4$.
- $X^{2^\Theta} \beta_1 = X^{1+2^\Theta} Q = X\beta_2$, will be cases of the trivial degree falls discussed in Lemma 2. The same is true for $X^{2^{d-\Theta}} \beta_1 = (X^{1+2^\Theta})^{2^{d-\Theta}} Q$ and $X^{2^{2\Theta}} \beta_2 = (X^{1+2^\Theta})^{2^\Theta} Q$. Lastly, the following is a sum of two trivial degree falls: $X\alpha = (X^{1+2^\Theta})^{2^{d-\Theta}} Q + X^{1+2^\Theta} Q^{2^{d-\Theta}}$.
- From $X^{2^{d-\Theta}} \alpha = X^{2^{d-\Theta+1}} Q + X^{2^{d-\Theta}+2^\Theta} Q^{2^{d-\Theta}} = X^{2^{d-\Theta+1}} Q + \left(X^{2^{2\Theta}} \beta_1\right)^{2^{d-\Theta}}$ we see that $X^{2^{d-\Theta}} \alpha$ can be written out as a polynomial generated by β_1, and one regular polynomial of degree 3. For this reason, the degree fall polynomials generated by either $X^{2^{d-\Theta}} \alpha$ or $X^{2^{2\Theta}} \beta_1$ do not bring anything new to the system once the other has been created, and so only one should be counted. The same is true for $X^{2^\Theta} \alpha = X^{2^{d-\Theta}} \beta_2 + X^{2^{\Theta+1}} Q^{2^{d-\Theta}}$.

There are two, five and two relations from the first to last bullet point, respectively, which do not count towards generating new degree fall polynomials made from $X^{2^i} \alpha$, $X^{2^i} \beta_1$ and $X^{2^i} \beta_2$. Summing these up we find that the adjusted number of degree fall polynomials at $a = 0$ should be $(3n - 9)d$.

It may initially seem like there are $a\binom{n}{2}$ removed polynomials of degree 4, namely all combinations $x_i x_j \hat{p}_k$, but this does not take into account the trivial syzygies arising from the fact that the $\hat{p}_k$'s are ultimately polynomials in the x_i-variables. Thus one should retract all combinations of trivial syzygies involving the $\hat{p}_k$-elements, namely the field syzygies; $\hat{p}_k^2 + \hat{p}_k = 0$ and Kozul syzygies of the types $\hat{p}_i \hat{p}_k + \hat{p}_k \hat{p}_i = 0$, for $i, k \in \{1, ..., a\}$, and $\hat{p}_k \bar{p}_j + \hat{p}_j \hat{p}_k = 0$, for $k \in \{1, ..., a\}$

and $j \in \{a+1, \ldots, d\}$. There are a such field equations, $\binom{a}{2}$ of the Kozul syzygies of the first type and $a(d-a)$ Kozul syzygies of the second type. This sums up to

$$a + \binom{a}{2} + a(d-a) = ad + \frac{a - a^2}{2},$$

which should be subtracted from $a\binom{n}{2}$ to give the precise number of degree fall polynomials lost due to τ. Similar to the case $D = 3$, we can now add together everything discussed so far to obtain an estimate of the number of linearly independent degree fall polynomials at $D = 4$:

$$N_4(n, d, a) = (3n - 9)d - a\binom{n}{2} + ad + \frac{a - a^2}{2}. \qquad (12)$$

Again, N_4 may become negative, so we take $\max\{N_4, 0\}$ to be our estimate for $\{\#P_{df}\}_4$.

5   Experimental Results

We now present experimental results to test the validity of the formulas from the previous section predicting the number of first fall polynomials. In the first set of experiments (Table 2) we vary the choices of parameters d, n, a and Θ. The numbers N_3 and N_4 have been calculated according to Eqs. (10) and (12), and the predicted first fall degree is the first degree where we expect a positive value. We then give the first fall degree and the number of first fall polynomials obtained at this step from the Gröbner basis routine in the MAGMA computer algebra system. In all our experiments the degree of the first fall polynomials were maximal, i.e. one less than the first fall degree. The solving degree is measured as the degree associated with the step having the largest matrix in the algorithm.

Table 2. Experimental results for EFLASH with varying parameters.

d	n	a	θ	N_3/N_4	D_{ff} (predicted)	D_{ff} (Magma)	$\{\#P_{df}\}_{D_{ff}}$ (Magma)	D_{solv}	$a+3$	D_{reg}
51	49	5	13	$-92/1403$	4	4	1403	4	8	9
51	49	3	13	$6/3660$	3	3	6	4	6	9
53	39	7	13	$-114/887$	4	4	887	5	10	7
56	40	9	8	$-192/-336$	≥ 5	4	20	5	12	7
56	40	4	8	$8/3314$	3	3	8	4	7	7
60	50	4	8	$-20/3794$	4	4	3794	4	7	8
63	50	3	7	$39/5394$	3	3	39	4*	6	8
63	50	3	5	$39/5394$	3	3	39	4*	6	8

* The highest degree reached in MAGMA was 5, but this step occurred after 50 linear relations were found, and consequently had little impact on the running time.

In Section 5.1 of [6] the authors note that smaller EFLASH–systems could be solved at degree equal to or one lower than for random systems of the same parameters (D_{reg} in our notation). As the systems (and hence also D_{reg}) grow in size, it was suggested to use the bound in Eq. (4), namely $a + 3$. We have included both D_{reg} and this bound in the last two columns of the table for comparison. One can notice that these values do not seem to be an adequate measure of the solving degree in our experiments.

Note that the first two entries satisfy the condition $n > d - a = m$. This is to emphasise that the validity of our theory is not only restricted to EFLASH (e.g. the parameters in the PFLASH signature scheme are taken to be $n > d - a$). There are several observations from Table 2 that we would like to point out. The first is that when at least one of the predictions N_3 and N_4 is positive, then our theory accurately predicts both the first fall degree and the number of polynomials obtained. An odd case in this regard happens in the fourth row, where we do not expect any degree fall polynomials at $D = 4$, but the GB algorithm is still able to find a small number of them. Secondly, we note that the recorded first fall degree and solving degrees are either the same or one apart in all the experiments. It is possible that this relation may be understood through the number of first fall polynomials. For example, a low $\{\#P_{df}\}_{D_{ff}}$ could imply $D_{solv} = D_{ff} + 1$, whereas a large $\{\#P_{df}\}_{D_{ff}}$ implies $D_{solv} = D_{ff}$, but any further exploration into this is beyond the scope of this paper.

The third point we wish to elaborate on from Table 2 is that the last two experiments differs only in $\Theta = 7$ and 5. Here 7 is a divisor of $d = 63$, while 5 is not. We obtain the same number of degree fall polynomials, indicating that for direct methods it does not seem to make a difference whether Θ divides d, as opposed to other attacks (see e.g. [17]).

In the next set of experiments we have fixed the value of the parameters $d = 56$, $n = 40$ and $\Theta = 8$, while only varying the number a of removed public polynomials. Note that when $a = 9$ this is the same case as presented in row 2 of Table 2. In these experiments we only present N_4 from Eq. (12) and the first fall degree and number of first fall polynomials measured by MAGMA.

For $6 \leq a \leq 8$ in Table 3 we find a positive value for N_4 and in these cases the theory exactly matches the experimental results. For $9 \leq a \leq 11$ the theory predicts no degree fall polynomials at $D = 4$, but MAGMA is still able to find a small number of degree fall polynomials here. We see that this number decreases by 9 as a is increased. When $a = 12$ public polynomials have been removed, no degree fall polynomials are detected at $D = 4$, but a substantial amount is found at $D = 5$.

This type of behaviour observed for $9 \leq a \leq 11$, with a small set of degree fall polynomials not predicted by Eq. (12) has also been observed for other sets of parameters, so we do not believe that the parameters considered in Table 3 form a special case with regards to this. At this point we are not able to explain what causes these degree fall polynomials.

Table 3. Effects of increasing a for $d = 56$, $n = 40$, $\Theta = 8$. The entry marked with * has been measured at $D = 5$.

a	Measured D_{ff}	N_4	$\{\#P_{df}\}_{D_{ff}}$
6	4	1857	1857
7	4	1127	1127
8	4	396	396
9	4	-336	20
10	4	-1069	11
11	4	-1803	2
12	5	-2538	8552*

6   Security Estimation for EFLASH

Based on our results from previous sections, we now examine the suggested 80–bit security parameters for EFLASH versus classical and quantum adversaries (Table 1), using our formula for $N_4(n, d, a)$ in Eq. (12). We find

$$N_4(80, 101, 5) = 8026 \quad \text{and} \quad N_4(160, 181, 5) = 22546,$$

which means that we expect that these sets of parameters will both admit a first fall degree of 4. From the experiments in the previous section we observed that when N_4 gives a positive number, it predicts the number of degree fall polynomials precisely. Furthermore, in all our experiments we find that the solving degree is at most one greater than the first fall degree. In Table 4 we have computed the complexity of solving the EFLASH equation system on these parameter sets using Eq. (2) when D_{solv} is 4 and 5. We have chosen to include two values that are typically used for ω: 2.4 corresponding to the smallest known value (here up to 1 decimal precision), and 2.8 which is the value from Strassen's algorithm. From Table 4 we find that both sets of parameters fail to achieve 80–bit security in all scenarios, with the exception of the parameters versus quantum adversaries under the most pessimistic (for an attacker) assumptions ($\omega = 2.8$ and $D_{solv} = 5$).

For the suggested 128–bit security parameters in Table 1 we get a negative number for N_4 and so we are not able to predict the first fall degree for these cases. We have however seen that the minus modifier does not work as effectively for EFLASH as initially believed, and so it is very likely that these parameters will also fail to achieve their proposed security level.

Table 4. The complexity of solving the 80–bit security parameters suggested with respect to a classical adversary (left table) and a quantum adversary (right table).

D_{solv} / ω	4	5
2.4	2^{50}	2^{59}
2.8	2^{58}	2^{69}

D_{solv} / ω	4	5
2.4	2^{59}	2^{71}
2.8	2^{69}	2^{83}

7 Further Work

Following the attack described in this paper, one may wonder whether it is possible to fix the EFLASH scheme. We have seen that the relations β_1 and β_2 play a crucial role in the low first fall degree for this system. They are a direct consequence of the small base field, so it seems natural to try and choose a larger base field to mitigate this. The problem with this approach is that the condition for the central map to be injective, $\gcd(q^d - 1, q^\Theta + 1) = 1$, can only be satisfied when q is even. Furthermore, if $\mathbb{F}_q$ is chosen to be a small extension field of $\mathbb{F}_2$, then the system can always be solved as a system over $\mathbb{F}_2$, and so the existence of β_1, β_2 ultimately seems unavoidable. The minus modifier does help, but as we have seen it also strongly affects the efficiency of decryption in EFLASH. Since q^a needs to be low in order for decryption to be efficient, the designer is limited in the use of this modifier. For these reasons we cannot think of parameters that would result in instances of EFLASH that seem both efficient and secure.

A related question is whether the analysis presented here would have an impact on the security of the signature scheme PFLASH. As mentioned earlier, EFLASH and PFLASH share the same central map, and so the latter will also suffer from the same degree fall generators α, β_1 and β_2. The main difference is that signature schemes can allow a significant number of public polynomials to be removed without becoming inefficient. This can be seen from the suggested parameters for PFLASH in [7], where roughly one third of the public polynomials are removed. We are at this point not able to conclude either way on the security of the current PFLASH parameters, but our work shows the need for an updated security analysis against direct attacks for this scheme.

It will also be interesting to see if the ideas presented in this work may have an impact on other multivariate big field schemes that also benefit from the minus modifier. We point out that our methods not only predict the first fall degree, but also the number of degree fall polynomials obtained at this degree. It remains to be seen if this information can be used in other ways by an attacker.

One idea is to use this information in conjunction with the Joux–Vitse algorithm [19]. For example, if we predict k degree fall polynomials at degree D, then it may be the case that combining Mac_{D-1} and the k degree fall polynomials of degree $\leq D - 1$ leads to optimal parameter choices for this algorithm (see [19] for notation and more details on this). This could be particularly interesting in cases where the first fall degree and solving degree may be far apart.

8 Conclusions

With the prospect of quantum computers becoming a reality, cryptographers have looked for quantum-safe public-key encryption algorithms that can replace RSA. The C^* scheme was proposed more than 30 years ago and is based on the MQ problem which is considered quantum-safe. However, the basic C^* scheme was quickly broken and cryptographers have since tried to find variants that may lead to secure quantum-safe public-key schemes. Some signature schemes built around the C^* construction have indeed withstood cryptanalysis; however it has proven to be much harder to come up with secure and efficient encryption algorithms based on it. EFLASH is one recent attempt.

However we have shown in this work that non-trivial degree fall polynomials arise rather early in a Gröbner basis attack when the central mapping is just a power-function and q is even (in particular when $q = 2$, as suggested for EFLASH). Two techniques that have been proposed for overcoming the deficiencies of the basic C^* system are to embed the plaintext space in a larger field, and to remove some of the polynomials in the public key before it is published. In this work we have seen that these two techniques to some extent work against each other, and we have shed some light on how much security is actually gained by the removal of some of the public polynomials.

During this work we were able to explain and give formulas for how many degree fall polynomials will appear at step degrees 3 and 4 in a solving algorithm. Experiments of fairly large instances show that our formulas give the exact number of degree fall polynomials when the predicted number is positive, giving confidence that we have captured the whole picture in our analysis. However, in some cases we get a few non-trivial degree fall polynomials when our formulas predict none, so more research is needed to explain these.

Based on our analysis we are very confident that we will indeed see a large number of non-trivial degree fall polynomials at step degree 4 for the suggested 80-bit security parameter sets for EFLASH. In all likelihood the solving degree for an actual EFLASH system will then be at most 5, giving solving complexities significantly lower than the claimed security. This means that EFLASH does not withstand direct Gröbner basis attacks, and should therefore be considered insecure.

References

1. Bardet, M., Faugère, J.-C., Salvy, B.: Complexity of Gröbner basis computation for Semi-regular overdetermined sequences over $\mathbb{F}_2$ with solutions in $\mathbb{F}_2$. [Research Report] RR-5049, INRIA, inria-00071534 (2003)
2. Bardet, M., et al.: Asymptotic behaviour of the degree of regularity of semi-regular polynomial systems. In: Proceedings of MEGA, vol. 5 (2005)
3. Bettale, L., Faugère, J.-C., Perret, L.: Cryptanalysis of HFE, multi-HFE and variants for odd and even characteristic. Des. Codes Cryptogr. **69**(1), 1–52 (2013). https://doi.org/10.1007/s10623-012-9617-2

4. Bouillaguet, C., Fouque, P.-A., Macario-Rat, G.: Practical key-recovery for all possible parameters of SFLASH. In: Lee, D.H., Wang, X. (eds.) ASIACRYPT 2011. LNCS, vol. 7073, pp. 667–685. Springer, Heidelberg (2011). https://doi.org/10.1007/978-3-642-25385-0_36

5. Cabarcas, D., Smith-Tone, D., Verbel, J.A.: Key recovery attack for ZHFE. In: Lange, T., Takagi, T. (eds.) PQCrypto 2017. LNCS, vol. 10346, pp. 289–308. Springer, Cham (2017). https://doi.org/10.1007/978-3-319-59879-6_17

6. Cartor, R., Smith-Tone, D.: EFLASH: a new multivariate encryption scheme. In: Cid, C., Jacobson Jr., M. (eds.) SAC 2018. Lecture Notes in Computer Science, vol. 11349, pp. 281–299. Springer, Cham (2019). https://doi.org/10.1007/978-3-030-10970-7_13

7. Chen, M.-S., Yang, B.-Y., Smith-Tone, D.: PFLASH - secure asymmetric signatures on smart cards. In: Lightweight Cryptography Workshop (2015). https://ws680.nist.gov/publication/get_pdf.cfm?pub_id=926103

8. Cox, D.A., Little, J., O'shea, D.: Using Algebraic Geometry, vol. 185. Springer, New York (2006). https://doi.org/10.1007/b138611

9. Diene, A., Ding, J., Gower, J.E., Hodges, T.J., Yin, Z.: Dimension of the linearization equations of the matsumoto-imai cryptosystems. In: Ytrehus, Ø. (ed.) WCC 2005. LNCS, vol. 3969, pp. 242–251. Springer, Heidelberg (2006). https://doi.org/10.1007/11779360_20

10. Ding, J., Hodges, T.J.: Inverting HFE systems is quasi-polynomial for all fields. In: Rogaway, P. (ed.) CRYPTO 2011. LNCS, vol. 6841, pp. 724–742. Springer, Heidelberg (2011). https://doi.org/10.1007/978-3-642-22792-9_41

11. Ding, J., Kleinjung, T.: Degree of regularity for HFE-. In: IACR Cryptology ePrint Archive 2011, p. 570 (2011)

12. Ding, J., Schmidt, D.: Solving degree and degree of regularity for polynomial systems over a finite fields. In: Fischlin, M., Katzenbeisser, S. (eds.) Number Theory and Cryptography. LNCS, vol. 8260, pp. 34–49. Springer, Heidelberg (2013). https://doi.org/10.1007/978-3-642-42001-6_4

13. Ding, J., Dubois, V., Yang, B.-Y., Chen, O.C.-H., Cheng, C.-M.: Could SFLASH be repaired? In: Aceto, L., Damgård, I., Goldberg, L.A., Halldórsson, M.M., Ingólfsdóttir, A., Walukiewicz, I. (eds.) ICALP 2008. LNCS, vol. 5126, pp. 691–701. Springer, Heidelberg (2008). https://doi.org/10.1007/978-3-540-70583-3_56

14. Faugère, J.C.: A new efficient algorithm for computing Gröbner bases (F4). J. Pure Appl. Algebra 139(1–3), 61–88 (1999)

15. Faugère, J.C.: A new efficient algorithm for computing Gröbner bases without reduction to zero (F 5). In: Proceedings of the 2002 International Symposium on Symbolic and Algebraic Computation, pp. 75–83. ACM (2002)

16. Faugère, J.-C., Joux, A.: Algebraic cryptanalysis of Hidden Field Equation (HFE) cryptosystems using Gröbner bases. In: Boneh, D. (ed.) CRYPTO 2003. LNCS, vol. 2729, pp. 44–60. Springer, Heidelberg (2003). https://doi.org/10.1007/978-3-540-45146-4_3

17. Felke, P.: On the affine transformations of HFE-cryptosystems and systems with branches. In: Ytrehus, Ø. (ed.) WCC 2005. LNCS, vol. 3969, pp. 229–241. Springer, Heidelberg (2006). https://doi.org/10.1007/11779360_19

18. Felke, P.: On the security of biquadratic C^* public-key cryptosystems and its generalizations. Crypt. Commun. 11, 1–16 (2018)

19. Joux, A., Vitse, V.: A crossbred algorithm for solving boolean polynomial systems. In: Kaczorowski, J., Pieprzyk, J., Pomykała, J. (eds.) NuTMiC 2017. LNCS, vol. 10737, pp. 3–21. Springer, Cham (2018). https://doi.org/10.1007/978-3-319-76620-1_1

20. Kipnis, A., Shamir, A.: Cryptanalysis of the HFE public key cryptosystem by relinearization. In: Wiener, M. (ed.) CRYPTO 1999. LNCS, vol. 1666, pp. 19–30. Springer, Heidelberg (1999). https://doi.org/10.1007/3-540-48405-1_2

21. Liu, J., et al.: Structural key recovery of simple matrix encryption scheme family. Comput. J. **61** (2018). https://doi.org/10.1093/comjnl/bxy093

22. Matsumoto, T., Imai, H.: Public quadratic polynomial-tuples for efficient signature-verification and message-encryption. In: Barstow, D., et al. (eds.) EUROCRYPT 1988. LNCS, vol. 330, pp. 419–453. Springer, Heidelberg (1988). https://doi.org/10.1007/3-540-45961-8_39

23. Patarin, J.: Cryptanalysis of the matsumoto and imai public key scheme of Eurocrypt'88. In: Coppersmith, D. (ed.) CRYPTO 1995. LNCS, vol. 963, pp. 248–261. Springer, Heidelberg (1995). https://doi.org/10.1007/3-540-44750-4_20

24. Patarin, J.: Hidden Fields Equations (HFE) and Isomorphisms of Polynomials (IP): two new families of asymmetric algorithms. In: Maurer, U. (ed.) EUROCRYPT 1996. LNCS, vol. 1070, pp. 33–48. Springer, Heidelberg (1996). https://doi.org/10.1007/3-540-68339-9_4

25. Patarin, J., Courtois, N., Goubin, L.: FLASH, a fast multivariate signature algorithm. In: Naccache, D. (ed.) CT-RSA 2001. LNCS, vol. 2020, pp. 298–307. Springer, Heidelberg (2001). https://doi.org/10.1007/3-540-45353-9_22

26. Perlner, R., Petzoldt, A., Smith-Tone, D.: Total break of the SRP encryption scheme. In: Adams, C., Camenisch, J. (eds.) SAC 2017. LNCS, vol. 10719, pp. 355–373. Springer, Cham (2018). https://doi.org/10.1007/978-3-319-72565-9_18

27. Porras, J., Baena, J., Ding, J.: ZHFE, a new multivariate public key encryption scheme. In: Mosca, M. (ed.) PQCrypto 2014. LNCS, vol. 8772, pp. 229–245. Springer, Cham (2014). https://doi.org/10.1007/978-3-319-11659-4_14

28. Tao, C., Diene, A., Tang, S., Ding, J.: Simple matrix scheme for encryption. In: Gaborit, P. (ed.) PQCrypto 2013. LNCS, vol. 7932, pp. 231–242. Springer, Heidelberg (2013). https://doi.org/10.1007/978-3-642-38616-9_16

29. Yasuda, T., Sakurai, K.: A multivariate encryption scheme with rainbow. In: Qing, S., Okamoto, E., Kim, K., Liu, D. (eds.) ICICS 2015. LNCS, vol. 9543, pp. 236–251. Springer, Cham (2016). https://doi.org/10.1007/978-3-319-29814-6_19

FPL: White-Box Secure Block Cipher
Using Parallel Table Look-Ups

Jihoon Kwon[1], Byeonghak Lee[2], Jooyoung Lee[2(✉)], and Dukjae Moon[1]

[1] Samsung SDS, Seoul, Korea
{jihoon.kwon,dukjae.moon}@samsung.com
[2] KAIST, Daejeon, Korea
{lbh0307,hicalf}@kaist.ac.kr

Abstract. In this work, we propose a new table-based block cipher structure, dubbed FPL, that can be used to build white-box secure block ciphers. Our construction is a balanced Feistel cipher, where the input to each round function determines multiple indices for the underlying table via a *probe* function, and the sum of the values from the table becomes the output of the round function. We identify the properties of the probe function that make the resulting block cipher white-box secure in terms of weak and strong space hardness against known-space and non-adaptive chosen-space attacks. Our construction, enjoying rigorous provable security without relying on any ideal primitive, provides flexibility to the block size and the table size, and permits parallel table look-ups.

We also propose a concrete instantiation of FPL, dubbed FPL$_{AES}$, using (round-reduced) AES for the underlying table and probe functions. Our implementation shows that FPL$_{AES}$ provides stronger security without significant loss of efficiency, compared to existing schemes including SPACE, WhiteBlock and WEM.

Keywords: Feistel cipher · White-box security · Space hardness · Provable security

1 Introduction

The white-box threat model in cryptography, introduced by Chow et al. [9] in 2002, assumes that the adversary is accessible to the entire information on the encryption process, and can even change parts of it at will. Numerous primitives claiming for security at the white-box model were proposed in the last few years. These primitives can be roughly divided into two classes.

The first class includes algorithms which take an existing block cipher (usually AES or DES), and use various methods (e.g., based on large look-up tables and random encodings) to obfuscate the encryption process, so that a white-box adversary

J. Lee was supported by a National Research Foundation of Korea (NRF) grant funded by the Korean government (Ministry of Science and ICT), No. NRF-2017R1E1A1A03070248.

© Springer Nature Switzerland AG 2020
S. Jarecki (Ed.): CT-RSA 2020, LNCS 12006, pp. 106–128, 2020.
https://doi.org/10.1007/978-3-030-40186-3_6

will not be able to extract the secret key. Pioneered by Chow et al. [9], this approach was followed by quite a few designers. Unfortunately, most of these designs were broken by practical attacks a short time after their presentation [3,14,17], and the remaining ones are very recent and have not been subjected to extensive cryptanalytic efforts yet.

The second class includes new cryptographic primitives designed with white-box protection in mind. Usually such designs are based on key-dependent tables, designed in such a way that even if a white-box adversary can recover the full dictionary of such a table, it still cannot use this knowledge to recover the secret key. Stronger security notions than *key extraction hardness* are also considered in the provable security setting. In this line of research, a number of block ciphers have been proposed, including ASASA [4], SPACE [6], SPNbox [7], WhiteBlock [12], and WEM [8].[1] Alternatively, key generators have also been proposed that are claimed to be secure in the white-box model. In this case, an initial vector is chosen uniformly at random, and it determines the corresponding secret key via the key generator. With this key, a plaintext is encrypted using a conventional block cipher such as AES, and the resulting ciphertext is sent to the recipient together with the initial vector. This approach has been rigorously analyzed in the bounded retrieval model [1,2]. However, key generators might not be suitable for protecting data at rest in any stable medium since an adversary might try to exploit the initial vector first, and then the corresponding table entries to recover the secret key.

As the white-box security notion for our construction, we will consider *space hardness* [6,7] (also called incompressibility [11] and weak white-box security [4]), meaning that an adversary with access to the white-box implementation cannot produce a functionally equivalent program of significantly smaller size. This property is needed, as a white-box adversary can perform code lifting, i.e., extract the entire code and use it as an equivalent secret key. While space hardness does not make code lifting impossible, it does make it harder to implement in practice. The attack models can be classified into three types: known-space attack, non-adaptive chosen-space attack and adaptive chosen-space attack (as described in Sect. 2 in detail).

1.1 Our Contribution

In this work, we propose a new table-based block cipher construction, dubbed FPL (Feistel cipher using Parallel table Look-ups), that can be used to build white-box secure block ciphers. FPL is a balanced Feistel cipher, where the input to each round function determines multiple indices for the underlying table via a probe function, and the sum of the values from the table becomes the output of the round function (see Fig. 1). The motivation behind our design (compared to existing constructions) can be listed as follows.

---

[1] Some instantiations of ASASA have been broken [13,16].

- The block size and the table size can be chosen flexibly, compared to substitution-permutation ciphers such as SPNbox, WhiteBlock and WEM using 128-bit dedicated block ciphers as their components. For this reason, FPL might be suitable for protecting database, e.g., format preserving encryption.[2]
- The underlying table is easy to generate (compared to substitution-permutation ciphers) since they do not need to be bijective.
- Encryption can be made faster in an environment where parallel or pipelined table look-ups are possible (compared to SPACE).

Provable security of FPL depends on the properties of the probe function; we identify such properties, dubbed *superposedness* and *linear independence*, that make the resulting block cipher white-box secure. Assuming these properties, we prove the security of FPL in terms of weak and strong space hardness against known-space and non-adaptive chosen-space attacks. Our security proof does not rely on the randomness of the probe function. On the other hand, we show that a random function satisfies the desirable properties except with negligible probability. This observation will be useful particularly when we use a pseudorandom function (e.g., a block cipher with a fixed key) to construct a probe function.

From a practical point of view, we propose a concrete instantiation of FPL, dubbed FPL_{AES}, using (round-reduced) AES for the underlying table and probe functions. Our implementation shows that FPL_{AES} provides stronger security without significant loss of efficiency, compared to existing schemes including SPACE, WhiteBlock and WEM. To make a fair comparison, we focused on AES-based constructions, not including SPNbox as it is a fully dedicated construction. We also remark that Lin et al. proposed an unbalanced Feistel-type white-box secure construction [15], while its security has not been proved nor claimed in terms of space hardness; their security model seems to be incomparable to space hardness.

DISCUSSION. The known-space attack models the limited control of the adversary over the platform and captures trojans, malwares and memory-leakage software vulnerability, while the chosen-space attack captures stronger adversarial ability to isolate a certain part of the underlying table and send it out via a communication channel with a limited capacity. In particular, the adaptive chosen-space attack, which is the most powerful attack, assumes an adversary with full access to the table at any time during the execution of the block cipher. However, it should be noted that strong space hardness cannot be achieved against adaptive chosen-space attacks for any (table-based) white-box design; an adversary would be able to fix an arbitrary plaintext, and exploit all the table entries needed to compute the corresponding ciphertext. As for weak space hardness of FPL against adaptive chosen-space attacks, we provides only a heuristic argument using the approach given in [7].

---

[2] It would also be possible to tweak the probe function when it is instantiated with a pseudorandom function such as AES.

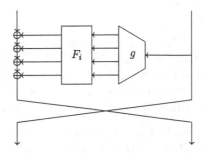

Fig. 1. The i-th round of FPL with four table look-ups. The probe function and the secret table of the i-th round are denoted by g and F_i, respectively.

2 Preliminaries

2.1 Table-Based Block Cipher

(CONVENTIONAL) BLOCK CIPHER. Let κ and n be positive integers. An n-bit *block cipher* using κ-bit keys is a function family

$$E : \{0,1\}^{\kappa} \times \{0,1\}^n \to \{0,1\}^n$$

such that for all $k \in \{0,1\}^{\kappa}$ the mapping $E(k, \cdot)$ is a permutation on $\{0,1\}^n$. TABLE-BASED BLOCK CIPHER. For positive integers s and t, a *table* with s-bit inputs and t-bit outputs can be viewed as a function

$$f : \{0,1\}^s \to \{0,1\}^t.$$

By viewing this table as a key of a block cipher, we will consider a *table-based block cipher*

$$\widetilde{E} : \mathcal{F}_{s,t} \times \{0,1\}^n \to \{0,1\}^n$$

where $\mathcal{F}_{s,t}$ denotes the set of all functions from $\{0,1\}^s$ to $\{0,1\}^t$ bits, and for each $f \in \mathcal{F}_{s,t}$ the mapping $\widetilde{E}(f, \cdot)$ is a permutation on $\{0,1\}^n$. A table-based block cipher $\widetilde{E}$ using a secret table $f \in \mathcal{F}_{s,t}$ will be written as $\widetilde{E}[f]$. A main difference of a table-based block cipher from conventional ones is that $\widetilde{E}[f]$ is assumed to make a fixed number of oracle queries (or table look-ups) to the underlying table f in its implementation. By a table-look up with an s-bit input x, $f(x)$ will be returned.

KEYED-TABLE-BASED BLOCK CIPHER. A pair of a table-based block cipher $\widetilde{E}$ and a family of tables

$$F : \{0,1\}^{\kappa} \times \{0,1\}^s \to \{0,1\}^t$$

will be called a *keyed-table-based block cipher*.[3] Each key $k \in \{0,1\}^{\kappa}$ defines an n-bit permutation $\widetilde{E}[F(k, \cdot)]$ as in a conventional block cipher, while in its white-box implementation, the keyed table $F(k, \cdot)$ will be stored instead of the key k.

---

[3] A table-based block cipher $\widetilde{E}$ can be regarded as keyed since each table in $\mathcal{F}_{s,t}$ can be indexed by $t \cdot 2^s$ bits.

2.2 Security Notions

Let $(\widetilde{E}, F)$ be a keyed-table-based block cipher. At the beginning of the attack, an adversary $\mathcal{A}$ is allowed access to the table $F(k, \cdot)$, where k is chosen uniformly at random from $\{0,1\}^\kappa$ and kept secret to the adversary. More precisely, we will assume that $\mathcal{A}$ makes q oracle queries to $F(k, \cdot)$ for a positive integer q. In this phase, we can distinguish three different types of attacks as follows.

1. Known-space attack (KSA): $\mathcal{A}$ obtains q pairs of inputs and the corresponding outputs of $F(k, \cdot)$, namely $(x_i, F(k, x_i))$, $i = 1, \ldots, q$, where x_i are randomly chosen from $\{0,1\}^s$ without replacement.
2. Non-adaptive chosen-space attack (NCSA): $\mathcal{A}$ chooses a priori q inputs x_i and obtains the corresponding outputs $F(k, x_i)$ for $i = 1, \ldots, q$.
3. Adaptive chosen-space attack (CSA): $\mathcal{A}$ adaptively chooses q inputs x_i and obtains the corresponding outputs $F(k, x_i)$ for $i = 1, \ldots, q$. (So $\mathcal{A}$ is allowed to choose x_j based on the previous responses $F(k, x_i)$, $i = 1, \ldots, j - 1$.)

After making all the oracle queries to the table, $\mathcal{A}$ is supposed to achieve a certain security goal. We will consider three different goals, defining three notions of security.

WEAK SPACE HARDNESS. $\mathcal{A}$ is given a random plaintext $u \in \{0,1\}^n$, and asked to encrypt $\widetilde{E}[F(k, \cdot)](u)$. Note that $\mathcal{A}$ makes oracle queries to $F(k, \cdot)$ without knowing the plaintext u. So in the definition of the adversarial advantage, $\mathcal{A}$ consists of two phases $\mathcal{A}_1$ and $\mathcal{A}_2$, where $\mathcal{A}_1$ relays a certain state σ to $\mathcal{A}_2$ after making oracle queries to the underlying table, and $\mathcal{A}_2$ tries to find v on receipt of σ and u.

$$\mathbf{Adv}_{\widetilde{E},F}^{\mathsf{atk\text{-}wsh}}(\mathcal{A})$$
$$= \Pr\left[k \xleftarrow{\$} \{0,1\}^\kappa, u \xleftarrow{\$} \{0,1\}^n, \sigma \leftarrow \mathcal{A}_1^{F(k,\cdot)}, v \leftarrow \mathcal{A}_2(\sigma, u) : v = \widetilde{E}[F(k,\cdot)](u)\right],$$

where $\mathsf{atk} \in \{\mathsf{ksa}, \mathsf{ncsa}, \mathsf{csa}\}$ represents the attack model.

STRONG SPACE HARDNESS. $\mathcal{A}$ is asked to come up with a valid plaintext-ciphertext pair (u, v) such that $v = \widetilde{E}[F(k, \cdot)](u)$. The adversarial advantage is formally defined as follows: for $\mathsf{atk} \in \{\mathsf{ksa}, \mathsf{ncsa}, \mathsf{csa}\}$,

$$\mathbf{Adv}_{\widetilde{E},F}^{\mathsf{atk\text{-}ssh}}(\mathcal{A}) = \Pr\left[k \xleftarrow{\$} \{0,1\}^\kappa, (u,v) \leftarrow \mathcal{A}^{F(k,\cdot)} : v = \widetilde{E}[F(k,\cdot)](u)\right].$$

KEY EXTRACTION HARDNESS. $\mathcal{A}$ is asked to recover the secret key k. The adversarial advantage is formally defined as

$$\mathbf{Adv}_{\widetilde{E},F}^{\mathsf{atk\text{-}keh}}(\mathcal{A}) = \Pr\left[k \xleftarrow{\$} \{0,1\}^\kappa, k' \leftarrow \mathcal{A}^{F(k,\cdot)} : k' = k\right].$$

For $q, \tau > 0$ and $(\mathsf{atk}, \mathsf{sec}) \in \{\mathsf{ksa}, \mathsf{ncsa}, \mathsf{csa}\} \times \{\mathsf{wsh}, \mathsf{ssh}, \mathsf{keh}\}$, we define

$$\mathbf{Adv}_{\widetilde{E},F}^{\mathsf{atk\text{-}sec}}(q, \tau) = \max_{\mathcal{A}} \mathbf{Adv}_{\widetilde{E},F}^{\mathsf{atk\text{-}sec}}(\mathcal{A}),$$

where the maximum is taken over all adversaries $\mathcal{A}$ running in time τ and making at most q queries.

PSEUDORANDOMNESS. Later, we will consider the security of F in terms of its pseudorandomness (as a keyed function family); in this notion of security, $\mathcal{A}$ would like to tell apart two worlds $F(k, \cdot)$ and a truly random function f by adaptively making (forward) queries to the function, where k is chosen uniformly at random from the key space and kept secret to $\mathcal{A}$, while f is chosen uniformly at random from $\mathcal{F}_{s,t}$. Formally, $\mathcal{A}$'s distinguishing advantage is defined by

$$\mathbf{Adv}_F^{\mathrm{prf}}(\mathcal{A}) = \left| \Pr\left[f \xleftarrow{\$} \mathcal{F}_{s,t} : 1 \leftarrow \mathcal{A}^f \right] - \Pr\left[k \xleftarrow{\$} \{0,1\}^\kappa : 1 \leftarrow \mathcal{A}^{F(k,\cdot)} \right] \right|.$$

For $q, \tau > 0$, we define

$$\mathbf{Adv}_F^{\mathrm{prf}}(q, \tau) = \max_{\mathcal{A}} \mathbf{Adv}_F^{\mathrm{prf}}(\mathcal{A}),$$

where the maximum is taken over all adversaries $\mathcal{A}$ running in time τ and making at most q queries.

3   FPL: Block Cipher Using Parallel Table Look-Ups

In this section, we define the FPL keyed-table-based block cipher. This construction is a Feistel cipher; let n and r denote the block size and the number of rounds, respectively. We will assume that n is even, writing $n = 2m$ for a positive integer m. For a (keyed) round function H from m-bits to m-bits, let $\Phi[H]$ denote a single-round Feistel cipher such that

$$\Phi[H](u_L, u_R) = (u_R, u_L \oplus H(u_R))$$

for $(u_L, u_R) \in \{0,1\}^m \times \{0,1\}^m$ (identifying $\{0,1\}^n$ with $\{0,1\}^m \times \{0,1\}^m$). The FPL block cipher is an r-round balanced Feistel cipher;

$$\mathsf{FPL} = \Phi[H_r] \circ \cdots \circ \Phi[H_2] \circ \Phi[H_1]$$

for r round functions H_i, $i = 1, \ldots, r$.

ROUND FUNCTIONS OF FPL. Once parameters κ, s, d are fixed, each round function H_i, $i = 1, \ldots, r$, is defined by a *probe function*

$$g : \{0,1\}^m \rightarrow (\{0,1\}^s)^d$$

and a keyed table

$$F : \{0,1\}^\kappa \times (\{1, \ldots, r\} \times \{1, \ldots, d\} \times \{0,1\}^s) \rightarrow \{0,1\}^m.$$

We separate this table into smaller ones by writing $F_{i,j} = F(\cdot, i, j, \cdot)$ for $i \in \{1, \ldots, r\}$ and $j \in \{1, \ldots, d\}$. Then for $x \in \{0,1\}^m$,

$$H_i(x) = F_{i,1}(y_1) \oplus F_{i,2}(y_2) \oplus \cdots \oplus F_{i,d}(y_d),$$

where we write $g(x) = (y_1, y_2, \ldots, y_d) \in (\{0,1\}^s)^d$. In this way, FPL becomes a keyed-table-based block cipher that encrypts n-bit blocks using a κ-bit key. The size of the underlying keyed table is $rdm2^s$ bits.

SECURITY REQUIREMENTS FOR PROBE FUNCTIONS. The (provable) security of FPL depends on the property of its probe function. We need the following definitions.

Definition 1. *Let p and q be positive integers, and let $g : \{0,1\}^m \to (\{0,1\}^s)^d$. If for any subsets $Y_1, \ldots, Y_d \subset \{0,1\}^s$ such that $|Y_1| + \cdots + |Y_d| \leq q$,*

$$|\{x \in \{0,1\}^m : g(x) \in Y_1 \times \cdots \times Y_d\}| < p,$$

then we will say that g is (p, q)-superposing.

Definition 2. *Given a function $g : \{0,1\}^m \to (\{0,1\}^s)^d$, the* incidence matrix *of g, denoted M_g, is a $2^m \times d2^s$ zero-one matrix, where the rows and the columns are indexed by $\{0,1\}^m$ and $\{1, \ldots, d\} \times \{0,1\}^s$, respectively, and $(M_g)_{x,(j,y_j)} = 1$ for $j = 1, \ldots, d$ if and only if $g(x) = (y_1, y_2, \ldots, y_d)$.*

Note that each row of M_g contains exactly d 1's.

Definition 3. *Let ℓ be a positive integer, and let $g : \{0,1\}^m \to (\{0,1\}^s)^d$. If any ℓ rows of M_g are linearly independent over $\mathbf{GF}(2)$, then g is called ℓ-independent.*

The superposedness and linear independence of the probe function will turn out to be essential in the security proof of FPL.

4   Probabilistic Construction of Secure Probe Functions

In this section, we will consider probabilistic construction of secure probe functions. This approach is relevant when we instantiate the probe function with a block cipher (adding a prefix to inputs and truncating its outputs) in practice, since a block cipher is typically modeled as a pseudorandom function. So we will see how the randomness of the probe function is related to the security requirements discussed in Sect. 3, namely the superposedness and the linear independence.

Once we fix an integer q such that $0 \leq q \leq d2^s$, and subsets $Y_1, \ldots, Y_d \subset \{0,1\}^s$ such that $|Y_1| + \cdots + |Y_d| = q$, then a random function $g : \{0,1\}^m \to (\{0,1\}^s)^d$ will map an element of $\{0,1\}^m$ to an element of $Y_1 \times \cdots \times Y_d$ with probability $\prod_{i=1}^{d} (|Y_i|/2^s)$, which is upper bounded by $q^d/(d2^s)^d$. So the number of $x \in \{0,1\}^m$ such that $g(x) \in Y_1 \times \cdots \times Y_d$ will be close to $2^m q^d/(d2^s)^d$. This intuition is formalized in the following lemma.

Lemma 1. *Let λ be a positive integer. A random function $g : \{0,1\}^m \to (\{0,1\}^s)^d$ is $(p(q), q)$-superposing for every q such that $0 \leq q \leq d2^s$ except with probability at most $2^{-\lambda}$, where*

$$p(q) = 3 \left(\frac{q}{d2^s} \right)^d 2^m + d2^s + \lambda.$$

Proof. Let $c = q/(d2^s)$, where $0 \le c \le 1$, and let

$$\delta = \frac{d2^s + \lambda}{c^d 2^m} + 2$$

as a function in c. So we have $p = (1+\delta)c^d 2^m$. We fix subsets $Y_1, \ldots, Y_d \subset \{0,1\}^s$ such that $|Y_1| + \cdots + |Y_d| = q$.

For each $x \in \{0,1\}^m$, let $\mathbf{Y}_x$ be a random variable, where $\mathbf{Y}_x = 1$ if $g(x) \in Y_1 \times \cdots \times Y_d$, and $\mathbf{Y}_x = 0$ otherwise. Random variables $\mathbf{Y}_x$, $x \in \{0,1\}^m$, are all independent, and $\Pr[\mathbf{Y}_x = 1] \le c^d$ for every $x \in \{0,1\}^m$. Let $\mathbf{Z}_x$, $x \in \{0,1\}^m$, be independent Bernoulli random variables such that $\Pr[\mathbf{Z}_x = 1] = c^d$ and $\Pr[\mathbf{Z}_x = 0] = 1 - c^d$. We can couple $\mathbf{Y}_x$ and $\mathbf{Z}_x$ so that $\mathbf{Z}_x = 1$ whenever $\mathbf{Y}_x = 1$.

Let $\mathbf{Y} = \sum_{x \in \{0,1\}^m} \mathbf{Y}_x$ and let $\mathbf{Z} = \sum_{x \in \{0,1\}^m} \mathbf{Z}_x$. Then $\mathbf{Y}$ counts the number of $x \in \{0,1\}^m$ such that $g(x) \in Y_1 \times \cdots \times Y_d$, while $\mathbf{Z}$ is the sum of independent Bernoulli random variables such that $\mathrm{Ex}[\mathbf{Z}] = c^d 2^m$. By applying the Chernoff bound to the variable $\mathbf{Z}$, we obtain

$$\Pr[\mathbf{Y} \ge p] \le \Pr\left[\mathbf{Z} \ge (1+\delta)c^d 2^m\right]$$

$$\le e^{-\frac{\delta^2 \cdot c^d \cdot 2^m}{2+\delta}} \le e^{-(\delta-2)c^d 2^m} = e^{-(d2^s+\lambda)}.$$

Since the number of possible choices for subsets $Y_1, \ldots, Y_d \subset \{0,1\}^s$ is upper bounded by

$$\sum_{q=0}^{d2^s} \binom{d2^s}{q} = 2^{d2^s},$$

we can use the union bound to conclude that a random function $g : \{0,1\}^m \to (\{0,1\}^s)^d$ is (p,q)-superposing for every q such that $0 \le q \le d2^s$ except with probability at most $2^{d2^s} \cdot e^{-(d2^s+\lambda)}$, where $2^{d2^s} \cdot e^{-(d2^s+\lambda)} \le 2^{-\lambda}$.   □

Lemma 2. *For a positive integer ℓ, a random function $g : \{0,1\}^m \to (\{0,1\}^s)^d$ is ℓ-independent except with probability at most*

$$\mathsf{P}_{m,s,d,\ell} \overset{\text{def}}{=} \sum_{j=1}^{\lfloor \frac{\ell}{2} \rfloor} \left(\frac{j^{d-2}}{2^{ds-2m-1}}\right)^j.$$

If $2^{ds-2m-2} \ge \left(\frac{e\ell}{2}\right)^{d-2}$, then we have $\mathsf{P}_{m,s,d,\ell} \le \frac{1}{2^{ds-2m-2}}$.

Proof. A probe function $g : \{0,1\}^m \to (\{0,1\}^s)^d$ defines a $2^m \times d2^s$ incidence matrix M_g. This matrix can be viewed as obtained by concatenating d matrices $M_g[i]$, $i = 1, \ldots, d$, where the rows and the columns of $M_g[i]$ are indexed by $\{0,1\}^m$ and $\{0,1\}^s$, respectively, and $(M_g)[i]_{x,y} = 1$ if the i-th entry of $g(x)$ is y and $(M_g)[i]_{x,y} = 0$ otherwise. When g is chosen uniformly at random, the position of the nonzero entry will also be random and independent for each row of $(M_g)[i]$, $i = 1, \ldots, d$.

Let $M_g[i]_x$ denote the row of $M_g[i]$ indexed by $x \in \{0,1\}^m$. If g is not ℓ-independent, then there will be indices $x_1, \ldots, x_{2j} \in \{0,1\}^m$ for a positive integer j such that $2j \leq \ell$, satisfying

$$M_g[i]_{x_1} \oplus M_g[i]_{x_2} \oplus \cdots \oplus M_g[i]_{x_{2j-1}} \oplus M_g[i]_{x_{2j}} = \mathbf{0} \tag{1}$$

for every $i = 1, \ldots, d$, where $\mathbf{0}$ denotes the zero vector. In order for (1) to hold for a fixed $i \in \{1, \ldots, d\}$ and a set of indices $X = \{x_1, \ldots, x_{2j}\} \subset \{0,1\}^m$, there should be a perfect matching in a complete graph on X (or equivalently an involution without fixed points on X) such that for any edge $\{x_\alpha, x_\beta\}$ the corresponding rows have "1" at the same position. For a fixed edge $\{x_\alpha, x_\beta\}$, the corresponding rows have "1" at the same position with probability $1/2^s$ over the randomness of g. Since the number of perfect matchings is

$$(2j-1) \cdot (2j-3) \cdots \cdots 3 \cdot 1 = \frac{(2j)!}{2^j j!},$$

and $M_g[1], \ldots, M_g[d]$ are chosen independently, the probability that g is *not* ℓ-independent is upper bounded by

$$\sum_{j=1}^{\lfloor \frac{\ell}{2} \rfloor} \binom{2^m}{2j} \left(\frac{(2j)_j}{2^{(s+1)j}} \right)^d \leq \sum_{j=1}^{\lfloor \frac{\ell}{2} \rfloor} \binom{2^m}{2j} \left(\frac{(2j)!}{2^j j!} \left(\frac{1}{2^s} \right)^j \right)^d$$

$$\leq \sum_{j=1}^{\lfloor \frac{\ell}{2} \rfloor} \left(\frac{e2^m}{2j} \right)^{2j} \left(\frac{j}{2^s} \right)^{dj}$$

$$\leq \sum_{j=1}^{\lfloor \frac{\ell}{2} \rfloor} \left(\frac{j^{d-2}}{2^{ds-2m-1}} \right)^j.$$

Let $p_j = \left(\frac{j^{d-2}}{2^{ds-2m-1}} \right)^j$ for $j = 1, \ldots, \lfloor \frac{\ell}{2} \rfloor$. One can easily show that $p_{j+1} \leq p_j/2$ if

$$2^{ds-2m-2} \geq \left(\frac{e\ell}{2} \right)^{d-2}. \tag{2}$$

In this case, we have

$$\mathsf{P}_{m,s,d,\ell} = \sum_{j=1}^{\lfloor \frac{\ell}{2} \rfloor} p_j \leq \sum_{j=1}^{\lfloor \frac{\ell}{2} \rfloor} \frac{p_1}{2^{j-1}} \leq \frac{1}{2^{ds-2m-2}}. \tag{3}$$

5   White-Box Security of FPL

Throughout this section, we will fix the parameters of FPL, namely, m, s, d, κ, r, where we assume $r \geq 7$. Furthermore, we suppose that an r-round FPL block cipher is based on a probe function

$$g : \{0,1\}^m \to (\{0,1\}^s)^d$$

and a keyed table

$$F : \{0,1\}^\kappa \times (\{1,\ldots,r\} \times \{1,\ldots,d\} \times \{0,1\}^s) \to \{0,1\}^m,$$

writing $F_{i,j} = F(\cdot,i,j,\cdot)$ for $i \in \{1,\ldots,r\}$ and $j \in \{1,\ldots,d\}$.

5.1 Key Extraction Hardness of FPL

Up to the pseudorandomness of the keyed table, one would not be able to recover the secret key by exploiting the table entries. More precisely, it is easy to see

$$\mathbf{Adv}^{\mathsf{csa\text{-}keh}}_{\mathsf{FPL},F}(q,\tau) = \mathbf{Adv}^{\mathsf{prf}}_F(q',\tau'),$$

where $q' = q + O(\kappa/n)$ and $\tau' = \tau + O(\kappa/n)$. So in the following, we will focus on the space hardness of FPL.

5.2 Space Hardness of FPL

Throughout this section, we will replace the underlying keyed tables $F_{i,j}$, $(i,j) \in \{1,\ldots,r\} \times \{1,\ldots,d\}$, by independent uniform random functions $f_{i,j}$ up to the pseudorandomness of F, so all the security bounds have an additional term $\mathbf{Adv}^{\mathsf{prf}}_F(q,\tau)$. In this setting, we will consider an information theoretic adversary $\mathcal{A}$ with unbounded computational power.

A USEFUL LEMMA. Note that for $x \in \{0,1\}^m$,

$$H_i(x) = F_{i,1}(y_1) \oplus F_{i,2}(y_2) \oplus \cdots \oplus F_{i,d}(y_d)$$

where $g(x) = (y_1, y_2, \ldots, y_d) \in (\{0,1\}^s)^d$. For i and j such that $1 \leq i \leq j \leq r$, let

$$\mathsf{FPL}_{i,j} = \Phi[H_j] \circ \cdots \circ \Phi[H_{i+1}] \circ \Phi[H_i]$$

be the subcipher of FPL containing rounds i to j, and for $w \in \{0,1\}^m$, let

$$\mathsf{FPL}^w_{i,j} : \{0,1\}^m \to \{0,1\}^m,$$

be a function such that $\mathsf{FPL}^w_{i,j}(u) = v$ if $\mathsf{FPL}_{i,j}(w,u) = (v',v)$ for some $v' \in \{0,1\}^m$. In other words, $\mathsf{FPL}^w_{i,j}$ sets the left half of the input to $\mathsf{FPL}_{i,j}$ to w, and takes only the right half of the output from $\mathsf{FPL}_{i,j}$.

In order to prove the strong space hardness of FPL, we need to prove the multi-collision security of $\mathsf{FPL}^w_{i,j}$ over the random choice of the underlying tables.

Lemma 3. *Let $1 \leq i \leq j \leq r$, let $\ell \geq 2$, and let $w \in \{0,1\}^m$. If a probe function g is ℓ-independent, then the probability that there are ℓ distinct elements $u_1, \ldots, u_\ell \in \{0,1\}^m$ such that $\mathsf{FPL}^w_{i,j}(u_1) = \cdots = \mathsf{FPL}^w_{i,j}(u_\ell)$ is upper bounded by*

$$2^m \left(\frac{e}{\ell}\right)^\ell.$$

Proof. We will first fix $v \in \{0,1\}^m$ and ℓ distinct elements $u_1, \ldots, u_\ell \in \{0,1\}^m$, and then upper bound the probability that

$$\mathsf{FPL}_{i,j}^w(u_\alpha) = v \tag{4}$$

for every $\alpha = 1, \ldots, \ell$. Let $(w_\alpha', u_\alpha') = \mathsf{FPL}_{i,j-1}(w, u_\alpha)$ (with arbitrary tables for rounds i to $j-1$) and let

$$g(u_\alpha') = (y_{\alpha,1}, y_{\alpha,2}, \ldots, y_{\alpha,d})$$

for $\alpha = 1, \ldots, \ell$. Then (4) implies the following ℓ equations:

$$H_j(u_\alpha') = F_{j,1}(y_{\alpha,1}) \oplus F_{j,2}(y_{\alpha,2}) \oplus \cdots \oplus F_{j,d}(y_{\alpha,d}) = w_\alpha' \oplus v \tag{5}$$

for $\alpha = 1, \ldots, \ell$. If $u_{\alpha_1}' = u_{\alpha_2}'$ for some $1 \le \alpha_1 < \alpha_2 \le \ell$, then it should be the case that $w_{\alpha_1}' \oplus v \ne w_{\alpha_2}' \oplus v$ since (w_α', u_α') are all distinct. Therefore we can assume that u_α' are all distinct.

Rewriting $F_{j,\beta}(y_{\alpha,\beta})$ by $z_{\beta, y_{\alpha,\beta}}$ for $1 \le \alpha \le \ell$ and $1 \le \beta \le d$, we obtain a system of equations in unknowns $z_{\beta, y_{\alpha,\beta}}$. If the number of the unknowns is denoted by L, then the number of solutions to this system is given as $2^{(L-\ell)m}$ since g is ℓ-independent. Furthermore, for each solution, say $(z_{\beta, y_{\alpha,\beta}}^*)$, the probability that $F_{j,\beta}(y_{\alpha,\beta}) = z_{\beta, y_{\alpha,\beta}}^*$ is given as $1/2^{Lm}$. Therefore, the probability of an ℓ-multicollision in $\mathsf{FPL}_{i,j}^w$ is upper bounded by

$$2^m \binom{2^m}{\ell} \frac{2^{(L-\ell)m}}{2^{Lm}} = 2^m \binom{2^m}{\ell} \frac{1}{2^{\ell m}} \le 2^m \left(\frac{e}{\ell}\right)^\ell. \qquad \square$$

SECURITY AGAINST KNOWN-SPACE ATTACKS. Weak and strong space hardness of FPL against known-space attacks is summarized by the following theorem.

Theorem 1. *Suppose that g is ℓ-independent for a positive integer ℓ. Then for any integers q, r_1 and r_2 such that $0 \le q \le rd2^s$, $r_1, r_2 \ge 3$ and $r_1 + r_2 < r$, we have*

$$\mathbf{Adv}_{\mathsf{FPL},F}^{\mathsf{ksa\text{-}wsh}}(q, \tau) \le \mathbf{Adv}_F^{\mathsf{prf}}(q, \tau) + \frac{2^m q^{r_1 d}}{(rd2^s)^{r_1 d}} + \frac{2^{2m} q^{r_2 d}}{(rd2^s)^{r_2 d}} + 2^m \left(\frac{e}{\ell}\right)^\ell + \frac{\ell}{2^{2m}}. \tag{6}$$

We also have

$$\mathbf{Adv}_{\mathsf{FPL},F}^{\mathsf{ksa\text{-}ssh}}(q, \tau) \le \mathbf{Adv}_F^{\mathsf{prf}}(q, \tau) + 2^{2m+1} \left(\frac{q}{rd2^s}\right)^{(\lceil \frac{r}{2} \rceil - 1)d} + 2^m \left(\frac{e}{\ell}\right)^\ell + \frac{\ell}{2^{2m}}. \tag{7}$$

Proof. We will give the proof of (6); The upper bound (7) is proved similarly.

In the first phase of the attack, $\mathcal{A}$ is given q queries $f_{i_\alpha, j_\alpha}(y_\alpha)$, $\alpha = 1, \ldots, q$, where $i_\alpha \in \{1, \ldots, r\}$, $j_\alpha \in \{1, \ldots, d\}$ and $y_\alpha \in \{0,1\}^s$ are chosen independently at random. In the second phase of the attack, $\mathcal{A}$ is given a random plaintext $u \in \{0,1\}^n$, where u is written as $u_L \| u_R$ for $u_L, u_R \in \{0,1\}^m$.

For $i \in \{1, \ldots, r\}$ and $j \in \{1, \ldots, d\}$, let $Y_{i,j} \subset \{0,1\}^s$ be a set of queries y such that $f_{i,j}(y)$ have been fixed (so $i = i_\alpha$, $j = j_\alpha$ and $y = y_\alpha$ for some $\alpha \in \{1, \ldots, q\}$). If there are $r_1 + 1$ elements, denoted $x_0, x_1, \ldots, x_{r_1} \in \{0,1\}^m$, such that

1. $x_0 = u_L$ and $x_1 = u_R$,
2. $g(x_i) \overset{\text{def}}{=} (y_{i,1}, \ldots, y_{i,d}) \in Y_{i,1} \times \cdots \times Y_{i,d}$ for $i = 1, \ldots, r_1$,
3. $x_{i-1} \oplus x_{i+1} = f_{i,1}(y_{i,1}) \oplus \cdots \oplus f_{i,1}(y_{i,d})$ for $i = 1, \ldots, r_1 - 1$,

then we will give a win to $\mathcal{A}$. For each $(r_1 + 1)$-tuple $(x_0, \ldots, x_{r_1}) \in (\{0,1\}^m)^{r_1 + 1}$, the probability that $x_0 = u_L$, $x_1 = u_R$, and $g(x_i) \in Y_{i,1} \times \cdots \times Y_{i,d}$ for $i = 1, \ldots, r_1$ is upper bounded by

$$\frac{1}{2^{2m}} \left(\frac{q}{rd2^s} \right)^{r_1 d}.$$

Furthermore, the probability that $x_{i-1} \oplus x_{i+1} = f_{i,1}(y_{i,1}) \oplus \cdots \oplus f_{i,1}(y_{i,d})$ for $i = 2, \ldots, r_1 - 1$ is upper bounded by

$$\left(\frac{1}{2^m} \right)^{r_1 - 2}$$

over the randomness of the underlying tables. Overall, the probability that $\mathcal{A}$ wins is upper bounded by

$$\frac{2^m q^{r_1 d}}{(rd2^s)^{r_1 d}}. \tag{8}$$

On the other hand, if there are r_2 elements $x_1, \ldots, x_{r_2} \in \{0,1\}^m$, such that

1. $g(x_i) \overset{\text{def}}{=} (y_{i,1}, \ldots, y_{i,d}) \in Y_{i,1} \times \cdots \times Y_{i,d}$ for $i = r - r_2 + 1, \ldots, r$,
2. $x_{i-1} \oplus x_{i+1} = f_{i,1}(y_{i,1}) \oplus \cdots \oplus f_{i,1}(y_{i,d})$ for $i = r - r_2 + 2, \ldots, r - 1$,

then we will also give a win to $\mathcal{A}$. The probability of $\mathcal{A}$'s winning in this game is upper bounded by

$$\frac{2^{2m} q^{r_2 d}}{(rd2^s)^{r_2 d}}. \tag{9}$$

Suppose that $\mathcal{A}$ outputs $v \in \{0,1\}^{2m}$ at the end of the attack, where we will write $v = v_L \| v_R$ for $v_L, v_R \in \{0,1\}^m$. Without the winning events above, one can find a sequence of $r' + 1$ elements, say $x_0, x_1, \ldots, x_{r'} \in \{0,1\}^m$, for some r_1 such that $1 \leq r' \leq r_1$, where

1. $x_0 = u_L$ and $x_1 = u_R$,
2. for $i = 1, \ldots, r' - 1$,

$$g(x_i) \overset{\text{def}}{=} (y_{i,1}, \ldots, y_{i,d}) \in Y_{i,1} \times \cdots \times Y_{i,d},$$
$$x_{i+1} = x_{i-1} \oplus f_{i,1}(y_{i,1}) \oplus \cdots \oplus f_{i,1}(y_{i,d}),$$

3. $g(x_{r'}) \notin Y_{r',1} \times \cdots \times Y_{r',d}$.

Similarly, there is a sequence of $r''+1$ elements, say $x_{r-r''+1}, x_{r-r''+2}, \ldots, x_{r+1} \in \{0,1\}^m$, for some r'' such that $1 \leq r'' \leq r_2$, where

1. $x_r = v_L$ and $x_{r+1} = v_R$,
2. for $i = r - r'' + 2, \ldots, r$,

$$
g(x_i) \overset{\text{def}}{=} (y_{i,1}, \ldots, y_{i,d}) \in Y_{i,1} \times \cdots \times Y_{i,d},
$$
$$
x_{i+1} = x_{i-1} \oplus f_{i,1}(y_{i,1}) \oplus \cdots \oplus f_{i,1}(y_{i,d}),
$$

3. $g(x_{r-r''+1}) \notin Y_{r-r''+1,1} \times \cdots \times Y_{r-r''+1,d}$.

Next, we focus on $r - r' - r''$ (≥ 1) rounds in the middle from round $r' + 1$ to $r - r''$. By Lemma 3, the number of inputs that collides on $x_{r-r''+1}$ under $\mathsf{FPL}^{x_{r'}}_{r'+1,r-r''}$ is at most ℓ except with probability

$$
2^m \left(\frac{e}{\ell}\right)^\ell. \tag{10}
$$

Without any ℓ-multicollision, we would have two sets of ℓ' different values, say $\{x^1_{r'+1}, \ldots, x^{\ell'}_{r'+1}\}$ and $\{x^1_{r-r''}, \ldots, x^{\ell'}_{r-r''}\}$, for some $\ell' \leq \ell$, such that

$$
\Phi[H_{r-r''}] \circ \cdots \circ \Phi[H_{r'+2}] \circ \Phi[H_{r'+1}](x_{r'}, x^j_{r'+1}) = (x^j_{r-r''}, x_{r-r''+1})
$$

for $j = 1, \ldots, \ell'$. Therefore, $\mathsf{FPL}(u) = v$ implies that

$$
\Phi[H_{r'}](x_{r'-1}, x_t) = (x_{r'}, x^j_{r'+1}),
$$
$$
\Phi[H_{r-r''+1}](x^j_{r-r''}, x_{r-r''+1}) = (x_{r-r''+1}, x_{r-r''+2})
$$

for some $j = 1, \ldots, \ell'$, which hold with probability at most

$$
\frac{\ell}{2^{2m}}. \tag{11}
$$

The proof of (6) is complete by (8), (9), (10) and (11). □

Security Against Non-adaptive Chosen-space Attacks. Weak and strong space hardness of FPL against non-adaptive chosen-space attacks is summarized by the following theorem.

Theorem 2. *Let ℓ be a positive integer and let $p(\cdot)$ be an increasing function defined on $\{0, \ldots, d2^s\}$. Suppose that $g : \{0,1\}^m \to (\{0,1\}^s)^d$ is ℓ-independent and $(p(q'), q')$-superposing for every $q' \in \{0, \ldots, d2^s\}$. For any $q \in \{0, \ldots, rd2^s\}$ and $r' \in \{1, \ldots, r\}$, let $p^*(q, r')$ be the maximum of $\prod_{i=1}^{r'} p(q_i)$ subject to the constraints $\sum_{i=1}^{r'} q_i = q$ and $0 \leq q_i \leq d2^s$ for $i = 1, \ldots, r'$. Then for any r_1 and r_2 such that $r_1, r_2 \geq 3$ and $r_1 + r_2 < r$, we have*

$$
\mathbf{Adv}^{\mathsf{ncsa\text{-}wsh}}_{\mathsf{FPL},F}(q, \tau) \leq \mathbf{Adv}^{\mathsf{prf}}_F(q, \tau) + \frac{p^*(q, r_1)}{2^{mr_1}} + \frac{p^*(q, r_2)}{2^{m(r_2-2)}} + 2^m \left(\frac{e}{\ell}\right)^\ell + \frac{\ell}{2^{2m}}. \tag{12}
$$

We also have

$$\mathbf{Adv}_{\mathsf{FPL},F}^{\mathsf{ncsa\text{-}ssh}}(q,\tau) \leq \mathbf{Adv}_F^{\mathsf{prf}}(q,\tau) + \frac{p^*\left(q, \lceil\frac{r}{2}\rceil - 1\right)}{2^{(\lceil\frac{r}{2}\rceil - 3)m-1}} + 2^m \left(\frac{e}{\ell}\right)^\ell + \frac{\ell}{2^{2m}}. \tag{13}$$

Proof. We will give the proof of (12); The upper bound (13) is proved similarly.

At the first phase of the attack, $\mathcal{A}$ chooses sets of queries $Y_{i,j} \subset \{0,1\}^s$ and obtains $f_{i,j}(y)$ for each $y \in Y_{i,j}$, where $i \in \{1,\ldots,r\}$ and $j \in \{1,\ldots,d\}$. At the second phase of the attack, $\mathcal{A}$ is given a random plaintext $u \in \{0,1\}^n$, where u is written as $u_L \| u_R$ for $u_L, u_R \in \{0,1\}^m$.

If there are $r_1 + 1$ elements, denoted $x_0, x_1, \ldots, x_{r_1} \in \{0,1\}^m$, such that

1. $x_0 = u_L$ and $x_1 = u_R$,
2. $g(x_i) \stackrel{\mathrm{def}}{=} (y_{i,1}, \ldots, y_{i,d}) \in Y_{i,1} \times \cdots \times Y_{i,d}$ for $i = 1, \ldots, r_1$,
3. $x_{i-1} \oplus x_{i+1} = f_{i,1}(y_{i,1}) \oplus \cdots \oplus f_{i,1}(y_{i,d})$ for $i = 1, \ldots, r_1 - 1$,

then we will give a win to $\mathcal{A}$. Since $|Y_{i,1}| + \cdots + |Y_{i,d}| = q_i$ and g is $(p(q_i), q_i)$-superposing, we have

$$|\{x \in \{0,1\}^m : g(x) \in Y_{i,1} \times \cdots \times Y_{i,d}\}| < p(q_i)$$

for $i = 1, \ldots, r_1$. Therefore the number of tuples $(x_0, x_1, \ldots, x_{r_1})$ such that $g(x_i) \in Y_{i,1} \times \cdots \times Y_{i,d}$ for $i = 1, \ldots, r_1$ is upper bounded by

$$2^m \prod_{i=1}^{r_1} p(q_i) \leq 2^m p^*(q, r_1),$$

since $q_1 + \cdots + q_{r_1} \leq q$; for each $(r_1 + 1)$-tuple $(x_0, \ldots, x_{r_1})$, the probability that $u_L = x_0$, $u_R = x_1$ and $x_{i-1} \oplus x_{i+1} = f_{i,1}(y_{i,1}) \oplus \cdots \oplus f_{i,1}(y_{i,d})$ for $i = 1, \ldots, r_1 - 1$ is upper bounded by

$$\left(\frac{1}{2^m}\right)^{r_1+1}$$

over the randomness of the underlying tables. Overall, the probability that $\mathcal{A}$ wins is upper bounded by

$$\frac{p^*(q, r_1)}{2^{mr_1}}. \tag{14}$$

Similarly, if there are r_2 elements $x_1, \ldots, x_{r_2} \in \{0,1\}^m$, such that

1. $g(x_i) \stackrel{\mathrm{def}}{=} (y_{i,1}, \ldots, y_{i,d}) \in Y_{i,1} \times \cdots \times Y_{i,d}$ for $i = r - r_2 + 1, \ldots, r$,
2. $x_{i-1} \oplus x_{i+1} = f_{i,1}(y_{i,1}) \oplus \cdots \oplus f_{i,1}(y_{i,d})$ for $i = r - r_2 + 2, \ldots, r - 1$,

then we will also give a win to $\mathcal{A}$. The probability of $\mathcal{A}$'s winning in this game is also upper bounded by

$$\frac{p^*(q, r_2)}{2^{m(r_2-2)}}. \tag{15}$$

Suppose that $\mathcal{A}$ outputs $v \in \{0,1\}^{2m}$ at the end of the attack, where we will write $v = v_L \| v_R$ for $v_L, v_R \in \{0,1\}^m$. Without the winning events above, one can find a sequence of $r' + 1$ elements, say $x_0, x_1, \ldots, x_{r'} \in \{0,1\}^m$, for some r' such that $1 \leq r' \leq r_1$, where

1. $x_0 = u_L$ and $x_1 = u_R$,
2. for $i = 1, \ldots, r' - 1$,

$$g(x_i) \stackrel{\text{def}}{=} (y_{i,1}, \ldots, y_{i,d}) \in Y_{i,1} \times \cdots \times Y_{i,d},$$
$$x_{i+1} = x_{i-1} \oplus f_{i,1}(y_{i,1}) \oplus \cdots \oplus f_{i,1}(y_{i,d}),$$

3. $g(x_{r'}) \notin Y_{r',1} \times \cdots \times Y_{r',d}$.

Similarly, there is a sequence of $r''+1$ elements, say $x_{r-r''+1}, x_{r-r''+2}, \ldots, x_{r+1} \in \{0,1\}^m$, for some r'' such that $1 \leq r'' \leq r_2$, where

1. $x_r = v_L$ and $x_{r+1} = v_R$,
2. for $i = r - r'' + 2, \ldots, r$,

$$g(x_i) \stackrel{\text{def}}{=} (y_{i,1}, \ldots, y_{i,d}) \in Y_{i,1} \times \cdots \times Y_{i,d},$$
$$x_{i+1} = x_{i-1} \oplus f_{i,1}(y_{i,1}) \oplus \cdots \oplus f_{i,1}(y_{i,d}),$$

3. $g(x_{r-r''+1}) \notin Y_{r-r''+1,1} \times \cdots \times Y_{r-r''+1,d}$.

Next, we focus on $r - r' - r''$ (≥ 1) rounds in the middle from round $r' + 1$ to $r - r''$. By Lemma 3, the number of inputs that collides on $x_{r-r''+1}$ under $\mathsf{FPL}_{r'+1,r-r''}^{x_{r'}}$ is at most ℓ except with probability

$$2^m \left(\frac{e}{\ell}\right)^\ell. \tag{16}$$

Without any ℓ-multicollision, we would have two sets of ℓ' different values, say $\{x_{r'+1}^1, \ldots, x_{r'+1}^{\ell'}\}$ and $\{x_{r-r''}^1, \ldots, x_{r-r''}^{\ell'}\}$, for some $\ell' \leq \ell$, such that

$$\varPhi[H_{r-r''}] \circ \cdots \circ \varPhi[H_{r'+2}] \circ \varPhi[H_{r'+1}](x_{r'}, x_{r'+1}^j) = (x_{r-r''}^j, x_{r-r''+1})$$

for $j = 1, \ldots, \ell'$. Therefore, $\mathsf{FPL}(u) = v$ implies that

$$\varPhi[H_{r'}](x_{r'-1}, x_t) = (x_{r'}, x_{r'+1}^j),$$
$$\varPhi[H_{r-r''+1}](x_{r-r''}^j, x_{r-r''+1}) = (x_{r-r''+1}, x_{r-r''+2})$$

for some $j = 1, \ldots, \ell'$, which hold with probability at most

$$\frac{\ell}{2^{2m}}. \tag{17}$$

The proof of (12) is complete by (14), (15), (16) and (17).   □

SECURITY AGAINST ADAPTIVE CHOSEN-SPACE ATTACKS. We claim weak space hardness of FPL against adaptive chosen-space attacks with a somewhat heuristic argument.

We first estimate how large space is necessary to compute L plaintexts in advance. When L plaintexts are encrypted, each table has L accesses, and for L

table accesses, the expected number of used entries in each table $F_{i,j}$ is estimated as $\left(1 - e_{in}^L\right) \cdot 2^s$, where $e_{in} \overset{\text{def}}{=} 1 - 1/2^s$. Therefore an adaptive chosen-space attack of table leakage $\delta\ (= q/rd2^s)$ enables to compute $\lceil \log_{e_{in}} (1 - \delta) \rceil$ pairs of plaintexts and the corresponding ciphertexts. A randomly-drawn plaintext will be included in the set of the prepared pairs with probability $\lceil \log_{e_{in}} (1 - \delta) \rceil / 2^n$. On the other hand, if the plaintext is not in the set of the prepared pairs, then the adversary is able to successfully guess its ciphertext with probability at most δ^{dr}. Overall, the adversarial success probability is upper bounded by

$$\frac{\lceil \log_{e_{in}} (1 - \delta) \rceil}{2^n} + \delta^{dr}.$$

For example, when the parameters are given as $(n, s, d, r) = (128, 12, 40, 11)$ (as used in Table 3) and when $\delta = 0.25$, the success probability is limited to 2^{-117}.

5.3 Numerical Interpretation

Table 1 compares the security of FPL for various sets of parameters when $n = 128$ and $n = 64$. In this table, FPL-(n, s, d, r) denotes the n-bit FPL cipher of r rounds using d table look-ups for each round, where each table has 2^s entries. We will assume that the probe function g is pseudorandom so that we can probabilistically guarantee its superposedness and linear independence using Lemmas 1 and 2, and this probability is represented by the security parameter λ. Since all the security bounds in Sect. 5 include the term $2^{\frac{n}{2}} \left(\frac{e}{\ell}\right)^\ell + \frac{\ell}{2^n}$, which is optimized when ℓ is close to n, we will set the target security level to $(n - \log n)$ bits, and compare the maximum table leakage $\delta\ (= q/rd2^s)$ that achieves this level of security.

For each set of parameters (n, s, d, r), the maximum table leakage is computed as follows.

1. Fix sufficiently large λ, and by Lemma 1, assume that the probe function g is $(Aq^d + B, q)$-superposing for every q such that $0 \leq q \leq d2^s$, where $A = \frac{3 \cdot 2^m}{(d2^s)^d}$ and $B = d2^s + \lambda$.

2. Find ℓ that minimizes $2^{\frac{n}{2}} \left(\frac{e}{\ell}\right)^\ell + \frac{\ell}{2^n}$ over positive integers ℓ such that $\mathsf{P}_{m,s,d,\ell}$ is sufficiently small, say $\leq 2^{-\lambda}$ for the fixed parameter λ.

3. In order to analyze the ncsa-wsh security, for each (r_1, r_2) such that $r_1, r_2 \geq 3$ and $r_1 + r_2 < r$, maximize $q \in \{0, \dots, rd2^s\}$ such that

$$\frac{p^*(q, r_1)}{2^{mr_1}} + \frac{p^*(q, r_2)}{2^{m(r_2-2)}} + 2^m \left(\frac{e}{\ell}\right)^\ell + \frac{\ell}{2^{2m}} \tag{18}$$

is upper bounded by $n/2^n$, where $p^*(\cdot, \cdot)$ is as defined in Theorem 2. Let $q^*_{r_1, r_2}$ denote this maximum.

4. Maximize $q^*_{r_1, r_2}$ over (r_1, r_2) such that $r_1, r_2 \geq 3$ and $r_1 + r_2 < r$. Let q^{**} denote this maximum. Then $q^{**}/rd2^s$ becomes the maximum table leakage that achieves $(n - \log n)$-bit security.

5. The ksa-wsh, ksa-ssh, ncsa-ssh security is analyzed similarly.

In the third step, we need to compute $p^*(q, r_1)$ and $p^*(q, r_2)$ for each q and (r_1, r_2), and see if (18) is upper bounded by $n/2^n$. For a fixed pair (q, r), $p^*(q, r)$ is the maximum of

$$\prod_{i=1}^{r} \left(A q_i^d + B \right)$$

subject to the constraints $\sum_{i=1}^{r} q_i = q$ and $0 \le q_i \le d2^s$ for $i = 1, \ldots, r$. We observe that

$$\ln \left(\prod_{i=1}^{r} \left(A q_i^d + B \right) \right) = \sum_{i=1}^{r} \ln \left(A q_i^d + B \right), \tag{19}$$

where

$$C(x) \stackrel{\text{def}}{=} \ln \left(A x^d + B \right)$$

is concave in $[(B/A)^{\frac{1}{d}}, rd2^s]$.[4] For simplicity of analysis, we upper bound $C(x)$ by $\overline{C}(x)$, where

$$\overline{C}(x) \stackrel{\text{def}}{=} \begin{cases} C((B/A)^{\frac{1}{d}}) & \text{if } x \le (B/A)^{\frac{1}{d}}, \\ C(x) & \text{if } x \ge (B/A)^{\frac{1}{d}}. \end{cases}$$

Once we fix the number of indices i, denoted r', such that $q_i \ge (B/A)^{\frac{1}{d}}$, then $\sum_{i=1}^{r} \ln \overline{C}(x)$ is upper bounded by

$$(r - r')C((B/A)^{\frac{1}{d}}) + r'C(q/r')$$

by Jensen's inequality.[5] So we conclude that

$$\ln p^*(q, r) \le \max_{0 \le r' \le r} \left\{ (r - r')C((B/A)^{\frac{1}{d}}) + r'C(q/r') \right\}.$$

For example, let $n = 128$ (i.e., $m = 64$) and let $(s, d, r) = (12, 20, 17)$. As a function of ℓ,

$$2^{\frac{n}{2}} \left(\frac{e}{\ell} \right)^{\ell} + \frac{\ell}{2^n}$$

is minimized when $\ell = 47$. We also see that $\mathsf{P}_{64,12,20,47} \le 1/2^{111}$, so we let $\lambda = 111$. This means that when we use AES with a fixed key as a probe function it would satisfy ℓ-linear independence except with probability $1/2^{111}$. When $q = 0.17 \cdot (rd2^s)$, we have

$$\mathbf{Adv}_{\mathsf{FPL},(F_{i,j})}^{\mathsf{ncsa\text{-}wsh}}(q, \tau) \le 2^{-122.2}$$

assuming that the underlying tables are truly random.

---

[4] We assume that $0 < (B/A)^{\frac{1}{d}} < rd2^s$. All the parameters in Table 1 satisfy this inequality.

[5] We let $r'C(q/r') = 0$ when $r' = 0$.

Table 1. Security of FPL

(a) Security of FPL with $n = 128$.

Cipher	Table size	λ	ksa		ncsa	
			wsh	ssh	wsh	ssh
FPL-$(128, 12, 20, 17)$	10.63 MB	111	0.38	0.33	0.17	0.12
FPL-$(128, 12, 20, 33)$	20.62 MB	111	0.61	0.58	0.28	0.26
FPL-$(128, 16, 16, 17)$	136.00 MB	127	0.30	0.25	0.13	0.09
FPL-$(128, 16, 16, 33)$	264.00 MB	127	0.54	0.50	0.24	0.22
FPL-$(128, 20, 12, 17)$	1.59 GB	111	0.20	0.16	0.09	0.05
FPL-$(128, 20, 12, 33)$	3.09 GB	111	0.44	0.40	0.22	0.22

(b) Security of FPL with $n = 64$.

Cipher	Table size	λ	ksa		ncsa	
			wsh	ssh	wsh	ssh
FPL-$(64, 8, 16, 9)$	144.00 KB	63	0.26	0.26	0.00	0.00
FPL-$(64, 8, 16, 17)$	272.00 KB	63	0.55	0.51	0.13	0.08
FPL-$(64, 8, 16, 33)$	528.00 KB	63	0.74	0.71	0.30	0.26
FPL-$(64, 16, 8, 17)$	34.00 MB	63	0.30	0.26	0.00	0.00
FPL-$(64, 16, 8, 33)$	66.00 MB	63	0.55	0.51	0.20	0.14
FPL-$(64, 16, 16, 17)$	68.00 MB	63	0.55	0.51	0.00	0.00

6   FPL$_{\mathsf{AES}}$: Concrete Instantiation

Given probabilistic construction of a secure probe function, one might want to use AES (with a fixed key) as the probe function, assuming AES is pseudorandom. In this section, we propose a concrete instantiation of FPL, dubbed FPL$_{\mathsf{AES}}$, using (round-reduced) AES for the underlying table and probe functions.

6.1   Specification

The FPL$_{\mathsf{AES}}$ cipher is defined by parameters r, m, d, s, where m is even and $s \leq 16$.[6] Let $n = 2m$, and let FPL$_{\mathsf{AES}}$-(n, s, d, r) denote the n-bit FPL$_{\mathsf{AES}}$ cipher of r rounds using d table look-ups for each round, where each table has 2^s entries. The probe function uses AES reduced to 5 rounds (without the linear mixing operation in the last round), denoted AES[5], while the table is generated using the full-round AES using 128-bit keys. In the following, $\mathsf{Tr}_a(\cdot)$ denotes truncation of the first a bits from the input, and $\langle x \rangle_a$ denotes the a-bit binary representation of integer x.

PROBE FUNCTIONS. The probe function $g : \{0,1\}^m \to (\{0,1\}^s)^d$ is computed as follows.

---

[6] The definition can be straightforwardly extended to $s > 16$.

1. On input $x \in \{0,1\}^m$, compute

$$y = \mathsf{AES}[5]_{\mathbf{0}_{128}}(\langle 1 \rangle_{128-m} \| x) \| \cdots \| \mathsf{AES}[5]_{\mathbf{0}_{128}}(\langle \lceil d/8 \rceil \rangle_{128-m} \| x),$$

where $\mathbf{0}_{128}$ denotes the zero vector of 128 bits,[7] and the input prefixes are represented by $128 - m$ bits.

2. Break down y as $y_1' \| \cdots \| y_d' \| *$, where $y_j' \in \{0,1\}^{16}$ for $j = 1, \ldots, d$ and $*$ denotes the remaining bits; the index y_j for the j-th table is defined as $\mathsf{Tr}_{16-s}(y_j')$ for $j = 1, \ldots, d$. So we have $g(x) = (y_1, \ldots, y_d)$.

TABLES. The $\mathsf{FPL}_{\mathsf{AES}}$ cipher uses a single keyed table

$$F : \{0,1\}^{128} \times \{1, \ldots, r\} \times \{1, \ldots, d\} \times \{0,1\}^s \longrightarrow \{0,1\}^m,$$

where $F(k, i, j, y) = \mathsf{Tr}_{128-m}(\mathsf{AES}_k(\langle i \rangle_{64} \| \langle j \rangle_{64-s} \| y))$.

6.2   Black-Box Security of $\mathsf{FPL}_{\mathsf{AES}}$

In this section, we analyze the differential and the linear properties of $\mathsf{FPL}_{\mathsf{AES}}$.

DIFFERENTIAL CRYPTANALYSIS. Fix an s-to-m bit function $f : \{0,1\}^s \to \{0,1\}^m$. Given an input difference α and an output difference β, the differential probability of f is defined as

$$\mathsf{DP}(\alpha, \beta) = |\{(u, v) | u \oplus v = \alpha \text{ and } f(u) \oplus f(v) = \beta\}|$$

for $u, v \in \{0,1\}^s$. The distribution of $\mathsf{DP}(\alpha, \beta)$ over all s-to-m bit functions has been shown to be binomial for sufficiently large s and m [5,10]. For a non-trivial differential (α, β) with fixed α and β, this distribution is binomial with the following probability;

$$\Pr[\mathsf{DP}(\alpha, \beta) = \lambda] = (2^{-m})^\lambda \cdot (1 - -2^{-m})^{2^{s-1} - \lambda} \cdot \binom{2^{s-1}}{\lambda}.$$

In [6], the probability p_B that $\mathsf{DP}(\alpha, \beta)$ is at most B over all non-trivial values of α and β is lower bounded by

$$\left(1 - \frac{(2^{s-1} \cdot 2^{-m})^{B+1}}{(B+1)!}\right)^{2^{s+m+1}}.$$

Table 2a shows p_B for f with $s = 12, 16, 20$ when $n = 128$ (so $m = 64$). By using this probability p_B, the differential probability of f is estimated as $B/2^s$. Suppose that the differential probability of f to be $2^{-10.4}$ $(= 3/2^{12})$, 2^{-14} $(= 4/2^{16})$ and 2^{-18} $(= 4/2^{20})$, since p_3, p_4 and p_5 are very close to 1 in f with $s = 12, 16$ and 20, respectively. Due to diffusion properties of the probe function, $\mathsf{FPL}_{\mathsf{AES}}$ with $s = 12, 16$ and 20 have at least 13, 10 and 8 active $F_{i,j}$ functions after 3 rounds.

---

[7] Any constant key will not affect the overall security (compared to $\mathbf{0}_{128}$).

When $n = 64$, the lower bounds on p_B are listed in Table 2b. The differential probability of f with $s = 8$ and 16 is $2^{-6.4}$ ($= 3/2^8$) and $2^{-13.4}$ ($= 6/2^{16}$), respectively. $\mathsf{FPL_{AES}}$ with $s = 8$ and 16 have at least 10 and 5 active $F_{i,j}$ functions after 3 rounds.

Table 2. Lower bounds on p_B

(a) Lower bounds on p_B with $n = 128$.

s	p_1	p_2	p_3	p_4	p_5	p_6
12	$1\text{-}2^{-30}$	$1\text{-}2^{-85}$	$\underline{1\text{-}2^{-140}}$	$1\text{-}2^{-195}$	$1\text{-}2^{-250}$	$1\text{-}2^{-306}$
16	$1\text{-}2^{-18}$	$1\text{-}2^{-69}$	$1\text{-}2^{-120}$	$\underline{1\text{-}2^{-171}}$	$1\text{-}2^{-222}$	$1\text{-}2^{-274}$
20	$1\text{-}2^{-6}$	$1\text{-}2^{-53}$	$1\text{-}2^{-100}$	$\underline{1\text{-}2^{-147}}$	$1\text{-}2^{-194}$	$1\text{-}2^{-242}$

(b) Lower bounds on p_B with $n = 64$.

s	p_1	p_2	p_3	p_4	p_5	p_6
8	$1\text{-}2^{-10}$	$1\text{-}2^{-37}$	$\underline{1\text{-}2^{-64}}$	$1\text{-}2^{-91}$	$1\text{-}2^{-118}$	$1\text{-}2^{-146}$
16	-	$1\text{-}2^{-5}$	$1\text{-}2^{-24}$	$1\text{-}2^{-43}$	$1\text{-}2^{-62}$	$\underline{1\text{-}2^{-82}}$

LINEAR CRYPTANALYSIS. Fix an s-to-m bit function $f : \{0,1\}^s \rightarrow \{0,1\}^m$. Given an input mask $\gamma \in \{0,1\}^s$ and an output mask $\delta \in \{0,1\}^m$, the correlation of a linear approximation with respect to (γ, δ) is defined as

$$\mathsf{Cor} = 2^s \cdot (|\{x \in \{0,1\}^s | \gamma \cdot x \oplus \delta \cdot f(x) = 0\}| - |\{x \in \{0,1\}^s | \gamma \cdot x \oplus \delta \cdot f(x) = 1\}|).$$

The linear probability LP for (γ, δ) is defined as Cor^2. If LP of f is assumed to be normally distributed, then LP of a non-trivial linear approximation of f has mean $\mu(\mathsf{LP}) = 2^{-s}$ and variance $\sigma^2(\mathsf{LP}) = 2 \times 2^{-2s}$ [10].

In [6], LP of f with a fixed key is upper bounded by $2^{-s} + 10\sigma$ with probability at least $1 - 2^{-148}$. Therefore, the maximum linear probabilities can be assumed to be 2^{-4}, 2^{-8}, 2^{-12} and 2^{-16} for $s = 8$, 12, 16 and 20, respectively. So $\mathsf{FPL_{AES}}$ with $s = 12, 16, 20$ and $n = 128$ have at least 16, 11 and 8 active $F_{i,j}$ functions after 3 rounds. When $n = 64$, $\mathsf{FPL_{AES}}$ with $s = 8$ and 16 have at least 16 and 6 active $F_{i,j}$ functions after 4 and 3 rounds, respectively.

6.3 Performance

In this section, all of our experiments are done in the Zen+ microarchitecture (AMD Ryzen 7 2700X @ 3.70 GHz) which supports AVX (including AVX2), SSE, and AES instructions. The machine has L1-data, L2, and L3 caches with 32 KB, 512 KB, and 8192 KB sizes as well as 64 GB DDR4 RAM with a clock frequency of 2400 MHz. The source codes have been compiled by the GNU C Compiler 7.4.0 in O2 optimization level.

Figure 2 compares the performance of FPL_{AES} in the white-box setting for a various number of rounds r. When s and d are fixed, the table size is proportional to the number of rounds, and so is the execution time (in cycles per byte). We also observe that FPL_{AES}-$(128, 12, 40, r)$ is significantly faster than FPL_{AES}-$(128, 12, 20, 2r)$ (e.g., when $r = 10$, 15), where FPL_{AES}-$(128, 12, 20, 2r)$ and FPL_{AES}-$(128, 12, 40, r)$ use tables of the same size with the same number of table look-ups. The reason is that FPL_{AES}-$(128, 12, 40, r)$ makes more tables looks-ups per round than FPL_{AES}-$(128, 12, 20, 2r)$, which can be pipelined minimizing latency.

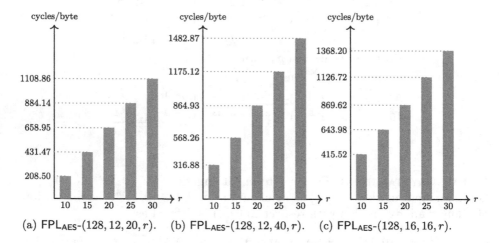

(a) FPL_{AES}-$(128, 12, 20, r)$.   (b) FPL_{AES}-$(128, 12, 40, r)$.   (c) FPL_{AES}-$(128, 16, 16, r)$.

Fig. 2. Performance of FPL_{AES}-(n, s, d, r) for a various number of rounds r.

Table 3 compares the performance of FPL_{AES} to SPACE, WhiteBlock and WEM with block size $n = 128$. The comparison has been made with table sizes around 13 MB.[8] The table size is not exactly the same as some constructions recommend only a small number of sets of parameters with their security analysis, while the table size affects both efficiency and security. That said, we observe that FPL_{AES}-$(128, 12, 40, 11)$ provides the strongest security without significant loss of efficiency; it provides ksa-wsh and ksa-ssh security up to the leakage of 44% and 41%, respectively. Note that SPACE uses a single table for every round, so its provable security is also heuristic.

BLACK BOX IMPLEMENTATION. A key owner might want to use a compact implementation of the encryption scheme by storing keys instead of the corresponding tables. For example, in an environment where a single server communicates with all the users, it would be infeasible to store all the keyed tables. Table 4 compares performance of FPL_{AES} to existing schemes in the black-box setting, where the underlying tables are all generated using the full AES block cipher.

---

[8] This is the table size of WEM for their recommended parameters.

Table 3. Comparison of FPL$_{AES}$ to existing schemes with block size $n = 128$. The security is compared in terms of weak space hardness against known-space attacks.

Cipher	Table size	Security	Table look-ups	Cycles per byte
SPACE-$(20, 64)$	13.50 MB	128 bits @ 0.25	64 RAM-TL	891.60
WhiteBlock-20	24.00 MB	108 bits @ 0.25	69 RAM-TL	582.62
WEM-$(16, 12)$	13.00 MB	112 bits @ 0.25	104 RAM-TL	356.49
FPL$_{AES}$-$(12, 40, 11)$	13.75 MB	121 bits @ 0.44	440 RAM-TL	357.52

This comparison does not include WEM, since the bijective S-boxes of the WEM are generated by the Fisher-Yates shuffle, which is too slow when implemented with AES. We see that FPL$_{AES}$ is comparable to existing schemes in the black box implementation.

Table 4. Black-box performance of FPL$_{AES}$ and existing schemes in cycles/byte.

SPACE-$(20, 64)$	WhiteBlock-20	WEM-$(16, 12)$	FPL$_{AES}$-$(12, 40, 11)$
166.40	93.30	–	200.35

References

1. Bellare, M., Dai, W.: Defending against key exfiltration: efficiency improvements for big-key cryptography via large-alphabet subkey prediction. In: Proceedings of the 22nd ACM SIGSAG Conference on Computer and Communications Security, pp. 923–940. ACM (2017)
2. Bellare, M., Kane, D., Rogaway, P.: Big-key symmetric encryption: resisting key exfiltration. In: Robshaw, M., Katz, J. (eds.) CRYPTO 2016. LNCS, vol. 9814, pp. 373–402. Springer, Heidelberg (2016). https://doi.org/10.1007/978-3-662-53018-4_14
3. Billet, O., Gilbert, H., Ech-Chatbi, C.: Cryptanalysis of a white box AES implementation. In: Handschuh, H., Hasan, M.A. (eds.) SAC 2004. LNCS, vol. 3357, pp. 227–240. Springer, Heidelberg (2004). https://doi.org/10.1007/978-3-540-30564-4_16
4. Biryukov, A., Bouillaguet, C., Khovratovich, D.: Cryptographic schemes based on the ASASA structure: black-box, white-box, and public-key (extended abstract). In: Sarkar, P., Iwata, T. (eds.) ASIACRYPT 2014. LNCS, vol. 8873, pp. 63–84. Springer, Heidelberg (2014). https://doi.org/10.1007/978-3-662-45611-8_4
5. Blondeau, C., Bogdanov, A., Leander, G.: Bounds in shallows and in miseries. In: Canetti, R., Garay, J.A. (eds.) CRYPTO 2013. LNCS, vol. 8042, pp. 204–221. Springer, Heidelberg (2013). https://doi.org/10.1007/978-3-642-40041-4_12
6. Bogdanov, A., Isobe, T.: White-box cryptography revisited: space-hard ciphers. In: Proceedings of the 22nd ACM SIGSAG Conference on Computer and Communications Security, pp. 1058–1069. ACM (2015)

7. Bogdanov, A., Isobe, T., Tischhauser, E.: Towards practical whitebox cryptography: optimizing efficiency and space hardness. In: Cheon, J.H., Takagi, T. (eds.) ASIACRYPT 2016. LNCS, vol. 10031, pp. 126–158. Springer, Heidelberg (2016). https://doi.org/10.1007/978-3-662-53887-6_5

8. Cho, J., Choi, K.Y., Dinur, I., Dunkelman, O., Keller, N., Moon, D., Veidberg, A.: WEM: a new family of white-box black ciphers based on the even-mansour construction. In: Handschuh, H. (ed.) Topics in Cryptology - CT-RSA 2017. LNCS, vol. 10159, pp. 293–308. Springer, Berlin (2017)

9. Chow, S., Eisen, P., Johnson, H., Van Oorschot, P.C.: White-box cryptography and an AES implementation. In: Nyberg, K., Heys, H. (eds.) SAC 2002. LNCS, vol. 2595, pp. 250–270. Springer, Heidelberg (2003). https://doi.org/10.1007/3-540-36492-7_17

10. Daemen, J., Rijmen, V.: Probability distributions of correlation and differentials in block ciphers. J. Math. Cryptol. 1(3), 221–242 (2007)

11. Delerablée, C., Lepoint, T., Paillier, P., Rivain, M.: White-box security notions for symmetric encryption schemes. In: Lange, T., Lauter, K., Lisoněk, P. (eds.) SAC 2013. LNCS, vol. 8282, pp. 247–264. Springer, Heidelberg (2014). https://doi.org/10.1007/978-3-662-43414-7_13

12. Fouque, P.-A., Karpman, P., Kirchner, P., Minaud, B.: Efficient and provable white-box primitives. In: Cheon, J.H., Takagi, T. (eds.) ASIACRYPT 2016. LNCS, vol. 10031, pp. 159–188. Springer, Heidelberg (2016). https://doi.org/10.1007/978-3-662-53887-6_6

13. Gilbert, H., Plût, J., Treger, J.: Key-recovery attack on the ASASA cryptosystem with expanding S-boxes. In: Gennaro, R., Robshaw, M. (eds.) CRYPTO 2015. LNCS, vol. 9215, pp. 475–490. Springer, Heidelberg (2015). https://doi.org/10.1007/978-3-662-47989-6_23

14. Lepoint, T., Rivain, M., De Mulder, Y., Roelse, P., Preneel, B.: Two attacks on a white-box AES implementation. In: Lange, T., Lauter, K., Lisoněk, P. (eds.) SAC 2013. LNCS, vol. 8282, pp. 265–285. Springer, Heidelberg (2014). https://doi.org/10.1007/978-3-662-43414-7_14

15. Lin, T.-T., Lai, X.-J., Xue, W.-J., Jia, Y.: A new feistel-type white-box encryption scheme. J. Comput. Sci. Technol. 32(2), 386–395 (2017)

16. Minaud, B., Derbez, P., Fouque, P.-A., Karpman, P.: Key-recovery attacks on ASASA. In: Iwata, T., Cheon, J.H. (eds.) ASIACRYPT 2015. LNCS, vol. 9453, pp. 3–27. Springer, Heidelberg (2015). https://doi.org/10.1007/978-3-662-48800-3_1

17. Wyseur, B., Michiels, W., Gorissen, P., Preneel, B.: Cryptanalysis of white-box DES implementations with arbitrary external encodings. In: Adams, C., Miri, A., Wiener, M. (eds.) SAC 2007. LNCS, vol. 4876, pp. 264–277. Springer, Heidelberg (2007). https://doi.org/10.1007/978-3-540-77360-3_17

Extending NIST's CAVP Testing of Cryptographic Hash Function Implementations

Nicky Mouha[(✉)] and Christopher Celi

National Institute of Standards and Technology, Gaithersburg, MD, USA
nicky@mouha.be, christopher.celi@nist.gov

Abstract. This paper describes a vulnerability in Apple's CoreCrypto library, which affects 11 out of the 12 implemented hash functions: every implemented hash function except MD2 (Message Digest 2), as well as several higher-level operations such as the Hash-based Message Authentication Code (HMAC) and the Ed25519 signature scheme. The vulnerability is present in each of Apple's CoreCrypto libraries that are currently validated under FIPS 140-2 (Federal Information Processing Standard). For inputs of about 2^{32} bytes (4 GiB) or more, the implementations do not produce the correct output, but instead enter into an infinite loop. The vulnerability shows a limitation in the Cryptographic Algorithm Validation Program (CAVP) of the National Institute of Standards and Technology (NIST), which currently does not perform tests on hash functions for inputs larger than 65 535 bits. To overcome this limitation of NIST's CAVP, we introduce a new test type called the Large Data Test (LDT). The LDT detects vulnerabilities similar to that in CoreCrypto in implementations submitted for validation under FIPS 140-2.

Keywords: CVE-2019-8741 · FIPS · CAVP · ACVP · Apple · CoreCrypto · Hash function · Vulnerability

1 Introduction

The security of cryptography in practice relies not only on the resistance of the algorithms against cryptanalytical attacks, but also on the correctness and robustness of their implementations. Software implementations are vulnerable to software faults, also known as bugs.

A (cryptographic) hash function turns a message of a variable length into an output of a fixed length, often called a message digest, or digest. This fixed-length output can then serve as a "fingerprint" for the message, in the sense that it should be computationally infeasible to construct two messages that result in the same digest. Hash functions are crucial to the security of many higher-level cryptographic algorithms and protocols.

In the context of digital signature schemes, hash functions are used to ensure that only the given message and the corresponding signature (along with the

© Springer Nature Switzerland AG 2020
S. Jarecki (Ed.): CT-RSA 2020, LNCS 12006, pp. 129–145, 2020.
https://doi.org/10.1007/978-3-030-40186-3_7

public key) passes the signature verification process. Digital signatures provide authentication in a similar manner to signatures in the real world. For example, a web browser can verify a package that is downloaded comes from a specific website by verifying the signature that was provided with the download using the known, trusted public key of the website. As a part of this verification process, the browser hashes the downloaded data so that the fixed-length digest can stand in place of the large variable-length data in the digital signature scheme.

A recent study by Mouha et al. [12] of the National Institute of Standards and Technology (NIST) SHA-3 (Secure Hash Algorithm) competition found that about half of the implementations submitted to the SHA-3 competition contained bugs, including two out of the five finalists. It appears that cryptographic algorithms can be difficult to implement, given that even the designers of the algorithm can have trouble to develop a correct implementation. Furthermore, even for a secure and well-designed cryptographic algorithm, bugs can be particularly severe with respect to the cryptographic properties of the algorithm's implementation.

For example, in the case of all submitted implementations of the BLAKE [4] algorithm to the SHA-3 competition, given one message and its corresponding hash function output, it is easy to construct another message that produces the same hash value. This "second preimage attack" is not due to a weakness in the BLAKE algorithm specification, but due to an implementation bug that remained undiscovered for seven years.

In [12], Mouha et al. did not find any bugs in the submission packages of Keccak [6], the hash function algorithm that won the SHA-3 competition and that is now standardized in Federal Information Processing Standard (FIPS) 202 [17]. In this paper, we explore whether implementations of hash functions that are standardized by NIST and currently used in commercial products may also contain bugs. Furthermore, we investigate how these bugs can impact more complex cryptographic operations such as digital signature schemes.

2   Testing Within NIST's CAVP

NIST maintains the Cryptographic Algorithm Validation Program (CAVP), which provides validation testing for the NIST-recommended cryptographic algorithms. The CAVP is a prerequisite for validating cryptographic implementations according to FIPS 140-2 under the Cryptographic Module Validation Program (CMVP). Since the Federal Information Security Management Act (FISMA) of 2002, U.S. Federal Agencies no longer have a statutory provision to waive FIPS 140-2. This means that commercial vendors must validate their cryptographic implementations, also known as modules, according to CAVP/CMVP before they can be deployed by U.S. Federal Agencies.

The CAVP testing methodology is derived directly from the algorithm specification, independent of the actual code that a vendor's implementation uses. Therefore, it is realistic to expect three main limitations of the CAVP:

1. The CAVP does not require that the internals of an implementation are known in order to generate tests, and is therefore restricted to black-box testing. For many widely-used cryptographic libraries, however, the software is either open source or available on the vendor's website, which may be used to reveal additional bugs through static analysis (including checking software coding standards), or white-box testing.
2. The CAVP tests only the capabilities of the implementation that are declared by the vendor. For example, a hash function implementation may declare that it can only process messages up to 65 535 bits, corresponding to the largest test vectors currently in the CAVP, even though it may encounter much larger inputs under typical use. When NIST introduces tests for larger inputs, it is therefore the vendor's responsibility to declare whether or not their implementation supports such inputs. However, it is in the vendor's interest to avoid bugs and therefore declare the capabilities of the implementations as broadly as possible.
3. The CAVP focuses mostly on the correct processing of valid inputs (positive testing), rather than the rejection of invalid inputs (negative testing). Because of the nature of black-box testing, the CAVP provides test vector data to the implementation. A developer of the module must program a test harness to submit this data to the interfaces of the cryptographic library itself and collect the output to send back to the CAVP. As the test harness is outside the bounds of the CAVP, it is difficult to know from a validation perspective whether invalid inputs are handled by the module, or by the test harness. There are a few notable exceptions to this, such as the CAVP tests for digital signature schemes that test whether the implementation can recognize valid versus invalid signatures.[1]

Furthermore, the focus of most cryptographic algorithm testing is on correctness towards common cases within the specification. This may leave cryptographic algorithms vulnerable to malicious inputs that manifest themselves very rarely under random testing. Notable examples exploit bugs in modular arithmetic [7], incorrect group order validation [21], or improper primality testing [1] to result in full or partial key recovery attacks on OpenSSL and other implementations. These examples show the importance to consider not just random but also "rare" and "unusual" inputs for cryptographic implementations, as they may lead to catastrophic security failures.

In spite of these limitations, the CAVP can be highly effective at detecting many types of bugs. This is because the CAVP test design is aware of the internals of "typical" implementations of cryptographic algorithms. The focus of the CAVP is not just conformance testing but also regression testing, as the CAVP test design is also aware of how changes to the implementations may lead to certain bugs. To see this, we now explain how the CAVP tests are generated.

The two test types in the CAVP are the Algorithm Functional Test (AFT), and the Monte Carlo Test (MCT). They were introduced in 1977 by the National

---

[1] For the signature verification operation, the CAVP also includes some invalid padding tests.

Bureau of Standards (NBS), the former name of NIST, in the (now-withdrawn) Special Publication (SP) 500-20 [13] to test the Data Encryption Standard (DES). In this standard, static AFTs known as Known Answer Tests (KATs) were provided in order to "fully exercise the non-linear substitution tables" (S-boxes), whereas MCTs contained "pseudorandom data to verify that the device has not been designed just to pass the [fixed] test set." Additionally, the large amount of data of the MCT was intended to detect whether it can "cause the device to hang or otherwise malfunction," for example due to a memory leak [8] in present-day implementations. The spirit and design of these tests was carried over to other algorithms such as the Advanced Encryption Standard (AES) in FIPS 197 [14] and hash functions.

This paper focuses on testing for hash functions within the CAVP at NIST. FIPS 180-4 [16] standardizes the hash functions SHA-1, SHA-224, SHA-256, SHA-384, SHA-512, SHA-512/224, and SHA-512/256. As these hash functions closely resemble each other, they are considered functionally equivalent for the purpose of this document. Testing for SHA-3 was added after the publication of FIPS 202 [16], and with the exception of the SHAKE extendable-output functions (XOFs), mimics the testing done for the FIPS 180-4 hash functions. As with the other CAVP tests, the Secure Hash Algorithm Validation System (SHAVS) [5] specifies both AFTs and MCTs.

Testing by the CAVP was done for many years using the Cryptographic Algorithm Validation System (CAVS) tool. An implementation under test (IUT) is accompanied with a declaration to the CAVS tool of which digest sizes it supports along with a couple of other properties such as whether or not it can hash an empty message, whether or not it can hash incomplete bytes (i.e. a 7-bit message), and the maximum message size. The maximum message size allowed by the tool is 65 535 bits.

As of 2019, the CAVP is undergoing a transition to use the Automated Cryptographic Validation Protocol (ACVP) to enable the generation and validation of standardized algorithm test vectors. This involves a shift of generating and validating tests at remote, approved laboratories, to performing these actions on NIST-hosted servers. The concept of first-party testing is introduced to allow vendors to test and validate their implementations without laboratories as intermediaries. This combined with hosting a demo server (a sandbox environment for algorithm testing), allows vendors to incorporate continuous testing of crypto implementations in their development process. The ACVP thereby significantly speeds up testing and validation.

The ACVP uses a JSON (JavaScript Object Notation) format to specify the test cases. The client to the NIST ACVP servers would then correspond to the test harness in the previous CAVS model, and is responsible for communicating with the server and exercising the proper interfaces on the module. In the JSON examples below, some of the original content has been trimmed for readability. For more information on the protocol itself, as well as the complete examples, we refer to the GitHub repository of the ACVP [11].

2.1   Algorithm Functional Test (AFT)

AFTs take a single message as input, and verify the correctness of the corresponding output. A JSON file is sent from the server to the client, which usually provides inputs to a cryptographic algorithm, and is very simple for an individual test case:

```
{
  "msg": "BCE7",
  "len": 16
}
```

where "msg" corresponds to the message represented as hexadecimal, and "len" corresponds to the length in bits of the message. The messages have fixed values that have been drawn uniformly at random from the space of messages of a certain bit length, ranging from the client's specified minimum to their specified maximum or 65 535, whichever comes first. The expected response to this test case is another simple JSON object:

```
{
  "md": "1FA29E9B23060562F9370453EF817E18C56AE844E5B85F2ED34B4B38"
}
```

where "md" corresponds to the message digest. The hash function in this example is SHA-224.

AFTs can vary in length from byte-oriented messages (i.e., "len" is a multiple of 8) or bit-oriented messages (with any bit lengths). This allows implementations to specify their properties to the CAVP to receive appropriate test cases.

These tests are intended to provide assurance that an implementation can handle messages of various sizes. However, the assurance that the AFTs currently offer may be limited, as they may not test more than one message of any specific bit length.

2.2   Monte Carlo Test (MCT)

MCTs, on the other hand, construct a chain of hash outputs by combining the previous three hash outputs into a single message, and use it to produce the next hash output. Each chain consists of 1000 iterations, and returns the hash output that is obtained at the end. This whole process is repeated 100 times with the original message replaced by the latest hash output.

The initial condition for an MCT is as follows:

```
{
  "msg": "B4FCB616B3A4A7C9E6AF1D836CF1576709A67F16141217B827E52611",
  "len": 224
}
```

where "msg" becomes the seed in the pseudocode of the MCT, which is given in Algorithm 1. The seed is not fixed, but is drawn uniformly at random for every invocation of the test.

Algorithm 1. The Monte Carlo Test (MCT) for hash functions

Require: seed (random string of same length as hash output)
    for $i = 1$ to 100 **do**
        MD[0] = MD[1] = MD[2] = seed;
        for $j = 3$ to 1002 **do**
            Msg[j] = MD[$j - 3$] ∥ MD[$j - 2$] ∥ MD[$j - 1$];
            MD[j] = Hash(Msg[j]);
        end for
        seed = MD[1002];
        Output seed;
    end for

The response is an array of 100 hash outputs as follows:

```
{
"resultsArray": [
 {
  "md": "7B893BC7322AA6578A2EC565593B86776FB8376AC16B0A354E6DA016"
 },
 {
  "md": "4BCB655F36D976ADAAE620B485DA7FD8ED321E0BF060E0FE2B5F9AFE"
 },
 {
  "md": "57AA388954B3D52645BFAC69E87F48B3D57A86CF385F38A2549FE957"
 }
]
}
```

shortened to only three outputs for brevity, and again using the SHA-224 hash function in the example. The CAVP makes an implicit assumption here that the client's implementation can handle a message that is three times the size of the hash output.

These tests are intended to provide assurance that an implementation is correct for valid inputs over thousands of iterations. However, the assurance that the MCTs currently offer may be limited, as the bit lengths of the messages do not vary between test cases. Furthermore, as this bit length is three times the digest size, the MCTs only cover a negligibly small percentage of the total input space of the given bit length.

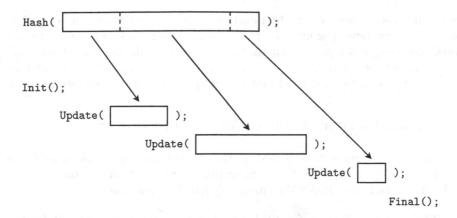

Fig. 1. Hash functions are commonly implemented using a `Hash` interface that takes a variable-length message, and returns a fixed-length output. It is common to also have an `Init-Update-Final` interface, which can be convenient to process large messages on the fly.

3   Common Hashing Interfaces

Although not mentioned in the NIST hash function standards [16,17], many cryptographic implementations have at least two distinct functional interfaces for hash operations, as shown in Fig. 1. One of the two interfaces, or both interfaces, may be available to a consumer of the module or to higher-level algorithms within the module. The first is an `Init-Update-Final` interface. This structure allows implementations to constantly stream smaller chunks of data into `Update()` repeatedly, rather than keep the message as a single large chunk. Perhaps the entire message is not available at once, or perhaps there is a limit to the capacity of a single `Update()` call.

The other interface is a more intuitive `Hash()` call that expects the whole message up front. This is different from the previous interface and the same module could potentially behave differently under these two interfaces [12].

In practice, the `Init-Update-Final` interface can be convenient to hash the concatenation of various elements. For example, the American National Standards Institute (ANSI) X9.63 Key Derivation Function (KDF) [2] computes the hash of a secret value Z, a counter, and an optional `SharedInfo` string that is shared between two entities. This hash can be computed using one `Init()` call, followed by an `Update()` call to process Z, another `Update()` call for the counter, and then an optional third `Update()` call for `SharedInfo`. The `Final()` call can then be used to compute the hash function output.

To hash the contents of a file, there are two approaches that are commonly encountered in practice. One approach is to loop through the contents of the file (e.g., using `fread()` in C), and process each chunk using a call to `Update()`. Another common approach is to map the file to the virtual address space (e.g., using `mmap()` in C), and then compute the hash by calling `Hash()`. This second approach must be used when the interface requires the data to be located in memory. For example, the interface of the Ed25519 signature scheme in Apple's CoreCrypto requires a pointer for the data to be hashed, therefore if an application wants to compute (or verify) a digital signature on a file (e.g., containing a large software update), it must first use `mmap()` to map this file into memory.

4   Vulnerability in Apple's CoreCrypto Library

We show how adding test cases beyond the current coverage of the CAVP can reveal previously undiscovered bugs in cryptographic implementations.

First, we look the SHAVS document [5], which states that:

> *"While the specification for SHA specifies that messages up to at least $2^{64} - 1$ bits are possible, these tests only test messages up to a limited size of approximately 100,000 bits. This is adequate for detecting algorithmic and implementation errors."*

In contrast, the SHA-3 Competition Test Suite [15] also contains an "Extremely Long Message Test," which contains a message of 2^{33} bits (1 GiB), with the intention of checking whether messages of more than 2^{32} bits were processed correctly. This test from the SHA-3 competition is not adopted by the CAVP however. We now explain how adding a similar test for large messages reveals a bug in the widely-used Apple CoreCrypto library.

Apple makes the source code of its CoreCrypto library publicly available [3] to allow for "verification of its security characteristics and correct functioning."[2] The CoreCrypto library provides low-level cryptographic primitives that are fundamental to the security of Apple's products, and is currently deployed in iPhone, iPad, and Mac devices worldwide. The library has also undergone rigorous testing, and is currently present in 20 FIPS 140-2-validated modules.

In the latest CoreCrypto library, the bug is present in the `ccdigest_update.c` file, which is located in the `ccdigest/src` subdirectory. This code is shared by all implemented hash functions except for MD2. The full code of the function is given in Appendix A. All the implemented hash functions are iterated hash functions, which means that an underlying compression function processes the message in multiples of a block size that is specific to the algorithm. Part of the code to process message in multiples of the block size is as follows:

```
1  //low-end processors are slow on division
2  if (di->block_size == 1<<6 ){ //sha256
3    nblocks = len >> 6;
4    nbytes = len & 0xFFFFFfC0;
5  } else if(di->block_size == 1<<7 ){ //sha512
```

---

[2] We refer to the latest CoreCrypto that is available online at the time of writing (November 25, 2019). It does not appear to have a version number, but can be identified by the year 2018 in the copyright notice.

```
6    nblocks = len >> 7;
7    nbytes = len & 0xFFFFff80;
8  } else {
9    nblocks = len / di->block_size;
10   nbytes = nblocks * di->block_size;
11 }
```

In this code, the variables `len`, `nblocks`, and `nbytes` are declared as `size_t`, which corresponds to a 64-bit unsigned integer on a 64-bit architecture. The `len` variable is the length of the message in bytes. In case `len` is less than 2^{32}, the value of `nblocks` is the number of complete blocks to be hashed: `len` divided by the block size (in bytes), whereas `nbytes` is the number of bytes of these complete blocks.

However, for block sizes of 64 or 128 bytes (i.e., when `di->block_size` is `1<<6` or `1<<7`), the calculation of `nbytes` contains a bug: the four highest bytes of `size_t` are incorrectly set to zero by the bitwise AND (`&`) operation. Consequently, when `len` is at least 2^{32} (corresponding to messages of at least 4 GiB), the value of `nbytes` does not contain the correct number of complete blocks. Therefore, later in the code, the statement `len -= nbytes` does not decrement `len` by the correct amount; instead `len` remains 2^{32} or larger. Given that all these statements are contained in a while-loop with condition `len > 0`, the program enters into an infinite loop.

A list of affected hash function implementations is given in Table 1.

Table 1. Hash function implementations in Apple's CoreCrypto library.

Algorithm	Block size (in bytes)	Vulnerable
MD2	16	✗
MD4	64	✓
MD5	64	✓
RIPEMD-128	64	✓
RIPEMD-160	64	✓
RIPEMD-256	64	✓
RIPEMD-320	64	✓
SHA-1	64	✓
SHA-224	64	✓
SHA-256	64	✓
SHA-384	128	✓
SHA-512	128	✓

When this code was written, perhaps the assumption was made that `size_t` corresponds to a 32-bit value, in which case the code would have been correct. When `size_t` is 64 bits, however, the integer constant used to perform the AND operation is incorrect.

One way to avoid this type of bug, could be to follow software coding standards, such as the Computer Emergency Response Team (CERT) C Coding Standard. This standard states in INT17-C: "Define integer constants in an implementation-independent manner" [19], and gives an example that is very similar to the bug in Apple's CoreCrypto library. Note that it is possible to avoid masks altogether, by using `nbytes = nblocks << 6` or `nbytes = nblocks << 7` for 64-byte and 128-byte blocks respectively.

4.1   Experimental Verification

We downloaded the latest CoreCrypto library from Apple's website [3], and compiled it using the Xcode IDE (Integrated Development Environment) on macOS 10.14 (Mojave) on a mid 2015 MacBook Pro, as well as using Clang 8 under Ubuntu 14.04 on an Intel Skylake processor. For Linux, the README.md file warns that the Linux Makefile is not up-to-date, therefore we needed to make some minor changes to the Makefile to allow compilation.

Because the bug is due to incorrect C code, we expect that the bug will manifest itself on any 64-bit platform for which the code is compiled. To confirm that the executable is stuck in an infinite loop, we added some source code instrumentation.

In our proof of concept code, we generated an input with a length of 2^{32} bytes. Because the actual value of the input is not relevant for the bug, we arbitrarily set all bits to zero in our experiments. When this input is provided to MD4, MD5, RIPEMD-128, RIPEMD-160, RIPEMD-256, RIPEMD-320, SHA-1, SHA-224, SHA-256, SHA-384, or SHA-512, we verified that the implementation enters into an infinite loop. We mentioned earlier that the MD2 implementation does not share the code of `ccdigest_update.c`, and we also confirmed that the same input does not cause an infinite loop for MD2. This provides experimental confirmation for the results of Table 1.

Then, we looked into higher-level cryptographic operations. We found that the implementation of the ANSI X9.63 KDF is not vulnerable when provided with a secret value Z of length 2^{32} bytes. This is due to a range check in the input length, which is documented by the following source code comment in CoreCrypto: "`ccdigest_update only supports 32bit length`."

However, such a range check is not applied to every hash function calculation, and most other cryptographic algorithms inside Apple's CoreCrypto library that use hash functions are vulnerable. We verified that HMAC enters into an infinite loop for all the vulnerable algorithms in Table 1 when provided with a message of 2^{32} bytes.

For the Ed25519 signature scheme, we found that a message of at least $2^{32} +$ 64 bytes is needed to trigger the bug. To explain this, note that the Ed22519 algorithm always prepends some data to the message before computing the hash value using SHA-512. This is implemented in Apple's CoreCrypto using the `Init-Update-Final` interface. When there are 64 bytes already in the buffer, the first 64 bytes of the message are used to complete a 128-byte block, which we recall is the block size for the SHA-512 algorithm. After processing the first

64 bytes of the message, if there are at least 2^{32} bytes or more left, then the bug is triggered. For details, we refer to the full code of the ccdigest_update() function in Appendix A.

We verified that the Ed25519 implementation indeed enters into an infinite loop when a message of $2^{32} + 64$ bytes is digitally signed or verified. Note that in order to trigger the bug in the verification operation, it is not necessary to provide a valid signature. Therefore, even if the private key is stored properly and never used to sign long messages, the verification operation still enters into an infinite loop for an incorrectly-signed message of $2^{32} + 64$ bytes or more. Note that digitally signed messages typically come from untrusted sources, because the concern that a message can be modified by an adversary is typically the reason to apply a digital signature in the first place.

Another cryptographic operation in Apple's CoreCrypto that uses hash functions, is the Secure Remote Password (SRP) protocol. This protocol is run between a client and a server, which can create additional security concerns when communication is done over a network and the adversary controls either the client or the server, and may therefore send malicious inputs. In CoreCrypto's SRP implementation, the username is provided as a null-terminated string.

We verified that when this string contains 2^{32} repetitions of the 'a' character followed by a null character, then the SRP implementation of both the client and the server enter into an infinite loop. Note that in contrast to the previous examples, the length in this case is not provided by the adversary as a separate parameter, but it is derived inside CoreCrypto using C's strlen() function. Therefore, range checking all input length values to CoreCrypto would not have been effective to avoid this attack using a long null-terminated string.

In Sect. 2, we recalled that an input that would "cause the device to hang" was already a concern when the MCT test was introduced for DES in 1977. But an infinite loop is also a security vulnerability, categorized under Common Weakness Enumeration (CWE) 835 [20], where it is also known as a "Loop with Unreachable Exit Condition." More specifically, an adversarially-crafted input that causes an implementation to enter an infinite loop, can lead to a "denial of service" (DoS) attack when it consumes excessive CPU resources.

5   Proposing the Large Data Test (LDT)

In the current CAVP tests, the length of the largest message is 65 535 bits. Such small testing sizes are not realistic towards normal usage. We propose a new Large Data Test (LDT) for the CAVP to provide a greater assurance for the implementations that undergo validation.

The LDT would be a type of AFT, and could be specified similarly to the example in Sect. 2.1. Implementations could specify the size of the largest message size that they can handle, for example on the order of 2 GiB to 8 GiB. The ACVP server can select one of many large supported arbitrary sizes to craft messages. However, a test for such messages may be impractical to communicate natively within the normal JSON structures. To work around this limitation, the LDT employs a simple function to generate the test input, as defined in Algorithm 2.

Algorithm 2. The Large Data Test (LDT)

Require: Msg (a non-zero number of bytes), fullLength (in bits)
  FullMsg = "";
  for i = 0 to ceil(fullLength / bitlength(Msg)) **do**
      FullMsg = FullMsg ‖ Msg;
  end for
  FullMsg = truncate(FullMsg, fullLength);
  Output FullMsg;

Due to the truncation at the end, it is possible for the LDT to output messages of any number of bits, instead of only multiples of the size of the repeating Msg pattern. The Msg pattern itself needs to be an integer number of bytes, in order to greatly simplify implementations in C-like programming languages. This is, however, not an actual restriction to the messages that can be output. The reason is that any 7-bit repeating pattern (for example) can also be written as a 56-bit (= 7-byte) repeating pattern, where 56 is the least common multiple of 7 and 8 (the number of bits in one byte).

With a generator function defined to expand a short message of a few bytes, into a large message of any arbitrary size, we can define the JSON structure for the LDT as the following:

```
{
  "largeMsg": {
    "content": "D6F7",
    "contentLength": 16,
    "fullLength": 34359738368,
    "expansionTechnique": "repeating"
  }
}
```

We define an "expansionTechnique" to allow extensibility in the future for other methods of producing a message of the proper size. In this example "repeating" corresponds to the repeating nature of Algorithm 2.

After the test generates a message of a specific number of bits, this message would then be hashed on the server to produce a single hash output similar to the AFTs. Once the test is sent to the client, this could flush out implementations for faults from long messages that produce incorrect outputs. As hashing is a core operation to many other cryptographic operations, it is important to consider scenarios where an adversary may maliciously generate large inputs.

Note that to unearth the bug in the Apple CoreCrypto library, it is necessary to use either the Hash() interface on a message of 4 GiB or more, or the Init-Update-Final interface where at least one of the Update() calls contains 4 GiB or more. In the latter case, it may be necessary to make the message a few bytes longer, as explained in Sect. 4.1.

Given that the LDT is designed to work with large data, we need to take into consideration that the implementation may run out of memory. When allocating dynamic memory (e.g., using `malloc()` in C) or mapping files to the virtual address space (e.g., using `mmap()` in C) are unsuccessful on the target platform, it may be an option to consider increasing the memory available to the platform or even simulating the environment for the purposes of testing.

6   Discussion

As hash functions are a core primitive within many other cryptographic algorithms, it is critically important to ensure correctness under all valid inputs. Yet the methods with which these algorithms are tested are still based on techniques from 1977. While the original tests are still valid, an automated system allows the CAVP to continually add test types and boost the assurances gained from the program. With a publicly standardized JSON protocol, and open-source test harnesses such as libacvp [9], the CAVP is in a good position to move forward with improved testing techniques. We suggest the LDT as a way to directly improve the assurances gained from the CAVP. Of course, one needs to design, specify, publicly review the tests, etc. before they can be used in a program such as CAVP. Openness and transparency are important for acceptance in this highly sensitive domain.

To test the limits of common variable types such as 32-bit unsigned integers, the LDT would need to be on the order of 2^{32} bytes or 4 GiB. This would be sufficient to detect the CoreCrypto bug, and potentially similar bugs in other cryptographic implementations.

However, an inherent limitation of the CAVP and of software testing in general, is that it is a selection process, where a very small subset is selected from the total number of possible test cases. Therefore, testing is not a method to prove the correctness over all types of inputs for an implementation. As stated by Dijkstra, "Program testing can be used to show the presence of bugs, but never to show their absence!" Indeed, the entire goal of software testing is to determine how to perform this selection process, in order to try to quantify the assurance that we get from testing.

Furthermore, the CAVP only tests the capabilities that are declared by the vendor, and would therefore not detect the bug if it only declares support for short messages. While this is reflected in the final validation certificate the vendor receives, this shows the potential need for a wider amount of negative testing. Negative tests are those that test not only well-defined inputs that may be beyond the advertised capabilities, but also invalid inputs.

We note the potential hazards of exposing multiple entry points to a single set of functionality. As mentioned, hash functions often provide at least two interfaces: an `Init-Update-Final` interface and a `Hash()` interface. Often both are exposed such as within CoreCrypto.

Lastly, it can be interesting to explore the parallels between different levels at which vulnerabilities can be handled, as we now explain.

A security vulnerability report to the vendor can allow for a rapid response to address a vulnerability. The FIPS 140-2 Implementation Guidance (IG) [18] encourages this process by providing the vendors with a "means to quickly fix, test and revalidate a module that is subject to a security-relevant CVE." A CVE (Common Vulnerability and Exposure) is security-relevant if it affects how the module meets the requirements of the FIPS 140-2 standard.

For FIPS 140-2 validated cryptographic modules, publishing a vulnerability with a CVE can accelerate the time for end users to obtain crucial security updates. Yet the very nature of the CVE system is an ad hoc procedure, and there is no mechanism in place to ensure that a vendor has learned from such a vulnerability. A vendor may implement test cases within their own development process to detect similar issues in the future, but this holds a very limited scope. The implementations of other vendors could be susceptible to similar issues, but there may be no incentive to react.

If the CAVP implements tests based on CVEs (e.g., as done by Project Wycheproof [10]), then lessons learned from a CVE are not restricted to a single implementation. The requirement of FIPS validation would then also provide stronger assurances to government and private entities that rely on the program. If a CVE can be detected via existing test types, a static test could be seamlessly included from the NIST server. By using an existing test type, no additional code is needed from a test harness to understand how to process the test. In addition, with the speed of testing under ACVP, it is mutually beneficial to constantly test while developing cryptographic implementations.

7   Conclusion

Apple's CoreCrypto library contains a bug due to the implementation-dependent manner in which integer constants are specified. Due to this bug, the MD4, MD5, and the RIPEMD and SHA family hash function implementations enter into an infinite loop for messages of 4 GiB or larger. The bug affects all implemented hash functions (except MD2), and higher-level operations such as HMAC, Ed25519, and SRP. To detect the bug in NIST's CAVP, we proposed a new Large Data Test (LDT) to calculate the hash value for large messages. We also pointed out that stricter coding standards might be helpful to avoid this type of bug.

Responsible Disclosure. The Apple Product Security team was notified of the vulnerability described in this paper on May 30, 2019, and has since taken steps to address the issue. In a conference call on July 17, 2019, Apple Product Security clarified that they do not object to the publication of the research results presented in this paper. On July 23, 2019, Apple Product Security informed us that they are planning to assign a CVE to this issue. On October 29, 2019, Apple publicly announced CVE-2019-8741 to address the vulnerability described in this paper for macOS Catalina 10.15, tvOS 13, watchOS 6, iOS 13, iTunes 12.10.1 for Windows, and iCloud for Windows 7.14.

Acknowledgments. The authors would like to thank the anonymous reviewers and their NIST colleagues for providing useful comments and suggestions. Special thanks go to Patrick Kamongi, Andrew Regenscheid, Apostol Vassilev, and Jeffrey Marron for their detailed feedback. Certain algorithms and commercial products are identified in this paper to foster understanding. Such identification does not imply recommendation or endorsement by NIST, nor does it imply that the algorithms or products identified are necessarily the best available for the purpose.

A   The `ccdigest_update()` function of Apple's CoreCrypto

Here, we provide the implementation of the `ccdigest_update()` in Apple Core-Crypto, which is made available to the public on Apple's website [3]. For readability, we made minor changes to the indentation, corrected the spelling of the word "division" and expanded the `CC_MEMCPY` macro to `memcpy`.

```
1   void ccdigest_update(const struct ccdigest_info *di, ccdigest_ctx_t ctx,
2                        size_t len, const void *data) {
3     const char * data_ptr = data;
4     size_t nblocks, nbytes;
5
6     while (len > 0) {
7       if (ccdigest_num(di, ctx) == 0 && len > di->block_size) {
8         //low-end processors are slow on division
9         if (di->block_size == 1<<6 ){ //sha256
10          nblocks = len >> 6;
11          nbytes = len & 0xFFFFffC0;
12        } else if(di->block_size == 1<<7 ){ //sha512
13          nblocks = len >> 7;
14          nbytes = len & 0xFFFFff80;
15        } else {
16          nblocks = len / di->block_size;
17          nbytes = nblocks * di->block_size;
18        }
19
20        di->compress(ccdigest_state(di, ctx), nblocks, data_ptr);
21        len -= nbytes;
22        data_ptr += nbytes;
23        ccdigest_nbits(di, ctx) += nbytes * 8;
24      } else {
25        size_t n = di->block_size - ccdigest_num(di, ctx);
26        if (len < n)
27          n = len;
28        memcpy(ccdigest_data(di, ctx) + ccdigest_num(di, ctx), data_ptr, n);
29        /* typecast: less than block size, will always fit into an int */
30        ccdigest_num(di, ctx) += (unsigned int)n;
31        len -= n;
32        data_ptr += n;
33        if (ccdigest_num(di, ctx) == di->block_size) {
34          di->compress(ccdigest_state(di, ctx), 1, ccdigest_data(di, ctx));
35          ccdigest_nbits(di, ctx) += ccdigest_num(di, ctx) * 8;
36          ccdigest_num(di, ctx) = 0;
37        }
38      }
39    }
40  }
```

References

1. Albrecht, M.R., Massimo, J., Paterson, K.G., Somorovsky, J.: Prime and prejudice: primality testing under adversarial conditions. In: Lie, D., Mannan, M., Backes, M., Wang, X. (eds.) Proceedings of the 2018 ACM SIGSAC Conference on Computer and Communications Security, CCS 2018, Toronto, ON, Canada, 15–19 October 2018, pp. 281–298. ACM (2018). https://doi.org/10.1145/3243734.3243787
2. American National Standards Institute: Public Key Cryptography for the Financial Services Industry - Key Agreement and Key Transport Using Elliptic Curve Cryptography. ANSI X9.63 (2017). https://webstore.ansi.org/standards/ascx9/ansix9632011r2017
3. Apple: Security - Apple Developer, September 2019. https://developer.apple.com/security/
4. Aumasson, J.P., Henzen, L., Meier, W., Phan, R.C.W.: SHA-3 proposal BLAKE. Submission to the NIST SHA-3 Competition (Round 3) (2010). http://131002.net/blake/blake.pdf
5. Bassham III, L.E., Hall, T.A.: The Secure Hash Algorithm Validation System (SHAVS), May 2014. https://csrc.nist.gov/CSRC/media/Projects/Cryptographic-Algorithm-Validation-Program/documents/shs/SHAVS.pdf
6. Bertoni, G., Daemen, J., Peeters, M., van Assche, G.: The Keccak SHA-3 submission. Submission to the NIST SHA-3 Competition (Round 3) (2011). http://keccak.noekeon.org/Keccak-submission-3.pdf
7. Brumley, B.B., Barbosa, M., Page, D., Vercauteren, F.: Practical realisation and elimination of an ECC-related software bug attack. In: Dunkelman, O. (ed.) CT-RSA 2012. LNCS, vol. 7178, pp. 171–186. Springer, Heidelberg (2012). https://doi.org/10.1007/978-3-642-27954-6_11
8. Celi, C.: ACVP Secure Hash Algorithm (SHA) JSON Specification. IETF Internet-Draft (2018). https://usnistgov.github.io/ACVP/artifacts/draft-celi-acvp-sha-00.html
9. Cisco: The libacvp library, September 2019. https://github.com/cisco/libacvp
10. Google: Project Wycheproof tests crypto libraries against known attacks, September 2019. https://github.com/google/wycheproof
11. Industry Working Group on Automated Cryptographic Algorithm Validation: ACVP, September 2019. https://usnistgov.github.io/ACVP/
12. Mouha, N., Raunak, M.S., Kuhn, D.R., Kacker, R.: Finding bugs in cryptographic hash function implementations. IEEE Trans. Reliab. **67**(3), 870–884 (2018). https://doi.org/10.1109/TR.2018.2847247
13. National Bureau of Standards: Validating the Correctness of Hardware Implementations of the NBS Data Encryption Standard. NBS Special Publication 500–20, November 1977. https://doi.org/10.6028/NBS.SP.500-20e1977
14. National Institute of Standards and Technology: Advanced Encryption Standard (AES). NIST Federal Information Processing Standards Publication 197, November 2001. https://doi.org/10.6028/NIST.FIPS.197
15. National Institute of Standards and Technology: Description of Known Answer Test (KAT) and Monte Carlo Test (MCT) for SHA-3 Candidate Algorithm Submissions, February 2008. https://csrc.nist.gov/CSRC/media/Projects/Hash-Functions/documents/SHA3-KATMCT1.pdf
16. National Institute of Standards and Technology: Secure Hash Standard (SHS). NIST Federal Information Processing Standards Publication 180–4, August 2015. https://doi.org/10.6028/NIST.FIPS.180-4

17. National Institute of Standards and Technology: SHA-3 Standard: Permutation-Based Hash and Extendable-Output Functions. NIST Federal Information Processing Standards Publication 202, August 2015. https://doi.org/10.6028/NIST.FIPS.202
18. National Institute of Standards and Technology and Canadian Centre for Cyber Security: Implementation Guidance for FIPS 140–2 and the Cryptographic Module Validation Program, August 2019. https://csrc.nist.gov/CSRC/media/Projects/cryptographic-module-validation-program/documents/fips140-2/FIPS1402IG.pdf
19. SEI CERT C Coding Standard: INT17-C. Define integer constants in an implementation-independent manner, September 2019. https://wiki.sei.cmu.edu/confluence/display/c/INT17-C.+Define+integer+constants+in+an+implementation-independent+manner
20. The MITRE Corporation: CWE-835: Loop with Unreachable Exit Condition ('Infinite Loop') (2019). https://cwe.mitre.org/data/definitions/835.html
21. Valenta, L., et al.: Measuring small subgroup attacks against Diffie-Hellman. In: 24th Annual Network and Distributed System Security Symposium, NDSS 2017, San Diego, California, USA, 26 February - 1 March, 2017. The Internet Society (2017). https://www.ndss-symposium.org/ndss2017/ndss-2017-programme/measuring-small-subgroup-attacks-against-diffie-hellman/

A Fast Characterization Method for Semi-invasive Fault Injection Attacks

Lichao Wu[1] , Gerard Ribera[2] , Noemie Beringuier-Boher[2] ,
and Stjepan Picek[1]([✉])

[1] Delft University of Technology, Delft, The Netherlands
picek.stjepan@gmail.com
[2] Amsterdam, The Netherlands

Abstract. Semi-invasive fault injection attacks are powerful techniques well-known by attackers and secure embedded system designers. When performing such attacks, the selection of the fault injection parameters is of utmost importance and usually based on the experience of the attacker. Surprisingly, there exists no formal and general approach to characterize the target behavior under attack. In this work, we present a novel methodology to perform a fast characterization of the fault injection impact on a target, depending on the possible attack parameters. We experimentally show our methodology to be a successful one when targeting different algorithms such as DES and AES encryption and then extend to the full characterization with the help of deep learning. Finally, we show how the characterization results are transferable between different targets.

Keywords: Physical attacks · Fault injection · Fast space characterization · Deep learning · Metrics

1 Introduction

A secure microcontroller or smartcard should be designed in such a way that no (or, as little as possible) secret information is leaked to the attacker and its integrity is protected. Still, there is an attack type that proved to be very powerful in the last decades and where, despite all the efforts, the attacker can obtain or modify the secret information. Such attacks are called implementation attacks as they do not target the algorithm's security but the weaknesses in its implementation. Two well-known types of implementation attacks are side-channel attacks (SCAs) and fault injection (FI) attacks. While those attacks are powerful, they can be also difficult to deploy due to a large number of choices one needs to make.

Semi-invasive attacks, a type of fault injection attacks, are widely used by attackers as well as during security evaluations in the industry due to their

---

G. Ribera and N. Beringuier-Boher—Independent Researcher.

S. Jarecki (Ed.): CT-RSA 2020, LNCS 12006, pp. 146–170, 2020.
https://doi.org/10.1007/978-3-030-40186-3_8

affordable and easy-to-repeat characteristics [1]. While semi-invasive attacks are powerful, they are not without limitations. First, the tuning of the parameters that play a role in the fault definition is a time-consuming and non-deterministic process. Using optical fault injection as an example, the required parameters to perform evaluation are numerous: laser pulse amplitude, laser pulse width, spot size, delays (attack time interval), and scan locations. As a complete analysis considering all possible parameter combinations is not practical, the decisions involved in the process of the parameter selection are usually based on intuition and personal criteria of an attacker. Additionally, due to the differences between FI setups, the measurement results obtained from one setup cannot be easily reproduced by another. An attacker is consequently bound to repeatedly search for the optimal parameters in every attack scenario, for every sample, and setup. Finally, the existence of countermeasures on both hardware and software levels can further increase the difficulties in defining parameters such as delays and scan locations.

To solve these problems, a characterization of the target of evaluation (TOE) for the optimal parameter searching is necessary as the preliminary step of evaluation. Surprisingly, there is no formal approach for doing this. Manual testing on parameter combinations based on the attacker's experience is a common method to get an impression of the target behavior. Still, this approach is not able to provide good coverage of the impact analysis for all the parameter combinations when the investigation is time-constrained. For example, the combinations of a shorter laser pulse width and stronger laser pulse amplitude could be more effective in manipulating some short execution of the command such as integrity check; in contrast with the opposite parameter combinations, long execution, such as Flash writing, would be more easily interfered. Unfortunately, these optimal parameters cannot be covered by manual tests. Exhaustive search, on the other hand, can be a solution if a full characterization is needed but will require more time as a trade-off. Finally, techniques coming from the artificial intelligence domain could work well but face issues like the uncertainty of parameter selection. In terms of the parameter optimization, researchers explored techniques such as genetic [2,3] and memetic algorithms [4] to improve the optimization approach. Although such approaches work well for voltage glitching or electromagnetic fault injection (EMFI), they are less universal for other fault injection approaches such as optical fault injection. More precisely, if the involved fault injection parameters are too strong, there is a high chance that the target will be damaged. Additionally, the obtained optimal parameters are limited to a certain fault injection setup as well as the sample under attack. Either the change of the setup or the sample will result in the change of the optimal parameters.

To speed-up the attack parameter identification while considering the coverage of the parameters, the development of strong and reproducible methodologies is of significant interest. Such methodologies should ensure a proper selection of the tested parameters and the effectiveness of an attack for various fault injection attack methods. Unfortunately, to the best of our knowledge, previous works only focused on optimizing the parameter selection for FI attacks. The methodology for the TOE characterization is still missing. Therefore, in this paper, we propose a methodology for the fast characterization of fault injection settings. The methodology is based on the construction of a sensitivity curve, which is then used by the attacker for a proper selection of the fault injection parameters and their assessment. To that end, we propose two metrics, one to be used in the measurement phase and one in the evaluation phase. Next, we use deep learning for the full estimation of the characterization space based on a limited number of measurements. Finally, we show that the obtained characterization results can be transferred to different samples with the same target. Throughout the paper, we use optical fault injection to perform the attack because of its popularity and difficulty in terms of characterization. Nevertheless, our characterization method is compatible with other semi-invasive fault injection approaches.

In conclusion, the methodology we propose can boost the characterization process while keeping track of useful information. This can eventually lead to (1) a better estimation of the target behavior, (2) a proper selection of the fault injection settings, (3) a good reference when attacking different devices, and (4) an informative archive for future attacks.

1.1 Related Work

Fault injection is a well-researched topic already spanning a range of more than 20 years [5,6]. Specifically, an optical fault injection attack is one of the most powerful attacks in this domain. Skorobogatov and Anderson introduced optical fault injection and attacked secure microcontrollers and smartcards [1]. There, the authors presented a countermeasure against such attacks (self-timed dual-rail circuit design technique) but concluded that such attacks are the most successful smartcard perturbation attacks as it is not easy to implement countermeasures. Although more advanced countermeasures have been developed in the later stage, optical FI attacks are still practical. S. Skorobogatov introduced a new optical fault attack type called fault masking attack [7]. Such attacks are aimed at disrupting the normal memory operation through preventing changes of the memory contents. Van Woudenberg et al. investigated optical fault injection on secure microcontrollers and concluded that the presence of countermeasures makes the attack more difficult but still possible [8,9]. Note, while being very powerful, optical fault injection attacks are usually considered very complex due to the high costs of equipment and the preparation of the sample. More recently, Guillen et al. presented a low-cost fault injection setup capable of producing localized faults in modern 8-bit and 32-bit microcontrollers [10]. The authors showed how even such a low-cost setup can be used to successfully attack the Speck cipher.

When considering implementation attacks and artificial intelligence techniques, most of the work concentrated on side-channel analysis. There, machine learning and more recently deep learning techniques are playing an important role in profiling attacks that can outperform template attacks but also break implementations protected with countermeasures [11–13]. When considering fault injection, several works are investigating how to find fault injection parameters with evolutionary algorithms, but to the best of our knowledge, none of these works consider machine learning nor optical fault injection. Carpi et al. considered the usage of evolutionary algorithms to find the fault injection parameters for supply voltage (VCC) glitching [2]. There, besides the evolutionary algorithms approach, the authors used three more search techniques. Next, Picek et al. extended this work by using a combination of an evolutionary algorithm and a local search to characterize the search space for voltage glitching as efficient as possible [4]. Maldini et al. used a genetic algorithm for finding fault injection parameters when considering electromagnetic fault injection (EMFI) [14]. There, the authors attacked the SHA-3 algorithm and reported 40 times more faulty measurements and 20 times more distinct fault measurements than by using a random search.

1.2 Our Contributions

In this paper, we consider semi-invasive fault injection attacks and fast characterization of the target behavior, which to the best of our knowledge, has not been explored before. More precisely, we introduce a methodology for semi-invasive fault injection that consists of:

1. New technique for searching for fault injection parameters consisting of a fast generation of a sensitivity curve and its evaluation, which is compatible with different FI techniques, attack scenarios, and TOEs.
2. Two metrics that enable us to properly guide the characterization and also assess it.
3. A novel approach based on deep learning classification that enables us to characterize the search space based on the limited number of actual measurements.

Besides these, from an attacker perspective, the use of the fast characterization method will significantly reduce the time needed to identify the optimal attack parameters. Additionally, because the characterization method increases the attack parameters coverage, the quality of the results will be improved and the chance of missing the optimal parameters will be reduced. To prove the efficiency of the proposed method, we provide detailed experimental results targeting the AES and DES ciphers implemented on a secured microcontroller. Finally, we then show that the characterization results are transferable towards different targets of the same type.

This paper is organized as follows. In Sect. 2, we discuss fault injection attacks, supervised machine learning, and neural networks. Next, in Sect. 3, we start by introducing our notation. Afterward, we present two new metrics we designed to help us better assess the performance of the attack and how to generate/evaluate the sensitivity curve. In Sect. 5, we discuss our experimental setup and results obtained after attacking samples with the AES and DES ciphers. Finally, in Sect. 6, we conclude the paper and present possible future research directions.

2   Preliminaries

In this section, we first describe the fault injection attacks, where we divide them into three types of attacks and discuss their major differences. We emphasize semi-invasive attacks due to their high-efficiency and low-cost properties. Subsequently, we briefly introduce the supervised learning paradigm, the general architecture of a neural network, and then broaden such a structure to the deep neural network. Finally, we discuss multilayer perceptron as the algorithm of choice in our experiments.

2.1   Fault Injection Attacks

Fault injection attacks aim at retrieving information or injecting faults to the target. Currently, many powerful techniques have been developed, all of which can be divided into three main categories - non-invasive, semi-invasive, and invasive attacks [15]. The main difference between the non-invasive and invasive attacks is in the approach of attacking the TOEs. To perform an invasive attack, it is required to remove at least part of the passivation layer to establish the contact between the probes and silicon [16]. Non-invasive attacks, on the other hand, mainly focus on investigating the settings that can be controlled externally [17], or passively measuring the running time, the cache behavior, the power consumption, and/or the electromagnetic radiation of the device through the package [18].

Semi-invasive attacks, standing in the middle of the two types of attacks discussed above, have their specific properties. Similar to the invasive attacks, they require direct access to the chip surface by removing the package, but the passivation layer is kept. A semi-invasive attack can be performed in a reasonably short time with much less expensive equipment than the invasive attacks. Finally, the skills and knowledge required to perform them also can be easily and quickly acquired [19]. From the approach perspective, semi-invasive attacks could be performed using a variety of tools such as IR light [20], X-rays [1] and other sources of ionizing radiation, electromagnetic fields [21], and body biasing [22].

2.2   Supervised Machine Learning

In the supervised learning paradigm, the goal is to learn a mapping f, such that $f : \mathcal{X} \rightarrow \mathcal{Y}$, given a training set of N pairs (x_i, y_i). Here, for each example x, there is a corresponding label y, where $y \in \mathcal{Y}$. This phase is commonly known as the training phase. The function f is an element of the space of all possible functions $\mathcal{F}$. Once the function f is obtained, the testing phase starts with the goal to predict the labels for new, previously unseen examples. In the case that Y takes values from a finite set (discrete labels), we conduct classification, while if the labels are continuous, we conduct regression.

2.3   Neural Networks and Deep Learning

A neural network is an interconnected assembly of simple processing elements, units or nodes, whose functionality is based on the biological process occurring in the brain [23]. In general, a neural network consists of three blocks: an input layer, one or more hidden layers, and an output layer, whose processing ability is represented by the strength (weight) of the inter-unit connections, learning from a set of training patterns from the input layer.

To improve computation ability, a standard approach is to add hidden layers to build a deep neural network. An example of the deep neural network is shown in Fig. 1. With the help of multiple layers, a deep neural network can map complicated low-level details to high-level features progressively. Thus, deep neural networks can make a proper estimation of the output, where this adaption process is referred to as deep learning.

In this paper, we applied a commonly-used deep learning structure, multilayer perceptron (MLP) in our methodology. MLP is a feed-forward neural network mapping sets of inputs onto sets of appropriate outputs. It consists of multiple layers of nodes in a directed graph, with each layer fully connected to the next one. Each node in one layer connects with a certain weight w to every node in the following layer. The MLP architecture consists of at least three layers: one input layer, one output layer, and one hidden layer. Those layers must consist of non-linearly activating nodes [24].

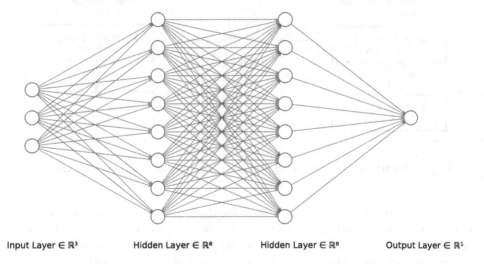

Input Layer ∈ ℝ³   Hidden Layer ∈ ℝ⁸   Hidden Layer ∈ ℝ⁸   Output Layer ∈ ℝ¹

Fig. 1. An example of deep neural network with 2 hidden layers and 8 neurons per hidden layer (created with NN-SVG [25]). Note that it is enough to have more than one hidden layer to consider a certain architecture as deep learning.

3   Fast Characterization Methodology

A reliable characterization methodology can be used to obtain a quick impression of the influence caused to the target for a different combination of attack parameters. An attacker will use the outcome to better choose the settings to perform the attack in a later stage. However, there are several obstacles to build such a characterization methodology:

1. How to quantify the effect of the FI settings?
2. How to obtain a characterization of the impact that can be generated in a short amount of time?
3. How to map the behavior of the target to the characterization?
4. How to make sure that the characterization result is transferable between different targets?

The solutions to these problems are summarized with a work-flow presented in Fig. 2. In general, one can observe that the attacker can divide his actions into two separate phases: (1) fast characterization of the target and (2) fault injection procedure. Our methodology concentrates on the fast characterization part as the fault injection procedure stems from it. To characterize the target in a fast and correct way, we first generate the sensitivity curve (described in Sect. 4). Next, we evaluate the measurements to further investigate the target behavior with different FI settings.

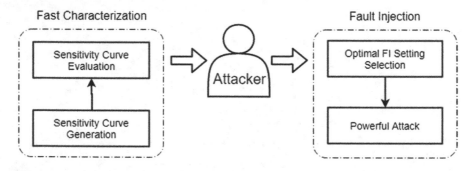

Fig. 2. An attack work-flow with proposed fast characterization methodology.

It should be noted that the attack location and time delay to inject the fault should be defined in advance, as they are initial conditions for the sensitivity curve generation. The attack location, for instance, can be inferred by reverse engineering techniques (i.e., IR-imaging) and a good understanding of the targeted fault model, while the Simple Power Analysis (SPA) can be used to define the attack time window. However, such analyses are out of the scope of this paper. Additionally, there are many other relevant parameters, such as the thickness of the silicon, that can influence the sensitivity of the target. However, it is a less interesting parameter in practice as it is difficult to control it precisely. In contrast, from an attacker perspective, the simplest and the most effective parameters to work with are the parameters that can directly influence the strength of the injected fault, such as laser pulse width and laser pulse amplitude for optical fault injection. In this paper, we focus on characterizing these two parameters.

In this section, we start by introducing the notation used in this paper when discussing the behavior of targets. Next, we present two different metrics that enable us to better evaluate the performance of a fault injection process. One of the metrics (Level of Influence) measures the fault injection process and we use it in the proposed search algorithm while the other one (Impact Score) is used to evaluate the results of the fault injection. Note that throughout the paper, we use interchangeably the notions target, the target of evaluation, and its abbreviation TOE.

3.1 Notations

Fault injection attacks impact the behavior of the target, which can be noticed when its response to a target command deviates from the expected one. Those faulty responses can be used to categorize them into verdict classes that correspond to the effectiveness of the measurement (i.e., attack attempt). The possible classes for each measurement are listed in the ascending order based on their relevance for the attacker.

1. NORMAL: TOE behaves as expected.
2. RESET: The attack is detected and TOE resets.
3. MUTE: TOE stops communication. This type of response can be caused either by hard failures caused by the attack (i.e., the chip doesn't work anymore) or can be the response when the attack is detected.
4. CHANGING: TOE fails to detect the injected faults and returns unexpected values.
5. SUCCESS: TOE fails to detect the injected faults and returns abnormal but exploitable values.

Note that an exploitable fault is a fault that can be used to obtain more critical information (e.g., retrieve encryption key with Differential Fault Analysis (DFA) [26]) or perform additional malicious activities (e.g., install unauthorized software). In this paper we attack two popular encryption algorithms: AES and DES, an exploitable fault is the faulty cipher output: with these outputs, the encryption key can be retrieved with DFA. A non-exploitable fault, on the other hand, can be any other outputs, such as status word or unrelated data stored in other addresses. It also worth to mention that when attacking a device with fault injection, different types of unexpected results can be outputted and are difficult to classify. The situation becomes even worse when targeting different types of devices as the implementations are also different. To simplify the characterization and to abstract from the underlying fault model, we classify the faults on the algorithmic level instead of on the hardware level.

In this paper, the optical FI technique is used for the experiments. The main attack parameters - the laser voltage (energy) and laser pulse width are denoted with upper-case letters X and Y, while their realizations are given in the lower-case letters x and y. More precisely, the search boundaries for these two FI settings are X_{min}/X_{max} and Y_{min}/Y_{max}. The search steps are represented by X_{step} and Y_{step}.

3.2   Metrics Definition

Level of Influence. The Level of Influence (LOI) represents the percentage of responses that are different from the expected (NORMAL response) in the total number of attempts, which can be used to quantify the impact of the attack parameter set. For instance, by decreasing the laser pulse amplitude or the duration, the fault injection is less effective and the target tends to behave normally, thus having a low influence. In contrast, by increasing these settings, there is a higher possibility that the target is influenced by the attack, which will eventually increase its influence on the target behavior. The LOI metric can be calculated as follows:

$$LOI = 1 - \frac{Quantity_{normal}}{\sum^{class} Quantity_{class}}. \tag{1}$$

Here, $Quantity_{normal}$ represents the number of NORMAL responses while $Quantity_{class}$ represents the number of the specific class occurrences during the whole measurement process.

Impact Score. The outputs of the TOE under fault injection are divided into several classes (see Sect. 3.1). To further clarify the effect of each FI settings and to optimize the parameter selection in the later attack phase, we assign weights to each class based on its significance and eventually come up with a score based on every measurement result. As this score directly reflects the effects of the FI with respect to the target behavior, we denote this metric Impact Score (IS).

The Impact Score metric aims to show the relevance of the measurements that are acquired during the generation of the sensitivity curve (see Sect. 4). By assigning different weights to the different classes obtained, an attacker can identify if some of the parts of the curve are more relevant and could potentially lead to a successful manipulation.

In practice, class SUCCESS has the highest priority of all the classes and is assigned the largest weight. Differing, the class NORMAL (indicating the target behaves normally) is linked to a small weight. The IS metric can be calculated as:

$$IS = \frac{\sum^{class} Quantity_{class} \cdot Weight_{class}}{\sum^{class} Quantity_{class}}, \tag{2}$$

where $Weight_{class}$ represents the assigned weight for a corresponding class. In the experiments presented in this paper, the classes SUCCESS, CHANGING, MUTE, RESET, and NORMAL have weights 20, 10, 2, 0.5, and 0, respectively. The weights are adjusted based on the experience of the attacker and the rationale behind is defined after an assessment of the hypothetical fault model that leads to such responses.

4   Sensitivity Curve

In this section, we start by introducing the concept of the sensitivity curve. Afterward, we discuss how to generate such a curve by first finding the "golden" point and then applying the sensitivity curve search algorithm. Finally, we discuss how to evaluate the sensitivity curve through Impact Score or deep learning classification process.

4.1 Setting

To obtain a characterization algorithm that has a good parameter coverage, is less time-consuming, and is universal for different scenarios, several methods from simple (e.g., exhaustive search with large scan step, binary search) to complicated (e.g., genetic algorithm, deep learning) have been tested. The comparison of different architectures is not shown due to the lack of space and redundancy in obtained results. We observed that simple algorithms are predictable which is ideal for the TOE characterization but normally less time-efficient. In contrast, complicated approaches tend to rely on the number and quality of the obtained data. However, these algorithms work unstable as the number of data sets we obtained is extremely limited. In the worst case, a non-converged model can lead to the target being damaged by the undesired parameter selection.

Therefore, the ideal algorithm for the characterization should stand in the middle of these two extremes. In other words, it should be deterministic, but not highly data-dependent. Fortunately, the sensitivity curve, which consists of a set of FI settings that cause a similar impact on the TOE, perfectly fulfills our requirements.

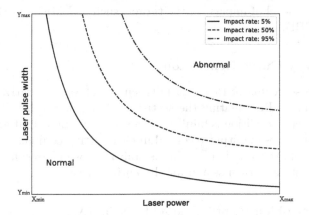

Fig. 3. An example of the sensitivity curves with different LOIs. From here, the normal and abnormal behaviour of the target can be estimated.

Three sensitivity curve with different LOI is given in Fig. 3; each point on the curve has a similar impact on the TOE behavior. There, with sensitivity curves, one can estimate that the injected fault (X and Y axes represent the FI settings) can be ignored at the left side of the curve with 5% LOI; while the target will behave almost always abnormally at the right side of the curve with

90% LOI. Moreover, the figure presents multiple possible selections of the fault injection settings that can lead to the same LOI. For instance, to achieve 50% of the LOI, besides choosing the parameters in the middle of the curve, an attacker can achieve a similar result by selecting smaller x and larger y or vice versa. It is possible that the sensitivity curve is not decreasing monotonically as shown in Fig. 3. Nevertheless, the sensitivity curves act as contour lines in the parametric coordinate system, which can be used to estimate the quantity of impact with different FI settings. Furthermore, the presence of the sensitivity curves provides the attacker with a multiple choice in setting selection: although the LOI is the same, appropriate selection of the FI settings based on the attack scenarios may lead to a more powerful attack. Therefore, we use the sensitivity curve for TOE characterization.

To conclude, if compared with other approaches, the advantages of the sensitivity curve-based characterization are the followings:

1. The sensitivity curve defines the natural boundary between the "weak" and "strong" FI settings, which present a rough overview of the target behavior.
2. The input of the sensitivity curve delimits the number of the parameter combinations to be examined, thus it is more time-efficient.
3. Since the LOI of a sensitivity curve is defined by an attacker, it resolves the problem of an FI setting selection through a genetic algorithm or random search.
4. The proposed methodology can be applied to other semi-invasive FI methods that follow the assumption that the strength of the setting is positively correlated to the level of impact on the target, such as EMFI and Body Biasing Injection (BBI).

4.2   Sensitivity Curve Generation

In general, the searching of the sensitivity curve relies on iterative performing of measurements and calculating the statistics to decide the next setting to be tested until the end condition is fulfilled. The statistics (LOI) that are calculated are based on the types of output recorded in each setting combinations. To make a clear description, the search algorithm is split into two phases: first, determine the "golden point" and then search for the entire curve.

Finding the "Golden Point". The golden point (X_{golden}, Y_{golden}) represents the first obtained FI setting that targets the LOI (C_{target}) defined by an attacker and acts as the reference for the curve searching in the later step. To find such a point, we use the diagonal search algorithm. The diagonal search algorithm is performed by increasing the values of the FI parameters simultaneously with a fixed step as shown in Fig. 4. Note how the search progresses in a number of steps (in our example, 6) before reaching a point on the sensitivity curve. The diagonal search algorithm ensures to start testing with weak laser settings and then gradually going stronger. Indeed, some approaches may lead to faster converge. However, during the experiments, we noticed that the chip sensitivity towards the laser can vary dramatically between targets (i.e., different types of microcontrollers). In other words, a laser setting that does not have any influence on one product may destroy another product immediately. Consequently, the diagonal search algorithm is selected to ensure the tested product being alive throughout the characterization process as well as to broaden the usage of our methodology towards different products.

It is worth to note that the diagonal search cannot always guarantee to find the FI settings with exact C_{target} value. In many cases, the LOI can exceed the target when performing the search. Therefore, we introduce the $C_{tolerance}$ to broaden the range search of the golden point: if the LOI of the tested FI setting is within the range of $C_{target} \pm C_{tolerance}$, the applied FI setting can be counted as the golden point. In cases when the current LOI exceeds the maximum range $(C_{target}+C_{tolerance})$ but no golden point is observed, a binary search is performed to trace back to lower settings and search for the golden point within the range of tolerance.

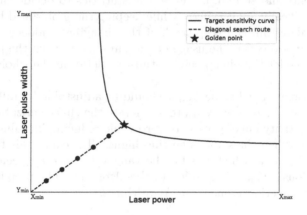

Fig. 4. A depiction of the diagonal search. The golden point represents the first obtained FI setting with the target LOI.

Curve Searching. Once the golden point is obtained from the diagonal search, the search for the sensitivity curve can be executed. As discussed in Sect. 4.2, the golden point is obtained in a diagonal route, but there are still areas on its left and right-hand side to be characterized. Therefore, to localize the sensitivity curve in the whole parameter plane, the curve search is performed in both directions individually, while they start with the golden point. As the search strategies for both directions are the same, the search algorithm to the left (X_{min}) direction is given in Algorithm 1. Curve search on the right-hand side can be realized by adjusting the *while* condition as well as the x increment step.

The function $DoTest(x,y)$ performs a measurement with a combination of the FI setting x and y. $BinarySearch(a,b)$ represents the binary search in the range from a to b. The main idea of Algorithm 1 is to first iteratively obtain

Algorithm 1. Sensitivity curve search.

1: **function** SEARCHING_LEFT($X_{golden}, Y_{golden}, C_{target}, C_{tolerance}$)
2:      $data \leftarrow []$
3:      $x \leftarrow X_{golden}$
4:      $y \leftarrow Y_{golden}$ ▷ Initialize (x, y)
5:      **while** $x - X_{step} > X_{min}$ **do**   ▷ Search from the left plane
6:          $x \leftarrow X_{prev} - X_{step}$
7:          $LOI \leftarrow \text{DoTest}(x, y)$ ▷ Test with setting (x, y)
8:          **if** $LOI < C_{target} + C_{tolerance}$ **then**
9:              $y \leftarrow \text{BinarySearch}(y, Y_{max})$ ▷ Search with stronger settings
10:          **else if** $LOI > C_{target} - C_{tolerance}$ **then**
11:              $y \leftarrow \text{BinarySearch}(y, Y_{min})$ ▷ Search with weaker settings
12:          $data \leftarrow data + [x, y, LOI]$
13:      **return** $data$ ▷ Return all of the tested data
---

the measurements and second, calculate the statistics to decide the next pairs of settings. Specifically, by varying x while keeping the y obtained by the previous steps, the algorithm can keep track of the changing tendency of the target sensitivity curve. Moreover, the usage of the parameters from the previous test delimits the range for the binary search, thus accelerating the whole characterization procedure.

Instead of using a fixed value, X_{step} should be adjustable for different conditions. For instance, increasing X_{step} to accelerate the characterization when the slope of the sensitivity curve is close to zero while reducing its value to evaluate more FI settings when the slope is getting higher. To realize this functionality, a new variable Y_{diff}, which stands for the value difference between the current y and the previous y (Y_{prev}), is added to the algorithm. The pseudocode of the step adjustment function is shown in Algorithm 2.

4.3   Sensitivity Curve Evaluation

The sensitivity curve provides the attacker with a quick impression of the target behavior (through the LOI metric) with different FI settings. To further benefit from the performed measurements, the attacker can use techniques to visualize the data differently with the Impact Score metric and to obtain an overview of the different setting relevance in FI. Additionally, he can even estimate the non-measured parameter combinations with a deep learning algorithm.

Algorithm 2. Step adjustment

1: **function** ADJUST_XSTEP($X_{step}, Y_{step}, Y_{prev}, y$)
2:      $Y_{diff} \leftarrow \text{absolute}(Y_{prev} - y)$
3:      **if** $Y_{diff} <= Y_{step}$ **then**
4:          **return** $X_{step} * 2$
5:      **else**
6:          **return** $X_{step} / 2$

Impact Score Evaluation. As described in Sect. 4.2, the generation of the sensitivity curve is based on searching the FI settings with a similar LOI. Although the target behavior can be estimated based on the curve, it is difficult to define the optimal parameters which can lead to more significant responses. Indeed, LOI only distinguishes between NORMAL and non-NORMAL responses. To fully evaluate the performance of one setting, the non-NORMAL response should be additionally classified based on its significance.

Taking advantage of its wide setting selection, the sensitivity curve is a good candidate for evaluating the effectiveness of the FI. Therefore, the curve is regenerated with the IS metric to obtain the optimal setting for fault injection. Specifically, by calculating IS for each parameter combination, the relevance of the measurement can be quantified: a larger Impact Score represents the existence of higher-priority responses, indicating that the corresponding setting is more preferable for the later attacks.

Impact Estimation with MLP. In practice, the assessment of attacking the non-measured area is a part of the evaluation and comes from the attacker's decision. Various advanced techniques can be used to help the attacker to estimate the impact in the non-measured areas. Here, function regression, realized by MLP with gradient descent, is used to build the relationship between its input (FI parameters) and output (LOI). A converged model can provide a proper estimation of the impact that can be caused in the target with different parameters.

However, the prediction accuracy highly relies on the training data. Indeed, the sensitivity curve provides several unique data sets, but the prediction of the untested locations is still challenging, as the number of the training sets is extremely limited while we aim at predicting huge amounts of parameter combinations in a wide range. We have evaluated several algorithms to find an optimal one that can provide sufficient prediction accuracy. Eventually, it turned out that the multilayer perceptron is the best candidate. Compared with other machine learning structures and statistic methods, MLP dramatically reduced the prediction error especially in the excessive area from weak to the strong parameter (the region an attacker cares about most) with the help of the deeper layers. Although higher precision of the prediction can be obtained by using more data (e.g., by generating another sensitivity curve with different LOI), MLP is the best solution to provide an overall estimation of the target behavior without additional tests (costs). Moreover, in our case, MLP is less sensitive to the distribution/number variation of the training sets and can always extract features from a limited amount of data and thus can improve the robustness of our methodology.

The cross-entropy is implemented as the loss function to classify the discrete data from the sensitivity curve. By minimizing the loss function during iterations, the MLP can estimate the LOI with different FI settings, whose accuracy is further evaluated by calculating the offset between the predicted and measured data. Note that we consider the prediction result as reasonable if the prediction error is small when compared with the test data and the plots fit the shape of the sensitivity curve. Although the sample's behavior under attack can vary from the prediction due to the prediction error and many other reasons, the presented prediction methodology can provide an attacker with a proper estimation of the overall sample behavior, which leads to a better selection of the parameters.

5   Results

In this section, we start by introducing our experimental setup. Then, we present the results obtained for DES and AES settings using the presented fast characterization methodology. Finally, we validate the transferability of the characterization result by repeating the characterization for a different sample of the same TOE.

5.1   Experimental Setup

In all our experiments, we use a TOE based on a high-performance 32-bit microcontroller realized in Complementary Metal Oxide Semiconductor (CMOS) technology with 4 MHz clock frequency. Due to confidentiality reasons, we are not able to disclose the details of the targets. Still, we are confident to note that the proposed method is compatible with various types of devices, as it was proved to be efficient with multiple devices that are not listed in the paper due to the page limit.

No FI specific countermeasures are implemented at the hardware level. For the experimental purpose, we present two different attack scenarios on software implementation of cryptographic algorithms, one targeting the beginning of the last round of Data Encryption Standard (DES) cipher and another one targeting the beginning of the last round of Advanced Encryption Standard (AES) cipher. Note that we used Single Power Analysis (SPA) to identify the encryption rounds. In both cases, we present a fast characterization that could be used by an attacker to perform the attack in a later stage to obtain faulty ciphers that can be used to run a DFA attack [27].

Experiments shown in this paper are performed on the Flash decoders as we assumed they are the most vulnerable part for light manipulation. The attack locations are uniformly distributed on the entire scan area. The FI setup used to perform the measurements is an optical fault injection setup using an IR light (1 024 nm) long-pulse laser which is one of the most powerful solutions for an optical fault injection attack. Since this light source is less effective when attacking the front-side of the sample as it cannot penetrate through the metal layers, we concentrated on attacking the backside (silicon side). To fully demonstrate as well to characterize the chip behavior with different laser settings, we selected a wide range of parameters that are used during the searching algorithm. The details are given in Table 1 while the MLP hyper-parameters for the LOI prediction are in Table 2.

Table 1. Parameters for the search algorithm.

Parameter	Value
Laser pulse width	[1, 50] μs in a step of 1 μs
Laser voltage (Pulse Amplitude)	[0.05, 0.6]V in a step of 0.01 V
Target LOI	0.5
Searching tolerance	0.05

Table 2. MLP hyper-parameters.

Parameter	Value
Architecture	[2, 8, 6, 6, 5, 1]
Activation	4 ReLU + 1 Sigmoid
Learning rate (α)	0.2
Decay rate	α * 0.97 per 1 000 epochs
Regularization	L2
Iterations	50 000

5.2 Characterization for the DES Encryption Attack

The DES encryption process is the target execution in this attack scenario. The attack time interval is delimited with SPA (Simple Power Analysis). The fast characterization is launched to assess the FI settings that might potentially lead to a successful attack (i.e., faulty ciphertexts).

Three steps are performed during the characterization procedure: first, generating the sensitivity curve, followed by the impact estimation using a deep learning algorithm, and finally evaluating the curve with the IS metric. During the first step, all the measurements are acquired. The second and third steps belong to the evaluation phase. The generation of the sensitivity curve and the impact estimation using deep learning are based on the LOI metric while the third step is based on the IS metric.

Level of Influence for DES. The characterization result based on the proposed algorithm is depicted in Fig. 5a. For comparison purposes, a full-characterization was performed and the LOI graph of an exhaustive scan with a full range of settings is shown in Fig. 5b. The color of the dots represents the value of the LOI metric. The test run of Algorithm 1 to perform the fast characterization (59 measurement points) was obtained within 2 h while the full-characterization (3 080 measurement points) took more than a week of measurement time.

As a remark, each training data consists of results from different attack locations. Attacking more locations can better represent the sample's behavior with certain laser parameters, but will spend more time as a trade-off. Here, we performed an exhaustive scan with more than 3 000 tests for the validation purpose, where due to the time constraints, we have to control the cost of the training data in an acceptable range (around 4 min per test).

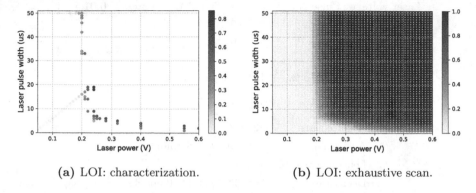

(a) LOI: characterization.   (b) LOI: exhaustive scan.

Fig. 5. LOI distribution with different fault injection settings.

From the result, the outline of the sensitivity curve, which acts as the boundary between "week" and "strong" parameters, can be estimated with the measured data. Based on this curve, the impact of the target on different FI settings can be estimated. Besides that, additional information can be extracted from the graph:

1. FI becomes effective when the laser voltage is larger than 0.2 V.
2. Similar LOI can be achieved with completely different setting combinations.
3. Laser voltage is more influential in FI than the laser pulse width.

The usage of this information depends on the attack scenario. For example, if the attack scenario is to skip an instruction execution, short pulses might be preferred; whereas to corrupt a memory write (long operation), longer pulses could be more appropriate. Nevertheless, an attacker can benefit from these inputs in the next phase of the attack.

The MLP (as described in Table 2) is used to predict the LOI with all FI setting combinations, trained by the data obtained during the characterization process. In this attack scenario, 59 training set pairs, with two FI settings as features and Level of Interest values as labels, are collected from the sensitivity curve. The plot of the loss with respect to the epoch numbers during the training is shown in Fig. 6.

As shown in Fig. 7a, the prediction result matches the measured data with the majority of the setting combinations. The prediction error plotted in Fig. 7b is also close to the sensitivity curve: the maximum error is 0.14 and the average error is 0.009. The prediction results indicate the capability of deep learning in predicting LOI with a limited number of training sets, which offers a proper estimation of the target behavior in significantly less time than a full characterization.

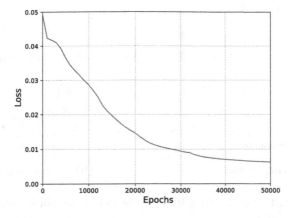

Fig. 6. LOI prediction for DES: loss versus epoch numbers.

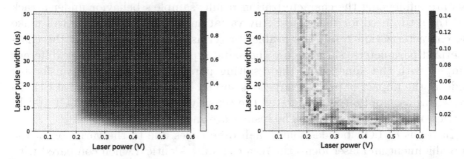

(a) Prediction result using a five-layer neu-   (b) Error plot when comparing with the
ral network.   full-characterization measured data.

Fig. 7. Prediction result with a deep neural network.

Impact Score for DES. To further investigate target behavior, Impact Scores
are calculated (Fig. 8a) based on the measurements performed during the generation of the sensitivity curve. The IS results from the exhaustive scan are shown
as the reference (Fig. 8b).

From Fig. 8a, a higher IS can be obtained with shorter laser pulse width
but stronger laser voltage, indicating the high probability in obtaining more
significant output in this region. Indeed, this assumption can be proved by Fig. 8b
with IS for all setting combinations. Since the IS-based sensitivity curve only
covers a few of the setting combinations, other, untested optimal settings could
still exist. Still, this curve provides a general layout for the settings with better
relevance from the measurements performed, which can eventually lead to a
better parameter selection for a later attack stage.

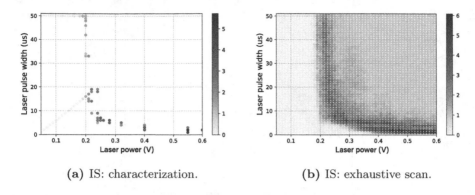

(a) IS: characterization.   **(b)** IS: exhaustive scan.

Fig. 8. IS distribution with different fault injection settings.

Transferability of the DES Characterization Results. In general, two factors are influencing the characterization result: sample's behavior under attack and the setup used for the attack. Any variation of these two factors will make the characterization result less usable. In terms of transferability of the characterized parameters, since we use the same type of TOE and attack different samples with the same setup, the resulting parameters should be transferable (indeed, the impact of process variations should be negligible for optical FI). To prove this assumption, we generated the sensitivity curve with the LOI and IS metrics on a different sample. The results are shown in Fig. 9.

In terms of LOI, besides some small differences due to the variation of the chip alignment and laser focus, the result is quite identical when compared with Fig. 5a. The IS, on the other hand, also shows its consistency when comparing with Fig. 8a, as it also indicates that the shorter laser pulse width with stronger laser voltage can lead to higher impact scores at the same parameter range. Therefore, since the shape of the curve, LOI, and the corresponding IS tested

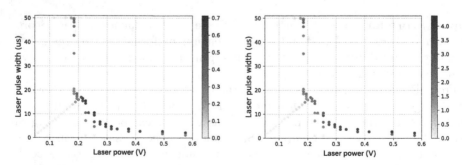

(a) LOI: characterization with a different sample.   **(b)** IS: characterization with a different sample.

Fig. 9. Characterization results with a different sample targeting DES encryption.

on two different samples match with each other, we conclude that the characterization result from one sample is transferable to a different sample of the same TOE.

5.3   Characterization for the AES Encryption Attack

To verify the proposed methodology in different conditions, we performed an additional FI experiment with another laser setup of the same type. This experiment aims to manipulate the encryption of AES software implementation. Similar to the previous experiment, SPA techniques are used to delimit the attack time interval. The building block to be targeted is kept the same (Flash decoders).

Level of Influence for AES. As for the DES cipher, a characterization was performed to obtain a LOI graph. The sensitivity curve is shown in Fig. 10a (47 measurements) while its full-characterization counterpart is presented in Fig. 10b (3 800 measurements). When comparing this characterization result with the one targeting the DES encryption (Fig. 5a), we can observe the differences in setting selections for comparable LOIs. This difference can be due either to the use of a different laser setup or to the different attack scenarios.

Once the LOI graph was obtained, the same MLP architecture was used to map the LOI with all the FI setting inputs from the data measured during the sensitivity curve generation. Again, we plot the loss with respect to the epoch numbers during the training. The result is shown in Fig. 11. By comparing the prediction results (Fig. 12a) with the full-characterization (Fig. 10b), we can confirm that the LOI tendency is properly estimated. To evaluate the prediction error, the difference between the two is plotted in Fig. 12b. Although the error can be further delimited by tuning the hyper-parameters of the network architecture or increasing the number of measurements during the sensitivity curve generation, the effectiveness of the MLP for LOI estimation is verified.

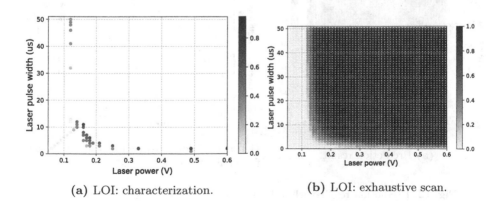

(a) LOI: characterization.   (b) LOI: exhaustive scan.

Fig. 10. LOI distribution with different fault injection settings.

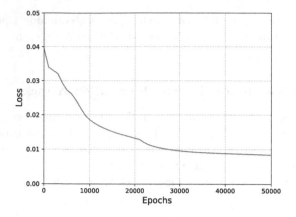

Fig. 11. LOI prediction for AES: loss versus epoch numbers.

Impact Score for AES. The IS-based sensitivity curve is shown in Fig. 13a while the full characterization reference is presented in Fig. 13b. Similar to the IS distribution shown in Fig. 8a, the fault injection is more effective with short laser pulse widths for AES encryption (Fig. 13a), as the points with high IS are accumulated at the bottom-right of the graph. Taking Fig. 13b as the reference, the IS-based sensitivity curve can cover the overall target behavior effectively with a limited amount of data, thus proving its capability in settings optimization in a short amount of time.

Transferability of the AES Characterization Results. Similar to the experiment performed in Sect. 5.2, we generated the sensitivity curve with the LOI and IS metrics on a new sample attacking the same locations and using the same laser setup. The results are shown in Fig. 14.

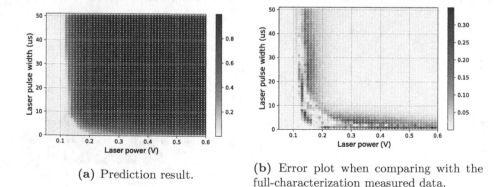

(a) Prediction result.

(b) Error plot when comparing with the full-characterization measured data.

Fig. 12. Prediction result with a deep neural network for AES encryption.

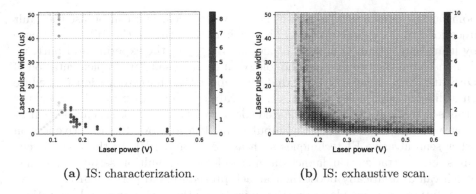

(a) IS: characterization.   (b) IS: exhaustive scan.

Fig. 13. IS distribution with different fault injection settings for AES encryption.

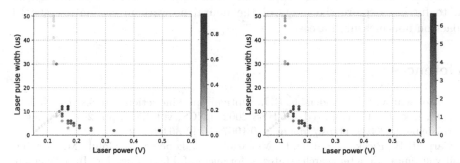

(a) LOI: characterization with a different (b) IS: characterization with a different
sample.   sample.

Fig. 14. Characterization results with a different sample targeting AES encryption.

From the figures, the LOI and IS distribution are identical to the previous characterization results (Figs. 10a and 13a). Therefore, we again show that the characterization result is transferable between different samples of the same TOE. We also conclude from this test on the AES that the fast characterization methodology presented in this paper applies to different attack scenarios.

6   Conclusions and Future Work

In this paper, we present a novel methodology for semi-invasive fault injection attacks that improves the identification (characterization) phase of an attack. This methodology consists of a fast generation of the sensitivity curve and a proper evaluation of the Level of Influence and Impact Score metrics. Instead of testing FI setting conditions randomly, we start by generating the sensitivity curve, which happens in two phases. First, we find the golden point, which is close to the target LOI and then, we depict the rest of the curve using this point as the reference. Finally, we show how deep learning can be used in fault injection attacks characterization phase where we estimate the full search space by using only a limited number of measurements. In the experimental part, we demonstrated the proposed methodology on running software implementation of DES and AES ciphers. Besides that, we repeat the characterization procedure on a different sample to verify its transferability. Not shown in this paper, the proposed method had been validated for a variety of attack scenarios such as program flow attack and data manipulations. It also showed its effectiveness on other semi-invasive FI techniques such as EMFI and BBI. In the realistic circumstances, attackers can launch our methodology on multiple setups in parallel, which can dramatically boost their attack procedure and performance.

In future work, we plan to further investigate the advantages and limitations of the fast characterization with different fault injection methods, setups, targets, and initial conditions such as temperature and supply voltage. Additionally, we aim to further explore the usage of the neural network in estimating the FI impact on non-measured areas.

References

1. Skorobogatov, S.P., Anderson, R.J.: Optical fault induction attacks. In: Kaliski, B.S., Koç, K., Paar, C. (eds.) CHES 2002. LNCS, vol. 2523, pp. 2–12. Springer, Heidelberg (2003). https://doi.org/10.1007/3-540-36400-5_2
2. Carpi, R.B., Picek, S., Batina, L., Menarini, F., Jakobovic, D., Golub, M.: Glitch it if you can: parameter search strategies for successful fault injection. In: Francillon, A., Rohatgi, P. (eds.) CARDIS 2013. LNCS, vol. 8419, pp. 236–252. Springer, Cham (2014). https://doi.org/10.1007/978-3-319-08302-5_16
3. Picek, S., Batina, L., Jakobović, D., Carpi, R.B.: Evolving genetic algorithms for fault injection attacks. In: 2014 37th International Convention on Information and Communication Technology, Electronics and Microelectronics (MIPRO), pp. 1106–1111. IEEE (2014)
4. Picek, S., Batina, L., Buzing, P., Jakobovic, D.: Fault injection with a new flavor: memetic algorithms make a difference. In: Mangard, S., Poschmann, A.Y. (eds.) COSADE 2014. LNCS, vol. 9064, pp. 159–173. Springer, Cham (2015). https://doi.org/10.1007/978-3-319-21476-4_11
5. Boneh, D., DeMillo, R.A., Lipton, R.J.: On the importance of checking cryptographic protocols for faults. In: Fumy, W. (ed.) EUROCRYPT 1997. LNCS, vol. 1233, pp. 37–51. Springer, Heidelberg (1997). https://doi.org/10.1007/3-540-69053-0_4
6. Kömmerling, O., Kuhn, M.G.: Design principles for tamper-resistant smartcard processors. In: Proceedings of the USENIX Workshop on Smartcard Technology on USENIX Workshop on Smartcard Technology, p. 2. Berkeley, CA, USA, USENIX Association (1999)
7. Skorobogatov, S.: Optical fault masking attacks. In: 2010 Workshop on Fault Diagnosis and Tolerance in Cryptography, pp. 23–29. August 2010
8. van Woudenberg, J.G.J., Witteman, M.F., Menarini, F.: Practical optical fault injection on secure microcontrollers. In: 2011 Workshop on Fault Diagnosis and Tolerance in Cryptography, pp. 91–99. September 2011

9. Leveugle, R., et al.: Laser-induced fault effects in security-dedicated circuits. In: 2014 22nd International Conference on Very Large Scale Integration (VLSI-SoC), pp. 1–6. IEEE (2014)
10. Guillen, O.M., Gruber, M., De Santis, F.: Low-cost setup for localized semi-invasive optical fault injection attacks. In: Guilley, S. (ed.) COSADE 2017. LNCS, vol. 10348, pp. 207–222. Springer, Cham (2017). https://doi.org/10.1007/978-3-319-64647-3_13
11. Cagli, E., Dumas, C., Prouff, E.: Convolutional neural networks with data augmentation against jitter-based countermeasures - profiling attacks without pre-processing. In: Proceedings of International Conference on Cryptographic Hardware and Embedded Systems - CHES 2017–19th, Taipei, Taiwan, 25–28 September 2017, pp. 45–68 (2017)
12. Picek, S., Heuser, A., Jovic, A., Bhasin, S., Regazzoni, F.: The curse of class imbalance and conflicting metrics with machine learning for side-channel evaluations. IACR Trans. Cryptogr. Hardw. Embed. Syst. 2019(1), 209–237 (2019)
13. Kim, J., Picek, S., Heuser, A., Bhasin, S., Hanjalic, A.: Make some noise. unleashing the power of convolutional neural networks for profiled side-channel analysis. IACR Trans. Cryptographic Hardware Embed. Syst. 2019(3), 148–179 (2019)
14. Maldini, A., Samwel, N., Picek, S., Batina, L.: Genetic algorithm-based electromagnetic fault injection. In: 2018 Workshop on Fault Diagnosis and Tolerance in Cryptography (FDTC), pp. 35–42. September 2018
15. Zhou, Y.B., Feng, D.G.: Side-channel attacks: ten years after its publication and the impacts on cryptographic module security testing. IACR Cryptol. ePrint Archive 2005, 388 (2005)
16. Tria, A., Choukri, H.: Invasive attacks. In: van Tilborg, H.C.A., Jajodia, S. (eds.) Encyclopedia of Cryptography and Security, pp. 623–629. Springer, Boston (2011). https://doi.org/10.1007/978-1-4419-5906-5
17. Kumar, R., Jovanovic, P., Polian, I.: Precise fault-injections using voltage and temperature manipulation for differential cryptanalysis. In: 2014 IEEE 20th International On-Line Testing Symposium (IOLTS), pp. 43–48. IEEE (2014)
18. Picek, S., et al.: Side-channel analysis and machine learning: a practical perspective. In: 2017 International Joint Conference on Neural Networks (IJCNN), pp. 4095–4102. IEEE (2017)
19. Skorobogatov, S.P.: Semi-invasive attacks: a new approach to hardware security analysis (2005)
20. Johnston, A.H.: Charge generation and collection in PN junctions excited with pulsed infrared lasers. IEEE Trans. Nuclear Sci. 40(6), 1694–1702 (1993)
21. Merli, D., Schuster, D., Stumpf, F., Sigl, G.: Semi-invasive EM attack on FGPA RO PUFs and countermeasures. In: Proceedings of the Workshop on Embedded Systems Security, WESS 2011, pp. 2:1–2:9, New York, NY, USA, ACM (2011)
22. Beringuier-Boher, N., Lacruche, M., El-Baze, D., Dutertre, J.-M., Rigaud, J.-B., Maurine, P.: Body biasing injection attacks in practice. In: Proceedings of the Third Workshop on Cryptography and Security in Computing Systems, pp. 49–54. ACM (2016)
23. Gurney, K.: An Introduction to Neural Networks. CRC Press, Boca Raton (2014)
24. Collobert, R., Bengio, S.: Links between perceptrons, MLPs and SVMs. In: Proceedings of the Twenty-First International Conference on Machine Learning, ICML 2004, p. 23. New York, NY, USA, ACM (2004)
25. LeNail, A.: NN-SVG: publication-ready neural network architecture schematics. J. Open Source Softw. 4(33), 747 (2019)

26. Biham, E., Shamir, A.: Differential fault analysis of secret key cryptosystems. In: Kaliski, B.S. (ed.) CRYPTO 1997. LNCS, vol. 1294, pp. 513–525. Springer, Heidelberg (1997). https://doi.org/10.1007/BFb0052259
27. Giraud, C.: DFA on AES. In: Dobbertin, H., Rijmen, V., Sowa, A. (eds.) AES 2004. LNCS, vol. 3373, pp. 27–41. Springer, Heidelberg (2005). https://doi.org/10.1007/11506447_4

Tightly Secure Two-Pass Authenticated Key Exchange Protocol in the CK Model

Yuting Xiao[1,2], Rui Zhang[1,2]([✉]), and Hui Ma[1]([✉])

[1] State Key Laboratory of Information Security, Institute of Information Engineering, Chinese Academy of Sciences, Beijing, China
{xiaoyuting,r-zhang,mahui}@iie.ac.cn
[2] School of Cyber Security, University of Chinese Academy of Sciences, Beijing, China

Abstract. Tightly secure authenticated key exchange (AKE), whose security is independent from the number of users and sessions (tight security), has been studied by Bader et al. [TCC 2015] and Gjøsteen-Jager [CRYPTO 2018] in the Bellare-Rogaway (BR) model. However, how to achieve tight security in stronger models (e.g., the Canetti-Krawczyk (CK) model and the extended Canetti-Krawczyk (eCK) model) were still left as an open problem by now.

In this paper, we investigate this problem in the CK model. We start from a generic construction [ACISP 2008] based on key encapsulated mechanisms (KEMs). We analyze the reason why it cannot achieve tight reduction, by merely assuming the underlying KEMs are secure in the *multi-user* and *multi-challenge* setting with *corruption* as Bader et al. [TCC 2015] and Gjøsteen-Jager [CRYPTO 2018] did. Then we put forward a new generic construction to overcome the potential obstacles.

In addition, we introduce a strong type of chosen ciphertext attack in the *multi-user* and *multi-challenge* setting with *corruption* for tag-based key encapsulated mechanism (TB-KEM), where adversaries are not only allowed to adaptively corrupt secret keys of users, generate multi-challenges with different coins, and open some challenges as well. We further prove that the Naor-Yung transform also works in this model, hence our generic construction can be instantiated.

Keywords: Tight security · Authenticated key exchange · The CK model · Multi-user · Multi-challenge · Corruption

1 Introduction

Authenticated Key exchange (AKE) is a fundamental cryptographic primitive, which enables each party to verify the identity of the other party with the help of some pre-shared information, such that only the honest players can obtain the final session keys after executions. Nowadays, AKE is widely and frequently used to achieve secure communications over public channels in daily life, e.g., TLS handshake protocol.

© Springer Nature Switzerland AG 2020
S. Jarecki (Ed.): CT-RSA 2020, LNCS 12006, pp. 171–198, 2020.
https://doi.org/10.1007/978-3-030-40186-3_9

As AKE protocols are executed over an open network and vulnerable to complicated cyber-attacks, provable security is an important design goal. Along with the development of modern cryptography, the provable security paradigm has become widely-accepted to analyze cryptographic schemes. The first formal security model (i.e., the BR model) for AKE was introduced by Bellare and Rogaway [7], which allows attackers to fully control the communication channel, corrupt the long-term secret keys of communicating parties and reveal session keys. After that, for capturing more practical attacks or providing more security guarantees, several strong security models were developed, e.g., the CK [11], eCK [23], CK+ [22] and eCK-PFS [15] models. Commonly, in a reduction, it is necessary to prove that if there exists an attacker $\mathcal{A}$ who is able to break the CK/eCK/CK+/eCK-PFS-security, there exists an another attacker $\mathcal{B}$ who is able to solve a hard problem. Denotes $\epsilon_{\mathcal{A}}$ and $\epsilon_{\mathcal{B}}$ as the success probabilities of the attacker $\mathcal{A}$ breaking the security experiment and the attacker $\mathcal{B}$ solving the underlying hard problem, respectively. A successful reduction ends up with an inequality like $\epsilon_{\mathcal{A}} \leq L \cdot \epsilon_{\mathcal{B}}$, where L is known as the reduction loss. In particular, the reduction is called *tight* when L is a small constant, which means $\epsilon_{\mathcal{A}} \approx \epsilon_{\mathcal{B}}$ and the difficulty for any attacker of breaking the protocol is almost equal to solve the underlying hard problem.

In the literature, a number of protocols [9,11,15,16,23,30] were proved in the CK, eCK, CK+ and eCK-PFS models, but almost all of them came with a loose reduction that depends on the number of users μ and sessions ℓ per user, e.g., $L = 1/(\mu \cdot \ell)$ or $L = 1/(\mu \cdot \ell)^2$. If the selected security parameters are kept unchanged, the concrete security of these protocols will degrade in their application scales, hence larger parameters should be selected to compensate their concrete security loss. Therefore, these protocols might not be suitable for applications in a large-scale setting, e.g., a web search engine with billions of HTTPs connections per day. *Protocols with tight security that does not degrade with the number of users or sessions, are more preferable.* The reason is that to embed its problem instance, in the beginning of the experiment the simulator has to guess the target of the attacker among all users and all the sessions.

The first construction with tight reduction was proposed by Bader et al. [5], in an enhanced version of the BR model. In a high-level view, their protocol follows a well-known paradigm: a key encapsulated mechanism (KEM) is used to transport shared keys, and a signature (SIG) scheme is used to authenticate exchanged messages, where the SIG scheme is existentially unforgeable in the *multi-user* setting with *corruption* (abbreviated as *mu-corr* setting) with tight security reduction, where adversaries are allowed to adaptively corrupt the secret keys of multi-users; the KEM scheme is tightly secure against chosen plaintext attack (CPA) in the *multi-user* and *multi-challenge* setting with *corruption*, where adversaries are allowed to adaptively corrupt the secret keys of multi-users and request multi-challenge using different coins. The simulator first carefully embeds KEM challenges into simulated sessions, then answers corruption queries of long-term secret keys (i.e., singing secret keys) and reveal queries of session keys (derived from encapsulated keys) using corresponding corruption oracles provided in the SIG and KEM security experiments, respectively. By doing so, it is no longer necessary to guess the target user session at the beginning of the experiment and a tight reduction is achieved. Later, Gjøsteen and Jager [19] proposed a more efficient protocol, but still merely proved secure in the BR model. Up to now, *how to achieve tight security in other stronger models is still left as an interesting open problem.*

As pointed out by Cremers [14], the existing strong security models (in particular, the CK, CK+ and eCK models) are incomparable, thus hard to choose. In a cloud or desktop environment, developers usually care less about the memory, and never erase memory after usage. Since the CK model captures such session state leakage, in this paper, we focus on tight reduction in the CK model.

1.1 Our Contributions

We give the first tightly secure generic construction of AKEs in the CK model, in addition, we take into account key-compromise impersonation (KCI) resistance [28] and weak perfect forward secrecy (wPFS) [22]. The construction follows the "$2\times$SIG$+2\times$TB-KEM $+2\times$OTS$+$wKEM" paradigm, where SIG is a deterministic signature that is existentially unforgeable in the *multi-user* setting with *corruption*, OTS is an one-time signature that is strongly existential unforgeable in the *multi-user* setting, TB-KEM is a tag-based key encapsulated mechanism that is secure against chosen ciphertext attack (CCA) in the *multi-user* and *multi-challenge* setting with *corruption*, and wKEM is a KEM that is CPA secure in the *multi-user* and *multi-challenge* setting with *corruption*, respectively.

We note that it is the first time that CCA security in the *multi-user* and *mu-mc-corr* setting for TB-KEM is considered. Different from [1,21], in our definition, adversaries are allowed to adaptively corrupt secret keys of multi-users, generate multi-challenge with different coins, and even open some challenges as long as the final target has not been opened and its corresponding secret key has not been corrupted. We prove that the classic Naor-Yung transform [26] is valid in this scenario.

Finally, we present a concrete instantiation based on the known modules. Compared with the existing tightly secure AKE constructions, our construction is proved secure in a stronger model, and achieves lower round complexity but higher communication and computation complexity.

1.2 Related Work

Tight security in the *multi-user* and *multi-challenge* setting for public key encryption (PKE) has been studied for a long time. Bellare, Boldyreva and Micali [6] first proved the ELGamal encryption meets tight CPA security in such setting. After that, the tight CCA security was kept as an open problem for decade, until Hofheinz and Jager [21] proposed the first tightly CCA secure scheme by applying the typical Naor-Young transform [26], where each ciphertext consists of two CPA secure PKE ciphertexts and one simulation-sound non-interactive zero-knowledge (NIZK) proof. Then Blazy et al. [8] presented an improved scheme for it with more compact ciphertext size. In another line, Abe et al. [1] and Wei et al. [29] proposed tightly CCA secure schemes based on simulation-extractable NIZK proof systems, where each ciphertext merely consists of one CPA secure PKE ciphertext and one proof.

Along the development of tight security, almost tight security was also studied, which allows reduction loss be dependent on the security parameter. For examples, Libert et al. [24,25], Hofheinz [20] and Gay et al. [17] proposed several almost tightly CCA secure schemes, and all these schemes have compact ciphertext sizes. In particular, each ciphertext of Gay et al. [17] only consists of 3 group elements, but which still suffers big public key. The work by Gay, Hofheinz and Kohl [18] further reduced the public key size to 6 group elements. As well known, identity based encryption (IBE) can be converted to CCA secure PKE by applying the CHK transform [10], thus the existing almost tightly secure IBE schemes [4,12,13] in the *multi-user* and *multi-challenge* setting also yields almost tightly CCA secure PKE schemes in the same setting.

2 Preliminaries

Notations. Let $-$ denote an empty string, while $*$ denotes an arbitrary but nonempty string. The operator $\oplus$ denotes bit-wise "XOR", and $\|$ denotes string concatenation. For $k \in \mathbb{N}$, 1^k denotes the string of k ones. For an integer m, $[m] = \{1, 2, \ldots, m\}$. For a distribution S, $x \leftarrow_{\$} S$ means randomly choosing an element according to the distribution S. For an arbitrary bit string s, $|s|$ denotes its bit-length. For an algorithm A, $y \leftarrow A(x) \ /y = A(x)$ means running the randomized/deterministic algorithm A with x as input gets the output y. A function $\mu(\cdot)$ is called negligible, if for every polynomial $p(\cdot)$, there exists some λ_0 such that $\mu(\lambda) \leq 1/p(\lambda)$, for every $\lambda > \lambda_0$.

Tag-Based Key Encapsulation Mechanism in the Multi-User Setting consists of four algorithms: $\mathsf{Setup}(1^\lambda) \to \Pi$, on input a security parameter 1^λ, outputs a public parameter Π; $\mathsf{Gen}(\Pi) \to (ek, dk)$, on input a public parameter Π, outputs an encryption key ek and a decryption key dk; $\mathsf{Enc}(ek, \tau) \to (c, k)$, on input an encryption key ek and a tag τ, outputs a ciphertext c and an encapsulated key $k \in \mathcal{K}$ (the key space); $\mathsf{Dec}(dk, c, \tau) = k/\bot$, on input a decryption key dk, a ciphertext c and a tag τ, outputs a key k or a special symbol $\bot$ indicating c is invalid. We require usual correctness properties. We will define a new type of CCA security in the *multi-user* and *multi-challenge* setting with *corruption*, which is called MU-IND-CCA^{Corr} security.

Definition 1 (MU-IND-CCA^{Corr}). *A tag-based key encapsulated mechanism* TB-KEM $=$ (Setup, Gen, Enc, Dec) *is called MU-IND-CCA^{Corr} secure, If for any PPT adversary $\mathcal{A}$,*

$$\mathsf{Adv}_{\mathsf{TB\text{-}KEM},\mathcal{A}}^{\mathsf{MU\text{-}IND\text{-}CCA}^{\mathrm{Corr}}}(\lambda) = |\Pr[\mathsf{Exp}_{\mathsf{TB\text{-}KEM},\mathcal{A}}^{\mathsf{MU\text{-}IND\text{-}CCA}^{\mathrm{Corr}}}(\lambda) = 1] - \frac{1}{2}|$$

is negligible in λ, where the experiment is defined as follows:

$\mathsf{Exp}_{\mathsf{TB\text{-}KEM},\mathcal{A}}^{\mathsf{MU\text{-}IND\text{-}CCA}^{\mathsf{Corr}}}(\lambda):$	$\mathcal{O}_E(i, \tau_{i,j})$: //the j-th query on ek_i
$\Pi \leftarrow \mathsf{Setup}(1^\lambda)$	$(c_{i,j}, k_{i,j,0}) \leftarrow \mathsf{Enc}(ek_i, \tau_{i,j}),\ k_{i,j,1} \leftarrow_{\$} \mathcal{K}$
$(ek_i, dk_i)_i \leftarrow \mathsf{Gen}(\Pi),\ \mathcal{Q} := \emptyset$	$b_{i,j} \leftarrow_{\$} \{0,1\},\ \mathcal{Q} = \mathcal{Q} \cup \{(i,j,b_{i,j})\}$
$(i^*, j^*, b') \leftarrow \mathcal{A}^{\mathcal{O}_E, \mathcal{O}_D, \mathcal{O}_C}(\Pi, (ek_i)_i)$	$return\ (c_{i,j}, k_{i,j,b_{i,j}})$
$return\ \mathsf{win}(i^*, j^*, b')$	$\mathcal{O}_D(i, c, \tau)$:
$\mathcal{O}_C(i)$:	$return\ k = \mathsf{Dec}(dk_i, c, \tau)$
$return\ dk_i$	

where $\mathsf{win}(\cdot, \cdot, \cdot)$ denotes a predicate function, for any input (i, j, b), which outputs 1 only when $(i, j, b) \in \mathcal{Q}$, and $\mathcal{A}$ has never performed $\mathcal{O}_D(i, c_{i,j}, \tau_{i,j})$ and $\mathcal{O}_C(i)$ queries.

Key Encapsulated Mechanism in the Multi-User Setting consists of four algorithms: $\mathsf{Setup}(1^\lambda) \to \Pi$, on input a security parameter 1^λ, outputs a public parameter Π; $\mathsf{Gen}(\Pi) \to (ek, dk)$, on input a public parameter Π, outputs an encryption key ek and a decryption key dk; $\mathsf{Enc}(ek) \to (c, k)$, on input an encryption key ek, outputs a ciphertext c and an encapsulated key $k \in \mathcal{K}$ (the key space); $\mathsf{Dec}(dk, c) = k/\bot$, on input a decryption key dk and a ciphertext c, outputs a key k or a special symbol $\bot$ indicating that c is invalid. We require usual correctness properties. We consider the CPA security notion in the *multi-user* and *multi-challenge* setting with *corruption* (called MU-IND-CPA^{Corr} security) in [5].

Definition 2 (MU-IND-CPA^{Corr}). *A key encapsulated mechanism* KEM $=$ (Setup, Gen, Enc, Dec) *is called MU-IND-CPA^{Corr} secure, if for any PPT adversary $\mathcal{A}$,*

$$\mathsf{Adv}_{\mathsf{KEM},\mathcal{A}}^{\mathsf{MU\text{-}IND\text{-}CPA}^{\mathsf{Corr}}}(\lambda) = |\Pr[\mathsf{Exp}_{\mathsf{KEM},\mathcal{A}}^{\mathsf{MU\text{-}IND\text{-}CPA}^{\mathsf{Corr}}}(\lambda) = 1] - \frac{1}{2}|$$

is negligible in λ, where the experiment is defined as follows:

$\mathsf{Exp}_{\mathsf{KEM},\mathcal{A}}^{\mathsf{MU\text{-}IND\text{-}CPA}^{\mathsf{Corr}}}(\lambda):$	$\mathcal{O}_E(i)$: //the j-th query on ek_i
$\Pi \leftarrow \mathsf{Setup}(1^\lambda)$	$(c_{i,j}, k_{i,j,0}) \leftarrow \mathsf{Enc}(ek_i),\ k_{i,j,1} \leftarrow_{\$} \mathcal{K}$
$(ek_i, dk_i)_i \leftarrow \mathsf{Gen}(\Pi),\ \mathcal{Q} := \emptyset$	$b_{i,j} \leftarrow_{\$} \{0,1\},\ \mathcal{Q} = \mathcal{Q} \cup \{(i,j,b_{i,j})\}$
$(i^*, j^*, b') \leftarrow \mathcal{A}^{\mathcal{O}_E, \mathcal{O}_C}(\Pi, (ek_i)_i)$	$return\ (c_{i,j}, k_{i,j,b_{i,j}})$
$return\ \mathsf{win}(i^*, j^*, b')$	$\mathcal{O}_C(i)$:
	$return\ dk_i$

where $\mathsf{win}(\cdot, \cdot, \cdot)$ denotes a predicate function, for any input (i, j, b), which outputs 1 only when $(i, j, b) \in \mathcal{Q}$, and $\mathcal{A}$ has never performed $\mathcal{O}_C(i)$ queries.

Public Key Encryption in the Multi-User Setting consists of four algorithms: $\mathsf{Setup}(1^\lambda) \to \Pi$, on input a security parameter 1^λ, outputs a public parameter Π; $\mathsf{Gen}(\Pi) \to (pk, sk)$, on input a public parameter Π, outputs a public key pk and a secret key sk; $\mathsf{Enc}(pk, m) \to c$, on input a public key pk and a message m, outputs a ciphertext c; $\mathsf{Dec}(sk, c) = m/\bot$, on input a secret key

sk and a ciphertext c, outputs a message m or a special symbol $\perp$ indicating c is invalid. We require usual correctness properties. Recall the CPA security definition in the *multi-user* setting and *multi-challenge* setting under single challenge bit in [21], which is called S-MU-IND-CPA security in this paper.

Definition 3 (S-MU-IND-CPA). *A public key encryption* PKE = (Setup, Gen, Enc, Dec) *is called S-MU-IND-CPA secure, if for any PPT adversary* $\mathcal{A}$,

$$\mathsf{Adv}_{\mathsf{PKE},\mathcal{A}}^{\mathsf{sMU\text{-}IND\text{-}CPA}}(\lambda) = |\Pr[\mathsf{Exp}_{\mathsf{PKE},\mathcal{A}}^{\mathsf{sMU\text{-}IND\text{-}CPA}}(\lambda) = 1] - \frac{1}{2}|$$

is negligible in λ, *where the experiment is defined as follows:*

$\mathsf{Exp}_{\mathsf{PKE},\mathcal{A}}^{\mathsf{sMU\text{-}IND\text{-}CPA}}(\lambda)$:	$\mathcal{O}_E(i, m_0, m_1)$:
$\Pi \leftarrow \mathsf{Setup}(1^\lambda), (pk_i, sk_i)_i \leftarrow \mathsf{Gen}(\Pi)$	$c_{i,0} \leftarrow \mathsf{Enc}(pk_i, m_0)$
$b \leftarrow_\$ \{0,1\}, b' \leftarrow \mathcal{A}^{\mathcal{O}_E}(\Pi, (pk_i)_i)$	$c_{i,1} \leftarrow \mathsf{Enc}(pk_i, m_1)$
return 1 if $b' = b$	*return* $c_{i,b}$

Signature in the Multi-User Setting consists of four algorithms: $\mathsf{Setup}(1^\lambda) \rightarrow \Pi$, on input a security parameter 1^λ, outputs a public parameter Π; $\mathsf{Gen}(\Pi) \rightarrow (vk, sk)$, on input a public parameter Π, outputs a verification key vk and a signing key sk; $\mathsf{Sig}(sk, m) \rightarrow \sigma$, on input a signing key sk and a message m, outputs a signature σ; $\mathsf{Vrfy}(vk, m, \sigma) = 0/1$, on input a verification key vk, a message m and a signature σ, outputs a bit 0 or 1 that indicating σ is valid or invalid. We require usual correctness properties. We consider the multi-user existential unforgeability under adaptive chosen-message attacks with adaptive corruptions (called MU-EUF-CMA^{Corr} security) and the multi-user strongly one-time existential unforgeability under adaptive chosen-message attacks (called MU-1-sEUF-CMA security) in [5].

Definition 4 (MU-EUF-CMA^{Corr}). *A signature* SIG = (Setup, Gen, Sig, Vrfy) *is called MU-EUF-CMA^{Corr} secure, if for any PPT forger* $\mathcal{F}$,

$$\mathsf{Adv}_{\mathsf{SIG},\mathcal{F}}^{\mathsf{MU\text{-}EUF\text{-}CMA}^{\mathsf{Corr}}}(\lambda) = |\Pr[\mathsf{Exp}_{\mathsf{SIG},\mathcal{F}}^{\mathsf{MU\text{-}EUF\text{-}CMA}^{\mathsf{Corr}}}(\lambda) = 1]|$$

is negligible in λ, *where the experiment is defined as follows:*

$\mathsf{Exp}_{\mathsf{SIG},\mathcal{F}}^{\mathsf{MU\text{-}EUF\text{-}CMA}^{\mathsf{Corr}}}(\lambda)$:	$\mathcal{O}_S(i, m)$:
$\Pi \leftarrow \mathsf{Setup}(1^\lambda)$	$\sigma \leftarrow \mathsf{Sig}(sk_i, m)$
$(vk_i, sk_i)_i \leftarrow \mathsf{Gen}(\Pi), \mathcal{Q} := \emptyset$	$\mathcal{Q} = \mathcal{Q} \cup \{(i, m)\}$
$(i^*, m^*, \sigma^*) \leftarrow \mathcal{A}^{\mathcal{O}_S, \mathcal{O}_C}(\Pi, (vk_i)_i)$	*return* σ
return $\mathsf{win}(i^*, m^*, \sigma^*)$	$\mathcal{O}_C(i)$:
	return sk_i

where $\mathsf{win}(\cdot, \cdot, \cdot)$ denotes a predicate function, for any input (i, m, σ), which outputs 1 only when $(i, m) \notin \mathcal{Q} \wedge \mathsf{Vrfy}(vk_i, m, \sigma) = 1$, and $\mathcal{A}$ has never performed $\mathcal{O}_C(i)$ queries.

Definition 5 (MU-1-sEUF-CMA). *A signature* $\mathsf{SIG} = (\mathsf{Setup}, \mathsf{Gen}, \mathsf{Sig}, \mathsf{Vrfy})$ *is called MU-1-sEUF-CMA secure, if for any PPT forger* $\mathcal{F}$,

$$\mathsf{Adv}_{\mathsf{SIG},\mathcal{F}}^{\mathsf{MU\text{-}1\text{-}EUF\text{-}CMA}}(\lambda) = |\Pr[\mathsf{Exp}_{\mathsf{SIG},\mathcal{F}}^{\mathsf{MU\text{-}1\text{-}EUF\text{-}CMA}}(\lambda) = 1]|$$

is negligible in λ, *where the experiment is defined similarly to* $\mathsf{Exp}_{\mathsf{SIG},\mathcal{F}}^{\mathsf{MU\text{-}EUF\text{-}CMA}^{\mathsf{Corr}}}(\lambda)$, *but where* $\mathcal{O}_C$ *queries are not allowed and* $\mathcal{O}_S$ *queries on each* i *can be asked once at most. Besides,* $\{(i, m, \sigma)\}$ *instead of* $\{(i, m)\}$ *is inserted into* $\mathcal{Q}$ *when answering each* $\mathcal{O}_S$ *query, and the predicate function* $\mathsf{win}(i, m, \sigma)$ *checks whether* $\{(i, m, \sigma)\} \in \mathcal{Q}$.

Quasi-Adaptive NIZK Proof is NIZK proof where the common reference string (crs) is allowed to depend on the specific language for which proofs have to be generated. It consists of four algorithms: $\mathsf{K}_0(1^\lambda) \rightarrow \Gamma$, on input a security parameter 1^λ, outputs a public parameter Γ; $\mathsf{K}_1(\Gamma, \rho) \rightarrow \psi$, on input a public parameter Γ and a language-specific parameter ρ, outputs a crs ψ; $\mathsf{P}(\psi, x, w, \mathsf{lbl}) \rightarrow \pi$, on input a crs ψ, a statement x, a witness w and a label lbl, outputs a proof π; $\mathsf{V}(\psi, x, \pi, \mathsf{lbl}) \rightarrow 0/1$, on input a crs ψ, a statement x, a proof π and a label lbl as input, outputs 1 indicating π is valid or 0 indicating invalid. For public parameters $\Gamma \leftarrow \mathsf{K}_0(1^\lambda)$, let $\mathcal{D}_\Gamma$ be a probability distribution over a collection of relations $\mathcal{R} = \{R_\rho\}$ parameterized by ρ with an associated language $\mathcal{L}_\rho = \{x | \exists w : R_\rho(x; w) = 1\}$. Here we recall the definition of unbounded simulation-sound QA-NIZK proof in the multi-crs setting in [25], which is called M-USS-QA-NIZK in this paper. A some difference is that we do not require the same enhanced version for unbounded simulation-soundness where $\mathcal{A}_4$ is also given trapdoors that allow deciding membership in the language $\mathcal{L}_\rho$.

Definition 6 (M-USS-QA-NIZK). *For* $\mathcal{R}$, *we say a tuple of efficient algorithms* $(\mathsf{K}_0, \mathsf{K}_1, \mathsf{P}, \mathsf{V})$ *is an M-USS-QA-NIZK proof, if there exists a PPT simulator* $\mathcal{S} = (\mathcal{S}_1, \mathcal{S}_2)$ *such that for any PPT adversaries* $\mathcal{A}_1, \mathcal{A}_2, \mathcal{A}_3, \mathcal{A}_4$, *we have:*

Quasi-Adaptive Completeness

$$\Pr[\Gamma \leftarrow \mathsf{K}_0(1^\lambda); \rho \leftarrow_\$ \mathcal{D}_\Gamma; \psi \leftarrow \mathsf{K}_1(\Gamma, \rho), (x, w, \mathsf{lbl}) \leftarrow \mathcal{A}_1(\Gamma, \psi, \rho); \pi \leftarrow \mathsf{P}(\psi, x, w, \mathsf{lbl}) :$$
$$\mathsf{V}(\psi, x, \pi, \mathsf{lbl}) = 1 \text{ if } R_\rho(x, w) = 1] = 1.$$

Quasi-Adptive Soundness

$$\Pr[\Gamma \leftarrow \mathsf{K}_0(1^\lambda); \rho \leftarrow_\$ \mathcal{D}_\Gamma; \psi \leftarrow \mathsf{K}_1(\Gamma, \rho); (x, w, \mathsf{lbl}) \leftarrow \mathcal{A}_2(\Gamma, \psi, \rho) :$$
$$\mathsf{V}(\psi, x, \pi, \mathsf{lbl}) = 1 \wedge \neg(\exists w : R_\rho(x, w) = 1] \leq \epsilon_\mathsf{S},$$

where ϵ_S *is negligible in* λ.

Quasi-Adptive Zero-Knowledge

$$|\Pr[\Gamma \leftarrow \mathsf{K}_0(1^\lambda); \rho \leftarrow_\$ \mathcal{D}_\Gamma; \psi \leftarrow \mathsf{K}_1(\Gamma, \rho) : \mathcal{A}_3^{\mathsf{P}(\psi,\cdot,\cdot,\cdot)}(\Gamma, \psi, \rho) = 1] - \Pr[\Gamma \leftarrow \mathsf{K}_0(1^\lambda);$$

$$\rho \leftarrow_\$ \mathcal{D}_\Gamma; (\psi, \tau_{sim}) \leftarrow \mathsf{S}_1(\Gamma, \rho) : \mathcal{A}_3^{\mathsf{S}_2(\psi,\tau_{sim},\cdot,\cdot,\cdot)}(\Gamma, \psi, \rho) = 1]| \leq \epsilon_{\mathsf{QA\text{-}ZK}},$$

where ϵ_S is negligible in λ and $\mathcal{A}_3$ is given two different oracles:

1. $\mathsf{P}(\psi, \cdot, \cdot, \cdot)$: on input $(x, w) \in R_\rho$ and a label lbl, outputs a proof generated by $\mathsf{P}(\psi, x, w, \mathsf{lbl})$. Otherwise, outputs $\perp$.
2. $\mathsf{S}(\psi, \tau_{sim}, \cdot, \cdot, \cdot)$: on input $(x, w) \in R_\rho$ and a label lbl, outputs a simulated proof generated by $\mathsf{S}_2(\psi, x, w, \mathsf{lbl})$. Otherwise, outputs $\perp$.

Unbounded Simulation-Soundness in the multi-crs setting

$$\Pr[\Gamma \leftarrow \mathsf{K}_0(1^\lambda); \{\rho_i\}_i \leftarrow_\$ \mathcal{D}_\Gamma; \{(\psi_i, \tau_{sim,i})\}_i \leftarrow \mathsf{S}_1(\Gamma, \{\rho_i\});$$

$$(i^*, x, \pi, \mathsf{lbl}) \leftarrow \mathcal{A}_4^{\hat{\mathsf{S}}_2(\psi_i, \tau_{sim,i}, \cdot, \cdot, \cdot)}(\Gamma, \{\psi_i, \rho_i\}_i):$$

$$\mathsf{V}(\psi_{i^*}, x, \pi, \mathsf{lbl}) = 1 \wedge \neg(\exists w : R_{\rho_{i^*}}(x, w) = 1) \wedge (i^*, x, \pi, \mathsf{lbl}) \notin \mathcal{Q}] \leq \epsilon_{\mathsf{USS}}.$$

where ϵ_USS is negligible in λ. $\mathcal{A}_4$ is given unbounded access to the oracle $\hat{\mathsf{S}}_2(\{\psi_i\}_i, \{\tau_{sim,i}\}_i, \cdot, \cdot, \cdot)$: on input (j, x, lbl) (where x may be outside $\mathcal{L}_{\rho_j}$, outputs a simulated proof generated by $\mathsf{S}_2(\psi_j, x, w, \mathsf{lbl})$ and updates $\mathcal{Q} = \mathcal{Q} \cup \{(j, x, \pi, \mathsf{lbl})\}$.

Definition 7 (Pseudo-Random Function). Let $\mathsf{PRF} : \{\mathsf{PRF}_\lambda : \mathcal{S}_\lambda \times Dom_\lambda \rightarrow Rng_\lambda\}_{\lambda \in \mathbb{N}}$ define a function family with families of key spaces $\{\mathcal{S}_\lambda\}_{\lambda \in \mathbb{N}}$, domains $\{Dom_\lambda\}_{\lambda \in \mathbb{N}}$ and ranges $\{Rng_\lambda\}_{\lambda \in \mathbb{N}}$, where λ denotes a security parameter. We say PRF is a secure PRF family if for any PPT adversary $\mathcal{A}$, $| \Pr[1 \leftarrow \mathcal{A}^{\mathsf{PRF}_\lambda(\cdot)}] - \Pr[1 \leftarrow A^{\mathsf{RF}_\lambda(\cdot)}] | \leq \epsilon_{\mathsf{PRF}}$ is negligible in λ, where $\mathsf{RF}_\lambda(\cdot) : Dom_\lambda \rightarrow Rng_\lambda$ is a truly random function.

3   Tightly Secure AKE Protocol in the CK Model

In this section, we first review the CK model [11] and slightly change its original definition to additionally provide KCI resistance and wPFS. We then present a new construction and prove its security in such model with a tight reduction.

3.1   The CK Model

A protocol $\mathcal{P}$ is modeled as a collection of m interactive PPT machine running at different parties, $P_1, \cdots, P_m$. Each invocation of $\mathcal{P}$ within a party is defined to be a session, and each party may have multiple sessions running concurrently. The i-th session on party P_j is denoted as a tuple $(P_j, i) \in \{P_1, \cdots, P_m\} \times \mathbb{N}$. For each session $s \in \{P_1, \cdots, P_m\} \times \mathbb{N}$, a quintuple of variables is set. E.g., a session owned by a party (P_i) is denoted as $s = (s_{actor}, s_{peer}, s_{role}, s_{sent}, s_{recv})$, where s_{actor} $(=P_i)$ denotes the owner of the session, s_{peer} the intended partner (of P_i), $s_{role} \in \{\mathcal{I}, \mathcal{R}\}$ (where $\mathcal{I}/\mathcal{R}$ denotes initiator/responder), and s_{sent}/s_{recv} denotes the message sent/received by the session owner (P_i). Two sessions $s = (s_{actor}, s_{peer}, s_{role}, s_{sent}, s_{recv})$ and $s' = (s'_{actor}, s'_{peer}, s'_{role}, s'_{sent}, s'_{recv})$ are called CK-matching session if $s_{actor} = s'_{peer}$, $s_{peer} = s'_{actor}$, $s_{role} \neq s'_{role}$, $s_{sent} = s'_{recv}$ and $s_{recv} = s'_{sent}$. Any PPT adversary is allowed to perform following queries:

- *active* session s, which consists of two forms:
  - *establish-session* (P_i, P_j). This query is answered by starting a new session s on P_i and a matching session of s on P_j, and the transcript is output. In particular, P_i is assumed be the initiator.
  - *incoming-message* (s, P_i, m). This query denotes a type of interaction that the adversary sends a message m to the session s in the name of P_i, and it is answered by strictly following the protocol description.

  Upon activation, the corresponding variables of each session are initialized, and each session may either be *uncompleted* or *completed*. If a session is completed, the party will erase all the intermediate states except for the session key k.

- *corrupt* (P_i). This query reveals the long term secret of party P_i.
- *session-key reveal* (s). This query reveals the session key of arbitrary completed session s.
- *session-state reveal* (s). This query reveals all the state information of the session s before it is completed. In particular, randomness and intermediate values that should be stored for moments (e.g., dk, k, k_i, k_j) to waiting for the computation of the final session key are included in the session-state.
- *session-expiration* (s). This query can only be queried for completed sessions. It will erase the session key k of this session from memory.
- *test-session* (s). A random bit b_s is selected, if $b_s = 0$ then the real session key is output; otherwise, a random key from the key space is output. This query is only allowed to completed, unexpired and unexposed sessions. In particular, this query is allowed to be asked for multiple times, but the answers for matched sessions s and s' should be kept consistent in case of trivially broken.

The security of a protocol $\mathcal{P}$ is defined based on an experiment played between a challenger and an adversary $\mathcal{A}$:

1. the challenger generates the system parameters and all long-term keys, and sends all public information to $\mathcal{A}$;
2. $\mathcal{A}$ adaptively performs *establish-session*$(\cdot)$, *incoming-message*$(\cdot)$, *corrupt*$(\cdot)$, *session-key reveal*$(\cdot)$, *session-state reveal*$(\cdot)$, *session-expiration*$(\cdot)$ and *test-session*$(\cdot)$ queries;
3. at the end, $\mathcal{A}$ outputs its guess (s^*, b') on whether the returned value of the *test-session*(s^*) was the real session key or a random value.

$\mathcal{A}$ wins the experiment if $b_{s^*} = b'$. Throughout the experiment, $\mathcal{A}$ is not allowed to expose s^*. In particular, a session s is said to be *exposed* if $\mathcal{A}$ has performed one of the following queries:

  ○ a *session-state reveal*$(\cdot)$ query on s or its matching session s' (if exists);
  ○ a *session-key reveal*$(\cdot)$ query on s or its matching session s' (if exists);
  ○ (the matching session s' does not exist) a *corrupt*$(\cdot)$ query on the claimed owner of the session s.

Remark 1. There are two special cases that do not lead to a session s *exposed*: (1) if its matching session s' exists, $\mathcal{A}$ performed *corrupt·* queries on both of the claimed owners of s and s'; (2) if its matching session s' does not exist, $\mathcal{A}$ performed *corrupt*($\cdot$) query on the claimed owner of s but not s'. The first case illustrates why our CK model provides wPFS, and the second corresponds to KCI resistance in the implicit authentication case (that inherently refers to the key indistinguishability under compromise of the partner's long-term secret key).

Remark 2. Our definition follows the original definition [5] for AKE in the *multi-challenge* case where each *test-session*($\cdot$) query has an independent challenge bit. There also exists a variant for it, where all *test-session*($\cdot$) queries have the same global challenge bit. As many other primitives in the *multi-challenge* case are defined in such single-bit challenge definition, single-bit challenge CK-security is useful when one want to actually use key exchange protocols as sub-protocols in other protocols, e.g., when one want to do a single game hop where the actually session key is replaced by a random key independent of the key exchange.

Definition 8. *A protocol* $\mathcal{P}$ *is said to be secure in the CK model, if and only if for any PPT adversary* $\mathcal{A}$ *as defined above, the following properties hold,*

1. *when two uncorrupted parties complete CK-matching sessions, they output the same key,*
2. *the advantage* $\mathsf{Adv}^{\mathsf{CK}}_{\mathcal{P},\mathcal{A}}(\lambda) = |\Pr[b' = b] - 1/2|$ *that* $\mathcal{A}$ *correctly guess the bit* b *of the test-session is negligible in the security parameter.*

3.2 Our Construction

In this section, we introduce our technique and construction.

Our Start Point. Review the "2×KEM+Diffie-Hellman" construction [9] with wPFS and KCI resistance in the CK model (Fig. 1). Without loss of generality, we substitute the "Diffie-Hellman" module by an equivalent "wKEM" module.

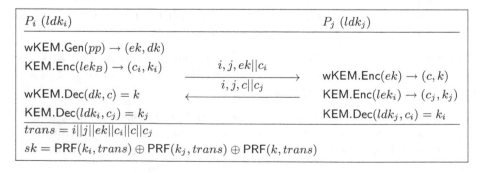

Fig. 1. The "2×KEM+wKEM" construction

Similar to Bader et al. [5], we use the underlying KEM/wKEM be CCA/CPA secure in the *multi-user* and *multi-challenge* setting with corruption. In a reduction, a simulator can embed different challenges into different sessions, and when *corruption* and *session-state/session-key reveal* queries arrive, the simulator just relays these queries to the underlying KEM and wKEM oracles. But the simulator may fail due to the following attack.

An adversary may impersonate P_i and send a message $ek^*||c_i^*$ to activate a session s^* on P_j who sends $c^*||c_j^*$ as reply, which will be finally selected as its target session. In this case, the matching session of the target session does not exist and the adversary should never corrupt P_i. Hence, only c_j^* is left for embedding the challenge. But before the adversary claiming its final target: it can interpose another session s' executed between P_i and P_j, where the reply message sent by P_j is replaced by $c'||c_j^*$; then perform a *session-state reveal* query on s'. This attack will cause the simulation to fail since no limitation is posed on *session-state reveal* query if a session is not the target session or its matching sessions. Thus, a simulator must answer real session-states for all *session-state reveal* queries before knowing the final target of the adversary, i.e., before the adversary performing the *test* query, the adversary may have corrupted the decapsulated key of c_j^*, such that he can compute the real session key of the target session by itself.

A Failed Attempt. One may try to limit an adversary by appending a signature SIG to "2×KEM+wKEM" as in Fig. 2. Though an adversary cannot pretend to be a specific party to send arbitrary messages without knowing the signing key, but replaying messages generated by a party is still possible.

$P_i\ (ldk_i, lsk_i)$		$P_j\ (ldk_j, lsk_j)$
wKEM.Gen$(pp) \rightarrow (ek, dk)$		
KEM.Enc$(lek_B) \rightarrow (c_i, k_i)$		
SIG.Sig$(lsk_i, i||j||ek||c_i) \rightarrow \sigma_i$	$\xrightarrow{\ i,j, ek||c_i||\sigma_i\ }$	
		SIG.Vrfy$(lvk_i, i||j||ek||c_i, \sigma_i) = b$
		if $b \neq 1$, reject it and output $\bot$
		else wKEM.Enc$(ek) \rightarrow (c, k)$
		KEM.Enc$(lek_i) \rightarrow (c_j, k_j)$
	$\xleftarrow{\ i,j, c||c_j||\sigma_j\ }$	SIG.Sig$(lsk_j, i||j||ek||c_i||c||c_j) \rightarrow \sigma_j$
SIG.Vrfy$(lvk_j, i||j||ek||c_i||c||c_j, \sigma_j) = b'$		
if $b' \neq 1$, reject it and output $\bot$		
else wKEM.Dec$(dk, c) = k$		
KEM.Dec$(ldk_i, c_j) = k_j$		KEM.Dec$(ldk_j, c_i) = k_i$
$trans = i||j||ek||c_i||\sigma_i||c||c_j||\sigma_j$		
$sk = \mathsf{PRF}(k_i, trans) \oplus \mathsf{PRF}(k_j, trans) \oplus \mathsf{PRF}(k, trans)$		

Fig. 2. Generic "2×SIG+2×KEM+wKEM" construction

If we further bundle each reply message to its initiation message, so that the adversary is limited to merely replay the initiation messages generated in other sessions. But again, the adversary $\mathcal{A}$ may manipulate multiple different execution instances between P_i and P_j according to the following strategies:

In the first instance, $\mathcal{A}$ passively observes the execution between P_i and P_j; in the second one, $\mathcal{A}$ replays the initiation message sent by P_i in the first execution to P_j. In the third one, $\mathcal{A}$ modifies the reply message sent by P_j. We present the execution details in the first row of Table 1. We assume that the long-term secret key of P_j has been corrupted by $\mathcal{A}$, such the last one execution also terminates normally without outputting $\perp$. Such three execution instances should have yielded six sessions in all. But the third and the sixth sessions are controlled by $\mathcal{A}$ in fact, which are regarded as "non-existent".

Table 1. Simulation failure example (KCI attack)

	P_i $\quad$ P_j	P_i $(\mathcal{A})$ $\quad$ P_j	P_i $\quad$ P_j $(\mathcal{A})$
execution instances	$\xrightarrow{ek\|\|c_i\|\|\sigma_i}$ $\quad$ $\xleftarrow{c\|\|c_j\|\|\sigma_j}$	$\xrightarrow{ek\|\|c_i\|\|\sigma_i}$ $\quad$ $\xleftarrow{c'\|\|c_j'\|\|\sigma_j'}$	$\xrightarrow{ek'\|\|c_i'\|\|\sigma_i'}$ $\quad$ $\xleftarrow{c''\|\|c_j'\|\|\sigma_j''}$
session-state	dk,k,k_i,k_j $\quad$ k,k_i,k_j	$\quad\quad\quad$ k',k_i,k_j'	dk',k'',k_i',k_j'
state reveal	✓		✓
challenge		$\quad\quad\quad$ $\star$	

Note that the two honest sessions involved in a single execution instance are mutually called matching session to each other. Assume the final target is the fourth one, whose matching session does not exist actually. In such case, $\mathcal{A}$ is essentially launching KCI attack. According to the definition of the CK model, this session is allowed to be the final target if only the long-term secret key of P_i is kept uncorrupted and $\mathcal{A}$ has never performed the *session-state reveal* and *session-key reveal* queries on it. But before $\mathcal{A}$ clamming his real target, he can perform *session-state reveal* queries on the first and the fifth sessions at will, thus learning the value of (k', k_i, k_j') and computing the target session key by itself. The simulation also fails.

Our Solution. In the above attempt, what accounts for the simulation failure is that $\mathcal{A}$ is able to replay the challenge ciphertexts (in particular c_j') embedded in the target session to activate other non-matching sessions. More straightforward, *session-state reveal* queries are allowed to be performed on these sessions, which is equivalent to giving $\mathcal{A}$ a free decryption oracle to open all embedded challenges.

To overcome it, we replace the "2KEM" module by "2TB-KEM+2OTS" as in Fig. 3. The key idea is a little bit like the CHK transform [10]: to generate a reply message, the party P_j should generate an extra OTS key-pair (vk_j, sk_j), and generate a TB-KEM (instead of KEM) ciphertext c_j with respect to vk_j as the "tag" and sign the partial initiation/reply message $ek\|\|c_i\|\|c\|\|c_j$ using sk_j

to obtain a signature $\sigma_{j,1}$. Only when $\sigma_{j,1}$ and $\sigma_{j,2}$ are both valid, the reply message can be accepted by P_i. Assuming the underlying OTS be strongly existential unforgeable, $\mathcal{A}$ can no longer replay the challenge c_j embedded in the target session to activate other non-matching sessions since he does not know the corresponding OTS secret key. Therefore, we achieve a tight reduction.

Concretely, our construction uses five building blocks, a wKEM = (Gen, Enc, Dec), a TB-KEM = (Gen, Enc, Dec), a deterministic SIG = (Gen, Sig, Vrfy), an OTS = (Gen, Sig, Vrfy) and a PRF family PRF. The construction mainly consists of the following three parts:

System Setup. Given a security parameter λ, select public parameters required for the underlying wKEM, TB-KEM, SIG, OTS and PRF. For ease of description, we use the string pp to denote the all system parameters in unified.

$P_i \ (ldk_i, lsk_i)$	$P_j \ (ldk_j, lsk_j)$
wKEM.Gen$(pp) \rightarrow (ek, dk)$	
OTS.Gen$(pp) \rightarrow (vk_i, sk_i)$	
TB-KEM.Enc$(lek_j, vk_i) \rightarrow (c_i, k_i)$	
OTS.Sig$(sk_i, ek\|\|c_i) \rightarrow \sigma_{i,1}$	
SIG.Sig$(lsk_i, i\|\|j\|\|vk_i\|\|\sigma_{i,1}) \rightarrow \sigma_{i,2}$	
$\xrightarrow{\quad i, j, ek\|\|vk_i\|\|c_i\|\|\sigma_{i,1}\|\|\sigma_{i,2} \quad}$	
	OT-SIG.Vrfy$(vk_i, ek\|\|c_i, \sigma_{i,1}) = b_0$
	SIG.Vrfy$(lvk_i, i\|\|j\|\|vk_i\|\|\sigma_{i,1}, \sigma_{i,2}) = b_1$
	if $b_0 \neq 1 \vee b_1 \neq 1$, output $\bot$
	else wKEM.Enc$(ek) \rightarrow (c, k)$
	OTS.Gen$(pp) \rightarrow (vk_j, sk_j B)$
	TB-KEM.Enc$(lek_i, vk_j) \rightarrow (c_j, k_j)$
	OTS.Sig$(sk_j, ek\|\|c_i\|\|c\|\|c_j) \rightarrow \sigma_{j,1}$
	SIG.Sig$(lsk_j, i\|\|j\|\|vk_j\|\|\sigma_{j,1}) \rightarrow \sigma_{j,2}$
$\xleftarrow{\quad i, j, c\|\|vk_j\|\|c_j\|\|\sigma_{j,1}\|\|\sigma_{j,2} \quad}$	
OTS.Vrfy$(vk_j, ek\|\|c_i\|\|c\|\|c_j, \sigma_{j,1}) = b_0'$	
SIG.Vrfy$(lvk_j, i\|\|j\|\|vk_j\|\|\sigma_{j,1}, \sigma_{j,2}) = b_1'$	
if $b_0' \neq 1 \vee b_1' \neq 1$, output $\bot$	
else wKEM.Dec$(dk, c) = k$	
TB-KEM.Dec$(ldk_i, c_j, vk_j) = k_j$	TB-KEM.Dec$(ldk_j, c_i, vk_i) = k_i$
$trans = i\|\|j\|\|ek\|\|vk_i\|\|c_i\|\|\sigma_{i,1}\|\|\sigma_{i,2}\|\|c\|\|vk_j\|\|c_j\|\|\sigma_{j,1}\|\|\sigma_{j,2}$	
$sk = \mathsf{PRF}(k_i, trans) \oplus \mathsf{PRF}(k_j, trans) \oplus \mathsf{PRF}(k, trans)$	

Fig. 3. Generic "$2\times$SIG$+2\times$TB-KEM$+2\times$OTS$+$wKEM" construction

Long-Term Secrets. Each party P_i is in possession of two key pairs $(lek_i, ldk_i) \leftarrow$ TB-KEM.Gen(pp) and $(lvk_i, lsk_i) \leftarrow$ SIG.Gen(pp). In particular, (lek_i, lvk_i) and (ldk_j, lsk_j) are denoted his long-term public and secret key, respectively.

Session Execution. To negotiate a fresh session key, two parties (e.g., P_i and P_j) should execute the steps shown in Fig. 3. We assume P_i as the initiator without loss of generality. In concrete,

Step 1. P_i first computes $(ek, dk) \leftarrow$ wKEM.Gen(pp), $(vk_i, sk_i) \leftarrow$ OTS.Gen(pp), $(k_i, c_i) \leftarrow$ TB-KEM.Enc(lek_j, vk_i), $\sigma_{i,1} \leftarrow$ OTS.Sig$(sk_i, ek\|c_i)$ and $\sigma_{i,2} \leftarrow$ SIG.Sig$(lsk_i, i\|j\|vk_i\|\sigma_{i,1})$ in order; then sends the initiation-message $(i, j, ek\|vk_i\|c_i\|\sigma_{i,1}\|\sigma_{i,2})$ to P_j.

Step 2. Upon receiving the initiation-message sent from P_i, P_j first checks the validity of both $\sigma_{i,1}$ and $\sigma_{i,2}$. Outputs $\perp$ if OTS.Vrfy$(vk_i, ek\|c_i, \sigma_{i,1}) \neq 1$ or SIG.Vrfy$(lvk_i, i\|j\|vk_i\|\sigma_{i,1}, \sigma_{i,2}) \neq 1$.
   Otherwise, computes $(c, k) \leftarrow$ wKEM.Enc(ek), $(vk_j, sk_j) \leftarrow$ OTS.Gen (pp), $(c_j, k_j) \leftarrow$ TB-KEM.Enc(lek_i, vk_j), $\sigma_{j,1} \leftarrow$ OTS.Sig$(sk_j, ek\|c_i\|c\|c_j)$ and $\sigma_{j,2} \leftarrow$ SIG.Sig$(lsk_j, i\|j\|vk_j\|\sigma_{j,1})$ in order, then sends back the reply-message $(i, j, c\|vk_j\|c_j\|\sigma_{j,1}\|\sigma_{j,2})$ to P_i.

Step 3. Upon receiving the reply-message sent from P_j, P_i first checks the validity of both $\sigma_{j,1}$ and $\sigma_{j,2}$. Outputs $\perp$ if OTS.Vrfy$(vk_j, ek\|c_i\|c\|c_j, \sigma_{j,1}) \neq 1$ or SIG.Vrfy$(lvk_j, i\|j\|vk_j\|\sigma_{j,1}, \sigma_{j,2}) \neq 1$.
   Otherwise, P_i computes $k =$ wKEM.Dec(dk, c) and $k_j =$ TB-KEM.Dec (ldk_i, c_j, vk_j). P_j also computes $k_i =$ TB-KEM.Dec(ldk_j, c_i, vk_i). Finally, lets $trans = i\|j\|ek\|vk_i\|c_i\|\sigma_{i,1}\|\sigma_{i,2}\|c\|vk_j\|c_j\|\sigma_{j,1}\|\sigma_{j,2}$ denote the session transcript, both P_i and P_j compute the session key as $sk = $ PRF$(k_i, trans) \oplus$ PRF$(k_j, trans) \oplus$ PRF$(k, trans)$.

Theorem 1. *If* wKEM *is* MU-IND-CPA^{Corr} *secure,* TB-KEM *is* MU-IND-CCA^{Corr} *secure,* SIG MU-EUF-CMA^{Corr} *secure,* OTS *is* MU-1-sEUF-CMA *secure and* PRF *is secure, the protocol* $\mathcal{P}$ *illustrated in Fig. 3 is secure in the* CK *model. In particular, for any PPT adversary* $\mathcal{A}$:

$$\mathsf{Adv}^{\mathsf{CK}}_{\mathcal{P}, \mathcal{A}}(\lambda) \leq \epsilon_{\mathsf{wKEM}} + \epsilon_{\mathsf{TB\text{-}KEM}} + \epsilon_{\mathsf{SIG}} + \epsilon_{\mathsf{OTS}} + \epsilon_{\mathsf{PRF}}.$$

Proof. It is obvious that two matching sessions executed by honest parties complete with the same session key. Next, a sequence of experiments will be put forwarded and let ϵ_δ denote the success advantage of $\mathcal{A}$ in Exp$_\delta$. For ease of description, we first introduce some notations, where the subscript S, E, D and C denote *signing, encapsulation, decapsulation* and *corruption* queries, respectively. In addition, $\mathcal{S}_1$ and $\mathcal{S}_2$ are two simulators will be used later.

Notations		
Challenger	**Experiment**	**Queries**
$\mathcal{C}$	$\mathsf{Exp}_{\mathcal{P},\mathcal{A}}^{\mathsf{CK}}$	all provided in the CK model
$\mathcal{C}_{\mathsf{OTS}}$	$\mathsf{Exp}_{\mathsf{OTS},\mathcal{C}}^{\mathsf{MU\text{-}sEUF\text{-}1\text{-}CMA}}(\lambda)$	$\mathcal{O}_{\mathsf{OTS},\mathsf{S}}(\cdot)$
$\mathcal{C}_{\mathsf{SIG}}$	$\mathsf{Exp}_{\mathsf{SIG},\mathcal{C}}^{\mathsf{MU\text{-}EUF\text{-}CMA}^{\mathsf{Corr}}}(\lambda)$	$\mathcal{O}_{\mathsf{SIG},\mathsf{S}}(\cdot), \mathcal{O}_{\mathsf{SIG},\mathsf{C}}(\cdot,\cdot)$
$\mathcal{C}_{\mathsf{wKEM}}$	$\mathsf{Exp}_{\mathsf{wKEM},\mathcal{S}_1}^{\mathsf{MU\text{-}IND\text{-}CPA}^{\mathsf{Corr}}}(\lambda)$	$\mathcal{O}_{\mathsf{wKEM},\mathsf{E}}(\cdot), \mathcal{O}_{\mathsf{wKEM},\mathsf{C}}(\cdot)$
$\mathcal{C}_{\mathsf{TB\text{-}KEM}}$	$\mathsf{Exp}_{\mathsf{TB\text{-}KEM},\mathcal{S}_2}^{\mathsf{MU\text{-}IND\text{-}CCA}^{\mathsf{Corr}}}(\lambda)$	$\mathcal{O}_{\mathsf{TB\text{-}KEM},\mathsf{E}}(\cdot), \mathcal{O}_{\mathsf{TB\text{-}KEM},\mathsf{D}}(\cdot,\cdot), \mathcal{O}_{\mathsf{TB\text{-}KEM},\mathsf{C}}(\cdot)$

Three lists $\mathcal{L}_{corr}$, $\mathcal{L}_{var}$ and $\mathcal{L}_{ss}$ will be used to record all corrupted parties (e.g., $(P_i, (lek_i, lvk_i), (ldk_i, lsk_i))$, sessions' corresponding variables (i.e., $(s_{actor}, s_{peer}, s_{role}, s_{sent}, s_{recv})$) and session states (e.g., $(s, (dk, k, k_i, k_j))$ for an initiation session or $(s, (-, k, k_i, k_j))$ for a response session), respectively. Upon a session is activated, two corresponding records are inserted into $\mathcal{L}_{var}$ and $\mathcal{L}_{ss}$, respectively. In particular, if a specific item (e.g., s_{recv}, dk, k, k_i or k_j) hasn't been assigned or determined yet, a placeholder "-" is used to represent it and will be automatically updated along with the experiment proceeding.

Exp$_0$. This experiment is same as the original security experiment, such that

$$\epsilon_0 = \mathsf{Adv}_{\mathcal{P},\mathcal{A}}^{\mathsf{CK}}(\lambda). \qquad \square$$

Exp$_1$. This experiment is same as Exp$_0$, except that we modify the ways of generating signatures and answering related queries as follows:

(1) collects all verification keys output by $\mathcal{C}_{\mathsf{SIG}}$ and $\mathcal{C}_{\mathsf{OTS}}$ into the sets $\mathcal{Q}_{lvk}$ and $\mathcal{Q}_{vk}$, respectively.
(2) assigns the long-term verification keys of all parties (e.g., lvk_i for P_i) using the items in $\mathcal{Q}_{lvk}$ without repetition.
(3) when answering $corrupt(\cdot)$ queries, performs corresponding $\mathcal{O}_{\mathsf{SIG},\mathsf{C}}(\cdot)$ queries for required long-term signing keys.
(4) when generating SIG signatures for uncorrupted parties (e.g., $P_i \notin \mathcal{L}_{corr}$), performs corresponding $\mathcal{O}_{\mathsf{OTS},\mathsf{S}}(\cdot,\cdot)$ queries.
(5) when generating a fresh pair of OTS verification key and signature, selects an unused item $vk \in \mathcal{Q}_{vk}$ and performs a corresponding $\mathcal{O}_{\mathsf{OTS},\mathsf{S}}(vk,\cdot)$ query.

The view of $\mathcal{A}$ remains identical, such that

$$\epsilon_1 = \epsilon_0. \qquad \square$$

Exp$_2$. This experiment is same as Exp$_1$, except that we adds two rejection rules when answering $incoming\text{-}message(\cdot,\cdot,\cdot)$ queries as follows:

$\star$ *taking a query on (s, P_i, m) as an example*

(1) s is an unused session on a party P_j but $P_i \notin \mathcal{L}_{corr} \wedge (P_i, P_j, \mathcal{I}, m, */-) \notin \mathcal{L}_{var}$. Namely, $\mathcal{A}$ generates a fresh initiation-message on behalf of P_i without corrupting it.

(2) s is an uncompleted session on a party P_j with a record $(P_j, P_i, \mathcal{I}, \bar{m}, -) \in \mathcal{L}_{var}$ but $P_i \notin \mathcal{L}_{corr} \wedge (P_i, P_j, \mathcal{R}, m, \bar{m}) \notin \mathcal{L}_{var}$. Namely, $\mathcal{A}$ generates a fresh response-message on behalf of P_i without corrupting it.

No matter in which cases, only when $\mathcal{A}$ is able to forge a valid SIG signature (without knowing lsk_i), a falsely rejected event occurs and $\mathcal{A}$ distinguishes Exp_2 from Exp_1. Thus,

$$\epsilon_2 \leq \epsilon_1 + \epsilon_{\mathsf{SIG}}.$$

□

Exp$_3$. This experiment is same as Exp_2, except that we adds two another rejection rules when answering *incoming-message*$(\cdot, \cdot, \cdot)$ queries as follows:
  ⋆ *taking a query on (s, P_i, m) as an example*

(1) s is an unused session on a party P_j, m is an initiation-message that can be phrased as $ek||vk_i||c_i||\sigma_{i,1}||\sigma_{i,2}$, $vk_i \in \mathcal{Q}_{vk}$ but $(ek||c_i, \sigma_{i,1})$ is not an output of performing $\mathcal{O}_{\mathsf{OTS,S}}(vk_i, ek||c_i)$ query.
(2) s is an uncompleted session on a party P_j with a record $(P_j, P_i, \mathcal{I}, \bar{m} = ek||vk_j||c_j||\sigma_{j,1}||\sigma_{j,2}, -) \in \mathcal{L}_{var}$, m is a response-message that can be phrased as $c||vk_i||c_i||\sigma_{i,1}||\sigma_{i,2}$, $vk_i \in \mathcal{Q}_{vk}$ but $(ek||c_j||c||c_i, \sigma_{i,1})$ is not an output of performing $\mathcal{O}_{\mathsf{OTS,S}}(vk_i, ek||c_j||c||c_i)$ query.

No matter in which cases, only when $\mathcal{A}$ is able to forge a valid OTS signature, a falsely rejected event occurs and $\mathcal{A}$ distinguishes Exp_3 from Exp_2. Thus,

$$\epsilon_3 \leq \epsilon_2 + \epsilon_{\mathsf{OTS}}.$$

□

Putting all rejection rules together, there exist two facts:

Fact.1. If $\mathcal{A}$ has not corrupted a party P_i, it is unable to generate any fresh message in the name of it. Such that $\mathcal{A}$ can only launch replay attacks. Besides, as each response-message is related to its corresponding initiation-message, $\mathcal{A}$ is unable to replay response-messages to make other non-matching sessions accept.

Fact.2. If $\mathcal{A}$ has corrupted a party P_i, it is able to generate any message to make other sessions accept. But, $\mathcal{A}$ has to choose OTS key pair by itself. Taking an initiation-message $ek||vk_i||c_i||\sigma_{i,1}||\sigma_{i,2}$ sent by P_i as an example, if $\mathcal{A}$ hasn't generated (vk_i, sk_i) by itself, $\sigma_{i,1}$ cannot be valid except that it is a successful forgery. Therefore, OTS verification keys used as "tags" in generating TB-KEM ciphertexts must be fresh every time.

Exp$_4$. This experiment is same as Exp_3, except that we modifies the way to compute the real session keys of tested sessions that are passively-activated, such that wKEM decapsulated keys are replaced by random keys.

Here, we introduce a simulator $\mathcal{S}_1$ who is simulating Exp_3 or Exp_4. On the basis of Exp_3, $\mathcal{S}_1$ modifies the way of generating wKEM ciphertexts and answering related queries:

(1) collects all public keys output by C_{wKEM} into the set $\mathcal{Q}_{ek}$;

(2) when answering *establish-message*$(\cdot,\cdot)$ queries, selects unused items from $\mathcal{Q}_{ek}$ and perform corresponding $\mathcal{O}_{\mathsf{wKEM,E}}(\cdot)$ queries for required wKEM encryption keys and ciphertexts, respectively.

(3) when answering *session-state/key reveal*$(\cdot)$ queries on passively-activated sessions, performs corresponding $\mathcal{O}_{\mathsf{wKEM,C}}(\cdot)$ queries to derive unknown wKEM secret keys, and computes session states or keys accordingly.

(4) when answering *test-session*$(\cdot)$ queries on passively-activated sessions, computes the real tested session keys using the corresponding challenge encapsulated keys output by $\mathcal{O}_{\mathsf{wKEM,E}}(\cdot)$.

Assuming the final output of $\mathcal{A}$ is (s^*, b'), s^* should never be exposed. Thus *session-key reveal*$(\cdot)$ and *session-state reveal*$(\cdot)$ queries were never performed on s^* and its matching-sessions. Therefore, the underlying wKEM challenge was never opened. Thus,

$$\epsilon_4 \leq \epsilon_3 + \epsilon_{\mathsf{wKEM}}.$$

$\square$

Exp$_5$. This experiment is same as Exp$_4$, except that we change the way to compute the real session keys of tested sessions that are actively-activated, such that TB-KEM decapsulated keys are replaced by random keys.

Here, we introduce a simulator $\mathcal{S}_2$ who is simulating Exp$_4$ or Exp$_5$. On the basis of Exp$_4$, $\mathcal{S}_2$ modifies the way of generating TB-KEM ciphertexts and answering related queries:

(1) collects all public keys output by $C_{\mathsf{TB\text{-}KEM}}$ into the set $\mathcal{Q}_{lek}$, and assigns the long-term encryption keys of all parties (e.g., lek_i for P_i) using the items in $\mathcal{Q}_{lek}$ without repetition.

(2) when answering *corrupt*$(\cdot)$ queries, performs corresponding $\mathcal{O}_{\mathsf{TB\text{-}KEM,C}}(\cdot)$ queries for required long-term decryption keys.

(3) when decrypting TB-KEM ciphertexts for uncorrupted parties (e.g., $P_i \notin \mathcal{L}_{corr}$), performs corresponding $\mathcal{O}_{\mathsf{TB\text{-}KEM,D}}(\cdot,\cdot,\cdot)$ queries.

(4) when answering *incoming-message*$(\cdot,\cdot,\cdot)$ queries, e.g., a query on (s, P_i, m) as an example: if s is a response-session on a party P_j, $P_i \notin \mathcal{L}_{corr}$, performs an $\mathcal{O}_{\mathsf{TB\text{-}KEM,E}}(lek_i, \cdot)$ query to derive the required TB-KEM ciphertext c_j. In this case, $(P_i, P_j, \mathcal{I}, m, *) \in \mathcal{L}_{var}$ must hold according to our rejection rules in Exp$_3$. Namely, $\mathcal{A}$ is actually launching replay attack.

(5) when answering *session-state/key reveal*$(\cdot)$ queries on actively-attacked sessions: performs corresponding $\mathcal{O}_{\mathsf{TB\text{-}KEM,D}}(\cdot,\cdot,\cdot)$ queries to derive unknown TB-KEM decapsulated keys, and computes session keys accordingly.

(6) when answering *test-session*$(\cdot)$ queries on actively-activated sessions: computes the real tested session keys using the corresponding challenge encapsulated keys output by $\mathcal{O}_{\mathsf{TB\text{-}KEM,E}}(\cdot,\cdot)$.

Assuming the final output of $\mathcal{A}$ is (s^*, b'), s^* should never be exposed. Thus *session-key reveal*$(\cdot)$ and *session-state reveal*$(\cdot)$ queries were never performed on s^*, and *corrupt*$(\cdot)$ query was also never performed on s^*_{peer}. In addition, according to Fact.1 and Fact.2, $\mathcal{A}$ cannot embed the underlying TB-KEM challenge into other non-matching sessions and utilize other queries (i.e., *session-key reveal*($\cdot$) and *session-state reveal*($\cdot$)) to open it. Thus,

$$\epsilon_5 \leq \epsilon_4 + \epsilon_{\text{TB-KEM}}. \qquad \square$$

Exp$_6$. This experiment is same as Exp$_5$, except that we modifies the way to answer *test-session*($\cdot$) queries, taking a query on s^* (whose real session state should include three decapsulated keys (k^*, k_1^*, k_2^*) and transcript is denoted as $trans^*$) as an example:

(1) if s^* is a passively-activated session, selectes $k \leftarrow_{\$} Rng_\lambda$ and computes the real target session key as $sk^* = k \oplus \text{PRF}(k_1^*, trans^*) \oplus \text{PRF}(k_2^*, trans^*)$.
(2) if s^* is an actively-activated session, selectes $k \leftarrow_{\$} Rng_\lambda$ and computes the real target session key as $sk^* = \text{PRF}(k^*, trans^*) \oplus \text{PRF}(k_1^*, trans^*) \oplus k$.

According to the security definition of PRF, we have

$$\epsilon_6 \leq \epsilon_5 + \epsilon_{\text{PRF}}. \qquad \square$$

Exp$_7$. This experiment is same as Exp$_6$ except that we further modifies the way to answer *test-session*($\cdot$) queries, such that the real session key is changed as choosing $sk^* \leftarrow_{\$} Rng_\lambda$. Since k is randomly chosen from Rng_λ, sk^* is also randomly distributed in Rng_λ. It means that Exp$_7$ is actually identical to Exp$_6$, thus

$$\epsilon_7 = \epsilon_6. \qquad \square$$

It is obvious that each real target session key sk^* in Exp$_7$ is randomly chose from $\mathcal{FS}$, the advantage of $\mathcal{A}$ is actually equal to 0, which means $\epsilon_7 = 0$. Summarizing all, the inequality is established. ∎

Remark 3. As the CK model has to answer *corrupt*($\cdot$) and *session-key/state reveal*($\cdot$) queries, which should be answered by opening secret keys or challenges. Thus, we have to require the underlying KEM security notions to be defined in the multi-bit challenge case. Otherwise, decrypting one challenge would reveal the global challenge. Which in turn to make our proof cannot be extended easily into the single-bit challenge variant of the CK model.

4   MU-IND-CCA^{Corr} Secure TB-KEM

The typical Naor-Yung transform [26] can be proved MU-IND-CCA^{Corr} secure, where adversaries are additionally allowed to adaptively corrupt long-term secret keys and open some challenges. Note that each ciphertext generated from the Naor-Yung transform consists of two CPA secure PKE ciphertexts and one NIZK proof, each public key consists of two PKE public key but each secret key merely consists of one of the two corresponding secret keys. In the simulation, for each public key, the simulator is able to generate one secret key by itself and embed the underlying PKE challenges into another one when answering corresponding encryption queries, and using the known secret key to answer the corruption query and open simulated challenges. As long as the adversary is unable to distinguish the simulated case from the real case, the security proof is established.

We first give a variant of the typical Naor-Yung transform. Let PKE = (Setup, Gen, Enc, Dec) be a PKE scheme with message space $\mathcal{M}$, and QA-NIZK = (K_0, K_1, P, V) be a QA-NIZK proof system. In particular, we consider the language $\mathcal{L}_{ek_0, ek_1} := \{(c_0, c_1) | c_0 = \text{PKE.Enc}(ek_0, m) \wedge c_1 = \text{PKE.Enc}(ek_1, m)$ for a message $m \in \mathcal{M}\}$. A TB-KEM scheme TB-KEM = (Setup, Gen, Enc, Dec) can be constructed as in Fig. 4:

TB-KEM.Setup(1^λ):	TB-KEM.Enc($\hat{ek}, \tau$):
$\Pi \leftarrow$ PKE.Setup(1^λ)	phrase $\hat{ek} = (ek_0, ek_1, \psi)$
$\Gamma \leftarrow$ QA-NIZK.$K_0(1^\lambda)$	$k \leftarrow_\$ \mathcal{M}$, $c_0 \leftarrow$ PKE.Enc($ek_0, k; r_0$)
return $\hat{\Pi} := (\Pi, \Gamma)$	$c_1 \leftarrow$ PKE.Enc($ek_1, k; r_1$), lbl $= (c_0, c_1, \tau)$
TB-KEM.Gen($\hat{\Pi}$):	$\pi \leftarrow$ QA-NIZK.P($\psi, (c_0, c_1), (r_0, r_1)$, lbl)
phrase $\hat{\Pi} := (\Pi, \Gamma)$, $\delta \leftarrow_\$ \{0,1\}$	return $(\hat{c} = (c_0, c_1, \pi), \hat{k} = k)$
$(ek_0, dk_0) \leftarrow$ PKE.Gen(Π)	TB-KEM.Dec($\hat{dk}, \hat{c}, \tau$):
$(ek_1, dk_1) \leftarrow$ PKE.Gen(Π)	phrase $\hat{dk} = (\delta, dk_\delta)$, $\hat{c} = (c_0, c_1, \pi)$
$\rho := (ek_0, ek_1)$	lbl $= (c_0, c_1, \tau)$
$\psi \leftarrow$ QA-NIZK.$K_1(\Gamma, \rho)$	$b = $ QA-NIZK.V($\psi, (c_0, c_1), \pi$, lbl)
return	$k \leftarrow$ PKE.Dec(dk_δ, c_δ)
$\hat{ek} := (ek_0, ek_1, \psi)$, $\hat{dk} := (\delta, dk_\delta)$	if $b = 1$ return $\hat{k} = k$, else return $\bot$

Fig. 4. A variant of the Naor-Yung transform

Theorem 2. *If* PKE *is* S-MU-IND-CPA *secure, and* QA-NIZK *is an* M-USS-QA-NIZK *proof, then* TB-KEM *is* MU-IND-CCA^{Corr} *secure. In particular, for any PPT adversary $\mathcal{A}$:*

$$\text{Adv}_{\mathcal{A},\text{TB-KEM}}^{\text{MU-IND-CCA}^{\text{Corr}}}(\lambda) \leq \epsilon_{\text{PKE}} + \epsilon_{\text{QA-ZK}} + 2\epsilon_{\text{USS}}.$$

Proof. The proof inherently follows the strategy of [27]. The correctness inherits from the underlying PKE and QA-NIZK schemes. For proving the security, a sequence of experiments will be put forwarded and ϵ_δ is used to denote the success advantage of $\mathcal{A}$ wining in the Exp_δ.

Exp$_0$. This experiment is the original security experiment. In particular, for each encryption query by (i, j) (i.e., the j-th query on the public key $\hat{ek}_i$), we denote $k_{i,j,0}$ as the real key while $k_{i,j,1}$ as a random key. It is obvious,

$$\epsilon_0 = \text{Adv}_{\text{TB-KEM},\mathcal{A}}^{\text{MU-IND-CCA}^{\text{Corr}}}(\lambda).$$

$\square$

Exp$_1$. This experiment is same as Exp$_0$ except that the way to generate QA-NIZK proofs is changed to use the QA-NIZK simulator $\mathcal{S} = (\mathcal{S}_1, \mathcal{S}_2)$. Due to the quasi adaptive zero-knowledge property of QA-NIZK,

$$\epsilon_1 - \epsilon_0 \leq \epsilon_{\mathsf{QA\text{-}ZK}}.$$

□

Exp$_2$. This experiment is same as Exp$_1$ except that the way to generate challenge ciphertexts is changed. For each ciphertext $c_{i,j} = (c_{i,j,0}, c_{i,j,1}, \pi)$ with tag $\tau_{i,j}$ under public key $\hat{ek}_i = (ek_{i,0}, ek_{i,1}, \psi_i)$, the challenger generates $c_{\delta_i} \leftarrow \mathsf{PKE.Enc}(ek_{i,\delta_i}, k_{i,j,0})$, $c_{1-\delta_i} \leftarrow \mathsf{PKE.Enc}(ek_{i,1-\delta_i}, k_{i,j,1})$ and a simulated proof π as before. Due to the CPA security of PKE,

$$\epsilon_2 - \epsilon_1 \leq \epsilon_{\mathsf{PKE}}.$$

□

Exp$_3$. This experiment is same as Exp$_2$ except that the way to answer corruption queries and decryption queries is changed. In this experiment, the challenger generates key pair for each user i as follows: first computes $(ek_{i,0}, dk_{i,0}) \leftarrow \mathsf{PKE.Gen}(\Pi)$ and $(ek_{i,1}, dk_{i,1}) \leftarrow \mathsf{PKE.Gen}(\Pi)$, then chooses $\delta_i \leftarrow_{\$} \{0, 1\}$, finally sets $(\hat{ek}, \hat{dk}) := ((ek_{i,0}, ek_{i,1}, \psi_i), (\delta_i, dk_{i,\delta_i}))$, where ψ_i is generated by $\mathcal{S}_1$. For answering corruption queries, corresponding $(\delta_i, dk_{i,\delta_i})$ is returned; for answering decryption queries:

⋄ If the query $(c_{i,j}, \tau_{i,j})$ is a challenge generated by the challenger before, returns the corresponding real encapsulated key $k_{i,j,0}$.
⋄ Else if the queried ciphertext $c_{i,j}$ is a challenge ciphertext generated by the challenger before, but with a different tag $\tau'_{i,j}$, returns $\perp$.
⋄ Otherwise, for a given ciphertext $c = (c_0, c_1, \pi)$ with tag τ under public key $\hat{ek}_i$. First checks the validity of π. If it is valid, computes $k \leftarrow \mathsf{PKE.Dec}(dk_{i,\delta_i}, c_{\delta_i})$ and returns $\hat{k} = k$. In other case, returns $\perp$.

For the second case, there exists a bad event that if $(c_{i,j}, \tau'_{i,j})$ is a valid ciphertext, but it is falsely rejected. As we define $\mathsf{lbl}_{i,j} = (c_{i,j}, \tau_{i,j})$, the adversary must generate a valid proof for a fresh label $\mathsf{lbl}'_{i,j} = (c_{i,j}, \tau'_{i,j}) \neq \mathsf{lbl}_{i,j}$. Due to the unbounded simulation-soundness of QA-NIZK, such bad event only occurs with ϵ_{USS} probability. Exclude this bad event: before launching corruption query on $\hat{ek}_i$, the adversary has no idea about the internal bit δ_i, except that he submits a ciphertext $c = (c_0, c_1, \pi)$ that proof π is accepted but $\mathsf{PKE.Dec}(dk_{i,\delta_i}, c_{\delta_i}) \neq \mathsf{PKE.Dec}(dk_{i,1-\delta_i}, c_{1-\delta_i})$. But in such case, the adversary has to provide a proof π for a false statement. Due to the unbounded simulation-soundness of QA-NIZK, it only occurs with ϵ_{USS} probability. Thus,

$$\epsilon_3 - \epsilon_2 \leq 2\epsilon_{\mathsf{USS}}.$$

□

Assume the final target of the adversary is (i^*, j^*) (related to a challenge ciphertext c^* with tag τ^*), $\mathcal{O}_D(i^*, c^*, \tau^*)$ and $\mathcal{O}_C(i^*)$ queries should never been queried in the experiment. Therefore, both δ_i^* and b_{i^*, j^*} are kept hidden for the adversary. Therefore, the advantage for the adversary in Exp$_3$ is zero, i.e., $\epsilon_3 = 0$. Summarizing all above statements, the inequality is established. ∎

5   Instantiation and Comparisons

We first instantiate our protocol using the following strategies:

- The MU-IND-CPA^{Corr} secure wKEM is instantiated using the double ELGamal encryptions. Bellare, Boldyreva and Micali [6] have proved the ELGamal encryption meets the S-MU-IND-CPA security. Thus, we can apply the generic construction (i.e., double encryption paradigm) in Section 3.3 of [5]. In particular, we optimize it using randomness reusing technique, such that each public key consists of 2 group elements (e.g., (g^{s_1}, g^{s_2}) for secret key $(s_1, s_2) \leftarrow_\$ \mathbb{Z}_p$) and each ciphertext consists of 3 group elements (e.g., $(g^r, g^{rs_1}k, g^{rs_2}k)$ for a randomness $r \leftarrow_\$ \mathbb{Z}_p$ and an encapsulated key k). Note that, even the randomness r is reused, the security reduction strategy used in [5] will not be affected, where simulator only needs to know a partial secret key to answer extra corruption queries.
- the MU-EUF-CMA^{Corr} secure SIG is instantiated using the construction in Section 3.2 of [19], which is based on the DDH and CDH problems and where each signature consists of 6 group elements plus a λ-bit nonce.
- The MU-1-sEUF-CMA secure OTS is instantiated using the discrete-log-based construction in Section 4.2 of [21], where each signature consists of 2 group elements and each verification key consists of 2 group elements.
- As for the MU-IND-CCA^{Corr} secure TB-KEM, we apply the generic construction presented in Fig. 4. In particular, the underlying PKE is instantiated using the ELGamal encryption once again, and the underlying QA-NIZK is instantiated using the construction in Appendix H of [25] (whose security is based on the DLIN assumption and a strongly unforgeable OTS). In particular, we use a proof system in the context of asymmetric pairings $e : \mathbb{G} \times \hat{\mathbb{G}} \to \mathbb{G}_T$, with $\mathbb{G} \neq \hat{\mathbb{G}}$. Using the OTS in Section 4.2 of [21] under the group $\mathbb{G}$ to instantiate QA-NIZK, we have a proof system where each proof consists of 30 elements of $\mathbb{G}$ and 12 elements of $\hat{\mathbb{G}}$. Combining with the optimized ELGamal double encryptions under the group $\mathbb{G}$, we have that each TB-KEM ciphertext consists of 33 elements of $\mathbb{G}$ and 12 elements of $\hat{\mathbb{G}}$.

Here, we analyze the communication overhead of our protocol when instantiated with the building blocks described above. In particular, wKEM, SIG, OTS are implemented on the group $\mathbb{G}$. The messages exchanged for each run of the protocol include $m_i = i||j||ek||vk_i||c_i||\sigma_{i,1}||\sigma_{i,2}$ and $m_j = i||j||c||vk_j||c_j||\sigma_{j,1}||\sigma_{j,2}$ two messages. In detail,

$$|m_i| = |i| + |j| + |ek_{\text{wKEM}}| + |vk_{\text{OTS}}| + |c_{\text{TB-KEM}}| + |\sigma_{\text{OTS}}| + |\sigma_{\text{SIG}}|$$

$$|m_j| = |i| + |j| + |c_{\text{wKEM}}| + |vk_{\text{OTS}}| + |c_{\text{TB-KEM}}| + |\sigma_{\text{OTS}}| + |\sigma_{\text{SIG}}|$$

Thus, the message sent by P_i consists of 45 elements of $\mathbb{G}$ and 12 elements of $\hat{\mathbb{G}}$ (plus a λ-bit nonce and two identities); while the message sent by P_j consists of 46 elements of $\mathbb{G}$ and 12 elements of $\hat{\mathbb{G}}$ (plus a λ-bit nonce and two identities). The concrete execution procedures are presented in Appendix A.

Table 2. Comparisons with exiting tightly secure constructions

Constructions	Model	Round	Communication overhead		
			m_i	m_j	m_i'
Bader et al. [5]	BR	3	$7 \times |\mathbb{G}|$	$9 \times |\mathbb{G}|$	$2 \times |\mathbb{G}|$
Gjøsteen-Jager [19]	BR	3	λ	$7 \times |\mathbb{G}| + \lambda$	$7 \times |\mathbb{G}| + \lambda$
Ours	CK	2	$45 \times |\mathbb{G}| + 12 \times |\hat{\mathbb{G}}| + \lambda$	$46 \times |\mathbb{G}| + 12 \times |\hat{\mathbb{G}}| + \lambda$	——

where λ denote the security parameter, $|\mathbb{G}|$ and $|\hat{\mathbb{G}}|$ denote the least bits required to express an element of $\mathbb{G}$ and $\hat{\mathbb{G}}$, respectively. We assume P_i playing the role of initiator while P_j playing the role of responder. The message m_i and m_i' denote the first and the second message sent by P_i, respectively.

We further compare our construction with exiting tightly secure schemes as in Table 2. Both Bader et al. [5] and Gjøsteen-Jager [19] achieve tight-security in the BR model, while our construction achieves tight-security in the CK model. Since the CK model is stronger than the BR model, such that our construction is more secure than the former two. In addition, our construction costs lower round complexity, which is more preferable in practical use since higher round complexity involves higher network latency (that is a key factor weakening the practical performance of communication protocols). An important reason for which is that our construction merely reaches implicit authentication.

What is less satisfying is that, our scheme suffers high communication cost, accompanying with high computation cost for generating and verifying QA-NIZK proofs. In particular, our concrete instantiation requires 125 exponentiations to generate a QA-NIZK proof, and 34 pairings as well as 4 exponentiations to validate it. Such that, in a single protocol execution, the initiator requires 158 exponentiations and 34 pairings, while the responder requires 157 exponentiations and 34 pairings. Comparing to the most efficient AKE protocol Gjøsteen-Jager [19], where each party requires 17 exponentiations, this instantiation is significant inefficient and cannot be directly applied for practical use.

Remark 4. In our construction, to improve the efficiency (i.e., reducing communication and computation costs), it is important to achieve more efficient (almost) tightly unbounded simulation-sound QA-NIZK in the *multi-crs* setting, which is an independent interest. As far as we know, there exist a number of works [2,3,17] with tighter reduction or more compact proof. However, their security proofs were merely given with respect to the *single-crs* setting. We notice that [2,3] directly applied their results to obtain PKEs with tight CCA security in the *multi-user, multi-challenge* setting. Actually, it requires adapting their schemes to the *multi-crs* setting. [3] claimed that their scheme readily adapts to the *multi-crs* setting, however, we have not seen the complete proof.

On the other hand, by assuming [2,3] achieve so, our construction can be instantiated more efficiently. For example, applying [2], we can derive a QA-NIZK proof where each proof consists of only 8 elements of $\mathbb{G}$ and 6 elements of $\hat{\mathbb{G}}$, and which requires 22 exponentiations and 18 pairings to generate and validate a proof, respectively. Hence in a single protocol execution, the initiator requires 52 exponentiations and 18 pairings, while the responder requires 51 exponentiations and 18 pairings in total.

Acknowledgements. This work was supported in part by National Natural Science Foundation of China (Grant Nos. 61772520, 61802392, 61972094, 61632020, 61472416), Key Research Project of Zhejiang Province (Grant No. 2017C01062), and Beijing Municipal Science and Technology Project (Grant Nos. Z191100007119007, Z191100007119002).

A   Concrete Instantiation

We instantiate our protocol using the strategies described in Sect. 5, which includes the following three parts.

System Setup. Invoke the algorithm $\mathsf{K}_0(\lambda)$ in Appendix H of [25] to obtain the common public parameters of $\mathsf{NIZK} = (\mathsf{K}_0, \mathsf{K}_1, \mathsf{P}, \mathsf{V})$, denoted as $\Gamma = ((\mathbb{G}, \hat{\mathbb{G}}, \mathbb{G}_T), f, g, h, \Sigma)$, where $(\mathbb{G}, \hat{\mathbb{G}}, \mathbb{G}_T)$ are asymmetric bilinear groups of prime order $p > 2^\lambda$ with $f, g, h \leftarrow_\$ \mathbb{G}$ and Σ describes a strongly unforgeable one-time signature scheme used as a subroutine. In addition, select a random element U from $\mathbb{G}$, a PRF family PRF and three hash functions $\mathsf{H}_0 : \{0,1\}^* \to \mathbb{Z}_p$, $\mathsf{H}_1 : \{0,1\}^* \to \mathbb{G}$ and $\mathsf{H}_2 : \{0,1\}^* \to \mathbb{Z}_p$. Define the distribution $\mathcal{Q} := \{0,1\}^\lambda$ and let $(\Gamma, U, \mathsf{PRF}, \mathsf{H}_0, \mathsf{H}_1, \mathsf{H}_2, \mathcal{Q})$ be the system public parameters pp.

Long-Term Secrets. Each party executes the following Long-term Key Generation procedure to generate their own key pairs and share public keys (through PKI, but we drop the details here). We elaborate with the party P_i.

Long-term Key Generation (P_i)

1. $b_i \leftarrow_\$ \{0,1\}, x_{i,b_i} \leftarrow_\$ \mathbb{Z}_p, X_{i,b_i} = g^{x_{i,b_i}}, X_{i,1-b_i} \leftarrow_\$ \mathbb{G}$
3. $\widetilde{H}_i = (X_{i,0}/X_{i,1}, g), \psi_i \leftarrow \mathsf{K}_1(\Gamma, \widetilde{H}_i)$
4. $lek_i := (X_{i,0}, X_{i,1}, \psi_i), ldk_i := (b_i, x_{i,b_i})$ //TB-KEM.Gen(pp) $\to (lek_i, ldk_i)$
5. $\bar{b}_i \leftarrow_\$ \{0,1\}, y_{i,\bar{b}_i} \leftarrow_\$ \mathbb{Z}_p, Y_{i,\bar{b}_i} = g^{y_{i,\bar{b}_i}}, Y_{i,1-\bar{b}_i} \leftarrow_\$ \mathbb{G}$
6. $lvk_i := (Y_{i,0}, Y_{i,1}), lsk_i := (\bar{b}_i, y_{i,\bar{b}_i})$ // SIG.Gen(pp) $\to (lvk_i, lsk_i)$

---

where K_1 is invoked to generate language-specific common reference strings.

Session Execution. If two parties (e.g., P_i and P_j) want to establish a fresh session key, they should execute the following Key Establishment procedure in the next page.

Key Establishment

P_i $\hspace{6cm}$ P_j

1. $\hat{b} \leftarrow_\$ \{0,1\}, w_{\hat{b}} \leftarrow_\$ \mathbb{Z}_p, W_{\hat{b}} = g^{w_{\hat{b}}}$

2. $W_{1-\hat{b}} \leftarrow_\$ \mathbb{G},\ \boxed{ek := (W_0, W_1), dk := (\hat{b}, w_{\hat{b}})}$ $\hspace{1.5cm}$ //wKEM.Gen$(pp) \rightarrow (ek, dk)$

3. $u_i, s_i \leftarrow_\$ \mathbb{Z}_p, U_i = g^{u_i}, S_i = g^{s_i}$

4. $\boxed{vk_i := (U_i, S_i), sk_i := (u_i, s_i)}$ $\hspace{3cm}$ //OTS.Gen$(pp) \rightarrow (vk_i, sk_i)$

5. $r_i \leftarrow_\$ \mathbb{Z}_p, K_i \leftarrow_\$ \mathbb{G}, R_i = g^{r_i}, D_{i,0} = X_{j,0}{}^{r_i} K_i$

6. $D_{i,1} = X_{j,1}{}^{r_i} K_i, \ell_i = (R_i, D_{i,0}, D_{i,1}, vk_i)$

7. $\pi_i \leftarrow \mathsf{P}(\Gamma, \psi_j, \widetilde{T}_i = (D_{i,0}/D_{i,1}, R_i), r_i, \ell_i)$ $\hspace{1.2cm}$ //prove $\widetilde{T}_i \in \mathrm{span}(X_{i,0}/X_{i,1}, g)$

8. $\boxed{c_i := (R_i, D_{i,0}, D_{i,1}, \pi_i)}$ $\hspace{3.5cm}$ //TB-KEM.Enc$(lek_j, vk_i) \rightarrow (c_i, k_i)$

9. $a_{i,0} \leftarrow_\$ \mathbb{Z}_p, E_i = g^{\mathsf{H}_0(ek||c_i)} U^{a_{i,0}}$

10. $a_{i,1} = (s_i - \mathsf{H}_0(E_i))/u_i,\ \boxed{\sigma_{i,1} := (a_{i,0}, a_{i,1})}$ $\hspace{1cm}$ //OTS.Sig$(sk_i, ek||c_i) \rightarrow \sigma_{i,1}$

11. $t \leftarrow_\$ \mathcal{Q}, F_i = \mathsf{H}_1(t, i||j||vk_i||\sigma_{i,1})$

12. $Z_{i,\bar{b}_i} = F_i{}^{y_{i,\bar{b}_i}}, Z_{i,1-\bar{b}_i} \leftarrow_\$ \mathbb{G}$

13. $\eta_i \leftarrow_\$ \mathbb{Z}_p, N_{i,\bar{b}_i} = g^{\eta_i}, \bar{N}_{i,\bar{b}_i} = F_i{}^{\eta_i}$

14. $\alpha_{1-\bar{b}_i}, \rho_{1-\bar{b}_i} \leftarrow_\$ \mathbb{Z}_p, N_{i,1-\bar{b}_i} = g^{\rho_{1-\bar{b}_i}} Y_{1-\bar{b}_i}{}^{\alpha_{1-\bar{b}_i}}$

15. $\bar{N}_{i,1-\bar{b}_i} = F_i{}^{\rho_{1-\bar{b}_i}} Z_{i,1-\bar{b}_i}{}^{\alpha_{1-\bar{b}_i}}$

16. $\alpha_{\bar{b}_i} = \mathsf{H}_2(g, F_i, N_{i,0}, \bar{N}_{i,0}, N_{i,1}, \bar{N}_{i,1}) - \alpha_{1-\bar{b}_i}$

17. $\rho_{\bar{b}_i} = \eta_i - \alpha_{\bar{b}_i} y_{i,\bar{b}_i}$

18. $\boxed{\sigma_{i,2} := (t, Z_{i,0}, Z_{i,1}, \alpha_0, \alpha_1, \rho_0, \rho_1)}$ $\hspace{1cm}$ //SIG.Sig$(lsk_i, i||j||vk_i||\sigma_{i,1}) \rightarrow \sigma_{i,2}$

19. $\xrightarrow{\hspace{2cm} i, j, ek||vk_i||c_i||\sigma_{i,1}||\sigma_{i,2} \hspace{2cm}}$

20. $\hspace{4.5cm} E_i = g^{\mathsf{H}_0(ek||c_i)} U^{a_{i,0}}, F_i = \mathsf{H}_1(t, i||j||vk_i||\sigma_{i,1})$

21. $\hspace{4.5cm} N_{i,0} = g^{\rho_0} Y_{i,0}{}^{\alpha_0}, \bar{N}_{i,0} = F_i{}^{\rho_0} Z_{i,0}{}^{\alpha_0}$

22. $\hspace{4.5cm} N_{i,1} = g^{\rho_1} Y_{i,1}{}^{\alpha_1}, \bar{N}_{i,1} = F_i{}^{\rho_1} Z_{i,1}{}^{\alpha_1}$

23. $\hspace{4.5cm} \textbf{output } \bot \textbf{ if } S_i \neq g^{\mathsf{H}_0(E_i)} U_i{}^{a_{i,1}}$

24. //check the validity of $\sigma_{i,1}$ and $\sigma_{i,2}$ $\hspace{1cm} \textbf{or } \alpha_0 + \alpha_1 \neq \mathsf{H}_2(g, F_i, N_{i,0}, \bar{N}_{i,0}, N_{i,1}, \bar{N}_{i,1})$

25. $\hspace{4.5cm} \textbf{else } v \leftarrow_\$ \mathbb{Z}_p, K \leftarrow_\$ \mathbb{G}, V = g^v$

26. //wKEM.Enc$(ek) \rightarrow (c, k)$ $\hspace{1.7cm} J_0 = W_0{}^v K, J_1 = W_1{}^v K, \boxed{c := (V, J_0, J_1)}$

27. $\hspace{4.5cm} u_j, s_j \leftarrow_\$ \mathbb{Z}_p, U_j = g^{u_j}, S_j = g^{s_j}$

28. //OTS.Gen$(par) \rightarrow (vk_j, sk_j)$ $\hspace{1cm} \boxed{vk_j := (U_j, D_j), sk_j := (u_j, s_j)}$

29. $\hspace{4.5cm} r_j \leftarrow_\$ \mathbb{Z}_p, K_j \leftarrow_\$ \mathbb{G}, R_j = g^{r_j}, D_{j,0} = X_{i,0}{}^{r_j} K_j$

30. $\hspace{4.5cm} D_{j,1} = X_{i,1}{}^{r_j} K_j, \ell_j = (R_j, D_{j,0}, D_{j,1}, vk_j)$

31. //prove $\widetilde{T}_j \in \mathrm{span}(X_{j,0}/X_{j,1}, g)$ $\hspace{0.5cm} \pi_j \leftarrow \mathsf{P}(\Gamma, \psi_i, \widetilde{T}_j = (D_{j,0}/D_{j,1}, R_j), r_j, \ell_j)$

32. //TB-KEM.Enc$(lek_j, ck_i) \rightarrow (c_j, k_j)$ $\hspace{0.3cm} \boxed{c_j := (R_j, D_{j,0}, D_{j,1}, \pi_j)}$

(to be continued)

Key Establishment - continued	
P_i	P_j
33.	$a_{j,0} \leftarrow_\$ \mathbb{Z}_p, E_j = g^{\mathsf{H}_0(ek\|c_i\|c\|c_j)} U^{a_{j,0}}$
34. $//\mathsf{OTS.Sig}(sk_j, ek\|c_i\|c\|c_j) \to \sigma_{j,1}$	$a_{j,1} = (s_j - \mathsf{H}_0(E_j))/u_j,\ \boxed{\sigma_{j,1} := (a_{j,0}, a_{j,1})}$
35.	$\bar{t} \leftarrow_\$ \mathcal{Q}, F_j = \mathsf{H}_1(\bar{t}, i\|j\|vk_j\|\sigma_{j,1})$
36.	$Z_{j,\bar{b}_j} = F_j{}^{y_{j,\bar{b}_j}}, Z_{j,1-\bar{b}_j} \leftarrow_\$ \mathbb{G}$
37.	$\eta_j \leftarrow_\$ \mathbb{Z}_p, N_{j,\bar{b}_j} = g^{\eta_j}, \bar{N}_{j,\bar{b}_j} = F_j{}^{\eta_j}$
38.	$\beta_{1-\bar{b}_j}, \mu_{1-\bar{b}_j} \leftarrow_\$ \mathbb{Z}_p$
39.	$N_{j,1-\bar{b}_j} = g^{\mu_{1-\bar{b}_j}} Y_{1-\bar{b}_j}{}^{\beta_{1-\bar{b}_j}}$
40.	$\bar{N}_{j,1-\bar{b}_j} = F_j{}^{\mu_{1-\bar{b}_j}} Z_{j,1-\bar{b}_j}{}^{\beta_{1-\bar{b}_j}}$
41.	$\beta_{\bar{b}_j} = \mathsf{H}_2(g, F_j, N_{j,0}, \bar{N}_{j,0}, N_{j,1}, \bar{N}_{j,1}) - \beta_{1-\bar{b}_j}$
42.	$\mu_{\bar{b}_j} = \eta_j - \beta_{\bar{b}_j} y_{j,\bar{b}_j}$
43. $//\mathsf{SIG.Sig}(lsk_j, i\|j\|vk_j\|\sigma_{j,1}) \to \sigma_{j,2}$	$\boxed{\sigma_{j,2} := (\bar{t}, Z_{j,0}, Z_{j,1}, \beta_0, \beta_1, \mu_0, \mu_1)}$
44.	$\xleftarrow{\quad i, j, c\|vk_j\|c_j\|\sigma_{j,1}\|\sigma_{j,2} \quad}$
45. $E_j = g^{\mathsf{H}_0(ek\|c_i\|c\|c_j)} U^{a_{i,0}}, F_j = \mathsf{H}_1(\bar{t}, i\|j\|vk_j\|\sigma_{j,1})$	
46. $N_{j,0} = g^{\mu_0} Y_{j,0}{}^{\beta_0}, \bar{N}_{j,0} = F_j{}^{\mu_0} Z_{j,0}{}^{\beta_0}$	
47. $N_{j,1} = g^{\mu_1} Y_{j,1}{}^{\beta_1}, \bar{N}_{j,1} = F_j{}^{\mu_1} Z_{j,1}{}^{\beta_1}$	
48. **output** $\perp$ if $S_j \neq g^{\mathsf{H}_0(E_j)} U_j{}^{a_{j,1}}$	
49. **or** $\beta_0 + \beta_1 \neq \mathsf{H}_2(g, F_j, N_{j,0}, \bar{N}_{j,0}, N_{j,1}, \bar{N}_{j,1})$ //check the validity of $\sigma_{j,1}$ and $\sigma_{j,2}$	
50. **else** $K = J_{\bar{b}}/V^{w_{\bar{b}}}$ //wKEM.Dec$(dk, c) = k$	
51. $\ell_j = (R_j, D_{j,0}, D_{j,1}, vk_j)$	
52. $\xi_j \leftarrow \mathsf{V}(\Gamma, \psi_i, \tilde{T}_j = (D_{j,0}/D_{j,1}, R_j), \pi_j, \ell_j)$	
53. **if** $\xi_j \neq 1$ **and output** $\perp$	
54. **else** $K_j = D_{j,b_i}/R_j{}^{x_{i,b_i}}$ //TB-KEM.Dec$(ldk_i, c_j, vk_j) = k_j$	
55.	$\ell_i = (R_i, D_{i,0}, D_{i,1}, vk_i)$
56.	$\xi_i \leftarrow \mathsf{V}(\Gamma, \psi_j, \tilde{T}_i = (D_{i,0}/D_{i,1}, R_i), \pi_j, \ell_i)$
57.	**if** $\xi_i \neq 1$ **output** $\perp$
58. $//\mathsf{TB\text{-}KEM.Dec}(ldk_j, c_i, vk_i) = k_i$	**else** $K_i = D_{i,b_j}/R_i{}^{x_{j,b_j}}$

$trans = i\|j\|ek\|vk_i\|c_i\|\sigma_{i,1}\|\sigma_{i,2}\|c\|vk_j\|c_j\|\sigma_{j,1}\|\sigma_{j,2}$

$SK = \mathsf{PRF}(K_i, trans) \oplus \mathsf{PRF}(K_j, trans) \oplus \mathsf{PRF}(K, trans)$

where P and V are invoked to generate QA-NIZK proofs and verify the validity of QA-NIZK proofs, respectively.

References

1. Abe, M., David, B., Kohlweiss, M., Nishimaki, R., Ohkubo, M.: Tagged one-time signatures: tight security and optimal tag size. In: Kurosawa, K., Hanaoka, G. (eds.) PKC 2013. LNCS, vol. 7778, pp. 312–331. Springer, Heidelberg (2013). https://doi.org/10.1007/978-3-642-36362-7_20

2. Abe, M., Jutla, C.S., Ohkubo, M., Pan, J., Roy, A., Wang, Y.: Shorter QA-NIZK and SPS with tighter security. In: Galbraith, S.D., Moriai, S. (eds.) ASIACRYPT 2019. LNCS, vol. 11923, pp. 669–699. Springer, Cham (2019). https://doi.org/10.1007/978-3-030-34618-8_23

3. Abe, M., Jutla, C.S., Ohkubo, M., Roy, A.: Improved (almost) tightly-secure simulation-sound QA-NIZK with applications. In: Peyrin, T., Galbraith, S. (eds.) ASIACRYPT 2018. LNCS, vol. 11272, pp. 627–656. Springer, Cham (2018). https://doi.org/10.1007/978-3-030-03326-2_21

4. Attrapadung, N., Hanaoka, G., Yamada, S.: A framework for identity-based encryption with almost tight security. In: Iwata, T., Cheon, J.H. (eds.) ASIACRYPT 2015. LNCS, vol. 9452, pp. 521–549. Springer, Heidelberg (2015). https://doi.org/10.1007/978-3-662-48797-6_22

5. Bader, C., Hofheinz, D., Jager, T., Kiltz, E., Li, Y.: Tightly-secure authenticated key exchange. In: Dodis, Y., Nielsen, J.B. (eds.) TCC 2015. LNCS, vol. 9014, pp. 629–658. Springer, Heidelberg (2015). https://doi.org/10.1007/978-3-662-46494-6_26

6. Bellare, M., Boldyreva, A., Micali, S.: Public-key encryption in a multi-user setting: security proofs and improvements. In: Preneel, B. (ed.) EUROCRYPT 2000. LNCS, vol. 1807, pp. 259–274. Springer, Heidelberg (2000). https://doi.org/10.1007/3-540-45539-6_18

7. Bellare, M., Rogaway, P.: Entity authentication and key distribution. In: Stinson, D.R. (ed.) CRYPTO 1993. LNCS, vol. 773, pp. 232–249. Springer, Heidelberg (1994). https://doi.org/10.1007/3-540-48329-2_21

8. Blazy, O., Kakvi, S.A., Kiltz, E., Pan, J.: Tightly-secure signatures from chameleon hash functions. In: Katz, J. (ed.) PKC 2015. LNCS, vol. 9020, pp. 256–279. Springer, Heidelberg (2015). https://doi.org/10.1007/978-3-662-46447-2_12

9. Boyd, C., Cliff, Y., Gonzalez Nieto, J., Paterson, K.G.: Efficient one-round key exchange in the standard model. In: Mu, Y., Susilo, W., Seberry, J. (eds.) ACISP 2008. LNCS, vol. 5107, pp. 69–83. Springer, Heidelberg (2008). https://doi.org/10.1007/978-3-540-70500-0_6

10. Canetti, R., Halevi, S., Katz, J.: Chosen-ciphertext security from identity-based encryption. In: Cachin, C., Camenisch, J.L. (eds.) EUROCRYPT 2004. LNCS, vol. 3027, pp. 207–222. Springer, Heidelberg (2004). https://doi.org/10.1007/978-3-540-24676-3_13

11. Canetti, R., Krawczyk, H.: Analysis of key-exchange protocols and their use for building secure channels. In: Pfitzmann, B. (ed.) EUROCRYPT 2001. LNCS, vol. 2045, pp. 453–474. Springer, Heidelberg (2001). https://doi.org/10.1007/3-540-44987-6_28

12. Chen, J., Gong, J., Weng, J.: Tightly secure IBE under constant-size master public key. In: Fehr, S. (ed.) PKC 2017. LNCS, vol. 10174, pp. 207–231. Springer, Heidelberg (2017). https://doi.org/10.1007/978-3-662-54365-8_9

13. Chen, J., Wee, H.: Fully, (almost) tightly secure IBE and dual system groups. In: Canetti, R., Garay, J.A. (eds.) CRYPTO 2013. LNCS, vol. 8043, pp. 435–460. Springer, Heidelberg (2013). https://doi.org/10.1007/978-3-642-40084-1_25

14. Cremers, C.: Examining indistinguishability-based security models for key exchange protocols: the case of CK, CK-HMQV, and eCK. In: ASIACCS 2011, pp. 80–91 (2011). https://doi.org/10.1145/1966913.1966925
15. Cremers, C., Feltz, M.: Beyond eCK: perfect forward secrecy under actor compromise and ephemeral-key reveal. In: Foresti, S., Yung, M., Martinelli, F. (eds.) ESORICS 2012. LNCS, vol. 7459, pp. 734–751. Springer, Heidelberg (2012). https://doi.org/10.1007/978-3-642-33167-1_42
16. Fujioka, A., Suzuki, K., Xagawa, K., Yoneyama, K.: Strongly secure authenticated key exchange from factoring, codes, and lattices. In: Fischlin, M., Buchmann, J., Manulis, M. (eds.) PKC 2012. LNCS, vol. 7293, pp. 467–484. Springer, Heidelberg (2012). https://doi.org/10.1007/978-3-642-30057-8_28
17. Gay, R., Hofheinz, D., Kiltz, E., Wee, H.: Tightly CCA-secure encryption without pairings. In: Fischlin, M., Coron, J.-S. (eds.) EUROCRYPT 2016. LNCS, vol. 9665, pp. 1–27. Springer, Heidelberg (2016). https://doi.org/10.1007/978-3-662-49890-3_1
18. Gay, R., Hofheinz, D., Kohl, L.: Kurosawa-desmedt meets tight security. In: Katz, J., Shacham, H. (eds.) CRYPTO 2017. LNCS, vol. 10403, pp. 133–160. Springer, Cham (2017). https://doi.org/10.1007/978-3-319-63697-9_5
19. Gjøsteen, K., Jager, T.: Practical and tightly-secure digital signatures and authenticated key exchange. In: Shacham, H., Boldyreva, A. (eds.) CRYPTO 2018. LNCS, vol. 10992, pp. 95–125. Springer, Cham (2018). https://doi.org/10.1007/978-3-319-96881-0_4
20. Hofheinz, D.: Algebraic partitioning: fully compact and (almost) tightly secure cryptography. In: Kushilevitz, E., Malkin, T. (eds.) TCC 2016. LNCS, vol. 9562, pp. 251–281. Springer, Heidelberg (2016). https://doi.org/10.1007/978-3-662-49096-9_11
21. Hofheinz, D., Jager, T.: Tightly secure signatures and public-key encryption. In: Safavi-Naini, R., Canetti, R. (eds.) CRYPTO 2012. LNCS, vol. 7417, pp. 590–607. Springer, Heidelberg (2012). https://doi.org/10.1007/978-3-642-32009-5_35
22. Krawczyk, H.: HMQV: a high-performance secure Diffie-Hellman protocol. In: Shoup, V. (ed.) CRYPTO 2005. LNCS, vol. 3621, pp. 546–566. Springer, Heidelberg (2005). https://doi.org/10.1007/11535218_33
23. LaMacchia, B., Lauter, K., Mityagin, A.: Stronger security of authenticated key exchange. In: Susilo, W., Liu, J.K., Mu, Y. (eds.) ProvSec 2007. LNCS, vol. 4784, pp. 1–16. Springer, Heidelberg (2007). https://doi.org/10.1007/978-3-540-75670-5_1
24. Libert, B., Peters, T., Joye, M., Yung, M.: Non-malleability from malleability: simulation-sound quasi-adaptive NIZK proofs and CCA2-secure encryption from homomorphic signatures. In: Nguyen, P.Q., Oswald, E. (eds.) EUROCRYPT 2014. LNCS, vol. 8441, pp. 514–532. Springer, Heidelberg (2014). https://doi.org/10.1007/978-3-642-55220-5_29
25. Libert, B., Peters, T., Joye, M., Yung, M.: Compactly hiding linear spans - tightly secure constant-size simulation-sound QA-NIZK proofs and applications. In: Iwata, T., Cheon, J.H. (eds.) ASIACRYPT 2015. LNCS, vol. 9452, pp. 681–707. Springer, Heidelberg (2015). https://doi.org/10.1007/978-3-662-48797-6_28
26. Naor, M., Yung, M.: Public-key cryptosystems provably secure against chosen ciphertext attacks. In: STOC 1990, pp. 427–437 (1990). https://doi.org/10.1145/100216.100273
27. Sahai, A.: Non-malleable non-interactive zero knowledge and adaptive chosen-ciphertext security. In: FOCS 1999, pp. 543–553 (1999). https://doi.org/10.1109/SFFCS.1999.814628

28. Strangio, M.A.: On the resilience of key agreement protocols to key compromise impersonation. In: Atzeni, A.S., Lioy, A. (eds.) EuroPKI 2006. LNCS, vol. 4043, pp. 233–247. Springer, Heidelberg (2006). https://doi.org/10.1007/11774716_19
29. Wei, P., Wang, W., Zhu, B., Yiu, S.M.: Tightly-secure encryption in the multi-user, multi-challenge setting with improved efficiency. In: Pieprzyk, J., Suriadi, S. (eds.) ACISP 2017. LNCS, vol. 10342, pp. 3–22. Springer, Cham (2017). https://doi.org/10.1007/978-3-319-60055-0_1
30. Xue, H., Lu, X., Li, B., Liang, B., He, J.: Understanding and constructing AKE via double-key key encapsulation mechanism. In: Peyrin, T., Galbraith, S. (eds.) ASIACRYPT 2018. LNCS, vol. 11273, pp. 158–189. Springer, Cham (2018). https://doi.org/10.1007/978-3-030-03329-3_6

Symmetric-Key Authenticated Key Exchange (SAKE) with Perfect Forward Secrecy

Gildas Avoine[1,2], Sébastien Canard[3], and Loïc Ferreira[1,3(✉)]

[1] Univ Rennes, INSA Rennes, CNRS, IRISA, Rennes, France
gildas.avoine@irisa.fr
[2] Institut Universitaire de France, Paris, France
[3] Orange Labs, Applied Crypto Group, Caen, France
{sebastien.canard,loic.ferreira}@orange.com

Abstract. Key exchange protocols in the asymmetric-key setting are known to provide stronger security properties than protocols in symmetric-key cryptography. In particular, they can provide *perfect forward secrecy*, as illustrated by key exchange protocols based on the Diffie-Hellman scheme. However public-key algorithms are too heavy for low-resource devices, which can then not benefit from forward secrecy. In this paper, we describe a scheme that solves this issue. Using a shrewd resynchronisation technique, we propose an authenticated key exchange protocol in the symmetric-key setting that guarantees perfect forward secrecy. We prove that the protocol is sound, and provide a formal proof of its security.

Keywords: Authenticated key agreement · Symmetric-key cryptography · Perfect forward secrecy · Key-evolving

1 Introduction

An authenticated key exchange (AKE) protocol executed between two parties aims at authenticating the parties, and computing a fresh shared session key. Well-known two-party authenticated key exchange protocols make use of digital signatures to provide authentication, and apply the Diffie-Hellman (DH) scheme [20] to compute a shared session key. However, such protocols are too heavy for low-resource devices. More suited protocols, solely based on symmetric-key functions, have been proposed (e.g., [12,16,23,26,29,30,33,34] to cite a few), including widely deployed ones (e.g., in 3G/UMTS [2] and 4G/LTE [3]). Such symmetric-key protocols are needed in various applications, ranging from Wireless Sensor Networks (WSNs), Radio Frequency Identification (RFID) tags, smart cards, Controller Area Networks (CANs) for vehicular systems, smart home, up to industrial Internet of Things (IoT). Yet, existing symmetric-key based protocols lack a fundamental security property usually provided by the

S. Jarecki (Ed.): CT-RSA 2020, LNCS 12006, pp. 199–224, 2020.
https://doi.org/10.1007/978-3-030-40186-3_10

DH scheme: *perfect forward secrecy* (PFS) [21,24]. PFS is a very strong form of long-term security which, informally, guarantees that future disclosures of some long-term secret keys do not compromise past session keys. It is widely accepted that PFS can only be provided by asymmetric schemes. Indeed, in protocols based on symmetric-key functions, the two parties must share a long-term symmetric key (which the session keys are computed from). Therefore the disclosure of this static long-term key allows an adversary to compute all the past (and future) session keys. In this paper, we introduce an AKE protocol in the *symmetric-key* setting, and, yet, that does guarantee PFS.

1.1   Related Work

Symmetric-key based protocols do not provide the same security guarantees as those based on asymmetric algorithms. In particular, they do not guarantee forward secrecy. Nonetheless, (a few) attempts aim at proposing symmetric-key protocols that incorporate forward secrecy, as illustrated by the following related work.

Dousti and Jalili [22] describe a key exchange protocol where the shared master key is updated based on time. Their protocol requires perfect synchronicity between the parties otherwise this leads to two main consequences. Firstly, in order to handle the key exchange messages, the parties may use different values of the master key corresponding to consecutive epochs, which causes the session to abort. Secondly, this allows an adversary to trivially break forward secrecy. Once a party deems the protocol run is correct and the session key can be safely used (i.e., once the party "accepts"), the adversary corrupts its partner (which still owns the previous, not updated yet, master key), and computes the current session key. Furthermore, achieving perfect time synchronisation may be quite complex in any context, in particular for low-resource devices. Contrary to Dousti et al., the protocol we propose explicitly deals with the issue of updating the master keys at both parties without requiring any additional functionality (such as a synchronised clock).

In the RFID field, the protocol proposed by Le, Burmester, and de Medeiros [28] aims at authenticating a tag to a server, and at computing a session key in order to establish a secure channel (which they do not describe). The master key is updated throughout the protocol run. To deal with the possible desynchronisation between the reader and the tag, the server keeps two consecutive values of the key: the current and the previous one. If the tag does not update its master key (which happens when the last message is dropped), the server is able to catch up during the next session. This implies that, in case of desynchronisation, the server computes the session key from the updated master key, whereas the tag still stores the previous value. Hence, an adversary that corrupts the tag can compute the previous session key with respect to the server. In fact, since the server always keeps the previous value of the master key, together with the current one, the scheme is intrinsically insecure in strong security models (i.e., models that allow the adversary to corrupt any of the partners, once the targeted party accepts). Yet, Le et al. analyse their protocol in a model where any server corruption is forbidden, and corrupting a tag is allowed only once it accepts. In our scheme, one of the parties also keeps in memory (a few) samples of a master key corresponding to different epochs (including a previous one). Yet the disclosure of all these values does *not* compromise past session keys. Furthermore, the (strong) security model we use allows the adversary to corrupt either partner as soon as the targeted party accepts.

Brier and Peyrin [17] propose a forward secret key derivation scheme in a client-server setting, that aims at improving a previous proposal [7]. In addition to forward secrecy, another constraint is that the amount of calculation to compute the master key (directly used as encryption key) on the server side must be low. Their solution implies the storage, on the client side, of several keys in parallel and to use a (short) counter, which is involved in the keys update. The keys belong to a tree whose each leaf (key) is derived from the previous one and the counter. The client must send the counter with the encrypted message for the server to be able to compute the corresponding key. The main drawback of this scheme is that the number of possible encryption keys is reduced. Increasing that limit implies increasing the counter size and the number of keys stored in parallel on the client side. Moreover, Brier et al. (as well as [7]) focus on forward secrecy with respect to the client only. The server is deemed as incorruptible, and is supposed to compute an encryption key only upon reception of a client's message (the secure channel is unidirectional, and the server does not need to send encrypted messages to the client). Therefore, the scheme does not need to deal with the issue of *both* parties being in sync (with respect to the key computation), and providing forward secrecy. In addition, the purpose of Brier et al. (as well as [7]) is not to provide mutual authentication. More generally sending additional information in order to resynchronise (such as a sufficiently large counter) is a simple (and inefficient) way to build a forward secret protocol. But this yields several drawbacks. Firstly, the size of such a counter must be large enough in order to avoid any exhaustion. Secondly, sending the counter (at least periodically) is necessary for the two parties to resynchronise, which consumes bandwidth. Thirdly, resynchronisation may imply multiple updates of the master keys at once (the scheme of Brier et al. and [7] aims at limiting that amount of calculation, but it leads to a narrowed number of possible encryption keys). Our scheme avoids all these drawbacks.

The more general question of forward security in symmetric cryptography has been also investigated by Bellare and Yee [14]. They propose formal definitions and practical constructions of forward secure primitives (e.g., MAC, symmetric encryption algorithm). Their constructions protect against decryption of past messages, or antedated forgeries of messages (i.e., previously authenticated messages are made untrustworthy). Their algorithms are based on key-evolving schemes [10]. Nonetheless, Bellare et al. consider only algorithms (but not protocols) and they do not deal with the issue of synchronising the evolution of the shared key at *both* parties. That is, they propose out-of-context (non-interactive) solutions with respect to our purpose.

Abdalla and Bellare [4] investigate a related question which is "re-keying". Their formal analysis show that appropriate re-keying techniques "increase" the lifetime of a key. They consider re-keying in the context of symmetric encryption (in order to thwart attacks based on the ability to get lots of encrypted messages under the same key), and forward security (in order to protect past keys). Yet, they confine their analysis to algorithms and not protocols. Hence, as Bellare et al. [14], they do not treat the synchronisation issues that arise from evolving a shared symmetric key.

The Signal messaging protocol [1] uses a key derivation scheme called "double ratchet algorithm" [31]. This scheme combines a DH based mechanism with a symmetric key-evolving mechanism (based on a one-way function). The first mechanism provides an asymmetric ratchet, whereas the second provides a symmetric ratchet. The asymmetric ratchet is applied when a fresh DH share is received (included in an application message) from the peer. The symmetric ratchet is applied when a party wants to send several successive messages without new incoming message from its partner. Thanks to the DH scheme, the asymmetric ratchet is supposed to provide forward secrecy.[1] Regarding the symmetric ratchet, each party is compelled to store the decryption keys of the not yet received messages. This is due to the asynchronous nature of the Signal protocol. Therefore, the symmetric ratchet in Signal does not provide forward secrecy, as stated in their security analysis by Cohn-Gordon, Cremers, Dowling, Garratt, and Stebila [19]: "*old but unused receiving keys are stored at the peer for an implementation dependent length of time, trading off forward security for transparent handling of outdated messages. This of course weakens the forward secrecy of the keys*". Consequently, Cohn-Gordon et al. choose not to model this weakened property. In turn, Alwen, Coretti, and Dodis [6] incorporate the latter in the security analysis of their "generalised Signal protocol". But the crucial difference in their notion of forward security is that, as soon as the receiver is compromised, no more security can be provided. On the contrary, we tackle the synchronisation issue, and solve it in our protocol. The security model we use captures forward secrecy and allows corrupting a party and its partner as soon as the targeted party "accepts" (i.e., deems the session key can be safely used). With regard to Signal, our protocol can be compared to the asymmetric ratchet (in synchronous mode), and yet does not implement asymmetric functions.

We stress that the goals of several of the aforementioned protocols are not the same as ours. Nonetheless, the small number of existing symmetric-key protocols that provide forward secrecy, and the lukewarm security level they achieve illustrate that combining symmetric-key cryptography and (a strong form of) forward secrecy is a non-trivial task.

1.2 Contributions

We describe the SAKE protocol, a two-party authenticated key exchange protocol in the *symmetric-key* setting with the following characteristics.

---

[1] In Signal, the DH exchanges can be asynchronous. This impairs the forward secrecy property usually ensured by this scheme.

- It guarantees forward secrecy.
- It is self-synchronising. That is, after a correct and complete session (and whatever the internal state of the parties prior to the session), the two parties involved in the protocol run share a new session key, and their internal state is updated and synchronised.
- It allows establishing an (virtually) unlimited number of sessions (as opposite to symmetric-key protocols that make use of a predefined list of master keys, each being used once only).
- The amount of calculation done by both parties in a single protocol run is strictly bounded. In particular we avoid the need of sending additional information in order to resynchronise, such as a (sufficiently large) counter that keeps track of the evolution of the master keys, and the subsequent drawbacks: periodically doing a great amount of computations at once (when resynchronisation is necessary), and consuming bandwidth (to transmit the additional data).

In addition, we provide a formal security proof for SAKE. We also present a complementary mode of SAKE (that we call SAKE-AM) which is an "aggressive mode" of the protocol. This mode inverts the role of the initiator and the responder in terms of calculations (in SAKE, the initiator performs – at most – two additional MAC computations compared to the responder). Using SAKE and SAKE-AM together results in an implementation (gathering all the aforementioned properties, starting with the forward secrecy property) that allows any party to be either initiator or responder of a session, and such that the smallest amount of calculation is always done by the same party. This is particularly convenient in the context of a set of (low-resource) end-devices communicating with a central server. In such a case, the end-device supports the smallest amount of calculation, whereas either the server or the end-device can initiate a session.

1.3   Our Approach

Key Concepts. The authenticated key exchange protocol we propose is *solely* based on symmetric-key functions. Not only does it provide mutual authentication and key agreement, but it guarantees perfect forward secrecy. We attain this very strong form of long-term security by using a key-evolving scheme. As soon as two parties make a shared (symmetric) key evolve, a synchronisation problem arises. We provide a simple and efficient solution to this issue. We require using neither a clock, nor an additional resynchronising procedure. Our solution is based on a second (independent) chain of master keys. These keys allow tracking the evolution of the internal state, and resynchronising the parties if necessary. The parties authenticate each other prior to updating their master keys. Hence the possible gap is bounded (as we prove it), and each party is always able to catch up in case of desynchronisation (of course, if the session is correct and complete). Mutual authentication, key exchange (with forward secrecy), and resynchronisation are done in the continuity of the protocol run.

Our protocol is based on two symmetric master keys: a derivation master key K and an authentication master key K'. The protocol makes use of symmetric-key functions only. Each pair of parties (A, B) shares distinct master keys. The main lines of the protocol are as follows. The two parties exchange pseudo-random values r_A, r_B which are used to

- authenticate each other: each party sends back the value it has received in a message that is MAC-ed with the authentication master key K'. For instance, if B receives r_A it replies with $r_B \| \tau_B$ where $\tau_B = \mathsf{Mac}(K', B\|A\|r_B\|r_A)$.
- Compute a session key: a pseudo-random function KDF is keyed with the derivation master key K and uses the pseudo-random values as input. That is, $sk \leftarrow \mathsf{KDF}(K, f(r_A, r_B))$. $f(r_A, r_B)$ is deliberately left undefined, and designates an operation between r_A and r_B such as the concatenation or the bitwise addition.

Providing Forward Secrecy. The shared key K is used to compute the session keys. If this key remains unchanged throughout all protocol runs, its disclosure allows computing all past (and future) session keys. To solve this issue we apply a key-evolving technique. We update the master key such that a previous master key cannot be computed from an updated one. Each of the two parties involved in a session updates its own copy of the derivation master key K with a non-invertible function update: $K \leftarrow \mathsf{update}(K)$. Hence this protects past sessions in case the (current value of) master key K is revealed. Each party authenticates its peer prior to updating the derivation master key. If the master key is updated throughout the session, it may happen that one of the two involved parties update its master key whereas the other does not. This leads to a *synchronisation problem*.

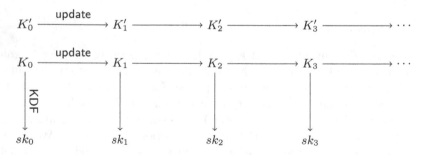

Fig. 1. Master key chains in SAKE. At epoch j, the initiator stores four keys: $K = K_j$, and K'_{j-1}, K'_j, K'_{j+1}. The responder stores two keys: $K = K_j$ and $K' = K'_j$. (Illustration with $j = 2$)

The Synchronisation Problem. If two parties use a different key K, they are obviously not able to compute a shared session key. Hence they must resynchronise first. More fundamentally, if a party initiates a session with some derivation master key K, and its partner stores a master key corresponding to an earlier epoch, then an adversary that corrupts the partner can compute past session keys with respect to the initiator, hence trivially break forward secrecy. Therefore, it is of paramount importance that the parties know if the master key of its partner has actually been updated. We provide a solution to both issues in the continuity of a *single* session. In particular, no extra procedure is needed in order for a desynchronised party to catch up. We avoid the need of sending additional information in order to resynchronise, such as a (sufficiently large) counter that keeps track of the evolution of the master keys, and the subsequent drawbacks: periodically doing a great amount of computations at once (when resynchronisation is necessary), and consuming bandwidth (to transmit the additional data). We base our solution on the second master key K' used to authenticate the messages exchanged during a session. The solution is to update K' at the same time as K (see Fig. 1). Therefore the evolution of K' follows that of K. The party that receives the first authenticated message uses the MAC tag to learn which epoch the sender belongs to. Of course, K' can also be desynchronised in the same way as K. This is why, whereas one party (responder B) stores only one sample of the key K', the other party (initiator A) stores several samples of the authentication master key K' corresponding to several consecutive epochs. We *prove* that only three keys K'_{j+1}, K'_j, K'_{j-1}, corresponding respectively to the next, the current, and the previous epochs, are sufficient in order for A and B to resynchronise. The initiator (A) is the one able to deal with the synchronisation issue, and consequently tells B how to behave. Each party "accepts" only after it has received a confirmation (final MAC-ed messages) that its partner has already updated its own master keys. In such a case, the party ending in accepting state deems that the fresh session key can be safely used. Otherwise (in particular when the parties are desynchronised), the session key is discarded.

Since two independent master keys are used (authentication and session key derivation), one can safely maintain a copy of K' corresponding to an earlier epoch (K'_{j-1}) without risk of threatening forward secrecy. Only one sample of the derivation master key K is kept: the most up-to-date.

1.4   Outline of the Paper

In Sect. 2 we detail the security model used to analyse the protocol we propose. Our authenticated key exchange protocol in symmetric-key setting with forward secrecy is described in Sect. 3. In Sect. 4, we investigate the feasibility of a variant based on our protocol. Formal proofs of soundness and security for the main protocol are presented in Sect. 5. The differences between our approach and the DH scheme are highlighted in Sect. 6. Finally, we conclude in Sect. 7.

2   Security Model

Before describing our symmetric-key protocol in Sect. 3 (which is self-sufficient and contains all the specifics required to understand the protocol), we present in this section the security model that we employ to formally prove its security.

In a nutshell, we use the model for authenticated key exchange protocols described by Brzuska, Jacobsen, and Stebila [18]. This model incorporates all the features that are usually considered when analysing key agreement protocols in the public-key setting (e.g., DH-based protocols with signature). In this model, the adversary has full control over the communication network. It can forward, alter, drop any message exchanged by honest parties, or insert new messages. Brzuska et al.'s model then captures adaptive corruptions but also perfect forward secrecy. This appears in the definition of the security experiment.

2.1   Execution Environment

In this section, we present the security model for authenticated key exchange protocols described by Brzuska et al. [18], and reuse the corresponding notation.

Parties. A two-party protocol is carried out by a set of parties $\mathcal{P} = \{P_0, \ldots, P_{n-1}\}$. Each party P_i has an associated long-term key ltk. Each pair of parties shares a distinct key ltk.[2]

Instances. Each party can take part in multiple sequential executions of the protocol. We prohibit *parallel* executions of the protocol. Indeed, since the protocol we propose is based on shared *evolving* symmetric keys, running multiple instances in parallel may cause some executions to abort (we elaborate more on this in Sect. 6). This is the only restriction we demand compared to AKE security models used in the public-key setting.

Each run of the protocol is called a session. To each session of a party P_i, an instance π_i^s is associated which embodies this (local) session's execution of the protocol, and has access to the long-term key of the party. In addition, each instance maintains the following state specific to the session.

- ρ: the role $\rho \in \{\mathsf{init}, \mathsf{resp}\}$ of the session in the protocol execution, being either the initiator or the responder.
- pid: the identity pid $\in \mathcal{P}$ of the intended communication partner of π_i^s.
- α: the state $\alpha \in \{\bot, \mathtt{running}, \mathtt{accepted}, \mathtt{rejected}\}$ of the instance.
- sk: the session key derived by π_i^s.
- κ: the status $\kappa \in \{\bot, \mathtt{revealed}\}$ of the session key π_i^s.sk.
- sid: the identifier of the session.
- b: a random bit $\mathsf{b} \in \{0, 1\}$ sampled at initialisation of π_i^s.

We put the following correctness requirements on the variables α, sk, sid and pid. For any two instances π_i^s, π_j^t, the following must hold:

$$(\pi_i^s.\alpha = \mathtt{accepted}) \Rightarrow (\pi_i^s.\mathsf{sk} \neq \bot \wedge \pi_i^s.\mathsf{sid} \neq \bot) \tag{1}$$

$$\left(\pi_i^s.\alpha = \pi_j^t.\alpha = \mathtt{accepted} \wedge \pi_i^s.\mathsf{sid} = \pi_j^t.\mathsf{sid}\right) \Rightarrow \begin{cases} \pi_i^s.\mathsf{sk} = \pi_j^t.\mathsf{sk} \\ \pi_i^s.\mathsf{pid} = P_j \\ \pi_j^t.\mathsf{pid} = P_i \end{cases} \tag{2}$$

---

[2] Note that ltk can be a set of master keys (e.g., each one used by the party for a different purpose).

Adversarial Queries. The adversary $\mathcal{A}$ is assumed to control the network, and interacts with the instances by issuing the following queries to them.

- NewSession$(P_i, \rho, \mathsf{pid})$: this query creates a new instance π_i^s at party P_i, having role ρ, and intended partner pid.
- Send(π_i^s, m): this query allows the adversary to send any message m to π_i^s. If $\pi_i^s.\alpha \neq \mathtt{running}$, it returns $\bot$. Otherwise π_i^s responds according to the protocol specification.
- Corrupt(P_i): this query returns the long-term key $P_i.\mathsf{ltk}$ of P_i. If Corrupt(P_i) is the ν-th query issued by the adversary, then we say that P_i is ν-*corrupted*. For a party that has not been corrupted, we define $\nu = +\infty$.
- Reveal(π_i^s): this query returns the session key $\pi_i^s.\mathsf{sk}$, and $\pi_i^s.\kappa$ is set to $\mathtt{revealed}$.
- Test(π_i^s): this query may be asked only once throughout the game. If $\pi_i^s.\alpha \neq \mathtt{accepted}$, then it returns $\bot$. Otherwise it samples an independent key $sk_0 \xleftarrow{\$} \mathcal{K}$, and returns sk_b, where $sk_1 = \pi_i^s.\mathsf{sk}$. The key sk_b is called the Test-*challenge*.

Definition 1 (Partnership). *Two instances π_i^s and π_j^t are partners if $\pi_i^s.\mathsf{sid} = \pi_j^t.\mathsf{sid}$.*

Definition 2 (Freshness). *An instance π_i^s is said to be* fresh *with intended partner P_j, if*

(a) $\pi_i^s.\alpha = \mathtt{accepted}$ and $\pi_i^s.\mathsf{pid} = P_j$ when $\mathcal{A}$ issues its ν_0-th query,
(b) $\pi_i^s.\kappa \neq \mathtt{revealed}$ and P_i is ν-corrupted with $\nu_0 < \nu$, and
(c) for any partner instance π_j^t of π_i^s, we have that $\pi_j^t.\kappa \neq \mathtt{revealed}$ and P_j is ν'-corrupted with $\nu_0 < \nu'$.

Note that the notion of freshness incorporates a requirement for forward secrecy.

An *authenticated key exchange protocol* (AKE) is a two-party protocol satisfying the correctness requirements 1 and 2, and where the security is defined in terms of an AKE experiment played between a challenger and an adversary. This experiment uses the execution environment described above. The adversary can win the AKE experiment in one of two ways: (i) by making an instance accept maliciously, or (ii) by guessing the secret bit of the Test-instance.

Definition 3 (Entity Authentication (EA)). *An instance π_i^s of a protocol Π is said to have* accepted maliciously *in the AKE security experiment with intended partner P_j, if*

(a) $\pi_i^s.\alpha = \mathtt{accepted}$ and $\pi_i^s.\mathsf{pid} = P_j$ when $\mathcal{A}$ issues its ν_0-th query,
(b) P_i and P_j are ν- and ν'-corrupted with $\nu_0 < \nu, \nu'$, and
(c) there is no unique instance π_j^t such that π_i^s and π_j^t are partners.

The adversary's advantage is defined as its winning probability:

$$\mathsf{adv}_{\Pi}^{\mathsf{ent\text{-}auth}}(\mathcal{A}) = \Pr[\mathcal{A} \text{ wins the EA game}].$$

Definition 4 (Key Indistinguishability). *An adversary $\mathcal{A}$ against a protocol* Π*, that issues its* Test*-query to instance* π_i^s *during the AKE security experiment, answers the* Test*-challenge correctly if it terminates with output* b'*, such that*

(a) π_i^s *is fresh with some intended partner* P_j*, and*
(b) $\pi_i^s.\mathsf{b} = b'$*.*

The adversary's advantage is defined as

$$\mathsf{adv}_\Pi^{\mathsf{key\text{-}ind}}(\mathcal{A}) = \left| \Pr[\pi_i^s.\mathsf{b} = b'] - \frac{1}{2} \right|.$$

Definitions 3 and 4 allow the adversary to corrupt an instance involved in the security experiment (once the targeted instance has accepted, in order to exclude trivial attacks). Therefore, protocols secure with respect to Definition 5 below provide *perfect forward secrecy*. Note that we do not allow the targeted instance to be corrupted before it accepts. This security model does not capture key-compromise impersonation attacks (KCI) [15] since that would allow trivially breaking key exchange protocols solely based on shared symmetric keys.

Definition 5 (AKE Security). *We say that a two-party protocol* Π *is a secure AKE protocol if* Π *satisfies the correctness requirements 1 and 2, and for all probabilistic polynomial time adversary* $\mathcal{A}$*,* $\mathsf{adv}_\Pi^{\mathsf{ent\text{-}auth}}(\mathcal{A})$ *and* $\mathsf{adv}_\Pi^{\mathsf{key\text{-}ind}}(\mathcal{A})$ *are a negligible function of the security parameter.*

2.2 Security Definitions of SAKE's Building Blocks

In this section, we recall the definitions of the main security notions we use in our results. The security definition of a pseudo-random function is taken from Bellare, Desai, Jokipii, and Rogaway [9], and that of a MAC strongly unforgeable under chosen-message attacks from Bellare and Namprempre [11]. We recall also the definition of matching conversations initially proposed by Bellare and Rogaway [12], and modified by Jager, Kohlar, Schäge, and Schwenk [27].

Secure PRF. A *pseudo-random function* (PRF) F is a deterministic algorithm which given a key $K \in \{0,1\}^\lambda$ and a bit string $x \in \{0,1\}^*$ outputs a string $y = F(K,x) \in \{0,1\}^\gamma$ (with γ being polynomial in λ). Let $Func$ be the set of all functions of domain $\{0,1\}^*$ and range $\{0,1\}^\gamma$. The security of a PRF is defined with the following experiment between a challenger and an adversary $\mathcal{A}$:

1. The challenger samples $K \xleftarrow{\$} \{0,1\}^\lambda$, $G \xleftarrow{\$} Func$, and $b \xleftarrow{\$} \{0,1\}$ uniformly at random.
2. The adversary may adaptively query values x to the challenger. The challenger replies to each query with either $y = F(K,x)$ if $b = 1$, or $y = G(x)$ if $b = 0$.
3. Finally, the adversary outputs its guess $b' \in \{0,1\}$ of b.

The adversary's advantage is defined as

$$\mathsf{adv}_F^{\mathsf{prf}}(\mathcal{A}) = \left| \Pr[b = b'] - \frac{1}{2} \right|.$$

Definition 6 (Secure PRF). *A function* $F\colon\{0,1\}^\lambda \times \{0,1\}^* \to \{0,1\}^\gamma$ *is said to be a* secure pseudo-random function (PRF) *if, for all probabilistic polynomial time adversary* $\mathcal{A}$*,* $\mathsf{adv}_F^{\mathsf{prf}}(\mathcal{A})$ *is a negligible function in* λ*.*

Secure MAC. A message authentication code (MAC) consists of two algorithms (Mac, Vrf). The tagging algorithm Mac takes as input a key $K \in \{0,1\}^k$ and a message $m \in \{0,1\}^*$ and returns a tag $\tau \in \{0,1\}^\gamma$ (with γ being polynomial in k). The verification algorithm Vrf takes as input the key K, a message m, and a candidate tag τ for m. It outputs 1 if τ is a valid tag on message m with respect to K. Otherwise, it returns 0. The notion of *strong unforgeability under chosen-message attacks* (SUF-CMA) for a MAC $G = (\mathsf{Mac}, \mathsf{Vrf})$ is defined with the following experiment between a challenger and an adversary $\mathcal{A}$:

1. The challenger samples $K \overset{\$}{\leftarrow} \{0,1\}^k$, and sets $S \leftarrow \emptyset$.
2. The adversary may adaptively query values m to the challenger. The challenger replies to each query with $\tau = \mathsf{Mac}(K, m)$ and records (m, τ): $S \leftarrow S \cup \{(m, \tau)\}$.
   In addition, the adversary may adaptively query values (m', τ') to the challenger. The challenger replies to each query with $\mathsf{Vrf}(K, m', \tau')$.
3. Finally, the adversary sends (m^*, τ^*) to the challenger.

The adversary's advantage is defined as

$$\mathsf{adv}_G^{\mathsf{suf\text{-}cma}}(\mathcal{A}) = \Pr[\mathsf{Vrf}(K, m^*, \tau^*) = 1 \wedge (m^*, \tau^*) \notin S].$$

Definition 7 (SUF-CMA). *A message authentication code* $G = (\mathsf{Mac}, \mathsf{Vrf})$ *with* $\mathsf{Mac}\colon\{0,1\}^k \times \{0,1\}^* \to \{0,1\}^\gamma$ *is said to be* strongly unforgeable under chosen-message attacks *(SUF-CMA) if, for all probabilistic polynomial time adversary* $\mathcal{A}$*,* $\mathsf{adv}_G^{\mathsf{suf\text{-}cma}}(\mathcal{A})$ *is a negligible function in* k*.*

Matching Conversations. Let $T_{i,s}$ be the sequence of all (valid) messages sent and received by an instance π_i^s in chronological order. For two transcripts $T_{i,s}$ and $T_{j,t}$, we say that $T_{i,s}$ is a prefix of $T_{j,t}$ if $T_{i,s}$ contains at least one message, and the messages in $T_{i,s}$ are identical to the first $|T_{i,s}|$ messages of $T_{j,t}$.

Definition 8 (Matching Conversations). *We say that* π_i^s *has a matching conversation to* π_j^t*, if*

- π_i^s *has sent all protocol messages and* $T_{j,t}$ *is a prefix of* $T_{i,s}$*, or*
- π_j^t *has sent all protocol messages and* $T_{i,s} = T_{j,t}$*.*

3 Our Symmetric-Key AKE Protocol with Perfect Forward Secrecy

In this section we describe our main protocol. Although all the calculations are based on shared master keys, forward secrecy is guaranteed by using a key-evolving scheme. More precisely, we use two types of keys: one to compute the session keys, the other to authenticate messages and resynchronise when necessary. This second type of keys allows tracking the master keys evolution, and limit the gap (in terms of keys update) between both parties. Mutual authentication, key exchange, and synchronised update of the master keys are done in the same session.

3.1 Description of the Protocol

The protocol is depicted by Fig. 2. The parameter δ_{AB} computed by A corresponds to the gap between A and B with respect to the evolution of the master keys. We prove that $\delta_{AB} \in \{-1, 0, 1\}$ (see Sect. 5.1). That is, A can only be either *one step* behind, or in sync, or *one step* ahead to B. During a session, A uses the keys K'_j, K'_{j-1}, K'_{j+1} (by order of likelihood) and the first message (m_B) sent by B to learn δ_{AB}. The message m_B is computed with the current value K' of B. Therefore m_B indicates the current synchronisation state of B. Then A informs B. One bit ϵ is enough (message m_A) because B takes two behaviours only: if $\delta_{AB} \in \{-1, 0\}$ ($\epsilon = 0$), and if $\delta_{AB} = 1$ ($\epsilon = 1$). A and B behave as follows.

- If A is in sync with B ($\delta_{AB} = 0$), A computes the new session key, and updates its master keys. Then, upon reception of m_A, B does the same.
- If A is in advance ($\delta_{AB} = 1$), A waits for B to resynchronise (i.e., B updates its master keys a first time), and to proceed with the regular operations (i.e., B computes the new session key, and updates its master keys a second time). Then, once A receives a confirmation that B is synchronised (message τ'_B), A performs the regular operations as well (session key computation, master keys update). Since A waits for B to resynchronise before proceeding, the gap between the parties is *bounded* (as proved in Sect. 5.1).
- If A is late ($\delta_{AB} = -1$), it resynchronises (i.e., it updates its master keys a first time), and then performs the regular operations (session key computation, master keys update). Then (upon reception of message m_A), B applies the regular operations.

Once a correct and complete session ends, three goals are achieved in the *same* protocol run: (i) the two parties have updated their master keys, (ii) they are synchronised (which stems in particular from the fact that the gap between A and B is bounded, i.e., $|\delta_{AB}| \leq 1$), and (iii) they share a new session key. In other words, the protocol is *self-synchronising*.

Before the first session between A and B, the master keys are initialised as follows:

1. K and K' are uniformly chosen at random.
2. $K'_{j-1} \leftarrow \perp$
3. $K'_j \leftarrow K'$
4. $K'_{j+1} \leftarrow \mathsf{update}(K')$

Since K'_{j+1} and K'_j can be computed from K'_{j-1}, it is possible to store only K'_{j-1}, and to compute the two other keys when necessary during the session. Then, with respect to the security model presented in Sect. 2, the long-term key of A and B corresponds respectively to $A.\mathsf{ltk} = (K, K'_{j-1})$ and $B.\mathsf{ltk} = (K, K')$.

Although this does not appear explicitly in Fig. 2, a party aborts the session if it receives a message computed with an invalid identity. For the responder B an invalid identity corresponds to an initiator party A it does not share master keys with. For an initiator A, the particular case $B = A$, among other possibilities, yields an error (each party must have a distinct identity).

Number of Rounds. The session can be reduced from five to four messages in some cases. Indeed, regarding the synchronisation state, in two cases (when $\delta_{AB} \in \{-1, 0\}$, that is $\epsilon = 0$), A and B are synchronised, and share a session key once B has received message m_A and executed the subsequent operations. Therefore, in such a case, the session can end upon reception of message τ'_B by A. More precisely

- if $\delta_{AB} = 1$ ($\epsilon = 1$), then A accepts upon reception of τ'_B, and B accepts upon reception of τ'_A;
- if $\delta_{AB} \in \{-1, 0\}$ ($\epsilon = 0$), then A accepts upon reception of τ'_B, and B accepts upon reception of m_A.

Each message of the protocol fulfills a specific task: party authentication, detecting desynchronisation, and then catching up. This eventually results in the forward secrecy property being ensured. Removing one message yields an attack, as shown by any of the numerous alternative versions we have analysed. Although we do not formally prove it, we do think that the figure of five rounds is the least achievable in order to take into account all cases.

3.2 Notation

For the sake of clarity, we use the following notation in Fig. 2:

- kdf corresponds to: $sk \leftarrow \mathsf{KDF}(K, f(r_A, r_B))$
- upd_A corresponds to
    1. $K \leftarrow \mathsf{update}(K)$
    2. $K'_{j-1} \leftarrow K'_j$
    3. $K'_j \leftarrow K'_{j+1}$
    4. $K'_{j+1} \leftarrow \mathsf{update}(K'_{j+1})$
- upd_B corresponds to
    1. $K \leftarrow \mathsf{update}(K)$
    2. $K' \leftarrow \mathsf{update}(K')$

A	B
$(K, K'_{j+1}, K'_j, K'_{j-1})$	(K, K')

$r_A \overset{\$}{\leftarrow} \{0,1\}^\lambda$

$$\xrightarrow{\quad A\|r_A \quad}$$

$r_B \overset{\$}{\leftarrow} \{0,1\}^\lambda$
$\tau_B \leftarrow \mathsf{Mac}(K', B\|A\|r_B\|r_A)$
$m_B \leftarrow r_B\|\tau_B$

$$\xleftarrow{\quad m_B \quad}$$

if $(\mathsf{Vrf}(K'_j, B\|A\|r_B\|r_A, \tau_B) = \mathtt{true})$
    $\delta_{AB} \leftarrow 0$
    $K' \leftarrow K'_j$; kdf; upd_A; $\epsilon \leftarrow 0$
else if $(\mathsf{Vrf}(K'_{j-1}, B\|A\|r_B\|r_A, \tau_B) = \mathtt{true})$
    $\delta_{AB} \leftarrow 1$
    $K' \leftarrow K'_{j-1}$; $\epsilon \leftarrow 1$
else if $(\mathsf{Vrf}(K'_{j+1}, B\|A\|r_B\|r_A, \tau_B) = \mathtt{true})$
    $\delta_{AB} \leftarrow -1$
    $K' \leftarrow K'_{j+1}$; upd_A; kdf; upd_A; $\epsilon \leftarrow 0$
else
    abort

$\tau_A \leftarrow \mathsf{Mac}(K', \epsilon\|A\|B\|r_A\|r_B)$
$m_A \leftarrow \epsilon\|\tau_A$

$$\xrightarrow{\quad m_A \quad}$$

if $(\mathsf{Vrf}(K', \epsilon\|A\|B\|r_A\|r_B, \tau_A) = \mathtt{false})$
    abort
if $(\epsilon = 1)$
    upd_B
kdf; upd_B
$\tau'_B \leftarrow \mathsf{Mac}(K', r_B\|r_A)$

$$\xleftarrow{\quad \tau'_B \quad}$$

if $(\epsilon = 0)$
    $K' \leftarrow K'_j$
    if $(\mathsf{Vrf}(K', r_B\|r_A, \tau'_B) = \mathtt{false})$
        abort
else if $(\epsilon = 1)$
    $K' \leftarrow K'_{j+1}$
    if $(\mathsf{Vrf}(K', r_B\|r_A, \tau'_B) = \mathtt{false})$
        abort
    kdf; upd_A

$\tau'_A \leftarrow \mathsf{Mac}(K', r_A\|r_B)$

$$\xrightarrow{\quad \tau'_A \quad}$$

if $(\mathsf{Vrf}(K', r_A\|r_B, \tau'_A) = \mathtt{false})$
    abort

Fig. 2. SAKE protocol

Moreover, $\mathsf{Vrf}(k, m, \tau)$ denotes the MAC verification function that takes as input a secret key k, a message m, and a tag τ. It outputs $\mathtt{true}$ if τ is a valid tag on message m with respect to k. Otherwise, it returns $\mathtt{false}$.

3.3 SAKE-AM: A Complementary Mode of SAKE

From SAKE, we can derive an aggressive mode that allows any party to be either initiator or responder, and such that the smallest amount of calculation is always done by the *same* party.

In SAKE the initiator A owns the three keys K'_{j+1}, K'_j, K'_{j-1}, and the responder B does the lightest computations. In this mode B owns the three keys, and A does the smallest amount of calculation. The main idea is to skip the first SAKE message $A\|r_A$. Hence the roles between the two parties are swapped. This leads to other minor changes in message format compared to SAKE. Despite these differences, the messages and the calculations are essentially the same as in SAKE. This mode remains a sound and secure AKE protocol (according to Definition 5).[3] We call this mode *SAKE in aggressive mode* (SAKE-AM).

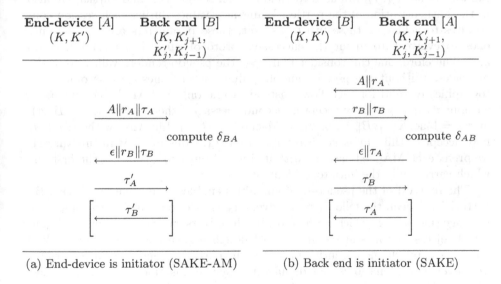

(a) End-device is initiator (SAKE-AM)   (b) Back end is initiator (SAKE)

Fig. 3. Symmetric-key authenticated key exchange with forward secrecy between a low-resource end-device and a back-end server. Both parties may initiate the session. In some cases, the last message can be skipped.

This can be applied in the context of industrial IoT when a set of end-devices (e.g., sensors, actuators) communicate with a central server. When the end-device wants to initiate a communication, protocol SAKE-AM is launched.

---

[3] The proofs of soundness and security for SAKE-AM are essentially the same as for SAKE (see Sect. 5). They are given in the full version of the paper [8].

Otherwise (the server is initiator), SAKE is used (see Fig. 3). Therefore, the end-device always does the lightest computations.

4   A Random-Free Variant of SAKE

From SAKE, one can devise several variants. First, the three authentication keys K'_{j-1}, K'_j, K'_{j+1} can be replaced by two local counters c_A, c_B (respectively stored by A and B) that keep track of the evolution of the derivation master key K, with one static authentication master key K'.[4] On the initiator' side, the MAC verifications are then done with consecutive values of the counter $j - 1$, j, $j + 1$. Overall, the sequence of operations and the computations are similar to that of SAKE. This means mainly replacing function $x \mapsto \mathsf{Mac}(K'_j, x)$ with $x \mapsto \mathsf{Mac}(K', j\|x)$. Yet, this alternative implies the storage of two keys and one counter: K, K' and c_A/c_B, instead of two keys only: K and K'_{j-1}/K' (and, one the initiator' side only, one or two additional calls to update in order to compute K'_j and, possibly, K'_{j+1}).

Another, more interesting, variant is the following.[5] In SAKE, the pseudo-random values r_A, r_B are used to yield a fresh session key, and participate also in the authentication of the parties. Using new values during each session contributes to achieving these two tasks. Yet, these parameters are not the only ones to evolve throughout the successive protocol runs. The master keys do also. Therefore, one can consider removing the pseudo-random values from the messages. Without the pseudo-random values, several messages become cryptographically valid for each flow (instead of one only in SAKE). For instance, without r_A, party A may accept as second message either $\tau_B = \mathsf{Mac}(K'_j, B\|A)$, or $\tau_B = \mathsf{Mac}(K'_{j-1}, B\|A)$, or $\tau_B = \mathsf{Mac}(K'_{j+1}, B\|A)$. Likewise, without r_B, B may accept as third message either $0\|\tau_A$ or $1\|\tau_A$. Consequently, in this variant, we prefix each MAC-ed message with its index from 1 to 4 (but not the first one which carries only the initiator's identity).

The removal of the pseudo-random values enables a "mismatch attack". By "attack" we mean the following: an adversary is able to compel B to compute a message (message 4) which is *unaltered* by the adversary and expected by A, and yet A rejects this message as invalid. Although unpleasant, this "attack" does not break any claimed security property (in particular entity authentication). Moreover, this scenario cannot damage the synchronisation of the two parties. That is, if they start a new session, the latter completes successfully (if the adversary remains passive), as in SAKE.

In this variant, the length of the messages is shortened, and this avoids also calling the pseudo-random generation function. This is advantageous for low-resource devices. Nonetheless, the possibility provided by the aforementioned scenario is not what one usually expects from a security protocol. Consequently, for the practitioners for whom this mismatch attack is unacceptable, the SAKE protocol is more adequate.

---

[4] This alternative has been suggested by anonymous reviewers of Crypto 2019.

[5] We describe it from SAKE, but the same holds for SAKE-AM.

5   Security and Soundness for SAKE

In this section we prove that (i) SAKE is *sound*, and (ii) it is a *secure AKE* protocol according to Definition 5 given above.

5.1   Soundness of SAKE

We want to show that SAKE is *sound*, which essentially means that, once a correct session is complete, both parties have updated their respective internal state, are synchronised, and share the same (new) session key. We call a "benign" adversary an adversary that faithfully forwards all messages between an initiator A and a responder B.

Lemma 1. *Let A and B be respectively the initiator and the responder of a SAKE session. Let δ_{AB} be the gap between A and B with respect to the evolution of the master keys of both parties. The following conditions always hold:*

1. *$\delta_{AB} \in \{-1, 0, 1\}$, and*
2. *whatever the synchronisation state of A and B (i.e., whatever A and B are synchronised or not) when a new session starts, when that session completes in presence of a benign adversary, then*
   (a) A and B have updated their master keys at least once, and
   (b) A and B are synchronised (with respect to their master keys), and
   (c) A and B share the same session key.

   In order to prove Lemma 1, we use the following notation. The messages exchanged during a session are numbered from 1 to 5. The notation "(i_A, i_B)" means that, when the session ends, the last valid message received by A is message of index i_A, and the last valid message received by B is message of index i_B. We call a (i_A, i_B)-*session* a session where the last message received by A is message i_A, and the last message received by B is message i_B. By convention $i_A = 0$ means that no message has been received by A.

   It may happen that A send a first message which is not received by B. B cannot know if it has missed a first message. But this is of no consequence regarding the synchronisation between A and B (A may simply run the protocol anew). Therefore we do not use the value $i_B = 0$ (it is equivalent to $i_B = 5$). At initialisation (i.e., before the first run of the protocol), (i_A, i_B) is set to $(4, 5)$. Since A sends message $i \in \{3, 5\}$ only upon reception of a valid message $i - 1$, and B sends message $j \in \{2, 4\}$ only upon reception of a valid message $j - 1$, the only possible values for (i_A, i_B) are: $(0, 1)$, $(2, 1)$, $(2, 3)$, $(4, 3)$, and $(4, 5)$.

Proof. We prove Lemma 1. We first prove item 1.

   Let c_A (resp. c_B) be a (virtual) monotonically increasing counter initialised to 0 that follows the evolution of the master keys held by A (resp. B). That is, c_A (resp. c_B) is increased each time the master keys K, K'_{j+1}, K'_j, K'_{j-1} (resp. K, K') are updated. The parameter δ_{AB} corresponds to the gap between A and B with respect to the evolution of their master keys, hence $\delta_{AB} = c_A - c_B$.

We prove item 1 by constructing iteratively Table 1b.

Before the first protocol run, A and B are synchronised. That is $\delta_{AB} = c_A - c_B = 0$, and $(c_A, c_B) = (i, i)$ (with $i = 0$). Therefore, A can validate τ_B (in message m_B) with the same key $K'_j = K'$ as B. Hence A computes $\delta_{AB} = 0$, and $\epsilon = 0$. Consequently, if one carries out the protocol run starting with $\delta_{AB} = 0$ and $\epsilon = 0$, for each possible value (i_A, i_B), one eventually gets the following:

- $(c_A, c_B) = (i, i)$ and $\delta_{AB} = 0$ after a $(0, 1)$-session,
- $(c_A, c_B) = (i + 1, i)$ and $\delta_{AB} = 1$ after a $(2, 1)$-session,
- $(c_A, c_B) = (i + 1, i + 1)$ and $\delta_{AB} = 0$ after a $(2, 3)$-session,
- $(c_A, c_B) = (i + 1, i + 1)$ and $\delta_{AB} = 0$ after a $(4, 3)$-session,
- $(c_A, c_B) = (i + 1, i + 1)$ and $\delta_{AB} = 0$ after a $(4, 5)$-session.

This corresponds to the first column of Tables 1a and b. As we can see, the only possible values for δ_{AB} after any session are 0 and 1. $\delta_{AB} = 0$ has already been investigated. Hence, starting with $\delta_{AB} = 1$ (i.e., $(c_A, c_B) = (i + 1, i)$), we look for all the values δ_{AB} may have when the session ends, considering any possible session.

$(c_A, c_B) = (i + 1, i)$ means that A is in advance with respect to B. In such a case, A succeeds in validating τ_B with K'_{j-1} (and, indeed, finds $\delta_{AB} = 1$). Then A uses $\delta_{AB} = 1$ and $\epsilon = 1$. If one carries out the protocol run using these two values, one gets three possible values for δ_{AB}: 1, 0, −1. This corresponds to the second column of Table 1b, and shows that a third value is possible for δ_{AB}, which is −1 (i.e., $(c_A, c_B) = (i, i + 1)$).

Then we restart the protocol with all possible sessions, assuming that $(c_A, c_B) = (i, i + 1)$ at the beginning of the run. This means that A is one step late with respect to B. In such a case, A succeeds in validating τ_B with key K'_{j+1} (and, indeed, finds $\delta_{AB} = -1$). Then A uses $\delta_{AB} = -1$ and $\epsilon = 0$. If one carries out the protocol run using these two values, we end with three possible values for δ_{AB} (third column of Table 1b): −1, 0 and 1, that have been explored already. This proves that, whatever the sequences of sessions, the only possible values for δ_{AB} are in $\{-1, 0, 1\}$.

Now we prove item 2 of Lemma 1.

We know that $\delta_{AB} \in \{-1, 0, 1\}$. For each possible value of δ_{AB} at the beginning of the session, the last line of Table 1b indicates the value of that parameter after a correct and complete session (i.e., a $(4, 5)$-session). As we can see, A and B are always synchronised (i.e., $\delta_{AB} = 0$) in such a case whatever the value of δ_{AB} when the session starts. Furthermore, the session key computation immediately precedes the last update of the derivation master key K. Hence, when a correct and complete session ends, A and B use the same derivation master key K to compute the session key. Therefore, using the same values r_A, r_B, A and B compute the same session key.

In addition, Table 1a shows that, whatever the synchronisation state of A and B (i.e., c_A and c_B) at the beginning of the session, after a correct and complete session, A and B have updated their internal state at least once (as the last line of the table, corresponding to a $(4, 5)$-session, indicates).   □

Table 1. Possible values for δ_{AB} and (c_A, c_B) among all sequences of sessions in SAKE

(a) Possible values for (c_A, c_B)

session \ (c_A, c_B)	(i, i)	$(i+1, i)$	$(i, i+1)$
$(0, 1)$	(i, i)	$(i+1, i)$	$(i, i+1)$
$(2, 1)$	$(i+1, i)$	$(i+1, i)$	$(i+2, i+1)$
$(2, 3)$	$(i+1, i+1)$	$(i+1, i+2)$	$(i+2, i+2)$
$(4, 3)$	$(i+1, i+1)$	$(i+2, i+2)$	$(i+2, i+2)$
$(4, 5)$	$(i+1, i+1)$	$(i+2, i+2)$	$(i+2, i+2)$

(b) Possible values for δ_{AB}

session \ δ_{AB}	0	1	-1
$(0, 1)$	0	1	-1
$(2, 1)$	1	1	1
$(2, 3)$	0	-1	0
$(4, 3)$	0	0	0
$(4, 5)$	0	0	0

5.2 Security of SAKE

In order to prove that the protocol SAKE is a secure AKE protocol, we use the execution environment described in Sect. 2.1. We define the partnering between two instances with the notion of *matching conversations* (see Definition 8). That is, we define sid to be the transcript, in chronological order, of all the (valid) messages sent and received by an instance during the key exchange, but, possibly, the last one. Furthermore, we choose the function update to be a PRF, that is update : $K \mapsto \mathsf{PRF}(K, x)$ for some (constant) value x.

Theorem 1. *The protocol SAKE is a secure AKE protocol, and for any probabilistic polynomial time adversary $\mathcal{A}$ in the AKE security experiment against protocol SAKE, we have*

$$\mathsf{adv}_{SAKE}^{\text{ent-auth}}(\mathcal{A}) \leq nq \left((nq - 1)2^{-\lambda} + (q + 1)\mathsf{adv}_{\text{update}}^{\text{prf}}(\mathcal{B}) + 2\mathsf{adv}_{\text{Mac}}^{\text{suf-cma}}(\mathcal{C}) \right)$$

$$\mathsf{adv}_{SAKE}^{\text{key-ind}}(\mathcal{A}) \leq nq \left((q - 1)\mathsf{adv}_{\text{update}}^{\text{prf}}(\mathcal{B}) + \mathsf{adv}_{\text{KDF}}^{\text{prf}}(\mathcal{D}) \right) + \mathsf{adv}_{SAKE}^{\text{ent-auth}}(\mathcal{A})$$

where n is the number of parties, q the maximum number of instances (sessions) per party, λ the size of the pseudo-random values (r_A, r_B), and $\mathcal{B}$ is an adversary against the PRF-security of update, $\mathcal{C}$ an adversary against the SUF-CMA-security of Mac, and $\mathcal{D}$ an adversary against the PRF-security of KDF.

Proof. In order for an initiator instance π_i^s at some party P_i to accept, two valid messages (i.e., with valid MAC tags) must be received by π_i^s (m_B and τ_B'). We reduce the security of the Mac function to the (in)ability to forge a valid output. Therefore we use the fact that the key K' is random. By assumption, the genuine value of K' (i.e., the value used during the first session between two same parties) is uniformly chosen at random. Yet K' (and K) is updated throughout the session with the function update. If K' is random, we can rely on the pseudo-randomness of update$(\cdot) = \mathsf{PRF}(\cdot, \cdot)$. In turn, since $\mathsf{PRF}(K', \cdot)$ can be replaced with a truly random function, its output (updated K') is random. Therefore, one can rely upon the pseudo-randomness of the function update keyed with this new value K', and so forth. Each transition (i.e., each update of K') implies a loss equal to $\mathsf{adv}^{\mathsf{prf}}_{\mathsf{update}}(\mathcal{B})$ corresponding to the ability of an adversary $\mathcal{B}$ to distinguish update from a random function.

If P_i is synchronised with the responder ($\delta_{AB} = 0$), P_i updates its master keys once (upon reception of m_B). If P_i is in advance ($\delta_{AB} = 1$), it updates its keys at most once (if a valid message τ'_B is received). If P_i is late ($\delta_{AB} = -1$), it updates its keys twice. Yet, in that case, P_i did not update its keys during the previous session. Therefore, on average, P_i updates its keys at most once per session. Hence, when the u-th session starts, P_i has updated its keys at most $u - 1$ times on average, and, upon reception of τ'_B, P_i updates the keys at most two times.

This is similar regarding the responder. A responder instance π^t_j at some party P_j accepts only if the two messages m_A and τ'_A are valid. Upon reception of a valid message m_A, the keys are updated once ($\epsilon = 0$) or twice ($\epsilon = 1$). In the latter case, the keys have not been updated during the previous session. This means that the keys are updated on average at most once per session. Therefore, when the u-th session starts, P_j has updated its keys at most $u - 1$ times on average, and, upon reception of m_A, the keys are updated at most two times.

We can now proceed with the proof. We proceed through a sequence of games [13,32], where each consecutive game aims at reducing the challenger's dependency on the functions Mac, update and KDF. We first prove the entity authentication security. Let E_i be the event that the adversary win the entity authentication experiment in Game i.

Game 0. This game corresponds to the entity authentication security experiment described in Sect. 2.1. Therefore

$$\Pr[E_0] = \mathsf{adv}^{\mathsf{ent\text{-}auth}}_{SAKE}(\mathcal{A})$$

Game 1. The challenger aborts if there exists any instance that chooses a random value r_A or r_B that is not unique. There is at most $n \times q$ random values, each uniformly drawn at random in $\{0,1\}^\lambda$. Therefore the probability that at least two random values be equal is at most $\frac{nq(nq-1)}{2^\lambda}$. Hence

$$\Pr[E_0] \leq \Pr[E_1] + \frac{nq(nq-1)}{2^\lambda}$$

Game 2. The challenger tries to guess which instance will be the first to accept maliciously. If the guess is wrong, the game is aborted. The number of instances is at most nq. Therefore

$$\Pr[E_2] = \Pr[E_1] \times \frac{1}{nq}$$

Game 3. Let π be the instance targeted by the adversary. In this game, we add an abort rule. The challenger aborts the experiment if π ever receives a valid message m_B (resp. m_A) if it is an initiator (resp. responder) instance, but no instance having a matching conversation to π has output that message. We reduce the probability of this event to the security of the functions Mac and update. As explained above, when the u-th session starts, the master keys have been updated at most $u - 1$ times already. The genuine value of K' is uniformly chosen at random. In order to be able to replace, during the current session, the key used to compute the MAC tag in m_A (resp. m_B) with a random value, one must rely upon the pseudo-randomness of the function update that outputs (the new value of) K'. In turn, this relies upon the (previous) key K' being random (and on the pseudo-randomness of update). Therefore, in order to replace K' with a random value one must take into account the successive losses $\mathsf{adv}^{\mathsf{prf}}_{\mathsf{update}}(\mathcal{B})$, each corresponding to the ability of an adversary $\mathcal{B}$ to distinguish the function update (keyed with a different key K') from a random function. Since there is at most q sessions, this loss is at most $(q - 1)\mathsf{adv}^{\mathsf{prf}}_{\mathsf{update}}(\mathcal{B})$. Then we reduce the probability of the adversary $\mathcal{A}$ to win this game to the ability of an adversary $\mathcal{C}$ to forge a valid tag τ_B (resp. τ_A).

Therefore, we replace each function $\mathsf{update}(K') = \mathsf{PRF}(K', x)$ (keyed with a different key K' throughout the, at most, $q - 1$ successive sessions established, prior to that current session, by the same party that owns π) with truly random functions $\mathsf{F}^{\mathsf{update}}_0, \ldots, \mathsf{F}^{\mathsf{update}}_{q-2}$. Moreover, if an instance uses the same key $K' = K'_i, 0 \le i < q - 1$, to key update, then we replace update with the corresponding random function $\mathsf{F}^{\mathsf{update}}_i$. Since, to that point, the key $K' = K'_{q-1}$ used to compute the authentication tag τ_B (resp. τ_A) is random, we reduce the ability of $\mathcal{A}$ to win to the security of the Mac function. Hence

$$\Pr[E_2] \le \Pr[E_3] + (q - 1)\mathsf{adv}^{\mathsf{prf}}_{\mathsf{update}}(\mathcal{B}) + \mathsf{adv}^{\mathsf{suf\text{-}cma}}_{\mathsf{Mac}}(\mathcal{C})$$

Game 4. The challenger aborts the experiment if π ever receives a valid message τ'_B (resp. τ'_A), but no instance having a matching conversation to π has output that message. Between the message m_B (resp. m_A) being received by π, and the message τ'_B (resp. τ'_A) being received by π, the master keys are updated at most twice. We reduce the probability of the adversary to win this game to the security of the Mac function used to compute the message τ'_B (resp. τ'_A). In turn we must rely on the randomness of the Mac key, hence on the security of the function update used to update the Mac key K' (recall that, due to Game 3, the current key K' is random). Therefore

$$\Pr[E_3] \le \Pr[E_4] + 2\mathsf{adv}^{\mathsf{prf}}_{\mathsf{update}}(\mathcal{B}) + \mathsf{adv}^{\mathsf{suf\text{-}cma}}_{\mathsf{Mac}}(\mathcal{C})$$

To that point, the only way for the adversary to make π accept maliciously is to send a valid message τ'_B (resp. τ'_A) different from all the messages sent by all the instances. However, in such a case, the challenger aborts. Therefore $\Pr[E_4] = 0$.

Collecting all the probabilities from Game 0 to 4, we get the indicated bound.

Now we prove the key indistinguishability security. Let E'_i be the event that an adversary win the key indistinguishability experiment in Game i, and $\mathsf{adv}_i = \Pr[E'_i] - \frac{1}{2}$.

Game 0. This game corresponds to the key indistinguishability experiment described in Sect. 2.1. Therefore

$$\Pr[E_0'] = \frac{1}{2} + \mathsf{adv}_{SAKE}^{\mathsf{key\text{-}ind}}(\mathcal{A}) = \frac{1}{2} + \mathsf{adv}_0$$

Game 1. The challenger aborts the experiment and chooses $b' \in \{0, 1\}$ uniformly at random if there exists an instance that accepts maliciously. In other words, in this game we make the same modifications as in the games performed during the entity authentication proof. Hence

$$\mathsf{adv}_0 \leq \mathsf{adv}_1 + \mathsf{adv}_{SAKE}^{\mathsf{ent\text{-}auth}}(\mathcal{A})$$

Game 2. The challenger tries to guess which instance is targeted by the adversary. If the guess is wrong, the game is aborted. The number of instances is at most nq. Therefore

$$\mathsf{adv}_2 = \mathsf{adv}_1 \times \frac{1}{nq}$$

Game 3. Let π be the instance targeted by the adversary. We reduce the advantage of the adversary to win this game to the security of the function KDF used to compute the session key. That is, we rely upon the pseudo-randomness of the KDF function. This is possible if the key K is random. The genuine value of K is uniformly chosen at random by assumption. Then K is updated with update at most once per session on average. Therefore, when the u-th session starts, K has been updated at most $u - 1$ times already. Therefore we must take into account the successive losses due to the key update with respect to the pseudo-randomness of update. Since there is at most q sessions per party (i.e., per original key K), this loss is at most $(q - 1)\mathsf{adv}_{\mathsf{update}}^{\mathsf{prf}}(\mathcal{B})$. Hence we replace each function $\mathsf{update}(K) = \mathsf{PRF}(K, x)$ (keyed with a different key K throughout the, at most, $q - 1$ successive sessions established, prior to that current session, by the same party that owns π) with truly random functions $\mathsf{G}_0^{\mathsf{update}}, \ldots, \mathsf{G}_{q-2}^{\mathsf{update}}$. Moreover, if an instance uses the same key $K = K_i$, $0 \leq i < q-1$, to key update, then we replace update with the corresponding random function $\mathsf{G}_i^{\mathsf{update}}$. Since, to that point, the key $K = K_{q-1}$ used to compute the session key is random, we reduce the ability of $\mathcal{A}$ to win to the security of KDF. Therefore

$$\mathsf{adv}_2 \leq \mathsf{adv}_3 + (q - 1)\mathsf{adv}_{\mathsf{update}}^{\mathsf{prf}}(\mathcal{B}) + \mathsf{adv}_{\mathsf{KDF}}^{\mathsf{prf}}(\mathcal{D})$$

To that point the session key is random, therefore the adversary has no advantage in guessing whether $\pi.\mathsf{b} = b'$. That is

$$\mathsf{adv}_3 = 0$$

Collecting all the probabilities from Game 0 to 3, we get the indicated bound.

$\square$

6   Comparison with the DH Paradigm

The protocol SAKE provides a strong form of forward secrecy. Despite this result, it differs from a DH scheme in several ways beyond the intrinsic distinction between public-key and symmetric-key cryptography.

Concurrent Executions. Our protocol does not allow parallel executions. Indeed, since it is based on shared evolving symmetric keys, running multiple instances in parallel may cause some sessions to abort. A way to relax this restriction is that each party use separate master keys for concurrent executions. On the contrary, the DH scheme allows an (virtually) unlimited number of parallel executions.

KCI Attacks. The ephemeral DH scheme is resistant against KCI attacks, whereas our protocol is not (due to the dependency between the (updated) master keys). Moreover if an adversary succeeds in getting the key K' (or K'_j), it can compute the subsequent key (corresponding to K'_{j+1}). Hence the adversary can forge a message m_B in SAKE that brings the initiator to update its master keys twice consecutively. Therefore, that party is desynchronised with respect to an honest partner, with no possibility to resynchronise.

Note that KCI attacks affect also the static DH scheme (when a party uses a fixed DH share, whereas the other generates a fresh ephemeral one [25]).

Another consequence of the dependency of the master keys in SAKE, is that once the keys are compromised, an adversary can passively compromise all subsequent session keys. This is not the case in general with ephemeral DH. Yet, this is also true regarding non-DH public-key protocols (e.g., TLS-RSA), but also ephemeral DH (in some pathological cases) when reduced size (fixed) public parameters are used [5].

Computations. The DH scheme implies heavier computations (modular exponentiations, elliptic curve point multiplication) than SAKE which is solely built on symmetric-key functions. In practice, SAKE is likely more suitable to be implemented on constrained devices which have limited computational (and communication) capabilities.

7   Conclusion

We have described SAKE, an authenticated key exchange protocol in the symmetric-key setting. Although this protocol is solely based on symmetric-key algorithms, it provides perfect forward secrecy without requiring any additional procedure (e.g., resynchronisation phase) or functionality (e.g., shared clock). The underlying idea is to make the shared master keys evolve. We solve the synchronisation problem that stems from this evolving principle with an elegant and efficient solution.

SAKE guarantees that, whatever the synchronisation state of the involved parties prior to the session, both parties share a new session key, and their internal state is updated and synchronised, once a correct session is complete: SAKE is self-synchronising. As in the public-key setting, our protocol allows an (virtually) unlimited number of sessions. Furthermore, we prove that SAKE is sound, and provide a formal proof of its security in a strong model.

Finally, we describe SAKE-AM, a complementary mode of our protocol, which, used in conjunction with SAKE, results in an implementation that gathers all the aforementioned properties (starting with forward secrecy). This implementation allows any party to be initiator or responder of a session, such that the smallest amount of calculation is always done by the same party. This is particularly convenient in the context of IoT where a set of (low-resource) end-devices communicates with a back-end server.

To the best of our knowledge, this is the first protocol with perfect forward secrecy in the symmetric-key setting that is comparable to the DH scheme, beyond the intrinsic distinction between public-key and symmetric-key cryptography.

Acknowledgment. We thank the anonymous reviewers for their valuable comments.

References

1. Signal. https://signal.org/
2. 3rd Generation Partnership Project: Technical Specifications 33. http://www.3gpp.org/DynaReport/33-series.htm
3. 3rd Generation Partnership Project: Technical Specifications 35. http://www.3gpp.org/DynaReport/35-series.htm
4. Abdalla, M., Bellare, M.: Increasing the lifetime of a key: a comparative analysis of the security of re-keying techniques. In: Okamoto, T. (ed.) ASIACRYPT 2000. LNCS, vol. 1976, pp. 546–559. Springer, Heidelberg (2000). https://doi.org/10.1007/3-540-44448-3_42
5. Adrian, D., et al.: Imperfect forward secrecy: how Diffie-Hellman fails in practice. In: Ray, I., Li, N., Kruegel, C. (eds.) ACM CCS 2015, pp. 5–17. ACM Press, October 2015. https://doi.org/10.1145/2810103.2813707
6. Alwen, J., Coretti, S., Dodis, Y.: The Double Ratchet: Security Notions, Proofs, and Modularization for the Signal Protocol. Cryptology ePrint Archive, Report 2018/1037 (2018). https://eprint.iacr.org/2018/1037
7. American National Standards Institute: ANSI X9.24-1:2009 Retail Financial Services Symmetric Key Management Part 1: Using Symmetric Techniques (2009)
8. Avoine, G., Canard, S., Ferreira, L.: Symmetric-key Authenticated Key Exchange (SAKE) with Perfect Forward Secrecy. Cryptology ePrint Archive, Report 2019/444 (2019). http://eprint.iacr.org/2019/444
9. Bellare, M., Desai, A., Jokipii, E., Rogaway, P.: A concrete security treatment of symmetric encryption. In: 38th FOCS, pp. 394–403. IEEE Computer Society Press, October 1997. https://doi.org/10.1109/SFCS.1997.646128
10. Bellare, M., Miner, S.K.: A forward-secure digital signature scheme. In: Wiener, M. (ed.) CRYPTO 1999. LNCS, vol. 1666, pp. 431–448. Springer, Heidelberg (1999). https://doi.org/10.1007/3-540-48405-1_28
11. Bellare, M., Namprempre, C.: Authenticated encryption: relations among notions and analysis of the generic composition paradigm. J. Cryptol. **21**(4), 469–491 (2008). https://doi.org/10.1007/s00145-008-9026-x

12. Bellare, M., Rogaway, P.: Entity authentication and key distribution. In: Stinson, D.R. (ed.) CRYPTO 1993. LNCS, vol. 773, pp. 232–249. Springer, Heidelberg (1994). https://doi.org/10.1007/3-540-48329-2_21

13. Bellare, M., Rogaway, P.: The security of triple encryption and a framework for code-based game-playing proofs. In: Vaudenay, S. (ed.) EUROCRYPT 2006. LNCS, vol. 4004, pp. 409–426. Springer, Heidelberg (2006). https://doi.org/10.1007/11761679_25

14. Bellare, M., Yee, B.: Forward-security in private-key cryptography. In: Joye, M. (ed.) CT-RSA 2003. LNCS, vol. 2612, pp. 1–18. Springer, Heidelberg (2003). https://doi.org/10.1007/3-540-36563-X_1

15. Blake-Wilson, S., Johnson, D., Menezes, A.: Key agreement protocols and their security analysis. In: Darnell, M. (ed.) Cryptography and Coding 1997. LNCS, vol. 1355, pp. 30–45. Springer, Heidelberg (1997). https://doi.org/10.1007/BFb0024447

16. Boyd, C., Mathuria, A.: Protocols for Authentication and Key Establishment. Information Security and Cryptography. Springer, Heidelberg (2003). https://doi.org/10.1007/978-3-662-09527-0

17. Brier, E., Peyrin, T.: A forward-secure symmetric-key derivation protocol. In: Abe, M. (ed.) ASIACRYPT 2010. LNCS, vol. 6477, pp. 250–267. Springer, Heidelberg (2010). https://doi.org/10.1007/978-3-642-17373-8_15

18. Brzuska, C., Jacobsen, H., Stebila, D.: Safely exporting keys from secure channels. In: Fischlin, M., Coron, J.-S. (eds.) EUROCRYPT 2016. LNCS, vol. 9665, pp. 670–698. Springer, Heidelberg (2016). https://doi.org/10.1007/978-3-662-49890-3_26

19. Cohn-Gordon, K., Cremers, C., Dowling, B., Garratt, L., Stebila, D.: A formal security analysis of the signal messaging protocol. In: 2017 IEEE European Symposium on Security and Privacy (EuroS&P), pp. 451–466. IEEE, April 2017. https://doi.org/10.1109/EuroSP.2017.27

20. Diffie, W., Hellman, M.E.: New directions in cryptography. IEEE Trans. Inf. Theory 22(6), 644–654 (1976)

21. Diffie, W., van Oorschot, P.C., Wiener, M.J.: Authentication and authenticated key exchanges. Des. Codes Crypt. 2(2), 107–125 (1992)

22. Dousti, M.S., Jalili, R.: FORSAKES: a forward-secure authenticated key exchange protocol based on symmetric key-evolving schemes. Cryptology ePrint Archive, Report 2014/123 (2014). http://eprint.iacr.org/2014/123

23. GlobalPlatform: GlobalPlatform - Card Specification - Version 2.3.1, reference GPC_SPE_034, March 2018. https://www.globalplatform.org/specificationscard.asp

24. Günther, C.G.: An identity-based key-exchange protocol. In: Quisquater, J.-J., Vandewalle, J. (eds.) EUROCRYPT 1989. LNCS, vol. 434, pp. 29–37. Springer, Heidelberg (1990). https://doi.org/10.1007/3-540-46885-4_5

25. Hlauschek, C., Gruber, M., Fankhauser, F., Schanes, C.: Prying open Pandora's box: KCI attacks against TLS. In: Proceedings of the 9th USENIX Conference on Offensive Technologies, WOOT 2015, USENIX Association (2015)

26. International Organization for Standardization: ISO/IEC 11770-2 - Information technology - Security techniques - Key Management - Part 2: Mechanisms using Symmetric Techniques (2008)

27. Jager, T., Kohlar, F., Schäge, S., Schwenk, J.: On the security of TLS-DHE in the standard model. Cryptology ePrint Archive, Report 2011/219 (2011). http://eprint.iacr.org/2011/219

224   G. Avoine et al.

28. Le, T.V., Burmester, M., de Medeiros, B.: Universally composable and forward-secure RFID authentication and authenticated key exchange. In: Bao, F., Miller, S. (eds.) ASIACCS 2007, pp. 242–252. ACM Press, March 2007
29. Park, T., Shin, K.G.: LiSP: a lightweight security protocol for wireless sensor networks. ACM Trans. Embed. Comput. Syst. $3(3)$, 634–660 (2004)
30. Perrig, A., Szewczyk, R., Tygar, J., Wen, V., Culler, D.E.: SPINS: security protocols for sensor networks. Wireless Netw. $8(5)$, 521–534 (2002)
31. Perrin, T., Marlinspike, M.: The Double Ratchet Algorithm (2016). https://signal.org/docs/specifications/doubleratchet/. Revision 1, 20/11/2016
32. Shoup, V.: Sequences of games: a tool for taming complexity in security proofs. Cryptology ePrint Archive, Report 2004/332 (2004). http://eprint.iacr.org/2004/332
33. Sornin, N., Luis, M., Eirich, T., Kramp, T.: LoRaWAN Specification, LoRa Alliance, version 1.0, July 2016
34. ZigBee Alliance: ZigBee specification. http://www.zigbee.org/download/standards-zigbee-specification/

TMPS: Ticket-Mediated Password Strengthening

John Kelsey[1,2] , Dana Dachman-Soled[3(✉)] , Sweta Mishra[1,4] ,
and Meltem Sönmez Turan[1]

[1] National Institute of Standards and Technology, Gaithersburg, MD, USA
[2] Department of Electrical Engineering, ESAT/COSIC, KU Leuven, Leuven, Belgium
[3] Department of Electrical and Computer Engineering,
University of Maryland, College Park, MD, USA
danadach@umd.edu
[4] Department of Computer Science and Engineering, Shiv Nadar University,
Greater Noida, India

Abstract. We introduce the notion of TMPS: Ticket-Mediated Password Strengthening, a technique for allowing users to derive keys from passwords while imposing a strict limit on the number of guesses of their password any attacker can make, and strongly protecting the users' privacy. We describe the security requirements of TMPS, and then a set of efficient and practical protocols to implement a TMPS scheme, requiring only hash functions, CCA2-secure encryption, and blind signatures. We provide several variant protocols, including an offline symmetric-only protocol that uses a local trusted computing environment, and online variants that use group signatures or stronger trust assumptions instead of blind signatures. We formalize the security of our scheme by defining an ideal functionality in the Universal Composability (UC) framework, and by providing game-based definitions of security. We prove that our protocol realizes the ideal functionality in the random oracle model (ROM) under adaptive corruptions with erasures, and prove that security with respect to the ideal/real definition implies security with respect to the game-based definitions.

Keywords: Dictionary attacks · TMPS · Key derivation

1 Introduction

Alice needs a cryptographic key on her device, but doesn't want to store it there directly, lest someone steal the device and access her private data. The key might be used to decrypt a hard drive, or a file, or a cryptographic key which

This work was supported in part by NSF grants #CNS-1933033, #CNS-1840893, #CNS-1453045 (CAREER), by a research partnership award from Cisco and by financial assistance award 70NANB15H328 from the U.S. Department of Commerce, National Institute of Standards and Technology.

© Springer Nature Switzerland AG 2020
S. Jarecki (Ed.): CT-RSA 2020, LNCS 12006, pp. 225–253, 2020.
https://doi.org/10.1007/978-3-030-40186-3_11

will in turn be used to do some other operation. If Bob were to learn this key, he could bypass Alice's cryptographic protections–read her files, sign arbitrary things with her private key, spend her bitcoins, etc.

The common solution to this problem involves password-based key derivation–Alice enters a password into her device, which is processed in some computationally expensive way, along with a salt (stored on her device), to get a symmetric key. Unfortunately for Alice, her device includes all the information needed to derive the key from a password and check whether the key is correct with a trial decryption. If Bob can steal her device, he can run an offline password search (a *dictionary attack*) on a machine set up for password cracking. Alice may not be able to remember a password strong enough to withstand such an attack.

1.1 Security Goals

To avoid this problem, we introduce TMPS: Ticket-Mediated Password Strengthening. Consider an attacker who has stolen the user's device and is trying to access her encrypted files–TMPS strictly limits the number of password guesses possible for that attacker. TMPS combines secret information stored on the user's device with an online server, to help the user decrypt her locally-stored files. However, simply incorporating an online server into the key derivation process does not provide a satisfactory solution.

TMPS prevents offline dictionary attacks, *even in the case where the server is compromised*. Note that this is *impossible* to achieve if the user (or user's device) does not hold some secret state that gets input to the protocol. Specifically, if the user's only input to the protocol is her password (and possibly other public information), then the user's only protection against a dictionary attack is rate-limiting by the server. If the server is compromised, the user's interaction with the server can be *fully simulated*, which means the attacker can run a dictionary attack against her password. Once the password is guessed correctly, the attacker obtains the corresponding payload key. This motivates our use of *tickets* which are locally stored on the user's device.

In fact, TMPS prevents offline password guessing attacks on Alice unless *both* Alice's local device and the server are compromised. Note that this is the best security possible for this kind of protocol, since if both Alice and the server are compromised, the protocol between Alice and the server can always be fully simulated, just by choosing password inputs for Alice. To achieve this stronger guarantee, we must create tickets that are tied to a specific user, password and payload key. This ensures that even if Charlie and the server are compromised, Charlie's tickets cannot be used to make password guesses on Alice's password.

Since tickets must be tied to a specific user, *privacy* now becomes a significant problem. We want to ensure that when the server receives a ticket, the server cannot link it to a specific user. Full user privacy requires anonymous communications with the server, however simply eliminating the need for the server to keep track of when each individual user accesses her files provides a privacy benefit–information that's never collected can never be leaked, subpoenaed, or sold.

Since the server can't determine which user is requesting its services, it becomes important to allow the server to *limit the service to only authorized users*. Naturally, this must be done in a way that still preserves the users' privacy.

1.2   Overview of TMPS

In TMPS, when the user wants to produce a new password-derived key, she runs a protocol with a server to produce a set of t *tickets*–bitstrings which she stores locally. Later, when she wants to unlock the key using her password, she runs another protocol with the server, providing (and expending) one of these tickets. The password can only be used to unlock the user's key with the server's help, and the server will not provide this help without a ticket that has never before been used.

The critical feature of TMPS is that *each ticket allows one guess of a password to unlock a particular key*. When Bob steals Alice's device, he gets t guesses at her password, one per ticket. Once he is out of tickets, the server will no longer help him check password guesses. Each ticket entitles the bearer to assistance computing one specific password-based decryption.

The result is that Alice can establish a hard limit on the number of possible guesses of the password Bob can make–if she has only 20 tickets on her device, then an attacker who compromises the device can never try more than 20 guesses of her password.

Our scheme gives users a security metric that is *human-meaningful*–the user can know the maximum number of guesses the attacker can ever have against their password. Hardness parameters of password hashes, or entropy estimates of a password, are meaningful only to security experts; the maximum number of attacker guesses that will be allowed is much easier to understand. Even rate-limiting parameters (e.g., no more than 10 tries per hour) are arguably less intuitive to users than a limit on the total number of password guesses. On the other hand, our scheme imposes the need to be online in order to unlock a key secured by a password[1].

TMPS also ensures that the server never learns anything about the user's password or keys or private data, or even which user is unlocking her data at which time[2]. As discussed above, no offline attack is possible against our scheme unless both the server and the user's device are compromised. On the other hand, this comes at a cost–our scheme works only on a specific device that has been set up by the user.

---

[1] In the full paper, we also provide an optional variant scheme for offline access–allowing a very computationally expensive key derivation when the server is unavailable, albeit at the cost of losing the limit on maximum number of guesses.

[2] Note that full user privacy requires the user to communicate with the server over an anonymous channel.

1.3   Related Work

Most work on password security focuses on password-based authentication systems. While there are similarities with earlier schemes, TMPS solves a different problem, mostly using different techniques.

Password Based Key Derivation (PBKDF) involves carrying out an expensive computation to derive a key from a password locally (e.g., [6,27]). Since PBKDFs do not need server access for key derivation, the privacy of the user is protected. However, although computationally- and memory-hard PBKDFs slow down dictionary attacks, such attacks can still be mounted. Note that TMPS uses a PBKDF as a component.

Remote Storage lets the user stores her secret information on some remote service, and retrieve it by logging in. This is in some sense the trivial solution to the problem of an attacker compromising the user's device. However, note that a server compromise in this case not only allows an offline attack on Alice's password, it reveals her secret data.

Password Authenticated Key Exchange (PAKE) protocols (e.g., [4,5, 16,28]) allow a user and server who share a password to securely establish a session key. These protocols have some similarities to our scheme, but they solve a very different problem–establishing a session key instead of rederiving a key for decrypting locally-stored data. Also, these protocols are vulnerable to offline dictionary attacks after server compromise, and the server inevitably knows who the user is when it establishes a key.

In [22], Mani describes a scheme that uses a server to assist in password hashing, but without any concern for user privacy–the goal in that scheme was to harden the password file by incorporating a pseudorandom function (PRF) computed on a single-purpose machine. Similarly, [2,23,24] describe a scheme with a separately-stored secret key in a crypto server to strengthen password hashing, an informal description of the concept of **Password Hardening**, later formally defined in [13,20,25]. Current password hardening schemes involve an outward-facing server into which the user logs in, and a rate-limiting server that assists in hashing passwords. Our scheme is somewhat related to password hardening, but is solving a different problem with different constraints and requirements.

A proposal by Lai et al. [19] defines a **Password Hardening Encryption** (PHE) scheme, which combines password hardening with encryption of user data. Our scheme is closely related to PHE, but there are important differences: TMPS uses locally stored data on the user's device, which means an offline attack can only be done when the user's device is compromised; for PHE, the outward-facing server plus the rate-limiting server can run offline dictionary attacks on the user's password[3]. Additionally, in PHE, the user is logging into a service, so there's no sense in trying to prevent the server learning when a given user

---

[3] Note that this is a straightforward engineering tradeoff–PHE avoids local storage, so it is more deployable, but the cost of that decision is that the user's data can be compromised even without compromising her device. TMPS makes the opposite tradeoff–the system is harder to deploy because it needs local storage, but it provides a corresponding security advantage.

is accessing her data–in TMPS, the user is accessing her own data on her own device, and so shouldn't have to leave a data trail with some external service.

In **Password-Protected Secret Sharing** [15], the user provides shares of a key to n servers, and requires some subset k of the servers to assist it in reconstructing the secret, in a way that will only work if the user provides the correct password. These schemes aren't focused on decrypting local storage, but could be adapted to such an application. However, because they avoid secret data stored on the user's device, an attacker who compromises k servers can run an offline dictionary attack. Further, servers know which user is reconstructing her secret data at any given time. A closely related line of work introduces the notion of password-based threshold authentication [1] for token-based authentication in single sign-on setting–in their scheme, any subset of ℓ of n servers participate in verifying the user's password and generating a token, which can then be used to authenticate to other devices on the network.

1.4   Our Results

- We introduce the notion of TMPS, a mechanism for allowing users to derive keys from passwords while imposing a strict limit on the number of guesses of their password any attacker can make, and strongly protecting the users' privacy.
- We formalize the security requirements of our new notion of TMPS, by defining a corresponding ideal functionality in the Universal Composability (UC) framework (See Sect. 5). In the full version of the paper [18], we also provide game-based proofs that show that the ideal functionality provides the desired level of security.
- We present efficient protocols realizing our new notion. Our basic protocol requires only hash functions, CCA2-secure encryption, and blind signatures (See Sect. 4).
- We prove that our protocol UC-realizes the aforementioned ideal functionality in the random oracle model (ROM) under adaptive corruptions with erasures (See Sect. 5.1) and prove that security with respect to the Ideal/Real definition implies security with respect to the game-based definitions (See the full version [18]).
- In the full version of the paper [18], we present several variants of our protocol, including an offline version of our protocol using a local hardware security module (HSM) or trusted execution environment, and variants that make use of group signatures, proofs of work, or weaker security assumptions to ensure user privacy while still preventing overuse of server resources.
- Finally, we discuss efficient implementations and performance, in Sect. 6, and consider some questions left open by this research in Sect. 7.

2   Preliminaries

2.1   Notation

Let $k \in \mathbb{N}$. The set of bitstrings of length k is denoted as $\{0,1\}^k$. The concatenation of two bitstrings x and y is denoted by $x \parallel y$. The exclusive-OR of two bitstrings x and y of same length is denoted as $x \oplus y$. We let b^k denote the string with k successive repetitions of bit b. If $\mathcal{X}$ is a set, we let $x \leftarrow_{\$} \mathcal{X}$ denote sampling a uniformly random element x from $\mathcal{X}$. The security parameter is denoted by $n \in \mathbb{N}$. Unless otherwise specified, we assume all symmetric keys and hash outputs to be n bits in length.

2.2   Underlying Primitives and Functions

We use the following primitives in our protocols:

- HASH(X): The cryptographic hash of input X.
- HMAC(K, X): The HMAC of X under key K.
- PH(S, P): Hash of the password P using salt S.
- KDF(K, D, ℓ): ℓ-bit key derived from the secret value K and public value D.
- $\Pi_{ENC} := $ (GEN, ENC, DEC): An encryption system where ENC(K, X) is encryption of plaintext X under the key K, and DEC(K, Y) is decryption of ciphertext Y under the key K.
- $\Pi_{BSIG} := $ (GEN, BLIND, UBLIND, SIGN, BVERIFY): A 2-move blind signature scheme where
    - $M^* \leftarrow$ BLIND(M): The user blinds the message M to obtain M^* and sends to the signer.
    - $\sigma^* \leftarrow$ SIGN$_{SK}$(M^*): The signer outputs a signature σ^* on input of message M^* and private key SK and sends to the user.
    - $F \leftarrow$ UBLIND(σ^*): The user unblinds the signature σ^* to obtain F. Note that the user inputs additional private state to the UBLIND algorithm, which we leave implicit.
    - BVERIFY$_{PK}$(M, F): Verification of signature F on message M under public key PK as valid/invalid.

Next, we define two internal functions: VE(D, K_P) provides verifiable encryption of K_P with D and DV(D, Z) decrypts K_P after checking the correctness of D. Both functions assume that D, K_P and hash outputs are n bits long. We remark that we use the special-purpose verifiable encryption scheme define here, as opposed to using a generic authenticated encryption scheme, for two reasons: First, our UC security proof requires use of a random oracle call here to allow for programmability; second, what is required here is not quite authenticated encryption–we only care about whether the *key* is correct, not about whether the decrypted plaintext is correct, and we only encrypt *once* under any key.

Formal definitions for the primitives used in our protocol appear in Appendix A.

Algorithm 1. Verifiably encrypt K_P with D.

1: **function** $\text{VE}(D, K_P)$
2:     $Z \leftarrow \text{HASH}(0 \parallel D) \parallel (\text{HASH}(1 \parallel D) \oplus K_P)$
3:     **return**(Z)

Algorithm 2. Verifiably decrypt Z with D.

1: **function** $\text{DV}(D, Z)$
2:     $X \leftarrow Z_{0...n-1}$
3:     $Y \leftarrow Z_{n...2n-1}$
4:     $X^* = \text{HASH}(0 \parallel D)$
5:     **if** $X == X^*$ **then**
6:         **return**$(\text{HASH}(1 \parallel D) \oplus Y)$
7:     **else**
8:         **return**$(\bot)$

---

3 Ticket-Mediated Password Strengthening

3.1 TMPS Overview

In *Ticket-Mediated Password Strengthening* (TMPS, for short), the user[4] first interacts with a server to get a set of *tickets*. Each ticket entitles the user to assistance from the server with one attempt to unlock a master secret (called the *payload key*) using a password. Later, users (or anyone else with access to the tickets) may use the tickets to attempt to unlock the payload key using the password.

TMPS requires a setup phase, and two protocols: REQUEST and UNLOCK. During setup, the server establishes public encryption and signing keys and makes them available to its users.

In order to get tickets, the user's device starts with a payload key (generated randomly) and a password, and runs the REQUEST protocol with the server, requesting t tickets. If the protocol terminates successfully, the user ends up with t tickets, each of which entitles her to one run of the UNLOCK protocol. Note that each ticket is bound to UNLOCKing a specific key with a specific password–Bob's tickets will not help with guessing Alice's password.

In order to use a password to unlock the payload key, the user must consume a ticket–she runs the UNLOCK protocol with the server, passing the server some information from the ticket and some information derived from her ticket and her password. The server will never accept the same ticket information twice. When the protocol runs successfully, the user recovers the payload key.

---

[4] For convenience, we refer to "the user" generating random values and running protocols in the rest of this paper when we really mean "software on the user's device." The user herself should only need to remember the password, and perhaps provide credentials to identify herself to the server when she requests new tickets.

The security requirements of a TMPS scheme are:

1. REQUEST
   (a) The server learns nothing about the password or payload key from the REQUEST protocol.
   (b) There is no way to get a ticket the server will accept, except by running the REQUEST protocol.
   (c) Each ticket is generated for a specific password and payload key; tickets generated for one password and payload key give no help in unlocking or learning any other password or payload key.
2. UNLOCK
   (a) An UNLOCK run will be successful (it will return the correct K_P) if and only if:
       i. This ticket came from a successful run of the REQUEST protocol.
       ii. This ticket has never been used in another UNLOCK call.
       iii. The same password used to REQUEST the ticket is used to UNLOCK it.
   (b) From an unsuccessful run of the UNLOCK protocol, the user gains no information about the payload key.
   (c) From an unsuccessful run of the UNLOCK protocol, the user learns (at most) that the password used to run the protocol was incorrect.
   (d) The server learns nothing about the payload key or password from the UNLOCK protocol.
   (e) The server learns nothing about which user ran the UNLOCK protocol with it at any given time.

Note that these requirements don't describe the generation of the payload key or the selection of the password. If the payload key is known or easily guessed, then TMPS can do nothing to improve the situation. In any real-world use, the payload key should be generated using a high-quality cryptographic random number generator.

The strength of the password matters for the security of ticket-mediated password strengthening, but in a very limited way–each run of UNLOCK consumes one ticket and allows the user to check one guess of the password. An attacker given N equally-likely passwords and t tickets thus has at most a t/N probability of successfully learning the password.

3.2   Discussion

The usual way password-based key derivation fails is that an offline attacker tries a huge number of candidate passwords, until he finally happens upon the user's password. He then derives the same key as the user derived, and may decrypt her files. A TMPS scheme avoids this attack by requiring the involvement of the server in each password guess, and (more importantly) by limiting the number of guesses that will ever be allowed. If the user of a TMPS scheme requests only 100 tickets from the server, then an attacker who compromises her machine and learns the tickets will never get more than 100 guesses of her password. If he cannot guess the password in his first 100 guesses, then he will never learn either the password or the payload key. Even if he is given the correct password after he has used up all the tickets, he cannot use that password to learn anything about the payload key.

The security of a TMPS scheme relies on the server being unwilling to allow anyone to reuse a ticket, and the inability of anyone to unlock a payload key with a password *without* running the UNLOCK protocol with a server, and consuming a fresh ticket in the process.

A corrupt server can weaken the security of TMPS, but only in limited ways. It cannot learn anything about the password or payload key. It cannot determine which user is associated with which ticket[5], or link REQUEST and UNLOCK runs. But it *can* enable an attacker who has already compromised a user's tickets to reuse those tickets as many times as he likes.

4 The Basic Protocol

In this section, we describe a set of protocols that implement Ticket-Mediated Password Strengthening in a concrete way. Our protocols require a secure cryptographic hash function, a public key encryption scheme providing CCA2 security[6], and a blind signature scheme[7]. Our scheme has some similarities to an online anonymous e-cash scheme–notably in the need to reject attempts to "double-spend." However, each ticket in our scheme is bound to a specific password hashing computation–it's as though each coin in an e-cash system could only be spent buying one particular item from one particular store.

A *ticket* gives a user enough information to enlist the server in helping carry out one password-based key derivation. Each ticket contains an *inside* part (which the user retains and does not share with the server) and an *outside* part (which the user sends to the server). The different parts of a ticket are bound together with each other and with the specific password and key derivation being carried out, and can't be used for a different key derivation.

We make two assumptions about this protocol: First, all messages in this protocol take place over an encrypted and authenticated channel. Second, the user somehow demonstrates that he is entitled to be given tickets by the server; we assume the user has already done this before the REQUEST protocol is run. There are many plausible ways this might be done, such as: (1) The user may

---

[5] To get a strong privacy guarantee, the user must communicate with the server over an anonymous communications channel. However, there's also a practical privacy benefit to a scheme in which the server has no reason to keep track of the times each user has unlocked a file.

[6] An attacker who can alter a ciphertext to get a new valid ciphertext for the same plaintext can attack our scheme.

[7] Variants which do not require a blind signature scheme appear in the full paper.

pay per ticket, (2) the user may demonstrate his membership in some group to whom the server provides this service, (3) the server may simply provide this service for all comers.

The specific method used is outside our scope. However the user demonstrates her authorization to receive tickets, it is very likely to involve revealing her identity. In order to protect the user's privacy from the server, the REQUEST protocol must thus prevent the server linking tickets with this identifying information, or linking tickets issued together.

4.1 Server Setup

The following steps are done once by the server[8]: (1) The server establishes an encryption keypair PK_S, SK_S for some algorithm that supports CCA2 security. Server distributes its public key to all users. (2) The server establishes a signature keypair PK_S', SK_S' for some algorithm that supports blind signatures. (3) The server establishes a list to store previously-seen tickets.

4.2 REQUEST: Protocol for Requesting Tickets

To request a ticket, the user starts out with a password P and a payload key K_P, and generates t tickets with the assistance of the server. In order to create a ticket without revealing any identifying information to the server, the user carries out the following steps:

1. Randomly generate an n-bit salt S and an n-bit secret value B.
2. Encrypt B using the public encryption key PK_S of the server, producing E.
3. Run a protocol to get a blind signature on E from the server–this is F.
4. Derive a one-time key from the password and the secret B:
$$D \leftarrow \text{HMAC}(B, \text{PH}(S, P))$$
5. Encrypt the payload key under the one-time key:
$$Z \leftarrow \text{VE}(D, K_P)$$

The ticket will consist of (S, E, F, Z); the user must irretrievably delete all the intermediate values above. The user repeats the steps t times to get t tickets. At the end of this protocol, the user has t tickets she can use to run the UNLOCK protocol. The server, on the other hand, knows only that it has issued t tickets to the user–it knows nothing else about them!

---

[8] Rolling over to new keys periodically can be done, but old decryption keys must be kept active until all tickets issued for them have been used–this could plausibly mean that old decryption keys never go away, and this does not allow for recovery from compromise of a decryption key.

Protocol: $\text{REQUEST}(P, K_P, t)$:

User	Server
for $i = 1 \ldots t$	

$\quad S \leftarrow_\$ \{0,1\}^n$

$\quad B \leftarrow_\$ \{0,1\}^n$

$\quad E \leftarrow \text{ENC}(PK_S, B)$

$\quad E^* \leftarrow \text{BLIND}(E)$

$$\xrightarrow{\quad E^* \quad}$$

$$\sigma^* \leftarrow \text{SIGN}_{SK'_S}(E^*)$$

$$\xleftarrow{\quad \sigma^* \quad}$$

$\quad F \leftarrow \text{UBLIND}(\sigma^*)$

$\quad C \leftarrow \text{PH}(S, P)$

$\quad D \leftarrow \text{HMAC}(B, C)$

$\quad Z \leftarrow \text{VE}(D, K_P)$

$\quad$ Forget B, C, D, E^*, σ^*

$\quad T_i \leftarrow (S, E, F, Z)$

endfor

return$(T_{1,2,\ldots,t})$

4.3   UNLOCK: Protocol for Unlocking a Ticket

In order to use a ticket along with a password $\hat{P}$ to unlock K_P, the user does the following steps:

1. Hash the password: $\hat{C} \leftarrow \text{PH}(S, \hat{P})$.
2. Send $(E, F, \hat{C})$ to the server.
3. If the signature is invalid or E is being reused, then the server returns $\perp$.
4. Otherwise:
   - (a) The server stores E, F as a used ticket.
   - (b) $B \leftarrow \text{DEC}(SK_S, E)$
   - (c) $D \leftarrow \text{HMAC}(B, \hat{C})$
   - (d) The server sends back D.
5. The user tries to decrypt Z with D. If this succeeds, she learns K_P. Otherwise, she learns that $\hat{P}$ was not the right password.

Note that in these two protocols, the server never learns anything about K_P, P, or $\hat{P}$, and has no way of linking a ticket between REQUEST and UNLOCK calls.

We also note that the UNLOCK protocol could be easily modified to enable creation of new tickets when the submitted password to UNLOCK is correct. This would ensure that a user who knows the password always has at least one valid ticket, which would improve usability of our scheme in real-world applications.

Protocol: UNLOCK$(S, E, F, Z, \hat{P})$:

User	Server
$\hat{C} \leftarrow \text{PH}(S, \hat{P})$	

$$\xrightarrow{\quad E, F, \hat{C} \quad}$$

IF
  E fresh AND
  $\text{VERIFY}_{SK'_S}(E, F)$
THEN
  $B \leftarrow \text{DEC}(SK_S, E)$
  $D \leftarrow \text{HMAC}(B, \hat{C})$
ELSE
  $D \leftarrow \perp$

$$\xleftarrow{\quad D \quad}$$

$K_P \leftarrow \text{DV}(D, Z)$
return(K_P)

---

5   Security Analysis

In this section, we provide a security analysis and some security proofs for our basic protocol. Our approach comes in three separate parts: First, we define an *ideal functionality* for the system. Second, we prove that our basic protocol is indistinguishable from the ideal functionality in the UC framework. In the full version of the paper, we also provide several game-based security definitions, and prove bounds on an attacker's probability of winning the games when they are interacting with the ideal functionality. These game-based definitions show that the ideal functionality we've defined actually provides the practical security we need from this scheme.

The ideal functionality makes use of a table τ—a key-value database indexed by a ticket T. T can be any n-bit string, or the special values $\perp$ and $*$.

A user calls REQUEST to get a new ticket[9]. We assume a two-sided authenticated and secure channel for REQUEST–the ideal functionality knows the user's identity, and the user knows she is talking with the ideal functionality. Also, REQUEST requires an interaction with the server, in which the server also learns the user's identity. At the end of the REQUEST call, the user either has a valid ticket, or knows she did not get a valid ticket. Note that in the case of a corrupted server, we allow the server to "override" the honest behavior of the ideal functionality by outputting a value R. If $R = 1$, the ideal functionality proceeds as normal. If $R = 0$, it indicates that the server does not wish to cooperate. In this case, the output to the user is $\perp$. Note that in the real world, we cannot prevent the corrupt server from issuing an invalid ticket. However, in this case, we require that the user can detect that the ticket is invalid. The strongest guarantees we can hope for in the real world are therefore captured by our ideal functionality.

Algorithm 3. Ideal Functionality: Initialize and REQUEST

    # *Initialize the table that will store passwords,*
    # *payload keys and aliases.*
1: **function** INITIALIZE(SID)
2:     SID.$\tau \leftarrow \{\}$
3: **function** REQUEST(U, SID, P, K_P)
    # *T corresponds to the "ideal" ticket.*
4:     $T \leftarrow_{\$} \{0,1\}^n$
    # *Insert $(P, K_P, \perp)$ into table τ with key T. The $\perp$*
    # *value indicates that the ticket T is fresh.*
5:     SID.$\tau[T] \leftarrow (P, K_P, \perp)$
6:     Send to server SID: (SID, REQUEST, U)
7:     **if** server SID compromised **then**
8:         Wait for response (SID, REQUEST, U, R).
9:     **else**
10:        $R \leftarrow 1$
11:     **if** $R = 1$ **then**
12:        Send to source U: (SID, REQUEST, T)
13:     **else**
14:        Send to source U: (SID, REQUEST, $\perp$)

---

[9] The ideal functionality is defined to return one ticket per REQUEST, but in our protocol description above, we define REQUEST to return t tickets at a time. This is equivalent to just rerunning the REQUEST ideal functionality t times.

The user makes use of a ticket and a password to recover her payload key with an UNLOCK call. We assume the UNLOCK call is made over a secure channel which is authenticated on one side–the user knows she is talking with the ideal functionality, but the ideal functionality doesn't know who is talking to it. UNLOCK also requires an interaction with the server, in which the server is not told the identity of the user. At the end of the UNLOCK call, the user either learns the payload key associated with the ticket she has used, or receives an error message ($\perp$) and knows the UNLOCK call has failed. Note that in the case of a corrupted server, we allow the server to "override" the honest behavior of the ideal functionality by outputting a value R. If $R = 1$, the ideal functionality responds with the payload key, in the case that the password is correct, *even if the ticket is not fresh*. If $R = 0$, it indicates that the server does not wish to cooperate. In this case, the output to the user is $\perp$. Note that in the real world, we cannot prevent the corrupt server from responding to unlock requests with tickets that are not fresh (this corresponds to the corrupt ideal server flipping R from 0 to 1). Moreover, in the real world, we cannot prevent a corrupt server from deviating from the protocol and computing the wrong payload key (this corresponds to the corrupt ideal server flipping R from 1 to 0). However, in this case, we require that the user can detect that the returned payload key is invalid. The strongest guarantees we can hope for in the real world are therefore captured by our ideal functionality.

Before stating our theorem, we note that we assume that the protocols for REQUEST and UNLOCK given in Sects. 4.2 and 4.3 are executed in a hybrid model, where an ideal functionality for secure, two (resp. one)-sided authenticated channels, $\mathcal{F}_{ac}$ (resp. $\mathcal{F}_{osac}$), (see e.g. [8]) is invoked each time a message is sent. We require that the VE scheme used is the one given in Algorithms 1 and 2. We assume three independent random oracles: H_{pw}, H_{KD}, H_{VE}. H_{pw} is the password hash. H_{KD} is used to model the HMAC key derivation as a random oracle[10] and H_{VE} is the random oracle for the verifiable encryption scheme given in Algorithms 1, 2.

Theorem 1. *Under the assumption that Π_{ENC} is a CCA2-secure encryption scheme (see Definition 5), Π_{BSIG} is a 2-move blind signature scheme (see Definition 7) and the assumptions listed above, the protocols for SETUP, REQUEST and UNLOCK given in Sects. 4.1, 4.2 and 4.3, UC-realize the ideal functionality provided in Algorithms 3 and 4 under adaptive corruptions, with erasures.*

---

[10] We remark that Dodis et al. [12] showed that HMAC is not indifferentiable from a random oracle. However, their attack only applies when one allows different sizes for the HMAC key. Since we require B to always be a fixed length, this attack does not apply to our setting–finding two values of B that give identical results from HMAC, implies finding collisions for the underlying hash function.

Algorithm 4. Ideal Functionality: UNLOCK

    # If ticket and password good, return K_P.
    # Otherwise, return $\perp$.
1: **function** UNLOCK(SID, T, $\hat{P}$)
2:    **if** $T \in$ SID.τ **then**
3:       $(P, K_P, \alpha) \leftarrow$ SID.$\tau[T]$
4:    **else**
      # $\alpha = *$ signals invalid ticket.
5:       $(P, K_P, \alpha) \leftarrow (\perp, \perp, *)$
6:       $R \leftarrow 0$
      # α corresponds to the alias for ticket T.
      # $\alpha = \perp$ indicates the ticket is fresh. $\alpha \neq \perp$ indicates
      # ticket T was previously assigned an alias so not fresh.
7:    **if** $\alpha = \perp$ **then**
      # Fresh ticket
8:       $\alpha \leftarrow_\$ \{0,1\}^n$
9:       $R \leftarrow 1$
10:   **else**
      # Reused or invalid ticket
11:       $R \leftarrow 0$
      # Server can see whether it's getting invalid,
      # repeated, or fresh ticket.
12:    Send to server SID: (SID, UNLOCK, α)
      # If server is NOT compromised, we know R.
      # If server IS compromised, we must ask it
      # how to respond.
13:    **if** Server SID compromised **then**
14:       Wait for (SID, UNLOCK, R)
      # $R \in \{0,1\}$
      # Send back the right response to the user.
15:    **if** $R = 0$ **then**
      # Server returns $\perp$, no decryption possible.
16:       Respond to caller: (SID, UNLOCK, $\perp$)
17:    **else if** $R = 1$ **then**
      # Server plays straight.
18:       **if** $\hat{P} = P$ **then**
19:          Respond to caller: (SID, UNLOCK, K_P)
20:       **else**
      # Server returns value, decryption fails.
21:          Respond to caller: (SID, UNLOCK, $\perp$)

5.1   Proof of Theorem 1

We also note that the only random oracle that gets programmed[11] in the proof is H_{VE}. We also assume that honest users securely erase their tickets after an unlock attempt with that ticket has been made (as well as any other part of their state which no longer needs to be stored).

To prove the Theorem 1, we provide a simulator Sim and prove that the resulting Ideal and Real distributions are computationally indistinguishable. Throughout, we assume that the same ticket (resp. alias) is never issued twice during a REQUEST (resp. UNLOCK) procedure in an Ideal execution with a single SID. Since each of these events occurs with at most $\lambda'^2/2^n$ probability, where λ' is the total number of tickets issued, this assumption can only reduce the adversarial distinguishing probability by at most $2 \cdot \lambda'^2/2^n$, which is negligible.

5.2   Description of Simulator Sim

Simulator Sim Under Adaptive Corruptions of Parties. Note that since we assume secure channels, Sim only needs to begin simulating the view at the moment that some party is corrupted.

Fix an environment Env, Server Server, users $\mathcal{U}_1, \ldots, \mathcal{U}_m$ and adversary $\mathcal{A}$. Recall that we allow the environment Env to choose the inputs of all parties. Simulator Sim does the following:

1. Initialization: Initialize tables $\mathcal{B}, \mathcal{E}, \mathcal{S}, \mathcal{Z}, \mathcal{T}_{\text{gen}}, \mathcal{T}_{\text{used}}$ to empty and counters count_i for $i \in [m]$ to 0.
2. Preprocessing: Let λ'_i be the maximum number of tickets for each party $\mathcal{U}_i$. For $i \in [m]$, $j \in [\lambda'_i]$: Generate $B^i_j \leftarrow \{0,1\}^n$, $S^i_j \leftarrow \{0,1\}^n$, $Z^i_j \leftarrow \{0,1\}^{2n}$. Add all generated B^i_j (resp. S^i_j, Z^i_j) values to $\mathcal{B}$ (resp. $\mathcal{S}, \mathcal{Z}$). Let λ' be the total number of (B^i_j, S^i_j, Z^i_j) tuples generated.
3. Responding to corruption requests:
   Corruption of a party $\mathcal{U}_i$: Sim corrupts the corresponding ideal party and obtains its internal state, consisting of unused tickets $t^i_1, \ldots, t^i_{\lambda_i}$. For $j \in [\text{count}_i]$, modify entry $(U^i, S^i_j, B^i_j, E^i_j, F^i_j, Z^i_j, \perp) \in \mathcal{T}_{\text{gen}}$ to $(U^i, S^i_j, B^i_j, E^i_j, F^i_j, Z^i_j, t^i_j)$. For $j \in \{\text{count}_i + 1, \ldots, \lambda_i\}$:

---

[11] We note that for UC composition to hold in the programmable random oracle model, one must, in general, assume that an independent random oracle is used for each SID instance. In our case, we essentially use the programmability of the random oracle to implement a non-committing encryption scheme (see [11]), by adjusting the outcome of H_{VE} to ensure that the string Z_i decrypts to the correct K_P value. Camenisch et al. [7] showed that some natural non-committing encryption schemes in the programmable random oracle model can be proven secure in the UC setting, since the simulator only needs to program the random oracle at random inputs, which have negligible chance of being already queried or programmed. We anticipate that a similar argument would work for our scheme, since D^i_j is unpredictable and with very high probability will not be queried in any other session before being programmed in the target session. However, our formal proof is only for the case where an independent random oracle is assumed for each session.

(a) Generate $E_j^i = \mathrm{ENC}_{PK_S}(B_j^i)$ and F_j^i as a blind signature of E_j^i using SK_S (note that since $\lambda_i - \mathrm{count}_i > 0$, Sim must have already generated $(PK_S, SK_S, PK_S', SK_S')$).

(b) Add $(U^i, S_j^i, E_j^i, F_j^i, Z_j^i, t_j^i)$ to $\mathcal{T}_{\mathrm{gen}}$ and E_j^i to set $\mathcal{E}$.
Sim releases tickets $(S_j^i, E_j^i, F_j^i, Z_j^i)$.

Corruption of Server: Sim corrupts the corresponding ideal party and obtains its ideal internal state If an Initialize query has not yet been submitted to the ideal functionality, Sim returns $\perp$. Otherwise, if the server's keys have not yet been sampled, Sim samples $(PK_S, SK_S, PK_S', SK_S')$. Let $\alpha_1, \ldots, \alpha_\lambda$ be the aliases in the ideal internal state (if any). Associate each row in $\mathcal{T}_{\mathrm{used}}$ with a random alias so each entry in $\mathcal{T}_{\mathrm{used}}$ contains a value from $\{\alpha_1, \ldots, \alpha_\lambda\}$ in its final column. For $i \in [\lambda - |\mathcal{T}_{\mathrm{used}}|]$, Generate $B_i \leftarrow \{0,1\}^n$, $E_i = \mathrm{ENC}_{PK_S}(B_i)$ and F_i as a blind signature of E_i. Add all tuples $(B_i, E_i, F_i, *, \alpha_i)$ to $\mathcal{T}_{\mathrm{used}}$. For each row of $\mathcal{T}_{\mathrm{used}}$, release (E_i, F_i).

4. Responding to random oracle queries to $H_{\mathrm{pw}}, H_{\mathrm{KD}}$: Sim forwards the query to the oracle and forwards the response back.

5. Responding to random oracle queries to H_{VE}: Sim maintains a table $\mathcal{T}_{H_{\mathrm{VE}}}$. The table is initialized as empty. Each time $\mathcal{A}$ queries H_{VE} on input x, Sim checks the table to see if an entry of the form (x, y) appears in the table for some y. If yes, Sim returns y. Otherwise, Sim chooses a random y, adds entry (x, y) to $\mathcal{T}_{H_{\mathrm{VE}}}$ and returns y to A.

6. When responding to oracle queries, Sim also does the following:
   - **Bad Event 1:** If Server is corrupted and $\mathcal{A}$ makes a query to H_{pw} with input of the form $S_j^i || \hat{P}_j^i$, where $S_j^i \in \mathcal{S}$ and $(\cdot, S_j^i, \cdot, \cdot, \cdot, \cdot, t_j^i) \notin \mathcal{T}_{\mathrm{gen}}$ (for $t_j^i \neq \perp$) then Sim aborts.
   - **Bad Event 2:** If Server is not corrupted and $\mathcal{A}$ makes a query to H_{KD} with input of the form $(B_j^i || \hat{C}_j^i)$, where $B_j^i \in \mathcal{B}$, then Sim aborts.
   - If Server is corrupted and $\mathcal{A}$ makes a query to H_{pw} with input of the form $S_j^i || \hat{P}_j^i$ where $S_j^i \in \mathcal{S}$, Sim finds the tuple of the form $(\cdot, S_j^i, \cdot, \cdot, \cdot, \cdot, t_j^i) \in \mathcal{T}_{\mathrm{gen}}$ and submits $\mathrm{UNLOCK}(\mathrm{SID}, t_j^i, \hat{P}_j^i)$ to the ideal functionality. Sim receives $(\mathrm{UNLOCK}, \mathrm{SID}, \alpha)$ from the ideal functionality, and returns $(\mathrm{SID}, \mathrm{UNLOCK}, 1)$. If the ideal functionality returns $\perp$, Sim forwards $\hat{C}_j^i = H_{\mathrm{pw}}(S_j^i || \hat{P}_j^i)$ to $\mathcal{A}$. If the ideal functionality returns K_P, Sim computes $\hat{C}_j^i = H_{\mathrm{pw}}(S_j^i || \hat{P}_j^i)$, $D_j^i = H_{\mathrm{KD}}(B_j^i || \hat{C}_j^i)$ and entries for $(0 || D_j^i, y_1), (1 || D_j^i, y_2)$ such that $y_1 || y_2 = Z_j^i \oplus (0^n, K_P))$ to $\mathcal{T}_{H_{\mathrm{VE}}}$. Sim returns $\hat{C}_j^i$ to A. **Bad Event 3:** If at this point $0 || D_j^i$ or $1 || D_j^i$ have already been queried to H_{VE}, Sim aborts.

7. Responding to messages from the REQUEST protocol issued by a corrupted $\mathcal{U}_i$ when Server is not corrupted. Sim does the following:
   (a) Generate $(PK_S, SK_S, PK_S', SK_S')$ if not yet generated.
   (b) Submit $\mathrm{REQUEST}(\mathcal{U}_i, \mathrm{SID}, 0, 0)$ to the ideal functionality and receive back ticket t.
   (c) Place $(U_i, *, *, *, *, *, t) \in \mathcal{T}_{\mathrm{gen}}$.
   (d) Play the part of an honest signer with secret key SK_S' in the blind signature protocol with the corrupted user.

8. Responding to $(\text{SID}, \text{REQUEST}, U_i)$ messages from Ideal Functionality. Sim does the following:
   (a) Set $\text{count}_i := \text{count}_i + 1$ and $j := \text{count}_i$.
   (b) Generate $E_j^i := \text{ENC}_{PK_S}(B_j^i)$.
   (c) Participate in a blind signature protocol on message E_j^i with the corrupted Server to obtain signature F_j^i.
   (d) Store $(U_i, S_j^i, B_j^i, E_j^i, F_j^i, Z_j^i, \bot) \in \mathcal{T}_{\text{gen}}$.
9. Responding to messages from the UNLOCK protocol issued by adversary $\mathcal{A}$ when Server is not corrupted. $\mathcal{A}$ sends $(\hat{E}, \hat{F}, \hat{C})$ to the server.
   – If a tuple of the form $(\cdot, \hat{E}, \cdot, \hat{t}, *) \in \mathcal{T}_{\text{used}}$, then send $\text{UNLOCK}(\text{SID}, \hat{t}, \bot)$ to the ideal functionality.
   – Otherwise, if the signature does not verify submit $\text{UNLOCK}(\text{SID}, \bot, \bot)$ to the ideal functionality.
   – Otherwise, if $\hat{E} = E_j^i \in \mathcal{E}$:
     (a) Find an entry of the form $(\cdot, \cdot, \cdot, \hat{E}, \cdot, \cdot, \hat{t}) \in \mathcal{T}_{\text{gen}}$. Add $(\hat{B}, \hat{E}, \hat{F}, \hat{t}, *)$ to $\mathcal{T}_{\text{used}}$.
     (b) **Bad Event 4:** If there is more than one oracle query that returned $\hat{C}$, Sim aborts.
     (c) If the unique query exists, extract the password guess $\hat{P}$ (with bit length at most n'). If it does not exist, set $\hat{P}$ to $\bot$. Send $\text{UNLOCK}(\text{SID}, \hat{t}, \hat{P})$ to the ideal functionality. **Bad Event 5:** If $\hat{C} = H_{\text{pw}}(S_j^i, \cdot)$, for some $S_j^i \in \mathcal{S}$, but $\mathcal{A}$ did not make an oracle query returning $\hat{C}$, Sim aborts.
     (d) If the ideal functionality returns a value K_P, then set $D_j^i = H_{\text{KD}}(B_j^i || \hat{C})$. Add $(0||D_j^i, y_1), (1||D_j^i, y_2)$ to $\mathcal{T}_{H_{\text{VE}}}$ such that $y_1 || y_2 = Z_j^i \oplus (0^n, K_P))$ Return D_j to $\mathcal{A}$. **Bad Event 6:** If $\mathcal{A}$ has already queried H_{VE} on $0||D_j^i$ or $1||D_j^i$, Sim aborts.
     (e) Otherwise, return $D_j^i = H_{\text{KD}}(B_j^i || \hat{C}_j^i)$.
   – Otherwise if $\hat{E} \notin \mathcal{E}$, Sim does the following:
     (a) **Bad Event 7:** If there is no entry of the form $(\cdot, *, *, *, *, *, \hat{t}) \in \mathcal{T}_{\text{gen}}$, Sim aborts.
     (b) Find an entry of the form $(\cdot, *, *, *, *, *, \hat{t}) \in \mathcal{T}_{\text{gen}}$ and remove it.
     (c) Decrypt $\hat{E}$ using SK_S to obtain $\hat{B}$. **Bad Event 8:** If $\hat{B} \in \mathcal{B}$, Sim aborts.
     (d) Make an UNLOCK request to the ideal functionality $\text{UNLOCK}(\text{SID}, \hat{t}, \bot)$
     (e) Continue the execution honestly to recover $\hat{D} = H_{\text{KD}}(\hat{B} || \hat{C})$. Return $\hat{D}$ to $\mathcal{A}$.
10. Responding to $(\text{UNLOCK}, \text{SID}, \alpha)$ messages from Ideal Functionality. If Sim receives a message $(\text{SID}, \text{UNLOCK}, \alpha)$ (which does not stem from an UNLOCK request submitted by Sim) then Sim does the following:
   (a) If there is some $(\hat{B}, \hat{E}, \hat{F}, *, \alpha) \in \mathcal{T}_{\text{used}}$. Then Sim forwards $(\hat{E}, \hat{F})$ to Server, along with a random value for $\hat{C}$.
   (b) If not, update the next tuple of the form $(\hat{B}, \hat{E}, \hat{F}, *, \bot) \in \mathcal{T}_{\text{used}}$, to $(\hat{B}, \hat{E}, \hat{F}, *, \alpha)$. Forward $(\hat{E}, \hat{F})$ to Server, along with a random value for $\hat{C}$.

(c) If Server returns $\perp$, then return 0 to the ideal functionality.

(d) Otherwise, Sim receives back a D value from Server and checks whether D was computed correctly with respect to $\hat{B}$ and $\hat{C}$. If yes, Sim sends (SID, UNLOCK, 1) to the ideal functionality. Otherwise, Sim sends (SID, UNLOCK, 0) to the ideal functionality. If tuples of the form $(0||D, y_1), (1||D, y_2)$ are not in $\mathcal{T}_{H_{\text{VE}}}$, Sim chooses random y_1, y_2 and adds $(0||D, y_1), (1||D, y_2)$ to $\mathcal{T}_{H_{\text{VE}}}$. **Bad Event 9:** If $(y_1||y_2) \oplus Z_j^i = 0^n||\cdot$, where $Z_j^i \in \mathcal{Z}$ and $(\cdot, \cdot, \cdot, Z_j^i, t_j^i) \notin \mathcal{T}_{\text{gen}}$ (for $t_j^i \neq \perp$), Sim aborts.

In Fig. 1, we list each of the Bad Events, its definition, an upperbound on its probability of occurrence, the underlying primitive that is relied upon (if any), and the corresponding lemma (if applicable). Recall that q is the total number of oracle queries made by the adversary $\mathcal{A}$ and Sim. λ' is the total number of tickets issued, ℓ is the total number of UNLOCK queries, n is the length of S_j^i, B_j^i as well as the output length of the random oracles, and n' is the bit-length of the password.

We begin by bounding the probability that the Bad Events occur. It is clear by inspection that Bad Event 1 occurs with probability at most $q \cdot \lambda' / 2^n$, and that Bad Event 4 occurs with probability at most $q^2 / 2^n$, where q is the total number of oracle queries made by the adversary and Sim. Moreover, it is clear that if Bad Event 2 does not occur, then Bad Events 3 and 6 occur with probability at most $q^2 / 2^n$ each. Bad Event 9 occurs with probability at most $\lambda' \cdot q / 2^n$. We proceed to bound the remaining events (Events 2, 5, 7, 8).

Lemma 1. *Bad Event 5 occurs with at most negligible probability in the Ideal experiment.*

We upper bound the probability of Bad Event 5 by analyzing the probability that $\hat{C} = H_{\text{pw}}(S_j^i, x)$, for some value of $x \in \{0,1\}^{n'}$. This probability can be upper bounded by $\frac{2^{n'}}{2^n}$, since there are $2^{n'}$ possible strings of the form $S_j^i||x$ and each of these gets mapped to a particular string $\hat{C}$ with probability $\frac{1}{2^n}$. Since there are at most ℓ number of unlock queries, the total probability is at most $\frac{\ell \cdot 2^{n'}}{2^n}$ Setting parameters appropriately, we have that $\frac{\ell \cdot 2^{n'}}{2^n}$ is negligible.

Lemma 2. *Assuming the CCA2 security of encryption scheme* ENC *(see Definition 7), the probability that Bad Event 2 or Bad Event 8 occurs is at most negligible in the Ideal experiment.*

The proof proceeds by showing that if Bad Event 2 or Bad Event 8 occurs with non-negligible probability, then there must be some $i \in [m]$, $j \in [\lambda_i']$ and efficient Env, $\mathcal{A}$ (who did not corrupt Server) such that $\mathcal{A}$ queries H_{KD} on the value, B_j^i, or, in an UNLOCK request, sends an encryption $\hat{E} \notin \mathcal{E}$ that decrypts to B_j^i, with non-negligible probability. We will use Env, $\mathcal{A}$ to obtain another efficient adversary $\mathcal{A}'$ who breaks the security of the CCA2 encryption scheme ENC.

The adversary $\mathcal{A}'$ breaking the CCA2 security of the encryption scheme ENC proceeds as follows: $\mathcal{A}'$ plays the part of Sim in the Ideal experiment, with the

Event	Definition	Probability	Primitive	Lemma
Bad Event 1	**Server** is corrupted and $\mathcal{A}$ queries $H_{\sf pw}$ with an input of the form $S_j^i\|\hat{P}_j^i$, where $S_j^i \in \mathcal{S}$ and there is no entry $(S_j^i, \cdot, \cdot, \cdot, t_j^i) \in \mathcal{T}$, with $t_j^i \neq \perp$.	$q \cdot \lambda'/2^n$	statistical	
Bad Event 2	**Server** is not corrupted and $\mathcal{A}$ makes a query to $H_{\sf KD}$ with input of the form $(B_j^i\|\hat{C}_j^i)$, where $B_j^i \in \mathcal{B}$.	negligible	CCA2 Enc Scheme	Lem 2
Bad Event 3	Server is corrupted and $(0\|D_j^i)$ or $(0\|D_j^i)$ have already been queried to $H_{\sf VE}$ at the point when Sim tries to program them.	$q^2/2^n$	statistical	
Bad Event 4	Two distinct oracle queries to $H_{\sf pw}$ returned the same value.	$q^2/2^n$	statistical	
Bad Event 5	UNLOCK query with $\hat{C} = H_{\sf pw}(S_j^i, \cdot)$ for some $S_j^i \in \mathcal{S}$, but $\mathcal{A}$ did not make an oracle query returning $\hat{C}$.	$\ell \cdot 2^{n'}/2^n$	statistical	Lem 1
Bad Event 6	Server is not corrupted and $(0\|D_j^i)$ or $(0\|D_j^i)$ have already been queried to $H_{\sf VE}$ at the point when Sim tries to program them.	$q^2/2^n$	statistical	
Bad Event 7	Server is not corrupted, $\mathcal{A}$ sends $(\hat{E}, \hat{F}, \hat{C})$ to Server, the signature verifies, $\hat{E} \notin \mathcal{E}$ and there is no unused entry in $\mathcal{T}_{\sf gen}$.	negligible	Unforg. of Blind Signature	Lem 3
Bad Event 8	Server is not corrupted, $\mathcal{A}$ sends $(\hat{E}, \hat{F}, \hat{C})$ to Server, the signature verifies, $\hat{E} \notin \mathcal{E}$ and $\hat{B} = {\sf DEC}_{SK_S}(\hat{E}) \in \mathcal{B}$.	negligible	CCA2 Enc Scheme	Lem 2
Bad Event 9	For some y_1, y_2 such that $(0\|D, y_1), (1\|D, y_2)$ are in $\mathcal{T}_{H_{\sf VE}}$, $(y_1\|y_2) \oplus Z_j^i = 0^n\|\cdot$, where $Z_j^i \in \mathcal{Z}$ and there is no entry $(\cdot, \cdot, \cdot, Z_j^i, t_j^i) \in \mathcal{T}_{\sf gen}$, with $t_j^i \neq \perp$.	$\lambda' \cdot q/2^n$	statistical	

Fig. 1. Table of Bad Events occurring in the simulation.

exception that (1) It knows all the honest users passwords and keys (since it controls Env); (2) It receives PK_S externally from its CCA2 challenger (and does not know the corresponding SK_S), (3) It aborts and outputs $0, 1$ with probability $1/2$ if $\mathcal{A}$ requests a Server corruption. Sim chooses random strings $B_j^i, B'^i_j \mathcal{B}$. Upon corruption of party $\mathcal{U}_i$, $\mathcal{A}'$ Sim sends B_j^i, B'^i_j back to its CCA2 challenger. The CCA2 challenger chooses $\tilde{b} \leftarrow \{0,1\}$ and returns an encryption of B_j^i if $\tilde{b} = 0$ and an encryption of B'^i_j if $\tilde{b} = 1$. Let E^* denote the challenge ciphertext that $\mathcal{A}'$ receives in return. $\mathcal{A}'$ continues to play the part of Sim, but includes challenge ciphertext E^* in the information returned for the corruption request for party $\mathcal{U}_i$, instead of a newly generated ciphertext. When responding to UNLOCK queries $(\hat{E}, \hat{F})$, Sim must decrypt using SK_S if $\hat{E} \notin \mathcal{E}$. But in this case, either (1) $\mathcal{A}'$ has not yet requested/received its challenge ciphertext from the CCA2 challenger or (2) $\hat{E} \neq E^*$, since $E^* \in \mathcal{E}$. So $\mathcal{A}'$ forwards the decryption query $\hat{E}$ to its CCA2 oracle. Recall that throughout the experiment, $\mathcal{A}'$ (playing the part of Sim) monitors all queries made to the random oracles. If an UNLOCK request is made with a valid ticket that includes E^* and a $\hat{C}_j^i$ value corresponding to the correct password, $\mathcal{A}'$ chooses a value for D_j^i at random (without querying oracle H_{KD}). If, at any point, **Case 1:** a query to H_{KD} of the form $(B_j^i, *)$ is made or some CCA2 decryption oracle query yields value B_j^i, then $\mathcal{A}'$ aborts the experiment and returns 0 to its challenger. If, at any point, **Case 2:** a query to H_{KD} of the form $(B'^i_j, *)$ is made or some CCA2 decryption oracle query yields value B'^i_j, then $\mathcal{A}'$ aborts the experiment and returns 1 to its challenger. If the experiment completes without the above cases occurring, $\mathcal{A}'$ flips a coin and returns the outcome to its challenger.

Now, note that if Bad Event 2 or 8 occur with non-negligible probability $\rho = \rho(n)$, then we must have that $\Pr[\tilde{b} = 0 \wedge \textbf{Case 1} \text{ occurs}] = \Pr[\tilde{b} = 1 \wedge \textbf{Case 2} \text{ occurs}] = \rho/2$.

On the other hand, it is always the case that $\Pr[\tilde{b} = 0 \wedge \textbf{Case 2} \text{ occurs}] = \Pr[\tilde{b} = 1 \wedge \textbf{Case 1} \text{ occurs}] = q/2^{n+1} + \lambda'/2^{n+1}$, where q is the total number of distinct oracle queries made during the experiment. This is because when $\tilde{b} = 0$, there is no information at all about B'^i_j contained in adversary $\mathcal{A}$'s view (unless $B'^i_j = B^{i'}_{j'}$ for some $(i', j') \neq (i, j)$, which occurs with probability at most $\lambda'/2^{n+1}$) and so $\mathcal{A}$ can only happen to query the oracle on B'^i_j at random. The case for $\tilde{b} = 1$ follows by identical reasoning.

Thus, the distinguishing advantage of CCA2 adversary $\mathcal{A}'$ is $\rho/2 - q/2^{n+1} - \lambda'/2^{n+1}$, which is non-negligible, since ρ is non-negligible. This implies a contradiction to the CCA2 security of the underlying encryption scheme.

Lemma 3. *Assuming the unforgeability of the blind signature scheme (see Definition 7), Bad Event 7 occurs with at most negligible probability in the Ideal experiment.*

The proof proceeds by showing that if Bad Event 7 occurs with non-negligible probability for some efficient adversary A, then, by definition, we obtain an efficient adversary $\mathcal{A}'$ who submits a larger number of valid UNLOCK requests than there are valid tickets obtained from the ideal functionality. But note that each valid UNLOCK request is accompanied by a fresh blind signature $\hat{F}$. Moreover, the number of valid signatures obtained from the signer corresponds to the number of valid tickets obtained. Thus, adversary $\mathcal{A}$ can be used to obtain adversary $\mathcal{A}'$ such that, according to Definition 7, breaks the security of the blind signature scheme.

Conditioned on the Bad Events not occurring, the only difference between a Real and Ideal execution, is that in the Ideal execution in Step (10b) the simulator submits the next available $(\hat{E}, \hat{F})$ pair, whereas in the Real execution the order of submitted $(\hat{E}, \hat{F})$ pairs depends on which party is making the UNLOCK request. However, the blindness property of the blind signature scheme ensures that given a set of interactions and message signature pairs, the signer cannot tell in which order the message signature pairs were generated. Indeed, this is the case even when (PK'_S, SK'_S) are adversarially generated. Thus, the view of the adversary is indistinguishable in the two cases. We therefore conclude with the following lemma.

Lemma 4. *Assuming the blindness of the blind signature scheme (see Definition 7), the Ideal and Real output distributions are computationally indistinguishable.*

6 Performance and Implementation

The TMPS protocol requires several primitives: (1) password hashing (e.g., PBKDF2 or Argon2), (2) public key encryption (e.g. RSA or El Gamal), (3) blind signatures (e.g. RSA or ElGamal), and (4) hash functions and HMAC (e.g., using SHA256 or Blake2).

The protocol permits a great deal of flexibility in choice of underlying cryptographic primitives. Notably, there are proposed post-quantum algorithms that meet these requirements.

We implemented our protocol in Python[12], using the Cryptography module, which provides a Python frontend for OpenSSL calls. The protocol allows a choice of underlying primitives; we used RSA with 3072-bit moduli for (blind) signatures and public key encryption, along with SHA256 for hashing, and PBKDF2_HMAC_SHA2 for password-hashing.

All measurements were performed on a Macbook Pro (3.5 GHz Intel Core i7)[13]. While this is not an optimized implementation, it allows us to obtain concrete performance numbers, and it demonstrates the practicality of the scheme.

6.1 Requesting a Ticket

On the user device, each ticket REQUEST requires the following operations: (1) one password hash computation, (2) generating $2n$ random bits, (3) one

---

[12] We will make source code available on a public-facing git repository.

[13] Any mention of commercial products within the paper is for information only; it does not imply recommendation or endorsement by NIST.

public key encryption, (4) blinding and unblinding one signature request, (5) one HMAC computation, and (6) two hash operations.

With RSA, this is comparable to the work needed to set up a TLS connection. Thus, devices that can set up a TLS connection can REQUEST tickets. The slowest part of this process on the user device is likely to be the password hash computation, which can be tuned by choosing its hardness parameters. In our implementation, each REQUEST required about 0.008 seconds on the user side.

On the server, each REQUEST requires only a blind signature. With RSA, this is approximately the same cost as a normal RSA signature[14]. In our implementation, each REQUEST required about 0.076 seconds on the server side.

6.2   Unlocking a Ticket

On the user device, each UNLOCK requires (1) one password hash, one HMAC and two hash computations. Again, the password hash is almost certain to be the slowest part of this process. In our implementation, each UNLOCK required about 0.0049s on the user side.

On the server, an UNLOCK call requires looking up a value in a list of previously-used tickets, a signature verification, a public key decryption and an HMAC computation. The cryptography used here is comparable to setting up a TLS connection, and so should be no problem for any server. In our implementation, each UNLOCK required about 0.002 seconds on the server side.

6.3   Storage

Keeping track of the previously-used tickets requires some storage, but not a huge amount. We can hash the value of E from the ticket (the public-key encrypted value) into 128 bits[15] (16 bytes), e.g., by truncating SHA256 outputs at 128 bits.

A user who makes ten UNLOCK calls per day will go through fewer than 4096 tickets in one year. The server needs 64 KiB to store one 16 byte hash for each of those tickets. If the server supports 1000 users, it will need about 64 MiB for a year's worth of tickets–a hash table with these values in it will fit into RAM.

Using 3072-bit RSA, each ticket requires less than 1 KiB on the user device. Thus, even low-end devices like tablets and smartphones can easily store a year's supply of tickets.

7   Conclusion and Open Questions

In this paper, we have introduced TMPS (Ticket-Mediated Password Strengthening), a new mechanism for strengthening password-based key derivation. We

---

[14] The extra work for getting a blind RSA signature is done by the person requesting the blind signature–they must blind the signature request, and unblind the value they get back from the signer.

[15] We can use a relatively short hash because we don't care about collisions–an attacker who forces two tickets to collide simply deprives himself of the use of one of his tickets.

have also proposed a set of protocols that implements a TMPS scheme, and proven its security in the UC model. In the full paper, we additionally provide a number of variant schemes which allow for different implementation constraints and tradeoffs.

There are several questions left open by this research.

- *Are there other settings where one can use tickets bound to a computation to obtain a novel functionality?* For example, could we use this kind of mechanism to limit accesses to a local encrypted database, or computations of a key derivation function?
- *Are there are more elaborate restrictions that can be imposed on these tickets, without losing the users' privacy?* For example, is it possible to rate-limit UNLOCK requests from a given user without revealing which user was using the scheme?
- A number of additional features would be useful in implementing this scheme on a large scale. Specifically:
  - Our TMPS protocol doesn't support key rollover well. The server can trivially switch to new encryption/signing keys for new tickets, but in practice, must keep the old decryption key active indefinitely. This means that rolling over the key in response to a suspected breach at the server isn't workable. An improved scheme for rolling over keys would be a valuable addition.
  - Our protocol doesn't have a nice way to resynchronize with the server when the user's device is restored from backup. Developing such a mechanism would make TMPS more practically useful.

Acknowledgements. The authors gratefully acknowledge Bart Preneel, Vincent Rijmen, Frank Piessens, Peihan Miao, Ray Perlner, Kristen Greene, and the many attendees of the Fall 2018 DC Area Crypto Day and NIST Crypto Reading Group for useful feedback and suggestions on this paper.

Appendix

A   Definitions

In this section, we mention the key definitions used in the security analysis of our protocol to facilitate better understanding. Our exposition closely follows [3, 14, 17, 26].

Definition 1 [Encryption System]. *An encryption system can be defined as a tuple of probabilistic polynomial-time algorithms* $\Pi_{ENC}(\text{GEN}, \text{ENC}, \text{DEC})$ *such that:*

1. *The key-generation algorithm* GEN *takes as input the security parameter* 1^n *and outputs a key* K.
2. *The encryption algorithm* ENC *takes as input a key* K *and a plaintext message* $M \in \{0, 1\}^*$, *and outputs a ciphertext* C *where* $C \leftarrow \text{ENC}_K(M)$.

3. *The decryption algorithm* DEC *takes as input a key and a ciphertext, and outputs a message. We assume without loss of generality that the decryption algorithm corresponding* ENC_K *is* DEC_K *such that* $M = \text{DEC}_K(C)$ *and for every* n, *every key* K *output by* GEN(1^n), *and every* $M \in \{0,1\}^*$, *it holds that* $\text{DEC}_K(\text{ENC}_K(M)) = M$.

The Chosen-Ciphertext Attack (CCA) Security Experiment $PrivK_{\mathcal{A},\Pi_{\text{ENC}}}^{cca}(n)$: Consider the following experiment for an encryption system $\Pi_{\text{ENC}} = (\text{GEN}, \text{ENC}, \text{DEC})$, adversary $\mathcal{A}$, and value n for the security parameter.

1. A random key K is generated by running GEN(1^n).
2. The adversary $\mathcal{A}$ is given input 1^n and oracle access to $\text{ENC}_K(\cdot)$ and $\text{DEC}_K(\cdot)$. It outputs a pair of messages M_0, M_1 of the same length.
3. A random bit $b \leftarrow \{0,1\}$ is chosen, and then a ciphertext $C \leftarrow \text{ENC}_K(M_b)$ is computed and given to $\mathcal{A}$. We call C the challenge ciphertext.
4. The adversary $\mathcal{A}$ continues to have oracle access to $\text{ENC}_K(\cdot)$ and $\text{DEC}_K(\cdot)$, but is not allowed to query the latter on the challenge ciphertext itself. Eventually, $\mathcal{A}$ outputs a bit b'
5. The output of the experiment is defined to be 1 if $b' = b$, and 0 otherwise.

Definition 2 *[CCA Security]*. *An encryption system* Π_{ENC} *has indistinguishable encryptions under a chosen-ciphertext attack (or is CCA-secure) if for all probabilistic polynomial-time adversaries* $\mathcal{A}$ *there exists a negligible function* negl *such that:*

$$Pr[PrivK_{\mathcal{A},\Pi_{\text{ENC}}}^{cca}(n) = 1] \leq \frac{1}{2} + negl(n),$$

where the probability is taken over all random coins used in the experiment.

Other variants of the CCA Security definition are defined below.

Definition 3 *[Chosen Plaintext Attack (CPA) Security]*. *Similar to the security experiment of CCA except that the Adversary* $\mathcal{A}$ *is not given access to decryption oracle at step 2 and step 4.*

Definition 4 *[Non-adaptive CCA or CCA1 Security]*. *Similar to the security experiment of CCA except that the Adversary* $\mathcal{A}$ *is not given access to decryption oracle at step 4.*

Definition 5 *[Adaptive CCA or CCA2 Security]*. *Similar to the security experiment of CCA where the Adversary* $\mathcal{A}$ *is allowed to perform a polynomially bounded number of encryptions, decryptions or other calculations over inputs of its choice except on the challenge ciphertext.*

Definition 6 *[Signature Scheme]*. *A signature scheme is a tuple of probabilistic polynomial-time algorithms* $\Pi_{SIG}(\text{GEN}, \text{SIGN}, \text{VERIFY})$ *such that:*

1. *The key-generation algorithm* GEN *takes as input a security parameter* 1^n *and outputs a pair of keys* (PK, SK). *These are called the public key and the private key, respectively.*

2. *The signing algorithm* SIGN *takes as input a private key SK and a message M from some underlying message space. It outputs a signature F represented as $F \leftarrow$ SIGN$_{SK}(M)$.*
3. *The deterministic verification algorithm* VERIFY *takes as input a public key PK, a message M, and a signature F. It outputs a bit b represented as $b =$ VERIFY$_{PK}(M, F)$ where $b = 1$ means valid and $b = 0$ means invalid.*

We require that for every n, every (PK, SK) output by GEN(1^n), and every message M in the appropriate underlying plaintext space, it holds that

$$\text{VERIFY}_{PK}(M, \text{SIGN}_{SK}(M)) = 1.$$

We say F is a valid signature on a message M if VERIFY$_{PK}(M, F) = 1$.

Definition 7 [Blind Signature]. *A 2-move blind signature scheme is an interactive signature scheme with signer $\mathcal{S}$ and user $\mathcal{U}$ and can be defined as a tuple of probabilistic polynomial-time algorithms $\Pi_{BSIG} =$ (GEN, BLIND, UBLIND, SIGN, BVERIFY) such that:*

1. *The key-generation algorithm Gen takes as input a security parameter 1^n and outputs a pair of keys (PK, SK). These are called the public key and the private key, respectively.*
2. *Signature Issuing. The parties execute the following protocol, denoted $\langle \mathcal{U}(PK, M), \mathcal{S}(SK) \rangle$:*
   (a) *$M^* \leftarrow$ BLIND(M): The user blinds the message M to obtain M^* and sends to the signer.*
   (b) *$F^* \leftarrow$ SIGN$_{SK}(M^*)$: The signer outputs a signature F^* on input of message M^* and private key SK and sends to the user.*
   (c) *$F \leftarrow$ UBLIND(F^*): The user unblinds the signature F^* to obtain F. Note that the user inputs additional private state to the UBLIND algorithm, which we leave implicit.*
3. *The deterministic verification algorithm* BVERIFY *takes as input a public key PK, a message M, and a signature F. It outputs a bit b where $b = 1$ means valid and $b = 0$ means invalid.*

We require that for every n, every (PK, SK) output by GEN(1^n), and every message $M \in \{0,1\}^n$ and any F output by $\mathcal{U}$ in the joint execution of $\langle \mathcal{U}(PK, M), \mathcal{S}(SK) \rangle$, it holds that

$$\text{BVERIFY}_{PK}(M, F) = 1.$$

The security of blind signature schemes requires two properties, namely unforgeability and blindness.

Definition 8 [Unforgeability]. *A 2-move blind signature scheme $\Pi_{BSIG} =$ (GEN, BLIND, UBLIND, SIGN, BVERIFY) is called unforgeable if for any efficient algorithm $\mathcal{A}$ the probability that experiment Unforge$_{\mathcal{A}}^{\Pi_{BSIG}}(n)$ evaluates to 1 is negligible (as a function of n) where*

Experiment $\boldsymbol{Forge^{\mathcal{A}}_{\Pi_{BSIG}}}$

1. $(SK, PK) \leftarrow \texttt{GEN}(1^n)$
2. $((M_1, F_1), \cdots, (M_{k+1}, F_{k+1})) \leftarrow \mathcal{A}^{\langle \cdot, \mathcal{S}(SK)\rangle^{\infty}}(PK)$ *Return 1 iff*
   (a) $M_i \neq M_j$ for $1 \leq i < j \leq k+1$ and
   (b) $\texttt{BVERIFY}_{PK}(M_i, F_i) = 1$ for all $i = 1, 2, \cdots, k+1$, and
   (c) at most k interactions with $\langle \cdot, \mathcal{S}(SK)\rangle^{\infty}$ were completed.

Definition 9 [Blindness]. *A 2-move blind signature scheme* $\Pi_{BSIG} =$ $(\texttt{GEN}, \texttt{BLIND}, \texttt{UBLIND}, \texttt{SIGN}, \texttt{BVERIFY})$ *is called blind if for any efficient algorithm* $\mathcal{A}$ *the probability that experiment* $Blind^{\Pi_{BSIG}}_{\texttt{BSIGN}^*}(n)$ *evaluates to 1 is negligibly close to* $\frac{1}{2}$ *where*

Experiment $\boldsymbol{Blind^{\Pi_{BSIG}}_{\texttt{BSIGN}^*}}$

1. $(PK, M_0, M_1, st_{find}) \leftarrow \mathcal{A}(find, 1^n)$
2. $b \leftarrow \{0, 1\}$
3. $st_{issue} \leftarrow \mathcal{A}^{\langle \mathcal{U}(PK, M_b), \cdot\rangle^1, \langle \mathcal{U}(PK, M_{1-b}), \cdot\rangle^1}(issue, st_{find})$ and let F_b, F_{1-b} denote the (possibly undefined) local outputs of $\mathcal{U}(PK, M_b)$ resp. $\mathcal{U}(PK, M_{1-b})$
4. set $(F_0, F_1) = (\bot, \bot)$ if $F_0 = \bot$ or $F_1 = \bot$
5. $b^* = \mathcal{A}(guess, F_0, F_1, st_{issue})$
6. return 1 iff $b = b^*$.

Definition 10 [Group Signature]. *A group signature scheme* $\Pi_{GSIG} =$ $(GK_g, \texttt{GSIGN}, \texttt{GVERIFY}, \texttt{OPEN})$ *consists of four polynomial-time algorithms:*

1. *The randomized group key generation algorithm* GK_g *takes input a security parameter* 1^n *and* 1^m *where* $m \in \mathbb{N}$ *is the group size and outputs a tuple* $(gPK, gmSK, gSK)$, *where* gPK *is the group public key,* $gmSK$ *is the group manager's secret key, and* gSK *is an n-vector of keys with* $gSK[i]$ *being a secret signing key for player* $i \in [m]$.
2. *The randomized group signing algorithm* $\texttt{GSIGN}$ *takes as input a secret signing key* $gSK[i]$ *and a message* M *to return a signature of M under* $gSK[i]$ $i \in [m]$.
3. *The deterministic group signature verification algorithm* $\texttt{GVERIFY}$ *takes as input the group public key* gPK, *a message* M, *and a candidate signature* F *for M to return either 1 or 0.*
4. *The deterministic opening algorithm* $\texttt{OPEN}$ *takes as input the group manager secret key* $gmSK$, *a message* M, *and a signature* F *of M to return an identity* i *or the symbol* $\bot$ *to indicate failure.*

Correctness: The scheme must satisfy the following correctness requirement. For all $n, m \in \mathbb{N}$, *all* $(gPK, gmSK, gSK) \in [GK_g(1^n, 1^m)]$, *all* $i \in [n]$ *and all* $M \in \{0, 1\}^*$

$$\texttt{GVERIFY}(gPK, M, \texttt{GSIGN}(gSK[i], M)) = 1 \text{ and}$$

$$\texttt{OPEN}(gmSK, M, \texttt{GSIGN}(gSK[i], M)) = i$$

Definitions of security in the Universal Composability (UC) framework. We refer to previous work [9, 10, 21] for definitions of UC secure computation in the adaptive-corruption setting.

References

1. Agrawal, S., Miao, P., Mohassel, P., Mukherjee, P.: PASTA: password-based threshold authentication. In: ACM Conference on Computer and Communications Security, pp. 2042–2059. ACM (2018)
2. Akhawe, D.: How dropbox securely stores your passwords (2016). https://blogs.dropbox.com/tech/2016/09/how-dropbox-securely-stores-your-passwords/. Accessed 4 January 2019
3. Bellare, M., Micciancio, D., Warinschi, B.: Foundations of group signatures: formal definitions, simplified requirements, and a construction based on general assumptions. In: Biham, E. (ed.) EUROCRYPT 2003. LNCS, vol. 2656, pp. 614–629. Springer, Heidelberg (2003). https://doi.org/10.1007/3-540-39200-9_38
4. Bellare, M., Pointcheval, D., Rogaway, P.: Authenticated key exchange secure against dictionary attacks. In: Preneel, B. (ed.) EUROCRYPT 2000. LNCS, vol. 1807, pp. 139–155. Springer, Heidelberg (2000). https://doi.org/10.1007/3-540-45539-6_11. http://dl.acm.org/citation.cfm?id=1756169.1756185
5. Bellovin, S.M., Merritt, M.: Encrypted key exchange: password-based protocols secure against dictionary attacks. In: IEEE Symposium on Research in Security and Privacy, pp. 72–84 (1992)
6. Biryukov, A., Dinu, D., Khovratovich, D.: Argon2: New generation of memory-hard functions for password hashing and other applications. In: IEEE European Symposium on Security and Privacy, EuroS&P 2016, Saarbrücken, Germany, 21–24 March 2016, pp. 292–302. IEEE (2016). https://doi.org/10.1109/EuroSP.2016.31, http://dx.doi.org/10.1109/EuroSP.2016.31
7. Camenisch, J., Drijvers, M., Gagliardoni, T., Lehmann, A., Neven, G.: The wonderful world of global random oracles. In: Nielsen, J.B., Rijmen, V. (eds.) EUROCRYPT 2018. LNCS, vol. 10820, pp. 280–312. Springer, Cham (2018). https://doi.org/10.1007/978-3-319-78381-9_11
8. Camenisch, J., Enderlein, R.R., Neven, G.: Two-server password-authenticated secret sharing UC-secure against transient corruptions. Cryptology ePrint Archive, Report 2015/006 (2015). http://eprint.iacr.org/2015/006
9. Canetti, R.: Security and composition of multiparty cryptographic protocols. J. Cryptology 13(1), 143–202 (2000). https://doi.org/10.1007/s001459910006
10. Canetti, R., Damgård, I., Dziembowski, S., Ishai, Y., Malkin, T.: On adaptive vs. non-adaptive security of multiparty protocols. In: Pfitzmann, B. (ed.) EUROCRYPT 2001. LNCS, vol. 2045, pp. 262–279. Springer, Heidelberg (2001). https://doi.org/10.1007/3-540-44987-6_17
11. Canetti, R., Feige, U., Goldreich, O., Naor, M.: Adaptively secure multi-party computation. In: 28th ACM STOC, pp. 639–648. ACM Press, May 1996. https://doi.org/10.1145/237814.238015
12. Dodis, Y., Ristenpart, T., Steinberger, J., Tessaro, S.: To hash or not to hash again? (In)Differentiability results for H^2 and HMAC. In: Safavi-Naini, R., Canetti, R. (eds.) CRYPTO 2012. LNCS, vol. 7417, pp. 348–366. Springer, Heidelberg (2012). https://doi.org/10.1007/978-3-642-32009-5_21
13. Everspaugh, A., Chaterjee, R., Scott, S., Juels, A., Ristenpart, T.: The pythia PRF service. In: 24th USENIX Security Symposium (USENIX Security 15), pp. 547–562. USENIX Association, Washington, D.C. (2015). https://www.usenix.org/conference/usenixsecurity15/technical-sessions/presentation/everspaugh
14. Hohenberger, S., Lewko, A., Waters, B.: Detecting dangerous queries: a new approach for chosen ciphertext security. Cryptology ePrint Archive, Report 2012/006 (2012). http://eprint.iacr.org/2012/006

15. Jarecki, S., Kiayias, A., Krawczyk, H., Xu, J.: TOPPSS: cost-minimal password-protected secret sharing based on threshold OPRF. In: Gollmann, D., Miyaji, A., Kikuchi, H. (eds.) ACNS 2017. LNCS, vol. 10355, pp. 39–58. Springer, Cham (2017). https://doi.org/10.1007/978-3-319-61204-1_3

16. Jarecki, S., Krawczyk, H., Xu, J.: OPAQUE: an asymmetric PAKE protocol secure against pre-computation attacks. In: Nielsen, J.B., Rijmen, V. (eds.) EUROCRYPT 2018. LNCS, vol. 10822, pp. 456–486. Springer, Cham (2018). https://doi.org/10.1007/978-3-319-78372-7_15

17. Katz, J., Lindell, Y.: Introduction to Modern Cryptography, 2nd edn. CRC Press, Boca Raton (2014)

18. Kelsey, J., Dachman-Soled, D., Mishra, S., Turan, M.S.: TMPS: ticket-mediated password strengthening. IACR Cryptology ePrint Archive 2019, 543 (2019). https://eprint.iacr.org/2019/543

19. Lai, R.W.F., Egger, C., Reinert, M., Chow, S.S.M., Maffei, M., Schröder, D.: Simple password-hardened encryption services. In: 27th USENIX Security Symposium (USENIX Security 18), pp. 1405–1421. USENIX Association, Baltimore, MD (2018). https://www.usenix.org/conference/usenixsecurity18/presentation/lai

20. Lai, R.W.F., Egger, C., Schröder, D., Chow, S.S.M.: Phoenix: rebirth of a cryptographic password-hardening service. In: 26th USENIX Security Symposium (USENIX Security 17), pp. 899–916. USENIX Association, Vancouver, BC (2017). https://www.usenix.org/conference/usenixsecurity17/technical-sessions/presentation/lai

21. Lindell, A.Y.: Adaptively secure two-party computation with erasures. In: Fischlin, M. (ed.) CT-RSA 2009. LNCS, vol. 5473, pp. 117–132. Springer, Heidelberg (2009). https://doi.org/10.1007/978-3-642-00862-7_8

22. Mani, A.: Life of a password. In: Real World Crypto 2015 (2015). https://rwc.iacr.org/2015/Slides/RWC-2015-Amani.pdf

23. Muffett, A.: Facebook: password hashing & authentication. Presentation at Passwords 2014 Conference, NTNU (2014). https://video.adm.ntnu.no/pres/54b660049af94

24. Muffett, A.: Life of a password. Presentation at Real World Crypto 2015 (2015)

25. Schneider, J., Fleischhacker, N., Schröder, D., Backes, M.: Efficient cryptographic password hardening services from partially oblivious commitments. In: Weippl, E.R., Katzenbeisser, S., Kruegel, C., Myers, A.C., Halevi, S. (eds.) Proceedings of the 2016 ACM SIGSAC Conference on Computer and Communications Security, Vienna, Austria, 24–28 October 2016, pp. 1192–1203. ACM (2016). http://dl.acm.org/citation.cfm?id=2976749

26. Schröder, D., Unruh, D.: Security of blind signatures revisited. In: Fischlin, M., Buchmann, J., Manulis, M. (eds.) PKC 2012. LNCS, vol. 7293, pp. 662–679. Springer, Heidelberg (2012). https://doi.org/10.1007/978-3-642-30057-8_39

27. Sönmez Turan, M., Barker, E.B., Burr, W.E., Chen, L.: SP 800–132. recommendation for password-based key derivation: Part 1: Storage applications. Technical report, National Institute of Standards & Technology, Gaithersburg, MD, United States (2010)

28. Wu, T.: The SRP authentication and key exchange system. RFC 2945, pp. 1–8 (2000). https://doi.org/10.17487/RFC2945

Overdrive2k: Efficient Secure MPC over $\mathbb{Z}_{2^k}$ from Somewhat Homomorphic Encryption

Emmanuela Orsini[1] (iD), Nigel P. Smart[1,2(✉)] (iD), and Frederik Vercauteren[1] (iD)

[1] imec-COSIC, KU Leuven, Leuven, Belgium
{emmanuela.orsini,nigel.smart,frederik.vercauteren}@kuleuven.be
[2] University of Bristol, Bristol, UK

Abstract. Recently, Cramer et al. (CRYPTO 2018) presented a protocol, SPDZ2k, for actively secure multiparty computation for dishonest majority in the pre-processing model over the ring $\mathbb{Z}_{2^k}$, instead of over a prime field $\mathbb{F}_p$. Their technique used oblivious transfer for the pre-processing phase, more specifically the MASCOT protocol (Keller et al. CCS 2016). In this paper we describe a more efficient technique for secure multiparty computation over $\mathbb{Z}_{2^k}$ based on somewhat homomorphic encryption. In particular we adapt the Overdrive approach (Keller et al. EUROCRYPT 2018) to obtain a protocol which is more like the original SPDZ protocol (Damgård et al. CRYPTO 2012). To accomplish this we introduce a special packing technique for the BGV encryption scheme operating on the plaintext space defined by the SPDZ2k protocol, extending the ciphertext packing method used in SPDZ to the case of $\mathbb{Z}_{2^k}$. We also present a more complete pre-processing phase for secure computation modulo 2^k by adding a new technique to produce shared random bits.

1 Introduction

The last ten years have seen a remarkable advance in practical protocols and systems to perform secure Multi-Party Computation (MPC). A major pillar of this advance has been in the case of a dishonest majority, in which one can obtain so-called active-security-with-abort. In this situation one is interested in MPC protocols for n parties, where $n \geq 2$, which are practical even for values of n in the tens (or potentially hundreds). Following the initial work of Bendlin et al. [4], the main breakthrough came with the SPDZ protocol by Damgård et al. [13] and its improvements, e.g. [12]. This protocol works in an offline/online manner over finite fields. In the offline phase, function-independent pre-processing is performed, typically to generate Beaver triples [3]. In the online phase, this pre-processing is consumed as the desired function is securely evaluated. Active security is obtained by parties not only sharing data, but also sharing a linear MAC on this data together with a share of the MAC key. Validation of correct behavior is done via a MAC check protocol which verifies that all opened data shares and all privately held MAC and key shares are consistent.

© Springer Nature Switzerland AG 2020
S. Jarecki (Ed.): CT-RSA 2020, LNCS 12006, pp. 254–283, 2020.
https://doi.org/10.1007/978-3-030-40186-3_12

Over the previous decade there has been a multitude of methods to produce the offline data needed for the SPDZ protocol. The initial protocol, [4], in this family used a linearly homomorphic encryption scheme, and pairwise zero-knowledge proofs to correctly generate the offline data. This approach works well for a small number of parties, but does not scale for larger values of n. The linearly homomorphic encryption method was replaced in the SPDZ paper [13] by a level-one Somewhat Homomorphic Encryption (SHE) scheme. The main efficiency improvement came from using the BGV [5] SHE scheme, and making extensive use of the packing technique of Smart and Vercauteren [21]. On the other hand, the main inefficiency was that, to obtain active security, one needed to prove knowledge of plaintexts and correctness of ciphertexts. These zero-knowledge proofs can (currently) only be done in a non-tight manner, and with a relatively large soundness error. This inefficiency in soundness error is usually overcome using standard amortization techniques. In [12], a different zero-knowledge proof was utilized which, whilst asymptotically better than that of [13], turned out to be impractical.

Attention then switched to Oblivious Transfer (OT) based pre-processing, such as the Tiny-OT [20] and MASCOT [18] protocols. Finally, in the last two years attention switched back to homomorphic encryption based protocols with the Overdrive paper by Keller et al. [19]. Overdrive gives two variants of the SPDZ protocol: Low-Gear and High-Gear. The Low-Gear variant uses the original linearly homomorphic encryption based methodology of [4], but implements it using a level-zero LWE-based SHE scheme (in this instance, BGV). The resulting method is very efficient for a small number of parties due to the inherent packing one can use. For two parties the authors of [19] suggest it is six to fourteen times faster than MASCOT [18, Tables 2 and 4] (with the precise figure depending on the network latency).

In the High-Gear variant of Overdrive the authors return to the original zero-knowledge proofs of [13], and make improvements by both reducing the lack of tightness (although not totally eliminating it), and enabling batching of the zero-knowledge proofs across all n parties on top of the usual amortization techniques. This last optimization results in an immediate improvement by a factor of n. Thus, for larger values of n, High-Gear is currently the best method for SPDZ-family style pre-processing over finite fields. In [19, Tables 2 and 4] the High-Gear protocol for two parties is shown to be up to six times faster than MASCOT (again depending on the network latency); whilst for 100 parties, [19, Table 7] implies a 13 fold improvement over MASCOT.

Very recently a new protocol was introduced to the SPDZ family in the work of Cramer et al. [10], referred to there, and here, by the shorthand SPDZ2k. Instead of defining MPC protocols over a finite field, SPDZ2k defines MPC protocols over a ring $\mathbb{Z}_{2^k}$. Designing MPC protocols over rings $\mathbb{Z}_{2^k}$ is potentially useful in many applications, and could significantly simplify implementations, such as in the case of evaluations of functions containing comparisons and bitwise operations. To enable computation over such rings, SPDZ2k makes changes to the way MACs are held, and verified, and more generally to how the pre-processing works. The paper [10] bases its pre-processing on a MASCOT-style methodology, hence the two protocols are inherently very similar. Indeed, recent work by Dåmgard et al. [11] implemented the SPDZ2k protocol showing that its performance is comparable to the MASCOT one.

Establishing whether an efficient pre-processing for MPC over $\mathbb{Z}_{2^k}$ can be provided via homomorphic encryption was left as an open problem by the authors of SPDZ2k. A quick naive investigation seems to imply that this is a non-starter. The main reason the SHE-based approach (either Low-Gear or High-Gear) is efficient is in the possibility of packing data into ciphertexts and performing many operations in parallel. For SPDZ over finite prime fields one selects the underlying ring in BGV (of degree N) to completely split over the finite field, thus one obtains N-fold parallelism. When extending the SHE schemes to work with a plaintext modulus of 2^k, instead of a prime p, the packing capacity decreases dramatically and one cannot approach anything like N-fold parallelism.

Our Contribution. In this paper we revisit the idea of using a SHE-based pre-processing, i.e. Overdrive-based, for the SPDZ2k family. We show that the above naive analysis, which would discount its applicability, is actually wrong.

Our *first contribution* is a new packing methodology which is particularly tailored to the pre-processing phase of SPDZ2k. In particular, we obtain (roughly speaking) a $N/5$ fold parallelism for High-Gear when mapped to working modulo 2^k. Since the High-Gear protocol is the state-of-the-art for the SPDZ family protocols in terms of efficiency for large numbers of parties, we focus our work on the High-Gear of Overdrive[1].

Using our new packing technique comes with difficulties. The main issue is that the packing for level-zero ciphertexts of a plaintext message is different from the packing used at level one. Thus there is a need to modify the distributed decryption procedure in one important case, namely when one needs to obtain a fresh encryption of the underlying plaintext rather than an additive secret sharing of it. This in turn raises another problem: the distributed decryption protocol requires pairs of ciphertexts with special properties associated to the packing. A party needs to generate two ciphertexts, one at level zero and one at level one, which encrypt the same value, but with different packings. Since parties could be adversarial, this means that we also need to adapt the zero-knowledge proofs associated with the High-Gear protocol to enable such pairs of ciphertexts to be produced correctly. Some of our amortized zero-knowledge proofs need to prove a more complex statement associated to our packing techniques, with an overall estimated factor $2/3$ loss in performance compared to HighGear.

Given that Overdrive is up to fourteen times faster that MASCOT, depending on the number of parties, and that MASCOT and SPDZ2k perform very

---

[1] Whilst writing this paper the TopGear [2] variant of High-Gear was published on e-print. This essentially allows the High-Gear protocol to be run at higher security levels for roughly the same performance. The TopGear improvements *cannot* be applied directly to our work, since the zero-knowledge proofs here require challenge spaces to be in $\mathbb{F}_q$ to ensure correctness.

similarly, we expect that our protocol is up to two times more efficient than the OT-based protocols in the two party setting. As the number of parties grows this gap will increase. Whilst these only indicate rough expected performance figures, we give a more concrete estimation of the communication complexity of our protocol in Sect. 7.

Our *second contribution* is in the construction of a more complete preprocessing phase for SPDZ-like protocols modulo 2^k, with active security in the dishonest majority setting. Other than a protocol for producing multiplication triples, we show how to efficiently produce random shared bits in the SPDZ2k framework using a trick similar to the one used in the SPDZ protocol over $\mathbb{F}_p$. Protocols over fields make use of the squaring operation over finite fields of odd characteristic which is a 2-to-1 map, whereas, modulo 2^k, this operation is a 4-to-1 map. We show a simple trick that permits to use essentially the same technique used mod p in the modulo 2^k setting.[2]

2 Preliminaries

In this section we introduce some important notation, describe the security model, recap on the SPDZ2k paper's requirements for the offline phase [10], plus the necessary background on the BGV Somewhat Homomorphic Encryption (SHE) scheme [5]. By way of notation we let $a \leftarrow A$ denote randomly assigning a value a from a set A, where we assume a uniform distribution on A. If A is an algorithm, we let $a \leftarrow A$ denote assignment of the output, where the probability distribution is over the random coins of A; we also let $a \leftarrow b$ be a shorthand for $a \leftarrow \{b\}$, i.e. to denote normal variable assignment. We denote by $[d]$ the set of integers $\{1, \ldots, d\}$.

Security Model. We prove security of our protocols in the universal composition (UC) framework of Canetti [7], and assume familiarity with this. Our protocols work with n parties, $P_1, \ldots, P_n$, and we consider security against malicious, static adversaries, i.e. corruption may only take place before the protocols start, corrupting up to $n - 1$ parties. Informally, when we say that a protocol Π securely implements a functionality $\mathcal{F}$ with computational (resp. statistical) security parameter κ (resp. s), our theorems guarantee that the advantage of any environment $\mathcal{Z}$ in distinguishing the ideal and real executions is in $O(2^{-\kappa})$ (resp. $O(2^{-s})$).

In some of our protocols we will need a coin-tossing functionality $\mathcal{F}_{\mathsf{Rand}}$, which given a set $\mathcal{D}$, outputs a uniformly random element r from $\mathcal{D}$. This functionality can be efficiently implemented in the random oracle model as described in [10].

---

[2] A similar trick for random shared bit generation is described in a concurrent and independent work [11].

2.1   The SPDZ2k Protocol

The SPDZ2k protocol [10] is parametrized by two integers k and s, where k defines the modulus 2^k over which the MPC protocol will run, and s is a statistical security parameter, for simplicity of exposition we will set $t = k + s$. For the reader who is new to the SPDZ2k protocol think of $k = s = 64$. As we are mainly focusing on the offline phase our complexity does not depend on whether $k < s$ or $k \geq s$, it only depends on the value of $t = k + s$.

The protocol performs MPC over the underlying ring $\mathbb{Z}_{2^k}$, however each value $x \in \mathbb{Z}_{2^k}$ is secret shared amongst the n parties via values $[x]_i \in \mathbb{Z}_{2^t}$, such that $x = \sum_{i=1}^{n} [x]_i \pmod{2^k}$. By abusing notation we also think of x as the sum $\sum_{i=1}^{n} [x]_i \pmod{2^t}$, since in the main SPDZ2k online protocol the upper s bits of x will be ignored.

Sometimes we will use $[x]_i$ to denote additive sharings of values $x \in \mathbb{Z}_{2^t}$, and sometimes with domains different from $\mathbb{Z}_{2^t}$. We will explicitly point this out when we do such alterations to the basic sharing.

Each of the n parties also holds a share $[\alpha]_i \in \mathbb{Z}_{2^s}$ of a global MAC key $\alpha = \sum_{i=1}^{n} [\alpha]_i \pmod{2^t}$. The global MAC key is used to authenticate the shares held by a party, in particular each party holds a value $[\gamma_x]_i = [\alpha \cdot x]_i \in \mathbb{Z}_{2^t}$ such that

$$\gamma_x = \sum_{i=1}^{n} [\alpha \cdot x]_i = \alpha \cdot x \pmod{2^t}.$$

A secret value $x \in \mathbb{Z}_{2^t}$ shared in this way is represented by $\langle x \rangle = \{[x]_i, [\gamma_x]_i\}_{i \in [n]}$, and we let $\langle x \rangle_i$ denote the pair of values $([x]_i, [\alpha \cdot x]_i)$ held by party P_i in this sharing.

Using this secret sharing scheme any *linear* function can be computed locally by the parties, i.e. without any interaction. This is done using the method in Fig. 1. We denote the process of executing this operation for a specific linear function as

$$\langle y \rangle \leftarrow c_0 + \sum_{i=1}^{k} c_i \cdot \langle x_i \rangle.$$

To perform non-linear operations the SPDZ2k protocol makes use of the offline-online paradigm. In the offline phase various generic pre-processed data items are produced which allow the online phase to proceed as a sequence of linear functions and opening operations. Each opening operation in the online phase needs to be checked for consistency, which can be done via the method introduced in [10] (which we recap on in the full version of the paper). The overall protocol achieves actively secure MPC with abort, with a statistical error probability of roughly $2^{-s + \log_2 s}$ (see [10, Lemma 1] for more details).

2.2   The BGV SHE Scheme and Associated Number Theory

In this section we outline the details of what we require of the BGV encryption scheme. Most of the details can be found in [5,14–16], although we will only require a variant, which supports circuits of multiplicative depth one.

Procedure LinearFuncShares

This procedure allows the computation of an arbitrary linear function $y = c_0 + \sum_{j=1}^{k} c_j \cdot x_j \mod 2^t$ given public inputs $c_0, c_1, \ldots, c_k$ and the parties shares $\langle x_j \rangle_i = \{[x_j]_i, [\gamma_{x_j}]_i\}_{j=1}^{k}, i \in [n]$. The output are the shares of $\langle y \rangle$.

1. Each $P_i, i \neq 1$, sets $[y]_i = \sum_{j=1}^{k} c_j \cdot [x_j]_i \pmod{2^t}$
2. Party P_1 sets $[y]_1 = c_0 + \sum_{j=1}^{k} c_j \cdot [x_j]_1 \pmod{2^t}$
3. Each party P_i sets $[\alpha \cdot y]_i = [\alpha]_i \cdot c_0 + \sum_{j=1}^{k} c_j \cdot [\alpha \cdot x_j]_i \pmod{2^t}$
4. Each party P_i sets $\langle y \rangle_i = \{[y]_i, [\alpha \cdot y]_i\}$

Fig. 1. Procedure to locally compute linear functions on shares

The Rings: The BGV encryption scheme, as we will use it, is built around the arithmetic of the cyclotomic ring $R = \mathbb{Z}[X]/(\Phi_m(X))$, where $\Phi_m(X)$ is the m-th cyclotomic polynomial. For an integer $q > 0$, we denote by R_q the ring obtained as reduction of R modulo q. In this work we will be taking m to be a prime p, and not the usual power of two as in most other papers. This is because we require that R factors modulo 2^t into a number r of distinct irreducible polynomials of degree d. To ensure better underlying geometry of the ring, i.e. the ring constant c_m is small (see [13]), we then select m to be prime.

Our main optimization to enable an efficient offline phase for SPDZ2k will rely on us looking at the plaintext space in different ways. The main plaintext space $\mathcal{P}$ we will use is equivalent to the 2-adic local ring, approximated to the t-th coefficient, namely

$$\mathcal{P} = \mathbb{Z}_{2^t}[X]/(\Phi_p(X)).$$

As can be found in [8], and used extensively in [14], the ring $\mathcal{P}$ decomposes into r irreducible factors each of degree d, as

$$\mathcal{P} \cong (\mathbb{Z}_{2^t}[X]/F_1(X)) \times \ldots \times (\mathbb{Z}_{2^t}[X]/F_r(X)) = \overline{\mathcal{P}},$$

where $\deg(F_i(X)) = d$ is the order of the element 2 in $\mathbb{F}_p^*$, and each $F_i(X)$ is the Hensel lift of the associated factor $f_i(X)$ of the factorization $\Phi_p(X) \equiv f_1(X) \cdots f_r(X) \pmod{2}$. We write $N = \deg(\Phi_p(X)) = \phi(p) = p - 1$ and so $N = r \cdot d$. We will denote by $\Gamma : \mathcal{P} \longrightarrow \overline{\mathcal{P}}$ the map which takes elements in $\mathcal{P}$ and maps them to the slot representation $\overline{\mathcal{P}}$, and by Ψ_{2^t} the map from the global polynomial ring R representation to the slot $\overline{\mathcal{P}}$ representation, i.e.

$$\Psi_{2^t} : R \longrightarrow \overline{\mathcal{P}}.$$

Note that this map takes a polynomial f in R, maps it to $\mathcal{P}$, via reduction modulo 2^t, and then turns the resulting polynomial into its slot representation, thus $\Psi_{2^t}(f) = \Gamma(f \pmod{2^t})$. We also let Γ^{-1} denote the inverse map of Γ, which maps an element in $\overline{\mathcal{P}}$ to its equivalent element in $\mathcal{P}$. See Fig. 2 for a summary of these, and other maps, we will be using[3].

---

[3] We will define the maps Θ_I, Θ_J and χ_I, χ_J in Fig. 2 in the next section.

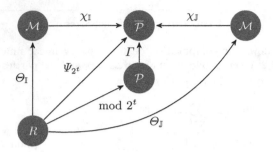

Fig. 2. Summary of the maps we use between different rings and representations

It is well known that the number of monic irreducible polynomials of degree d over a finite field $\mathbb{F}_q$ is equal to

$$\frac{1}{d} \sum_{i|d} \mu(d/i) \cdot q^i,$$

where $\mu(\cdot)$ is the Möbius function. This means that the number of SIMD "slots" r, using the packing technique of Smart and Vercauteren [21], is bounded by this value. In particular $r < 2^d$, and hence as N gets bigger we get progressively less efficient if we perform packing in a naive manner.

The problem occurs because we are interested in the plaintext space $\mathbb{Z}_{2^t}$, but the packing technique of [21] will only use the degree zero coefficient of each slot. Thus as d becomes larger for large N, the density of useful packing becomes smaller, and the ratio of data to plaintext space from this naive packing is $r/N = 1/d$.

The Distributions: Following [16, Full version, Appendix A.5] and [1, Documentation] we need different distributions in our protocol.

- HWT(h, N): This generates a vector of length N with elements chosen at random from $\{-1, 0, 1\}$ subject to the condition that the number of non-zero elements is equal to h.
- ZO$(0.5, N)$: This generates a vector of length N with elements chosen from $\{-1, 0, 1\}$ such that the probability of each coefficient is $p_{-1} = 1/4$, $p_0 = 1/2$ and $p_1 = 1/4$.
- dN(σ^2, N): This generates a vector of length N with elements chosen according to an approximation to the discrete Gaussian distribution with variance σ^2.
- RC$(0.5, \sigma^2, N)$: This generates a triple of elements (v, e_0, e_1) where v is sampled from ZO$_s(0.5, N)$ and e_0 and e_1 are sampled from dN$_s(\sigma^2, N)$.
- U(q, N): This generates a vector of length N with elements generated uniformly modulo q.

In the full version of the paper we present the traditional noise analysis for the BGV scheme adapted to our specific application; this is adapted from [16], using the above distributions.

The Two Level BGV Scheme: We consider a two-leveled homomorphic scheme, given by three algorithms/protocols $\mathcal{E}_{\mathsf{BGV}} = \{\mathsf{BGV.KeyGen}, \mathsf{BGV.Enc}, \mathsf{BGV.Dec}\}$, which is parametrized by a security parameter κ, and defined as follows. First we fix two moduli q_0 and q_1 such that $q_1 = p_0 \cdot p_1$ and $q_0 = p_0$, where p_0, p_1 are prime numbers. Encryption generates level one ciphertexts, i.e. with respect to the largest modulo q_1, and level one ciphertexts can be moved to level zero ciphertexts via the modulus switching operation. We require

$$p_1 \equiv 1 \pmod{2^t} \quad \text{and} \quad p_0 - 1 \equiv p_1 - 1 \equiv 0 \pmod{p}.$$

The first condition is to enable modulus switching to be performed efficiently, whereas the second is to enable fast arithmetic using Number Theoretic Fourier Transforms.

- BGV.KeyGen(1^κ): It outputs a secret key $\mathfrak{st}$ which is randomly selected from a distribution with Hamming weight h, i.e. $\mathsf{HWT}(h, N)$, much as in other systems, e.g. HELib [17] and SCALE [1] etc. The public key, $\mathfrak{pt}$, is of the form (a, b), such that

$$a \leftarrow \mathsf{U}(q_1, N) \quad \text{and} \quad b = a \cdot \mathfrak{st} + 2^t \cdot \epsilon \pmod{q_1},$$

where $\epsilon \leftarrow \mathsf{dN}(\sigma^2, N)$. This algorithm also outputs the relinearisation data $(a_{\mathfrak{st}, \mathfrak{st}^2}, b_{\mathfrak{st}, \mathfrak{st}^2})$ [6], where

$$a_{\mathfrak{st}, \mathfrak{st}^2} \leftarrow \mathsf{U}(q_1, N) \quad \text{and} \quad b_{\mathfrak{st}, \mathfrak{st}^2} = a_{\mathfrak{st}, \mathfrak{st}^2} \cdot \mathfrak{st} + 2^t \cdot e_{\mathfrak{st}, \mathfrak{st}^2} - p_1 \cdot \mathfrak{st}^2 \pmod{q_1},$$

with $e_{\mathfrak{st}, \mathfrak{st}^2} \leftarrow \mathsf{dN}(\sigma^2, N)$. We fix $\sigma = 3.16$ in what follows.
- BGV.Enc($m, \mathbf{r}; \mathfrak{pt}$): Given a plaintext $m \in \mathcal{P}$, the encryption algorithm samples $\mathbf{r} = (v, e_0, e_1) \leftarrow \mathsf{RC}(0.5, \sigma^2, n)$, i.e.

$$v \leftarrow \mathsf{ZO}(0.5, N) \quad \text{and} \quad e_0, e_1 \leftarrow \mathsf{dN}(\sigma^2, N),$$

and then sets

$$c_0 = b \cdot v + 2^t \cdot e_0 + m \pmod{q_1}, \quad c_1 = a \cdot v + 2^t \cdot e_1 \pmod{q_1}.$$

Hence the initial ciphertext is $\mathsf{ct} = (1, c_0, c_1)$, where the first index denotes the level (initially set to be equal to one). We define a modulus switching operation which allows us to move from a level one to a level zero ciphertext, *without altering* the plaintext polynomial, that is

$$(0, c_0', c_1') \leftarrow \mathsf{SwitchMod}((1, c_0, c_1)), \quad c_0', c_1' \in R_{q_0}.$$

- BGV.Dec$((c_0, c_1); \mathfrak{st})$: Decryption is obtained by switching the ciphertext to level zero (if it is not already at level zero) and then decrypting $(0, c_0, c_1)$ via the equation

$$(c_0 - \mathfrak{st} \cdot c_1 \quad (\mathrm{cmod}\, q_0)) \quad (\mathrm{mod}\, 2^t),$$

which results in an element of $\mathcal{P}$. The notation cmod refers to centered modular reduction, i.e. the resulting coefficients are taken in the interval $(-q/2, q/2]$. In the next sections, we will extend the decryption algorithm to enable distributed decryption.

- *Homomorphic Operations:* Ciphertexts at the same level ℓ can be added,

$$(\ell, c_0, c_1) \boxplus (\ell, c_0', c_1') = (\ell, (c_0 + c_0' \quad (\mathrm{mod}\, q_\ell)), (c_1 + c_1' \quad (\mathrm{mod}\, q_\ell)),$$

with the result being a ciphertext, which encodes a plaintext that is the sum of the two plaintexts of the initial ciphertexts.

Ciphertexts at level one can be multiplied together to obtain a ciphertext at level zero, where the output ciphertext encodes a plaintext which is the product of the plaintexts encoded by the input plaintexts. We do not present the method here, although it is pretty standard consisting of a modulus-switch, tensor-operation, then relinearization. We write the operation as

$$(1, c_0, c_1) \odot (1, c_0', c_1') = (0, c_0'', c_1''), \quad \text{with} \quad c_0'', c_1'' \in R_{q_0}.$$

3   Modified SHE Scheme

In this section we present a modified form of the previously presented "standard" BGV scheme. The main difference is that we introduce a new form of packing, where at each ciphertext level we interpret the naive BGV plaintext space $\mathcal{P}$ in a different manner. This modification enables us to obtain a final pre-processing phase for our MPC protocol which is less inefficient than one would naively expect.

3.1   Our New Packing Technique

The standard packing method of using only the degree zero coefficient in each slot will result in a very inefficient use of resources, as we have already mentioned. Thus we introduce a new packing technique which uses more coefficients in each slot. To do so, we first define two sets $\mathbb{I} = \{i_1, \dots, i_{|\mathbb{I}|}\}$ and $\mathbb{J} = \{j_1, \dots, j_{|\mathbb{I}|}\}$, such that $|\mathbb{I}| = |\mathbb{J}|$, and $j_\ell = 2 \cdot i_\ell$, for all $\ell = 1, \dots, |\mathbb{I}|$. The idea is to encode (in each slot) $|\mathbb{I}|$ messages as coefficients of the powers X^i, with $i \in \mathbb{I}$, as follows. We define a map $\omega_{\mathbb{I}}$ for the set $\mathbb{I}$, as

$$\omega_{\mathbb{I}} : \begin{cases} (\mathbb{Z}_{2^t})^{|\mathbb{I}|} & \longrightarrow \quad \mathbb{Z}_{2^t}[X] \\ (m_1, \dots, m_{|\mathbb{I}|}) & \longmapsto m_1 \cdot X^{i_1} + \dots + m_{|\mathbb{I}|} \cdot X^{i_{|\mathbb{I}|}}, \end{cases}$$

and a similar one $\omega_{\mathbb{J}}$ for the set $\mathbb{J}$. The reason why we require $j_\ell = 2 \cdot i_\ell$, for all $\ell = 1, \dots, |\mathbb{I}|$, is that the $\mathbb{J}$-encoding will typically be used to hold the result of a product of two $\mathbb{I}$-encodings. As such we are only interested in the product of two terms of the same degree (giving rise to the $2 \cdot i_\ell$) and will ignore all other cross-products that appear in the product of two $\mathbb{I}$-encodings (all terms of degree $i_j + i_k$ for $j \neq k \in [|\mathbb{I}|]$). For level one ciphertexts (namely fresh ciphertexts), we will pack a message value from $\mathcal{M} = (\mathbb{Z}_{2^t})^{r \times |\mathbb{I}|}$ into the plaintext space $\overline{\mathcal{P}}$ as follows

$$\chi_\mathbb{I} : \begin{cases} \mathcal{M} & \longrightarrow & \overline{\mathcal{P}} \\ (\mathbf{m}_1, \ldots, \mathbf{m}_r) & \longmapsto & (\omega_\mathbb{I}(\mathbf{m}_1), \ldots, \omega_\mathbb{I}(\mathbf{m}_r)), \end{cases}$$

with a similar map being defined for the set $\mathbb{J}$. It is straightforward to see that this is a valid packing, and will be consistent for all ciphertexts at level one, since linear operations on elements in $\mathsf{Im}(\chi_\mathbb{I})$ also lie in $\mathsf{Im}(\chi_\mathbb{I})$.

For ease of convenience, we also define an "inverse" map, $\chi_\mathbb{I}^{-1}$, of the map above, which is defined on $\overline{\mathcal{P}}$ and simply selects the correct coefficients, producing a final output in $\mathcal{M}$. We also define $\mathsf{Supp}(\mathbb{I})$, to be the set of (potentially) non-zero coefficients in each slot in the image of $\omega_\mathbb{I}$, in particular elements in $\mathsf{Supp}(\mathbb{I})$ are the only values which affect the value of $\chi_\mathbb{I}^{-1}$. Thus we have

$$\mathsf{Supp}(\mathbb{I}) = \{(1, i_1), \ldots, (1, i_{|\mathbb{I}|}), (2, i_1), \ldots, (r, i_{|\mathbb{I}|})\},$$

where the first element of each pair refers to which slot we are considering and the second element to the power of X in that particular slot. Given an element u in the global polynomial ring R we can define an element in $\mathcal{M}$ by reducing the polynomial u modulo 2^t then taking its image under one of the inverse maps above. Thus we have the map

$$\Theta_\mathbb{I} : \begin{cases} R & \longrightarrow & \mathcal{M} \\ u & \longmapsto & \chi_\mathbb{I}^{-1}(\Psi_{2^t}(u)) \end{cases}$$

Given an element $m \in \mathcal{M}$, there are infinitely many preimages under the map $\Theta_\mathbb{I}$. At various points we will need to select one subject to a given bound B on the coefficients of the polynomial in R. We therefore define, in Fig. 3, a procedure which outputs an element in R, uniformly at random, subject to the constraint that its image under $\Theta_\mathbb{I}$ is equal to a given element $\mathbf{m} \in \mathcal{M}$ and its coefficients are bounded by B. Clearly, all of the above considerations apply also to the set $\mathbb{J}$.

3.2 The BGV Encryption Scheme with Double Packing Set

We are now ready to define our modified BGV scheme, $\mathcal{E}_{\mathsf{mBGV}} = \{\mathsf{mBGV.KeyGen}, \mathsf{mBGV.Enc}, \mathsf{mBGV.Dec}\}$, which uses plaintext space $\mathcal{M} = (\mathbb{Z}_{2^t})^{r \times |\mathbb{I}|}$. The key generation algorithm $\mathsf{mBGV.KeyGen}$ is the same as in the original BGV scheme presented earlier, i.e. given a security parameter κ, it outputs a public/private key pair $(\mathfrak{pk}, \mathfrak{sk})$ and the relinearisation data.

The encryption algorithm differs as it now encrypts using one of the two sets $\mathbb{I}$ or $\mathbb{J}$. To make the dependence clear on which set we are encrypting a message under, we write either

$$\mathfrak{ct}^\mathbb{I} = (1, c_0, c_1)^\mathbb{I} = \mathsf{mBGV.Enc}(\mathbf{m}, \mathbf{r}; \mathbb{I}, \mathfrak{pk}) = \mathsf{BGV.Enc}(\Gamma^{-1}(\chi_\mathbb{I}(\mathbf{m})), \mathbf{r}; \mathfrak{pk})$$

The Function $\Theta_{\mathbb{I}}^{-1}(m, B)$

1. Compute $m_{\overline{\mathcal{P}}} \in \overline{\mathcal{P}}$, the image of $\mathbf{m}$ under the map $\chi_{\mathbb{I}}$.
2. For all entries *not in* $\mathsf{Supp}(\mathbb{I})$, replace the zero coefficient in each slot by a uniformly random element selected from $[0, \ldots, 2^t]$, resulting in a uniformly random element $m'_{\overline{\mathcal{P}}} \in \overline{\mathcal{P}}$ whose image under $\chi_{\mathbb{I}}^{-1}$ is also $\mathbf{m}$.
3. Pull back $m'_{\overline{\mathcal{P}}}$ to R by computing the element $m'_R \leftarrow \Psi_{2^t}^{-1}(m'_{\overline{\mathcal{P}}})$ subject to all coefficients lying in $[0, \ldots, 2^t]$.
4. Select a uniformly random polynomial $u \in R$ whose coefficient infinity norm is bounded by $B/2^t$.
5. Output $m_R \leftarrow m'_R + 2^t \cdot u$.

Fig. 3. The procedure $\Theta_{\mathbb{I}}^{-1}(\mathbf{m}, B)$ from R to $\mathcal{M}$

or

$$\mathfrak{ct}^{\mathbb{J}} = (1, c_0, c_1)^{\mathbb{J}} = \mathsf{mBGV.Enc}(\mathbf{m}, \mathbf{r}; \mathbb{J}, \mathfrak{pt}) = \mathsf{BGV.Enc}(\Gamma^{-1}(\chi_{\mathbb{J}}(\mathbf{m})), \mathbf{r}; \mathfrak{pt}),$$

where $\mathbf{m} \in \mathcal{M}$. Similarly, the decryption algorithm is defined as

$$\mathbf{m} = \mathsf{mBGV.Dec}(\mathfrak{ct}^{\mathbb{I}}; \mathfrak{st}) = \chi_{\mathbb{I}}^{-1}(\Gamma(\mathsf{BGV.Dec}(\mathfrak{ct}^{\mathbb{I}}; \mathfrak{st})))$$

and

$$\mathbf{m} = \mathsf{mBGV.Dec}(\mathfrak{ct}^{\mathbb{J}}; \mathfrak{st}) = \chi_{\mathbb{J}}^{-1}(\Gamma(\mathsf{BGV.Dec}(\mathfrak{ct}^{\mathbb{J}}; \mathfrak{st}))).$$

Addition and multiplication of ciphertexts are accomplished as in the "standard" BGV scheme, but with some notable differences. Notice we can now only add ciphertexts at the same level when they are with respect to the same encoding. Thus we have (say)

$$(1, c_0, c_1)^{\mathbb{I}} \boxplus (1, c'_0, c'_1)^{\mathbb{I}} = (1, c''_0, c''_1)^{\mathbb{I}}.$$

The idea is that the $\mathbb{I}$ encoding is used for messages at level one, and the $\mathbb{J}$ encoding is used for messages at level zero, typically obtained as the result of multiplying two level one ciphertexts.

In the following sections we will use the bracked exponent $\mathfrak{ct}^{(\ell)}$ on a ciphertext to denote the "level" which the ciphertext is at, with fresh ciphertext always being at level one. Hence, following the discussion above we will usually have:

$$\mathfrak{ct}^{(1)} = (1, c_0, c_1)^{\mathbb{I}} = \mathfrak{ct}^{\mathbb{I}} \quad \text{and} \quad \mathfrak{ct}^{(0)} = (0, c_0, c_1)^{\mathbb{J}} = \mathfrak{ct}^{\mathbb{J}}.$$

However we might need to encrypt some messages using index set $\mathbb{J}$, for example if we wish to encrypt a fresh message and then move it directly to level zero using a $\mathsf{SwitchMod}$ operation, as in $(0, c'_0, c'_1)^{\mathbb{J}} \leftarrow \mathsf{SwitchMod}((1, c_0, c_1)^{\mathbb{J}})$, where $(1, c_0, c_1)^{\mathbb{J}} = \mathsf{Enc.mBGV}(\mathbf{m}, \mathbf{r}; \mathbb{J}, \mathfrak{pt})$. The reason we switch encodings as we transfer between level one and level zero is that when two ciphertexts are multiplied at level one to produce a level zero ciphertext, the $\mathbb{I}$ packing will no longer be valid. So we switch to index set $\mathbb{J}$ at this point. Our multiplication is now an operation of the form

$$(1, c_0, c_1)^{\mathbb{I}} \odot (1, c_0', c_1')^{\mathbb{I}} = (0, c_0'', c_1'')^{\mathbb{J}}.$$

We will clarify the dependence on $\mathbb{I}$ or $\mathbb{J}$ and the encryption level ℓ when it is not clear from the context. More formally, in our MPC protocol, we will denote addition and multiplication of ciphertexts as follows:

$$\mathsf{ct}^{(\ell, \cdot)}_{m_1 + m_2} \leftarrow \mathsf{ct}^{(\ell, \cdot)}_{m_1} \boxplus \mathsf{ct}^{(\ell, \cdot)}_{m_2},$$
$$\mathsf{ct}^{(\ell, \cdot)}_{a \cdot m} \leftarrow a \odot \mathsf{ct}^{(\ell, \cdot)}_{m}, \quad \text{for } a \in \mathcal{M},$$
$$\mathsf{ct}^{(0, \mathbb{J})}_{m_1 \cdot m_2} \leftarrow \mathsf{ct}^{(1, \mathbb{I})}_{m_1} \odot \mathsf{ct}^{(1, \mathbb{I})}_{m_2}.$$

Correctness. To have correctness we need to ensure that multiplication of two elements in $\mathsf{Im}(\chi_{\mathbb{I}})$ results in something correct when we restrict $\overline{\mathcal{P}}$ to the image of the $\chi_{\mathbb{J}}$ map, i.e. by ignoring coefficients which are not in the image of $\chi_{\mathbb{J}}$. This is because a product of two elements in $\mathsf{Im}(\chi_{\mathbb{I}})$ is *not* an element of $\mathsf{Im}(\chi_{\mathbb{J}})$. Looking ahead, when we use this packing technique in our MPC protocol we need to ensure that ignoring coefficients that are not in $\mathsf{Im}(\chi_{\mathbb{I}})$ does not leak information. We shall deal with this security issue in the next sections, so for now we consider only the correctness concern.

To select $\mathbb{I}$ we have two conditions: The first obvious correctness guarantee is that the product term does not wrap around modulo each factor $F_i(X)$, so that we require

$$\forall i \in \mathbb{I}, \quad 2 \cdot i < d.$$

Secondly, we need that any cross-product terms do not interfere with any of the desired slot terms. This is implied by the equation

$$\forall i_1, i_2, j \in \mathbb{I}, \quad i_1 + i_2 \neq 2 \cdot j, \text{ with } i_1 \neq j, i_2 \neq j.$$

In Fig. 4 we plot the growth of the maximum size of $|\mathbb{I}|$ versus the size of d. As one can see, it grows in a step wise manner, looking like about $d^{0.6}$ in the range under consideration here.

This analysis gives the amount of packing we can produce in a given standard slot. To see what is the total packing ratio we can achieve, we need to look at the number theoretic properties of the polynomials $\Phi_p(X)$ for p prime. As remarked earlier these factor modulo 2 into r factors of degree d, where d is equal to the order of the element 2 in $\mathbb{F}_p^*$. We can then take the maximum value of $|\mathbb{I}|$ from the above calculations and compute the ratio of "useful" slots, in our application, as

$$\pi_p = \frac{r \cdot |\mathbb{I}|}{p - 1}.$$

For security reasons in our MPC applications we will be taking p in the range $8192 < p < 65536$, so in Table 1 we present the prime values in this range which

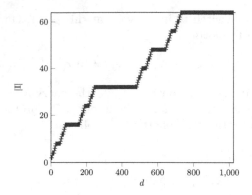

Fig. 4. Growth of $|\mathbb{I}|$ with d

Table 1. Primes with a packing density ratio greater than 0.15 in the range $8192 < p < 65536$

p	r	d	$|\mathbb{I}|$	$r \cdot |\mathbb{I}|$	π_p
9719	226	43	8	1808	.186
11119	218	51	8	1744	.156
11447	118	97	16	1888	.164
13367	326	41	8	2608	.195
14449	172	84	16	2752	.190
20857	316	66	12	3792	.181
23311	518	45	8	4144	.177
26317	387	68	12	4644	.176
29191	278	105	16	4448	.152
30269	329	92	16	5264	.173
32377	568	57	10	5680	.175
38737	538	72	13	6994	.180
43691	1285	34	8	10280	.235
61681	1542	40	8	12336	.200

give us a ratio greater than 0.15. We see that it is possible to select p so that the packing ratio π_p approaches 0.2. Thus we can obtain an efficiency of packing of around $\phi(p)/5$, as mentioned in the introduction. All that remains is to adapt the MPC protocols to deal with this new packing methodology.

4   OverDrive Global ZKPoKs

Given a SHE scheme (in our case either $\mathcal{E}_{\mathsf{mBGV}}$ or $\mathcal{E}_{\mathsf{BGV}}$), we denote by $\mathcal{C}$ the set of admissible circuits for the SHE scheme, the exact choice of $\mathcal{C}$ will depend on the underlying construction. In our protocol the decryption function will be always correct assuming the input ciphertext is the evaluation of an admissible circuit from $\mathcal{C}$ applied to ciphertexts which are marked "correct enough". We shall call a ciphertext valid if it is either "correct enough", or is the output of a circuit in $\mathcal{C}$ applied to "correct enough" ciphertexts.

Looking ahead, in Sect. 5 we will extend the scheme $\mathcal{E}_{\mathsf{mBGV}}$, introduced in the previous section, to allow distributed decryption. The reason for using the term "correct enough" is that our distributed decryption protocol will be proved correct even if some ciphertexts are not completely valid, namely they are not generated using the standard encryption algorithm.

In describing our protocol, we assume a key generation functionality $\mathcal{F}_{\mathsf{KeyGen}}$. It runs BGV.KeyGen and outputs for each party P_i the public key $\mathfrak{pt}$ and an additive share $[\mathfrak{st}]_i$ of $\mathfrak{st}$ for performing distributed decryption. This means that given a public ciphertext, parties can use their shares of the $\mathfrak{st}$ and collaborate to decrypt it. Just as in Overdrive, SPDZ and SCALE [1,13,19], we will assume a trusted dealer that implements the distributed key generation, possibly in practice via HSMs. Our goal here is to focus on the main part of the protocol and not on set-up assumptions, thus we do not discuss how to securely realise the ideal functionality $\mathcal{F}_{\mathsf{KeyGen}}$, as was done in the aforementioned works.

4.1 Bounded Linearly Homomorphic Predicates

Here we show how to ensure that all the ciphertexts used in our protocol are valid. Compared to similar protocols in previous works, other than prove that our ciphertexts decrypt correctly, we also need to show that the underlying plaintexts satisfy a given predicate P which we call *bounded linearly homomorphic*.

Definition 4.1. *We say that a given predicate* P *is* bounded linearly homomorphic *if, given a bound B and values $\mathbf{x}_1, \ldots, \mathbf{x}_\nu$, where*

$$\mathbf{x}_1 = (x_{1,1}, \ldots, x_{u,1}) \in R^u, \ldots, \mathbf{x}_\nu = (x_{1,\nu}, \ldots, x_{u,\nu}) \in R^u,$$

such that

1. *$\forall j \in [u]$, $\mathsf{P}(x_{j,1}, \ldots, x_{j,\nu}) = \mathsf{true}$, and*
2. *the coefficient norm of each $x_{j,k}$ is bounded by B,*

then, for all $\mathbf{a} \in \{0,1\}^u$, $\mathsf{P}(\mathbf{a} \cdot \mathbf{x}_1, \ldots, \mathbf{a} \cdot \mathbf{x}_v) = \mathsf{true}$.

We will give two different instantiations of this definition. The first one is with the diagonal predicate P = Diag also used in [13]. This takes as input a single element $\mathbf{x}_1 \in R^u$, i.e. $\nu = 1$, and checks whether each of the slot entries in $\mathbf{x}_1$ (when mapped to $\overline{\mathcal{P}}$ via the map Ψ_{2^b} for $b = \lceil \log_2(u \cdot B) \rceil$), are identical to each other. Clearly if the predicate holds for input ciphertexts with plaintext coefficient norms bounded by B, then it also holds for a sum of u ciphertexts with plaintext coefficient norms bounded by $u \cdot B$.

The second instantiation works with $\nu = 2$. We recall from Sect. 3 that the maps $\Theta_\mathbb{I}$ and $\Theta_\mathbb{J}$ map an element $x \in R$ to an element in $\mathcal{M}$ according to $\chi_\mathbb{I}$ and $\chi_\mathbb{J}$, respectively. The predicate P = Pack is then defined as follows:

- Let $\mathbf{m}_\mathbb{I} = \Theta_\mathbb{I}(x_1, B)$ and $\mathbf{m}_\mathbb{J} = \Theta_\mathbb{J}(x_2, B)$. The elements in $\mathsf{Supp}_{2^b}(\mathbf{m}_\mathbb{I})$, for $b = \lceil \log_2(u \cdot B) \rceil$, are indexed by $\mathsf{Supp}(\mathbb{I})$.
- If $\mathsf{Supp}_{2^b}(\mathbf{m}_\mathbb{I}) = \{c_{i,i_j}\}$, for $i \in [r]$ and $i_j \in \mathbb{I}$, then the coefficients in $\Psi_{2^b}(m_\mathbb{J})$ indexed by $(i, 2 \cdot i_j)$ are equal to c_{i,i_j}, and are uniformly random elsewhere. Being uniformly random in locations not indexed by $\mathbb{J}$ will be important for security of our distributed decryption protocol later.

Again it is straightforward to prove that this predicate is bounded linearly homomorphic.

4.2   Amortized Zero Knowledge Proof

Given the definition of a *bounded linearly homomorphic* predicate on the plaintexts, we are now ready to define what we mean by a *valid ciphertext* which encrypts such a plaintext. We recall that a ciphertext $\mathfrak{ct} = \mathsf{BGV.Enc}(x, \mathbf{r}; \mathfrak{pk})$ encrypts a plaintext value $x \in \mathcal{P}$ under randomness $\mathbf{r} = (v, e_0, e_1) \in R^3$. In our protocol we assume that $x = \Theta_\mathbb{I}^{-1}(\mathbf{m})$, for some $\mathbf{m} \in \mathcal{M}$. In a legitimate ciphertext, the plaintext x lies in $\mathcal{P}$ and the randomness values come from specific distributions (see Sect. 3). An adversarially chosen ciphertext may not be generated in this way, however, as long as the adversarial plaintexts and random coins are selected from some restricted set, the ciphertexts will correctly decrypt. A ciphertext which comes from this restricted set (no matter how it is generated) is said to be **valid**.

Suppose we have $u \cdot \nu$ BGV ciphertexts $\mathfrak{ct}_j \leftarrow \mathsf{BGV.Enc}(x_j, \mathbf{r}_j, \mathfrak{pk}), j \in [u \cdot \nu]$, such that

$$\mathfrak{ct}_j = \sum_{i \in [n]} \mathfrak{ct}_j^i, \quad x_j = \sum_{i \in [n]} x_j^i, \quad \mathbf{r}_j = \sum_{i \in [n]} \mathbf{r}_j^i, \quad \forall j \in [u \cdot \nu],$$

i.e. $\mathfrak{ct}_j^i \leftarrow \mathsf{BGV.Enc}(x_j^i, \mathbf{r}_j^i, \mathfrak{pk})$, x_j^i and $\mathbf{r}_j^i$ are respectively the ciphertext, the plaintext and the randomness held by party P_i. The protocol $\Pi_{\mathsf{gZKPoK}}^{\nu,\mathsf{flag}}$ (Figs. 5 and 6) guarantees that each ciphertext $\mathfrak{ct}_j$ is both **valid** and satisfies the bounded linearly homomorphic predicate P. Our zero-knowledge proof is very similar to the one given in [19], with some modifications due to our new packing technique, and it is a generalization to the multiparty setting of the amortized proof described in [13] and [9]. Note that as done in Overdrive, our protocol does not check the correctness of every single share $\mathfrak{ct}_j^i$, but just of their sum since it is sufficient for our purpose.

To understand the proof $\Pi_{\mathsf{gZKPoK}}^{\nu,\mathsf{flag}}$, first, let us assume $\nu = 1$ and flag = Diag. Following Cramer et al. [9]'s blueprint, the protocol $\Pi_{\mathsf{gZKPoK}}^{1,\mathsf{Diag}}$ simultaneously *tries* to prove that u ciphertexts $\mathfrak{ct}_j$ are generated such that:

$$\|v_j\|_\infty \leq n \cdot \rho_1, \quad \|e_{0,j}\|_\infty, \|e_{1,j}\|_\infty \leq n \cdot \rho_2, \quad \|x_j\|_\infty \leq n \cdot \tau, \quad \forall j \in [u], \quad (2)$$

for $\tau = 2^{t-1}, \rho_1 = 1$ and $\rho_2 = 20$. This is done using an amortized Σ protocol that samples commitments $\bar{\mathfrak{ct}}_j \leftarrow \mathsf{BGV.Enc}(y_j, \bar{\mathbf{r}}_j, \mathfrak{pk}), j \in [u], \bar{\mathbf{r}}_j = (\bar{v}_j, \bar{e}_{0,j}, \bar{e}_{1,j})$,

Protocol $\Pi_{\text{gZKPoK}}^{\nu,\text{flag}}$ - Part I

PARAMETERS: an integer ν, $u = \text{ZK\_sec}$, $V = 2 \cdot \text{ZK\_sec} - 1$, a flag $\in \{\text{Diag}, \text{Pack}, \perp\}$ such that if flag $= \text{Diag}$ then $P = \text{Diag}$; if flag $= \text{Pack}$ then $P = \text{Pack}$ and if flag $=\perp$ then $P = \emptyset$.

INPUT: Each P_i inputs $u \cdot \nu$ BGV ciphertexts $\mathfrak{ct}_{j,k}^i, j \in [u], k \in [\nu]$, such that

$$\|v_{j,k}^i\|_\infty \leq \rho_1, \quad \|e_{0,j,k}^i\|_\infty, \|e_{1,j,k}^i\|_\infty \leq \rho_2, \quad \|x_{j,k}^i\|_\infty \leq \tau,$$

where $x_{j,k}^i \in R$ is the plaintext corresponding to $\mathfrak{ct}_{j,k}^i$, satisfying $P(x_{j,1}^i, \ldots, x_{j,\nu}^i) = \text{true}$, and for each $k \in [\nu]$, set:

$$\mathbf{r}_k^i = (v_{1,k}^i, \ldots, v_{u,k}^i, e_{0,1,k}^i, \ldots, e_{0,u,k}^i, e_{1,1,k}^i, \ldots, e_{1,u,k}^i) \in R^{u \times 3},$$
$$\mathbf{x}_k^i = (x_{1,k}^i, \ldots, x_{u,k}^i) \in R^u$$
$$\mathbf{c}_k^i = \mathfrak{ct}_k^i = (\mathfrak{ct}_{1,k}^i, \ldots, \mathfrak{ct}_{u,k}^i) \in R^{u \times 2}.$$

gZKPoK: If flag $\in \{\text{Diag}, \perp\}$ parties execute the following steps.
- For each $k \in [\nu]$ execute:

Commit:
- Each P_i broadcasts $\mathbf{c}_k^i = \text{BGV.Enc}(\mathbf{x}_k^i, \mathbf{r}_k^i; \mathfrak{pe})$
- Each party P_i samples a new set of "plaintexts" $\mathbf{y}_k^i \in R^V$ and "randomness vectors" $\bar{\mathbf{r}}_k^i \in R^{V \times 3}$, such that, for $j \in [u]$ and $P(y_{j,1}, \ldots, y_{j,\nu}) = \text{true}$,

$$\|y_{j,k}^i\|_\infty \leq 2^{\text{ZK\_sec}} \cdot \tau, \quad \|\bar{v}_{j,k}^i\|_\infty \leq 2^{\text{ZK\_sec}} \cdot \rho_1,$$
$$\|\bar{e}_{0,j,k}^i\|_\infty, \quad \|\bar{e}_{1,j,k}^i\|_\infty \leq 2^{\text{ZK\_sec}} \cdot \rho_2.$$

- Each P_i computes and broadcasts $\mathbf{a}_k^i \leftarrow \text{BGV.Enc}(\mathbf{y}_k^i, \bar{\mathbf{r}}_k^i; \mathfrak{pe})$, for $k \in [\nu]$.

Challenge: Parties call $\mathcal{F}_{\text{Rand}}$ to get a random $\hat{\mathbf{e}}_k = (\hat{e}_{k,1}, \ldots, \hat{e}_{k,u}) \in \{0,1\}^u$.

Prove:
- Parties define $M_{\hat{\mathbf{e}}_k} \in \{0,1\}^{V \times u}$ to be the matrix such that $(M_{\hat{\mathbf{e}}_k})_{r,c} = \hat{e}_{k,r-c+1}$, for $1 \leq r - c + 1 \leq u$, and 0 in all other entries.
- Each P_i computes and broadcasts the values $(\mathbf{z}_k^i, T_k^i)$, where $\mathbf{z}_k^{i\mathsf{T}} = \mathbf{y}_k^{i\mathsf{T}} + M_{\hat{\mathbf{e}}_k} \cdot \mathbf{x}_k^{i\mathsf{T}}$ and $T_k^i = \bar{\mathbf{r}}_k^i + M_{\hat{\mathbf{e}}_k} \cdot \mathbf{r}_k^i$.

Verify:
- Each party P_i computes $\mathbf{d}_k^i = \text{BGV.Enc}(\mathbf{z}_k^i, T_k^i; \mathfrak{pe})$ and then stores the sum $\mathbf{d}_k = \sum_{i=1}^n \mathbf{d}_k^i$.
- The parties compute the values

$$\mathbf{c}_k = \sum_{i \in [n]} \mathbf{c}_k^i, \quad \mathbf{a}_k = \sum_{i \in [n]} \mathbf{a}_k^i, \quad \mathbf{z}_k = \sum_i \mathbf{z}_k^i, \quad T_k = \sum_{i \in [n]} T_k^i,$$

and conduct the following checks, where $t_{i,j,k}$ is the (i,j)-th element of T_k,

$$\mathbf{d}_k^\mathsf{T} = \mathbf{a}_k^\mathsf{T} + (M_{\hat{\mathbf{e}}_k} \cdot \mathbf{c}_k), \quad \|\mathbf{z}_k\|_\infty \leq 2 \cdot n \cdot 2^{\text{ZK\_sec}} \cdot \tau \qquad (1)$$

$$\|t_{i,1,k}\|_\infty \leq 2 \cdot n \cdot 2^{\text{ZK\_sec}} \cdot \rho_1, \quad \|t_{i,2,k}\|_\infty, \quad \|t_{i,3,k}\|_\infty \leq 2 \cdot n \cdot 2^{\text{ZK\_sec}} \cdot \rho_2.$$

- If $P = \text{Diag}$ the proof is rejected if $P(z_{j,1}^i) \neq \text{true}$ for any $j \in [u]$. If the check passes, the parties output $\sum_{i \in [n]} \mathbf{c}_1^i, \ldots, \sum_{i \in [n]} \mathbf{c}_\nu^i$.

Fig. 5. Protocol for global proof of knowledge of a ciphertext - Part I

such that

$$\|\bar{v}_j\|_\infty \leq n \cdot 2^{\mathsf{ZK\_sec}} \cdot \rho_1,$$
$$\|\bar{e}_{0,j}\|_\infty, \|\bar{e}_{1,j}\|_\infty \leq n \cdot 2^{\mathsf{ZK\_sec}} \cdot \rho_2,$$
$$\|y_j\|_\infty \leq n \cdot 2^{\mathsf{ZK\_sec}} \cdot \tau, \quad \forall j \in [u],$$

for some large enough $2^{\mathsf{ZK\_sec}}$. In this way we can form the responses $\mathbf{z}$ and T such that the terms $\mathbf{y}$ and $\bar{\mathbf{r}}$ statistically hide $M_e \cdot \mathbf{x}$ and $M_e \cdot \mathbf{r}$ respectively, for some challenge matrix M_e. The bounds on $\mathbf{z}$ and T imply bounds on $\mathbf{x}$ and $\mathbf{r}$. This implies that, instead of obtaining a proof that the input ciphertexts satisfy Eq. 2, we get a proof that those values satisfy the following relationships:

$$\|v_j\|_\infty \leq n \cdot S \cdot \rho_1, \quad \|e_{j,0}\|_\infty, \|e_{j,1}\|_\infty \leq n \cdot S \cdot \rho_2, \quad \|x_j\|_\infty \leq n \cdot S \cdot \tau, \quad \forall j \in [u], \tag{3}$$

where $S = 2 \cdot 2^{3 \cdot \mathsf{ZK\_sec}/2+1}$. These bounds are clearly not tight and the value S is called the *soundness slack*.

When $\nu = 2$ and $\mathsf{P} = \mathsf{Pack}$, we need to repeat the above proof twice, or equivalently sample the challenge in $\{0,1\}^{2 \cdot \mathsf{ZK\_sec}}$, and add the proof for the predicate P. Line 2 of Fig. 6 is checked by a verifier only that required equality between coefficients in the predicate holds. That the other coefficients are uniformly distributed is not checked, indeed this is impossible to do. However, if the other coefficients are not uniformly distributed then the prover will loose the desired zero-knowledge property, thus it is not in the provers interest to produce values which are not uniformly distributed. In the case of our application an honest verifier is actually one of the n provers, and this is enough to ensure the desired uniform property holds on the required subset of coefficients.

Thus in both cases the protocol $\Pi_{\mathsf{gZKPoK}}^{\nu,\mathsf{flag}}$ is an honest-verifier zero-knowledge proof of knowledge for the relation

$$\mathcal{R}_{\mathsf{gZKPoK}} = \big\{(x,w) \mid x = (\mathbf{c}, \mathfrak{pk}), w = ((x_1, \mathbf{r}_1) \ldots, (x_{\nu \cdot u}, \mathbf{r}_{\nu \cdot u}))$$
$$: \{u = \mathsf{ZK\_sec}, \|x_j\|_\infty \leq n \cdot S \cdot \tau, \mathbf{m}_j = \Theta_{\mathbb{I}}(x_j) \in \mathcal{M},$$
$$\mathbf{c} = (\mathfrak{ct}_1, \ldots, \mathfrak{ct}_u), \|v_j\|_\infty \leq n \cdot S \cdot \rho_1, \|e_{0,j}\|_\infty, \|e_{1,j}\|_\infty \leq n \cdot S \cdot \rho_2\}$$
$$\wedge \{\mathsf{P}(x_{j,1}, \ldots, x_{j,\nu}) = \mathsf{true}, \forall j \in [u]\}\big\}$$

Theorem 4.1. *The protocol $\Pi_{\mathsf{gZKPoK}}^{\nu,\mathsf{flag}}$ is an honest-verifier zero-knowledge proof of knowledge for the relation $\mathcal{R}_{\mathsf{gZKPoK}}$ with error probability $2^{-\mathsf{ZK\_sec}}$ and soundness slack $S = 2 \cdot 2^{3 \cdot \mathsf{ZK\_sec}/2+1}$.*

We do not follow the Overdrive proof approach in our MPC protocol, i.e. we do not give an ideal functionality for $\Pi_{\mathsf{gZKPoK}}^{\nu,\mathsf{flag}}$. The reason is that a security proof for $\Pi_{\mathsf{gZKPoK}}^{\nu,\mathsf{flag}}$ would require rewinding the adversary to extract corrupt parties' inputs in the simulation, breaking the UC security of the protocol. Instead, we will use $\Pi_{\mathsf{gZKPoK}}^{\nu,\mathsf{flag}}$ inside our MPC protocol, as done in [13], and prove UC security for this latter protocol. The complete proof of the theorem above is however still similar to the one in [19]. It is given in in the full version of this paper.

Protocol $\Pi_{\text{gZKPoK}}^{\nu,\text{flag}}$ - Part II

If flag = Pack then apply the proof for flag $=\perp$ above, making sure the sampling in Step 4.1 follows the predicate P for Pack. Then, perform the following steps (using the values obtained whilst executing the above proof).

1. Each P_i computes and broadcasts the values

$$\mathbf{z}_2^{i\mathsf{T}} = \mathbf{y}_2^{i\mathsf{T}} + M_{\hat{\mathbf{e}}_2} \cdot \mathbf{x}_2^{i\mathsf{T}} \in R^V.$$

2. The proof is rejected if $\mathsf{P}(z_{j,1}^i, z_{j,2}^i) \neq$ true for any $j \in [u]$. If the check passes, the parties output $\sum_{i\in[n]} \mathbf{c}_1^i, \ldots, \sum_{i\in[n]} \mathbf{c}_\nu^i$.

Fig. 6. Protocol for global proof of knowledge of a ciphertext - Part II

5   Distributed Somewhat Homomorphic Encryption

We are now ready to describe and implement the functionality $\mathcal{F}_{\text{DistrDec}}$ (Fig. 7) that extends the scheme $\mathcal{E}_{\text{mBGV}}$ introduced in the previous sections to allow distributed decryption. It will be the main building block of our MPC protocol in the next section.

As mentioned before, our protocol ensures that all the ciphertexts that are input of $\mathcal{F}_{\text{DistrDec}}$ correctly decrypt. For this purpose we use the ideal functionality $\mathcal{F}_{\text{GenValidCiph}}^{\nu,\text{flag}}$ (see Fig. 11). Given the procedures $\overline{\Gamma}_{\mathbb{I}}$ and $\overline{\Gamma}_{\mathbb{J}}$ described in Fig. 8, and on inputs $[\mathbf{m}]_i \in \mathcal{M}$ from each P_i, where $\mathcal{M} = \mathbb{Z}_{2^t}^{r \times |\mathbb{I}|}$ is the plaintext space of our encryption scheme, and $r \times |\mathbb{I}|$ is the number of supported slots, the functionality $\mathcal{F}_{\text{GenValidCiph}}^{\nu,\text{flag}}$ returns:

- If $\nu = 1$ and flag $=\perp$, a valid ciphertext $\mathfrak{ct}_{\mathbf{m}}^{\mathbb{I}} \leftarrow \text{BGV.Enc}(\overline{\Gamma}_{\mathbb{I}}^{-1}(\chi_{\mathbb{I}}(\mathbf{m})), \mathbf{r}; \mathfrak{p}^{\mathfrak{e}})$, such that $\mathbf{m} = \sum_{i\in[n]}[\mathbf{m}]_i$; If $\nu = 1$ and flag = Diag a valid ciphertext computed as before and satisfying the predicate P = Diag;
- If $\nu = 2$ and flag = Pack, two ciphertexts $\mathfrak{ct}_{\mathbf{m}}^{\mathbb{I}} \leftarrow \text{BGV.Enc}(\overline{\Gamma}_{\mathbb{I}}^{-1}(\chi_{\mathbb{I}}(\mathbf{m})), \mathbf{r}; \mathfrak{p}^{\mathfrak{e}})$ and $\mathfrak{ct}_{\mathbf{m}}^{\mathbb{J}} \leftarrow \text{BGV.Enc}(\overline{\Gamma}_{\mathbb{J}}^{-1}(\chi_{\mathbb{J}}(\mathbf{m})), \mathbf{r}; \mathfrak{p}^{\mathfrak{e}})$ satisfying the predicate P = Pack.

The ideal functionality $\mathcal{F}_{\text{GenValidCiph}}^{\nu,\text{flag}}$ is implemented by $\Pi_{\text{GenValidCiph}}^{\nu,\text{flag}}$ (see the full version).

5.1   Distributed Decryption Protocols

Here we give two distributed decryption protocols, $\Pi_{\text{DistrDec1}}$ and $\Pi_{\text{DistrDec2}}$, in Figs. 9 and 10, respectively. The protocols $\Pi_{\text{DistrDec1}}$ and $\Pi_{\text{DistrDec2}}$ implement the functionality $\mathcal{F}_{\text{DistrDec}}$ (Fig. 7) on commands **D1** and **D2**, respectively. Notice that we do not perform a proper full distributed decryption, because the way we pack entries into a ciphertext would result in information leakage if we allowed all the parties to recover the plaintext corresponding to the public input ciphertext

---

Functionality $\mathcal{F}_{\mathsf{DistrDec}}$

Let A be the set of corrupt parties.

PARAMETERS: B_{DDec}, a bound on the coefficients of the mask values, and B_{noise} a bound on the noise of ciphertexts before decryption.

COMMON INPUT: A single valid level-zero ciphertext $\mathsf{ct}_{\mathbf{m}}^{(0,\mathbb{J})} = (0, c_0, c_1)^{\mathbb{J}}$ from all the parties.

Initialize: On receiving (Init) from all parties the functionality, run $(\mathfrak{pe}, \mathfrak{se}) \leftarrow$ mBGV.KeyGen(1^κ), sending the value $\mathfrak{pe}$ to the adversary and all the parties.

D1: On receiving the public input (D1, $\mathsf{ct}_{\mathbf{m}}^{(0,\mathbb{J})}$) from all the parties, where $\mathsf{ct}_{\mathbf{m}}^{(0,\mathbb{J})}$ is valid level-zero ciphertext, the functionality performs the following steps.
- Execute $\mathbf{m} \leftarrow \mathsf{Dec}(\mathsf{ct}_{\mathbf{m}}^{(0,\mathbb{J})}; \mathfrak{se})$ and handle this value to the adversary.
- If P_1 *is honest*: Wait for the adversary to input either abort or δ. If abort, then forward abort to the honest parties and halt. Otherwise sample the honest shares $[\mathbf{m}]_i \leftarrow \mathcal{M}, i \notin A, i \neq 1$, at random and set $[\mathbf{m}]_1 = -\sum_{i \notin A, i \neq 1} [\mathbf{m}]_i + \mathbf{m} + \delta$. Send $[\mathbf{m}]_i$ to $P_i, \forall i \notin A$.
- If P_1 *is corrupt*: Send $\mathbf{m}$ to the adversary. Wait for an input from the adversary. If this input is abort, then forward abort to the honest parties and halt. Otherwise receive $\mathbf{b}$. Sample the honest shares $[\mathbf{m}]_i \leftarrow \mathcal{M}, i \notin A$, at random but subject to the condition $\sum_{i \notin A} [\mathbf{m}]_i = \mathbf{b}$. Send these values $\mathbf{m}_i, i \notin A$ to the honest parties.

D2: On receiving (D2, $\mathsf{ct}_{\mathbf{m}}^{(0,\mathbb{J})}$) from all parties, the functionality performs the following steps.
- Execute $\mathbf{m} \leftarrow \mathsf{Dec}(\mathsf{ct}_{\mathbf{m}}^{(0,\mathbb{J})}; \mathfrak{se})$ and send $\mathbf{m}$ to the adversary.
- Wait for an input from the adversary: if abort is received, then abort.
- Otherwise receive $\mathbf{m}'$ and $\{[\mathbf{m}']_i\}_{i \in A}$. Sample random shares $\{[\mathbf{m}']_i\}_{i \notin A}$ such that $\sum_{i \in [n]} \{[\mathbf{m}']_i\} = \mathbf{m}'$.
- Output $\{[\mathbf{m}']_i\}_{i \notin A}$ to honest parties and $\hat{\mathsf{ct}}_{\mathbf{m}'}^{(1,\mathbb{I})}$ to all parties.

Fig. 7. The functionality for distributed decryption

The Procedures $\overline{\Gamma}_{\mathbb{I}}^{-1}(\mathbf{m})$ **(resp.** $\overline{\Gamma}_{\mathbb{J}}^{-1}(\mathbf{m})$**)**

1. If computing $\overline{\Gamma}_{\mathbb{I}}^{-1}(\mathbf{m})$ set all entries in $\mathbf{m}$ *not in* $\mathsf{Supp}(\mathbb{I})$ to zero.
2. If computing $\overline{\Gamma}_{\mathbb{J}}^{-1}(\mathbf{m})$ set all entries in $\mathbf{m}$ *not in* $\mathsf{Supp}(\mathbb{J})$ to a uniformly random element selected from $[0, \ldots, 2^t]$.
3. Output $\Gamma^{-1}(\mathbf{m})$.

Fig. 8. The procedure $\overline{\Gamma}_{\mathbb{I}}^{-1}(\mathbf{m})$ (resp. $\overline{\Gamma}_{\mathbb{J}}^{-1}(\mathbf{m})$) from $\overline{\mathcal{P}}$ to $\mathcal{P}$

$\mathsf{ct}_{\mathbf{m}}^{(0,\mathbb{J})}$, but both our protocols output to each party P_i an additive share $[\mathbf{m}]_i$ of $\mathbf{m}$. Both protocols depend on a constant B_{noise} which represents a bound on the ciphertext noise before a decryption occurs. For example, in case of fresh ciphertexts we have that $B_{\mathsf{noise}} = B_{\mathsf{clean}}^{\mathsf{dishonest}}$ (see the full version of the paper).

There are two main differences between the two protocols. The first one is in the way the shares $[\mathbf{m}]_i$ are computed. The protocol $\Pi_{\mathsf{DistrDec2}}$ is essentially the same as the Reshare protocol of [12,13], where a masking ciphertext is used before the distributed decryption is performed. More precisely, parties call the functionality $\mathcal{F}_{\mathsf{GenValidCiph}}^{2,\mathsf{Pack}}$ which produces two ciphertexts $(\mathfrak{ct}_{\mathbf{f}}^{(1,\mathbb{I})}, \mathfrak{ct}_{\mathbf{f}}^{(1,\mathbb{J})})$, with $\mathbf{f} = \sum_{i \in [n]} [\mathbf{f}]_i$; then they decrypt $\mathfrak{ct}_{\mathbf{m}+\mathbf{f}}^{(0,\mathbb{J})} = \mathfrak{ct}_{\mathbf{m}}^{(0,\mathbb{J})} \oplus \mathfrak{ct}_{\mathbf{f}}^{(0,\mathbb{J})}$, where $\mathfrak{ct}_{\mathbf{f}}^{(0,\mathbb{J})} = $ SwitchMod($\mathfrak{ct}_{\mathbf{f}}^{(1,\mathbb{J})}$), so that each P_i can compute a share $[\mathbf{m}+\mathbf{f}]_i - [\mathbf{f}]_i$ of $\mathbf{m}$.

On the other hand, the protocol $\Pi_{\mathsf{DistrDec1}}$ uses random masks $f_i, i \in [n]$, inside the actual decryption to mask the decryption shares, so it does not require to perform any expensive zero-knowledge proof. Note that this approach cannot be used if the parties need to generate a new fresh ciphertext of $\mathbf{m}$ after the decryption, as happens in $\Pi_{\mathsf{DistrDec2}}$, where this fresh encryption is computed using the first ciphertext $\mathfrak{ct}_{\mathbf{f}}^{(1,\mathbb{I})}$ given by $\mathcal{F}_{\mathsf{GenValidCiph}}^{2,\mathsf{Pack}}$.

Protocol $\Pi_{\mathsf{DistrDec1}}$

PARAMETERS: The protocol is parametrized by two bounds: B_{DDec}, a bound on the coefficients of the mask values, and B_{noise} a bound on the noise of ciphertexts before decryption.

COMMON INPUT: A single valid level-zero ciphertext $\mathfrak{ct}_{\mathbf{m}}^{(0,\mathbb{J})} = (0, c_0, c_1)^{\mathbb{J}}$.

Initialize: Each party P_i calls $\mathcal{F}_{\mathsf{KeyGen}}$ receiving $(\mathfrak{pt}, [\mathfrak{st}]_i)$.

D1:   On input $(\mathsf{D1}, \mathfrak{ct}_{\mathbf{m}}^{(0,\mathbb{J})})$, where $\mathfrak{ct}_{\mathbf{m}}^{(0,\mathbb{J})} = (0, c_0, c_1)^{\mathbb{J}}$ is a (single) ciphertext, parties do as follows.

1. Each P_i samples $f_i \leftarrow [0, B_{\mathsf{DDec}}]^N$ (i.e. a polynomial in R with bounded coefficients).
2. P_1 computes $v_1 \leftarrow ((c_0 - [\mathfrak{st}]_1 \cdot c_1) + f_1 \pmod{q_0}) = w_1 + f_1 \pmod{q_0}$. Each $P_i, i \neq 1$ computes $v_i \leftarrow (-[\mathfrak{st}]_i \cdot c_1 + f_i \pmod{q_0}) = w_i + f_i \pmod{q_0}$. All parties broadcast these values.
3. Parties check that $(\sum_i v_i \pmod{q_0})$ is bounded by $B_{\mathsf{noise}} + n \cdot B_{\mathsf{DDec}}$, if not abort.
4. P_1 computes $u_1 \leftarrow (\sum_{i=1}^{n} v_i \pmod{q_0}) - f_1 \pmod{2^t}$. Each $P_i, i \neq 1$ computes $u_i \leftarrow -f_i \mod 2^t$.
5. Each $P_i, i \in [n]$, sets $[\mathbf{m}]_i \leftarrow \chi_{\mathbb{J}}^{-1}(\Gamma(u_i))$.

Fig. 9. Protocol implementing the command D1 on $\mathcal{F}_{\mathsf{DistrDec}}$

Protocol $\Pi_{\mathsf{DistrDec1}}$. Given a public input ciphertext $\mathfrak{ct}_{\mathbf{m}}^{(0,\mathbb{J})}$, each party P_i samples a random polynomial f_i in R, with coefficients bounded by some fixed, large enough value B_{DDec} to avoid any leakage of information in the secret key, which is used to mask the decryption share.

Note that the correctness holds only if the values f_i introduced by the parties during the protocol are sampled from the right set, i.e. $\|f_i\|_\infty < B_{\mathsf{DDec}}$, and

$\| \sum_{i \in [n]} v_i \pmod{q_0} \|_\infty < B_{\text{noise}} + n \cdot B_{\text{DDec}} < q_0/2$. We will derive the precise value B_{DDec} in the security proof.

In terms of protocol security, the intuition is that the polynomial f_i masks not only the values in $\text{Supp}(\mathbb{J})$ which contain information, but also values not in $\text{Supp}(\mathbb{J})$ which could contain residual information from prior homomorphic operations. So, the fact that the honest party effectively "forgets" the values corresponding to slot terms not in $\text{Im}(\omega_{\mathbb{J}})$ results in the protocol not leaking information on these terms. A complete proof of this intuition can be found in the full version.

Theorem 5.1. *The protocol $\Pi_{\text{DistrDec1}}$ (Fig. 9) implements the functionality $\mathcal{F}_{\text{DistrDec}}.\text{D1}$ (Fig. 7) against any static, active adversary corrupting up to $n-1$ parties in the $\mathcal{F}_{\text{KeyGen}}$-hybrid model with statistical security $2^{-\text{DDec}}$ if $\big(B_{\text{noise}} + 2^{\text{DDec}} \cdot n \cdot (B_{\text{noise}} + 2^t)\big) < q_0/2$.*

Protocol $\Pi_{\text{DistrDec2}}$

PARAMETERS: The protocol is parametrized by B_{DDec}.
COMMON INPUT: A single valid level-zero ciphertext $\mathfrak{ct}_{\mathsf{m}}^{(0,\mathbb{J})} = (0, c_0, c_1)^{\mathbb{J}}$.

Initialize: Each party P_i calls $\mathcal{F}_{\text{KeyGen}}$ receiving $(\mathfrak{pk}, [\mathfrak{sk}]_i)$

D2: On input $(\text{D2}, \mathfrak{ct}_{\mathsf{m}}^{(0,\mathbb{J})})$ from all parties, where $\mathfrak{ct}_{\mathsf{m}}^{(0)} = (0, c_0, c_1)^{\mathbb{J}}$ is a (single) ciphertext.

1. Parties call the functionality $\mathcal{F}_{\text{GenValidCiph}}^{2,\text{Pack}}$ on input $[\mathbf{f}]_i, \forall i \in [n]$, which returns the ciphertexts $(\mathfrak{ct}_{\mathbf{f}}^{(1,\mathbb{I})}, \mathfrak{ct}_{\mathbf{f}}^{(1,\mathbb{J})})$ to *all* parties.
2. All the parties locally compute $\mathfrak{ct}_{\mathbf{f}}^{(0,\mathbb{J})} = \text{SwitchMod}(\mathfrak{ct}_{\mathbf{f}}^{(1,\mathbb{J})})$.
3. The parties homomorphically compute $\mathfrak{ct}_{\mathsf{m}+\mathbf{f}}^{(0,\mathbb{J})} = \mathfrak{ct}_{\mathsf{m}}^{(0)} \oplus \mathfrak{ct}_{\mathbf{f}}^{(0,\mathbb{J})}$, and let $\mathfrak{ct}_{\mathsf{m}+\mathbf{f}}^{(0,\mathbb{J})}$ be $(0, c_0, c_1)$.
4. P_1 computes $v_1 \leftarrow (c_0 - \mathfrak{sk}_1 \cdot c_1) \pmod{q_0} \in R_{q_0}$.
5. $P_i, i \neq 1$ computes $v_i \leftarrow -\mathfrak{sk}_i \cdot c_1 \pmod{q_0} \in R_{q_0}$.
6. All parties compute and broadcast $t_i = v_i + 2^t \cdot r_i$ for some random element $r_i \in R_{q_0}$ with infinity norm bound B_{DDec}.
7. The parties compute $(\mathbf{m}+\mathbf{f}) = \chi_{\mathbb{J}}^{-1}(\Psi_{2^t}(\sum t_i \pmod{q_0})) \in \mathcal{M}$.
8. Party P_1 sets $[\mathbf{m}]_1 \leftarrow (\mathbf{m}+\mathbf{f}) - [\mathbf{f}]_1$, party $P_i, i \neq 1$ sets $[\mathbf{m}]_i \leftarrow -[\mathbf{f}]_i$.
9. All parties compute, using some default value $\mathbf{0}$ for the randomness,

$$\hat{\mathfrak{ct}}_{\mathsf{m}}^{(1,\mathbb{I})} \leftarrow \text{BGV.Enc}(\Psi_{2^t}^{-1}(\chi_{\mathbb{I}}(\mathbf{m}+\mathbf{f})), \mathbf{0}, \mathfrak{pk}) \ominus \mathfrak{ct}_{\mathbf{f}}^{(1,\mathbb{I})}.$$

Fig. 10. Protocol implementing the command **D2** on $\mathcal{F}_{\text{DistrDec}}$

Protocol $\Pi_{\text{DistrDec2}}$. Given a public ciphertext $\mathfrak{ct}_{\mathsf{m}}^{(0,\mathbb{J})}$, the protocol $\Pi_{\text{DistrDec2}}$ outputs a share $[\mathbf{m}]_i$ of the plaintext $\mathbf{m}$ and a fresh ciphertext $\mathfrak{ct}_{\mathsf{m}}^{(1,\mathbb{I})}$ to each party P_i. The protocol makes use of the command **Gen-2** of the functionality $\mathcal{F}_{\text{GenValidCiph}}^{2,\text{Pack}}$ (Fig. 11), for which an implementation is given in the full version of the paper. This command outputs two level-1 ciphertexts $\mathfrak{ct}_{\mathbf{f}}^{(1,\mathbb{I})}$ and $\mathfrak{ct}_{\mathbf{f}}^{(1,\mathbb{J})}$ of the same plaintext $\mathbf{f}$ corresponding to the set $\mathbb{I}$ and $\mathbb{J}$, respectively.

The ciphertext $\mathfrak{ct}_{\mathbf{f}}^{(1,\mathbb{J})}$, corresponding to the set $\mathbb{J}$, is used as a mask in the distributed decryption, and $\mathfrak{ct}_{\mathbf{f}}^{(1,\mathbb{I})}$, corresponding to the set $\mathbb{I}$, is used to create a fresh encryption $\hat{\mathfrak{ct}}_{\mathbf{m}}^{(1,\mathbb{I})}$ of $\mathbf{m}$.

The proof of security for this protocol is similar to the corresponding protocol in SPDZ [13]. The major changes from SPDZ are that we need to produce two auxiliary ciphertexts per party $(\mathfrak{ct}_{\mathbf{f}_i}^{(1,\mathbb{I})}, \mathfrak{ct}_{\mathbf{f}_i}^{(1,\mathbb{J})})$, since we have different encodings at level zero and level one of the underlying message space. Intuitively, the protocol reveals no more information about the BGV plaintext inside $\mathfrak{ct}_{\mathbf{m}}^{(0,\mathbb{J})}$ because the honest parties are masking the coefficients not in $\mathsf{Supp}(\mathbb{J})$ using the coefficients from the plaintext inside $\mathfrak{ct}_{\mathbf{f}_i}^{(1,\mathbb{J})}$, which have been chosen to be uniformly random for coefficients not in $\mathsf{Supp}(\mathbb{J})$, using the procedure $\overline{\Gamma}_{\mathbb{J}}^{-1}$. A proof for this result is given in the full version.

Theorem 5.2. *The protocol $\Pi_{\mathsf{DistrDec2}}$ implements the functionality $\mathcal{F}_{\mathsf{DistrDec}}$.D2 (Fig. 7) against any static, active adversary corrupting up to $n-1$ parties in the $(\mathcal{F}_{\mathsf{KeyGen}}, \mathcal{F}_{\mathsf{GenValidCiph}}^{2,\mathsf{Pack}})$-hybrid model with statistical security $2^{-\mathsf{DDec}}$ if $(B_{\mathsf{noise}} + 2^{\mathsf{DDec}} \cdot n \cdot (B_{\mathsf{noise}} + 2^t)) < q_0/2$.*

Functionality $\mathcal{F}_{\mathsf{GenValidCiph}}^{\nu,\mathsf{flag}}$

Let A be the set of corrupt parties.

PARAMETERS: an integer ν, a security parameter ZK_sec, a flag $\in \{\mathsf{Diag}, \mathsf{Pack}, \perp\}$ such that: If flag $= \mathsf{Diag}$, then $\mathsf{P} = \mathsf{Diag}$; If flag $= \mathsf{Pack}$, then $\mathsf{P} = \mathsf{Pack}$ and if flag $= \perp$, then $\mathsf{P} = \emptyset$.

Initialize: On receiving (Init) from all parties run $(\mathfrak{pk}, \mathfrak{sk}) \leftarrow \mathsf{BGV.KeyGen}(1^\kappa)$, sending the value $\mathfrak{pk}$ to the adversary and all the parties.

Gen-1: On input $(\mathsf{Gen\text{-}1}, \mathsf{flag}, [\mathbf{m}]_i)$ from all parties $P_i, i \in [n]$, do the following:
- If the adversary sends **abort**, return **abort**
- Otherwise receive $\mathfrak{ct}_{\mathbf{m}}^{(1,\mathbb{I})}$ and send this value to the parties

Gen-2: On input $(\mathsf{Gen\text{-}2}, \mathsf{flag}, [\mathbf{m}]_i)$ from all parties, proceed as follows:
- If the adversary sends **abort**, return **abort**
- Otherwise receive $\mathfrak{ct}_{\mathbf{m}}^{(1,\mathbb{I})}$ and $\mathfrak{ct}_{\mathbf{m}'}^{(1,\mathbb{J})}$ and send these values to all parties

---

Fig. 11. The functionality $\mathcal{F}_{\mathsf{GenValidCiph}}^{\nu,\mathsf{flag}}$ to generate valid ciphertexts

5.2   Generating Valid Ciphertexts

Here we implement the ideal functionality $\mathcal{F}_{\mathsf{GenValidCiph}}^{\nu,\mathsf{flag}}$ to create valid ciphertexts, see Fig. 12. To prove the security of $\Pi_{\mathsf{GenValidCiph}}^{\nu,\mathsf{flag}}$ we proceed like in [13], that is

---

Protocol $\Pi_{\mathsf{GenValidCiph}}^{\nu,\mathsf{flag}}$

PARAMETERS: an integer ν, a security parameter $\mathsf{ZK\_sec}$, a flag $\in \{\mathsf{Diag}, \mathsf{Pack}, \perp\}$ such that: If flag $= \mathsf{Diag}$, then $P = \mathsf{Diag}$; If flag $= \mathsf{Pack}$, then $P = \mathsf{Pack}$ and if flag $= \perp$, then $P = \emptyset$.

Initialize: Each party P_i calls $\mathcal{F}_{\mathsf{KeyGen}}$ receiving $(\mathfrak{pk}, [\mathfrak{sk}]_i)$.

Gen-1: Each P_i inputs $(\mathsf{Gen\text{-}1}, \mathsf{flag}, [\mathbf{m}]_i)$, where flag $\in \{\mathsf{Diag}, \perp\}$ and $[\mathbf{m}]_i$ are private inputs and if flag $= \mathsf{Diag}$ then all slots of $[\mathbf{m}]_i$ are equal.

    1. Each P_i sets $[m_\mathbb{I}]_i \leftarrow \chi_\mathbb{I}([\mathbf{m}]_i) \in \overline{\mathcal{P}}$ and computes $\mathfrak{ct}_{m_i}^\mathbb{I} \leftarrow$ $\mathsf{BGV.Enc}(\overline{\varGamma}_\mathbb{I}^{-1}([m_\mathbb{I}]_i), \mathbf{r}_i; \mathfrak{pk})$.

    2. Parties run the protocol $\Pi_{\mathsf{gZKPoK}}^{1,\mathsf{flag}}$ receiving either $\mathfrak{ct}_m^\mathbb{I}$ or abort.

Gen-2: Each P_i inputs $(\mathsf{Gen\text{-}2}, \mathsf{flag}, [\mathbf{m}]_i)$, where flag $= \mathsf{Pack}$ and $[\mathbf{m}]_i$ are private inputs :

    1. Each P_i sets $[m_\mathbb{I}]_i \leftarrow \chi_\mathbb{I}([\mathbf{m}]_i) \in \overline{\mathcal{P}}$ and $[m_\mathbb{J}]_i \leftarrow \chi_\mathbb{J}([\mathbf{m}]_i) \in \overline{\mathcal{P}}$, then they compute $\mathfrak{ct}_{m_i}^\mathbb{I} \leftarrow \mathsf{Enc.BGV}(\overline{\varGamma}_\mathbb{I}^{-1}([m_\mathbb{I}]_i), \mathbf{r}_i; \mathfrak{pk})$ and $\mathfrak{ct}_{m_i}^{'\mathbb{J}} \leftarrow$ $\mathsf{Enc.BGV}(\overline{\varGamma}_\mathbb{J}^{-1}([m_\mathbb{J}]_i), \mathbf{r}_i'; \mathfrak{pk})$.

    2. Parties run the protocol $\Pi_{\mathsf{gZKPoK}}^{1,\mathsf{flag}}$ receiving either $(\mathfrak{ct}_m^\mathbb{I}, \mathfrak{ct}_m^{'\mathbb{J}})$ to all the parties or abort.

Fig. 12. Protocol for generating valid encryption on random shared values

we assume that the encryption scheme $\mathcal{E}_{\mathsf{mBGV}}$ has an additional key generation algorithm $\widetilde{\mathsf{KeyGen}}()$ that outputs a meaningless public key $\widetilde{\mathfrak{pk}}$ such that

- $\mathsf{Enc}(m, \widetilde{\mathfrak{pk}})) \overset{s}{\approx} \mathsf{Enc}(0, \widetilde{\mathfrak{pk}})$, i.e. an encryption of any message m is statistically indistinguishable from an encryption of 0;
- If $\widetilde{\mathfrak{pk}} \leftarrow \widetilde{\mathsf{KeyGen}}()$ and $(\mathfrak{pk}, \mathfrak{sk}) \leftarrow \mathsf{KeyGen}()$, then $\mathfrak{pk} \overset{c}{\approx} \widetilde{\mathfrak{pk}}$, namely the two public keys are computationally indistinguishable.

In $\mathcal{E}_{\mathsf{BGV}}$ the algorithm $\widetilde{\mathsf{KeyGen}}()$ just samples $\widetilde{\mathfrak{pk}} = (\tilde{a}, \tilde{b})$ uniformly at random mod q_1.

The high level idea of the proof is then the following. We describe a simulator $\mathcal{S}$ and show that if an environment $\mathcal{Z}$ can distinguish the simulation from the real protocol execution, then we can construct a distinguisher that by rewinding the environment together with the adversary can distinguish between a public key $\mathfrak{pk}$ generated by KeyGen and a meaningless $\widetilde{\mathfrak{pk}}$ with non negligible probability. To this purpose we need to generalise the proof in [13] to our multiparty global zero knowledge of plaintext knowledge.

Theorem 5.3. *The protocol $\Pi_{\mathsf{GenValidCiph}}^{\nu,\mathsf{flag}}$ securely implements the functionality $\mathcal{F}_{\mathsf{GenValidCiph}}^{\nu,\mathsf{flag}}$ (Fig. 7) against any static, active adversary corrupting up to $n-1$ parties in the $(\mathcal{F}_{\mathsf{KeyGen}}, \mathcal{F}_{\mathsf{Rand}})$-hybrid model.*

6   SPDZ$_{2^k}$ from Somewhat Homomorphic Encryption - Pre-processing Phase

We now present our offline protocol based on the homomorphic scheme $\mathcal{E}_{\mathsf{mBGV}}$ described in Sect. 3. Even if the online computation is assumed to be performed over $\mathbb{Z}_{2^k}$, we produce random authenticated data over $\mathbb{Z}_{2^{k+s}}$. We use the same MAC scheme (and MACCheck procedure) used in SPDZ2k, with the difference that in our protocol also the shares $[\alpha]_i, i \in [n]$, of the secret global key α are in $\mathbb{Z}_{2^{k+s}}$. We set $k + s = t$ and $\mathcal{M} = (\mathbb{Z}_{2^t})^\rho$, where ρ is the number of packing slots.

The main task of the pre-processing protocol, which implements the ideal functionality $\mathcal{F}_{\mathsf{Prep}}$, given in the full version of the paper, is to produce the following type of random authenticated values:

Input masks: $(\langle r \rangle, P_i)$, with the authenticated shared valued r known by P_i.
Triples: $(\langle a \rangle, \langle b \rangle, \langle c \rangle)$, where $a, b, c \in \mathbb{Z}_{2^t}$ are random shared values and $c = a \cdot b$.
Squares: $(\langle a \rangle, \langle b \rangle)$, where $a \in \mathbb{Z}_{2^t}$ is a random secret shared value and $b = a^2$.
Bits: $\langle b \rangle$, where b is a random secret shared bit.

We first implement a weaker form of pre-processing functionality $\mathcal{F}_{\mathsf{wPrep}}$ (in the full version of the paper), that might output incorrect values. After that, in protocol Π_{Prep} (see the full version of the paper), we will bootstrap outputs from $\mathcal{F}_{\mathsf{wPrep}}$ to implement the desired functionality preprocessing functionality $\mathcal{F}_{\mathsf{Prep}}$ which returns different types of correct random authenticated values to be used in the online evaluation.

6.1   Weak Offline Protocol

We only describe our new protocol for producing random authenticated bits, the remaining commands are implemented similarly to the SPDZ2k paper and are given in the full version. In all steps we produce $\rho = r \cdot |\mathbb{I}|$ random pre-processed values at a time, since values are produced in the set $\mathcal{M}$. As before, given $\mathbf{m} \in \mathcal{M}$ we write $[\mathbf{m}]_i$ to denote an additive share of $\mathbf{m}$ and $[\alpha \cdot \mathbf{m}]_i$ to denote an additive share of the scalar multiplication of $\mathbf{m}$ by the scalar α, and reserve the notation $\langle x \rangle$ for authenticated sharings of values $x \in \mathbb{Z}_{2^t}$.

Authenticated Bits. The standard trick in the modulo p setting, see [12], is to use the 2-to-1 map induced by squaring modulo p, inverting it, and taking an element in the kernel by dividing the initial value by the obtained square root, i.e. $x/\sqrt{x^2} \in \{-1, 1\}$. When working modulo 2^t this is no longer possible, as the squaring map is 4-to-1. However, by temporarily working modulo 2^{t+1} and then reducing the roots modulo 2^t we can again obtain a 2-to-1 map. Furthermore, since we need to be able to divide by the $\sqrt{x^2}$, we will limit ourselves to invertible x's, i.e. such that $x = 1 \pmod{2}$. The protocol to generate a random element in $\{-1, 1\}$ is therefore as follows:

1. Given $a \leftarrow \mathbb{Z}_{2^t}$, compute $b \leftarrow 1 + 2a \pmod{2^{t+1}}$ (b is determined mod 2^{t+1})

Protocol Π_{wPrep} - Part 1

PARAMETERS: Let $\rho = r \times |\mathbb{I}|$ be the number of random authenticated data we produce for each call of the following commands.

Initialize: On command (Init) the parties do as follows.
  1. Call $\mathcal{F}_{\mathsf{DistrDec}}.\mathsf{Init}$ to obtain $\mathfrak{p}\mathfrak{k}$
  2. Parties sample random $[\alpha]_i \leftarrow \mathbb{Z}_{2^t}, i \in [n]$. Let $[\alpha]_i \leftarrow \mathcal{M}$ denote a plaintext with all the slots set to $[\alpha]_i$. Set $\alpha = \sum_{i \in [n]} [\alpha]_i$.
  3. The parties call the functionality $\mathcal{F}_{\mathsf{GenValidCiph}}^{1,\mathsf{Diag}}$ on private inputs $[\alpha]_i$ so that each party P_i receives ct_α.

Input: On input (Input, P_i) from all other parties, this commands produces ρ random masks for P_i.
  1. P_i samples a random $\mathbf{r} \in \mathcal{M}$, creates random additive shares $[\mathbf{r}]_j$ of $\mathbf{r}$ and sends them to the designated party P_j
  2. Parties call the functionality $\mathcal{F}_{\mathsf{GenValidCiph}}^{1,\perp}$ on input $(\mathsf{Gen\text{-}1}, \perp, [\mathbf{r}]_i)$, $\forall i \in [n]$, receiving $\mathsf{ct}_{\mathbf{r}}^{(1,\mathbb{I})}$
  3. Parties call the subprotocol Π_{Auth} on input $\mathsf{ct}_{\mathbf{r}}^{(1,\mathbb{I})}$, so to obtain $\langle \gamma_{\mathbf{r}} \rangle$.

wTriple: On input (wTriple), this command produces ρ triples in one execution.
  1. The parties call $\mathcal{F}_{\mathsf{GenValidCiph}}^{1,\perp}$ on random inputs $[\mathbf{a}]_i, [\mathbf{b}]_i$, so that each party receives $\mathsf{ct}_{\mathbf{a}}$ and $\mathsf{ct}_{\mathbf{b}}$.
  2. Parties locally compute $\mathsf{ct}_{\mathbf{c}} \leftarrow \mathsf{ct}_{\mathbf{a}} \odot \mathsf{ct}_{\mathbf{b}}$
  3. The parties call $\mathcal{F}_{\mathsf{DistrDec}}.\mathsf{D2}$ on input $\mathsf{ct}_{\mathbf{c}}$, so that each P_i receives $[\mathbf{c}]_i$ and a fresh ciphertext $\mathsf{ct}_{\mathbf{c}}'$
  4. Parties run Π_{Auth} on inputs $\mathsf{ct}_{\mathbf{a}}, \mathsf{ct}_{\mathbf{b}}, \mathsf{ct}_{\mathbf{c}}'$ to obtain $\langle \gamma_{\mathbf{a}} \rangle, \langle \gamma_{\mathbf{b}} \rangle, \langle \gamma_{\mathbf{c}} \rangle$.

wSquare: On input (wSquare), this command produces ρ random authenticated squares.
  1. This is exactly the same as wTriple above, except that we only sample the messages/ciphertexts for $\mathbf{a}$ and then set $\mathbf{b} = \mathbf{a}^2$.

Fig. 13. Weak offline protocol Π_{wPrep} - Part 1

2. $v \leftarrow b^2 \pmod{2^{t+2}}$ (note that v is determined modulo 2^{t+2} since $b + 2^{t+1}$ has the same square as b).
3. $\hat{b} \leftarrow \sqrt{v} \pmod{2^{t+1}}$ (A fixed square root is taken. Notice since v is a square, square roots exist, and there are four such square roots modulo 2^{t+2}, namely: $b, -b, b + 2^{t+1}$ and $-b + 2^{t+1}$. However, when reduced modulo 2^{t+1} there are only two possibilities, namely b and $-b$.
4. $d \leftarrow b/\hat{b} \pmod{2^{t+1}} \in \{-1, 1\}$.

Since we are interested in sharing bits in $\{0, 1\}$, not in $\{-1, 1\}$, we have to convert d. To perform the conversion in the large prime case of "standard" SPDZ, one can simply add one and then divide by two, but in our case division by two is impossible. However, we have a well defined division-by-2 map from $\mathbb{Z}_{2^{t+1}}$ to $\mathbb{Z}_{2^t}$ that maps $x \in \mathbb{Z}_{2^{t+1}}$ with $x = 0 \pmod 2$ to $x/2 \in \mathbb{Z}_{2^t}$, losing one bit of precision in the process. As such we can replace step 5 by:

5. $d \leftarrow (b/\hat{b} + 1)/2 \pmod{2^t} = (a/\hat{b} + (1 + \hat{b})/2\hat{b}) \pmod{2^t} \in \{0, 1\}$.

Note that since $\hat{b}$ is odd, the expression $(1 + \hat{b})/2$ is well defined modulo 2^t. We are now ready to give the wBit procedure of Π_{wPrep}, where we map these operations to the ciphertext space and the shares of a so as to produce shared bits in $\{0, 1\}$. In particular, given a sharing $[a]_i$ of a, it is easy to compute a sharing of d by defining $[d]_1 = [a]_1/\hat{b} + (1 + \hat{b})/(2\hat{b})$ (mod 2^t) and $[d]_i = [a]_i/\hat{b}$ (mod 2^t) for $i > 1$.

Protocol Π_{wPrep} - Part 2

PARAMETERS: Let $\rho = r \times |\mathbb{I}|$ be the number of random authenticated data we produce for each call of the following commands.

wBit: This command produces ρ random authenticated bits in one execution.
  1. Parties call $\mathcal{F}_{\mathsf{GenValidCiph}}^{1,\perp}$ on command (Gen-1, $\perp$) with random inputs $[\mathbf{a}]_i \in \mathcal{M}, i \in [n]$, so that each P_i receives $\mathsf{ct_a}$. Parties locally compute $\mathsf{ct_b} = \mathsf{ct_a} \boxplus \mathsf{ct_a} \boxplus \mathsf{ct_1}$, where $\mathsf{ct_1}$ a trivial encryption of the all one vector.
  2. Parties set $\mathsf{ct_v} \leftarrow \mathsf{ct_b} \odot \mathsf{ct_b}$.
  3. The parties call $\mathcal{F}_{\mathsf{DistrDec}}.\mathsf{D1}$ on input $\mathsf{ct_v}$ and so each party P_i obtains $[\mathbf{v}]_i \in \mathcal{M}'$. Note $\mathcal{M}'$ is mod 2^{t+2}.
  4. The parties broadcast $[\mathbf{v}]_i$ and set $\mathbf{v} \leftarrow [\mathbf{v}]_1 + \ldots + [\mathbf{v}]_n$ (mod 2^{t+2}).
  5. Parties set $\hat{\mathbf{b}} \leftarrow \sqrt{\mathbf{v}}$ (mod 2^{t+1}), where a fixed square root value is taken in each slot position modulo 2^{t+1}. If a square root does not exists, abort.
  6. Parties locally set

$$\mathsf{ct_d} \leftarrow \mathsf{ct_a}/\hat{\mathbf{b}} \boxplus \mathsf{ct}_{(\hat{\mathbf{b}}+1)/2\hat{\mathbf{b}}},$$

$$[\mathbf{d}]_1 \leftarrow [\mathbf{a}]_1/\hat{\mathbf{b}} + (\hat{\mathbf{b}} + 1)/2\hat{\mathbf{b}} \quad (\text{mod } 2^t),$$

$$[\mathbf{d}]_i \leftarrow [\mathbf{a}]_i/\hat{\mathbf{b}} \quad (\text{mod } 2^t), \text{ for } i > 1,$$

  where $\mathsf{ct}_{(\hat{\mathbf{b}}+1)/2\hat{\mathbf{b}}}$ is a deterministic encryption of the public value $(\hat{\mathbf{b}}+1)/2\hat{\mathbf{b}}$.
  7. Parties run Π_{Auth} on input $\mathsf{ct_d}^{(1,\mathbb{I})}$, so to obtain $[\boldsymbol{\gamma}_\mathbf{d}]_i, \forall i \in [n]$, i.e. each party P_i obtains $[\boldsymbol{\alpha} \cdot \mathbf{d}]_i$.
  8. For each slot in the plaintext space $\mathcal{M}$ each party P_i can obtain a value of $\langle d_j \rangle_i$, $j \in [\rho]$, (a sharing modulo 2^t) from the plaintexts $([\mathbf{d}]_i, [\boldsymbol{\alpha} \cdot \mathbf{d}]_i)$.
  9. Each party P_i's output is $\langle d_j \rangle_i, j \in [\rho]$.

Fig. 14. Weak offline protocol Π_{wPrep} - wBit

Note that since we do not expose a direct distributed decryption operation on the $\mathcal{F}_{\mathsf{DistrDec}}$ functionality we need to obtain the clear value of $\mathbf{v}$ via sharing and opening, unlike in [12]. Also note again unlike in [12], we produce exactly the given number of slots in each call to Bit, as we do not need to cope with the case of square roots of zero in this method. The following theorem then follows, with the proof given in the full version of the paper.

Theorem 6.1. *The Protocol Π_{wPrep} (Figs. 13 and 14) securely realises the ideal functionality $\mathcal{F}_{\mathsf{wPrep}}$ in the $(\mathcal{F}_{\mathsf{GenValidCiph}}, \mathcal{F}_{\mathsf{DistrDec}})$-hybrid model.*

Table 2. Amortized communication cost (in kbit) of producing triples of our protocol and SPDZ2k

Protocol	N	$\log_2 q$	k	s	sec	Triple cost
This paper	14449	270	32	32	26	**72.8**
SPDZ2k	–	–	32	32	26	79.87
This paper	32377	520	64	64	57	**153.3**
SPDZ2k	–	–	64	64	57	319.488
This paper	32377	720	128	64	57	**212.2**
SPDZ2k	–	–	128	64	57	557.06

6.2   From $\mathcal{F}_{\mathsf{wPrep}}$ to $\mathcal{F}_{\mathsf{Prep}}$ - Sacrificing

We can now show how to turn the Π_{wPrep} protocol into a protocol which realises the $\mathcal{F}_{\mathsf{Prep}}$ functionality. As said before, the authenticated shared data generated by $\mathcal{F}_{\mathsf{wPrep}}$ are incorrect if corrupt parties cheated in the distributed decryption, i.e. the output of $\mathcal{F}_{\mathsf{wPrep}}$ is a set of sharings $\{\langle a \rangle, \langle b \rangle, \langle c \rangle\}$ (resp. $\{\langle a \rangle, \langle b \rangle\}$ or $\{\langle a \rangle\}$) where we have $c = a \cdot b + \delta_c$ (resp. $b = a^2 + \delta_b$ or $a \in \{a, a + \delta_a\}$) for some adversarially chosen error value $\delta \in \mathbb{Z}_{2^t}$ and shared values $a, b, c \in \mathbb{Z}_{2^t}$. In a nutshell, the protocol of Π_{Prep} takes the output of Π_{wPrep} and ensures that the adversarially chosen values δ's are all equal to zero using the standard technique of sacrificing.

However, also the MACs on these values might be incorrect, i.e. we might have $\gamma_a = \sum_i [\alpha \cdot a]_i + \delta_{\gamma_a}$ for each authenticated value a. We can check the MAC on all the opened values at the end of the offline phase, and also check that the input masks are correctly MAC'd, by performing a MACCheck on a random linear combination of them. We add these checks in our preprocessing protocol, but in practice we do no worry about the errors δ_γ's on the MAC equations, since they can be dealt with later during the online phase, when all the values opened during the circuit evaluation are checked. We obtain the following theorem, whose proof is again given in the full version.

Theorem 6.2. *The protocol Π_{Prep} securely implements the ideal functionality $\mathcal{F}_{\mathsf{Prep}}$ against any static, active adversary corrupting up to $n - 1$ parties in the $(\mathcal{F}_{\mathsf{wPrep}}, \mathcal{F}_{\mathsf{Rand}})$-hybrid model.*

7   Communication Efficiency Analysis

Here we analyse the communication efficiency of our preprocessing protocol, when compared to the method of [10]. To simplify matters we focus just on the cost of our triple generation procedure as it is the most expensive step of the preprocessing phase. The entire protocol we want to maintain the same level of statistical security, which is equal to $\mathsf{sec} = s - \log_2 s$.

The most expensive step in our protocol is the zero-knowledge proof that proves that ZK_sec ciphertexts are valid with ZK_sec bits of statistical security. Once this parameter is fixed, to sec, the protocol $\Pi_{\mathsf{gZKPoK}}^{1,\mathsf{flag}}$ requires $2 \times$ ZK_sec broadcasts of ciphertexts in R^2 and the broadcast of $\mathbf{z}^i$ and T_i, which gives a total cost of $4 \cdot$ ZK_sec $\cdot N \cdot \log(q) + 8 \cdot$ ZK_sec $\cdot N - 4 \cdot N \cdot$ ZK_sec bits.

To generate ZK_sec $\cdot \rho$ triples $\langle \mathbf{a} \rangle, \langle \mathbf{b} \rangle, \langle \mathbf{c} \rangle$ we need two calls to $\mathcal{F}_{\mathsf{GenValidCiph}}^{1,\perp}$, to create ZK_sec ciphertexts $\mathfrak{ct}_{\mathbf{a}}, \mathfrak{ct}_{\mathbf{b}}$, after that one call to $\mathcal{F}_{\mathsf{DistrDec}}$.D2, to produce shares of $\mathfrak{ct}_{\mathbf{c}}$ and ZK_sec fresh ciphertexts $\mathfrak{ct}'_{\mathbf{c}}$. These are used later to produce the MAC shares $[\gamma_{\mathbf{a}}]_i, [\gamma_{\mathbf{b}}]_i, [\gamma_{\mathbf{c}}]_i$, obtained by running $3 \times$ ZK_sec times the sub-protocol Π_{Auth}. Notice that, as done in [10], we are ignoring here the cost of the MACCheck, as it can be done in the online phase and, in any case, it is independent of the number of generated triples, and the cost of $\mathcal{F}_{\mathsf{Rand}}$ and sacrificing, as it is negligible compared to the cost of the rest of the protocol. This gives a total cost (amortized) of roughly $4 \cdot (12 \cdot \log(q) \cdot N/\rho + N/\rho \cdot q)$ bits per triple, where ρ is the amount of packing in a single ciphertext.

We then estimate for various values of (k, s) the values of N and q and which give the best values for packing from Table 1. We select parameters which give us roughly 128 bits of computational security according to the tool obtained from https://bitbucket.org/malb/lwe-estimator. This allows us to give an estimation of the communication complexity of our protocol and SPDZ2k in the case of two parties creating one triple, see Table 2. In the important cases of statistical security of 64 bits in SPDZ2k over 64 and 128-bit data types we have a reduction in communication of over a half. In addition our protocol will get progressively more efficient than the OT-based pre-processing of SPDZ2k as the number of parties increases.

Acknowledgments. We thank Cyprien Delpech de Saint Guilhem for many helpful discussions. This work has been supported in part by ERC Advanced Grant ERC-2015-AdG-IMPaCT, by the Defense Advanced Research Projects Agency (DARPA) and Space and Naval Warfare Systems Center, Pacific (SSC Pacific) under contract No. N66001-15-C-4070, and by the FWO under an Odysseus project GOH9718N.

References

1. Aly, A., et al.: SCALE-MAMBA v1.6: Documentation (2019). https://homes.esat.kuleuven.be/~nsmart/SCALE/Documentation.pdf
2. Baum, C., Cozzo, D., Smart, N.P.: Using TopGear in Overdrive: a more efficient ZKPoK for SPDZ. Cryptology ePrint Archive, Report 2019/035 (2019). http://eprint.iacr.org/2019/035
3. Beaver, D.: Foundations of secure interactive computing. In: Feigenbaum, J. (ed.) CRYPTO 1991. LNCS, vol. 576, pp. 377–391. Springer, Heidelberg (1992). https://doi.org/10.1007/3-540-46766-1_31
4. Bendlin, R., Damgård, I., Orlandi, C., Zakarias, S.: Semi-homomorphic encryption and multiparty computation. In: Paterson, K.G. (ed.) EUROCRYPT 2011. LNCS, vol. 6632, pp. 169–188. Springer, Heidelberg (2011). https://doi.org/10.1007/978-3-642-20465-4_11

5. Brakerski, Z., Gentry, C., Vaikuntanathan, V.: (Leveled) fully homomorphic encryption without bootstrapping. In: Goldwasser, S. (ed.) ITCS 2012, pp. 309–325. ACM, New York (2012)
6. Brakerski, Z., Vaikuntanathan, V.: Efficient fully homomorphic encryption from (standard) LWE. In: Ostrovsky, R. (ed.) 52nd FOCS, pp. 97–106. IEEE Computer Society Press, October 2011
7. Canetti, R.: Universally composable security: a new paradigm for cryptographic protocols. In: 42nd FOCS, pp. 136–145. IEEE Computer Society Press, October 2001
8. Cassels, J.W.: Local Fields. Cambridge University Press, Cambridge (1986)
9. Cramer, R., Damgård, I.: On the amortized complexity of zero-knowledge protocols. In: Halevi, S. (ed.) CRYPTO 2009. LNCS, vol. 5677, pp. 177–191. Springer, Heidelberg (2009). https://doi.org/10.1007/978-3-642-03356-8_11
10. Cramer, R., Damgård, I., Escudero, D., Scholl, P., Xing, C.: SPD$\mathbb{Z}_{2^k}$: efficient MPC mod 2^k for dishonest majority. In: Shacham, H., Boldyreva, A. (eds.) CRYPTO 2018, Part II. LNCS, vol. 10992, pp. 769–798. Springer, Cham (2018). https://doi.org/10.1007/978-3-319-96881-0_26
11. Damgård, I., Escudero, D., Frederiksen, T.K., Keller, M., Scholl, P., Volgushev, N.: New primitives for actively-secure MPC over rings with applications to private machine learning. In: 2019 IEEE Symposium on Security and Privacy, pp. 1102–1120. IEEE Computer Society Press, May 2019
12. Damgård, I., Keller, M., Larraia, E., Pastro, V., Scholl, P., Smart, N.P.: Practical covertly secure MPC for dishonest majority – or: breaking the SPDZ limits. In: Crampton, J., Jajodia, S., Mayes, K. (eds.) ESORICS 2013. LNCS, vol. 8134, pp. 1–18. Springer, Heidelberg (2013). https://doi.org/10.1007/978-3-642-40203-6_1
13. Damgård, I., Pastro, V., Smart, N., Zakarias, S.: Multiparty computation from somewhat homomorphic encryption. In: Safavi-Naini, R., Canetti, R. (eds.) CRYPTO 2012. LNCS, vol. 7417, pp. 643–662. Springer, Heidelberg (2012). https://doi.org/10.1007/978-3-642-32009-5_38
14. Gentry, C., Halevi, S., Smart, N.P.: Better bootstrapping in fully homomorphic encryption. In: Fischlin, M., Buchmann, J., Manulis, M. (eds.) PKC 2012. LNCS, vol. 7293, pp. 1–16. Springer, Heidelberg (2012). https://doi.org/10.1007/978-3-642-30057-8_1
15. Gentry, C., Halevi, S., Smart, N.P.: Fully homomorphic encryption with polylog overhead. In: Pointcheval, D., Johansson, T. (eds.) EUROCRYPT 2012. LNCS, vol. 7237, pp. 465–482. Springer, Heidelberg (2012). https://doi.org/10.1007/978-3-642-29011-4_28
16. Gentry, C., Halevi, S., Smart, N.P.: Homomorphic evaluation of the AES circuit. In: Safavi-Naini, R., Canetti, R. (eds.) CRYPTO 2012. LNCS, vol. 7417, pp. 850–867. Springer, Heidelberg (2012). https://doi.org/10.1007/978-3-642-32009-5_49
17. Halevi, S., Shoup, V.: Algorithms in HElib. In: Garay, J.A., Gennaro, R. (eds.) CRYPTO 2014, Part I. LNCS, vol. 8616, pp. 554–571. Springer, Heidelberg (2014). https://doi.org/10.1007/978-3-662-44371-2_31
18. Keller, M., Orsini, E., Scholl, P.: MASCOT: faster malicious arithmetic secure computation with oblivious transfer. In: Weippl, E.R., Katzenbeisser, S., Kruegel, C., Myers, A.C., Halevi, S. (eds.) ACM CCS 2016, pp. 830–842. ACM Press, New York (2016)
19. Keller, M., Pastro, V., Rotaru, D.: Overdrive: making SPDZ great again. In: Nielsen, J.B., Rijmen, V. (eds.) EUROCRYPT 2018, Part III. LNCS, vol. 10822, pp. 158–189. Springer, Cham (2018). https://doi.org/10.1007/978-3-319-78372-7_6

20. Nielsen, J.B., Nordholt, P.S., Orlandi, C., Burra, S.S.: A new approach to practical active-secure two-party computation. In: Safavi-Naini, R., Canetti, R. (eds.) CRYPTO 2012. LNCS, vol. 7417, pp. 681–700. Springer, Heidelberg (2012). https://doi.org/10.1007/978-3-642-32009-5_40

21. Smart, N.P., Vercauteren, F.: Fully homomorphic SIMD operations. Des. Codes Crypt. **71**(1), 57–81 (2014)

SoK: A Consensus Taxonomy in the Blockchain Era

Juan Garay[1](✉) and Aggelos Kiayias[2]

[1] Texas A&M University, College Station, TX, USA
garay@cse.tamu.edu
[2] University of Edinburgh and IOHK, Edinburgh, UK
akiayias@inf.ed.ac.uk

Abstract. Consensus is arguably one of the most fundamental problems in distributed computing, playing also an important role in the area of cryptographic protocols as the enabler of a secure broadcast functionality. While the problem has a long and rich history and has been analyzed from many different perspectives, recently, with the advent of blockchain protocols like Bitcoin, it has experienced renewed interest from a much wider community of researchers and has seen its application expand to various novel settings.

One of the main issues in consensus research is the many different variants of the problem that exist as well as the various ways the problem behaves when different setup, computational assumptions and network models are considered. In this work we perform a systematization of knowledge in the landscape of consensus research in the Byzantine failure model starting with the original formulation in the early 1980s up to the present blockchain-based new class of consensus protocols. Our work is a roadmap for studying the consensus problem under its many guises, classifying the way it operates in the various settings and highlighting the exciting new applications that have emerged in the blockchain era.

1 Introduction

The consensus problem—reaching agreement distributedly in the presence of faults—has been extensively studied in the literature starting with the seminal work of Shostak, Pease and Lamport [88,108]. The traditional setting of the problem involves parties connected by point-to-point channels, possibly using digital signatures in order to ensure the integrity of the information that is exchanged in the course of the protocol. For a relatively recent overview of the many variants of consensus that are considered in the distributed systems literature see Cachin *et al.* [25]. Tolerating "Byzantine" behavior, i.e., the presence of parties that may behave arbitrarily, possibly in malicious ways, has been one of the hallmark features in the study of the problem.

Bitcoin was introduced by Nakamoto in 2008–2009 [95,97], with the objective of providing a payment system that is decentralized in the sense of not

The full version of this paper can be found in the Cryptology ePrint Archive [65].

© Springer Nature Switzerland AG 2020
S. Jarecki (Ed.): CT-RSA 2020, LNCS 12006, pp. 284–318, 2020.
https://doi.org/10.1007/978-3-030-40186-3_13

relying on a central authority that should be trusted for transactions to be considered as final. Expectedly, the fundamental enabling component of the Bitcoin system is a consensus mechanism that facilitates agreement on the history of transactions. Given the conflicting interests of the Bitcoin protocol participants, such a system should be resilient to Byzantine behavior, which brings us to the main contribution of Bitcoin in the context of the consensus problem, namely. a non-traditional and novel approach from the perspective of distributed computing to solve the problem in a setting that until then had not received sufficient attention.

In light of these developments, it is important to rethink the consensus problem in the blockchain era and organize the landscape that is currently being formed, acknowledging all the new directions and novel tools that have become available in the context of consensus protocol design.

One main aspect of our work is to look into the consensus problem from a modeling perspective providing the definitions needed to understand the problem and the solutions that have been developed over the years both in the traditional and the newer blockchain settings. In the course of this, we provide a taxonomy of protocols and impossibility results that comprehensively outline what is currently known about consensus and which questions continue to remain open. Also important is to "extract" the relevant consensus question that is particular to Bitcoin, which we term "ledger consensus" (sometimes referred to as "Nakamoto consensus"), and which is an instance of the state machine replication problem that has been long-studied in distributed systems [111].

Consequently, in this paper we provide precise definitions of the relevant versions of consensus that have been investigated and systematize the existing knowledge about the problem with respect to (i) the network model, (ii) trusted setup assumptions, and (iii) computational assumptions under which, and at what cost in terms of running time and communication overhead, the problem can be solved.

We emphasize that our approach is problem-centric and the results being overviewed conceptual and fundamental in nature, with a *feasibility focus* with respect to the "resources" mentioned above, which means that in the case of classical consensus, a very active area of research in the distributed systems community, we might only mention in passing (if at all) the more recent results on practical Byzantine fault tolerance, for example. As such, our systematization complements the various other enumerative surveys of results and publications on the subject (e.g., [10, 25, 112]).

Organization of the Paper. We start in Sect. 2 by specifying a model of multi-party protocol execution and how protocols' properties will be deemed satisfied, as well as presenting the definition of (variants of) the consensus problem. We then specify the available resources and assumptions mentioned above under which the problem has been studied: Network assumptions (communication primitives, synchrony) in Sect. 3; trusted setup assumptions (no setup, public-state setup, private-state setup) in Sect. 4; and computational assumptions (none, one-way functions, proofs-of-work, random oracle) in Sect. 5.

We then overview possibility (i.e., constructions) and impossibility results for consensus with respect to number of parties as a function of misbehaving parties (resp., honest vs malicious computational power), trusted setup, running time and communication costs in the traditional (point-to-point communication) setting (Sect. 6), and in the Bitcoin (peer-to-peer) setting (Sect. 7).

We present ledger consensus in Sect. 8. After defining the problem, we proceed to the evaluation of existing results through a similar lens as in the case of (standard) consensus, including an adaptation to ledger consensus of the impossibility of standard consensus for dishonest majorities.

Due to space limitations, supplementary material including the ideal specification of some of the resources available to the protocol can be found in the full version of the paper [65].

2   Model and Definitions

2.1   Protocol Execution

In order to provide a description of protocols and their executions it is useful to consider a formal model of computation. We choose the Interactive Turing Machine (ITM)-based model put forth by [30, 76]. An ITM is like a Turing Machine but with the addition of an incoming and an outgoing communication tape as well as an identity tape and a "subroutine" tape. When an instance of an ITM is generated (we will henceforth call this an ITI, for interactive Turing machine *instance*), the identity tape is initialized to a specific value that remains constant throughout the instance's execution. The ITI may communicate with other ITI's by writing to its outgoing communication tape.

Let us consider a protocol Π that is modeled as an ITM. Ideally, we would like to consider the execution of this protocol in an arbitrary setting, i.e., with an arbitrary set of parties and arbitrary configuration. A common way to model this in distributed cryptographic protocols is to consider that a certain program, thought of as an adversary, produces this configuration and therefore the properties of the protocol should hold for any possible choice of that program, potentially with some explicitly defined restrictions. The advantage of this particular modeling approach is that it obviates the need to quantify over all the details that concern the protocol (and substitutes them with a single universal quantification over all such "environments").

Suppose now that we have a protocol Π that is specified as an ITM and we would like to consider all possible executions of this protocol in the presence of an adversary $\mathcal{A}$, that is also modeled as an ITM. We capture this by specifying a pair of ITMs $(\mathcal{Z}, C)$, called the *environment* and the *control program*, respectively. The environment $\mathcal{Z}$ is given some input which may be trivial (such as a security parameter 1^κ) and is allowed to "spawn" new ITIs using the programs of Π and $\mathcal{A}$. By convention, only a single instance of $\mathcal{A}$ will be allowed. Spawning such new instances is achieved by writing a single message to its outgoing tape which is read by C. The control program is responsible for approving such spawning requests by $\mathcal{Z}$. Subsequently, all communication of the instances that are created will be routed via C, i.e., C will be receiving the instances' outgoing messages and will be approving whether they can be forwarded to the receiving parties' incoming tape. Note that this may be used to simulate the existence of point-to-point channels; nevertheless, we will take a more general approach. Specifically, the control function C, will by definition only permit outgoing messages of running ITIs to be sent to the adversary $\mathcal{A}$ (with instructions for further delivery). This captures the fact that the network cannot be assumed to be *de facto* safe for the instances that are communicating during the protocol execution (see below where we explain how the adversarial influence in the network may be constrained). Beyond writing messages that are routed though $\mathcal{A}$, ITIs can also spawn additional ITIs as prescribed by the rules hardcoded in C. This enables instances of a protocol Π to invoke subroutines that can assist in its execution. These subroutines can be sub-protocols or instances of "ideal functionalities" that may be accessible by more than a single running instance.

Given those features, the above approach provides a comprehensive framework for reasoning about protocol executions. In case a polynomial-time bound is required, in the setting where a computational assumption is employed that holds only for polynomial-time bounded programs, for example, some care needs to be applied to ensure that the total execution run time of the $(\mathcal{Z}, C)$ system remains polynomial-time. This is because even if all ITIs are assumed to be polynomially bounded, the total execution run time may not be. We refer to Proposition 3 in [30] for more details regarding enforcing an overall polynomial-time bound.

Functionalities. We will next need to specify the "resources" that may be available to the instances running protocol Π. For example, access to reliable point-to-point channels or a "diffuse" channel (see below). To allow for the most general way to specify such resources we will follow the approach of describing them as "ideal functionalities" in the terminology of [30]. In simple terms, an ideal functionality is another ITM that may interact with instances running concurrently in the protocol execution. A critical feature of ideal functionalities is that they can be spawned by ITIs running protocol Π. In such case, the protocol Π is defined with respect to the functionality $\mathcal{F}$. The ideal functionality may interact with the adversary $\mathcal{A}$ as well as other ITIs running the protocol. One main advantage of using the concept of an ideal functionality in our setting, is that we can capture various different communication resources that may be available to the participants running the protocol. For instance, a secure channel functionality may be spawned to transmit a message between two instances of Π that will only leak the length of the message to the adversary. As another example, a message-passing functionality may ensure that all parties are activated prior to advancing to the next communication round (see below in synchronous vs. asynchronous executions).

Execution of Multiparty Protocols. When protocol instances are spawned by $\mathcal{Z}$ they will be initialized with an identity which is available to the program's code, as well as, possibly, with the identities of other instances that may run concurrently (this is at the discretion of the environment program $\mathcal{Z}$). The identities themselves may be useful to the program instance, as they may be used by the instance to address them. We will use the notation $\mathsf{VIEW}_{\Pi,\mathcal{A},\mathcal{Z}}$ to denote an *execution* of the protocol Π with an adversary $\mathcal{A}$ and an environment $\mathcal{Z}$. The execution is a string that is formed by the concatenation of all messages and all ITI states at each step of the execution of the system $(\mathcal{Z}, C)$. The parties' inputs are provided by the environment $\mathcal{Z}$ which also receives the parties' outputs. Parties that receive no input from the environment remain inactive. We denote by INPUT() the input tape of each party.

We note that by adopting the computational modeling of systems of ITMs by [30] we obviate the need of imposing a strict upper bound on the number of messages that may be transmitted by the adversary in each activation. In our setting, honest parties, at the discretion of the environment, are given sufficient time to process all messages delivered by any communication functionality available to them as a resource. It follows that denial of service attacks cannot be used to the adversary's advantage in the analysis – i.e., they are out of scope from our perspective of studying the consensus problem.

Properties of Protocols. In our statements we will be concerned with *properties* of protocols Π. Such properties will be defined as predicates over the random variable $\mathsf{VIEW}_{\Pi,\mathcal{A},\mathcal{Z}}$ by quantifying over all adversaries $\mathcal{A}$ and environments $\mathcal{Z}$.

Definition 1. *Given a predicate Q we say that* the protocol Π *satisfies property Q provided that for all $\mathcal{A}$ and $\mathcal{Z}$, $Q(\mathsf{VIEW}_{\Pi,\mathcal{A},\mathcal{Z}})$ holds.*

Note that in some cases, protocols may only satisfy properties with a small probability of error over all possible executions. The probability space is determined by the private coins of all participants and the functionalities they employ. In such cases, we may indicate that the protocol satisfies the property with some (small, typically negligigle in a security parameter) error probability. We will only consider properties that are polynomial-time computable predicates. Our notion of execution will capture the single-session, stand-alone execution setting for protocols, hence properties will be single-session properties.

Asynchronous vs. Synchronous Execution. The model above is able to capture various flavors of synchrony. This is achieved by abstracting the network communication as a functionality and specifying how the adversary may interfere with message delivery. The functionality may keep track of parties' activations and depending on the case ensure that parties will be given a chance to act as the protocol execution advances.

Static vs. Dynamic Environments. In terms of protocol participants, the model we present captures both static and dynamic environments. Specifically, it is suitable for protocols that run with a fixed number of parties that should be known to all participants in advance, but it also allows protocols for which the number of participants is not known beforehand and, in fact, it may not even be known during the course of the execution. Note that in order to allow for proper ITI intercommunication we will always assume that the *total* set of parties is known, but, nevertheless, only a small subset of them may be active in a particular moment during the protocol execution.

Setup Assumptions. In a number of protocols, there is a need to have some pre-existing configuration (such as the knowledge of a common reference string [CRS], or a public-key infrastructure [PKI]). Such setup assumptions can be also captured as separate functionalities $\mathcal{F}$ that are available to the protocol ITIs.

Permissioned vs. Permissionless Networks. In the context of the consensus problem, this terminology became popular with the advent of blockchain protocols. The Bitcoin blockchain protocol is the prototypical "permissionless" protocol where read access to the ledger is unrestricted and write access (in the form of posting transactions) can be obtained by anyone that possesses BTC (which may be acquired, in principle, by anyone that is running the Bitcoin client and invests computational power solving proofs of work). On the other hand, a permissioned protocol imposes more stringent access control on the read and write operations that are available as well as with respect to who can participate in the protocol. Extrapolating from the terminology as applied in the ledger setting, a permissionless consensus protocol would enable any party to participate and contribute input for consideration of the other parties. With this in mind, the traditional setting of consensus is permissioned, since only specific parties are allowed to participate; on the other hand, consensus in the blockchain setting can be either permissioned or permissionless.

Cryptographic Primitives. We now overview some standard cryptographic primitives, as they are employed by some of the consensus protocols. A *digital signature scheme* consists of three PPT algorithms (Gen, Sign, Verify) such that $(vk, sk) \leftarrow$ Gen(1^κ) generates a public-key/secret-key pair; $\sigma \leftarrow$ Sign(sk, m) signs a message m; and Verify(vk, m, σ) returns 1 if and only if σ is a valid signature for m given vk. A digital signature scheme is *existentially unforgeable*, if for any PPT adversary $\mathcal{A}$ that has access to a Sign$(sk, \cdot)$ oracle, the event that $\mathcal{A}$ returns some (m, σ) such that Verify$(vk, m, \sigma) = 1$ has measure negl(κ), where the probability is taken over the coin tosses of the algorithms, negl() denotes a negligible function, and κ is the security parameter. A *collision resistant (keyed) hash function family* $\{H_k\}_{k \in K}$ has the property that $H_k : \{0,1\}^* \rightarrow \{0,1\}^\kappa$, it is efficiently computable and the probability to produce $x \neq y$ with $H_k(x) = H_k(y)$ given k is negl(κ). Another, less standard primitive that has been widely deployed in consensus protocol design with the advent of the Bitcoin blockchain is *proof of work* (PoW); see Sect. 5 for more information on the primitive.

2.2 The Consensus Problem

As mentioned earlier, *consensus* (aka *Byzantine agreement*), formulated by Shostak, Pease and Lamport [88,108], is one of the fundamental problems in the areas of fault-tolerant distributing computing and cryptographic protocols, in particular secure multi-party computation [18, 36, 77, 115]. In the consensus problem, n parties attempt to reach agreement on a value from some fixed domain V, despite the malicious behavior of up to t of them. More specifically, every party P_i starts the consensus protocol with an initial value $v \in V$, and every run of the protocol must satisfy (except possibly for some negligible probability) the following conditions (we note that all properties below are expressible as Q predicates according to Definition 1).

- *Termination:* All honest parties decide on a value.
- *Agreement:* If two honest parties decide on v and w, respectively, then $v = w$.
- *Validity:* If all honest parties have the same initial value v, then all honest parties decide on v.

The domain V can be arbitrary, but frequently the case $V = \{0, 1\}$ is considered given the efficient transformation of binary agreement protocols to the multi-valued case cf. [113].[1]

There exist various measures of quality of a consensus protocol: its *resiliency*, expressed as the fraction $(\frac{t}{n})$ of misbehaving parties a protocol can tolerate; its running time—worst number of rounds by which honest parties terminate; and its communication complexity—worst total number of bits/messages communicated during a protocol run.

In the consensus problem, all the parties start with an initial value. A closely related variant is the single-source version of the problem (aka the *Byzantine Generals* problem [88], or simply (reliable or secure) "broadcast"), where only a distinguished party—the *sender*—has an input. In this variant, both the Termination and Agreement conditions remain the same, and Validity becomes:

- *Validity:* If the sender is honest and has initial value v, then all honest parties decide on v.

A stronger, albeit natural, version of the consensus problem requires that the output value be one of the honest parties' inputs, a distinction that is only important in the case of non-binary inputs. In this version, called *strong consensus* [99], the Validity condition becomes:

- *Strong Validity:* If the honest parties decide on v, then v is the input of some honest party.

Note that the distinction with the standard version of the problem is only relevant in the case of non-binary inputs. Further, the resiliency bounds for this version also depend on $|V|$ (see Sect. 6).

Another way to enhance validity is to require that the output of an honest party conforms to an *external* predicate Q [26]. In this setting, each input v is

---

[1] Refer to Sect. 6 for more efficient transformations, where in particular the longer message is only transmitted $O(n)$ times, as opposed to $O(n^2)$.

accompanied by a proof π and is supposed to satisfy $Q(v, \pi) = 1$ (for instance, π can be a digital signature on v and Q would be verifying its validity). Note that the resulting guarantee is weaker than strong validity (since it could be the case that the decision is made on an input suggested by a corrupted party), but nevertheless it can be suitable in a multi-valued setting where only externally validated inputs are admissible as outputs.

Finally, we point out that, traditionally, consensus problems have been specified as above, in a *property-based* manner. Protocols for the problem are then proven secure/correct by showing how the properties (e.g., the Agreement, Validity and Termination conditions) are met. Nowadays, however, it is widely accepted to formulate the security of a protocol via the "trusted-party paradigm" (cf. [76,77]), where the protocol execution is compared with an ideal process where the outputs are computed by a trusted party that sees all the inputs. A protocol is then said to securely carry out the task if running the protocol with a realistic adversary amounts to "emulating" the ideal process with the appropriate trusted party. One advantage of such a simulation-based approach is that it simultaneously captures *all* the properties that are guaranteed by the ideal world, without having to enumerate some list of desired properties. Simulation-based definitions are also useful for applying *composition theorems* (e.g., [29,30]) that enable proving the security of protocols that use other protocols as sub-routines, which typically would be the case for consensus and/or broadcast protocols.

The above captures the classical definition of the consensus problem. A related and recently extensively studied version of the problem is state-machine replication or "ledger" consensus that we will treat in Sect. 8.

On the Necessity of an Honest Majority. Regardless of the resources available to the parties in the protocol execution, an upper bound of (less than) $n/2$ can be shown for resiliency (see, for example, [59]). Specifically, consider a set n of parties that are equally divided with respect to their initial values between inputs 0 and 1, and an adversary that with $1/3$ probability corrupts no one (case 1), with $1/3$ probability corrupts the parties that have input 0 (case 2) and with $1/3$ probability corrupts the parties that have input 1 (case 3). In any case, the adversarial parties follow the protocol. Observe that case 1 requires from the honest parties to converge to a common output (due to Agreement), while in the other two cases the honest parties should output 0 (case 2) and 1 (case 3). However, all three cases are perfectly indistinguishable in the view of the honest parties and as a result a logical contradiction ensues.

3 Network Assumptions

Communication Primitives. Consensus protocols are described with respect to a network layer that enables parties to send messages to each other. An important distinction we will make is between point-to-point connectivity vs. message "diffusion" as it manifests in a peer-to-peer communication setting.

Point-to-Point Channels. In this setting parties are connected with pairwise reliable and authentic channels. We call that resource RMT, for *reliable message transmission.* When a party sends a message it specifies its recipient as well as the message contents and it is guaranteed that the recipient will receive it. The recipient can identify the sender as the source of the message. In such fixed connectivity setting, all parties are aware of the set of parties running the protocol. Full connectivity has been the standard communication setting for consensus protocols, see [88], although sparse connectivity has also been considered (cf. [53,114]). We present the functionality for RMT in the full version of the paper [65].

In terms of measuring communication costs in this model, it will be simpler for us to use the (maximum) total number of messages in a protocol run, rather than the total number of communicated bits, assuming a suitable message size. See, e.g., [59] (Chap. 3) for a detailed account of the communication complexity of consensus (and broadcast) protocols.

Peer-to-Peer Diffusion. This setting is motivated by peer-to peer message transmission that happens via "gossiping," i.e., messages received by a party are passed along on to the party's peers. We refer to this basic message passing operation as "Diffuse." Message transmission is not authenticated and it does not preserve the order of messages in the views of different parties. When a message is diffused by an honest party, there is no specific recipient and it is guaranteed that all activated honest parties will receive the same message. Nonetheless, the source of the message may be "spoofed" and thus the recipient may not reliably identify the source of the message,[2] and when the sender is malicious not everyone is guaranteed to receive the same message. Contrary to the point-to-point channels setting, parties may neither be aware of the identities of the parties running the protocol nor their precise number. The ideal functionality capturing the diffuse operation is also presented in the full version of the paper.

In order to measure the total communication costs of peer-to-peer diffusion, one needs to take into account the underlying network graph. The typical deployment setting will be a sparse constant-degree graph for which it holds that the number of edges equals $O(n)$. In such setting, each invocation of the primitive requires $O(n)$ messages to be transmitted in the network.

Relation Between the Communication Primitives. It is easy to see that given RMT, there is a straightforward, albeit inefficient, protocol that simulates Diffuse; given a message to be diffused, the protocol using RMT will send the message to each party in the set of parties running the protocol. On the other hand, it is not hard to establish that no protocol can simulate RMT given Diffuse. The argument is as follows, and it works no matter how the protocol using Diffuse may operate. When a party A transmits a message M to party B, it is possible for the adversary in the Diffuse setting to simulate a "fake" party A that sends a

---

[2] Note that in contrast to a sender-anonymous channel (cf. [35]), a diffuse channel will leak the identity of the sender to the adversary.

message $M' \neq M$ to B concurrently. Invariably, this will result to a setting where B has to decide which is the correct message to output and will have to produce the wrong message with non-negligible probability. It follows that Diffuse is a weaker communication primitive: one would not be able to substitute Diffuse for RMT in a protocol setting.

Other Models. The above models may be extended in a number of ways to capture various real world considerations in message passing. For instance, in point-to-point channels, the communication graph may change over the course of protocol execution with edges being added or removed adversarially, something that may also result in temporary network partitions. Another intermediate model between point-to-point channels and diffusion, formulated by Okun [101], is to have a diffusion channel with "port awareness," i.e., the setting where messages from the same source are linkable, or without port awareness, but where each party is restricted to sending one message per round (see Sect. 3 for the notion of round) and their total number is known. Yet another intermediate model in terms of partial knowledge of parties and authentication has been treated, e.g., in [4,13] and follow-up works.

Synchrony. The ability of the parties to synchronize in protocol execution is an important aspect in the design of consensus protocols. Synchrony in message passing can be captured by dividing the protocol execution in rounds where parties are activated in some sequence and each one of them has the opportunity to send messages which are received by the recipients at the onset of the next round. This reflects the fact that in real world networks messages are delivered most of the time in a timely fashion and thus parties can synchronize the protocol execution in discrete rounds.

A first important relaxation to the synchronous model is to allow the adversary to control the activation of parties so that it acts last in each round having access to all messages sent by honest participants before it decides on the actions of the adversarial participants and the ordering of message delivery for the honest parties in the next round. This concept is standard in the secure mult-iparty computation literature [18,37,78] and is commonly referred to as the "rushing adversary" [30]. This is captured by the corresponding communication functionalities. A second relaxation is to impose a time bound on message delivery that is not known to the protocol participants. We shall refer to this as the "partially synchronous setting" [50]. The partial synchronous setting is easy to capture by the communication functionalities as follows: a parameter $\Delta \in \mathbb{N}$ is introduced in each functionality that determines the maximum time a message can remain "in limbo." For each message that is sent, a counter is introduced that is initially 0 and counts the number of rounds that have passed since its transmission (note that this concept of round is not any more a "message passing" round). When this counter reaches Δ the message is copied to the inbox$(\cdot)$ strings for the active participants.

An even weaker setting than partial synchrony is that of message transmission with eventual message delivery, where all messages between honest parties are guaranteed to be delivered but there is no specific time bound that mandates their delivery in the course of the protocol execution. This is the classical model in fault tolerant distributed computing that is referred to as asynchronous [58, 90]. Again, it is easy to adapt the communication functionalities to accomodate eventual delivery, following the recent formalization of this model in [44]. Note that it is proven that no deterministic consensus protocol exists in this setting [58], and the impossibility can be overcome by randomization [15,39,55,110].

Finally, in the "fully asynchronous setting" (cf. [30]), where messages may be arbitrarily delayed *or dropped* consensus is trivially impossible.

4   Setup Assumptions

In the context of protocol design, a setup assumption refers to information that can be available at the onset of the protocol to each protocol participant. Consensus protocols are designed with respect to a number of different setup assumptions that we outline below.

No Setup. In this setting we consider protocols that parties do not utilize any setup functionality beyond the existence of the communication functionality. Note that the communication functionality may already provide some information to the participants about the environment of the protocol; nevertheless, this setting is distinguished from other more thorough setup assumptions that are described below. We note that in this setting it may be of interest to consider protocol executions wherein the adversary is allowed a certain amount of precomputation prior to the onset of execution that involves the honest parties.

Public-State Setup. A public-state setup is parameterized by a probability ensemble $\mathcal{D}$. For each input size κ, the ensemble $\mathcal{D}$ specifies a probability distribution that is sampled a single time at the onset of the protocol execution to produce a string denoted by s that is of length polynomial in κ. All protocol parties, including adversarial ones, are assumed to have access to s. In this setting, the consensus protocol will be designed for a specific ensemble $\mathcal{D}$.

The concept of a public-state setup can be further relaxed in a model that has been called "sun-spots" [32], where the ensemble is further parameterized by an index a. The definition is the same as above but now the protocol execution will be taken for some arbitrary choice of a. Intuitively, the parameter a can be thought as an adversarial influence in the choice of the public string s. In this setting, the consensus protocol will be designed with respect to the ensemble class $\{\mathcal{D}_a\}_a$.

Private-State Setup. As in the public state case, a private state setup is parameterized by an ensemble $\mathcal{D}$. For each input size κ and number of parties n, $\mathcal{D}$ specifies a probability distribution that is sampled a single time to produce a sequence of values $(s_1, \ldots, s_n)$. The length of each value s_i is polynomial in κ. At the onset of the protocol execution, the ensemble is sampled once and each protocol participant will receive one of the values s_i following some predetermined order. The critical feature of this setting is that each party will have private access to s_i. Observe that, trivially, the setting of private-state setup subsumes the setting of public-state setup.

As in the case of a public-state setup, it is important to consider the relaxation where the ensemble $\mathcal{D}$ is parameterized by string a. As before sampling from $\mathcal{D}_a$ will be performed from some arbitrary choice of a. It is in this sense where private-state setup has been most useful. In particular, we can use it to express the concept of a public-key infrastructure (PKI). In this setting the ensemble $\mathcal{D}$ employs a digital signature algorithm (Gen, Sign, Verify) and samples a value $(vk_i, sk_i) \leftarrow \mathsf{Gen}(1^\kappa)$ independently for each honest participant. For each participant which is assumed to be adversarial at the onset of the execution, its public and secret key pair is set to a predetermined value that is extracted from a. The private input s_i for the i-th protocol participant will be equal to $(vk_1, \ldots, vk_n, sk_i)$, thus giving access to all parties' public (verification) keys and its own private key. Other types of private setup include "correlated randomness" [12], where parties get correlated random strings $(r_1, r_2, ..., r_n)$ drawn from some predetermined distribution, which has been used to implement a random beacon [110].

One may consider more complicated interactive setups, such as for example the adversary choosing a somehow based on public information available about $(s_1, \ldots, s_n)$, but we will refrain from considering those here. An alternative (and subsumed by the above) formulation of a private setup includes the availability of a broadcast channel prior to the protocol execution, which enables participants to exchange shared keys [109].

5 Computational Assumptions

The assumptions used to prove the properties of consensus protocols can be divided into two broad categories. In the information-theoretic (aka "unconditional") setting, the adversary is assumed to be unbounded in terms of its computational resources. In the computational setting, on the other hand, a polynomial-time bound is assumed.

Information-Theoretic Security. In the information-theoretic setting the adversarial running time is unbounded. It follows that the adversary may take arbitrary time to operate in each invocation. Note that the protocol execution may continue to proceed in synchronous rounds, nevertheless the running time of the adversary within each round will dilate sufficiently to accomodate its complete operation. When proving the consensus properties in this setting we can further consider two variations: perfect and statistical. When a property, Agreement for example, is perfectly satisfied this means that in all possible executions the honest parties never disagree on their outputs. On the other hand, in the statistical variant, there will be certain executions where the honest parties are allowed to disagree. Nevertheless, these executions will have negligible density in a security parameter (in this case, n) among all executions. We observe that the statistical setting is only meaningful for a probabilistic consensus protocol, where the honest parties may be "unlucky" in their choices of coins.

Computational Security. In the computational setting the adversarial running time, and/or the computational model within which the adversary (and the parties running the protocol) are expressed becomes restricted. We distinguish the following variants.

One-Way functions. A standard computational assumption is the existence of one-way functions. A one-way function is a function $f : X \rightarrow Y$ for which it holds that f is polynomial-time computable, but the probability $\mathcal{A}(1^{|x|}, f(x)) \in f^{-1}(f(x))$ for a randomly sampled x, is negligible in $|x|$ for any polynomial time bounded program $\mathcal{A}$. One-way functions, albeit quite basic, are a powerful primitive that enables the construction of more complex cryptographic algorithms that include symmetric-key encryption, target collision-resistant hash functions and digital signatures [98]; the latter in particular play an important role when categorizing consensus protocols as we see below.

Proof of Work. A proof of work (PoW) [52] is a cryptographic primitive that enables a verifier to be convinced that certain amount of computational effort has been invested with respect to a certain context, e.g., a plaintext message or a nonce that the verifier has provided. A number of properties have been identified as important for the application of the primitive specifically to blockchain protocols, including amortization resistance, sampleability, fast verification, hardness against tampering and message attacks, and almost k-wise independence [71]. Some variants of PoWs have been shown to imply one-way functions [22].

The Random Oracle Model. In the previous subsections the level of security described was captured in the standard computational model where all parties are assumed to be Interactive Turing machines. In many cases, including consensus protocol design, it is proven useful to describe properties in the random oracle model, [14]. The random oracle model can be captured as an ideal functionality $\mathcal{F}_{RO}$ (see the full version of the paper). In a relevant adaptation of the $\mathcal{F}_{RO}$ model for the consensus setting, the access to the oracle is restricted by a quota of $q \geq 1$ queries per party per round of protocol execution [67]. This bound is also imposed on the adversary who is assumed to control t parties. In case $t < n/2$, the execution will be said to impose honest majority in terms of "computational power."

6   Consensus in the Point-to-Point Setting

In the traditional network model of point-to-point reliable channels between every pair of parties, the problem was formulated in [88] in the two settings described in Sect. 5: the information-theoretic setting and the computational (also called *cryptographic*, or *authenticated*) setting. As mentioned above, in the former no assumptions are made about the adversary's computational power, while the latter relies on the hardness of computational problems (such as factoring large integers or computing discrete logs), and requires a trusted setup in the form of a PKI. Depending on the setting, some of the bounds on the

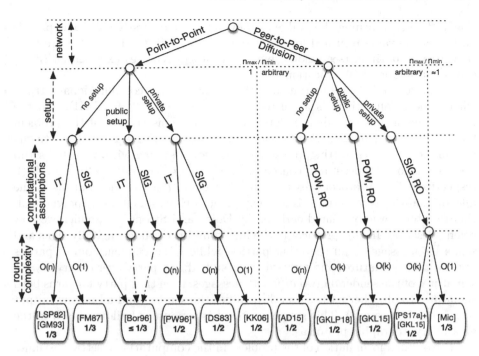

Fig. 1. The taxonomy of consensus protocols and impossibility results in the synchronous setting. The dotted arrows leading to [23] mean that even though those cases were not explicitly considered, a similar reasoning would lead to that impossibility result. $n_{\max}/n_{\min}$ refers to *participation tolerance* (cf. Sect. 7).

problems' quality measures differ. Refer to Fig. 1 (specifically, the left subtree) as we go through the classification below.

Number of Parties. For the information-theoretic setting, $n > 3t$ is both necessary and sufficient for the problem to have a solution. The necessary condition is presented in [88] for the broadcast problem (see [57] for the consensus version of the impossibility result), as the special case of 3 parties ("generals"), having to agree on two values ('attack', 'retreat'), with one of them being dishonest. As in the information-theoretic setting (with no additional setup) the parties are not able to forward messages in an authenticated manner, it is easily shown that an honest receiver cannot distinguish between a run where the sender is dishonest and sends conflicting messages, and a run where a receiver is dishonest and claims to have received the opposite message, which leads to the violation of the problem's conditions (Agreement and Validity, respectively). The general case (arbitrary values of n) reduces to the 3-party case. The (broadcast) protocol presented in [88] matches this bound ($n > 3t$), and essentially consists in recursively echoeing messages received in a round while excluding the messages' senders. (In the first round, only the sender sends messages.) This is done for $t + 1$ rounds, at which point the parties take majority of the values received for that instance, returning that value as they exit that recursive step. The party's output is the value returned for the first recursive call. $t + 1$ rounds were later shown to be optimal (see below), but the protocol requires exponential (in n) computation and communication.

Lamport et al. [88] also formulated the problem in the computational setting, where, specifically, there is a trusted private-state setup (of a PKI), and the parties have access to a digital signature scheme. This version of the problem has been referred to as *authenticated* Byzantine agreement. In contrast to the information-theoretic setting, in the computational setting with a trusted setup the bounds for broadcast and consensus differ: $n > t$ [88] and $n > 2t$ (e.g., [59]), respectively. The protocol presented in [88] runs in $t + 1$ rounds but, as in the information-theoretic setting, is also exponential-time; an efficient (polynomial-time) protocol was presented early on by Dolev and Strong [49], which we now briefly describe. In this protocol in the first round the sender digitally signs and sends his message to all the other parties, while in subsequent rounds parties append their signatures and forward the result. If any party ever observes valid signatures of the sender on two *different* messages, then that party forwards both signatures to all other parties and disqualifies the sender (and all parties output some default message). This simple protocol is a popular building block in the area of cryptographic protocols.

The original formulation of the problem in the computational setting assumes a PKI. In [23], Borcherding considered the situation where no PKI is available, which he refers to as "local authentication," meaning that no agreement on the parties' keys is provided, as each party distributes its verification key by itself. Borcherding shows that in this case, as in the information-theoretic setting above, broadcast and consensus are not possible if $n \leq 3t$, even though this setting is strictly stronger, as a dishonest party cannot forge messages sent by honest parties. The gist of the impossibility is that the adversary can always confuse honest parties about the correct protocol outcome and digital signatures cannot help if they are not pre-associated with the parties running the protocol in advance (something only ensured given a private setup).

Regarding the "strong" version of the problem (the decision value must be one of the honest parties' input values), Fitzi and Garay [60] showed that the problem has a solution if and only if $n > \max(3, |V|)t$ in the unconditional setting[3], where V is the domain of input/output values, and $n > |V|t$ in the computational setting with a trusted setup, giving resiliency-optimal and polynomial-time protocols that run in $t + 1$ rounds.

Running Time. Regarding the running time of consensus protocols, a lower bound of $t + 1$ rounds for deterministic protocols was established by Fischer and Lynch [56] for the case of benign ("crash") failures, and extended to the setting with malicious failures where messages are authenticated by Dolev and Strong [49]. As mentioned above, the original protocols by Lamport et al. already achieved this bound, but required exponential computation and communication.

---

[3] The lower bound was in fact shown by Neiger, who formulated this version of the problem [99].

In contrast to the computational setting, where a polynomial-time resiliency-and round-optimal protocol was found relatively soon [49], in the information-theoretic setting this took quite a bit longer, and was achieved by Garay and Moses [72]. In a nutshell, the [72] result builds on the "unraveled" version of the original protocol, presented and called *Exponential Information Gathering* by Bar-Noy *et al.* [11], applying a suite of "early-stopping" (see more on this below) and fault-detection techniques to prune the tree data structure to polynomial size. Regarding strong consensus, the $t + 1$-round lower bound also applies to this version of the problem, which the protocols by Fitzi and Garay [60] achieve (as well as being polynomial-time and resiliency-optimal).

In the $t + 1$-round lower bound for deterministic protocols, t is the maximum number of corruptions that can be tolerated in order to achieve consensus in a given model. Dolev, Reischuk and Strong [48] asked what would the running time be when the *actual* number of corruptions, say, f is smaller than t, and showed a lower bound of $\min\{t+1, f+2\}$ for any consensus protocol, even when only crash failures occur, which is important when f is very small. They called a consensus protocol satisfying this property *early-stopping*. Faster termination, however, comes at a price of non-simultaneous termination, as they also showed that if simultaneous termination is required, then $t + 1$ rounds are necessary. (See also [51].)

Optimal early stopping for the optimal number of parties (i.e., $n > 3t$) was achieved in the information-theoretic setting by Berman and Garay [21]; the protocol, however, is inefficient, as it requires exponential communication and computation. Relatively recently, an efficient (polynomial-time) optimal early-stopping consensus protocol was presented by Abraham and Dolev [2].

The above $t + 1$-round lower bound applies to deterministic protocols. A major breakthrough in fault-tolerant distributed algorithms was the introduction of randomization to the field by Ben-Or [15] and Rabin [110], which, effectively, showed how to circumvent the above limitation by using randomization. Rabin [110], in particular, showed that linearly resilient consensus protocols in expected *constant* rounds were possible, provided that all parties have access to a "common coin" (i.e., a common source of randomness). Essentially, the value of the coin can be adopted by the honest parties in case disagreement at any given round is detected, a process that is repeated multiple times. This line of research culminated with the work of Feldman and Micali [55], who showed how to obtain a shared random coin with constant probability from "scratch," yielding a probabilistic consensus protocol tolerating the maximum number of misbehaving parties ($t < n/3$) that runs in expected constant number of rounds.

The [55] protocol works in the information-theoretic setting; these results were later extended to the computational setting by Katz and Koo [82], who showed that assuming a PKI and digital signatures there exists an (expected-)constant-round consensus protocol tolerating $t < n/2$ corruptions. Recall that broadcast protocols in the computational setting with setup tolerate an arbitrary number (i.e., $n > t$) of dishonest parties; in contrast, the protocol in [82] assumes $n > 2t$ (as it is based on VSS—*verifiable secret sharing* [40]). In [63], Garay *et al.*

consider the case of a dishonest majority (i.e., $n \leq 2t$), presenting an expected-constant-round protocol for $t = \frac{n}{2} + O(1)$ dishonest parties (more generally, expected $O(k^2)$ running time when $t = \frac{n}{2} + k$), and showing the impossibility of expected-constant-round broadcast protocols when $n - t = o(n)$.

The speed-up on the running time of probabilistic consensus protocols comes at the cost of uncertainty, as a party that terminates can never be sure that other parties have also terminated—i.e., there cannot be *simultaneous* termination [48], which is an issue when these protocols are invoked from a higher-level protocol, as a party cannot be sure how long after he receives his output from a call to such a *probabilistic termination* (PT) consensus protocol (cf. [42]) he can safely carry out with the execution of the calling protocol. The sequential composition of PT consensus protocols was addressed by Lindell *et al.* [89] while the parallel composition of such protocols by Ben-Or and El-Yaniv [17]. (The issue in the case of parallel invocations of expected-constant-round PT protocols is that the overall running time of the parallel executions is not necessarily expected constant.) The above results on sequential and parallel composition, however, do not use simulation-based security, and it was therefore unclear how (or if) one would be able to use them to instantiate consensus (and/or broadcast) from a higher-level protocol. Such formal simulation-based (and therefore composable) definition and constructions of consensus protocols with probabilistic termination has been recently presented in [42].

Trusted Setup. We already covered this aspect above while describing the protocols achieving the different bounds on the number of parties; here we briefly summarize it. There is no trusted setup in the unconditional setting, although in the case of randomized protocols there is the additional requirement of the point-to-point channels being private in addition to reliable, while the "authenticated" consensus protocols assume a PKI. Related to a trusted setup assumption, we remark that if a *pre-computation* phase is allowed in the information-theoretic setting where reliable broadcast is guaranteed, then Pfitzmann and Waidner showed that broadcast and consensus are achievable with the same bounds on the number of parties as in the computational setting, using a tool known as a "pseudo-signatures" [109].

Communication Cost. A lower bound of $\Omega(n^2)$ on the number of messages (in fact, $\Omega(nt)$) was shown by Dolev and Reischuk for consensus for both information-theoretic and computational security [47]; for the latter, what they showed was that the number of signatures that are required by any protocol is $\Omega(nt)$, resulting in an $\Omega(nt|\sigma|)$ bit complexity (for a constant-size domain), where $|\sigma|$ represents the maximum signature size. The first information-theoretically secure protocols to match this bound were given by Berman *et al.* [20] and independently by Coan and Welch [41]; regarding computational security, the protocol presented by Dolev and Strong [49] requires that many messages. By relaxing the model and allowing for a small probability of error, King and Saia [85], presented a protocol that circumvents the impossibility result (with message complexity $\tilde{O}(n^{1.5})$).

The above bounds (except for [85]) reflect the fact that in typical protocols messages are communicated at least $\Omega(n^2)$ times, resulting in an overall communication complexity of at least $\Omega(\ell n^2)$ for ℓ-bit messages. In [61,80], Fitzi and Hirt and Hirt and Raykov show protocols for consensus and broadcast, respectively, where the long message is communicated $O(n)$ times, which is optimal as no protocol can achieve consensus or broadcast of an ℓ-bit message with communication complexity $o(\ell n)$. See also [62,106] for further improvements.

Beyond Synchrony. The case of partial synchrony, introduced in [50], considers the existence of an unknown bound Δ that determines the maximum delay of a message that is unknown to the protocol participants.[4] As shown in [50], the resiliency bounds presented in the point-to-point subtree of Fig. 1 remain unaltered in the no setup and public setup cases, but it degrades to $n/3$ in the private setup case.

In the eventual delivery setting, as mentioned above, deterministic consensus is impossible but it is still feasible to obtain protocols with probabilistic guarantees. Furthermore, note that in this setting it is not possible to account for all of the honest parties' inputs since parties cannot afford to wait for all the parties to engage (since corrupt parties may never transmit their messages and it is impossible to set a correct time-out). In more detail, without a setup in the information-theoretic setting, it is possible to adapt the protocol in [55] and achieve $n/4$ resilience [54] (see Fig. 1). By allowing the protocol not to terminate with negligible probability, Canetti and Rabin showed how to bring the resiliency to $n/3$ [33], which was later on improved to guarantee termination with probability 1 by Abraham et al. [3]. Efficiency improvements to the above two results (specifically, communication of the first one, and running time of the second one) were more recently presented in [9,107], respectively.

In the private-setup setting, assuming one-way functions, it is possible to obtain an always-terminating protocol with $n/3$ resiliency (cf. [54]). We note that it is infeasible to go beyond $n/3$ resiliency, as shown in [16,28], where this bound is argued for fail-stop failures, and thus the above results are optimal in this sense.

Most protocols mentioned above demonstrate the feasibility of the respective bounds. Much effort has also been dedicated to achieving practical Byzantine fault tolerance (BFT) in the eventual message delivery model. For completeness, here we mention some relevant results, with the work by Castro and Liskov [34] as a notable instance, where they focus on a fault-tolerant replicated transactions service in the cryptographic setting with the corresponding Safety and Liveness properties (see Sect. 8), achieving $n/3$ resiliency. Cachin et al. [27] study consensus in the same model, showing an efficient coin tossing protocol assuming a random oracle. Other related works focusing on practical efficiency include the work by Kursawe and Shoup on "asynchronous" atomic broadcast [87] (atomicity means that broadcast executions are ordered in such a way that two broadcast

---

[4] In [50] partial synchrony between the clocks of the processors is also considered as a separate relaxation to the model. In the present treatment we only focus on partial synchrony with respect to message passing.

requests are received in the same order by any two honest parties), following the "optimistic" approach presented in [34] where first only a "Bracha broadcast" protocol [24] is first attempted, reverting to the use of cryptography if things go wrong. Finally, Miller *et al.* [93] improve on the communication complexity of the protocol in [26], and guarantee Liveness without any timing assumptions, which was the case in [34].

Property-Based vs. Simulation-Based Proofs. As mentioned in Sect. 2.2, consensus and broadcast protocols have been typically proven secure/correct following a *property-based* approach. It turns out, as pointed out by Hirt and Zikas [81] (see also [64]), that in the case of *adaptive* adversaries who can choose which parties to corrupt dynamically, during the course of the protocol execution (cf. [31]), most existing broadcast and consensus protocols cannot be proven secure in a simulation-based manner. The reason, at a high level, is that when the adversary (having corrupted a party) receives a message from an honest party, can corrupt that party and make him change his message to other parties. This creates an inconsistency with the ideal process, where the party has already provided his input to the trusted party/ideal functionality that abstracts consensus. To be amenable to a simulation-based proof, instead of sending its initial message "in the clear," the sender in a broadcast protocol sends a *commitment* to the message, allowing the simulator in the ideal process to "equivocate" when the committed value becomes known in case the party has been corrupted and the initial value changed [64,81].

7   Consensus in the Peer-to-Peer Setting

Consensus in the peer-to-peer setting is the consensus problem when the available communication resource is peer-to-peer diffusion (cf. Sect. 3), a weaker communication primitive compared to point-to-point channels. (For this section, refer to the right subtree of Fig. 1.) This setting arose with the advent of the Bitcoin blockchain protocol, and was formally studied for the first time in [67]. In a nutshell, it constitutes an unauthenticated model of communication where no correlation of message sources across rounds can be established and the exact number of parties that participate may be unknown to the protocol participants. Moreover, since the adversary may inject messages in the network, an honest party cannot infer the number of participants from a message count.

We note that in a precursor model, where there is no correlation of message sources, but the point-to-point structure is still in place albeit without authentication, Okun showed that deterministic consensus algorithms are impossible for even a single failure [101,102], but that probabilistic consensus is still feasible by suitably adapting the protocols of [15,55][5]; the protocol, however, takes exponentially many rounds.

The consensus problem in the peer-to-peer setting has mostly been considered in the computational setting utilizing one-way functions and the proof-of-work

---

[5] Hence, consensus in this setting shares a similar profile with consensus in the asynchronous network model [58].

(PoW) primitive (Sect. 5). The first suggestion for a solution was informally described in [6], where it was suggested that PoWs can be used as an "identity assignment" tool, which subsequently can be used to bootstrap a standard consensus protocol like [49]. Nevertheless, the viability of this plan was never fully analyzed until an alternative approach to the problem was informally described by Nakamoto in an email exchange [96], where he argued that the "Byzantine Generals" problem can be solved by a blockchain/PoW approach tolerating a number of misbehaving parties strictly below $n/2$. As independently observed in [66,92], however, with overwhelming probability the Validity property is not satisfied by Nakamoto's informal suggestion.

The blockchain approach suggests to string PoWs together in a hash chain and achieve agreement using a rule that favors higher concentrations of computational effort as reflected in the resulting hash chains. The inputs to the consensus problem are "entangled" within the PoWs themselves and the final output results from a processing of the hash chain. The approach was first formalized in [67] where also two constructions were provided that satisfy all properties assuming a public setup.

Without access to a public setup, it is also possible to obtain a construction based on the results of [5], who were the first to formalize the [6] informal approach of using PoWs for identity assignment. Moreover, a blockchain-based approach is also possible as shown in [70]. Using a private setup, it becomes feasible to use primitives such as digital signatures and verifiable random functions (by storing the public key information as part of the public part of the setup, while the secret key information is the private part of the setup) and obtain even more efficient constructions such as the consensus sub-protocol of [38].

Number of Parties. One of the most important characteristics of consensus in the peer-to-peer setting is that the actual number of parties that are running the protocol is not assumed to be known in advance. Instead, the actual number of parties becomes a run-time execution parameter and the protocol is supposed to be able to tolerate a range of different of possible choices for the number of parties. We capture this by posing a range of possible operational values $[n_{min}, n_{max}]$, and posit that if the actual number of parties falls within the range then the properties will be guaranteed. We call the ratio n_{max}/n_{min} for a given protocol a protocol's *participation tolerance*. We note that this notion is somewhat related to models that have been considered in fault-tolerant distributed computing and secure multiparty computation (see, e.g., [73] and [79], respectively). In such scenarios the parties are subject to two types of faults, Byzantine and benign, such as "going to sleep," but adversarially scheduled. In the latter type, the parties will cease participating in the protocol execution.

In the convention introduced in [67], each party has a fixed quota of hashing queries that is allowed per round. As a result, the number of parties is directly proportional to the "computational power" that is present in the system and the total number of PoWs produced by the honest parties collectively would exceed that of the adversary assuming honest majority with very high probability. Given this it is tempting to imagine a direct translation of computational power to a set of identities [6]. The main problem is that the set of identities as perceived by the honest participants in the protocol execution might be inconsistent. This was resolved with the protocol of [5] where PoWs are used to build a "graded" PKI, where keys have ranks. The graded PKI is an instance of the *graded agreement* problem [55], or partial consistency problem [43], where honest parties do not disagree by much, according to some metric. Subsequently, it is possible to morph this graded consistency to global consistency by running multiple instances of [49]. This can be used to provide a consensus protocol with resiliency $n/2$ without a trusted setup.

It is unnecessary though for the parties to reach consensus by establishing identities. In the first consensus protocol presented in [67], the parties build a blockchain where each block contains a value that matches the input of the party that produced the block. The protocol continues for a certain number of rounds that ensures that the blockchain has grown to a certain length. In the final round, the parties remove a k-block suffix from their local blockchain, and output the majority bit from the remaining prefix. Based on the property called "common prefix" in [67], it is shown that with overwhelming probability in the security parameter, the parties terminate with the same output, while using the "chain quality" property, it is shown that if all the honest parties start with the same input, the corrupt parties cannot overturn the majority bit, which corresponds to the honest parties' input. The number of tolerated misbehaving parties in this protocol is strictly below $n/3$, a sub-optimal resiliency due to the low chain quality of the underlying blockhain protocol. The maximum resiliency that can be expected is $n/2$, something that can be shown by easily adapting the standard argument for the necessity of honest majority shown in Sect. 2.

Optimal resiliency can be reached by the second consensus protocol of [67] as follows: The protocol substitutes Bitcoin transactions with a type of transactions that are *themselves* based on PoWs, and hence uses PoWs in two distinct ways: for the maintenance of the ledger and for the generation of the transactions themselves. The protocol requires special care in the way it employs PoWs since the adversary should be incapable of "shifting" work between the two PoW tasks that it faces in each round. To solve this problem, a special strategy for PoW-based protocol composition is introduced in [67] called "2-for-1 PoWs." In the second solution presented in [67] the number of tolerated misbehaving parties is strictly below $n/2$.

We note that all these protocols come with a hard-coded difficulty level for PoWs which is assumed to be correlated with the number of parties n. If f is the probability that at least one honest party will produce a PoW in a round of protocol execution, it holds that f approaches 0 for small n while it approaches 1 for large n. It follows that the choice of PoW difficulty results in an operational range of values $[n_{min}, n_{max}]$ and it is possible to set the difficulty for any constant ratio n_{max}/n_{min}, so the participation tolerance of the protocol can be set to any arbitrary constant. We note that the lower bound n_{min} can be arbitrarily small as long as we are able to assume that even a single party has sufficient computational power to ensure that finding PoWs is not very rare. In case this is not true and $n < n_{\min}$, the protocol cannot be guaranteed to satisfy Validity with high probability, while on the other hand, if $n > n_{\max}$, the protocol cannot be guaranteed to achieve agreement with high probability.

Using digital signatures and verifiable random functions (VRFs) (or just digital signatures and a hash function modeled as a random oracle), it is possible to implement the second consensus protocol in [67] over an underlying blockchain protocol that uses a public-key infrastructure as opposed to PoWs, and allows for arbitrary participation tolerance such as [104] for optimal resiliency of $n/2$. The idea is as follows: one can use VRFs for each participant to enable a random subset of elected transaction issuers in each round. The ledger will then incorporate such transactions within a window of time following the same technique and counting argument as in the second consensus protocol of [67]. In Fig. 1 this is the protocol referred to in the second leaf from the right.

Running Time. In order to measure the running time that the protocols require in the peer-to-peer setting assuming PoW, one will have to also take into account that periods of silence, i.e., rounds without any message passing, may also be required for ensuring the required properties with high probability in κ, a security parameter. In the consensus protocol derived from the protocol of [5], $O(n)$ rounds are required where n is the number of parties. This can be improved to $O(\kappa)$ by, e.g., using a blockchain-based approach [70]. In the public-setup setting, assuming that the number of parties fall within the operational range, the protocols of [67] run also in time $O(\kappa)$.

It is worth noting the contrast to the approach used in randomized solutions to the problem in the standard setting (cf. Sect. 6), where achieving consensus is reduced to (the construction of) a shared random coin, and comparable guarantees are obtained after a poly-logarithmic number of rounds in the number of parties. The probabilistic aspect in the blockchain setting stems from the parties' likelihood of being able to provide proofs of work.

In the private setup setting it is possible to improve the running time to expected constant, e.g., by deploying the consensus sub-protocol of Algorand [38] for $1/3$ resiliency.

Trusted Setup. The relevant trusted setup assumption in the above protocols include a fresh random string, that can be incorporated as part of a "genesis block" in the blockchain protocol setting, or in general as part of the PoWs[6]. The objective of this public setup is to prevent a pre-computation attack by the adversary that will violate the relative superiority of honest parties which would be derived by the honest majority assumption. Note that protocols that require no trusted setup such as [5,70] take advantage of a special randomness exchange phase prior to PoW calculation that guarantees freshness without the need of a common random string.

It is worth to emphasize the fundamental advantage of the PoW setting compared to other computational assumptions that have been used for consensus.

---

[6] Alternatively, the protocols would consider as valid any chain that extends the empty chain, and where the adversary is not allowed any pre-computation.

Specifically, it is known that without a private setup, consensus is not possible with more than $n/3$ corruptions [23] even assuming digital signatures. The $n/3$ impossibility result does not apply here since, essentially, proofs of work can make it infeasible for the adversary to present diverging protocol transcripts without investing effort for distinct PoW calculations.

Another observation is that assuming a private setup in the peer-to-peer setting, one can simulate point-to-point connectivity, and thus run any consensus protocol from the previous section; nevertheless, this reduction is not efficient and in the peer-to-peer setting with private-setup one can still obtain protocols that are more efficient (e.g., with subquadratic communication complexity).

Communication Cost. The total number of transmitted messages in the consensus protocols described above is, in expectation, $O(n^2\kappa)$ for the case of [5,70] counting each invocation of the diffuse channel as costing $O(n)$ messages. For the two protocols of [67] the number of messages is $O(n\kappa)$ in the public setup setting. In the private setup setting it can be possible to reduce this further using techniques from [38].

We recall that an important difference with randomized consensus protocols in the standard setting is that parties send messages in every round, while in the PoW setting (honest) parties only communicate whenever they are able to produce a proof of work; otherwise, they remain silent. This also suggests that there may be honest parties that never diffuse a message[7] and thus it is feasible to drop communication costs to below n^2 (with a probabilistic guarantee; cf. Sect. 6).

Beyond Synchrony. The consensus protocols of [67] in Fig. 1 can be analyzed in the partial synchronous setting as well (refer to the full version of [66] as a starting point). Recall that the way the protocols operate in this setting is that a parameterisation of difficulty is hardcoded that provides a reasonable PoW production rate over message passing time. The security of the protocols will then be at the theoretical maximum in terms of resiliency as long as the original estimate is close to being safe (network delay is low) and will degrade if the estimate is worse, dissipating entirely when the delay gets larger (for the full argument, see [103], where it is shown how the blockchain protocol's consistency collapses when delay is arbitrarily large).

Property-Based vs. Simulation-Based Proofs. To our knowledge, there is no simulation-based treatment of consensus in the peer-to-peer setting, however it is easy to infer a functionality abstracting the problem. The only essential difference is that the actual number of parties involved in the execution are to be decided on the fly and will be unknown to the protocol participants.

---

[7] Note the similarity with standard consensus in the eventual-delivery setting (Sect. 6), where not all honest parties' inputs may be accounted for.

8   Ledger Consensus

Ledger consensus (aka "Nakamoto consensus") is the problem where a set of servers (or nodes) operate continuously accepting inputs ("transactions") that belong to a set $\mathbb{T}$ and incorporate them in a public data structure called the *ledger*. We assume that the language of all valid ledgers $\mathbb{L}$ has an efficient membership test and moreover for all tx there is an $\mathcal{L} \in \mathbb{L}$ such that tx $\in \mathcal{L}$. We call a language $\mathbb{L}$ *trivial* if it holds that for all $tx_1, tx_2 \in \mathbb{T}$ there exists $\mathcal{L} \in \mathbb{L}$ that contains both tx_1, tx_2. The purpose of ledger consensus is to provide a unique view of the ledger to anyone asking to see it. The ledger view of a party P is denoted by $\widetilde{\mathcal{L}_P}$ while the "settled" portion of the ledger in the view of P is denoted by $\mathcal{L}_P$. Note that it always holds $\mathcal{L}_P \preceq \widetilde{\mathcal{L}_P}$, where $\preceq$ denotes the standard prefix operation. The properties that a ledger consensus protocol must satisfy are as follows:

- *Consistency* (or *Persistence*): This property mandates that if a client queries an honest node's ledger at round r_1 and receives the response $\widetilde{\mathcal{L}_1}$, then a client querying an honest node's ledger at round $r_2 \geq r_1$ will receive a response $\widetilde{\mathcal{L}_2}$ that satisfies $\mathcal{L}_1 \preceq \widetilde{\mathcal{L}_2}$.
- *Liveness:* If a transaction tx is given as input to all honest nodes at a round r and it holds that tx is valid w.r.t. $\widetilde{\mathcal{L}_P}$ for every honest party P, then at round $r + u$ it holds that $\mathcal{L}_P$ includes tx for any honest party P.

In classical distributed systems literature, such problem is often referred to as *state machine replication* [111]. Consistency ensures that parties have the same view of the log of transactions, while Liveness ensures the quick incorporation of transactions. Furthermore, a third property, called "order" in [111], is introduced which, in our notation, can be expressed as follows.

- *Serializability:* For transactions tx, tx′, if tx is given as input to all honest nodes at a round r and it holds that tx is valid w.r.t. $\widetilde{\mathcal{L}_P}$ and tx′ $\notin \widetilde{\mathcal{L}_P}$ for every honest party P, then it holds that for any $r' > r$, the ledger $\mathcal{L}_P$ of any honest party cannot include tx′, tx in this order.

Given a consensus protocol it is tempting to apply it in sequential composition in order to solve ledger consensus. The reduction indeed holds but some special care is needed. First, let us consider the case where no setup is available. The construction in the synchronous network model is as follows. First, suppose that we have at our disposal a consensus protocol that satisfies Agreement, (Strong) Validity, and Termination after u rounds. The protocol has all nodes collect transactions and then run the consensus protocol with the set of transactions as their input. When the protocol terminates after u rounds, the nodes assign an index to the output (call it the i-th entry to the ledger) and move on to the next consensus instance. It is easy to see that Consistency is satisfied because of Agreement, while Liveness is satisfied with parameter u because of Strong Validity and Termination. It is worth noting that "plain" Validity by itself is not enough, since a ledger protocol is supposed to run for any given set of transactions and as a result it is possible that no two honest nodes would ever agree on a set of inputs. In this case, Validity might just provide that honest parties' agree on an adversarial value, which might be the empty string. As a result the ledger would be empty and Liveness would be violated. However it is possible to deal with this problem without resorting to the full power of Strong Validity. For instance, it is sufficient to consider a variant of consensus where each party has an input set X_i and the joint output set S satisfies that $X_i \subseteq S$. We note that such a "union" consensus protocol can be implied by Interactive Consistency, as defined in [108], and it has also recently been considered explicitly as a consensus variant [46]. Other intermediate notions of Validity such as a *predicate-based* notion [26] can be useful here as well.

Let us now comment how the reduction can be performed under different setup and network assumptions. First, if a setup assumption is used, observe that the above reduction will require the availability of the setup every u rounds. Given this might be impractical, one may consider how to emulate the sequence of setups using a single initial setup. This approach is non-black-box on the underlying protocol and may not be straightforward. For instance, when sequentially composing a PoW-based consensus protocol that relies on a public setup, the security of the protocol may non-trivially rely on the unpredictability of the i-th setup. Techniques related to sequential composition of a basic building block protocol have appeared in a number of ledger protocols, including [19,38,84]. Regarding network aspects, we observe that the reduction can proceed in essentially the same way in the peer-to-peer setting as in the point-to-point setting. Finally, note that when simultaneous termination is not available in the underlying consensus protocol, special care is needed in applying composition (cf. [42]).

Ledger consensus was brought forth as an objective of the Bitcoin blockchain protocol. For this reason, in the remaining of the paper, we only consider the problem in the peer-to-peer setting, although we note that in the point-to-point setting it is possible to adapt standard BFT methods to solve the problem. We refer to, e.g., [75,93] for some recent examples. We remark also that combining private setup and the peer-to-peer setting, it is straightforward to simulate the point-to-point setting by relying on the authentication information that can be made available by the setup. A pictorial overview of our protocol classification is presented in Fig. 2.

Number of Parties. We start with an adaptation of the impossibility result for dishonest majority as shown in [59]. The result shows that in all the relevant cases for practice, specifically, ledger consensus with non-trivial ledgers, or providing serializability as defined above, honest majority is a necessary requirement.

Theorem 1. *Suppose that the transaction set $\mathbb{T}$ satisfies $|\mathbb{T}| \geq 2$. Ledger consensus is impossible in case the adversary controls $n/2$ nodes, assuming either (i) the language $\mathbb{L}$ is non-trivial or (ii) Serializability holds.*

Proof. For simplicity we describe the impossibility result in a setting where the properties are perfectly satisfied. The same argument can be easily extended to the setting where the properties are satisfied with overwhelming probability.

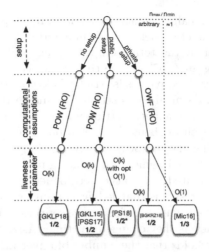

Fig. 2. The taxonomy of ledger consensus protocols (peer-to-peer setting).

Suppose all parties are split in two sets A_1, A_2 of size exactly $n/2$. We describe an environment and an adversary. The environment prepares two transactions $tx_1, tx_2 \in \mathbb{T}$ that are in conflict, i.e., it holds that no valid $\mathcal{L}$ exists for which it holds that both $tx, tx' \in \mathcal{L}$ but they can be both validly added to some ledger since they are members of $\mathbb{T}$. The environment provides at round 1 the appropriate sequence of transactions so that parties in A_b receive transaction tx_b respectively and advances the execution for at least u rounds, the Liveness parameter. We consider three adversaries $\mathcal{A}_0, \mathcal{A}_1, \mathcal{A}_2$. The $\mathcal{A}_0$ adversary corrupts no party and allows the execution to advance normally. On the other hand, the adversary $\mathcal{A}_b$ with $b \in \{1, 2\}$ corrupts the set of parties A_b and simulates honest operation. Consider a party $P_1 \in A_1$ and a party $P_2 \in A_2$. In case $b \in \{1, 2\}$, by Liveness, at the end of the execution it should be the case that $tx_b \in \mathcal{L}_b$. In case $b = 0$, by Consistency, it should be that $\mathcal{L}_1 \preceq \widetilde{\mathcal{L}_2}$. Given that in the three cases the executions are perfectly indistinguishable, this means that $tx_1 \in \widetilde{\mathcal{L}_2}$ which is a contradiction since $tx_2 \in \mathcal{L}_2 \preceq \widetilde{\mathcal{L}_2}$.

The argument for the case of Serializability is similar to the above. In this case, we just assume that transactions $tx_1, tx_2 \in \mathbb{T}$ are just distinct (they do not have to be in conflict). Observe that by Liveness in the experiments above we will have that $tx_b \in \mathcal{L}_b$ for party P_b. Moreover, due to Serializability, for P_b it must be the case that transactions cannot be in the order tx_{3-b}, tx_b. This leads to a contradiction due to Consistency. $\qquad\square$

As in the case of peer-to-peer consensus (Sect. 7), the actual number of parties n is not known in advance and may be assumed to fall within a range of operational parameters $n \in [n_{\min}, n_{\max}]$. This is also related to the concept of "sporadic participation" that was considered in [104], where certain honest parties may "go to sleep" for arbitrary amounts of time.

In the PoW setting, recall that each party has a fixed quota of queries that it can perform to a hash function per unit of time and thus the number of parties is directly proportional to the total computational or hashing power that is available. In this setting, first [67] showed that ledger consensus can be achieved when the number of corrupted parties is strictly below $n/2$. This bound was also preserved in the partially synchronous setting, as shown by Pass *et al.* [103].

The above results refer to a static setting where there are no large deviations in the number of parties throughout the execution. The setting where the population of parties running the protocol can dynamically (and quite drastically) change over time with the environment introducing new parties and deactivating parties that have participated was considered for ledger consensus for the first time in [68]. Their main result is that ledger consensus can be achieved in the PoW setting, assuming an honest majority appropriately restated by considering the number of parties as they change over time: Assuming n_i are the active parties at time unit i, it holds that the number of adversarial parties is bounded away from $n_i/2$.

Assuming a private setup and a setting where the adversary gets t Byzantine corruptions and s asleep parties, in [104] it is shown that ledger consensus can be achieved as long as t is strictly bounded by $a/2$ where $a = n - s$ is the number of "alert" parties, i.e., the number of asleep parties may be larger than $n/2$ and hence an arbitrary participation ratio can also be achieved in this setting without resorting to PoWs. With respect to lower bounds, in the case of sleep corruptions the bound can be generalized to $a/2$; see [104]. A dynamic setting of parties was also considered in [19,45,84], providing a similar type of results assuming a PKI with honest "stake" majority. An important deficiency shared by these works is that new parties have to be chaperoned into the system by receiving advice consistent with the views of the honest parties. This was highlighted as the "bootstrapping from genesis" problem in [7] which resolved it via a suitable chain selection rule; in the same work, a more refined model of dynamic participation was put forth, called *dynamic availability*. This model allows finer control from the environment's perspective in terms of disconnecting parties, or having parties lose access to resources such as the clock or the hash function.

Finally, in terms of participation tolerance, we observe that an arbitrary n_{max}/n_{min} can be achieved by protocols such as [7,104] while Algorand [38,91] requires n_{max}/n_{min} to be (approximately) 1 since the expected participation is a hardcoded value in the protocol (it is worth noting that despite this limitation, Algorand still qualifies as a peer-to-peer protocol, since the identities of the parties engaging in the protocol need not be known in advance).

Transaction Processing Time. Contrary to a consensus protocol, a ledger consensus protocol is a protocol that is supposed to be running over an arbitrary, potentially long, period of time. Thus, the relevant measure in this context is the amount of time that it takes for the system to insert a transaction in the log that is maintained by the participants. This relates to the parameter u introduced as part of the Liveness property, which determines the number of rounds needed in the execution model for a transaction to be included in the log. Observe that

Liveness is only provided for transactions that are produced by honest participants or are otherwise unambiguously provided to the honest parties running the protocol.

In this setting we observe that [67] achieves ledger consensus with processing time $O(\kappa)$ rounds of interaction, where κ is the security parameter. This result is replicated in the partially synchronous setting, where processing time takes $O(\kappa\Delta)$ rounds, and where Δ is the maximum delay that is imposed on message transmission. The above results assume the adversarial bounds consistent with honest majority which are tight (cf. [105]). Considering a weaker adversarial setting it is possible to improve Liveness; for instance, Algorand [38] achieves expected-constant number of rounds while, Thunderella [105], shows that the processing time can be dropped to $O(1)$ rounds worst-case, assuming an honest super-majority (i.e., adversarially controlled number of parties strictly below $n/4$) and the existence a specific party called the *accelerator* to be honest.

Trusted Setup. Ledger consensus can be achieved in the public- or private-state setup setting. Protocols falling in the former category are [67, 68, 103], whereas protocols consistent with the latter are [19, 38, 74, 84, 104]. In the absence of a trusted setup, it has been shown that it is possible to "bootstrap" a ledger consensus protocol from "scratch," either directly [70] or via setting up a public-key directory using proofs of work [5]. An important further consideration between public and private setup is that in the peer-to-peer setting, the former represents what typically is consistent with the so-called persmissionless setting, while the latter is consistent with the permissioned setting. This follows from the fact that anyone that has access to the peer-to-peer channel is free to participate in the protocol, if no setup or a public setup is assumed. On the other hand, in the private setup setting, a higher level of permissioning is implied: The parties that are eligible to run the protocol need to get authorized either by the setup functionaliy so that they receive the private information that is related to the protocol execution, or, alternatively, interact with the parties that are already part of the protocol execution so they can be inducted. Note that the point-to-point setting is—by definition—permissioned via access to the RMT functionality.

Communication Cost. Given that ledger consensus is an ongoing protocol that processes incoming transactions, defining communication costs requires some care. To our knowledge, no formal definitions of communication costs for ledger consensus have been proposed. A first approach to the problem is to consider a type of "communication overhead" on top of the transactions that are transmitted in the system. It follows that the minimum communication necessary for each bit of transaction transmitted is the diffusion of this bit. Given the above, the communication costs of ledger consensus protocols based on blockchain protocols can be seen to be constant in the sense that parties transmit, up to constant factors, more data.

Beyond Synchrony. Initial work in ledger consensus protocols in the public setup [67, 68] and the no setup setting [69, 70] assumed a rushing adversary and synchronous operation. This can be extended to the partial synchrony setting as shown in [103] as well as in the full version of [66] with the same limitations explained in Sect. 7.

Property-Based vs. Simulation-Based Proofs. The first simulation-based definition of ledger consensus was presented by Badertscher et al. [8]. A refinement of this definition was presented in [7], where it was also shown how to adapt it in a setting where a private setup is available. In terms of composability, an (expected) disadvantage for PoW-based protocols highlighted in the work of [8] is that access to the random oracle should be specific to the current ledger protocol session.

References

1. Proceedings of the 48th Annual IEEE Symposium on Foundations of Computer Science (FOCS 2007), Providence, RI, USA, 20–23 October 2007. IEEE Computer Society (2007)
2. Abraham, I., Dolev, D.: Byzantine agreement with optimal early stopping, optimal resilience and polynomial complexity. In: Servedio, R.A., Rubinfeld, R. (eds.) Proceedings of the Forty-Seventh Annual ACM on Symposium on Theory of Computing, STOC 2015, Portland, OR, USA, 14–17 June 2015, pp. 605–614. ACM (2015)
3. Abraham, I., Dolev, D., Halpern, J.Y.: An almost-surely terminating polynomial protocol for asynchronous byzantine agreement with optimal resilience. In: Bazzi, R.A., Patt-Shamir, B. (eds.) Proceedings of the Twenty-Seventh Annual ACM Symposium on Principles of Distributed Computing, PODC 2008, Toronto, Canada, 18–21 August 2008, pp. 405–414. ACM (2008)
4. Alchieri, E.A.P., Bessani, A.N., da Silva Fraga, J., Greve, F.: Byzantine consensus with unknown participants. In: Baker, T.P., Bui, A., Tixeuil, S. (eds.) OPODIS 2008. LNCS, vol. 5401, pp. 22–40. Springer, Heidelberg (2008). https://doi.org/10.1007/978-3-540-92221-6_4
5. Andrychowicz, M., Dziembowski, S.: PoW-based distributed cryptography with no trusted setup. In: Gennaro, R., Robshaw, M. (eds.) CRYPTO 2015, Part II. LNCS, vol. 9216, pp. 379–399. Springer, Heidelberg (2015). https://doi.org/10.1007/978-3-662-48000-7_19
6. Aspnes, J., Jackson, C., Krishnamurthy, A.: Exposing computationally-challenged Byzantine impostors. Technical report YALEU/DCS/TR-1332, Yale University Department of Computer Science, July 2005
7. Badertscher, C., Gazi, P., Kiayias, A., Russell, A., Zikas, V.: Ouroboros genesis: composable proof-of-stake blockchains with dynamic availability. In: Lie, D., Mannan, M., Backes, M., Wang, X. (eds.) Proceedings of the 2018 ACM SIGSAC Conference on Computer and Communications Security, CCS 2018, Toronto, ON, Canada, 15–19 October 2018, pp. 913–930. ACM (2018)
8. Badertscher, C., Maurer, U., Tschudi, D., Zikas, V.: Bitcoin as a transaction ledger: a composable treatment. In: Katz and Shacham [83], pp. 324–356
9. Bangalore, L., Choudhury, A., Patra, A.: Almost-surely terminating asynchronous byzantine agreement revisited. In: Newport, C., Keidar, I. (eds.) Proceedings of the 2018 ACM Symposium on Principles of Distributed Computing, PODC 2018, Egham, United Kingdom, 23–27 July 2018, pp. 295–304. ACM (2018)

10. Bano, S., et al.: Consensus in the age of blockchains. CoRR, abs/1711.03936 (2017)
11. Bar-Noy, A., Dolev, D., Dwork, C., Strong, H.R.: Shifting gears: changing algorithms on the fly to expedite byzantine agreement. Inf. Comput. **97**(2), 205–233 (1992)
12. Beaver, D.: Correlated pseudorandomness and the complexity of private computations. In: Miller [94], pp. 479–488
13. Beimel, A., Franklin, M.K.: Reliable communication over partially authenticated networks. Theor. Comput. Sci. **220**(1), 185–210 (1999)
14. Bellare, M., Rogaway, P.: Random oracles are practical: a paradigm for designing efficient protocols. In: CCS 1993, Proceedings of the 1st ACM Conference on Computer and Communications Security, Fairfax, Virginia, USA, 3–5 November 1993, pp. 62–73 (1993)
15. Ben-Or, M.: Another advantage of free choice: completely asynchronous agreement protocols (extended abstract). In: Probert, R.L., Lynch, N.A., Santoro, N. (eds.) PODC, pp. 27–30. ACM (1983)
16. Ben-Or, M., Canetti, R., Goldreich, O.: Asynchronous secure computation. In Kosaraju et al. [86], pp. 52–61
17. Ben-Or, M., El-Yaniv, R.: Resilient-optimal interactive consistency in constant time. Distrib. Comput. **16**(4), 249–262 (2003)
18. Ben-Or, M., Goldwasser, S., Wigderson, A.: Completeness theorems for non-cryptographic fault-tolerant distributed computation (extended abstract), pp. 1–10 (1988)
19. Bentov, I., Pass, R., Shi, E.: Snow white: provably secure proofs of stake. IACR Cryptology ePrint Archive, 2016:919 (2016)
20. Berman, P., Garay, J.A., Perry, K.J.: Bit optimal distributed consensus. In: Baeza-Yates, R., Manber, U. (eds.) Computer Science, pp. 313–321. Springer, Boston (1992). https://doi.org/10.1007/978-1-4615-3422-8_27
21. Berman, P., Garay, J.A., Perry, K.J.: Optimal early stopping in distributed consensus. In: Segall, A., Zaks, S. (eds.) WDAG 1992. LNCS, vol. 647, pp. 221–237. Springer, Heidelberg (1992). https://doi.org/10.1007/3-540-56188-9_15
22. Bitansky, N., Goldwasser, S., Jain, A., Paneth, O., Vaikuntanathan, V., Waters, B.: Time-lock puzzles from randomized encodings. In: Sudan, M. (ed.) Proceedings of the 2016 ACM Conference on Innovations in Theoretical Computer Science, Cambridge, MA, USA, 14–16 January 2016, pp. 345–356. ACM (2016)
23. Borcherding, M.: Levels of authentication in distributed agreement. In: Babaoğlu, Ö., Marzullo, K. (eds.) WDAG 1996. LNCS, vol. 1151, pp. 40–55. Springer, Heidelberg (1996). https://doi.org/10.1007/3-540-61769-8_4
24. Bracha, G.: An asynchronou [(n-1)/3]-resilient consensus protocol. In: Kameda, T., Misra, J., Peters, J.G., Santoro, N. (eds.) Proceedings of the Third Annual ACM Symposium on Principles of Distributed Computing, Vancouver, B. C., Canada, 27–29 August 1984, pp. 154–162. ACM (1984)
25. Cachin, C., Guerraoui, R., Rodrigues, L.: Introduction to Reliable and Secure Distributed Programming, 2nd edn. Springer, Heidelberg (2011). https://doi.org/10.1007/978-3-642-15260-3
26. Cachin, C., Kursawe, K., Petzold, F., Shoup, V.: Secure and efficient asynchronous broadcast protocols. In: Kilian, J. (ed.) CRYPTO 2001. LNCS, vol. 2139, pp. 524–541. Springer, Heidelberg (2001). https://doi.org/10.1007/3-540-44647-8_31
27. Cachin, C., Kursawe, K., Shoup, V.: Random oracles in constantinople: practical asynchronous byzantine agreement using cryptography. J. Cryptol. **18**(3), 219–246 (2005)

28. Canetti, R.: Studies in secure multiparty computation and applications. Ph.D. thesis, Weizmann Institute of Science (1996)
29. Canetti, R.: Security and composition of multiparty cryptographic protocols. J. Cryptol. **13**(1), 143–202 (2000)
30. Canetti, R.: Universally composable security: a new paradigm for cryptographic protocols. In: 42nd Annual Symposium on Foundations of Computer Science, FOCS 2001, Las Vegas, Nevada, USA, 14–17 October 2001, pp. 136–145. IEEE Computer Society (2001)
31. Canetti, R., Feige, U., Goldreich, O., Naor, M.: Adaptively secure multi-party computation. In: Miller [94], pp. 639–648
32. Canetti, R., Pass, R., Shelat, A.: Cryptography from sunspots: how to use an imperfect reference string. In: 48th Annual IEEE Symposium on Foundations of Computer Science (FOCS 2007), Providence, RI, USA, 20–23 October 2007, Proceedings [1], pp. 249–259
33. Canetti, R., Rabin, T.: Fast asynchronous byzantine agreement with optimal resilience. In: Kosaraju et al. [86], pp. 42–51
34. Castro, M., Liskov, B.: Practical byzantine fault tolerance and proactive recovery. ACM Trans. Comput. Syst. **20**(4), 398–461 (2002)
35. Chaum, D.: Untraceable electronic mail, return addresses, and digital pseudonyms. Commun. ACM **24**(2), 84–88 (1981)
36. Chaum, D., Crépeau, C., Damgård, I.: Multiparty unconditionally secure protocols (abstract) (informal contribution), p. 462 (1987)
37. Chaum, D., Crépeau, C., Damgård, I.: Multiparty unconditionally secure protocols (extended abstract). In: Simon, J. (ed.) Proceedings of the 20th Annual ACM Symposium on Theory of Computing, Chicago, Illinois, USA, 2–4 May 1988, pp. 11–19. ACM (1988)
38. Chen, J., Micali, S.: Algorand: a secure and efficient distributed ledger. Theor. Comput. Sci. **777**, 155–183 (2019)
39. Chor, B., Dwork, C.: Randomization in byzantine agreement. Adv. Comput. Res. **5**, 443–497 (1989)
40. Chor, B., Goldwasser, S., Micali, S., Awerbuch, B.: Verifiable secret sharing and achieving simultaneity in the presence of faults (extended abstract). In: 26th Annual Symposium on Foundations of Computer Science, Portland, Oregon, USA, 21–23 October 1985, pp. 383–395. IEEE Computer Society (1985)
41. Coan, B.A., Welch, J.L.: Modular construction of nearly optimal byzantine agreement protocols. In: Rudnicki, P. (ed.) Proceedings of the Eighth Annual ACM Symposium on Principles of Distributed Computing, Edmonton, Alberta, Canada, 14–16 August 1989, pp. 295–305. ACM (1989)
42. Cohen, R., Coretti, S., Garay, J., Zikas, V.: Probabilistic termination and composability of cryptographic protocols. In: Robshaw, M., Katz, J. (eds.) CRYPTO 2016, Part III. LNCS, vol. 9816, pp. 240–269. Springer, Heidelberg (2016). https://doi.org/10.1007/978-3-662-53015-3_9
43. Considine, J., Fitzi, M., Franklin, M., Levin, L.A., Maurer, U., Metcalf, D.: Byzantine agreement given partial broadcast. J. Cryptol. **18**(3), 191–217 (2005)
44. Coretti, S., Garay, J., Hirt, M., Zikas, V.: Constant-round asynchronous multiparty computation based on one-way functions. In: Cheon, J.H., Takagi, T. (eds.) ASIACRYPT 2016, Part II. LNCS, vol. 10032, pp. 998–1021. Springer, Heidelberg (2016). https://doi.org/10.1007/978-3-662-53890-6_33
45. David, B., Gazi, P., Kiayias, A., Russell, A.: Ouroboros praos: an adaptively-secure, semi-synchronous proof-of-stake blockchain. In: Nielsen and Rijmen [100], pp. 66–98

46. Dold, F., Grothoff, C.: Byzantine set-union consensus using efficient set reconciliation. EURASIP J. Inf. Secur. **2017**(1), 14 (2017)
47. Dolev, D., Reischuk, R.: Bounds on information exchange for byzantine agreement. J. ACM **32**(1), 191–204 (1985)
48. Dolev, D., Reischuk, R., Strong, H.R.: Early stopping in byzantine agreement. J. ACM **37**(4), 720–741 (1990)
49. Dolev, D., Strong, H.R.: Authenticated algorithms for Byzantine agreement. SIAM J. Comput. **12**(4), 656–666 (1983)
50. Dwork, C., Lynch, N.A., Stockmeyer, L.J.: Consensus in the presence of partial synchrony. J. ACM **35**(2), 288–323 (1988)
51. Dwork, C., Moses, Y.: Knowledge and common knowledge in a byzantine environment: crash failures. Inf. Comput. **88**(2), 156–186 (1990)
52. Dwork, C., Naor, M.: Pricing via processing or combatting junk mail. In: Brickell, E.F. (ed.) CRYPTO 1992. LNCS, vol. 740, pp. 139–147. Springer, Heidelberg (1993). https://doi.org/10.1007/3-540-48071-4_10
53. Dwork, C., Peleg, D., Pippenger, N., Upfal, E.: Fault tolerance in networks of bounded degree. SIAM J. Comput. **17**(5), 975–988 (1988)
54. Feldman, P.: Optimal algorithms for Byzantine agreement. Ph.D. thesis, Massachusetts Institute of Technology (1988)
55. Feldman, P., Micali, S.: An optimal probabilistic protocol for synchronous Byzantine agreement. SIAM J. Comput. **26**(4), 873–933 (1997)
56. Fischer, M.J., Lynch, N.A.: A lower bound for the time to assure interactive consistency. Inf. Process. Lett. **14**(4), 183–186 (1982)
57. Fischer, M.J., Lynch, N.A., Merritt, M.: Easy impossibility proofs for distributed consensus problems. Distrib. Comput. **1**(1), 26–39 (1986)
58. Fischer, M.J., Lynch, N.A., Paterson, M.: Impossibility of distributed consensus with one faulty process. J. ACM **32**(2), 374–382 (1985)
59. Fitzi, M.: Generalized communication and security models in Byzantine agreement. Ph.D. thesis, ETH Zurich, Zürich, Switzerland (2003)
60. Fitzi, M., Garay, J.A.: Efficient player-optimal protocols for strong and differential consensus. In: PODC, pp. 211–220 (2003)
61. Fitzi, M., Hirt, M.: Optimally efficient multi-valued byzantine agreement. In: Ruppert, E., Malkhi, D. (eds.) Proceedings of the Twenty-Fifth Annual ACM Symposium on Principles of Distributed Computing, PODC 2006, Denver, CO, USA, 23–26 July 2006, pp. 163–168. ACM (2006)
62. Ganesh, C., Patra, A.: Broadcast extensions with optimal communication and round complexity. In: Giakkoupis, G. (ed.) Proceedings of the 2016 ACM Symposium on Principles of Distributed Computing, PODC 2016, Chicago, IL, USA, 25–28 July 2016, pp. 371–380. ACM (2016)
63. Garay, J.A., Katz, J., Koo, C., Ostrovsky, R.: Round complexity of authenticated broadcast with a dishonest majority. In: 48th Annual IEEE Symposium on Foundations of Computer Science (FOCS 2007), Providence, RI, USA, 20–23 October 2007, Proceedings [1], pp. 658–668
64. Garay, J.A., Katz, J., Kumaresan, R., Zhou, H.: Adaptively secure broadcast, revisited. In: Gavoille, C., Fraigniaud, P. (eds.) Proceedings of the 30th Annual ACM Symposium on Principles of Distributed Computing, PODC 2011, San Jose, CA, USA, 6–8 June 2011, pp. 179–186. ACM (2011)
65. Garay, J.A., Kiayias, A.: SoK: a consensus taxonomy in the blockchain era. IACR Cryptology ePrint Archive, 2018:754 (2018)
66. Garay, J.A., Kiayias, A., Leonardos, N.: The Bitcoin Backbone Protocol: Analysis and Applications. IACR Cryptology ePrint Archive, 2014:765 (2014)

67. Garay, J.A., Kiayias, A., Leonardos, N.: The bitcoin backbone protocol: analysis and applications. In: Oswald, E., Fischlin, M. (eds.) EUROCRYPT 2015, Part II. LNCS, vol. 9057, pp. 281–310. Springer, Heidelberg (2015). https://doi.org/10.1007/978-3-662-46803-6_10

68. Garay, J.A., Kiayias, A., Leonardos, N.: The bitcoin backbone protocol with chains of variable difficulty. In: Katz and Shacham [83], pp. 291–323

69. Garay, J.A., Kiayias, A., Leonardos, N., Panagiotakos, G.: Bootstrapping the blockchain - directly. IACR Cryptology ePrint Archive, 2016:991 (2016)

70. Garay, J.A., Kiayias, A., Leonardos, N., Panagiotakos, G.: Bootstrapping the blockchain, with applications to consensus and fast PKI setup. In: Abdalla, M., Dahab, R. (eds.) PKC 2018, Part II. LNCS, vol. 10770, pp. 465–495. Springer, Cham (2018). https://doi.org/10.1007/978-3-319-76581-5_16

71. Garay, J.A., Kiayias, A., Panagiotakos, G.: Proofs of work for blockchain protocols. IACR Cryptology ePrint Archive, 2017:775 (2017)

72. Garay, J.A., Moses, Y.: Fully polynomial byzantine agreement for n ¿ 3t processors in t + 1 rounds. SIAM J. Comput. $27(1)$, 247–290 (1998)

73. Garay, J.A., Perry, K.J.: A continuum of failure models for distributed computing. In: Segall, A., Zaks, S. (eds.) WDAG 1992. LNCS, vol. 647, pp. 153–165. Springer, Heidelberg (1992). https://doi.org/10.1007/3-540-56188-9_11

74. Gilad, Y., Hemo, R., Micali, S., Vlachos, G., Zeldovich, N.: Algorand: scaling byzantine agreements for cryptocurrencies. In: Proceedings of the 26th Symposium on Operating Systems Principles, Shanghai, China, 28–31 October 2017, pp. 51–68. ACM (2017)

75. Golan-Gueta, G., et al.: SBFT: a scalable decentralized trust infrastructure for blockchains. CoRR, abs/1804.01626 (2018)

76. Goldreich, O.: The Foundations of Cryptography - Volume 1, Basic Techniques. Cambridge University Press, Cambridge (2001)

77. Goldreich, O., Micali, S., Wigderson, A.: Proofs that yield nothing but their validity and a methodology of cryptographic protocol design (extended abstract), pp. 174–187 (1986)

78. Goldreich, O., Micali, S., Wigderson, A.: How to play any mental game or A completeness theorem for protocols with honest majority. In: Aho, A.V. (ed.) Proceedings of the 19th Annual ACM Symposium on Theory of Computing, 1987, New York, USA, pp. 218–229. ACM (1987)

79. Halevi, S., Lindell, Y., Pinkas, B.: Secure computation on the web: computing without simultaneous interaction. In: Rogaway, P. (ed.) CRYPTO 2011. LNCS, vol. 6841, pp. 132–150. Springer, Heidelberg (2011). https://doi.org/10.1007/978-3-642-22792-9_8

80. Hirt, M., Raykov, P.: Multi-valued byzantine broadcast: the t < n case. In: Sarkar, P., Iwata, T. (eds.) ASIACRYPT 2014. LNCS, vol. 8874. Springer, Heidelberg (2014). https://doi.org/10.1007/978-3-662-45608-8_24

81. Hirt, M., Zikas, V.: Adaptively secure broadcast. In: Gilbert, H. (ed.) EUROCRYPT 2010. LNCS, vol. 6110, pp. 466–485. Springer, Heidelberg (2010). https://doi.org/10.1007/978-3-642-13190-5_24

82. Katz, J., Koo, C.-Y.: On expected constant-round protocols for Byzantine agreement. J. Comput. Syst. Sci. $75(2)$, 91–112 (2009)

83. Katz, J., Shacham, H. (eds.): CRYPTO 2017, Part I. LNCS, vol. 10401. Springer, Cham (2017). https://doi.org/10.1007/978-3-319-63688-7

84. Kiayias, A., Russell, A., David, B., Oliynykov, R.: Ouroboros: a provably secure proof-of-stake blockchain protocol. In: Katz and Shacham [83], pp. 357–388

85. King, V., Saia, J.: Byzantine agreement in expected polynomial time. J. ACM **63**(2), 13:1–13:21 (2016)
86. Kosaraju, S.R., Johnson, D.S., Aggarwal, A. (eds.): Proceedings of the Twenty-Fifth Annual ACM Symposium on Theory of Computing, San Diego, CA, USA, 16–18 May 1993. ACM (1993)
87. Kursawe, K., Shoup, V.: Optimistic asynchronous atomic broadcast. In: Caires, L., Italiano, G.F., Monteiro, L., Palamidessi, C., Yung, M. (eds.) ICALP 2005. LNCS, vol. 3580, pp. 204–215. Springer, Heidelberg (2005). https://doi.org/10.1007/11523468_17
88. Lamport, L., Shostak, R.E., Pease, M.C.: The Byzantine generals problem. ACM Trans. Program. Lang. Syst. **4**(3), 382–401 (1982)
89. Lindell, Y., Lysyanskaya, A., Rabin, T.: On the composition of authenticated byzantine agreement. J. ACM **53**(6), 881–917 (2006)
90. Lynch, N.A.: Distributed Algorithms. Morgan Kaufmann Publishers Inc., San Francisco (1996)
91. Micali, S.: ALGORAND: the efficient and democratic ledger. CoRR, abs/1607.01341 (2016)
92. Miller, A., LaViola, J.J.: Anonymous Byzantine consensus from moderately-hard puzzles: a model for bitcoin. University of Central Florida. Tech report, CS-TR-14-01, April 2014
93. Miller, A., Xia, Y., Croman, K., Shi, E., Song, D.: The honey badger of BFT protocols. In: Weippl, E.R., Katzenbeisser, S., Kruegel, C., Myers, A.C., Halevi, S. (eds.) Proceedings of the 2016 ACM SIGSAC Conference on Computer and Communications Security, Vienna, Austria, 24–28 October 2016, pp. 31–42. ACM (2016)
94. Miller, G.L. (ed.) Proceedings of the Twenty-Eighth Annual ACM Symposium on the Theory of Computing, Philadelphia, Pennsylvania, USA, 22–24 May 1996. ACM (1996)
95. Nakamoto, S.: Bitcoin: A peer-to-peer electronic cash system (2008). http://bitcoin.org/bitcoin.pdf
96. Nakamoto, S.: The proof-of-work chain is a solution to the Byzantine Generals' problem. The Cryptography Mailing List, November 2008. https://www.mail-archive.com/cryptography@metzdowd.com/msg09997.html
97. Nakamoto, S.: Bitcoin open source implementation of p2p currency, February 2009. http://p2pfoundation.ning.com/forum/topics/bitcoin-open-source
98. Naor, M., Yung, M.: Universal one-way hash functions and their cryptographic applications. In: Johnson, D.S. (ed.) Proceedings of the 21st Annual ACM Symposium on Theory of Computing, Seattle, Washington, USA, 14–17 May 1989, pp. 33–43. ACM (1989)
99. Neiger, G.: Distributed consensus revisited. Inf. Process. Lett. **49**(4), 195–201 (1994)
100. Nielsen, J.B., Rijmen, V. (eds.): EUROCRYPT 2018, Part II. LNCS, vol. 10821. Springer, Cham (2018). https://doi.org/10.1007/978-3-319-78375-8
101. Okun, M.: Agreement among unacquainted byzantine generals. In: Fraigniaud, P. (ed.) DISC 2005. LNCS, vol. 3724, pp. 499–500. Springer, Heidelberg (2005). https://doi.org/10.1007/11561927_40
102. Okun, M.: Distributed computing among unacquainted processors in the presence of Byzantine failures. Ph.D. thesis, Hebrew University of Jerusalem (2005)

103. Pass, R., Seeman, L., Shelat, A.: Analysis of the blockchain protocol in asynchronous networks. In: Coron, J.-S., Nielsen, J.B. (eds.) EUROCRYPT 2017, Part II. LNCS, vol. 10211, pp. 643–673. Springer, Cham (2017). https://doi.org/10.1007/978-3-319-56614-6_22

104. Pass, R., Shi, E.: The sleepy model of consensus. In: Takagi, T., Peyrin, T. (eds.) ASIACRYPT 2017, Part II. LNCS, vol. 10625, pp. 380–409. Springer, Cham (2017). https://doi.org/10.1007/978-3-319-70697-9_14

105. Pass, R., Shi, E.: Thunderella: blockchains with optimistic instant confirmation. In: Nielsen and Rijmen [100], pp. 3–33

106. Patra, A.: Error-free multi-valued broadcast and byzantine agreement with optimal communication complexity. In: Fernàndez Anta, A., Lipari, G., Roy, M. (eds.) OPODIS 2011. LNCS, vol. 7109, pp. 34–49. Springer, Heidelberg (2011). https://doi.org/10.1007/978-3-642-25873-2_4

107. Patra, A., Choudhury, A., Rangan, C.P.: Asynchronous byzantine agreement with optimal resilience. Distrib. Comput. 27(2), 111–146 (2014)

108. Pease, M.C., Shostak, R.E., Lamport, L.: Reaching agreement in the presence of faults. J. ACM 27(2), 228–234 (1980)

109. Pfitzmann, B., Waidner, M.: Unconditional byzantine agreement for any number of faulty processors. In: STACS, vol. 577, pp. 339–350. Springer, Heidelberg (1992)

110. Rabin, M.O.: Randomized byzantine generals. In: FOCS, pp. 403–409. IEEE Computer Society (1983)

111. Schneider, F.B.: Implementing fault-tolerant services using the state machine approach: a tutorial. ACM Comput. Surv. 22(4), 299–319 (1990)

112. Stifter, N., Judmayer, A., Schindler, P., Zamyatin, A., Weippl, E.R.: Agreement with satoshi - on the formalization of nakamoto consensus. IACR Cryptology ePrint Archive, 2018:400 (2018)

113. Turpin, R., Coan, B.A.: Extending binary byzantine agreement to multivalued byzantine agreement. Inf. Process. Lett. 18(2), 73–76 (1984)

114. Upfal, E.: Tolerating linear number of faults in networks of bounded degree. In: Hutchinson, N.C. (ed.) Proceedings of the Eleventh Annual ACM Symposium on Principles of Distributed Computing, Vancouver, British Columbia, Canada, 10–12 August 1992, pp. 83–89. ACM (1992)

115. Yao, A.C.-C.: Protocols for secure computations (extended abstract), pp. 160–164 (1982)

Consensus from Signatures of Work

Juan A. Garay[1], Aggelos Kiayias[2,3], and Giorgos Panagiotakos[2(✉)]

[1] Department of Computer Science and Engineering, Texas A&M University,
College Station, USA
garay@cse.tamu.edu
[2] School of Informatics, University of Edinburgh, Edinburgh, UK
akiayias@inf.ed.ac.uk, giorgos.pan@ed.ac.uk
[3] IOHK, Edinburgh, UK

Abstract. Assuming the existence of a public-key infrastructure (PKI), digital signatures are a fundamental building block in the design of secure consensus protocols with optimal resilience. More recently, with the advent of blockchain protocols like Bitcoin, consensus has been considered in the "permissionless" setting where no authentication or even point-to-point communication is available. Yet, despite some positive preliminary results, all attempts to formalize a building block that is sufficient for designing consensus protocols in this setting, rely on a very strong independence assumption about adversarial accesses to the underlying computational resource.

In this work, we relax this assumption by putting forth a primitive, which we call *signatures of work* (SoW). Distinctive features of our new notion are a lower bound on the number of steps required to produce a signature; fast verification; *moderate unforgeability*—producing a sequence of SoWs, for chosen messages, does not provide an advantage to an adversary in terms of running time; and *honest* signing time independence—most relevant in concurrent multi-party applications, as we show.

Armed with SoW, we then present a new permissionless consensus protocol which is secure assuming an honest majority of computational power, thus in a sense providing a blockchain counterpart to the classical Dolev-Strong consensus protocol. The protocol is built on top of a SoW-based blockchain and standard properties of the underlying hash function, thus improving on the known provably secure consensus protocols in this setting, which rely on the strong independence property mentioned above in a fundamental way.

1 Introduction

The consensus problem—reaching agreement distributedly in the presence of faults—has been extensively studied in the literature starting with the seminal work of Shostak, Pease and Lamport [38,44]. The problem formulation has a

A. Kiayias—Research partly supported by Horizon 2020 project PANORAMIX, No. 653497.

© Springer Nature Switzerland AG 2020
S. Jarecki (Ed.): CT-RSA 2020, LNCS 12006, pp. 319–344, 2020.
https://doi.org/10.1007/978-3-030-40186-3_14

number of servers (parties) starting with an individual input which should agree at the end to a joint output that has to match the input in the case where all non-faulty servers happened to have the same input value. One of the critical measures of effectiveness for consensus protocols is maximizing their resilience to Byzantine faults, typically denoted by t. It is known that $t < n/2$ is necessary to achieve consensus, where n is the total number of parties, while protocols have been designed that reach that level of resilience assuming synchrony and a way to authenticate messages using digital signatures [20][1] (or "pseudosignatures" [45]). This result is known to be tight since lack of synchrony would imply $t < n/3$ [22] (as well as randomization [25]), while lack of a message authentication mechanism has a similar effect [17].

Recently, with the advent of blockchain protocols like Bitcoin, the problem has experienced renewed interest from a much wider community of researchers and has seen its application expand to various novel settings, such as the so-called "permissionless" setting, where participation in the protocol is both unrestricted and unauthenticated. In fact, this setting was initially studied in [41,42], where it was shown that deterministic consensus algorithms are impossible for even a single failure but that probabilistic consensus is still feasible by suitably adapting the protocols of [12,24]. Nevertheless, the resulting protocol required exponentially many rounds in n.

The first efficient solutions for the consensus problem in the permissionless setting were formally shown to be possible utilizing an abstraction of the Bitcoin blockchain protocol in [29], against adversaries controlling less than half of the computational power which, in a uniform configuration (meaning parties are endowed with the same computational power), corresponds to a number of Byzantine faults $t < n/2$ in the original setting. At a high level, these protocols (as well as the Bitcoin blockchain protocol itself) rely on a concept known as *proofs of work* (PoW), which, intuitively, enables one party to convince others that he has invested some computational effort for solving a given task. While being formulated a while back [23] and used for a variety of purposes—e,g, spam mitigation [23], sybil attacks [21], and denial of service protection [4,35]—their role in the design of permissionless blockchain protocols [40], is arguably their most impactful application.

In the context of permissionless blockchain protocols, the way a PoW-like primitive helps is by *slowing down* message generation for all parties indiscriminately, thus generating opportunities for honest parties to converge to a unique view under the assumption that the aggregate computational power of honest parties sufficiently exceeds that of the adversary. Now, while this intuition matches the more rigorous analyses of the Bitcoin protocol that have been carried out so far [6,29,30,43], these works have refrained from formally defining such enabling functionality as a stand-alone cryptographic primitive, and

---

[1] Recall that the protocol in [20] tolerates an arbitrary number of Byzantine faults $(n > t)$, but in the version of the problem of a single sender (a.k.a. "Byzantine Generals," or just broadcast); in the case of consensus, $t < n/2$ is necessary regardless of the resources available to the parties in the protocol execution (see, e.g., [26,27]).

relied instead on the random oracle (RO) model [10] or similar idealized assumptions (cf. the $\mathcal{F}_{\text{TREE}}$ functionality in [43]) to prove *directly* the properties of the blockchain protocol. The same is true for other provably secure PoW-based distributed protocols [3,31,36].

The core of the hardness (or even impossibility [19]) of implementing the assumed idealized resources is that they satisfy a strong independence property: Each bit output on a new query to the resource is independently sampled, even if the adversary is the one who is accessing the resource. This is indeed a very strong property, as it directly implies that the best way to compute a PoW for both an honest party and the adversary is brute force. Moreover, the same property is explicitly used to argue the security of the proposed consensus protocols in the PoW setting [3,29], as we explain in detail later.

In this work we make progress in relaxing this assumption, by putting forth a formalization of a PoW-like primitive, which we call *signatures of work* (SoW). An SoW can be implemented in the RO model or by using $\mathcal{F}_{\text{TREE}}$, but the adversarial SoW computation process does *not* necessarily satisfy such strong guarantees as the ones mentioned above. Indeed, in contrast to previous approaches, only an upper bound on the rate at which the adversary generates SoWs needs to be assumed. We then present a new permissionless consensus protocol based on SoWs that can be proven secure without relying on such strong independence guarantees. The protocol utilizes a SoW-based blockchain and standard properties of the underlying hash function, and is secure assuming an honest majority of computational power. As a result, this protocol can be seen as an exemplar of how a permissionless signature-like primitive enables honest majority consensus in the same way that classical digital signatures imply honest-majority consensus protocols in the traditional setting.

Why *Signatures* of Work? We first provide some intuition behind the relevance of SoW as a useful primitive for the design of permissionless distributed protocols. Recall the main property of a digital signature in the design of classical consensus protocols: It enables parties to communicate to each other their protocol view and inputs at a certain stage of the protocol execution in a way that is transferable and non-repudiable. Indeed, Bob, upon receiving Alice's signed message, can show it to Charlie in a way that the latter is unequivocally convinced of the message's origin. It follows that Bob cannot modify Alice's messages, playing man-in-the-middle between Alice and Charlie, and thus Alice can be held accountable in case she provides conflicting views to the two parties. A SoW scheme provides a similar capability: Using a SoW, a party like Alice can invest effort into a specific protocol view and inputs, so that when Bob is presented with a SoW produced by Alice it will be infeasible for Alice to provide a conflicting view and inputs to Charlie, *unless she invests twice the effort*. Moreover, the above argument holds without establishing any set of identities among the parties, so for example Bob does not need to know he talks to Alice *per se* but rather to an arbitrary party that invested some effort with respect to a specific protocol view. Furthermore, exactly like digital signatures, SoWs can be chained recursively, enabling the parties to build on each other's protocol view.

While the above functionalities hint to the usefulness of SoWs in the distributed permissionless setting, formalizing and applying them properly is no simple task. Firstly, in contrast with classical signatures, there is no secret key involved in this primitive. This make sense, since in a permisionless setting signing messages using some kind of secret information is meaningless, as parties do no have any secret setup to begin with. Hence, if they are to sign any message, they should use some other kind of resource that only they have access to, such as their computational power. Secondly, in classical signatures, the exact time when the verification key becomes available to different parties is irrelevant; The key is only useful for verification, up to polynomial-time differences. In the context of SoWs, however, this time is of great importance. For example, allowing a party to learn the verification key, say, two days earlier than other parties, means that this party will be able to compute two days worth of signatures more than them. Hence, in contexts where *counting* the number of generated signatures matters, as is the case in blockchain protocols, great care should be taken on guaranteeing that the verification key is "fresh" enough for the relevant application.

Our Results. Our contributions are as follows:

(1) Formalization of an SoW scheme. The syntax of an SoW scheme entails four algorithms: Public parameter generation, key generation, signing and verification—PPub, KeyGen, Sign and Verify, respectively. PPub is invoked on input 1^λ, where λ is the security parameter, and outputs public security parameters pp. KeyGen is invoked on input pp, and outputs a random verification key vk. Sign is invoked on input (pp, vk, msg, h), where msg is the message to be signed, and h is the *hardness* level of the signature generation. Expectedly, Verify is invoked on input (pp, vk, msg, h, σ), where σ is (possibly) an output of Sign. We require a SoW scheme to be:

- **Correct:** As in the case of classical signatures, we require that signatures produced by Sign should be accepted by the Verify algorithm.
- (t, α)**-Successful:** This property lower-bounds the probability that an honest signer will successfully produce a SoW in a certain number of steps t; α is a function of the hardness level h.
- t**-Verifiable:** The verifier should be able to verify a SoW in t steps. (Typically, t is a lot smaller than the time need to produce a signature.)
- **Moderately Unforgeable against Tampering and Chosen-Message Attacks $((\beta, \epsilon)$-MU-TCMA):** This property is akin to the property of *existential unforgeability under chosen-message attacks* of digital signatures (EU-CMA). It captures the fact that producing a *sequence* of SoWs, for chosen messages, does not provide an advantage to an adversary in terms of running time. Specifically, the chances to produce more than $\beta \cdot t$ SoWs in t steps

(for any t) are less than ϵ.[2] Further, this should hold against an adversary able to *tamper* with the keys, and even in the presence of a Sign oracle.

- **Run-time independent:** This final property captures the setting where honest signers are potentially invoked on adversarial inputs and ensures that their running time enjoys some degree of independence. Specifically, the random variables defined as the running time of each Sign invocation is a set of almost independent random variables (cf. [1]). We stress that the adversarial signing algorithm may *not* satisfy this property.

As a "sanity check," we show in the full version of the paper that a SoW scheme can be easily designed and proven secure in the random oracle model (or by using $\mathcal{F}_{\text{TREE}}$), and hence in practice can be instantiated by a cryptographic hash function such as SHA-256.

(2) Consensus from SoW. Next, we design a consensus protocol for an honest majority of computational power that can be reduced to the SoW primitive above. The core idea behind our new protocol is as follows. First, the parties build a blockchain using SoWs in a way reminiscent of the Bitcoin blockchain. Using SoWs we show how to emulate the Bitcoin backbone protocol [29] by having parties compute a SoW in parallel, "on top" of the current view that incorporates the largest number of SoWs, i.e., the longest chain. However, in contrast with the consensus protocol of [29], to generate a block, the parties include not only their input to the consensus protocol, but also the headers of "orphan" blocks that exist in forks stemming off their main chain and which have not been included so far, where the header of a block contains the hash of the previous block in the chain, the signature, the input to the consensus protocol, and a hash of the block's contents.

Using this mechanism, as shown in Fig. 1, we prove that it is possible to reconstruct the whole tree of block headers from the blockchain contents, and thus in this way preserve all block headers produced by the honest parties. This ensures that the resulting ledger will reflect the number of parties and hence a consensus protocol may now be easily reduced to this blockchain protocol.

Our new consensus protocol relying on the SoW primitive in the setting where no PKI is available, exemplifies the contrast with consensus in the classical setting, relying on standard signatures and a PKI setup [20] (cf. [27]). It is worth noting that the only known blockchain-based provably secure and optimally resilient consensus protocol is given in [29], using a technique called "2-for-1 PoW" where two PoW-based protocols can be run concurrently and create a blockchain where the number of honest-party contributions is proportional to their actual number, but which relies on the strong independence property of the RO model, discussed earlier, in a fundamental way. Indeed, in the RO model,

---

[2] Note that, unlike previous unforgeability definitions (e.g, [11]), this definition is parameterized by the *rate* β at which the adversary can produce signatures, instead of the number of steps it needs to compute one. We feel that this formulation is more appropriate for the moderate unforgeability game where the adversary tries to produce multiple signatures. For further details, see Definition 7.

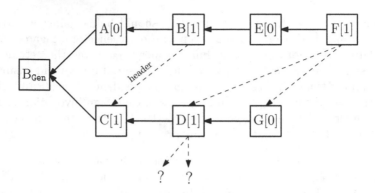

Fig. 1. The data structure maintained by the consensus protocol. Block F has consensus input 1, and includes the headers of blocks D and G, with input 1 and 0, respectively. Block D includes the headers of invalid blocks. This is not a problem, since any chain that contains D will be invalid and not selected by any party, while D's consensus input is correctly counted as a valid block header.

each witness for a PoW can be rearranged in a certain way so as to obtain a test for a witness for *another* PoW in a way that is independent from the first solution. Our new protocol gets rid of this need. The only other (non-blockchain) PoW-based consensus protocol [3] also relies on the RO model.

As intermediate steps in our analysis, we first introduce an appropriate adaptation of the model of [29] that allows for a standard model analysis and which may be of independent interest. We then recall the three basic properties of the blockchain data structure presented in [29]: (strong) common prefix, chain quality and chain growth, and show how our SoW-based blockchain protocol satisfies them assuming, beyond the security of SoW, standard collision resistance from the underlying hash function that is used to "glue" the blocks together. This is achieved as follows: We first prove that using the MU-TCMA property and assuming the adversarial hashing power is suitably bounded, it is unlikely in any sufficiently long time window for the adversary to exceed the number of SoWs of the honest parties. Then, using the (t, α)-Successful and (β, ϵ)-MU-TCMA properties in conjunction with run-time independence, we establish that summations of running times of successive Sign invocations have the *variance* needed to ensure that "uniquely successful rounds" (i.e., rounds where exactly one of the honest parties produces a SoW) happen with high density in any sufficiently long time window. Using these last two core results, and under suitable constraints for the basic SoW parameters $\alpha, \beta, \epsilon, h$ and number of parties n, we prove that the security of the Bitcoin backbone protocol implements a robust transaction ledger [29]. Further, and as a sanity check, in the full version of the paper, we argue that the results we get from our black-box analysis (and the RO-based SoW construction mentioned earlier), are similar to those from the random-oracle analysis of [29].

Our analysis is carried out in the synchronous setting. It is relatively straight-forward to extend our results to the Δ-synchronous setting of [43], by using the same techniques as in [[28] (Section 7)]. We leave as an open question extending our results to the variable difficulty setting of [30].

(3) Other applications. In addition to the blockchain and consensus applications of SoW, we note that the security properties we put forth are suitable for the more traditional DDOS setting, with considerable advantages over existing approaches (cf. [50]). The problem is as follows: A server wants to protect itself from malicious actors in the network which send network packets to eat up its resources. The canonical defense for this attack is for the server to run a PoW challenge-response protocol with the sender, in order to make sending a message costly. The MU-TCMA property, we have defined, directly implies exactly this property in the strongest sense: For any, adaptively selected, set of messages sent, the adversary must consume computational resources proportional to the number of messages, even if it can also see SoWs sent by other parties. Moreover, this process can be made non-interactive by delegating the generation of the ver-ification key to some public randomness service, e.g., the NIST beacon, and only accept messages that include a SoW with respect to this key. Finally, note that the same security guarantees can be easily extended to multiple servers who use the same beacon, by requiring that the sent messages contain some unique identification string.

Prior and Related Work. We have already mentioned above relevant related work regarding classical and blockchain-based consensus protocols. For a more exhaustive recent survey, refer to [27]. We also note that the focus of the paper is the original consensus problem [38, 44], and not so-called "ledger consensus" (sometimes referred to as "Nakamoto consensus"), which is an instance of the state machine replication problem [47]; see also [27] for an overview of such protocols. The idea of referencing off-chain blocks has been considered early on in the ledger consensus literature (see, e.g., [13, 39, 48, 49]) as a way to obtain fairness, better throughput and faster confirmation times. Our novelty is that we leverage this technique along with the new SoW notion to build a provably secure consensus protocol, which, unlike prior results, is not based on the "2-for-1 PoW" technique described earlier.

There have been a number of attempts to formalize a proof of work (PoW) primitive that it is also sufficient to imply the security of a blockchain protocol. Nevertheless, such works were either informal [5, 46], or they did not produce a correctness proof for a blockchain or consensus protocol, focusing instead on other applications [2, 7, 15, 16, 33]. More specifically, in [33], Garay *et al.* study the necessary hardness condition that the underlying computational problem should satisfy in order for Bitcoin to implement a public ledger. In contrast to our work, an enhanced version of that security notion is shown to be sufficient to implement a public ledger against an adversary controlling only 1/3 (as opposed to 1/2) of the computational power. Further, it is unclear whether such notion can be used to solve the original consensus problem.

Another effort to formalize an intermediate PoW-like building block for the Bitcoin protocol was made in [43]. The proposed ideal functionality, $\mathcal{F}_{\mathrm{TREE}}^p$, keeps track of a tree of messages, which both the honest parties and the adversary can extend with probability p. The outcome of each such trial is independent of the others, even if it is made by the adversary. $\mathcal{F}_{\mathrm{TREE}}^p$ satisfies the strong independence property mentioned before, and hence it is not suitable for the goals of this paper. Moreover, we note that any protocol instantiating this functionality must necessarily be *interactive*, as two parties can use $\mathcal{F}_{\mathrm{TREE}}^p$ to communicate at least one bit. Finally, in [43], it was shown how to implement a transaction ledger, but not how to achieve consensus; the techniques introduced in this paper can be adapted to implement a consensus protocol using $\mathcal{F}_{\mathrm{TREE}}$. Additional related work is mentioned in the full version of the paper.

Organization of the Paper. The basic computational model, definitions and cryptographic building blocks used by our constructions are presented in Sect. 2. Formal definition of the SoW primitive and its security properties are presented in Sect. 3. Section 4 is dedicated to applications of SoW: First, we introduce an appropriate model for our applications (Sect. 4.1). We then analyze the Bitcoin backbone protocol based on (and reducing its security to) SoW (Sect. 4.2), followed by the new blockchain-based consensus protocol (Sect. 4.3). Due to space limitations, some of the proofs and other supplementary material are presented in the full version of the paper [32].

2   Preliminaries

In this section we introduce basic notation and definitions that are used in the rest of the paper. For $k \in \mathbb{N}^+$, $[k]$ denotes the set $\{1, \ldots, k\}$. For strings x, z, $x \| z$ is the concatenation of x and z, and $|x|$ denotes the length of x. We denote sequences by $(a_i)_{i \in I}$, where I is the index set. For a set X, $x \leftarrow X$ denotes sampling a uniform element from X. For a distribution $\mathcal{U}$ over a set X, $x \leftarrow \mathcal{U}$ denotes sampling an element of X according to $\mathcal{U}$. By $\mathcal{U}_\lambda$ we denote the uniform distribution over $\{0, 1\}^\lambda$. We denote the statistical distance between two random variables X, Z with range $\mathcal{U}$ by $\Delta[X, Y]$, i.e., $\Delta[X, Z] = \frac{1}{2} \sum_{v \in \mathcal{U}} |\Pr[X = v] - \Pr[Z = v]|$. For $\epsilon > 0$, we say that X, Y are ϵ-*close* when $\Delta(X, Y) \leq \epsilon$.

We let λ denote the security parameter. In this paper we will follow a more concrete ("exact") approach [8,11,14,34] to security evaluation rather than an asymptotic one. We will use functions t, ϵ, whose ranges are $\mathbb{N}, \mathbb{R}$, respectively, and have possibly many different arguments, to denote concrete bounds on the running time (number of steps) and probability of adversarial success of an algorithm in some fixed computational model, respectively. When we speak about running time this will include the execution time plus the length of the code (cf. [14]; note also that we will be considering uniform machines). We will always assume that t is a polynomial in the security parameter λ, although we will sometimes omit this dependency for brevity.

Instead of using interactive Turing machines (ITMs) as the underlying model of distributed computation, we will use (interactive) RAMs. The reason is that we need a model where subroutine access and simulation do not incur a significant overhead. ITMs are not suitable for this purpose, since one needs to account for the additional steps to go back-and-forth all the way to the place where the subroutine is stored. A similar choice was made by Garay $et\ al.$ [34]; refer to [34] for details on using interactive RAMs in a UC-like framework, as well as to Sect. 4.1. Given a RAM M, we will denote by $\mathsf{Steps}_M(1^\lambda, x)$ the random variable that corresponds to the number of steps of M given as input the security parameter 1^λ and x. We will say that M is t-bounded if it holds that $\Pr[\mathsf{Steps}_M(1^\lambda, x) \le t(\lambda)] = 1$.

Finally, we remark that in our analyses there will be asymptotic terms of the form $\mathsf{negl}(\lambda)$ and concrete terms; throughout the paper, we will assume that λ is large enough to render the asymptotic terms insignificant compared to the concrete terms.

Cryptographic Hash Functions. We will make use of the following notion of security for cryptographic hash functions:

Definition 1. *Let* $\mathcal{H} = \{\{H_k : M(\lambda) \to Y(\lambda)\}_{k \in K(\lambda)}\}_{\lambda \in \mathbb{N}}$ *be a hash-function family, and* $\mathcal{A}$ *be a PPT adversary. Then* $\mathcal{H}$ *is* collision resistant *if and only if for any* $\lambda \in \mathbb{N}$ *and corresponding* $\{H_k\}_{k \in K}$ *in* $\mathcal{H}$,

$$\Pr[k \leftarrow K; (m, m') \leftarrow \mathcal{A}(1^\lambda, k); (m \neq m') \wedge (H_k(m) = H_k(m'))] \le \mathsf{negl}(\lambda).$$

Robust Public Transaction Ledgers. The notion of a *public transaction ledger* was introduced in [29] to describe the functionality implemented by the Bitcoin protocol. It is defined with respect to a set of valid ledgers $\mathcal{L}$ and a set of valid transactions $\mathcal{T}$, each one possessing an efficient membership test. A ledger $\mathbf{x} \in \mathcal{L}$ is a vector of sequences of transactions $\mathsf{tx} \in \mathcal{T}$. Ledgers correspond to chains in the Bitcoin protocol. It is possible for the adversary to create two transactions that are conflicting; valid ledgers must not contain conflicting transaction. Moreover, it is assumed that in the protocol execution there also exists an oracle Txgen that generates valid transactions, and is unambiguous, i.e., the adversary cannot create transactions that come in 'conflict' with the transactions generated by the oracle. A transaction is called *neutral* if there does not exist any transactions that comes in conflict with it.

Definition 2. *A protocol* Π *implements a* robust public transaction ledger *if it organizes the ledger as a chain of blocks of transactions and satisfies the following two properties:*

- **Persistence:** *Parameterized by* $k \in \mathbb{N}$ *(the "depth" parameter), if in a certain round an honest player reports a ledger that contains a transaction* tx *in a block more than* k *blocks away from the end of the ledger, then* tx *will always be reported in the same position in the ledger by any honest player from this round on.*
- **Liveness:** *Parameterized by* $u, k \in \mathbb{N}$ *(the "wait time" and "depth" parameters, resp.), provided that a transaction either (i) issued by* Txgen, *or (ii) is*

neutral, is given as input to all honest players continuously for u consecutive rounds, then all honest parties will report this transaction at a block more than k blocks from the end of the ledger.

The Consensus Problem. Next, we give the definition of the well-known consensus problem (a.k.a. Byzantine agreement) [38, 44]. There are n parties, $t < n$ of which might be corrupted, taking an initial input $x \in V$ (without loss of generality, we can assume $V = \{0, 1\}$).

Definition 3. *A protocol* Π *solves the consensus problem provided it satisfies the following properties:*

- **Agreement.** *All honest parties will output the same value eventually.*
- **Validity.** *If all the honest parties have the same input, then they all output this value.*

3   Signatures of Work

The main goal of this paper is to implement consensus in the permissionless setting without relying on the strong independence property of the underlying computational resource. Towards that goal, in this section we introduce the *signature of work* (SoW) primitive. At a high level, a SoW enables one party to convince others that she has invested some computational power during some specific time interval and with respect to a "message." Next, we formalize this notion and present its desired security properties.

SoW Syntax. Given a security parameter λ, let PP be the public parameter space, $HP \subseteq \mathbb{N}$ the hardness parameter space, K the key space, M the message space, and S the signature space. With foresight, the role of the key is to provide "freshness" for the signature computation, thus certifying that the signature was computed in the given time interval.

Definition 4. *A SoW scheme consists of four algorithms* SoW $=$ (PPub, KeyGen, Sign, Verify), *where:*

- PPub(1^λ) *is a randomized algorithm that takes as input the security parameter* λ, *and returns a set of public parameters* $pp \in PP$.
- KeyGen(pp) *is a randomized algorithm that takes as input the public parameters* pp, *and returns a key* $vk \in K$. *(See Remark 1 below on the role of keys in* SoW *schemes.)*
- Sign(pp, vk, msg, h) *is a randomized algorithm that takes as input public parameters* $pp \in PP$, *a key* $vk \in K$, *a message* $msg \in M$ *and hardness parameter* $h \in HP$, *and returns a signature (of work)* $\sigma \in S$.
- Verify(pp, vk, msg, h, σ) *is a deterministic algorithm that takes as input public parameters* $pp \in PP$, *a key* $vk \in K$, *message* $msg \in M$, *hardness parameter* $h \in HP$ *and a signature* $\sigma \in S$, *and returns* true *or* false *to indicate the validity of the signature.*

Remark 1. SoW schemes only have a public verification key. The role of this key is to guarantee that the computational work spent in order to create a signature of work is "fresh," i.e., executed during a specific time interval (say, from the time the key became known to the signer). In contrast, classical digital signatures also have a secret key that serves as a trapdoor to compute signatures. In the applications we consider, the existence of trapdoor information is not meaningful, and in fact may hurt the security of the respective constructions.

Security Properties. Next, we present a number of security properties that we will require SoW schemes to satisfy. We start with the correctness property.

Definition 5. *We say that a SoW scheme is* correct *if for every* $\lambda \in \mathbb{N}, pp \in PP, vk \in K, h \in HP,$ *and* $msg \in M:$

$$\Pr\left[\, \mathsf{Verify}(pp, vk, msg, h, \mathsf{Sign}(pp, vk, msg, h)) = \mathsf{true} \,\right] \geq 1 - \mathsf{negl}(\lambda).$$

Next, we require that the time to verify a signature be upper bounded.

Definition 6. *We say that a SoW scheme is* t-verifiable, *if* Verify *takes time at most* t *(on all inputs).*

Next, we capture the case of a malicious signer (resp., verifier) in the context of SoWs. In the first case, the adversary's objective is to compute a number of signatures a lot faster than an honest signer would, while in the second case it is to make the honest signer take too much time to generate a signature.

We deal with malicious signers first. We put forth an attack that we will use to express a class of adversaries that attempt to forge signatures faster than expected. Intuitively, this constitutes an attack against an honest verifier that may be trying to gauge a certain measure using the number of signatures. The game defining the attack is shown in Fig. 2; we call the corresponding security property *Moderate Unforgeability against Tampering and Chosen Message Attack* (MU-TCMA). As in the security definitions of standard signatures (e.g., EU-CMA), we allow the adversary to have access to a signing oracle $\mathcal{S}$. Every time the oracle is queried, we assume that it runs the Sign procedure with uniformly sampled randomness. A subtle point in the modeling of security in the presence of such oracle is that $\mathcal{S}$ should also "leak" the number of steps it took for a query to be processed. In an actual execution while interacting with honest parties that are producing signatures, time is a side channel that may influence the adversarial strategy; in order to preserve the dependency on this side channel we will require from $\mathcal{S}$ to leak this information. We note that in the classical signatures literature, timing attacks have also been a serious consideration [37].

In addition, we require that the key used by the adversary to construct signatures be fresh, i.e., we want to avoid situations where the adversary outputs signatures that he has precomputed a long time ago. We model this by providing the fresh key after the adversary has finished running his precomputation phase.

$$\text{Exp}_{\mathcal{A},\mathcal{F}}^{\text{MU-TCMA}}(1^\lambda, h, \ell)$$

$\Sigma \leftarrow U_\lambda; \; pp \leftarrow \text{PPub}(1^\lambda);$	*(Public parameters)*
$st \leftarrow \mathcal{A}_1(1^\lambda, \Sigma, pp);$	*(Precomputation)*
$vk \leftarrow \text{KeyGen}(pp);$	*(Verification key)*
$(f_i, msg_i, \sigma_i)_{i \in [\ell]} \leftarrow \mathcal{A}_2^{\mathcal{S}(\cdot,\cdot)}(1^\lambda, vk, st);$	*(SoW computation)*

$$\text{return } \bigwedge_{i=1}^{\ell} \left(\begin{array}{l} \text{Verify}(pp, f_i(\Sigma, vk), msg_i, \sigma_i) \wedge \neg\text{Asked}(f_i(\Sigma, vk), msg_i, \sigma_i) \\ \wedge \, (f_i \in F_\lambda) \wedge (\forall j \in [\ell] : f_i(\Sigma, vk) = f_j(\Sigma, vk) \Rightarrow i = j) \end{array} \right)$$

Fig. 2. The Moderate Unforgeability against Tampering and Chosen-Message Attack (MU-TCMA) experiment for a SoW scheme.

Further, we allow the adversary to tamper with the key by manipulating it via tampering functions belonging to a family of functions $\mathcal{F}$.

Looking ahead, the tampering function in our applications will be related to a keyed hash function, where the key of the hash is part of a *common random string* (CRS). Hence, we choose to model functions in $\mathcal{F}$ to have two inputs: Σ (the CRS) and vk. Moreover, the output of the adversary is deemed invalid if he tampers vk with functions f_1, f_2 in such a way that $f_1(\Sigma, vk) = f_2(\Sigma, vk)$. Otherwise, the adversary could launch a generic attack that is unrelated to the SoW scheme, and produce signatures at twice the rate of an honest signer, as follows. The adversary first finds f_1, f_2 that have this property, and then computes signatures using the tampered key $f_1(\Sigma, vk)$. The trick is that each of them will also correspond to a signature with key $f_2(\Sigma, vk)$. Hence, he effectively can double the rate at which he produces signatures.

Formally, the adversary will have access to $\mathcal{S}(\cdot, \cdot)$, an SoW oracle that on input (vk', msg), where $vk' \in K$ and $msg \in M$, returns the pair (σ, t) where σ is the output of $\text{Sign}(pp, vk', msg, h)$ and t is the number of steps taken by the Sign algorithm on these parameters. Function $\text{Asked}(vk', msg, \sigma)$ is true if σ was the response of $\mathcal{S}$ to some query (vk', msg).

We are now ready to formulate the security property of *Moderate Unforgeability against Tampering and Chosen Message Attacks* (MU-TCMA). It has two parameters, β and ϵ, and, informally, it states that no adversary $\mathcal{A}$ exists in the experiment of Fig. 2 that takes at most t steps after receiving key vk and produces $\ell \geq \beta \cdot t$ signatures with probability better than ϵ. Note that in total we allow $\mathcal{A}$ to take any polynomial number of steps, i.e., the adversary is allowed to execute a precomputation stage that permits it to obtain an arbitrary number of signatures before learning vk. In the definition below, we allow β to depend on the hardness level h, and ϵ on h, t and $q_\mathcal{S}$, the number of queries the adversary makes to the signing oracle.

Definition 7. *Let $\mathcal{F} = \{F_\lambda\}_{\lambda\in\mathbb{N}}$, where F_λ is a family of functions $f : \{0,1\}^\lambda \times K \to K$.[3] A SoW scheme is (β, ϵ)-Moderately Unforgeable against Tampering and Chosen-Message Attacks (MU-TCMA) with respect to tampering function class $\mathcal{F}$, if for any polynomially large t_1, t_2, any adversary $\mathcal{A} = (\mathcal{A}_1, \mathcal{A}_2)$, where $\mathcal{A}_1$ is t_1-bounded and $\mathcal{A}_2$ is t_2-bounded and makes at most q_S queries to oracle $\mathcal{S}$, for any $\lambda \in \mathbb{N}$, and any $h \in HP$, the probability of $\mathcal{A}$ winning in $\mathsf{Exp}_{\mathcal{A},\mathcal{F}}^{MU\text{-}TCMA}(1^\lambda, h, \lfloor \beta(h) \cdot t_2 \rfloor)$ (Fig. 2) is less than $\epsilon(h, t_2, q_S)$.*

Remark 2. As mentioned in Sect. 1, unlike previous unforgeability definitions (e.g, [11]), Definition 7 is parameterized by the *rate* at which the adversary can produce signatures, instead of the number of steps it needs to compute one, which is more appropriate for the moderate unforgeability game where the adversary tries to produce multiple signatures.

In the MU-TCMA definition we are going to consider tampering functions classes that at the very least preserve the unpredictability of vk. Otherwise, the adversary can generically attack any SoW scheme by predicting the tampered key and precomputing signatures. Formally, we will say that $\mathcal{F}$ is *computationally unpredictable* if the adversary, given the CRS Σ, cannot guess a value y that he will be able to "hit" when he gains access to vk through some $f \in \mathcal{F}$.

Definition 8. *Let $\mathcal{F} = \{F_\lambda\}_{\lambda\in\mathbb{N}}$, where F_λ is a family of functions $f : \{0,1\}^\lambda \times K \to K$. We say that $\mathcal{F}$ is computationally unpredictable with respect to a SoW scheme SoW, if for any PPT RAM $\mathcal{A} = (\mathcal{A}_1, \mathcal{A}_2)$, and for any $\lambda \in \mathbb{N}$, it holds that:*

$$\Pr_{\substack{pp\leftarrow\mathsf{PPub}(1^\lambda); \\ vk\leftarrow\mathsf{KeyGen}(pp); \\ \Sigma\leftarrow\mathcal{U}_\lambda}} \left[\begin{array}{l} (st, y) \leftarrow \mathcal{A}_1(1^\lambda, \Sigma, pp); f \leftarrow \mathcal{A}_2(1^\lambda, st, vk) : \\ f \in F_\lambda \wedge f(\Sigma, vk) = y \end{array} \right] \leq \mathsf{negl}(\lambda).$$

Next, we consider the case of attacking an honest signer. Attacking an honest signer amounts to finding a certain set of keys over which the honest signer algorithm fails to produce SoWs sufficiently fast and regularly. We say that a SoW scheme is (t, α)-*successful* when the probability that the signer computes a signature in t steps is at least α.

Definition 9. *We say that SoW scheme is (t, α)-successful if for any $\lambda \in \mathbb{N}$ and any $h \in HP$, it holds that:*

$$\Pr_{\substack{pp\leftarrow\mathsf{PPub}(1^\lambda); \\ vk\leftarrow\mathsf{KeyGen}(pp); \\ msg\leftarrow M}} \left[\mathsf{Steps}_{\mathsf{Sign}}(pp, vk, msg, h) \leq t \right] \geq \alpha(h).$$

Finally, in the same corrupt-verifier setting, we will require the signing time of honest signers to have some (limited) *independence*, which will be important for the applications we have in mind. This property, in combination with the

---

[3] K is the key space of the SoW scheme.

efficiency and MU-TCMA properties, will prove crucial in ensuring that when multiple signers work together, the distribution of the number of them who succeed in producing a signature has some "good" variance and concentration properties.

Definition 10. *We say that a SoW scheme has* almost-independent runtime *iff for any polynomial $p(\cdot)$, any $\lambda \in \mathbb{N}$, any $h \in HP$, there exists a set of mutually independent random variables $\{Y_i\}_{i \in [p(\lambda)]}$ such that for any $pp \in PP, ((vk_i, m_i))_{i \in [p(\lambda)]} \in (K \times M)^{p(\lambda)}$ it holds that $\Delta[(\mathsf{Steps}_{\mathsf{Sign}}(pp, vk_i, m_i, h))_i, (Y_i)_i] \leq \mathsf{negl}(\lambda)$.*

Independence Assumptions. As mentioned earlier, MU-TCMA does not enforce any independence assumption, and only bounds the probability that the rate at which the adversary computes SoWs is high. In contrast, the independent-runtime property does so, but only for honest signers. We remark that achieving such property is considerably easier for the honest case, as we can be sure that signers will use independently sampled coins if instructed; a guarantee that we cannot have for the adversary.

Parameters' Range. Let SoW be a scheme that is $(t_{\mathsf{sign}}, \alpha)$-Successful. SoW trivially satisfies the MU-TCMA property for $\beta(h) > 1$, since the adversary does not have enough time to output the signatures it has computed. On the other hand, assuming $\epsilon(h, t, q_S)$ is a negligible function of t, $\alpha(h)$ must be smaller than $\beta(h) \cdot t_{\mathsf{sign}}$, otherwise the expected number of SoWs computed by the Sign function would exceed that allowed by the MU-TCMA property. Hence, for optimal security, it should hold that $\alpha(h)$ is close to $\beta(h) \cdot t_{\mathsf{sign}}$.

Next, we turn to applications of our SoW primitive.

4   Applications

In this section we showcase applications of SoWs, the first one being implementing robust transaction ledgers: Using our primitive and standard properties of the underlying hash function, we establish the security of the Bitcoin backbone protocol [29]. The second application is realizing consensus in the permisionless setting: We construct a new blockchain-based consensus protocol for an honest majority provably secure under the same assumptions as above, thus providing a blockchain counterpart to the classical result in the cryptographic setting with a trusted (PKI) setup [20].

In both applications we assume the existence of a SoW scheme with the security properties defined below.

Assumption 1. (SoW Assumption). *For parameters $\beta, \epsilon, t'_{\mathcal{H}}, \alpha$ and t_{ver} we assume that* SoW = (PPub, KeyGen, Sign, Verify) *is:*

- *Correct;*
- *(β, ϵ)-MU-TCMA with respect to any computationally unpredictable tampering function class (cf. Definition 8);*

- $(t'_{\mathcal{H}}, \alpha)$-*successful*;[4]
- *almost run-time independent; and*
- t_{ver}-*verifiable,*

where $\epsilon(h, t, q_S) \in \text{negl}(\beta(h) \cdot t)$. *Moreover, we assume that the parameter spaces* K, M, S *of the scheme are equal to* $\{0, 1\}^{\log |K|}, \{0, 1\}^*, \{0, 1\}^{\log |S|}$, *respectively.*

For a SoW scheme to be used in the context of the Bitcoin protocol, choosing K, M, S as above is important due to the underlying hash-chain structure of the blockchain: The hash of each block acts as a key of the SoW scheme, thus the output of the hash function should match the key space of the SoW.

We start with some pertinent details about the model that the two applications mentioned above will be analyzed under.

4.1 The Permissionless Model, Revisited

All the security models proposed for the analysis of PoW-based blockchain protocols [29,43] rely on bounding the number of queries to an idealized functionality to model limited computational resources. In contrast, we do not wish to restrict the way the adversary accesses the computational resource, and thus we model limited computational resources in a more general manner, i.e., by limiting the exact number of steps parties take. Next, we present a revised version of the model of [29] that captures our considerations.

For the reasons explained in Sect. 2, we substitute IRAMs for ITMs. The execution of a protocol Π is driven by an "environment" program $\mathcal{Z}$ that may spawn multiple instances running the protocol Π. The programs in question can be thought of as "interactive RAMs" communicating through registers in a well-defined manner, with instances and their spawning at the discretion of a control program which is also an IRAM and is denoted by C. In particular, the control program C forces the environment to perform a "round-robin" participant execution sequence for a fixed set of parties.

Specifically, the execution driven by $\mathcal{Z}$ is defined with respect to a protocol Π, an adversary $\mathcal{A}$ (also an IRAM) and a set of parties $P_1, ..., P_n$; these are hardcoded in the control program C. The protocol Π is defined in a "hybrid" setting and has access to one "ideal functionality," called the *diffusion channel* (see below). It is used as subroutine by the programs involved in the execution (the IRAMs of Π and $\mathcal{A}$) and is accessible by all parties once they are spawned.

Initially, the environment $\mathcal{Z}$ is restricted by C to spawn the adversary $\mathcal{A}$. Each time the adversary is activated, it may communicate with C via messages of the form (Corrupt, P_i). The control program C will register party P_i as corrupted, only provided that the environment has previously given an input of the form (Corrupt, P_i) to $\mathcal{A}$ and that the number of corrupted parties is less or equal t, a bound that is also hardcoded in C. The first party to be spawned running protocol Π is restricted by C to be party P_1. After a party P_i is activated, the

---

[4] Parameter $t'_{\mathcal{H}}$ corresponds to a lower bound on the running time of honest parties that we introduce in detail later.

environment is restricted to activate party P_{i+1}, except when P_n is activated in which case the next party to be activated is always the adversary $\mathcal{A}$. Note that when a corrupted party P_i is activated the adversary $\mathcal{A}$ is activated instead.

Next, we describe how different parties communicate. Initially, the diffusion functionality sets the variable round to be 1. It also maintains a Receive() string defined for each party P_i. A party is allowed at any moment to fetch the messages sent to it at the previous round that are contained in its personal Receive() string. Moreover, when the functionality receives an instruction to diffuse a message m from party P_i it marks the party as complete for the current round and forwards the message to the adversary; note that m is allowed to be empty. At any moment, the adversary $\mathcal{A}$ is allowed to specify the contents of the Receive() string for each party P_i. The adversary has to specify when it is complete for the current round. When all parties are complete for the current round, the functionality inspects the contents of all Receive() strings and includes any messages that were diffused by the parties in the current round but not contributed by the adversary to the Receive() tapes. The variable round is then incremented.

Based on the above, we denote by $\{\text{VIEW}_{\Pi,\mathcal{A},\mathcal{Z}}^{P,t,n}(z)\}_{z\in\{0,1\}^*}$ the random variable ensemble that corresponds to the view of party P at the end of an execution where $\mathcal{Z}$ takes z as input. We will consider stand-alone executions, hence z will always be of the form 1^λ, for $\lambda \in \mathbb{N}$. For simplicity, to denote this random variable ensemble we will use $\text{VIEW}_{\Pi,\mathcal{A},\mathcal{Z}}^{P,t,n}$. By $\text{VIEW}_{\Pi,\mathcal{A},\mathcal{Z}}^{t,n}$ we denote the concatenation of the views of all parties. The probability space where these variables are defined depends on the coins of all honest parties, $\mathcal{A}$ and $\mathcal{Z}$.

Next, we consider the complications in the modeling due to the analysis of Bitcoin in the concrete security setting. Both in [29] and [43] a modified version of the standard simulation-based paradigm of [18] is followed, where there exist both a malicious environment and a malicious adversary. In addition, the SoW scheme (called PoW in [29,43]) is modeled in a non black-box way using a random oracle (RO), and the computational power of the adversary is then bounded by limiting the number of queries it can make to the RO per round. Since in this work the SoW scheme is modeled in a black-box way, an alternative approach to bound the adversary's power is needed.

A naïve first approach is to only bound the computational power of $\mathcal{A}$. Unfortunately this will not work for several reasons. Firstly, nothing stops the environment from aiding the adversary, i.e., computing signatures, and then communicating with it through their communication channel or some other subliminal channel. Secondly, even if we bound the *total* number of steps of $\mathcal{A}$, it is not clear how to bound the steps it is taking per round in the model of [18], which we build on. Lastly, another issue arising is that if the adversary is able to send, say, θ messages in each round, it can force each honest party to take $\theta \cdot t_{\text{ver}}$ extra steps per round. If we don't bound θ, then the adversary will be able to launch a DOS attack and spend all the resources the honest parties have[5].

---

[5] This problem is extensively discussed in [3], Section 3.4.

In order to capture these considerations we are going to define a predicate on executions and prove our properties in disjunction with this predicate, i.e., either the property holds or the execution is not good.

Definition 11. *Let $(t_\mathcal{A}, \theta)$-good be a predicate defined on executions in the hybrid setting described above. Then E is $(t_\mathcal{A}, \theta)$-good, where E is one such execution, if*

- *the total number of steps taken by $\mathcal{A}$ and $\mathcal{Z}$ per round is no more than $t_\mathcal{A}$;*[6]
- *the adversary sends at most θ messages per round.*

Finally, we assume the existence of a *common reference string* (CRS), that becomes available to all parties at the start of the execution. This is also implicitly assumed in previous models, where either parties have access to a special "genesis" block at the beginning of the execution [43], or they do not have access to the RO before the beginning of the execution [29].

Definition 12. *Given a predicate Q and bounds $t_\mathcal{A}, \theta, t, n \in \mathbb{N}$, with $t < n$, we say that protocol Π satisfies property Q for n parties assuming the number of corruptions is bounded by t, provided that for all PPT $\mathcal{Z}, \mathcal{A}$, the probability that $Q(\mathrm{VIEW}_{\Pi,\mathcal{A},\mathcal{Z}}^{t,n})$ is false and the execution is $(t_\mathcal{A}, \theta)$-good is negligible in λ.*

4.2   Public Transaction Ledger from Signatures of Work

Next, we take a reduction approach to the underlying cryptographic primitive—SoW, as defined in Sect. 3—to prove the security of the Bitcoin backbone protocol [29]. We start with a description of the protocol based on SoW, and then continue with the security proof.

The Bitcoin Backbone Protocol. The Bitcoin backbone protocol [29], parameterized by functions $V(\cdot), R(\cdot), I(\cdot)$, is an abstraction of the Bitcoin protocol. First, we introduce some notation needed to understand the description of the algorithms, and then cast the protocol making use of our SoW primitive.

We will use the terms *block* and *chain* to refer to tuples of the form $\langle s, x, \sigma \rangle$ and sequences of such tuples, respectively. The rightmost (resp. leftmost) block of chain $\mathcal{C}$ is denoted by $\mathrm{head}(\mathcal{C})$ (resp. $\mathrm{tail}(\mathcal{C})$). Each block contains a seed, data, and a signature denoted by s, x, σ, respectively. As mentioned, all parties have access to a CRS at the beginning of the execution that contains: the public parameter pp of the SoW scheme, a verification key vk generated by $\mathsf{KeyGen}(pp)$, and the key k of the hash functions H, G used later. We will refer to $\langle 0^\lambda, pp\|vk\|k, 0^\lambda \rangle$ as the *genesis* block B_{Gen}. A chain $\mathcal{C} = B_1 \ldots B_m$ is *valid* with respect to the CRS if and only if (i) B_1 is the

---

[6] The adversary cannot use the running time of honest parties that it has corrupted; it is activated instead of them during their turn. Also, note that it is possible to compute this number by counting the number of configurations that $\mathcal{A}$ or $\mathcal{Z}$ are activated per round.

genesis block, (ii) for any two consecutive blocks $\langle s_i, x_i, \sigma_i \rangle, \langle s_{i+1}, x_{i+1}, \sigma_{i+1} \rangle$ it holds that $H_k(s_i, G_k(x_i), \sigma_i) = s_{i+1}$, (iii) each block, besides B_{Gen}, contains a valid SoW, i.e., $\mathsf{Verify}(pp, s_i, x_i, \sigma_i) = \mathsf{true}$, and (iv) the content validation predicate $V(\langle x_1, \ldots, x_m \rangle)$ outputs true. We call $H_k(s_i, G_k(x_i), \sigma_i)$ the *hash of block* B_i and denote it by $H_k(B_i)$. Moreover, we define $H(\mathcal{C})$ to be equal to the hash of the head of chain $\mathcal{C}$.

At each round, each party chooses the longest valid chain amongst the ones it has received and tries to extend it by computing (mining) another valid block. If it succeeds, it diffuses the new block to the network. In more detail, each party will run the Sign procedure, with the message parameter being determined by the input contribution function $I(\cdot)$, and the key parameter being the hash of the last block. We assume that the hardness parameter h is fixed for all executions. Finally, if the party is queried by the environment, it outputs $R(\mathcal{C})$ where $\mathcal{C}$ is the chain selected by the party; the chain reading function $R(\cdot)$ interprets $\mathcal{C}$ differently depending on the higher-level application running on top of the backbone protocol. Each honest party runs for at most $t_{\mathcal{H}}$ steps per round. For a full description of the protocol refer to the full version of the paper

In order to turn the backbone protocol into a protocol realizing a public transaction ledger suitable definitions were given for functions $V(\cdot), R(\cdot), I(\cdot)$ in [29]. We change these definitions slightly as shown in Table 1, to ensure two things: Firstly, that the data contained in the hash chain is encoded with a suffix-free code; this is important to ensure that no collisions occur [9] as we show later. And, secondly, to ensure that any block created by an honest party contains sufficient entropy, thus the adversary will not be able to use blocks that it has precomputed to extend this block. We call the resulting protocol $\Pi_{\mathsf{PL}}^{\mathsf{SoW}}$.

Table 1. The instantiation of functions $I(\cdot), V(\cdot), R(\cdot)$ for protocol $\Pi_{\mathsf{PL}}^{\mathsf{SoW}}$.

Content validation predicate $V(\cdot)$	$V(\cdot)$ is true if its input $\langle x_1, \ldots, x_m \rangle$ is a valid ledger, i.e., it is in $\mathcal{L}$, and each x_i starts with a neutral transaction of the form $r\|i$, where r is a string of length $\log|K|$ and i is the "height" of the respective block
Chain reading function $R(\cdot)$	$R(\cdot)$ returns the contents of the chain if they constitute a valid ledger, otherwise it is undefined
Input contribution function $I(\cdot)$	$I(\cdot)$ returns the largest subsequence of transactions in the input and receive registers that constitute a valid ledger, with respect to the contents of the chain $|C|$ the party already has, preceded by a neutral transaction of the form $\mathsf{KeyGen}(pp)\|\|C\|$

Security Proof. We now prove that $\Pi_{\mathsf{PL}}^{\mathsf{SoW}}$ implements a robust public transaction ledger (Definition 2), assuming the underlying SoW scheme satisfies
Assumption 1 for appropriate parameters, related to the running time of honest
parties and the adversary. First, we formalize this relation.

Let t_{bb} (bb for backbone) be an upper bound on the number of steps needed
to run the code of an honest party in one round, besides the Sign and Verify calls.
By carefully analyzing the backbone protocol one can extract an upper bound
on this value.[7] To aid our presentation, we will use $t'_{\mathcal{A}}$ and $t'_{\mathcal{H}}$ to denote: (i) the
time needed by a RAM machine to simulate one round in the execution of the
Bitcoin protocol, without taking into account calls made to the Sign routine by
the honest parties, and (ii) the minimum number of steps that an honest party
takes running the Sign routine per round, respectively.

$$t'_{\mathcal{A}} = t_{\mathcal{A}} + n \cdot t_{\mathsf{bb}} + \theta t_{\mathsf{ver}} \quad \text{and} \quad t'_{\mathcal{H}} = t_{\mathcal{H}} - t_{\mathsf{bb}} - \theta t_{\mathsf{ver}}$$

It holds that at least $n - t$ (non-corrupted) parties will run the Sign routine for
at least $t'_{\mathcal{H}}$ steps at every round.

In previous works [29,31,43], the security assumptions regarding the computational power of the parties participating in the protocol were twofold: (1)
The total running time of honest parties per round should exceed that of the
adversary, and (2) the rate at which parties produce blocks at each round should
be bounded. More realistically, in our approach the running time of the adversary and the running time of honest parties do not have the same *quality*, as the
adversary may use a superior signing algorithm. To take this into account, we
additionally need to assume that the efficiency of the adversarial signing algorithm, i.e., β, is close to that of the honest parties. Finally, note that if SoW
is close to optimal, i.e., $\alpha(h) \approx \beta t'_{\mathcal{H}}$, and the block generation rate is a lot less
than 1, our assumption holds as long as the honest parties control the majority
of the computational power.

We now state the computational power assumption formally. The second
and the third conditions are similar to the ones already found in previous works,
while the first one is the new condition we introduce regarding the underlying
computational primitive.

Assumption 2 (Computational Power Assumption). *There exist*
$\delta_{\mathsf{SoW}}, \delta_{\mathsf{Steps}}, \delta \in (0,1)$, *such that for sufficiently large* $\lambda \in \mathbb{N}$, *there exists an*
$h \in HP$, *such that:*

- $\alpha(h) \geq (1 - \delta_{\mathsf{SoW}})\beta t'_{\mathcal{H}} > \mathsf{negl}(\lambda)$ *(signatures generation rate gap)*
- $(n - t)t'_{\mathcal{H}}(1 - \delta_{\mathsf{Steps}}) \geq t'_{\mathcal{A}}$ *(steps gap)*
- $\frac{\delta_{\mathsf{Steps}} - \delta_{\mathsf{SoW}}}{2} \geq \delta > \beta(h)(t'_{\mathcal{A}} + nt_{\mathcal{H}})$ *(bounded block generation rate)*

---

[7] Note that t_{bb} depends on the running time of three external functions: $\mathrm{V}(\cdot), \mathrm{I}(\cdot)$
and $\mathrm{R}(\cdot)$. For example, in Bitcoin these functions include the verification of digital
signatures, which would require doing modular exponentiations. In any case t_{bb} is at
least linear in λ.

From now on, we will assume that the hardness parameter used in our protocols, is one satisfying the above conditions.

Remark 3. The better the adversarial signing algorithm may be compared to the honest one, the closer δ_{SoW} is to 0, while the closer the number of adversarial steps $t'_{\mathcal{A}}$ are to that of the honest parties, the closer δ_{Steps} is to 0. Assumption 2 implies, in a quantitative manner, that the better the adversarial signing algorithm, the smaller the computational power of the adversary we can tolerate.

Based now on Assumptions 1 and 2, we can prove that Π_{PL}^{SoW} implements a transaction ledger. Our main technical contribution is showing that an adversary that computes blocks fast in an execution of Π_{PL}^{SoW}, can be used to construct another adversary that breaks the moderate unforgeability property of the SoW scheme. Hence, the rate at which the adversary computes blocks is bounded by the parameters of the MU-TCMA property. After that step, we follow the proving strategy of [29], to prove three blockchain level properties: common prefix, chain quality and chain growth. In order to do that we take advantage of the Successful and Runtime Independence properties of the SoW scheme, to establish a lower bound on the rate of uniquely successful rounds, i.e., rounds that only a single honest party computes a block, which then show to be larger than the rate at which the adversary computes blocks. Our analysis also crucially depends on the collision resistance property of the underlying hash function, to ensure that each chain corresponds to a single history of transactions that cannot be altered in the future. Due to lack of space, we point to the full version of the paper for the detailed analysis.

Theorem 1. *Assuming the existence of a collision-resistant hash function and a SoW scheme that complies with Assumptions 1 and 2, there exists a protocol that implements a robust public transaction ledger except with negligible probability in λ.*

As a "sanity check," we show in the full version of the paper that the Bitcoin SoW scheme we outline there, is secure both in the random oracle and the $\mathcal{F}_{TREE}$ model [43] according to our definitions; moreover, according to the security parameters we obtain for the scheme, the security guarantees we get from our black-box analysis of the Bitcoin backbone are similar to those proved in [29,43].

4.3   Consensus from Signatures of Work

In this section we show how to achieve consensus (a.k.a. Byzantine agreement [38,44]) under exactly the same assumptions used for proving the security of the Bitcoin backbone protocol in Sect. 4.2.

As mentioned earlier, in [29] consensus is achieved under the Honest Majority Assumption by using a proof-of-work construction in a *non-black-box* way, through a mining technique called "2-for-1 PoWs." In more detail, the technique shows how miners can compute proofs of work for two different PoW schemes at the cost of one, while at the same time ensuring that their resources cannot be used in favor of one of the two schemes. However, the security proof for the resulting protocol crucially relies on the fact that each of the bits of the strings output by the random oracle are independently sampled, and thus goes again our stated goal of designing a SoW scheme that does not make such a strong independence assumption.

Here we get rid of this requirement, by showing how blockchain-based consensus can be achieved by only using the security properties we have defined, directly, and without the extra non-black-box machinery used in [29]. This yields the first consensus protocol for honest majority reducible to a SoW primitive in the permissionless setting. The protocol is based on the Bitcoin backbone protocol, and formally specified by providing adequate definitions for the V, R, I functions presented in Sect. 4.2.

First, we define some additional notation and terminology that will be used in the remainder of the section. We will use the terms "input" and "vote" interchangeably, referring to the parties' input to the consensus problem. We will use $header(\langle s, x || vote, \sigma \rangle)$ to denote the "compressed" version of block $\langle s, x || vote, \sigma \rangle$[8], equal to $\langle s, G(x) || vote, \sigma \rangle$. Note that, as defined, the header of any block is of a fixed size. We also extend the definition of our hash function H as applied to headers of blocks. The hash of the header of some block B will be equal to the hash of B, i.e., $H((header(B)) = H(B) = H(s, G(x) || vote, \sigma)$ (note that the header of B provides all the information needed to calculate the hash of B).

We now present a high-level description of the protocol. The basic idea is that during block mining, parties are going to include in their blocks not only their own votes, but also headers of other blocks that they have seen and that *are not* part of their chain. Then, after a predetermined number of rounds, the parties will count the votes "referenced" in a prefix of their chain, including the votes found in the headers of the blocks referenced. In this way, they can take advantage of the robust transaction ledger built in Sect. 4.2. The Persistence property implies that the honest parties will all agree on *which* votes should be counted, while the Liveness property guarantees that the majority of the counted votes come from honest parties.

The reader may wonder about the reason behind honest parties including in their blocks also headers of other blocks that they have seen but that are not part of their chain. It's because, as shown in [29], the adversary is able to add more blocks in the main chain than his ratio of mining power (e.g., using a selfish-mining attack). This does not hold if the honest parties are able to also count off-chain blocks as our protocol does.

---

[8] We augment the block content x with a vote bit. This does not change the results of the analysis of the previous section.

Algorithm 1. The *content validation predicate*. The input is the contents of the blocks of some chain.

```
 1: function V(⟨x₁,...,xₘ⟩)
 2:     D ← new AVL()                                    ▷ Create a new (empty) AVL tree.
 3:     D.add(H(B_Gen))                          ▷ Add the hash of the genesis block on the tree.
 4:     for i = 1, ..., m do
 5:         queue ← references(xᵢ)                    ▷ Add all block references in a queue.
 6:         ⟨r||height⟩ ← queue.top()
 7:         if  height ≠ i then
 8:             return False                          ▷ Check for the correct block "height".
 9:         end if
10:         while queue ≠ ∅ do
11:             ⟨s, G(x)||vote, w⟩ ← queue.top()
12:             if ((D.exists(s)) ∧ Verify(s, G(x)||vote, h, w)) then
13:                 D.add(H(⟨s, G(x)||vote, w⟩))           ▷ Add new entry on the tree.
14:                 queue.pop()
15:             else
16:                 return False                          ▷ If not, the chain is invalid.
17:             end if
18:         end while
19:     end for
20:     return True
21: end function
```

A main technical challenge is to be able to add the block references without making the honest parties' chains grow too large, and at the same time to ensure that the number of honest votes exceeds the adversarial ones. To overcome this challenge, we modify the Sign algorithm so that it is run on the header of the block, i.e., $\mathsf{Sign}(pp, s, G(x)||vote, h)$ and $\mathsf{Verify}(pp, s, G(x)||vote, h, \sigma)$, respectively. This way we are able to verify the validity of a block as a SoW and determine the block's vote by only knowing its header. These are exactly the properties we need for the consensus application.

Moreover, we should be able to tell whether the referenced blocks are "fresh"; that is, the adversary should not be able to reference blocks that it has precomputed and are not related to the genesis block. We achieve this by requiring blockchain contents to have a special structure in order to be considered valid by the content validation predicate $V(\cdot)$ (Algorithm 1). A chain will be *valid* when the referenced blocks on every prefix of the chain form a *tree* that has the genesis block at its root. In order to check this efficiently, we require that the block headers listed in each block are ordered, so that each entry extends some block header found in previous entries of the same or parent blocks.

In more detail, to efficiently check for membership in the hash tree, in line 2 of Algorithm 1 we use an AVL tree. (Any other data structure supporting efficient updates and search would also work.) In line 5 the referenced blocks are extracted and pushed into a queue. We note that during this process it is checked that:

Table 2. The instantiation of functions $I(\cdot), V(\cdot), R(\cdot)$ for protocol $\Pi_{\mathsf{BA}}^{\mathsf{SoW}}$.

Content validation predicate $V(\cdot)$	As defined in Algorithm 1
Chain reading function $R(\cdot)$	$R(\cdot)$ outputs the majority of the votes found in the block headers of the first M blocks of the selected chain
Input contribution function $I(\cdot)$	The input function $I(\cdot)$ maintains state of which blocks have been received, and outputs an input value x that contains (i) the headers of all valid blocks that extend the genesis and are not mentioned in the chain $\mathcal{C}$ that the party is currently extending, (ii) a neutral transaction of the form $\mathsf{KeyGen}(pp)\|\|\mathcal{C}\|$, and (iii) the party's input (i.e., 0 or 1)

(i) the contents of the block have a correct format, i.e., a vote field and list of block headers, (ii) each header in the list is a valid SoW and extends a chain starting from the genesis block, and (iii) that the first reference includes a string r and the height of the block as required in the security analysis of Sect. 4.2 and described in Table 1.

The algorithm runs for L rounds, after which it outputs the majority of the votes found in a prefix of the selected chain, of a predetermined length M. We call the resulting protocol $\Pi_{\mathsf{BA}}^{\mathsf{SoW}}$ ("BA" for Byzantine agreement). A description of the consensus protocol (specifically, the V, R, I functions) is presented in Table 2, and also recall the example in Fig. 1. Note that all parties terminate the protocol simultaneously. For the full proof of the theorem refer to the full version of the paper.

Theorem 2. *Assuming the existence of a collision-resistant hash function and a SoW scheme that complies with Assumptions 1 and 2. Protocol $\Pi_{\mathsf{BA}}^{\mathsf{SoW}}$ solves consensus with overwhelming probability in λ.*

References

1. Alon, N., Goldreich, O., Håstad, J., Peralta, R.: Simple construction of almost k-wise independent random variables. Random Struct. Algorithms **3**(3), 289–304 (1992)
2. Alwen, J., Tackmann, B.: Moderately hard functions: definition, instantiations, and applications. In: Kalai, Y., Reyzin, L. (eds.) TCC 2017. LNCS, vol. 10677, pp. 493–526. Springer, Cham (2017). https://doi.org/10.1007/978-3-319-70500-2_17
3. Andrychowicz, M., Dziembowski, S.: PoW-based distributed cryptography with no trusted setup. In: Gennaro, R., Robshaw, M. (eds.) CRYPTO 2015. LNCS, vol. 9216, pp. 379–399. Springer, Heidelberg (2015). https://doi.org/10.1007/978-3-662-48000-7_19

4. Back, A.: Hashcash-a denial of service counter-measure (2002)
5. Back, A., et al.: Enabling blockchain innovations with pegged sidechains (2014). http://www.opensciencereview.com/papers/123/enablingblockchain-innovations-with-pegged-sidechains
6. Badertscher, C., Maurer, U., Tschudi, D., Zikas, V.: Bitcoin as a transaction ledger: a composable treatment. In: Katz, J., Shacham, H. (eds.) CRYPTO 2017. LNCS, vol. 10401, pp. 324–356. Springer, Cham (2017). https://doi.org/10.1007/978-3-319-63688-7_11
7. Ball, M., Rosen, A., Sabin, M., Vasudevan, P.N.: Proofs of work from worst-case assumptions. In: Shacham, H., Boldyreva, A. (eds.) CRYPTO 2018. LNCS, vol. 10991, pp. 789–819. Springer, Cham (2018). https://doi.org/10.1007/978-3-319-96884-1_26
8. Bellare, M., Desai, A., Jokipii, E., Rogaway, P.: A concrete security treatment of symmetric encryption. In: 38th Annual Symposium on Foundations of Computer Science, FOCS 1997, Miami Beach, Florida, USA, 19–22 October 1997, pp. 394–403 (1997)
9. Bellare, M., Jaeger, J., Len, J.: Better than advertised: improved collision-resistance guarantees for MD-based hash functions. In: Proceedings of the 2017 ACM SIGSAC Conference on Computer and Communications Security, CCS 2017, pp. 891–906. ACM, New York (2017)
10. Bellare, M., Rogaway, P.: Random oracles are practical: a paradigm for designing efficient protocols. In: Proceedings of the 1st ACM Conference on Computer and Communications Security, CCS 1993, Fairfax, Virginia, USA, 3–5 November 1993, pp. 62–73 (1993)
11. Bellare, M., Rogaway, P.: The exact security of digital signatures-how to sign with RSA and rabin. In: Maurer, U. (ed.) EUROCRYPT 1996. LNCS, vol. 1070, pp. 399–416. Springer, Heidelberg (1996). https://doi.org/10.1007/3-540-68339-9_34
12. Ben-Or, M.: Another advantage of free choice: completely asynchronous agreement protocols (extended abstract). In: Probert, R.L., Lynch, N.A., Santoro, N. (eds.) Proceedings of the Second Annual ACM SIGACT-SIGOPS Symposium on Principles of Distributed Computing, Montreal, Quebec, Canada, 17–19 August 1983, pp. 27–30. ACM (1983)
13. Bentov, I., Hub'avcek, P., Moran, T., Nadler, A.: Tortoise and hares consensus: the meshcash framework for incentive-compatible, scalable cryptocurrencies. IACR Cryptology ePrint Archive 2017:300 (2017)
14. Bernstein, D.J., Lange, T.: Non-uniform cracks in the concrete: the power of free precomputation. In: Sako, K., Sarkar, P. (eds.) ASIACRYPT 2013. LNCS, vol. 8270, pp. 321–340. Springer, Heidelberg (2013). https://doi.org/10.1007/978-3-642-42045-0_17
15. Bitansky, N., Goldwasser, S., Jain, A., Paneth, O., Vaikuntanathan, V., Waters, B.: Time-lock puzzles from randomized encodings. In: Sudan, M. (ed.) Proceedings of the 2016 ACM Conference on Innovations in Theoretical Computer Science, Cambridge, MA, USA, 14–16 January 2016, pp. 345–356. ACM (2016)
16. Boneh, D., Bonneau, J., Bünz, B., Fisch, B.: Verifiable delay functions. In: Shacham, H., Boldyreva, A. (eds.) CRYPTO 2018. LNCS, vol. 10991, pp. 757–788. Springer, Cham (2018). https://doi.org/10.1007/978-3-319-96884-1_25
17. Borcherding, M.: Levels of authentication in distributed agreement. In: Babaoğlu, Ö., Marzullo, K. (eds.) WDAG 1996. LNCS, vol. 1151, pp. 40–55. Springer, Heidelberg (1996). https://doi.org/10.1007/3-540-61769-8_4
18. Canetti, R.: Security and composition of multiparty cryptographic protocols. J. Cryptol. **13**(1), 143–202 (2000)

19. Canetti, R., Goldreich, O., Halevi, S.: The random oracle methodology, revisited. J. ACM **51**(4), 557–594 (2004)
20. Dolev, D., Strong, H.R.: Authenticated algorithms for Byzantine agreement. SIAM J. Comput. **12**(4), 656–666 (1983)
21. Douceur, J.R.: The sybil attack. In: Druschel, P., Kaashoek, F., Rowstron, A. (eds.) IPTPS 2002. LNCS, vol. 2429, pp. 251–260. Springer, Heidelberg (2002). https://doi.org/10.1007/3-540-45748-8_24
22. Dwork, C., Lynch, N.A., Stockmeyer, L.J.: Consensus in the presence of partial synchrony. J. ACM **35**(2), 288–323 (1988)
23. Dwork, C., Naor, M.: Pricing via processing or combatting junk mail. In: Brickell, E.F. (ed.) CRYPTO 1992. LNCS, vol. 740, pp. 139–147. Springer, Heidelberg (1993). https://doi.org/10.1007/3-540-48071-4_10
24. Feldman, P., Micali, S.: An optimal probabilistic protocol for synchronous Byzantine agreement. SIAM J. Comput. **26**(4), 873–933 (1997)
25. Fischer, M.J., Lynch, N.A., Paterson, M.: Impossibility of distributed consensus with one faulty process. J. ACM **32**(2), 374–382 (1985)
26. Fitzi, M.: Generalized communication and security models in Byzantine agreement. Ph.D. thesis, ETH Zurich, Zürich, Switzerland (2003)
27. Garay, J.A., Kiayias, A.: SoK: a consensus taxonomy in the blockchain era. IACR Cryptology ePrint Archive 2018:754 (2018)
28. Garay, J.A., Kiayias, A., Leonardos, N.: The bitcoin backbone protocol: analysis and applications. IACR Cryptology ePrint Archive 2014:765 (2014)
29. Garay, J., Kiayias, A., Leonardos, N.: The bitcoin backbone protocol: analysis and applications. In: Oswald, E., Fischlin, M. (eds.) EUROCRYPT 2015. LNCS, vol. 9057, pp. 281–310. Springer, Heidelberg (2015). https://doi.org/10.1007/978-3-662-46803-6_10
30. Garay, J., Kiayias, A., Leonardos, N.: The bitcoin backbone protocol with chains of variable difficulty. In: Katz, J., Shacham, H. (eds.) CRYPTO 2017. LNCS, vol. 10401, pp. 291–323. Springer, Cham (2017). https://doi.org/10.1007/978-3-319-63688-7_10
31. Garay, J.A., Kiayias, A., Leonardos, N., Panagiotakos, G.: Bootstrapping the blockchain, with applications to consensus and fast PKI setup. In: Abdalla, M., Dahab, R. (eds.) PKC 2018. LNCS, vol. 10770, pp. 465–495. Springer, Cham (2018). https://doi.org/10.1007/978-3-319-76581-5_16
32. Garay, J.A., Kiayias, A., Panagiotakos, G.: Consensus from signatures of work. Cryptology ePrint Archive, Report 2017/775 (2017). https://eprint.iacr.org/2017/775
33. Garay, J.A., Kiayias, A., Panagiotakos, G.: Iterated search problems and blockchain security under falsifiable assumptions. Cryptology ePrint Archive, Report 2019/315 (2019). https://eprint.iacr.org/2019/315
34. Garay, J.A., MacKenzie, P., Prabhakaran, M., Yang, K.: Resource fairness and composability of cryptographic protocols. J. Cryptol. **24**(4), 615–658 (2011)
35. Juels, A., Brainard, J.G.: Client puzzles: a cryptographic countermeasure against connection depletion attacks. In: Proceedings of the Network and Distributed System Security Symposium, NDSS 1999, San Diego, California, USA. The Internet Society (1999)
36. Katz, J., Miller, A., Shi, E.: Pseudonymous secure computation from time-lock puzzles. IACR Cryptology ePrint Archive 2014:857 (2014)
37. Kocher, P.C.: Timing attacks on implementations of Diffie-Hellman, RSA, DSS, and other systems. In: Koblitz, N. (ed.) CRYPTO 1996. LNCS, vol. 1109, pp. 104–113. Springer, Heidelberg (1996). https://doi.org/10.1007/3-540-68697-5_9

38. Lamport, L., Shostak, R.E., Pease, M.C.: The Byzantine generals problem. ACM Trans. Program. Lang. Syst. **4**(3), 382–401 (1982)
39. Lewenberg, Y., Sompolinsky, Y., Zohar, A.: Inclusive block chain protocols. In: Böhme, R., Okamoto, T. (eds.) FC 2015. LNCS, vol. 8975, pp. 528–547. Springer, Heidelberg (2015). https://doi.org/10.1007/978-3-662-47854-7_33
40. Nakamoto, S.: Bitcoin: a peer-to-peer electronic cash system (2008). http://bitcoin.org/bitcoin.pdf
41. Okun, M.: Agreement among unacquainted Byzantine generals. In: Fraigniaud, P. (ed.) DISC 2005. LNCS, vol. 3724, pp. 499–500. Springer, Heidelberg (2005). https://doi.org/10.1007/11561927_40
42. Okun, M.: Distributed computing among unacquainted processors in the presence of Byzantine distributed computing among unacquainted processors in the presence of Byzantine failures. Ph.D. thesis, Hebrew University of Jerusalem (2005)
43. Pass, R., Seeman, L., Shelat, A.: Analysis of the blockchain protocol in asynchronous networks. In: Coron, J.-S., Nielsen, J.B. (eds.) EUROCRYPT 2017. LNCS, vol. 10211, pp. 643–673. Springer, Cham (2017). https://doi.org/10.1007/978-3-319-56614-6_22
44. Pease, M.C., Shostak, R.E., Lamport, L.: Reaching agreement in the presence of faults. J. ACM **27**(2), 228–234 (1980)
45. Pfitzmann, B., Waidner, M.: Unconditional Byzantine agreement for any number of faulty processors. In: Finkel, A., Jantzen, M. (eds.) STACS 1992. LNCS, vol. 577, pp. 337–350. Springer, Heidelberg (1992). https://doi.org/10.1007/3-540-55210-3_195
46. Poelstra, A.: On stake and consensus (2015). https://download.wpsoftware.net/bitcoin/pos.pdf
47. Schneider, F.B.: Implementing fault-tolerant services using the state machine approach: a tutorial. ACM Comput. Surv. **22**(4), 299–319 (1990)
48. Sompolinsky, Y., Lewenberg, Y., Zohar, A.: SPECTRE: a fast and scalable cryptocurrency protocol. IACR Cryptology ePrint Archive 2016:1159 (2016)
49. Sompolinsky, Y., Zohar, A.: Secure high-rate transaction processing in bitcoin. In: Böhme, R., Okamoto, T. (eds.) FC 2015. LNCS, vol. 8975, pp. 507–527. Springer, Heidelberg (2015). https://doi.org/10.1007/978-3-662-47854-7_32
50. Stebila, D., Kuppusamy, L., Rangasamy, J., Boyd, C., Gonzalez Nieto, J.: Stronger difficulty notions for client puzzles and denial-of-service-resistant protocols. In: Kiayias, A. (ed.) CT-RSA 2011. LNCS, vol. 6558, pp. 284–301. Springer, Heidelberg (2011). https://doi.org/10.1007/978-3-642-19074-2_19

Faster Homomorphic Encryption is not Enough: Improved Heuristic for Multiplicative Depth Minimization of Boolean Circuits

Pascal Aubry[2(✉)], Sergiu Carpov[1], and Renaud Sirdey[1]

[1] CEA, LIST, Point Courrier 172, 91191 Gif-sur-Yvette Cedex, France
[2] CEA, LIST, 38054 Grenoble Cedex, France
p.aubry@cea.fr

Abstract. In somewhat homomorphic encryption schemes (e.g. B/FV, BGV) the size of ciphertexts and the execution performance of homomorphic operations depends heavily on the multiplicative depth. The multiplicative depth is the maximal number of consecutive multiplications for which the homomorphic encryption scheme was parameterized.

In this work we improve a heuristic for multiplicative depth minimization of Boolean circuits found in the literature. In particular, a new circuit rewriting operator is introduced, the so called cone rewrite operator. The results we obtain using the new method are relevant in terms of accuracy and performance. The multiplicative depths for a benchmark of Boolean circuits is highly improved and the execution time of the new heuristic is significantly lower. The proposed rewrite operator and heuristic are not limited to Boolean circuits, but can also be used for arithmetic circuits.

Keywords: Somewhat homomorphic encryption · Multiplicative depth · Boolean functions · Heuristic

1   Introduction and Related Works

We denote by *encryption scheme* the way to encrypt plaintext messages and to decrypt ciphertexts such that discovering the plaintext message from encrypted data is either computationally very hard or even impossible without a secret. An *homomorphic encryption scheme* (HE) allows some operations to be performed directly in the ciphertext space, i.e. without decrypting ciphertexts. An homomorphic encryption is said to be functionally complete when both addition and multiplication operations are supported. Since the seminal work of Gentry [16], many other simpler and more efficient homomorphic encryption schemes have been proposed [5,6]. A HE scheme with a binary plaintext space allows to execute any Boolean circuit directly over encrypted data.

This work was funded in part under French FUI project ANBLIC.

© Springer Nature Switzerland AG 2020
S. Jarecki (Ed.): CT-RSA 2020, LNCS 12006, pp. 345–363, 2020.
https://doi.org/10.1007/978-3-030-40186-3_15

A common characteristic of HE schemes ciphertexts is the noise component, which is added to the ciphertexts during the encryption for security reasons. Each homomorphic operation applied on ciphertexts increases this noise component. After a predefined number of homomorphic operations, decryption correctness cannot be ensured as the noise component becomes too large to guarantee exact decryption. Usually, the noise growth induced by the multiplication operation is greater than the noise growth induced by addition. This is why in most cases the *multiplicative depth* of Boolean circuits to be evaluated is considered when HE schemes are parametrized. The multiplicative depth is the maximal number of sequential homomorphic multiplications which can be performed on fresh ciphertexts such that once decrypted we retrieve the result of these multiplications. For an equivalent security level, the increase of circuit multiplicative depth implies larger size ciphertexts and by consequence the cost of homomorphic operations increases also.

Several solutions to ciphertext size increase exist. One of them is the ciphertext bootstrapping procedure introduced in [17]. The bootstrapping procedure consists in executing homomorphically the HE scheme decryption algorithm with a noisy ciphertext as input. The noise of the resulting "bootstrapped" ciphertext is lower and independent of the input ciphertext noise. The bootstrapping, being a heavy procedure, is typically applied on many plaintext messages at once after executing as many homomorphic operations as possible. Several works [2,20,22] study the problem of minimizing the number bootstrappings in Boolean circuits.

Further improvements to the bootstrapping were proposed in [11,14] where the bootstrapping procedure is applied after each operation. This procedure is fast (compared to first constructions) but it allows bootstrapping only one message at a time. An optimization problem for fast-bootstrapping schemes is circuit size minimization, a well know problem in the hardware synthesis field. In batched homomorphic applications (i.e. applications executing the same circuit over multiple input data) a trade-off between executing a multiplicative depth-optimized circuit once (on all input data) or executing a size-optimized circuit for each input data element is to be made.

Reducing the multiplicative depth of Boolean circuits is a major impediment in the practical use of somewhat homomorphic encryption. HE scheme parameters increase in size with every multiplicative level. The execution time for the whole Boolean circuit increases accordingly. Many works in the literature treat problems of Boolean circuit optimization for hardware targets or more generally the problem of hardware synthesis. We refer to the open-source software system used for hardware synthesis ABC [3]. It is an open-source environment providing implementations of state-of-the-art circuit optimization algorithms. These algorithms are mainly designed for minimizing circuit area or latency but, currently, none of them is designed for multiplicative depth minimization.

Several works in the cryptographic literature [4] and more specifically the secure multi-party computation (MPC) literature [19,23] focus on the study of Boolean circuits with minimal number of AND gates. The authors of [7] deal with the minimization of the depth of Boolean circuits. This paper presents depth minimization techniques in the context of MPC, with no differentiation between AND and XOR gates. We shall note that several MPC protocols (e.g. GMW [18], SPDZ [13]) would benefit from circuit multiplicative depth minimization when used in high-latency settings.

The authors of the Cingulata toolchain [10] proposed a multi-start priority based heuristic [9] based on multiplicative depth-2 path rewriting operators. These operators decrease locally the multiplicative depth of the circuit. In average, their algorithm managed to lower by more than 3 times the multiplicative depth. Nonetheless, the computational cost of the overall algorithm is very large as the base heuristic is executed several times with different priority functions. None of the proposed priority functions ensures smallest multiplicative depth for all benchmark circuits. Sometimes better results were obtained with a random priority function than with a non-random one.

The heuristic and local circuit rewrite operator described in [9] is the starting point of the current study. We start by recalling the multiplicative depth-2 path rewrite operator from [9] and then we generalize it to cone rewriting operator. Afterwards, we propose an improved heuristic using the cone rewrite operator. Experimental studies show that smaller multiplicative depth circuits and better computational performances are obtained by the new heuristic. We finalize the paper with concluding remarks and give some perspectives for future works.

2   Rewrite Operators

2.1   Preliminary Definitions

We represent a Boolean circuit as a directed acyclic graph $C = (V, E)$ with a set of nodes V and a set of edges E. Circuit nodes represent Boolean functions (gates) and circuit edges are connections between nodes. The set of nodes can be split into 3 independent sub-sets:

- Nodes without a predecessor define circuit inputs. An input can be either a Boolean input variable or a Boolean constant (i.e. logic "0" or logic "1" inputs c_i).
- Nodes without successors (and necessarily with 1 predecessor) define circuit outputs c_o.
- Nodes representing a gate applying a basic Boolean function to the value of its predecessors. The input degree of gates is 2 and the output degree is at least 1. In this work, we suppose that the Boolean circuit is built of AND and XOR operators only. The set {AND,XOR} together with the constant "1" is functionally complete [25]. Any Boolean function can be expressed by these operators.

Let pred : $V \rightarrow 2^V$ and succ : $V \rightarrow 2^V$ be the functions giving the set of predecessors, respectively successors, of a node $v \in V$ in a Boolean circuit C. We denote anc : $V \rightarrow 2^V$ (resp. desc $\rightarrow 2^V$) the functions giving the set of ancestors (resp. descendants) of a node $v \in V$.

The *multiplicative depth* is defined as the number of successively executed AND gates. It influences the parameters of HE schemes which heavily influences their performance. The minimization of the multiplicative depth allows not only to obtain smaller ciphertext sizes but also to minimize the overall execution time of the Boolean circuit. Let us define the function $d : V \rightarrow \{0, 1\}$ which return 1 for AND nodes and zero otherwise. The multiplicative depth is influenced only by nodes $v \in V$ such that $d(v) = 1$.

The *multiplicative depth* of nodes is given by $l : V \rightarrow \mathbb{N}^+$. The *multiplicative depth* of a node is the maximum number of AND gates on any path beginning at an input node and ending at node v. The function l is defined by:

$$l(v) = \begin{cases} 0 & \text{if } |\text{pred}(v)| = 0, \\ \max_{u \in \text{pred}(v)} l(u) + d(v) & \text{otherwise.} \end{cases}$$

The *reverse multiplicative depth* of nodes is given by $r : V \rightarrow \mathbb{N}$. The *reverse multiplicative depth* is the maximum number of AND gates on any path beginning at a successor of v and ending at an output node. The function r is defined by:

$$r(v) = \begin{cases} 0 & \text{if } |\text{succ}(v)| = 0, \\ \max_{u \in \text{succ}(v)} (r(u) + d(u)) & \text{otherwise.} \end{cases}$$

Both l and r can be computed recursively. The overall *multiplicative depth* of a circuit C is the maximal multiplicative depth of its nodes:

$$l^{\max} = \max_{v \in V} l(v) = \max_{v \in V} r(v).$$

A node is said to be *critical* if relation (1) is verified.

$$l(v) + r(v) = l^{\max}, \ v \in V \tag{1}$$

We define the *critical circuit* C^* as the sub-circuit containing all the critical nodes of circuit C. A *critical path* is a path in this circuit and a *critical cone* is a subset of connected *critical nodes* with a common descendant.

The overall multiplicative depth of circuit C is equal to the multiplicative depth of the critical circuit C^*. Decreasing the multiplicative depth of the *critical circuit* is expected to decrease the overall multiplicative depth (and never to increase it).

2.2   Multiplicative Depth-2 Path Rewriting

In this section, we recall the local circuit rewrite operators given in [9] and improve their method by combining these two operators into a single one. The application of these operators allows to reorder circuit gates such that the multiplicative depth is locally reduced. We start by introducing the combined multiplicative depth-2 path rewriting operator and afterwards describe its limitations when applied to arbitrary depth-2 paths.

Let $p = (v_1, U_y, v_t)$ be a path starting and ending with AND gates v_1 and v_t. Between these two gates there is a multi-input XOR[1] gate U_y having inputs v_1 and $y_1, \ldots, y_m$. We denote a_1, a_2 the inputs of node v_1 with $l(a_1) \geq l(a_2)$ and a_t is the input of v_t other than U_y. Refer to the left-hand side of Fig. 1 for an illustration. The Boolean formula of path p is $((a_1 \cdot a_2) \oplus \bigoplus_i y_i) \cdot a_t$.

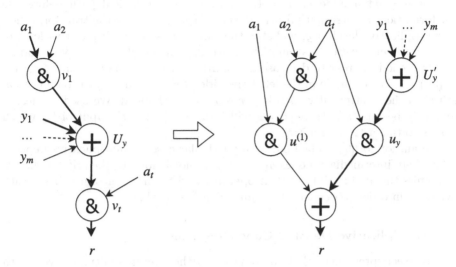

Fig. 1. Rewriting operator for multiplicative depth-2 paths. Bold lines denote critical paths.

The multiplicative depth-2 path rewrite operator we propose rewrites this path as $((a_2 \cdot a_t) \cdot a_1) \oplus (a_t \cdot \bigoplus_i y_i)$. Figure 1 illustrates this transformation. Once applied the multiplicative depth *locally* decreases by one (on the path from a_1 to r) if relation (2) is verified.

$$\min_{u \in \mathrm{pred}(v)} l(u) < l(v_1) - 1, \ v \in \{v_1, v_t\}. \tag{2}$$

Entries y_i can be rearranged in a tree structure of 2-input XOR gates after the rewriting in order to obtain again a 2-input gate circuit. Their order does not matter. Nonetheless, it would be more interesting to reuse existing XORs for lowering the number of newly created gates. Some special cases need more explanation. If path p does not have any XOR node, then the final path reformulation will be $(a_2 \cdot a_3) \cdot a_1$. If U_y is a 2-input XOR gate, then it will disappear in the transformed circuit and the AND gate u_y will have y_1 and a_3 as inputs.

---

[1] For the sake of simplicity and without loss of generality, we have grouped intermediary 2-input XOR gates from the initial circuit into a single multi-input XOR gate.

In the initial path the multiplicative depth of output r is $l(a_1) + 2$. When relation (2) is verified we have $l(a_1) > l(a_2)$ and $l(a_1) > l(a_3)$. After the depth-2 path transformation the multiplicative depth of r becomes:

$$\max(l(a_1), l(y_1), \ldots, l(y_m)) + 1.$$

Suppose that a node y_i, $i = 1, \ldots, m$, is on the critical path before the transformation, i.e. its multiplicative level is $l(y_i) + 1$. After the transformation the multiplicative level of y_i will stay the same, thus the multiplicative level of r does not decrease. *At least* another depth-2 path rewriting on a path ending in u_y is needed in order to decrease the multiplicative depth of r from $l(a_1) + 2$ to $l(a_1) + 1$. For example in the left-hand side of Fig. 1 if node y_1 is on a critical path then the multiplicative depth of r remains unchanged. We used "at least" previously because a path rewriting will be needed for each input of U_y which belongs to the critical circuit.

The authors of [9] studied only the particular case of multiplicative depth-2 paths where intermediary nodes $y_1, \ldots, y_m$ do not belong to the critical circuit. This limits the applicability of their operator and the number of necessary path rewritings in order to decrease the multiplicative depth.

2.3   Multiplicative Depth-2 Cone Rewriting

We have seen previously that in some cases the overall multiplicative depth does not decrease after a single application of the multiplicative depth-2 path operator. In order to address this issue we generalize the multiplicative depth-2 path operator to cones of multiplicative depth 2. We traverse upwards the circuit starting from the sub-set of nodes of $y_1, \ldots, y_m$ which are critical and stop at the first found AND gate. In this way, a cone of multiplicative depth-2 is obtained. In what follows, we introduce a method to rewrite these types of cones such that the overall multiplicative depth decreases.

The cone rewriting operator is equivalent (in terms of multiplicative depth decrease) with the application of the depth-2 path rewriting operator for each critical input of XOR gate U_y (refer to Fig. 1) as it has been stated earlier. A unified rewrite operator allows to perform a single transformation reducing the multiplicative depth and not several rewrite operators for each critical input of U_y. Also, we seek to reduce the number of newly created nodes after the transformation. The new heuristic we propose is based on that cone rewriting operator. We firstly present the transformation for multiplicative depth-2 critical cones and we further generalize it to cones of arbitrary depth.

A multiplicative depth-2 critical cone δ^2 is a Boolean structure ending by an AND gate v_t and beginning with AND gates $v_1, \ldots, v_n$, such that $v_i \in \text{anc}(v_t)$ and $l(v_i) = l(v_t) - 1$, for any $i = 1, \ldots, n$. The left-hand side of Fig. 2 illustrates such a cone. The outputs of $v_1, \ldots, v_n$ are combined by a XOR gate U_y (as previously we merged intermediary 2-input XOR gates into one multi-input gate) and connected to one input of node v_t. Let a_t be the input of v_t other than U_y. We denote $a_1^{(i)}$ and $a_2^{(i)}$ the 2 inputs of v_i such that $l\left(a_1^{(i)}\right) \geq l\left(a_2^{(i)}\right)$ and by

$y_1, \ldots, y_m$ the inputs of XOR gate U_y which are not critical. By construction we have $l(y_i) < l(v_t)$ for any y_i.

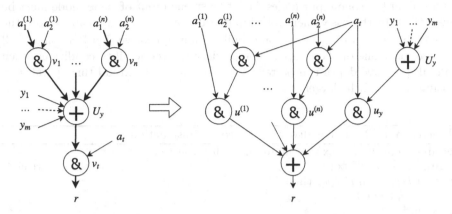

Fig. 2. Rewriting operation for multiplicative depth-2 cone. Bold lines denote critical paths.

Figure 2 illustrates the transformation to be performed in order to decrease the multiplicative depth of cone δ^2. It follows the same idea as the depth-2 path rewriting operator presented earlier. The Boolean formula of the illustrated multiplicative depth-2 cone is:

$$\left(\bigoplus_{i=1}^{n} \left(a_1^{(i)} \cdot a_2^{(i)} \right) \oplus \bigoplus_{i=1}^{m} y_i \right) \cdot a_t.$$

After the rewrite operation the formulation becomes:

$$\left(\bigoplus_{i=1}^{n} \left(a_t \cdot a_2^{(i)} \right) \cdot a_1^{(i)} \right) \oplus \left(a_t \cdot \bigoplus_{i=1}^{m} y_i \right).$$

Thus each AND gate v_i from the input cone is rewritten as $u^{(i)} = \left(a_2^{(i)} \cdot a_t \right) \cdot a_1^{(i)}$ using 2 AND gates and has a smaller multiplicative depth. A new XOR gate U_y' is added for non critical inputs y_i. The output of this gate and a_t are the inputs of a new AND gate u_y. The outputs of gates $u^{(1)}, \ldots, u^{(n)}$ and u_y are finally combined together using a multi-input XOR gate. The multiplicative depth of r is reduced by 1 because the following relations are verified (as a consequence of the cone construction procedure):

$$\min_{u \in \mathrm{pred}(v_k)} l(u) < l(v_t) - 2, \forall v_k, k \in \{1, .., n, t\} \tag{3}$$

The main benefit of multiplicative depth-2 cone rewriting is that the multiplicative depth of r is reduced if relations 3 are verified. A single cone transformation is needed instead of n depth-2 path transformations and only n new AND gates are created (a new gate for each v_i).

2.4   Cone Rewriting

Multiplicative depth-2 cone rewrite operators require that condition (3) is satisfied for all of the cone input nodes, i.e. at least one input of the v_i node must be non-critical. In the case when both inputs of v_i are critical we can explore the cones starting with $a_1^{(i)}$ and $a_2^{(i)}$ and build a multiplicative depth-3 cone. If all inputs of only one of these input cones satisfy the reducibility conditions, then the multiplicative depth can be reduced. We can easily extend this operator to multiplicative depths larger than 3.

Algorithm 1. Recursive algorithm for cone construction.

Require: $minDepth$ – explore up to this multiplicative depth
1: **function** CONEREC(v)   ▷ v – start node
2:     **if** $l(v) = minDepth$ **then**
3:         **return** $\emptyset$
4:     **end if**
5:     $P \leftarrow \{p \in \text{pred}(v) \mid l(p) = l(v) - d(v)\}$
6:     **if** $|P| < 2$ and v is an AND node **then**
7:         **return** $\{v\}$
8:     **else**
9:         $\Delta_r \leftarrow \{\text{CONEREC}(p) \mid p \in P\}$
10:         $\Delta_r \leftarrow \{\delta_r \in \Delta_r \mid \delta_r \neq \emptyset\}$ ▷ reducible input cones
11:         **if** v is an AND node **then**
12:             **if** $|\Delta_r| = 0$ **then**   ▷ no cone is reducible
13:                 **return** $\emptyset$
14:             **else**
15:                 $\delta \leftarrow$ choose randomly from Δ_r
16:             **end if**
17:         **else**   ▷ v is a XOR node
18:             **if** $|\Delta_r| = |P|$ **then**   ▷ critical cones are reducible
19:                 $\delta \leftarrow \bigcup_{\delta_r \in \Delta_r} \delta_r$
20:             **else**
21:                 **return** $\emptyset$
22:             **end if**
23:         **end if**
24:         **return** $\delta \cup \{v\}$
25:     **end if**
26: **end function**

Our cone construction procedure CONEREC is given in Algorithm 1. It recursively explores the set of critical predecessor nodes starting from node v and incrementally constructs a reducible cone (as the procedure output). If the minimal multiplicative depth to explore is reached (line 2) or at least one predecessor of an AND node v is not critical (line 6) then the exploration stops. Otherwise there are two possibilities as a function of node v type:

AND node If at least one predecessor is reducible then the cone corresponding to this predecessor (or a random one if both are reducible) is added to the result, otherwise the exploration is complete.

XOR node If both predecessors are reducible then the respective cones are added to the result, otherwise exploration is also complete.

To summarize, an AND node is reducible if at least one of its ancestor is reducible and a XOR node is reducible if both its ancestors are reducible.

The CONEREC procedure is called on a circuit node v. If the procedure returns an empty set then the cone ending at v cannot be reduced. Otherwise the procedure output represents the cone to be rewritten and it ensures that the multiplicative depth of this cone can be reduced. We use a $minDepth$ value equal to $l(p) + 1$, where p is the non-critical input of node v.

Observe that the CONEREC procedure when applied to the ending node of a reducible multiplicative depth-2 cone will find exactly that cone. In the case when no reducible multiplicative depth-2 cone ending at v exists the CONEREC procedure will return a cone with a multiplicative depth larger than 2. Rewriting such a cone is very similar to the depth-2 cone rewriting method presented previously. Multiplicative depth cone rewriting is a powerful tool for minimizing the multiplicative depth of Boolean circuits.

3 Improved Heuristic

3.1 Overview

In the this section, we introduce the heuristic we have developed to minimize the multiplicative depth of Boolean circuits. In [9] the authors propose a multi-start heuristic based on multiplicative depth-2 path rewriting operator. This operator is the simplest way to locally reduce the multiplicative depth of a Boolean circuit. Their heuristic uses a priority function in order to select the multiplicative depth-2 path to be reduced. None of the priority functions seems to give better results than the others in general as the structure of the Boolean circuit appears to play an important role in which of the priority functions is the most appropriate. Therefore, the authors execute the heuristic with all the priority functions and output the minimal multiplicative depth circuit they obtain. The computational cost of all these executions is therefore high and can be prohibitive for large size Boolean circuits.

The heuristic presented in Algorithm 2 aims at minimizing the multiplicative depth of a given Boolean circuit in a single pass. Indeed, the number of times critical circuits have to be computed is reduced thanks to the proposed cone rewriting operator. At each iteration a set Δ^{min} of cones to minimize is computed. More details about how this set is constructed are given in the next section. If the set Δ^{min} is not empty then the cones from this set are transformed. Afterwards, the multiplicative depths of circuit nodes are updated. If the multiplicative depth of the new circuit becomes smaller then the output circuit C_{out} is updated. Otherwise, a new set Δ^{min} of cones is computed and the process starts over.

Indeed transforming cones from Δ^{min} does not guarantee that the multiplicative depth is globally reduced as some of the performed reductions may affect the inputs of critical AND gates. Thus, additional cone transformations may be applicable after this step. The algorithm terminates when the set Δ^{min} is empty. Other termination criteria (e.g. run time, iteration count, multiplicative depth to achieve) can also be considered.

Algorithm 2. Multiplicative depth minimization heuristic based on cone rewriting.

Require: C – input Boolean circuit
Ensure: C_{out} – multiplicative depth optimized
 1: $C_{out} \leftarrow C$
 2: $\Delta^{min} \leftarrow$ compute reducible cones set
 3: **while** Δ^{min} is not empty **do**
 4:     Rewrite cones from Δ^{min}
 5:     Update multiplicative depth of C
 6:     **if** $l_{\max}(C_{out}) > l_{\max}(C)$ **then**
 7:         $C_{out} \leftarrow C$
 8:     **end if**
 9:     $\Delta^{min} \leftarrow$ compute reducible cones set
10: **end while**

3.2   Cone Selection Method

The goal of the cone selection method is to find a minimal set of cones which rewriting is likely to lead to a decrease in the overall multiplicative depth of the circuit at hand, C. Yet, as we have seen earlier any cone rewriting operator adds new nodes to the circuit. So minimizing the cardinality of the set of cones is also beneficial in order to limit the number of newly created nodes.

Thus, we need to find a minimal size set Δ^{min} of cones such that each critical path in C contains the ending node of at least one cone from this set. Hence, under this condition, we are guaranteed that the overall multiplicative depth decreases after the cones from Δ^{min} are rewritten. This problem is known as the DVD (DAG Vertex Deletion) problem [21] in the combinatorial optimization community. The DVD problem is $\mathcal{UG}$-hard [24], thus efficiently finding an optimal Δ^{min} in the general case is not possible and we therefore propose a heuristic for finding an approximate solution to this problem.

Our cone selection heuristic starts by finding the set Δ of all reducible cones (under the CONEREC procedure). Then, a graph C^{AND} containing the critical AND nodes is built. Two AND nodes are connected in C^{AND} if there is a depth-2 critical path between them in the initial circuit. An AND node is said to be reducible if it is the (topological) last node of a reducible cone (note that for each cone $\delta \in \Delta$, there is a unique terminal AND node in C^{AND}).

We then use the following network-flow inspired Algorithm 3 to find a set of cones Δ^{min} of small cardinality. The algorithm visits all the nodes v of C^{AND} in topological order. Then, for each node v, node flow $f^+(v)$ is computed by setting $f^+(v)$ to the sum of the flows on the input edges of v or to 1 for input nodes. For each output edge of v, we define the edge flow $g^+(v, u)$, $u \in \text{succ}(v)$, as the node flow $f^+(v)$ split equally between node v outputs.

We then perform the same computations on graph C^{AND} where the edge directions have been reversed (i.e. in the initial circuit this corresponds to starting from outputs and traversing C^{AND} in reverse topological order) and compute the ascending node flows $f^-(v)$ for each node v. Afterwards, we compute the node weight $f(v)$ defined as the product between its descending and ascending node flows. The node u with the highest weight is selected and deleted from graph C^{AND}. The critical cone terminating in u is added to Δ^{min}. This process (ascending, descending flow computation, etc.) is repeated until C^{AND} is empty.

Finally, the critical cones from Δ^{min} are then rewritten by means of Algorithm 2.

Algorithm 3. Cone selection algorithm.

Require: C^{AND} – input circuit
Ensure: Δ^{min} – minimal set of cones
 1: **function** COMPFLOW(C) $\triangleright$ C – input circuit
 2:     **for** $v \in C$ in topological order **do**
 3:         **if** v is input **then**
 4:             $f(v) = 1$
 5:         **else**
 6:             $f(v) = \sum_{u \in \text{pred}(v)} g(u, v)$
 7:         **end if**
 8:         $g(v, u) = \frac{f(v)}{|\text{succ}(v)|}$ for all $u \in \text{succ}(v)$
 9:     **end for**
10:     **return** f
11: **end function**
12: $\Delta^{min} \leftarrow \emptyset$
13: **while** C^{AND} is not empty **do**
14:     $f^+ \leftarrow$ COMPFLOW(C^{AND})
15:     Reverse circuit C^{AND} edge directions
16:     $f^- \leftarrow$ COMPFLOW(C^{AND})
17:     $f(v) = f^-(v) \cdot f^+(v)$ for all $v \in C^{AND}$
18:     $u = \arg\max_{v \in C^{AND}} f(v)$
19:     Remove node u from C^{AND}
20:     Add critical cone ending at node u to Δ^{min}
21: **end while**

3.3   Reductions on Non-critical Circuits

In some cases, no more reducible cones are available in the critical circuit C^{AND}. Yet, this does not mean that the multiplicative depth of C cannot be further reduced as we could further rewrite non-critical parts of circuit C. This may decrease the multiplicative depth of certain nodes and, as a consequence, some cones which did not fulfill the reducibility conditions before may become reducible.

For this purpose, we construct a sub-circuit C_v which contains all the ancestors of a node v. Observe that by computing the critical circuit of C_v and applying Algorithm 2 on this circuit we can reduce the multiplicative depth of v. Afterwards, we verify if there are new reducible cones in C and transform them if this is the case.

In this work, we only reduce sub-circuits C_v such that v is a non-critical input of a critical AND node. We could imagine to extend these reductions to other nodes of C. Still, as we wanted to limit the number of created nodes, we did not explore this idea. Nevertheless, we think it is an interesting perspective for further decreasing the multiplicative depth.

4 Experimental Results

We used for our experimentations the Boolean circuits from the EPFL Combinational Benchmark Suite. Three types of combinational circuits are provided: arithmetic, random/control and very large (multi-million gate designs). One can refer to [1] for more details about these benchmarks. In our experiments, only two types of benchmarks are used: 10 arithmetic and 10 random/control circuits. Benchmark circuits have been beforehand optimized and mapped with ABC commands `resyn2` and `map`. `map` command is used to obtain circuit representations with only AND and XOR gates. Table 1 shows the characteristics of the obtained benchmarks after these commands were performed. The same benchmarks were used in [9].

We firstly present results on the minimization of multiplicative depth and afterwards we try to estimate the induced acceleration factor for an homomorphic execution of these circuits.

4.1 Multiplicative Depth Minimization

The heuristic described in previous section was implemented in C. The binary uses ABC as a helper library. We have executed the new heuristic on a single core of an Intel Core™ i7-7600U CPU @ 2.80 GHz. The obtained solutions by the new heuristic and the results from work [9] are shown in Table 2.

The initial characteristics of circuits are also recalled (column "initial"). The notations we use are the multiplicative depth ("×depth"), the number of AND gates ("#AND"), the ratio between the multiplicative depth of the input circuit and the optimized one ("ratio") and the execution time in seconds ("time(s)").

The new heuristic presented in this paper gives better results for almost every circuits in the benchmark. The multiplicative depth is reduced when compared to solutions from [9] for all the arithmetic circuits and lower or equal for all random/control circuits. When the multiplicative depths are equal the number

Table 1. EPFL Combinational Benchmark Suite characteristics after initial optimization with ABC.

Circuit name	#input	#output	×depth	#AND
adder	256	129	255	509
bar	135	128	12	3141
div	128	128	4253	25219
hyp	256	128	24770	120203
log2	32	32	341	20299
max	512	130	204	2832
multiplier	128	128	254	14389
sin	24	25	161	3699
sqrt	128	64	4968	15571
square	64	128	247	9147
arbiter	256	129	87	11839
ctrl	7	26	8	108
cavlc	10	11	16	658
dec	8	256	3	304
i2c	147	142	15	1161
int2float	11	7	15	213
mem_ctrl	1204	1231	110	44795
priority	128	8	203	676
router	60	30	21	167
voter	1001	1	36	4229

of AND nodes is lower for cavlc, priority and router benchmarks. The voter and ctrl circuit are the only case where the multi-start heuristic [9] gives a better result in terms of AND gate count, although the differences are only 27 gates and 1 gate respectively. On the other side, the output circuits found by our heuristic for sin and arbiter contain less AND gates and have a lower multiplicative depth.

In term of computational performance the new heuristic is clearly faster than the multi-start heuristic and this for example allows to minimize the multiplicative depth of complex circuits such as arbiter, div or sqrt in a reasonable time. For the hyp circuit, the minimal multiplicative depth for the circuits has not been found after 48 h of execution. Nonetheless, the multiplicative depth has been significantly reduced compared to the multi-start heuristic.

4.2 Homomorphic Execution Acceleration

In this subsection we study the influence of multiplicative depth minimization on an homomorphic execution of the benchmark circuits. The homomorphic multiplication operation (i.e. the AND gate) is the heaviest one in the somewhat

Table 2. Solutions obtained by the heuristic proposed in this work (column "this work") and best obtained solutions for the multi-start heuristic [9] (combined priority functions, random and non-random ones). Bold font is used to emphasize the best solutions in terms of multiplicative depth as well as number of AND gates. The ratio between multiplicative depths of the input circuit and the optimized one is shown in columns "ratio". The "time" columns represents the execution time for both methods.

Circuit	Initial		This work				Multi-start [9]			
	× depth	#AND	× depth	#AND	ratio	time(s)	× depth	#AND	ratio	time(s)
adder	255	509	**9**	16378	28.3	125	11	1125	23.2	**40.0**
bar	12	3141	**10**	4193	1.2	**0.7**	12	3141	1.0	10.4
div	4253	25219	**532**	190855	8	**3731**	1463	31645	2.9	72000
hyp	24770	120203	**15230**	135433	1.6	172000	24562	120307	1.0	72000
log2	341	20299	**129**	31573	2.6	**94**	141	27362	2.4	14690
max	204	2832	**26**	7666	7.8	**14.5**	27	4660	7.6	1712
multiplier	254	14389	**57**	23059	4.5	**30.7**	59	17942	4.3	14810
sin	161	3699	**74**	5507	2.2	**4.5**	76	5922	2.1	652.8
sqrt	4968	15571	**2084**	321555	2.4	107814	4225	18435	1.2	72000
square	247	9147	**26**	11306	9.3	**12.5**	28	10478	8.8	9840
arbiter	87	11839	**10**	**5183**	8.7	**43**	42	8582	2.1	72000
ctrl	8	108	**5**	110	1.6	0.0	**5**	**109**	1.6	0.0
cavlc	16	658	**9**	**667**	1.8	**0.0**	9	669	1.8	3.8
dec	3	304	**3**	304	1.0	0.0	**3**	304	1.0	0.0
i2c	15	1161	**7**	1213	2.1	**0.1**	8	1185	1.9	7.3
int2float	15	213	**7**	216	2.1	**0.0**	8	216	1.9	0.2
mem_ctrl	110	44795	**40**	54816	2.4	**85.0**	45	49175	2.4	66222
priority	203	676	**102**	**876**	2.0	**0.5**	102	1106	2.0	22.2
router	21	167	**11**	**198**	1.9	0.0	11	204	1.9	0.5
voter	36	4229	**30**	4315	1.2	**1.6**	30	**4288**	1.2	112.4

homomorphic encryption schemes described in the introduction. We start by explaining how we estimate the complexity of a multiplication operation.

An in-depth study of parameters for homomorphic encryption schemes ha been performed in [12]. The authors provide in the appendices several samples of HE scheme parameters for different multiplicative depths, plaintext spaces, etc. Table 3 shows a sample of parameters for the FV scheme [15] and a Boolean plaintext space[2]. A power regression model is fitted onto this data and used afterwards to extrapolate ciphertext size as a function of multiplicative depth. The power regression model we obtain is $y = 1.2215 \cdot x^{2.0179}$ where x is the multiplicative depth and y is the ciphertext size in kBytes. The obtained model is highly accurate (coefficient of determination > 0.9999 and root mean squared

---

[2] We have performed the same estimations for other HE schemes (Yashe and BGV) and similar results, as the ones described in what follows, were obtained.

Table 3. Multiplicative depth and ciphertext size (kBytes) for FV scheme instances from [12].

× depth	2	5	10	20	30
Size	5	31	127	513	1180
Estimated size	4.95	31.4	127.3	515.5	1168.2

relative error $< 1\%$). Estimated ciphertext sizes are given in the third row of Table 3.

Using this model we are able to estimate the size of ciphertext for a given multiplicative depth. The asymptotic complexity of ciphertext multiplication in HE schemes is comparable to the complexity of multiplying arbitrary-precision numbers. One of the best known algorithms for multiplying arbitrary-precision numbers is the Schönhage–Strassen algorithm. It has an asymptotic run-time bit complexity of $O\left(n \cdot \log\left(n\right) \cdot \log\left(\log\left(n\right)\right)\right)$. So, to find the run-time complexity of multiplying 2 HE ciphertexts we use the ciphertext bit-size as n in the above complexity formula. We consider that the run-time complexity of a Boolean circuit HE execution is equal to the number of AND gates in the circuit scaled by the complexity of ciphertext multiplication at the multiplicative depth of this circuit. For example the run-time complexity of the adder circuit is equal to 509 (number of AND gates) multiplied by $\alpha \cdot \log\left(\alpha\right) \cdot \log\left(\log\left(\alpha\right)\right)$, where $\alpha = 8192 \cdot 1.2215 \cdot x^{2.0179}$. Here, the 8192 factor corresponds to the number of bits in 1 kByte (i.e. power regression model units).

We have computed run-time complexities for input circuits, circuits from [9] and circuits generated by the heuristic proposed in this paper. Table 4 shows the ratios between the run-time complexity of optimized circuits and the initial ones. These ratios give an estimation of the acceleration factor between the homomorphic execution of an optimized circuit when compared to the homomorphic execution of the input one. We note that these estimates of the acceleration factor only provide orders of magnitude since other factors (ciphertext key-switch, memory complexity, circuit XOR gates, etc.) which influence the execution time were not considered. Moreover, not considering the size (by consequence memory access times on a real machine) of ciphertexts is advantageous for large ciphertexts (i.e. high multiplicative depth circuits). The third column ("best") provides the best expected run-time acceleration ratio obtained during the execution of the heuristic proposed in this paper. For this purpose, our heuristic returns the circuit with the best run-time complexity instead of the circuit with the lowest depth.

Homomorphic execution times of Boolean circuits depend not only on the multiplicative depth but also on the number of AND gates to be executed. The results presented in Table 4 suggests that circuit optimization heuristics for HE execution should consider other objectives complementary to solely the multiplicative depth. For example, even if the multiplicative depth, 9, of the adder circuit found by our heuristic is smaller compared to the multiplicative depth,

Table 4. Run-time complexity of optimized circuits compared to initial ones, i.e. how many times faster the execution of an optimized circuit will be.

Circuit	Acceleration factor		
	This work		Multi-start [9]
	Lowest depth	Best	
adder	44.92	408.29	**419.52**
bar	**1.17**	**1.17**	1.00
div	10.98	**40.26**	7.66
hyp	**2.47**	**2.47**	1.02
log2	5.19	**5.45**	4.95
max	32.04	**61.03**	48.53
multiplier	15.68	17.46	**18.70**
sin	3.60	**3.80**	3.16
sqrt	0.31	**2.05**	1.19
square	105.81	**109.34**	97.10
arbiter	**257.93**	**257.93**	6.69
ctrl	2.80	2.80	**2.82**
cavlc	**3.51**	**3.51**	3.50
dec	1.00	1.00	1.00
i2c	**5.16**	**5.16**	3.93
int2float	3.93	3.93	3.95
mem_ctrl	**7.43**	**7.43**	6.32
priority	**3.40**	**3.40**	2.69
router	**3.50**	**3.50**	3.40
voter	1.47	1.47	1.47

11, of the same circuit from [9] the acceleration factor of our circuit HE execution is 10 times smaller (44.92 vs 419.52). The homomorphic execution of the optimized circuit will be slower than a circuit with a larger multiplicative depth. The best run-time complexity is obtained by our algorithm for a multiplicative depth of 12. Thus, the ratio is below but close the acceleration factor obtained by [9] (408.29 vs 419.52). For several other examples such as sqrt, div or max, the acceleration factor is much higher when choosing the Boolean circuit with the best acceleration ratio.

5   Conclusion and Perspectives

In this work, we proposed an improved method for minimizing the multiplicative depth of Boolean circuits. In order to do so, we introduced new advanced operators for rewriting critical paths and cones. The presented heuristic is based on these rewriting operators. The multiplicative depth of Boolean circuits is reduced by searching for a set of reducible cones and then rewriting them. This heuristic gives better results compared to the method from [9] in terms of multiplicative depth and execution time. For a majority of benchmarks we have obtained smaller multiplicative depth circuits within a much smaller computational budget. We have also asymptotically demonstrated that, in the context of an homomorphic execution of Boolean circuits, the minimization of multiplicative depth is beneficial only if the number of newly created AND gates is below a threshold.

We recall that Boolean circuit execution is a particular case of ring-based somewhat homomorphic encryption schemes where a binary plaintext space is employed. More generally, somewhat HE schemes allow to execute arbitrary arithmetic circuits (with a predefined multiplicative depth) over a finite field $\mathbb{F}_{p^k}$. The heuristic proposed in this work, as well as the one from [9], can be easily adapted to minimize the multiplicative depth of arithmetic circuits. Many more applications of somewhat HE which use other than binary plaintext space exist and will benefit from these optimization heuristics.

Some further improvements of the heuristic are envisaged as perspectives. For example, the trade-off between reduction of multiplicative depth and the number of newly created AND gates must be made more precise in the context of HE execution. An interesting approach would be to determine a budget of AND gates to be created at each iteration of our algorithm. Indeed, we can compute the cost, in terms of number of newly added AND gates, of a cone transformation before performing it. Another approach would be to try to minimize the number of AND gates between two iteration of our heuristic.

In the literature, some HE implementations of algorithms with a low multiplicative depth and small number of AND gates can be found but with a huge amount of XOR gates [8]. In such circuits, the computational time and the influence on ciphertext noise of XOR gates must be taken into account too. An interesting perspective would be to measure the noise increase incurred by the homomorphic execution of a Boolean circuit, and, to propose heuristics which try to optimize this noise instead of the multiplicative depth (or an estimation of the acceleration factor).

References

1. Amarú, L., Gaillardon, P.E., De Micheli, G.: The EPFL combinational benchmark suite. In: Proceedings of the 24th International Workshop on Logic & Synthesis (IWLS) (2015)
2. Benhamouda, F., Lepoint, T., Mathieu, C., Zhou, H.: Optimization of bootstrapping in circuits. In: SODA, pp. 2423–2433. SIAM (2017)
3. Berkeley Logic Synthesis and Verification Group: ABC: A System for Sequential Synthesis and Verification. Release 30308. http://www.eecs.berkeley.edu/~alanmi/abc/, http://www.eecs.berkeley.edu
4. Boyar, J., Peralta, R.: Concrete multiplicative complexity of symmetric functions. In: Královič, R., Urzyczyn, P. (eds.) MFCS 2006. LNCS, vol. 4162, pp. 179–189. Springer, Heidelberg (2006). https://doi.org/10.1007/11821069_16

5. Brakerski, Z.: Fully homomorphic encryption without modulus switching from classical GapSVP. In: Safavi-Naini, R., Canetti, R. (eds.) CRYPTO 2012. LNCS, vol. 7417, pp. 868–886. Springer, Heidelberg (2012). https://doi.org/10.1007/978-3-642-32009-5_50
6. Brakerski, Z., Gentry, C., Vaikuntanathan, V.: (Leveled) fully homomorphic encryption without bootstrapping. In: Proceedings of the 3rd Innovations in Theoretical Computer Science Conference, ITCS 2012, pp. 309–325 (2012)
7. Buescher, N., Holzer, A., Weber, A., Katzenbeisser, S.: Compiling low depth circuits for practical secure computation. In: Askoxylakis, I., Ioannidis, S., Katsikas, S., Meadows, C. (eds.) ESORICS 2016. LNCS, vol. 9879, pp. 80–98. Springer, Cham (2016). https://doi.org/10.1007/978-3-319-45741-3_5
8. Canteaut, A., et al.: Stream ciphers: a practical solution for efficient homomorphic-ciphertext compression. J. Cryptol. **31**(3), 885–916 (2018)
9. Carpov, S., Aubry, P., Sirdey, R.: A multi-start heuristic for multiplicative depth minimization of boolean circuits. In: Brankovic, L., Ryan, J., Smyth, W.F. (eds.) IWOCA 2017. LNCS, vol. 10765, pp. 275–286. Springer, Cham (2018). https://doi.org/10.1007/978-3-319-78825-8_23
10. Carpov, S., Dubrulle, P., Sirdey, R.: Armadillo: A compilation chain for privacy preserving applications. In: Proceedings of the 3rd International Workshop on Security in Cloud Computing, SCC 2015, pp. 13–19 (2015)
11. Chillotti, I., Gama, N., Georgieva, M., Izabachène, M.: Faster fully homomorphic encryption: bootstrapping in less than 0.1 seconds. In: Cheon, J.H., Takagi, T. (eds.) ASIACRYPT 2016. LNCS, vol. 10031, pp. 3–33. Springer, Heidelberg (2016). https://doi.org/10.1007/978-3-662-53887-6_1
12. Costache, A., Smart, N.P.: Which ring based somewhat homomorphic encryption scheme is best? In: Sako, K. (ed.) CT-RSA 2016. LNCS, vol. 9610, pp. 325–340. Springer, Cham (2016). https://doi.org/10.1007/978-3-319-29485-8_19
13. Damgård, I., Pastro, V., Smart, N., Zakarias, S.: Multiparty computation from somewhat homomorphic encryption. In: Safavi-Naini, R., Canetti, R. (eds.) CRYPTO 2012. LNCS, vol. 7417, pp. 643–662. Springer, Heidelberg (2012). https://doi.org/10.1007/978-3-642-32009-5_38
14. Ducas, L., Micciancio, D.: FHEW: bootstrapping homomorphic encryption in less than a second. In: Oswald, E., Fischlin, M. (eds.) EUROCRYPT 2015. LNCS, vol. 9056, pp. 617–640. Springer, Heidelberg (2015). https://doi.org/10.1007/978-3-662-46800-5_24
15. Fan, J., Vercauteren, F.: Somewhat practical fully homomorphic encryption. IACR Cryptol. ePrint Arch. **2012**, 144 (2012)
16. Gentry, C.: Fully homomorphic encryption using ideal lattices. In: Proceedings of the Forty-first Annual ACM Symposium on Theory of Computing STOC 2009, pp. 169–178 (2009)
17. Gentry, C., Halevi, S., Smart, N.P.: Better bootstrapping in fully homomorphic encryption. In: Fischlin, M., Buchmann, J., Manulis, M. (eds.) PKC 2012. LNCS, vol. 7293, pp. 1–16. Springer, Heidelberg (2012). https://doi.org/10.1007/978-3-642-30057-8_1
18. Goldreich, O., Micali, S., Wigderson, A.: How to play any mental game. In: Proceedings of the Nineteenth Annual ACM Symposium on Theory of Computing, pp. 218–229. ACM (1987)
19. Kolesnikov, V., Sadeghi, A.-R., Schneider, T.: Improved garbled circuit building blocks and applications to auctions and computing minima. In: Garay, J.A., Miyaji, A., Otsuka, A. (eds.) CANS 2009. LNCS, vol. 5888, pp. 1–20. Springer, Heidelberg (2009). https://doi.org/10.1007/978-3-642-10433-6_1

20. Lepoint, T., Paillier, P.: On the minimal number of bootstrappings in homomorphic circuits. In: Adams, A.A., Brenner, M., Smith, M. (eds.) FC 2013. LNCS, vol. 7862, pp. 189–200. Springer, Heidelberg (2013). https://doi.org/10.1007/978-3-642-41320-9_13
21. Paik, D., Reddy, S., Sahni, S.: Deleting vertices to bound path length. IEEE Trans. Comput. **9**, 1091–1096 (1994)
22. Paindavoine, M., Vialla, B.: Minimizing the number of bootstrappings in fully homomorphic encryption. In: Dunkelman, O., Keliher, L. (eds.) SAC 2015. LNCS, vol. 9566, pp. 25–43. Springer, Cham (2016). https://doi.org/10.1007/978-3-319-31301-6_2
23. Schneider, T., Zohner, M.: GMW vs. Yao? efficient secure two-party computation with low depth circuits. In: Sadeghi, A.-R. (ed.) FC 2013. LNCS, vol. 7859, pp. 275–292. Springer, Heidelberg (2013). https://doi.org/10.1007/978-3-642-39884-1_23
24. Svensson, O.: Hardness of vertex deletion and project scheduling. In: Gupta, A., Jansen, K., Rolim, J., Servedio, R. (eds.) APPROX/RANDOM -2012. LNCS, vol. 7408, pp. 301–312. Springer, Heidelberg (2012). https://doi.org/10.1007/978-3-642-32512-0_26
25. Wernick, W.: Complete sets of logical functions. Trans. Am. Math. Soc. **51**(1), 117–132 (1942)

Better Bootstrapping for Approximate Homomorphic Encryption

Kyoohyung Han[1]($\boxtimes$)(iD) and Dohyeong Ki[2](iD)

[1] Coinplug Inc., Seongnam-si, Republic of Korea
kyoohyunghan@coinplug.com
https://kyoohyunghan.github.io
[2] Seoul National University, Seoul, Republic of Korea
wooki7098@snu.ac.kr

Abstract. After Cheon et al. (Asiacrypt' 17) proposed an approximate homomorphic encryption scheme, HEAAN, for operations between encrypted real (or complex) numbers, the scheme is widely used in a variety of fields with needs on privacy-preserving in data analysis. After that, a bootstrapping method for HEAAN is proposed by Cheon et al. (Eurocrypt' 18) with modulus reduction being replaced by a sine function. In this paper, we generalize the Full-RNS variant of HEAAN proposed by Cheon et al. (SAC, 19) to reduce the number of temporary moduli used in key-switching. As a result, our scheme can support more depth computations without bootstrapping while ensuring the same level of security.

We also propose a new polynomial approximation method to evaluate a sine function in an encrypted state, which is specialized for the bootstrapping for HEAAN. Our method considers a ratio between the size of a plaintext and the size of a ciphertext modulus. Consequently, it requires a smaller number of non-scalar multiplications, which is about half of the Chebyshev method.

With our variant of the Full-RNS scheme and a new sine evaluation method, we firstly implement bootstrapping for a Full-RNS variant of approximate homomorphic encryption scheme. Our method enables bootstrapping for a plaintext in the space $\mathbb{C}^{16384}$ to be completed in 52 s while preserving 11 bit precision of each slot.

Keywords: Homomorphic encryption · Bootstrapping

1 Introduction

After the Gentry's first blueprint for a fully homomorphic encryption scheme [9], homomorphic encryption is regarded as one of the most important tools for privacy-preserving. In various applications that need privacy-protection, homomorphic operations between encrypted real number data are necessary. In 2017,

K. Han—This work was done when the first author was in Seoul National University (SNU).

© Springer Nature Switzerland AG 2020
S. Jarecki (Ed.): CT-RSA 2020, LNCS 12006, pp. 364–390, 2020.
https://doi.org/10.1007/978-3-030-40186-3_16

Cheon et al. proposed a new homomorphic encryption scheme for efficient operations between real number data, which is called HEAAN [8]. Through homomorphic operations on encrypted real numbers, a lot of methodologies, such as logistic regression and Genome-side association study (GWAS), can be done in encrypted states [4,11,13,14,16–18].

Recently, a lot of data analysis tools and methods come out into the world, and they become more and more complicated. For examples, machine-learning algorithms such as convolutional neural network (CNN) and deep neural network (DNN) are extremely complicated. Therefore, modern data analysis algorithms require faster homomorphic operations and huge depth, which makes them hard to display their all ability in encrypted states without bootstrapping, since only a limited number of levels is provided by homomorphic encryption schemes. For example, since *nGraph-HE* [3], a deep-learning prediction on encrypted data, does not use bootstrapping, it only supports a limited number of layers. Also, in the case of logistic regression, solutions without bootstrapping [16,18] support only a small number of iterations. For these reasons, importance of efficient homomorphic operations and bootstrapping become greater nowadays.

To solve these problems, a full-RNS variant of HEAAN (HEAAN-RNS) is proposed by Cheon et al. [6]. The key idea of their work comes from the fast base conversion in the full-RNS variant of the FV scheme [2]. By using the conversion, they can expand and reduce basis without going through Chinese Remainder Theorem (CRT) composition process. Since it does not need to use big integer arithmetic, overall speed of its homomorphic operations becomes 4 to 10 times faster than that of the original HEAAN scheme. After that, SEAL includes an implementation of this scheme in version 3.0. To avoid using temporary moduli, they combined the bit-decomposition technique and the RNS-decomposition technique[1]. Recently, an improved method for the fast base conversion is introduced in [11], which requires floating point operations to predict quotient parts.

In the case of the bootstrapping for HEAAN, the first method is proposed by Cheon et al. [7] with modulus reduction being replaced by a sine function. More precisely, they approximate the modulo q operation by the function $\frac{q}{2\pi}\sin(\frac{2\pi x}{q})$. Since HEAAN is an approximate homomorphic encryption scheme, additive noise in bootstrapping, which is not that big, is acceptable. To evaluate the function $\frac{q}{2\pi}\sin(\frac{2\pi x}{q})$ efficiently, they apply the Taylor approximation method to the function in a small range and use double-angle formula. This method requires a small number of homomorphic multiplications, but it needs the degree of an approximate polynomial to be large $(= O(\log Kq))$, when $x/q \in (-K, K)$. After that, improved methods for linear transformation in the bootstrapping are suggested in [5,12], and another method for sine evaluation via the Chebyshev polynomial approximation is proposed in [5]. By using the Chebyshev polynomial approximation, they reduce the degree of an approximate polynomial a lot without increasing the number of homomorphic multiplications much.

---

[1] After version 3.2, they use one temporary modulus instead of bit-decomposition as in [17].

In this paper, to make the bootstrapping more practical, we generalize the Full-RNS variant of HEAAN and improve a sine evaluation method for the bootstrapping. Moreover, we implement our generalized HEAAN-RNS scheme and it's bootstrapping using a newly computed approximate polynomial which is optimized for the bootstrapping.

1.1 Our Contribution

- We suggest a generalized key-switching method for the Full-RNS variant of HEAAN. We combine the RNS-decomposition method in [2] and the temporary modulus technique in [10]. Compared to the HEAAN-RNS scheme, we use a smaller number of temporary moduli while consuming lower complexity. As a result, our scheme requires about half complexity for homomorphic multiplication even with a larger security parameter.
- We propose a method which considers the size of a message in sine evaluation. More precisely, we evaluate a sine function by considering a ratio between the size of a message and the size of a ciphertext modulus. As a result, our method only requires $\mathsf{Max}(\log K + 3 + \frac{1}{K}(\log \epsilon - 1), \log \log q)$ levels, where ϵ is a ratio between the size of a message and the size of a ciphertext modulus. Furthermore, by using cosine instead of sine, we combine double-angle formula for cosine with our approximation method. As a result, the number of non-scalar multiplications is almost reduced by half compared to the previous work [5].
- We put every technique together and implement the bootstrapping for our Full-RNS variant of HEAAN. As a result, our bootstrapping only takes 52 s for a plaintext in the space $\mathbb{C}^{16384}$ while preserving 11 bit precision of each slot.

1.2 Road Map

In Sect. 2, we briefly introduce the Chebyshev approximation, the HEAAN-RNS scheme with its fast base conversion, and the bootstrapping for HEAAN. In Sect. 3, we discuss a generalized key-switching method for the Full-RNS variant of HEAAN. In Sect. 4, we propose a better way of approximating a sine function for the bootstrapping. In Sect. 5, we implement our Full-RNS variant of HEAAN and its bootstrapping, and analyze results of our experiments. We complete the paper with a suggestion of future works for improving the bootstrapping.

2 Preliminary

2.1 Chebyshev Approximation

For the range $[a, b]$ and $n > 0$, choose $n + 1$ Chebyshev points $\{t_i\}_{1 \leq i \leq n+1}$ as

$$t_i = \frac{b + a}{2} + \frac{b - a}{2} \cdot \cos\left(\frac{2i - 1}{2n + 2}\pi\right).$$

For these points, the goal of the Chebyshev approximation of $f(x)$ is to find the degree n polynomial $p_n(t)$ satisfying $p_n(t_i) = f(t_i)$ for all $1 \leq i \leq n+1$. Due to the property of the Chebyshev points, there exists some $\psi_t \in [a, b]$ which makes the following inequality hold for $t \in [a, b]$.

$$||f(t) - p_n(t)|| \leq \frac{|f^{(n+1)}(\psi_t)|}{(n+1)!} \cdot \frac{1}{2^n} \cdot \left(\frac{b-a}{2}\right)^{n+1} \tag{1}$$

Note that the additional term $\frac{1}{2^n}$ is the reason why the Chebyshev method is much better than the Taylor approximation method when the degree n is large.

2.2   Full-RNS HEAAN

In this section, we introduce the fast base conversion in [2] and the HEAAN-RNS scheme in [6]. By using the fast base conversion which does not require CRT decomposition, we can keep ciphertexts of the HEAAN-RNS scheme in residue number systems (RNS) throughout homomorphic operations.

Fast Base Conversion. In the HEAAN-RNS scheme, a RNS representation

$$[a]_{\mathcal{C}} = (a^{(0)}, \ldots, a^{(\ell-1)}) \in \mathbb{Z}_{q_0} \times \cdots \times \mathbb{Z}_{q_{\ell-1}}$$

of an integer a with respect to $\mathbb{Z}_Q$ can be easily converted into its RNS representation with respect to $\mathbb{Z}_P$ by the equation

$$\text{Conv}_{\mathcal{C} \to \mathcal{B}}([a]_{\mathcal{C}}) = \left(\sum_{j=0}^{\ell-1} [a^{(j)} \cdot \hat{q}_j^{-1}]_{q_j} \cdot \hat{q}_j \pmod{p_i}\right)_{0 \leq i < k},$$

where $\hat{q}_j = \prod_{j' \neq j} q_{j'} \in \mathbb{Z}$, $P = \prod_{i=0}^{k} p_i$ and $Q = \prod_{j=0}^{l-1} q_j$. Since $a + Qe \in \mathbb{Z}_P$ for some small e is given as a result of this conversion, it includes the noise which can be ignored in the case of the HEAAN-RNS scheme. Even though the effect of this noise is negligible, we can reduce its size further by adapting the algorithms introduced in [11].

In [6], authors introduce two algorithms called ModUp and ModDown to expand and to reduce a modulus space, respectively (Algorithm 1 and 2 in [6]):

$$\text{ModUp}_{\mathcal{C} \to \mathcal{D}}(\cdot) : \prod_{j=0}^{\ell-1} R_{q_j} \to \prod_{i=0}^{k-1} R_{p_i} \times \prod_{j=0}^{\ell-1} R_{q_j}$$

$$: [a]_{\mathcal{C}} \to (\text{Conv}_{\mathcal{C} \to \mathcal{B}}([a]_{\mathcal{C}}), [a]_{\mathcal{C}}),$$

$$\text{ModDown}_{\mathcal{D} \to \mathcal{C}}(\cdot) : \prod_{i=0}^{k-1} R_{p_i} \times \prod_{j=0}^{\ell-1} R_{q_j} \to \prod_{j=0}^{\ell-1} R_{q_j}$$

$$: ([a]_{\mathcal{B}}, [b]_{\mathcal{C}}) \to ([b]_{\mathcal{C}} - \text{Conv}_{\mathcal{B} \to \mathcal{C}}([a]_{\mathcal{B}})) \cdot [P^{-1}]_{\mathcal{C}},$$

where $\mathcal{D} = \{p_0, \ldots, p_{k-1}, q_0, \ldots, q_{\ell-1}\}$, $\mathcal{B} = \{p_0, \ldots, p_{k-1}\}$, $\mathcal{C} = \{q_0, \ldots, q_{\ell-1}\}$, and $P = \prod_{i=0}^{k-1} p_i$. Note that ModUp expands the modulus space of a from $\mathcal{C}$ to $\mathcal{D}$, and ModDown reverts the modulus space of a to the original and divide its value further by $P = \prod p_i$. These algorithms are used for modulus switching before and after key-switching, respectively.

Scheme Description. In this section, K is a $(2N)$-th cyclotomic field $\mathbb{Q}[X]/(X^N+1)$ and R is its ring of integers $(= \mathbb{Z}[X]/(X^N+1))$ for a power-of-two integer N. The residue ring modulo an integer q is denoted by $R_q = R/qR$.

<u>Setup</u>$(q, L, \eta; 1^\lambda)$. As a base integer q, a number of levels L, a bit precision η, and a security parameter λ are given as inputs, we choose the followings according to them.

- A power-of-two integer N.
- A secret key distribution χ_{key}, an encryption key distribution χ_{enc}, and an error distribution χ_{err} over R.
- A basis $\mathcal{D} = \{p_0, \ldots, p_{k-1}, q_0, q_1, \ldots, q_L\}$ for which $q_j/q \in (1 - 2^{-\eta}, 1 + 2^{-\eta})$ for $1 \leq j \leq L$.

Next, we let $\mathcal{B} = \{p_0, \ldots, p_{k-1}\}$, $\mathcal{C}_\ell = \{q_0, \ldots, q_\ell\}$, and $\mathcal{D}_\ell = \mathcal{B} \cup \mathcal{C}_\ell$ for $0 \leq \ell \leq L$. Also, we let $P = \prod_{i=0}^{k-1} p_i$, $Q = \prod_{j=0}^L q_j$, $\hat{p}_i = \prod_{0 \leq i' < k, i' \neq i} p_{i'}$ for $0 \leq i < k$, and $\hat{q}_{\ell,j} = \prod_{0 \leq j' \leq \ell, j' \neq j} q_{j'}$ for $0 \leq j \leq \ell \leq L$. As the last step of Setup, we compute the followings.

- $[\hat{p}_i]_{q_j}$ and $[\hat{p}_i^{-1}]_{p_i}$ for $0 \leq i < k$, $0 \leq j \leq L$.
- $[P^{-1}]_{q_j} = \left(\prod_{i=0}^{k-1} p_i\right)^{-1} \pmod{q_j}$ for $0 \leq j \leq L$.
- $[\hat{q}_{\ell,j}]_{p_i}$ and $[\hat{q}_{\ell,j}^{-1}]_{q_j}$ for $0 \leq i < k$, $0 \leq j \leq \ell \leq L$.

<u>KSGen</u>(s_1, s_2). Sample $(a'^{(0)}, \ldots, a'^{(k+L)}) \leftarrow U\left(\prod_{i=0}^{k-1} R_{p_i} \times \prod_{j=0}^L R_{q_j}\right)$ and an error $e' \leftarrow \chi_{\text{err}}$ first. With secret polynomials $s_1, s_2 \in R$ given as inputs, compute the switching key swk by

$$\left(\text{swk}^{(0)} = (b'^{(0)}, a'^{(0)}), \ldots, \text{swk}^{(k+L)} = (b'^{(k+L)}, a'^{(k+L)})\right) \in \prod_{i=0}^{k-1} R_{p_i}^2 \times \prod_{j=0}^L R_{q_j}^2,$$

where $b'^{(i)} \leftarrow -a'^{(i)} \cdot s_2 + e' \pmod{p_i}$ for $0 \leq i < k$ and $b'^{(k+j)} \leftarrow -a'^{(k+j)} \cdot s_2 + [P]_{q_j} \cdot s_1 + e' \pmod{q_j}$ for $0 \leq j \leq L$.

<u>KeyGen</u>. First, sample $s \leftarrow \chi_{\text{key}}$ and set the secret key as $\text{sk} \leftarrow (1, s)$ and the evaluation key as $\text{evk} \leftarrow \text{KSGen}(s^2, s)$. Next, sample $(a^{(0)}, \ldots, a^{(L)}) \leftarrow U\left(\prod_{j=0}^L R_{q_j}\right)$ and $e \leftarrow \chi_{\text{err}}$ and set the public key as

$$\text{pk} \leftarrow \left(\text{pk}^{(j)} = (b^{(j)}, a^{(j)}) \in R_{q_j}^2\right)_{0 \leq j \leq L},$$

where $b^{(j)} \leftarrow -a^{(j)} \cdot s + e \pmod{q_j}$ for $0 \leq j \leq L$.

$\underline{\mathsf{Enc}_{\mathsf{pk}}(m)}$. First, sample $v \leftarrow \chi_{\mathsf{enc}}$ and $e_0, e_1 \leftarrow \chi_{\mathsf{err}}$. With a plaintext $m \in R$ given as a input, obtain the ciphertext $\mathsf{ct} = \left(\mathsf{ct}^{(j)}\right)_{0 \leq j \leq L} \in \prod_{j=0}^{L} R_{q_j}^2$, where $\mathsf{ct}^{(j)} \leftarrow v \cdot \mathsf{pk}^{(j)} + (m + e_0, e_1) \pmod{q_j}$ for $0 \leq j \leq L$.

$\underline{\mathsf{Dec}_{\mathsf{sk}}(\mathsf{ct})}$. Given a ciphertext $\mathsf{ct} = \left(\mathsf{ct}^{(j)}\right)_{0 \leq j \leq \ell} \in \prod_{j=0}^{\ell} R_{q_j}^2$, compute $\langle \mathsf{ct}^{(0)}, \mathsf{sk} \rangle$ $\pmod{q_0}$.

$\underline{\mathsf{Add}(\mathsf{ct}, \mathsf{ct}')}$. Given two ciphertexts $\mathsf{ct} = \left(\mathsf{ct}^{(0)}, \ldots, \mathsf{ct}^{(\ell)}\right), \mathsf{ct}' = \left(\mathsf{ct}'^{(0)}, \ldots, \mathsf{ct}'^{(\ell)}\right) \in \prod_{j=0}^{\ell} R_{q_j}^2$, obtain the ciphertext $\mathsf{ct}_{\mathsf{add}} = \left(\mathsf{ct}_{\mathsf{add}}^{(j)}\right)_{0 \leq j \leq \ell}$, where $\mathsf{ct}_{\mathsf{add}}^{(j)} \leftarrow \mathsf{ct}^{(j)} + \mathsf{ct}'^{(j)} \pmod{q_j}$ for $0 \leq j \leq \ell$.

$\underline{\mathsf{Mult}_{\mathsf{evk}}(\mathsf{ct}, \mathsf{ct}')}$. Given two ciphertexts $\mathsf{ct} = \left(\mathsf{ct}^{(j)} = (c_0^{(j)}, c_1^{(j)})\right)_{0 \leq j \leq \ell}$ and $\mathsf{ct}' = \left(\mathsf{ct}'^{(j)} = (c_0'^{(j)}, c_1'^{(j)})\right)_{0 \leq j \leq \ell}$, perform the following computations in turn and obtain the ciphertext $\mathsf{ct}_{\mathsf{mult}} \in \prod_{j=0}^{\ell} R_{q_j}^2$.

- $d_0^{(j)} \leftarrow c_0^{(j)} c_0'^{(j)} \pmod{q_j}$, $d_1^{(j)} \leftarrow c_0^{(j)} c_1'^{(j)} + c_1^{(j)} c_0'^{(j)} \pmod{q_j}$, and $d_2^{(j)} \leftarrow c_1^{(j)} c_1'^{(j)} \pmod{q_j}$ for $0 \leq j \leq \ell$.
- $\mathsf{ModUp}_{\mathcal{C}_\ell \to \mathcal{D}_\ell}(d_2^{(0)}, \ldots, d_2^{(\ell)}) = (\tilde{d}_2^{(0)}, \ldots, \tilde{d}_2^{(k-1)}, d_2^{(0)}, \ldots, d_2^{(\ell)})$.
- $\tilde{\mathsf{ct}} = (\tilde{\mathsf{ct}}^{(0)} = (\tilde{c}_0^{(0)}, \tilde{c}_1^{(0)}), \ldots, \tilde{\mathsf{ct}}^{(k+\ell)} = (\tilde{c}_0^{(k+\ell)}, \tilde{c}_1^{(k+\ell)})) \in \prod_{i=0}^{k-1} R_{p_i}^2 \times \prod_{j=0}^{\ell} R_{q_j}^2$, where $\tilde{\mathsf{ct}}^{(i)} = \tilde{d}_2^{(i)} \cdot \mathsf{evk}^{(i)} \pmod{p_i}$ and $\tilde{\mathsf{ct}}^{(k+j)} = d_2^{(j)} \cdot \mathsf{evk}^{(k+j)} \pmod{q_j}$ for $0 \leq i < k, 0 \leq j \leq \ell$.
- $\left(\hat{c}_0^{(0)}, \ldots, \hat{c}_0^{(\ell)}\right) \leftarrow \mathsf{ModDown}_{\mathcal{D}_\ell \to \mathcal{C}_\ell}\left(\tilde{c}_0^{(0)}, \ldots, \tilde{c}_0^{(k+\ell)}\right)$ and $\left(\hat{c}_1^{(0)}, \ldots, \hat{c}_1^{(\ell)}\right) \leftarrow \mathsf{ModDown}_{\mathcal{D}_\ell \to \mathcal{C}_\ell}\left(\tilde{c}_1^{(0)}, \ldots, \tilde{c}_1^{(k+\ell)}\right)$.
- $\mathsf{ct}_{\mathsf{mult}} = (\mathsf{ct}_{\mathsf{mult}}^{(j)})_{0 \leq j \leq \ell}$, where $\mathsf{ct}_{\mathsf{mult}}^{(j)} \leftarrow (\hat{c}_0^{(j)} + d_0^{(j)}, \hat{c}_1^{(j)} + d_1^{(j)}) \pmod{q_j}$ for $0 \leq j \leq \ell$.

$\underline{\mathsf{RS}(\mathsf{ct})}$. Given a ciphertext $\mathsf{ct} = \left(\mathsf{ct}^{(j)} = (c_0^{(j)}, c_1^{(j)})\right)_{0 \leq j \leq \ell} \in \prod_{j=0}^{\ell} R_{q_j}^2$, compute the ciphertext $\mathsf{ct}' \leftarrow \left(\mathsf{ct}'^{(j)} = (c_0'^{(j)}, c_1'^{(j)})\right)_{0 \leq j \leq \ell-1} \in \prod_{j=0}^{\ell-1} R_{q_j}^2$, where $c_i'^{(j)} \leftarrow q_\ell^{-1} \cdot \left(c_i^{(j)} - c_i^{(\ell)}\right) \pmod{q_j}$ for $i = 0, 1$ and $0 \leq j < \ell$.

2.3   Bootstrapping for HEAAN

In this section, we briefly describe the overall process of the bootstrapping for HEAAN suggested in [7], and the improvements introduced in [5,12]. As in the previous section, we let $R = \mathbb{Z}[X]/(X^N + 1)$ for a power-of-two integer N and $R_q = R/qR$. For $a \in \mathbb{Z}_q$, assign a the unique integer, which is equivalent to a $\pmod{q}$ and is contained in $\mathbb{Z} \cap (-q/2, q/2]$, and denote it by $[a]_q$. Extend this definition to R_q by applying it component-wisely.

Let ct be a ciphertext of $m(X)$ relative to the secret key sk and the ciphertext modulus q. Note that $m(X) = [\langle \mathsf{ct}, \mathsf{sk} \rangle]_q$. The goal of the bootstrapping is to find an encryption of $m(X)$ with a bigger ciphertext modulus. In other words, we hope to find ct' and a modulus $Q > q$ satisfying $m(X) = [\langle \mathsf{ct}', \mathsf{sk} \rangle]_Q$. The overall process can be divided into four steps; Modulus Raising, Coefficients to Slots, Sine Evaluation and Slots to Coefficients.

Modulus Raising. Consider a polynomial $t(X) = \langle \mathsf{ct}, \mathsf{sk} \rangle$ of $\deg < N$. Under the assumption that the message m is much smaller than the ciphertext modulus q, $t(X)$ can be represented as $t(X) = qI(X) + m(X)$, where $I(X) \in R$ and all the coefficients of I are bounded by a constant K which is determined by the secret key distribution of the scheme. If we choose $Q_0 \gg q$, then it follows that $t(X) = [\langle \mathsf{ct}, \mathsf{sk} \rangle]_{Q_0}$. Therefore, ct can be regarded as an encryption of $t(X)$ with respect to the modulus Q_0.

Coefficients to Slots. Before introducing about this step, we need to recall encoding and decoding procedures of HEAAN. Let ξ be a primitive $2N$-th root of unity and $\xi_i = \xi^{5i}$ for $0 \le i < N/2$. Since 5 has the order $N/2$ modulo $2N$ and spans $\mathbb{Z}_{2N}^*$ with -1, $\{\xi_i, \bar{\xi}_i : 0 \le i < N/2\}$ is the set of all primitive $2N$-th roots of unity. Now, we can define a decoding map $\tau : \mathbb{R}[X]/(X^N + 1) \to \mathbb{C}^{N/2}$ by $\tau(m(X)) = (m(\xi_j))_{0 \le j < N/2}$. We say $m(X)$ has values $m(\xi_0), \cdots, m(\xi_{\frac{N}{2}-1})$ in its slots or $m(X)$ is the plaintext of $(m(\xi_j))_{0 \le j < N/2}$ in this case. If we identifying each element $m(X) = m_0 + m_1 X + \cdots + m_{N-1} X^{N-1}$ of $\mathbb{R}[X]/(X^N + 1)$ with $\mathbf{m} = (m_0, \cdots, m_{N-1}) \in \mathbb{R}^N$, the decoding map can be considered as a linear transformation from $\mathbb{R}^N$ to $\mathbb{C}^{N/2}$, which is characterized by the matrix

$$
\mathbf{U} = \begin{pmatrix} 1 & \xi_0 & \xi_0^2 & \cdots & \xi_0^{N-1} \\ 1 & \xi_1 & \xi_1^2 & \cdots & \xi_1^{N-1} \\ \vdots & \vdots & \vdots & \ddots & \vdots \\ 1 & \xi_{\frac{N}{2}-1} & \xi_{\frac{N}{2}-1}^2 & \cdots & \xi_{\frac{N}{2}-1}^{N-1} \end{pmatrix}.
$$

With this identification, the decoding process can be simply written as $\mathbf{m} \mapsto \mathbf{U} \cdot \mathbf{m}$ for $\mathbf{m} \in \mathbb{R}^N$. Moreover, an encoding map is just an inverse map of the decoding map, and it can be checked that the encoding process can be written as $\mathbf{z} \mapsto \frac{1}{N}(\bar{\mathbf{U}}^T \mathbf{z} + \mathbf{U}^T \bar{\mathbf{z}})$ for $\mathbf{z} \in \mathbb{C}^{N/2}$.

Given a polynomial $t(X) = t_0 + t_1 X + \cdots + t_{N-1} X^{N-1}$ from the previous step, this step aims to get the ciphertext whose corresponding plaintext has values $t_0, \cdots, t_{N-1}$ in its slots. Since each plaintext can have at most $N/2$ values, it is impossible that just one plaintext has those values. Thus, we will find two ciphertexts that correspond to plaintexts of the vectors $\mathbf{z_1} = (t_0, \cdots, t_{\frac{N}{2}-1})$ and $\mathbf{z_2} = (t_{\frac{N}{2}}, \cdots, t_{N-1})$, respectively.

Let $\mathbf{z} = \tau(t) \in \mathbb{C}^{N/2}$ be the vector that corresponds to the ciphertext ct. If we divide the matrix $\mathbf{U}$ into following two square matrices

$$
\mathbf{V} = \begin{pmatrix} 1 & \xi_0 & \cdots & \xi_0^{\frac{N}{2}-1} \\ 1 & \xi_1 & \cdots & \xi_1^{\frac{N}{2}-1} \\ \vdots & \vdots & \ddots & \vdots \\ 1 & \xi_{\frac{N}{2}-1} & \cdots & \xi_{\frac{N}{2}-1}^{\frac{N}{2}-1} \end{pmatrix} \quad \text{and} \quad \mathbf{W} = \begin{pmatrix} \xi_0^{\frac{N}{2}} & \xi_0^{\frac{N}{2}+1} & \cdots & \xi_0^{N-1} \\ \xi_1^{\frac{N}{2}} & \xi_1^{\frac{N}{2}+1} & \cdots & \xi_1^{N-1} \\ \vdots & \vdots & \ddots & \vdots \\ \xi_{\frac{N}{2}-1}^{\frac{N}{2}} & \xi_{\frac{N}{2}-1}^{\frac{N}{2}+1} & \cdots & \xi_{\frac{N}{2}-1}^{N-1} \end{pmatrix},
$$

it follows that $\mathbf{z_1} = \frac{1}{N}(\bar{\mathbf{V}}^T\mathbf{z}+\mathbf{V}^T\bar{\mathbf{z}})$ and $\mathbf{z_2} = \frac{1}{N}(\bar{\mathbf{W}}^T\mathbf{z}+\mathbf{W}^T\bar{\mathbf{z}})$. These equations mean that $\mathbf{z_1}$ and $\mathbf{z_2}$ can be obtained by applying linear transformations to $\mathbf{z}$, and thus we can also get corresponding ciphertexts by applying the same linear transformations homomorphically to ct.

Sine Evaluation. This step is the hardest part of the bootstrapping for HEAAN. This step aims to perform the function $f(t) = [t]_q$ homomorphically. More precisely, given two ciphertexts ct_1 and ct_2 corresponding to $\mathbf{z_1}$ and $\mathbf{z_2}$, respectively, we hope to obtain ciphertexts corresponding to the plaintexts of $\mathbf{z_1'} = (m_0, \cdots, m_{\frac{N}{2}-1})$ and $\mathbf{z_2'} = (m_{\frac{N}{2}}, \cdots, m_{N-1})$, where $t_j = qI_j + m_j$ for $0 \le j < N$, by applying the function f to ct_1 and ct_2. However, the problem is that the function f is hard to approximate by a polynomial. Therefore, the function $g(t) = \frac{q}{2\pi} \sin(\frac{2\pi t}{q})$ is used as an approximation of f. Since t can be represented as $t = qI + m$, where $|I| < K$ and $m \ll q$, the difference between $f(t)$ and $g(t)$ is given as

$$
|f(t) - g(t)| = \frac{q}{2\pi}\left| \frac{2\pi m}{q} - \sin(\frac{2\pi m}{q}) \right| \le \frac{q}{2\pi} \cdot \frac{1}{6} \left| \frac{2\pi m}{q} \right|^3,
$$

which is small enough due to $m \ll q$. Also, since g is a smooth function, it is easier to approximate it by a polynomial. For these reasons, the sine function g is a good approximation of the modulus reduction function f, and the main interest of this step becomes how to approximate g by a polynomial.

The ways to approximate g by a polynomial differ in previous works [5,7]. In [7], to evaluate $\sin(t)$, they first scale down t by a power of two to make it locate close enough to the origin, and they use the Taylor polynomial approximation for the evaluation of sine in a small interval around the origin. After that, they compute the original sine value at t by using double angle formula. On the other hand, in [5], they use the Chebyshev polynomial approximation instead of the Taylor approximation.

Slots to Coefficients. This is the final step, and it is just a reverse process of Coefficients to Slots. Given two ciphertexts ct_1' and ct_2' corresponding to $\mathbf{z_1'} = (m_0, \cdots, m_{\frac{N}{2}-1})$ and $\mathbf{z_2'} = (m_{\frac{N}{2}}, \cdots, m_{N-1})$, respectively, the goal of this step is to find the ciphertext whose plaintext is $m(X) = m_0 + m_1 X + \cdots + m_{N-1}X^{N-1}$.

If we let $\mathbf{z}' = \tau(m)$, it follows that $\mathbf{z}' = \mathbf{U}m = \mathbf{V}\mathbf{z}_1' + \mathbf{W}\mathbf{z}_2'$. Therefore, we can get the ciphertext that we want by taking the same linear combination homomorphically to ct_1' and ct_2'. As a result, through the bootstrapping process, we can get a ciphertext ct' which is an encryption of $m(X)$ relative to a ciphertext modulus Q, which is smaller than Q_0, but much bigger enough than q.

Remark 1. Improved linear transformation. Applying linear transformation to a ciphertext with n slots originally requires $O(n)$ homomorphic operations, and it can be improved a lot by using special structure of the matrix $\mathbf{U}$ [5,12]. In [5,12], they decompose the linear transformation part (including "Coefficients to Slots" and "Slots to Coefficients") and reduce the complexity to $O(r \log_r n)$ while consuming $O(\log_r n)$ depth.

3   Full-RNS Variant of HEAAN

Before starting this section, we note that we use the same notation as in Sect. 2. In the HEAAN-RNS scheme, since the decomposition methods are not used for key-switching, it only requires one evaluation key for key-switching. Also, since $P = \prod_{i=0}^{k} p_i$ should be much bigger than $Q = \prod_{j=0}^{L-1} q_j$ to effectively reduce the size of noise added through key-switching, k, which indicates the number of temporary moduli, should be $\simeq L^2$. On the other hand, SEAL (v 3.3) uses one temporary modulus and the RNS-decomposition technique, which will be introduced later, to perform key-switching. In other words, they set the number of temporary moduli k to 1.

Using large k ($k \simeq L$) and small k ($k = 1$) has pros and cons, respectively. By using large $k \simeq L$, we only need one evaluation key for key-switching, and thus smaller complexity for key-switching is required. However, since the security of the scheme depends on the largest ciphertext modulus $\prod_{i=0}^{k-1} p_i \cdot \prod_{i=0}^{L} q_i$, the bit size of $\prod_{i=0}^{k-1} p_i \cdot \prod_{i=0}^{L} q_i$ should be fixed when we assume the same security level. Therefore, using large $k \simeq L$ forces us to use a smaller number of q_j's, and it follows that the less depth computations are supported by the scheme.

As noted above, there is a trade-off between the complexity of key-switching and the number of levels supported by the scheme. Therefore, in many cases, it is better to choose an appropriate value of k between 1 and L rather than using extremely large k ($k \simeq L$) and extremely small k ($k = 1$). However, the HEAAN-RNS scheme and SEAL (v 3.3) only support $k \simeq L$ and $k = 1$ case, respectively. Hence, the main goal of our scheme is to propose a generalized HEAAN-RNS scheme, which also includes the scheme of SEAL (v.3.3), to make it possible to use optimal k for each situation.

---

[2] In practice, p_i's are chosen to have maximum sizes within the word size (<64 bits). On the other hand, sizes of q_j's are depend on the precision of applications, and usually they are 40–45 bits.

Full-RNS Decomposition. First, we will introduce the RNS-decomposition technique in [2]. The RNS-decomposition method can be represented by the following equations:

$$\text{RNS-Decomp}_{\mathcal{C}}(a(x)) = ([a(x) \cdot \hat{q}_0^{-1}]_{q_0}, \ldots, [a(x) \cdot \hat{q}_L^{-1}]_{q_L}) \in R^{L+1}$$

$$\text{RNS-Power}_{\mathcal{C}}(b(x)) = (b(x) \cdot \hat{q}_0, b(x) \cdot \hat{q}_1, \ldots, b(x) \cdot \hat{q}_L) \in R^{L+1},$$

where $\mathcal{C} = \{q_0, q_1, \ldots, q_L\}$, $\hat{q}_i = \prod_{j \neq i} q_j$ and $a(x), b(x) \in R$. Here, $f(x) \cdot c$ indicates the multiplication between each coefficient of polynomial $f(x)$ and c. Those functions work similarly as the bit-decomposition and power of two technique:

$$a(x) \cdot b(x) = \langle \text{RNS-Decomp}_{\mathcal{C}}(a(x)), \text{RNS-Power}_{\mathcal{C}}(b(x)) \rangle \in R_Q,$$

where $Q = \prod_{i=0}^{L} q_i$. Since the sizes of coefficients of $\text{RNS-Decomp}_{\mathcal{C}}(a(x))$ are less than $\max_{0 \leq i \leq L}(q_i) \ll Q$, the functions can be used for key-switching. More precisely, we can replace the multiplication of $a(x)$ and $s(x)^2$ in key-switching with

$$\langle \text{RNS-Decomp}_{\mathcal{C}}(a(x)), \text{RNS-Power}_{\mathcal{C}}(s(x)^2) + \text{Enc}_{s(x)}(0) \rangle \mod Q.$$

Here, we add the term $\text{Enc}_{s(x)}(0)$ not to reveal information on $s(x)^2$. In this method, since both vectors have length $L+1$, the complexity of the inner product is quadratic to L, which is not favorable. Furthermore, the noise growth through key-switching is about $\|e_{\text{fresh}}\| \cdot \max(\|q_i\|)$, which is quite large compared to the size of a plaintext.

Overview of Idea. To solve those problems stated above, we will reduce the length of the vectors and control the noise growth using temporary moduli[3]. First, we use the partial products $\{Q_j\}_{0 \leq j < \text{dnum}} = \{\prod_{i=j\alpha}^{(j+1)\alpha - 1} q_i\}_{0 \leq j < \text{dnum}}$, where $\alpha = (L+1)/\text{dnum}$ for a pre-fixed parameter dnum, instead of using $\{q_i\}_{0 \leq i \leq L}$ in the RNS-decomposition. Then, it follows that $P = \prod_{i=0}^{k-1} p_i$ only needs to be bigger than $\max_{0 \leq j < \text{dnum}} Q_j$ to effectively reduce the size of noise added through key-switching. Therefore, we can set the number of temporary moduli k to α. In addition, we apply the fast base conversion to avoid CRT composition in re-linearization (key-switching in multiplication). The brief sketch about our re-linearization method can be represented as follows:

0. For $k = (L+1)/\text{dnum}$, set an evaluation key as $\text{evk} = \text{RNS-Power}_{\mathcal{C}'}(s(x)^2) + \text{Enc}_{s(x)}(0) \mod PQ$, where $P = \prod_{i=0}^{k-1} p_i$, $Q = \prod_{i=0}^{L} q_i$ and $\mathcal{C}' = \{Q_j\}_{0 \leq j < \text{dnum}}$.

---

[3] In the case of SEAL v3.2, they use the bit-decomposition technique with the RNS-decomposition to reduce the noise growth. But, this method also has a drawback. It increases the length of the public key vector for key-switching further, which is directly related to the complexity of the process.

1. For a given ciphertext $(c(x), b(x), a(x))$ such that $c(x) + b(x) \cdot s(x) + a(x) \cdot s(x)^2 = m + e \mod Q$, we compute

$$(b'(x), a'(x)) = \langle \text{RNS-Decomp}_{\mathcal{C}'}(a(x)), \text{evk} \rangle \mod PQ.$$

   In $\text{RNS-Decomp}_{\mathcal{C}'}(a(x)) \mod PQ$ computation, we avoid CRT composition using the fast base conversion.
2. We apply modulus-switching using ModDown to reduce the size of noise:

$$(b''(x), a''(x)) = \lfloor (b'(x), a'(x))/P \rceil \mod Q$$

3. Return $(c(x) + b''(x), b(x) + a''(x))$.

Since we just make differences in key-switching, we only need to revise $\text{KSGen}(s_1, s_2)$, KeyGen, and $\text{Mult}_{\text{evk}}(\text{ct}, \text{ct}')$ in Sect. 2. We remark that the case of $\text{dnum} = 1$ is same as the HEAAN-RNS scheme. Using larger dnum increases the number of evaluation keys, but it reduces the dimension of ring or increases the parameter L when we assume the same level of security. Detailed comparisons with HEAAN-RNS and SEAL (v.3.3) are contained in Sect. 3.2.

3.1   Scheme Description

We will focus on differences between the HEAAN-RNS scheme and ours. The other parts which are not mentioned in this section are same as the scheme in Sect. 2. In this section, let

$$\mathcal{C}' = \{Q_j\}_{0 \le j < \text{dnum}} = \left[\prod_{i=j\alpha}^{(j+1)\alpha - 1} q_i \right]_{0 \le j < \text{dnum}}$$

for a given integer $\text{dnum} > 0$ and $\alpha = (L+1)/\text{dnum}$. Also, let $\hat{Q}_j = \prod_{i \neq j} Q_i$ and $P = \prod_{i=0}^{k-1} p_i$, and assume $|P| \ge \max_{0 \le j < \text{dnum}}(Q_j)$.

$\text{KSGen}(s_1, s_2, \text{dnum})$. For given secret polynomials $s_1, s_2 \in R$, sample $(a'^{(0)}, \ldots, a'^{(k+L)}) \leftarrow U\left(\prod_{i=0}^{k-1} R_{p_i} \times \prod_{j=0}^{L} R_{q_j}\right)$ and sample an error $e' \leftarrow \chi_{\text{err}}$. Output switching keys $\{\text{swk}_j\}_{0 \le j < \text{dnum}}$ as

$$\left(\text{swk}_j^{(0)} = (b'^{(0)}_j, a'^{(0)}_j), \ldots, \text{swk}_j^{(k+L)} = (b'^{(k+L)}_j, a'^{(k+L)}_j) \right) \in \prod_{i=0}^{k-1} R_{p_i}^2 \times \prod_{i=0}^{L} R_{q_i}^2,$$

where $b'^{(i)}_j \leftarrow -a'^{(i)}_j \cdot s_2 + e' \pmod{p_i}$ for $0 \le i < k$ and $b'^{(k+i)}_j \leftarrow -a'^{(k+i)}_j \cdot s_2 + [P]_{q_i} \cdot [\hat{Q}_j]_{q_i} \cdot s_1 + e' \pmod{q_i}$ for $0 \le i \le L$.

KeyGen. First, sample $s \leftarrow \chi_{\text{key}}$ and set a secret key as $\text{sk} \leftarrow (1, s)$ and evaluation keys as $\{\text{evk}_i\}_{0 \le j < \text{dnum}} \leftarrow \text{KSGen}(s^2, s)$.

   For convenience, let $\mathcal{C}_i = \{q_0, \ldots, q_i\}$, $\mathcal{C}'_i = \{q_{i\alpha}, \ldots, q_{((i+1)\alpha - 1)}\}$ and let $\mathcal{D}_i = (\cup_{0 \le j < i} \mathcal{C}'_j) \cup \{p_0, \ldots, p_{k-1}\}$.

$\underline{\text{Mult}_{\text{evk}}(\text{ct}, \text{ct}')}$. Given two ciphertexts $\text{ct} = \left(\text{ct}^{(j)} = (c_0^{(j)}, c_1^{(j)})\right)_{0 \le j \le \ell}$ and $\text{ct}' = \left(\text{ct}'^{(j)} = (c_0'^{(j)}, c_1'^{(j)})\right)_{0 \le j \le \ell}$, perform the followings and return the ciphertext $\text{ct}_{\text{mult}} \in \prod_{j=0}^{\ell} R_{q_j}^2$.

1. For $0 \le j \le \ell$, compute

$$d_0^{(j)} \leftarrow c_0^{(j)} c_0'^{(j)} \pmod{q_j},$$
$$d_1^{(j)} \leftarrow c_0^{(j)} c_1'^{(j)} + c_1^{(j)} c_0'^{(j)} \pmod{q_j},$$
$$d_2^{(j)} \leftarrow c_1^{(j)} c_1'^{(j)} \pmod{q_j}.$$

2. RNS-Decompose:
   2-1. Zero-padding and Split: Let $\beta = \lceil (\ell+1)/\alpha \rceil$,

$$d'^{(i)}_{2,j} = \begin{cases} d_2^{(j\alpha+i)} \cdot [Q']_{q_{j\alpha+i}} & \text{if } j\alpha + i \le \ell \\ 0 & \text{otherwise} \end{cases}$$

   for $0 \le i < \alpha$, $0 \le j < \beta$ and $Q' = \prod_{i=\ell+1}^{\alpha\beta-1} q_i$.
   2-2. RNS-Decompose:

$$d'^{(i)}_{2,j} \leftarrow d'^{(i)}_{2,j} \cdot [\hat{Q}_j^{-1}]_{q_{j\alpha+i}}$$

   for $0 \le i < \alpha$ and $0 \le j < \beta$ with $j\alpha + i \le \ell$.
3. Modulus-Raise: compute $d_{2,j} = \text{ModUp}_{\mathcal{C}'_j \to \mathcal{D}_\beta}(d'_{2,j})$.
4. Inner Product: compute

$$\tilde{\text{ct}} = (\tilde{\text{ct}}^{(0)} = (\tilde{c}_0^{(0)}, \tilde{c}_1^{(0)}), \ldots, \tilde{\text{ct}}^{(k+\ell)} = (\tilde{c}_0^{(k+\ell)}, \tilde{c}_1^{(k+\ell)})) \in \prod_{i=0}^{k-1} R_{p_i}^2 \times \prod_{j=0}^{\ell} R_{q_j}^2,$$

where $\tilde{\text{ct}}^{(i)} = \sum_{j=0}^{\beta-1} \tilde{d}_{2,j}^{(i)} \cdot \text{evk}_j^{(i)} \pmod{p_i}$ for $0 \le i < k$ and $\tilde{\text{ct}}^{(k+i)} = \sum_{j=0}^{\beta-1} \tilde{d}_{2,j}^{(k+i)} \cdot \text{evk}_j^{(k+i)} \pmod{q_i}$ for $0 \le i < \alpha\beta$.
5. Modulus-Down: compute

$$\left(\hat{c}_0^{(0)}, \ldots, \hat{c}_0^{(\ell)}\right) \leftarrow \text{ModDown}_{\mathcal{D}_\beta \to \mathcal{C}_\ell}\left(\tilde{c}_0^{(0)}, \ldots, \tilde{c}_0^{(k+\alpha\beta-1)}\right),$$
$$\left(\hat{c}_1^{(0)}, \ldots, \hat{c}_1^{(\ell)}\right) \leftarrow \text{ModDown}_{\mathcal{D}_\beta \to \mathcal{C}_\ell}\left(\tilde{c}_1^{(0)}, \ldots, \tilde{c}_1^{(k+\alpha\beta-1)}\right).$$

6. Output the ciphertext $\text{ct}_{\text{mult}} = (\text{ct}_{\text{mult}}^{(j)})_{0 \le j \le \ell}$, where $\text{ct}_{\text{mult}}^{(j)} \leftarrow (\hat{c}_0^{(j)} + d_0^{(j)}, \hat{c}_1^{(j)} + d_1^{(j)}) \pmod{q_j}$ for $0 \le j \le \ell$.

Figure 1 shows the overall process of our multiplication algorithm from Step 2 to Step 4, which are the key parts of our algorithm. The gray area in Fig. 1 indicates temporary moduli $\{p_0, p_1, \ldots, p_{k-1}\}$.

Remark 2 (Correctness). The correctness of our scheme is directly followed from the correctness of ModUp, ModDown, RNS-Decomp, RNS-Power. Detailed proof for the correctness and noise growth is contained in Appendix.

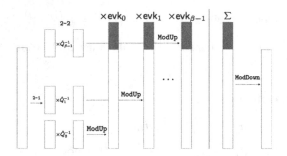

Fig. 1. Overview of our algorithm from Step 2 to Step 5.

Remark 3 (Security). In our scheme, we change the key generation and the multiplication algorithm. A way of generating evaluation key is changed, but our evaluation key is also an addition of information about secret key and encryption of zero. Therefore, the security of our scheme is also based on the Ring-LWE problem (same as HEAAN-RNS).

Remark 4 (Quantization and Batching). The homomorphic encryption scheme in Sect. 2 is described for a plaintext $m(x) \in R = \mathbb{Z}[X]/(X^N + 1)$. To encrypt a vector of complex numbers, we use an isomorphism between $\mathbb{C}^{N/2}$ and $\mathbb{R}[X]/(X^N + 1)$. Choose an isomorphism $\rho : \mathbb{C}^{N/2} \to \mathbb{R}[X]/(X^N + 1)$ and define $\mathsf{Encode}(m, \Delta) = \lceil \Delta \cdot \rho^{-1}(m) \rfloor = m(x) \in R$. The HEAAN-RNS scheme uses the same scaling factor Δ for all levels by letting $q_i \simeq \Delta$ for all i. However, this method yields additional noise in Rescale process. Therefore, as in SEAL, we use different scaling factors for each level, which means that we just regard Rescale process as dividing scaling factor by q_i.

3.2 Comparison

In this section, we compare our scheme with HEAAN-RNS and SEAL v3.3. We note that the HEAAN-RNS scheme and SEAL v3.3 can be regarded as (dnum = 1)-case and (dnum = L+1)-case of our scheme, respectively. Before comparison, we check the complexity of the homomorphic multiplication of our scheme.

Complexity of Homomorphic Multiplication. We assume that ciphertexts and evaluation keys are NTT (Number-theoretic transform) transformed in advance. Also, we only count the number of multiplications in $\mathbb{Z}_{p_i}$ or $\mathbb{Z}_{q_i}$ for complexity. The followings are complexity for each step of the multiplication. Here, we ignore the last step which only needs some additions (no multiplication).

Step 1. This step computes tensor product of two vectors (with length 2). By performing in the sense of Karatsuba multiplication, it only requires 3 polynomial multiplications. Therefore, this step requires 3 Hadamard multiplications and 3 inverse NTT transformations for each ring R_{q_i}[4]: $3(\ell + 1)N + 3(\ell + 1)N \log N$.

---

[4] In Step 1, inverse NTT transform is needed for the next step (modulus raising).

Step 2-2. Step 2-1 just rearranges the vector and zero-padding, which requires no complexity, and the multiplications in Step 2-1 can be merged into the multiplications in Step 2-2. Hence, we can ignore this part. In Step 2-2, ℓ modulus multiplications are needed: $\ell \cdot N$.

Step 3. ModUp requires $n(m - n)$ multiplications for input vector size n and output vector size m. Hence, the complexity for $\text{ModUp}_{\mathcal{C}_j \to \mathcal{D}_\beta}$ is $\alpha(\alpha\beta + k - \alpha)$. Since we have to perform it β times for each coefficient, the total complexity is $\alpha\beta(\alpha\beta + k - \alpha)N$.

Step 4. This step can be divided into the following 4 sub-steps:

1. NTT transform: we need to apply the NTT algorithm for each $\{\tilde{d}_{2,j}^{(i)}\}_{0 \leq i < k+\alpha\beta}$:
$$\beta(k + \alpha\beta)N \log N$$

2. Hadamard Mult.: $2\beta(k + \alpha\beta)N$.
3. Summation: there is no multiplication.
4. Inverse NTT transform: $(k + \alpha\beta)N \log N$.

Step 5. ModDown requires $m(n - m)$ multiplications for input vector size n and output vector size m. Hence, the complexity for $\text{ModDown}_{\mathcal{D}_\beta \to \mathcal{C}_\ell}$ is $\ell(k + \alpha\beta - \ell)$. Since we have to perform it for each coefficient, the total complexity of this step is $\ell \cdot (k + \alpha\beta - \ell) \cdot N$.

If we set k to α and regard all parameters except k as constants, the total complexity of the multiplication is approximately

$$N\left\{(l + \log N) \cdot k + (2 + \log N)l^2 \cdot (1/k)\right\} + (\text{constant})$$

since $\alpha \cdot \beta \simeq l$. Hence, the total complexity is minimized when $k = \sqrt{\frac{2+\log N}{1+\log N}} \cdot l$. As a result, from the point of view of complexity, it is better to use proper k between 1 and l.

Comparison. Now, we compare various parameter sets for our scheme, which have different k values. First, Table 1 shows parameter sets with various k for fixed ℓ, and corresponding complexity of homomorphic multiplication. Note that the first and the last row correspond to SEAL v3.3 and HEAAN-RNS scheme[5], respectively. Suppose that we need an optimal parameter set which has $\ell+1 = 24$ and ensures $\lambda > 128$. Then, it is better to set k to 8, which requires the lowest complexity among the values that ensure enough security.

Table 2 shows parameter sets with various ℓ and k for fixed $\log_2 PQ$, and corresponding complexity of homomorphic multiplication. As seen from the table, HEAAN-RNS can only support depth 14 computation without bootstrapping. On the other hand, SEAL v3.3 supports depth 28 computation, but it requires the largest complexity and public key size for re-linearization. Since there is a trade-off between supported depth computation and complexity, it is important to choose proper k depending on the situation that we are in.

---

[5] Here, SEAL v.3.3 and HEAAN-RNS indicate the scheme corresponding to each paper and library.

Table 1. Complexity of homomorphic multiplication for fixed ℓ.

N	$\ell+1$	k	$\log_2 PQ$	λ	$\log_2(\text{Total Complexity})$	
65536	24	1	1136	147.6	29.67	SEAL v3.3
		2	1181	144.2	28.94	
		3	1227	141.3	28.60	
		4	1272	138.3	28.39	
		6	1363	132.4	28.16	
		8	1454	128.3	28.05	$\lambda > 128$
		12	1635	118.2	27.96	
		24	2180	94.3	27.97	HEAAN-RNS

Table 2. Complexity of homomorphic multiplication for fixed $\log_2 PQ$ and λ.

N	$\log_2 PQ$	λ	$\ell+1$	k	$\log_2(\text{Total Complexity})$	
65536	1450	133.7	15	15	27.13	HEAAN-RNS
			20	10	27.64	
			24	6	28.16	
			27	3	28.88	
			29	1	30.17	SEAL v3.3

4   Better Homomorphic Sine Evaluation

As mentioned in Sect. 2.3, the key part of the bootstrapping for HEAAN is a homomorphic evaluation of a sine function. In other words, the way to approximate a sine function by a polynomial is important in the bootstrapping for HEAAN. Also, all the previous works [5,7] can be simply represented by

$$[t]_q \simeq \frac{q}{2\pi} \sin(\tfrac{2\pi}{q} t) \simeq p(t)$$

for some suitable polynomial $p(t) \in \mathbb{R}[X]$, and the difference between those works [5,7] occurs in the step of approximating a sine function by a polynomial.

Recall that an input value t can be represented as $t = qI + m$ for some $|I| < K$ and $m \ll q$. Hence, $\frac{t}{q}$ locates close enough to some integer, and it is the reason why the first approximation of the modulus operation with the sine function is reasonable. However, all the previous works [5,7] do not use this property in the second approximation. In other words, they just find a polynomial that approximates a sine function well in a global sense. Therefore, there is a room for finding a better approximate polynomial $p(t)$ based on the property.

From now on, by scaling and shifting t, we approximate $\cos(2\pi t)$ instead of $\sin(\frac{2\pi t}{q})$. This enables us to use the hybrid method that combines polynomial approximation and double angle formula. Now, the condition for an input t changes to $t \in \cup_{i=-K+1}^{K-1} I_i$, where $I_i = [i - \tfrac{1}{4} - \epsilon, i - \tfrac{1}{4} + \epsilon]$.

4.1   Our Method

When a sufficiently smooth function is estimated by an interpolation polynomial, an error, difference between a real value and an estimated value, can be simply represented due to the following theorem.

Theorem 1 (polynomial interpolation). *Let f be a function in $C^{n+1}[a,b]$ and p_n be a polynomial of degree $\leq n$ that interpolates the function f at $n+1$ distinct points $t_0, t_1, \cdots, t_n \in [a,b]$, i.e. $p_n(t_i) = f(t_i)$ for all $0 \leq i \leq n$. Then, for each $t \in [a,b]$, there exists a point $\psi_t \in [a,b]$ such that*

$$f(t) - p_n(t) = \frac{f^{(n+1)}(\psi_t)}{(n+1)!} \cdot \prod_{i=0}^{n}(t - t_i). \tag{2}$$

Let $p_n(t)$ be the interpolation polynomial of degree $\leq n$ that interpolates $\cos(2\pi t)$ at $n+1$ distinct points. Then, the error bound between $\cos(2\pi t)$ and $p_n(t)$ can be computed through Eq. 2. Even though the term $\frac{f^{(n+1)}(\psi_t)}{(n+1)!}$ in Eq. 2 is hard to be estimated exactly, it is bounded by the constant when f is $\cos(2\pi t)$. Thus, the error bound of polynomial approximation mainly depends on the other term

$$w(t) = \prod_{i=0}^{n}(t - t_i)$$

for pre-determined $t_0, t_1, \ldots, t_n \in [a,b]$ which are called *nodes*. Therefore, we need to choose $\{t_i\}_{1 \leq i \leq n}$ appropriately to minimize the maximum value of $w(t)$ in a specified domain of t. In the case of the Chebyshev method, the nodes are chosen by $t_i = \frac{b+a}{2} + \frac{b-a}{2} \cdot \cos(\frac{2i-1}{2n+2}\pi)$ for $1 \leq i \leq n+1$ in the range $[a,b]$, and these nodes make the upper bound of $w(t)$ in the whole interval $\frac{1}{2^n} \cdot (\frac{b-a}{2})^{n+1}$ (which is $(\frac{b-a}{2})^{n+1}$ in the case of the Taylor approximation).

Although the Chebyshev method gives fairly good error bound in a global sense, it is not appropriate for our purpose because it does not consider the condition that t is near one of the points. Therefore, we focus on the bound of $w(t)$ for $t \in \cup_{i=-K+1}^{K-1} I_i$, where $I_i = [i - \frac{1}{4} - \epsilon, i - \frac{1}{4} + \epsilon]$, and propose a better method for this setting.

Our Optimized Nodes. We choose nodes as the Chebyshev method in each interval $I_i = [i - \frac{1}{4} - \epsilon, i - \frac{1}{4} + \epsilon]$ for all $-K < i < K$. More precisely, in the interval I_i, we choose d_i nodes $t_{i,j} = i - \frac{1}{4} + \epsilon \cdot \cos\left(\frac{2j-1}{2d_i}\pi\right)$ for $1 \leq j \leq d_i$. Let $n = \sum d_i - 1$ and p_n be the polynomial of degree $\leq n$ that interpolates the function $\cos(2\pi t)$ at $n+1$ distinct points $t_{i,j}$ ($-K < i < K, 1 \leq j \leq d_i$). In other words, p_n satisfies the following equation:

$$p_n(t_{i,j}) = \cos(2\pi t_{i,j}) \quad \text{for } -K < i < K, 1 \leq j \leq d_i$$

Then, as in Eq. 1, we can deduce the following upper bound of $||w(t)||$:

$$||w(t)|| \leq \frac{1}{2^{d_i-1}} \cdot \epsilon^{d_i} \cdot \prod_{j=1}^{K-1-i} (j+\epsilon)^{d_{i+j}} \cdot \prod_{j=1}^{K-1+i} (j+\epsilon)^{d_{i-j}},$$

when $t \in I_i = [i - \frac{1}{4} - \epsilon, i - \frac{1}{4} + \epsilon]$. Therefore, $||\cos(2\pi t) - p_n(t)|| = O(\epsilon^{d_i})$ on I_i, which means that the error bound decreases as ϵ, representing the ratio between the size of a message and the size of a ciphertext modulus, gets smaller. In contrast, the error between $\cos(2\pi t)$ and $p_n(t)$ obtained from the Chebyshev method is bounded by $\frac{(2\pi)^{n+1}}{(n+1)!} \cdot \frac{K^{n+1}}{2^n}$, which is not affected by ϵ. In sum, let $M_i = \mathsf{Max}_{t \in I_i} ||w(t)||$, then we obtain

$$||\cos(2\pi t) - p_n(t)|| \leq \frac{(2\pi)^{n+1}}{(n+1)!} \cdot \mathsf{Max}\{M_{-K+1}, M_{-K+2}, \dots, M_{K-1}\} \quad (3)$$

for $t \in \cup_{i=-K+1}^{K-1} I_i$, where $I_i = [i - \frac{1}{4} - \epsilon, i - \frac{1}{4} + \epsilon]$.

How to Choose $d_{-K+1,\dots,d_{K-1}}$. For each integer i, we have to decide d_i, the number of nodes in the interval $I_i = [i - \frac{1}{4} - \epsilon, i - \frac{1}{4} + \epsilon]$, and it is done by the following algorithmical way. We first initialize $d_i = 1$ for all i. With these d_i's, we compute each M_i and find the index that has a maximum M_i value. Then, if $i_0 = \mathrm{argmax} M_i$, we increase d_{i_0} by 1. We repeat this process until the total degree $(= \sum d_i - 1)$ becomes target degree.

Comparison. We conduct an experiment to compare our method and the Chebyshev method. We compare the experimental error bound of our method with that of the other method. Figure 2 shows experimental error bounds between the function $\cos(2\pi t)$ and its approximate polynomials obtained from each method. Figure 2(a) is obtained by fixing $n = 76$ and varying ϵ and Fig. 2(b)

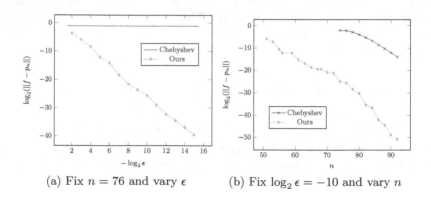

(a) Fix $n = 76$ and vary ϵ (b) Fix $\log_2 \epsilon = -10$ and vary n

Fig. 2. Error bounds $\log_2(||f - p_n||)$ for our optimized interpolation ($K = 12$).

is obtained by fixing $\log_2 \epsilon = -10$ and varying n. Since we bound the term $\frac{f^{(n+1)}(\psi_t)}{(n+1)!}$ in Eq. 2 by a constant, an exact error bound is smaller than the theoretical error bound explained above.

As seen in Fig. 2, our method far outperforms the Chebyshev method. For fixed $n = 76$, for example, $\log_2$ value of the experimental error bound of ours is about -25.6 when $\log_2 \epsilon = -10$, but that of the Chebyshev method is about -1.1 independent of ϵ. Also, for fixed $\log_2 \epsilon = -10$, the degree of an interpolation polynomial of the Chebyshev method needs to be greater than 103 to yield the same level of the experimental error bound as the interpolation polynomial of degree 76 of ours.

4.2   Homomorphic Evaluation of $p_n(t)$

After we get an approximate polynomial of degree $\leq n$ using our optimized method, we need to evaluate a value of the function at t in a homomorphic way. Naive approach is to compute t^i for all $i \in \{0, 1, \dots, n\}$ first and then evaluate $p_n(t) = \sum_{i=0}^{n} p_i \cdot t^i$. Unfortunately, due to the un-stability of the coefficients, this way of computation not only can yield a lot of numerical errors but also make homomorphic evaluation difficult. Especially, extremely small p_i values make homomorphic evaluation inept since we need to multiply a huge modulus to encrypt these values. To avoid this problem, we represent the polynomial with the Chebyshev basis instead of t^i's.

The Chebyshev polynomials T_i's on $[-1, 1]$ are defined recursively by

$$T_0(t) = 1, T_1(t) = t,$$
$$T_i(t) = 2t T_{i-1}(t) - T_{i-2}(t) \text{ for } i \geq 2$$

Then, T_i satisfies the equation $T_i(\cos \theta) = \cos(i\theta)$ for all θ, thus $|T_i(t)| \leq 1$ for all $|t| \leq 1$. Since the domain of our approximate polynomial is $[-K, K]$, we use $\tilde{T}_i(t) = T_i(\frac{t}{K})$ instead of T_i for each i. Note that $|\tilde{T}_i(t)| \leq 1$ for all $|t| \leq K$.

Since each $\tilde{T}_i$ is a polynomial of degree i, $\{\tilde{T}_i\}_{i=0}^{n}$ forms a basis for the vector space of polynomials of degree $\leq n$. Hence, $p_n(t)$ can be represented by a linear combination of $\{\tilde{T}_i\}_{i=1}^{n}$ as $p_n(t) = \sum_{i=0}^{n} c_i \cdot \tilde{T}_i(t)$ for some $c_0, \cdots, c_n \in \mathbb{R}$. Well, these c_i values also can be un-stable as in the case of the original t^i basis representation. However, since $|\tilde{T}_i(t)| \leq 1$ for all $|t| \leq K$, the term $c_i \cdot \tilde{T}_i(t)$ with extremely small c_i has little effect on the value of $p_n(t)$. Therefore, we can simply ignore the term having extremely small c_i, which not only causes numerical errors but also makes the homomorphic evaluation inefficient.

Algorithm 1. Baby-step Giant-step algorithm

1: **Input** : A polynomial of degree n, $p = \sum_{i=0}^{n} c_i T_i$.
2: Let m be the smallest integer satisfying $2^m > n$ and $l \approx m/2$.
3: Evaluate $T_2(t), T_3(t) \cdots, T_{2^l}(t)$ inductively.
4: Evaluate $T_{2^l+1}(t) \cdots, T_{2^m-1}(t)$ using the equation $T_{2i}(t) = 2T_i(t)^2 - 1$.
5: Find polynomials q and r of degree $< 2^{m-1}$ which satisfy $p = q \cdot T_{2^m-1} + r$ in forms of a linear combination of Chebyshev basis.
6: Evaluate $q(t)$ and $r(t)$ recursively. (Repeat 5 with p being replaced by q and r until the degree of a quotient and a remainder become smaller than 2^l)
7: Evaluate $p(t)$ with $q(t)$, $r(t)$ and $T_{2^m-1}(t)$.
8: **Output** : $p(t)$

Next, we can use the Baby-step Giant-step algorithm (Algorithm 1) to evaluate the polynomial $p_n(t)$. This algorithm enables us to evaluate $p_n(t)$ in $2\sqrt{2n} + \frac{1}{2}\log_2 n + O(1)$ non-scalar multiplications and $\lceil \log_2 n \rceil$ depth consumption. More precisely, with m the smallest integer satisfying $2^m > n$ and $l \approx m/2$, we can evaluate $p_n(x)$ with $2^l + 2^{m-l} + m - l - 3$ non-scalar multiplications while consuming m depth.

Also, we can use the Paterson-Stockmeyer algorithm for Chebyshev polynomials suggested in [5]. In [5], authors modify the original Paterson-Stockmeyer algorithm [19] to evaluate polynomials represented in the Chebyshev basis. They propose an algorithm that enables evaluating a polynomial of degree n represented in the Chebyshev basis with $\sqrt{2n} + \log_2 n + O(1)$ non-scalar multiplications, see [5] for more details. By using this algorithm, we can evaluate $p_n(t)$ with $\sqrt{2n} + \log_2 n + O(1)$ non-scalar multiplications while consuming $\lceil \log_2 n \rceil$ depth. More precisely, with $k \approx \sqrt{n/2}$ and the smallest integer m satisfying $(2^m - 1)k > n$, we can evaluate $p_n(t)$ with $2^{m-1} + 2m + k - 4$ non-scalar multiplications while consuming $\lceil \log_2 k \rceil + m$ depth.

Even though the Paterson-Stockmeyer algorithm is asymptotically better than the Baby-step Giant-step algorithm, it does not mean that the Paterson-Stockmeyer algorithm outperforms the Baby-step Giant-step algorithm in a practical sense. The degree of an approximate polynomial that we use is not so big in practical, and we can reduce it further by using the hybrid method which will be introduced in the next section. Moreover, when the degree n is small, the effect of the term $\log_2 n$ becomes greater, especially in the Paterson-Stockmeyer algorithm. In fact, the Baby-step Giant-step algorithm shows the better performance based on our experiment when degree n is small. For these reasons, we use the Baby-step Giant-step algorithm instead of the Paterson-Stockmeyer algorithm.

4.3 Hybrid Method

Recall that, in [7], authors scale down an input t by a power of two and use double-angle formula to make it locate close enough to the origin before they use the Taylor approximation. We can also apply this idea to our method simply by using double angle formula of cosine[6].

Suppose we scale down t by 2^r before using our method and let $t' = t/2^r$. We say the number of scaling is r in this case. Then, we need to approximate $\cos(2\pi t')$ based on the fact that t' is contained in one of the intervals $\tilde{I}_i = [\frac{1}{2^r}(i - \frac{1}{4} - \epsilon), \frac{1}{2^r}(i - \frac{1}{4} + \epsilon)]$. Naturally, we choose d_i nodes in each interval $\tilde{I}_i$ by $\tilde{t}_{i,j} = \frac{1}{2^r}\left(i - \frac{1}{4} + \epsilon \cdot \cos\left(\frac{2j-1}{2d_i}\pi\right)\right)$ for $1 \leq j \leq d_i$ and $|i| < K$ to apply our method. Then, we can see from Eq. 2 that all the terms in $w(t) = \prod_{i=0}^{n}(t - t_i)$ decrease by a factor of 2^r compared to before, and thus degree n can be smaller while ensuring the same level of error bounds as before. However, since the other term $1/(n + 1)!$ is difficult to predict how it changes as n varies, it is hard to predict an exact value of degree that yields the same level of error bounds as the method without scaling.

We conduct an experiment to find the degree that gives the same level of error bound as the original method (the method without scaling) for each number of scaling. The result of the experiment is given in Table 3. The first column indicates the degree of approximate polynomials from the original method and the other columns represents the minimum degree of approximate polynomials that ensure the same level of error bounds for each number of scaling and corresponding depth consumption. Note that we need to consume $\lceil \log_2 n \rceil$ depth to evaluate $p_n(t)$ in a homomorphic way and require r more depth for double angle formula for a cosine function when the number of scaling is r. As our expectation, the degree of an approximate polynomial gradually decreases as the number of scaling increases. However, even the coefficients of the Cheby-

Table 3. Minimum degree of an approximate polynomials to ensure the same level of error bound for each number of scaling and corresponding depth consumption. ($K = 12$ and $\log_2 \epsilon = -10$)

Degree	Depth	# of scaling					
		1		2		3	
		Degree	Depth	Degree	Depth	Degree	Depth
76	7	49	6+1	31	5+2	24	5+3
86	7	57	6+1	40	6+2	28	5+3
96	7	65	7+1	45	6+2	34	6+3
106	7	72	7+1	51	6+2	38	6+3
116	7	80	7+1	57	6+2	43	6+3
126	7	88	7+1	63	6+2	49	6+3
136	8	94	7+1	70	7+2	55	6+3

---

[6] Previous method uses a sine function and double angle formula for a sine function needs both $\cos(t)$ and $\sin(t)$ to compute $\sin(2t)$.

shev basis representation become more stabilized and the number of non-scalar multiplications decreases, it does not necessarily mean that the scaling is always favorable because depth consumption can increase.

In the case of degree 76, if we scale by a factor of 4, we can compute the approximate polynomial with depth consumption 7 as the original while the number of non-scalar multiplications based on Algorithm 1 decreases from 24 to 13. Therefore, the scaling is unconditionally favorable in this case. However, in the case of degree 116, if we scale by a factor of 2, even the number of non-scalar multiplications decreases, we need to consume one more depth compared to the original method. Therefore, in this case, we need to consider the trade-off between the number of non-scalar multiplications and the depth consumption. In conclusion, we need to conduct an experiment to decide whether we use the hybrid method or not, and decision will depend on the trade-off between the number of non-scalar multiplications and the depth consumption[7].

4.4   Overall Comparison

In this section, we compare our method with the previous work [5]. In [5], authors use the approximate polynomial of degree 119 obtained from the Chebyshev method.[8] In our case, we choose degree 74 because the approximate polynomial of degree 74 obtained from our method gives the same level of error as the inevitable error occurs between t and $\frac{1}{2\pi}\sin(2\pi t)$ under the parameter sets that used by the previous work [5]. The comparison between our method and the previous work [5] is given in Table 4. As seen from the table, by using the hybrid method with the number of scaling 2 and evaluating the obtained approximate polynomial of degree 30 with Algorithm 1, we can decrease the number of non-scalar multiplications almost by half while consuming the same depth.

Table 4. Comparison between our method and the previous work. [5] ($K = 12$ and $\log_2 \epsilon = -10$)

Method	Degree	# of Scaling	Degree (after scaling)	Non-scalar multiplication	Depth
Ours	74	0	74	24 (Algorithm 1)	7
		1	49	16 + 1 (Algorithm 1)	6 + 1
		2	**30**	**11 + 2 (Algorithm 1)**	**5 + 2**
[5]	119	–	–	20 (PS alg)	7

---

[7] The code for finding an approximate polynomial for the cosine function can be found at [15].

[8] In fact, they use the nodes $t_i = K\cos(i\pi/n)$ for $0 \le i \le n$ instead of nodes $t_i = K\cos((2i-1)\pi/(2n+2))$ for $1 \le i \le n+1$. But, there is no big difference.

4.5 Put Everything Together

Using the scheme in Sect. 3 and the above sine evaluation method, we can do a better bootstrapping for Full-RNS variant of HEAAN. Recall that the bootstrapping can be divided into four steps: modular raising, linear transformation, sine evaluation, and inverse linear transformation. For linear transformation and the inverse part, we used the techniques proposed in [5, 12].

Sine Evaluation. To approximate a sine function, we use the polynomial interpolation method with our optimized nodes, which performs better than the other methods because an input for a sine function is restricted to some small intervals. Also, we further improve it by using the hybrid method, which combines our method with double angle formula of cosine, and it can decrease the number of non-scalar multiplications a lot while consuming the same depth.

With the approximate polynomial obtained from our method, we evaluate it with the Baby-step Giant-step algorithm, which shows better performance when the degree of an approximate polynomial is small. In our implementation, we fix $\log_2 \epsilon = -10$ and use the approximate polynomial of degree 30 obtained from the hybrid method with the number of scaling 2.

Scaling Factor Control. After each homomorphic multiplication and rescaling, the scaling factor changes. Therefore, the bootstrapping process can also change the scaling factor, and this can be a problem when we want to do some operations with an output of the bootstrapping and fresh ciphertexts. Even though they are in the same level, their scaling factor can be different, and thus, for example, homomorphic addition between these two ciphertexts can yield an un-expected result.

To solve this problem, at the last step of the bootstrapping, evaluation, we multiply Δ' and perform $\mathsf{RS}(\cdot)$ with a constant Δ' for which $(\Delta' \cdot \Delta)/q_{L'} = \Delta_{L'-1}$, where $\Delta_{L'-1}$ is the scaling factor at level $L' - 1$ and Δ is the current scaling factor. This requires one level consumption, but we can optimize it by merging this process with the last step of linear transformation in the bootstrapping.

5 Implementation

We implement our full-RNS variant of HEAAN in Sect. 3 and its bootstrapping. The experiments are conducted in PC with Intel(R) Core(TM) i9-9820X CPU @ 3.30 GHz using single-thread.

5.1 Performance of Basic Homomorphic Operations.

First, the performance of the basic homomorphic operations is given in Table 5. The results again show why it is better to use a proper dnum. By using $1 < $ dnum $< L + 1$, we can reduce the complexity of the homomorphic multiplication.

For example, in Table 5, the best timing result is almost two times faster than the dnum = 24 case which is used in the SEAL library. In addition, the first row (dnum = 1), which corresponds to the HEAAN-RNS scheme, not only does not satisfy the 128-bit security condition based on the Martin's LWE estimator [1], but also gives a 1.8 times slower result compared to the second row[9].

Table 5. Performance of our Full-RNS variant of HEAAN with 2^{15} slots.

	$\log q_i$	L	dnum	Enc	Dec	Mult	Rescale	
$N = 2^{16}$	45	23	1	103 ms	5 ms	773 ms	60 ms	HEAAN-RNS
			4			**436 ms**		
			6			487 ms		
			12			660 ms		
			24			958 ms		SEAL v3.3

5.2 Bootstrapping Performance

For an experiment on the bootstrapping, we set two parameter sets as in Table 6 using the Martin's LWE estimator. The bit size of each prime in modulus chain is set to 40 for Param 1 and 45 for Param 2, and $\log q_0$ is 50 and 55, respectively. In the case of Param 1, we used large dnum = 10 to make the security parameter >100. This enables us to use $\log_2 N = 15$ which should be 16 if we use dnum = 1. In our experiment, we use the approximate polynomial of degree 30 with 2 times of scaling for sine evaluation (See 3rd parameters of our method in Table 4).

Table 6. Parameter sets

	L	dnum	N	$\log Q$	$\log Q + \log P$	Security
Param 1	19	10	32768	810	910	110.4
Param 2	27	7	65536	1270	1452	127.2

Using those two parameter sets, we ran our bootstrapping with various number of slots ns. Here, Amortized Time indicates bootstrapping time per each slot. Because of computational errors generated in the linear transformation part, large ns implies lower precision. Here, the precision means $- \log_2 e$, where e is average noise generated through the bootstrapping. For example, precision 15.5 in the first row in Table 7 means that noise with average size $2^{-15.5}$ is added through the bootstrapping.

---

[9] Here, SEAL v.3.3 and HEAAN-RNS indicate the schemes corresponding to each library and paper.

Table 7. Performance of the bootstrapping in our scheme

	ns	Boot Time	Precision	After Level	Amortized Time
Param 1	2^0	6.8 s	15.5	5	7.1 s
	2^1	7.0 s	16.8	3	3.5 s
	2^2	7.5 s	15.0	3	1.87 s
Param 2	2^5	28 s	18.5	9	0.87 s
	2^{10}	37.6 s	15.3	7	0.036 s
	2^{14}	52.8 s	10.8	7	0.0032 s

In our experiment, we used fixed $\epsilon = 2^{-10}$. Because of the difference between t and $\sin t^{10}$, the maximum precision for the bootstrapping is limited to $\simeq \epsilon^2 = 2^{-20}$. From the ns $= 2^5$ case with Param 2, which ensures 18.5 precision, we can see that sine evaluation with our method yields an accurate enough result.

Comparison. The last row of Table 4 in [5] and Table 2 in [12] use similar parameter sets to the last row of Table 7. Timing results were 158 s in [5] and 127 s in [12], which is just 52.8 s in our experiment. In other words, using the Full-RNS variant with proper dnum and the improved method for sine approximation gives a 3 and 2.5 times faster result than the previous works, respectively.

6   Conclusion

In this work, we suggest the generalized key-switching method for Full-RNS variant of HEAAN and propose a better method for approximating a sine function. With these improvements, we increase the efficiency of the bootstrapping for Full-RNS variant of HEAAN. Our method of approximating a sine function is specialized in the setting when inputs for a function are restricted to union of small intervals. Hence, we can also apply our method effectively to another functions which has a restricted domain as in the case of the bootstrapping for HEAAN.

So far, the research on approximating a modulus function is based on a sine function. Therefore, it has the limitation because of the inevitable error generated from the approximation of $[t]_q$ with $\frac{1}{2\pi}\sin(2\pi t)$. We expect that we can overcome this limitation by finding another approximation of $[\cdot]_q$ operation. We think it can be a new breakthrough of improving the bootstrapping.

A   Correctness and Noise Growth of Homomorphic Multiplication

Before proving the correctness of the homomorphic multiplication, first remind the properties of ModUp and ModDown with the following three equations:

$$\|\text{CRT}_{\mathcal{C} \cup \mathcal{B}}(\text{ModUp}([a(x)]_{q_0}, [a(x)]_{q_1}, \ldots, [a(x)]_{q_\ell}))\|_\infty \leq (\ell + 1) \cdot Q, \qquad (A.1)$$

---

10 $|t - \sin t| < O(t^3)$ for t near the origin.

$$\text{CRT}_{\mathcal{C} \cup \mathcal{B}}(\text{ModUp}([a(x)]_{q_0}, [a(x)]_{q_1}, \ldots, [a(x)]_{q_\ell})) \equiv a(x) \bmod Q, \tag{A.2}$$

$$\left\| \text{CRT}_{\mathcal{C}}(\text{ModDown}([a(x)]_{q_0}, \ldots, [a(x)]_{q_\ell}, [a(x)]_{p_0}, \ldots, [a(x)]_{p_{k-1}})) - \left\lfloor \frac{a(x)}{P} \right\rceil \right\|_\infty < k, \tag{A.3}$$

where $\mathcal{B} = \{p_0, \ldots, p_{k-1}\}$ and $\mathcal{C} = \{q_0, \ldots, q_\ell\}$. With the above three equations and properties of RNS-Decompose and RNS-Power, we can prove the correctness of the homomorphic multiplication in our scheme.

Theorem 2. *The algorithm* $\underline{\text{Mult}_{\text{evk}}(\text{ct}_0, \text{ct}_1)}$ *returns* $(b_3(x), a_3(x))$ *such that*

$$b_3(x) + a_3(x) \cdot s(x) = M_1(x) \cdot M_2(x) + M_0(x) \cdot e_1(x) + M_1(x) \cdot e_0(x) + \epsilon(x),$$

where $\|\epsilon(x)\|_\infty < \|s(x)\|_1$, *when* $P > 2\beta N e_{\text{fresh}} \cdot (\max_{0 \leq i < \beta} Q_i)$. *Here,* $\text{ct}_i = (b_i(x), a_i(x)) \in R_Q^2$, *and* $b_i(x) + a_i(x) \cdot s(x) = M_i(x) + e_i(x)$ *for* $i = 0, 1$.

Proof. *For simplicity, we assume that* $\ell = L$ *and* $(\ell+1)$ *is a multiple of* α. *First, a vector* $(d_0(x), d_1(x), d_2(x))$ *which satisfies*

$$\begin{aligned} d_0(x) + d_1(x) \cdot s(x) + d_2(x) \cdot s(x)^2 &= (M_0(x) + e_0(x)) \cdot (M_1(x) + e_0(x)) \\ &= M_0(x) \cdot M_1(x) + M_0(x) \cdot e_1(x) + M_1(x) \cdot e_0(x) + e_0(x) \cdot e_1(x) \\ &= M_0(x) \cdot M_1(x) + e_2(x) \in R_Q. \end{aligned}$$

is obtained after Step 1.

In Step 2, since $\ell = L$ *and* $(L + 1)$ *is a multiple of* α, β *equals to* dnum *and the zero-padding part can be omitted. Then,*

$$([d_2(x) \cdot \hat{Q}_0^{-1}]_{Q_0}, \ldots, [d_2(x) \cdot \hat{Q}_{dnum-1}^{-1}]_{Q_{dnum-1}}) = \textit{RNS-Decomp}_{\mathcal{C}'}(d_2(x))$$

is returned after RNS-Decompose step.

Also, Modulus-Raise step returns vectors of length $k + \ell + 1$,

$$\begin{aligned} &([\tilde{d}_2^{(i)}(x)]_{q_0}, \ldots, [\tilde{d}_2^{(i)}(x)]_{q_\ell}, [\tilde{d}_2^{(i)}(x)]_{p_0}, \ldots, [\tilde{d}_2^{(i)}(x)]_{p_{k-1}}) \\ &= \text{ModUp}_{\mathcal{C}_i \to \mathcal{C} \cup \mathcal{B}}([d_2(x) \cdot \hat{Q}_i^{-1}]_{q_{i\alpha}}, \ldots, [d_2(x) \cdot \hat{Q}_i^{-1}]_{q_{(i+1)\alpha-1}}), \end{aligned}$$

where $\tilde{d}_2^{(i)}(x) \in R_{PQ}$, *for* $0 \leq i < $ dnum. *From Eqs.* A.1–A.2, *we can check that* $\tilde{d}_2(x)$ *satisfies the following equations:*

$$\tilde{d}_2^{(i)}(x) \equiv d_2(x) \cdot \hat{Q}_i^{-1} \bmod Q_i \text{ and } \left\| \tilde{d}_2^{(i)}(x) \right\|_\infty \leq (\alpha + 1) \cdot Q_i. \tag{A.4}$$

Note that the norm of $\tilde{d}_2^{(i)}(x)$ *is still much smaller than* PQ, *and for this reason,* ModUp *does not harm the functionality of RNS-Decompose and RNS-Power.*

Next, we suppose that evaluation keys $\text{evk}_i = (B_i(x), A_i(x)) \in R_{PQ}^2$ *which satisfy* $B_i(x) + A_i(x) \cdot s(x) = P \cdot \hat{Q}_i \cdot s^2(x) + E_i(x) \in R_{PQ}$, *where* $\|E_i(x)\|_\infty < e_{\text{fresh}}$, *are generated in the key generation step. Then, the inner product step returns* $(B'(x), A'(x)) = \sum_{i=0}^{\beta-1} \left[\tilde{d}_2^{(i)}(x) \cdot (B_i(x), A_i(x)) \right]$ *and it satisfies the following equation:*

$$B'(x) + A'(x) \cdot s(x) = P \sum_{i=0}^{\beta-1} \left(\tilde{d}_2^{(i)}(x) \cdot \hat{Q}_i \cdot s^2(x) \right) + \sum_{i=0}^{\beta-1} \left(\tilde{d}_2^{(i)}(x) \cdot E_i(x) \right)$$

$$= P \cdot d_2(x) \cdot s^2(x) + E'(x) \in R_{PQ},$$

where $\|E'(x)\|_\infty < N \sum_{0 \le i < \beta} Q_i \cdot e_{fresh} \le N \cdot \beta \cdot e_{fresh} \cdot (\max_{0 \le i < \beta} Q_i)$ *and* N *is the dimension of the ring.*

After that, we apply modulus-down process to revert the modulus space from R_{PQ} to R_Q and to reduce the size of $E'(x)$. Let $(\tilde{B}(x), \tilde{A}(x))$ be the return of modulus-down step with CRT decomposed representation. From the modulus switching technique and Equation A.3, we can see that $(\tilde{B}(x), \tilde{A}(x))$ has the following property:

$$\tilde{B}(x) + \tilde{A}(x) \cdot s(x) = d_2(x) \cdot s^2(x) + \left\lceil \frac{E'(x)}{P} \right\rfloor + \epsilon(x) \in R_Q,$$

where $\|\epsilon(x)\|_\infty < \|s(x)\|_1$. *Since* $P > 2 \cdot N \cdot \beta \cdot e_{fresh} \cdot (\max_{0 \le i < \beta} Q_i)$, *each coefficient of* $E'(x)/P$ *is in the range* $(-0.5, 0.5)$, *and thus rounding of the polynomial becomes a zero polynomial. Therefore, it follows that* $\tilde{B}(x) + \tilde{A}(x) \cdot s(x) = d_2(x) \cdot s(x)^2 + \epsilon(x) \in R_Q$.

At the last step, we compute and return $(b_3(x), a_3(x)) = (d_0(x) + \tilde{B}(x), d_1(x) + \tilde{A}(x))$. Then, from the equation

$$b_3(x) + a_3(x) \cdot s(x) = d_0(x) + d_1(x) \cdot s(x) + d_2(x) \cdot s(x)^2 + \epsilon(x)$$

$$= M_0(x) \cdot M_1(x) + e_2(x) + \epsilon(x),$$

the correctness of homomorphic multiplication is followed. Furthermore, the size of the noise after multiplication is given by $M_0(x) \cdot e_1(x) + M_1(x) \cdot e_0(x) + e_0(x) \cdot e_1(x) + \epsilon(x)$, *where* $\|\epsilon(x)\|_\infty < \|s(x)\|_1$. □

References

1. Albrecht, M.R., Player, R., Scott, S.: On the concrete hardness of learning with errors. J. Math. Cryptol. **9**(3), 169–203 (2015)
2. Bajard, J.-C., Eynard, J., Hasan, M.A., Zucca, V.: A full RNS variant of FV like somewhat homomorphic encryption schemes. In: Avanzi, R., Heys, H. (eds.) SAC 2016. LNCS, vol. 10532, pp. 423–442. Springer, Cham (2017). https://doi.org/10.1007/978-3-319-69453-5_23
3. Boemer, F., Lao, Y., Wierzynski, C.: nGraph-HE: a graph compiler for deep learning on homomorphically encrypted data. arXiv preprint arXiv:1810.10121 (2018)
4. Carpov, S., Gama, N., Georgieva, M., Troncoso-Pastoriza, J.R.: Privacy-preserving semi-parallel logistic regression training with Fully Homomorphic Encryption. Cryptology ePrint Archive, Report 2019/101 (2019). https://eprint.iacr.org/2019/101

5. Chen, H., Chillotti, I., Song, Y.: Improved bootstrapping for approximate homomorphic encryption. In: Ishai, Y., Rijmen, V. (eds.) EUROCRYPT 2019. LNCS, vol. 11477, pp. 34–54. Springer, Cham (2019). https://doi.org/10.1007/978-3-030-17656-3_2

6. Cheon, J.H., Han, K., Kim, A., Kim, M., Song, Y.: A full RNS variant of approximate homomorphic encryption. In: Cid, C., Jacobson Jr., M. (eds.) SAC 2018. LNCS, vol. 11349, pp. 347–368. Springer, Cham (2018). https://doi.org/10.1007/978-3-030-10970-7_16

7. Cheon, J.H., Han, K., Kim, A., Kim, M., Song, Y.: Bootstrapping for approximate homomorphic encryption. In: Nielsen, J.B., Rijmen, V. (eds.) EUROCRYPT 2018. LNCS, vol. 10820, pp. 360–384. Springer, Cham (2018). https://doi.org/10.1007/978-3-319-78381-9_14

8. Cheon, J.H., Kim, A., Kim, M., Song, Y.: Homomorphic encryption for arithmetic of approximate numbers. In: Takagi, T., Peyrin, T. (eds.) ASIACRYPT 2017. LNCS, vol. 10624, pp. 409–437. Springer, Cham (2017). https://doi.org/10.1007/978-3-319-70694-8_15

9. Gentry, C.: Fully homomorphic encryption using ideal lattices. In: STOC, vol. 9, pp. 169–178 (2009)

10. Gentry, C., Halevi, S., Smart, N.P.: Homomorphic evaluation of the AES circuit. In: Safavi-Naini, R., Canetti, R. (eds.) CRYPTO 2012. LNCS, vol. 7417, pp. 850–867. Springer, Heidelberg (2012). https://doi.org/10.1007/978-3-642-32009-5_49

11. Halevi, S., Polyakov, Y., Shoup, V.: An improved RNS variant of the BFV homomorphic encryption scheme. In: Matsui, M. (ed.) CT-RSA 2019. LNCS, vol. 11405, pp. 83–105. Springer, Cham (2019). https://doi.org/10.1007/978-3-030-12612-4_5

12. Han, K., Hhan, M., Cheon, J.H.: Improved homomorphic discrete Fourier transforms and FHE bootstrapping. IEEE Access **7**, 57361–57370 (2019)

13. Han, K., Hong, S., Cheon, J.H., Park, D.: Efficient logistic regression on large encrypted data. Cryptology ePrint Archive, Report 2018/662 (2018)

14. Jiang, Y., Wang, C., Wu, Z., Du, X., Wang, S.: Privacy-preserving biomedical data dissemination via a hybrid approach. In: AMIA Annual Symposium Proceedings, vol. 2018, p. 1176. American Medical Informatics Association (2018)

15. Ki, D.: (2019). https://github.com/DohyeongKi/better-homomorphic-sine-evaluation

16. Kim, A., Song, Y., Kim, M., Lee, K., Cheon, J.H.: Logistic regression model training based on the approximate homomorphic encryption. BMC Med. Genomics **11**(4) (2018). Article number: 83

17. Kim, M., Song, Y., Li, B., Micciancio, D.: Semi-parallel logistic regression for GWAS on encrypted data. Cryptology ePrint Archive, Report 2019/294 (2019). https://eprint.iacr.org/2019/294

18. Kim, M., Song, Y., Wang, S., Xia, Y., Jiang, X.: Secure logistic regression based on homomorphic encryption: Design and evaluation. JMIR Med. Inform. **6**(2), e19 (2018)

19. Paterson, M.S., Stockmeyer, L.J.: On the number of nonscalar multiplications necessary to evaluate polynomials. SIAM J. Comput. **2**(1), 60–66 (1973)

Improved Secure Integer Comparison via Homomorphic Encryption

Florian Bourse[1], Olivier Sanders[1(✉)], and Jacques Traoré[2]

[1] Orange Labs, Applied Crypto Group, Cesson-Sévigné, France
`olivier.sanders@orange.com`
[2] Orange Labs, Applied Crypto Group, Caen, France

Abstract. Secure integer comparison has been one of the first problems introduced in cryptography, both for its simplicity to describe and for its applications. The first formulation of the problem was to enable two parties to compare their inputs without revealing the exact value of those inputs, also called the Millionaires' problem [45]. The recent rise of fully homomorphic encryption has given a new formulation to this problem. In this new setting, one party blindly computes an encryption of the boolean $(a < b)$ given only ciphertexts encrypting a and b.

In this paper, we present new solutions for the problem of secure integer comparison in both of these settings. The underlying idea for both schemes is to avoid decomposing the integers in binary in order to improve the performances. On the one hand, our fully homomorphic based solution is inspired by [9], and makes use of the fast bootstrapping techniques developed by [12,14,23] to obtain scalability for large integers while preserving high efficiency. On the other hand, our solution to the original Millionaires' problem is inspired by the protocol of [10], based on partially homomorphic encryption. We tweak their protocol in order to minimize the number of interactions required, while preserving the advantage of comparing non-binary integers.

Both our techniques provide efficient solutions to the problem of secure integer comparison for large (even a-priori unbounded in our first scenario) integers with minimum interactions.

1 Introduction

Evaluation of algorithms over encrypted data is a major topic in cryptography which has known very important results over the past decade (*e.g.* [27]). Generic solutions supporting any operation exist but they usually require to represent the algorithm as a boolean circuit and incur very large complexity. Conversely, solutions specifically designed for a particular algorithm are more efficient, but require a large amount of work that must be started over each time the algorithm is updated.

In this context, an interesting middle-way is the one consisting in designing efficient protocols for simple tasks (but still more complex than basic operations) that are frequently used as subroutines by other algorithms. Indeed, in this case,

© Springer Nature Switzerland AG 2020
S. Jarecki (Ed.): CT-RSA 2020, LNCS 12006, pp. 391–416, 2020.
https://doi.org/10.1007/978-3-030-40186-3_17

the resulting protocol will be more efficient than the one generated by applying generic solutions and, at the same time, the widespread use of this subroutine will ensure that the efforts invested in the design of this protocol will benefit to a very large number of algorithms.

Perhaps the most prominent example of this approach (for both historical and practical reasons) is the one of secure integer comparison, where two parties knowing respectively secret integers m_1 and m_2 want to compare them without leaking any information beyond the result ($m_1 \leq m_2$).

Introduced in 1982 by Yao [45] who presented it as the problem encountered by two millionaires wanting to secretly compare their respective wealth (hence its name of *Millionaires' problem*), this problem is of utter importance in many areas, especially since the rise of machine learning. Indeed, several classifiers require to sort (and therefore to compare) elements and thus need appropriate protocols when the latter are encrypted, as illustrated in [8]. More generally, the fact that most algorithms run integers comparison as subroutines emphasizes the need for counterparts handling encrypted data.

In his seminal paper [45], Yao proposed a first protocol for secure comparison based on garbled circuits, a by-now standard tool in cryptography which has become a subject on its own. However, this kind of techniques, despite several improvements (*e.g.* [5,6,16,32]), implies rather important communication complexity, which can be problematic in contexts where communications are slow.

In [2,24], the authors follow a different strategy, based on the Legendre symbol, which leads to very elegant protocols. Unfortunately, the latter can only handle integers of limited size, and it does not seem possible to extend them to support large inputs.

Another approach for secure comparison is the one based on homomorphic encryption, starting from Fischlin's work [25]. The ability to perform operations on encrypted data can remove some interactions but at the cost of greater computational complexity. Here again, several improvements followed [7,20,21,26,30,34,42] but they involve bitwise encryption of the integers, leading to a complexity of at least $\log_2(M)$ operations where M is a bound on the integers to compare.

Comparing the solutions based on garbled circuits with the ones based on homomorphic encryption is not always relevant as they are very different constructions. Garbled circuits mostly rely on symmetric primitives and thus usually offer good performance. Homomorphic encryption is a more complex tool but seems to be a promising solution to go beyond the $\log_2(M)$ barrier. Indeed, two homomorphic-based constructions [9,10] overcoming this limation have recently been introduced for different settings.

The first one (CEK), proposed by Carlton, Essex and Kapulkin [10], corresponds exactly to the Millionaires' problem scenario where two parties want to compare their respective secret values m_1 and m_2. It is based on an homomorphic threshold encryption system allowing to directly compare small integers, leading to less computations, but at the cost of more interactions compared to the DGK protocol [20]. Indeed, in their protocol, the party A knowing the decryption keys received either an encryption of 0 (if $m_1 \geq m_2$) or of some value related to m_1 and m_2 (if $m_1 < m_2$). This forces the other party B to blind the plaintext with some random value s leading to the following problem: in any case A decrypts randomness. To bypass this problem, both parties run a plaintext equality test (PET) at the end of the protocol to decide whether the randomness is s (in which case $m_1 \geq m_2$) or not. This PET implies at least one additional pass and the use of another homomorphic encryption scheme. In some way, the result of Carlton $et\ al.$ can thus be seen as a new tradeoff between computation and communication complexity.

In the second setting, one party is given two ciphertexts for values m_1 and m_2 and has to produce a ciphertext for the boolean $(m_1 > m_2)$, whereas the other party is the only one having the secret key that allows decryption of these ciphertexts. One way to solve this problem has been to reduce it to the Millionaires' problem, as done in [41,42]. More interestingly, this problem can even be solved non-interactively, by using fully homomorphic encryption. However, the current state-of-the-art in FHE doesn't provide a fully satisfactory solution to the homomorphic evaluation of the comparison. The two main techniques are either based on somewhat homomorphic encryption, which is not suitable because the comparison cannot a priori be represented by a low degree polynomial, so the noise growth would be unmanageable, or have to deal with the bit decomposition of the messages ($e.g.$ [11,19]). In [44], the authors proposed a solution based on Wilson's theorem to avoid binary decomposition. However, it requires to perform $(2M)^2$ homomorphic multiplications to compare integers smaller than M, which rapidly becomes prohibitive as M increases.

At Crypto 18, Bourse $et\ al.$ [9] proposed a modified FHE system enabling to efficiently evaluate the sign function. This can be used to compare two encrypted values by subtracting and evaluating the sign. However, this scheme only supports a bounded message space, and the sizes of the bootstrapping key and ciphertexts grow exponentially in the size of the messages (or superlinear in the value of bound on the messages). This result is enough to work on very small sized input, or on computation that are inherently fault-tolerant, as they show with neural network evaluations, but is hardly usable in practice for less specific applications. Moreover, this requires the bound on the messages to be chosen at setup time, because the parameters of the scheme depend on it.

1.1   Our Contribution

In this work we propose two protocols that respectively improve [9] and [10] and thus the state-of-the-art of secure integer comparison.

In a first part, we describe a new FHE-based solution in the setting where B wants to blindly compare two encrypted integers. Starting from [9], we show how (1) to modify it in order to output 0 whenever the two inputs are equal, and (2) to scale the output by any chosen factor. The first part requires a careful modification of the testVector from [9] because the function to be computed must verify some anticyclic properties, and ternary sign doesn't satisfy those.

Hence, we had to add a slot never used into the message space. The second part might seem trivial for FHE because scaling can be performed by multiplying the output ciphertext by the chosen factor. However, this would yield too much noise. We then here again need to modify the `testVector` to take into account the scaling factor before returning the output ciphertext.

Then, relying on those two properties, we construct recursively an algorithm to compare unbounded integers, by decomposing them in some basis that can be handled by our modified scheme for bounded integers. The resulting scheme combines the generality of bitwise encryption comparisons, because we can compare unbounded integers using a fixed bootstrapping key that can be generated without knowledge of the integers to compare, together with the improved efficiency, both in computation time and in ciphertext expansion factor, of the schemes that support non-binary message spaces.

In a second part, we propose a new protocol to address the Millionaires' problem that combines (almost) all the best features of the DGK and CEK protocols. Starting from the latter, we introduce several modifications to avoid the costly PET that constitutes the last step of CEK. More specifically, we manage to replace the whole PET by a simple hash value sent by the party B in the second pass. This digest will indeed be enough for A to decide whether the decrypted plaintext is the blind factor or not. However, this idea cannot be directly applied to the CEK protocol because a simple exhaustive search on the message space enables A to recover B's value whenever $m_2 > m_1$. We therefore consider different RSA parameters to introduce new random elements in the protocol to thwart (with overwhelming probability) exhaustive searches. The point is that all these modifications do not significantly hamper the main feature of CEK, namely the ability to compare several bits at once, which means that our protocol still compares favourably to DGK (and its predecessors).

Concretely, compared to DGK, our protocol also requires two passes but divides both the computation and the communication cost by a factor up to 4. Compared to CEK, the speedup factor is harder to assess because it heavily depends on the security parameter (see Sect. 4.2) but we manage anyway to divide by up to two the number of passes. This comes at the cost of a security proof in the random oracle model (ROM) but this model is widely used in cryptography, especially to design practical constructions.

We stress that these improvements must not be measured just for one run of our protocols but must rather be put in perspective with the massive use of comparisons in algorithms. For example, the classifiers considered in [8] require to find the greater value of a list $a_1, \ldots, a_k$ of encrypted elements and so to run k secure comparison protocols. In such a case, the impact of our protocols will be multiplied by at least k.

1.2 Organization

Our paper addresses two different versions of the Millionaires' problem and is thus divided in two parts that can be read independently. In Sect. 2, we describe a solution based on fully homomorphic encryption that outputs an encrypted boolean $(m_1 > m_2)$ given two ciphertexts encrypting respectively m_1 and m_2. In Sect. 3, we consider the original scenario of the Millionaires' problem and provide a solution that enables two parties to secretly compare their respective entries.

2   Homomorphic Comparison of Integers

In this section, we build a new technique to homomorphically compare two integers. We first start by recalling all necessaries preliminaries about lattice-based cryptography and fully homomorphic encryption that we will use. Then, we start our construction by extending the work of [9] to allow ternary sign computation, and add as an input a scaling factor that will multiply the output. Finally, we show how to compare two unbounded integers by calling recursively our comparison procedure for small integers.

2.1   Preliminaries

As in [14], we present the learning with errors problem and assumptions using the torus $\mathbb{T} = \mathbb{R}/\mathbb{Z}$ (i.e., the real modulo 1), and binary vectors as the secret keys. The same results hold for the formulation over $\mathbb{Z}_q$ for any q instead of $\mathbb{T}$. However, to the best of our knowledge, binary secret keys are required for the techniques allowing a fast bootstrapping.

Learning With Errors (LWE). This problem was introduced by Regev [38] as a candidate problem that is hard to solve, even for quantum computers. Let n be a positive integer, and χ a probability distribution over $\mathbb{R}$. For any vector[1] $\mathbf{s} \in \{0,1\}^n$, we define the LWE distribution $\mathsf{LWE}_{n,\mathbf{s},\chi}$ as $(\mathbf{a}, b)$, where $\mathbf{a} \xleftarrow{\$} \mathbb{T}^n$, $e \xleftarrow{\$} \chi$, and $b = \langle \mathbf{s}, \mathbf{a} \rangle + e$.

The LWE assumption states that for $\mathbf{s} \xleftarrow{\$} \{0,1\}^n$, it is hard to distinguish between $\mathsf{LWE}_{n,\mathbf{s},\chi}$ and the uniform distribution over $\mathbb{T}^n$.

Ring Learning With Errors (RLWE). We also extend the ring variant [35] of LWE to the special case where $\mathcal{R}_N = \mathbb{R}_N[X]/\mathbb{Z}_N[X]$, with $\mathbb{R}_N[X] = \mathbb{R}[X]/(X^N + 1)$ (respectively, $\mathbb{Z}_N[X] = \mathbb{Z}[X]/(X^N + 1)$), i.e., the $\mathbb{Z}_N[X]$ module of polynomials of degree up to $N - 1$ with coefficients in $\mathbb{T}$, with the operations done modulo $X^N + 1$ and modulo 1. Let N be a power of two, and χ be a distribution over $\mathbb{R}_N[X]$ for the noise. For any polynomial s of degree up to $N - 1$ with binary coefficients, we define the RLWE distribution $\mathsf{RLWE}_{N,s,\chi}$ as (a, b), where $a \xleftarrow{\$} \mathcal{R}_N$, $e \xleftarrow{\$} \chi$, and $b = s \cdot a + e$.

The RLWE assumption states that for a uniformly random polynomial s of degree up to $N - 1$ with binary coefficients, it is hard to distinguish between $\mathsf{RLWE}_{N,s,\chi}$ and the uniform distribution over $\mathcal{R}_N^2$.

---

[1] This is not exactly the original LWE definition since we here consider binary coefficients for the secret key, as in [9,12,13]. Nevertheless, we will still refer to it as LWE for sake of simplicity.

LWE Encryption Scheme. As in [9] and in some previous works [1,3,31,37], we use a variant of Regev's secret key encryption scheme which supports a non-binary message space. It can easily be transformed into a public key encryption scheme using standard techniques. Let B be an integer. The message space will be $\{-B+1, \ldots, B-1\}$. We define the encryption scheme as follows:

Setup(1^λ): on input a security parameter λ, fix $n = n(\lambda)$, samples and returns $\mathbf{s} \xleftarrow{\$} \{0,1\}^n$;

Encrypt$(\mathbf{s}, m)$: on input secret key $\mathbf{s}$ and message m, samples $(\mathbf{a}, b) \xleftarrow{\$}$ $\mathsf{LWE}_{n,\mathbf{s},\chi}$, and returns $ct = (\mathbf{ct}_0, ct_1) = (\mathbf{a}, b + \frac{m}{2B})$;

Decrypt$(\mathbf{s}, ct)$: computes x the representative of $ct_1 - \langle \mathbf{ct}_0, \mathbf{s} \rangle \mod 1$ in $[-\frac{1}{2}, \frac{1}{2}[$, and returns $\lfloor 2B \cdot x \rceil$.

We note that using $2B - 1$ as denominator would be enough to support the message space $\{-B+1, \ldots, B-1\}$. However, we require one extra unused slot in the message space for technical reasons during the sign computation.

Some of our protocols involve LWE encryption schemes of different dimensions. In such a case, we will refer to some ciphertexts as n-LWE ciphertexts, where n is the dimension, to avoid confusion with the other ciphertexts.

This encryption scheme generalizes to RLWE in a straightforward manner.

Bootstrapping Procedure. Our construction relies on three functions **BlindRotate**, **Extract** and **KeySwitch** that are defined in [9,12]. A proper definition of these functions requires to introduce many technical details along with the ring variant of the GSW encryption scheme [28]. However, such a definition is not necessary for the understanding of our work. For sake of clarity, we then only provide an informal definition that is sufficient for our paper.

BlindRotate: on input an LWE encryption ct encrypted with key $\mathbf{s}$, and a bootstrapping key bk, returns an RLWE encryption of $X^{\bar{b} - \langle \bar{\mathbf{a}}, \mathbf{s} \rangle}$, where $\bar{b} = \lfloor 2N \cdot ct_1 \rceil$ and $\bar{\mathbf{a}} = \lfloor 2N \cdot ct_0 \rceil$;

Extract: on input an RLWE encryption of a polynomial $p(X)$, returns an LWE encryption of $p(0)$;

KeySwitch: on input an LWE encryption c of m under a certain key $\mathbf{s}$ and a keyswitching key ksk (which consists of LWE encryptions of the bits s_i of $\mathbf{s}$ under secret key $\mathbf{s}'$), returns an LWE encryption of m under secret key $\mathbf{s}'$.

The key switching algorithm is not required for the construction to work, but it brings a lot of improvement in efficiency by reducing the dimension of the LWE ciphertext.

2.2   Strategy Overview

Before presenting our construction in more details, we give a high level overview of the underlying idea.

Let us assume that we are given an algorithm to compute the sign of integers in $\{-B+1, \ldots, B-1\}$. It can be used to compare two numbers x and y in $[0, B-1]$ as follows:

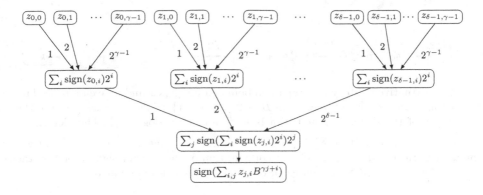

Fig. 1. Strategy to compare unbounded integers x and y given a procedure to compute the sign of integers in $\{-B+1, \ldots, B-1\}$. Here, $z_{i,j} = x_{i,j} - y_{i,j}$ are the differences of the digits of x and y in base B and $\delta = \lceil k/\gamma \rceil$. Arrows indicate computation of the ternary sign, scaled by the factor labelling it, and nodes consist of the sums of their incoming arrows.

1. take the difference $z = x - y$;
2. compute the sign of z.

If z is positive, it means x was greater than y, and vice versa.

Now let us say we are given bigger integers x and y such that we cannot use our sign function directly. What we can do is to decompose x and y in basis B, in order to obtain numbers in $[0, B-1]$. Let $(x_i)_{i \in [0,k]}$ and $(y_i)_{i \in [0,k]}$ be the digits of x and y in base B, for some integer k. For each i in $[0, k]$, we can compute the sign of $z_i = x_i - y_i$. However, we need a trick to combine those results to obtain the comparison of x and y, which is the sign of $z = \sum_{i \in [0,k]} z_i B^i$.

In order to continue, our main observation is that the sign of z is the same as the sign of $\sum_{i \in [0,k]} \text{sign}(z_i) 2^i$. Thus, we can pack the values z_i by groups of $\gamma = \lfloor \log_2(B) \rfloor$ values, scale each of them by a factor 2^i, depending on their position, and carry on computing the signs in a tree-like fashion as illustrated on Fig. 1.

Intuitively, the sign of each node will be the same as the sign of the rightmost non-zero node pointing to it, assuming the digits are ordered from the least significant on the left to the most significant on the right. Hence, by induction, the final value will be the sign of the rightmost non-zero z_i, i.e., -1 if $x < y$, 0 if $x = y$, and 1 if $x > y$.[2]

This construction requires two new features that are not present in [9]:

- it requires the sign to be ternary, *i.e.* $\text{sign}(0) = 0$;
- the output has to be scaled by a factor 2^i given as input.

---

[2] The binary sign can be obtained by applying the techniques of [9] instead of our ternary sign in the last step.

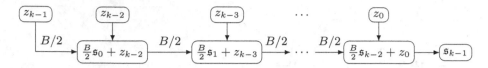

Fig. 2. Alternative strategy to compare unbounded integers x and y given a procedure to compute the sign of integers in $\{-B+1,\ldots,B-1\}$. Here, $z_i = x_i - y_i$ are the differences of the digits of x and y in base $\frac{B}{2}$ and $k = \lceil \log_{\frac{B}{2}}(x) \rceil$. The element $\mathfrak{s}_i$ denotes the ternary sign of $\sum_{j \in \{0,\ldots,i\}} z_{k-1-j} \left(\frac{B}{2}\right)^{k-1-j}$, the $(i+1)$ most significant digits of z. Horizontal arrows indicate computation of the ternary sign, scaled by the factor labelling it, and nodes consist of the sums of their incoming arrows.

The former is required in order to propagate the comparison of least significant digits whenever the most significant digits are equal. The latter cannot be accomplished by scaling the output ciphertext, because this would yield too much noise, thus preventing correct decryption of the resulting ciphertext. We will then explain how to take this scaling factor into account before returning the ciphertext, which leads to better noise management.

We also suggest another way to bootstrap such a technique to unbounded integers that has better noise management, at the cost of slightly larger ciphertexts, and sequential computations. We give an illustration of this on Fig. 2.

The idea is now to only have one addition in order to minimize the noise growth and optimize the parameters. We thus decompose the integers in basis $\frac{B}{2}$ and start from the most significant digits. At each step, we compute the ternary sign, and scale it by $\frac{B}{2}$ before adding it to the next digits. That way, the sign of our accumulator is always the sign of the difference, up to that point.

In the following, we first build an algorithm to compute the sign with the two additional features required, and then we present a recursive algorithm for each of our strategies.

Remark 1. At first sight, a simpler solution to compare x and y could be to select a bound B greater than these two integers, to generate keys compatible with this message space and then to directly run the protocol from [9] on $z = x - y$. However, there are two problems with this solution. First, the complexity of [9] is exponential in the size of the messages so selecting large B is not a good strategy (see Sect. 2.5 for more details). Second, this solution leads to the following dilemma. Either we select a bound B large enough to handle any integers x and y or we select, for each comparison, the smallest possible value for B. The former option makes the previous complexity issue even worse. The second option makes key management quite cumbersome because it implies several keys, one for each possible range of values of x and y.

Algorithm 1. HomomorphicCompare$_{B,0}$

Input: two LWE ciphertexts c_1, c_2 encrypting messages $m_1, m_2 \in [0, B-1]$, a bootstrapping key bk and a scaling factor k

Output: an N-LWE encryption of $k \cdot \text{sign}(m_1 - m_2)$

1: $P(X) := -k \cdot \sum_{i \in \{\lceil \frac{N}{2B} \rceil, \ldots, \lfloor N - \frac{N}{2B} \rfloor \}} X^i$
2: $c := c_1 - c_2$ (the task is now to find the sign of the plaintext in c)
3: $\tilde{c} := \text{BlindRotate}(c, bk)$
4: $x := \text{Extract}(P(X) \cdot \tilde{c})$
5: **return** x

2.3 Homomorphic Comparison of Small Integers

In this subsection, we show how to compare small integers, which will be the base case for our induction. While the techniques from [9] could be used directly to compare small integers, they do not fit our strategies for larger integers. We therefore modify their scheme in order to output 0 whenever the plaintexts are equal. This will be required in order to compare unbounded integers using this simple construction as a building block.

Our homomorphic comparison for small values HomomorphicCompare$_{B,0}$ is defined in Algorithm 1. For simplicity, we chose to define it without keyswitching to reduce the number of parameters, but it can easily be introduced as an optimization before returning the result. The scaling factor for the output is not important for the comparison of small integers, but will be needed to efficiently compute the comparison of larger integers in the next section. Correctness of this protocol is proved below.

Correctness. If c_1 encrypted m_1 and c_2 encrypted m_2, x encrypts k if $m_1 > m_2$, $-k$ if $m_1 < m_2$, and 0 if $m_1 = m_2$ with overwhelming probability, for well chosen parameters. Indeed, c encrypts $m_1 - m_2$, $\tilde{c}$ encrypts $X^{\bar{m}_1 - \bar{m}_2 + e}$, where $\bar{m}_i = m_i \cdot \frac{N}{B}$, and e is the error resulting from c_1, c_2, and the scalings and roundings during BlindRotate. Then, $P(X) \cdot \tilde{c}$ encrypts $-k \cdot \sum_{i \in \{\lceil \frac{N}{2B} \rceil, \ldots, \lfloor N - \frac{N}{2B} \rfloor \}} X^i \cdot X^{\bar{m}_1 - \bar{m}_2 + e}$, the constant term of which is

$$k \text{ if } \lceil \frac{N}{2B} \rceil \leq \bar{m}_1 - \bar{m}_2 + e \leq \lfloor N - \frac{N}{2B} \rfloor$$

$$-k \text{ if } -\lfloor N - \frac{N}{2B} \rfloor \leq \bar{m}_1 - \bar{m}_2 + e \leq -\lceil \frac{N}{2B} \rceil$$

$$0 \text{ otherwise}$$

Now let us assume that $m_1 > m_2$ and that the parameters are chosen such that $|e| < \frac{N}{2B}$, we have:

$$1 \leq m_1 - m_2 \leq B - 1$$

$$\Leftrightarrow \frac{N}{B} \leq \frac{N(m_1 - m_2)}{B} \leq \frac{N \cdot (B-1)}{B}$$

$$\Leftrightarrow \frac{N}{B} + e \leq \bar{m}_1 - \bar{m}_2 + e \leq \frac{N \cdot (B-1)}{B} + e$$
$$\Rightarrow \left\lceil \frac{N}{2B} \right\rceil \leq \bar{m}_1 - \bar{m}_2 + e < \frac{N \cdot (B-1)}{B} + \frac{N}{2B}$$

where the first inequality comes from the fact that $|e| < \frac{N}{2B}$ and that $\bar{m}_1 - \bar{m}_2 + e$ is an integer. Now, if we write:

$$\frac{N \cdot (B-1)}{B} + \frac{N}{2B} = N - \frac{N}{2B}$$

we get

$$\left\lceil \frac{N}{2B} \right\rceil \leq \bar{m}_1 - \bar{m}_2 + e \leq \left\lfloor N - \frac{N}{2B} \right\rfloor$$

which ensures that x encrypts k if $m_1 - m_2 \geq 1$.

Conversely, if $m_1 < m_2$, we get

$$-\frac{N}{B} + e \geq \bar{m}_1 - \bar{m}_2 + e \geq -\frac{N \cdot (B-1)}{B} + e$$

which implies that

$$-\left\lceil \frac{N}{2B} \right\rceil \geq \bar{m}_1 - \bar{m}_2 + e \geq -\left\lfloor N - \frac{N}{2B} \right\rfloor$$

and so that x encrypts $-k$.

2.4   Homomorphic Comparison of Unbounded Integers

In Sect. 2.2, we have described two strategies for comparing unbounded integers. The first one will be referred to as *tree-based*, whereas the latter one will be referred to as *sequential*. Informally, the tree-based approach is suitable for parallel computing whereas the sequential one offers better parameters but requires sequential computations (hence its name).

Tree-Based Strategy. Let us denote $\gamma = \lfloor \log_2(B) \rfloor$. Assuming that $B \geq 4$ (i.e., $\gamma \geq 2$), we can define a family of algorithms that can homomorphically compute the comparison of unbounded integers (that is, for any size of messages, there exists an algorithm in the family that can handle it) by decomposing the number in basis B, and do the comparison recursively in a bottom-up tree fashion, where each node has up to γ children. For each of them, we use the small integer homomorphic comparison with scaling factor 2^i, with i the position of the child, starting from 0 for the least significant. By adding the resulting values and then running again the small integer comparison protocol, we get the sign of the most significant non-zero child, as illustrated in Fig. 1.

Algorithm 2. HomomorphicCompare$_{B,\ell+1}$ for message space $[0, B^{\gamma^{\ell+1}} - 1]$

Input: two ciphertexts c_1, c_2 encrypting messages $m_1, m_2 \in [0, B^{\gamma^{\ell+1}} - 1]$, a bootstrapping key bk and a scaling factor k

Output: an N-LWE encryption of $k \cdot \text{sign}(m_1 - m_2)$

1: **for** $i = 0 \ldots \gamma - 1$ **do**
2:     $\overline{c_i} := \text{HomomorphicCompare}_{B,\ell}(c_{1,i}, c_{2,i}, bk, 2^i)$
3: **end for**
4: $P(X) := -k \cdot \sum_{i \in \{\lceil \frac{N}{2B} \rceil, \ldots, \lfloor N - \frac{N}{2B} \rfloor\}} X^i$
5: $c := \sum_{i \in [0, \gamma-1]} \overline{c_i}$ (the task is now to find the sign of the plaintext in c)
6: $\tilde{c} := \text{BlindRotate}(c, bk)$
7: $x := \text{Extract}(P(X) \cdot \tilde{c})$
8: **return** x

Before defining our algorithm to compare larger integers homomorphically, we need to specify how we encrypt those. Our encryption scheme is also defined by induction:

Enc$_B$: we use LWE.Encrypt as defined in Sect. 2.1;
Enc$_{B^{\gamma^{\ell+1}}}$: on input $m = \sum_{i \in [0, \gamma-1]} m_i (B^{\gamma^\ell})^i$, returns $(Enc_{B^{\gamma^\ell}}(m_i))_{i \in [0, \gamma-1]}$.

A ciphertext c encrypting a message $m \in [0, B^{\gamma^{\ell+1}}]$ thus contains γ ciphertexts c_i encrypting messages $m_i \in [0, B^{\gamma^\ell}]$. We are now ready to describe our family of algorithms to homomorphically compare large integers in Algorithm 2. By induction, this defines algorithms for homomorphic comparison with message spaces $[0, B^{\gamma^\ell} - 1]$, for any positive integer ℓ.

Correctness. By induction hypothesis, c_i encrypts $2^i \cdot \text{sign}(m_{1,i} - m_{2,i})$. Then c encrypts $\sum_{i \in [0, \gamma-1]} 2^i \cdot \text{sign}(m_{1,i} - m_{2,i})$, the sign of which is the sign of the last non-zero $m_{1,i} - m_{2,i}$, which is the sign of $m_1 - m_2$. Then, assuming the error does not grow too much, we can use the same analysis as previously to conclude that we correctly evaluate to $k \cdot \text{sign}(m_1 - m_2)$. The noise now comes from the sum of γ ciphertexts instead of 2.

Sequential Strategy. In order to minimize the noise growth during the computation, we apply the technique described in Sect. 2.2. First, we encrypt the messages by decomposing them in basis $\frac{B}{2}$ as follows:

$\overline{\text{Enc}_{(\frac{B}{2})^\ell}}$: on input $m = \sum_{i \in [0, \ell-1]} m_i (\frac{B}{2})^i$, returns $(\text{LWE.Encrypt}(m_i))_{i \in [0, \ell-1]}$.

As previously, we describe our alternative technique as a family of algorithms $\overline{\text{HomomorphicCompare}_{B,\ell}}$ in Algorithm 3, for homomorphic comparison with message spaces $[0, (\frac{B}{2})^\ell - 1]$, for any positive integer ℓ.

Algorithm 3. $\mathsf{HomomorphicCompare}_{B,\ell}$ for message space $[0, (\frac{B}{2})^\ell - 1]$

Input: two ciphertexts c_1, c_2 encrypting messages $m_1, m_2 \in [0, (\frac{B}{2})^\ell - 1]$, a bootstrapping key bk and a scaling factor k
Output: an N-LWE encryption of $k \cdot \mathrm{sign}(m_1 - m_2)$
1: $acc = 0$
2: **for** $i = \ell - 1, \ldots, 1$ **do**
3:     $acc := \mathsf{HomomorphicCompare}_{B,0}(acc + c_{1,i}, c_{2,i}, bk, \frac{B}{2})$
4: **end for**
5: **return** $\mathsf{HomomorphicCompare}_{B,0}(acc + c_{1,0}, c_{2,0}, bk, k)$

Correctness. After the i-th iteration of the loop, the accumulator acc contains the sign of $m_1^{(i)} - m_2^{(i)}$ scaled by $\frac{B}{2}$, where $m_b^{(i)} = \sum_{j \in \{0,\ldots,i\}} m_{b,\ell-1-j} \left(\frac{B}{2}\right)^{\ell-1-j}$ for $b \in \{0,1\}$. Indeed, observe that for all $i \in \{1, \ldots, \ell - 1\}$, $\left(m_1^{(i)} - m_2^{(i)}\right)$ has the same sign as

$$\frac{B}{2} \cdot \mathrm{sign}\left(m_1^{(i-1)} - m_2^{(i-1)}\right) + m_{1,\ell-1-i} - m_{2,\ell-1-i},$$

because $|m_{1,\ell-1-i} - m_{2,\ell-1-i}| < \frac{B}{2}$. The correctness then follows from the one of $\mathsf{HomomorphicCompare}_{B,0}$.

2.5 Efficiency

In order to test the efficiency of our technique, we implemented our protocol and ran it on a Core i7-3630QM laptop, on which a bootstrapping from the TFHE library takes about 33 ms. For such a processor supporting parallel computations, the tree-based approach significantly outperforms the sequential one. We will then only consider this strategy in the following. We nevertheless note that our sequential strategy offers better noise management and thus better parameters, making it more efficient if evaluated on a single core.

The fact that our protocol allows to process $\log_2(B)$ bits at once might lead to select large B. Unfortunately, the size of B impacts the parameters of our system and thus its efficiency. A careful noise analysis is therefore necessary to select optimal values for B.

Let σ_{bs}^2 be the variance of the noise at the end of the bootstrapping, as defined in [15], theorem 6.3:

$$\sigma_{bs}^2 = n(k+1)\ell N \beta^2 \sigma_{bk}^2 + n(1 + kN)\varepsilon^2 + n2^{-2(t+1)} + tn\sigma_{ks}^2$$

We use the same notation as in [15]. σ_{bk}^2 (resp. σ_{ks}^2) is the variance of the error of the bootstrapping key (resp. the key-switching key). k, ℓ, N, β and ε are parameters of the encryption schemes involved in **BlindRotate** whereas t and n are parameters of **KeySwitch**.

We have to correctly handle a message space of $2B$ slots even after adding $\gamma = \lfloor \log_2(B) \rfloor$ ciphertexts. We also have to take into account the noise resulting from rounding to multiples of $\frac{1}{2N}$.

Table 1. Timings obtained with three different sets of parameters for comparing 32 bits integers. For all of them, we have $k = 1$.

	B	N	n	σ_{ks}	σ_{bk}	β	t	Bootstr.	32bits comp.		
									1 core	8f cores	Max parall.
Set 1	4	2048	500	2^{-20}	2^{-50}	2048	17	72 ms	2232 ms	648 ms	360 ms
Set 2	4	4096	400	2^{-14}	2^{-70}	4096	13	126 ms	3902 ms	1137 ms	620 ms
Set 3	6	4096	750	2^{-18}	2^{-70}	4096	17	240 ms	3840 ms	1200 ms	960 ms

We thus get the following probability of correctness

$$\mathrm{erf}\left(\left(\frac{1}{4B} - \frac{n+1}{4N}\right)\frac{1}{\sigma_{bs}\sqrt{2\log_2(B)}}\right),$$

where erf is the Gauss error function.

This probability shows that increasing B requires to increase N, which is not a good strategy since the complexity of the bootstrapping is superlinear in N. For a given set of parameters (selected to ensure some level of security), one then simply has to choose the largest possible value for B. Interestingly, this means that, compared to binary decomposition, the efficiency of our protocol will increase with the security level.

We note that the flexibility in the choice of B (we can choose any value $B \geq 4$) allows a better noise management than in [9]. This means that our technique can probably be adapted to improve parameters of [9] for evaluation of neural networks where the message space is large.

We have tested our implementation for different sets of parameters. The results are presented in Table 1.

These three sets of parameters respectively yield a security [4] of 90/109/211 bits for the key switching key, and 230/378/378 bits for the bootstrapping key. The probability of error for a bootstrapping is respectively less than $2^{-50}/2^{-47}/2^{-89}$. Table 1 shows that our first set of parameters, with $B = 4$ and $N = 2048$, provides the best performances.

We note that the improvements from [9,46] halve the rounding cost by slightly unfolding the loop in BlindRotate. This allows us to basically double the message space at a very small cost. With the same noise analysis technique, we suggest to modify our first set of parameters as follows:

$$(N, n, \sigma_{ks}, \sigma_{bk}, \beta, t, k, \epsilon) = (1024, 500, 2^{-20}, 2^{-38}, 2048, 17, 1, 2^{-25})$$

This set of parameters yields a security of ≈ 90 bits for the key switching key, and ≈ 107 bits for the bootstrapping key. The probability of error for a bootstrapping is less than 2^{-50}. The running time for these parameters should be roughly 33 ms, given the experiments conducted in [9,46], which yields comparison of 32 bits integers in 1023 ms on a single core, 297 ms on 8 cores, and 165 ms with maximum parallelization.

For elements of comparison, using a binary decomposition requires 128 gates [32] for greater than comparison of 32 bits integers (what we are achieving is stronger, because we test equality as well), which would yield 4224 ms on the same laptop.

3   A Protocol for the Millionaires' Problem

In this section, we improve on the CEK protocol by avoiding one round induced by the plaintext equality test. This allows us to reduce the interaction to the minimum, while preserving efficiency. We first describe the more efficient protocol for small integers, before showing how it can easily be extended to larger integers by following the techniques in [10]. Even the protocol for larger messages only deals with bounded messages, however that bound grows really fast with the size of the RSA modulus chosen.

3.1   Preliminaries

The security of our protocol will rely on the Small RSA Subgroup Decision Assumption, defined in [10], inspired by [29]. Informally, it states that it is hard to distinguish a random element in a subgroup of $\mathbb{Z}_N^*$ from a random element. Let us introduce the following notation for our RSA quintuples (u, p_0, d, N, g):

- u is an integer such that the Discrete Logarithm Problem is infeasible in a subgroup of $\mathbb{Z}_N^*$ whose order is a prime of bit-length u;
- p_0 is a prime;
- d is an integer greater than 1;
- N is an integer of the form $N = pq$, whose factorisation is infeasible, where $p = 2 \cdot p_0^d \cdot p_s \cdot p_t + 1$ and $q = 2 \cdot p_0^d \cdot q_s \cdot q_t + 1$, with p_s and q_s primes of bit-length u, and p_t and q_t primes whose bit-length is not u;
- g is an element of order p_0^d in $\mathbb{Z}_N^*$;
- $\mathbb{QR}_N$ is the set of quadratic residues mod N.

Definition 2. *We say that the small RSA subgroup decision assumption holds if given an RSA quintuple (u, p_0, d, N, g), the distributions x and $x^{p_0^d \cdot p_t \cdot q_t}$ are computationally indistinguishable, for $x \xleftarrow{\$} \mathbb{QR}_N$ a uniformly random quadratic residue mod N.*

In other words, the small RSA subgroup assumption states that it is hard to distinguish an element of order $p_s \cdot q_s$ from a random quadratic residue in $\mathbb{Z}_N^*$. Since pinpointing the optimal parameters for security and efficiency is not trivial in this setting, we discuss in more details our choices of parameters in Sect. 4.1.

3.2   Protocol for Small Integers

We describe in this section our protocol for secure integer comparison but first start by providing the intuition behind it.

Intuition. As in [10], our protocol makes use of the threshold properties of prime power subgroups of $\mathbb{Z}_N^*$. We will then assume that there exist a prime p_0 and an integer $d > 0$ such that p_0^d divides $\phi(N)$. Let g be an element of order p_0^d in $\mathbb{Z}_N^*$ and $\mathbb{G}$ be the cyclic subgroup generated by g.

In [10], the core idea is that the element $C = g^{p_0^{d+m_1-m_2}}$ can be used to compare the integers m_1 and m_2. Indeed, this element is equal to 1 if and only if $m_1 \geq m_2$. However, to prevent any leakage of information on its secret integer m_2, the second party B has to blind C using a random element $g^s \in \mathbb{G}$ leading to the following problem for the first party A : in all cases (namely $m_1 \geq m_2$ or $m_1 < m_2$) it receives a random element $g^{s'}$. To compare m_1 and m_2, Carlton et al. therefore propose (1) to recover s' from $g^{s'}$ (i.e. to compute a discrete logarithm) and (2) to run a plaintext equality test (PET) between A and B to compare s' and s. It implies at least another pass and involves additional primitives (e.g. homomorphic encryption in [10]).

The goal of our protocol is to remove these last steps and so to reduce the number of passes while avoiding the computational overhead of PET protocols.

Let $0 < a \leq d$ be a public integer such that $p_0^a \geq 2^\lambda$ where λ is the security parameter[3]. Of course, this requirement implies larger subgroups $\mathbb{G}$ but, as we will explain, this is not a significant problem for us since we will no longer need to compute discrete logarithms in $\mathbb{G}$. Let $\mathbb{H}$ be a subgroup of order coprime with p_0, generated by some element h.

To compare $m_1, m_2 \leq d/a$, the party A computes $C = g^{p_0^{a \cdot m_1}} \cdot h^{r_1}$, for some random scalars r_1, and sends it to B. The latter then selects three random scalars: $u \in [0, p_0^a - 1]$, $v \in [0, p_0^d - 1]$ and $r_2 \in [0, \bar{b} - 1]$ where $\bar{b}$ is some bound on the order of $\mathbb{H}$. It then computes and sends to A two elements:

$$D \leftarrow C^{u \cdot p_0^{d-a \cdot m_2}} \cdot g^v \cdot h^{r_2} \text{ and } D' \leftarrow \mathcal{H}(g^v)$$

where $\mathcal{H}$ is some hash function. One can note that $D = g^{u \cdot p_0^{d+a(m_1-m_2)}+v} \cdot h^*$ for some random element $h^* \in \mathbb{H}$. By using its knowledge of the factorization of N, A can easily remove h^* and recover $C' = g^{u \cdot p_0^{d+a(m_1-m_2)}+v}$. There are then two different cases:

1. If $m_1 \geq m_2$, then $C' = g^v$ which can easily be detected by A since $\mathcal{H}(C') = D'$ in such a case.
2. Else, $\mathcal{H}(C')$ differs from D' with overwhelming probability, leading A to conclude that $m_1 < m_2$.

From the security point of view, one can note that B always received values masked by a random element h of $\mathbb{H}$. It is thus unable to learn information on m_1 unless it can solve the small RSA subgroup problem. In the case where $m_1 \geq m_2$ the pair (D, D') received by A is independent of m_2 so this entity cannot learn any information on this value. In the case where $m_1 < m_2$, the element C' is a random element of $\mathbb{G}$ (since v is random) but A has an information on the

---

[3] We will provide more details on the parameters in Sect. 4.1.

Party A $(pp, sp, m_1 \in [0, d/a])$	**Party B** $(pp, m_2 \in [0, d/a])$

$r_1 \xleftarrow{\$} [1, \bar{b} - 1]$

$C = g^{p_0^{a \cdot m_1}} h^{r_1}$

$\xrightarrow{\quad C \quad}$ $u \xleftarrow{\$} [1, p_0^a - 1]$, $v \xleftarrow{\$} [1, p_0^d - 1]$,

$\qquad\qquad\qquad\qquad r_2 \xleftarrow{\$} [1, \bar{b} - 1]$

$\qquad\qquad\qquad\qquad D \leftarrow C^{u \cdot p_0^{d - a \cdot m_2}} \cdot g^v \cdot h^{r_2}$

$\xleftarrow{\quad (D, D') \quad}$ $D' \leftarrow \mathcal{H}(g^v)$

$C' \leftarrow D^c$

If $D' = \mathcal{H}(C')$, return $(m_1 \geq m_2)$

Else, return $(m_1 < m_2)$.

Fig. 3. A two-pass protocol for secure comparison of small integers.

blinding factor g^v since it knows $D' = \mathcal{H}(g^v)$. Since a hash function is assumed to be one-way, A cannot recover g^v directly from D but can try to guess it either directly (with probability $1/p_0^d$) or by guessing the cofactor $g^{u \cdot p_0^{d + a(m_1 - m_2)}}$. However, the latter element is of order a least $p_0^a > 2^\lambda$ which makes a correct guess very unlikely when u is random.

Our Construction. Our protocol is described in Fig. 3 and makes use of the following parameters:

- $N = p \cdot q$ is a product of two primes p and q
- p_0, p_s and q_s are prime numbers such that $p_s|p - 1$, $q_s|q - 1$ and p_0^d divides both $p - 1$ and $q - 1$ for some integer $d > 0$
- $0 < a \leq d$ is an integer smaller than d
- $g \in \mathbb{Z}_N^*$ is an element of order p_0^d in both $\mathbb{Z}_p^*$ and $\mathbb{Z}_q^*$ while $h \in \mathbb{Z}_N^*$ is an element of order $p_s \cdot q_s$
- $\bar{b}$ is an upper bound on $p_s \cdot q_s$
- c is an integer such that $c = p_s \cdot q_s \cdot [(p_s \cdot q_s)^{-1}]_{p_0^d}$, where $[x]_{p_0^d}$ denotes x mod p_0^d.
- $\mathcal{H} : \mathbb{Z}_N^* \to \{0,1\}^*$ is a cryptographic hash function.

The public parameters pp are defined as $\{N, a, p_0, d, g, h, \bar{b}\}$ whereas the secret parameters sp, only known to A, are $\{p, q, c\}$.

Correctness. As explained above, the element C' computed by A is exactly $g^{u \cdot p_0^{d + a(m_1 - m_2)} + v}$. If $m_1 \geq m_2$, then $C' = g^v$ and $D' = \mathcal{H}(C')$. Else, $m_1 - m_2 < 0$ and p_0^a divides the order of $g^{p_0^{d + a(m_1 - m_2)}}$. Since $u \in [1, p_0^a - 1]$, $g^{u \cdot p_0^{d + a(m_1 - m_2)}} \neq 1$ and $C' \neq g^v$. Therefore, $D = \mathcal{H}(C')$ would imply a collision of the hash function $\mathcal{H}$, which is very unlikely.

3.3 Security of the Protocol for Small Integers

We prove the security for both A and B against honest-but-curious adversaries in the random oracle model. This means that A (respectively B) will not learn any information about m_2 (resp. m_1), except whether it is bigger or smaller than m_1 (resp. m_2).

Privacy of A. We first show that B learns nothing about m_1 in this protocol. More formally, we have the following security theorem.

Theorem 3. *Under the Small RSA Subgroup Decision Assumption, B's view is computationally indistinguishable from a uniformly random element in $\mathbb{QR}_N$ for any message m_1.*

Proof. We show that we can use an adversary that has probability ϵ of distinguishing B's view from a uniformly random element in $\mathbb{Z}_N^*$ to break the Small RSA Subgroup Decision Assumption with the same probability.

Let us define a first game where the reduction $\mathcal{R}$ publishes a valid set of parameters $\{N, a, p_0, d, g, h, \bar{b}\}$ (here valid means in particular that h is of order $p_s \cdot q_s$) and plays the role of A as defined in Fig. 3.

In a second game, $\mathcal{R}$ proceeds as in the previous game except that it generates a random element $z \xleftarrow{\$} \mathbb{Z}_N^*$ and sets $h = z^2$. In such a case, the element C received by B is a uniformly random element in $\mathbb{QR}_N$ for any message m_1.

Now let us assume that an adversary $\mathcal{A}$ is able to distinguish these two games with probability ϵ. On input an RSA quintuple (u, p_0, d, N, g) and an instance x to the small RSA subgroup decision problem, $\mathcal{R}$ defines the public parameters as $\{N, a, p_0, d, g, h, \bar{b}\}$, where a and $\bar{b}$ are selected as usual, but where $h = x$. If x is of order $p_s \cdot q_s$, then this is exactly our first game. Else, x is a uniformly random quadratic residue and $\mathcal{A}$ is playing our second game. Therefore, $\mathcal{A}$ will succeed in breaking the Small RSA Subgroup Decision Assumption with probability ϵ, which implies that ϵ is negligible.

Privacy of B. We now show that A only learns the output of the protocol $(m_1 \geq m_2)$ and nothing else about m_2.

Theorem 4. *There exists an efficient simulator $\mathcal{S}$, such that $\mathcal{S}(1^\lambda, (m_1 \geq m_2))$ is statistically indistinguishable from A's view for any messages m_1 and m_2 in the random oracle model.*

Proof. The simulator S works as follows:

- If $m_1 < m_2$ pick random elements $v, v' \xleftarrow{\$} [1, p_0^d - 1], r \xleftarrow{\$} [1, \bar{b} - 1]$ and return $\left(g^v \cdot h^r, \mathcal{H}(g^{v'}) \right)$.
- Else pick random elements $v \xleftarrow{\$} [1, p_0^d - 1], r \xleftarrow{\$} [1, \bar{b} - 1]$ and return $(g^v \cdot h^r, \mathcal{H}(g^v))$.

In the first case, we show that the statistical distance between the view of A and the output of S is negligible: The two distribution only differ when the adversary queries the random oracle with input $g^{v - u \cdot p_0^{d + a(m_1 - m_2)}}$ and realizes that it's different from $\mathcal{H}(g^{v'})$. However, this can never happen with non-negligible

Party A $(pp, sp, m_1 = \sum_{i=0}^{\ell} m_{1,i} \cdot b^i)$	**Party B** $(pp, m_2 = \sum_{i=0}^{\ell} m_{2,i} \cdot b^i)$

For $i \in [0, \ell]$: $r_{1,i} \overset{\$}{\leftarrow} [1, \overline{b} - 1]$

$$C_i = g^{-m_1^{(i)}} g_{p_0}^{a(m_{1,i})} h^{r_{1,i}} \quad \xrightarrow{\{C_i\}_{i=0}^{\ell}}$$

For $i \in [0, \ell]$:
$$u_i \overset{\$}{\leftarrow} [1, p_0^a - 1], \ v_i \overset{\$}{\leftarrow} [1, p_0^d - 1],$$
$$r_{2,i} \overset{\$}{\leftarrow} [1, \overline{b} - 1], \ D_i' \leftarrow \mathcal{H}(g^{v_i})$$
$$D_i \leftarrow (C_i \cdot g^{m_2^{(i)}})^{u_i \cdot p_0^{d-a(m_{2,i}+1)}} \cdot g^{v_i} \cdot h^{r_{2,i}}$$

$$\xleftarrow{\pi(\{(D_i, D_i')\}_{i=0}^{\ell})}$$

For $i \in [0, \ell]$:
  $C_i' \leftarrow D_i^c$
If $\exists i$ s.t. $D_i' = \mathcal{H}(C_i')$,
    return $(m_1 > m_2)$
Else, return $(m_1 \le m_2)$.

Fig. 4. A two-pass protocol for secure integer comparison. π is a random permutation of the symmetric group $S_{\ell+1}$.

probability because $g^{u \cdot p_0^{d+a(m_1+m_2)}}$ is uniform in a subgroup of order at least p_0^a, which is exponential in the security parameter for the parameters we suggest in Sect. 4.1.

In the second case, the distribution is exactly the same as in the protocol.

3.4   A Protocol for Large Integers

As we explain in Sect. 4.1, the constraints that apply on the different parameters imply that the protocol of Fig. 3 can only be used to compare small messages. However, our protocol can be extended to compare larger integers by adapting a technique used in previous works (e.g. [10,20]). Let $m_1 = \sum_{i=0}^{\ell} m_{1,i} \cdot b^i$ and $m_2 = \sum_{i=0}^{\ell} m_{2,i} \cdot b^i$ be the rewriting of the messages m_1 and m_2 in base $b = \lfloor d/a \rfloor$ (i.e. $m_{j,i} \in [0, b-1]$ for $i \in [0, \ell]$ and $\ell = \lceil \log_b(M) \rceil$, where $M < p_0^a$ is a bound on the messages m_1 and m_2). For $i \in [0, \ell]$, we define $m_j^{(i)} = \sum_{k=i+1}^{\ell} m_{j,k} b^k$. Our protocol is described in Fig. 4 and uses the same parameters as in Sect. 3.2.

Remark 5. The bound $M < p_0^a$ is not a strong constraint for most applications since $p_0^a > 2^\lambda$ (see Sect. 4.1 below). This protocol is therefore sufficient to compare integers of reasonable size but, if need be, it can easily be extended for even larger integers. Indeed, instead of including $g^{m_i^{(i)}}$ in C_i, the party A can encrypt it separately as $E_i = g^{-m_i^{(1)}} h^{r'_{1,i}}$ and sends it along with C_i. The party B will now compute D_i as $(C^{p_0^{d-a(m_2+1)}} E_i \cdot g^{m_2^{(i)}})^{u_i} \cdot g^{v_i} \cdot h^{r_{2,i}}$ leading to a much larger bound of $B < p_0^d \sim N^{1/4}$.

Correctness. We prove that $m_1 > m_2 \Leftrightarrow \exists i \in [0, \ell]$ such that $D_i' = \mathcal{H}(C_i')$.

First note that if $m_1 > m_2$, then $\exists i \in [0, \ell]$ such that (1) $m_1^{(i)} = m_2^{(i)}$ and (2) $m_{1,i} > m_{2,i}$, or equivalently $(m_{1,i} - m_{2,i}) \geq 1$. For such an index i, we have:

$$C_i' = g^{u_i [(m_2^{(i)} - m_1^{(i)}) p_0^{d-a(m_{2,i}+1)} + p_0^{d+a(m_{1,i} - m_{2,i} - 1)}] + v_i} = g^{v_i}$$

which means that $D_i' = \mathcal{H}(C_i')$. Now, let us assume that $\exists i \in [0, \ell]$ such that $D_i' = \mathcal{H}(C_i')$. Due to the collision resistance of $\mathcal{H}$, this means (with overwhelming probability) that $g^{v_i} = C_i'$ and so that:

$$u_i [(m_2^{(i)} - m_1^{(i)}) p_0^{d-a(m_{2,i}+1)} + p_0^{d+a(m_{1,i} - m_{2,i} - 1)}] = 0 \bmod p_0^d$$

One can note that the powers of p_0 between the square brackets are either multiples of p_0^d or of the form p_0^t with $t \leq d - a$. Since $0 < u_i < p_0^a$, this implies that:

$$[(m_2^{(i)} - m_1^{(i)}) p_0^{d-a(m_{2,i}+1)} + p_0^{d+a(m_{1,i} - m_{2,i} - 1)}] = 0 \bmod p_0^d$$
$$\Leftrightarrow p_0^{d-a(m_{2,i}+1)} [(m_2^{(i)} - m_1^{(i)}) + p_0^{a \cdot m_{1,i}}] = 0 \bmod p_0^d$$
$$\Leftrightarrow (m_2^{(i)} - m_1^{(i)}) + p_0^{a \cdot m_{1,i}} = 0 \bmod p_0^{a(m_{2,i}+1)} \quad (\mathrm{I})$$

For all $i \in [0, \ell]$, we have $m_2^{(i)} - m_1^{(i)} \leq M - (b - 1) \leq M - 1 < p_0^a - 1$. We can therefore distinguish two cases.

- Case 1: $m_{2,i} \geq m_{1,i}$. From $(m_2^{(i)} - m_1^{(i)}) + p_0^{a \cdot m_{1,i}} < p_0^a - 1 + p_0^{a \cdot m_{2,i}} \leq p_0^{a \cdot m_{2,i} + 1}$ and the Equation (I), we can deduce that $(m_2^{(i)} - m_1^{(i)}) + p_0^{a \cdot m_{1,i}} \leq 0$ and in particular that $m_1^{(i)} > m_2^{(i)}$. The latter inequality means that $m_1 > m_2$, which concludes our proof.
- Case 2: $m_{2,i} < m_{1,i}$. The Equation (I) then becomes:

$$(m_2^{(i)} - m_1^{(i)}) = 0 \bmod p_0^{a(m_{2,i}+1)}.$$

However, we know that $-p_0^a < m_2^{(i)} - m_1^{(i)} < p_0^a$, so the previous equation can only hold if $m_2^{(i)} = m_1^{(i)}$. Here again, this means that $m_1 > m_2$.

Therefore, $m_1 > m_2 \Leftrightarrow \exists i \in [0, \ell]$ such that $D_i' = \mathcal{H}(C_i')$, which proves the correctness of our protocol.

4 Security of the Protocol for Large Integers

The proof of security for this protocol is very similar to the previous one, and the claims are similar: A's data will be computationally secure, while B's data will be statistically secure. One key observation is that each pair (D_i, D_i') proves or disproves the statement $m_1^{(i)} = m_2^{(i)} \wedge m_{1,i} > m_{2,i}$. At most one of them can be satisfied, and one is satisfied if and only if $m_1 > m_2$.

Privacy of A. We first show that B learns nothing about m_1 in this protocol. More formally, we have the following security theorem.

Theorem 6. *Under the Small RSA Subgroup Decision Assumption, B's view is computationally indistinguishable from a uniformly random element in $\mathbb{QR}_N^{\ell+1}$ for any message m_1.*

Proof. As in the previous case, we can show this indistinguishability by replacing the element h by a small RSA subgroup decision challenge. If the element has order $p_s \cdot q_s$, then the view of B is identical to the real protocol. Otherwise, B only receives a uniformly random element in $\mathbb{QR}_N^{\ell+1}$. Thus, any adversary breaking the privacy of A can be used to solve the Small RSA Subgroup Decision problem.

Privacy of B. We now show that A only learns the output of the protocol ($m_1 > m_2$) and nothing else about m_2.

Theorem 7. *There exists an efficient simulator $\mathcal{S}$, such that $\mathcal{S}(1^\lambda, (m_1 > m_2))$ is statistically indistinguishable from A's view for any messages m_1 and m_2 in the random oracle model.*

Proof. The simulator $\mathcal{S}$ works as follows:

- If $m_1 \leq m_2$, for each $i \in [0, \ell]$ pick random elements $v_i, v_i' \xleftarrow{\$} [1, p_0^d - 1], r_i \xleftarrow{\$} [1, \overline{b} - 1]$ and sets $\left(D_i = g^{v_i} \cdot h^{r_i}, D_i' = \mathcal{H}(g^{v_i'}) \right)$. Then it returns $\{(D_i, D_i')\}_{i=0}^{\ell}$;
- Else pick a random index $j \in [0, \ell]$, random elements $v_j \xleftarrow{\$} [1, p_0^d - 1], r_j \xleftarrow{\$} [1, \overline{b} - 1]$ and sets $\left(D_j = g^{v_j} \cdot h^{r_j}, D_j' = \mathcal{H}(g^{v_j}) \right)$. Then, for each $i \in [0, \ell]$, $i \neq j$, pick random elements $v_i, v_i' \xleftarrow{\$} [1, p_0^d - 1], r_i \xleftarrow{\$} [1, \overline{b} - 1]$ and sets $\left(D_i = g^{v_i} \cdot h^{r_i}, D_i' = \mathcal{H}(g^{v_i'}) \right)$. Finally, returns $\{(D_i, D_i')\}_{i=0}^{\ell}$

As previously, in the first case, we show that the statistical distance between the view of B and the output of S is negligible: The two distribution can only differ when the adversary queries the random oracle with input $g^{\tilde{v}_{k,i}}$ for some indices $i, k \in [0, \ell]$, where

$$\tilde{v}_{k,i} = v_k - u_i \cdot (m_2^{(i)} - m_1^{(i)}) \cdot p_0^{d-a(m_{2,i}+1)} + u_i \cdot p_0^{d-a(m_{1,i}-m_{2,i}+1)}.$$

However, as we have shown for correctness,

$$(m_2^{(i)} - m_1^{(i)}) \cdot p_0^{d-a(m_{2,i}+1)} + p_0^{d-a(m_{1,i}-m_{2,i}+1)} \neq 0 \bmod p_0^d,$$

unless $m_2^{(i)} = m_1^{(i)}$ and $m_{i,1} > m_{i,2}$. Thus, the $\tilde{v}_{k,i}$ are uniformly random in an exponentially big subgroup for parameters suggested in Sect. 4.1 (of order at least p_0^a). Since the adversary runs in polynomial time, the probability that he queries the random oracle on one of these input is negligible.

In the second case, the distribution is exactly the same as in the protocol for the index j that satisfies $m_2^{(j)} = m_1^{(j)}$ and $m_{j,1} > m_{j,2}$. For all the other indices, we use the same argument as in the first case: the two distributions can only differ when the adversary queries the random oracle with input $g^{\tilde{v}_{k,i}}$ for some indices $i, k \in [0, \ell]$, $k \neq j$.

4.1 Parameters

One must be careful when using RSA modulus whose prime factors have unusual decomposition, as shown in [17,18,36,39]. We discuss in this section the bounds on the different parameters to ensure the security of our protocols and their impact on efficiency.

There are several attacks that we must take into account due to the special form of our RSA modulus. One of them is the Coron et al. attack [18] that gives us a bound on the order of h: $\log_2(p_s) = \log_2(q_s) \geq 2\lambda$.

The condition $p_0^d | p - 1$ and $p_0^d | q - 1$ makes our protocol vulnerable to the McKee's and Pinch's attack [36] and thus imposes the upper bound $N^{1/4}/2^\lambda$ on the value of p_0^d, where λ is the security parameter. We must therefore have:

$$d \cdot \log(p_0) \leq \frac{1}{4}\log(N) - \lambda\log(2).$$

This gives us a bound on the messages m that can be compared in a single execution of our protocol:

$$m \leq d/a \leq \frac{\log(N)/4 - \lambda\log(2)}{\log(p_0) \cdot a}$$

Ideally, we would like to choose $p_0 = 2$ and $a = 1$ to get the largest bound. However, we must additionally ensure that the random scalar u cannot be guessed with non-negligible probability. This means that:

$$a \cdot \log(p_0) \geq \lambda\log(2)$$

Combining these two constraints leads to the following bound on the messages:

$$m \leq \frac{\log(N)/4 - \lambda\log(2)}{\log(p_0) \cdot a} \leq \frac{\log(N)/4 - \lambda\log(2)}{\lambda\log(2)}$$

One can note that this bound on m is independent of p_0 and a. This means that there is a great flexibility in the choice of these parameters provided that the requirement $a \cdot \log(p_0) \geq \lambda\log(2)$ is fulfilled.

Interestingly, the fact that N grows more quickly than the security parameter λ [33,40] implies that this bound depends on the security parameter. In particular, compared to previous protocols (e.g. [20,42,43]) that work with bit-wise encrypted values, the speedup factor will be larger for $\lambda = 256$ than for $\lambda = 128$.

4.2 Efficiency

As we mention in the introduction, there is a wide range of solutions to the Millionaire's problem from garbled circuits to homomorphic encryption. And even among solutions based on homomorphic encryption, one can find different tradeoffs such as the two-passes protocol proposed by Damgård et al. [20] and the protocol proposed by Carlton et al. [10] that allows to process several bits

Table 2. Efficiency comparison between related works and our protocol. E_t refers to the cost of an exponentiation whose exponent is smaller than t. $\text{dlog}_{\mathbb{G}}$ refers to the cost of computing a discrete logarithm in the group $\mathbb{G}$. $\text{Enc}_{\oplus}$, $\text{Dec}_{\oplus}$ and $\text{Rand}_{\oplus}$ respectively refer to the cost of encrypting, decrypting and re-randomizing with the additively homomorphic encryption scheme Π used for the PET. Finally, $C_{\oplus}$ refers to a ciphertext generated using Π and H to a digest generated by $\mathcal{H}$.

Schemes	DGK [20]	CEK [10]	Our work
Computational Cost (A)	$\log_2(M)[1\ E_{\bar{b}} + 1\ E_{\bar{b}p_0^d}]$	$\log_{b'}(M)[1\ E_{\bar{b}} + 1\ E_{\bar{b}p_0^d} + 1\ \text{dlog}_{\mathbb{G}} + 1\ \text{Rand}_{\oplus}]$	$\log_b(M)[1\ E_{\bar{b}} + 1\ E_{\bar{b}p_0^d}]$
Computational Cost (B)	$\log_2(M)[1\ E_{\bar{b}}]$	$\log_{b'}(M)[1\ E_{\bar{b}} + 2\ E_{p_0^d} + 1\ \text{Enc}_{\oplus} + 1\ \text{Dec}_{\oplus}]$	$\log_b(M)[1\ E_{\bar{b}} + 2\ E_{p_0^d}]$
Communication Cost	$\log_2(M)[2\ \mathbb{Z}_N^*]$	$\log_{b'}(M)[2\ \mathbb{Z}_N^* + 2\ C_{\oplus}]$	$\log_b(M)[2\ \mathbb{Z}_N^* + 1\ H]$
Passes	2	$3-4^a$	

^{a} Carlton *et al.* explain how to combine the last pass of their protocol with the first one of the PET, leading to a protocol with 3 passes instead of 4. However, in such a case, the entity (A) that initiated the protocol does not know the result of the comparison (only B knows it), contrarily to our protocol or to the DGK one.

at once but at the cost of an extra plaintext equality check (PET) involving additional passes. We therefore choose to compare our protocol with both solutions by providing in Table 2 an assessment of the different respective costs. In particular, we stress that the cost of additional passes, and more generally the communication cost, should not be underestimated. It can indeed be very high for some devices such as smartcards, and even exceeds computational cost in some cases (see *e.g.* [22]).

For the sake of clarity, we do not consider additions, multiplications and hash evaluations whose costs are negligible compared to the other operations. We also assume, for all protocols, that the elements only depending on the messages m_1 or m_2 and on the system parameters (*e.g.* $g^{p_0^{a \cdot m_{1,i}}}$) have been pre-computed.

For proper comparison, we need to specify the values of the factors $\log_{b'}(M)$ and $\log_b(M)$ respectively used in the evaluation of the complexity of the CEK protocol and ours. This is not a trivial task as the constraints placed on our parameters prevent us from using conventional RSA moduli. This is done in Sect. 4.1 where we show that:

$$b = \left\lfloor \frac{\log(N)/4 - \lambda\log(2)}{\lambda\log(2)} \right\rfloor$$

A similar analysis for the CEK protocol shows that:

$$b' = \left\lfloor \frac{\log(N)/4 - \lambda\log(2)}{\log(p_0)} \right\rfloor$$

Our protocol can easily be compared to the DGK one since they both involve 2 passes and do not need PET. Actually, one can note that our protocol is roughly $\frac{\log(b)}{\log(2)}$ more efficient than the DGK one. For a security parameter λ of respectively 128, 192 and 256, we have $b = 5$, $b = 9$ and $b = 14$ (see [40]), which means that the speedup factor is always greater than 2 and will increase with the security level.

Conversely, comparing our solution with the CEK one is more complex, as they are very different protocols. Ours only requires 2 passes and does not require a PET, thus avoiding additional interactions and the costs associated with an homomorphic encryption system. Regarding computational costs, a single execution of our comparison protocol is more efficient than the CEK one, but this is offset by the fact that CEK requires to run less individual comparison tests because $\log_{b'}(M) < \log_b(M)$. However, we note that the ratio $\frac{\log_b(M)}{\log_{b'}(M)}$ decreases towards 1 as λ increases due to the existence of subexponential factorization algorithms (see [33,40] and references therein), meaning that the number of comparison tests for both solutions will tend to be similar in the future.

5 Conclusion

More than three decades after its introduction by Yao, the Millionaires' problem has proved very important in cryptography, and more generally in most use-cases involving secure computation (*e.g.* machine learning on private data). It has drawn attention from many researchers that have provided a wide range of solutions, based on different primitives or addressing different versions of the original problem. However, despite all this work, secure integer comparison remains a complex issue, all the existing solutions entailing either a large amount of computations or a large amount of communication.

In this work, we have introduced new solutions to the Millionaires' problem in two different settings. Our first one extends the recent FHE construction of Bourse *et al.* [9] to enable efficient computation of the encrypted boolean $(m_1 \leq m_2)$ given only the encryption of (a-priori unbounded) integers m_1 and m_2. Our second solution leverages the threshold homomorphic encryption scheme of Carlton *et al.* [10] to construct a two-passes integer comparison protocol that improves over the state-of-the art. Although these constructions are very different, they both share the same guiding principles, namely reducing as much as possible the number of interactions and avoiding bitwise decomposition of the integers. Regarding the latter point, this concretely means that our protocols achieve a $\log_2(b)$ speedup factor compared to most homomorphic-based solutions, where $b > 4$ is some integer depending on the parameters of our constructions.

Acknowledgements. This work is supported by the European Union PROMETHEUS project (Horizon 2020 Research and Innovation Program, grant 780701) and PAPAYA project (Horizon 2020 Innovation Program, grant 786767). The authors are also grateful for the support of the ANR through project ANR-16-CE39-0014 PERSOCLOUD.

References

1. Abdalla, M., Bourse, F., De Caro, A., Pointcheval, D.: Simple functional encryption schemes for inner products. In: Katz, J. (ed.) PKC 2015. LNCS, vol. 9020, pp. 733–751. Springer, Heidelberg (2015). https://doi.org/10.1007/978-3-662-46447-2_33
2. Abspoel, M., Bouman, N.J., Schoenmakers, B., de Vreede, N.: Fast secure comparison for medium-sized integers and its application in binarized neural networks. In: Matsui, M. (ed.) CT-RSA 2019. LNCS, vol. 11405, pp. 453–472. Springer, Cham (2019). https://doi.org/10.1007/978-3-030-12612-4_23
3. Agrawal, S., Libert, B., Stehlé, D.: Fully secure functional encryption for inner products, from standard assumptions. In: Robshaw, M., Katz, J. (eds.) CRYPTO 2016, Part III. LNCS, vol. 9816, pp. 333–362. Springer, Heidelberg (2016). https://doi.org/10.1007/978-3-662-53015-3_12
4. Albrecht, M.R., Player, R., Scott, S.: On the concrete hardness of learning with errors. J. Math. Cryptol. **9**(3), 169–203 (2015)
5. Bellare, M., Hoang, V.T., Keelveedhi, S., Rogaway, P.: Efficient garbling from a fixed-key blockcipher. In: 2013 IEEE SSP, pp. 478–492 (2013)
6. Bellare, M., Hoang, V.T., Rogaway, P.: Foundations of garbled circuits. In: ACM CCS 2012, pp. 784–796 (2012)
7. Blake, I.F., Kolesnikov, V.: Conditional encrypted mapping and comparing encrypted numbers. In: Di Crescenzo, G., Rubin, A. (eds.) FC 2006. LNCS, vol. 4107, pp. 206–220. Springer, Heidelberg (2006). https://doi.org/10.1007/11889663_18
8. Bost, R., Popa, R.A., Tu, S., Goldwasser, S.: Machine learning classification over encrypted data. In: NDSS (2015)
9. Bourse, F., Minelli, M., Minihold, M., Paillier, P.: Fast homomorphic evaluation of deep discretized neural networks. In: Shacham, H., Boldyreva, A. (eds.) CRYPTO 2018, Part III. LNCS, vol. 10993, pp. 483–512. Springer, Cham (2018). https://doi.org/10.1007/978-3-319-96878-0_17
10. Carlton, R., Essex, A., Kapulkin, K.: Threshold properties of prime power subgroups with application to secure integer comparisons. In: Smart, N.P. (ed.) CT-RSA 2018. LNCS, vol. 10808, pp. 137–156. Springer, Cham (2018). https://doi.org/10.1007/978-3-319-76953-0_8
11. Cheon, J.H., Kim, M., Kim, M.: Search-and-compute on encrypted data. In: Brenner, M., Christin, N., Johnson, B., Rohloff, K. (eds.) FC 2015. LNCS, vol. 8976, pp. 142–159. Springer, Heidelberg (2015). https://doi.org/10.1007/978-3-662-48051-9_11
12. Chillotti, I., Gama, N., Georgieva, M., Izabachène, M.: Faster fully homomorphic encryption: bootstrapping in less than 0.1 s. In: Cheon, J.H., Takagi, T. (eds.) ASIACRYPT 2016, Part I. LNCS, vol. 10031, pp. 3–33. Springer, Heidelberg (2016). https://doi.org/10.1007/978-3-662-53887-6_1
13. Chillotti, I., Gama, N., Georgieva, M., Izabachène, M.: A homomorphic LWE based E-voting scheme. In: Takagi, T. (ed.) PQCrypto 2016. LNCS, vol. 9606, pp. 245–265. Springer, Cham (2016). https://doi.org/10.1007/978-3-319-29360-8_16
14. Chillotti, I., Gama, N., Georgieva, M., Izabachène, M.: Faster packed homomorphic operations and efficient circuit bootstrapping for TFHE. In: Takagi, T., Peyrin, T. (eds.) ASIACRYPT 2017, Part I. LNCS, vol. 10624, pp. 377–408. Springer, Cham (2017). https://doi.org/10.1007/978-3-319-70694-8_14
15. Chillotti, I., Gama, N., Georgieva, M., Izabachène, M.: TFHE: fast fully homomorphic encryption over the torus. Cryptology ePrint Archive, Report 2018/421 (2018). https://eprint.iacr.org/2018/421

16. Chou, T., Orlandi, C.: The simplest protocol for oblivious transfer. In: Lauter, K., Rodríguez-Henríquez, F. (eds.) LATINCRYPT 2015. LNCS, vol. 9230, pp. 40–58. Springer, Cham (2015). https://doi.org/10.1007/978-3-319-22174-8_3

17. Coppersmith, D.: Small solutions to polynomial equations, and low exponent RSA vulnerabilities. J. Cryptol. 10(4), 233–260 (1997)

18. Coron, J.-S., Joux, A., Mandal, A., Naccache, D., Tibouchi, M.: Cryptanalysis of the RSA subgroup assumption from TCC 2005. In: Catalano, D., Fazio, N., Gennaro, R., Nicolosi, A. (eds.) PKC 2011. LNCS, vol. 6571, pp. 147–155. Springer, Heidelberg (2011). https://doi.org/10.1007/978-3-642-19379-8_9

19. Crawford, J.L.H., Gentry, C., Halevi, S., Platt, D., Shoup, V.: Doing real work with FHE: the case of logistic regression. In: WAHC@CCS 2018, pp. 1–12 (2018)

20. Damgård, I., Geisler, M., Krøigaard, M.: Efficient and secure comparison for on-line auctions. In: Pieprzyk, J., Ghodosi, H., Dawson, E. (eds.) ACISP 2007. LNCS, vol. 4586, pp. 416–430. Springer, Heidelberg (2007). https://doi.org/10.1007/978-3-540-73458-1_30

21. Damgård, I., Geisler, M., Krøigaard, M.: A correction to 'efficient and secure comparison for on-line auctions'. IJACT 1(4), 323–324 (2009)

22. Desmoulins, N., Lescuyer, R., Sanders, O., Traoré, J.: Direct anonymous attestations with dependent basename opening. In: Gritzalis, D., Kiayias, A., Askoxylakis, I. (eds.) CANS 2014. LNCS, vol. 8813, pp. 206–221. Springer, Cham (2014). https://doi.org/10.1007/978-3-319-12280-9_14

23. Ducas, L., Micciancio, D.: FHEW: bootstrapping homomorphic encryption in less than a second. In: Oswald, E., Fischlin, M. (eds.) EUROCRYPT 2015, Part I. LNCS, vol. 9056, pp. 617–640. Springer, Heidelberg (2015). https://doi.org/10.1007/978-3-662-46800-5_24

24. Feige, U., Kilian, J., Naor, M.: A minimal model for secure computation (extended abstract). In: 26th ACM STOC, pp. 554–563 (1994)

25. Fischlin, M.: A cost-effective pay-per-multiplication comparison method for millionaires. In: Naccache, D. (ed.) CT-RSA 2001. LNCS, vol. 2020, pp. 457–471. Springer, Heidelberg (2001). https://doi.org/10.1007/3-540-45353-9_33

26. Garay, J., Schoenmakers, B., Villegas, J.: Practical and secure solutions for integer comparison. In: Okamoto, T., Wang, X. (eds.) PKC 2007. LNCS, vol. 4450, pp. 330–342. Springer, Heidelberg (2007). https://doi.org/10.1007/978-3-540-71677-8_22

27. Gentry, C.: Fully homomorphic encryption using ideal lattices. In: 41st ACM STOC, pp. 169–178 (2009)

28. Gentry, C., Sahai, A., Waters, B.: Homomorphic encryption from learning with errors: conceptually-simpler, asymptotically-faster, attribute-based. In: Canetti, R., Garay, J.A. (eds.) CRYPTO 2013, Part I. LNCS, vol. 8042, pp. 75–92. Springer, Heidelberg (2013). https://doi.org/10.1007/978-3-642-40041-4_5

29. Groth, J.: Cryptography in subgroups of $\mathbb{Z}_n^*$. In: Kilian, J. (ed.) TCC 2005. LNCS, vol. 3378, pp. 50–65. Springer, Heidelberg (2005). https://doi.org/10.1007/978-3-540-30576-7_4

30. Joye, M., Salehi, F.: Private yet efficient decision tree evaluation. In: Kerschbaum, F., Paraboschi, S. (eds.) DBSec 2018. LNCS, vol. 10980, pp. 243–259. Springer, Cham (2018). https://doi.org/10.1007/978-3-319-95729-6_16

31. Kawachi, A., Tanaka, K., Xagawa, K.: Concurrently secure identification schemes based on the worst-case hardness of lattice problems. In: Pieprzyk, J. (ed.) ASIACRYPT 2008. LNCS, vol. 5350, pp. 372–389. Springer, Heidelberg (2008). https://doi.org/10.1007/978-3-540-89255-7_23

32. Kolesnikov, V., Sadeghi, A.-R., Schneider, T.: Improved garbled circuit building blocks and applications to auctions and computing minima. In: Garay, J.A., Miyaji, A., Otsuka, A. (eds.) CANS 2009. LNCS, vol. 5888, pp. 1–20. Springer, Heidelberg (2009). https://doi.org/10.1007/978-3-642-10433-6_1
33. Lenstra, A.K.: Key lengths. In: The Handbook of Information Security (2004)
34. Lin, H.-Y., Tzeng, W.-G.: An efficient solution to the millionaires' problem based on homomorphic encryption. In: Ioannidis, J., Keromytis, A., Yung, M. (eds.) ACNS 2005. LNCS, vol. 3531, pp. 456–466. Springer, Heidelberg (2005). https://doi.org/10.1007/11496137_31
35. Lyubashevsky, V., Peikert, C., Regev, O.: On ideal lattices and learning with errors over rings. In: Gilbert, H. (ed.) EUROCRYPT 2010. LNCS, vol. 6110, pp. 1–23. Springer, Heidelberg (2010). https://doi.org/10.1007/978-3-642-13190-5_1
36. McKee, J., Pinch, R.: Further attacks on server-aided RSA cryptosystems (1998)
37. Peikert, C., Waters, B.: Lossy trapdoor functions and their applications. In: 40th ACM STOC, pp. 187–196 (2008)
38. Regev, O.: On lattices, learning with errors, random linear codes, and cryptography. In: 37th ACM STOC, pp. 84–93
39. Rivest, R.L., Shamir, A.: Efficient factoring based on partial information. In: Pichler, F. (ed.) EUROCRYPT 1985. LNCS, vol. 219, pp. 31–34. Springer, Heidelberg (1986). https://doi.org/10.1007/3-540-39805-8_3
40. Smart, N.P.: Algorithms, key size and protocols report, ECRYPT - CSA (2018). http://www.ecrypt.eu.org/csa/documents/D5.4-FinalAlgKeySizeProt.pdf
41. Veugen, T.: Encrypted integer division. In: 2010 IEEE International Workshop on Information Forensics and Security, pp. 1–6 (2010)
42. Veugen, T.: Improving the DGK comparison protocol. In: WIFS 2012, pp. 49–54 (2012)
43. Veugen, T.: Encrypted integer division and secure comparison. IJACT **3**(2), 166–180 (2014)
44. Wang, S., et al.: HEALER: homomorphic computation of exact logistic regression for secure rare disease variants analysis in GWAS. Bioinformatics **32**(2), 211–218 (2016)
45. Yao, A.C.-C.: Protocols for secure computations (extended abstract). In: 23rd FOCS, pp. 160–164. IEEE Computer Society Press, November 1982
46. Zhou, T., Yang, X., Liu, L., Zhang, W., Ding, Y.: Faster bootstrapping with multiple addends. Cryptology ePrint Archive, report 2017/735 (2017). http://eprint.iacr.org/2017/735

Efficient FPGA Implementations
of LowMC and Picnic

Daniel Kales[1], Sebastian Ramacher[2], Christian Rechberger[1],
Roman Walch[1,3(✉)], and Mario Werner[1]

[1] Graz University of Technology, Graz, Austria
{daniel.kales,christian.rechberger,roman.walch,
mario.werner}@iaik.tugraz.at
[2] AIT Austrian Institute of Technology, Vienna, Austria
sebastian.ramacher@ait.ac.at
[3] Know-Center GmbH, Graz, Austria

Abstract. Post-quantum cryptography has received increased attention in recent years, in particular, due to the standardization effort by NIST. One of the second-round candidates in the NIST post-quantum standardization project is PICNIC, a post-quantum secure signature scheme based on efficient zero-knowledge proofs of knowledge. In this work, we present the first FPGA implementation of PICNIC. We show how to efficiently calculate LowMC, the block cipher used as a one-way function in PICNIC, in hardware despite the large number of constants needed during computation. We then combine our LowMC implementation and efficient instantiations of KECCAK to build the full PICNIC algorithm. Additionally, we conform to recently proposed hardware interfaces for post-quantum schemes to enable easier comparisons with other designs. We provide evaluations of our PICNIC implementation for both, the standalone design and a version wrapped with a PCIe interface, and compare them to the state-of-the-art software implementations of PICNIC and similar hardware designs. Concretely, signing messages on our FPGA takes 0.25 ms for the L1 security level and 1.24 ms for the L5 security level, beating existing optimized software implementations by a factor of 4.

Keywords: LowMC · FPGA · Digital signatures · NIST PQC · Picnic

1 Introduction

Cryptographic primitives with low multiplicative complexity have many interesting applications in higher-level protocols.[1] Recently, the post-quantum secure digital signature scheme PICNIC [19,20] used zero-knowledge proof of knowledge

---

[1] For example, they find use as pseudo-random functions (PRF) in secure multiparty computation (MPC) [5,31,45] to handle encrypted data, as oblivious PRFs in private set intersection (PSI) [28,37], but also enable the elimination of ciphertext expansion in homomorphic encryption schemes [5,42].

© Springer Nature Switzerland AG 2020
S. Jarecki (Ed.): CT-RSA 2020, LNCS 12006, pp. 417–441, 2020.
https://doi.org/10.1007/978-3-030-40186-3_18

schemes to build a signature based on the knowledge of a pre-image of a one-way function (OWF). Since the size of the proof of knowledge is directly related to the number of AND gates in the OWF, PICNIC employed block ciphers with low multiplicative complexity. In particular, the designers of PICNIC chose LowMC [5], a very parameterizable block cipher design, to build the OWF. PICNIC is currently a round 2 candidate in the NIST post-quantum cryptography project [1] and, since the construction lends itself to design more complex statements, it has also been extended to other signature variants including ring and EPID signatures [14, 22, 38] as well as double-authentication preventing signatures [21]. All of those signatures only rely on symmetric-key primitives for their security guarantees.

LowMC allows its users to select parameters suitable for the intended application. For the use in PICNIC, this means that one can select instances with a reduced data complexity and thereby reducing the number of required rounds. More importantly, it can also be parametrized in such a way that the number of multiplication gates – in this case AND gates – is minimized. For classical security of 128 bits, LowMC only requires 861 AND gates for full security and 546 AND gates in the reduced data complexity case. In comparison to that, other candidates for lightweight cipher designs require significantly more AND gates to achieve full data security: Simon requires 4352 AND gates [10], Kreyvium requires 1537 AND gates [17], and Fantomas requires 2112 AND gates [32] (cf. [20, Section 6.1] and [3, Table 1]). None of them come close to the numbers of LowMC. Only recently, GMiMC [2] was proposed, which can be reduced to 783 AND gates and can compete in the low data complexity scenario. For reference, AES-128 implemented over $GF(2)$ requires more than 5000 AND gates [16] and a round reduced version for the low data complexity case would amount to 3200 AND gates (including key schedule) [15].

While the choice of LowMC with small multiplicative complexity significantly reduces the signature size of PICNIC, the number of LowMC rounds has to be increased for security. Conversely, with higher multiplicative complexity, fewer rounds are required to achieve a secure design. Since each round consists of a matrix multiplication involving the full state, the number of rounds essentially define the runtime characteristics of PICNIC. Additionally, one matrix is sampled uniformly at random for each round during instance generation. In practice, this means that the size of the constants stored in implementations also grows linearly in the number of rounds. For the instances selected for NIST's L5 security level of 128-bit post-quantum security, the constants sum up to 621 KB. Recent optimizations of the linear layer by Dinur et al. [23] reduced the storage requirements for the constants down to 129 KB. Even with these optimizations, the sheer size of involved matrices seems to prohibit an implementation on resource-constrained devices, like microcontrollers or FPGAs. While the size of constants is less of a problem for software implementations running on desktops, servers or mobile phones, the size of these constants has a direct impact on the area of a hardware design or the hardware utilization of FPGA designs, respectively.

As the NIST post-quantum project progressed into the second round, the performance of the candidates is becoming a more important criterion. Consequently, NIST published targets for optimized implementations. Since optimized software implementations of LowMC and Picnic already exist, we focus on the implementation of several variants on FPGA platforms, including the Xilinx Kintex-7 as well as the Xilinx Artix-7. The latter is one of the optimization platforms recommended by NIST.

1.1 Contribution

Our contribution can be summarized as follows. We provide the first FPGA implementation of LowMC using a state machine design. Due to the structure of LowMC, the evaluation of the encryption algorithm requires a large number of constants in the form of uniformly random matrices and vectors. We adapt the recent result of Dinur et al. [23] to our FPGA implementation and are thereby able to significantly reduce the hardware utilization of our design compared to a naïve implementation.

We combine the LowMC implementation and custom KECCAK modules to instantiate the complete Picnic design on a Xilinx Kintex-7 board. This implementation conforms to the round 2 submission of the Picnic signature scheme [19] and supports the L1 and L5 parameter sets. Additionally, we port our implementation of Picnic-L1 to the Xilinx Artix-7 board. The implementation is flexible enough to support signing only and verification only versions besides the full version without significant overhead. However, our implementation focuses on the Fiat-Shamir transformed version of Picnic due to recent results [18,24] improving the confidence in its post-quantum security. Furthermore, the implementation also conforms to the proposed guidelines for hardware designs [26] of post-quantum schemes in the NIST standardization project to facilitate easier comparisons with other designs.

We evaluate the performance of our FPGA design and provide comparisons to optimized software implementations of Picnic. Our design performs up to a factor 4 faster for signing and up to a factor 3 faster for verification than SIMD optimized software implementations. We also compare our design to other hardware designs of signature schemes including SPHINCS [11]. While the Picnic design has a higher hardware utilization, it performs significantly better in run time than the SPHINCS design.

We discuss potential modifications to the LowMC cipher design that would benefit the FPGA implementation of Picnic. In particular, the suggested changes improve the hardware utilization by up to 30% and makes it possible to fit a Picnic implementation for the 128-bit post-quantum security level on the NIST recommended Artix-7 evaluation board.

Finally, we also provide a pipeline design of LowMC for high throughput scenarios. This design may also be of interest in other contexts such as PSI protocols [37], or fast database joins on secret shared data [40].

1.2   Related Work

Efficient hardware implementations are a very active point of research, and the NIST post-quantum standardization project only amplifies this [1]. In the following, we discuss other works in this area, with a focus on hardware implementations of post-quantum algorithms. We still want to mention that for a wide variety of primitives and schemes, hardware implementations have been proposed over the years [6,41,47,48], among others.

Basu et al. [9] provide an evaluation of 11 of the second-round candidates of the NIST post-quantum standardization project. Their approach is based on an automated synthesis of post-quantum accelerators based on the C code provided by the submissions to NIST. They analyze the designs for both FPGA and ASIC targets and compare their runtime and hardware utilization. But since PICNIC is a fairly complex design with a large number of individual primitives and constants, an FPGA implementation is not straightforward and can not be synthesized easily from the software implementation. Therefore, Basu et al. do not include PICNIC in their evaluation.

Besides this generic approach, Amiet et al. [7] presented an FPGA accelerator for SPHINCS-256 [11], a predecessor of SPHINCS+ [12], another candidate in the NIST post-quantum standardization project. Their implementation provides a highly optimized CHACHA12 pipeline, which is the core of the SPHINCS design. They report signing times of 1.53 ms on the same FPGA we target in our work.

Wang et al. [50] presented FPGA implementations of the Niederreiter cryptosystem using binary Goppa codes. For key encapsulation mechanisms and key exchange, Howe et al. [34] presented implementations of FrodoKEM, a post-quantum key encapsulation mechanism, for FPGAs and microcontrollers. Roy et al. [46] give an optimized implementation of SIKE, a post-quantum key exchange algorithm based on supersingular isogenies, for FPGA platforms. In a different approach, Albrecht et al. [4] repurpose existing RSA coprocessors to speed up computations of RLWE-based schemes, concretely for KEM Kyber.

2   Preliminaries

We will give an overview of LowMC, PICNIC and its main building blocks.

2.1   LowMC

LowMC [5] is a block cipher designed to reduce the number of AND gates needed for symmetric encryption. The design of the cipher is based on the substitution-permutation network (SPN) design strategy, with the choice to move to a partial substitution layer instead of applying the Sbox on the full state. The parameters block size (n), key size (k), number of Sboxes per round (m), allowed data complexity (d) and the number of rounds (r) are parameterizable according to the LowMC v3 round formula [44]. This formula calculates the lowest number of rounds necessary to provide secure encryption for the given parameter set. The script for determining the number of rounds for a given set of LowMC parameters can be found in the official GitHub repository [39].

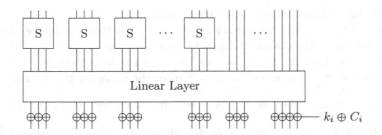

Fig. 1. One round of encryption with LowMC (modified from [5]).

A LowMC encryption starts with an initial whitening by XORing the first round key to the plaintext, followed by r rounds. As depicted in Fig. 1, one round consists of four steps: (i) SBOXLAYER, (ii) LINEARLAYER, (iii) CONSTANTADDITION and (iv) KEYADDITION. In the SBOXLAYER, m 3-bit Sboxes are applied to the first $s = 3 \cdot m$ bits of the state. The remaining bits of the state are not affected by the SBOXLAYER. The Sbox is defined as

$$S(a, b, c) = (a \oplus b \cdot c, a \oplus b \oplus a \cdot c, a \oplus b \oplus c \oplus a \cdot b),$$

with three GF(2) inputs and outputs. From this definition, it is obvious that only 3 AND gates are required per Sbox. In the LINEARLAYER, the state is multiplied with a pseudorandomly generated matrix $L_r \in \mathrm{GF}(2)^{n \times n}$, where r is the current round. The matrices are chosen pseudorandomly from the set of all invertible binary $n \times n$ matrices during the instantiation of LowMC. During the CONSTANTADDITION the vector $C_r \in \mathrm{GF}(2)^n$ is XORed to the state, where r describes the current round. The vectors are chosen pseudorandomly during the instantiation of LowMC. During KEYADDITION, the round key of the current round is XORed to the state. All round keys are generated as a result of the multiplication of the master key with the matrix $K_r \in \mathrm{GF}(2)^{n \times k}$, where r is the current round. The matrices are chosen pseudorandomly from the set of all full-rank binary $n \times k$ matrices during the instantiation of LowMC.

2.2 Picnic and ZKB++

The PICNIC signature scheme is based on zero-knowledge proofs of knowledge of pre-images of one-way functions. Currently, PICNIC supports two proof systems: ZKB++ [20] and KKW [38]. They both improve on the "MPC-in-the-head" paradigm [36], which describes a generic way to turn MPC protocols into zero-knowledge proofs. In this work we focus on the parameter set using ZKB++, since it is more efficient in runtime.

ZKB++ builds the zero-knowledge proof system from $(2,3)$-circuit decomposition, which we describe in more detail. Let ϕ be some circuit and $y = \phi(x)$, where x is some secret input and y is the publicy-known output. Within $(2,3)$-circuit decomposition, the computation is decomposed in the following way [29]:

- SHARE splits the input into three input shares.
- UPDATE advances the computation one gate at a time, computes the wire values for the next gate and returns the updated view.
- OUTPUT produces the output shares based on the final view.
- RECONSTRUCT recomputes the output from the three output shares.

The decomposition of the circuit has to satisfy correctness and 2-privacy [29]:

Correctness: The reconstruction of the output shares y_i must always be the result of the original relation $y = \phi(x)$.

2-Privacy: It should not be possible to reveal information about the private key x by publishing any information on any two players.

In ZKB++, $(2,3)$-circuit decomposition is constructed as follows: Let R be an arbitrary finite ring and ϕ a function such that $\phi: R^m \to R^\ell$ can be expressed by an n-gate arithmetic circuit over the ring using addition (respectively multiplications) by constants, and binary addition and binary multiplication gates. A $(2,3)$-decomposition of ϕ is then given by:

Share(x, k_1, k_2, k_3): Samples random $x_1, x_2 \in R^m$ from k_1 and k_2 and computes x_3 such that $x_1 + x_2 + x_3 = x$. Returns views containing x_1, x_2, x_3.

Update$_i^{(j)}$(view$_i^{(j)}$, view$_{i+1}^{(j)}$, k_i, k_{i+1}) : Computes player P_i's view of the output wire of gate g_j and appends it to the view. For the k-th wire w_k where $w_k^{(i)}$ denotes P_i's view, the update operation is defined as follows:

Addition by constant $(w_b = w_a + c)$: $w_b^{(i)} = w_a^{(i)} + c$ if $i = 1$ and $w_b^{(i)} = w_a^{(i)}$ otherwise.

Multiplication by constant $(w_b = c \cdot w_a)$: $w_b^{(i)} = c \cdot w_a^{(i)}$

Binary addition $(w_c = w_a + w_b)$: $w_c^{(i)} = w_a^{(i)} + w_b^{(i)}$

Binary multiplication $(w_c = w_a \cdot w_b)$: $w_c^{(i)} = w_a^{(i)} \cdot w_b^{(i)} + w_a^{(i+1)} \cdot w_b^{(i)} + w_a^{(i)} \cdot w_b^{(i+1)} + R_i(c) - R_{i+1}(c)$ where $R_i(c)$ is the c-th output of a pseudorandom generator seeded with k_i.

Output$_i$(view$_i^{(n)}$): Return the ℓ output wires stored in the view view$_i^{(n)}$.

Reconstruct(y_1, y_2, y_3): Computes $y = y_1 + y_2 + y_3$ and returns y.

Note that the player P_i can compute all gate types except for binary multiplication gates locally as the latter requires inputs from P_{i+1}. In other words, only outputs of binary multiplication gates need to be serialized as part of the communication transcript, and thus the view size and consequentially the signature size of PICNIC depend on the size of the ring R and the number of these gates.

To create a proof the prover repeats the $(2,3)$-circuit decomposition protocol T times. For each run, the prover commits to the view of each player P_i consisting of the input share, a communication transcript, and the output share. After all

T runs, the prover sends all the output shares and commitments for each run and player to the verifier, who responds with a challenge vector c. The challenge tells the prover which two of the three players should be corrupted per run and therefore which views should be published as part of the proof. Since the decomposition satisfies the 2-privacy property, no information is leaked on the secret key by publishing the views of two players. The verifier then recalculates the two opened views and checks, (1) whether the opened views were calculated correctly, (2) and if the three output shares can be reconstructed to y.

Each run gives some assurance that the prover knows the secret key x, therefore increasing the number of runs T decreases the probability that the prover can cheat without the verifier catching him at least once. Due to the nature of the circuit decomposition, the prover could potentially cheat in 2 of the 3 possible challenges per run; therefore we calculate the probability for him to cheat without getting caught as $(2/3)^T$.

ZKB++ is a Σ-protocol, i.e., an interactive proof, that can be made non-interactive by applying standard techniques such as the Fiat-Shamir (FS) transformation [27]. FS transformed Σ-protocols compute the challenge c as the output of a random oracle on the first message from the prover to the verifier, which contains the commitments to the shares of the circuit evaluation. This results in a non-interactive zero-knowledge proof protocol secure in the random oracle model. To obtain a signature scheme the message is included in the call to the random oracle as well.

In PICNIC, the circuit used for the circuit decomposition is $C = \text{LowMC}_k(p)$, where k is a LowMC secret key and (p, C), a corresponding plain-/ciphertext pair, which is known publicly and constitutes the public key. A signature is then a proof of knowledge of a k satisfying this relation.

2.3 Picnic Instances and Parameters

For each of the three security levels $S \in \{128, 192, 256\}$, there exist two variants of the PICNIC algorithms differing in the choice of transformations turning the Σ-protocol into a signature scheme: one variant is based on the Fiat-Shamir (FS) transformation, and the other is based on the Unruh (UR) transformation [49]. In contrary to the FS transformation, which makes the resulting non-interactive Σ-protocol secure in the random oracle model, the UR transformation is provably secure in the quantum random oracle model (QROM) [13], where an adversary can query the random oracle in quantum superposition. However, recent results by Don et al. [24] and Chailloux [18] show that the specific use of the FS transformation in PICNIC is also secure in the quantum random oracle model. Therefore, we focus our implementations on the variants of PICNIC using the FS transformation and ignore the more costly variants based on the Unruh transformation, that would require additional KECCAK instances to be fitted into the FPGA design.

PICNIC uses LowMC to reduce the size of the overall proof and thus the signature. The proof contains a transcript of a party, i.e., the view of the party for each AND gate in the circuit. Due to the additive secret-sharing used, XOR gates can be computed locally and do not influence the signature size. Therefore, LowMC is used instead of other lightweight ciphers, since, as discussed in Sect. 1, alternatives to LowMC require significantly more AND gates. Table 1 shows the LowMC instances that are used in PICNIC and their AND gate counts. We note that those instances are selected to provide a trade-off between signature size and runtime [20]. We want to note though, that even when the instances are selected based on this trade-off, they can still be represented with a lower number of AND gates than alternative cipher designs.

Table 1. PICNIC parameters with LowMC instances (block size n, key size k, # of Sboxes m, rounds r), sizes of public key pk, secret key sk and signatures σ.

Parameter set	S	T	LowMC				Hash/KDF		Sizes		
			n	k	m	r	Algorithm	ℓ	pk	sk	σ
PICNIC-L1-FS	128	219	128	128	10	20	SHAKE128	256	32	16	≤ 34032
PICNIC-L3-FS	192	329	192	192	10	30	SHAKE256	384	48	24	≤ 76772
PICNIC-L5-FS	256	438	256	256	10	38	SHAKE256	512	64	32	≤ 132856

Table 1 shows the parameters of the different PICNIC versions based on the Fiat-Shamir transformation. The expected security of the various instances corresponds to S bits against classical attacks and $S/2$ bits against quantum attacks. The parameter T describes the number of repetitions of ZKB++ required to reduce the soundness error to the desired security level [19]. Additionally, Table 1 shows the different key and signature sizes for the PICNIC instances. One particular optimization of ZKB++ [20] has the result that the signature size is dependent on the challenge, because for one of the players in the MPC protocol we need to include some auxiliary information in the proof. Therefore, the expected signature size will be smaller than values specified in the table.

In the remainder of this work, we focus our implementation on the PICNIC instances with security levels $S \in \{128, 256\}$ based on the FS transformation, namely PICNIC-L1-FS and PICNIC-L5-FS. Similarly, for LowMC the focus lies on instances with 128 and 256-bit block and key sizes.

PICNIC2 *Instances.* In the second round of the NIST post-quantum standardization project, the PICNIC team introduced an additional new parameter set, called PICNIC2. The main difference in the new parameter set is the choice of the underlying proof system. In PICNIC2, ZKB++ was complemented with KKW [38], which is also based on the "MPC-in-the-head" paradigm, but uses a different MPC protocol with precomputation. The nature of the new proof system allows for shorter signatures, but it has an increased number of players in the simulated MPC protocol resulting in longer signing and verification times when compared to PICNIC. An evaluation of these additional parameter sets on FPGA platforms is an interesting topic for future work.

3   Implementation

We will now describe our implementations[2] of LowMC and the Picnic signature algorithm on an FPGA platform. We first give insight into the design of the main module of Picnic, the computation of LowMC. Following that, we show how to combine this module with several SHAKE modules to instantiate the full Picnic signature scheme for the L1 and L5 security levels. In our implementation, we use the dual-port RAM module available as in the open-source framework MEMSEC [51,52].

Target Platform. For our design, we target a Xilinx Kintex-7 board – concretely we use a Xilinx Kintex-7 FPGA KC705 Evaluation Kit. Our target FPGA has 203800 lookup-tables (LUTs), 407600 flip-flops (FF) and 445 BRAMs available. In an announcement on the official mailing list of the NIST post-quantum standardization project, it was specified that implementors should target the Artix-7 platform due to its widespread use. Since the toolchain we use, Xilinx Vivado, also supports Artix-7 platforms as a target, adaptation to this platform is straightforward, and we discuss the resulting Artix-7 resource utilization in Sect. 4.1.

3.1   Optimized VHDL Implementation of LowMC

One of the major modules in our Picnic design is the evaluation of the LowMC block cipher. During Picnic's signing process, a proof of knowledge is generated by evaluating the LowMC encryption function in an MPC protocol. As discussed in Sect. 2.2, this is done by applying the $(2,3)$-circuit decomposition as defined by ZKB++ to the LowMC circuit. In terms of the matrix multiplications, the sharing of the circuit requires the 3-fold evaluation for signing.

In this section, we discuss our design choices and the difficulty of a LowMC VDHL implementation and compare a straightforward standalone implementation of LowMC with a standalone implementation using the optimizations by Dinur et al. [23]. We shortly give an intuition of these optimizations in the following Sections and refer the reader to [23] for a more detailed explanation.

Design Choices. The difficulty in implementing LowMC (and consequently Picnic) in VHDL arises from the high number of constants involved in the matrix multiplications in LowMC's linear layer and round key schedule. For the LowMC instance in Picnic-L5, 621 kB of constants are required which can be reduced to 129 kB by using the optimizations in [23]. Usually, we consider using block RAM (BRAM), RAM cells directly located on FPGAs, for storing a large amount of constants. The Kintex-7 FPGA comes with dual-port BRAM cells with a capacity of 36 kB each, which are capable of providing at most 72 bits during one clock cycle at each port. During one round we multiply the inner state of LowMC to an $S \times S$ bit (256×256 for Picnic-L5) matrix.

---

[2] All implementations are available at https://github.com/IAIK/Picnic-FPGA.

Considering a high-performance implementation, where we want to perform the matrix multiplication in one clock cycle, we would have to use $\approx$455 BRAM cells in parallel, which exceeds the number of available cells. The alternative multi-cycle approach would, therefore, necessarily lower the performance of the implementation. Furthermore, in the case of high BRAM cell usage, additional clock frequency penalties have to be expected due to increasing routing delays.

In our implementation, we decided to encode the constants for the matrices in lookup-tables (LUTs). This decision implies a high hardware utilization of our design, but comes with the advantage of fast matrix multiplications (1 clock cycle each) and therefore with the best performance. A low area implementation of LowMC (and consequently Picnic) using BRAMs instead of LUTs for constants could be an interesting topic for future work.

LowMC *Optimizations.* The main idea behind the optimizations proposed in [23] is that all operations except the Sbox layer are linear. Furthermore, only part of the state is affected by the Sbox layer. For example, consider the key addition: we can swap the order of the linear layer and the key addition by multiplying the round key with the inverse of the linear layer. Subsequently, we can move part of the key addition through the identity part of the Sbox layer and combine this part of the key addition with the key addition of the previous round. This process can be repeated recursively until we have combined a large part of the key additions in the initial key addition before the first round. The same process can be repeated for the round constants. Using some more advanced linear algebra properties, we can also move parts of the linear layer matrix multiplication to the next or previous round, again repeating this process to combine parts of the linear layer in the last or first round.

Figure 2a shows the VHDL design of LowMC without the optimizations. In Fig. 2b, we present the design with the optimizations applied. Without the optimizations, there is only one implementation for all the rounds, and the matrix multiplications affect the entire state. In the optimized implementation, there are 5 different matrix multiplication modules, each for a matrix with different dimensions. The Sbox layer, round key, and constants of the new implementation only affect the first s bits of the state, and the linear layer matrix multiplication follows the algorithm in [23].

Optimized Hardware Utilization. The impact of the optimizations depends on the concrete LowMC instance. It especially depends on the number of Sboxes m and the resulting size of the non-linear layer. The fewer Sboxes per round, the more significant is the effect of the optimizations. The concrete effect of the optimizations can be seen in Table 2, where the required lookup-tables (LUTs) of the LowMC VHDL implementation are shown for the two different LowMC instances used in Picnic-L1-FS and Picnic-L5-FS. The instance for security level L1 only requires about a third of the LUTs required before, and the instance for security level L5 only requires about a fifth of the LUTs of the straightforward version. Without the optimizations, it would not even be possible to synthesize one LowMC instance for security level L5 on our FPGA board, whereas we require several instances for the PICNIC implementation. The improvement for LowMC instances with larger non-linear layers is smaller, though.

3.2 Pipeline versus State Machine

Besides the implementation of LowMC using a simple state machine, we also provide an alternative implementation using a pipelined design. While both designs have a latency of r cycles to get a specific ciphertext, the pipelined design has a much higher throughput with 1 ciphertext per cycle. The state machine design, on the other hand, has to wait for an encryption to be finished before it can process another plaintext and therefore has a throughput of 1 ciphertext per

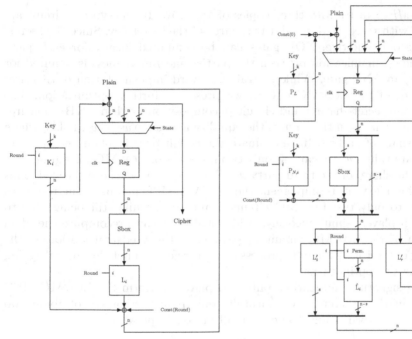

(a) LowMC implementation without optimizations of the round key and linear layer computations.

(b) LowMC implementation with optimized round key computation and linear layer evaluation.

Fig. 2. State diagrams of different LowMC implementations.

Table 2. LUTs of one LowMC with/without optimizations (203800 available).

LowMC instance	LowMC				Without opt.		With opt.		Improv. %
	n	k	m	r	LUTs	% LUTs	LUTs	% LUTs	
PICNIC-L1-FS	128	128	10	20	42395	20.80%	13558	6.65%	68.02%
PICNIC-L5-FS	256	256	10	38	209348	102.72%	44431	21.8%	78.78%

r rounds. However, the state machine design requires fewer lookup tables on an FPGA, because the LowMC round only needs to be instantiated once. For the Picnic coprocessor, we use the state machine design due to smaller hardware utilization. When interested in higher throughput, for example, when it is used as an oblivious pseudo-random function in a PSI protocol, the pipeline design is the better choice.

3.3   Optimized VHDL Implementation of Picnic

We now use the LowMC implementation as a building block for our Picnic coprocessors. In the following, we shortly describe the other different submodules and finally, the high-level design of the Picnic coprocessors.

LowMC-*MPC*. In Picnic, three copies of the LowMC encryption circuit are evaluated with three random additive shares of the secret key. Since the secret-sharing used is additive, XOR gates can be computed locally for each part, while some communication between the parties and randomness is required for computing an AND gate. While a straightforward implementation of this uses three copies of the LowMC circuit, we present a further optimization. The nature of the secret-sharing and circuit decomposition used in ZKB++ ensures that for each wire w in the circuit, the equality $w = w_1 \oplus w_2 \oplus w_3$, holds, where w_i is the share of party i. If we evaluate the circuit once in plain and store all intermediate values w, we can use only two instances of LowMC for signing and compute the shares of the third party $w_3 = w \oplus w_1 \oplus w_2$ whenever needed. This optimization allows us to implement the LowMC-MPC module using resources equivalent to only two LowMC circuit evaluations, while still being able to evaluate all players simultaneously. Additionally, we can precompute the plain evaluation of the LowMC circuit in parallel to the Seeds calculation at the beginning of the Picnic signing process and, therefore, do not slow down signing while using this optimization.

During signature verification, only two players perform the LowMC-MPC circuit evaluation; therefore, we naturally only require resources of about two LowMC circuit evaluations to perform all players in parallel.

SHAKE. In Picnic, instances of SHAKE are used for different purposes, both as a hash function with fixed output or as an extensible output function to generate pseudorandom tapes of arbitrary size. Therefore, we implemented a custom, flexible Keccak design, supporting many different configurations while maintaining efficiency and small hardware utilization.

Seeds, Tapes, and Commitments. In the beginning, one master seed is pseudo-randomly generated and expanded into seeds for each of the T runs. We use three instances of SHAKE to expand the seeds for each player's current run into its random tape and three more instances to commit to the transcript of the current run for each player. We are capable of calculating the randomness required for run $t+1$ of PICNIC's circuit decomposition in parallel to calculating the commitments of run t, reducing the overall number of clock cycles for signing and verification. However, due to limited routing freedom due to high resource utilization of our synthesized PICNIC-L5 design, this optimization would significantly increase the critical path of the design and, therefore, this optimization is only used for PICNIC-L1.

Challenge Generation (H3). Based on the Fiat-Shamir transformation, we instantiate the random oracle for the challenge generation using SHAKE. All commitments for all T runs are hashed together with some additional parameters to produce the challenge vector. Since the challenge vector consists of entries in $\{0, 1, 2\}$ to denote the player that is not revealed for this run, the H3 module takes care to filter the output bits of the SHAKE call according to the PICNIC specification.

Serialization and Deserialization. We also implemented small submodules to assemble the final signature as a byte array conforming to the PICNIC specification. For verification, we parse incoming signatures and store all the intermediate values of the opened views in the block RAM cells of the FPGA. These modules

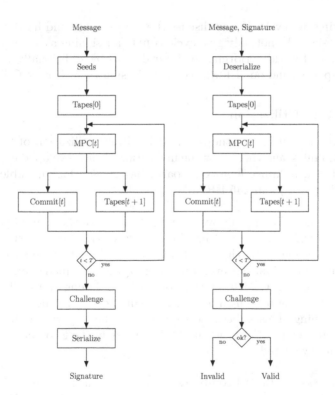

Fig. 3. High-level design of PICNIC signing (left) and verification (right).

are implemented to be able to handle the variable signature length of PICNIC internally.

High-Level Design. We developed several different VHDL designs for PICNIC-L1-FS and PICNIC-L5-FS. We implemented a standalone version for message signing or signature verification only, as well as a version which is capable of doing both.

The overall design of the implementations is a nested state machine, where the high-level design connects the inputs and outputs of all the described submodules. Figure 3 shows a diagram of the high-level design, with the signing process shown on the left side and the verification process on the right. In the designs which are capable of doing both signing and verification, both processes are implemented. Most of the submodules can be reused for both signing and verification, only the MPC module has to implement two different Sbox calculations, and the combined design has to include both the *Serialize* and *Deserialize* submodules. Therefore, the difference in hardware utilization between a sign-only design and a sign/verify design is quite low.

4   Evaluation

In the following, we evaluate and discuss the performance and hardware utilization of our design. We not only give cycle counts for signing and verification but also show the real-world performance of our designs by additionally synthesizing a PCIe wrapper around our PICNIC cores and using them from a C library.

4.1   Hardware Utilization

First, we give an overview of the required hardware utilization of the different PICNIC submodules, and then show the utilization of the developed coprocessors. The used FPGA, a Xilinx Kintex-7 board, has 203800 lookup-tables (LUTs), 407600 flip-flops (FF) and 445 BRAMs available.

PICNIC *Submodules.* To give an overview of the costs of the individual submodules, we present their hardware utilization for PICNIC-L1-FS and PICNIC-L5-FS in Table 3. This table shows that the LowMC-MPC modules require by far the most hardware utilization. However, observe that the combined submodule which is able to do the LowMC-MPC encryption for both signing and verification only requires less than one percent more LUTs than the submodule which can only be used for signing. This is because we can reuse large parts of the circuit for both signing and verification, the only difference is in the Sbox layer, where the AND gates are evaluated.

PICNIC *Coprocessors.* Table 4 compares the hardware utilization of the different submodules of the final coprocessors, including our 6 different PICNIC cores synthesized for the Kintex-7. Our PICNIC cores require a lot of LUTs on the

Table 3. Hardware utilization for different parts of the L1 and L5 designs on Kintex-7.

Design Part	L1				L5			
	LUTs	%	FF	%	LUTs	%	FF	%
Keccak	3726	1.83%	1606	0.39%	3726	1.83%	1606	0.39%
Tapes (3× Keccak)	9574	4.70%	5589	1.37%	9420	4.62%	9621	2.36%
Commits (3× Keccak)	12221	6.00%	5589	1.37%	14160	6.95%	6357	1.56%
Seeds (1× Keccak)	5867	2.88%	1846	0.45%	8974	4.40%	2640	0.65%
H3 (1× Keccak)	7236	3.55%	3641	0.89%	8815	4.33%	4085	1.00%
Serialize	1962	0.96%	125	0.03%	1608	0.79%	172	0.79%
Deserialize	2025	0.99%	125	0.03%	2317	1.14%	155	0.04%
LowMC-MPC Sign	31837	15.62%	3060	0.75%	97066	47.63%	5940	1.46%
LowMC-MPC Verify	29756	14.60%	1126	0.28%	93959	46.10%	2246	0.55%
LowMC-MPC	32224	15.81%	3061	0.75%	98319	48.24%	5958	1.46%

Table 4. Hardware utilization for different parts of the coprocessor for Kintex-7.

Design Part	LUTs	%	FF	%	BRAM	%
PCIe/DMA	22216	10.90%	22692	5.57%	42.5	9.55%
Picnic-L1	90037	44.18%	23105	5.67%	52.5	11.80%
Picnic-L1-sign	76472	37.52%	21061	5.17%	52.5	11.80%
Picnic-L1-verify	68614	33.67%	16821	4.13%	33.5	7.53%
Picnic-L5	167530	82.20%	33164	8.14%	98.5	22.13%
Picnic-L5-sign	149456	73.33%	30441	7.47%	98.5	22.13%
Picnic-L5-verify	138547	67.98%	24278	5.96%	62.5	14.04%

Table 5. Hardware utilization on Artix-7.

Design Part	LUTs	%	FF	%	BRAM	%
Picnic-L1	90037	67.29%	23105	8.63%	52.5	14.38%
Picnic-L1-sign	76472	57.15%	21061	7.87%	52.5	14.38%
Picnic-L1-verify	68614	51.28%	16821	6.29%	33.5	9.18%

used FPGA, especially the Picnic-L5-FS implementations. The PCIe/DMA Subsystem which connects the Picnic cores to the PCIe port of the used FPGA board adds about 22 000 additional LUTs to the design.

On the Artix-7, the picture is quite different, as we only have 133 800 LUTs, 267 600 flip-flops and 365 BRAMs available. Consequently, neither Picnic-L5 Picnic-L5-sign, nor Picnic-L5-verify fit on this board. The hardware utilization of the Artix implementations of L1 are depicted in Table 5.

Table 6. Clock Cycles per Submodule.

Design Part	PICNIC-L1-FS	PICNIC-L5-FS
LowMC-MPC	40	76
Tapes	51	75
Commits	51	100
Seeds	1 732	7 904
H3 (absorb)	6 490	26 220
Deserialize	1 per 128 bit	1 per 128 bit
Serialize	1 per 128 bit	1 per 128 bit
$T\times$ LowMC-MPC	8 760	31 844
$T\times$ Tapes	11 169	31 425
$T\times$ Commits	11 169	41 900

Critical Path. The critical path of the synthesized design is across the matrix multiplications in LowMC's linear layer and round key schedule, due to the high number of constants involved. But we also observed, that since the PICNIC-L5 design has a considerable hardware utilization, the synthesizer has much less freedom in routing the design and, therefore, naturally produces long paths between registers. These long paths make it very difficult to optimize the design for high frequencies.

4.2 Clock Cycles

Table 6 lists the number of clock cycles each submodule of our PICNIC implementation requires. The LowMC-MPC module performs the evaluation of a round in two clock cycles and, therefore, requires $2 \cdot r$ cycles in total. Evaluating a round in one cycle would have drastically increased the critical path of the design since two matrix multiplications (linear layer and round key schedule) would have been performed sequentially in this case.

Our KECCAK implementation performs one round of the state transformation function during one clock cycle, which leads to 24 cycles for one absorbing/squeezing phase. The number of absorbing/squeezing phases, therefore, determines the number of clock cycles required for the *Tapes, Commits, Seeds,* and the first part of the *H3* submodules. The duration of the second part of the *H3* submodule depends on the generated challenge and differs for every signature.

In PICNIC we have T runs of the FS transformed ZKB++ proof system, in contrary to the *Seeds, H3, Serialize* and *Deserialize* modules which are only required once. In Table 6 we, therefore, also show the overall runtime of each submodule involved in the proof creation and it can be seen, that the proof system dominates the overall runtime of the signature creation and verification process.

Table 7. Runtime comparison of the coprocessors on benchmark platform A.

Coprocessor	Clock frequency (MHz)	Clock cycles	FPGA	C-Access
			Runtime (ms)	
PICNIC-L1-SIGN	125	≈ 31300	0.250	0.349
PICNIC-L1-VERIFY	125	≈ 29600	0.237	0.395
PICNIC-L5-SIGN	125	≈ 154500	1.236	1.383
PICNIC-L5-VERIFY	125	≈ 146600	1.173	2.128

4.3 Benchmarks

To verify the performance characteristics of our implementation, we compared the runtime of the coprocessors running on a Kintex-7 board to the state-of-the-art optimized software implementations of PICNIC. The platforms used for the benchmarks are as follows:

Platform A Intel i7-960, 3.2 GHz with 16 GB RAM, Debian 9
Platform B Intel i7-4790, 3.6 GHz with 16 GB RAM, Ubuntu 18.04.1
Platform C Intel E31230, 3.2 GHz with 8 GB RAM, Ubuntu 18.04.2

We used platform A to test our coprocessors, platforms B and C were used in the PICNIC design document [19] to test their optimized software implementations.

Table 7 shows the average runtime of the developed coprocessors for signing and verification. The column *FPGA runtime* is the calculated time resulting from the clock frequency and the number of clock cycles (including 1 cycle per 128 bit of data transmission) and therefore is the actual runtime of the FPGA. The column *C-Access runtime* is the measured runtime using our developed C library on platform A.

As Table 7 shows, the C library developed to interface with the coprocessor adds some overhead to the signing and verification process. For signing, the overhead is about 0.1 ms in runtime, but for verification, the overhead is a bit larger. Especially for PICNIC-L5-FS the measured runtime is much bigger than the raw verification runtime of the coprocessor. We suspect that this is due to the driver for the PCIe/DMA Subsystem being slower for writing large amounts of data, like the PICNIC-L5-FS signature, from the PC to the FPGA board and that this overhead could be optimized further.

For comparison, Table 8 shows the runtime of the optimized implementation of PICNIC in C and an optimized version which uses processor-specific compiler intrinsics on two different benchmark platforms as described in the official PICNIC design document [19]. This table shows, that the runtime of PICNIC highly depends on the underlying hardware and if the CPU supports *single instruction, multiple data* (SIMD) instruction sets, like SSE2 and AVX2, which further improve execution time. However, in any case, our developed coprocessors are faster than the corresponding software counterparts and do not rely on specific CPU instructions. For PICNIC-L1-FS signing is ≈ 4 times faster than the fastest

Table 8. Runtime comparison of optimized software implementations [19].

Platform	Parameters	Using SIMD	Sign	Verify
B	Picnic-L1-FS	✓	1.44 ms	1.15 ms
B	Picnic-L5-FS	✓	5.87 ms	4.92 ms
B	Picnic-L1-FS	✗	2.82 ms	2.34 ms
B	Picnic-L5-FS	✗	12.37 ms	10.59 ms
C	Picnic-L1-FS	✓	4.20 ms	3.40 ms
C	Picnic-L5-FS	✓	17.67 ms	14.67 ms
C	Picnic-L1-FS	✗	4.41 ms	3.56 ms
C	Picnic-L5-FS	✗	19.52 ms	16.81 ms

Table 9. Comparison of FPGA implementations (modified from [7]).

Scheme	Security			Area	f	t
	Classic	PQ	FPGA	LUT/FF/BRAM	MHz	ms
SPHINCS-256 [7]	256	128	K7	19067/38132/36	525	1.53
SPHINCS+-128 [9]	128	64	V7	11438/3335/?	100	9.38
BLISS-IV [43]	192	?	S6	6438/6198/7	135	0.35
ECDSA-256 [6]	128	✗	V7	6816/4442/0	225	1.49
ECDSA-256 [33]	128	✗	V4	34869/32430/176	375	0.04
ECDSA-521 [6]	256	✗	V7	8273/7689/0	161	5.02
RSA-2048 [47]	112	✗	V7	3558 slices/0	399	5.68
Picnic-L1-FS	128	64	K7	90037/23105/52.5	125	0.25
Picnic-L5-FS	256	128	K7	167530/33164/98.5	125	1.24

software implementation, verification is ≈ 3 times faster. For Picnic-L5-FS our implementations are ≈ 4 times faster for signing and ≈ 2.3 times faster for verification. For CPUs which do not support AVX2 instructions and for portable C-only implementations the speedup of our coprocessors is even more significant.

4.4   Comparison to FPGA Implementations of Other Signature Schemes

To put our FPGA implementation in context of other signature schemes, we compare our Picnic coprocessors to implementations of ECDSA [6] and RSA coprocessors [47] as well as implementations of SPHINCS-256 [7] and BLISS-IV [43]. Table 9 compares several different FPGA implementations of various signature schemes, the runtime for signing t is calculated from the clock frequency and the number of clock cycles and therefore does not take the overhead of any transmission of data via a C-program into account. Thus this value compares to the column *FPGA runtime* of Table 7.

As Table 9 shows, our PICNIC-L5-FS coprocessors, which have the same security level as a SPHINCS-256 [7] coprocessor, have a slightly better runtime for signing on the Kintex-7 (K7) FPGA. Similar, for the SPHINCS+ design obtained from the high-level synthesis design flow [9], our coprocessor has a significant better runtime at the cost of higher hardware utilization. The implementations of the traditional signature schemes RSA [47] and ECDSA [6] on a Virtex-7 (V7) FPGA are also slower than our coprocessors. The ECDSA implementation in [33] occupies more area but uses high parallelism to drastically increase their throughput. The implementation of BLISS-IV [43], another post-quantum signature scheme based on lattices, on a Spartan-6 (S6) FPGA is very efficient regarding area and runtime for signing. However, it has a lower security level, and its security against a quantum adversary is not as well understood as for schemes based on symmetric primitives like SPHINCS and PICNIC.

However, even though our coprocessors are very competitive with regards to signing times, the hardware utilization is significantly higher in comparison to implementations of other signature schemes. This is due to the nature of PICNIC relying on a high number of different KECCAK and LowMC primitives, where especially the LowMC instances have a high hardware utilization on their own. In comparison, the coprocessor of SPHINCS-256, a hash-based post-quantum signature scheme, can be built efficiently using only one pipelined CHACHA12 instance and one instance of BLAKE-256 [8] and as a result, requires less hardware utilization [7].

4.5   Evaluation of the LowMC Pipeline Design

Finally, we evaluate our pipelined design. After r cycles, the design is capable of producing one ciphertext per cycle (cf. Section 3.2), a feature which is of particular interest for high throughput use cases. We compare our coprocessor ($f = 125$ MHz) for a LowMC instance with 128 bit block size and full data complexity to AES-128 accelerated with the AES-NI instruction set [35]. For this comparison we choose a LowMC instance with $n = 128$, $k = 128$, $m = 25$, $r = 11$. This instance provides a trade-off between costs in the linear layer and the number of AND gates. The comparison of the coprocessor, including C-access times, the raw FPGA runtime, the SIMD-optimized LowMC software implementation and AES-NI is depicted in Table 10. These benchmarks were recorded on a PC running Ubuntu 16.05 with an Intel i7-4790 CPU, 3.6 GHz. As the table shows, the coprocessor speeds up encryption by a factor of ≈ 84 compared to the LowMC software implementation, and when considering the C-access time, the improvement is still up to a factor of ≈ 14. Compared to AES-NI, the raw performance on the FPGA is better by a factor of ≈ 2.75, but the access time adds significant overhead. Therefore, we expect this design to render LowMC an alternative for PSI protocols [37] or database joins on secret shared data [40].

This speed up direct translates to the same performance gain in the setup phase of the PSI protocol as proposed in [37]. Thus, the excellent performance of our coprocessor makes it feasible to use LowMC in the PSI protocol. Thereby,

Table 10. Performance of LowMC ($n = 128, k = 128, m = 25, r = 11$) implemented in software and in our pipeline coprocessor, as well as AES-NI.

# Encryptions	Size	LowMC			AES
		FPGA-Raw	FPGA-C	Software	AES-NI
2^{20}	16 MB	0.008 s	0.046 s	0.677 s	0.022 s
2^{24}	256 MB	0.134 s	0.771 s	10.78 s	0.359 s
2^{26}	1024 MB	0.537 s	3.11 s	43.31 s	1.436 s
2^{28}	4096 MB	2.15 s	12.57 s	182.65 s	5.743 s

the PSI protocol can profit from reduced communication overhead during the online phase due to the reduced multiplicative complexity of LowMC without requiring the tradeoff of having a slower setup phase.

5   Reducing the Hardware Utilizations

The large size of the constants needed for LowMC is one of the limiting factors to implement PICNIC on FPGAs. Even after applying the optimizations to the round key and linear layer computations, the constants are still too large to fit an implementation on an Artix-7 board. To fit an implementation of PICNIC suitable for the 128-bit post-quantum security level on this board, different LowMC instances with fewer rounds could be selected. Conversely, as this change requires the number of Sboxes to be increased to retain the security guarantees, the signature size will increase. In addition to fitting PICNIC on smaller FPGA boards, the performance of the optimized implementations would also improve, since fewer rounds are required to achieve the same level of security when more Sboxes are used. Alternatively, further improvements are required to reduce the size of LowMC constants. We envision multiple alternatives that could make this possible.

The current design of PICNIC was chosen to have an acceptable trade-off between area and runtime and, therefore, evaluates the LowMC-MPC simulation concurrently for all three players by using two instances of the LowMC matrices. By doing the MPC simulation consecutively, we would be able to reduce the instances used to only one and reduce the hardware utilization. However, this optimization would result in more clock cycles per LowMC-MPC rounds and longer critical paths after synthesis reducing the clock frequency, and, therefore, would produce a very high performance penalty of at least a factor 2 if not more.

Another possibility to reduce the hardware utilization by modifying our design would be to reuse KECCAK instances for different purposes in the design. However, this would again result in longer critical paths after synthesis, and since our KECCAK design is very small in comparison to the LowMC design, the resulting performance penalty is too big in comparison to the actual reduction of the hardware utilization.

Table 11. Hardware utilization (LUTs) with reduced LowMC.

Design Part	LUTs	Improvement	Utilization	
			Kintex-7	Artix-7
LowMC MPC-L1	17751	44.91%	8.71%	13.27%
LowMC MPC-L5	47615	51.57%	23.36%	35.59%
Picnic-L1	75662	15.97%	37.13%	56.55%
Picnic-L1-sign	62272	18.57%	30.56%	46.54%
Picnic-L1-verify	55321	19.37%	27.14%	41.35%
Picnic-L5	121299	27.60%	59.52%	90.66%
Picnic-L5-sign	103688	30.62%	50.88%	77.49%
Picnic-L5-verify	92910	32.94%	45.59%	69.44%

The use of LowMC in Picnic is relatively unique in the sense that it uses LowMC instances with low data complexity. Only recently, LowMC in this setting has seen more security analysis [44], leading to LowMC version 3 with a higher number of rounds. While the higher number of rounds on its own is not a problem for the FPGA implementation, the size of the constants also increases as more and more unique matrices are required. However, new designs [30] that are also optimized for a low multiplicative complexity make use of a single matrix for the linear layer. We propose to apply this idea also to LowMC, that is, the same uniformly random matrix is re-used for all linear layers.[3] Thereby we can significantly reduce the hardware utilization as can be seen in Table 11. With this change, the Picnic-L5 design fits on the Artix-7.

Furthermore, with this change in place, one could go a step further and remove the constants from the implementation altogether. The matrices and round constants could then be derived from the LFSR as specified in the LowMC instance generation algorithm. It would be necessary to store the intermediate states of the LFSR where it is known to produce invertible matrices, though, but then no invertible checks would need to be implemented. While deriving the matrices during runtime would come with a performance penalty, we expect it the reduce the hardware utilization significantly.

Alternatively, LowMC could be replaced by recently proposed cipher designs such as GMiMC [2]. Similarly to LowMC, GMiMC – and in particular its ERF variant – can be parameterized for the low data complexity scenario. It can be parameterized in a way leading to roughly similar sized signatures with better performance (in software). However, for an FPGA implementation, we expect it to use a lot less area since the size of the constants is significantly smaller. For the GMiMC instance over $GF(2^{17})$ with 63 rounds, the constants would consist

---

[3] The LowMC designers confirmed in private communication that they do not expect this change to enable a new attack vector. However, more security analysis on this case would be required before this can be integrated into Picnic itself.

of only 63 field elements in total. The additional multipliers required for $GF(2^{17})$ are cheap [25] when compared to the size of LowMC matrices.

6   Conclusion

In this work, we presented two LowMC designs for FPGAs. The first design relying on a simple state machine shows the feasibility of implementing the post-quantum signature scheme PICNIC on FPGA platforms. The resulting FPGA design can sign messages for the L1 security level in $\approx$31300 cycles and verify signatures in $\approx$29600 cycles. Using our concrete FPGA board, a Xilinx Kintex-7 FPGA KC705 evaluation kit, this allows signing of a message using a C library communicating with our board connected via PCIe in 0.35 ms.

Acknowledgements. This work was partially supported by the EU's Horizon 2020 ECSEL Joint Undertaking project SECREDAS under grant agreement n°783119, by the European Research Council (ERC) under Horizon 2020 grant agreement n°681402, by EU's Horizon 2020 project Safe-DEED under grant agreement n°825225, and by the IoT4CPS project which is partially funded by the "ICT of the Future" Program of the FFG and the BMVIT. D. Kales was supported by iov42 Ltd.

References

1. Alagic, G., et al.: Status report on the first round of the NIST post-quantum cryptography standardization process (2019). https://doi.org/10.6028/NIST.IR.8240
2. Albrecht, M.R., et al.: Feistel structures for MPC, and more. In: Sako, K., Schneider, S., Ryan, P.Y.A. (eds.) ESORICS 2019. LNCS, vol. 11736, pp. 151–171. Springer, Cham (2019). https://doi.org/10.1007/978-3-030-29962-0_8
3. Albrecht, M.R., Grassi, L., Rechberger, C., Roy, A., Tiessen, T.: MiMC: efficient encryption and cryptographic hashing with minimal multiplicative complexity. In: Cheon, J.H., Takagi, T. (eds.) ASIACRYPT 2016. LNCS, vol. 10031, pp. 191–219. Springer, Heidelberg (2016). https://doi.org/10.1007/978-3-662-53887-6_7
4. Albrecht, M.R., Hanser, C., Höller, A., Pöppelmann, T., Virdia, F., Wallner, A.: Implementing RLWE-based schemes using an RSA co-processor. IACR Trans. Cryptogr. Hardw. Embed. Syst. **2019**(1), 169–208 (2019)
5. Albrecht, M.R., Rechberger, C., Schneider, T., Tiessen, T., Zohner, M.: Ciphers for MPC and FHE. In: Oswald, E., Fischlin, M. (eds.) EUROCRYPT 2015. LNCS, vol. 9056, pp. 430–454. Springer, Heidelberg (2015). https://doi.org/10.1007/978-3-662-46800-5_17
6. Amiet, D., Curiger, A., Zbinden, P.: Flexible FPGA-based architectures for curve point multiplication over $GF(p)$. In: DSD, pp. 107–114. IEEE Computer Society (2016)
7. Amiet, D., Curiger, A., Zbinden, P.: FPGA-based accelerator for post-quantum signature scheme SPHINCS-256. IACR Trans. Cryptogr. Hardw. Embed. Syst. **2018**(1), 18–39 (2018)
8. Aumasson, J.-P., Neves, S., Wilcox-O'Hearn, Z., Winnerlein, C.: BLAKE2: simpler, smaller, fast as MD5. In: Jacobson, M., Locasto, M., Mohassel, P., Safavi-Naini, R. (eds.) ACNS 2013. LNCS, vol. 7954, pp. 119–135. Springer, Heidelberg (2013). https://doi.org/10.1007/978-3-642-38980-1_8

9. Basu, K., Soni, D., Nabeel, M., Karri, R.: NIST post-quantum cryptography-a hardware evaluation study. ePrint 2019, 47 (2019)

10. Beaulieu, R., Shors, D., Smith, J., Treatman-Clark, S., Weeks, B., Wingers, L.: The SIMON and SPECK families of lightweight block ciphers. ePrint 2013, 404 (2013)

11. Bernstein, D.J., et al.: SPHINCS: practical stateless hash-based signatures. In: Oswald, E., Fischlin, M. (eds.) EUROCRYPT 2015. LNCS, vol. 9056, pp. 368–397. Springer, Heidelberg (2015). https://doi.org/10.1007/978-3-662-46800-5_15

12. Bernstein, D.J., Hülsing, A., Kölbl, S., Niederhagen, R., Rijneveld, J., Schwabe, P.: The SPHINCS$^+$ signature framework. In: CCS, pp. 2129–2146. ACM (2019)

13. Boneh, D., Dagdelen, Ö., Fischlin, M., Lehmann, A., Schaffner, C., Zhandry, M.: Random oracles in a quantum world. In: Lee, D.H., Wang, X. (eds.) ASIACRYPT 2011. LNCS, vol. 7073, pp. 41–69. Springer, Heidelberg (2011). https://doi.org/10.1007/978-3-642-25385-0_3

14. Boneh, D., Eskandarian, S., Fisch, B.: Post-quantum EPID signatures from symmetric primitives. In: Matsui, M. (ed.) CT-RSA 2019. LNCS, vol. 11405, pp. 251–271. Springer, Cham (2019). https://doi.org/10.1007/978-3-030-12612-4_13

15. Bouillaguet, C., Derbez, P., Fouque, P.-A.: Automatic search of attacks on round-reduced AES and applications. In: Rogaway, P. (ed.) CRYPTO 2011. LNCS, vol. 6841, pp. 169–187. Springer, Heidelberg (2011). https://doi.org/10.1007/978-3-642-22792-9_10

16. Boyar, J., Matthews, P., Peralta, R.: Logic minimization techniques with applications to cryptology. J. Cryptol. **26**(2), 280–312 (2013)

17. Canteaut, A., et al.: Stream ciphers: a practical solution for efficient homomorphic-ciphertext compression. In: Peyrin, T. (ed.) FSE 2016. LNCS, vol. 9783, pp. 313–333. Springer, Heidelberg (2016). https://doi.org/10.1007/978-3-662-52993-5_16

18. Chailloux, A.: Quantum security of the Fiat-Shamir transform of commit and open protocols. ePrint 2019, 699 (2019)

19. Chase, M., et al.: The picnic signature scheme design document (version 2) (2019). https://github.com/microsoft/Picnic/blob/master/spec/design-v2.0.pdf

20. Chase, M., et al.: Post-quantum zero-knowledge and signatures from symmetric-key primitives. In: ACM CCS, pp. 1825–1842. ACM (2017)

21. Derler, D., Ramacher, S., Slamanig, D.: Generic double-authentication preventing signatures and a post-quantum instantiation. In: Baek, J., Susilo, W., Kim, J. (eds.) ProvSec 2018. LNCS, vol. 11192, pp. 258–276. Springer, Cham (2018). https://doi.org/10.1007/978-3-030-01446-9_15

22. Derler, D., Ramacher, S., Slamanig, D.: Post-quantum zero-knowledge proofs for accumulators with applications to ring signatures from symmetric-key primitives. In: Lange, T., Steinwandt, R. (eds.) PQCrypto 2018. LNCS, vol. 10786, pp. 419–440. Springer, Cham (2018). https://doi.org/10.1007/978-3-319-79063-3_20

23. Dinur, I., Kales, D., Promitzer, A., Ramacher, S., Rechberger, C.: Linear equivalence of block ciphers with partial non-linear layers: application to LowMC. In: Ishai, Y., Rijmen, V. (eds.) EUROCRYPT 2019. LNCS, vol. 11476, pp. 343–372. Springer, Cham (2019). https://doi.org/10.1007/978-3-030-17653-2_12

24. Don, J., Fehr, S., Majenz, C., Schaffner, C.: Security of the Fiat-Shamir transformation in the quantum random-oracle model. In: Boldyreva, A., Micciancio, D. (eds.) CRYPTO 2019. LNCS, vol. 11693, pp. 356–383. Springer, Cham (2019). https://doi.org/10.1007/978-3-030-26951-7_13

25. El-Razouk, H., Reyhani-Masoleh, A.: New bit-level serial GF (2^m) multiplication using polynomial basis. In: ARITH, pp. 129–136. IEEE (2015)

26. Ferozpuri, A., Farahmand, F., Dang, V., Sharif, M.U., Kaps, J.P., Gaj, K.: Hardware API for Post-Quantum Public Key Cryptosystems (2018). https://cryptography.gmu.edu/athena/PQC/PQC_HW_API.pdf
27. Fiat, A., Shamir, A.: How to prove yourself: practical solutions to identification and signature problems. In: Odlyzko, A.M. (ed.) CRYPTO 1986. LNCS, vol. 263, pp. 186–194. Springer, Heidelberg (1987). https://doi.org/10.1007/3-540-47721-7_12
28. Freedman, M.J., Ishai, Y., Pinkas, B., Reingold, O.: Keyword search and oblivious pseudorandom functions. In: Kilian, J. (ed.) TCC 2005. LNCS, vol. 3378, pp. 303–324. Springer, Heidelberg (2005). https://doi.org/10.1007/978-3-540-30576-7_17
29. Giacomelli, I., Madsen, J., Orlandi, C.: ZKBoo: faster zero-knowledge for Boolean circuits. In: USENIX Security Symposium, pp. 1069–1083. USENIX Association (2016)
30. Grassi, L., Kales, D., Khovratovich, D., Roy, A., Rechberger, C., Schofnegger, M.: Starkad and poseidon: new hash functions for zero knowledge proof systems. ePrint 2019, 458 (2019)
31. Grassi, L., Rechberger, C., Rotaru, D., Scholl, P., Smart, N.P.: MPC-friendly symmetric key primitives. In: ACM CCS, pp. 430–443. ACM (2016)
32. Grosso, V., Leurent, G., Standaert, F.-X., Varıcı, K.: LS-Designs: bitslice encryption for efficient masked software implementations. In: Cid, C., Rechberger, C. (eds.) FSE 2014. LNCS, vol. 8540, pp. 18–37. Springer, Heidelberg (2015). https://doi.org/10.1007/978-3-662-46706-0_2
33. Güneysu, T.: Utilizing hard cores of modern FPGA devices for high-performance cryptography. J. Cryptogr. Eng. **1**(1), 37–55 (2011)
34. Howe, J., Oder, T., Krausz, M., Güneysu, T.: Standard lattice-based key encapsulation on embedded devices. IACR Trans. Cryptogr. Hardw. Embed. Syst. **2018**(3), 372–393 (2018)
35. Intel Corporation: Securing the enterprise with intel® AES-NI (2010). https://www.intel.com/content/dam/doc/white-paper/enterprise-security-aes-ni-white-paper.pdf
36. Ishai, Y., Kushilevitz, E., Ostrovsky, R., Sahai, A.: Zero-knowledge from secure multiparty computation. In: STOC, pp. 21–30. ACM (2007)
37. Kales, D., Rechberger, C., Schneider, T., Senker, M., Weinert, C.: Mobile private contact discovery at scale. In: USENIX Security Symposium, pp. 1447–1464. USENIX Association (2019)
38. Katz, J., Kolesnikov, V., Wang, X.: Improved non-interactive zero knowledge with applications to post-quantum signatures. In: ACM CCS, pp. 525–537. ACM (2018)
39. LowMC: Official LowMC Github Repository. https://github.com/LowMC/lowmc
40. Mohassel, P., Rindal, P., Rosulek, M.: Fast database joins for secret shared data. ePrint 2019, 518 (2019)
41. Moradi, A., Poschmann, A., Ling, S., Paar, C., Wang, H.: Pushing the limits: a very compact and a threshold implementation of AES. In: Paterson, K.G. (ed.) EUROCRYPT 2011. LNCS, vol. 6632, pp. 69–88. Springer, Heidelberg (2011). https://doi.org/10.1007/978-3-642-20465-4_6
42. Naehrig, M., Lauter, K.E., Vaikuntanathan, V.: Can homomorphic encryption be practical? In: CCSW, pp. 113–124. ACM (2011)
43. Pöppelmann, T., Ducas, L., Güneysu, T.: Enhanced lattice-based signatures on reconfigurable hardware. In: Batina, L., Robshaw, M. (eds.) CHES 2014. LNCS, vol. 8731, pp. 353–370. Springer, Heidelberg (2014). https://doi.org/10.1007/978-3-662-44709-3_20
44. Rechberger, C., Soleimany, H., Tiessen, T.: Cryptanalysis of low-data instances of full LowMCv2. IACR Trans. Symmetric Cryptol. **2018**(3), 163–181 (2018)

45. Rotaru, D., Smart, N.P., Stam, M.: Modes of operation suitable for computing on encrypted data. IACR Trans. Symmetric Cryptol. **2017**(3), 294–324 (2017)
46. Roy, D.B., Mukhopadhyay, D.: Post quantum ECC on FPGA platform. ePrint 2019, 568 (2019)
47. San, I., At, N.: Improving the computational efficiency of modular operations for embedded systems. J. Syst. Archit. Embed. Syst. Des. **60**(5), 440–451 (2014)
48. Sasdrich, P., Güneysu, T.: Implementing curve25519 for side-channel-protected elliptic curve cryptography. TRETS **9**(1), 3:1–3:15 (2015)
49. Unruh, D.: Non-interactive zero-knowledge proofs in the quantum random oracle model. In: Oswald, E., Fischlin, M. (eds.) EUROCRYPT 2015. LNCS, vol. 9057, pp. 755–784. Springer, Heidelberg (2015). https://doi.org/10.1007/978-3-662-46803-6_25
50. Wang, W., Szefer, J., Niederhagen, R.: FPGA-based niederreiter cryptosystem using binary goppa codes. In: Lange, T., Steinwandt, R. (eds.) PQCrypto 2018. LNCS, vol. 10786, pp. 77–98. Springer, Cham (2018). https://doi.org/10.1007/978-3-319-79063-3_4
51. Werner, M., Unterluggauer, T.: Transparent memory encryption and authentication. https://github.com/IAIK/memsec
52. Werner, M., Unterluggauer, T., Schilling, R., Schaffenrath, D., Mangard, S.: Transparent memory encryption and authentication. In: FPL, pp. 1–6. IEEE (2017)

Traceable Ring Signatures
with Post-quantum Security

Hanwen Feng[1,2], Jianwei Liu[1], Qianhong Wu[1(✉)], and Ya-Nan Li[3]

[1] Key Laboratory of Aerospace Network Security,
Ministry of Industry and Information Technology,
School of Cyber Science and Technology,
Beihang University, Beijing, China
{feng_hanwen,liujianwei,qianhong.wu}@buaa.edu.cn
[2] State Key Laboratory of Information Security,
Institute of Information Engineering,
Chinese Academy of Sciences, Beijing 100093, China
[3] New Jersey Institute of Technology, Newark, USA
ly252@njit.edu

Abstract. Traceable ring signature (TRS), a variant of ring signature, allows a signer to sign a message anonymously labeled with a tag on behalf of a group of users, but may reveal the signer's identity if he creates two signatures with the same tag. TRS provides accountable anonymity for users, and serves as an important role in e-voting systems and e-coupon services. However, current TRS schemes are built on hard problems in number theory that cannot resist quantum attackers. To address this issue, first, we propose a general framework of TRS, by using a non-interactive zero-knowledge proof of knowledge, a collision-resistant hash function, and a pseudorandom function with some additional properties. Then, we construct an efficient TRS scheme in the quantum random oracle model, by instantiating the framework with appropriate lattice-based building blocks. Moreover, the signature size of the lattice-based TRS is logarithmic in the ring size.

1 Introduction

Traceable ring signature (TRS) [20] is a cryptographic primitive for achieving accountable anonymity. TRS is essentially a tag-based ring signature [33]. Here, the tag consists of a *ring*, that is a signer-chosen group of users, and an *issue*, that is a string referring to a social problem or a vote in practice. A signer can anonymously sign a message on behalf of the ring, but his identity may be revealed if he produces two signatures with the same tag. More precisely, with the same tag, if the two signatures are generated for different messages, everyone can extract the signer's identity from the signatures; if they are for the same message, everyone knows they are created by the same signer. In many information systems like e-voting [13] and anonymous off-line coupon service [19], the signature represents the signer's use of his rights, e.g., voting for someone and

S. Jarecki (Ed.): CT-RSA 2020, LNCS 12006, pp. 442–468, 2020.
https://doi.org/10.1007/978-3-030-40186-3_19

spending a coupon. In such cases, signing twice with the same tag often refers to some unexpected behavior such as multiple voting and double spending. TRS can protect an honest user's privacy and keep users away from these dishonest behaviors, and thus it becomes an important tool in these scenarios.

Since Fujisaki et al. [20] proposed the first TRS scheme in 2007, several works have been proposed for improving security or performance. Fujisaki [19] presented a TRS scheme with sub-linear size in the standard model. Au et al. [3] adapted TRS to the identity-based setting. However, all these schemes are based on computational problems in number theory that can be efficiently solved by quantum computers [34]. As TRS serves as an essential building block in many applications, there is a strong interest to build a post-quantum secure TRS scheme.

Post-quantum Security. Since Shor's seminal work [34] on efficient quantum algorithms for factoring and discrete logarithm problems, post-quantum cryptography has become a hot topic in cryptography community.

The early efforts are mainly about building cryptographic schemes on alternative hard problems that are conjectured to be quantum-resistant. Among them, lattice-based cryptography is emerging as a substantial branch of post-quantum cryptography, and has received intensive interests, since it has better asymptotic efficiency, and supports many advanced functionalities such as fully homomorphic encryption [22].

In the last decade, it is also realized that some classical security proof techniques are not available in the quantum world [8]. The most notable example is the random oracle model (ROM), in which hash functions are treated as truly random functions and can only be evaluated through querying random oracles. Since hash functions are executed off-line in the real world, a quantum attacker can evaluate a hash function on some quantum superposition states. To adapt to this ability, the ROM should be adjusted to the quantum random oracle model (QROM), where superposition queries are allowed. However, this simple adjustment makes the traditional simulation technique for ROM does not work, as discussed in [8]. Moreover, Ambainis et al. [2] have pointed out that the Fiat-Shamir construction [17], which produces secure signatures in the ROM, is insecure in the QROM under assumptions that are sufficient in classical security. Therefore, it is essential to provide a reasonable security proof for a cryptography scheme in the quantum world.

1.1 Our Results

In this paper, we are interested in building a lattice-based TRS scheme with a reasonable security proof against quantum adversaries.

General Construction of TRS. First, we propose a general construction of TRS schemes, and show that its security can be built upon the existence of some basic primitives such as general non-interactive zero-knowledge (computational) proof of knowledge (NIZKPoK) [15,30] and collision-resistant hash functions. Since these basic primitives have post-quantum secure implementations [12,30], the general construction also implies a TRS scheme can be secure against quantum attackers.

There exists a general framework for a related primitive called *unique ring signatures* [18]. The primitive is a variant of ring signatures, where every two signatures under the same tag created by the same signer will share a common component, and then everyone can link them. This general construction utilizes the "PRF made public" paradigm [6], and is built upon a pseudorandom function (PRF) family and a non-interactive zero-knowledge (NIZK) proof system. However, it does not support tracing the identity of a dishonest user, and thus cannot subsume the notion of TRS.

The main obstacle to present a general construction for TRS is that how to ensure the correctness and security of the tracing function from the properties of the basic primitives. We address this challenge by making it clear what properties of the underlying PRF are necessary in Fujisaki *et al.*'s TRS scheme [20], and integrating their design principle with the framework of unique ring signatures [18]. Then, we obtain a general construction of TRS that takes building blocks as an NIZKPoK, a collision-resistant hash function and a PRF with certain properties. More concretely, we show that a *unique* PRF with an *intersection-free* range is sufficient for Fujisaki *et al.*'s paradigm. We state the requirements on PRF in the following.

- **Uniqueness.** It says that given the same input, evaluating the PRF with different keys can output identical values with only negligible probability.
- **Intersection-free Range.** We call a range is intersection-free, if (i) it is a vector space of the rational number field $\mathbb{Q}$; (ii) for every two distinct elements y_1, y_2, every two uniformly randomly chosen elements δ_1, δ_2, and any polynomial $N(\cdot)$, the probability, that there exists an integer $i \leq N(\lambda)$ *s.t.* $y_1 + i\delta_1 = y_2 + i\delta_2$, is negligible. This property guarantees that two signatures generated by different signers will not be wrongly traced.

To base our general construction on quantum-resistant assumptions, we analyze how to build a unique PRF with an intersection-free range. We consider Goldreich *et al.*'s PRF construction [23], which takes the building block as a pseudorandom generator (PRG) with expansion factor $2n$. We show this PRF is unique if the underlying PRG is *two-layer collision-resistant*, i.e., for this PRG, no PPT algorithm can find two different seeds *s.t.* their outputs have either the same first n bits or the same last n bits. Further, we show that $\mathbb{Z}_q^n$ is an intersection-free set, where q is prime and n is an integer. Since a binary string can be combined into a vector in $\mathbb{Z}_q^n$, it is then straightforward to construct a PRF with an intersection-free range from a PRF that outputs binary strings. In addition, previous works [30,31] have shown that an NIZKPoK exists if the learning with errors (LWE) problem [32] is hard. Therefore, the general construction of TRS also implies that the existence of TRS can be reduced to the existence of collision-resistant hash functions and two-layer collision-resistant PRG, as well as the hardness assumption of the LWE problem.

An Efficient Lattice-Based TRS Scheme. Then, given the general framework, we construct an efficient lattice-based TRS scheme in the QROM, which is also the first TRS scheme that is conjectured to be post-quantum secure.

The first challenge is to find or construct a post-quantum secure PRF that has an efficient proof system to show the correct evaluation while preserving pseudorandomness. We address this challenge by proving the post-quantum pseudorandomness of a lattice-based PRF $F^H(T, \mathbf{s}) = \lfloor H(T) \cdot \mathbf{s} \rceil_p$, that is initially presented in [4]. To demonstrate the correct evaluation of this function, Libert et al. [26] developed an efficient lattice-based proof system that belongs to Stern protocols, a widely-used class of sigma protocols in lattice-based cryptography. The pseudorandomness of this function can be reduced to the hardness of LWE problems in the ROM [9]. Although not stated in detail, the random oracle in this proof is simulated by generating $\mathbf{R}_x \leftarrow \{-1, 1\}^{m \times m}$ for each query x and answering $H(x) := \mathbf{R}_x \cdot \mathbf{A}$ with a prefixed matrix $\mathbf{A} \in \mathbb{Z}_q^{m \times n}$. However, as discussed in [8], this simulation technique is not reasonable in the QROM, since it has to know the value of a query before responding and will disturb a quantum superposition query. We adapt this proof to the one in the QROM by providing an alternative simulation for $H(\cdot)$ through Zhandry's technique [41], which can answer to quantum superposition inputs. Concretely, $H(\cdot)$ is simulated as $K(\cdot) \cdot \mathbf{A}$, where $K(\cdot)$ is a uniformly chosen $2q$-wise independent function that is identical to a uniform random function for any algorithm performing at most q queries.

The second obstacle is to construct an NIZKPoK for a specific relation $R_{TRS} = \{\mathbf{A}, \mathbf{B}, (\mathbf{y}_i, \mathbf{t}_i)_{[L]}; \mathbf{s} \in \mathbb{Z}_q^n : \exists i \in [L] s.t. \mathbf{y}_i = \lfloor \mathbf{A} \cdot \mathbf{s} \rceil_p$ and $\mathbf{t}_i = \lfloor \mathbf{B} \cdot \mathbf{s} \rceil_p\}$. Observe that a post-quantum secure NIZKPoK can be obtained by applying a general transform such as the Unruh transform [37] to post-quantum secure sigma protocols. Building such a sigma protocol for R_{TRS} is sufficient. Utilizing the general Stern protocol and LWR transforming techniques introduced in [26], we first build a Stern protocol for the relation $R_0 = \{(pk_i, t_i); \mathbf{s}_i : pk_i = \lfloor H(g) \cdot \mathbf{s}_i \rceil_p \wedge t_i = \lfloor H(T) \cdot \mathbf{s}_i \rceil_p\}$. Clearly, R_{TRS} is an **OR** composition of R_0. The most well-known method to build sigma protocols for an **OR** composition is Cramer et al.'s technique [14], but it requires the standard special soundness of the underlying sigma protocol, while Stern protocols do not have this property. To address this challenge, we use an alternative method to build sigma protocol for an **OR** relation, that is completed with an accumulator scheme [25]. We first hash the pair (pk_i, t_i) to an element d_i for all $i \in [L]$ via a collision-resistant hash function h, and take $R = (d_1, \cdots, d_L)$ as the set to be accumulated. We then compute the accumulator value u. Assuming the security of the accumulator scheme, it is sufficient to prove the relation R'_{TRS} that there are an sk_j and d_j s.t. (i) $d_j \in R$, and (ii) $d_j = h(pk_j, t_j)$, and (iii) $pk_j = \lfloor H(g) \cdot \mathbf{s}_j \rceil_p$ and $t_j = \lfloor H(T) \cdot \mathbf{s}_j \rceil_p$. In our TRS scheme, we implement the accumulator scheme with the Merkle-tree-based accumulator scheme in [25], and implement the hash function with the one used to build the accumulator. Since there already exists a Stern protocol for the accumulator scheme, a Stern protocol for the relation R'_{TRS} can be constructed through a combinatorial way.

Benefiting from the logarithmic size of the proof for this accumulator scheme [25], the signature size in our scheme is also logarithmic in the ring size.

1.2   Related Work

Linkable Ring Signatures. Linkable ring signature (LRS) is a closely-related primitive, which is proposed by Liu *et al.* [28] in 2004. The definition of LRS is only slightly different from the previously mentioned *unique ring signatures* [18], and people tend to use the notion of LRS. In an LRS scheme, every two signatures produced by the same signer with the same tag should be just linked, but the identity of the signer will not be revealed. Thus, it is not applicable to some scenarios such as off-line e-cash systems [11], where we wish to find dishonest users. Recently, several lattice-based LRS schemes [5,29,36,39,42] are proposed, while all of them only achieve a weaker property called one-time linkability, namely every two signatures generated by the same signer will be linked regardless of whether they are with the same tag. Baum *et al.*'s construction [5] and Torres *et al.*'s construction [36] are very similar, and both can be regarded as the lattice-based counterparts of Liu *et al.*'s LRS scheme [28]. The signature size of the two constructions is a few KB when the ring has fewer than ten members, but grows linearly with the ring size. Zhang *et al.*'s LRS scheme [42] is a lattice-based analogue of Groth and Kohlweiss's one-out-of-many proofs [24], and the signature size is logarithmic in the ring size. All the three constructions cannot be simply extended to standard LRS schemes, since the component used for linking in a signature is generated by using one-way functions instead of PRFs, and then extra information of the secret key may be leaked when generating the components with different tags. Yang *et al.* [39] almost follows the framework in [18] to construct a lattice-based LRS scheme. Their construction relies on a lattice-based weak Pseudorandom Random Function (wPRF) and a Merkle-tree-based accumulator [25] that is also used in our TRS scheme, and thus achieves logarithmic signature size. Recently, Lu *et al.* [29] developed a new paradigm to achieve one-time linkability in RS schemes, which was subsequently formalized in [38]. Their construction takes a one-time signature scheme as a building block, and uses the public key of the one-time signature as the linking component. This construction has a better practical performance than previous constructions since it does not need a zero-knowledge proof to guarantee the validity of linking components. The signature size of this scheme is linear in the ring size, and it is still unknown how to achieve standard linkability, rather than one-time linkability, under this paradigm. All these lattice-based LRS schemes only provide a security proof in the ROM, instead of in the QROM.

Previous Attempt on Post-quantum Secure TRS. Very recently, we note that [10] (accepted by PQCrypto 2019) attempts to build a post-quantum secure TRS scheme based on coding theory. However, this construction suffers from some security flaws. In detail, this work leverages the Stern protocols to prove the knowledge on a binary vector $\mathbf{e}$ with a fixed hamming weight *s.t.* $\mathbf{G}\mathbf{e}^T = \mathbf{s}^T$

and $\mathbf{He}^T = \mathbf{r}^T$, where $\mathbf{G}$, $\mathbf{H}$, $\mathbf{s}$, $\mathbf{r}$ are public binary matrices or vectors. Then, it applies Cramer $et\ al.$'s OR-composition method [14] to this Stern protocol. However, Cramer $et\ al.$'s OR-composition method is only applicable to sigma protocols with standard special soundness [21], but the Stern protocols do not have this property. Moreover, the misuse of Cramer $et\ al.$'s technique cannot give a sound proof (or argument) system. We analyze it in the full version of this paper.

2 Preliminaries

2.1 Notations

For arrow using, $x \hookleftarrow X$ denotes sampling x from the uniform distribution over X or sampling x from distribution X, which is determined by the case X is either a set or a distribution; $\mathcal{X} \leftarrow \mathcal{Y}$ or $\mathcal{Y} \rightarrow \mathcal{X}$ denotes that $\mathcal{Y}$ is the range of some map with the domain $\mathcal{X}$; $a \leftarrow T(b)$ or $T(b) \rightarrow a$ denotes that a is an output of the algorithm $T(b)$; $A \Leftrightarrow B$ denotes that the two events A and B are equivalent.

For matrices and vectors, $[\mathbf{A}|\mathbf{B}] \in \mathbb{Z}^{n \times (m_1 + m_2)}$ denotes the concatenation of matrices $\mathbf{A} \in \mathbb{Z}^{n \times m_1}$ and $\mathbf{B} \in \mathbb{Z}^{n \times m_2}$; $\mathbf{a}[i]$ denotes the i-th component of the vector $\mathbf{a}$; $\|x\|$ and $\|x\|_\infty$ denote the Euclidean norm and infinity norm, respectively. For sets, we use $[i, n]$ to denote the set $\{i, i+1, \cdots, n\}$ and abbreviate it as $[n]$ if $i = 1$. We use $(a_i)_{[n]}$ to denote $(a_i)_{i \in [n]}$, that is, the sequence $(a_1, \cdots, a_n)$.

We say a function $f(n)$ is negligible in n if $\lim_{n \to \infty} n^c f(n) = 0$ for any $c > 0$, denoting by $f(n) \in \mathrm{negl}(n)$. A function $f(n)$ is non-negligible in n if $f(n) \notin \mathrm{negl}(n)$. We use $\lambda \in \mathbb{N}$ to denote the security parameter, and say that two distributions ϕ and φ are statistically close, also denoted by $\phi \approx \varphi$, if their statistical distance belongs to $\mathrm{negl}(\lambda)$. We say two distributions ϕ and φ are computational indistinguishable, denoted by $\phi \approx_c \varphi$, if there is no PPT algorithm can distinguish them with non-negligible advantage. We say a distribution χ is B-bounded for some positive integer B, if $\Pr[\|x\| > B : x \leftarrow \chi] \in \mathrm{negl}(\lambda)$. For any $\mathbf{x} \in \mathbb{Z}_q^m$, we define $\lfloor \mathbf{x} \rceil_p = \lfloor (p/q) \cdot \mathbf{x} \rceil \bmod q$.

Throughout the whole paper, we define matrices $\mathbf{G}_{n,q} = \mathbf{I}_n \otimes [1| \cdots |2^{\lceil \log q \rceil - 1}]$ $\in \mathbb{Z}_q^{n \times n \lceil \log q \rceil}$, and a map bin : $\mathbb{Z}_q^n \to \{0, 1\}^{n \lceil \log q \rceil}$, which is obtained by replacing each entry of a vector by its binary expansion. For every $\mathbf{v} \in \mathbb{Z}_q^n$, we have that $\mathbf{G}_{n,q} \cdot \mathrm{bin}(\mathbf{v}) = \mathbf{v}$.

The learning with errors (LWE) [32] assumption and the short integer solution (SIS) [1] assumption are basic assumptions of our construction. They are recalled in the full version of this paper.

2.2 Stern Protocols

Stern protocols [35] are a special class of sigma protocols. In each execution of a Stern protocol, the transcript between the prover and verifier consists of three messages $(com, ch, resp)$. The first message com called commitment and the third message $resp$ called response are sent by the prover, and the second message ch called challenge is uniformly sampled from a fixed domain by the verifier. The Stern protocols were originally proposed for demonstrating the possession of a short vector w.r.t. a syndrome matrix [35], and recently were used to prove many relations appearing in the lattice-based cryptography [27]. More precisely, Stern protocols can prove relations that can be transformed to the following relation which we call the *Stern relation*.

Definition 1 (Stern Relation). *Let* $\mathbb{V} \subset \{-1, 0, 1\}^d$, n_i, d_i, q_i *be positive integers for* $i \in [N]$, *where* $\sum_{i=1}^{N} d_i = d$, *the Stern relation is defined as*

$$R_S = \{\{(\mathbf{M}_i \in \mathbb{Z}_{q_i}^{n_i \times d_i}, \mathbf{v}_i \in \mathbb{Z}_{q_i}^{n_i})\}_{[N]}; \Upsilon_i \in \{-1, 0, 1\}^{d_i} :$$
$$\mathbf{M}_i \cdot \Upsilon_i = \mathbf{v}_i \bmod q_i, \forall i \in [N], (\Upsilon_1^T | \cdots | \Upsilon_N^T) \in \mathbb{V}\}.$$

Permutations are the main techniques used in Stern protocols. To handle a Stern relation, we need an *eligible set of permutations* (ESP) for the set $\mathbb{V}$, defined as follows.

Definition 2 (Eligible Set of Permutations (ESP)). *Let* $\mathbb{S}$ *be a finite set s.t. each element* $\varphi \in \mathbb{S}$ *can be associated with a permutation* Φ_φ *over d elements. We call* $\mathbb{E}_S = \{\Phi_\varphi | \varphi \in \mathbb{S}\}$ *is an* **eligible set of permutations** *for* $\mathbb{V}$, *if*

$$\begin{cases} \Upsilon \in \mathbb{V} \Longleftrightarrow \Phi_\varphi(\Upsilon) \in \mathbb{V}; \\ \text{if } \Upsilon \in \mathbb{V} \text{ and } \varphi \text{ is uniform in } \mathbb{S}, \text{ then } \Phi_\varphi(\Upsilon) \text{ is uniform in } \mathbb{V}. \end{cases}$$

For a Stern relation R_S with an ESP $\mathbb{E}_S$, Libert *et al.* [26] presented a Stern protocol, to demonstrate the knowledge of $\{\Upsilon_i\}_{[N]}$ for the public tuple $\{(\mathbf{M}_i, \mathbf{v}_i)\}_{[N]}$. Their results can be summarized in the following lemma.

Lemma 1 ([26]). *Assuming an ESP* $\mathbb{E}_S = \{\Phi_\varphi | \varphi \in \mathbb{S}\}$ *for the set* $\mathbb{V}$ *of the Stern relation* R_S, *there is a Stern protocol for* R_S *with transcript size of* $\widetilde{\mathcal{O}}(\sum_i d_i \cdot \log q_i)$. *In particular, the Stern protocol is perfectly complete, and has the following properties.*

1. ***Statistical Honest-Verifier Zero-knowledge.*** *There exists a PPT algorithm called simulator, that takes as inputs* $\{\mathbf{M}_i, \mathbf{v}_i\}_{[N]}$, *and outputs an accepted transcript statistically close to that produced by the real prover and the real verifier.*
2. ***3-Special Soundness.*** *There exists a PPT algorithm called extractor, that takes as inputs a commitment com and valid responses* $(resp_1, resp_2, resp_3)$ *to three distinct challenges* (ch_1, ch_2, ch_3), *and outputs a witness* $W = (\Upsilon_1^T | \cdots | \Upsilon_N^T) \in \mathbb{V}$ *s.t.* $\mathbf{M}_i \cdot \Upsilon_i = \mathbf{v}_i$, $\forall i \in [N]$.

2.3 Merkle-Tree-Based Accumulator

An accumulator is a one-way membership function that takes as input a set R, and outputs a constant-size value u. Meanwhile, a value $d \in R$ has a short witness w to convince verifiers that d was accumulated to u. In this section, we introduce a lattice-based accumulator scheme [25] which is a building block of our TRS scheme.

This accumulator scheme is Merkle-tree-based, built upon a carefully designed hash function $\mathcal{H} = (Gen, h)$. In detail,

$$Gen(\lambda) := \mathbf{A} = [\mathbf{A}_0 | \mathbf{A}_1] \hookleftarrow \mathbb{Z}_q^{n \times (m+m)}, \quad h_{\mathbf{A}}(\mathbf{u}_0, \mathbf{u}_1) := \mathrm{bin}(\mathbf{A}_0 \mathbf{u}_0 + \mathbf{A}_1 \mathbf{u}_1), \tag{1}$$

where $n, q, m \in \mathbb{N}$, $\mathbf{u}_0, \mathbf{u}_1 \in \{0,1\}^m$, and the map $\mathrm{bin} : \mathbb{Z}_q^n \to \{0,1\}^{n\lceil \log q \rceil}$ is obtained by replacing each entry of a vector by its binary expansion. In particular, we set $m = n\lceil \log q \rceil$ when $\mathcal{H}$ is used in the accumulator.

Lemma 2 ([25]). *The function family $\mathcal{H}$ is collision-resistant, if the $SIS_{n,2m,q,1}$ problem is hard.*

This accumulator scheme consists of four algorithms (A-Setup, A-Acc, A-Witness, A-Verify). **A-Setup**(λ) generates a key for the hash function, as the public parameter pp. **A-Acc**(pp, R) accumulates all elements in R, by taking each element as a leaf node of a Merkle tree and outputting the root node u as the accumulator value. **A-Witness**(pp, R, u, d) outputs the hash path of d in the Merkle tree as the witness w. **A-Verify**(pp, u, d, w) just checks whether w is the hash path for d or not.

Roughly speaking, the correctness of an accumulator scheme means that

$$1 \leftarrow \text{A-Verify}(pp, \text{A-Acc}(pp, R), \mathbf{d}, \text{A-Witness}(pp, R, d)), \text{ for all } d \in R$$

holds for all $pp \leftarrow$ A-Setup(λ). We call an accumulator scheme secure if there is no PPT adversary can forge a witness w^* for some $d^* \notin R$ s.t. A-Verify$(pp, u, d^*, w^*) = 1$. Formal definitions refer to [25].

Lemma 3 ([25]). *The accumulator scheme is correct and secure, assuming the hardness of $SIS_{n,2m,q,1}$ problem.*

Libert *et al.* [25] also presented a Stern protocol Ψ_A with proof size $\widetilde{\mathcal{O}}(n \log L \cdot \log q)$ to demonstrate that there is secret element $\mathbf{d} \in \mathbb{Z}_q^n$ that was accumulated to a public accumulator value $\mathbf{u}$ which is computed from a set R with L elements.

2.4 Traceable Ring Signatures

A TRS scheme consists of five polynomial time algorithms, defined as follows.

- $pp \leftarrow$ **Setup**(1^λ): take the security parameter $\lambda \in \mathbb{N}$ as input, and output public parameter pp.
- $(pk, sk) \leftarrow$ **KeyGen**(pp): take the public parameter pp as input, and output a public/secret key pair (pk, sk).
- $\sigma \leftarrow$ **Sign**(pp, sk_π, T, M): take as inputs the public parameter pp, a secret key sk_π of user U_π, a tag $T = ((pk_i)_{[L]}, issue)$ and a message $M \in \{0,1\}^*$. It outputs a signature σ on the message M with the tag T. Here, L is the ring size, and $(pk_i)_{[L]}$ is required to contain pk_π.

- $ok \leftarrow$ **Verify**(pp, T, σ, M): take as inputs the public parameter pp, a tag T, a signature σ, and a message M. This algorithm outputs $ok = 1$ if accepting this signature or $ok = 0$ if not accepting it.
- $\xi \leftarrow$ **Trace**$(pp, T, M, \sigma, M', \sigma')$: take as inputs the public parameter pp, a tag T, and two message/signature pairs (M, σ) and (M', σ'), and output $\xi \in \{\texttt{accept}, \texttt{reject}, \texttt{linked}, pk\}$.

A TRS scheme is correct if it satisfies *completeness* and *public traceability*. The *completeness* property is the generic requirement of any signature scheme, capturing that a signature produced by an honest signer can always be accepted by an honest verifier. The *public traceability* property mandates the *correctness* of the tracing function.

Definition 3 (Completeness). *A TRS scheme is complete, if for all $pp \leftarrow$* ***Setup***(λ)*, all $(pk_i, sk_i) \leftarrow$* ***KeyGen***(pp) *for $i \in [L]$, all $T = ((pk_i)_{[L]}, issue)$ for some issue, all M and all $\sigma \leftarrow$* ***Sign***(pp, sk_π, T, M)*, it always holds that* ***Verify***$(pp, T, \sigma, M) = 1$.

Definition 4 (Public Traceability). *A TRS scheme is public traceable, if for all $pp \leftarrow$* ***Setup***(λ)*, all $(pk_i, sk_i) \leftarrow$* ***KeyGen***(pp) *for $i \in [L]$, all $T = ((pk_i)_{[L]}, issue)$ for some issue, all M, M', all $\sigma \leftarrow$* ***Sign***(pp, sk_π, T, M) *and $\sigma' \leftarrow$* ***Sign***$(pp, sk_{\pi'}, T, M')$*, it holds that*

$$\textbf{Trace}(pp, T, M, \sigma, M', \sigma') = \begin{cases} \texttt{accept}, & \textit{if } \pi \neq \pi', \\ \texttt{linked}, & \textit{else if } M = M', \\ pk_\pi, & \textit{otherwise } (M \neq M'), \end{cases}$$

with overwhelming probability.

We use the security definitions of [19], which formalize security requirements called *tag-linkability, anonymity* and *exculpability*.

Informally, *tag-linkability* is to defend the system, requiring that the total number of unlinked signatures with one tag cannot exceed the total number of ring members. *Anonymity* mandates that, when a signature is signed by either of two signers, an attacker (even with access to the two signing oracles) cannot infer anything as to by whom this signature is signed. *Exculpability* captures that an honest signer cannot be accused of being dishonest by breaking the rule, even if every ring member except him is corrupted. The formal definitions of these properties are recalled in the full version of this paper.

3 General Construction

In this section, we give a general construction of TRS schemes, mainly by integrating Fujisaki *et al.*'s design principle [20] into the framework of unique ring signatures [18].

Recall the framework of unique ring signatures. With a tag $T = ((pk_i)_{[L]}, issue)$, a signature σ consists of an element t, along with a non-interactive proof ϑ which guarantees that t is an evaluation of F_{sk_i} on T, where sk_i is the secret key of pk_i for some $i \in [L]$. Since t is determined by sk_i and the tag T, with the same tag T, two signatures generated by sk_i have the same t, and then everyone knows that they are signed by the same user. Consider a straightforward way to achieve the tracing function. A signature is required to contain a sequence $(t_i)_{[N]}$, as well as a non-interactive proof ensuring that some t_i is an evaluation of F_{sk_i} on T, where sk_i is the secret key of the i-th public key pk_i in the tag T. Then, two signatures generated by the same sk_i both have t_i, and the identity of signer can be publicly traced to pk_i.

However, this straightforward construction cannot provide a reliable tracing function, due to no restriction on other components t_j, $j \neq i$. Assume an honest user U_j (w.r.t. pk_j) generates a signature σ_j (with the tag T) which contains a component t_j. A dishonest user U_i (w.r.t. pk_i) can use his secret key to create a valid signature σ^* which also takes t_j as its j-th component. From previous argument, σ^* and σ_j will be judged to be generated by U_j. To defend against this attack, Fujisaki et al. [20] requires that all components t_j are determined by the used secret key sk_i, along with the tag T and message M. In their scheme, the range of the PRF is a cyclic group $\mathbb{G}$. Let the signature σ be signed by sk_i, and t_i be an evaluation of F_{sk_i} on T. Let $t_0 \in \mathbb{G}$ is a hash value of (T, M). The remaining components are generated as $t_j = t_0(\frac{t_i}{t_0})^{j/i}$. In this section, we will show how to employ their techniques to a generic PRF.

3.1 Building Blocks

Our construction has three main building blocks: a PRF, an NIZKPoK and a collision-resistant hash function.

Pseudorandom Function Family. A PRF family $F : \mathcal{K} \times \mathcal{X} \rightharpoonup \mathcal{Y}$ can be described by the following two algorithms.

- $k \leftarrow \text{Gen}(1^\lambda)$. Take as input the security parameter 1^λ, and output a key $k \in \mathcal{K}$.
- $y \leftarrow F_k(x)$. Evaluate the input x on the PRF with key k.

In our TRS construction, we require $\mathcal{Y} = \{0,1\}^*$. The standard security definition of a PRF is *pseudorandomness*.

Definition 5 (Pseudorandomness, [40]). *A function $F : \mathcal{K} \times \mathcal{X} \rightharpoonup \mathcal{Y}$ is pseudorandom, if no PPT adversary making polynomial-bounded queries can distinguish between a truly random function in $\mathcal{F}[\mathcal{X} : \mathcal{Y}]$ and the function F_k for a random k, where $\mathcal{F}[\mathcal{X} : \mathcal{Y}]$ is the set of all functions with the domain $\mathcal{X}$ and range $\mathcal{Y}$. Formally, for any PPT $\mathcal{A}$, we have*

$$\Pr[\mathcal{A}^{F_k}(1^\lambda) = 1, k \leftarrow Gen(1^\lambda)] - \Pr[\mathcal{A}^O(1^\lambda) = 1, O \leftarrow \mathcal{F}[\mathcal{X} : \mathcal{Y}]] \in negl(\lambda).$$

In addition, we require that the PRF F satisfies the following conditions.

1. *Uniqueness.* For a uniformly chosen message $x \hookleftarrow \mathcal{X}$, we have that

$$\Pr[\exists k_1, k_2 \in \mathcal{K}, k_1 \neq k_2 \wedge F_{k_1}(x) = F_{k_2}(x)] \in \mathrm{negl}(\lambda).$$

2. *Intersection-Free Range.* The range $\mathcal{Y}$ is a vector space of the rational number field $\mathbb{Q}$. For every two different elements $y_1, y_2 \in \mathcal{Y}$ and any polynomial $N(\cdot)$, we have that $\Pr[\exists i \leq N(\lambda), y_1 + i\delta_1 = y_2 + i\delta_2 : \delta_1, \delta_2 \hookleftarrow \mathcal{Y}] \in \mathrm{negl}(\lambda)$.

In the definition of the intersection-free range, δ_1 and δ_2 are required to be uniformly chosen. However, as we are considering the range of a PRF, it will be more desirable to consider the scenario where δ_1 and δ_2 are only pseudorandomly generated. Fortunately, we have the following result.

Lemma 4. *Let $\mathcal{Y}$ be an intersection-free range for some PRF $F1$. Let $F2 : \mathcal{K} \times \mathcal{X} \to \mathcal{Y}$ be a PRF, and let $k \leftarrow \mathrm{Gen}_2(1^\lambda)$, where Gen_2 is the key generation of $F2$. Then, for any efficient algorithm $\mathcal{A}$, and any polynomial $N(\cdot)$, we have*

$$\Pr[\exists i \leq N(\lambda), y_1 + i \cdot F2_k(a) = y_2 + i \cdot F2_k(b) : (y_1, y_2, a, b) \leftarrow \mathcal{A}^{F2_k(\cdot)}(1^\lambda)] \in \mathit{negl}(\lambda),$$

where the probability space is over the random flips of the algorithms $\mathcal{A}$ and Gen_2.

Proof (sketch). If there exists an efficient algorithm $\mathcal{A}$ which outputs (y_1, y_2, a, b) s.t. $y_1 + i \cdot F2_k(a) = y_2 + i \cdot F2_k(b)$ for some $i \leq N(\lambda)$ with non-negligible probability, we can construct an efficient distinguisher D to break the pseudorandomness of $F2$. D's strategies are (1) forwards all queries of $\mathcal{A}$ to $\mathcal{O}$, and (2) given $\mathcal{A}$'s outputs (y_1, y_2, a, b), it checks all $i \leq N(\lambda)$, and guesses that $\mathcal{O}$ is $F2_k(\cdot)$ if there exists i s.t $y_1 + i \cdot \mathcal{O}(a) = y_2 + i \cdot \mathcal{O}(b)$; otherwise, it guesses that $\mathcal{O}$ is a random oracle.

Non-interactive Zero-Knowledge Proof of Knowledge. An NIZKPoK $\Psi = (\mathcal{P}, \mathcal{V})$ for a relation R allows users to prove the knowledge of the witness W for a statement X s.t. $R(X, W) = 1$. More precisely, it consists of the following three algorithms.

- $pp \leftarrow \mathrm{Setup}_\Psi(1^\lambda)$. Only take as input the security parameter 1^λ, and output the public parameter pp.
- $\vartheta \leftarrow \mathcal{P}(pp, X, W)$. Take as inputs pp, a public statement X and its associated witness W. It outputs a proof ϑ.
- $\nu \leftarrow \mathcal{V}(pp, X, \vartheta)$. Take as inputs the public parameter pp, a statement x and a proof ϑ. It outputs $\nu = 1$ if the ϑ is a valid proof. Otherwise, it outputs $\nu = 0$.

The correctness of an NIZKPoK means that the verifier $\mathcal{V}$ always outputs 1 for an honestly generated proof when $R(X, W) = 1$. We consider the *zero-knowledge* property and *simulation-extractability* of the NIZKPoK.

Zero-knowledge property says that a malicious verifier cannot infer anything except validity of the statement through interacting with the prover.

Definition 6 (Zero-knowledge). *A non-interactive protocol $\Psi = (\mathcal{P}, \mathcal{V})$ for a relation R is zero-knowledge, if there exists a pair of PPT algorithms called simulator (S_O, S_P) s.t. for every PPT adversary $\mathcal{A}$, we have that*

$$|\Pr[b = 1 : pp \leftarrow Setup_\Psi(1^\lambda), b \leftarrow \mathcal{A}^{\mathcal{O}_1(pp, \cdot, \cdot)}(pp)] -$$
$$\Pr[b = 1 : (pp, \tau) \leftarrow S_O(1^\lambda), b \leftarrow \mathcal{A}^{\mathcal{O}_2(pp, \tau, \cdot)}(pp)]| \in negl(\lambda).$$

where $\mathcal{O}_1$ and $\mathcal{O}_2$ first check that the input $(X, W) \in R$, else return $\perp$; otherwise $\mathcal{O}_1$ returns $\pi \leftarrow \mathcal{P}(pp, X, W)$, and $\mathcal{O}_2$ returns $\pi \leftarrow S_P(pp, \tau, X)$.

Simulation-extractability captures that if a prover with access to simulation oracle can produce a valid proof, then there is an extractor that can extract a witness by interacting with the prover.

Definition 7 (Simulation-extractability). *A non-interactive protocol $\Psi = (\mathcal{P}, \mathcal{V})$ is simulation-extractable w.r.t a simulator (S_O, S_P), if there exists a PPT algorithm (called extractor) $\mathcal{E}$ s.t. for every PPT adversary $\mathcal{A}$, we have that*

$$\Pr[R(X, W) \neq 1 \wedge \vartheta^* \notin \mathbb{S} \wedge \nu = 1 : (pp, \tau, e) \leftarrow S_O(1^\lambda),$$
$$(X, \vartheta^*) \leftarrow \mathcal{A}^{\mathcal{O}(pp, \tau, \cdot)}(pp), \nu \leftarrow \mathcal{V}(pp, X, \vartheta^*), W \leftarrow \mathcal{E}^{\mathcal{A}}(X, \vartheta^*, e)] \in negl(\lambda),$$

where $\mathbb{S}$ denotes all proofs output by the simulator S_P, and $\mathcal{O}(pp, \tau, \cdot)$ on the input X returns $S_P(pp, \tau, X)$.

Specifically, we will use an NIZKPoK Ψ for a relation R_{OR}^L. Let $F : \mathcal{K} \times \mathcal{X} \rightarrow \mathcal{Y}$ be a PRF discussed above. The relation R_{OR}^L can be defined as follows:

$$R_{OR}^L := \{(a, b) \in \mathcal{X}^2, \{(y_i, t_i) \in \mathcal{Y}^2\}_{[L]}; \exists j \in [L]$$
$$\text{and } k \in \mathcal{K} : F_k(a) = y_j \wedge F_k(b) = t_j\}.$$

Collision-Resistant Hash Function. A hash function $H : \{0, 1\}^* \rightarrow \mathcal{Y}$ is collision-resistant, if it is hard to find $x_1 \neq x_2$ s.t. $H(x_1) = H(x_2)$. We require H has the same range as the PRF F.

3.2   Our Construction

We now describe our construction. Let F, $\Psi = (\mathcal{P}, \mathcal{V})$ and H be the PRF, the NIZKPoK and the hash function defined as above, respectively. We construct a secure TRS scheme $\Pi = $ (Setup, KeyGen, Sign, Verify, Trace) as follows.

Setup(1^λ). The setup algorithm invokes $pp_\Psi \leftarrow Setup_\Psi(1^\lambda)$, and uniformly samples $a \leftarrow \mathcal{X}$ at random. It outputs the public parameter as $pp = (pp_\Psi, a)$.

KeyGen(pp). The key generation algorithm calls $k \leftarrow Gen(1^\lambda)$, and evaluates the PRF $y \leftarrow F_k(a)$. It outputs $sk := k$ and $pk := y$.

Sign(pp, sk_π, T, M). It parses the tag T as $((pk_i)_{[L]}, issue)$, $pp = (pp_\Psi, a)$, and executes the following procedures.

- Compute $t_0 = H(T, M)$ and $t_\pi = F_{sk_\pi}(T)$.
- Compute $\delta = \frac{t_\pi - t_0}{\pi}$ and $t_i = t_0 + \delta \cdot i$ for all $i \neq \pi$.
- Set $X = (a, T, (pk_i, t_i)_{[L]})$ and $W = (\pi, sk_\pi)$, and invoke $\vartheta \leftarrow \mathcal{P}(pp, X, W)$.
- Output the signature $\sigma = (\delta, \vartheta)$.

Verify(pp, T, σ, M). It first parses $T = ((pk_i)_{[L]}, issue)$, $pp = (pp_\Psi, a)$, and $\sigma = (\delta, \vartheta)$. Then, it computes $t_0 = H(T, M)$ and $t_i = t_0 + i \cdot \delta$. It sets $X = (a, T, (pk_i, t_i)_{[L]})$ and invokes $\mathcal{V}(pp_\Psi, X, \vartheta)$ to check the validity of ϑ. It returns 1 if ϑ is valid; otherwise it returns 0.

Trace$(pp, T, M, \sigma, M', \sigma')$. It first parses $T = ((pk_i)_{[L]}, issue)$, $pp = (pp_\Psi, a)$, $\sigma = (\delta, \vartheta)$ and $\sigma' = (\delta', \vartheta')$. Then, it invokes the verification algorithm **Verify** to check the validity of both σ and σ'. If either is invalid, it returns reject. Otherwise, it compares the two tuples $(t_i)_{[L]}$ (w.r.t. σ) and $(t'_i)_{[L]}$ (w.r.t. σ') that are generated when invoking **Verify**. If $t_j = t'_j$ for all $j \in [L]$, it returns linked. If there is only one index $i \in [L]$ s.t. $t_i = t'_i$, it returns the associated pk_i. Otherwise, it returns accept.

3.3   Correctness Analysis

A TRS scheme is correct if it is *complete* and *public traceable*.

Completeness. The *completeness* of our construction is easy to verify. Since the range $\mathcal{Y}$ of the PRF F is a vector space of rational number filed $\mathbb{Q}$, and $1/\pi$ is a rational number, the operation $\frac{t_\pi - t_0}{\pi}$ is a scalar multiplication on $(t_\pi - t_0)$ by the scalar $1/\pi$, which will give an element in $\mathcal{Y}$. Therefore, the signer can always generate δ and $(t_i)_{[L]}$ as in the signing algorithm, and the verifier can reconstruct all $(t_i)_{[L]}$ using (t_0, δ). Then, from the completeness of the NIZKPoK Ψ, the verification algorithm **Verify**(pp, T, σ, M) always output 1, for the honestly generated σ.

Public Traceability. Now, we analyze the *public traceability* in all possible cases.

For the first case that $M = M'$ and $\pi = \pi'$, we have $t_0 = H(T, M) = H(T, M') = t'_0$ and $t_\pi = F_{sk_\pi}(T) = t'_{\pi'}$. Thus, it holds that $t_j = t'_j$ for all $j \in [L]$. In this case, **Trace** algorithm always returns linked.

For the second case that $M \neq M'$ and $\pi = \pi'$, we have $t_\pi = t_{\pi'}$. $H(T, M) = H(T, M')$ means (T, M) and (T, M') are a collision for H, and thus it happens with negligible probability. In other words, we have $t_0 \neq t'_0$ with overwhelming probability. Then, the two sequences $(t_i)_{[L]}$ and $(t'_i)_{[L]}$ have only one common component $\mathbf{t}_\pi$. Therefore, the algorithm **Trace** returns pk_π with overwhelming probability.

For the last case that $\pi' \neq \pi$, the inequality $F_{sk_\pi}(T) \neq F_{sk_{\pi'}}(T)$ holds with overwhelming probability, from uniqueness of the PRF. If $M = M'$, we have $t_0 = t'_0$, thus it holds that $t_j \neq t'_j$ with overwhelming probability for all $j \in [L]$.

If $M \neq M'$, we have $t_0 \neq t'_0$. Consider the $\delta = \frac{t_\pi - t_0}{\pi}$ and $\delta_{t'} = \frac{t'_{\pi'} - t'_0}{\pi'}$. We show δ and $\delta_{t'}$ are pseudorandom variables, where the probability space is over the random flips in $\text{Gen}(1^\lambda)$. Let $k \leftarrow \text{Gen}(1^\lambda)$, $r \leftarrow \mathcal{Y}$ and let T and a be an arbitrary element in $\mathcal{X}$. Then, from a simple argument, if F is pseudorandom, we have

$$(F_k(T), T, F_k(a), a) \approx_c (r, T, F_k(a), a).$$

Then, since δ can be computed from the $(F_k(T), T, F_k(a), a)$ (more specifically, $t_0 = H(T, m)$ and π is the index of $F_k(a)$ in the ring), we have $\delta \approx_c \frac{r - H_1(T)}{\pi}$. Thus, δ is a pseudorandom variable. This result also applies to $\delta_{t'}$. From the *intersection-free* assumption on the vector space $\mathcal{Y}$ and Lemma 4, it is infeasible to find t_0 and t'_0 s.t. $\exists i \leq N(\lambda)$, $t_0 + i\delta = t'_0 + i\delta_{t'}$. Therefore, in this case, with overwhelming probability, there exists no $i \in [L]$ s.t. $t_i = t'_i$, and the algorithm **Trace** will return accept.

As a conclusion, we have the following lemma.

Lemma 5. *If general construction is correct, in terms of completeness and public traceability, if the non-interactive protocol Ψ is complete, the hash function H is collision-resistant, and the function F is unique and pseudorandom.*

3.4 Security Analysis

The security of our general construction relies on the security of the underlying building blocks. Formally, we have the following results.

Theorem 1. *The general construction is secure, in terms of tag-linkability, anonymity, and exculpability, if the non-interactive protocol Ψ is zero-knowledge and simulation-extractable, and the function F is unique and pseudorandom.*

Proof for the Tag-Linkability. The main idea behind this proof is to show the contradiction between the uniqueness of F and a successful attack. Assume the adversary $\mathcal{A}$ outputs $L + 1$ valid signatures $\{\sigma^{(j)} = (\delta^{(j)}, \vartheta^{(j)})\}_{[L+1]}$ with the tag $T = ((pk_i)_{[L]}, issue)$, and either pair of them can be **accepted** by the **Trace** algorithm. Let $(t_i^{(j)})_{i \in [L]}$ be the sequence associated with $\sigma^{(j)}$. Then, from the description of the **Trace** algorithm, we have $t_i^{(j_0)} \neq t_i^{(j_1)}$ holds for all $i \in [L]$ and every $j_0 \neq j_1$.

Since the underlying non-interactive protocol Ψ is simulation-extractable, given any valid signature $(\delta^{(j)}, \vartheta^{(j)})$ we can extract a secret key sk and an index $\tau \in [L]$ s.t. $F_{sk}(a) = pk_\tau \wedge F_{sk}(T) = t_\tau^{(j)}$. From the uniqueness of the PRF, we know that the value of $t_\tau^{(j)}$ is uniquely determined by pk_τ. Since the tag T only contains L public keys, there must exist $j_1 \neq j_2$ s.t. $t_\tau^{(j_1)} = t_\tau^{(j_2)}$, which contradicts the above conclusion that $t_i^{(j_0)} \neq t_i^{(j_1)}$ holds for all $i \in [L]$ and every $j_0 \neq j_1$.

Proof for the Anonymity. The anonymity of the TRS scheme follows the zero-knowledge property of Ψ and the pseudorandomness of F. Consider a signature $\sigma = (\delta, \vartheta)$ that was created by using sk_0 or sk_1. We build a simulator $\mathcal{S}$ as follows. It randomly samples $\delta' \leftarrow \mathcal{Y}$, and computes $t_i' = H(T, M) + i\delta'$ for all $i \in [L]$ where T is the tag and M is the message. Then, $\mathcal{S}$ runs the simulator S_P of Ψ to generate a simulated proof ϑ'. From the zero-knowledge property of Ψ and pseudorandomness of F, it is infeasible to distinguish between the simulated signature $\sigma' = (\delta', \vartheta')$ and the signature $\sigma = (\delta, \vartheta)$, whether σ is generated by using sk_0 or sk_1. Therefore, it is also infeasible to guess the real signer of the signature σ.

Proof for the Exculpability. First, we build a simulator that (1) generates the public key pk by uniformly picking an element from $\mathcal{Y}$; and (2) answers the Sign_{sk} oracle by randomly choose t_π from uniform distribution on $\mathcal{Y}$ and generating a simulated proof ϑ. From definitions, if (T, M, σ) and (T, M', σ') lead to a successful attack, there is at least one tuple not linked to any one contained in the querying history list. We can extract a secret key sk s.t. $F_{sk}(a) = pk$ with overwhelming probability. It means that we can construct a algorithm that can inverse the PRF F, which contracts its pseudorandomness.

A detailed proof is presented in the full version of this paper.

3.5   Constructions of Unique PRF with Intersection-Free Range

In our general framework of TRS, we require that the underlying PRF is unique and has an intersection-free range. Although these requirements seem to be somewhat restrictive, they are not hard to be fulfilled. In the following, we show that the PRF in Fujisaki *et al.*'s construction [20] satisfies the two requirements, and a PRF with these properties can also be constructed from basic primitives.

PRF in Fujisaki *et al.*'s Scheme. Let $\mathbb{G}$ be a multiplicative group of prime order q, where $q = q(\lambda)$ is an exponential function, and let $H : \{0,1\}^* \rightharpoonup \mathbb{G}$ be a random oracle. The PRF $F' : \mathbb{Z}_q \times \{0,1\}^* \rightharpoonup \mathbb{G}$, used in Fujisaki *et al.*'s scheme, can be described as:

$$k \leftarrow \mathbb{Z}_q \text{ and } F_k'(x) := H(x)^k.$$

It is easy to verify that this F' is pseudorandom under the Decisional Diffie-Hellman assumption in the random oracle model. The uniqueness of F' comes from the fact that $\mathbb{G}$ is a group with prime order. In detail, assuming there are two distinct numbers $k_1, k_2 \in \mathbb{Z}_q$ s.t. $H(m)^{k_1} = H(m)^{k_2}$ for some message m, we have $H(m)^{k_1 - k_2} = e$ where e is the identity element of $\mathbb{G}$, which means either $H(m) = e$ or $k_1 - k_2 = 0 \bmod q$. Since $k_1 \neq k_2$ and H is a random oracle, $H(m)^{k_1} = H(m)^{k_2}$ only happens with negligible probability.

Now, we turn to show $\mathbb{G}$ is an intersection-free range. Define the vector addition and scalar multiplication as follows.

1. **Vector Addition.** Let $g, h \in \mathbb{G}$ be two group elements, the result of vector addition is $f = g \cdot h$, where $\cdot$ denotes the multiplication in the group $\mathbb{G}$.

2. **Scalar Multiplication.** Let $g \in \mathbb{G}$ be a group element, and $r = t/s$ be a rational number where t and s are integers. The result of scalar multiplication is $c = g^{t \cdot r^{-1}}$, where r^{-1} is the inverse of r in $\mathbb{Z}_q$ and $\cdot$ is the multiplication in $\mathbb{Z}_q$.

It can be easily checked that the two operations satisfies all axioms of the vector space, and thus $\mathbb{G}$ is a vector space of $\mathbb{Q}$. Let y_1, y_2 be two distinct elements in $\mathbb{G}$, then we have

$$\Pr[\exists i \leq N(\lambda), y_1 \cdot \delta_1^i = y_2 \cdot \delta_2^i : \delta_1, \delta_2 \hookleftarrow \mathbb{G}]$$
$$\leq \Pr[\exists i \leq N(\lambda), y_1/y_2 = \delta^i : \delta \hookleftarrow \mathbb{G}] \leq \frac{N(\lambda)}{q(\lambda)} \in \mathrm{negl}(\lambda).$$

Therefore, $\mathbb{G}$ is an intersection-free range.

Construction from Basic Primitives. *Unique PRF.* Our starting point is the Goldreich et al's construction [23] that builds a PRF from a PRG. More precisely, let $\mathcal{G} : \{0,1\}^n \rightarrow \{0,1\}^{2n}$ be a PRG, and denote $\mathcal{G}(s) = \mathcal{G}_1(s) | \mathcal{G}_2(s)$ where $\mathcal{G}_1(s), \mathcal{G}_2(s) \in \{0,1\}^n$. Goldreich et al.'s PRF F is constructed as $F_k(x) := \mathcal{G}_{x_\ell}(\ldots(\mathcal{G}_{x_2}(\mathcal{G}_{x_1}(k))))$, where $k \in \{0,1\}^n$ is the key and $x = x_0 \cdots x_\ell \in \{0,1\}^\ell$ is the input. We observe that the PRF F is unique if both $\mathcal{G}_0$ and $\mathcal{G}_1$ are collision-resistant. If there exists $k \neq k'$ s.t. $F_k(x) = F_{k'}(x)$ for some input x, then there is an index $j \in [\ell-1]$ s.t. $\mathcal{G}_{x_j}(\ldots \mathcal{G}_{x_1}(k)) \neq \mathcal{G}_{x_j}(\ldots \mathcal{G}_{x_1}(k'))$ but $\mathcal{G}_{x_{j+1}}(\ldots \mathcal{G}_{x_1}(k)) = \mathcal{G}_{x_{j+1}}(\ldots \mathcal{G}_{x_1}(k'))$, which implies a collision of $\mathcal{G}_{x_{j+1}}$. Formally, we define such a property as *two-layer collision-resistant*.

Definition 8 (Two-layer collision-resistant PRG). *A PRG $\mathcal{G} := \mathcal{G}_0 | \mathcal{G}_1$ with expansion factor $2n$ is two-layer collision-resistant, if $\mathcal{G}_0$ and $\mathcal{G}_1$ are both collision-resistant.*

We remark that a collision-resistant PRG can be constructed from any one-way permutation as shown by Blum and Micali [7]. More precisely, the first n-bit output of Blum and Micali's PRG is always a permutation of the seed, i.e., $\mathcal{G}_0$ is a permutation and thus it is collision-resistant. Intuitively, $\mathcal{G}_1$ should be also collision-resistant, since both $\mathcal{G}_0$ and $\mathcal{G}_1$ are parts of a PRG, and the outputs of them cannot be distinguished by a PPT adversary, but it still lacks a formal proof.

Intersection-Free Range. Another requirement is that the PRF should has an *intersection-free* range. We address it by showing the range $\mathbb{Z}_q^n$ is intersection-free if q is a prime and n is an integer. First, define the vector addition and scalar multiplication operations as follows.

1. **Vector Addition.** Let $\mathbf{a}, \mathbf{b} \in \mathbb{Z}_q^n$ be two vectors, the sum of them is $\mathbf{c} \in \mathbb{Z}_q^n$ where $\mathbf{c}[i] = \mathbf{a}[i] + \mathbf{b}[i] (\mathrm{mod}\, q)$ for all $i \in [n]$.
2. **Scalar Multiplication.** Let $\mathbf{a} \in \mathbb{Z}_q^n$ be a vector, and let $r = t/s$ be a rational number where t, s are integers. The result of the scalar multiplication is $\mathbf{d} \in \mathbb{Z}_q^n$, where $\mathbf{d}[i] = t \cdot s^{-1} \cdot \mathbf{a}[i] (\mathrm{mod}\, q)$ and s^{-1} is the inverse of $s \bmod q$.

It is easy to verify the two operations satisfy all axioms of the vector space, and thus $\mathbb{Z}_q^n$ (with operations defined above) is a vector space of $\mathbb{Q}$. In addition, in $\mathbb{Z}_q^n$, the case $y_1 + i\delta_1 = y_2 + i\delta_2$ means that the four points $y_1, y_2, \delta_1, \delta_2$ lay in one plane, which happens with probability at most q^{2-n} that is negligible for $n = O(\lambda)$. Therefore, $\mathbb{Z}_q^n$ is intersection free.

For an arbitrary PRF $\bar{F}$ with range $\{0,1\}^\iota$ where $\iota = n \cdot \lceil \log q \rceil$ for some $n \in \mathbb{Z}$ and some prime p, we can always convert $\bar{F}$ to F, one with range $\mathbb{Z}_q^n$, through the following public transformation.

$$F_k(x) := \mathbf{G}_{n,q} \cdot [\bar{F}_k(x)],$$

where $\mathbf{G}_{n,q} := \mathbf{I}_n \otimes [1| \cdots |2^{\lceil \log q \rceil - 1}] \in \mathbb{Z}_q^{n \times n \lceil \log q \rceil}$. Since this transformation is public and a bijection, F is still a PRF. Thus, the requirement on the intersection-free range of a PRF can be trivially satisfied.

Basing TRS on Quantum-Resistant Assumptions. We review all materials used in the our general construction. Following results are known in previous work.

– Assuming the hardness of the LWE problem, there exists an NIZK proof system for any NP language, in the common reference string model [30]. As discussed in [31], an NIZKPoK can be obtained from an NIZK proof system and a semantically secure dense public key encryption (PKE) scheme. Therefore, from the existence of LWE-based PKE schemes [32], we know a general NIZKPoK can also be based on the LWE assumptions.

Since a unique PRF with intersection-free range can be constructed from basic primitives, our general construction also indicate

Theorem 2. *There is a secure TRS scheme, assuming the existence of a two-layer collision-resistant PRG and a collision-resistant hash function, as well as the hardness of the LWE problem.*

4 Traceable Ring Signature Schemes from Lattices

We have shown the security of our general construction can be deduced from the existence of some basic primitives, as discussed in Theorem 2, instead of concrete cryptographic hard problems. Thus, a TRS can be secure against quantum attackers. However, instantiating a TRS scheme with the basic primitives requires expensive NP-reduction, and thus it will lead to a very inefficient construction. In this section, we present an efficient post-quantum secure TRS scheme from lattices, by instantiating the framework with a lattice-based PRF along with an associated lattice-based NIZKPoK.

Firstly, we prove the security of a lattice-based PRF F, which is compatible with an efficient zero-knowledge proof system, in the QROM. Then, we construct a proof system to demonstrate the knowledge on the secret key k

s.t. $F_k(x_1) = y_1 \land F_k(x_2) = y_2$ for public (x_1, y_1, x_2, y_2). After that, we use the Merkle-tree-based accumulator [25] to construct an OR-composition of the above proof system, and then get the desired NIZKPoK through the Unruh transformation [37]. Due to the use of Merkle tree, the signature size of our TRS scheme is logarithmic in the corresponding ring size.

4.1 Efficient PRF in QROM

We are interested in post-quantum secure PRFs with efficient proof systems, to avoid the computational burden of using general NIZK proof systems. The LWE-based PRF [4] is the only known one with an efficient proof system. However, given a message of length n, this PRF [4] will perform n times of large dimension matrix multiplication, which makes it far away from the practical use.

In this section, we consider the following function,

$$F^H : \mathbb{Z}_q^n \times \{0,1\}^* \to \mathbb{Z}_p^m \text{ with } F^H(T, \mathbf{s}) = \lfloor H(T) \cdot \mathbf{s} \rceil_p, \tag{2}$$

where $H : \{0,1\}^* \to \mathbb{Z}_q^{m \times n}$ is a random oracle. Its running time is almost independent from the input length, and it only requires one matrix multiplication and one rounding. A Stern protocol has also been proposed in [26] to prove the correct evaluation of this PRF, which makes it easy to construct an efficient TRS scheme upon this PRF. In addition, this function is also unique with proper parameter, as discussed in [39]. However, although its security can be deduced from the LWE assumption in the ROM [9], its security in the QROM has not been rigorously examined.

We note that there are two definitions of security for a PRF against a quantum adversary, as discussed in [40]. The difference between the two definitions is whether the adversary can query the PRF on a quantum superposition input. Recall our general framework for TRS schemes. The evaluation of a PRF is an inner step of the signing algorithm, and thus in the security proof the PRF is only evaluated on the classical queries to signing oracles. Therefore, throughout this paper, we only need to consider the security of PRF, so called standard security in [40], where a quantum adversary makes classical queries to the PRF. However, it does not mean that we can restrict an adversary only to make classical queries to a random oracle, since in the real world hash functions can always be executed off-line. Therefore, providing a security proof in the QROM for the PRF is also necessary even if we only need the *standard security*.

We will prove the security of this function Eq. 2 in the QROM. Before that, we present the definition of PRF in the QROM.

Definition 9 (PRF in the QROM). *Let $F^H : \mathcal{K} \times \mathcal{X} \to \mathcal{Y}$ be an efficient keyed function, and H be a quantum random oracle. We say F^H is pseudorandom in the QROM, if for all quantum-polynomial-time adversary $\mathcal{A}$, we have*

$$\Pr[\mathcal{A}^{F^H(k,\cdot),H(\cdot)}(1^\lambda) = 1 : k \leftarrow \mathcal{K}] -$$
$$\Pr[\mathcal{A}^{O(\cdot),H(\cdot)}(1^\lambda) = 1 : O \leftarrow \mathcal{F}[\mathcal{X} : \mathcal{Y}]] \in negl(\lambda),$$

where $\mathcal{F}[\mathcal{X}, \mathcal{Y}]$ denotes all functions from $\mathcal{K}$ to $\mathcal{Y}$.

Theorem 3. *Let n, m, q, p be positive integers, χ be a B-bounded error distribution s.t. $m > (n+1)\log q$, $q \geq p \cdot \sqrt{m} \cdot B \cdot n^{\omega(1)}$. The function F^H is a pseudorandom function in the QROM, assuming the hardness of $LWE_{n,q,\chi}$ problem.*

Proof (sketch). To prove this result, we build a sequence of games. In each game, the adversary $\mathcal{A}$ interacts with a simulator that answers the queries of $\mathcal{A}$ to $H(\cdot)$ and $F^H(k, \cdot)$. The simulator $\mathcal{S}_0$ in the first game forwards all queries to $H(\cdot)$ and answers queries to $F^H(k, \cdot)$ by evaluating it using k. Thus, $\Pr[\mathcal{A}^{\mathcal{S}_0}(1^\lambda) = 1] = \Pr[\mathcal{A}^{F^H(k,\cdot), H(\cdot)}(1^\lambda) = 1 : k \leftarrow \mathcal{K}]$. We show that (i) every two games in this sequence are indistinguishable for any quantum-polynomial-time $\mathcal{A}$; and (ii) the probability of $\mathcal{A}$ outputting 1 in the last game is statistically close to $\Pr[\mathcal{A}^{O(\cdot), H(\cdot)}(1^\lambda) = 1 : O \leftarrow \mathcal{F}[\mathcal{X} : \mathcal{Y}]]$. We list all games in the following, and give a detailed proof in the full version of this paper.

Game 0: The simulator $\mathcal{S}_0^H$ has quantum access to $H(\cdot)$. It first uniformly picks a secret key $k := \mathbf{s} \in \mathbb{Z}_q^n$ at random, answers all queries of $\mathcal{A}$ to $H(\cdot)$ by forwarding them, and answers all queries to $F^H(k, \cdot)$ by running this function with k.

Game 1: The simulator $\mathcal{S}_1^K$ works as the $\mathcal{S}_0^H$ except that it only has access to another random oracle $K : \mathcal{X} \to \{-1, 1\}^{m \times m}$, instead of that to H, and simulates H by responding $H'(x) := K(x) \cdot \mathbf{A} \bmod q$ for each query x. Here $\mathbf{A}$ is randomly picked from the uniform distribution by $\mathcal{S}_1^K$.

Game 2: The simulator $\mathcal{S}_2$ works as the $\mathcal{S}_1^K$, except that it does not has access to any random oracle, and simulates K by responding $K'(x)$ for each query x: (1) $p_{K'} \leftarrow \mathrm{GF}(2^{\ell^*})[X]$ with $\partial p_{K'} \leq 2q_{H_1} - 1$; and (2) $\bar{K}(x) := p_{K'}(\iota(x))_{1\cdots mm}$; and (3) $K'(x) := \mathrm{S2M}(\bar{K}(x))$. Here, $\iota : \{0, 1\}^\ell \to \{0, 1\}^{\ell^*}$ is an injection, and $\mathrm{S2M} : \{0, 1\}^{mm} \to \{-1, 1\}^{m \times m}$ is a function s.t. $r_{i,j} = (-1)^{x[i(m-1)+j]+1}$, where $x[i]$ denotes the i-th bit of the input x, and $\mathbf{R} = (r_{i,j})_{i,j}$ is the output of S2M. We denote $K'(x)\mathbf{A}$ by $H''(x)$, which is a simulation for H'.

Game 3: The simulator $\mathcal{S}_3$ works as $\mathcal{S}_2$, except that

1. $\mathcal{S}_3$ is given a pair $(\mathbf{A}, \mathbf{b} = \mathbf{A} \cdot \mathbf{s} + \mathbf{e})$, where $\mathbf{A}$ is from the uniform distribution over $\mathbb{Z}_q^{m \times n}$, $\mathbf{s} \leftarrow \mathbb{Z}_q^n$ and $\mathbf{e} \leftarrow \chi^m$.
2. It uses the given matrix $\mathbf{A}$ to simulate H trough the method in Game 2.
3. It dose not generate a secret key k, but answers a query x to $F^H(\cdot, k)$ by returning $\lfloor \mathbf{R} \cdot \mathbf{b} \rceil_p$, where $\mathbf{R} = K'(x)$.

Game 4: The simulator $\mathcal{S}_4$ is sampled from $\mathcal{S}_3$, except that the given pair $(\mathbf{A}, \mathbf{b})$ is drawn from the uniform distribution over $\mathbb{Z}_q^{m \times n} \times \mathbb{Z}_q^m$.

4.2   Stern Protocol for PRF

A Stern protocol to demonstrate the knowledge of k s.t. $F^H(k, x) = y$ has been proposed in [26]. In this section, we extend this protocol to prove the knowledge of k s.t. $F^H(k, x_1) = y_1 \wedge F^H(k, x_2) = y_2$ for public inputs and outputs (x_1, y_1, x_2, y_2). More exactly, we construct a Stern protocol for the relation R_0 defined as follows.

Definition 10 (Relation R_0). *Let* $\mathbf{A}, \mathbf{B} \in \mathbb{Z}_q^{m \times n}$, *and* $\mathbf{y} \in \mathbb{Z}_p^m, \mathbf{t} \in \mathbb{Z}_p^m$. *The* R_0 *is defined as*

$$R_0 = \{(\mathbf{A}, \mathbf{y}, \mathbf{B}, \mathbf{t}) \in (\mathbb{Z}_q^{m \times n} \times \mathbb{Z}_p^m)^2; \mathbf{s} \in \mathbb{Z}_q^n : \quad \mathbf{y} = \lfloor \mathbf{A} \cdot \mathbf{s} \rfloor_p \text{ and } \mathbf{t} = \lfloor \mathbf{B} \cdot \mathbf{s} \rfloor_p\}.$$

Our strategy is to transform R_0 to the standard form that the general Stern protocol can handle.

First, recall that the LWR rounding function $\lfloor \cdot \rfloor_p : \mathbb{Z}_q^m \to \mathbb{Z}_p^m$ is defined as $\lfloor \mathbf{x} \rfloor_p := \lfloor (p/q) \cdot \mathbf{x} \rfloor \mod p$. As discussed in [26], one knows $\mathbf{x} \in [0, q-1]^m$ s.t. $\lfloor \mathbf{x} \rfloor_p = \mathbf{y}$, iff one knows $\mathbf{x} \in [0, q-1]^m$ and $\mathbf{z} \in [-B', B']$ where $B' = \lfloor \frac{q-1}{2} \rfloor$ s.t. $p \cdot \mathbf{x} = q \cdot \mathbf{y} + \mathbf{z} \mod pq$. Therefore, to prove a tuple $(\mathbf{A}, \mathbf{y}, \mathbf{B}, \mathbf{t}) \in R_0$ is equivalent to prove that the tuple satisfies the condition that

$$\begin{cases} \mathbf{A} \cdot \mathbf{s} = \mathbf{x}_1 \mod q \\ p \cdot \mathbf{x}_1 = q \cdot \mathbf{y} + \mathbf{z}_1 \mod pq \\ \mathbf{B} \cdot \mathbf{s} = \mathbf{x}_2 \mod q \\ p \cdot \mathbf{x}_2 = q \cdot \mathbf{t} + \mathbf{z}_2 \mod pq \end{cases} \quad \begin{aligned} &\text{for some } \mathbf{s}, \mathbf{x}_1, \mathbf{x}_2 \in [0, q-1]^m \\ &\text{and, } \mathbf{z}_1, \mathbf{z}_2 \in [-B', B']^m. \end{aligned} \quad (3)$$

Let

$$\mathbf{M}_1 = \begin{bmatrix} \mathbf{A} & -\mathbf{I}_m & \\ \mathbf{B} & & -\mathbf{I}_m \end{bmatrix} \in \mathbb{Z}_q^{2m \times (n+2m)}, \quad \mathbf{M}_2 = \begin{bmatrix} p\mathbf{I}_m & -\mathbf{I}_m & \\ & & p\mathbf{I}_m & -\mathbf{I}_m \end{bmatrix} \in \mathbb{Z}_{pq}^{2m \times 4m}.$$

Let $\mathbf{v}_1 = \mathbf{0} \in \mathbb{Z}_q^{2m}$ and $\mathbf{v}_2 = (\mathbf{y}, \mathbf{t})^T \in \mathbb{Z}_{pq}^{2m}$. Define the set $\mathbb{V}$ as

$$\{(\mathbf{s}^T, \mathbf{x}_1^T, \mathbf{x}_2^T, \mathbf{x}_1^T, \mathbf{z}_1^T, \mathbf{x}_2^T, \mathbf{z}_2^T)^T : \mathbf{s}, \mathbf{x}_1, \mathbf{x}_2 \in [0, q-1]^m, \mathbf{z}_1, \mathbf{z}_2 \in [-B', B']^m\}.$$

The Eq. 3 can also be expressed as

$$\mathbf{M}_1 \cdot \Upsilon_1 = \mathbf{v}_1 \mod q, \text{ and } \mathbf{M}_2 \cdot \Upsilon_2 = \mathbf{v}_2 \mod pq, \text{ for some } (\Upsilon_1^T | \Upsilon_2^T) \in \mathbb{V}. \quad (4)$$

Clearly, it is equivalent to prove that there is $\Upsilon = (\Upsilon_1^T | \Upsilon_2^T)$ s.t. the Eq. 4 holds and to prove that there is a vector $\mathbf{s}$ s.t. $(\mathbf{A}, \mathbf{y}, \mathbf{B}, \mathbf{y}; \mathbf{s}) \in R_0$. Through standard techniques used in Stern protocols, such as *permutations, decompositions* and *extensions*, we show that

Lemma 6. *There is a public transformation* Γ, *which can transform the tuple* $(\mathbf{M}_1, \mathbf{v}_1, \mathbf{M}_2, \mathbf{v}_2, \mathbb{V})$ *to* $(\bar{\mathbf{M}}_1, \mathbf{v}_1, \bar{\mathbf{M}}_2, \mathbf{v}_2, \mathbb{V}^*)$ *with an ESP* $\mathbb{E}_S$ *for* $\mathbb{V}^* \in \{-1, 0, 1\}^d$ *s.t. one knows* $(\Upsilon_1^T | \Upsilon_2^T) \in \mathbb{V}$ *satisfying Eq. 4, if an only if he knows* $(\bar{\Upsilon}_1^T | \bar{\Upsilon}_2^T) \in \mathbb{V}^*$ *satisfying*

$$\bar{\mathbf{M}}_1 \cdot \bar{\Upsilon}_1^T = \mathbf{v}_1 \mod q, \quad \bar{\mathbf{M}}_2 \cdot \bar{\Upsilon}_2^T = \mathbf{v}_2 \mod pq$$

Proof. The main idea is to transform the secret vector Υ to a vector $\bar{\Upsilon} \in \mathbb{V}^* = \{\mathbf{x} \in \{-1, 0, 1\}^d : \mathbf{x}$ has the same number of $-1, 0, 1\}$. Clearly, the set $\mathbb{V}^*$ has an ESP. To achieve this goal, first we decompose each positive component into a binary vector over $\{0, 1\}$ and each negative component into $\{0, -1\}$, and concatenate all of them to a vector in $\{-1, 0, 1\}^{d'}$. Let $d = 3d'$. Then, we pad many $-1, 0, 1$ bits to the this vector and get the desired vector $\bar{\Upsilon}$. After that, we need to modify the matrix $\mathbb{M}$ to $\bar{\mathbb{M}}$ s.t. $\mathbb{M}\Upsilon = \bar{\mathbb{M}}\bar{\Upsilon}$. The basic idea is multiplying $\mathbb{M}$ by a matrix $\mathbf{G}$, where $\mathbf{G}$ satisfies $\mathbf{G} \cdot \text{bin}(\mathbf{v}) = \mathbf{v}$ for arbitrary $\mathbf{v}$.

We give a detailed description for this transformation in the full version of this paper.

Instantiating the general Stern protocol with the $(\bar{\mathbb{M}}_1, \mathbf{v}_1, \bar{\mathbb{M}}_2, \mathbf{v}_2, \mathbb{V}^*)$ with an ESP $\mathbb{E}_S$, we can get a concrete Stern protocol for R_0. Implied by Lemma 1, we have the following corollary.

Corollary 1. *Let (n, m, p, q) be parameters specified in R_0. Based on the hardness of $SIVP_{\widetilde{\mathcal{O}}(n)}$, there is a Stern protocol Ψ_0 for the relation R_0, with proof size $\widetilde{\mathcal{O}}(m \cdot \log^2 q)$.*

4.3 OR-Composition from Accumulators

When we instantiate our general construction with the PRF F^H given in Eq. 2, the underlying NIZKPoK is used to prove the following relation R_{TRS}.

$$R_{TRS} = \{\mathbf{A}, \mathbf{B}, (\mathbf{y}_i, \mathbf{t}_i)_{[L]}; \mathbf{s} \in \mathbb{Z}_q^n : \mathbf{y}_1 = \lfloor \mathbf{A} \cdot \mathbf{s} \rfloor_p \text{ and } \mathbf{t}_1 = \lfloor \mathbf{B} \cdot \mathbf{s} \rfloor_p \vee \cdots$$
$$\vee \mathbf{y}_L = \lfloor \mathbf{A} \cdot \mathbf{s} \rfloor_p \text{ and } \mathbf{t}_L = \lfloor \mathbf{B} \cdot \mathbf{s} \rfloor_p\}$$

Obviously, the relation R_{TRS} is the OR composition of L instances of R_0. One may think that a desirable proof system for R_{TRS} can be easily constructed by applying Cramer *et al.*'s OR-composition techniques [14] to the protocol Ψ_0. However, Ψ_0 does not satisfy the standard special soundness property that is required by the techniques.

We build a Stern protocol Ψ_{TRS} for R_{TRS} via finding a proper combination of the accumulator scheme (see Sect. 2.3) and the protocol Ψ_0. Recall the notion of accumulators. Every element in the accumulated set has a witness that can validate its membership, while any element outside the set does not have such a witness. A typical application of accumulators is ring signatures, where every element in the accumulated set is a public key. Set the accumulated set as $\{pk_i\}_{i \in [n]}$ and the accumulator value as u. If someone can prove the knowledge of the secret key for some pk_i and the corresponding witness w_i w.r.t. u in a zero-knowledge manner, the prover actually convinces the verifier that he knows a secret key for pk_1, or $pk_2, \ldots$, or pk_n.

The main obstacle to applying accumulators to our construction is that each instance in the OR-composition is a pair of vectors instead of one element. We solve this challenge by hashing each pair $(\mathbf{y}_i, \mathbf{t}_i)$ through an algebraic hash function to a single vector before applying the accumulator scheme. Concretely, we utilize the underlying hash function of the accumulator scheme, and thus it is easy to prove the correct evaluation of it. Let $m' = 2m \cdot \lceil \log p \rceil$ and $m'' =$

$2n \cdot \lceil \log q_1 \rceil$ for some $q_1 \in \mathbb{N}$. Assume $L = 2^\ell$ for some $\ell \in \mathbb{N}$, without loss of generality. We define a relation R'_{TRS} as follows.

$$R'_{TRS} = \{\mathbf{A}, \mathbf{B}, \mathbf{D}', \mathbf{D}, \mathbf{u}\}; (\mathbf{s}, \mathbf{y}_i, \mathbf{t}_i, \mathbf{d}_i, w_A) : \mathbf{A}\text{-Verify}((\mathbf{D}, \mathbf{u}, \mathbf{d}_i, \mathbf{t}_i), w_A) = 1$$
$$\wedge \mathbf{d}_i = \mathrm{bin}(\mathbf{D}'_1\mathrm{bin}(\mathbf{y}_i) + \mathbf{D}'_2\mathrm{bin}(\mathbf{t}_i)) \wedge \mathbf{y}_i = \lfloor \mathbf{A} \cdot \mathbf{s} \rceil_p \wedge \mathbf{t}_i = \lfloor \mathbf{B} \cdot \mathbf{s} \rceil_p\}.$$

where $\mathbf{D}' = [\mathbf{D}'_1 | \mathbf{D}'_2]$ and $\mathbf{D}$ are sampled from the uniform distributions over $\mathbb{Z}_{q_1}^{n \times 2m'}$ and $\mathbb{Z}_{q_1}^{n \times 2m''}$ at random respectively, $\mathbf{d}_i = \mathrm{bin}(\mathbf{D}'_1\mathrm{bin}(\mathbf{y}_i) + \mathbf{D}'_2\mathrm{bin}(\mathbf{t}_i))$, $\mathbf{u} = \mathbf{A}\text{-Acc}(\mathbf{D}, R = (\mathbf{d}_i)_{[L]})$, and $w_A = \mathbf{A}\text{-Witness}(\mathbf{D}, R, \mathbf{d}_i)$. Ensured by the correctness and security of the accumulator scheme, it is easy to see the equivalence of R_{TRS} and R'_{TRS}.

A Stern protocol for the language R'_{TRS} can be obtained from the protocol denoted by Ψ_A for the accumulator scheme [25], by adding one more layer: apart from proving that there is a secret $\mathbf{d}_i$ which was accumulated to the root $\mathbf{u}$, the prover also convinces the verifier that there are two vector $\mathbf{y}_i = \lfloor \mathbf{A} \cdot \mathbf{s} \rceil_p$, $\mathbf{t}_i = \lfloor \mathbf{B} \cdot \mathbf{s} \rceil_p$ for a secret $\mathbf{s}$, s.t. $\mathbf{d}_i = \mathrm{bin}(\mathbf{D}'_1\mathrm{bin}(\mathbf{y}_i) + \mathbf{D}'_2\mathrm{bin}(\mathbf{t}_i))$. Yang et al. [39] show that if there are two relations with the Stern protocols, then the Stern protocol for any linear combination of the two relations can be easily constructed. Notice that R'_{TRS} is a linear combination of R_0 and $R_A := \{(pp, u, d); w : \mathbf{A}\text{-Verify}(pp, u, d, w) = 1\}$, then there is a Stern protocol for $R_{abstract}$. Recall the proof size of Ψ_A is $\widetilde{\mathcal{O}}(n \cdot \log q_1 \cdot \log L)$, we have the following corollary.

Corollary 2. *Let* (n, m, p, q, q_1, ℓ) *be parameters specified in* R'_{TRS}. *Based on the hardness of* $SIVP_{\widetilde{\mathcal{O}}(n)}$, *there is a Stern protocol* Ψ_{TRS} *for the language* R_{TRS}, *with communication cost* $\widetilde{\mathcal{O}}(m \cdot \log^2 q + n \cdot \log q_1 \cdot \log L)$.

From Stern Protocols to NIZKPoK. The Fiat-Shamir [17] is the most well-known method to transform a sigma protocol to an NIZKPoK. However, the post-quantum security of this transform in general is not clear so far [2]. In this paper, we use an alternative transform, the Unruh transform [37]. As discussed in [16], the Unruh transform can give an NIZKPoK in the QROM from a Stern protocol.

A detailed description of the Unruh transform is beyond the scope of this paper. Roughly speaking, the Unruh transform runs the underlying sigma protocol for many times to generate t different commitments and m challenge-response pair for every commitment. For each commitment, the proof only reveals a specific response, the position of which is determined by a random oracle. It is required that (i) $t \cdot m = \omega(\log \lambda)$, and (ii) m is not smaller than the number of transcripts that are needed to extract the witness. For example, 3 transcripts are needed to extract the witness for a Stern protocol, see Lemma 1. So, when applying the Unruh transform to the Stern protocol Ψ'_{TRS}, we can set $m = 3$ and $t = \omega(\log \lambda)$. Formally, we have the following result.

Corollary 3. *If there is a Stern protocol for* R'_{TRS} *with proof size* v, *then there is an NIZKPoK for* R'_{TRS} *with proof size* $3t \cdot v$.

4.4   Description of the Scheme

We take the NIZKPoK $\Phi = (\mathcal{P}, \mathcal{V})$ for the relation R'_{TRS} and the PRF $F^H()$ as ingredients. We build our TRS scheme as follows.

Setup(λ): Choose a lattice parameter $n = \mathcal{O}(\lambda)$; a B-bounded distribution χ; a prime number q and an integer p *s.t.* $q \geq p \cdot B \cdot n^{\omega(1)}$ and $\mathrm{LWE}_{n,q,\chi}$ problem is hard; $q_1 = \widetilde{\mathcal{O}}(\lambda)$; $m > (n+1) \cdot (\log q)$; $m' = m \cdot \lceil \log p \rceil$; $m'' = n \cdot \lceil \log q_1 \rceil$; $t = \omega(\log \lambda)$. Set $params = (n, m, m', m'', p, q, q_1, t)$. Let $H_1 : \{0,1\}^* \rightarrow \mathbb{Z}_q^{m \times n}$, $H_2 : \{0,1\}^* \rightarrow \mathbb{Z}_p^m$ and $H_3 : \{0,1\}^* \rightarrow \{1,2,3\}^t$ be three distinct hash functions, and let H_1 and H_3 be modeled as random oracles. Choose random matrices $\mathbf{A} \leftarrow \mathbb{Z}_q^{m \times n}$, $\mathbf{D}' = [\mathbf{D}'_1 | \mathbf{D}'_2] \leftarrow \mathbb{Z}_{q_1}^{n \times 2m'}$, $\mathbf{D} \leftarrow \mathbb{Z}_{q_1}^{n \times 2m''}$, and output the public parameters: $pp = (params, H_1, H_2, H_3, \mathbf{A}, \mathbf{D}', \mathbf{D})$.

KeyGen(pp): Parse $pp = (params, H_1, H_2, H_3, \mathbf{A}, \mathbf{D}', \mathbf{D})$, and randomly choose an vector $\mathbf{s}$ from the uniform distribution over $\mathbb{Z}_q^n$. Then, compute a vector $\mathbf{y} = \lfloor \mathbf{A} \cdot \mathbf{s} \rfloor_p$. Output $sk := \mathbf{s}$ and $pk := \mathbf{y}$.

Let the tag $T = \{(pk_i)_{[L]}, issue\}$, and $M \in \{0,1\}^*$. Without loss of generality, we assume that $L = 2^\ell$ for some $\ell \in \mathbb{N}$. Let the index number π belong to $[L]$. The algorithms **Sign**, **Verify**, and **Trace** proceed as follows.

Sign(pp, sk_π, T, M): Parse $pp = (params, H_1, H_2, H_3, \mathbf{A}, \mathbf{D}', \mathbf{D})$, $T = \{(pk_i)_{[L]}, issue\}$, and $sk_\pi = \mathbf{s}_\pi$. Then, do the following procedures.

- Compute $\mathbf{B}_T = H_1(T) \in \mathbb{Z}_q^{m \times n}$.
- Compute $\mathbf{t}_\pi = \lfloor \mathbf{B}_T \cdot \mathbf{s}_\pi \rfloor_p$, and $\mathbf{t}_0 = H_2(T, M)$.
- Compute $\delta = \frac{\mathbf{t}_\pi - \mathbf{t}_0}{\pi}$, and $\mathbf{t}_j = \mathbf{t}_0 + \delta \cdot j$ for all $j \neq i$.
- Compute $\mathbf{d}_i = \mathrm{bin}(\mathbf{D}'_1 \cdot \mathrm{bin}(\mathbf{y}_i) + \mathbf{D}'_2 \cdot \mathrm{bin}(\mathbf{t}_i))$ for all $i \in [L]$, and define $R = (\mathbf{d}_i)_{[L]}$.
- Compute $\mathbf{u} = \text{A-Acc}(\mathbf{D}, R)$ and $w_A = \text{A-Witness}(\mathbf{D}, R, \mathbf{u}, \mathbf{d}_\pi)$.
- Take $X := (\mathbf{A}, \mathbf{B}_T, \mathbf{D}', \mathbf{D}, \mathbf{u})$ as public inputs of the protocol Φ, and take $W := (\mathbf{d}_\pi, w_A, \mathbf{y}_\pi, \mathbf{t}_\pi, \mathbf{s}_\pi)$ as the private inputs. Run $\mathcal{P}^{H_3}(X, W)$ to generate a non-interactive proof ϑ.
- Output the signature $\sigma = (\delta, \vartheta)$.

Verify(pp, T, σ, M): Parse $pp = (params, H_1, H_2, H_3, \mathbf{A}, \mathbf{D}', \mathbf{D})$, $\sigma = (\delta, \vartheta)$, and $T = \{(pk_i)_{[L]}, issue\}$. Then, do the following procedures.

- Compute $\mathbf{B}_T = H_1(T)$ and $\mathbf{t}_0 = H_2(T, M)$.
- Compute $\mathbf{t}_j = \mathbf{t}_0 + \delta \cdot j$, for all $j \in [L]$.
- Compute $\mathbf{d}_j = \mathrm{bin}(\mathbf{D}'_1 \cdot \mathrm{bin}(\mathbf{y}_j) + \mathbf{D}'_2 \cdot \mathrm{bin}(\mathbf{t}_j))$, and let $R = (\mathbf{d}_i)_{[L]}$.
- Compute $\mathbf{u} = \text{A-Acc}(\mathbf{D}, R)$.
- Take $X := (\mathbf{A}, \mathbf{B}_T, \mathbf{D}', \mathbf{D}, \mathbf{u})$ as the public input of the protocol Φ. Then run $\nu \leftarrow \mathcal{V}^{H_3}(X, \vartheta)$.
- Output 1 if $\nu = 1$. Otherwise, output 0.

Trace$(pp, T, M, \sigma, M', \sigma')$: Parse $pp = (params, H_1, H_2, H_3, \mathbf{A}, \mathbf{D}', \mathbf{D})$, $T = \{(pk_i)_{[L]}, issue\}$, $\sigma = (\delta, \vartheta)$ and $\sigma' = (\delta'_t, \vartheta')$. Then proceed as follows.

- Run $d \leftarrow$ **Verify**(pp, T, σ, M) and $d' \leftarrow$ **Verify**(pp, T, σ', M'). Return **reject** if $d = 0$ or $d' = 0$. Otherwise, continue.
- Compare two tuples $(\mathbf{t}_i)_{[L]}$ and $(\mathbf{t}'_i)_{[L]}$, which are generated in the inner step **Verify** algorithm, by using $(\delta, \mathbf{t}_0)$ and $(\delta', \mathbf{t}'_0)$ respectively.
  - If $\mathbf{t}_j = \mathbf{t}'_j$ for all $j \in [L]$, return linked;
  - Else if there is only one index $i \in [L]$ s.t. $\mathbf{t}_i = \mathbf{t}'_i$, return $pk_i = \mathbf{y}_i$, which is the public key located at the i-th position in T.
  - Otherwise, return accept.

Efficiency. We evaluate the efficiency of our scheme in terms of the sizes of public keys, secret keys and signatures.

- The public key of a user is a vector $\mathbf{y} \in \mathbb{Z}_p^m$, the bit length of which is $m \cdot \lceil \log p \rceil$. Under the parameters specified in our scheme, we have that $m \cdot \lceil \log p \rceil = \widetilde{\mathcal{O}}(\lambda)$.
- The secret key of a user is a vector $\mathbf{s} \in \mathbb{Z}_q^n$, the bit length of which is $n \cdot \lceil \log q \rceil$. Thus, the size of secret key of our scheme is also $\widetilde{\mathcal{O}}(\lambda)$.
- The size of a signature $\sigma = (\delta, \Pi)$ in our scheme is dominated by the proof Π. As mentioned in Corollary 3, the size of π is $3t \cdot v$, where v is the transcript size of the Stern protocol Ψ_{TRS} for R_{TRS}. From Corollary 2, we have $v = \mathcal{O}(m \cdot \log^2 pq + \ell n \cdot \log q_1)$. Under the parameters in our scheme, the size of Π is $\widetilde{\mathcal{O}}(\lambda \cdot \log L)$, which is also the asymptotic upper bound for the size of σ.

Security. Regarding the security of our scheme, we have the following result.

Theorem 4. *The proposed TRS scheme is secure in the QROM, in terms of tag-linkability, anonymity, and exculpability, under the hardness assumption of the SIS problem and the LWE problem.*

Proof (sketch). The hardness of the SIS and LWE problems (under some parameters) implies that (i) the underlying accumulator scheme is secure; (ii) the hash function h_D is collision-resistant; and (iii) the underlying non-interactive protocol Φ is an NIZKPoK, while adversaries are allowed to issue quantum queries to $H_3(\cdot)$; and (iv) the function $\lfloor H_1(\cdot) \cdot k \rceil_p$ is pseudorandom in the QROM, while adversaries are allowed to issue quantum queries to $H_1(\cdot)$. Then, the proposed TRS scheme is secure, from the results on the security of our general construction.

Acknowledgement. This paper is supported by the National Key R&D Program of China through project 2017YFB0802502, by the National Cryptography Development Fund through project MMJJ20170106, by the foundation of Science and Technology on Information Assurance Laboratory through project 1421120305162112006, the Natural Science Foundation of China through projects 61972019, 61932011, 61772538, 61672083, 61532021, 61472429, 91646203 and 61402029. We thank all the anonymous reviewers whose comments have greatly improved this paper.

References

1. Ajtai, M.: Generating hard instances of lattice problems (extended abstract). In: STOC 1996, pp. 99–108. ACM (1996)
2. Ambainis, A., Rosmanis, A., Unruh, D.: Quantum attacks on classical proof systems: the hardness of quantum rewinding. In: FOCS 2014, pp. 474–483. IEEE Computer Society (2014)
3. Au, M.H., Liu, J.K., Susilo, W., Yuen, T.H.: Secure ID-based linkable and revocable-iff-linked ring signature with constant-size construction. Theor. Comput. Sci. **469**, 1–14 (2013)
4. Banerjee, A., Peikert, C., Rosen, A.: Pseudorandom functions and lattices. In: Pointcheval, D., Johansson, T. (eds.) EUROCRYPT 2012. LNCS, vol. 7237, pp. 719–737. Springer, Heidelberg (2012). https://doi.org/10.1007/978-3-642-29011-4_42
5. Baum, C., Lin, H., Oechsner, S.: Towards practical lattice-based one-time linkable ring signatures. In: Naccache, D., et al. (eds.) ICICS 2018. LNCS, vol. 11149, pp. 303–322. Springer, Cham (2018). https://doi.org/10.1007/978-3-030-01950-1_18
6. Bellare, M., Goldwasser, S.: New paradigms for digital signatures and message authentication based on non-interactive zero knowledge proofs. In: Brassard, G. (ed.) CRYPTO 1989. LNCS, vol. 435, pp. 194–211. Springer, New York (1990). https://doi.org/10.1007/0-387-34805-0_19
7. Blum, M., Micali, S.: How to generate cryptographically strong sequences of pseudorandom bits. SIAM J. Comput. **13**(4), 850–864 (1984)
8. Boneh, D., Dagdelen, Ö., Fischlin, M., Lehmann, A., Schaffner, C., Zhandry, M.: Random oracles in a quantum world. In: Lee, D.H., Wang, X. (eds.) ASIACRYPT 2011. LNCS, vol. 7073, pp. 41–69. Springer, Heidelberg (2011). https://doi.org/10.1007/978-3-642-25385-0_3
9. Boneh, D., Lewi, K., Montgomery, H., Raghunathan, A.: Key homomorphic PRFs and their applications. In: Canetti, R., Garay, J.A. (eds.) CRYPTO 2013. LNCS, vol. 8042, pp. 410–428. Springer, Heidelberg (2013). https://doi.org/10.1007/978-3-642-40041-4_23
10. Branco, P., Mateus, P.: A traceable ring signature scheme based on coding theory. In: Ding, J., Steinwandt, R. (eds.) PQCrypto 2019. LNCS, vol. 11505, pp. 387–403. Springer, Cham (2019). https://doi.org/10.1007/978-3-030-25510-7_21
11. Camenisch, J., Hohenberger, S., Lysyanskaya, A.: Compact e-cash. In: Cramer, R. (ed.) EUROCRYPT 2005. LNCS, vol. 3494, pp. 302–321. Springer, Heidelberg (2005). https://doi.org/10.1007/11426639_18
12. Canetti, R., et al.: Fiat-shamir: from practice to theory. In: STOC 2019, pp. 1082–1090. ACM (2019)
13. Chow, S.S.M., Liu, J.K., Wong, D.S.: Robust receipt-free election system with ballot secrecy and verifiability. In: NDSS 2008. The Internet Society (2008)
14. Cramer, R., Damgård, I., Schoenmakers, B.: Proofs of partial knowledge and simplified design of witness hiding protocols. In: Desmedt, Y.G. (ed.) CRYPTO 1994. LNCS, vol. 839, pp. 174–187. Springer, Heidelberg (1994). https://doi.org/10.1007/3-540-48658-5_19
15. Feige, U., Lapidot, D., Shamir, A.: Multiple non-interactive zero knowledge proofs based on a single random string (extended abstract). In: FOCS 1990, pp. 308–317. IEEE Computer Society (1990)

16. Feng, H., Liu, J., Wu, Q.: Secure Stern signatures in quantum random oracle model. In: Lin, Z., Papamanthou, C., Polychronakis, M. (eds.) ISC 2019. LNCS, vol. 11723, pp. 425–444. Springer, Cham (2019). https://doi.org/10.1007/978-3-030-30215-3_21

17. Fiat, A., Shamir, A.: How to prove yourself: practical solutions to identification and signature problems. In: Odlyzko, A.M. (ed.) CRYPTO 1986. LNCS, vol. 263, pp. 186–194. Springer, Heidelberg (1987). https://doi.org/10.1007/3-540-47721-7_12

18. Franklin, M.K., Zhang, H.: A framework for unique ring signatures. IACR Cryptology ePrint Archive 2012, 577 (2012)

19. Fujisaki, E.: Sub-linear size traceable ring signatures without random oracles. In: Kiayias, A. (ed.) CT-RSA 2011. LNCS, vol. 6558, pp. 393–415. Springer, Heidelberg (2011). https://doi.org/10.1007/978-3-642-19074-2_25

20. Fujisaki, E., Suzuki, K.: Traceable ring signature. In: Okamoto, T., Wang, X. (eds.) PKC 2007. LNCS, vol. 4450, pp. 181–200. Springer, Heidelberg (2007). https://doi.org/10.1007/978-3-540-71677-8_13

21. Garay, J.A., MacKenzie, P., Yang, K.: Strengthening zero-knowledge protocols using signatures. In: Biham, E. (ed.) EUROCRYPT 2003. LNCS, vol. 2656, pp. 177–194. Springer, Heidelberg (2003). https://doi.org/10.1007/3-540-39200-9_11

22. Gentry, C.: Fully homomorphic encryption using ideal lattices. In: STOC 2009, pp. 169–178. ACM (2009)

23. Goldreich, O., Goldwasser, S., Micali, S.: How to construct random functions (extended abstract). In: FOCS 1984, pp. 464–479. IEEE Computer Society (1984)

24. Groth, J., Kohlweiss, M.: One-out-of-many proofs: or how to leak a secret and spend a coin. In: Oswald, E., Fischlin, M. (eds.) EUROCRYPT 2015. LNCS, vol. 9057, pp. 253–280. Springer, Heidelberg (2015). https://doi.org/10.1007/978-3-662-46803-6_9

25. Libert, B., Ling, S., Nguyen, K., Wang, H.: Zero-knowledge arguments for lattice-based accumulators: logarithmic-size ring signatures and group signatures without trapdoors. In: Fischlin, M., Coron, J.-S. (eds.) EUROCRYPT 2016. LNCS, vol. 9666, pp. 1–31. Springer, Heidelberg (2016). https://doi.org/10.1007/978-3-662-49896-5_1

26. Libert, B., Ling, S., Nguyen, K., Wang, H.: Zero-knowledge arguments for lattice-based PRFs and applications to e-cash. In: Takagi, T., Peyrin, T. (eds.) ASIACRYPT 2017. LNCS, vol. 10626, pp. 304–335. Springer, Cham (2017). https://doi.org/10.1007/978-3-319-70700-6_11

27. Ling, S., Nguyen, K., Stehlé, D., Wang, H.: Improved zero-knowledge proofs of knowledge for the ISIS problem, and applications. In: Kurosawa, K., Hanaoka, G. (eds.) PKC 2013. LNCS, vol. 7778, pp. 107–124. Springer, Heidelberg (2013). https://doi.org/10.1007/978-3-642-36362-7_8

28. Liu, J.K., Wei, V.K., Wong, D.S.: Linkable spontaneous anonymous group signature for ad hoc groups. In: Wang, H., Pieprzyk, J., Varadharajan, V. (eds.) ACISP 2004. LNCS, vol. 3108, pp. 325–335. Springer, Heidelberg (2004). https://doi.org/10.1007/978-3-540-27800-9_28

29. Lu, X., Au, M.H., Zhang, Z.: Raptor: a practical lattice-based (linkable) ring signature. In: Deng, R.H., Gauthier-Umaña, V., Ochoa, M., Yung, M. (eds.) ACNS 2019. LNCS, vol. 11464, pp. 110–130. Springer, Cham (2019). https://doi.org/10.1007/978-3-030-21568-2_6

30. Peikert, C., Shiehian, S.: Noninteractive zero knowledge for NP from (plain) learning with errors. In: Boldyreva, A., Micciancio, D. (eds.) CRYPTO 2019. LNCS, vol. 11692, pp. 89–114. Springer, Cham (2019). https://doi.org/10.1007/978-3-030-26948-7_4

31. Rackoff, C., Simon, D.R.: Non-interactive zero-knowledge proof of knowledge and chosen ciphertext attack. In: Feigenbaum, J. (ed.) CRYPTO 1991. LNCS, vol. 576, pp. 433–444. Springer, Heidelberg (1992). https://doi.org/10.1007/3-540-46766-1_35
32. Regev, O.: On lattices, learning with errors, random linear codes, and cryptography. In: STOC 2005, pp. 84–93. ACM (2005)
33. Rivest, R.L., Shamir, A., Tauman, Y.: How to leak a secret. In: Boyd, C. (ed.) ASIACRYPT 2001. LNCS, vol. 2248, pp. 552–565. Springer, Heidelberg (2001). https://doi.org/10.1007/3-540-45682-1_32
34. Shor, P.W.: Algorithms for quantum computation: discrete logarithms and factoring. In: FOCS 1994, pp. 124–134. IEEE Computer Society (1994)
35. Stern, J.: A new paradigm for public key identification. IEEE Trans. Inf. Theory **42**(6), 1757–1768 (1996)
36. Alberto Torres, W.A., et al.: Post-quantum one-time linkable ring signature and application to ring confidential transactions in blockchain (Lattice RingCT v1.0). In: Susilo, W., Yang, G. (eds.) ACISP 2018. LNCS, vol. 10946, pp. 558–576. Springer, Cham (2018). https://doi.org/10.1007/978-3-319-93638-3_32
37. Unruh, D.: Non-interactive zero-knowledge proofs in the quantum random oracle model. In: Oswald, E., Fischlin, M. (eds.) EUROCRYPT 2015. LNCS, vol. 9057, pp. 755–784. Springer, Heidelberg (2015). https://doi.org/10.1007/978-3-662-46803-6_25
38. Wang, X., Chen, Y., Ma, X.: Adding linkability to ring signatures with one-time signatures. In: Lin, Z., Papamanthou, C., Polychronakis, M. (eds.) ISC 2019. LNCS, vol. 11723, pp. 445–464. Springer, Cham (2019). https://doi.org/10.1007/978-3-030-30215-3_22
39. Yang, R., Au, M.H., Lai, J., Xu, Q., Yu, Z.: Lattice-based techniques for accountable anonymity: composition of abstract Stern's protocols and weak PRF with efficient protocols from LWR. IACR Cryptology ePrint Archive 2017, 781 (2017)
40. Zhandry, M.: How to construct quantum random functions. In: FOCS 2012, pp. 679–687. IEEE Computer Society (2012)
41. Zhandry, M.: Secure identity-based encryption in the quantum random oracle model. In: Safavi-Naini, R., Canetti, R. (eds.) CRYPTO 2012. LNCS, vol. 7417, pp. 758–775. Springer, Heidelberg (2012). https://doi.org/10.1007/978-3-642-32009-5_44
42. Zhang, H., Zhang, F., Tian, H., Au, M.H.: Anonymous post-quantum cryptocash. IACR Cryptology ePrint Archive 2017, 716 (2017)

Post-quantum Provably-Secure Authentication and MAC from Mersenne Primes

Houda Ferradi[1] and Keita Xagawa[2]($\boxtimes$)

[1] The Hong Kong Polytechnic University, Hung Hom, Hong Kong
houda.ferradi@ens.fr
[2] NTT Secure Platform Laboratories, Tokyo, Japan
keita.xagawa.zv@hco.ntt.co.jp

Abstract. This paper presents a novel, yet efficient secret-key authentication and MAC, which provide post-quantum security promise, whose security is reduced to the quantum-safe conjectured hardness of Mersenne Low Hamming Combination (MERS) assumption recently introduced by Aggarwal, Joux, Prakash, and Santha (CRYPTO 2018). Our protocols are very suitable to weak devices like smart card and RFID tags.

Keywords: Secret-key authentication · MAC · MERS assumption · Man-in-the-middle security

1 Introduction

1.1 Motivation

SECRET-KEY AUTHENTICATION AND HB FAMILY. *Secret-key unilateral authentication* protocol is a process by which a *prover* authenticates itself to a *verifier*, where they share a secret. The current best way to construct such a protocol is a challenge-response protocol by a strong pseudo-random function, e.g., AES. A verifier sends a random challenge m and a prover answers its ciphertext $c = \mathsf{AES}_K(m)$.

In recent years such protocols have become an important mechanism for low-cost device authentication with small computational power such as smart cards or radio-frequency identification (RFID) tags. Unfortunately, it is hard to implement the blockcipher-based authentication protocol in such constrained devices. Hopper and Blum [24] introduced a two-round secret-key authentication protocol, denoted by HB. The advantages of HB are that implementation requires only bit-wise operations and that the security is based on the hardness of the Learning Parity with Noise (LPN) problem [8]. Therefore, HB is attractive for

Houda Ferradi—This work was done while the first author was at NTT Secure Platform Laboratories – Tokyo

© Springer Nature Switzerland AG 2020
S. Jarecki (Ed.): CT-RSA 2020, LNCS 12006, pp. 469–495, 2020.
https://doi.org/10.1007/978-3-030-40186-3_20

low-cost devices. Juels and Weis [25] pointed out that HB is insecure against active adversary and proposed HB$^+$ built upon the HB protocol, a three-round secret-key authentication protocol.[1] Soon after, HB$^+$ was shown vulnerable to a *man-in-the-middle* (MIM) attack proposed by Gilbert, Robshaw, and Silbert [22]. The line of researches [12,13,16,21,23,28] proposed variants of HB/HB$^+$ and some of them are secure against MIM attacks.

Their underlying problems are the LPN problem and its variants. Several attacks on the LPN problem have been proposed over the last years [17,29]. Most of them are variants of the BKW algorithm [9] whose running time is $2^{\mathcal{O}(\frac{k}{\log k})}$. In addition, [17] introduced an algorithm solving the LPN problem running in the quantum setting. They make the HB family very inefficient in practice either in classical or quantum setting. Moreover, Bernstein and Lange [6] discussed the comparison of Lapin [23] and (light-weight) block-ciphers on RFID tags and smart cards. Armknecht, Hamann, and Mikhalev [4] also discussed the hardware limits of low-cost RFID tags in the range of \$0.05–\$0.10. They concluded that all LPN-based authentication protocols cannot be implemented in the low-cost RFID tags in this range.

Hence, it is desirable to come up with a new proposal for secret-key authentication and MAC that provides provable security with better efficiency in terms of key-size, communication, and rounds, while providing post-quantum security promise.

THE MERSENNE LOW-HAMMING COMBINATION (MERS) PROBLEM AND ITS APPLICATION. In 2017, Aggarwal, Joux, Prakash, and Santha proposed the *Mersenne Low Hamming Combination* (MERS) problem [1,2]: Given a Mersenne prime in the form $p = 2^n - 1$ (where n is prime), samples of the MERS$_{n,h}$ distribution are constructed as $(a, b = as + e)$, where $a \in \mathbb{Z}_p$ is chosen uniformly at random, the secret s and the error e are chosen uniformly at random from the elements in $\mathbb{Z}_p$ of the Hamming weight h. The decisional version of the MERS assumption states that any efficient adversary cannot distinguish the MERS$_{n,h}$ distribution from the uniform distribution over $\mathbb{Z}_p^2$. Aggarwal et al. proposed a public-key encryption scheme based on the MERS$_{n,h}$ problem [1,2].

Regarding the practical aspect, MERS assumption provides efficiency due to its reliance on Mersenne primes [11]. The potential benefit of MERS-based scheme is a subject of several ongoing research [1,2,18,36]. Unfortunately, because of their constraint that $n = \Theta(h^2)$ from the correctness of the key-encapsulation mechanisms, the mechanisms in [1,2,18,36] set $n = 216091$ or 756839. This impacts the sizes of public key and ciphertext, which are approximately n bits, 26.41 KiB – 100.39 KiB. Thus, the main motivation behind MERS-based authentication scheme and MAC is their potential suitability for lightweight devices such as Radio Frequency Identification (RFID) tags and smart card.

1.2   Our Contribution

There are three main contributions in this paper:

---

[1] Later, Katz, Shin, and Smith gave simplified security proofs of them [26].

Table 1. Authentication Protocols based on Weak-PRFs, the LPN-related assumptions, and the MERS assumption. A family of weak PRFs is denoted by $\mathcal{F} :=$ $\{F\colon \mathbb{K} \times \mathbb{D} \to \mathbb{F}\}$. A family of pairwise independent hash functions is denoted by $\mathcal{H} := \{H\colon \mathbb{H} \times \mathbb{D} \to \mathbb{F}\}$. ℓ and γ defines the dimension and the error rate of the LPN problem. $\eta = O(\ell)$ defines the number of parallel repetitions. n and h are parameters for MERS$_{n,h}$.

Protocol	# of rounds	Assumption	Security	Key size	Comm
Auth$_{\mathsf{wprf}}$ [15]	3	Weak PRF	Active	$\|\mathbb{K}\| + \|\mathbb{H}\|$	$2\|\mathbb{D}\| + \|\mathbb{F}\|$
Auth$_{\mathsf{wprf}}$ [30, Fig. 2]	3	Weak PRF	S-MIM	$\|\mathbb{K}\| + \|\mathbb{H}\|$	$\|\mathbb{D}\| + 2\|\mathbb{F}\|$
Auth$_{\mathsf{wprf}}$ [13]	2	Weak PRF	S-MIM	$2\ell\|\mathbb{K}\| + \|\mathbb{H}\|$	$\|\mathbb{D}\| + \|\mathbb{F}\|$
Auth [28]	2	LPN$_{\ell,\gamma}$	Active	2ℓ	$2\ell + (\ell+1)\eta$
Lapin [23]	2	Ring-LPN$_{\ell,\gamma}$	Active	2ℓ	3ℓ
Auth$_{\mathsf{LPN}}$ [13]	2	LPN$_{\ell,\gamma}$	S-MIM	5ℓ	$(\eta + 2)\ell$
AuthT$_{\mathsf{LPN}}$ [13]	2	LPN$_{\ell,\gamma}$	S-MIM	$(2\eta + 2)\ell$	$2\ell + \eta$
Auth$_{\mathsf{Field\text{-}LPN}}$ [13]	2	Field-LPN$_{\ell,\gamma}$	S-MIM	4ℓ	3ℓ
Auth$_{\mathsf{s\text{-}mim}}$ [Sect. 6]	2	MERS$_{n,h}$	S-MIM	$4n$	$3n$

New version of MERS problem: The first contribution of this work is MERS-U, which is the MERS problem assuming that the secret is *uniform*. We formally prove that the MERS-U problem is as hard as the MERS problem is hard as in the case of the LWE problem [3].

Two-round authentication with S-MIM security: The second contribution is a two-round authentication protocol secure against sequential man-in-the-middle (S-MIM) attacks with tight reductions to the MERS problem. Our construction need not require $n = \Theta(h^2)$ as in KEMs/PKEs in [1,2,18,36] and we can set $n = \Theta(h)$, say, $n = 4h$. Thus, we can set $n = 521$ and $h = 128$, and this makes our protocol efficient and compact, say, the communication complexity is at most $3n = 1563$ bits (Tables 1 and 2).

Message Authentication Code (MAC): The third contribution is to construct a MAC scheme that is existentially unforgeable under chosen message attacks (UF-CMA) assuming that the MERS problem is hard. Our MAC improves upon the key size, communication and computation complexity with respect to prior works [15,28]. Again, we can set $n = \Theta(h)$ as in the authentication.

1.3 Related Works

SECURITY NOTIONS. Bellare and Rogaway [5] gave the formal security definition of *mutual* authentication schemes. Their security model captures MIM attack and more. Vaudeney [38] gave the formal security and privacy definitions of RFID authentications. In this paper, we only consider *unilateral* authentication scheme and do not consider any corruption. Mol and Tessaro [31] gave

Table 2. MACs based on the LPN-related assumptions and the MERS assumption. ℓ and γ defines the dimension and the error rate of the LPN problem. $\eta = O(\ell)$ defines the number of parallel repetitions. n and h are parameters for $\mathsf{MERS}_{n,h}$. A family of pairwise independent hash functions is denoted by $\mathcal{H} := \{H \colon \mathbb{M} \times \{0,1\}^\nu \to \{0,1\}^\mu\}$. A family of pairwise independent permutations is denoted by $\mathcal{P} := \{\pi \colon \{0,1\}^z \to \{0,1\}^z\}$, where $z = \ell\eta + \eta + \nu$ for LPN case and $z = 2n + \nu$ for MERS case.

Protocol	Assumption	Security	Key size	Comm
MAC_1 [28]	$\mathsf{LPN}_{\ell,\gamma}$	UF-CMA	$2\ell + \lvert H \rvert + \lvert \pi \rvert$	$\ell\eta + \eta + \nu$
MAC_2 [28]	$\mathsf{LPN}_{\ell,\gamma}$	UF-CMA	$(\mu+1)\ell + \eta + \lvert H \rvert + \lvert \pi \rvert$	$\ell\eta + \eta + \nu$
$\mathsf{MAC}_{\mathsf{MERS}}$ [Sect. 7]	$\mathsf{MERS}_{n,h}$	UF-CMA	$(\mu+2)n + \lvert H \rvert + \lvert \pi \rvert$	$2n + \nu$

the security definitions for *unilateral* authentication scheme that captures from passive attacks to MIM attacks. Lyubashevsky and Masny [30] introduced an interesting notion of security against Man-In-the-Middle (MIM) attacks, which slightly weakens MIM to only allow the attacker to interfere with *non-overlapping sequential sessions*. This seems sufficient for real-world application in which the keys do not allow parallel sessions. Cash, Kiltz, and Tessaro [13] also defined Sequential MIM (S-MIM) security. We adopt the following definition of S-MIM security.

AUTHENTICATION FROM LPN/LWE. Hopper and Blum [24] introduced a secret-key authentication protocol that is proven secure against passive adversaries from the hardness of the LPN problem. Since then, a family of LPN-based authentication protocols has been developed. Juels and Weis [25] proposed an efficient three-round variant of HB, called HB^+, which they proved to be secure against active attacks. Later, Gilbert et al. [22] show that HB^+ is not secure against a MIM attack, resulting in several variants [16,32]. However, most of these variants lack security proofs [20]. Recent proposals [13,21,23,28,30] have proofs for active security or variants of MIM security.

LPN-based protocols have gained some popularity since they require only small number of primitive bit-wise operations (e.g., "XOR" and "AND") for their implementation. However, all LPN-based protocols require huge security parameters. Esser, Kübler, and May [17] estimates the hardness of $\mathsf{LPN}_{\ell,\tau}$. According to their estimation, for $\tau = 1/8$, $\ell = 670, 1060, 1410$ corresponds to 128, 192, and 256 bit security assuming that the memory is constrained to 2^{80} bits. If we set $\tau = 1/20$ as in [28], then ℓ should be larger than 1280 for 128-bit security.

AUTHENTICATION FROM NUMBER-THEORETIC PROBLEMS. Concurrently to above, there is another type of protocols based on number-theoretic assumptions, which are DDH-based protocols introduced in [13,15,30]. Unfortunately, same for RSA, the DDH implementation is not suitable for low-cost device. Besides that, factoring and the DDH assumption are known to be threatened by Shor's algorithm that runs by quantum computer [35].

AUTHENTICATION FROM WEAK PRFs. Dodis et al. [15] show how to construct a three-round authentication from any weak PRFs, which is secure against active attacks. Later, Lyubashevaky and Masny [30] constructs a three-round authentication from any weak PRFs with MIM security in sequential sessions.

MAC. Message Authentication Code (MAC) is one of the most fundamental primitive in cryptography, used to authenticate a message. Similarly to secret-key authentication, most of MAC schemes have been based on PRFs. This is achieved either by using secure block ciphers [33] or number-theoretic constructions as shown in [15,28]; the latter provides provably (weakly) MIM-secure[2] authentication scheme and MAC based on LPN/LWE and their ring/field variants.

1.4 Organization of the Paper

In Sect. 2, we review the basic notion and notations, secret-key authentication, and MAC. In Sect. 3, we review the MERS problem and assumption. In Sect. 4, we construct a two-round secret-key authentication scheme that is secure against passive adversaries. Next, we build an efficient two-round authentication protocol that has special properties (ROR-CMA security) in Sect. 5. We then build an efficient two-round authentication protocol secure against S-MIM attacks upon it in Sect. 6, by applying the transformation of [13]. Finally, we obtain a MAC scheme from the MERS problem in Sect. 7.

2 Preliminaries

2.1 Notation

We denote by $\|x\|$ the Hamming weight of an n-bit string x, which is the total number of 1's in x. Let $\mathfrak{H}_{n,h}$ be the set of all n-bit strings of Hamming weight h.

Let n be a positive integer and let $p = 2^n - 1$. We call p a Mersenne number if n is prime. If p is itself a prime number then p is called a Mersenne prime.[3]

Let $\mathbb{Z}_p$ be the integer ring modulo p, where p is a Mersenne prime. We have the following properties [1]: For any $x, y \in \mathbb{Z}_p$, we have

Lemma 2.1. *Let $x, y \in \mathbb{Z}_p$, then the following properties hold:*

- *Property 1: $\|x + y \ (\mathrm{mod} \ p)\| \le \|x\| + \|y\|$*
- *Property 2: $\|x \cdot y \ (\mathrm{mod} \ p)\| \le \|x\| \cdot \|y\|$*
- *Property 3: If $x \ne 0$, then $\| -x \ (\mathrm{mod} \ p)\| = n - \|x\|$*

The proof of this lemma is in [1].

---

[2] "MIM security" in [15] is defined by two-phase games. This is $(\{P, V\}, \{V\})$-auth security, while the MIM security is $(\{\}, \{P, V\})$-auth security using [31]'s terminology.

[3] For example, n can be 2, 3, 5, 7, 13, 17, 19, 31, 61, 89, 107, 127, 521, 607, 1279, 2203, 2281, 3217, 4253, 4423, 9689, 9941, 11213, 19937, 21701, 23209, 44497, 86243, 110503, 132049, 216091, 756839, 859433, and so on. Mersenne-756839 employed $n = 756839$ and Ramstake employed $n = 216091$ and 756839.

2.2   Secret-Key Authentication Syntax

Secret-key authentication protocol $\mathsf{Auth} = (\mathsf{KeyGen}, \mathsf{P}, \mathsf{V})$ is an interactive protocol in which P and V share the same secret key SK (in the context of RFID, we
consider P as a *tag* and V as a *reader*). More formally, a secret-key authentication
protocol proceeds in two phases:

- **Key-generation algorithm**: The key-generation algorithm $\mathsf{KeyGen}(1^\kappa)$ is
  executed on the security parameter κ and outputs a secret key SK.
- **Authentication Protocol**: The interactive algorithm between P and V takes
  as input the shared secret key SK and is executed r rounds. And finally, V
  outputs either `Accept` or `Reject`.

In this paper, we only consider *two-round random-challenge* secret-key authentication protocols, in which the protocol is run as follows; the verifier chooses
a challenge c from the challenge space $\mathcal{C}$ uniformly at random and sends it as
the first message; the prover receives c, computes a response $\tau \leftarrow \mathsf{P}_{\mathsf{SK}}(c)$, and
sends it as the second message; the verifier receives τ and outputs its decision
$d \leftarrow \mathsf{V}_{\mathsf{SK}}(c, \tau)$.

We say that the authentication protocol has *completeness error* α if for
all secret keys SK generated by $\mathsf{KeyGen}(1^\kappa)$ the honestly executed protocol
returns reject with probability at most α. More formally, for all $1^\kappa \in \mathbb{N}, \mathsf{SK} \leftarrow$
$\mathsf{KeyGen}(1^\kappa)$:

$$\Pr[c \leftarrow_\$ \mathcal{C}; \tau \leftarrow \mathsf{P}_{\mathsf{SK}}(c); d \leftarrow \mathsf{V}_{\mathsf{SK}}(c, \tau) : d = \texttt{Reject}] \leq \alpha.$$

2.3   Security Models

As for public-key authentication [19], several security notions have been introduced for secret-key authentication. There are three main security models against
impersonation attacks that are: *passive*, *active*, and *man-in-the-middle*. All three
models proceed in two steps: In the first step, the adversary interacts with P and
V and then in the second step, it starts interacting only with V in order to get
accepted. The weakest notion, which is the passive security, is when the adversary should not be able to interact with V after eavesdropping several sessions
in the authentication protocol between P and V. A stronger notion, which is the
active security, is when the adversary should not be able to interact with V after
interacting *arbitrarily* with P and eavesdropping passively several sessions in the
authentication protocol between P and V.

Finally, the strongest and most realistic security model of adversary is a
man-in-the-middle attack (MIM), where the adversary, in the first phase, can
arbitrarily interact with P and V before making verification queries to the reader.

Passive Security. As the basic security notion, we review the definition of
passive security for *two-round random-challenge* secret-key authentication protocols.

Definition 2.1 (Passive security). *Let* Auth = (KeyGen, P, V) *be a two-round random-challenge secret-key authentication protocol. Define the security game* $\mathsf{Exp}^{pa}_{\mathsf{Auth},\mathcal{A}}(\kappa)$ *between a challenger and an adversary* $\mathcal{A}$ *as in Fig. 1. For any adversary* $\mathcal{A}$, *we define its advantage against* Auth *as the quantity*

$$\mathsf{Adv}^{pa}_{\mathsf{Auth},\mathcal{A}}(\kappa) := \Pr[\mathsf{Exp}^{pa}_{\mathsf{Auth},\mathcal{A}}(\kappa) \Rightarrow \mathsf{True}].$$

We say Auth *is* (t, Q, ϵ)-*passively-secure if for all t-time adversary* $\mathcal{A}$ *querying to* T *at most* Q *times, we have* $\mathsf{Adv}^{pa}_{\mathsf{Auth},\mathcal{A}}(\kappa) \leq \epsilon$.

$\mathsf{Exp}^{pa}_{\mathsf{Auth},\mathcal{A}}(\kappa)$

$\mathsf{SK} \leftarrow_\$ \mathsf{KeyGen}(1^\kappa)$

$st \leftarrow \mathcal{A}^{T(\cdot)}(1^\kappa)$

$c^* \leftarrow_\$ \mathcal{C}$

$\tau^* \leftarrow \mathcal{A}(st, c^*)$

return $(\mathsf{V}_{\mathsf{SK}}(c^*, \tau^*) = \mathsf{Accept})$

Oracle $T()$

$c \leftarrow_\$ \mathcal{C}$

$\tau \leftarrow \mathsf{P}_{\mathsf{SK}}(c)$

return (c, τ)

Fig. 1. Definition of $\mathsf{Exp}^{pa}_{\mathsf{Auth},\mathcal{A}}(\kappa)$

2.4   Tag Sparsity Definition and Security

In this section we define an important tool that our construction relies on, which is *tag sparsity* [13].

This is the property of an authentication protocol Auth = (KeyGen, P, V) for which the tag τ is composed into two distinct components, which are $\tau_1 \in \mathcal{T}_1$ and $\tau_2 \in \mathcal{T}_2$.

Informally speaking, this notion says that for any challenge c, a secret SK, and a left tag τ_1, the number of right tags τ_2 that makes $\tau = (\tau_1, \tau_2)$ accepted is negligible.

Definition 2.2 (Right Tag-Sparsity [13, Definition 4]). *Let* Auth = (KeyGen, P, V) *be a two-round random-challenge secret-key authentication protocol with tags in* $\mathcal{T}_1 \times \mathcal{T}_2$ *and challenge space* $\mathcal{C}$. *For* $\epsilon = \epsilon(1^\kappa)$, *we say that* Auth *has* ϵ-*sparse right tags (or* Auth *has* ϵ-*right tag sparsity) if*

$$\Pr[\tau_2 \leftarrow_\$ \mathcal{T}_2; d \leftarrow \mathsf{V}_{\mathsf{SK}}(c, (\tau_1, \tau_2)) : d = \mathsf{Accept}] \leq \epsilon$$

for all $c \in \mathcal{C}, \mathsf{SK}$, *and* $\tau_1 \in \mathcal{T}_1$.

ROR-CMA Security. In our construction we are also considering a new property introduced in [13], called *real-or-random right-tag chosen-message security* (ROR-CMA) suitable to tag-sparsity notion. Roughly speaking, the scheme is

ROR-CMA-secure if, given a random challenge c^*, any efficient adversary cannot distinguish a real prover from the fake prover that returns the random right tag τ_2 on all challenge except c^* even if it can finally access to the verification oracle on the challenge c^* and τ^* of its choice. The formal statement follows:

Definition 2.3 (ROR-CMA security). *Let* $\mathsf{Auth} = (\mathsf{KeyGen}, \mathsf{P}, \mathsf{V})$ *be a two-round random-challenge secret-key authentication protocol. For* $b \in \{0,1\}$*, we define the security game* $\mathsf{Exp}_{\mathsf{Auth},\mathcal{A}}^{\mathrm{ror\text{-}cma},b}(\kappa)$ *between a challenger and an adversary* $\mathcal{A}$ *as in Fig. 2. For any adversary* $\mathcal{A}$*, we define its* ROR-CMA *advantage against* Auth *as the quantity*

$$\mathsf{Adv}_{\mathsf{Auth},\mathcal{A}}^{\mathrm{ror\text{-}cma}}(\kappa) := \left| \Pr[\mathsf{Exp}_{\mathsf{Auth},\mathcal{A}}^{\mathrm{ror\text{-}cma},0}(\kappa) \Rightarrow 1] - \Pr[\mathsf{Exp}_{\mathsf{Auth},\mathcal{A}}^{\mathrm{ror\text{-}cma},1}(\kappa) \Rightarrow 1] \right|.$$

We say Auth *is* (t, Q, ϵ)*-ROR-CMA-secure if for all t-time adversary $\mathcal{A}$ issuing at most Q queries to the oracle $T_b(\cdot)$, we have* $\mathsf{Adv}_{\mathsf{Auth},\mathcal{A}}^{\mathrm{ror\text{-}cma}}(\kappa) \leq \epsilon$.

$\mathsf{Exp}_{\mathsf{Auth},\mathcal{A}}^{\mathrm{ror\text{-}cma},b}(\kappa)$	Oracle $T_b(c)$
$\mathsf{SK} \leftarrow_\$ \mathsf{KeyGen}(1^\kappa)$	$(\tau_1, \tau_2^1) \leftarrow_\$ \mathsf{P}_{\mathsf{SK}}(c); \tau_2^0 \leftarrow_\$ \mathcal{T}_2$
$c^* \leftarrow_\$ \mathcal{C}$	if $c = c^*$ then
$(\tau^*, state) \leftarrow_\$ \mathcal{A}^{T_b(\cdot)}(1^\kappa, c^*)$	return $\tau := (\tau_1, \tau_2^1)$
$d \leftarrow_\$ \mathsf{V}_{\mathsf{SK}}(c^*, \tau^*)$	else
return $\mathcal{A}(state, d)$	return $\tau := (\tau_1, \tau_2^b)$

Fig. 2. Definition of $\mathsf{Exp}_{\mathsf{Auth},\mathcal{A}}^{\mathrm{ror\text{-}cma},b}(\kappa)$

2.5 Security Against Sequential Man-in-the-Middle Adversary

In this paper, we target a weaker notion of the man-in-the-middle security, which is Sequential MIM (S-MIM) security, of [13,30]; in which the adversary can first interact *sequentially* with P and V in independent sessions and then makes verification queries to V in order to make the latter accept.

Cash, Kiltz, and Tessaro [13] defined S-MIM security notion for two-round random-challenge secret-key authentication protocols. We invoke the adversary $\mathcal{A}$ who access to three oracles: C, P, and V. To synchronize the sessions, each of these oracles use a variable sid associated to a given session. For every session, $\mathcal{A}$ invokes $C()$ to get a new random challenge c, and then invokes the oracle $P()$ on input c' that runs $\mathsf{P}_{\mathsf{SK}}(c')$ and returns a response τ. Finally, given τ' from $\mathcal{A}$, $V()$ checks whether τ' is a valid response on a session challenge $c[\mathsf{sid}]$ or not, and then increases the session number sid. $\mathcal{A}$ wins if it makes V accepts in some session and has changed at least one of messages in the session sent by P and V.

Definition 2.4 (S-MIM security [13, Section 2]). *Let* Auth $=$ (KeyGen, P, V) *be a two-round random-challenge secret-key authentication protocol. Define the security game* $\mathsf{Exp}^{\mathsf{s\text{-}mim}}_{\mathsf{Auth},\mathcal{A}}(\kappa)$ *between a challenger and an adversary* $\mathcal{A}$ *as in Fig. 3. For any adversary* $\mathcal{A}$, *we define its* S-MIM *advantage against* Auth *as the quantity*

$$\mathsf{Adv}^{\mathsf{s\text{-}mim}}_{\mathsf{Auth},\mathcal{A}}(\kappa) := \Pr[\mathsf{Exp}^{\mathsf{s\text{-}mim}}_{\mathsf{Auth},\mathcal{A}}(\kappa) \Rightarrow \mathsf{True}].$$

We say Auth *is* (t, Q, ϵ)-S-MIM-*secure if for all t-time adversary* $\mathcal{A}$ *invoking at most Q sessions, we have* $\mathsf{Adv}^{\mathsf{s\text{-}mim}}_{\mathsf{Auth},\mathcal{A}}(\kappa) \leq \epsilon$.

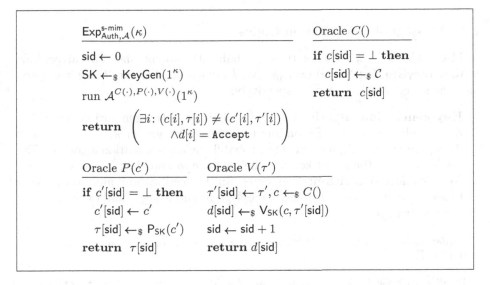

Fig. 3. Definition of $\mathsf{Exp}^{\mathsf{s\text{-}mim}}_{\mathsf{Auth},\mathcal{A}}(\kappa)$

Let Auth$'$ $=$ (KeyGen$'$, P$'$, V$'$) be two-round random-challenge authentication protocol with challenge space $\mathcal{C}$ and split tag space $\mathcal{T} = \mathcal{T}_1 \times \mathcal{T}_2$. We assume that $\mathcal{T}_2 = \mathbb{F}$ is a finite field with addition $+$ and multiplication $\circ$. Let $H := \{H_{K_H}: \mathcal{T}_1 \rightarrow \mathbb{F}\}$ be a family of pairwise independent hash functions. Cash et al. [13] turn Auth$'$ satisfying ROR-CMA security into Auth $=$ (KeyGen, P, V) as follows:

- **Public parameters**: The same as Auth$'$.
- **Key generation**: The key-generation algorithm KeyGen picks $K_H \leftarrow_\$ \mathcal{K}_H$, $K_F \leftarrow_\$ \mathbb{F} \setminus \{0\}$, and $K' \leftarrow_\$ \mathsf{KeyGen}'(1^\kappa)$. The key is $K := (K_H, K_F, K')$.
- **Challenge**: The challenge is $c \leftarrow_\$ \mathcal{C}$.
- **Response**: The response is $\sigma = (\sigma_1, \sigma_2)$; the prover first computes $\tau = (\tau_1, \tau_2) \leftarrow_\$ \mathsf{P}'_{K'}(c)$ and

$$\sigma = (\sigma_1, \sigma_2) := \left(\tau_1, \tau_2 \circ K_F + H_{K_H}(\tau_1)\right) \in \mathcal{T}_1 \times \mathbb{F}.$$

– **Verification:** Given a challenge c and response $\sigma = (\sigma_1, \sigma_2)$, the verifier first computes

$$\tau = (\tau_1, \tau_2) := \left(\sigma_1, (\sigma_2 - H_{K_H}(\sigma_1)) \circ K_F^{-1} \right)$$

and returns the decision $d \leftarrow_\$ V'_{K'}(c, \tau)$.

Theorem 2.1 ([13, **Theorem 5**]). *Suppose that H is δ-almost universal and that* Auth' *is* (t, Q, ϵ)-ROR-CMA-*secure, satisfies β-right tag sparsity, and has completeness error α. then* Auth *is* $\left(t', Q, Q \cdot (\epsilon + Q/|\mathcal{C}| + \beta\delta|\mathbf{F}|/(|\mathbf{F}| - 1) + Q\alpha \right)$-S-MIM-*secure, where* $t' \approx t$.

2.6   Message Authentication Codes

A MAC scheme is a tuple of three probabilistic polynomial-time algorithms MAC = (KeyGen, Tag, Verify) over $(\mathcal{K}, \mathcal{M}, \mathcal{T})$ where $\mathcal{K}$, $\mathcal{M}$, and $\mathcal{T}$ are key space, message space, and tag space, respectively:

– **Key-generation algorithm:** The probabilistic key-generation algorithm KeyGen gives secret key SK on input a security parameter κ.
– **Tag-generation algorithm:** The probabilistic authentication algorithm Tag takes as inputs the secret key SK, the message m and then outputs a tag σ.
– **Verification algorithm:** The deterministic verification algorithm Verify takes as inputs a secret key SK, a message m and a tag σ and outputs either Accept or Reject.

Completeness. We say that MAC has a completeness error α, if for all $m \in \mathcal{M}$ and $1^\kappa \in \mathbb{N}$:

$$\Pr[\mathsf{SK} \leftarrow_\$ \mathsf{KeyGen}(1^\kappa); \sigma \leftarrow_\$ \mathsf{Tag}(\mathsf{SK}, m); d \leftarrow \mathsf{Verify}(\mathsf{SK}, m, \sigma) : d = \texttt{Reject}] \le \alpha.$$

We often say that MAC is *perfectly correct* if $\alpha = 0$.

UF-CMA Security. The standard security notion for MAC scheme is *unforgeability under chosen-message attacks* (UF-CMA), captured by the experiment described in Fig. 4.

Definition 2.5. *Let* MAC = (KeyGen, Tag, Verify) *be a MAC scheme. We define the security game* $\mathsf{Exp}^{\mathsf{uf\text{-}cma}}_{\mathsf{MAC}, \mathcal{A}}(\kappa)$ *between a challenger and an adversary $\mathcal{A}$ as in Fig. 4. For any adversary $\mathcal{A}$, we define* UF-CMA *advantage against* MAC *as the quantity*

$$\mathsf{Adv}^{\mathsf{uf\text{-}cma}}_{\mathsf{MAC}, \mathcal{A}}(\kappa) := \Pr[\mathsf{Exp}^{\mathsf{uf\text{-}cma}}_{\mathsf{MAC}, \mathcal{A}}(\kappa) \Rightarrow \mathsf{True}].$$

We say that a MAC *is* (t, Q, ϵ)-UF-CMA-*secure if for all t-time adversary* $\mathsf{Adv}^{\mathsf{uf\text{-}cma}}_{\mathsf{MAC}, \mathcal{A}}(\kappa)$ *issuing at most Q queries to the oracles $T(\cdot)$ and $V(\cdot, \cdot)$, we have* $\mathsf{Adv}^{\mathsf{uf\text{-}cma}}_{\mathsf{MAC}, \mathcal{A}}(\kappa) \le \epsilon$.

2.7   Hash Functions

Our construction relies on pairwise-independent hash functions and is defined as following:

Definition 2.6 (Pairwise-independent hash functions). *A function* $h \colon \mathcal{K} \times \mathcal{N} \to \mathcal{M}$ *is called pairwise-independent hash function if for* $x_1 \neq x_2 \in \mathcal{N}$, $y_1, y_2 \in \mathcal{M}$,

$$\Pr_{\mathsf{SK} \leftarrow \mathcal{K}}[h_{\mathsf{SK}}(x_1) = y_1 \wedge h_{\mathsf{SK}}(x_2) = y_2] \leq \frac{1}{|\mathcal{M}|^2}.$$

$\mathsf{Exp}_{\mathsf{MAC},\mathcal{A}}^{\mathsf{uf\text{-}cma},b}(\kappa)$	Oracle $T(m)$
$\mathcal{Q}_T, \mathcal{Q}_V \leftarrow \emptyset$	$\mathcal{Q}_T \leftarrow \mathcal{Q}_T \cup \{m\}$
$\mathsf{SK} \leftarrow_\$ \mathsf{KeyGen}(1^\kappa)$	$\sigma \leftarrow_\$ \mathsf{Tag}(\mathsf{SK}, m)$
run $\mathcal{A}^{T(\cdot), V(\cdot, \cdot)}(1^\kappa)$	**return** σ
return $\begin{pmatrix} \exists (m, \sigma) \in \mathcal{Q}_V \text{ s.t. } m \notin \mathcal{Q}_T \\ \wedge \mathsf{Verify}(\mathsf{SK}, m, \sigma) = \mathtt{Accept} \end{pmatrix}$	Oracle $V(m, \sigma)$
	$\mathcal{Q}_V \leftarrow \mathcal{Q}_V \cup \{(m, \sigma)\}$
	return $\mathsf{Verify}(\mathsf{SK}, m, \sigma)$

Fig. 4. Definition of $\mathsf{Exp}_{\mathsf{MAC},\mathcal{A}}^{\mathsf{uf\text{-}cma}}(\kappa)$

Concrete Construction. We now consider the following construction of pairwise independent function based on ring of integers modulo prime $(\mathbb{Z}_p)$:

Lemma 2.2. *For every* $n \in \mathbb{N}$, *define:* $h : \mathbb{Z}_p^2 \times \mathbb{Z}_p \to \mathbb{Z}_p$ *by* $h_{a,b}(x) = a \cdot x + b$. *Then the function* h *is pairwise-independent. That is, for all* $x_1 \neq x_2$ *and* $y_1, y_2 \in \mathbb{Z}_p$,

$$\Pr_{(a,b) \leftarrow \mathbb{Z}_p^2}[h_{a,b}(x_1) = y_1 \wedge h_{a,b}(x_2) = y_2] \leq 1/p^2.$$

The proof can be found in [34].

3   The MERS Problem

Aggarwal et al. introduced new assumptions [1] mimicking NTRU/Ring-LWE with short secret over integers, relying on the properties of Mersenne primes in the ring $\mathbb{Z}_p$ instead of polynomial ring $\mathbb{Z}_q[x]/(x^n - 1)$. We here employ their latter assumption mimicking Ring-LWE with short secret and extend it to that mimicking Ring-LWE with uniform secret.

For two integers $n > h$ and for n-bit Mersenne prime $p = 2^n - 1$, and for integer $s \in \mathbb{Z}_p$, we define an oracle $\mathcal{O}_{s,n,h}$ as follows: choose $a \leftarrow_\$ \mathbb{Z}_p$ and $e \leftarrow_\$ \mathfrak{H}_{n,h}$ and return $(a, a \cdot s + e \bmod p)$. We also define a uniform oracle $\mathcal{U}$ as follows: choose $(a, b) \leftarrow_\$ \mathbb{Z}_p^2$ and return it.[4]

Let us define the *Mersenne Low-Hamming Combination Assumption* (the MERS assumption).

Definition 3.1 (MERS problem). *For two positive integers $n > h$ and for an adversary $\mathcal{A}$, we introduce the* $\mathsf{MERS}_{n,h}$ *advantage as the quantity:*

$$\mathsf{Adv}_{\mathcal{A}}^{\mathsf{MERS}_{n,h}}(\kappa) := \left| \Pr[\mathcal{A}^{\mathcal{O}_{s,n,h}()}(1^\kappa) \Rightarrow \mathsf{True}] - Pr[\mathcal{A}^{\mathcal{U}()}(1^\kappa) \Rightarrow \mathsf{True}] \right|,$$

where $s \leftarrow_\$ \mathfrak{H}_{n,h}$. We say that the $\mathsf{MERS}_{n,h}$ *problem is (t, Q, ϵ)-hard if all t-time attacker $\mathcal{A}$ with time complexity t, making at most Q queries, we have* $\mathsf{Adv}_{\mathcal{A}}^{\mathsf{MERS}_{n,h}}(\kappa) \leq \epsilon$.

The original definition [1, Definition 5] allows an adversary to query at most twice. We generalize the assumption by allowing polynomially-many queries.

3.1   MERS Problem with Uniform Secret

We next define the $\mathsf{MERS}\text{-}\mathsf{U}_{n,h}$ problem with $n > h$

Definition 3.2 (MERS problem with uniform secret). *For two positive integers $n > h$ and for an adversary $\mathcal{A}$, we define the* $\mathsf{MERS}\text{-}\mathsf{U}_{n,h}$ *advantage as the quantity:*

$$\mathsf{Adv}_{\mathcal{A}}^{\mathsf{MERS}\text{-}\mathsf{U}_{n,h}}(\kappa) := \left| \Pr[\mathcal{A}^{\mathcal{O}_{s,n,h}()}(1^\kappa) \Rightarrow \mathsf{True}] - \Pr[\mathcal{A}^{\mathcal{U}()}(1^\kappa) \Rightarrow \mathsf{True}] \right|, \quad (1)$$

where $s \leftarrow_\$ \mathbb{Z}_p$. We say that the $\mathsf{MERS}\text{-}\mathsf{U}_{n,h}$ *problem is (t, Q, ϵ)-hard if all attacker $\mathcal{A}$ with time complexity t, making at most Q queries, we have* $\mathsf{Adv}_{\mathcal{A}}^{\mathsf{MERS}\text{-}\mathsf{U}_{n,h}}(\kappa) \leq \epsilon$.

It is easy to show that if $\mathsf{MERS}_{n,h}$ is (t', Q, ϵ')-hard, then $\mathsf{MERS}\text{-}\mathsf{U}_{n,h}$ is also (t, Q, ϵ)-hard with $t' \approx t$ and $\epsilon' \approx \epsilon$ (by a simple randomization of the secret s). We note that the converse is also true.

Proposition 3.1. *If the* $\mathsf{MERS}\text{-}\mathsf{U}_{n,h}$ *problem is $(t', Q + 1, \epsilon')$-hard, then the* $\mathsf{MERS}_{n,h}$ *problem is (t, Q, ϵ')-hard, where $t' \approx t$ and $\epsilon' \approx \epsilon$.*

We omit the proof because this is very similar to that in [3, Lemma 2]. See the full version of this paper for the details.

---

[4] In the original definition, a is chosen from $\{0, 1\}^n$. This change introduces only negligible distance.

3.2 Hardness and Concrete Parameters

MEET-IN-THE-MIDDLE ATTACK. de Boer et al. [10] presented a meet-in-the-middle attack for solving the MERS problem. Their classical attack runs in the time $\tilde{O}\left(\binom{n-1}{h-1}^{1/2}\right)$. The quantum version runs in the time $\tilde{O}\left(\binom{n-1}{h-1}^{1/3}\right)$. They correspond to roughly $\frac{1}{4}h\lg n$ and $\frac{1}{6}h\lg n$ bits security, respectively.

LLL-ATTACK. The authors of [7,10] presented an LLL-based algorithm for solving the ratio version of MERS assumption[5] and the MERS problem used in the present paper. For small $h = O(\sqrt{n})$, the running time of the LLL attack is $O(2^{2h})$ on Turing machine and $O(2^h)$ on quantum machine.

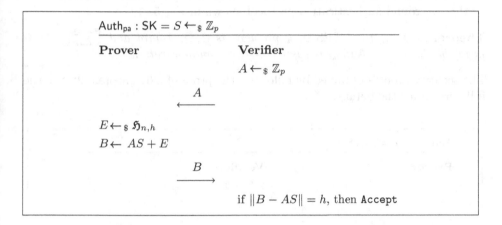

Fig. 5. Passively-secure authentication protocol $\mathsf{Auth_{pa}}$

Coron and Gini [14] also gave an LLL-based attack to solve the MERS problem. The (expected) running time of their attack is $O(2^{1.75h})$.

Tiepelt and Szepieniec [37] analyzed an quantum-LLL algorithm and applied it to the MERS problem.

Thus, it is reasonable to assume that attacks against MERS cannot exceed the complexity of the order 2^h where h is the hamming weight parameter, as claimed in [1]. When considering the security and implementation of our protocols, one should choose the parameter h at least half of the desired security level κ.

PRIMALITY OF n IN MERSENNE PRIMES. Aggarwal et al. discussed that $p = 2^n - 1$ and n should be primes to avoid an attack on composite n. For the details, see Aggarwal et al. [1].

PARAMETERS. Assuming the attacks and constraints above, we choose parameter values as $(\kappa, h, n) = (256, 128, 521)$. It will serve classical 256-bit sec. and quantum 192-bit sec.

---

[5] The Mersenne Low Hamming Ratio Assumption states that, given an n-bit Mersenne prime $p = 2^n - 1$ and an integer h, any PPT adversary cannot distinguish between $F/G \bmod p$ with $F, G \leftarrow_\$ \mathfrak{H}_{n,h}$, and $R \leftarrow \mathbb{Z}_p$ with non-negligible advantage.

4   Passively-Secure Authentication Based on MERS

In this section we introduce our new two-round authentication protocol based on $\mathsf{MERS}_{n,h}$ problem with passive security. Our $\mathsf{Auth}_{\mathsf{pa}}$ is defined as follows:

- **Public parameters**: The authentication protocol has the following public parameters that depend on the security parameter κ.
  - $n \in \mathbb{N}$: the length of A, S, and E
  - $h \in \mathbb{N}$: the Hamming weight of E
- **Key generation**: The key-generation algorithm $\mathsf{KeyGen}(1^\kappa)$ outputs $\mathsf{SK} = S \leftarrow_\$ \mathbb{Z}_p$.
- **Authentication protocol**: To be authenticated by a verifier, a prover follows the two-round authentication protocol shown in Fig. 5.

Theorem 4.1. *If the MERS-$\mathsf{U}_{n,h}$ problem is (t, Q, ϵ)-hard and $\frac{1}{p} \sum_{i=0}^{2h} \binom{n}{i}$ is negligible in κ, then $\mathsf{Auth}_{\mathsf{pa}}$ is passively-secure authentication.*

The security proof is obtained by following the proof of [26, Theorem 2]. See the full version for the details.

$\mathsf{Auth}_{\mathsf{ror}} : \mathsf{SK} = (S_1, S_2) \leftarrow_\$ \mathbb{Z}_p^2$

Prover	Verifier
	$A \leftarrow_\$ \mathbb{Z}_p$
$\xleftarrow{\quad A \quad}$	
$R \leftarrow_\$ \mathbb{Z}_p, E \leftarrow_\$ \mathfrak{H}_{n,h}$	
$B \leftarrow R(S_1 A + S_2) + E$	
$\xrightarrow{\quad R, B \quad}$	
	if $R \neq 0$ and $\|B - R(S_1 A + S_2)\| = h$,
	then Accept

Fig. 6. ROR-CMA-secure authentication protocol $\mathsf{Auth}_{\mathsf{ror}}$

ACTIVE ATTACK AGAINST $\mathsf{Auth}_{\mathsf{pa}}$. The active attack against $\mathsf{Auth}_{\mathsf{pa}}$ based on $\mathsf{MERS}_{n,h}$ is quite similar to the active attack against HB^+ [22]. It consists for an arbitrary fixed A, the adversarial verifier can send fixed A ,e.g., $A = 1$, repeatedly and obtain

$$B_1 \equiv AS + E_1 \pmod{p}, \ldots, B_k \equiv AS + E_k \pmod{p},$$

where each E_i's Hamming weight is at most h. If $h < n/2$ and k is sufficiently large, then the adversary can determine AS's bits from LSB to MSB as follows:

(1) taking the majority of LSB of B_i, which is AS's LSB, (2) taking the majority of 2nd bits of B_i- LSB of AS, which is AS's 2nd bit, and so on. It then learns $AS \bmod p$ and obtains S by computing A^{-1}.

5   ROR-CMA-Secure Authentication Based on MERS

Our Auth$_{\mathsf{ror}}$ is defined as follows:

- **Public parameters:** n and h as in Sect. 4.
- **Key generation:** The key-generation algorithm $\mathsf{KeyGen}_{\mathsf{ror}}(1^\kappa)$ outputs $\mathsf{SK} = (S_1, S_2) \leftarrow_\$ \mathbb{Z}_p^2$.
- **Authentication protocol:** To be authenticated by V, P follows the 2-round authentication protocol shown on Fig. 6.

Theorem 5.1. Auth$_{\mathsf{ror}}$ *has $\binom{n}{h}/p$-sparse right tags.*

Proof. For any secret (S_1, S_2), challenge A, and left tag $R \neq 0$, we have $\Pr[\mathsf{V}_{(S_1,S_2)}(A, (R, B)) \Rightarrow \texttt{Accept} : B \leftarrow_\$ \mathbb{Z}_p] = |\mathfrak{H}_{n,h}|/p = \binom{n}{h}/p.$ □

Theorem 5.2. *If the MERS-U$_{n,h}$ problem is (t, Q, ϵ)-hard, then* Auth$_{\mathsf{ror}}$ *is (t', Q, ϵ)-ROR-CMA-secure, where $t' \approx t$.*

Proof (Proof of Theorem 5.2). We follow the proof of the ROR-CMA security of the LPN-based authentication scheme in Cash, Kiltz, and Tessaro [13, Theorem 7].

The security of the MERS-based Auth$_{\mathsf{ror}}$ essentially builds on the ROR-CMA notion. Let us consider an adversary $\mathcal{A}$ who plays the security game $\mathsf{Exp}^{\mathsf{ror\text{-}cma},b}_{\mathsf{Auth}_{\mathsf{ror}},\mathcal{A}}(\kappa)$. We build an adversary $\mathcal{B}$ who solves the MERS-U$_{n,h}$ problem, where n and h are known, by using $\mathcal{A}$ as in Fig. 7.

$\mathcal{B}^{\mathrm{oracle}}()$	Procedure $\tilde{T}(A)$
$S_2' \leftarrow_\$ \mathbb{Z}_p$	**if** $A = A^*$ **then**
$A^* \leftarrow_\$ \mathbb{Z}_p$	$\quad R \leftarrow_\$ \mathbb{Z}_p$
$(\tau^*, state) \leftarrow \mathcal{A}^{\tilde{T}(\cdot)}(1^\kappa, A^*)$	$\quad \tilde{B} \leftarrow_\$ \mathfrak{H}_{n,h}$
Parse $\tau^* = (R^*, B^*)$	**else**
$d \leftarrow (\|B^* - R^* \cdot S_2'\|? = h)$	$\quad (\tilde{R}, \tilde{B}) \leftarrow$ oracle
return $\mathcal{A}(state, d)$	$\quad R \leftarrow \tilde{R} \cdot (A - A^*)^{-1}$
	$\quad B \leftarrow \tilde{B} + R \cdot S_2'$
	$\quad$ **return** $\tau = (R, B)$

Fig. 7. Definition of $\mathcal{B}$

Assume that S_1 is the secret of the MERS-$U_{n,h}$ problem. $\mathcal{B}$ chooses $S_2' \leftarrow_\$ \mathbb{Z}_p$ and $A^* \leftarrow_\$ \mathbb{Z}_p$. It implicitly defines $S_2 := -A^* \cdot S_1 + S_2' \bmod p$. Since S_2' is uniform over $\mathbb{Z}_p$, S_2 is also. In addition, we have

$$B^* - R^* \cdot (S_1 \cdot A^* + S_2) \equiv B^* - R^* \cdot S_2' \pmod{p}.$$

Thus, the decision by $\mathcal{B}$ is always correct.

We assume that oracle returns $(\tilde{R}, \tilde{B} = \tilde{R}S_1 + E)$, where $E \leftarrow_\$ \mathfrak{H}_{n,h}$ or $\mathbb{Z}_p$.

Let us consider $\bar{T}(\cdot)$, the simulation of $T(\cdot)$. If $A = A^*$, then the simulation is perfect, since $S_2' = S_1 A^* + S_2 \bmod p$ and $B = R \cdot S_2' + \tilde{B}$ where $\tilde{B} \leftarrow_\$ \mathfrak{H}_{n,h}$. Otherwise, that is, if $A \neq A^*$, we have

$$B = \tilde{B} + R \cdot S_2' = \tilde{R}S_1 + E + R \cdot S_2' = R \cdot (A - A^*)S_1 + E + R \cdot S_2'$$
$$= R \cdot (AS_1 - A^* S_1 + S_2') + E = R \cdot (AS_1 + S_2) + E,$$

where E is chosen from $\mathfrak{H}_{n,h}$ or $\mathbb{Z}_p$ uniformly at random.

If E is chosen from $\mathfrak{H}_{n,h}$, then (R, B) is distributed as a response computed by the honest prover with secret key (S_1, S_2). On the other hand, if E is chosen from $\mathbb{Z}_p$, then (R, B) is uniformly distributed over $\mathbb{Z}_p^2$. Therefore, $\mathcal{B}$'s simulations are perfect in both cases. This completes the proof.   □

S-MIM ATTACK AGAINST Auth$_{\text{ror}}$. Flip B's two bits. With probability $\approx 1/h(n-h)$, it will modify E while keeping its Hamming weight.

6   S-MIM-Secure Authentication Based on MERS

Now we turn our ROR-CMA-secure protocol into a S-MIM-secure protocol by using the transformation described in Sect. 2.5 by using the pairwise independent hash function in Sect. 2.7.

We set $\mathbb{F} := \mathbb{Z}_p$ and employ the family of pairwise independent hash functions $\{H_{K_1,K_2} \colon \mathbb{Z}_p \to \mathbb{Z}_p \mid K_1, K_2 \in \mathbb{Z}_p\}$, where $H_{K_1,K_2}(R) = K_1 \cdot R + K_2$. Applying the transformation, the key consists of $K = (S_1, S_2, K_F, K_1, K_2)$. The response to a challenge c is computed as $\sigma = (\sigma_1, \sigma_2)$, where

$$\sigma_1 = R \text{ and } \sigma_2 = \underbrace{(R \cdot (S_1 \cdot A + S_2) + E)}_{=\tau_2} \cdot K_F + \underbrace{K_1 \cdot R + K_2}_{=H_{K_H}(\tau_1)}.$$

We can apply the compression technique in [13]. Prover sends $\sigma = (R, Z)$, where

$$Z = (R \cdot (S_1 \cdot A + S_2) + E) \cdot K_F + (K_1 \cdot R + K_2)$$
$$= R(S_1 K_F \cdot A + S_2 K_F + K_1) + K_F \cdot E + K_2$$
$$= R(X_1 \cdot A + X_2) + X_3 \cdot E + X_4,$$

by substituting $X_1 = S_1 K_F$, $X_2 = S_2 K_F + K_1$, $X_3 = K_F$, and $X_4 = K_2$. The verifier also checks if

$$R \neq 0 \wedge \|(Z - R(X_1 A + X_2) - X_4) \cdot X_3^{-1}\| = h$$

or not. (We can choose them as $X_1 \leftarrow_\$ \mathbb{Z}_p^*$, $X_2 \leftarrow \mathbb{Z}_p$, $X_3 \leftarrow \mathbb{Z}_p^*$, and $X_4 \leftarrow \mathbb{Z}_p$.)

The compressed authentication systems, denoted by $\mathsf{Auth}_{\text{s-mim}}$, is summarized as follows:

- **Public parameters**: n and h as in Sect. 4.
- **Key generation**: The key-generation algorithm $\mathsf{KeyGen}_{\text{ror}}(1^\kappa)$ outputs $\mathsf{SK} = (X_1, X_2, X_3, X_4) \leftarrow_\$ \mathbb{Z}_p^* \times \mathbb{Z}_p \times \mathbb{Z}_p^* \times \mathbb{Z}_p$.
- **Authentication protocol**: To be authenticated by V, P follows the 2-round authentication protocol shown in Fig. 8.

Combining Theorems 5.1, 5.2, and 2.1, we get the following corollary.

Corollary 6.1. *If* MERS-U$_{n,h}$ *is* (t, Q, ϵ)-*hard, then* $\mathsf{Auth}_{\text{s-mim}}$ *is* (t', Q, ϵ')-S-MIM-*secure, where* $t' \approx t$ *and* $\epsilon' = Q \cdot \left(\epsilon + Q/p + \binom{n}{h}/(p-1) \right)$.

$\mathsf{Auth}_{\text{s-mim}} : \mathsf{SK} = (X_1, X_2, X_3, X_4) \leftarrow_\$ \mathbb{Z}_p^* \times \mathbb{Z}_p \times \mathbb{Z}_p^* \times \mathbb{Z}_p$

Prover   **Verifier**

$\qquad\qquad\qquad\qquad\qquad\qquad A \leftarrow_\$ \mathbb{Z}_p$

$\qquad\qquad\qquad \xleftarrow{\quad A \quad}$

$R \leftarrow_\$ \mathbb{Z}_p, E \leftarrow_\$ \mathfrak{H}_{n,h}$
$Z \leftarrow R(X_1 A + X_2)$
$\qquad + X_3 E + X_4$

$\qquad\qquad\qquad \xrightarrow{\quad R, Z \quad}$

$\qquad\qquad\qquad\qquad\qquad\qquad$ if $R \neq 0$
$\qquad\qquad\qquad\qquad\qquad\qquad$ and $\left\| X_3^{-1} \cdot (Z - R(X_1 A + X_2) - X_4) \right\| = h$
$\qquad\qquad\qquad\qquad\qquad\qquad$ then $\mathtt{Accept}$

Fig. 8. S-MIM-secure authentication protocol $\mathsf{Auth}_{\text{s-mim}}$

---

7   MAC from MERS

In this section, we introduce MAC based on MERS-U. Our construction is an analogue to that in [28]. The scheme $\mathsf{MAC} = (\mathsf{KeyGen}, \mathsf{Tag}, \mathsf{Verify})$ is summarized as follows:

- **Public parameters**: The public parameters $\mathsf{p}(1^\kappa)$ on the security parameter κ, outputs the public parameters n and h as in Sect. 4. We introduce new parameters $\mu = \nu = \Theta(\kappa)$.

- **Key generation**: The algorithm KeyGen, given public parameters p, samples $s'_0, s_0, s_1, \ldots, s_\mu \leftarrow_\$ \mathbb{Z}_p$, h: $\{0,1\}^* \times \{0,1\}^\nu \to \{0,1\}^\mu$, and pairwise-independent permutation π over $\mathbb{Z}_p \times \mathbb{Z}_p \times \{0,1\}^\nu$, and outputs SK := $(s'_0, s_0, s_1, \ldots, s_\mu, h, \pi)$.
- **Tagging**: The algorithm Tag is given a secret key SK and a message $m \in \mathcal{M}$. This probabilistic authentication algorithm proceeds as follows:
  1. Sample $R \leftarrow_\$ \mathbb{Z}_p$, $E \leftarrow_\$ \mathfrak{H}_{n,h}$ and $\beta \leftarrow_\$ \{0,1\}^\nu$.
  2. Compute $A := h(m, \beta)$.
  3. Compute $S_A = s_0 + \sum_{i=1}^\mu A[i] \cdot s_i$.
  4. Compute $B := R \cdot S_A + E + s'_0$.
  5. Output $\sigma = \pi(R, B, \beta)$.
- **Verification**: The algorithm Verify is given a secret key SK, a message m, and a tag σ. It proceeds as follows:
  1. Parse $\pi^{-1}(\sigma)$ as (R, B, β). If $R = 0$, then Reject.
  2. Compute $A := h(m, \beta)$ and $S_A := s_0 + \sum_{i=1}^\mu A[i] \cdot s_i$.
  3. If $\|B - (R \cdot S_A + s'_0)\| = h$ then return Accept; otherwise, return Reject.

Our scheme is perfectly correct.

$\underline{\text{Real}_\mathcal{B}(\kappa), \text{Rand}_\mathcal{B}(\kappa)}$

$L := \emptyset$

$s'_0, s_0, s_1, \ldots, s_\mu \leftarrow_\$ \mathbb{Z}_p$

$d \leftarrow^{\text{Eval}(\cdot), \text{Chal}(\cdot, \cdot)}(1^\kappa)$

return $d \wedge (A^* \notin L)$

$\underline{\text{Oracle Chal}(R^*, A^*) \text{ // one query}}$

$S_{A^*} := s_0 + \sum_{j=1}^\mu A^*[j] \cdot s_j$

$B^* := s'_0 + R^* \cdot S_{A^*}$

return B^*

$\underline{\text{Oracle Eval}(A)}$

if $A \in L$ **then**

    return $\perp$

$L \leftarrow L \cup \{A\}$

$S_A := s_0 + \sum_{j=1}^\mu A[j] \cdot s_j$

$R \leftarrow_\$ \mathbb{Z}_p; E \leftarrow_\$ \mathfrak{H}_{n,h}$

if Real **then**

    $B := s'_0 + R \cdot S_A + E$

if Rand **then**

    $B \leftarrow_\$ \mathbb{Z}_p$

    return $\tau = (R, B)$

Fig. 9. Definition of Real and Rand

Theorem 7.1. *If the* MERS-$U_{n,h}$ *problem is* (t, Q, ϵ)-*hard, then* MAC *is* (t', Q, ϵ')-UF-CMA-*secure, where* $t \approx t'$ *and*

$$\epsilon = \min\left\{\epsilon'/2 - Q^2/2^\mu, \epsilon'/(8\mu Q_{\text{Verify}}) - Q_{\text{Verify}}\binom{n}{h}/p\right\},$$

where $Q_{\text{Verify}} \leq Q$ *is the number of verification queries.*

7.1   Proof of Theorem 7.1

Let $\alpha_{n,h} := \binom{n}{h}/p$. In what follows, we say a forgery (m, σ) is *fresh* if the A contained in (m, σ) is different from all A's contained in all the previous queries to V and T. For our proof, we are distinguishing two cases: the case where the probability that A is fresh is sufficiently low as $\Pr[\mathsf{Fresh}] \leq \epsilon'/2$, or the complement case where $\Pr[\mathsf{Fresh}] > \epsilon'/2$.

Before proving our main theorem, we review a useful lemma for fresh case, whose proof is in Appendix A.

Lemma 7.1. *Consider the two games* Real *and* Rand *between a challenger and an adversary* $\mathcal{B}$ *defined in Fig. 9. Assume that the* MERS-$\mathsf{U}_{n,h}$ *problem is* (t, Q, ϵ)-*hard. Then, for all* (t', Q)-*adversary* $\mathcal{B}$ *with* $t' \approx t$, *we have*

$$|\Pr[\mathsf{Real}_{\mathcal{B}}(\kappa) \Rightarrow 1] - \Pr[\mathsf{Rand}_{\mathcal{B}}(\kappa) \Rightarrow 1]| \leq 2\mu\epsilon.$$

Fresh Case

Lemma 7.2. *Suppose that there exists an adversary* $\mathcal{A}$ *that breaks* (t', Q, ϵ')-UF-CMA-*security of* MAC. *If the probability that the first forgery found by the adversary is more likely to be fresh:* $\Pr[\mathsf{Fresh}] > \epsilon'/2$, *then we have another* (t, Q, ϵ)-*adversary* $\mathcal{B}$ *that breaks* MERS-$\mathsf{U}_{n,h}$ *with*

$$t \approx t' \text{ and } \epsilon \geq \epsilon'/(4\mu Q_{\mathsf{Verify}}) - Q_{\mathsf{Verify}}\alpha_{n,h},$$

where $Q_{\mathsf{Verify}} \leq Q$ *is the number of verification queries.*

Proof. (Proof of Lemma 7.2). We define the following games:

- Let G_0 be the original security game $\mathsf{Exp}^{\text{uf-cma}}$.
- Let G_j for $j = 1, \ldots, Q_{\mathsf{Verify}}$ denote the games where the adversary is allowed to ask only j verification queries.
- We also define G_j' as same as the game G_j except that the tag oracle will use random R, B, β to compute σ instead of the real computation.

As [28], we have

$$\epsilon'/2 < \Pr[\mathsf{Fresh}] = \Pr[G_0 = 1] \leq \sum_{j}^{Q_{\mathsf{Verify}}} \Pr[G_j = 1].$$

Thus, what we should do is bounding $\Pr[G_j = 1]$.

Claim. Assume that $\mathcal{A}$ is a (t, Q)-adversary for all j, there exists a (t', Q)-adversary $\mathcal{B}$ such that $t' \approx t$ and

$$|\Pr[G_j = 1] - \Pr[G_j' = 1]| \leq |\Pr[\mathsf{Real}_{\mathcal{B}}(\kappa) \Rightarrow 1] - \Pr[\mathsf{Rand}_{\mathcal{B}}(\kappa) \Rightarrow 1]|.$$

Proof (Proof of Claim). We construct $\mathcal{B}$ as follows:

1. $\mathcal{B}$ samples h and π.
2. $\mathcal{B}$ runs $\mathcal{A}$ on input 1^κ and simulates the oracles as follows:
   - $T(m)$:
     (a) sample a random $\beta \leftarrow_\$ \{0,1\}^\nu$ and compute $A = \mathsf{h}(m, \beta)$.
     (b) query A to oracle Eval and obtain a pair (R, B).
     (c) return $\sigma := \pi(R, B, \beta)$.
   - $V(m, \sigma)$:
     (a) if (m, σ) is previously returned to $\mathcal{A}$, then $\mathcal{B}$ returns Accept.
     (b) if (m, σ) is not j-th verification query, then $\mathcal{B}$ returns Reject.
     (c) if (m, σ) is the j-th verification query; we call it (m^*, σ^*). let $(R^*, B^*, \beta^*) := \pi^{-1}(\sigma^*)$; compute $A^* := \mathsf{h}(m^*, \beta^*)$; send (R^*, A^*) to oracle Chal and obtain B'. If $\|B^* - B'\| = h$, then return Accept. otherwise, return Reject.

The j-th verification query is fresh by the definition. In addition, since the oracle Chal returns $B' := s_0' + R^* \cdot S_{A^*}$, this simulated verification procedure correctly checks the Hamming weight of $\|B^* - (s_0' + R^* \cdot S_{A^*})\|$ as the correct verification. Therefore, the simulation is perfect if A^* is fresh as we wanted. □

Claim. For all j, $\Pr[G_j' = 1] \le \alpha_{n,h}$.

Proof (Proof of Claim). Fix a value $j \in \{1, \ldots, Q_{\mathsf{Verify}}\}$. In game G_j', the adversary obtains no information on $(s_0', s_0, s_1, \ldots, s_\mu)$ from the tagging oracle $T(\cdot)$ because the oracle returns random values (R, B). Therefore, the value $X := B^* - B' = B^* - (R^* \cdot S_{A^*} + s_0')$ should be uniformly at random over $\mathbb{Z}_p$, since s_0' is kept secret. Thus, the probability that the verification $\|B^* - B'\| = h$ passes is at most $\Pr[X \leftarrow \mathbb{Z}_p : \|X\| = h] = \binom{n}{h}/p = \alpha_{n,h}$. □

Combining those two claims, we obtain the following result: If $\mathcal{A}$ is (t, Q)-adversary, then there is a (t', Q)-adversary $\mathcal{B}$ such that $t' \approx t$ and

$$\Pr[G_j = 1] \le \Pr[G_j' = 1] + |\Pr[G_j = 1] - \Pr[G_j' = 1]|$$
$$\le \alpha_{n,h} + |\Pr[\mathsf{Real}_{\mathcal{B}}(\kappa) \Rightarrow 1] - \Pr[\mathsf{Rand}_{\mathcal{B}}(\kappa) \Rightarrow 1]|$$

as we wanted. Applying Lemma 7.1, we have $\Pr[G_j = 1] \le \alpha_{n,h} + 2\mu\epsilon$ under the assumption that the MERS-$U_{n,h}$ problem is (t, Q, ϵ)-hard. Therefore, we have

$$\epsilon'/2 \le \sum_{j}^{Q_{\mathsf{Verify}}} \Pr[G_j = 1] \le Q_{\mathsf{Verify}}\alpha_{n,h} + 2Q_{\mathsf{Verify}}\mu\epsilon.$$

This yields $\epsilon \ge \epsilon'/(4Q_{\mathsf{Verify}}\mu) - Q_{\mathsf{Verify}}\alpha_{n,h}$ as we wanted. □

Non-Fresh Case

Lemma 7.3. *Let $\mu = \nu$. Suppose that there exists an adversary $\mathcal{A}$ that breaks (t', Q, ϵ')-UF-CMA-security of MAC. If the probability that the first forgery found by the adversary is more likely to be non-fresh, that is, $\Pr[\mathsf{Fresh}] \le \epsilon'/2$, then we have $\mathcal{B}$ that breaks the (t, Q, ϵ)-hardness of the MERS-$U_{n,h}$ problem, where*

$$t \approx t' \text{ and } \epsilon \ge \epsilon'/2 - Q^2/2^\mu.$$

Proof. This proof is similar to the proof of the ROR-CMA security in Sect. 5.

Let us construct an adversary $\mathcal{B}^{\mathsf{oracle}}$ who will distinguish between two oracles $\mathcal{O}$ and $\mathcal{U}$.

$\mathcal{B}$ samples $\pi, \mathsf{h}, s_0', s_1, \dots, s_\mu$ except s_0 as defined in KeyGen. It then runs $\mathcal{A}$ and simulates the oracles as follows:

- $T(m)$: On a query m,
    1. Sample β and compute $A := \mathsf{h}(m, \beta)$
    2. Call the oracle and obtain $(\tilde{R}, \tilde{B})$
    3. Compute $B := \tilde{B} + \tilde{R} \cdot (\sum_{i=1}^{\mu} A[i] \cdot s_i) + s_0'$
    4. Return $\sigma := \pi(\tilde{R}, B, \beta)$
- $V(m, \sigma)$: On a query (m, σ), $\mathcal{B}$ always answers Reject.

Finally, $\mathcal{B}^{\mathsf{oracle}}$ outputs 1 if any query to T or V contains β that has appeared in a previous query to T or V. It outputs 0 otherwise.

We note that if oracle $= \mathcal{O}_{s,n,h}$, then $\tilde{B} = \tilde{R} \cdot s + e$, where $e \leftarrow_{\$} \mathfrak{H}_{n,h}$ and the simulation of T is perfect by letting $s_0 := s$.

Claim. If oracle $= \mathcal{O}_{s,n,h}$, then the probability that $\mathcal{B}^{\mathsf{oracle}}$ outputs 1 is $\geq \epsilon'/2$.

Proof (Proof of Claim). The proof is the same as that in [28, Proof of Claim 4.5]. The simulation of T is perfect. In addition, until $\mathcal{A}$ makes a valid forgery, the simulation of V is also perfect. The probability that $\mathcal{A}$ output his first forgery which is *not* fresh is simply lower bounded by $\epsilon' - \epsilon'/2 = \epsilon'/2$. Thus, we obtain the lower bound in the claim.   □

Claim If oracle $= \mathcal{U}$, then the probability that $\mathcal{B}^{\mathsf{oracle}}$ outputs 1 is at most $Q^2/2^\mu$.

Proof (Proof of Claim). The proof is the same as that in [28, Proof of Claim 4.6].

We have $A_i = A_j$ if and only if $\mathsf{h}(m_i, \beta_i) = \mathsf{h}(m_j, \beta_j)$. Now we will upper bound the probability that an adversary find such collision which imply the same probability that $\mathcal{B}^{\mathsf{oracle}}$ outputs 1, assuming that an adversary makes at most q queries and fixing that up to the $(i-1)$-th query by which we assume that all the $\mathcal{A}$'s were distinct. Then we obtain two cases of collision:

- The probability of collision that the i-th query in which β_i will collide with a previous β_j is at most $(i-1)/2^\nu$.
- If the first collision does not happen then the probability of collision in $\mathsf{h}(m_i, \beta_i) = \mathsf{h}(m_j, \beta_j)$ will be $(i-1)/2^\mu$.

Then similarly to the proof in [27] we obtain $\sum_{n=1}^{q}((i-1)/2^\nu + (i-1)/2^\mu) \leq Q^2/2^\mu$ where $\mu = \nu$.   □

Combining two claims, we have $\epsilon \geq \epsilon'/2 - Q^2/2^\mu$ as we wanted.   □

Acknowledgment. The first author would like thank to Krzysztof Pietrzak for fruitful discussions during the first stage of this project.

A   Proof of Lemma 7.1

Lemma A.1 (Lemma 7.1, restated). *Consider the two games* Real *and* Rand *between a challenger and an adversary $\mathcal{B}$ defined in Fig. 9. Assume that the* MERS-U$_{n,h}$ *problem is (t, Q, ϵ)-hard. Then, for all (t', Q)-adversary $\mathcal{B}$ with $t' \approx t$, we have*

$$|\Pr[\mathsf{Real}_{\mathcal{B}}(\kappa) \Rightarrow 1] - \Pr[\mathsf{Rand}_{\mathcal{B}}(\kappa) \Rightarrow 1]| \le 2\mu\epsilon.$$

The proof is almost same as that in [28].

For $i = 0, \ldots, \mu$ and $A \in \{0, 1\}^\mu$, we define $A[1..i]$ as the i-bit string $A_1 \ldots A_i \in \{0, 1\}^i$. (We let $A[1..0] = \bot$.) For $i = 0, \ldots, \mu$, $\mathsf{RF}_i, \mathsf{RF}'_i \colon \{0, 1\}^i \to \mathbb{Z}_p$ be two random functions. (If $i = 0$, then $\mathsf{RF}_0(\bot) = b'$ for some random $b' \leftarrow_\$ \mathbb{Z}_p$.)

We define the line of games as follows:

- G_0: this game is the same as Real except that
  - in the beginning, we sample 2μ elements $s_{1,0}, \ldots, s_{\mu,0}, s_{1,1}, \ldots, s_{\mu,1}$ from $\mathbb{Z}_p$ instead of $\mu + 1$ elements $s_0, s_1, \ldots, s_\mu$ from $\mathbb{Z}_p$.
  - in the computation of S_A, we compute $S_A := \sum_{j=1}^\mu s_{j,A[j]}$ instead of $S_A := s_0 + \sum_{j=1}^\mu A[j] \cdot s_j$. (We also replace the computation of S_{A^*}.)
- $G_{1,i}$ for $i = 0, \ldots, \mu$: this game is the same as G_0 except that
  - in the oracle Chal, we let $s'_0 := \mathsf{RF}_i(A^*[1..i])$
  - in the oracle Eval, we compute $B := \mathsf{RF}_i(A[1..i]) + RS_A + E$ instead of $B := s'_0 + RS_A + E$.
- G_2: this game is the same as $G_{1,\mu}$ except that
  - in the oracle Chal, we sample $B^* \leftarrow_\$ \mathbb{Z}_p$ instead of $B^* := s'_0 + R^* \cdot S_{A^*}$
  - in the oracle Eval, we compute $B := \mathsf{RF}_\mu(A)$ instead of $B := \mathsf{RF}_\mu(A) + RS_A + E$.

Lemma A.2. $\Pr[G_0 = 1] = \Pr[\mathsf{Real} \Rightarrow 1]$.

Proof. In G_0, we replace the computation of S_A. We note that if we set $s_0 := \sum_{j=1}^\mu s_{j,0}$ and $s_j := s_{j,1} - s_{j,0}$, we have $S_A = s_0 + \sum_{j=1}^\mu A[j] \cdot s_j = \sum_j^\mu s_{j,A[j]}$. In addition, if we choose $s_{j,k}$ uniformly at random, then $s_0, s_1, \ldots, s_\mu$ are also distributed according to the uniform distribution over $\mathbb{Z}_p$. Hence, the two games are equivalent. $\square$

Lemma A.3. *We have $\Pr[G_0 = 1] = \Pr[G_{1,0} = 1]$.*

Proof. G_0 is the same as $G_{1,0}$, since s'_0 can be interpreted as $\mathsf{RF}_0(\bot)$ [28]. $\square$

Lemma A.4. *Let $\mathcal{B}$ be a (t, Q)-adversary in Fig. 9. For all $i \in \{0, \ldots, \mu - 1\}$, there exists a (t', Q)-adversary $\mathcal{D}$ such that*

$$t' \approx t \ and \ |\Pr[G_{1,i} = 1] - \Pr[G_{1,i+1} = 1]| \le 2 \cdot \mathsf{Adv}_{\mathcal{D}}^{\mathsf{MERS\text{-}U}_{n,h}}(\kappa).$$

Proof. Notice that for arbitrarily fixed $b \in \{0,1\}$ and two random functions RF_i and RF'_i, we can define a new random function RF_{i+1} by

$$\mathsf{RF}_{i+1}(A[1..i+1]) := \begin{cases} \mathsf{RF}_i(A[1..i]) & \text{if } A[i+1] = b \\ \mathsf{RF}_i(A[1..i]) + \mathsf{RF}'_i(A[1..i]) & \text{o.w.} \end{cases}$$

Our adversary $\mathcal{D}$ guesses $b \leftarrow_\$ \{0,1\}$ as the prediction of $A^*[i+1]$ and simulates the oracles by using the above observation. We construct a distinguisher $\mathcal{D}$ as follows:

1. Given 1^κ, $\mathcal{D}$ prepares parameter values as follows:
   - Sample $b \leftarrow \{0,1\}$ and initialize $L := \emptyset$ and $L_i := \emptyset$.
   - Choose $s_{j,\beta} \leftarrow \mathbb{Z}_p$ for all $j \in [1,\mu]$ and $\beta \in \{0,1\}$ except for $s_{i+1,1-b}$.
   - Query to its oracle for Q times and obtain the answers (R_j, B'_j) for $j \in \{1,2,\ldots,Q\}$.
2. $\mathcal{D}$ runs $\mathcal{B}$ and simulates Eval and Chal as follows:
   - Simulation of Eval on input $A \in \{0,1\}^\mu$:
     (a) Update $L := L \cup \{A\}$
     (b) If $A[i+1] = b$, then $R \leftarrow_\$ \mathbb{Z}_p$, $E \leftarrow_\$ \mathfrak{H}_{n,h}$, compute $B := \mathsf{RF}_i(A[1..i]) + R \cdot (\sum_{j=1}^{\mu} s_{j,A[j]}) + E$ and return (R,B).
     (c) Else, that is, if $A[i+1] = 1-b$, then
       i. If L_i contains $(A[1..i], (R_j, B'_j))$ for some j, then let $(R,B') := (R_j, B'_j)$.
       ii. Else, use a next fresh pair, that is, $(R,B') := (R_j, B'_j)$ for the first j. Add $(A[1..i], (R_j, B'_j))$ to the list L_i.
       iii. Compute $B := \mathsf{RF}_i(A[1..i]) + R \cdot (\sum_{j=1, j\neq i+1}^{\mu} s_{j,A[j]}) + B'$ and return (R,B).
   - Simulation of Chal on input R^* and A^*:
     (a) If $A^*[i+1] \neq b$, abort.
     (b) Else, define $S_{A^*} := \sum_j^\mu s_{j,A^*[j]}$.
     (c) Return $B^* := R^* \cdot S_{A^*} + \mathsf{RF}_i(A^*[1..i])$.
3. Finally, $\mathcal{B}$ will outputs its decision d and stops. $\mathcal{D}$ outputs $d \wedge (A^* \notin L)$.

Suppose that the guess b is correct. This happens with probability $1/2$. If so, $\mathcal{D}$ perfectly simulates Chal, since $\mathsf{RF}_{i+1}(A^*[1..(i+1)]) = \mathsf{RF}_i(A^*[1..i])$ if $A^*[i+1] = b$. We next analyze the simulation of Eval: If $A[i+1] = b$, then we have $\mathsf{RF}_{i+1}(A[1..(i+1)]) = \mathsf{RF}_i(A[1..i])$. Thus, the distributions of E are the same in both games. Otherwise, that is, if $A[i+1] = 1-b$, then we consider two cases: If the oracle outputs $B' := Rs + E$ with $E \leftarrow_\$ \mathfrak{H}_{n,h}$, then we have

$$B := \mathsf{RF}_i(A[1..i]) + R \cdot \left(\sum_{j=1, j\neq i+1}^{\mu} s_{j,A[j]} \right) + R \cdot s + E$$

$$= \mathsf{RF}_i(A[1..i]) + R \cdot \left(\sum_{j=1}^{\mu} s_{j,A[j]} \right) + E$$

by letting $s_{i+1,1-b} := s$. Therefore, if the oracle is $\mathcal{O}_{s,n,h}$, then $\mathcal{D}$ perfectly simulates G_i. On the other hand, if the oracle is $\mathcal{U}$, that is, $B' = Rs + E + U$ with $E \leftarrow_\$ \mathfrak{H}_{n,h}$ and $U \leftarrow_\$ \mathbb{Z}_p$, then we have

$$B := \mathsf{RF}_i(A[1..i]) + R \cdot \left(\sum_{j=1, j \neq i+1}^{\mu} s_{j,A[j]} \right) + R \cdot s + E + U$$

$$= \mathsf{RF}_i(A[1..i]) + U + R \cdot \left(\sum_{j=1}^{\mu} s_{j,A[j]} \right) + E.$$

By letting $U := \mathsf{RF}'_i(A[1..i])$, we observe that $\mathcal{D}$ perfectly simulates G_{i+1}. Therefore, we have

$$t' \approx t \text{ and } |\Pr[G_{1,i} = 1] - \Pr[G_{1,i+1} = 1]| = 2 \cdot \mathsf{Adv}_{\mathcal{D}}^{\mathsf{MERS}\text{-}\mathsf{U}_{n,h}}(\kappa)$$

as we wanted.   □

Lemma A.5. *We have* $\Pr[G_{1,\mu} = 1] = \Pr[G_2 = 1]$.

Proof. This is almost obvious. Notice that every query A to Eval and Chal should be fresh. Thus, in both cases, $\mathsf{RF}_\mu(A)$ makes B (and B^*) random.   □

Lemma A.6. *We have* $\Pr[G_2 = 1] = \Pr[\mathsf{Rand} \Rightarrow 1]$.

Proof. In G_2, all returned values (R, B) from Eval and B^* from Chal are fresh and random if $A^* \notin L$. We also know that in Rand, all values are fresh and random if $A^* \notin L$, because s'_0 is random and kept secret. Therefore, there are no difference between G_2 and Rand if $A^* \notin L$. This completes the proof.   □

References

1. Aggarwal, D., Joux, A., Prakash, A., Santha, M.: A new public-key cryptosystem via Mersenne numbers. In: Shacham, H., Boldyreva, A. (eds.) CRYPTO 2018. LNCS, vol. 10993, pp. 459–482. Springer, Cham (2018). https://doi.org/10.1007/978-3-319-96878-0_16
2. Aggarwal, D., Joux, A., Prakash, A., Santha, M.: Mersenne-756839. Technical report, National Institute of Standards and Technology (2017). https://csrc.nist.gov/projects/post-quantum-cryptography/round-1-submissions
3. Applebaum, B., Cash, D., Peikert, C., Sahai, A.: Fast cryptographic primitives and circular-secure encryption based on hard learning problems. In: Halevi, S. (ed.) CRYPTO 2009. LNCS, vol. 5677, pp. 595–618. Springer, Heidelberg (2009). https://doi.org/10.1007/978-3-642-03356-8_35
4. Armknecht, F., Hamann, M., Mikhalev, V.: Lightweight authentication protocols on ultra-constrained RFIDs - myths and facts. In: Saxena, N., Sadeghi, A.-R. (eds.) RFIDSec 2014. LNCS, vol. 8651, pp. 1–18. Springer, Cham (2014). https://doi.org/10.1007/978-3-319-13066-8_1

5. Bellare, M., Rogaway, P.: Entity authentication and key distribution. In: Stinson, D.R. (ed.) CRYPTO 1993. LNCS, vol. 773, pp. 232–249. Springer, Heidelberg (1994). https://doi.org/10.1007/3-540-48329-2_21

6. Bernstein, D.J., Lange, T.: Never trust a bunny. In: Hoepman, J.-H., Verbauwhede, I. (eds.) RFIDSec 2012. LNCS, vol. 7739, pp. 137–148. Springer, Heidelberg (2013). https://doi.org/10.1007/978-3-642-36140-1_10

7. Beunardeau, M., Connolly, A., Géraud, R., Naccache, D.: On the hardness of the Mersenne low hamming ratio assumption. In: Lange, T., Dunkelman, O. (eds.) LATINCRYPT 2017. LNCS, vol. 11368, pp. 166–174. Springer, Cham (2019). https://doi.org/10.1007/978-3-030-25283-0_9

8. Blum, A., Furst, M., Kearns, M., Lipton, R.J.: Cryptographic primitives based on hard learning problems. In: Stinson, D.R. (ed.) CRYPTO 1993. LNCS, vol. 773, pp. 278–291. Springer, Heidelberg (1994). https://doi.org/10.1007/3-540-48329-2_24

9. Blum, A., Kalai, A., Wasserman, H.: Noise-tolerant learning, the parity problem, and the statistical query model. J. ACM 50(4), 506–519 (2003). https://doi.org/10.1145/792538.792543

10. de Boer, K., Ducas, L., Jeffery, S., de Wolf, R.: Attacks on the AJPS Mersenne-based cryptosystem. In: Lange, T., Steinwandt, R. (eds.) PQCrypto 2018. LNCS, vol. 10786, pp. 101–120. Springer, Cham (2018). https://doi.org/10.1007/978-3-319-79063-3_5

11. Bos, J.W., Kleinjung, T., Lenstra, A.K., Montgomery, P.L.: Efficient SIMD arithmetic modulo a Mersenne number. In: Proceedings of the 2011 IEEE 20th Symposium on Computer Arithmetic, ARITH 2011, pp. 213–221. IEEE Computer Society, Washington, DC (2011). https://doi.org/10.1109/ARITH.2011.37

12. Bringer, J., Chabanne, H., Dottax, E.: HB$^+$: a lightweight authentication protocol secure against some attacks. In: Proceedings of the Second International Workshop on Security, Privacy and Trust in Pervasive and Ubiquitous Computing, SECPERU 2006, pp. 28–33. IEEE Computer Society, Washington, DC (2006). https://doi.org/10.1109/SECPERU.2006.10

13. Cash, D., Kiltz, E., Tessaro, S.: Two-round man-in-the-middle security from LPN. In: Kushilevitz, E., Malkin, T. (eds.) TCC 2016. LNCS, vol. 9562, pp. 225–248. Springer, Heidelberg (2016). https://doi.org/10.1007/978-3-662-49096-9_10

14. Coron, J.S., Gini, A.: Improved cryptanalysis of the AJPS Mersenne based cryptosystem. In: Number-Theoretic Methods in Cryptology 2019 - NutMiC 2019 (2019). https://eprint.iacr.org/2019/610

15. Dodis, Y., Kiltz, E., Pietrzak, K., Wichs, D.: Message authentication, revisited. In: Pointcheval, D., Johansson, T. (eds.) EUROCRYPT 2012. LNCS, vol. 7237, pp. 355–374. Springer, Heidelberg (2012). https://doi.org/10.1007/978-3-642-29011-4_22

16. Duc, D.N., Kim, K.: Securing HB$^+$ against GRS man-in-the-middle attack. In: SCIS 2007, The 2007 Symposium on Cryptography and Information Security, pp. 2B3-4. IEICE, Sasebo, 23–26 January 2007

17. Esser, A., Kübler, R., May, A.: LPN decoded. In: Katz, J., Shacham, H. (eds.) CRYPTO 2017. LNCS, vol. 10402, pp. 486–514. Springer, Cham (2017). https://doi.org/10.1007/978-3-319-63715-0_17

18. Ferradi, H., Naccache, D.: Integer reconstruction public-key encryption. Cryptology ePrint Archive, Report 2017/1231 (2017). https://eprint.iacr.org/2017/1231

19. Fiat, A., Shamir, A.: How to prove yourself: practical solutions to identification and signature problems. In: Odlyzko, A.M. (ed.) CRYPTO 1986. LNCS, vol. 263, pp. 186–194. Springer, Heidelberg (1987). https://doi.org/10.1007/3-540-47721-7_12

20. Gilbert, H., Robshaw, M.J.B., Seurin, Y.: Good variants of HB$^+$ are hard to find. In: Tsudik, G. (ed.) FC 2008. LNCS, vol. 5143, pp. 156–170. Springer, Heidelberg (2008). https://doi.org/10.1007/978-3-540-85230-8_12

21. Gilbert, H., Robshaw, M.J.B., Seurin, Y.: HB$^{\#}$: increasing the security and efficiency of HB$^+$. In: Smart, N. (ed.) EUROCRYPT 2008. LNCS, vol. 4965, pp. 361–378. Springer, Heidelberg (2008). https://doi.org/10.1007/978-3-540-78967-3_21

22. Gilbert, H., Robshaw, M.J.B., Sibert, H.: Active attack against HB+: a provably secure lightweight authentication protocol. Electron. Lett. **41**(21), 1169–1170 (2005). https://doi.org/10.1049/el:20052622. https://eprint.iacr.org/2005/237

23. Heyse, S., Kiltz, E., Lyubashevsky, V., Paar, C., Pietrzak, K.: Lapin: an efficient authentication protocol based on ring-LPN. In: Canteaut, A. (ed.) FSE 2012. LNCS, vol. 7549, pp. 346–365. Springer, Heidelberg (2012). https://doi.org/10.1007/978-3-642-34047-5_20

24. Hopper, N.J., Blum, M.: Secure human identification protocols. In: Boyd, C. (ed.) ASIACRYPT 2001. LNCS, vol. 2248, pp. 52–66. Springer, Heidelberg (2001). https://doi.org/10.1007/3-540-45682-1_4

25. Juels, A., Weis, S.A.: Authenticating pervasive devices with human protocols. In: Shoup, V. (ed.) CRYPTO 2005. LNCS, vol. 3621, pp. 293–308. Springer, Heidelberg (2005). https://doi.org/10.1007/11535218_18

26. Katz, J., Shin, J.S., Smith, A.: Parallel and concurrent security of the HB and HB+ protocols. J. Cryptol. **23**(3), 402–421 (2010). https://doi.org/10.1007/s00145-010-9061-2

27. Kiltz, E., Pietrzak, K., Cash, D., Jain, A., Venturi, D.: Efficient authentication from hard learning problems. In: Paterson, K.G. (ed.) EUROCRYPT 2011. LNCS, vol. 6632, pp. 7–26. Springer, Heidelberg (2011). https://doi.org/10.1007/978-3-642-20465-4_3

28. Kiltz, E., Pietrzak, K., Venturi, D., Cash, D., Jain, A.: Efficient authentication from hard learning problems. J. Cryptol. **30**(4), 1238–1275 (2017). https://doi.org/10.1007/s00145-016-9247-3

29. Levieil, É., Fouque, P.-A.: An improved LPN algorithm. In: De Prisco, R., Yung, M. (eds.) SCN 2006. LNCS, vol. 4116, pp. 348–359. Springer, Heidelberg (2006). https://doi.org/10.1007/11832072_24

30. Lyubashevsky, V., Masny, D.: Man-in-the-middle secure authentication schemes from LPN and weak PRFs. In: Canetti, R., Garay, J.A. (eds.) CRYPTO 2013. LNCS, vol. 8043, pp. 308–325. Springer, Heidelberg (2013). https://doi.org/10.1007/978-3-642-40084-1_18

31. Mol, P., Tessaro, S.: Secret-key authentication beyond the challenge-response paradigm: definitional issues and new protocols. unpublished manuscripts (2012). https://homes.cs.washington.edu/~tessaro/

32. Munilla, J., Peinado, A.: HB-MP: a further step in the HB-family of lightweight authentication protocols. Comput. Netw. **51**(9), 2262–2267 (2007). https://doi.org/10.1016/j.comnet.2007.01.011

33. Preneel, B.: Hash functions and MAC algorithms based on block ciphers. In: Darnell, M. (ed.) Cryptography and Coding 1997. LNCS, vol. 1355, pp. 270–282. Springer, Heidelberg (1997). https://doi.org/10.1007/BFb0024473

34. Rubinfeld, R.: Randomness and computation. Course, MIT (2012). https://people.csail.mit.edu/ronitt/COURSE/S12/handouts/lec5.pdf

35. Shor, P.W.: Polynomial-time algorithms for prime factorization and discrete logarithms on a quantum computer. SIAM J. Comput. **26**(5), 1484–1509 (1997). https://doi.org/10.1137/S0097539795293172

36. Szepieniec, A.: Ramstake. Technical report. National Institute of Standards and Technology (2017). https://csrc.nist.gov/projects/post-quantum-cryptography/round-1-submissions
37. Tiepelt, M., Szepieniec, A.: Quantum LLL with an application to Mersenne number cryptosystems. In: Schwabe, P., Thériault, N. (eds.) LATINCRYPT 2019. LNCS, vol. 11774, pp. 3–23. Springer, Cham (2019). https://doi.org/10.1007/978-3-030-30530-7_1
38. Vaudenay, S.: On privacy models for RFID. In: Kurosawa, K. (ed.) ASIACRYPT 2007. LNCS, vol. 4833, pp. 68–87. Springer, Heidelberg (2007). https://doi.org/10.1007/978-3-540-76900-2_5

Another Look at Some Isogeny Hardness Assumptions

Simon-Philipp Merz[1]($\boxtimes$), Romy Minko[2], and Christophe Petit[3]

[1] Royal Holloway, University of London, Egham, England
Simon-philipp.merz.2018@rhul.ac.uk
[2] University of Oxford, Oxford, England
[3] University of Birmingham, Birmingham, England

Abstract. The security proofs for isogeny-based undeniable signature schemes have been based primarily on the assumptions that the One-Sided Modified SSCDH problem and the One-More SSCDH problem are intractable. We challenge the validity of these assumptions, showing that both the decisional and computational variants of these problems can be solved in polynomial time. We further demonstrate an attack, applicable to two undeniable signature schemes, one of which was proposed at PQCrypto 2014. The attack allows to forge signatures in $2^{4\lambda/5}$ steps on a classical computer. This is an improvement over the expected classical security of 2^λ, where λ denotes the chosen security parameter.

Keywords: Elliptic curves · Isogenies · Undeniable signatures

1 Introduction

Most currently deployed cryptographic schemes are based on mathematical problems that are assumed to be hard on classical computers, but can be solved in polynomial time using quantum algorithms. Continuous progress in quantum computing therefore requires the development of "post-quantum secure" cryptography relying on problems that will (at least to the best of our knowledge) remain hard for quantum algorithms. To achieve quantum resistance some directions currently being explored include lattice-based, multivariate, code-based, and hash-based cryptography and, most recently, cryptography based on isogeny problems. While the latter is appealing for relatively small key sizes compared to other candidates, it requires further optimization and scrutiny.

Isogeny-based cryptography was first proposed by Couveignes in 1997 in a seminar at the ENS [7], but he did not publish his ideas at the time. Almost a decade later Rostovtsev and Stolbunov rediscovered and further developed the same idea independently [20]. While these cryptosystems were based on "ordinary curves", "supersingular curves" were first put to use in the construction of a hash function by Charles, Goren and Lauter [4]. Jao and De Feo introduced another cryptosystem in the supersingular case, the so called Supersingular Isogeny Diffie-Hellman (SIDH) [11]. Instead of using the action of the class

© Springer Nature Switzerland AG 2020
S. Jarecki (Ed.): CT-RSA 2020, LNCS 12006, pp. 496–511, 2020.
https://doi.org/10.1007/978-3-030-40186-3_21

group on certain isomorphism classes of ordinary elliptic curves like Couveignes, Rostovtsev and Stolbunov, SIDH relies on the simple observation that it does not matter in which order we divide out two non-intersecting subgroups of an elliptic curve. One promising submissions to NIST's post-quantum standardization project [18] is the SIDH-based key exchange protocol called SIKE [1].

For a nice introduction to different computational problems in supersingular isogeny-based cryptography we refer to Galbraith and Vercauteren [10]. The template for isogeny-based cryptography is the general isogeny problem. That is, to find an isogeny $\phi : E_1 \to E_2$, for two randomly chosen isogenous curves E_1 and E_2. A variant of this problem includes the additional information of the degree of ϕ. This reduces the problem space from an infinite to a finite number of isogenies while simultaneously reducing the search space. Hence, it is not clear whether it makes the problem harder or easier. Another related problem is the computation of endomorphism rings of supersingular elliptic curves. Assume you know the endomorphism ring of a supersingular curve E_1 and you want to compute the endomorphism ring of E_2. This is computationally broadly equivalent to computing an isogeny $\phi : E_1 \to E_2$ [15,16].

However, more practical supersingular isogeny constructions give more information to a potential attacker. For example, the SIDH protocol, which we will describe in Sect. 3 in more detail, reveals the image of certain torsion points under some secret isogenies in addition to the origin and image curves. It was observed that this additional information might make the problem *a priori* easier and a framework for a potential attack under additional assumptions was given by Petit [19].

Various other versions of isogeny problems have been suggested and conjectured to be hard by other authors to provide security proofs for their cryptographic constructions.

Our Contribution: In this work, we will review some of the isogeny problems that have been suggested in the construction of isogeny-based undeniable signatures [12] published at PQCrypto 2014. While this construction has been used and extended by other authors [22], we show that the assumptions used to make the security proofs work are not valid and the proposed isogeny problems lack the conjectured hardness. This does not immediately lead to an attack on the signature scheme itself. However, we propose an attack on the cryptographic construction as well.

Outline: In Sect. 2 we recall some mathematical background on isogeny-based cryptography. In Sect. 3 we give the definitions of some isogeny problems that have been used in the literature and we give an attack on two of them. The following Sect. 4 describes how the problems have been used in the construction of isogeny-based undeniable signatures of [12]. We provide an attack on the signature scheme combining a near-collision search in the hash function and the attack on the underlying isogeny problem. Before concluding the paper, we mention other constructions that are affected by our attacks in Sect. 5.

2   Mathematical Background

For a full treatment of background information on elliptic curves and a detailed introduction to isogeny-based cryptography we refer to Silverman [21] and De Feo [9], respectively.

Let $\mathbb{F}_q$ be a finite field of characteristic p. In the following we assume $p \geq 3$ and therefore an elliptic curve E over $\mathbb{F}_q$ can be defined by its short Weierstrass form

$$E(\mathbb{F}_q) = \{(x,y) \in \mathbb{F}_q^2 \mid y^2 = x^3 + Ax + B\} \cup \{\mathcal{O}_E\}$$

where $A, B \in \mathbb{F}_q$ and $\mathcal{O}_E$ is the point $(X : Y : Z) = (0 : 1 : 0)$ on the projective curve $Y^2 Z = X^3 + AXZ^2 + BZ^3$. The set of points on an elliptic curve is an abelian group under the "chord and tangent rule" with $\mathcal{O}_E$ being the identity element. The number of points on an elliptic curve is $\#E(\mathbb{F}_q) = q+1-t$ for some integer $t \leq 2\sqrt{q}$. A curve E is called *supersingular* if $p|t$ and *ordinary* otherwise. The *j-invariant* of an elliptic curve is

$$j(E) = 1728 \frac{4A^3}{4A^3 + 27B^2}$$

and there is an isomorphism $f : E \rightarrow E'$ if and only if $j(E) = j(E')$.

Given two elliptic curves E_1 and E_2 over a finite field $\mathbb{F}_q$, an *isogeny* is a morphism $\phi : E_1 \rightarrow E_2$ such that $\phi(\mathcal{O}_{E_1}) = \mathcal{O}_{E_2}$. One can show that isogenies are morphisms both in the sense of algebraic geometry and group theory. If there exists a non-constant isogeny between them, two curves are called *isogenous*. The *degree* of an isogeny ϕ is its degree when treated as an algebraic map. This is equal to the size of the kernel of ϕ if the isogeny is separable (which is always the case in this work).

Since an isogeny defines a group homomorphism $E_1 \rightarrow E_2$, its kernel is a subgroup of E_1. Conversely, any subgroup $S \subset E_1$ determines a (separable) isogeny $\phi : E_1 \rightarrow E_2$ with $\ker(\phi) = S$ and $E_2 = E_1/S$. Since all isogenies in the following will have cyclic groups as kernels, knowledge of the isogeny and knowledge of the kernel of the isogeny are equivalent.

A basic example of an isogeny is the multiplication by n map on an elliptic curve $[n] : E \rightarrow E$. The kernel of the multiplication by n map over the algebraic closure $\overline{\mathbb{F}_q}$ of $\mathbb{F}_q$ is the n-torsion subgroup

$$E[n] = \{P \in E(\overline{\mathbb{F}_q}) : [n]P = \mathcal{O}_E\}.$$

Whenever n and q are relatively prime, the group $E[n]$ is isomorphic to $(\mathbb{Z}/n\mathbb{Z})^2$.

Given any isogeny $\phi : E_1 \rightarrow E_2$, there exists another isogeny $\hat{\phi}$, called the *dual isogeny*, satisfying $\phi \circ \hat{\phi} = \hat{\phi} \circ \phi = [\deg(\phi)]$.

3   The One-More Isogeny Problem

We begin this section by recalling the SIDH protocol and a problem underlying its security. Then, we define and illustrate the somewhat more artificial isogeny problems that were conjectured to be hard and that are used in the security proofs of [12,22]. However, at the end of this section we present our polynomial time attack against these more artificial problems and show that no confidence in them is justified.

3.1 Problem Statements

Even though we do not attack SIDH, it is useful to recall this fundamental key exchange protocol as it contains some ideas upon which the undeniable signature schemes we cryptanalyze are based.

Let p be a prime of the form $\ell_A^{e_A} \ell_B^{e_B} \cdot f \pm 1$ where ℓ_A and ℓ_B are small distinct primes, e_A and e_B are positive integers and f is some (usually small) cofactor. Moreover, we fix a supersingular elliptic curve E defined over $\mathbb{F}_{p^2}$ together with bases $\{P_A, Q_A\}$, $\{P_B, Q_B\}$ of the $\ell_A^{e_A}$ and $\ell_B^{e_B}$ torsion of E, $E[\ell_A^{e_A}]$ and $E[\ell_B^{e_B}]$, respectively.

Suppose Alice and Bob wish to establish a shared secret. Alice's secret is an integer $a \in \{0, \ldots, \ell_A^{e_A} - 1\}$, defining the subgroup $A := \langle P_A + [a]Q_A \rangle$ of $E[\ell_A^{e_A}]$. Her public key is the curve $E_A := E/A$ together with the images $\phi_A(P_B), \phi_A(Q_B)$ of Bob's public basis under her secret isogeny $\phi_A : E \to E/A$. Analogously, Bob chooses his secret key $b \in \{0, \ldots, \ell_B^{e_B} - 1\}$ defining the cyclic subgroup $B := \langle P_B + [b]Q_B \rangle \subset E[\ell_B^{e_B}]$, and his public key is the tuple $(E_B, \phi_B(P_A), \phi_B(Q_A))$.

The key exchange proceeds as follows: Upon receipt of Bob's public key, Alice uses the points to push her secret $A \subset E[\ell_A^{e_A}]$ to E/B, i.e. Alice computes an isogeny $\phi'_A : E_B \to E_{AB}$ with kernel $\langle \phi_B(P_A) + [a]\phi_B(Q_A) \rangle \subset E/B[\ell_A^{e_A}]$. Bob proceeds *mutatis mutandis*. We have

$$E_{AB} = \phi'_A(\phi_B(E)) = \phi'_B(\phi_A(E)) = E/\langle P_A + [a]Q_A, P_B + [b]Q_B \rangle,$$

where the equality holds up to isomorphism. Since the j-invariant is the same for all curves in one isomorphism class, both Alice and Bob can compute the shared secret $j(E_{AB})$ (Fig. 1).

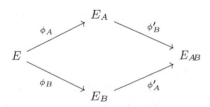

Fig. 1. The commutative diagram of the SIDH key exchange

The hardness of the following problem underlies the security of the SIDH protocol.

Definition 1 (Supersingular Computational Diffie-Hellman (SSCDH) Problem). *Let m_A, n_A be chosen at random from $\{0,\ldots,\ell_A^{e_A}-1\}$ not both divisible by ℓ_A. Analogously, let m_B, n_B be randomly chosen from $\{0,\ldots,\ell_B^{e_B}-1\}$ not both divisible by ℓ_B. Furthermore, let $\phi_A : E \to E_A$ and $\phi_B : E \to E_B$ denote the isogenies with kernel $\langle [m_A]P_A+[n_A]Q_A\rangle$ and $\langle [m_B]P_B+[n_B]Q_B\rangle$ respectively.*

Given the curves E_A, E_B and the points $\phi_A(P_B)$, $\phi_A(Q_B)$, $\phi_B(P_A)$ and $\phi_B(Q_A)$, find the j-invariant of

$$E_{AB} = E/\langle [m_A]P_A + [n_A]Q_A, [m_B]P_B + [n_B]Q_B\rangle.$$

For the following, we fix the notation of Definition 1.

Definition 2 (Modified SSCDH (MSSCDH) Problem). *[12] Given E_A, E_B and $\ker(\phi_B)$, determine E_{AB} up to isomorphism, i.e. $j(E_{AB})$.*

Note that knowledge of $\ker(\phi_B)$ is equivalent to knowledge of ϕ_B, but the lack of information on the auxiliary points in the image of ϕ_A in the MSSCDH problem prevents to *shift* $\ker(\phi_B)$ into E_A.

Definition 3 (One-sided Modified SSCDH (OMSSCDH) Problem). *[12] For fixed E_A, E_B, given an oracle to solve MSSCDH for any E_A, $E_{B'}$, $\ker(\phi_{B'})$ with $E_{B'}$ not isomorphic to E_B and $\ell_B^{e_B}$-isogenous to E, solve MSSCDH for E_A, E_B and $\ker(\phi_B)$.*

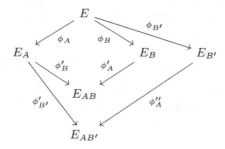

Fig. 2. The oracle provides $E_{AB'}$ for any E_B' and $\phi_{B'}$, while E_{AB} needs to be found in OMSSCDH

While the OMSSCDH assumption seems somewhat more artificial, it arises naturally in the security analysis of undeniable signatures proposed in [12]. Moreover, the authors proposing the problem conjectured it to be computationally infeasible, in the sense that for any polynomial-time solver algorithm, the advantage of the algorithm is a negligible function in the security parameter $\log p$. However, we will see in the next subsection that a polynomial time attacker will have a non-negligible advantage to solve the OMSSCDH problem (Fig. 2).

A decisional variant of this problem is also defined in [12]; our attack will apply to it in the obvious way as well.

Our results furthermore break other strongly related problems, such as the following slightly weaker problem used in the construction of undeniable blind signatures [22].

Definition 4 (One-More SSCDH (1MSSCDH) Problem). *Let E be some base curve of the form as in the SIDH protocol and let m_A, n_A be secret integers in $\{0, \ldots, \ell_A^{e_A} - 1\}$.*

Let a signing oracle respond $E_{AB} \cong E_B/\langle [m_A]P_B + [n_A]Q_B \rangle$ upon receipt of a curve E_B isogenous to E and points P_B, Q_B spanning $E_B[\ell_B^{e_B}]$.

The 1MSSCDH problem is to produce at least $q + 1$ distinct pairs of curves (E_{B_i}, E_{AB_i}), where E_{B_i} are $\ell_B^{e_B}$-isogenous to E, P_{B_i} and Q_{B_i} span $E_{B_i}[\ell_B^{e_B}]$ and E_{AB_i} is isomorphic to $E_{B_i}/\langle [m_A]P_{B_i} + [n_A]Q_{B_i} \rangle$ for $1 \le i \le q + 1$, after q queries to the signing oracle.

Compared to the OMSSCDH problem it leaves the choice of the additional MSSCDH instance which needs to be solved to the attacker. Both problems are somewhat natural variants of the SSCDH problem underlying the security of SIDH. However, variants of computational problems used in cryptography are not always as hard as the original problems themselves [13,14].

3.2 Basic Attack

Now, we describe our attacks on the OMSSCDH and 1MSSCDH problems.

Theorem 1. *A solution to the OMSSCDH problem (Definition 3) can be guessed with probability $\frac{1}{(\ell_B+1)\ell_B}$ after a single query to the signing oracle.*

Proof. Assume an attacker wants to solve OMSSCDH given E_A, E_B and $\ker(\phi_B)$. Let $E_{B'}$ be another curve ℓ_B^2-isogenous to E_B and $\ell_B^{e_B}$-isogenous to E. That is, one gets from E_B to $E_{B'}$ via backtracking the last ℓ_B-isogeny step of ϕ_B. One could guess such an $E_{B'}$ with probability $\frac{\ell_B - 1}{(\ell_B + 1)\ell_B}$ even without knowing ϕ_B .

Then, the attacker can query the oracle on $E_{B'}$ to receive $E_{AB'}$. Now, any curve in the isomorphism class of E_{AB} is ℓ_B^2-isogenous to $E_{AB'}$ as depicted in Fig. 3. Therefore an attacker can guess the isomorphism class of E_{AB} correctly with probability $((\ell_B + 1)\ell_B)^{-1}$ finishing the proof. $\qquad\square$

In practice the prime ℓ_B is chosen to be small (usually 2 or 3) and thus Theorem 1 breaks the OMSSCDH problem completely.

Remark 1. Without the condition on the degree of the isogeny between the curves submitted to the OMSSCDH oracle and the base curve, the attack can be made even more efficient. Namely, an attacker can always solve this modified version of the OMSSCDH problem after two queries to the oracle as follows.

The attacker computes two curves E_{B_1}, E_{B_2} of different isomorphism classes that are ℓ_B-isogenous to E_B. Knowing $\ker(\phi_B)$ the attacker can compute

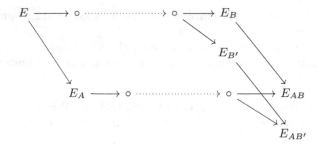

Fig. 3. Query of OMSSCDH oracle on ℓ_B^2-isogenous curve via backtracking one step yields elliptic curve close to target curve

$\ker(\phi_{B_i})$ and they can query the oracle to solve MSSCDH for E_A, E_{B_i} and $\ker(\phi_{B_i})$ for $i = 1, 2$. The oracle sends back E_{AB_i} which are ℓ_B-isogenous to the unknown E_{AB} as shown in Fig. 4. Listing all $\ell_B + 1$ isomorphism classes which are ℓ_B-isogenous to E_{AB_1} and E_{AB_2} respectively, we find the isomorphism class of E_{AB} as it is the only one appearing in both lists.

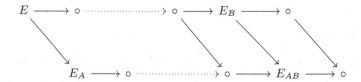

Fig. 4. Diagonal maps are the signing oracle sending ℓ_B-isogenous curves of E_B to ℓ_B-isogenous curves of target curve E_{AB}

Clearly, the attack described in Theorem 1 can be generalised to OMSSDDH, the decisional variant of OMSSCDH. Furthermore, a solution to the OMSSCDH problem implies a solution to the 1MSSCDH problem which yields the following theorem.

Theorem 2. *A solution to the 1MSSCDH problem (Definition 4) can be guessed with probability $\frac{1}{(\ell_B+1)\ell_B}$ after a single query to the signing oracle.*

4   Application to Jao-Soukharev's Construction

We now describe the application of our attack against Jao-Soukharev's undeniable signature scheme [12]. For background knowledge on undeniable signature schemes we refer the reader to [5,8,17].

4.1   Jao-Soukharev Undeniable Signatures

An undeniable signature scheme is a scheme in which signatures can only be verified with cooperation from the signer [5]. Upon receipt of a signature σ from a verifier, the signer engages in a zero-knowledge confirmation (or disavowal) protocol to prove the validity (or invalidity) of σ. The security properties required by an undeniable signature scheme are undeniability, unforgeability and invisibility. Undeniability ensures that a signer cannot repudiate a valid signature. Unforgeability is the notion that an adversary cannot compute a valid message-signature pair without knowledge of the signer's secret key. Invisibility requires that an adversary cannot distinguish between a valid signature and a signature produced by a simulator with non-negligible probability. We refer to Appendix A for a full definition of all security games for undeniable signature schemes.

The Jao-Soukharev protocol takes p as a prime of the form $\ell_A^{e_A} \ell_B^{e_B} \ell_C^{e_C} \cdot f \pm 1$. We fix a supersingular curve E over $\mathbb{F}_{p^2}$ and bases $\{P_A, Q_A\}$, $\{P_B, Q_B\}$ and $\{P_C, Q_C\}$ of the $\ell_A^{e_A}, \ell_B^{e_B}$ and $\ell_C^{e_C}$ torsion of E, $E[\ell_A^{e_A}], E[\ell_B^{e_B}]$ and $E[\ell_C^{e_C}]$, respectively. The public parameters of the scheme are p, E and the three torsion bases, together with a hash function H. The signer generates random integers $m_A, n_A \in \mathbb{Z}/\ell_A^{e_A}\mathbb{Z}$ and computes the isogeny $\phi_A : E \to E_A$, as defined in Definition 1. The public key consists of the curve E_A together with the points $\{\phi_A(P_C), \phi_A(Q_C)\}$ and the integers m_A, n_A constitute the private key. Note that this is equivalent to taking ϕ_A as the private key.

To sign a message M, the signer computes the hash $h = H(M)$ of the message and the isogenies

$$\phi_B : E \to E_B = E/\langle P_B + [h]Q_B \rangle$$
$$\phi_{AB} : E_A \to E_{AB} = E_A/\langle \phi_A(P_B + [h]Q_B) \rangle$$
$$\phi_{BA} : E_B \to E_{AB} = E_B/\langle \phi_B([m_A]P_A + [n_A]Q_A) \rangle.$$

The signer then outputs E_{AB} in addition to the set of two auxiliary points $\{\phi_{BA}(\phi_B(P_C)), \phi_{BA}(\phi_B(Q_C))\}$ as the signature.

Given a signature $\sigma = (E_\sigma, P, Q)$, the first step in the confirmation and disavowal protocols is for the signer to select $m_C, n_C \in \mathbb{Z}/\ell_C^{e_C}\mathbb{Z}$ and compute the curves $E_C = E/\langle [m_C]P_C + [n_C]Q_C \rangle$, $E_{BC} = E_B/\langle \phi_B([m_C]P_C + [n_C]Q_C) \rangle$, $E_{AC} = E_A/\langle \phi_A([m_C]P_C + [n_C]Q_C) \rangle$ and $E_{ABC} = E_{BC}/\langle \phi_B([m_A]P_A + [n_A]Q_A) \rangle$. The signer outputs these curves and $\ker(\phi_{CB})$ as the commitment, where ϕ_{CB} is the isogeny from E_C to E_{BC}. In addition to the auxiliary points of the signature, this commitment gives the verifier enough information to compute E_{ABC} and $E_{\sigma C} = E_\sigma/\langle [m_C]P + [n_C]Q \rangle$, to check whether $E_{\sigma C} = E_{ABC}$. Further details of the confirmation and disavowal protocols can be found in [12].

In the Jao-Soukharev construction, the adversary knows E_A and can compute E_{B_i} and $\ker(\phi_{B_i})$, corresponding to message M_i, from H. The signing oracle then essentially solves MSSCDH for any of the adversary's input messages M_i. The paper claims that under the assumption that the confirmation and disavowal protocols of the signature scheme are zero-knowledge, the unforgeability game describes the OMSSCDH problem. We will show that this claim is incorrect.

4.2   Another Look at the Security Proof of [12]

In [12] the claim is made that forging a signature for this construction is equivalent to solving OMSSCDH, so one would expect our attack to directly break unforgeability. However, equivalence would only be true if an attacker had the freedom to submit arbitrary curves to the signing oracle. In the protocol, an adversary wishing to forge a signature can only query the signing oracle with messages, M_i. In the Jao-Soukharev signing protocol the curves E_{B_i} are computed from message hashes, rather than the messages themselves. Thus, an adversary would need to find a message mapping to some specific curve first for the scheme to be equivalent to OMSSCDH and thus an adversary would need to break the hash function. Forging messages seems therefore actually harder than breaking OMSSCDH.

As a consequence the attack of Sect. 3 applies to the hardness assumption but not the actual protocol in [12]. However, in this section we will demonstrate how a hybrid version of our attack on OMSSCDH and finding "near-collisions" in the hash function allows to reduce the security of the construction for the given parameters.

In accounting for the scheme's loss of malleability due to the hash function we make use of the following Lemma.

Lemma 1. *Let E be a supersingular elliptic curve, let ℓ be a prime, let e be an integer, and let $\{P, Q\}$ be a basis for $E[\ell^e]$. Let $n, m < \ell^e$ be positive integers congruent modulo ℓ^k for some integer $k < e$. Then the ℓ-isogeny paths from E to $E_A = E/\langle P + [n]Q\rangle$ and $E_B = E/\langle P + [m]Q\rangle$ are equal up to the k-th step.*

Proof. Let $m = n + \alpha\ell^k$, for some $\alpha > 0$. Let $\phi_A : E \to E_A$ be a separable, cyclic isogeny of $\deg(\phi_A) = \ell^e$ and $\ker(\phi_A) = \langle P + [n]Q\rangle$. We can express ϕ_A as the composition of e ℓ-isogenies such that $\phi_A = \phi_1^A \circ \ldots \phi_e^A$. Likewise, $\phi_B : E \to E_B$ can be expressed as $\phi_B = \phi_1^B \circ \ldots \phi_e^B$. The single ℓ-isogenies correspond to the single steps in the ℓ-isogeny graph. We will show that $\phi_i^A = \phi_i^B$ for $1 \le i \le k$.

For $i = 1, \ldots, e$, let $\phi_i^A : E_{i-1} \to E_i$ be an isogeny with kernel $\langle \ell^{e-i} S_{i-1}^A\rangle$, where $E_0 = E$, $S_0^A = P + [n]Q$ and $S_{i-1}^A = \phi_{i-1}^A(S_{i-2}^A)$. Define the ϕ_i^B similarly, with B substituted for A and m for n. A proof can be found in [6] that these are ℓ-isogenies and that $\phi_1^A \circ \cdots \circ \phi_e^A = \phi_A$ up to composition with an automorphism on E_A (similarly for ϕ_B). We also have the recursion

$$\ell^{e-i} S_{i-1}^A = \ell^{e-i}\phi_{i-1}^A(S_{i-2}^A) = \phi_{i-1}^A \circ \cdots \circ \phi_1^A(\ell^{e-i} S_0^A)$$

with the analogous result for $\ell^{e-i} S_{i-1}^B$. For $1 \le i \le k$, we have $e - i + k \ge e$ and so

$$\begin{aligned}
\ell^{e-i} S_0^B &= \ell^{e-i}(P + [m]Q) \\
&= \ell^{e-i}(P + [n]Q) + \ell^{e-i+k}[\alpha]Q \\
&= \ell^{e-i}(P + [n]Q) \\
&= \ell^{e-i} S_0^A
\end{aligned}$$

using that isogenies are group homomorphisms and $Q \in E[\ell^e]$. It follows that $\phi_i^A = \phi_i^B$ for $1 \le i \le k$.

Let M be the message upon which the adversary wishes to forge a signature. Let $H : \{0,1\}^* \to \mathbb{Z}$ be the public hash function used in the signature scheme. The hash function determines a coefficient of a point in the $E[\ell_i^{e_i}]$ torsion group and can therefore be treated as a function to a group of size $2^{2\lambda}$ for classical security levels and $2^{3\lambda}$ for quantum security levels. Let 2^L denote the size of this group in the image.

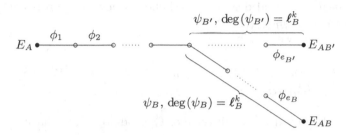

Fig. 5. Isogeny paths between E_A, E_{AB} and $E_{AB'}$. In our attack we use $\psi = \psi_B \circ \hat{\psi}_{B'}$ and have $\phi_{AB'} = \phi_{e_{B'}} \circ \phi_{e_{B'}-1} \circ \cdots \circ \phi_1$.

The attack proceeds as follows:

1. Build a near-collision on H with respect to the ℓ_B-adic metric. More precisely, find two messages M and M' such that the difference between $H(M)$ and $H(M')$ is divisible by a large power of ℓ_B, say a power of size roughly 2^{L_1}.
2. Submit M' to the signing oracle to obtain the signature

$$\sigma' = \big(E_{AB'}, P_1 := \phi_{B'A}(\phi_{B'}(P_C)), P_2 := \phi_{B'A}(\phi_{B'}(Q_C))\big).$$

3. Guess the ℓ_B^{2k}-isogeny $\psi : E_{AB'} \to E_{AB}$, where E_{AB} is the unknown curve corresponding to M. Let $\psi = \psi_B \circ \hat{\psi}_{B'}$, the composition of two degree $\ell_B^k \approx 2^{L_2}$ isogenies with $L_2 = L - L_1$, where $\hat{\psi}_{B'}$ corresponds to k backwards steps on the isogeny path from $E_{AB'}$ and ψ_B corresponds to k forward steps to E_{AB}. This is illustrated in Fig. 5. The probability of correctly identifying ψ in a single guess is $\frac{1}{(\ell_B+1)\ell_B^{2k-1}}$.
4. Find s such that $s\ell_B^k \equiv 1 \bmod \ell_C^{e_C}$. Compute the auxilary points of the signature as $\{[s] \cdot \psi(P_1), [s] \cdot \psi(P_2)\}$.
5. Output $\sigma = (E_{AB}, [s] \cdot \psi(P_1), [s] \cdot \psi(P_2))$.

Theorem 3. *Let* s, ψ, P_1 *and* P_2 *be defined as in our attack. Moreover, let* σ *be the signature* $(E_{AB}, [s] \cdot \psi(P_1), [s] \cdot \psi(P_2))$ *computed in the attack. Assuming that* E_{AB} *is guessed correctly,* σ *is a valid signature.*

Proof. Since ψ takes points on $E_{AB'}$ to points on E_{AB}, we have that $\psi(P_1), \psi(P_2)$ both lie on the target curve. Moreover, as $\psi(P_1) = \psi(\phi_{B'A}(\phi_{B'}(P_C)))$, the point lies in the $\ell_C^{e_C}$ torsion of E_{AB}, $E_{AB}[\ell_C^{e_C}]$. The same holds for $\psi(P_2)$. Although these points would already pass the validation for the signature scheme, they can be easily distinguished from the honestly generated points. The factor $[s]$ in our signature ensures that forged and honest signatures are identically distributed as described in the following.

Recall that $\psi = \psi_B \circ \hat{\psi}_{B'}$ and $P_1 = \phi_{B'A}(\phi_{B'}(P_C))$. Since the order of P_C is coprime to $\deg(\phi_{B'A})$ and $\deg(\phi_{B'})$, and the isogeny diagram is commutative, we can write $P_1 = \phi_{AB'}(\phi_A(P_C))$.
By expanding $\phi_{AB'}$ we obtain

$$\hat{\psi}_{B'} \circ \phi_{AB'} = \hat{\phi}_{e_{B'}-k} \circ \cdots \circ \hat{\phi}_{e_{B'}} \circ \phi_{e_{B'}} \circ \cdots \circ \phi_{e_{B'}-k} \circ \dots \phi_{e_B-k} \circ \cdots \circ \phi_1$$
$$= [\ell_B^k] \circ \phi_{e_{B'}-k-1} \circ \cdots \circ \phi_1.$$

Since s is the multiplicative inverse of ℓ_B^k modulo $\ell_C^{e_C}$, we have

$$[s] \cdot \psi(P_1) = \phi_{AB}(\phi_A(P_C)) \in E_{AB}[\ell_C^{e_C}].$$

Analogously, we have $[s] \cdot \psi(P_2) = \phi_{AB}(\phi_A(Q_C)) \in E_{AB}[\ell_C^{e_C}]$.

Let $P = \phi_{BA}(\phi_B(P_C)) \in E_{AB}[\ell_C^{e_C}]$ and $Q = \phi_{BA}(\phi_B(Q_C)) \in E_{AB}[\ell_C^{e_C}]$. These are the points we expect in an honest signature. In both the confirmation and disavowal protocols of the Jao-Soukharev scheme, the verifier uses the auxiliary points to compute an isogeny from E_{AB} to a curve E_σ defined as $E_{AB}/\langle [m_C \cdot s]\psi(P_1) + [n_C \cdot s]\psi(P_2)\rangle$, where $m_C, n_C \in \mathbb{Z}/\ell_C^{e_C}\mathbb{Z}$ are integers chosen by the signer. This curve is checked against $E_{ABC} = E_{AB}/\langle [m_C]P + [n_C]Q\rangle$ to determine the validity of σ. The two points obtained in our attack span the subgroup $E_{AB}[\ell_C^{e_C}]$, and we have E_{AB} as the correct signature curve, so it follows that $E_\sigma = E_{ABC}$ up to isomorphism and thus the signature is accepted as valid.

Finding a near-collision of L_1 bits on H classically has cost $2^{L_1/2}$. In Step 3 we can then guess the correct isogeny and curve E_{AB} with probability approximately $2^{-2L_2} = 2^{-2(L-L_1)}$. Taking $L_1 = 4L/5$ the attack then has a total classical cost of $2^{2L/5}$, as opposed to the expected $2^{L/2}$.

Assuming that we can find (near)-collisions of the hash function with lower quantum complexity [3], the first step of our attack costs $2^{L_1/3}$ on a quantum computer. Taking $L_1 = 6L/7$, this could lower the complexity on a quantum computer to $2^{2L/7}$, as opposed to the expected $2^{L/3}$. However, it has been argued that quantum collision search might be inferior to classical collision search because of the expensive memory access and quantum memory. For a general discussion on the impracticality of known quantum algorithms for collision search we refer to Bernstein [2].

Clearly, our attack breaks the unforgeability property of the scheme. Moreover, we are also able to break invisibility, since any adversary with the ability to forge signatures with higher probability can simply check whether the challenge signature obtained in the invisibility game (see Appendix A) matches a potential forgery.

5   Srinath and Chandrasekaran Undeniable Blind Signatures

Srinath and Chandrasekaran [22] extend the Jao-Soukharev construction to an undeniable *blind* signature scheme, introducing a third actor, the requestor, to the scheme. It is a four-prime variant of the original scheme, taking the prime p to be of the form $\ell_A^{e_A} \ell_B^{e_B} \ell_C^{e_C} \ell_D^{e_D} \cdot f \pm 1$ and adding the public parameter $\{P_D, Q_D\}$, a basis for $E[\ell_D^{e_D}]$. The requestor computes the message curve $E_B = E/\langle P_B + [H(m)]Q_B \rangle$ using the public hash function, as before. They then blind the curve by taking a random integer $0 < d < \ell_D^{e_D}$ to compute $E_{BD} = E_B/\langle \phi_B(P_D) + [d]\phi_B(Q_D)\rangle$. The blinded curve is then sent to the signer. The $\mathtt{Sign}$ algorithm of the scheme functions in the same way as for the Jao-Soukharev construction. Upon receipt of the blinded signature curve E_{BDA}, the requestor uses an unblinding algorithm to obtain the unblinded signature E_{BA}. The resulting signature is the same as the Jao-Soukharev signature. Thus, signatures as in Srinath and Chandrasekaran are just Jao-Soukharev signatures shifted through another coprime isogeny graph and the scheme is vulnerable to our attack. As before, both unforgeability and invisibility can be broken.

6   Conclusion

In this paper, we investigate the hardness of some isogeny problems used in cryptography. In particular, we show that the OMSSCDH and 1MSSCDH problems can be solved with non-negligible probability by a polynomial time attacker. This contribution is particularly relevant to isogeny-based undeniable signature schemes, as the security proofs for unforgeability and invisibility of currently known schemes assume the hardness of these problems. We give basic attacks against both OMSSCDH and 1MSSCDH, which are also applicable to their decisional variants.

Jao and Soukharev [12] proposed the first quantum-resistant undeniable isogeny-based signature scheme, which was extended to include blindness by Srinath and Chandrasekaran [22]. We present an attack against the unforgeability and invisibility properties of the Jao-Soukharev protocol, showing that an adversary with access to a signing oracle is able to forge arbitrary signatures at lower cost than expected for a given security parameter, λ. To summarise, this is achieved by computing a near-collision on the public hash function H and guessing an ℓ_B^{2k}-isogeny between an honest signature produced by the oracle for one message to the target forgery curve. The classical cost for this attack is

$2^{4\lambda/5}$, with the hash function length equal to 2λ. We postulate that the quantum cost for this attack is $2^{6\lambda/7}$. These attacks imply that parameters should now be increased by 25% to achieve the same classical security level (17% for quantum security). Furthermore, we argue that the equivalence drawn in [12] between unforgeability and the OMSSCDH problem is incorrect, and hence the security proofs in the paper are incorrect. We note that the inclusion of a hash function increases the difficulty of forgery, assuming the hash function is 'cryptographically secure', as the adversary is forced to search for a message that will result in a specific curve, rather than querying the oracle indiscriminately.

Finally, we review the Srinath-Chandrasekaran signature scheme and show that our attack is applicable against it. We also note the same problem with the security proofs.

Acknowledgements. We thank David Jao for his comments on a preliminary version of this paper. Moreover, we thank Neal Koblitz and Alfred Menezes for their inspiring work [13,14]. The work of all three authors was supported by the EPSRC and the UK government as part of the grants EP/P009301/1, EP/P00881X/1 and EP/S01361X/1 for the first, second and third author respectively.

A   Undeniable (Blind) Signature Schemes

Undeniable signature schemes were introduced by Chaum and van Antwerpen [5], differing from traditional signature schemes in that verification of a signature cannot be completed without cooperation from the signer. Following the notation of [17] we denote an undeniable signature scheme Σ by

$$\Sigma = \{\texttt{KeyGen}, \texttt{Sign}, \texttt{Check}, \texttt{Sim}, \pi_{con}, \pi_{dis}\}.$$

$\texttt{KeyGen}$ is the PPT (probabalistic polynomial time) key generation algorithm, which outputs (vk, sk) - a verification and signing key, respectively. $\texttt{Sign}$ is the PPT signing algorithm, taking a message m and sk as input to generate a signature σ. $\texttt{Check}$ is a deterministic validity checking algorithm, such that $\texttt{Check}((vk,m,\sigma),sk)$ returns 1 if (m,σ) is a valid message-pair and 0 if not. $\texttt{Sim}$ is a PPT algorithm outputting a simulated signature σ' on input of vk and m. Finally, π_{con} and π_{dis} are confirmation and disavowal protocols, respectively, with which the signer can prove the validity (or invalidity) of a signature to the verifier. These are zero-knowledge interactive protocols.

An undeniable signature scheme must satisfy undeniability, unforgeability and invisibility. We use the definitions as stated in [5,8,17]. An undeniable blind signature scheme must also satisfy blindness, as defined in [22].

Undeniability requires that a signer cannot use the disavowal protocol to deny a valid signature. A signer is also unable to convince the verifier that an invalid signature is valid.

Unforgeability is the notion that an adversary cannot compute a valid message-signature pair with non-negligible probability. It is defined using the following security game:

1. The challenger generates a key pair, giving the verification key to the adversary.
2. The adversary is given access to a signing oracle and makes queries adaptively with messages m_i, for $i = 1, 2, \ldots, k$, for some k, receiving corresponding signatures σ_i.
   (a) The adversary additionally has access to a confirmation/disavowal oracle for the protocol, which they can query adaptively with message-signature pairs throughout step 2.
3. The adversary outputs a pair (m, σ).

The adversary wins the game (i.e. successfully forges a signature) if (m, σ) is a valid message-signature pair and $m \neq m_i$ for any $i = 1, 2, \ldots k$. A signature scheme is *unforgeable* if any PPT adversary wins with only negligible probability.

Invisibility requires that an adversary cannot distinguish between a valid signature and a simulated signature with non-negligible probability. It is defined by the following security game:

1. The challenger generates a a key pair, giving the verification key to the adversary.
2. The adversary is given access to a signing oracle and makes queries adaptively with messages m_i, for $i = 1, 2, \ldots, k$, for some k, receiving corresponding signatures σ_i.
   (a) The adversary additionally has access to a confirmation/disavowal oracle for the protocol, which they can query adaptively with message-signature pairs throughout step 2.
3. The adversary sends a new message m_j to the challenger.
4. The challenger computes a random bit b. If $b = 1$, the challenger computes $\sigma = \texttt{Sign}(m_j, sk)$. If $b = 0$ the challenger computes $\sigma = \texttt{Sim}(m_j, vk)$. The challenger sends σ to the adversary.
5. The adversary is able to query the signing oracle again, with access to the confirmation/disavowal oracles. They cannot submit (m_j, σ) to either oracle.
6. The adversary outputs a bit b^*.

The adversary wins the game if $b^* = b$. An undeniable signature scheme is *invisible* if $|\Pr(b = b^*) - 1/2\,|$ is negligible.

Blindness requires that an adversary cannot relate message-signature pairs with their associated blind versions with non-negligible probability. It is defined by the following security game:

1. The adversary generates a key pair (sk, vk).
2. The adversary chooses two messages, m_0 and m_1, and sends them to the challenger.
3. The challenger computes a random bit b and reorders the messages as (m_b, m_{b-1}).
4. The challenger blinds the messages and sends them to the adversary.

5. The adversary signs the blinded messages, generating the signatures σ_b^{blind} and σ_{b-1}^{blind}, which are returned to the challenger.
6. The challenger applies an unblinding algorithm to σ_b^{blind} and σ_{b-1}^{blind} and reveals the unblinded signatures, σ_b and σ_{b-1}, to the adversary.
7. The adversary outputs a bit b'.

The adversary wins if $b' = b$. A signatures scheme is *blind* if $|\Pr(b = b^*) - 1/2|$ is negligible.

References

1. Azarderakhsh, R., et al.: Supersingular isogeny key encapsulation. Submission to the NIST Post-Quantum Standardization Project (2017)
2. Bernstein, D.J.: Cost analysis of hash collisions: will quantum computers make sharcs obsolete. In: SHARCS, vol. 9, p. 105 (2009)
3. Brassard, G., Hoyer, P., Tapp, A.: Quantum algorithm for the collision problem. arXiv preprint quant-ph/9705002 (1997)
4. Charles, D.X., Lauter, K.E., Goren, E.Z.: Cryptographic hash functions from expander graphs. J. Cryptol. **22**(1), 93–113 (2009)
5. Chaum, D., van Antwerpen, H.: Undeniable signatures. In: Brassard, G. (ed.) CRYPTO 1989. LNCS, vol. 435, pp. 212–216. Springer, New York (1990). https://doi.org/10.1007/0-387-34805-0_20
6. Costache, A., Feigon, B., Lauter, K., Massierer, M., Puskás, A.: Ramanujan graphs in cryptography. arXiv preprint arXiv:1806.05709 (2018)
7. Couveignes, J.M., Jean Marc Couveignes: Hard homogeneous spaces. IACR Cryptol. ePrint Arch. **2006**, 291 (2006)
8. Damgård, I., Pedersen, T.: New convertible undeniable signature schemes. In: Maurer, U. (ed.) EUROCRYPT 1996. LNCS, vol. 1070, pp. 372–386. Springer, Heidelberg (1996). https://doi.org/10.1007/3-540-68339-9_32
9. De Feo, L.: Mathematics of isogeny based cryptography. arXiv preprint arXiv:1711.04062 (2017)
10. Galbraith, S.D., Vercauteren, F.: Computational problems in supersingular elliptic curve isogenies. Quantum Inf. Process. **17**(10), 265 (2018)
11. Jao, D., De Feo, L.: Towards quantum-resistant cryptosystems from supersingular elliptic curve isogenies. In: Yang, B.-Y. (ed.) PQCrypto 2011. LNCS, vol. 7071, pp. 19–34. Springer, Heidelberg (2011). https://doi.org/10.1007/978-3-642-25405-5_2
12. Jao, D., Soukharev, V.: Isogeny-based quantum-resistant undeniable signatures. In: Mosca, M. (ed.) PQCrypto 2014. LNCS, vol. 8772, pp. 160–179. Springer, Cham (2014). https://doi.org/10.1007/978-3-319-11659-4_10
13. Koblitz, N., Menezes, A.: Another look at "provable security". IACR Cryptol. ePrint Arch. **2004**, 152 (2004)
14. Koblitz, N., Menezes, A.: Critical perspectives on provable security: fifteen years of "another look" papers. Adv. Math. Commun. **13**(4), 517–558 (2019)
15. Kohel, D.: Endomorphism rings of elliptic curves over finite fields. Ph.D. thesis, University of California, Berkeley (1996)
16. Kohel, D., Lauter, K., Petit, C., Tignol, J.-P.: On the quaternion ℓ- isogeny path problem. LMS J. Comput. Math. **17**(A), 418–432 (2014)

17. Kurosawa, K., Furukawa, J.: Universally composable undeniable signature. In: Aceto, L., Damgård, I., Goldberg, L.A., Halldórsson, M.M., Ingólfsdóttir, A., Walukiewicz, I. (eds.) ICALP 2008. LNCS, vol. 5126, pp. 524–535. Springer, Heidelberg (2008). https://doi.org/10.1007/978-3-540-70583-3_43
18. National Institute for Standards and Technology (NIST). Post-quantum crypto standardization (2016). https://csrc.nist.gov/projects/post-quantum-cryptography
19. Petit, C.: Faster algorithms for isogeny problems using torsion point images. In: Takagi, T., Peyrin, T. (eds.) ASIACRYPT 2017. LNCS, vol. 10625, pp. 330–353. Springer, Cham (2017). https://doi.org/10.1007/978-3-319-70697-9_12
20. Rostovtsev, A., Stolbunov, A.: Public-key cryptosystem based on isogenies. IACR Cryptol. ePrint Arch. **2006**, 145 (2006)
21. Silverman, J.H.: The Arithmetic of Elliptic Curves, vol. 106. Springer, Heidelberg (2009)
22. Seshadri Srinath, M., Chandrasekaran, V.: Isogeny-based quantum-resistant undeniable blind signature scheme. Int. J. Netw. Secur. **20**(1), 9–18 (2018)

How to Construct CSIDH on Edwards Curves

Tomoki Moriya[✉], Hiroshi Onuki, and Tsuyoshi Takagi

Department of Mathematical Informatics, The University of Tokyo, Bunkyō, Japan
{tomoki_moriya,onuki,takagi}@mist.i.u-tokyo.ac.jp

Abstract. CSIDH is an isogeny-based key exchange protocol proposed by Castryck, Lange, Martindale, Panny, and Renes in 2018. CSIDH is based on the ideal class group action on $\mathbb{F}_p$-isomorphism classes of Montgomery curves. In order to calculate the class group action, we need to take points defined over $\mathbb{F}_{p^2}$. The original CSIDH algorithm requires a calculation over $\mathbb{F}_p$ by representing points as x-coordinate over Montgomery curves. Meyer and Reith proposed a faster CSIDH algorithm in 2018 which calculates isogenies on Edwards curves by using a birational map between a Montgomery curve and an Edwards curve. There is a special coordinate on Edwards curves (the w-coordinate) to calculate group operations and isogenies. If we try to calculate the class group action on Edwards curves by using the w-coordinate in a similar way on Montgomery curves, we have to consider points defined over $\mathbb{F}_{p^4}$. Therefore, it is not a trivial task to calculate the class group action on Edwards curves with w-coordinates over only $\mathbb{F}_p$.

In this paper, we prove a number of theorems on the properties of Edwards curves. By using these theorems, we extend the CSIDH algorithm to that on Edwards curves with w-coordinates over $\mathbb{F}_p$. This algorithm is as fast as (or a little bit faster than) the algorithm proposed by Meyer and Reith.

Keywords: Isogeny-based cryptography · Montgomery curves · Edwards curves · CSIDH · Post-quantum cryptography

1   Introduction

Currently, there are two popular public-key cryptosystems: RSA [23], whose security is based on the computational complexity of the Prime Factorization Problem, and Elliptic Curve Cryptography [14,17], whose security is based on the computational complexity of the Discrete Logarithm Problem. However, Shor pointed out in 1994 that both the Prime Factorization Problem and the Discrete Logarithm Problem can be solved in polynomial time by using a quantum computer [24,25]. This means we should develop new cryptosystems which cannot be broken by quantum computers. We call such cryptosystems post quantum cryptography (PQC).

© Springer Nature Switzerland AG 2020
S. Jarecki (Ed.): CT-RSA 2020, LNCS 12006, pp. 512–537, 2020.
https://doi.org/10.1007/978-3-030-40186-3_22

Isogeny-based cryptography is a branch of public-key cryptography based on the computational complexity of the Isogeny Problem, which is a problem arising when we calculate isogenies between two given elliptic curves. It is considered as a candidate of PQC. Jao and De Feo proposed a Diffie-Hellman type isogeny-based key exchange protocol, called SIDH (Supersingular Isogeny Diffie-Hellman), in 2011 [12]. SIKE (Supersingular Isogeny Key Encapsulation) [1], which is derived from SIDH, is a round 2 candidate in the NIST PQC standardization competition [21]. The SIDH calculation uses supersingular elliptic curves over $\mathbb{F}_{p^2}$. Castryck, Lange, Martindale, Panny, and Renes proposed another Diffie-Hellman type of isogeny-based key exchange protocol, called CSIDH (Commutative Supersingular Isogeny Diffie-Hellman), in 2018 [4]. Its calculation uses supersingular elliptic curves over $\mathbb{F}_p$.

CSIDH is based on a commutative group action on $\mathbb{F}_p$-isomorphism classes of supersingular Montgomery curves defined over $\mathbb{F}_p$. In order to calculate this group action, we need to generate a point in $\ker(\pi_p - 1)$ or in $\ker(\pi_p + 1)$ and determine which set the point belongs to, where π_p is the p-Frobenius map. Castryck, Lange, Martindale, Panny, and Renes showed that if we take a random element from $\mathbb{F}_p$ as an x-coordinate of a point in a Montgomery curve and determine whether y-coordinate of the point belongs to $\mathbb{F}_p$ or not [4], then we can get a point in $\ker(\pi_p - 1)$ or in $\ker(\pi_p + 1)$ and determine which set the point belongs to. They also showed that a Montgomery coefficient is unique up to $\mathbb{F}_p$-isomorphism [4]. Since it is known that a group operation of a Montgomery curve can be calculated using only the x-coordinates of the points [18] and that isogenies between Montgomery curves can be also calculated by using only the x-coordinates of the points of the kernel [6,16], we can compute a CSIDH group action using only $\mathbb{F}_p$-arithmetic.

Table 1. Comparing CSIDH algorithms on Montgomery curves and Edwards curves

	Group operations	Calculation of isogenies	Kernel points
Montgomery	✓	✓	✓
Edwards (y-coordinate)	✓	✓	✓
Edwards (w-coordinate)	✓	✓	Not trivial

Meyer and Reith proposed a faster CSIDH algorithm in 2018 [16]. This algorithm calculates isogenies over Edwards curves instead of Montgomery curves, by using a birational map between a Montgomery curve and an Edwards curve. In this algorithm, a method for generating a point in $\ker(\pi_p - 1)$ or in $\ker(\pi_p + 1)$ and determining which set the point belongs to is the same as in the original CSIDH algorithm [4]. Hence, a question arises: How do we calculate the CSIDH algorithm on *purely* Edwards curves over $\mathbb{F}_p$?

There are two special coordinates (the y-coordinate and the w-coordinate) on Edwards curves for efficiently calculating the group operation [5,10] and isogenies [5,13,19] respectively. For a point P in an Edwards curve, if the y-coordinate of P is in $\mathbb{F}_p$, then P always belongs to $\ker(\pi_p - 1)$ or $\ker(\pi_p + 1)$.

Therefore, it is not difficult to construct the CSIDH algorithm on Edwards curves with y-coordinates. We detail this algorithm in the full paper of this paper [20, Appendix C]. However, if we take a random element from $\mathbb{F}_p$ as the w-coordinate of a point on an Edwards curve, the point is sometimes defined outside of $\mathbb{F}_{p^2}$ (defined over $\mathbb{F}_{p^4}$). Since the points in $\ker(\pi_p - 1)$ and those in $\ker(\pi_p + 1)$ are defined over $\mathbb{F}_{p^2}$, it is not a trivial task to run the CSIDH algorithm using only Edwards curves over $\mathbb{F}_p$ with w-coordinates.

We summarize the above discussion in Table 1.

1.1   Our Results

In this paper, we prove four important theorems about the w-coordinate on Edwards curves and use them to construct a new implementation of the CSIDH key exchange. First, we show that if we take a random element from the set of square elements in $\mathbb{F}_p$ as the w-coordinate of a point P and determine whether the w-coordinate of $2P$ is square in $\mathbb{F}_p$ or not, then we can generate a point in $\ker(\pi_p - 1)$ or in $\ker(\pi_p + 1)$ and determine which set the point belongs to. Specifically, if the w-coordinate of $2P$ is square, then this coordinate represents a point in $\ker(\pi_p + 1)$, and if the w-coordinate of $2P$ is not square, then the reciprocal of this coordinate represents a point in $\ker(\pi_p - 1)$. Second, we show that there is no difference between the probability of generating a point in $\ker(\pi_p - 1)$ and the probability of generating a point in $\ker(\pi_p + 1)$ in the previous way. Third, we prove the probability that we get a point of order ℓ_i is $1 - 1/\ell_i$, like Montgomery curves. Finally, we show that an Edwards coefficient is unique up to an $\mathbb{F}_p$-isomorphism, like a Montgomery coefficient.

By using these theorems, we construct a non-trivial new implementation of the CSIDH key exchange that uses w-coordinates on Edwards curves non-trivially (Algorithm 2). We show that our algorithm is as fast as (or a little bit faster than) the algorithm proposed by Meyer and Reith [16], which as far as we know, is the state of the art. This fact can be also confirmed from data obtained by the implementation (Table 2).

2   Preliminaries

2.1   Basic Mathematical Concepts

Here, we explain basic mathematical concepts behind isogeny-based cryptography.

Let $\mathbb{L}$ be a field, and $\mathbb{L}'$ be an algebraic extension field of $\mathbb{L}$. An elliptic curve E defined over $\mathbb{L}$ is a non-singular algebraic curve defined over $\mathbb{L}$ of genus one. Denote by $E(\mathbb{L}')$ the $\mathbb{L}'$-rational points of the elliptic curve E. $E(\mathbb{L}')$ is an abelian group [26, III. 2]. A supersingular elliptic curve E over a finite field $\mathbb{L}$ of characteristic p is defined as an elliptic curve which satisfies $\#E(\mathbb{L}) \equiv 1 \pmod{p}$, where $\#E(\mathbb{L})$ is the cardinality of $E(\mathbb{L})$.

Let E, E' be elliptic curves defined over $\mathbb{L}$. Define an isogeny $\phi\colon E \to E'$ over $\mathbb{L}'$ to be a morphism over $\mathbb{L}'$ which is a non-zero group homomorphism from $E(\overline{\mathbb{L}})$ to $E'(\overline{\mathbb{L}})$, where $\overline{\mathbb{L}}$ is the algebraic closure of $\mathbb{L}$. A separable isogeny with $\# \ker \phi = \ell$ is called an ℓ-isogeny. Denote by $\mathrm{End}_{\mathbb{L}'}(E)$ the endomorphism ring of E over $\mathbb{L}'$. It is represented as $\mathrm{End}_p(E)$ when $\mathbb{L}'$ is a prime field $\mathbb{F}_p$. An isogeny $\phi\colon E \to E'$ defined over $\mathbb{L}'$ is called an isomorphism over $\mathbb{L}'$ if ϕ has an inverse isogeny over $\mathbb{L}'$.

If G is a finite subgroup of $E(\overline{\mathbb{L}})$, then there exists an isogeny $\phi\colon E \to E'$ whose kernel is G, and E' is unique up to an $\overline{\mathbb{L}}$-isomorphism [26, Proposition I II.4.12]. This isogeny can be efficiently calculated by using Vélu formulas [27]. We denote a representative of E' by E/G.

$E[k]$ ($k \in \mathbb{Z}_{>0}$) is defined as the k-torsion subgroup of $E(\overline{\mathbb{L}})$. For an endomorphism ϕ of E, we sometimes denote $\ker \phi$ by $E[\phi]$.

Let $\mathbb{L}$ be a number field, and $\mathcal{O}$ be an order in $\mathbb{L}$. A fractional ideal $\mathfrak{a}$ of $\mathcal{O}$ is a finitely generated $\mathcal{O}$-submodule of $\mathbb{L}$ which satisfies $\alpha\mathfrak{a} \subset \mathcal{O}$ for some $\alpha \in \mathcal{O} \setminus \{0\}$. An invertible fractional ideal $\mathfrak{a}$ of $\mathcal{O}$ is defined as a fractional ideal of $\mathcal{O}$ which satisfies $\mathfrak{a}\mathfrak{b} = \mathcal{O}$ for some fractional ideal $\mathfrak{b}$ of $\mathcal{O}$. The fractional ideal $\mathfrak{b}$ is represented as $\mathfrak{a}^{-1}$. If a fractional ideal $\mathfrak{a}$ is contained in $\mathcal{O}$, then $\mathfrak{a}$ is called an integral ideal of $\mathcal{O}$.

Let $I(\mathcal{O})$ be a set of invertible fractional ideals of $\mathcal{O}$. $I(\mathcal{O})$ is an abelian group derived from multiplication of ideals with the identity $\mathcal{O}$. Let $P(\mathcal{O})$ be a subgroup of $I(\mathcal{O})$ defined by $P(\mathcal{O}) = \{\mathfrak{a} \mid \mathfrak{a} = \alpha\mathcal{O} \text{ (for some } \alpha \in \mathbb{L}^{\times})\}$. We call the abelian group $\mathrm{cl}(\mathcal{O})$ defined by $I(\mathcal{O})/P(\mathcal{O})$ the ideal class group of $\mathcal{O}$.

The $\mathbb{F}_p$-endomorphism ring $\mathrm{End}_p(E)$ of a supersingular elliptic curve E defined over $\mathbb{F}_p$ is isomorphic to an order in an imaginary quadratic field [8]. Denote by $\mathcal{E}\ell\ell_p(\mathcal{O})$ the set of $\mathbb{F}_p$-isomorphism classes of elliptic curves E whose $\mathbb{F}_p$-endomorphism ring $\mathrm{End}_p(E)$ is isomorphic to $\mathcal{O}$.

2.2 Montgomery Curves

Let $\mathbb{L}$ be a field whose characteristic is odd. An elliptic curve E defined by the following equation is called a Montgomery curve:

$$E\colon bY^2Z = X^3 + aX^2Z + XZ^2 \quad (a, b \in \mathbb{L} \text{ and } b(a^2 - 4) \neq 0).$$

In this paper, we denote the Montgomery curve $Y^2Z = X^3 + aX^2Z + XZ^2$ by $E_{M,a}$. The identity of E is $(0 : 1 : 0)$, and the inverse of $(X : Y : Z)$ is $(X : -Y : Z)$.

Montgomery showed that the group operations on Montgomery curves can be efficiently computed by using x-coordinates [18]. Define a function x as

$$x(X : Y : Z) = \frac{X}{Z}.$$

The function x is not defined at the point $(0 : 1 : 0)$. If P and Q satisfy $x(P) = x(Q)$, then $P = Q$ or $P = -Q$. Next define a function $\mathbf{x}$ as $\mathbf{x}(X : Y : Z) = (X : Z)$. We call $\mathbf{x}(P)$ the projective x-coordinates of P.

Let P be a point on E. Let $A/C = a$ and $B/C = b$. Let $(X : Z) = \mathbf{x}(P)$. The projective x-coordinates $(X' : Z')$ of $2P$ are calculated as follows [18]:

$$X' = 4C(X + Z)^2(X - Z)^2, \quad Z' = 4XZ(4C(X - Z)^2 + (A + 2C)4XZ). \quad (1)$$

The computational cost is $4\mathbf{M} + 2\mathbf{S} + 4\mathbf{a}$. If $Z = 1$, the computational cost is $4\mathbf{M} + 1\mathbf{S} + 5\mathbf{a}$. (We denote field multiplications by $\mathbf{M}$, field squarings by $\mathbf{S}$, and field additions or subtractions or doublings by $\mathbf{a}$.)

Let P_1 and P_2 be points on E, and $(X_1 : Z_1) = \mathbf{x}(P_1)$, $(X_2 : Z_2) = \mathbf{x}(P_2)$. Let $(X_0 : Z_0) = \mathbf{x}(P_1 - P_2)$. The projective x-coordinates $(X_3 : Z_3)$ of $P_1 + P_2$ are calculated as follows [18]:

$$X_3 = Z_0(X_1 X_2 - Z_1 Z_2)^2, \quad Z_3 = X_0(X_1 Z_2 - X_2 Z_1)^2. \tag{2}$$

The computational cost is $4\mathbf{M} + 2\mathbf{S} + 6\mathbf{a}$. If $Z_0 = 1$, the computational cost is $3\mathbf{M} + 2\mathbf{S} + 6\mathbf{a}$.

Costello and Hisil proposed efficient calculations for odd-degree isogenies by using x-coordinates [6], and Meyer and Reith improved them [16]. Let ℓ be an odd integer and s be the integer which satisfies that $\ell = 2s + 1$. Let P be a point on E, and $(X : Z) = \mathbf{x}(P)$. Let Q be an ℓ-order point on E, and $(X_1 : Z_1) = \mathbf{x}(Q)$. Let $(X_k : Z_k) = \mathbf{x}(kQ)$. Let $E' = E/\langle Q \rangle$ and ϕ be an isogeny $\phi \colon E \to E'$ with $\ker \phi = \langle Q \rangle$. The projective x-coordinates $(X' : Z')$ of $\phi(P)$ are calculated as follows [6]:

$$X' = X \cdot \prod_{i=1}^{s}(XX_i - ZZ_i)^2, \quad Z' = Z \cdot \prod_{i=1}^{s}(XZ_i - ZX_i)^2. \tag{3}$$

The computational cost is $(4s)\mathbf{M} + 2\mathbf{S} + (4s + 2)\mathbf{a}$. Let $A/C = a$. The curve coefficient $a' = A'/C'$ of E' is calculated as follows [16]:

$$\tilde{a} = A + 2C, \quad \tilde{d} = A - 2C, \quad \tilde{a}' = \tilde{a}^\ell \cdot \prod_{i=1}^{s}(X_i + Z_i)^8,$$

$$\tilde{d}' = \tilde{d}^\ell \cdot \prod_{i=1}^{s}(X_i - Z_i)^8, \quad A' = 2(\tilde{a}' + \tilde{d}'), \quad C' = \tilde{a}' - \tilde{d}'. \tag{4}$$

The computational cost is $(2s + 2)\mathbf{M} + 6\mathbf{S} + (2s + 6)\mathbf{a}$ and that of the two s-th powers. Since $X_i + Z_i$ and $X_i - Z_i$ are also used for calculating $\phi(P)$, the computational cost of calculating $\phi(P)$ and E' is $(6s + 2)\mathbf{M} + 8\mathbf{S} + (4s + 8)\mathbf{a}$ and that of the two s-th powers.

Appendix A.1 describes why the computational costs are as above.

2.3 Edwards Curves

In 2007, Edwards introduced a new form of an elliptic curve [9]. Bernstein and Lange extended these curves to another form in 2007, called Edwards curves [3]. For representing points at infinity, Hisil, Wong, Carter, and Dawson proposed projective closures of Edwards curves in $\mathbb{P}^3$ in 2008 [11].

Let $\mathbb{L}$ be a field. If an elliptic curve E is defined by the following equations, E is called an Edwards curve [11]:

$$E \colon X^2 + Y^2 = Z^2 + dT^2, \quad XY = ZT \quad (d \in \mathbb{L} \text{ and } d \neq 0, 1).$$

In this paper, we denote the Edwards curve $X^2 + Y^2 = Z^2 + dT^2$, $XY = ZT$ by E_d. The identity of E_d is $(0 : 1 : 1 : 0)$, which we will denote by 0_d for simplicity, while the inverse of $(X : Y : Z : T)$ is $(-X : Y : Z : -T)$. We obtain the group addition formulas as follows [11]:

$$(X_1 : Y_1 : Z_1 : T_1) + (X_2 : Y_2 : Z_2 : T_2)$$
$$= ((X_1 Y_2 + Y_1 X_2)(Z_1 Z_2 - dT_1 T_2) : (Y_1 Y_2 - X_1 X_2)(Z_1 Z_2 + dT_1 T_2) \qquad (5)$$
$$: (Z_1 Z_2 - dT_1 T_2)(Z_1 Z_2 + dT_1 T_2) : (Y_1 Y_2 - X_1 X_2)(X_1 Y_2 + Y_1 X_2)).$$

For simplicity, we will sometimes consider an Edwards curve to be an affine curve defined by the following equation:

$$E: x^2 + y^2 = 1 + dx^2 y^2 \quad (d \in \mathbb{L} \text{ and } d \neq 0, 1),$$

where $x = X/Z$ and $y = Y/Z$. In this equation, only $(\pm\sqrt{d} : 0 : 0 : 1)$ and $(0 : \pm\sqrt{d} : 0 : 1)$ are points at infinity. $(\pm\sqrt{d} : 0 : 0 : 1)$ are points of order 2, and $(0 : \pm\sqrt{d} : 0 : 1)$ are points of order 4. Hence, if the order of a point P on E_d is neither 2 nor 4, P can be represented in affine coordinates (x, y).

In [5,19] it was showed that the group calculations of Edwards curves can be efficiently performed by using the y-coordinate. Define a function y as

$$y(X : Y : Z : T) = \begin{cases} \frac{Y}{Z} & (\text{if } Z \neq 0) \\ \infty & (\text{if } Z = 0 \text{ (points at infinity)}) \end{cases}.$$

We call $y(P)$ the y-coordinate of P. If P and Q satisfy that $y(P) = y(Q)$, then $P = Q$ or $P = -Q$. Define a function $\mathbf{y}$ as $\mathbf{y}(X : Y : Z : T) = (Y : Z)$. We call $\mathbf{y}(P)$ the projective y-coordinates of P.

Let P be a point on E_d, and $(Y : Z) = \mathbf{y}(P)$. Let $D/C = d$. The projective y-coordinates $(Y' : Z')$ of $2P$ are calculated as follows [5]:

$$\begin{aligned} Y' &= (C - D)Y^2 Z^2 - (Z^2 - Y^2) \cdot ((C - D)Y^2 + C(Z^2 - Y^2)), \\ Z' &= (C - D)Y^2 Z^2 + (Z^2 - Y^2) \cdot ((C - D)Y^2 + C(Z^2 - Y^2)). \end{aligned} \qquad (6)$$

The computational cost is $4\mathbf{M} + 2\mathbf{S} + 5\mathbf{a}$. If $Z = 1$, the computational cost is $3\mathbf{M} + 1\mathbf{S} + 5\mathbf{a}$.

Let P_1 and P_2 be points on E_d, and $(Y_1 : Z_1) = \mathbf{y}(P_1)$, $(Y_2 : Z_2) = \mathbf{y}(P_2)$. Let $(Y_0 : Z_0) = \mathbf{y}(P_1 - P_2)$. The projective y-coordinates $(Y_3 : Z_3)$ of $P_1 + P_2$ are calculated as follows [5]:

$$\begin{aligned} Y_3 &= (Z_0 - Y_0)(Y_1 Z_2 + Y_2 Z_1)^2 - (Z_0 + Y_0)(Y_1 Z_2 - Y_2 Z_1)^2, \\ Z_3 &= (Z_0 - Y_0)(Y_1 Z_2 + Y_2 Z_1)^2 + (Z_0 + Y_0)(Y_1 Z_2 - Y_2 Z_1)^2. \end{aligned} \qquad (7)$$

The computational cost is $4\mathbf{M} + 2\mathbf{S} + 6\mathbf{a}$. In the case that $Z_0 = 1$, the computational cost is also $4\mathbf{M} + 2\mathbf{S} + 6\mathbf{a}$.

In [5] efficient calculations were proposed for odd-degree isogenies by using projective y-coordinates. Let ℓ be an odd integer and s be the integer which satisfies $\ell = 2s + 1$. Let P be a point on E_d, and $(Y : Z) = \mathbf{y}(P)$. Let Q be an ℓ-order point on E_d, and $(Y_1 : Z_1) = \mathbf{y}(Q)$. Let $(Y_k : Z_k) = \mathbf{y}(kQ)$. Let $E_{d'} = E_d/\langle Q \rangle$, and ϕ be an isogeny $\phi \colon E_d \to E_{d'}$ with $\ker \phi = \langle Q \rangle$. The projective y-coordinates $(Y' : Z')$ of $\phi(P)$ are calculated as follows [5]:

$$Y' = (Z + Y) \cdot \prod_{i=1}^{s}(ZY_i + Z_iY)^2 - (Z - Y) \cdot \prod_{i=1}^{s}(ZY_i - Z_iY)^2,$$
$$Z' = (Z + Y) \cdot \prod_{i=1}^{s}(ZY_i + Z_iY)^2 + (Z - Y) \cdot \prod_{i=1}^{s}(ZY_i - Z_iY)^2. \tag{8}$$

The computational cost is $(4s)\mathbf{M} + 2\mathbf{S} + (2s+4)\mathbf{a}$. The projective curve coefficient $d' = D'/C'$ is calculated as follows [19]:

$$D' = D^{\ell} \cdot \prod_{i=1}^{s}(Y_i)^8, \quad C' = C^{\ell} \cdot \prod_{i=1}^{s}(Z_i)^8. \tag{9}$$

The computational cost is $(2s + 2)\mathbf{M} + 6\mathbf{S}$ and that of the two s-th powers. The computational cost of calculating $\phi(P)$ and $E_{d'}$ is $(6s + 2)\mathbf{M} + 8\mathbf{S} + (2s + 4)\mathbf{a}$ and that of the two s-th powers.

Farashahi and Hosseini showed that the group calculations of Edwards curves can be efficiently performed by using the w-coordinate [10]. Define a function w as

$$w(X : Y : Z : T) = \begin{cases} \frac{dT^2}{Z^2} & (\text{if } Z \neq 0) \\ \infty & (\text{if } Z = 0 \text{ (points at infinity)}) \end{cases}.$$

In affine coordinates, $w(x, y) = dx^2y^2$. We call $w(P)$ the w-coordinate of P. If P and Q satisfy that $w(P) = w(Q)$, then $P + Q$ or $P - Q$ is an element of

$$\{0_d, (0 : -1 : 1 : 0), (1 : 0 : 1 : 0), (-1 : 0 : 1 : 0)\}.$$

In this paper, we will denote $\{0_d, (0 : -1 : 1 : 0), (1 : 0 : 1 : 0), (-1 : 0 : 1 : 0)\}$ by $\mathcal{G}_4$ for simplicity. Note that $\mathcal{G}_4$ is a cyclic group of order 4. Define a function $\mathbf{w}$ as $\mathbf{w}(X : Y : Z : T) = (dT^2 : Z^2)$. We call $\mathbf{w}(P)$ the projective w-coordinates of P.

Let P be a point on E_d, and $(W : Z) = \mathbf{w}(P)$. Let $D/C = d$. The projective w-coordinates $(W' : Z')$ of $2P$ are calculated as follows [10]:

$$W' = 4WZ(D(W + Z)^2 - 4CWZ), \quad Z' = D(W + Z)^2(W - Z)^2. \tag{10}$$

The computational cost is $4\mathbf{M} + 2\mathbf{S} + 4\mathbf{a}$. If $Z = 1$, the computational cost is $4\mathbf{M} + 1\mathbf{S} + 5\mathbf{a}$.

Let P_1 and P_2 be points on E_d, and $(W_1 : Z_1) = \mathbf{w}(P_1)$, $(W_2 : Z_2) = \mathbf{w}(P_2)$. Let $(W_0 : Z_0) = \mathbf{w}(P_1 - P_2)$. The projective w-coordinates $(W_3 : Z_3)$ of $P_1 + P_2$ are calculated as follows [10]:

$$W_3 = Z_0(W_1Z_2 - W_2Z_1)^2, \quad Z_3 = W_0(W_1W_2 - Z_1Z_2)^2. \tag{11}$$

The computational cost is $4\mathbf{M} + 2\mathbf{S} + 6\mathbf{a}$. If $Z_0 = 1$, the computational cost is $3\mathbf{M} + 2\mathbf{S} + 6\mathbf{a}$.

Kim, Yoon, Park, and Hong proposed efficient calculations for odd-degree isogenies by using projective w-coordinates [13]. Let ℓ be an odd integer and s be the integer which satisfies $\ell = 2s + 1$. Let P be a point on E_d, and $(W : Z) = \mathbf{w}(P)$. Let Q be an ℓ-order point on E_d, and $(W_1 : Z_1) = \mathbf{w}(Q)$. Let $(W_k : Z_k) = \mathbf{w}(kQ)$. Let $E_{d'} = E_d/\langle Q \rangle$, and ϕ be an isogeny $\phi \colon E_d \to E_{d'}$ with $\ker \phi = \langle Q \rangle$. The projective w-coordinates $(W' : Z')$ of $\phi(P)$ are calculated as follows [13]:

$$W' = W \cdot \prod_{i=1}^{s}(ZW_i - Z_iW)^2, \quad Z' = Z \cdot \prod_{i=1}^{s}(WW_i - ZZ_i)^2. \tag{12}$$

The computational cost is $(4s)\mathbf{M}+2\mathbf{S}+(4s+2)\mathbf{a}$. The projective curve coefficient $d' = D'/C'$ is calculated as follows [13]:

$$D' = D^\ell \cdot \prod_{i=1}^{s}(W_i + Z_i)^8, \quad C' = C^\ell \cdot \prod_{i=1}^{s}(2Z_i)^8. \tag{13}$$

The computational cost is $(2s + 2)\mathbf{M} + 6\mathbf{S} + (s + 4)\mathbf{a}$ and that of the two s-th powers. Since $W_i + Z_i$ is also used for calculating $\phi(P)$, the computational cost of calculating $\phi(P)$ and $E_{d'}$ is $(6s + 2)\mathbf{M} + 8\mathbf{S} + (4s + 6)\mathbf{a}$ and that of the two s-th powers.

Appendix A.2 describes why the computational costs are as above.

An Edwards curve has a following property.

Theorem 1. *Let p be a prime and $p \geq 3$. The Edwards curve E_d defined over $\mathbb{F}_p$ is $\mathbb{F}_p$-isomorphic to the Montgomery curve,*

$$E_\mathcal{M} \colon \frac{4}{1-d}Y^2Z = X^3 + \frac{2(1+d)}{1-d}X^2Z + XZ^2.$$

Proof. Bernstein, Birkner, Joye, Lange, and Peters show that there is a birational map between E_d and $E_\mathcal{M}$ [2]. This birational map becomes an isomorphism.

The precise proof of this theorem is given in the full paper of this paper [20, Appendix B]. □

It is known that there is a birational map between a Montgomery curve and an Edwards curve [2]. However, we need an isomorphism for constructing the CSIDH algorithm using only Edwards curves.

Corollary 1. *Let p be a prime, $p \geq 3$, and $p \equiv 3 \pmod 4$. An Edwards curve E_d defined over $\mathbb{F}_p$ is $\mathbb{F}_p$-isomorphic to the Montgomery curve,*

$$E_\mathcal{M} \colon Y^2Z = X^3 + \left(\frac{1-d}{p}\right) \cdot \frac{2(1+d)}{1-d}X^2Z + XZ^2,$$

where $\left(\frac{1-d}{p}\right)$ is the Legendre symbol.

Corollary 1 is easily proven from Theorem 1.

Corollary 2. *Let p be a prime, $p \geq 3$, and $p \equiv 3$ (mod 8). Let $E_{\mathcal{M},a}$ be a supersingular Montgomery curve $Y^2 Z = X^3 + aX^2 Z + XZ^2$ defined over $\mathbb{F}_p$. If $a - 2$ is square, then $E_{\mathcal{M},a}$ is $\mathbb{F}_p$-isomorphic to the Edwards curve,*

$$E_{\frac{a+2}{a-2}} : X^2 + Y^2 = Z^2 + \frac{a+2}{a-2} T^2, \quad XY = ZT,$$

and if $a - 2$ is not square, then $E_{\mathcal{M},a}$ is $\mathbb{F}_p$-isomorphic to the Edwards curve,

$$E_{\frac{a-2}{a+2}} : X^2 + Y^2 = Z^2 + \frac{a-2}{a+2} T^2, \quad XY = ZT.$$

Proof. As $E_{\mathcal{M},a}$ is supersingular, $\#E_{\mathcal{M},a}(\mathbb{F}_p) = \#\tilde{E}_{\mathcal{M},a}(\mathbb{F}_p) = p + 1 \equiv 4$ (mod 8), where $\tilde{E}_{\mathcal{M},a}$ is a quadratic twist of $E_{\mathcal{M}}$. From Table 1 of [7], $(a - 2)$ $(a + 2)$ is not square.

If $a - 2$ is square, the Edwards curve $E_{\frac{a+2}{a-2}}$ is $\mathbb{F}_p$-isomorphic to $E_{\mathcal{M},a}$ by Corollary 1. If $a - 2$ is not square, since $a + 2$ is square, the Edwards curve $E_{\frac{a-2}{a+2}}$ is $\mathbb{F}_p$-isomorphic to $E_{\mathcal{M},a}$ by Corollary 1.

This completes the proof of Corollary 2. $\qquad\qquad\qquad\qquad\qquad\qquad\square$

By using Corollarys 1 and 2, it is easy to convert an Edwards curve into a Montgomery curve and convert a Montgomery curve into an Edwards curve.

3   CSIDH [4]

CSIDH (Commutative Supersingular Isogeny Diffie-Hellman) was proposed by Castryck, Lange, Martindale, Panny, and Renes in 2018 [4].

CSIDH is based on the action of $cl(\mathbb{Z}[\pi_p])$ on $\mathcal{E}\ell\ell_p(\mathbb{Z}[\pi_p])$. Let the prime p be $4 \cdot \ell_1 \cdots \ell_n - 1$, where the $\ell_1, \ldots, \ell_n$ are small distinct odd primes, for Alice and Bob to calculate the action efficiently. Alice and Bob let random elements of $cl(\mathbb{Z}[\pi_p])$ be secret keys and calculate the actions on $E_{\mathcal{M},0} : Y^2 Z = X^3 + XZ^2$. They publish the obtained elliptic curves as public keys. Finally, they calculate the actions on the public keys, respectively. The obtained elliptic curves are identical up to $\mathbb{F}_p$-isomorphism by the commutativity of $cl(\mathbb{Z}[\pi_p])$; therefore, the values of the Montgomery coefficients are the same from Theorem 3. Let their values be SK_{shared}.

3.1   CSIDH Protocol

Before explaining the protocol of CSIDH, we should state the following important theorems.

Theorem 2 ([28, Theorem 4.5]). *Let $\mathcal{O}$ be an order of an imaginary quadratic field and E be an elliptic curve defined over $\mathbb{F}_p$. If $\mathcal{Ell}_p(\mathcal{O})$ contains the $\mathbb{F}_p$-isomorphism class of supersingular elliptic curves, then the action of the ideal class group $\mathrm{cl}(\mathcal{O})$ on $\mathcal{Ell}_p(\mathcal{O})$,*

$$\mathrm{cl}(\mathcal{O}) \times \mathcal{Ell}_p(\mathcal{O}) \longrightarrow \mathcal{Ell}_p(\mathcal{O})$$
$$([\mathfrak{a}], E) \longmapsto E/E[\mathfrak{a}]$$

is free and transitive, where $\mathfrak{a}$ is an integral ideal of $\mathcal{O}$, and $E[\mathfrak{a}]$ is the intersection of the kernels of elements in the ideal $\mathfrak{a}$.

Denote a representative of $E/E[\mathfrak{a}]$ by $[\mathfrak{a}]E$.

Theorem 3 ([4, Proposition 8]). *Let p be a prime satisfying $p \equiv 3 \pmod 8$. Let E be a supersingular elliptic curve defined over $\mathbb{F}_p$. Then, $\mathrm{End}_p(E) = \mathbb{Z}[\pi_p]$ holds if and only if there uniquely exists $a \in \mathbb{F}_p$ such that E is $\mathbb{F}_p$-isomorphic to a Montgomery curve $E_{\mathcal{M},a}$, where π_p is the p-Frobenius map.*

The exact protocol is as follows. Suppose that Alice and Bob want to share a secret key denoted by $\mathrm{SK}_{\mathrm{shared}}$.

Setup. Let p be a prime which satisfies $p = 4 \cdot \ell_1 \cdots \ell_n - 1$, where $\ell_1, \ldots, \ell_n$ are small distinct odd primes. Let the public parameters be p and $E_{\mathcal{M},0}$.

Key generation. One randomly chooses a integer vector $(e_1, \ldots, e_n)$ from $\{-m, \ldots, m\}^n$. Define $[\mathfrak{a}] = [\mathfrak{l}_1^{e_1} \cdots \mathfrak{l}_n^{e_n}] \in \mathrm{cl}(\mathbb{Z}[\pi_p])$, where $\mathfrak{l}_i = (\ell_i, \pi_p - 1)$, $\mathfrak{l}_i^{-1} = (\ell_i, \pi_p + 1)$, and m is the smallest integer which satisfies $2m + 1 \geq \sqrt[n]{\#\mathrm{cl}(\mathbb{Z}[\pi_p])} \approx p^{1/2n}$. One calculates the action of $[\mathfrak{a}]$ on $E_{\mathcal{M},0}$ and the Montgomery coefficient $a \in \mathbb{F}_p$ of $[\mathfrak{a}]E_{\mathcal{M},0}$: $Y^2 Z = X^3 + aX^2 Z + XZ^2$.

Let the integer vector $(e_1, \ldots, e_n)$ be the secret key, and $a \in \mathbb{F}_p$ be the public key.

Key exchange. Alice and Bob have pairs of keys, $([\mathfrak{a}], a)$ and $([\mathfrak{b}], b)$, respectively. Alice calculates the action $[\mathfrak{a}]E_{\mathcal{M},b} = [\mathfrak{a}][\mathfrak{b}]E_{\mathcal{M},0}$. Bob calculates the action $[\mathfrak{b}]E_{\mathcal{M},a} = [\mathfrak{b}][\mathfrak{a}]E_{\mathcal{M},0}$. Denote the Montgomery coefficient of $[\mathfrak{a}][\mathfrak{b}]E_{\mathcal{M},0}$ by SK_{Alice} and the Montgomery coefficient of $[\mathfrak{b}][\mathfrak{a}]E_{\mathcal{M},0}$ by SK_{Bob}.

From the commutativity of $\mathrm{cl}(\mathbb{Z}[\pi_p])$ and Theorem 3, $\mathrm{SK}_{Alice} = \mathrm{SK}_{Bob}$ holds. Let these values be the shared key $\mathrm{SK}_{\mathrm{shared}}$.

3.2   Evaluating the Class Group Action on Montgomery Curves [4]

In this subsection, we explain how to evaluate the class group action on Montgomery curves. Algorithm 1 is the algorithm for evaluating the class group action.

The inputs of the algorithm are a Montgomery coefficient $a \in \mathbb{F}_p$ and a list of integers $(e_1, \ldots, e_n)$. The output is a Montgomery coefficient $a' \in \mathbb{F}_p$ that satisfies $E_{\mathcal{M},a'} = [\mathfrak{l}_1^{e_1} \cdots \mathfrak{l}_n^{e_n}]E_{\mathcal{M},a}$. Let p be a prime satisfying $p = 4 \cdot \ell_1 \cdots \ell_n - 1$, where $\ell_1, \ldots, \ell_n$ are small distinct odd primes.

We calculate a' by repeating the calculations of the actions of $[\mathfrak{l}_i]$ or $[\mathfrak{l}_i]^{-1}$ (i.e., repeating the calculations of ℓ_i-isogenies).

Sampling Points (Line 2–8 in Algorithm 1). For calculating the class group action, we first sample a point which belongs to $\ker(\pi_p - 1)$ or $\ker(\pi_p + 1)$. We take a uniformly random element of $\mathbb{F}_p$. Let the element be x, and P be a point in $E_{\mathcal{M},a}$ such that $x(P) = x$. We calculate $x^3 + ax^2 + x$, which is a square of $y(P)$, where $y(P)$ is the y-coordinate of P. If $x^3 + ax^2 + x$ is square in $\mathbb{F}_p$, then $P \in \ker(\pi_p - 1)$, and if $x^3 + ax^2 + x$ is not square in $\mathbb{F}_p$, then $P \in \ker(\pi_p + 1)$. If $x^3 + ax^2 + x$ is square, we define S to be a set of i such that the sign of e_i is $+1$, and if $x^3 + ax^2 + x$ is not square, we define S to be a set of i such that the sign of e_i is -1. If $S = \emptyset$, we repeat this procedure with another sample point.

Scalar Multiplication (Line 9 in Algorithm 1). Next, we calculate $P_1 = \frac{p+1}{k}(P)$, where $k = \prod_{i \in S} \ell_i$. The calculation uses the Montgomery ladder algorithm [18].

Calculation of Isogenies (Line 10–16 in Algorithm 1). We calculate $P_2 = \frac{k}{\ell_i} P_1$. The order of P_2 is 1 or ℓ_i. The probability that P_2 is not the identity is $1 - \frac{1}{\ell_i}$ [4]. Therefore, with high probability, we get a point of order ℓ_i. Then, we calculate an ℓ_i-isogeny,

$$\phi \colon E_{\mathcal{M},a} \longrightarrow E_{\mathcal{M},a}/\langle P_2 \rangle,$$

by using the formulas in [6,16]. Denote the Montgomery coefficient of $E_{\mathcal{M},a}/\langle P_2 \rangle$ by $a' \in \mathbb{F}_p$. From Theorem 3, a' is unique. We redefine e_i as $e_i - 1$ (if $e_i > 0$) or $e_i + 1$ (if $e_i < 0$), k as k/ℓ_i, P_1 as $\phi(P_1)$, and a as a'.

We repeat this calculation for all $i \in S$. After that, if the list of integers $(e_1, \ldots, e_n)$ is not the zero vector, we return to the **Sampling points** part.

Output (Line 18 in Algorithm 1). If the list of integers $(e_1, \ldots, e_n)$ is the zero vector, we output the Montgomery coefficient $a' \in \mathbb{F}_p$.

4   Main Theorems Used for Our Algorithm

Here, we state and prove four theorems needed to construct the algorithm for evaluating the class group action based on Edwards curves.

First, we state important lemmas in order to prove four main theorems. Refer to the full paper of this paper [20] for proofs of lemmas without proofs.

Let E_d be a supersingular Edwards curve defined over $\mathbb{F}_p$, and p be a prime.

Lemma 1. *Let $p \equiv 3 \pmod 8$. If E_d satisfies $\mathrm{End}_p(E_d) \cong \mathbb{Z}[\pi_p]$, then d is not square.*

Proof. There exists a Montgomery curve $E_{\mathcal{M}}$ which is $\mathbb{F}_p$-isomorphic to E_d, by Corollary 1. If $E_{\mathcal{M}}[2] \subset E_{\mathcal{M}}(\mathbb{F}_p)$, Table 1 of [7] shows that the order of $E_{\mathcal{M}}$ or its quadratic twist can be divided by 8; however, both orders are $p+1 \equiv 4 \pmod 8$.

Algorithm 1. Evaluating the class group action on Montgomery curves [4]

Input: $a \in \mathbb{F}_p$ such that $E_{\mathcal{M},a}$ is supersingular and a list of integers $(e_1, \ldots, e_n)$
Output: a' such that $[\mathfrak{l}_1^{e_1} \cdots \mathfrak{l}_n^{e_n}] E_{\mathcal{M},a} = E_{\mathcal{M},a'}$

1: **while** some $e_i \neq 0$ **do**
2:     Sample a random $x \in \mathbb{F}_p$
3:     $\mathbf{x}(P) \leftarrow (x : 1)$
4:     Set $s \leftarrow +1$ if $x^3 + ax^2 + x$ is a square in $\mathbb{F}_p$, else $s \leftarrow -1$
5:     Let $S = \{i \mid \text{sign}(e_i) = s\}$
6:     **if** $S = \emptyset$ **then**
7:         Go to line 2
8:     **end if**
9:     $k \leftarrow \prod_{i \in S} \ell_i$, $\mathbf{x}(P) \leftarrow \mathbf{x}(((p+1)/k)P)$
10:     **for all** $i \in S$ **do**
11:         $\mathbf{x}(Q) \leftarrow \mathbf{x}((k/\ell_i)P)$
12:         **if** $Q \neq (0 : 1 : 0)$ **then**
13:             Compute an ℓ_i-isogeny $\phi \colon E_{\mathcal{M},a} \to E_{\mathcal{M},a'}$ with $\ker \phi = \langle Q \rangle$
14:             $a \leftarrow a'$, $\mathbf{x}(P) \leftarrow \mathbf{x}(\phi(P))$, $k \leftarrow k/\ell_i$, $e_i \leftarrow e_i - s$
15:         **end if**
16:     **end for**
17: **end while**
18: **return** a

$E_{\mathcal{M}}$ has the only one point of order 2 over $\mathbb{F}_p$. Therefore, E_d also has only one point of order 2 over $\mathbb{F}_p$.

Points of order 2 in E_d are $(0 : -1 : 1 : 0)$ and $(\pm\sqrt{d} : 0 : 0 : 1)$. Since $(0 : -1 : 1 : 0)$ is a $\mathbb{F}_p$-rational point, d is not square.   □

Lemma 2. *Let $p \equiv 3 \pmod 8$. If E_d satisfies $\text{End}_p(E_d) \cong \mathbb{Z}[\pi_p]$, then $1 - d$ is not square.*

Proof. As $p \equiv 3 \pmod 8$, $\#E_d(\mathbb{F}_p) = p + 1 \equiv 4 \pmod 8$.

By Lemma 1, there are no points at infinity on $E_d(\mathbb{F}_p)$. Hence, in this proof, we consider E_d to be an affine curve.

If a point (x, y) belongs to $E_d(\mathbb{F}_p)$, the points,

$$(-x, y), (x, -y), (-x, -y), (y, x), (-y, x), (y, -x), (-y, -x),$$

also belong to $E_d(\mathbb{F}_p)$. If $x \neq 0$, $y \neq 0$, $x \neq y$, and $x \neq -y$ hold, these eight points are different. If $x = 0$ or $y = 0$, the four points,

$$(0, 1), (0, -1), (1, 0), (-1, 0),$$

are different. If $x = y$ or $x = -y$, x is a root of the equation, $2x^2 = 1 + dx^4$. Therefore,

$$x^2 = \frac{1 \pm \sqrt{1 - d}}{d}.$$

Assume that $1 - d$ is square. Note that

$$\frac{1 + \sqrt{1 - d}}{d} \cdot \frac{1 - \sqrt{1 - d}}{d} = \frac{1 - (1 - d)}{d^2} = \frac{1}{d}.$$

By Lemma 1, d is not square. Hence, one of $\frac{1+\sqrt{1-d}}{d}$ or $\frac{1-\sqrt{1-d}}{d}$ is square, and the other one is not square. Therefore, if $x = y$ or $x = -y$, the four points,

$$(x, x), (x, -x), (-x, x), (-x, -x),$$

are different, where x is $\sqrt{\frac{1+\sqrt{1-d}}{d}}$ or $\sqrt{\frac{1-\sqrt{1-d}}{d}}$.

From the above, $\#E_d(\mathbb{F}_p) \equiv 4+4 \equiv 0 \pmod 8$ holds. This is a contradiction. Therefore, $1 - d$ is not square. $\qquad\square$

Lemma 3. *If P is a point of E_d such that $w(P) \in \mathbb{F}_p$, then $(\pi_p + 1)(P) \in \mathcal{G}_4$ or $(\pi_p - 1)(P) \in \mathcal{G}_4$.*

Proof. Since $\pi_p(w(P)) = w(\pi_p(P))$, $w(\pi_p(P)) = w(P)$. Therefore, $(\pi_p+1)(P) \in \mathcal{G}_4$ or $(\pi_p - 1)(P) \in \mathcal{G}_4$. $\qquad\square$

Lemma 4. *Let $p \equiv 3 \pmod 8$. Let P be a point of E_d, not a point at infinity, and $w(P) \neq 0$. Let E_d satisfy $\mathrm{End}_p(E_d) \cong \mathbb{Z}[\pi_p]$. If $P \in E_d[\pi_p + 1]$, then $w(P) \in \mathbb{F}_p$ and is square in $\mathbb{F}_p$, and if $P \in E_d[\pi_p - 1]$, then $w(P) \in \mathbb{F}_p$ and is not square in $\mathbb{F}_p$.*

Lemma 5. *Let $p \equiv 3 \pmod 8$. Let $P \in E_d[\pi_p - 1]$ or $E_d[\pi_p + 1]$, not a point at infinity, and $w(P) \neq 0$. Let E_d satisfy $\mathrm{End}_p(E_d) \cong \mathbb{Z}[\pi_p]$. If $w(P)$ is square in $\mathbb{F}_p$, then $P \in E_d[\pi_p + 1]$, and if $w(P)$ is not square in $\mathbb{F}_p$, then $P \in E_d[\pi_p - 1]$.*

Lemma 6. *Let P be a point of E_d. Then, points P_{odd} and P_{2power} uniquely exist such that $P = P_{odd} + P_{2power}$, the order of P_{odd} is odd, and the order of P_{2power} is a power of 2.*

Lemma 7. *Let P be a point of E_d such that $w(P) \in \mathbb{F}_p$. Let P_{odd} and P_{2power} be points of E_d such that $P = P_{odd} + P_{2power}$, the order of P_{odd} is odd, and the order of P_{2power} is a power of 2. Then, one of the following holds.*

- $P_{odd} \in E_d[\pi_p - 1]$ and $(\pi_p - 1)(P_{2power}) \in \mathcal{G}_4$.
- $P_{odd} \in E_d[\pi_p + 1]$ and $(\pi_p + 1)(P_{2power}) \in \mathcal{G}_4$.

Proof. By Lemma 3, $(\pi_p \pm 1)(P) \in \mathcal{G}_4$. In the case that $(\pi_p - 1)(P) \in \mathcal{G}_4$, $(\pi_p - 1)(P_{odd}) = 0_d$, since the order of P_{odd} is odd and $\mathcal{G}_4$ is a cyclic group of order 4. Then, $(\pi_p - 1)(P_{2power}) = (\pi_p - 1)(P) \in \mathcal{G}_4$.

Similarly, in the case that $(\pi_p + 1)(P) \in \mathcal{G}_4$, $P_{odd} \in E_d[\pi_p + 1]$ and $(\pi_p + 1)(P_{2power}) \in \mathcal{G}_4$ hold. $\qquad\square$

Lemma 8. *Let P be a point in E_d whose order is not a power of 2. Then, the number of points Q which satisfies $w(Q) = w(P)$ is 8.*

Lemma 9. *Let $p \equiv 3 \pmod 8$. There exists a bijection,*

$$f \colon E_d[\pi_p + 1] \cap E_d[(p + 1)/4] \longrightarrow E_d[\pi_p - 1] \cap E_d[(p + 1)/4],$$

such that $f(0_d) = 0_d$.

We now prove four main theorems.

Theorem 4. *Let $p \equiv 3 \pmod 8$. Let P be a point on an Edwards curve E_d such that the w-coordinate $w(P) \in \mathbb{F}_p$, the order of P is not a power of 2, and $w(P)$ is square. If $w(2P)$ is square, there exists P' such that $P' \in E_d[\pi_p + 1]$, $w(2P) = w(P')$, and $\frac{p+1}{4} P' = 0_d$. If $w(2P)$ is not square, there exists P' such that $P' \in E_d[\pi_p - 1]$, $1/w(2P) = w(P')$, and $\frac{p+1}{4} P' = 0_d$.*

Proof. Let (x, y) be the coordinates of P. Let P_{odd} and P_{2power} be points of E_d such that $P = P_{odd} + P_{2power}$, the order of P_{odd} is odd, and the order of P_{2power} is a power of 2. The existence of P_{odd} and P_{2power} are guaranteed by Lemma 6. By Lemma 7, one of the following holds.

- $(\pi_p - 1)(P_{2power}) \in \mathcal{G}_4$ and $P_{odd} \in E[\pi_p - 1]$.
- $(\pi_p + 1)(P_{2power}) \in \mathcal{G}_4$ and $P_{odd} \in E[\pi_p + 1]$.

It is easy to check that $(\pi_p + 1)\mathcal{G}_4 = \{0_d, (0, -1)\}$ and $(\pi_p - 1)\mathcal{G}_4 = \{0_d\}$. Therefore,

$$(\pi_p^2 - 1)(P_{2power}) = \begin{cases} 0_d & (\text{if } P_{odd} \in E[\pi_p + 1]), \\ 0_d \text{ or } (-1, 0) & (\text{if } P_{odd} \in E[\pi_p - 1]). \end{cases}$$

As $\pi_p^2 + p = 0$, $\pi_p^2 - 1 = -p - 1$. Since P_{2power} is a point whose order is a power of 2,

$$4P_{2power} = \begin{cases} 0_d & (\text{if } P_{odd} \in E[\pi_p + 1]), \\ 0_d \text{ or } (-1, 0) & (\text{if } P_{odd} \in E[\pi_p - 1]). \end{cases}$$

Hence, if $P_{odd} \in E[\pi_p + 1]$, then

$$2P_{2power} = 0_d, (0, -1), (\pm\sqrt{d} : 0 : 0 : 1),$$

and if $P_{odd} \in E[\pi_p - 1]$, then

$$2P_{2power} = 0_d, (0, -1), (\pm\sqrt{d} : 0 : 0 : 1), (1, 0), (-1, 0), (0 : \pm\sqrt{d} : 0 : 1).$$

It is easy to check that if $w(2P_{2power}) = 0$, then $w(2P) = w(2P_{odd})$, and if $w(2P_{2power}) = \infty$, then $w(2P) = 1/w(2P_{odd})$. Therefore, if $w(2P)$ is square, then $w(2P_{odd})$ is square, and if $w(2P)$ is not square, then $w(2P_{odd})$ is not square. By Lemma 5, if $w(2P)$ is square, then $2P_{odd} \in E_d[\pi_p + 1]$, and if $w(2P)$ is not square, then $2P_{odd} \in E_d[\pi_p - 1]$.

Denote $w(P)$ by w. By the Edwards addition formula (5), we have

$$w(2P) = \frac{4dx^2y^2(y^2 - x^2)^2}{(1 - dx^2y^2)^2(1 + dx^2y^2)^2} = \frac{4w(y^2 - x^2)^2}{(1 - w)^2(1 + w)^2}.$$

Since w is square, if $w(2P)$ is square, then $y^2 - x^2 \in \mathbb{F}_p$, and if $w(2P)$ is not square, then $y^2 - x^2 \notin \mathbb{F}_p$. As

$$2P = \left(\frac{2xy}{1 + dx^2y^2}, \frac{y^2 - x^2}{1 - dx^2y^2} \right),$$

if $w(2P)$ is square, then the y-coordinate of $2P$ is an element of $\mathbb{F}_p$, and if $w(2P)$ is not square, then the y-coordinate of $2P$ is not an element of $\mathbb{F}_p$.

In the case that $w(2P)$ is square, $y(2P) \in \mathbb{F}_p$ and $2P_{odd} \in E_d[\pi_p + 1]$. Therefore, $y(2P_{odd}) \in \mathbb{F}_p$. Assume that $2P_{2power} = (\sqrt{d} : 0 : 0 : 1)$ or $(-\sqrt{d} : 0 : 0 : 1)$. It is easy to check that

$$y(2P) = \pm \frac{1}{\sqrt{d} \cdot y(2P_{odd})}.$$

As $y(2P_{odd}) \in \mathbb{F}_p$, $y(2P) \notin \mathbb{F}_p$ by Lemma 1. This is a contradiction. We conclude that $2P_{2power}$ is 0_d or $(0, -1)$. Therefore, $w(2P) = w(2P_{odd})$. As $(\pi_p^2 - 1)(2P_{odd}) = 0_d$,

$$\frac{p+1}{4}(2P_{odd}) = 0_d.$$

In the case that $w(2P)$ is not square, $y(2P) \notin \mathbb{F}_p$ and $2P_{odd} \in E_d[\pi_p - 1]$. Therefore, $y(2P_{odd}) \in \mathbb{F}_p$. Assume that

$$2P_{2power} = 0_d, (0, -1), (1, 0), (-1, 0).$$

It is easy to check that $y(2P) = \pm y(2P_{odd})$. As $y(2P_{odd}) \in \mathbb{F}_p$, $y(2P) \in \mathbb{F}_p$. This is a contradiction. We conclude that $2P_{2power}$ is $(\pm\sqrt{d} : 0 : 0 : 1)$ or $(0 : \pm\sqrt{d} : 0 : 1)$. Therefore, it is easy to check that $w(2P) = 1/w(2P_{odd})$. As $(\pi_p^2 - 1)(2P_{odd}) = 0_d$,

$$\frac{p+1}{4}(2P_{odd}) = 0_d.$$

Let P' be $2P_{odd}$. This completes the proof of Theorem 4. $\qquad\square$

Theorem 5. *Let $p \equiv 3 \pmod 8$. Let P be a point on an Edwards curve E_d such that the w-coordinate $w(P) \in \mathbb{F}_p$, the order of P is not a power of 2, and $w(P)$ is square. The number of $w(P)$ such that $w(2P)$ is square is the same as the number of $w(P)$ such that $w(2P)$ is not square.*

Proof. Let the coordinates of P be (x, y). Let P_{odd} and P_{2power} be points of E_d such that $P = P_{odd} + P_{2power}$, the order of P_{odd} is odd, and the order of P_{2power} is a power of 2. The existence of P_{odd} and P_{2power} are guaranteed by Lemma 6. As shown in the proof of Theorem 4, we have

$$2P_{2power} = 0_d, (0, -1), (\pm\sqrt{d} : 0 : 0 : 1), (0 : \pm\sqrt{d} : 0 : 1).$$

If $2P_{2power}$ is 0_d or $(0, -1)$, $w(P_{2power})$ is 0 or ∞, since it is easy to check that

$$P_{2power} = 0_d, (0, -1), (\pm 1, 0), (\pm\sqrt{d} : 0 : 0 : 1), (0 : \pm\sqrt{d} : 0 : 1).$$

If $2P_{2power}$ is $(\pm\sqrt{d} : 0 : 0 : 1)$ or $(0 : \pm\sqrt{d} : 0 : 1)$, $w(P_{2power})$ is ± 1 since

$$w(2P_{2power}) = \frac{4w(P_{2power})((1 + w(P_{2power}))^2 - 4w(P_{2power})/d)}{(1 - w(P_{2power}))^2(1 + w(P_{2power}))^2}.$$

Assume that $w(P_{2power})$ is -1. $w(2P_{2power}) = \infty$. As shown in the proof of Theorem 4, $(\pi_p - 1)(P_{odd}) = 0_d$. Let the coordinates of P_{odd} be (x_o, y_o). It is easy to check that

$$P_{2power} = \left(\sqrt{\sqrt{\frac{1}{d}}}, \sqrt{-\sqrt{\frac{1}{d}}} \right) + Q',$$

where Q' is a point of E_d such that $w(Q') = 0$ or $w(Q') = \infty$. From the addition formula of Edward curves,

$$P = P_{odd} + P_{2power} = \left(\frac{x_o\sqrt{-\sqrt{\frac{1}{d}}} + y_o\sqrt{\sqrt{\frac{1}{d}}}}{1 + dx_oy_o\sqrt{\frac{-1}{d}}}, \frac{y_o\sqrt{-\sqrt{\frac{1}{d}}} - x_o\sqrt{\sqrt{\frac{1}{d}}}}{1 - dx_oy_o\sqrt{\frac{-1}{d}}} \right) + Q'.$$

Therefore,

$$w(P) = \frac{(2x_oy_o + (y_o^2 - x_o^2)\sqrt{-1})^2}{(1 + dx_o^2y_o^2)^2} \quad \text{or} \quad \frac{(1 + dx_o^2y_o^2)^2}{(2x_oy_o + (y_o^2 - x_o^2)\sqrt{-1})^2}.$$

As $p \equiv 4 \pmod 3$, -1 is not square. Since P_{odd} is not 0_d, $x_o \neq 0$ and $y_o \neq 0$. If we assume that $x_o^2 = y_o^2$, then it is easy to check that $2x_o^2 = 1 + dx_o^4$, and

$$x_o^2 = \frac{1 \pm \sqrt{1-d}}{d} \notin \mathbb{F}_p \quad \text{(by Lemma 2)}.$$

Since $x_o^2 \in \mathbb{F}_p$, $x_o^2 \neq y_o^2$. Therefore, $(2x_oy_o + (y_o^2 - x_o^2)\sqrt{-1})^2$ does not belong to $\mathbb{F}_p$. Hence, $w(P) \notin \mathbb{F}_p$. This is a contradiction. We conclude $w(P_{2power})$ is 0 or ∞ or 1.

If $w(2P)$ is square, as shown in the proof of Theorem 4, $w(P_{odd})$ is square and $2P_{2power} = 0_d$ or $(0, -1)$. Therefore, $w(P_{2power})$ is 0 or ∞. If $w(2P)$ is not square, as shown in the proof of Theorem 4, $w(P_{odd})$ is not square and $2P_{2power} = (\pm\sqrt{d} : 0 : 0 : 1)$ or $(0 : \pm\sqrt{d} : 0 : 1)$. Therefore, $w(P_{2power})$ is 1.

We prove that if $P_{odd} \in E_d[\pi_p - 1]$, then $w(P_{odd} + Q)$ is square for all points Q at which $w(Q)$ is 1. It is easy to check that

$$Q = \left(\sqrt{1 + \sqrt{-1}r}, \sqrt{1 - \sqrt{-1}r} \right) + Q',$$

where $r = \sqrt{\frac{1-d}{d}}$, and Q' is a point such that $w(Q') = 0$ or $w(Q') = \infty$. By Lemmas 1 and 2, $r \in \mathbb{F}_p$. Let the coordinates of P_{odd} be (x_o, y_o). Denote $\left(\sqrt{1 + \sqrt{-1}r}, \sqrt{1 - \sqrt{-1}r} \right)$ by R. Note that

$$P_{odd} + R = \left(\frac{x_o\sqrt{1 - \sqrt{-1}r} + y_o\sqrt{1 + \sqrt{-1}r}}{1 + \sqrt{d}x_oy_o}, \frac{y_o\sqrt{1 - \sqrt{-1}r} - x_o\sqrt{1 + \sqrt{-1}r}}{1 - \sqrt{d}x_oy_o} \right).$$

Therefore,

$$w\left(P_{odd} + R\right) = \frac{d(-2x_oy_o\sqrt{-1}r + (y_o^2 - x_o^2)\sqrt{1+r^2})^2}{(1 - dx_o^2y_o^2)^2} = \frac{(-2x_oy_o\sqrt{-d}r + (y_o^2 - x_o^2))^2}{(1 - dx_o^2y_o^2)^2}.$$

By Lemma 1, $\sqrt{-d} \in \mathbb{F}_p$. As $P_{odd} \in E_d[\pi_p - 1]$, $x_o, y_o \in \mathbb{F}_p$. Therefore, $w\left(P_{odd} + R\right)$ belongs to $\mathbb{F}_p$ and is square. Since $w(P_{odd} + Q) = w(P_{odd} + R)$ or $1/w(P_{odd} + R)$, $w(P_{odd} + Q)$ belongs to $\mathbb{F}_p$ and is square.

Let S_+ be the set of points P of E_d such that both $w(P)$ and $w(2P)$ are square and the order of P is not a power of 2, and let S_- be the set of points P of E_d such that $w(P)$ is square, $w(2P)$ is not square, and the order of P is not a power of 2. From Lemma 8, it suffices to prove that there is a bijection $\phi \colon S_+ \to S_-$. Define $\phi \colon S_+ \to S_-$ as follows.

$$\phi(P) := f(P_{odd}) + P_{2power} + R,$$

where P_{odd} and P_{2power} are points of E_d such that $P = P_{odd} + P_{2power}$, the order of P_{odd} is odd, the order of P_{2power} is a power of 2, R is defined as above, and f is the bijection in Lemma 9. As has already been shown, if $P \in S_+$, then $w(P_{2power})$ is 0 or ∞. As $f(P_{odd}) \in E_d[\pi_p - 1]$ and $w(P_{2power} + R) = 1$, $w(\phi(P))$ is square. Since $w(2\phi(P)) = 1/w(2f(P_{odd}))$ and $2f(P_{odd}) \in E_d[\pi_p - 1]$, $w(2\phi(P))$ is not square. As $f(P_{odd})$ is not 0_d, the order of $\phi(P)$ is not a power of 2. From Lemma 6 and the above, ϕ is well-defined. Define $\psi \colon S_- \to S_+$ as follows.

$$\psi(P) := f^{-1}(P_{odd}) + P_{2power} - R,$$

where P_{odd} and P_{2power} are points of E_d such that $P = P_{odd} + P_{2power}$, the order of P_{odd} is odd, and the order of P_{2power} is a power of 2. As has already been shown, if $P \in S_-$, then $w(P_{2power}) = 1$. As $w(P_{2power} - R)$ is 0 or ∞, $w(\psi(P)) = w(f^{-1}(P_{odd}))$ or $1/w(f^{-1}(P_{odd}))$. Since $f^{-1}(P_{odd}) \in E_d[\pi_p + 1]$, $w(f^{-1}(P_{odd}))$ is square by Lemma 4. Hence, $w(\psi(P))$ and $w(2\psi(P))$ are square. As $f^{-1}(P_{odd})$ is not 0_d, the order of $\psi(P)$ is not a power of 2. From Lemma 6 and the above, ψ is well-defined. It is easy to check that $\psi = \phi^{-1}$.

This completes the proof of Theorem 5. □

Theorem 6. *Let p be $4 \cdot \ell_1 \cdots \ell_n - 1$, where the $\ell_1, \ldots, \ell_n$ are small distinct odd primes. Let P be a point on an Edwards curve E_d such that the w-coordinate $w(P) \in \mathbb{F}_p$, the order of P is not a power of 2, and $w(P)$ is square. The probability that $\frac{p+1}{4\ell_i} P'$ is a point of order ℓ_i is $\frac{(\ell_i - 1)\frac{N}{\ell_i}}{N-1} \approx 1 - \frac{1}{\ell_i}$, where P' is a point in Theorem 4, and $N = \ell_1 \cdot \ell_2 \cdots \ell_n$.*

Proof. Let P_{odd} and P_{2power} be points of E_d such that $P = P_{odd} + P_{2power}$, the order of P_{odd} is odd, and the order of P_{2power} is a power of 2. As shown in the proof of Theorem 4, $P' = 2P_{odd}$. As shown in the proof of Theorem 5, for each point $Q \neq 0_d$ in $E_d[\pi_p + 1] \cap E_d[(p+1)/4]$ or $E_d[\pi_p - 1] \cap E_d[(p+1)/4]$, there is a point $\tilde{Q}$ that satisfies $w(\tilde{Q}) \in \mathbb{F}_p$, $w(\tilde{Q})$ is square, and $2\tilde{Q}_{odd} = Q$. It is easy to check that if $Q_1 \neq Q_2$, then $w(\tilde{Q}_1) \neq w(\tilde{Q}_2)$. Therefore, if we uniform randomly take P that satisfies $w(P)$ is square, then P' is a uniformly random point of $E_d[\pi_p + 1] \cap E_d[(p+1)/4] \setminus \{0_d\}$ or $E_d[\pi_p - 1] \cap E_d[(p+1)/4] \setminus \{0_d\}$. Since

$$E_d[\pi_p + 1] \cap E_d[(p+1)/4] \cong \mathbb{Z}/((p+1)/4)\mathbb{Z} \cong \mathbb{Z}/\ell_1\mathbb{Z} \times \cdots \times \mathbb{Z}/\ell_n\mathbb{Z},$$

$$E_d[\pi_p - 1] \cap E_d[(p+1)/4] \cong \mathbb{Z}/((p+1)/4)\mathbb{Z} \cong \mathbb{Z}/\ell_1\mathbb{Z} \times \cdots \times \mathbb{Z}/\ell_n\mathbb{Z},$$

Theorem 6 holds.   □

Theorem 7. *Let $p \equiv 3 \pmod 8$ and E be a supersingular elliptic curve defined over $\mathbb{F}_p$. Then $\mathrm{End}_p(E) \cong \mathbb{Z}[\pi_p]$ holds if and only if there exists $d \in \mathbb{F}_p$ such that E is $\mathbb{F}_p$-isomorphic to an Edwards curve E_d. Moreover, if such a d exists, then it is unique.*

Proof. The first half of this theorem follows from Corollarys 1, 2, and Theorem 3.

Let us prove the uniqueness of d. Let $d_1, d_2 \in \mathbb{F}_p$ such that E_{d_1} and E_{d_2} are supersingular Edwards curves, $\mathrm{End}_p(E_{d_1}) \cong \mathbb{Z}[\pi_p]$, $\mathrm{End}_p(E_{d_2}) \cong \mathbb{Z}[\pi_p]$, and $E_{d_1} \cong E_{d_2}$ over $\mathbb{F}_p$. As $1 - d_1$ and $1 - d_2$ are not square by Lemma 2,

$$E_{d_i} \cong Y^2 Z = X^3 - \frac{2(1+d_i)}{1-d_i} X^2 Z + XZ^2 \quad (i = 1, 2)$$

holds by Corollary 1. Therefore,

$$\frac{2(1+d_1)}{1-d_1} = \frac{2(1+d_2)}{1-d_2}$$

holds by the uniqueness of coefficients in Theorem 3. This equation reduces to $d_1 = d_2$.

This completes the proof of Theorem 7.   □

Now we proved all main theorems. Though the following lemma is not important essentially, we use it to reject points whose order is a power of 2 in the **Sampling points** calculation of Algorithm 2.

Lemma 10. *Let $p \equiv 3 \pmod 8$. Let P be a point on E_d such that $w(P) \in \mathbb{F}_p$ and the order of P is a power of 2. Then, $w(P)$ is 0 or ± 1.*

Proof. Refer to the full paper of this paper [20].   □

5   Evaluating the Class Group Action on Edwards Curves

In this section, we propose a method for evaluating the class group action based on Edwards curves. The theorems proved in the previous section will be used to construct the method. The algorithm is described in Algorithm 2. All of its calculations are done over $\mathbb{F}_p$.

The inputs of the algorithm are an Edwards coefficient $d \in \mathbb{F}_p$ and a list of integers $(e_1, \ldots, e_n)$. The output of this algorithm is an Edwards coefficient $d' \in \mathbb{F}_p$ such that $E_{d'} = [\mathfrak{l}_1^{e_1} \cdots \mathfrak{l}_n^{e_n}]E_d$. Let p be a prime which satisfies $p = 4 \cdot \ell_1 \cdots \ell_n - 1$, where the $\ell_1, \ldots, \ell_n$ are small distinct odd primes.

Algorithm 2. Evaluating the class group action on Edwards curves

---

Input: $d \in \mathbb{F}_p$ such that Edwards curve E_d is supersingular and a list of integers $(e_1, \ldots, e_n)$

Output: d' such that $[\mathfrak{l}_1^{e_1} \cdots \mathfrak{l}_n^{e_n}]E_d = E_{d'}$

1: **while** some $e_i \neq 0$ **do**
2:     $w \leftarrow 0$
3:     **while** $w = 0$ or $w = 1$ or $w = -1$ **do**
4:         Sample a random $w \in \mathbb{F}_p$
5:     **end while**
6:     $w \leftarrow w^2$ (**Theorem 4, 5**)
7:     $\mathbf{w}(P) \leftarrow (w : 1)$
8:     Compute $\mathbf{w}(2P)$ (**Theorem 4**)
9:     $(W : Z) \leftarrow \mathbf{w}(2P)$
10:    Set $s \leftarrow +1$ if W is a square in $\mathbb{F}_p$, else $s \leftarrow -1$
11:    Let $S = \{i \mid \text{sign}(e_i) = s\}$
12:    **if** $S = \emptyset$ **then**
13:        Go to line 2
14:    **end if**
15:    $\mathbf{w}(P) \leftarrow (W : Z)$, $k \leftarrow \prod_{i \in S} \ell_i$
16:    $\mathbf{w}(P) = (W : Z) \leftarrow \mathbf{w}(((p+1)/4k)P)$ (**Theorem 4, 6**)
17:    **if** $s = 1$ **then**
18:        $\mathbf{w}(P) \leftarrow (Z : W)$ (**Theorem 4**)
19:    **end if**
20:    **for all** $i \in S$ **do**
21:        $\mathbf{w}(Q) \leftarrow \mathbf{w}((k/\ell_i)P)$
22:        **if** $Q \neq 0_d$ **then**
23:            Compute an ℓ_i-isogeny $\phi \colon E_d \to E_{d'}$ with $\ker \phi = \langle Q \rangle$
24:            $d \leftarrow d'$, $\mathbf{w}(P) \leftarrow \mathbf{w}(\phi(P))$, $k \leftarrow k/\ell_i$, $e_i \leftarrow e_i - s$
25:        **end if**
26:    **end for**
27: **end while**
28: **return** d (**Theorem 7**)

Sampling Points (Line 2–14 in Algorithm 2). To sample a point that belongs to $E_d[\pi_p - 1]$ or $E_d[\pi_p + 1]$, we take a uniformly random element of $\mathbb{F}_p$. Denote this element by w. If w is 0 or ± 1, we take a random element again. (We reject any point whose order is a power of 2 by Lemma 10). Then, we calculate w^2. Let P be a point in E_d such that $w(P) = w^2$. By Theorem 4, if $w(2P)$ is square in $\mathbb{F}_p$, then there exists a point P' such that $w(P') = w(2P)$, $\frac{p+1}{4}P' = 0_d$, and $P' \in E_d[\pi_p + 1]$. If $w(2P)$ is not square in $\mathbb{F}_p$, then there exists a point P' such that $w(P') = 1/w(2P)$, $\frac{p+1}{4}P' = 0_d$, and $P' \in E_d[\pi_p - 1]$. Thus, we calculate $w(2P)$ by using the doubling formulas on Edwards curves and determine whether $w(2P)$ is square or not. If $w(2P)$ is square, we can use $w(2P)$ as an element of $E_d[\pi_p + 1]$. If $w(2P)$ is not square, we can use $1/w(2P)$ as an element of $E_d[\pi_p - 1]$. If $w(2P)$ is square, we define S as a set of i such that the sign of e_i is -1. If $w(2P)$ is not square, we define S as a set of i such that the sign of e_i is $+1$. If $S = \emptyset$, we go back to the **Sampling points** calculation.

From Theorem 5, the probability of getting points in $E_d[\pi_p - 1]$ is equal to the probability of getting points in $E_d[\pi_p + 1]$.

Scalar Multiplication (Line 15–19 in Algorithm 2). From Theorem 4, it suffices to calculate $w(\frac{p+1}{4k}(P'))$ instead of $w(\frac{p+1}{k}(P))$, where $k = \prod_{i \in S} \ell_i$. To calculate $w(\frac{p+1}{4k}(P'))$ efficiently, we use Algorithm 3.

Algorithm 3. The Edwards ladder using P and $2P$

Input: E_d, $k = \sum_{i=0}^{\ell-1} k_i 2^i$ with $k_{\ell-1} = 1$, $(W_0 : 1) = \mathbf{w}(P)$, and $(W : Z) = \mathbf{w}(2P)$
    s.t. $P \in E_d$
Output: $(W' : Z') = \mathbf{w}(kP)$
1: $(W_1 : Z_1) \leftarrow (W_0 : 1)$ and $(W_2 : Z_2) \leftarrow (W : Z)$
2: **for** $i = \ell - 2$ **down to** 0 **do**
3:     **if** $k_i = 0$ **then**
4:         $(W_1 : Z_1) \leftarrow 2(W_1 : Z_1)$ (doubling on E_d)
5:         $(W_2 : Z_2) \leftarrow (W_1 : Z_1) + (W_2 : Z_2)$ (addition on E_d with $Z_0 = 1$)
6:     **else**
7:         $(W_2 : Z_2) \leftarrow 2(W_1 : Z_1)$ (doubling on E_d)
8:         $(W_1 : Z_1) \leftarrow (W_1 : Z_1) + (W_2 : Z_2)$ (addition on E_d with $Z_0 = 1$)
9:     **end if**
10: **end for**
11: **return** $(W_1 : Z_1)$

If $w(2P)$ is not square, the proof of Theorem 4 indicates that $P' = 2P + Q$, where Q is a point at infinity. Since $\frac{p+1}{4k}$ is odd and an odd multiple of Q is also a point at infinity, $w(\frac{p+1}{4k}(P')) = 1/w(\frac{p+1}{4k}(2P))$.

Calculation of Isogenies (Line 20–26 in Algorithm 2). By Theorem 6 and 7, we can calculate isogenies by using the same strategy as the original CSIDH algorithm. To do so, we can use the formulas on Edwards curves [13].

Output (Line 28 in Algorithm 2). If the list of integers $(e_1, \ldots, e_n)$ is the zero vector, we output the Edwards coefficient $d' \in \mathbb{F}_p$.

Remark 1. To determine whether $w(2P)$ is square or not, we only need to consider W, where $(W : Z) = \mathbf{w}(2P)$.

Recall the isogenies formulas on Edwards curves:

$$D' = D^\ell \cdot \prod_{i=1}^{s}(W_i + Z_i)^8, \quad C' = C^\ell \cdot \prod_{i=1}^{s}(2Z_i)^8.$$

As ℓ is odd, if D is not square, then D' is also not square. At the beginning of the algorithm, we let $(D : C) = (d : 1)$. Hence, we can assume that D is not square. Let the projective w-coordinates of P be $(W' : Z')$, the projective w-coordinates of $2P$ be $(W : Z)$, and the projective coordinates of d be $(D : C)$. Z is not square, since

$$\mathbf{w}(2P) = (4W'Z'(D(W' + Z')^2 - 4CW'Z') : D(W' + Z')^2(W' - Z')^2).$$

Therefore, if W is square, then $w(2P)$ is not square. Moreover, if W is not square, then $w(2P)$ is square.

6   Computational Costs

In this section, we compare computational costs of our proposed CSIDH algorithm and that of the algorithm proposed by Meyer and Reith [16], theoretically. Moreover, we show our result of implementation on three different CSIDH algorithms: the algorithm on Montgomery curves proposed by Meyer and Reith [16] (Algorithm 1), that on Edwards curves with y-coordinates (Algorithm 4 in the full paper of this paper [20, Appendix C]), and that on Edwards curves with w-coordinates (Algorithm 2). The results are summarized in Table 2.

6.1   Comparing Computational Costs Theoretically

Our proposed CSIDH algorithm using only w-coordinates on Edwards curves is as fast as (or a little bit faster than) the algorithm proposed by Meyer and Reith [16]. In this subsection, we explain computational savings of our algorithm relative to the algorithm of Meyer and Reith.

On Edwards curves, the **Sampling points** calculation costs 1S for taking a uniformly random element of $(\mathbb{F}_p)^2$ and requires one doubling on Edwards curves with $Z = 1$ (the cost of $4\mathbf{M} + 1\mathbf{S} + 5\mathbf{a}$) for determining the set which the point belongs to. On the other hand, on Montgomery curves, **Sampling points** calculation entails calculating $Cx^3 + Ax^2 + Cx$ (the cost of $3\mathbf{M} + 1\mathbf{S} + 2\mathbf{a}$) for determining the set which the point belongs to, where $(A : C)$ is a projective coordinates of a. Therefore, our algorithm saves a cost of $-\mathbf{M} - \mathbf{S} - 3\mathbf{a}$ per **Sampling points** calculation.

The **Scalar multiplication** part entails multiplication by $\frac{p+1}{4k}$ on Edwards curves and multiplication by $\frac{p+1}{k}$ on Montgomery curves. Therefore, per **Scalar multiplication**, the proposed algorithm saves the cost of a doubling on Edwards curves with $Z = 1$ and the cost of doubling on Edwards curves with $Z \neq 1$ (i.e., $8\mathbf{M} + 3\mathbf{S} + 9\mathbf{a}$).

The probability that $S = \emptyset$ after performing the **Sampling points** calculation is at most $\frac{1}{2}$, by Theorem 5. Hence, we expect the proposed algorithm to save at least

$$\frac{1}{2}(-\mathbf{M} - \mathbf{S} - 3\mathbf{a}) + \frac{1}{2}(8\mathbf{M} + 3\mathbf{S} + 9\mathbf{a} - \mathbf{M} - \mathbf{S} - 3\mathbf{a}) = 3\mathbf{M} + \frac{1}{2}\mathbf{S} + \frac{3}{2}\mathbf{a},$$

per **Sampling points** and **Scalar multiplication** calculation.

Table 2. Computational costs on each CSIDH algorithm

	Montgomery [16]	Edwards (y-coordinate)	Edwards (w-coordinate)
M	328195	332707	328055
S	116915	116893	116857
a	332822	355533	331844
M + 0.8 × **S** + 0.05 × **a**	438368	443999	438133

The difference between **Calculation of isogenies** on Edwards curves and on Montgomery curves is only in calculating the isogenies. The computational cost of calculating $(2s + 1)$-degree isogenies on Edwards curves is $(6s + 2)\mathbf{M} + 8\mathbf{S} + (4s + 6)\mathbf{a}$ and that of the two s-th powers, while the computational cost on Montgomery curves is $(6s + 2)\mathbf{M} + 8\mathbf{S} + (4s + 8)\mathbf{a}$ and that of the two s-th powers. Therefore, the proposed algorithm saves $2\mathbf{a}$ per isogeny calculation.

From the above, we conclude that our proposed CSIDH algorithm using only Edwards curves is as fast as or a little bit faster than the algorithm proposed by Meyer and Reith.

6.2 Implementations

We measured average of computational costs of 50000 times, respectively. The results are summarized in Table 2. Here, p was chosen as $4 \cdot \ell_1 \cdots \ell_{74} - 1$, where ℓ_1 through ℓ_{73} were the smallest 73 odd primes and $\ell_{74} = 587$, and m was chosen as 5. These are parameters proposed in [4]. Secret keys were randomly taken for 50000 times.

As shown in Table 2, there is no big difference of computational costs among the three different algorithms. The algorithm on Edwards curves with w-coordinates is slightly faster than the other one in our implementation.

Remark 2. Our implementation of the algorithm on Montgomery curves is based on the algorithm proposed by Meyer and Reith [16]. There are some techniques to make the CSIDH algorithm faster [5,15]. We did not implement these techniques. However, as far as we know, these techniques affect only a little or can be also adapted to the our proposed algorithms. Therefore, even if we consider these techniques, we can conclude that there is no big difference of computational costs among the above three different algorithms.

7 Conclusion and Future Work

7.1 Conclusion

We proved four important theorems (Theorems 4, 5, 6 and 7) on Edwards curves and used them to construct a CSIDH algorithm on Edwards curves with w-coordinates. Theorem 4 shows that if $w(P)$ and $w(2P)$ are square, then $w(2P)$ can be treated as a point in $E_d[\pi_p + 1]$, and if $w(P)$ is square and $w(2P)$ is not square, then $1/w(2P)$ can be treated as a point in $E_d[\pi_p - 1]$. Theorem 5 claims that the number of $w(P)$ such that $w(P)$ and $w(2P)$ are square is equal to the number of $w(P)$ such that $w(P)$ is square and $w(2P)$ is not square. Theorem 6 shows the probability that $w\left(\frac{p+1}{4\ell_i}2P\right)$ represents a point of order ℓ_i is almost $1 - \frac{1}{\ell_i}$. Theorem 7 proves that an Edwards coefficient d is unique up to $\mathbb{F}_p$-isomorphism. From these four theorems, we extended the CSIDH algorithm to that on Edwards curves with w-coordinates over $\mathbb{F}_p$.

We compared complexities of the our proposed algorithm and the sate of the art one of Meyer and Reith. We showed that our proposed algorithm is as fast as (or a little bit faster than) the one of Meyer and Reith. Moreover, we implemented three different CSIDH algorithms (the algorithm on Montgomery curves [16], that on Edwards curves with y-coordinates, and that on Edwards curves with w-coordinates), and compared computational costs of them. There was no big difference of computational costs among the three different algorithms. The algorithm on Edwards curves with w-coordinates was slightly faster than the other one in our implementation.

7.2   Future Work

In this paper, we succeeded in extending the simple CSIDH algorithm to that on Edwards curves with w-coordinates. On the other hand, it is important to consider a constant time CSIDH algorithm. There are some proposals for constant CSIDH time algorithms [5, 15, 22]. It is a future work to extend these constant CSIDH algorithms to that on Edwards curves with w-coordinates.

Acknowlegements. This work was supported by JST CREST Grant Number JPM JCR14D6, Japan.

A   Compute group operations and isogenies

Here, we explain how to compute group operations and isogenies on Montgomery curves and Edwards curves.

A.1   Montgomery curves

The doublings formula (1) can be computed as

$$t_1 \leftarrow X + Z, \quad t_2 \leftarrow X - Z, \quad t_1 \leftarrow t_1^2, \quad t_2 \leftarrow t_2^2, \quad s \leftarrow t_1 - t_2, \quad t_2 \leftarrow t_2 \cdot (4C),$$

$$X' \leftarrow t_1 \cdot t_2, \quad t_1 \leftarrow (A + 2C) \cdot s, \quad t_1 \leftarrow t_1 + t_2, \quad Z' \leftarrow s \cdot t_1.$$

If $Z = 1$, the doublings formula (1) can be computed as

$$t_1 \leftarrow X + 1, \quad t_1 \leftarrow t_1^2, \quad s \leftarrow 2 \cdot X, \quad s \leftarrow 2 \cdot s, \quad t_2 \leftarrow t_1 - s, \quad t_2 \leftarrow t_2 \cdot (4C),$$

$$X' \leftarrow t_1 \cdot t_2, \quad t_1 \leftarrow (A + 2C) \cdot s, \quad t_1 \leftarrow t_1 + t_2, \quad Z' \leftarrow s \cdot t_1.$$

The addition formula (2) can be computed as

$$t_1 \leftarrow X_1 + Z_1, \quad s_1 \leftarrow X_2 + Z_2, \quad t_2 \leftarrow X_1 - Z_1, \quad s_2 \leftarrow X_2 - Z_2, \quad t \leftarrow t_1 \cdot s_2,$$

$$s \leftarrow t_2 \cdot s_1, \quad X_3 \leftarrow t + s, \quad Z_3 \leftarrow t - s, \quad X_3 \leftarrow X_3^2 \cdot Z_0, \quad Z_3 \leftarrow Z_3^2 \cdot X_0.$$

The formula for calculating $\phi(P)$ (3) can be computed as

$$t_i \leftarrow X_i + Z_i, \quad s_i \leftarrow X_i - Z_i, \quad t_i \leftarrow t_i \cdot (X - Z), \quad s_i \leftarrow s_i \cdot (X + Z),$$

$$X' \leftarrow \prod_{i=1}^{s}(t_i - s_i), \quad Z' \leftarrow \prod_{i=1}^{s}(t_i + s_i), \quad X' \leftarrow X \cdot (X')^2, \quad Z' \leftarrow Z \cdot (Z')^2.$$

The formula for calculating E' (4) can be computed as

$$c \leftarrow 2 \cdot C, \quad a \leftarrow A + c, \quad d \leftarrow A - c, \quad a' \leftarrow \prod_{i=1}^{s}(X_i + Z_i),$$

$$d' \leftarrow \prod_{i=1}^{s}(X_i - Z_i), \quad a' \leftarrow (a')^4, \quad d' \leftarrow (d')^4, \quad a' \leftarrow a^s \cdot a', \quad d' \leftarrow d^s \cdot d',$$

$$a' \leftarrow a \cdot (a')^2, \quad d' \leftarrow d \cdot (d')^2, \quad A' \leftarrow 2 \cdot (a' + d'), \quad C' \leftarrow a' - d'.$$

A.2 Edwards curves

The doublings formula (6) can be computed as

$$t_1 \leftarrow Y^2, \quad t_2 \leftarrow Z^2, \quad t_3 \leftarrow C - D, \quad t_4 \leftarrow t_2 - t_1, \quad t_1 \leftarrow t_3 \cdot t_1, \quad t_5 \leftarrow C \cdot t_4,$$

$$t_6 \leftarrow t_1 + t_5, \quad t_6 \leftarrow t_4 \cdot t_6, \quad t_1 \leftarrow t_1 \cdot t_2, \quad Y' \leftarrow t_1 - t_6, \quad Z' \leftarrow t_1 + t_6.$$

If $Z = 1$, the doublings formula (6) can be computed as

$$t_1 \leftarrow Y^2, \quad t_3 \leftarrow C - D, \quad t_4 \leftarrow 1 - t_1, \quad t_1 \leftarrow t_3 \cdot t_1, \quad t_5 \leftarrow C \cdot t_4,$$

$$t_6 \leftarrow t_1 + t_5, \quad t_6 \leftarrow t_4 \cdot t_6, \quad Y' \leftarrow t_1 - t_6, \quad Z' \leftarrow t_1 + t_6.$$

The addition formula (7) can be computed as

$$t_1 \leftarrow Y_1 \cdot Z_2, \quad t_2 \leftarrow Y_2 \cdot Z_1, \quad s_1 \leftarrow t_1 + t_2, \quad s_2 \leftarrow t_1 - t_2, \quad s_1 \leftarrow s_1^2, \quad s_2 \leftarrow s_2^2,$$

$$s_1 \leftarrow (Z_0 - Y_0) \cdot s_1, \quad s_2 \leftarrow (Z_0 + Y_0) \cdot s_2, \quad Y_3 \leftarrow s_1 - s_2, \quad Z_3 \leftarrow s_1 + s_2.$$

The formula for calculating $\phi(P)$ (8) can be computed as

$$t_i \leftarrow Z \cdot Y_i, \quad t_i' \leftarrow Z_i \cdot Y, \quad s_1 \leftarrow \prod_{i=1}^{s}(t_i + t_i'), \quad s_2 \leftarrow \prod_{i=1}^{s}(t_i - t_i'), \quad s_1 \leftarrow s_1^2,$$

$$s_2 \leftarrow s_2^2, \quad s_1 \leftarrow (Z + Y) \cdot s_1, \quad s_2 \leftarrow (Z - Y) \cdot s_2, \quad Y' \leftarrow s_1 - s_2, \quad Z' \leftarrow s_1 + s_2.$$

The formula for calculating E' (9) can be computed as

$$D' \leftarrow \prod_{i=1}^{s} Y_i, \quad C' \leftarrow \prod_{i=1}^{s} Z_i, \quad D' \leftarrow (D')^4, \quad C' \leftarrow (C')^4,$$

$$D' \leftarrow D^s \cdot D', \quad C' \leftarrow C^s \cdot C', \quad D' \leftarrow D \cdot (D')^2, \quad C' \leftarrow C \cdot (C')^2.$$

The formulas (10, 11, 12) can be computed similarly as the formulas on Montgomery curves. The formula for calculating E' (13) can be computed as

$$D' \leftarrow \prod_{i=1}^{s} (W_i + Z_i), \quad C' \leftarrow \prod_{i=1}^{s} Z_i, \quad D' \leftarrow (D')^4, \quad C' \leftarrow (C')^4,$$

$$D' \leftarrow D^s \cdot D', \quad C' \leftarrow (2 \cdot 2 \cdot 2 \cdot 2 \cdot C)^s \cdot C', \quad D' \leftarrow D \cdot (D')^2, \quad C' \leftarrow C \cdot (C')^2.$$

References

1. Azarderakhsh, R., et al.: Supersingular isogeny key encapsulation. Submission to the NIST Post-Quantum Standardization Project (2017)
2. Bernstein, D.J., Birkner, P., Joye, M., Lange, T., Peters, C.: Twisted edwards curves. In: Vaudenay, S. (ed.) AFRICACRYPT 2008. LNCS, vol. 5023, pp. 389–405. Springer, Heidelberg (2008). https://doi.org/10.1007/978-3-540-68164-9_26
3. Bernstein, D.J., Lange, T.: Faster addition and doubling on elliptic curves. In: Kurosawa, K. (ed.) ASIACRYPT 2007. LNCS, vol. 4833, pp. 29–50. Springer, Heidelberg (2007). https://doi.org/10.1007/978-3-540-76900-2_3
4. Castryck, W., Lange, T., Martindale, C., Panny, L., Renes, J.: CSIDH: an efficient post-quantum commutative group action. In: Peyrin, T., Galbraith, S. (eds.) ASIACRYPT 2018. LNCS, vol. 11274, pp. 395–427. Springer, Cham (2018). https://doi.org/10.1007/978-3-030-03332-3_15
5. Cervantes-Vázquez, D., Chenu, M., Chi-Domínguez, J.-J., De Feo, L., Rodríguez-Henríquez, F., Smith, B.: Stronger and faster side-channel protections for CSIDH. In: Schwabe, P., Thériault, N. (eds.) LATINCRYPT 2019. LNCS, vol. 11774, pp. 173–193. Springer, Cham (2019). https://doi.org/10.1007/978-3-030-30530-7_9
6. Costello, C., Hisil, H.: A simple and compact algorithm for sidh with arbitrary degree isogenies. In: Takagi, T., Peyrin, T. (eds.) ASIACRYPT 2017. LNCS, vol. 10625, pp. 303–329. Springer, Cham (2017). https://doi.org/10.1007/978-3-319-70697-9_11
7. Costello, C., Smith, B.: Montgomery curves and their arithmetic: the case of large characteristic fields. IACR Cryptology ePrint Archive, 2017:212 (2017). https://ia.cr/2017/212
8. Delfs, C., Galbraith, S.D.: Computing isogenies between supersingular elliptic curves over $\mathbb{F}_p$. Designs Codes Cryptogr. **78**, 425–440 (2016)
9. Edwards, H.: A normal form for elliptic curves. Bull. Am. Math. Soc. **44**, 393–422 (2007)
10. Farashahi, R.R., Hosseini, S.G.: Differential addition on twisted edwards curves. In: Pieprzyk, J., Suriadi, S. (eds.) ACISP 2017. LNCS, vol. 10343, pp. 366–378. Springer, Cham (2017). https://doi.org/10.1007/978-3-319-59870-3_21

11. Hisil, H., Wong, K.K.-H., Carter, G., Dawson, E.: Twisted Edwards curves revisited. In: Pieprzyk, J. (ed.) ASIACRYPT 2008. LNCS, vol. 5350, pp. 326–343. Springer, Heidelberg (2008). https://doi.org/10.1007/978-3-540-89255-7_20
12. Jao, D., De Feo, L.: Towards quantum-resistant cryptosystems from supersingular elliptic curve isogenies. In: Yang, B.-Y. (ed.) PQCrypto 2011. LNCS, vol. 7071, pp. 19–34. Springer, Heidelberg (2011). https://doi.org/10.1007/978-3-642-25405-5_2
13. Kim, S., Yoon, K., Park, Y.-H., Hong, S.: Optimized method for computing odd-degree isogenies on Edwards curves. IACR Cryptology ePrint Archive, 2019:110 (2019). https://ia.cr/2019/110. (to appear at ASIACRYPT 2019)
14. Koblitz, N.: Elliptic curve cryptosystems. Math. Comput. **48**, 203–209 (1987)
15. Meyer, M., Campos, F., Reith, S.: On lions and elligators: an efficient constant-time implementation of CSIDH. In: Ding, J., Steinwandt, R. (eds.) PQCrypto 2019. LNCS, vol. 11505, pp. 307–325. Springer, Cham (2019). https://doi.org/10.1007/978-3-030-25510-7_17
16. Meyer, M., Reith, S.: A faster way to the CSIDH. In: Chakraborty, D., Iwata, T. (eds.) INDOCRYPT 2018. LNCS, vol. 11356, pp. 137–152. Springer, Cham (2018). https://doi.org/10.1007/978-3-030-05378-9_8
17. Miller, V.S.: Use of elliptic curves in cryptography. In: Williams, H.C. (ed.) CRYPTO 1985. LNCS, vol. 218, pp. 417–426. Springer, Heidelberg (1986). https://doi.org/10.1007/3-540-39799-X_31
18. Montgomery, P.L.: Speeding the pollard and elliptic curve methods of factorization. Math. Comput. **48**, 243–264 (1987)
19. Moody, D., Shumow, D.: Analogues of Vélu's formulas for isogenies on alternate models of elliptic curves. Math. Comput. **85**, 1929–1951 (2016)
20. Moriya, T., Onuki, H., Takagi, T.: How to construct CSIDH on Edwards curves. IACR Cryptology ePrint Archive, 2019:843 (2019). https://ia.cr/2019/843
21. National Institute of Standards and Technology. Post-quantum cryptography standardization, December 2016. https://csrc.nist.gov/Projects/Post-Quantum-Cryptography/Post-Quantum-Cryptography-Standardization
22. Onuki, H., Aikawa, Y., Yamazaki, T., Takagi, T.: (Short Paper) A faster constant-time algorithm of CSIDH keeping two points. In: Attrapadung, N., Yagi, T. (eds.) IWSEC 2019. LNCS, vol. 11689, pp. 23–33. Springer, Cham (2019). https://doi.org/10.1007/978-3-030-26834-3_2
23. Rivest, R.L., Shamir, A., Adleman, L.: A method for obtaining digital signatures and public-key cryptosystems. Commun. ACM **21**, 120–126 (1978)
24. Shor, P.W.: Algorithms for quantum computation: discrete logarithms and factoring. In: Proceedings 35th Annual Symposium on Foundations of Computer Science, pp. 124–134. IEEE (1994)
25. Shor, P.W.: Polynomial-time algorithms for prime factorization and discrete logarithms on a quantum computer. SIAM Rev. **41**, 303–332 (1999)
26. Silverman, J.H.: The Arithmetic of Elliptic Curves, vol. 106. Springer, Heidelberg (2009). https://doi.org/10.1007/978-0-387-09494-6
27. Vélu, J.: Isogénies entre courbes elliptiques. CR Acad. Sci. Paris Sér. A 305–347 (1971)
28. Waterhouse, W.C.: Abelian varieties over finite fields. In: Annales scientifiques de l'École Normale Supérieure, pp. 521–560 (1969)

Policy-Based Sanitizable Signatures

Kai Samelin[1(✉)] and Daniel Slamanig[2]

[1] TÜV Rheinland i-sec GmbH, Hallbergmoos, Germany
kaispapers@gmail.com
[2] AIT Austrian Institute of Technology, Vienna, Austria
daniel.slamanig@ait.ac.at

Abstract. Sanitizable signatures are a variant of signatures which allow a single, and signer-defined, sanitizer to modify signed messages in a controlled way without invalidating the respective signature. They turned out to be a versatile primitive, proven by different variants and extensions, e.g., allowing multiple sanitizers or adding new sanitizers one-by-one. However, existing constructions are very restricted regarding their flexibility in specifying potential sanitizers. We propose a different and more powerful approach: Instead of using sanitizers' public keys directly, we assign attributes to them. Sanitizing is then based on policies, i.e., access structures defined over attributes. A sanitizer can sanitize, if, and only if, it holds a secret key to attributes satisfying the policy associated to a signature, while offering full-scale accountability.

1 Introduction

Unforgeability of a digital signature scheme prevents deriving signatures for a message not explicitly endorsed by the signer. This is a desired property in many use cases of signatures. However, it turned out that certain *controlled* modifications of signed messages are beneficial in many scenarios [ABC+15, BPS17, DDH+15, GGOT16]. Over the years, different types of signature schemes supporting such modifications have been proposed, including homomorphic signatures [ABC+15, BFKW09], redactable signatures [DPSS15, JMSW02, SBZ01], and sanitizable signatures [ACdMT05, BFF+09, BFLS10]. In this paper, we focus on sanitizable signatures (3S henceforth). In a nutshell, a *standard* 3S [ACdMT05] allows for altering signer-chosen (so called admissible) blocks of signed messages by a *single* semi-trusted entity, called the sanitizer, which is specified by the signer when generating the signature. The sanitizer holds its own key pair. By using the secret key, the sanitizer can derive modified messages with modifiable parts (called admissible blocks) arbitrarily updated, along with corresponding valid signatures. Moreover, given a sanitizable signature, there is a (virtual) entity, dubbed the judge, who can determine whether a signature

The project leading to this work has received funding from the European Union's Horizon 2020 research and innovation programme under grant agreement No 783119 SECREDAS.

comes from the original signer or has been sanitized, providing accountability. Even though allowing arbitrary modification of signer-specified blocks seems to give too much power to the sanitizer, 3Ss have proven to be useful in numerous use-cases, as exhaustively discussed by Bilzhause et al. [BPS17].

After 3Ss were introduced by Ateniese et al. [ACdMT05], they received a lot of attention in the recent past. The first thorough security model was given by Brzuska et al. [BFF+09] (later slightly modified by Gong et al. [GQZ10]). Their work was later extended for multiple signers/sanitizers [BFLS09, CJL12], unlink-ability (meaning derived signatures cannot be linked to its origin) [BFLS10, BPS13, BL17, BLL+19, FKM+16], non-interactive public-accountability (every party can determine which party is accountable for a given valid mes-sage/signature pair) [BPS12], limiting the sanitizer to signer-chosen val-ues [CJ10, DS15], invisibility (meaning that an outsider cannot determine which blocks of a message are sanitizable) [BCD+17, BLL+19, CDK+17, FH18], the case of strongly unforgeable signatures [KSS15], and generalizations such as merging the functionality from sanitizable and redactable signatures [KPSS18b, KPSS19]. All these extensions make 3Ss suitable for an even broader field of use-cases of (cf. [BPS17] for a discussion), and are directly applicable to our contribution.

In all of the aforementioned work on sanitizable signatures, the sanitizer(s) need(s) to be known *in advance* at signature generation, and there is no possibil-ity to control sanitizing capabilities in a fine-grained way. We note that there is the concept of trapdoor 3Ss [CLM08, LDW13, YSL10]. Although here the signer can grant the possibility to sanitize to different entities even after generating the initial signature, existing constructions do either not provide accountability, a central feature of 3S, or require obtaining the trapdoor from the original signer before sanitizing [LDW13]. This drastically restricts the applicability of 3Ss, their flexibility, and may lead to severe problems when the specified sanitizer is not available.

Motivation and Applications. To illustrate the problem, let us consider an enterprise scenario where policies are associated to different types of documents and documents of some type can be sanitized if the person performing the saniti-zation fullfills the respective policy. For simplicity, assume that sanitizing should be possible if the sanitizer satisfies the policy $P = (\text{IT department} \land \text{admin}) \lor (\text{team leader})$. Now, let's say that the head of IT department has previously signed a document, e.g., an order, which urgently needs to be sent to reseller but some information needs to be sanitized before, e.g., fixing the number of new PCs ordered. Unfortunately, the original signer is not available, e.g., due to vacation. Now, everyone satisfying P should be able to sanitize. Since this covers a potentially large set of persons, there is no availability issue, and the document can be sent in time. Still, the department head (the "group manager") can control via P who is trusted to sanitize the document if required, and there must be means to determine who performed the sanitization in case of a dispute. Realizing this scenario with the state-of-the-art 3S, such as using a sanitizer key per policy and giving the key to everyone satisfying it clearly destroys account-ability, i.e., there is no means identifying the accountable party later on, and thus no satisfying solution can be achieved. To tackle this situation, we intro-duce a primitive denoted policy-based sanitizable signatures (P3S), that allows to sanitize if, and only if, the attributes associated to a sanitizer satisfy the pol-icy associated to the signature, while at the same time providing accountability. We also want to discuss one application of P3S extending the scope of the one discussed in [DSSS19]. In particular, [DSSS19] discusses an application to updat-ing/rewriting transactions (or more generally speaking objects) in blockchains by selectively replacing the hash function used to aggregate transactions (e.g., within a Merkle-tree) by a novel chameleon hash. This adds flexibility to the ini-tial proposal of a redactable blockchain (where entire blocks can be rewritten) due to Ateniese et al. in [AMVA17]. In [DSSS19], everyone who wants a trans-action that can be updated/rewritten can distribute attribute-keys to users who can potentially update the transactions of this entity. Using P3S instead of this novel chameleon hash allows to not only hash transactions/objects but combine it with a signature (as usual for transactions and typically also for other objects in blockchains), we can thus achieve stronger guarantees than in [DSSS19]. In addition to transparency, meaning that no outsider sees whether updates hap-pened (as also achieved in [DSSS19]), using P3S provides accountability, i.e., it can be determined who conducted the update.

Contribution and Our Techniques. We introduce the notion of policy-based sanitizable signatures (P3S). The main idea is the following: At signing, the signer assigns some access-policy P with each generated signature. A sanitizer can sanitize such signatures, if, and only if, that sanitizer has a secret key sat-isfying the associated policy P. Sanitizers can obtain new secret keys for some attributes in a dynamic fashion by a special entity named the "group man-ager", essentially playing the same role as the *"issuer"* in dynamic group signa-tures [BSZ05].[1] The reason for this design choice stems from practical consider-ations: Generated sanitizing keys must only be valid for a single group; In our example mentioned above, the sanitization rights must not work for signatures for another company. However, we also allow that signers and sanitizers can re-use their keys across different groups, e.g., in an enterprise every employee can hold a single key-pair and can participate in multiple groups without generating fresh keys for every group. In our running example, this also means that, e.g., a supplier for our company could sanitize certain signatures using its long-term key (if it received the corresponding secret keys).

We provide a natural formal framework for such P3S by extending the one for 3S. We note that in the case of P3S, with a potentially large sets of sanitizers and different sanitization keys (depending on attributes), make the formal defi-nition much trickier and somewhat involved. Still, we believe that our proposed definitions are clean and easy to comprehend. We also consider a notion analo-

---

[1] If wanted, a signer can also be a group manager *simultaneously, without* sacrificing accountability.

gous to opening-soundness [SSE+12]. Moreover, we propose very strict privacy notions, where even (most of) the keys are generated by the adversary, further strengthening already existing definitions [dMPPS14,FF15,KSS15].

Finally, we provide a construction of P3S which we rigorously analyze in the proposed framework. Technically, the heart of our construction is a recent primitive called policy-based chameleon hash (PCH) [DSSS19], which is a trapdoor collision-resistant hash-function, where the hash computation in addition to the message takes a description of a policy as input. Loosely speaking, there are many different trapdoors and collisions can be found if, and only if, a trapdoor satisfying the policy used for the computation of the hash is known. Looking ahead, the PCH proposed in [DSSS19] combines chameleon-hashes with ephemeral trapdoors (CHET) [CDK+17] and CCA2-secure ciphertext-policy attribute-based encryption (CP-ABE) scheme. In contrast to the original PCH definition in [DSSS19], however, we have to make some minor, yet important, alterations and show that a modified construction from [DSSS19] satisfies our stronger notions. In this regard, we also strengthen the CH and CHET definitions by Camenisch et al. [CDK+17] to also cover keys generated by the adversary. We believe that this strengthened definitions are also useful in many other scenarios. The concrete PCH construction then requires some additional tools and tricks; In order to achieve accountability, we use an "OR-trick", and attach a non-interactive zero-knowledge proof of knowledge, demonstrating that either the signer or a sanitizer performed the signing, or the sanitization, respectively. The expressiveness of the policies supported by the P3S are determined by that of the PCH and in particular by that of the underlying CP-ABE scheme. We chose to build upon the existing PCH framework which covers (monotone) access structures as policies as this seems to be the most interesting setting for practical applications.[2] For a detailed intuition on the construction, see Sect. 4.

2   Preliminaries

Notation. With $\kappa \in \mathbb{N}$ we denote our security parameter. All algorithms implicitly take 1^κ as an additional input. We write $a \leftarrow A(x)$ if a is assigned to the output of algorithm A with input x. An algorithm is efficient, if it runs in probabilistic polynomial time (PPT) in the length of its input. All algorithms are PPT, if not explicitly mentioned otherwise. If we make the random coins r explicit, we use the notation $a \leftarrow A(x; r)$. Otherwise, we assume that the random coins are drawn internally. For $m = (m^1, m^2, \ldots, m^l)$, we call $m^i \in \mathcal{M}$, where $\mathcal{M} = \{0,1\}^*$, a block. Most algorithms may return a special error symbol $\perp \notin \{0,1\}^*$, denoting an exception. Returning output ends execution of an algorithm or an oracle. If S is a set, we write $a \leftarrow_r S$ to denote that a is chosen uniformly at random from S. For a list we require that there is an injective, and efficiently reversible, encoding, mapping the list to $\{0,1\}^*$. A function $\nu : \mathbb{N} \to \mathbb{R}_{\geq 0}$ is negligible, if it vanishes faster than every inverse polynomial, i.e., $\forall k \in \mathbb{N}, \exists n_0 \in \mathbb{N}$ such that $\nu(n) \leq n^{-k}, \forall n > n_0$.

---

[2] PCHs and P3S could be defined for richer policies, e.g., polynomial sized circuits.

Assumptions and Primitives. For our construction to work, we need a one-way function (OWF) f, an unforgeable digital signature scheme $\Sigma = \{\mathsf{PPGen}_\Sigma, \mathsf{KGen}_\Sigma, \mathsf{Sign}_\Sigma, \mathsf{Verf}_\Sigma\}$, and an IND-CCA2 secure, as well as key-verifiable, encryption scheme $\Pi = \{\mathsf{PPGen}_\Pi, \mathsf{KGen}_\Pi, \mathsf{Enc}_\Pi, \mathsf{Dec}_\Pi, \mathsf{KVrf}_\Pi\}$. Key-verifiability means that for each public key exactly only one matching secret key can be found (e.g., Cramer-Shoup (CS) encryption [CS98] in a setting with common group parameters suffices), while KVrf_Π checks whether a given secret key sk belongs to a pk. Moreover, we require a (labeled) simulation-sound extractable non-interactive zero-knowledge proof system $\Omega = \{\mathsf{PPGen}_\Omega, \mathsf{Prove}_\Omega, \mathsf{Verify}_\Omega\}$, and a recent primitive dubbed policy-based chameleon-hash (PCH), recently introduced by Derler et al. [DSSS19].

For the sake of readability, a somewhat informal Camenisch and Stadler notation [CS97] is used. For example, the notation

$$\pi \leftarrow_r \mathsf{Prove}_\Omega\{(g_1) : C = \mathsf{Enc}_\Pi(g_1)\}(\ell)$$

denotes the computation of a simulation-sound extractable non-interactive zero-knowledge proof (NIZK for short) of the plaintext g_1 contained in C (which is assumed to be public), with a non-malleable attached label $\ell \in \{0, 1\}^*$. Sometimes only "verify π" is used for verification of a proof π. It is assumed that the public parameters, and the statement to be proven, are also input to the proof system as the label, and are public (all those values are assumed to be part of π as well). This is not made explicit to increase readability.

All primitives, but PCHs, are rather standard and well-known; We give the full formal definitions of the standard building blocks in the full version of this paper, and only fully restate PCHs. In a nutshell, a PCH = ($\mathsf{PPGen}_{\mathsf{PCH}}$, $\mathsf{MKeyGen}_{\mathsf{PCH}}$, $\mathsf{KGen}_{\mathsf{PCH}}$, $\mathsf{Hash}_{\mathsf{PCH}}$, $\mathsf{Verify}_{\mathsf{PCH}}$, $\mathsf{Adapt}_{\mathsf{PCH}}$) is a trapdoor collision-resistant hash-function, where the hash computation in addition to the message takes a description of a policy as input. Loosely speaking there can be many different trapdoors and collisions can be found if, and only if, a trapdoor satisfying the policy used for the computation of the hash is known.

Before we recall PCHs, we need to define what an access structure is.

Definition 1 (Access Structure). *Let $\mathbb{U}$ denote the universe of attributes. A collection $\mathbb{A} \in 2^{\mathbb{U}} \setminus \{\emptyset\}$ of non-empty sets is an access structure on $\mathbb{U}$. The sets in $\mathbb{A}$ are called the authorized sets, and the sets not in $\mathbb{A}$ are called the unauthorized sets. A collection $\mathbb{A} \in 2^{\mathbb{U}} \setminus \{\emptyset\}$ is called monotone if $\forall\, B, C \in \mathbb{A} : $ if $B \in \mathbb{A}$ and $B \subseteq C$, then $C \in \mathbb{A}$.*

Definition 2 (Policy-Based Chameleon-Hashes). *A policy-based chameleon-hash PCH consists of the following six algorithms ($\mathsf{PPGen}_{\mathsf{PCH}}$, $\mathsf{MKeyGen}_{\mathsf{PCH}}$, $\mathsf{KGen}_{\mathsf{PCH}}$, $\mathsf{Hash}_{\mathsf{PCH}}$, $\mathsf{Verify}_{\mathsf{PCH}}$, $\mathsf{Adapt}_{\mathsf{PCH}}$), which are defined as follows [DSSS19].*

$\mathsf{PPGen}_{\mathsf{PCH}}$. *On input a security parameter κ, $\mathsf{PPGen}_{\mathsf{PCH}}$ outputs the public parameters:*

$$\mathsf{pp}_{\mathsf{PCH}} \leftarrow_r \mathsf{PPGen}_{\mathsf{PCH}}(1^\kappa)$$

We assume that $\mathsf{pp}_{\mathsf{PCH}}$ contains 1^κ and is implicit input to all other algorithms.

MKeyGen$_{\mathsf{PCH}}$. *On input of some global parameters* pp$_{\mathsf{PCH}}$, MKeyGen$_{\mathsf{PCH}}$ *outputs the master private and public key* (sk$_{\mathsf{PCH}}$, pk$_{\mathsf{PCH}}$) *of the scheme:*

$$(\mathsf{sk_{PCH}}, \mathsf{pk_{PCH}}) \leftarrow_r \mathsf{MKeyGen_{PCH}}(\mathsf{pp_{PCH}})$$

KGen$_{\mathsf{PCH}}$. *On input a secret key* sk$_{\mathsf{PCH}}$ *and a set of attributes* $\mathbb{S} \subseteq \mathbb{U}$ *(*$\mathbb{U}$ *is the universe), the key generation algorithm outputs a secret key* sk$_{\mathbb{S}}$:

$$\mathsf{sk_{\mathbb{S}}} \leftarrow_r \mathsf{KGen_{PCH}}(\mathsf{sk_{PCH}}, \mathbb{S})$$

Hash$_{\mathsf{PCH}}$. *On input a public key* pk$_{\mathsf{PCH}}$, *access structure* $\mathbb{A} \subseteq 2^{\mathbb{U}}$ *and a message* m, *this algorithm outputs a hash* h *and some randomness (sometimes referred to as "check value")* r:

$$(h, r) \leftarrow_r \mathsf{Hash_{PCH}}(\mathsf{pk_{PCH}}, m, \mathbb{A})$$

Verify$_{\mathsf{PCH}}$. *On input a public key* pk, *a message* m, *a hash* h, *and a randomness* r, *it outputs a bit* $b \in \{1, 0\}$.

$$b \leftarrow \mathsf{Verify_{PCH}}(\mathsf{pk_{PCH}}, m, h, r)$$

Adapt$_{\mathsf{PCH}}$. *On input a secret key* sk$_{\mathbb{S}}$, *messages* m *and* m', *a hash* h, *and randomness value* r, *the adaptation algorithm outputs a new randomness* r':

$$r' \leftarrow_r \mathsf{Adapt_{PCH}}(\mathsf{pk_{PCH}}, \mathsf{sk_{\mathbb{S}}}, m, m', h, r)$$

We assume that the KGen$_{\mathsf{PCH}}$ outputs $\perp$, if $\mathbb{S}$ is not contained in $\mathbb{U}$.

Note, we have added an additional algorithm PPGen$_{\mathsf{PCH}}$ which outputs some additional global parameters, which was not part of the original description in [DSSS19], as we work in a slightly different setting. Correctness is straightforward and given in the full version of this paper.

Furthermore, we require the following security properties, where our notion of indistinguishability below is stronger than the one introduced in [DSSS19]. We also restate the black-box construction from [DSSS19] (with some minor rephrasing and slightly stronger primitives) in the full version of this paper. The security proof in our stronger model is given in the full version of this paper.

Full Indistinguishability. Informally, indistinguishability requires that it be intractable to decide whether for a chameleon-hash its randomness is fresh or was created using the adaption algorithm. Full indistinguishability even lets the adversary choose the secret key used in the HashOrAdapt oracle. The security experiment grants the adversary access to a left-or-right style HashOrAdapt oracle and requires that the randomnesses r does not reveal whether it was obtained through Hash$_{\mathsf{PCH}}$ or Adapt$_{\mathsf{PCH}}$. The messages and secret keys are adaptively chosen by the adversary.

Definition 3 (PCH **Full Indistinguishability**). *We say a PCH scheme is fully indistinguishable, if for every PPT adversary* $\mathcal{A}$, *there exists a negligible function* ν *such that:*

$$\Pr\left[\mathbf{Exp}_{\mathcal{A},\mathsf{PCH}}^{\mathsf{FIndistinguishability}}(\kappa) = 1\right] - \tfrac{1}{2} \leq \nu(\kappa).$$

The corresponding experiment is depicted in Fig. 1.

$$\mathbf{Exp}_{\mathcal{A},\mathsf{PCH}}^{\mathsf{FIndistinguishability}}(\kappa)$$

$\qquad \mathsf{pp}_{\mathsf{PCH}} \leftarrow_r \mathsf{PPGen}_{\mathsf{PCH}}(1^\kappa)$

$\qquad b \leftarrow_r \{0,1\}$

$\qquad b^* \leftarrow_r \mathcal{A}^{\mathsf{HashOrAdapt}(\cdot,\cdot,\cdot,\cdot,\cdot,b)}(\mathsf{pp}_{\mathsf{PCH}})$

$\qquad\qquad$ where HashOrAdapt on input $\mathsf{pk}_{\mathsf{PCH}}, m, m', \mathsf{sk}_\mathbb{S}, \mathbb{A}, b$:

$\qquad\qquad\qquad (h_0, r_0) \leftarrow_r \mathsf{Hash}_{\mathsf{PCH}}(\mathsf{pk}_{\mathsf{PCH}}, m', \mathbb{A})$

$\qquad\qquad\qquad (h_1, r_1) \leftarrow_r \mathsf{Hash}_{\mathsf{PCH}}(\mathsf{pk}_{\mathsf{PCH}}, m, \mathbb{A})$

$\qquad\qquad\qquad r_1 \leftarrow_r \mathsf{Adapt}_{\mathsf{PCH}}(\mathsf{pk}_{\mathsf{PCH}}, \mathsf{sk}_\mathbb{S}, m, m', h_1, r_1)$

$\qquad\qquad\qquad$ return $\bot$, if $r_0 = \bot \vee r_1 = \bot$

$\qquad\qquad\qquad$ return (h_b, r_b)

$\qquad$ return 1, if $b = b^*$

$\qquad$ return 0

Fig. 1. PCH Full Indistinguishability

Insider Collision-Resistance. Insider collision-resistance addresses the requirement that not even insiders who possess secret keys with respect to some attributes can find collisions for hashes which were computed with respect to policies which are not satisfied by their keys (oracle $\mathsf{KGen}'_{\mathsf{PCH}}$). Intuitively, this notion enforces the attribute-based access-control policies, even if the adversary sees collisions for arbitrary attributes (oracles $\mathsf{KGen}''_{\mathsf{PCH}}$ and $\mathsf{Adapt}'_{\mathsf{PCH}}$).

Definition 4 (PCH Insider Collision-Resistance). *We say a PCH scheme is insider collision-resistant, if for every PPT adversary $\mathcal{A}$, there exists a negligible function ν such that:*

$$\Pr\left[\mathbf{Exp}_{\mathcal{A},\mathsf{PCH}}^{\mathsf{CRIns}}(\kappa) = 1\right] \le \nu(\kappa).$$

The corresponding experiment is depicted in Fig. 2.

Uniqueness. We also introduce the new notion of uniqueness for PCHs, which basically requires that it is hard to find different randomness yielding the same hash for an adversarial chosen message and public key.

Definition 5 (PCH Uniqueness). *We say a PCH scheme is unique, if for every PPT adversary $\mathcal{A}$, there exists a negligible function ν such that:*

$$\Pr\left[\mathbf{Exp}_{\mathcal{A},\mathsf{PCH}}^{\mathsf{Uniqueness}}(\kappa) = 1\right] \le \nu(\kappa).$$

The corresponding experiment is depicted in Fig. 3.

Note, we do not require the outsider collision-resistance notion from [DSSS19].

3 Our Framework for P3Ss

Additional Notation. We need to introduce some additional notation, to make our representation more compact. Our notation is taken from existing work, making reading more accessible [BCD+17, BFF+09, CDK+17]. The variable A

$\mathbf{Exp}_{\mathcal{A},\mathsf{PCH}}^{\mathsf{CRIns}}(\kappa)$

   $\mathsf{pp}_\mathsf{PCH} \leftarrow_r \mathsf{PPGen}_\mathsf{PCH}(1^\kappa)$

   $(\mathsf{sk}_\mathsf{PCH}, \mathsf{pk}_\mathsf{PCH}) \leftarrow_r \mathsf{MKeyGen}_\mathsf{PCH}(\mathsf{pp}_\mathsf{PCH})$

   $\mathcal{S} = \mathcal{H} = \mathcal{Q} \leftarrow \emptyset$

   $i \leftarrow 0$

   $(m^*, r^*, m'^*, r'^*, h^*) \leftarrow_r \mathcal{A}^{\mathsf{KGen}'_\mathsf{PCH}(\mathsf{sk}_\mathsf{PCH},\cdot),\mathsf{KGen}''_\mathsf{PCH}(\mathsf{sk}_\mathsf{PCH},\cdot),\mathsf{Hash}'_\mathsf{PCH}(\mathsf{pk}_\mathsf{PCH},\cdot,\cdot),\mathsf{Adapt}'_\mathsf{PCH}(\mathsf{pk}_\mathsf{PCH},\cdot,\cdot,\cdot,\cdot)}(\mathsf{pk}_\mathsf{PCH})$

     where $\mathsf{KGen}'_\mathsf{PCH}$ on input sk_PCH, $\mathbb{S}$:

       $\mathsf{sk}_\mathbb{S} \leftarrow_r \mathsf{KGen}_\mathsf{PCH}(\mathsf{sk}, \mathbb{S})$

       $\mathcal{S} \leftarrow \mathcal{S} \cup \{\mathbb{S}\}$

       return $\mathsf{sk}_\mathbb{S}$

     and $\mathsf{KGen}''_\mathsf{PCH}$ on input sk_PCH, $\mathbb{S}$:

       $\mathsf{sk}_\mathbb{S} \leftarrow_r \mathsf{KGen}_\mathsf{PCH}(\mathsf{sk}, \mathbb{S})$

       $\mathcal{Q} \cup \{(i, \mathsf{sk}_\mathbb{S})\}$

       $i \leftarrow i + 1$

       return $\perp$

     and $\mathsf{Hash}'_\mathsf{PCH}$ on input $\mathsf{pk}_\mathsf{PCH}, m, \mathbb{A}$:

       $(h, r) \leftarrow_r \mathsf{Hash}_\mathsf{PCH}(\mathsf{pk}_\mathsf{PCH}, m, \mathbb{A})$

       if $r \neq \perp$, $\mathcal{H} \leftarrow \mathcal{H} \cup \{(h, \mathbb{A}, m)\}$

       return (h, r)

     and $\mathsf{Adapt}'_\mathsf{PCH}$ on input $\mathsf{pk}_\mathsf{PCH}, m, m', h, r, j$:

       return $\perp$, if $(j, \mathsf{sk}_\mathbb{S}) \notin \mathcal{Q}$ for some $\mathsf{sk}_\mathbb{S}$

       $r' \leftarrow_r \mathsf{Adapt}_\mathsf{PCH}(\mathsf{pk}_\mathsf{PCH}, \mathsf{sk}_\mathbb{S}, m, m', h, r)$

       if $r' \neq \perp \wedge (h, \mathbb{A}, m) \in \mathcal{H}$ for some $\mathbb{A}$, $\mathcal{H} \leftarrow \mathcal{H} \cup \{(h, \mathbb{A}, m')\}$

       return r'

   return 1, if

     $\mathsf{Verify}_\mathsf{PCH}(\mathsf{pk}, m^*, h^*, r^*) = \mathsf{Verify}_\mathsf{PCH}(\mathsf{pk}, m'^*, h^*, r'^*) = 1 \wedge$

     $(h^*, \mathbb{A}, \cdot) \in \mathcal{H}$, for some $\mathbb{A} \wedge m^* \neq m'^* \wedge \mathbb{A} \cap \mathcal{S} = \emptyset \wedge (h^*, \cdot, m^*) \notin \mathcal{H}$

   return 0

Fig. 2. PCH Insider Collision-Resistance

$\mathbf{Exp}_{\mathcal{A},\mathsf{PCH}}^{\mathsf{Uniqueness}}(\kappa)$

   $\mathsf{pp}_\mathsf{PCH} \leftarrow_r \mathsf{PPGen}_\mathsf{PCH}(1^\kappa)$

   $(\mathsf{pk}^*, m^*, r^*, r'^*, h^*) \leftarrow_r \mathcal{A}(\mathsf{pp}_\mathsf{PCH})$

   return 1, if $\mathsf{Verify}_\mathsf{PCH}(\mathsf{pk}^*, m^*, h^*, r^*) = \mathsf{Verify}_\mathsf{PCH}(\mathsf{pk}^*, m^*, h^*, r'^*) = 1 \wedge r^* \neq r'^*$

   return 0

Fig. 3. PCH Uniqueness

contains the set of indices of the modifiable blocks, as well as l denoting the total number of blocks in the message m. We write $\mathbb{A}(m) = 1$, if $\mathbb{A}$ is valid w.r.t. m, i.e., $\mathbb{A}$ contains a fitting l, i.e., the correct length of m, and the indices of the admissible blocks are actually part of m. For example, let $\mathbb{A} = (\{1, 2, 3, 5\}, 5)$. Then, m must contain five blocks, and all but the fourth can be modified. If we write $m^i \in \mathbb{A}$, we mean that m^i is admissible. We also use $m_\mathbb{A}$ for the list of blocks in m which are admissible w.r.t. $\mathbb{A}$. Likewise, we use $m_{!\mathbb{A}}$ for the list of blocks of m which are not admissible w.r.t. to $\mathbb{A}$. Moreover, M is a set containing pairs (i, m'^i) for those blocks that are modified, meaning that m^i is replaced with m'^i. We write $M(\mathbb{A}) = 1$, if M is valid w.r.t. $\mathbb{A}$, meaning that the indices to be modified are contained in $\mathbb{A}$, i.e., admissible.

Definitional Framework. We now introduce our definitional framework. It is based on existing work [BCD+17, BFF+09, CDK+17]. The main idea is following the line of reasoning of group signatures. Namely, a designated entity, which we name "the group manager" generates a key pair for its group. The group manager can use its secret key to assign secret keys to sanitizers which are identified by their own key pair. In contrast, signers can create signatures for a signer-chosen group, identified by a public key. Moreover, signers do not require any prior interaction, i.e., knowledge of the group public-key is sufficient, which is a major difference to group signatures, and any sanitizer "authorized" by the manager of that group can then sanitize the generated signatures. Moreover, in contrast to group signatures, *only the signer* can decide which party has generated a signature, essentially it is also the "opener" in group signatures, but the group manager has no opening capabilities. These proofs, however, can be verified by anyone. We keep the wording of the algorithms mostly consistent with existing work to ease readability [BFF+09].

Definition 6 (P3S). *A sanitizable signature with attribute-based sanitizing P3S consists of the algorithms* {$\mathsf{ParGen_{P3S}}, \mathsf{Setup_{P3S}}, \mathsf{KGenSig_{P3S}}, \mathsf{KGenSan_{P3S}}, \mathsf{Sign_{P3S}}, \mathsf{AddSan_{P3S}}, \mathsf{Sanitize_{P3S}}, \mathsf{Verify_{P3S}}, \mathsf{Proof_{P3S}}, \mathsf{Judge_{P3S}}$} *such that:*

$\mathsf{ParGen_{P3S}}$. *The algorithm* $\mathsf{ParGen_{P3S}}$ *generates the public parameters:*

$$\mathsf{pp_{P3S}} \leftarrow_r \mathsf{ParGen_{P3S}}(1^\kappa)$$

We assume that $\mathsf{pp_{P3S}}$ *contains* 1^κ *and is implicit input to all other algorithms.*

$\mathsf{Setup_{P3S}}$. *The algorithm* $\mathsf{Setup_{P3S}}$ *outputs the global public key* $\mathsf{pk_{P3S}}$ *of a P3S, and some master secret key* $\mathsf{sk_{P3S}}$, *i.e., it generates the group manager's key pair:*

$$(\mathsf{sk_{P3S}}, \mathsf{pk_{P3S}}) \leftarrow_r \mathsf{Setup_{P3S}}(\mathsf{pp_{P3S}})$$

$\mathsf{KGenSig_{P3S}}$. *The algorithm* $\mathsf{KGenSig_{P3S}}$ *generates a key-pair for a signer:*

$$(\mathsf{sk_{P3S}^{Sig}}, \mathsf{pk_{P3S}^{Sig}}) \leftarrow_r \mathsf{KGenSig_{P3S}}(\mathsf{pp_{P3S}})$$

$\mathsf{KGenSan_{P3S}}$. *The algorithm* $\mathsf{KGenSan_{P3S}}$ *generates a key-pair for a sanitizer:*

$$(\mathsf{sk_{P3S}^{San}}, \mathsf{pk_{P3S}^{San}}) \leftarrow_r \mathsf{KGenSan_{P3S}}(\mathsf{pp_{P3S}})$$

$\mathsf{Sign_{P3S}}$. *The algorithm* $\mathsf{Sign_{P3S}}$ *generates a signature* σ, *on input of a master public key* $\mathsf{pk_{P3S}}$, *a secret key* $\mathsf{sk_{P3S}^{Sig}}$, *a message* m, A, *and some access structure* $\mathbb{A}$:

$$\sigma \leftarrow_r \mathsf{Sign_{P3S}}(\mathsf{pk_{P3S}}, \mathsf{sk_{P3S}^{Sig}}, m, \mathsf{A}, \mathbb{A})$$

$\mathsf{AddSan_{P3S}}$. *The algorithm* $\mathsf{AddSan_{P3S}}$ *allows to the group manager to generate a secret sanitizing key* $\mathsf{sk_S}$ *for a particular sanitizer, on input of* $\mathsf{sk_{P3S}}$, *a public key* $\mathsf{pk_{P3S}^{San}}$, *and some set of attributes* $\mathbb{S} \subseteq \mathbb{U}$:

$$\mathsf{sk_S} \leftarrow_r \mathsf{AddSan_{P3S}}(\mathsf{sk_{P3S}}, \mathsf{pk_{P3S}^{San}}, \mathbb{S})$$

$\mathsf{Verify}_{\mathsf{P3S}}$. *The deterministic algorithm* $\mathsf{Verify}_{\mathsf{P3S}}$ *allows to verify a signature* σ *on input of a master public key* $\mathsf{pk}_{\mathsf{P3S}}$, *a signer public key* $\mathsf{pk}_{\mathsf{P3S}}^{\mathsf{Sig}}$, *and a message* m. *It outputs a decision* $b \in \{0, 1\}$:

$$b \leftarrow \mathsf{Verify}_{\mathsf{P3S}}(\mathsf{pk}_{\mathsf{P3S}}, \mathsf{pk}_{\mathsf{P3S}}^{\mathsf{Sig}}, \sigma, m)$$

$\mathsf{Sanitize}_{\mathsf{P3S}}$. *The algorithm* $\mathsf{Sanitize}_{\mathsf{P3S}}$ *allows to derive a new signature on input of a master public key* $\mathsf{pk}_{\mathsf{P3S}}$, *a signer's public key* $\mathsf{pk}_{\mathsf{P3S}}^{\mathsf{Sig}}$, *a sanitizer's secret key* $\mathsf{sk}_{\mathsf{P3S}}^{\mathsf{San}}$, *a token* $\mathsf{sk}_{\mathbb{S}}$, *some modification instruction* M, *a message* m, *and a signature* σ:

$$(\sigma', m') \leftarrow_r \mathsf{Sanitize}_{\mathsf{P3S}}(\mathsf{pk}_{\mathsf{P3S}}, \mathsf{pk}_{\mathsf{P3S}}^{\mathsf{Sig}}, \mathsf{sk}_{\mathsf{P3S}}^{\mathsf{San}}, \mathsf{sk}_{\mathbb{S}}, m, \sigma, \mathsf{M})$$

$\mathsf{Proof}_{\mathsf{P3S}}$. *The algorithm* $\mathsf{Proof}_{\mathsf{P3S}}$ *allows to generate a proof* π_{P3S} *and some public* pk, *used by the next algorithm, to find the accountable party, on input of a master public key* $\mathsf{pk}_{\mathsf{P3S}}$, *a signer's secret key* $\mathsf{sk}_{\mathsf{P3S}}^{\mathsf{Sig}}$, *a signature* σ, *and a message* m:

$$(\pi_{\mathsf{P3S}}, \mathsf{pk}) \leftarrow_r \mathsf{Proof}_{\mathsf{P3S}}(\mathsf{pk}_{\mathsf{P3S}}, \mathsf{sk}_{\mathsf{P3S}}^{\mathsf{Sig}}, \sigma, m)$$

$\mathsf{Judge}_{\mathsf{P3S}}$. *The algorithm* $\mathsf{Judge}_{\mathsf{P3S}}$ *allows to verify whether a proof* π_{P3S} *is valid. The inputs are a master public key* $\mathsf{pk}_{\mathsf{P3S}}$, *a signer's public key* $\mathsf{pk}_{\mathsf{P3S}}^{\mathsf{Sig}}$, *some other public key* pk, *a proof* π_{P3S}, *a signature* σ, *and a message* m. *It outputs a decision* $b \in \{0, 1\}$, *stating whether* π_{P3S} *is a valid proof that the holder of* pk *is accountable for* σ:

$$b \leftarrow_r \mathsf{Judge}_{\mathsf{P3S}}(\mathsf{pk}_{\mathsf{P3S}}, \mathsf{pk}_{\mathsf{P3S}}^{\mathsf{Sig}}, \mathsf{pk}, \pi_{\mathsf{P3S}}, \sigma, m)$$

For each P3S it is required that the correctness properties hold. In particular, it is required that for all $\kappa \in \mathbb{N}$, for all $\mathsf{pp}_{\mathsf{P3S}} \leftarrow_r \mathsf{ParGen}_{\mathsf{P3S}}(1^{\kappa})$, for all $(\mathsf{pk}_{\mathsf{P3S}}, \mathsf{sk}_{\mathsf{P3S}}) \leftarrow_r \mathsf{Setup}_{\mathsf{P3S}}(\mathsf{pp}_{\mathsf{P3S}})$, for all $(\mathsf{sk}_{\mathsf{P3S}}^{\mathsf{Sig}}, \mathsf{pk}_{\mathsf{P3S}}^{\mathsf{Sig}}) \leftarrow_r \mathsf{KGenSig}_{\mathsf{P3S}}(\mathsf{pp}_{\mathsf{P3S}})$, for all $l \in \mathbb{N}$, for all $m \in \mathcal{M}^l$, for all $\mathbb{A} \in 2^{\mathbb{U}}$, for all $A \in \{A_i \mid A_i(m) = 1\}$, for all $\sigma \leftarrow_r \mathsf{Sign}_{\mathsf{P3S}}(\mathsf{pk}_{\mathsf{P3S}}, \mathsf{sk}_{\mathsf{P3S}}^{\mathsf{Sig}}, m, A, \mathbb{A})$, we have that $\mathsf{Verify}_{\mathsf{P3S}}(\mathsf{pk}_{\mathsf{P3S}}, \mathsf{pk}_{\mathsf{P3S}}^{\mathsf{Sig}}, \sigma, m) = 1$ and for all $(\pi_{\mathsf{P3S}}, \mathsf{pk}) \leftarrow_r \mathsf{Proof}_{\mathsf{P3S}}(\mathsf{pk}_{\mathsf{P3S}}, \mathsf{sk}_{\mathsf{P3S}}^{\mathsf{Sig}}, \sigma, m)$ we have that $\mathsf{Judge}_{\mathsf{P3S}}(\mathsf{pk}_{\mathsf{P3S}}, \mathsf{pk}_{\mathsf{P3S}}^{\mathsf{Sig}}, \mathsf{pk}_{\mathsf{P3S}}^{\mathsf{Sig}}, \pi_{\mathsf{P3S}}, \sigma, m) = 1$ and $\mathsf{pk} = \mathsf{pk}_{\mathsf{P3S}}^{\mathsf{Sig}}$. We also require that for all $(\mathsf{sk}_{\mathsf{P3S}}^{\mathsf{San}}, \mathsf{pk}_{\mathsf{P3S}}^{\mathsf{San}}) \leftarrow_r \mathsf{KGenSan}_{\mathsf{P3S}}(\mathsf{pp}_{\mathsf{P3S}})$, for all $\mathbb{S} \in \mathbb{A}$, for all $\mathsf{sk}_{\mathbb{S}} \leftarrow_r \mathsf{AddSan}_{\mathsf{P3S}}(\mathsf{sk}_{\mathsf{P3S}}^{\mathsf{San}}, \mathsf{pk}_{\mathsf{P3S}}^{\mathsf{San}}, \mathbb{S})$, for all $\mathsf{M} \in \{\mathsf{M}_i \mid \mathsf{M}_i(A) = 1\}$, for all $(\sigma', m') \leftarrow_r \mathsf{Sanitize}_{\mathsf{P3S}}(\mathsf{pk}_{\mathsf{P3S}}, \mathsf{pk}_{\mathsf{P3S}}^{\mathsf{Sig}}, \mathsf{sk}_{\mathsf{P3S}}^{\mathsf{San}}, \mathsf{sk}_{\mathbb{S}}, m, \sigma, \mathsf{M})$ we have that $\mathsf{Verify}_{\mathsf{P3S}}(\mathsf{pk}_{\mathsf{P3S}}, \mathsf{pk}_{\mathsf{P3S}}^{\mathsf{Sig}}, \sigma', m') = 1$ and that for all $(\pi'_{\mathsf{P3S}}, \mathsf{pk}') \leftarrow_r \mathsf{Proof}_{\mathsf{P3S}}(\mathsf{pk}_{\mathsf{P3S}}, \mathsf{sk}_{\mathsf{P3S}}^{\mathsf{Sig}}, \sigma', m')$, we have that $\mathsf{Judge}_{\mathsf{P3S}}(\mathsf{pk}_{\mathsf{P3S}}, \mathsf{pk}_{\mathsf{P3S}}^{\mathsf{Sig}}, \mathsf{pk}_{\mathsf{P3S}}^{\mathsf{San}}, \pi'_{\mathsf{P3S}}, \sigma', m') = 1$ and $\mathsf{pk}' = \mathsf{pk}_{\mathsf{P3S}}^{\mathsf{San}}$.

Security Definitions. We now introduce our security definitions. To increase readability, we keep the naming close to the already existing definitions for standard 3Ss [BFF+09]. However, due to the increased expressiveness of our new primitive, this is not always possible. Namely, we require new unforgeability and privacy definitions not considered before. This also has the effect that the implications and separations by Brzuska et al. [BFF+09] have to be revisited.

Overview. We first briefly introduce each security notion to ease understanding of the formal definitions given afterwards.

- **Unforgeability.** Unforgeability requires that an adversary cannot (except with negligible probability) generate any valid signature, if it does not hold enough attributes to do so. We explicitly include the case that the adversary can be group manager of other groups, but the challenge one.
- **Immutability.** Immutability requires that an adverserial group manager cannot (except with negligible probability) create signatures with altered immutable parts. This also includes appending or removing blocks.
- **Privacy.** Privacy requires that an adversary does not learn (except with negligible probability) anything about sanitized parts, even if it can generate all keys.
- **Transparency.** Transparency requires that an adversary cannot decide (except with negligible probability) whether it sees a freshly signed signature or a sanitized one, even if it can generate all keys, but the signer's one.
- **Pseudonymity.** Pseudonymity requires that an adversary does not learn (except with negligible probability) which party is accountable for a given sanitized signatures, even if it can generate all keys, but the signer's one.
- **Signer-Accountability.** Signer-Accountability requires that an adversary cannot (except with negligible probability) blame an honest sanitizer for a signature it did not create, even if it can generate all keys but the sanitizer's one.
- **Sanitizer-Accountability.** Sanitzer-Accountability requires that an adversary cannot (except with negligible probability) blame an honest signer for a signature it did not create, even if it can generate all keys but the signer's one.
- **Proof-Soundness.** Proof-Soundness requires that an adversary cannot (except with negligible probability) generate a proof for an adverserially chosen signature/message pair that points to different entities, even if it can generate all keys.
- **Traceability.** Traceability requires that an adversary cannot (except with negligible probability) generate a verifying signature such that an honest signer cannot identify the accountable party, even if it can generate all keys, but the signer's one.

Unforgeability. The property of unforgeability prohibits that an adversary, which is not a signer, or the entity holding sk_{P3S}, i.e., the group manager, can generate any validating signature which verifies for honestly generated keys. This also includes messages for which the adversary does not hold enough attributes for, even if it sees sanitizations of such signatures. We define it in such a way that (pk_{P3S}, sk_{P3S}), and $(sk_{P3S}^{Sig}, pk_{P3S}^{Sig})$, are generated honestly. The adversary gets access to the following oracles: (1) $Sign'_{P3S}$ (where it can even use different $pk_{P3S}s$, which models the case that secret signing keys can be re-used across multiple "groups"), (2) $GetSan$ which generates a new sanitizer (tracked by $\mathcal{S}$), (3) $AddSan'_{P3S}$ which allows to decide which attributes a given sanitizer holds (tracked by $\mathcal{R}$), (4) $\mathsf{Sanitize}'_{\mathsf{P3S}}$ which allows sanitizing signatures for an honest sanitizer (generated by GetSan) for the challenge group, and (5) $\mathsf{Sanitize}''_{\mathsf{P3S}}$ which allows sanitizing for signatures from any other group (i.e., where the adversary is the group manager). The adversary wins, if it can generate a valid signature for the defined group which has never been output by either $\mathsf{Sign}'_{\mathsf{P3S}}$ or $\mathsf{Sanitize}'_{\mathsf{P3S}}$ (tracked by the set $\mathcal{M}$; Note, this set may be exponential in size, but membership is trivial to decide by checking whether the element could have been derived using A and $\mathbb{A}$), and the adversary $\mathcal{A}$ does not hold enough attributes itself.

Definition 7 (P3S Unforgeability). *We say a* P3S *scheme is unforgeable, if for every PPT adversary $\mathcal{A}$, there exists a negligible function ν such that:*

$$\Pr\left[\mathbf{Exp}_{\mathcal{A},\mathsf{P3S}}^{\mathsf{Unforgeability}}(\kappa) = 1\right] \leq \nu(\kappa).$$

The corresponding experiment is depicted in Fig. 4.

Immutability. The above unforgeability definition assumes that the holder of $\mathsf{sk}_{\mathsf{P3S}}$ (the group manager) is honest. If this is not the case, however, the adversary can generate its own key pair for a sanitizer and can generate sk_{S} for any attribute-set it likes. Still, in such a case, we want to prohibit that an adversary generates any signatures which are outside the span the honest signer has endorsed for *any* combination of attributes. This is captured by the immutability definition — if a block is marked as non-admissible by a signer, no one must be able to change this block. This also includes that an adversary must not be able to redact or append a block. Clearly, we cannot limit the adversary to change admissible blocks, as it can grant sanitizing rights to itself.

This is modeled in such a way that the challenger draws $\mathsf{pp}_{\mathsf{P3S}}$ honestly, along with a key-pair for the signer. The adversary only receives $\mathsf{pp}_{\mathsf{P3S}}$ and $\mathsf{pk}_{\mathsf{P3S}}^{\mathsf{Sig}}$. Then, the adversary gains adaptive access to signing-oracle (where the adversary can choose $\mathsf{pk}_{\mathsf{P3S}}$, m, A, $\mathbb{A}$, but not $\mathsf{sk}_{\mathsf{P3S}}^{\mathsf{Sig}}$), and access to a proof-oracle. We keep a set $\mathcal{M}$ which contains all possible messages which can "legally" be derived by the adversary (bound to $\mathsf{pk}_{\mathsf{P3S}}$, also chosen by the adversary, and tracked by $\mathcal{M}$; Again, this set may be exponential in size, but membership is trivial to decide). If, and only if, the adversary finds a valid signature σ^* w.r.t. $\mathsf{pk}_{\mathsf{P3S}}^{\mathsf{Sig}}$ and pk^*, which could never been derived from any input, it wins.

Definition 8 (P3S Immutability). *We say a* P3S *scheme is immutable, if for every PPT adversary $\mathcal{A}$, there exists a negligible function ν such that:*

$$\Pr\left[\mathbf{Exp}_{\mathcal{A},\mathsf{P3S}}^{\mathsf{Immutability}}(\kappa) = 1\right] \leq \nu(\kappa).$$

The corresponding experiment is depicted in Fig. 5.

Privacy. Privacy prohibits that an adversary can derive any useful information from a sanitized signature. We define a very strong version, where all values can be generated by the adversary, making our definition even stronger than existing ones [dMPPS14, FF15].

$\mathbf{Exp}_{\mathcal{A},\mathsf{P3S}}^{\mathsf{Unforgeability}}(\kappa)$

$\quad \mathsf{pp}_{\mathsf{P3S}} \leftarrow_r \mathsf{ParGen}_{\mathsf{P3S}}(1^\kappa)$

$\quad (\mathsf{sk}_{\mathsf{P3S}}, \mathsf{pk}_{\mathsf{P3S}}) \leftarrow_r \mathsf{Setup}_{\mathsf{P3S}}(\mathsf{pp}_{\mathsf{P3S}})$

$\quad (\mathsf{sk}_{\mathsf{P3S}}^{\mathsf{Sig}}, \mathsf{pk}_{\mathsf{P3S}}^{\mathsf{Sig}}) \leftarrow_r \mathsf{KGenSig}_{\mathsf{P3S}}(\mathsf{pp}_{\mathsf{P3S}})$

$\quad \mathcal{Q} = \mathcal{S} = \mathcal{R} = \mathcal{M} = \mathcal{Z} \leftarrow \emptyset$

$\quad i \leftarrow 0$

$\quad (m^*, \sigma^*) \leftarrow_r \mathcal{A}^{\mathsf{Sign}_{\mathsf{P3S}}'(\cdot,\mathsf{sk}_{\mathsf{P3S}}^{\mathsf{Sig}},\cdot,\cdot,\cdot),\mathsf{GetSan}(),\mathsf{AddSan}_{\mathsf{P3S}}'(\mathsf{sk}_{\mathsf{P3S}},\cdot,\cdot),\mathsf{Sanitize}_{\mathsf{P3S}}'(\mathsf{pk}_{\mathsf{P3S}},\cdot,\cdot,\cdot,\cdot,\cdot)}_{\mathsf{,Sanitize}_{\mathsf{P3S}}''(\cdot,\cdot,\cdot,\cdot,\cdot,\cdot,\cdot),\mathsf{Proof}_{\mathsf{P3S}}(\cdot,\mathsf{sk}_{\mathsf{P3S}}^{\mathsf{Sig}},\cdot,\cdot)}(\mathsf{pk}_{\mathsf{P3S}}, \mathsf{pk}_{\mathsf{P3S}}^{\mathsf{Sig}})$

$\quad\quad$ where $\mathsf{Sign}_{\mathsf{P3S}}'$ on input $\mathsf{pk}_{\mathsf{P3S}}', \mathsf{sk}_{\mathsf{P3S}}^{\mathsf{Sig}}, m, \mathbb{A}, \mathcal{A}$:

$\quad\quad\quad \sigma \leftarrow_r \mathsf{Sign}_{\mathsf{P3S}}(\mathsf{pk}_{\mathsf{P3S}}', \mathsf{sk}_{\mathsf{P3S}}^{\mathsf{Sig}}, m, \mathbb{A}, \mathcal{A})$

$\quad\quad\quad$ if $\mathsf{pk}_{\mathsf{P3S}}' = \mathsf{pk}_{\mathsf{P3S}} \;\wedge\; \sigma \neq \bot$:

$\quad\quad\quad\quad \mathcal{Q} \leftarrow \mathcal{Q} \cup \{(\sigma, m, \mathbb{A}, \mathcal{A})\}$

$\quad\quad\quad\quad$ if $\mathbb{A} \in \mathcal{R}, \; \mathcal{M} \leftarrow \mathcal{M} \cup \{\mathsf{M}(m) \mid \mathsf{M}(\mathbb{A}) = 1\}$

$\quad\quad\quad$ return σ

$\quad\quad$ and GetSan:

$\quad\quad\quad (\mathsf{sk}_{\mathsf{P3S}}^{\mathsf{San}}, \mathsf{pk}_{\mathsf{P3S}}^{\mathsf{San}}) \leftarrow_r \mathsf{KGenSan}_{\mathsf{P3S}}(\mathsf{pp}_{\mathsf{P3S}})$

$\quad\quad\quad \mathcal{S} \leftarrow \mathcal{S} \cup \{(\mathsf{sk}_{\mathsf{P3S}}^{\mathsf{San}}, \mathsf{pk}_{\mathsf{P3S}}^{\mathsf{San}})\}$

$\quad\quad\quad$ return $\mathsf{pk}_{\mathsf{P3S}}^{\mathsf{San}}$

$\quad\quad$ and $\mathsf{AddSan}_{\mathsf{P3S}}'$ on input $\mathsf{sk}_{\mathsf{P3S}}, \mathsf{pk}_{\mathsf{P3S}}^{\mathsf{San}}, \mathbb{S}$

$\quad\quad\quad$ if $\neg\exists(\cdot, \mathsf{pk}_{\mathsf{P3S}}^{\mathsf{San}}) \in \mathcal{S}$:

$\quad\quad\quad\quad \mathsf{sk}_{\mathbb{S}} \leftarrow_r \mathsf{AddSan}_{\mathsf{P3S}}(\mathsf{sk}_{\mathsf{P3S}}, \mathsf{pk}_{\mathsf{P3S}}^{\mathsf{San}}, \mathbb{S})$

$\quad\quad\quad\quad$ return $\bot$, if $\mathsf{sk}_{\mathbb{S}} = \bot$

$\quad\quad\quad\quad \mathcal{R} \leftarrow \mathcal{R} \cup \{\mathbb{S}\}$

$\quad\quad\quad\quad$ for all $(\sigma_i, m_i, \mathbb{A}_i, \mathcal{A}_i) \in \mathcal{Q}$, where $\mathbb{S} \in \mathbb{A}_i, \; \mathcal{M} \cup \{\mathsf{M}(m_i) \mid \mathsf{M}(\mathbb{A}_i) = 1\}$

$\quad\quad\quad\quad$ return $\mathsf{sk}_{\mathbb{S}}$

$\quad\quad\quad \mathsf{sk}_{\mathbb{S}} \leftarrow_r \mathsf{AddSan}_{\mathsf{P3S}}(\mathsf{sk}_{\mathsf{P3S}}, \mathsf{pk}_{\mathsf{P3S}}^{\mathsf{San}}, \mathbb{S})$

$\quad\quad\quad \mathcal{Z} \leftarrow \mathcal{Z} \cup \{(i, \mathsf{sk}_{\mathbb{S}})\}$

$\quad\quad\quad i \leftarrow i + 1$

$\quad\quad$ and $\mathsf{Sanitize}_{\mathsf{P3S}}'$ on input $\mathsf{pk}_{\mathsf{P3S}}, \mathsf{pk}_{\mathsf{P3S}}^{\mathsf{Sig}}, \mathsf{pk}_{\mathsf{P3S}}^{\mathsf{San}}, j, m, \sigma, \mathsf{M}$:

$\quad\quad\quad$ return $\bot$, if $\neg\exists(\mathsf{sk}_{\mathsf{P3S}}^{\mathsf{San}}, \mathsf{pk}_{\mathsf{P3S}}^{\mathsf{San}}) \in \mathcal{S}$ for some $\mathsf{sk}_{\mathsf{P3S}}^{\mathsf{San}}$

$\quad\quad\quad (\sigma', m') \leftarrow_r \mathsf{Sanitize}_{\mathsf{P3S}}(\mathsf{pk}_{\mathsf{P3S}}, \mathsf{pk}_{\mathsf{P3S}}^{\mathsf{Sig}}, \mathsf{sk}_{\mathsf{P3S}}^{\mathsf{San}}, \mathsf{sk}_{\mathbb{S}}, m, \sigma, \mathsf{M})$, where $\mathsf{sk}_{\mathbb{S}}$ is taken from $(j, \mathsf{sk}_{\mathbb{S}}) \in \mathcal{Z}$

$\quad\quad\quad$ if $\sigma' \neq \bot$:

$\quad\quad\quad\quad \mathcal{Q} \leftarrow \mathcal{Q} \cup \{(\sigma', m', \bot, \bot)\}$

$\quad\quad\quad\quad$ return σ'

$\quad\quad$ and $\mathsf{Sanitize}_{\mathsf{P3S}}''$ on input $\mathsf{pk}_{\mathsf{P3S}}', \mathsf{pk}_{\mathsf{P3S}}^{\mathsf{Sig}}, \mathsf{pk}_{\mathsf{P3S}}^{\mathsf{San}}, \mathsf{sk}_{\mathbb{S}}, m, \sigma, \mathsf{M}$:

$\quad\quad\quad$ return $\bot$, if $\neg\exists(\mathsf{sk}_{\mathsf{P3S}}^{\mathsf{San}}, \mathsf{pk}_{\mathsf{P3S}}^{\mathsf{San}}) \in \mathcal{S} \;\vee\; \mathsf{pk}_{\mathsf{P3S}}' = \mathsf{pk}_{\mathsf{P3S}}$

$\quad\quad\quad (\sigma', m') \leftarrow_r \mathsf{Sanitize}_{\mathsf{P3S}}(\mathsf{pk}_{\mathsf{P3S}}', \mathsf{pk}_{\mathsf{P3S}}^{\mathsf{Sig}}, \mathsf{sk}_{\mathsf{P3S}}^{\mathsf{San}}, \mathsf{sk}_{\mathbb{S}}, m, \sigma, \mathsf{M})$

$\quad\quad\quad$ return σ'

$\quad$ return 0, if $\mathsf{Verify}_{\mathsf{P3S}}(\mathsf{pk}_{\mathsf{P3S}}, \mathsf{pk}_{\mathsf{P3S}}^{\mathsf{Sig}}, \sigma^*, m^*) = 0 \;\vee\; m^* \in \mathcal{M}$

$\quad\quad$ return 1, if $(\sigma^*, m^*, \cdot, \cdot) \notin \mathcal{Q}$

$\quad$ return 0

Fig. 4. P3S Unforgeability

In more detail, the challenger draws a bit $b \leftarrow_r \{0, 1\}$, while the parameters $\mathsf{pp}_{\mathsf{P3S}}$ are generated honestly. The adversary gains access to a LoRSanit-oracle, where it can input $\mathsf{pk}_{\mathsf{P3S}}, \mathsf{sk}_{\mathsf{P3S}}^{\mathsf{Sig}}, \mathsf{sk}_{\mathsf{P3S}}^{\mathsf{San}}, \mathbb{A}, m_0, m_1, \mathsf{M}_0, \mathsf{M}_1, \mathcal{A}$, and $\mathsf{sk}_{\mathbb{S}}$ (b is input by the challenger). The oracle then signs m_b with $\mathbb{A}$ and $\mathcal{A}$. Then, the resulting signature is sanitized to $\mathsf{M}_b(m_b)$, while $\mathsf{M}_0(m_0) = \mathsf{M}_1(m_1)$ must hold to prevent trivial attacks. The goal of the adversary is to guess the bit b.

We stress that this definition seems to be overly strong. However, it also preserves privacy in case of bad randomness at key generation, completely leaked keys, and even corrupt group managers.

$$\mathbf{Exp}_{\mathcal{A},\mathsf{P3S}}^{\mathsf{Immutability}}(\kappa)$$

$\quad \mathsf{pp_{P3S}} \leftarrow_r \mathsf{ParGen_{P3S}}(1^\kappa)$

$\quad (\mathsf{sk_{P3S}^{Sig}}, \mathsf{pk_{P3S}^{Sig}}) \leftarrow_r \mathsf{KGenSig_{P3S}}(\mathsf{pp_{P3S}})$

$\quad \mathcal{M} \leftarrow \emptyset$

$\quad (\mathsf{pk}^*, \sigma^*, m^*) \leftarrow_r \mathcal{A}^{\mathsf{Sign'_{P3S}}(\cdot, \mathsf{sk_{P3S}^{Sig}}, \cdot, \cdot, \cdot), \mathsf{Proof_{P3S}}(\cdot, \mathsf{sk_{P3S}^{Sig}}, \cdot, \cdot)}(\mathsf{pk_{P3S}^{Sig}})$

$\quad\quad$ where $\mathsf{Sign'_{P3S}}$ on input $\mathsf{pk_{P3S}}, \mathsf{sk_{P3S}^{Sig}}, m, \mathsf{A}, \mathbb{A}$:

$\quad\quad\quad \sigma \leftarrow_r \mathsf{Sign_{P3S}}(\mathsf{pk_{P3S}}, \mathsf{sk_{P3S}^{Sig}}, m, \mathsf{A}, \mathbb{A})$

$\quad\quad\quad$ return $\bot$, if $\sigma = \bot$

$\quad\quad\quad \mathcal{M} \cup \{(\mathsf{pk_{P3S}}, \mathsf{M}(m)) \mid \mathsf{M}(\mathsf{A}) = 1\}$

$\quad\quad\quad$ return σ

$\quad$ return 1, if:

$\quad\quad \mathsf{Verify_{P3S}}(\mathsf{pk}^*, \mathsf{pk_{P3S}^{Sig}}, \sigma^*, m^*) = 1 \wedge (\mathsf{pk}^*, m^*) \notin \mathcal{M}$

$\quad$ return 0

Fig. 5. P3S Immutability

$$\mathbf{Exp}_{\mathcal{A},\mathsf{P3S}}^{\mathsf{Privacy}}(\kappa)$$

$\quad \mathsf{pp_{P3S}} \leftarrow_r \mathsf{ParGen_{P3S}}(1^\kappa)$

$\quad b \leftarrow_r \{0,1\}$

$\quad b^* \leftarrow_r \mathcal{A}^{\mathsf{LoRSanit}(\cdot, \cdot, \cdot, \cdot, \cdot, \cdot, \cdot, \cdot, \cdot, \cdot, b)}(\mathsf{pp_{P3S}})$

$\quad\quad$ where $\mathsf{LoRSanit}$ on input of $\mathsf{pk_{P3S}}, \mathsf{sk_{P3S}^{Sig}}, \mathsf{sk_{P3S}^{San}}, \mathbb{A}, m_0, m_1, \mathsf{M}_0, \mathsf{M}_1, \mathsf{A}, \mathsf{sk_S}, b$:

$\quad\quad\quad \sigma \leftarrow_r \mathsf{Sign_{P3S}}(\mathsf{pk_{P3S}}, \mathsf{sk_{P3S}^{Sig}}, m_b, \mathsf{A}, \mathbb{A})$

$\quad\quad\quad$ for $b' \in \{0,1\}$, $(\sigma'_{b'}, \cdot) \leftarrow_r \mathsf{Sanitize_{P3S}}(\mathsf{pk_{P3S}}, \mathsf{pk_{P3S}^{Sig}}, \mathsf{sk_{P3S}^{San}}, \mathsf{sk_S}, m_{b'}, \sigma, \mathsf{M}_{b'})$

$\quad\quad\quad$ return $\bot$, if $\sigma'_0 = \bot \vee \sigma'_1 = \bot \vee \mathsf{A}(m_0) = 0 \vee \mathsf{A}(m_1) = 0 \vee \mathsf{M}_0(m_0) \neq \mathsf{M}_1(m_1)$

$\quad\quad\quad$ return σ'_b

$\quad$ return 1, if $b = b^*$

$\quad$ return 0

Fig. 6. P3S Privacy

Definition 9 (P3S Privacy). *We say a P3S scheme is private, if for every PPT adversary $\mathcal{A}$, there exists a negligible function ν such that:*

$$\Pr\left[\mathbf{Exp}_{\mathcal{A},\mathsf{P3S}}^{\mathsf{Privacy}}(\kappa) = 1\right] - \tfrac{1}{2} \leq \nu(\kappa).$$

The corresponding experiment is depicted in Fig. 6.

Transparency. Transparency prohibits that an adversary can decide whether a signature is fresh or the result of a sanitization. As for privacy, we define a very strong version, where all values, but the signer's key pair $(\mathsf{sk_{P3S}^{Sig}}, \mathsf{pk_{P3S}^{Sig}})$, can be generated by the adversary, making our definition even stronger than existing ones [dMPPS14, FF15, KSS15]. The reason why the signer's key pair must be generated honestly is that the signer can always pinpoint the accountable party due to correctness.

In more detail, the challenger draws a bit $b \leftarrow_r \{0,1\}$, while the parameters $\mathsf{pp_{P3S}}$ and the signer's key pair $(\mathsf{sk_{P3S}^{Sig}}, \mathsf{pk_{P3S}^{Sig}})$ are generated honestly. The adversary gains access to three oracles: $\mathsf{Sign_{P3S}}$, $\mathsf{SignOrSanit}$, and $\mathsf{Proof'_{P3S}}$. The $\mathsf{Sign_{P3S}}$-oracle allows the adversary to generate new signatures; the only fixed

552 K. Samelin and D. Slamanig

input is sk_{P3S}^{Sig}. The SignOrSanit-oracle is the challenge oracle. It allows the adversary $\mathcal{A}$ to input pk_{P3S}, sk_{P3S}^{Sig}, $\mathbb{A}$, m, M, A, and sk_S (b and sk_{P3S}^{Sig} are input by the challenger). The oracle then signs m with A and $\mathbb{A}$. Then, the resulting signature is sanitized to $\mathsf{M}(m)$. If $b = 1$, however, a fresh signature on $\mathsf{M}(m)$ is generated. The resulting signature is returned to the adversary. However, we also log the signatures generated by this oracle in a list $\mathcal{Q}$. The list $\mathcal{Q}$ is required to prohibit that the adversary $\mathcal{A}$ can generate a proof using the Proof'_{P3S}-oracle with signatures generated by the SignOrSanit-oracle, which directly returns the accountable party. Thus, the adversary can only input pk_{P3S}, sk_{P3S}^{Sig}, σ, m for which $(\mathsf{pk}_{P3S}, \sigma, m)$ was never input/output to the SignOrSanit-oracle. The goal of the adversary is to guess the bit b.

We stress that this definition also seems to be overly strong. However, it also preserves transparency in case of bad randomness at key generation, leaked keys, and even corrupt group managers.

Definition 10 (P3S Transparency). *We say a P3S scheme is transparent, if for every PPT adversary $\mathcal{A}$, there exists a negligible function ν such that:*

$$\Pr\left[\mathbf{Exp}_{\mathcal{A},P3S}^{Transparency}(\kappa) = 1\right] - \tfrac{1}{2} \leq \nu(\kappa).$$

The corresponding experiment is depicted in Fig. 7.

Pseudonymity. Pseudonymity prohibits that an adversary can decide which sanitizer actually is responsible for a given signature, if it does not have access to sk_{P3S}^{Sig}. This is related to the anonymity of group signatures [CvH91]. We formalize it in the following way. The challenger draws a bit $b \leftarrow_r \{0,1\}$, generates the public parameters pp_{P3S} and the signer's key pair $(\mathsf{sk}_{P3S}^{Sig}, \mathsf{pk}_{P3S}^{Sig})$ honestly. The adversary

---

$\mathbf{Exp}_{\mathcal{A},P3S}^{Transparency}(\kappa)$

  $\mathsf{pp}_{P3S} \leftarrow_r \mathsf{ParGen}_{P3S}(1^\kappa)$
  $(\mathsf{sk}_{P3S}^{Sig}, \mathsf{pk}_{P3S}^{Sig}) \leftarrow_r \mathsf{KGenSig}_{P3S}(\mathsf{pp}_{P3S})$
  $b \leftarrow_r \{0,1\}$
  $\mathcal{Q} \leftarrow \emptyset$
  $b^* \leftarrow_r \mathcal{A}^{\mathsf{Sign}_{P3S}(\cdot,\mathsf{sk}_{P3S}^{Sig},\cdot,\cdot,\cdot),\mathsf{SignOrSanit}(\cdot,\mathsf{sk}_{P3S}^{Sig},\cdot,\cdot,\cdot,\cdot,\cdot,\cdot,b),\mathsf{Proof}'_{P3S}(\cdot,\mathsf{sk}_{P3S}^{Sig},\cdot,\cdot)}(\mathsf{pk}_{P3S}^{Sig})$
      where SignOrSanit on input of pk_{P3S}, sk_{P3S}^{Sig}, sk_{P3S}^{San}, $\mathbb{A}$, m, M, A, sk_S, b:
        $\sigma \leftarrow_r \mathsf{Sign}_{P3S}(\mathsf{pk}_{P3S}, \mathsf{sk}_{P3S}^{Sig}, m, \mathsf{A}, \mathbb{A})$
        $(\sigma', m') \leftarrow_r \mathsf{Sanitize}_{P3S}(\mathsf{pk}_{P3S}, \mathsf{pk}_{P3S}^{Sig}, \mathsf{sk}_{P3S}^{San}, \mathsf{sk}_S, m, \sigma, \mathsf{M})$
        if $b = 1$:
          $\sigma' \leftarrow_r \mathsf{Sign}_{P3S}(\mathsf{pk}_{P3S}, \mathsf{sk}_{P3S}^{Sig}, m', \mathsf{A}, \mathbb{A})$
          $\mathcal{Q} \leftarrow \mathcal{Q} \cup \{(\mathsf{pk}_{P3S}, \sigma', m')\}$
        return σ'
      and Proof'_{P3S} on input of pk_{P3S}, sk_{P3S}^{Sig}, σ, m:
        return $\perp$, if $(\mathsf{pk}_{P3S}, \sigma, m) \in \mathcal{Q}$
        return $\mathsf{Proof}_{P3S}(\mathsf{pk}_{P3S}, \mathsf{sk}_{P3S}^{Sig}, \sigma, m)$
    return 1, if $b = b^*$
    return 0

Fig. 7. P3S Transparency

gains access to three oracles: $\mathsf{Sign}_{\mathsf{P3S}}$, $\mathsf{LoRSanit}$, and $\mathsf{Proof}'_{\mathsf{P3S}}$. The $\mathsf{Sign}_{\mathsf{P3S}}$-oracle allows the adversary to generate new signatures; the only fixed input is $\mathsf{sk}_{\mathsf{P3S}}^{\mathsf{Sig}}$. The $\mathsf{LoRSanit}$-oracle is the challenge oracle. It allows the adversary $\mathcal{A}$ to input $\mathsf{pk}_{\mathsf{P3S}}$, $\mathsf{pk}_{\mathsf{P3S}}^{\mathsf{Sig}}$, $\mathsf{sk}_{\mathsf{P3S},0}^{\mathsf{San}}$, $\mathsf{sk}_{\mathsf{P3S},1}^{\mathsf{San}}$, $\mathsf{sk}_{\mathbb{S}0}$, $\mathsf{sk}_{\mathbb{S}1}$, m, and σ (b and $\mathsf{sk}_{\mathsf{P3S}}^{\mathsf{Sig}}$ are input by the challenger). The oracle then signs m with A and $\mathbb{A}$. Then, the resulting signature is sanitized to $\mathsf{M}(m)$, using keys $\mathsf{sk}_{\mathsf{P3S},b}^{\mathsf{San}}$ and $\mathsf{sk}_{\mathbb{S},b}$. The resulting signature is given to the adversary. As done for transparency, we also log the signatures generated by this oracle in a list $\mathcal{Q}$. The list $\mathcal{Q}$ is required to prohibit that the adversary $\mathcal{A}$ wants to generate a proof using the $\mathsf{Proof}'_{\mathsf{P3S}}$-oracle with signatures generated by the $\mathsf{LoRSanit}$-oracle, which clearly contradicts pseudonymity. Thus, the adversary can only input $\mathsf{pk}_{\mathsf{P3S}}$, $\mathsf{sk}_{\mathsf{P3S}}^{\mathsf{Sig}}$, σ, m for which $(\mathsf{pk}_{\mathsf{P3S}}, \sigma, m)$ was never input/output to the $\mathsf{LoRSanit}$-oracle. The goal of the adversary is to guess the bit b.

Again, we stress that this definition also seems to be overly strong. However, as also done for group signatures, secrets keys may leak over time. This definition protects even against bad randomness at key generation.

Definition 11 (P3S Pseudonymity). *We say a P3S scheme is pseudonymous, if for every PPT adversary $\mathcal{A}$, there exists a negligible function ν such that:*

$$\Pr\left[\mathbf{Exp}_{\mathcal{A},\mathsf{P3S}}^{\mathsf{Pseudonymity}}(\kappa) = 1\right] - \tfrac{1}{2} \leq \nu(\kappa).$$

The corresponding experiment is depicted in Fig. 8.

Signer-Accountability. Signer-accountability prohibits that an adversary can generate a bogus proof that makes $\mathsf{Judge}_{\mathsf{P3S}}$ decide that a sanitizer is responsible for a given signature/message pair (m^*, σ^*), but that sanitizer has never generated this pair. This is even true, if the adversary can generate the signer's key pair, the global group key pair, while receiving full adaptive access to a sanitization-oracle.

$\mathbf{Exp}_{\mathcal{A},\mathsf{P3S}}^{\mathsf{Pseudonymity}}(\kappa)$
  $\mathsf{pp}_{\mathsf{P3S}} \leftarrow_r \mathsf{ParGen}_{\mathsf{P3S}}(1^\kappa)$
  $(\mathsf{sk}_{\mathsf{P3S}}^{\mathsf{Sig}}, \mathsf{pk}_{\mathsf{P3S}}^{\mathsf{Sig}}) \leftarrow_r \mathsf{KGenSig}_{\mathsf{P3S}}(\mathsf{pp}_{\mathsf{P3S}})$
  $\mathcal{Q} \leftarrow \emptyset$
  $b \leftarrow_r \{0,1\}$
  $b^* \leftarrow_r \mathcal{A}^{\mathsf{Sign}_{\mathsf{P3S}}(\cdot,\mathsf{sk}_{\mathsf{P3S}}^{\mathsf{Sig}},\cdot,\cdot,\cdot),\mathsf{Proof}'_{\mathsf{P3S}}(\cdot,\mathsf{sk}_{\mathsf{P3S}}^{\mathsf{Sig}},\cdot,\cdot),\mathsf{LoRSanit}(\cdot,\mathsf{pk}_{\mathsf{P3S}}^{\mathsf{Sig}},\cdot,\cdot,\cdot,\cdot,\cdot,\cdot,\cdot,b)}(\mathsf{pk}_{\mathsf{P3S}}^{\mathsf{Sig}})$
      where $\mathsf{Proof}'_{\mathsf{P3S}}$ on input of $\mathsf{pk}_{\mathsf{P3S}}$, $\mathsf{sk}_{\mathsf{P3S}}^{\mathsf{Sig}}$, σ, m:
        return $\bot$, if $(\mathsf{pk}_{\mathsf{P3S}}, \sigma, m) \in \mathcal{Q}$
        return $\mathsf{Proof}_{\mathsf{P3S}}(\mathsf{pk}_{\mathsf{P3S}}, \mathsf{sk}_{\mathsf{P3S}}^{\mathsf{Sig}}, \sigma, m)$
      and $\mathsf{LoRSanit}$ on input of $\mathsf{pk}_{\mathsf{P3S}}$, $\mathsf{pk}_{\mathsf{P3S}}^{\mathsf{Sig}}$, $\mathsf{sk}_{\mathsf{P3S},0}^{\mathsf{San}}$, $\mathsf{sk}_{\mathsf{P3S},1}^{\mathsf{San}}$, $\mathsf{sk}_{\mathbb{S}0}$, $\mathsf{sk}_{\mathbb{S}1}$, m, σ, M, b:
        for $b' \in \{0,1\}$, $(\sigma'_{b'}, m'_{b'}) \leftarrow_r \mathsf{Sanitize}_{\mathsf{P3S}}(\mathsf{pk}_{\mathsf{P3S}}, \mathsf{pk}_{\mathsf{P3S}}^{\mathsf{Sig}}, \mathsf{sk}_{\mathsf{P3S},b'}^{\mathsf{San}}, \mathsf{sk}_{\mathbb{S},b'}, m, \sigma, \mathsf{M})$
        return $\bot$, if $\sigma'_0 = \bot \vee \sigma'_1 = \bot$
        $\mathcal{Q} \leftarrow \mathcal{Q} \cup \{(\mathsf{pk}_{\mathsf{P3S}}, \sigma'_b, m'_b)\}$
        return σ'_b
  return 1, if $b = b^*$
  return 0

Fig. 8. P3S Pseudonymity

$$\mathbf{Exp}_{\mathcal{A},\mathsf{P3S}}^{\mathsf{Signer\text{-}Accountability}}(\kappa)$$

$\mathsf{pp}_{\mathsf{P3S}} \leftarrow_r \mathsf{ParGen}_{\mathsf{P3S}}(1^\kappa)$

$(\mathsf{sk}_{\mathsf{P3S}}^{\mathsf{San}}, \mathsf{pk}_{\mathsf{P3S}}^{\mathsf{San}}) \leftarrow_r \mathsf{KGenSan}_{\mathsf{P3S}}(\mathsf{pp}_{\mathsf{P3S}})$

$b \leftarrow_r \{0,1\}$

$\mathcal{Q} \leftarrow \emptyset$

$(\mathsf{pk}_0^*, \mathsf{pk}_1^*, \sigma^*, m^*, \pi^*) \leftarrow_r \mathcal{A}^{\mathsf{Sanitize}_{\mathsf{P3S}}'(\cdot,\cdot,\mathsf{sk}_{\mathsf{P3S}}^{\mathsf{San}},\cdot,\cdot,\cdot,\cdot)}(\mathsf{pk}_{\mathsf{P3S}}^{\mathsf{San}})$

    where $\mathsf{Sanitize}_{\mathsf{P3S}}'$ on input of $\mathsf{pk}_{\mathsf{P3S}}, \mathsf{pk}_{\mathsf{P3S}}^{\mathsf{Sig}}, \mathsf{sk}_{\mathsf{P3S}}^{\mathsf{San}}, \mathsf{sk}_{\mathsf{S}}, m, \sigma, \mathsf{M}$:

      $(\sigma', m') \leftarrow_r \mathsf{Sanitize}_{\mathsf{P3S}}(\mathsf{pk}_{\mathsf{P3S}}, \mathsf{pk}_{\mathsf{P3S}}^{\mathsf{Sig}}, \mathsf{sk}_{\mathsf{P3S}}^{\mathsf{San}}, \mathsf{sk}_{\mathsf{S}}, m, \sigma, \mathsf{M})$

      if $\sigma \neq \bot$, $\mathcal{Q} \leftarrow \mathcal{Q} \cup \{(\mathsf{pk}_{\mathsf{P3S}}, \mathsf{pk}_{\mathsf{P3S}}^{\mathsf{Sig}}, \sigma', m')\}$

      return σ'

    return 1, if $\mathsf{Judge}_{\mathsf{P3S}}(\mathsf{pk}_0^*, \mathsf{pk}_1^*, \mathsf{pk}_{\mathsf{P3S}}^{\mathsf{San}}, \pi^*, \sigma^*, m^*) = 1 \;\wedge\; (\mathsf{pk}_0^*, \mathsf{pk}_1^*, \sigma^*, m^*) \notin \mathcal{Q}$

    return 0

Fig. 9. P3S Signer-Accountability

Definition 12 (P3S Signer-Accountability). *We say a P3S scheme is signer-accountable, if for every PPT adversary $\mathcal{A}$, there exists a negligible function ν such that:*

$$\Pr\left[\mathbf{Exp}_{\mathcal{A},\mathsf{P3S}}^{\mathsf{Signer\text{-}Accountability}}(\kappa) = 1\right] \leq \nu(\kappa).$$

The corresponding experiment is depicted in Fig. 9.

Sanitizer-Accountability. Sanitizer-accountability prohibits that an adversary can generate a bogus signature/message pair (m^*, σ^*) that makes $\mathsf{Proof}_{\mathsf{P3S}}$ outputs a (honestly generated) generated proof π_{P3S} which points to the signer, but (m^*, σ^*) has never been generated by the signer. This is even true, if the adversary can generate all sanitizers key pairs, while receiving full adaptive access to a signing-oracle and a proof-oracle.

$$\mathbf{Exp}_{\mathcal{A},\mathsf{P3S}}^{\mathsf{Sanitizer\text{-}Accountability}}(\kappa)$$

$\mathsf{pp}_{\mathsf{P3S}} \leftarrow_r \mathsf{ParGen}_{\mathsf{P3S}}(1^\kappa)$

$(\mathsf{sk}_{\mathsf{P3S}}^{\mathsf{Sig}}, \mathsf{pk}_{\mathsf{P3S}}^{\mathsf{Sig}}) \leftarrow_r \mathsf{KGenSig}_{\mathsf{P3S}}(\mathsf{pp}_{\mathsf{P3S}})$

$b \leftarrow_r \{0,1\}$

$\mathcal{Q} \leftarrow \emptyset$

$(\mathsf{pk}^*, \sigma^*, m^*, \pi^*) \leftarrow_r \mathcal{A}^{\mathsf{Sign}_{\mathsf{P3S}}'(\cdot,\mathsf{sk}_{\mathsf{P3S}}^{\mathsf{Sig}},\cdot,\cdot,\cdot),\mathsf{Proof}_{\mathsf{P3S}}(\cdot,\mathsf{sk}_{\mathsf{P3S}}^{\mathsf{Sig}},\cdot,\cdot)}(\mathsf{pk}_{\mathsf{P3S}}^{\mathsf{Sig}})$

    where $\mathsf{Sign}_{\mathsf{P3S}}'$ on input of $\mathsf{pk}_{\mathsf{P3S}}, \mathsf{sk}_{\mathsf{P3S}}^{\mathsf{Sig}}, m, \mathsf{A}, \mathbb{A}$:

      $\sigma \leftarrow_r \mathsf{Sign}_{\mathsf{P3S}}(\mathsf{pk}_{\mathsf{P3S}}, \mathsf{sk}_{\mathsf{P3S}}^{\mathsf{Sig}}, m, \mathsf{A}, \mathbb{A})$

      if $\sigma \neq \bot$, $\mathcal{Q} \leftarrow \mathcal{Q} \cup \{(\mathsf{pk}_{\mathsf{P3S}}, \sigma', m')\}$

      return σ'

    $(\pi_{\mathsf{P3S}}, \mathsf{pk}) \leftarrow_r \mathsf{Proof}_{\mathsf{P3S}}(\mathsf{pk}^*, \mathsf{sk}_{\mathsf{P3S}}^{\mathsf{Sig}}, \sigma^*, m^*)$

    return 1, if $\mathsf{Judge}_{\mathsf{P3S}}(\mathsf{pk}^*, \mathsf{pk}_{\mathsf{P3S}}^{\mathsf{Sig}}, \mathsf{pk}_{\mathsf{P3S}}^{\mathsf{Sig}}, \pi_{\mathsf{P3S}}, \sigma^*, m^*) = 1 \;\wedge\; (\mathsf{pk}^*, \sigma^*, m^*) \notin \mathcal{Q}$

    return 0

Fig. 10. P3S Sanitizer-Accountability

Definition 13 (P3S Sanitizer-Accountability). *We say a P3S scheme is sanitizer-accountable, if for every PPT adversary $\mathcal{A}$, there exists a negligible function ν such that:*

$$\Pr\left[\mathbf{Exp}_{\mathcal{A},\text{P3S}}^{\text{Sanitizer-Accountability}}(\kappa) = 1\right] \leq \nu(\kappa).$$

The corresponding experiment is depicted in Fig. 10.

Proof-Soundness. Proof-soundness essentially only handles the case that a signature σ can only be opened in an unambiguous way. Thus, the adversary's goal is to output two proofs which "prove" different statements for the same signature/message pair. It is related to the property of opening-soundness introduced by Sakai et al. [SSE+12] for group signatures.

Definition 14 (P3S Proof-Soundness). *We say a P3S scheme is proof-sound, if for every PPT adversary $\mathcal{A}$, there exists a negligible function ν such that:*

$$\Pr\left[\mathbf{Exp}_{\mathcal{A},\text{P3S}}^{\text{Proof-Soundness}}(\kappa) = 1\right] \leq \nu(\kappa).$$

The corresponding experiment is depicted in Fig. 11.

$\mathbf{Exp}_{\mathcal{A},\text{P3S}}^{\text{Proof-Soundness}}(\kappa)$

$\quad \text{pp}_{\text{P3S}} \leftarrow_r \text{ParGen}_{\text{P3S}}(1^\kappa)$

$\quad ((\text{pk}_i^*)_{0\leq i\leq 5}, \sigma^*, m^*, \pi_0^*, \pi_1^*) \leftarrow_r \mathcal{A}(\text{pp}_{\text{P3S}})$

$\quad \text{return } 1, \text{ if } \text{Judge}_{\text{P3S}}(\text{pk}_0^*, \text{pk}_1^*, \text{pk}_2^*, \pi_0^*, \sigma^*, m^*) = \text{Judge}_{\text{P3S}}(\text{pk}_3^*, \text{pk}_4^*, \text{pk}_5^*, \pi_1^*, \sigma^*, m^*) = 1 \wedge$

$\quad\quad (\text{pk}_0^*, \text{pk}_1^*, \text{pk}_2^*) \neq (\text{pk}_3^*, \text{pk}_4^*, \text{pk}_5^*)$

$\quad \text{return } 0$

Fig. 11. P3S Proof-Soundness

Traceability. Traceability requires that an adversary cannot generate a signature which cannot be opened, i.e., it can be seen as the "dual" to proof-soundness. In more detail, the adversary's goal is to generate a verifying signature for which an honest signer cannot generate $(\pi_{\text{P3S}}, \text{pk})$ for which $\text{Judge}_{\text{P3S}}$ outputs correct.

$\mathbf{Exp}_{\mathcal{A},\text{P3S}}^{\text{Traceability}}(\kappa)$

$\quad \text{pp}_{\text{P3S}} \leftarrow_r \text{ParGen}_{\text{P3S}}(1^\kappa)$

$\quad (\text{sk}_{\text{P3S}}^{\text{Sig}}, \text{pk}_{\text{P3S}}^{\text{Sig}}) \leftarrow_r \text{KGenSig}_{\text{P3S}}(\text{pp}_{\text{P3S}})$

$\quad (\text{pk}^*, \sigma^*, m^*) \leftarrow_r \mathcal{A}^{\text{Sign}_{\text{P3S}}(\cdot,\text{sk}_{\text{P3S}}^{\text{Sig}},\cdot,\cdot,\cdot),\text{Proof}_{\text{P3S}}(\cdot,\text{sk}_{\text{P3S}}^{\text{Sig}},\cdot,\cdot)}(\text{pk}_{\text{P3S}}^{\text{Sig}})$

$\quad \text{return } 0, \text{ if } \text{Verify}_{\text{P3S}}(\text{pk}^*, \text{pk}_{\text{P3S}}^{\text{Sig}}, \sigma^*, m^*) = 0$

$\quad (\pi_{\text{P3S}}, \text{pk}) \leftarrow_r \text{Proof}_{\text{P3S}}(\text{pk}^*, \text{sk}_{\text{P3S}}^{\text{Sig}}, \sigma^*, m^*)$

$\quad \text{return } 1, \text{ if } \text{Judge}_{\text{P3S}}(\text{pk}^*, \text{pk}_{\text{P3S}}^{\text{Sig}}, \text{pk}, \pi_{\text{P3S}}, \sigma^*, m^*) = 0$

$\quad \text{return } 0$

Fig. 12. P3S Traceability

Definition 15 (P3S Traceability). *We say a* P3S *scheme is traceable, if for every PPT adversary $\mathcal{A}$, there exists a negligible function ν such that:*

$$\Pr\left[\mathbf{Exp}_{\mathcal{A},\mathsf{P3S}}^{\mathsf{Traceability}}(\kappa) = 1\right] \leq \nu(\kappa).$$

The corresponding experiment is depicted in Fig. 12.

Relationship of Properties. In the full version of this paper, we show that all defined properties are independent of each other.

4   Construction

In this section we present our P3S construction. The key ingredients are our strengthened version of a policy-based chameleon-hash PCH, a labeled simulation-sound extractable non-interactive zero-knowledge proof system Ω (NIZK for short), a one-way function f as well as a key-verifiable IND-CCA2 secure public key encryption scheme[3] Π and an eUNF-CMA-secure signature scheme Σ. The intuition behind our construction, given in Construction 1, is as follows.

The global parameters of the scheme are a one-way function f, the CRS of the NIZK, and the parameters for the encryption scheme, the signature scheme and the policy-based chameleon hash. The group setup generates the keys of the policy-based chameleon-hash, and a key pair of the signature scheme. The signer generates a signature key pair and publishes the public key together with an image y_1 of a random pre-image x_1 of the OWF f. The sanitizer chooses a random pre-image x_2 of the OWF as secret key and as public key $y_2 = f(x_2)$. If a sanitizers joins a group, i.e., obtains secret keys for a set of attributes $\mathbb{S}$, the group manager signs the sanitizer's public key and additionally issues a secret key for the PCH for attributes $\mathbb{S}$.

For signing, the signer hashes the message using the PCH and signs the hash (along with some additional information). Moreover, it computes a NIZK for the relation R (using as label ℓ some additional information like the admissible changes).

$$((y_1, c, y_2, \mathsf{pk}_\Pi, \mathsf{pk}_\Sigma), (x, r, \sigma_{\mathsf{sks}})) \in R \iff (y_1 = f(x) \ \wedge \ c = \mathsf{Enc}_\Pi(\mathsf{pk}_\Pi, y_1; r))$$
$$\vee \ (y_2 = f(x) \ \wedge \ c = \mathsf{Enc}_\Pi(\mathsf{pk}_\Pi, y_2; r) \ \wedge \ \mathsf{Verf}_\Sigma(\mathsf{pk}_\Sigma, y_2, \sigma_{\mathsf{sks}}) = 1).$$

Sanitizing amounts to computing a collision for the PCH hash, updating the respective message blocks, and again attaching a NIZK for relation R. Verification is straightforward. Relation R is used within signing and sanitizing to force the signer or the sanitizer to commit to having performed the action. Intuitively, when determining whether a signer or sanitizer has performed the action,

---

[3] Although key-verifiability is no property often explicitly used within IND-CCA2 encryption schemes, most encryption schemes are key-verifiable.

the Proof$_{P3S}$ algorithm (having access to the signer's secret key) can simply decrypt c and prove correct decryption.

It may be tempting to think that the weaker notion of witness indistinguishability is sufficient for our construction, but it turns out that one requires zero-knowledge. Moreover, we stress that due to the underlying construction paradigm, we do not consider the strong privacy notion of unlinkability [BFLS10], i.e., that sanitized signatures cannot be linked to its origin, which seems to be very hard to achieve with the current construction paradigm. However, finding such a construction may have its merits. Formally, for our construction, we can show the following:

Theorem 1. *If f is a one-way function, Π is IND-CCA2 secure and key-verifiable, Σ is eUNF-CMA secure, Ω is zero-knowledge and simulation-sound extractable, while PCH is fully indistinguishable, insider collision-resistant, and unique, the construction of a P3S given in Construction 1 is unforgeable, immutable, private, transparent, pseudonymous, signer-accountable, sanitizer-accountable, proof-sound, and traceable. Likewise, the construction is correct, if the underlying primitives are correct (and sound, resp.).*

The proof of the theorem is given in the full version of this paper. We give a sketch below.

Proof (Sketch). Unforgeability follows from the zero-knowledge and extractability property of the used proof system, the insider collision-resistance of the used PCH, as well as the one-wayness of f, and unforgeability of the used signature scheme. Immutability directly follows from the unforgeability of the used signature scheme. Privacy follows from the zero-knowledge property of the used proof system, the full indistinguishability of the used PCH, and somewhat surprisingly, the uniqueness of PCH. Likewise, transparency follows from the zero-knowledge property of the used proof system, and the IND-CCA2 security of the used encryption scheme. The same is true for pseudonymity, but we also require, again somewhat surprising, the uniqueness of the used PCH. Both signer-accountability, and sanitizer-accountability, follow from the extractability of the used proof system, and the one-wayness of f. Proof-soundness follows from key-verifiability of the used encryption scheme, and the extractability of the used proof system. Finally, traceability follows from the extractability of the used proof system.

Instantiation. The description of Construction 1 is as compact as reasonable. For a concrete instantiation, there are some aspects which can be optimized. Currently, it seems to be advisable to stick to elliptic curves and in particular to the type-3 bilinear group setting (a setting where we assume the SXDH assumption to hold), due to the efficiency of the CP-ABE schemes in this setting (used by the PCH). Consequently, we consider the OWF f to be simply the function $f(x) = g^x$ for $x \in \mathbb{Z}_q$ and g being a generator of a group $\mathbb{G}$ of prime order q (and in particular one of the base groups of a bilinear group). Then, as an encryption

---

$\mathsf{ParGen_{P3S}}(1^\kappa)$: On input a security parameter κ, let $\mathsf{pp}_\Pi \leftarrow_r \mathsf{PPGen}_\Pi(1^\kappa)$, $\mathsf{crs}_\Omega \leftarrow_r \mathsf{PPGen}_\Omega(1^\kappa)$.[a] Finally, choose a one-way function f, let $\mathsf{pp}_\Sigma \leftarrow_r \mathsf{PPGen}_\Sigma(1^\kappa)$, and $\mathsf{pp}_{\mathsf{PCH}} \leftarrow_r \mathsf{PPGen}_{\mathsf{PCH}}(1^\kappa)$. Return $\mathsf{pp}_{\mathsf{P3S}} \leftarrow (\mathsf{crs}_\Omega, \mathsf{pp}_\Pi, \mathsf{pp}_\Sigma, \mathsf{pp}_{\mathsf{PCH}}, f)$.

$\mathsf{Setup_{P3S}}(\mathsf{pp}_{\mathsf{P3S}})$: Let $(\mathsf{sk}_{\mathsf{PCH}}, \mathsf{pk}_{\mathsf{PCH}}) \leftarrow_r \mathsf{MKeyGen}_{\mathsf{PCH}}(\mathsf{pp}_{\mathsf{PCH}})$ and $(\mathsf{sk}_\Sigma, \mathsf{pk}_\Sigma) \leftarrow_r \mathsf{KGen}_\Sigma(\mathsf{pp}_\Sigma)$. Return $(\mathsf{sk}_{\mathsf{P3S}}, \mathsf{pk}_{\mathsf{P3S}}) \leftarrow ((\mathsf{sk}_{\mathsf{PCH}}, \mathsf{sk}_\Sigma), (\mathsf{pk}_{\mathsf{PCH}}, \mathsf{pk}_\Sigma))$.

$\mathsf{KGenSig_{P3S}}(\mathsf{pp}_{\mathsf{P3S}})$: Draw $x_1 \leftarrow_r D_f$, $(\mathsf{sk}_\Pi, \mathsf{pk}_\Pi) \leftarrow_r \mathsf{KGen}_\Pi(\mathsf{pp}_\Pi)$, let $y_1 \leftarrow f(x_1)$ and $(\mathsf{sk}'_\Sigma, \mathsf{pk}'_\Sigma) \leftarrow_r \mathsf{KGen}_\Sigma(\mathsf{pp}_\Sigma)$.
Return $(\mathsf{sk}_{\mathsf{P3S}}^{\mathsf{Sig}}, \mathsf{pk}_{\mathsf{P3S}}^{\mathsf{Sig}}) \leftarrow ((x_1, \mathsf{sk}'_\Sigma, \mathsf{sk}_\Pi), (y_1, \mathsf{pk}'_\Sigma, \mathsf{pk}_\Pi))$.

$\mathsf{KGenSan_{P3S}}(\mathsf{pp}_{\mathsf{P3S}})$: Draw $x_2 \leftarrow_r D_f$. Let $y_2 \leftarrow f(x_2)$. Return (x_2, y_2).

$\mathsf{Sign_{P3S}}(\mathsf{pk}_{\mathsf{P3S}}, \mathsf{sk}_{\mathsf{P3S}}^{\mathsf{Sig}}, m, \mathsf{A}, \mathbb{A})$: If $\mathbb{A} = \emptyset$, return $\perp$. Let $(h, r) \leftarrow_r \mathsf{Hash}_{\mathsf{PCH}}(\mathsf{pk}_{\mathsf{PCH}}, m, \mathbb{A})$, $\sigma_m \leftarrow_r \mathsf{Sign}_\Sigma(\mathsf{sk}'_\Sigma, (\mathsf{pk}_{\mathsf{P3S}}, \mathsf{pk}_{\mathsf{P3S}}^{\mathsf{Sig}}, \mathsf{A}, m_{!\mathsf{A}}, h, \mathbb{A}))$, and $c \leftarrow_r \mathsf{Enc}_\Pi(\mathsf{pk}_\Pi, y_1)$. Let $\pi \leftarrow_r \mathsf{Prove}_\Omega\{(x_1, x_2, \sigma_{\mathsf{sk_S}}) : (y_1 = f(x_1) \wedge c = \mathsf{Enc}_\Pi(\mathsf{pk}_\Pi, y_1)) \vee (y_2 = f(x_2) \wedge c = \mathsf{Enc}_\Pi(\mathsf{pk}_\Pi, y_2) \wedge \mathsf{Verf}_\Sigma(\mathsf{pk}_\Sigma, (y_2, \mathsf{pk}_{\mathsf{P3S}}), \sigma_{\mathsf{sk_S}}) = 1)\}(\ell)$, where $\ell = (\mathsf{pp}_{\mathsf{P3S}}, \mathsf{pk}_{\mathsf{P3S}}, \mathsf{pk}_{\mathsf{P3S}}^{\mathsf{Sig}}, h, r, m, \mathsf{A}, \mathbb{A}, m_{\mathsf{A}}, m_{!\mathsf{A}}, \sigma_m, c)$. Return $\sigma \leftarrow (h, r, \mathsf{A}, \sigma_m, \mathbb{A}, \pi, c)$.

$\mathsf{AddSan_{P3S}}(\mathsf{sk}_{\mathsf{P3S}}, \mathsf{pk}_{\mathsf{P3S}}^{\mathsf{San}}, \mathbb{S})$: If $\mathbb{S} \notin 2^\mathsf{U}$, return $\perp$. Let $\sigma_{\mathsf{sk_S}} \leftarrow_r \mathsf{Sign}_\Sigma(\mathsf{sk}_\Sigma, (\mathsf{pk}_{\mathsf{P3S}}^{\mathsf{San}}, \mathsf{pk}_{\mathsf{P3S}}))$ and $\mathsf{sk}'_\mathbb{S} \leftarrow_r \mathsf{KGen}_{\mathsf{PCH}}(\mathsf{sk}_{\mathsf{PCH}}, \mathbb{S})$. Return $\mathsf{sk}_\mathbb{S} \leftarrow (\sigma_{\mathsf{sk_S}}, \mathsf{sk}'_\mathbb{S})$.

$\mathsf{Verify_{P3S}}(\mathsf{pk}_{\mathsf{P3S}}, \mathsf{pk}_{\mathsf{P3S}}^{\mathsf{Sig}}, \sigma, m)$: If π or σ_m is not valid, return $\perp$. Check that $m_{!\mathsf{A}}$ is contained in m in the correct sequence at the right positions (derivable from A). If $\mathsf{Verify}_{\mathsf{PCH}}(\mathsf{pk}_{\mathsf{PCH}}, m, r, h) = 1$, return 1. Otherwise, return 0.

$\mathsf{Sanitize_{P3S}}(\mathsf{pk}_{\mathsf{P3S}}, \mathsf{pk}_{\mathsf{P3S}}^{\mathsf{Sig}}, \mathsf{sk}_{\mathsf{P3S}}^{\mathsf{San}}, \mathsf{sk}_\mathbb{S}, m, \sigma, \mathsf{M})$: If $\sigma_{\mathsf{sk_S}}$ or σ is not valid, return $\perp$. Let $r' \leftarrow_r \mathsf{Adapt}_{\mathsf{PCH}}(\mathsf{pk}_{\mathsf{PCH}}, \mathsf{sk}'_\mathbb{S}, m, \mathsf{M}(m), h, r)$, $c' \leftarrow_r \mathsf{Enc}_\Pi(\mathsf{pk}_\Pi, y_2)$, and $\pi' \leftarrow_r \mathsf{Prove}_\Omega\{(x_1, x_2, \sigma_{\mathsf{sk_S}}) : (y_1 = f(x_1) \wedge c' = \mathsf{Enc}_\Pi(\mathsf{pk}_\Pi, y_1)) \vee (y_2 = f(x_2) \wedge c' = \mathsf{Enc}_\Pi(\mathsf{pk}_\Pi, y_2) \wedge \mathsf{Verf}_\Sigma(\mathsf{pk}_\Sigma, (y_2, \mathsf{pk}_{\mathsf{P3S}}), \sigma_{\mathsf{sk_S}}) = 1)\}(\ell)$, where $\ell = (\mathsf{pp}_{\mathsf{P3S}}, \mathsf{pk}_{\mathsf{P3S}}, \mathsf{pk}_{\mathsf{P3S}}^{\mathsf{Sig}}, h, r', \mathsf{M}(m), \mathsf{A}, \mathbb{A}, m_{\mathsf{A}}, m_{!\mathsf{A}}, \sigma_m, c')$. Let $(\sigma', m') \leftarrow ((h, r', \mathsf{A}, \sigma_m, \mathbb{A}, \pi', c'), \mathsf{M}(m))$. If (σ', m') is not valid, return $\perp$. Return (σ', m').

$\mathsf{Proof_{P3S}}(\mathsf{pk}_{\mathsf{P3S}}, \mathsf{sk}_{\mathsf{P3S}}^{\mathsf{Sig}}, \sigma, m)$: If σ is not valid, return $\perp$. Let $\mathsf{pk} \leftarrow \mathsf{Dec}_\Pi(\mathsf{sk}_\Pi, c)$. Let $\pi_{\mathsf{P3S}} \leftarrow_r \mathsf{Prove}_\Omega\{(\mathsf{sk}_\Pi) : \mathsf{pk} = \mathsf{Dec}_\Pi(\mathsf{sk}_\Pi, c) \wedge \mathsf{KVrf}_\Pi(\mathsf{sk}_\Pi, \mathsf{pk}_\Pi) = 1\}(\ell)$, where $\ell = (\mathsf{pp}_{\mathsf{P3S}}, \mathsf{pk}_{\mathsf{P3S}}, \mathsf{pk}_{\mathsf{P3S}}^{\mathsf{Sig}}, \sigma, \mathsf{pk}, m)$. Return $(\pi_{\mathsf{P3S}}, \mathsf{pk})$.

$\mathsf{Judge_{P3S}}(\mathsf{pk}_{\mathsf{P3S}}, \mathsf{pk}_{\mathsf{P3S}}^{\mathsf{Sig}}, \mathsf{pk}, \pi_{\mathsf{P3S}}, \sigma, m)$: If σ or π_{P3S} is not valid, return 0. Return 1.

---

[a] Note, we need a different CRS for each language L involved. However, we keep the description short, and thus do not make this explicit.

Construction 1. Our P3S

scheme to encrypt images under f and that is key-verifiable, we can use Cramer-Shoup encryption in either of the two base groups. For completeness, we show key-verifiability of CS-encryption where keys are generated with respect to a common group description (including both generators) in the full version of this paper. Now, the signature keys $(\mathsf{sk}'_\Sigma, \mathsf{pk}'_\Sigma)$ used by signer to produce signatures can be any arbitrary eUNF-CMA-secure scheme. In contrast, the signature scheme associated to keys $(\mathsf{sk}_\Sigma, \mathsf{pk}_\Sigma)$ used by the group manager in $\mathsf{AddSan_{P3S}}$ to certify the y_2

values of sanitizers need to be chosen with care: we need a signature scheme with message space being one of the base groups of the bilinear group and thus the natural choice is a structure preserving signature scheme [AFG+10]. Moreover, the SPS (e.g., Groth [Gro15]) needs to be compatible with efficient labeled NIZK; the latter can be instantiated from standard Σ-protocols using the compiler by Faust et al. [FKMV12] and supporting labels is straightforward (cf. [ABM15]). As PCH instantiation we can use a strengthened version of the PCH by Derler et al. [DSSS19]. See the full version of this paper.

Efficiency. Our scheme is reasonably efficient. The group manager only needs to create a key-pair for a PCH, while the sanitizer only needs to evaluate a one-way functions (the signer additionally needs to draw a key-pair for an encryption scheme Π). For signing, the signer needs to generate a hash, a signature, an encryption, and a simple NIZK. For sanitizing, the sanitizer has to create an encryption, adapt a hash, and attaches a simple NIZK. Granting sanitizing rights boils down to creating a signature and creating a key for the PCH. Verification is also straightforward: A verifier checks a signature and the NIZK. Likewise, proof-generation is a simple decryption and a NIZK proving that decryption was done honestly. Checking a proof is verifying a proof and a signature. Thus, ignoring the NIZK and the encryptions, our scheme is comparable to existing, way less expressive, constructions.

5   Conclusion

We have introduced the notion of policy-based sanitizable signatures, which are an extension to standard sanitizable signature schemes, along with a provably secure construction. Our construction features, for the first time, full accountability. In our new primitive, a sanitizer is no longer appointed by the signer at signature generation, but rather can sanitize based on a set attributes it has.

References

[ABC+15] Ahn, J.H., et al.: Computing on authenticated data. J. Cryptol. **28**, 2 (2015). https://doi.org/10.1007/s00145-014-9182-0

[ABM15] Abdalla, M., Benhamouda, F., MacKenzie, P.: Security of the J-PAKE password-authenticated key exchange protocol. In: 2015 IEEE Symposium on Security and Privacy (SP 2015), pp. 571–587 (2015)

[ACdMT05] Ateniese, G., et al.: Sanitizable signatures. ESORICS 2005. LNCS, vol. 3679, pp. 159–177. Springer, Heidelberg (2005). https://doi.org/10.1007/11555827_10

[ADK+13] Abe, M., et al.: Tagged one-time signatures: tight security and optimal tag size. PKC 2013. LNCS, vol. 7778, pp. 312–331. Springer, Heidelberg (2013). https://doi.org/10.1007/978-3-642-36362-7_20

[AdM04] Ateniese, G., de Medeiros, B.: On the key exposure problem in chameleon hashes. In: Blundo, C., Cimato, S. (eds.) SCN 2004. LNCS, vol. 3352, pp. 165–179. Springer, Heidelberg (2005). https://doi.org/10.1007/978-3-540-30598-9_12

[AFG+10] Abe, M., Fuchsbauer, G., Groth, J., Haralambiev, K., Ohkubo, M.: Structure-preserving signatures and commitments to group elements. In: Rabin, T. (ed.) CRYPTO 2010. LNCS, vol. 6223, pp. 209–236. Springer, Heidelberg (2010). https://doi.org/10.1007/978-3-642-14623-7_12

[AMVA17] Ateniese, G., Magri, B., Venturi, D., Andrade, E.R..: Redactable blockchain - or - rewriting history in bitcoin and friends. In: EuroS&P, pp. 111–126 (2017)

[BCD+17] Beck, M.T., et al.: Practical strongly invisible and strongly accountable sanitizable signatures. ACISP 2017. LNCS, vol. 10342, pp. 437–452. Springer, Cham (2017). https://doi.org/10.1007/978-3-319-60055-0_23

[BFF+09] Brzuska, C., et al.: Security of sanitizable signatures revisited. PKC 2009. LNCS, vol. 5443, pp. 317–336. Springer, Heidelberg (2009). https://doi.org/10.1007/978-3-642-00468-1_18

[BFKW09] Boneh, D., et al.: Signing a linear subspace: signature schemes for network coding. PKC 2009. LNCS, vol. 5443, pp. 68–87. Springer, Heidelberg (2009). https://doi.org/10.1007/978-3-642-00468-1_5

[BFLS09] Brzuska, C., Fischlin, M., Lehmann, A., Schröder, D..: Santizable signatures: how to partially delegate control for authenticated data. In: BIOSIG, pp. 117–128 (2009)

[BFLS10] Brzuska, C., et al.: Unlinkability of sanitizable signatures. PKC 2010. LNCS, vol. 6056, pp. 444–461. Springer, Heidelberg (2010). https://doi.org/10.1007/978-3-642-13013-7_26

[BL17] Bultel, X., Lafourcade, P.: Unlinkable and strongly accountable sanitizable signatures from verifiable ring signatures. In: Capkun, S., Chow, S.S.M. (eds.) CANS 2017. LNCS, vol. 11261, pp. 203–226. Springer, Cham (2018). https://doi.org/10.1007/978-3-030-02641-7_10

[BLL+19] Bultel, X., et al.: Efficient invisible and unlinkable sanitizable signatures. PKC 2019, Part 1. LNCS, vol. 11442, pp. 159–189. Springer, Cham (2019). https://doi.org/10.1007/978-3-030-17253-4_6

[BNPS03] Bellare, M., Namprempre, C., Pointcheval, D., Semanko, M.: The one-more-RSA-inversion problems and the security of Chaum's blind signature scheme. J. Cryptol. **16**(3), 185–215 (2003). https://doi.org/10.1007/s00145-002-0120-1

[BPS12] Brzuska, C., Pöhls, H.C., Samelin, K.: Non-interactive public accountability for sanitizable signatures. In: De Capitani di Vimercati, S., Mitchell, C. (eds.) EuroPKI 2012. LNCS, vol. 7868, pp. 178–193. Springer, Heidelberg (2013). https://doi.org/10.1007/978-3-642-40012-4_12

[BPS13] Brzuska, C., Pöhls, H.C., Samelin, K.: Efficient and perfectly unlinkable sanitizable signatures without group signatures. In: Katsikas, S., Agudo, I. (eds.) EuroPKI 2013. LNCS, vol. 8341, pp. 12–30. Springer, Heidelberg (2014). https://doi.org/10.1007/978-3-642-53997-8_2

[BPS17] Bilzhause, A., Pöhls, H.C., Samelin, K.: Position paper: the past, present, and future of sanitizable and redactable signatures. In: Ares, pp. 87:1–87:9 (2017)

[BR93] Bellare, M., Rogaway, P.: Random oracles are practical: a paradigm for designing efficient protocols. In: CCS, 62–73 (1993)

[BSW07] Bethencourt, J., Sahai, A., Waters, B.: Ciphertext-policy attribute-based encryption. In: 2007 IEEE Symposium on Security and Privacy (SP 2007), pp. 321–334 (2007)

[BSZ05]   Bellare, M., Shi, H., Zhang, C.: Foundations of group signatures: the case of dynamic groups. In: Menezes, A. (ed.) CT-RSA 2005. LNCS, vol. 3376, pp. 136–153. Springer, Heidelberg (2005). https://doi.org/10.1007/978-3-540-30574-3_11

[CDK+17] Camenisch, J., et al.: Chameleon-hashes with ephemeral trapdoors - and applications to invisible sanitizable signatures. In: PKC, Part II (2017). https://doi.org/10.1007/978-3-662-54388-7_6

[CJ10]   Canard, S., Jambert, A.: On extended sanitizable signature schemes. In: Pieprzyk, J. (ed.) CT-RSA 2010. LNCS, vol. 5985, pp. 179–194. Springer, Heidelberg (2010). https://doi.org/10.1007/978-3-642-11925-5_13

[CJL12]   Canard, S., Jambert, A., Lescuyer, R.: Sanitizable signatures with several signers and sanitizers. In: Mitrokotsa, A., Vaudenay, S. (eds.) AFRICACRYPT 2012. LNCS, vol. 7374, pp. 35–52. Springer, Heidelberg (2012). https://doi.org/10.1007/978-3-642-31410-0_3

[CLM08]   Canard, S., et al.: *Trapdoor* sanitizable signatures and their application to content protection. ACNS 2008. LNCS, vol. 5037, pp. 258–276. Springer, Heidelberg (2008). https://doi.org/10.1007/978-3-540-68914-0_16

[CS97]   Camenisch, J., Stadler, M.: Efficient group signature schemes for large groups. In: Kaliski, B.S. (ed.) CRYPTO 1997. LNCS, vol. 1294, pp. 410–424. Springer, Heidelberg (1997). https://doi.org/10.1007/BFb0052252

[CS98]   Cramer, R., Shoup, V.: A practical public key cryptosystem provably secure against adaptive chosen ciphertext attack. In: Krawczyk, H. (ed.) CRYPTO 1998. LNCS, vol. 1462, pp. 13–25. Springer, Heidelberg (1998). https://doi.org/10.1007/BFb0055717

[CvH91]   Chaum, D., van Heyst, E.: Group signatures. In: Davies, D.W. (ed.) EUROCRYPT 1991. LNCS, vol. 547, pp. 257–265. Springer, Heidelberg (1991). https://doi.org/10.1007/3-540-46416-6_22

[DDH+15] Demirel, D., et al.: PRISMACLOUD D4.4: overview of functional and malleable signature schemes. Technical report, H2020 Prismacloud (2015). www.prismacloud.eu

[DHLW10] Dodis, Y., Haralambiev, K., López-Alt, A., Wichs, D.: Efficient public-key cryptography in the presence of key leakage. In: Abe, M. (ed.) ASIACRYPT 2010. LNCS, vol. 6477, pp. 613–631. Springer, Heidelberg (2010). https://doi.org/10.1007/978-3-642-17373-8_35

[dMPPS14] De Meer, H., et al.: On the relation between redactable and sanitizable signature schemes. ESSoS 2014. LNCS, vol. 8364, pp. 113–130. Springer, Cham (2014). https://doi.org/10.1007/978-3-319-04897-0_8

[DPSS15] Derler, D., et al.: A general framework for redactable signatures and new constructions. ICISC 2015. LNCS, vol. 9558, pp. 3–19. Springer, Cham (2016). https://doi.org/10.1007/978-3-319-30840-1_1

[DS15]   Derler, D., Slamanig, D.: Rethinking privacy for extended sanitizable signatures and a black-box construction of strongly private schemes. In: Au, M.-H., Miyaji, A. (eds.) ProvSec 2015. LNCS, vol. 9451, pp. 455–474. Springer, Cham (2015). https://doi.org/10.1007/978-3-319-26059-4_25

[DS19]   Derler, D., Slamanig, D.: Key-homomorphic signatures: definitions and applications to multiparty signatures and non-interactive zero-knowledge. Des. Codes Cryptogr. **87**(6), 1373–1413 (2019). https://doi.org/10.1007/s10623-018-0535-9

[DSSS19] Derler, D., Samelin, K., Slamanig, D., Striecks, C.: Fine-grained and controlled rewriting in blockchains: chameleon-hashing gone attribute-based. In: NDSS (2019)

[FF15] Fehr, V., Fischlin, M.: Sanitizable signcryption: sanitization over encrypted data (full version) (2015, ePrint)

[FH18] Fischlin, M., Harasser, P.: Invisible sanitizable signatures and public-key encryption are equivalent. In: Preneel, B., Vercauteren, F. (eds.) ACNS 2018. LNCS, vol. 10892, pp. 202–220. Springer, Cham (2018). https://doi.org/10.1007/978-3-319-93387-0_11

[FKM+16] Fleischhacker, N., et al.: Efficient unlinkable sanitizable signatures from signatures with re-randomizable keys. PKC 2016. LNCS, vol. 9614, pp. 301–330. Springer, Heidelberg (2016). https://doi.org/10.1007/978-3-662-49384-7_12

[FKMV12] Faust, S., et al.: On the non-malleability of the Fiat-Shamir transform. INDOCRYPT 2012. LNCS, vol. 7668, pp. 60–79. Springer, Heidelberg (2012). https://doi.org/10.1007/978-3-642-34931-7_5

[GGOT16] Ghosh, E., et al.: Verifiable zero-knowledge order queries and updates for fully dynamic lists and trees. SCN 2016. LNCS, vol. 9841, pp. 216–236. Springer, Cham (2016). https://doi.org/10.1007/978-3-319-44618-9_12

[GQZ10] gong, J., et al.: Fully-secure and practical sanitizable signatures. Inscrypt 2010. LNCS, vol. 6584, pp. 300–317. Springer, Heidelberg (2011). https://doi.org/10.1007/978-3-642-21518-6_21

[Gro06] Groth, J.: Simulation-sound NIZK proofs for a practical language and constant size group signatures. In: Lai, X., Chen, K. (eds.) ASIACRYPT 2006. LNCS, vol. 4284, pp. 444–459. Springer, Heidelberg (2006). https://doi.org/10.1007/11935230_29

[Gro15] Groth, J.: Efficient fully structure-preserving signatures for large messages. In: Iwata, T., Cheon, J.H. (eds.) ASIACRYPT 2015. LNCS, vol. 9452, pp. 239–259. Springer, Heidelberg (2015). https://doi.org/10.1007/978-3-662-48797-6_11

[JMSW02] Johnson, R., Molnar, D., Song, D., Wagner, D.: Homomorphic signature schemes. In: Preneel, B. (ed.) CT-RSA 2002. LNCS, vol. 2271, pp. 244–262. Springer, Heidelberg (2002). https://doi.org/10.1007/3-540-45760-7_17

[KPSS18a] Krenn, S., et al.: Chameleon-hashes with dual long-term trapdoors and their applications. AFRICACRYPT 2018. LNCS, vol. 10831, pp. 11–32. Springer, Cham (2018). https://doi.org/10.1007/978-3-319-89339-6_2

[KPSS18b] Krenn, S., et al.: Protean signature schemes. CANS 2018. LNCS, vol. 11124, pp. 256–276. Springer, Cham (2018). https://doi.org/10.1007/978-3-030-00434-7_13

[KPSS19] Krenn, S., Pöhls, H.C., Samelin, K., Slamanig, D.: Fully invisible protean signatures schemes (2019, ePrint)

[KR00] Krawczyk, H., Rabin, T.: Chameleon signatures. In: NDSS, pp. 143–154 (2000)

[KSS15] Krenn, S., Samelin, K., Sommer, D.: Stronger security for sanitizable signatures. In: DPM/QASA, pp. 100–117 (2015). https://doi.org/10.1007/978-3-319-29883-2_7

[LDW13] Lai, J., Ding, X., Wu, Y.: Accountable trapdoor sanitizable signatures. In: Deng, R.H., Feng, T. (eds.) ISPEC 2013. LNCS, vol. 7863, pp. 117–131. Springer, Heidelberg (2013). https://doi.org/10.1007/978-3-642-38033-4_9

[LOS+10] Lewko, A., Okamoto, T., Sahai, A., Takashima, K., Waters, B.: Fully secure functional encryption: attribute-based encryption and (hierarchical) inner product encryption. In: Gilbert, H. (ed.) EUROCRYPT 2010. LNCS, vol. 6110, pp. 62–91. Springer, Heidelberg (2010). https://doi.org/10.1007/978-3-642-13190-5_4

[SBZ01] Steinfeld, R., Bull, L., Zheng, Y.: Content extraction signatures. In: Kim, K. (ed.) ICISC 2001. LNCS, vol. 2288, pp. 285–304. Springer, Heidelberg (2002). https://doi.org/10.1007/3-540-45861-1_22

[SSE+12] Sakai, Y., et al.: On the security of dynamic group signatures: preventing signature hijacking. PKC 2012. LNCS, vol. 7293, pp. 715–732. Springer, Heidelberg (2012). https://doi.org/10.1007/978-3-642-30057-8_42

[YAHK11] Yamada, S., et al.: Generic constructions for chosen-ciphertext secure attribute based encryption. PKC 2011. LNCS, vol. 6571, pp. 71–89. Springer, Heidelberg (2011). https://doi.org/10.1007/978-3-642-19379-8_5

[YSL10] Yum, D.H., Seo, J.W., Lee, P.J.: Trapdoor sanitizable signatures made easy. In: Zhou, J., Yung, M. (eds.) ACNS 2010. LNCS, vol. 6123, pp. 53–68. Springer, Heidelberg (2010). https://doi.org/10.1007/978-3-642-13708-2_4

Traceable Inner Product Functional Encryption

Xuan Thanh Do[1,2]($\boxtimes$), Duong Hieu Phan[2], and David Pointcheval[3,4]

[1] Department of Mathematics, Vietnam National University, Hanoi, Vietnam
{xuan-thanh.do,duong-hieu.phan}@unilim.fr
[2] XLIM, University of Limoges, CNRS, Limoges, France
[3] DIENS, École Normale Supérieure, CNRS, PSL University, Paris, France
[4] Inria, Paris, France
david.pointcheval@ens.fr

Abstract. Functional Encryption (FE) has been widely studied in the last decade, as it provides a very useful tool for restricted access to sensitive data: from a ciphertext, it allows specific users to learn a function of the underlying plaintext. In practice, many users may be interested in the same function on the data, say the mean value of the inputs, for example. The conventional definition of FE associates each function to a secret *decryption functional key* and therefore all the users get the same secret key for the same function. This induces an important problem: if one of these users (called a *traitor*) leaks or sells the decryption functional key to be included in a *pirate* decryption tool, then there is no way to trace back its identity. Our objective is to solve this issue by introducing a new primitive, called *Traceable Functional Encryption*: the functional decryption key will not only be specific to a function, but to a user too, in such a way that if some users collude to produce a pirate decoder that successfully evaluates a function on the plaintext, from the ciphertext only, one can trace back at least one of them.

We propose a concrete solution for Inner Product Functional Encryption (IPFE). We first remark that the ElGamal-based IPFE from Abdalla *et al.* in PKC '15 shares many similarities with the Boneh-Franklin traitor tracing from CRYPTO '99. Then, we can combine these two schemes in a very efficient way, with the help of pairings, to obtain a Traceable IPFE with black-box confirmation.

Keywords: Functional Encryption · IPFE · Traceability

1 Introduction

Public Key Encryption (PKE) enables people to securely communicate and share sensitive data to others over public channels. Functional Encryption (FE) [9, 25], proposed by Boneh, Sahai and Waters, overcomes some limitations of PKE. It allows recipients to recover encrypted data in a more fine grained manner. Instead of revealing all-or-nothing of the original encrypted data as in PKE,

© Springer Nature Switzerland AG 2020
S. Jarecki (Ed.): CT-RSA 2020, LNCS 12006, pp. 564–585, 2020.
https://doi.org/10.1007/978-3-030-40186-3_24

recipients can get the evaluation of (statistical) functions on the data. As the function can contain an access control that checks some relation between the identity in the functional decryption key and the authorized identity in the plaintext, this primitive generalizes Identity Based Encryption (IBE) and Attribute Based Encryption (ABE), and actually received a large interest from the community. However, there is still no efficient construction of functional encryption for general functions. Currently, there are only simple and effective constructions for linear and quadratic functions [1, 4, 6].

In many practical applications, it is common that people only care about several specific functions on the data, for example the mean value of the data. Allowing many people to get access to the same function, with possible malicious users, has not been really covered by the previous works: the functional decryption key is derived from the function and the master secret key, but independently of the user. Therefore, all the users are given the same key, and if this key is leaked, no one can identify the origin of the leakage. The tracing problem becomes critical for this situation. We define a new primitive, called Traceable Functional Encryption (TFE).

Traitor tracing is a mechanism enabling an authority or an arbitrary party (who is a delegated party in the system to perform tracing tasks) can identify malicious users (traitors) who possibly colluded to produce a pirate decoder that behaves the same as a normal decryption. The very first traitor tracing scheme has been introduced by Chor, Fiat and Naor [13] and made use of combinatorial tools. The first algebraic traitor tracing scheme has been introduced by Boneh and Franklin [7], and is the basis for many subsequent schemes. A large number of schemes, in pairing-based setting or in lattice-based setting, have been introduced, we list a few of them [3, 8, 10–12, 14, 15, 17, 18, 23]. A taxonomy of the traitor tracing schemes can be found in [3, 15]. The classical tracing notion requires that the pirate decoder is able to decrypt random messages for being traced. In [15], it is shown that there is a flaw in some tracing systems with this notion and a fix is proposed with a stronger notion which only requires the decoder to distinguish two messages of its choice. This is a very strong notion and we will consider it in this work.

Concerning advanced primitives, traceability in IBE [2, 5, 16, 24] and in ABE [19–22] have been considered. Achieving traceability is usually very expensive. Adding traitor tracing to public-key encryption indeed requires a very high extra cost: even in the bounded model, the cost grows proportionally with the number of traitors. Interestingly, in the case of inner-product functional encryption, we can hope for a better deal. Indeed, in IPFE, as the number of corrupted keys is anyway bounded by the dimension of the plaintext vector and the ciphertext size is linear in this dimension, we can hope that adding traceability does not need such a huge extra cost. This is also what we achieve in this paper: adding certain level of traceability for inner-product functional encryption does not cost much. We achieve this in the discrete logarithm setting where we can note a clear similarity in the design of the first inner-product functional encryption scheme [1] and the Boneh-Franklin traitor tracing [7] and thus can combine them into a traceable inner-product functional encryption. It leaves as an open problem to get any level of traceability in other settings of inner-product functional encryption.

We eventually provide a construction for traceable inner-product functional encryption with black-box confirmation. Our construction is semantically secure in a more general setting than in IPFE as the adversary can choose both identity and function to query the corresponding functional secret key. Concerning traceability, it achieves *one-target tracing*: an adversary $\mathcal{A}$ is allowed to ask secret keys for one target function only, but many identities, and then produces a pirate decoder for this function. This is a basic step to be able to achieve higher level of traceability. Note that this is the security level we manage to prove, but this is still an open problem to prove it secure when the adversary can ask keys for several functions. At least, we did not find any attack in this stronger setting either.

This notion captures already useful real-life applications: suppose a group of users possesses decryption keys for the average functionality and leaks them to the pirate, if the pirate can produce a new decoder for this average function then one can trace one of the traitors. One might worry that a pirate decoder outputting an altered function (say $2F(x)$ instead of $F(x)$) might not be traced. However, as far as the target function can be computed (from public information) from the outputted function of the pirate decoder, then the traitors can still be traced. In fact, if the target function is $F^\star$ and if the pirate can output a decoder D that computes $F = 2F^\star$ then the tracer can still consider as if the decoder would output $F^\star$ because anyone can compute $F^\star$ from F. More formally, one can define a new decoder $D^\star$ for $F^\star$ (computable from F) from D for F and do tracing on $D^\star$ instead of D. We also notice that one-target tracing defeats cloned pirate decoders. In fact, the most popular way in practice to produce a pirate decoder is to clone a legitimate one with its secret key. By using the existing IPFE, one cannot trace a cloned decoder as the functional secret key does not depend on the identities of users. With one-target tracing, one can trace back the identity of the users who participated for the cloned decoder. This is indeed covered by the case that the adversary makes many queries but for one target function only, as the same function is implemented in the various decoders but for different identities. Eventually, in the theoretical sense, one-target tracing for IPFE is a stronger model than a bounded traitor tracing. Indeed if we fix a function $(1, x_2, \ldots, x_k)$, give secret keys for this function to the users, and then send the message $(m, 0, 0, \ldots, 0)$, then legitimates users can decrypt to the message m and the one-target tracing corresponds to a classical traitor tracing.

Our Technique. We exploit the similarities between the Boneh and Franklin's traitor tracing scheme [7] and the Abdalla *et al.*'s IPFE scheme [1] to integrate the Boneh-Franklin tracing technique into the IPFE scheme of Abdalla *et al.* [1] which allows in particular to personalize functional decryption keys. Interestingly, our method of personalizing keys and adding traceability does not need a huge extra cost as it is usually required for others primitives such as broadcast encryption.

We first informally recall the main ingredients of the IPFE of Abdalla *et al.* [1], that encrypts a plaintext vector $\boldsymbol{y} = (y_1, \ldots, y_k)$ as follows: the master secret key $\mathsf{MSK} = \boldsymbol{s} = (s_1, \ldots, s_k)$ and the public key $\mathsf{PK} = \left(\mathbb{G}, \left(h_i = g^{s_i}\right)_{i \in [k]}\right)$ respectively allow to generate functional decryption keys and ciphertexts:

$$\mathsf{sk}_{\boldsymbol{x}} = \langle \boldsymbol{s}, \boldsymbol{x} \rangle = \sum_{i \in [k]} s_i \cdot x_i, \qquad \mathsf{CT}_{\boldsymbol{y}} = \left(g^r, \left(h_i^r \cdot g^{y_i}\right)_{i \in [k]}\right).$$

Here, we are working in a cyclic $\mathbb{G}$ of prime order q, with a generator g. The master secret key MSK is a vector $\boldsymbol{s}$ with components s_i are taken from $\mathbb{Z}_q$. The public key PK consists of k group elements h_i. The vector $\boldsymbol{x} = (x_1, \ldots, x_k)$ with components x_i is taken from $\mathbb{Z}_q$ is used to extract a functional decryption key $\mathsf{sk}_{\boldsymbol{x}}$. A ciphertext, which is generated for a plaintext $\boldsymbol{y}$, denoted by $\mathsf{CT}_{\boldsymbol{y}}$. The Decrypt algorithm computes

$$\prod_{i \in [k]} \left(h_i^r \cdot g^{y_i}\right)^{x_i} \times \left(g^r\right)^{-\mathsf{sk}_{\boldsymbol{x}}} = \frac{g^{\langle \boldsymbol{s}, \boldsymbol{x} \rangle r} \cdot g^{\langle \boldsymbol{x}, \boldsymbol{y} \rangle}}{g^{\langle \boldsymbol{s}, \boldsymbol{x} \rangle r}} = g^{\langle \boldsymbol{x}, \boldsymbol{y} \rangle}$$

and gets $\langle \boldsymbol{x}, \boldsymbol{y} \rangle$, which is supposed to be relatively small, to allow the computation of the discrete logarithm.

For the mean value, the vector $\boldsymbol{x}$ is $(1, \ldots, 1)$. If many users are interested in the mean value then they all get the same functional decryption key $\mathsf{sk}_{\boldsymbol{x}}$ and there will be no way to trace the source of the leakage if this secret key is used somewhere. In order to personalize functional decryption keys for each vector $\boldsymbol{x}$, we have got inspired from the seminal technique of Boneh-Franklin: we associate to each user a representation of $g^{\langle \boldsymbol{s}, \boldsymbol{x} \rangle}$ in the basis of $\left(b_i = g^{t_i}\right)_{i \in [k]}$, with t_i is taken from $\mathbb{Z}_q$. Therefore, by adding b_i^r in the ciphertext, each user can compute $g^{\langle \boldsymbol{s}, \boldsymbol{x} \rangle r}$ as above and the decryption works in the same manner. Concretely, each user ID is associated to a public codeword $\boldsymbol{\theta}_{\mathsf{ID}} = (\theta_1, \ldots, \theta_k)$ and then, the personal secret key will be simply set to: $\mathsf{tk}_{\boldsymbol{x}, \mathsf{ID}} = \langle \boldsymbol{s}, \boldsymbol{x} \rangle / \langle \boldsymbol{t}, \boldsymbol{\theta}_{\mathsf{ID}} \rangle$. The master secret key MSK consists of two vectors $\boldsymbol{s} = (s_1, \ldots, s_k)$ and $\boldsymbol{t} = (t_1, \ldots, t_k)$. The public key $\mathsf{PK} = \left(\mathbb{G}, \left(b_i = g^{t_i}\right)_{i \in [k]}, \left(h_i = g^{s_i}\right)_{i \in [k]}\right)$. For each plaintext $\boldsymbol{y}$, the ciphertext is

$$\mathsf{CT}_{\boldsymbol{y}} = \left(\left(b_i^r\right)_{i \in [k]}, \left(h_i^r \cdot g^{y_i}\right)_{i \in [k]}\right).$$

The Decrypt algorithm then outputs

$$\prod_{i \in [k]} \left(h_i^r \cdot g^{y_i}\right)^{x_i} \times \prod_{i \in [k]} \left(b_i^r\right)^{-\mathsf{tk}_{\boldsymbol{x}, \mathsf{ID}} \theta_i} = \frac{g^{\langle \boldsymbol{s}, \boldsymbol{x} \rangle r} \cdot g^{\langle \boldsymbol{x}, \boldsymbol{y} \rangle}}{g^{\langle \boldsymbol{s}, \boldsymbol{x} \rangle r}} = g^{\langle \boldsymbol{x}, \boldsymbol{y} \rangle}.$$

The Use of Pairings. The above technique of personalizing secret keys seems to work well as in the Boneh-Franklin traitor tracing. However, there exists an issue specific to the setting of the functional encryption, that goes beyond the framework of Boneh-Franklin traitor tracing. Suppose that we are considering a scheme for two users with identities ID_1 and ID_2. The first user queries the secret keys corresponding to vectors $\boldsymbol{x}_1$ and $\boldsymbol{x}_2$ and gets $\mathsf{tk}_{\boldsymbol{x}_1,\mathsf{ID}_1} = \frac{\langle s,\boldsymbol{x}_1\rangle}{\langle t,\theta_{\mathsf{ID}_1}\rangle}$ and $\mathsf{tk}_{\boldsymbol{x}_2,\mathsf{ID}_1} = \frac{\langle s,\boldsymbol{x}_2\rangle}{\langle t,\theta_{\mathsf{ID}_1}\rangle}$. The second user only queries secret key to vector $\boldsymbol{x}_1$ and gets $\mathsf{tk}_{\boldsymbol{x}_1,\mathsf{ID}_2} = \frac{\langle s,\boldsymbol{x}_1\rangle}{\langle t,\theta_{\mathsf{ID}_2}\rangle}$. From these three secret keys $\mathsf{tk}_{\boldsymbol{x}_1,\mathsf{ID}_1}, \mathsf{tk}_{\boldsymbol{x}_2,\mathsf{ID}_1}$ and $\mathsf{tk}_{\boldsymbol{x}_1,\mathsf{ID}_2}$, it is possible to compute the secret key $\mathsf{tk}_{\boldsymbol{x}_2,\mathsf{ID}_2} = \frac{\mathsf{tk}_{\boldsymbol{x}_2,\mathsf{ID}_1}\cdot\mathsf{tk}_{\boldsymbol{x}_1,\mathsf{ID}_2}}{\mathsf{tk}_{\boldsymbol{x}_1,\mathsf{ID}_1}}$ for the vector $\boldsymbol{x}_2$ and identity ID_2. To avoid this attack, we will put the scalar $t_{\boldsymbol{x},\mathsf{ID}}$ in the exponent $\mathsf{sk}_{\boldsymbol{x},\mathsf{ID}} = g^{\mathsf{tk}_{\boldsymbol{x},\mathsf{ID}}}$ and the decryption will then be performed in the target group of the pairing. The goal of the rest of the paper is to prove this modification actually leads to a secure scheme.

Enhancing the Security of IPFE. It is worth noticing that, by putting the secret key in the exponent, we may enhance the security of the functional encryption. In the Abdalla *et al.*'s scheme [1], whenever the adversary queries more than k secret keys, it can get the whole MSK by solving a system of linear equations. In our scheme, there is no way, unless breaking discrete logarithm, to get this master key as it is only put in the exponent. We will though not exploit further this advantage in this work, as we will focus on traceability.

Tracing Algorithm. We rely on the classical linear tracing technique but we will adapt this technique into the functional encryption setting and with the strongest notion of pirate, namely pirate distinguisher introduced in [15].

Organization. In Sect. 2, we will recall some classical assumptions (DDH and BDDH), required for the security of our constructions. In Sect. 3, we introduce a new concept: Traceable functional encryption (TFE). We then define security game of TFE against adaptively-chosen plaintext attacks and security game of the Tracing algorithm. A concrete TFE construction for inner product will be presented in Sect. 4. We will prove that our construction achieves selective security. Section 5 will be intended to present a tracing algorithm which achieves one-target security as stated in Theorem 13. The black-box confirmation property of the Tracing algorithm will be proven in the Lemmas 11 and 12.

2   Preliminaries

We denote $[k]$ the set of integers between 1 and k. Given two vectors $\boldsymbol{x} = (x_1,\ldots,x_k)$ and $\boldsymbol{y} = (y_1,\ldots,y_k)$, where $x_i, y_i \in \mathbb{Z}_q$ for all $i \in [k]$, we define $\langle \boldsymbol{x},\boldsymbol{y}\rangle = \sum_{i=1}^{k} x_i y_i$. Next we recall classical assumptions as follows.

Definition 1 (Decisional Diffie-Hellman Assumption). *Given a cyclic group $\mathbb{G} = \langle g\rangle$ of prime order q, the Decision Diffie Hellman (DDH) problem consists in distinguishing the following distributions*

$$\mathcal{D}_0 = \{(g^a, g^b, g^{ab}) \mid a,b \xleftarrow{\$} \mathbb{Z}_q\} \qquad \mathcal{D}_1 = \{(g^a, g^b, g^c) \mid a,b,c \xleftarrow{\$} \mathbb{Z}_q\}.$$

The distribution $\mathcal{D}_0$ consists of Diffie-Hellman tuples whereas $\mathcal{D}_1$ consists of random tuples. Roughly speaking, the DDH problem consists in distinguishing

DH tuples from random tuples. The DDH assumption states that the two above distributions $\mathcal{D}_0$ *and* $\mathcal{D}_1$ *are indistinguishable.*

Let $\mathbb{G}_1, \mathbb{G}_2, \mathbb{G}_T$ be multiplicatively written groups of prime order q, and let g_1, g_2 be generators of $\mathbb{G}_1, \mathbb{G}_2$, respectively. We write 1_T to denote the unit element of $\mathbb{G}_T$. Let $e : \mathbb{G}_1 \times \mathbb{G}_2 \to \mathbb{G}_T$ be a function sending two elements from $\mathbb{G}_1$ and $\mathbb{G}_2$ into the group $\mathbb{G}_T$. We say that the tuple $(\mathbb{G}_1, \mathbb{G}_2, \mathbb{G}_T, q, e)$ is an asymmetric bilinear group if the following properties hold:

- **Bilinearity**: for all $h_1 \in \mathbb{G}_1, h_2 \in \mathbb{G}_2$ and $a, b \in \mathbb{Z}_q^*$, we have $e(h_1^a, h_2^b) = e(h_1, h_2)^{ab}$.
- **Non-degeneracy**: $e(g_1, g_2) \neq 1_T$.
- The function e can be efficiently computed.

Definition 2 (Bilinear Decisional Diffie-Hellman Assumption). *Given an asymmetric bilinear group* $(\mathbb{G}_1, \mathbb{G}_2, \mathbb{G}_T, q, e)$, *the Bilinear Decisional Diffie-Hellman (BDDH) problem consists in distinguishing the following distributions, for generators* g_1 *and* g_2

$$\mathcal{D}_0 = \left\{ \left(g_1^a, g_1^b, g_2^a, g_2^c, e\,(g_1, g_2)^{abc} \right) | a, b, c \xleftarrow{\$} \mathbb{Z}_q \right\}$$

$$\mathcal{D}_1 = \left\{ (g_1^a, g_1^b, g_2^a, g_2^c, e\,(g_1, g_2)^z) | a, b, c, z \xleftarrow{\$} \mathbb{Z}_q \right\}.$$

The BDDH assumption states that no PPT adversary can distinguish $\mathcal{D}_0$ *and* $\mathcal{D}_1$ *with non negligible advantage.*

Lemma 3 (Two-tailed Chernoff Bound). *Let* $X_1, X_2, \ldots, X_n$ *be independent Poisson trials (yes/no experiments) with success probabilities* $p_1, p_2, \ldots, p_n$. *Let* $X = \sum_{i=1}^{n} X_i$ *and* $\mu = \sum_{i=1}^{n} p_i$. *For* $0 < \delta < 1$, *we have*

$$\Pr[|X - \mu| \geq \delta\mu] \leq 2e^{-\mu\delta^2/3}.$$

3   Traceable Functional Encryption

We begin by describing the syntactic definition of traceable functional encryption (TFE) for circuits. A functionality (circuit) $F \in \mathcal{F}_\lambda$ describes the function of a plaintext that can be derived from the ciphertext. More precisely, a functionality is defined as follows.

Definition 4. *Let* $\mathcal{Y} = \{\mathcal{Y}_\lambda\}_{\lambda \in \mathbb{N}}$ *and* $\mathcal{S} = \{\mathcal{S}_\lambda\}_{\lambda \in \mathbb{N}}$ *denote ensembles where each* $\mathcal{Y}_\lambda$ *and* $\mathcal{S}_\lambda$ *is a finite set. Let* $\mathcal{F} = \{\mathcal{F}_\lambda\}_{\lambda \in \mathbb{N}}$ *denotes an ensemble where each* $\mathcal{F}_\lambda$ *is a finite collection of circuits, and each circuit* $F \in \mathcal{F}_\lambda$ *takes as input a message* $y \in \mathcal{Y}_\lambda$ *and outputs* $F(y) \in \mathcal{S}_\lambda$.

Definition 5. *A traceable functional encryption scheme* $\mathcal{T} - \mathcal{FE}$ *for an ensemble* $\mathcal{F}$ *consists of five algorithms* (Setup, Extract, Encrypt, Decrypt, Tracing) *defined as follows:*

Setup(1^λ): *Takes as input a security parameter λ and outputs a master key pair* (PK, MSK).

Extract(ID, MSK, F): *Given an identity* ID *of a user, a circuit $F \in \mathcal{F}_\lambda$ and the master secret key* MSK, *this algorithm outputs an individual functional secret key* $\mathsf{sk}_{F,\mathsf{ID}}$.

Encrypt(PK, y): *Takes as input the public key* PK *and a message $y \in \mathcal{Y}_\lambda$, this randomized algorithm outputs a ciphertext* CT.

Decrypt(PK, $\mathsf{sk}_{F,\mathsf{ID}}$, CT): *Given the public key* PK, *a secret key* $\mathsf{sk}_{F,\mathsf{ID}}$ *and a ciphertext* CT, *this algorithm outputs $F(y) \in \mathcal{S}_\lambda$, if* CT *encrypts y, or an invalid symbol* $\perp$.

Tracing$^{\mathcal{D}_F}$(MSK, F, $\mu(.)$, y^0, y^1): *The tracing algorithm takes as input the master secret key* MSK, *a circuit $F \in \mathcal{F}_\lambda$, two messages $y^0, y^1 \in \mathcal{Y}_\lambda$ which are obtained from $\mathcal{D}_F$ and a function $\mu(.)$ representing the probability that the decoder can distinguish between the ciphertexts of y^0 and of y^1. The algorithm interacts with a confiscated pirate decoder $\mathcal{D}_F$, as a black-box, and outputs an identity or an invalid symbol* $\perp$.

For correctness, we require that for all (PK, MSK) $\leftarrow$ Setup(1^λ), all $y \in \mathcal{Y}_\lambda$, each $F \in \mathcal{F}_\lambda$ and all identities ID, $\mathsf{sk}_{F,\mathsf{ID}} \leftarrow$ Extract(ID, MSK, F), if CT $\leftarrow$ Encrypt(PK, y), then one should get Decrypt(PK, $\mathsf{sk}_{F,\mathsf{ID}}$, CT) $= F(y)$, with overwhelming probability.

Requirement on the Pirate Decoder

- The classical requirement is that the pirate decoder $\mathcal{D}_F$ is a device that is able to decrypt successfully any normal ciphertext generated by the Encrypt algorithm with high probability. Yet, in another approach, the tracer is only able to interact with $\mathcal{D}_F$ through an oracle $\mathcal{O}_F^{\mathcal{D}}$ by sending a message-ciphertext pair (tracing signal) to $\mathcal{O}_F^{\mathcal{D}}$ and gets a response that is a bit indicating whether $\mathcal{D}_F$ can successfully decrypt the ciphertext into the provided message (evaluated with the function F). We say that the tracing algorithm is executing in minimal access black-box mode.

$$\mathcal{O}_F^{\mathcal{D}}(\mathsf{CT}, y) = \begin{cases} 1 & \text{if } \mathcal{D}_F(\mathsf{CT}) = F(y) \\ 0 & \text{otherwise.} \end{cases}$$

- We consider the same setting for the pirate as in [15]: of course, this is not required the pirate decoder $\mathcal{D}_F$ to output entire message (or an indicator bit as in minimal access model) nor to decrypt with high probability every ciphertexts which are taken from random messages. Instead, it is enough that the pirate decoder can distinguish the encryption of two messages y^0, y^1 which are chosen by itself (see [15]): Adapted from [15], we define a μ-useful Pirate Distinguisher $\mathcal{D}_F$ associated to a unique function F as below

$$\left| \Pr \left[\mathcal{D}_F\left(\mathsf{CT}_b\right) = b : \begin{array}{l} (\mathsf{MSK}, \mathsf{PK}) \leftarrow \mathsf{Setup}(\cdot) \\ \{\mathsf{sk}_{F,i} \leftarrow \mathsf{Extract}(i, \mathsf{MSK}, F)\}_{i \in [n]} \\ \left(\mathcal{D}_F, y^0, y^1\right) \leftarrow \mathcal{A}(\mathsf{PK}, \{\mathsf{sk}_{F,i}\}_{i \in [t]}) \\ \mathrm{st}.F(y^0) \neq F(y^1) \\ b \xleftarrow{\$} \{0,1\}, \mathsf{CT}_b \leftarrow \mathsf{Encrypt}(\mathsf{PK}, y^b) \end{array} \right] - \frac{1}{2} \right| \geq \mu(\lambda),$$

where the function $\mu(\cdot)$ is a non-negligible function in λ.

This very strong notion of Pirate Distinguisher has been introduced in [15]. It requires the pirate distinguisher to be able to distinguish the encryption of two different messages y^0, y^1. To adapt to the functional encryption, as the goal of the pirate is to compute the function on the message, we require that the pirate distinguisher be able to distinguish the encryption of y^0, y^1 such that $F(y^0) \neq F(y^1)$.

As shown in [15], this notion is stronger than the classical Pirate Decoder which is able to correctly decrypt random messages with non-negligible probability. When considering the case of functional encryption, a pirate decoder for a function F is useful if it can compute $F(y)$ from the encryption of y, for a random message y. Clearly, pirate distinguisher is also stronger than pirate decoder in this case. Indeed, one can build a distinguisher $\mathcal{D}_F$ from a decoder Dec_F: randomly choose y^0, y^1 such that $F(y^0) \neq F(y^1)$, then when receiving the challenge ciphertext CT, call Dec_F and check whether this is $F(y^0)$ or $F(y^1)$ to output the correct guess, if this is none of them, output a random guess. In this work, we will deal with this notion of pirate distinguisher which is actually the strongest notion (*i.e.*, minimal requirement) about the usefulness of pirate decoders.

Security: Indistinguishability. We consider the IND security game between an adversary $\mathcal{A}$ and a challenger $\mathcal{B}$ as follows:

Definition 6. *A traceable functional encryption scheme $\mathcal{T} - \mathcal{FE}$ for an ensemble $\mathcal{F}$, $\mathcal{T} - \mathcal{FE}$ = (Setup, Extract, Encrypt, Decrypt, Tracing) is semantically secure under chosen-plaintext attacks (or IND−CPA security) if no PPT adversary has non-negligible advantage in the following game:*

- *The challenger $\mathcal{B}$ runs $(\mathsf{PK}, \mathsf{MSK}) \leftarrow \mathsf{Setup}(1^\lambda)$ and the public key PK is given to the adversary $\mathcal{A}$.*
- *The adversary adaptively makes secret key queries to the challenger. That is, the adversary $\mathcal{A}$ chooses some pairs of identities ID and functions $F \in \mathcal{F}_\lambda$. $\mathcal{A}$ sends them to $\mathcal{B}$ and then obtains $\mathsf{sk}_{F,\mathsf{ID}} \leftarrow \mathsf{Extract}(\mathsf{ID}, \mathsf{MSK}, F)$ from $\mathcal{B}$.*
- *The adversary $\mathcal{A}$ chooses distinct messages $y_0, y_1 \in \mathcal{Y}_\lambda$ such that $F(y_0) = F(y_1)$ for all F already asked. This restriction is required in all functional encryption to avoid trivial attacks. Whenever $\mathcal{B}$ receives the messages, it randomly picks $\beta \xleftarrow{\$} \{0,1\}$ and then transfers to $\mathcal{A}$ a ciphertext $\mathsf{CT}_\beta = \mathsf{Encrypt}(\mathsf{PK}, y_\beta)$.*
- *Adversary $\mathcal{A}$ continues making further decryption key queries for other pairs of identities ID and functions F, and receives $\mathsf{sk}_{F,\mathsf{ID}}$ from $\mathcal{B}$. Again, it is also required that $F(y_0) = F(y_1)$ to avoid trivial attacks.*

– *Adversary $\mathcal{A}$ eventually returns a guess β' for a bit β and wins if $\beta' = \beta$.*

A weaker version has been defined, when the messages y_0, y_1 for the challenge ciphertext are chosen before the Setup algorithm started, then the $\mathcal{T} - \mathcal{FE}$ scheme is said selectively-security against chosen-plaintext attacks, which is denoted by sel−IND−CPA.

Traceability. The security game between the attacker $\mathcal{A}$ and the challenger $\mathcal{B}$ takes place as follows:

1. The challenger $\mathcal{B}$ runs $(\mathsf{PK}, \mathsf{MSK}) \leftarrow \mathsf{Setup}(1^\lambda)$ and the public key PK sent to the adversary $\mathcal{A}$. $\mathcal{B}$ also creates a table $\mathcal{T}$ to store pairs of identities of users who queried keys and functions F, for all $F \in \mathcal{F}_\lambda$. It means that the table $\mathcal{T}$ stores (ID, F). Initially $\mathcal{T}$ is set empty.
2. The adversary adaptively makes secret key queries to the challenger. Concretely, the adversary $\mathcal{A}$ chooses some pairs of identities ID and functions $F \in \mathcal{F}_\lambda$ to query functional secret keys. The challenger $\mathcal{B}$ stores all these pairs in the table $\mathcal{T}$ and replies with the secret keys $\mathsf{sk}_{F,\mathsf{ID}}$ for those pairs.
3. The adversary $\mathcal{A}$ outputs $(F^*, \mathcal{D}_{F^*})$ and two messages y^0, y^1, where $\mathcal{D}_{F^*}$ is a pirate distinguisher for the function F^*.
4. After receiving the messages y^0, y^1 from $\mathcal{A}$, the challenger $\mathcal{B}$ runs the algorithm $\mathsf{Tracing}^{\mathcal{D}_{F^*}}(\mathsf{MSK}, F^*, 1^\mu, y^0, y^1)$ and outputs an identity ID^*.

We say that the adversary $\mathcal{A}$ wins the game if the output of Tracing is either an invalid symbol $\mathsf{ID}^* = \perp$ or the identity ID^* did not ask for F^*: $(\mathsf{ID}^*, F^*) \notin \mathcal{T}$.

   When the adversary $\mathcal{A}$ is allowed to ask secret keys for the only target function F^* (but for any ID), and so for (ID, F^*), the security of Tracing algorithm will then be called *one-target security*.

   As explained in the introduction, this one-target security also covers the case where the adversary outputs any function F such that the target function F^* is computable from F with public information. In such a case, when the pirate outputs the function F and the decoder $\mathcal{D}_F$ (together with two messages), one can define a decoder $\mathcal{D}_{F^*}$ that calls $\mathcal{D}_F$ and then applies the computation of F^* from F on the output, then do tracing on this $\mathcal{D}_{F^*}$, applying also the public transformation to the messages.

4   Our Inner-Product Functional Encryption

We will describe concretely a traceable functional encryption for inner product scheme $(\mathcal{T} - \mathcal{FE})$ for n users. Let $\mathbb{G}$ be a bilinear group of large prime of order q. Additionally, let $e : \mathbb{G}_1 \times \mathbb{G}_2 \rightarrow \mathbb{G}_T$ denote a bilinear map, where $\mathbb{G}_1, \mathbb{G}_2$ and $\mathbb{G}_T$ are cyclic groups of order q, written multiplicatively.

Setup($1^\lambda, 1^k$): This algorithm generates a bilinear setting $\mathbb{G} = (\mathbb{G}_1, \mathbb{G}_2, \mathbb{G}_T, q, e)$ for sufficiently large prime order q and g_1, g_2 respectively are generators of the groups $\mathbb{G}_1$ and $\mathbb{G}_2$. The bilinear map e over $\mathbb{G}_1$, $\mathbb{G}_2$ can be calculated efficiently.

- Randomly choose $t_1, \ldots, t_k \xleftarrow{\$} \mathbb{Z}_q$, set $\boldsymbol{t} = (t_1, \ldots, t_k)$ and $b_1 = g_1^{t_1}, \ldots,$ $b_k = g_1^{t_k}$.
- For each $i \in \{1, \ldots, k\}$, randomly choose $s_i \xleftarrow{\$} \mathbb{Z}_q$. We set $\boldsymbol{s} = (s_1, \ldots, s_k)$ and set $G = e(g_1, g_2) \in \mathbb{G}_T$ and $H_i = G^{s_i} \in \mathbb{G}_T$ for all $i = 1, \ldots, k$.
- We consider a linear code $\boldsymbol{\Gamma}$ over the alphabet $\mathbb{Z}_q$ with n codewords $\boldsymbol{\Gamma} = \{\boldsymbol{\theta}_1, \ldots, \boldsymbol{\theta}_n\}$, corresponding to n users in our system. Each codeword has the length k.
- The public key is $\mathsf{PK} = \Big(\mathbb{G}, \boldsymbol{\Gamma}, g_1, g_2, G, H_1, \ldots, H_k, b_1, \ldots, b_k\Big)$.
- The master secret key is $\mathsf{MSK} = \{\boldsymbol{s}, \boldsymbol{t}\}$.

$\mathsf{Extract}(\mathsf{ID}, \mathsf{MSK}, \boldsymbol{x})$: Takes as input an identity ID, the master secret key MSK and a characteristic vector $\boldsymbol{x} = (x_1, \ldots, x_k) \in \mathbb{Z}_q^k$. Choose a (new) vector (codeword) $\boldsymbol{\theta}_{\mathsf{ID}} = (\theta_1, \ldots, \theta_k) \in \boldsymbol{\Gamma}$. A secret key is an element $g_2^{\mathsf{tk}_{\boldsymbol{x}}, \mathsf{ID}} \in \mathbb{G}_2$ such that $\mathsf{tk}_{\boldsymbol{x}, \mathsf{ID}} \cdot \boldsymbol{\theta}_{\mathsf{ID}}$ is a representation of $g_1^{\langle \boldsymbol{s}, \boldsymbol{x} \rangle}$ in the basis of $(b_1, b_2, \ldots, b_k)$. That is $g_1^{\langle \boldsymbol{s}, \boldsymbol{x} \rangle} = \prod_{i=1}^k b_i^{\mathsf{tk}_{\boldsymbol{x}}, \mathsf{ID}\theta_i} = b_1^{\mathsf{tk}_{\boldsymbol{x}}, \mathsf{ID}\theta_1} \cdots b_k^{\mathsf{tk}_{\boldsymbol{x}}, \mathsf{ID}\theta_k}$. Concretely, set $\mathsf{tk}_{\boldsymbol{x}, \mathsf{ID}} = \dfrac{\langle \boldsymbol{s}, \boldsymbol{x} \rangle}{\langle \boldsymbol{t}, \boldsymbol{\theta}_{\mathsf{ID}} \rangle}$ and define $\mathsf{sk}_{\boldsymbol{x}, \mathsf{ID}} = g_2^{\mathsf{tk}_{\boldsymbol{x}}, \mathsf{ID}}$ for $\boldsymbol{\theta}_{\mathsf{ID}}$.

$\mathsf{Encrypt}(\mathsf{PK}, \boldsymbol{y})$: Takes as input the public key PK and a message $\boldsymbol{y} = (y_1, \ldots, y_k) \in \mathbb{Z}_q^k$. To encrypt $\boldsymbol{y}$, sample $r \xleftarrow{\$} \mathbb{Z}_q$ and compute

$$\mathsf{CT} = (H_1^r G^{y_1}, \ldots, H_k^r G^{y_k}, b_1^r, \ldots, b_k^r).$$

$\mathsf{Decrypt}(\mathsf{PK}, \mathsf{sk}_{\boldsymbol{x}, \mathsf{ID}}, \mathsf{CT})$: Takes as input the public key PK, the secret key $\mathsf{sk}_{\boldsymbol{x}, \mathsf{ID}} = g_2^{\mathsf{tk}_{\boldsymbol{x}}, \mathsf{ID}}$ for $\boldsymbol{\theta}_{\mathsf{ID}} = (\theta_1, \ldots, \theta_k)$ and a ciphertext CT, the algorithm computes

$$E = \frac{\left(H_1^r G^{y_1}\right)^{x_1} \cdots \left(H_k^r G^{y_k}\right)^{x_k}}{e\left(\left(b_1^r\right)^{\theta_1} \cdots \left(b_k^r\right)^{\theta_k}, g_2^{\mathsf{tk}_{\boldsymbol{x}}, \mathsf{ID}}\right)}.$$

Finally, it returns the discrete logarithm of E in basis $G = e(g_1, g_2)$.

Correctness: For all $(\mathsf{PK}, \mathsf{MSK}) \leftarrow \mathsf{Setup}(1^\lambda, 1^k)$, all $\boldsymbol{y} \in \mathbb{Z}_q^k$ and $\boldsymbol{x} \in \mathbb{Z}_p^k$, for $\mathsf{sk}_{\boldsymbol{x}, \mathsf{ID}} = (g_2^{\mathsf{tk}_{\boldsymbol{x}}, \mathsf{ID}}, \boldsymbol{\theta}_{\mathsf{ID}}) \leftarrow \mathsf{Extract}(\mathsf{ID}, \mathsf{MSK}, \boldsymbol{x})$ and $\mathsf{CT} \leftarrow \mathsf{Encrypt}(\mathsf{PK}, \boldsymbol{y})$, we have that

$$\frac{\left(H_1^r G^{y_1}\right)^{x_1} \cdots \left(H_k^r G^{y_k}\right)^{x_k}}{e\left(\left(b_1^r\right)^{\theta_1} \cdots \left(b_k^r\right)^{\theta_k}, g_2^{\mathsf{tk}_{\boldsymbol{x}}, \mathsf{ID}}\right)} = \frac{G^{\langle \boldsymbol{x}, \boldsymbol{y} \rangle} \cdot \left(G^{x_1 s_1 + \cdots + x_k s_k}\right)^r}{e\left(g_1^{t_1 r \theta_1} \cdots g_1^{t_k r \theta_k}, g_2^{\frac{\langle \boldsymbol{s}, \boldsymbol{x} \rangle}{\langle \boldsymbol{t}, \boldsymbol{\theta}_{\mathsf{ID}} \rangle}}\right)}$$

$$= \frac{G^{\langle \boldsymbol{x}, \boldsymbol{y} \rangle} \cdot G^{r \langle \boldsymbol{s}, \boldsymbol{x} \rangle}}{e(g_1, g_2)^{r \langle \boldsymbol{s}, \boldsymbol{x} \rangle}} G^{\langle \boldsymbol{x}, \boldsymbol{y} \rangle} = e(g_1, g_2)^{\langle \boldsymbol{x}, \boldsymbol{y} \rangle}.$$

Theorem 7. *The above $\mathcal{T} - \mathcal{FE}$ achieves the selective security ($\mathsf{sel-IND-CPA}$) under the BDDH assumption*

Proof. We assume that there exists an adversary $\mathcal{A}$ can distinguish distributions of ciphertexts in the real game with non-negligible advantage. We build a simulator $\mathcal{B}$ that solves the BDDH problem. It means that $\mathcal{B}$ takes as input a tuple

$(g_1^a, g_1^b, g_2^a, g_2^c, T) \in \mathbb{G}_1^2 \times \mathbb{G}_2^2 \times \mathbb{G}_T$, it must decide whether the input is BDDH tuple where $T = e(g_1, g_2)^{abc}$ or random tuple where $T = e(g_1, g_2)^z$. We set

$$\mathcal{D}_0 = \left\{ \left(g_1^a, g_1^b, g_2^a, g_2^c, e(g_1, g_2)^{abc} \right) | a, b, c \xleftarrow{\$} \mathbb{Z}_q \right\}$$
$$\mathcal{D}_1 = \left\{ \left(g_1^a, g_1^b, g_2^a, g_2^c, e(g_1, g_2)^z \right) | a, b, c, z \xleftarrow{\$} \mathbb{Z}_q \right\}.$$

The algorithm $\mathcal{B}$ progresses as follows:

- Firstly, $\mathcal{B}$ is provided two distinct messages $\boldsymbol{y}_0$ and $\boldsymbol{y}_1$.
- $\mathcal{B}$ chooses $\boldsymbol{\Gamma} = \{\boldsymbol{\theta}_1, \dots, \boldsymbol{\theta}_n\}$ is a linear code of size n and length k, as well as $t_1, \dots, t_k \xleftarrow{\$} \mathbb{Z}_q$. Set $\boldsymbol{t} = (t_1, \dots, t_k)$ and $b_i = g_1^{t_i}$, for $i = 1$ to k.
- $\mathcal{B}$ finds a $(k-1)$-basis of subspace $(\boldsymbol{y}_0 - \boldsymbol{y}_1)^{\perp}$ because the adversary $\mathcal{A}$ can only ask secret keys for vectors $\boldsymbol{x}$ in $(\boldsymbol{y}_0 - \boldsymbol{y}_1)^{\perp}$. We denote this basis by $(\boldsymbol{z}_1, \dots, \boldsymbol{z}_{k-1})$. For $i = 1, \dots, k-1$, $\mathcal{B}$ randomly chooses $u_i \xleftarrow{\$} \mathbb{Z}_q$.
- We consider the canonical basis $(\boldsymbol{e}_1, \dots, \boldsymbol{e}_k)$ of $\mathbb{Z}_q^k$. A linear transformation from basis $(\boldsymbol{z}_1, \dots, \boldsymbol{z}_{k-1}, (\boldsymbol{y}_0 - \boldsymbol{y}_1))$ to $(\boldsymbol{e}_1, \dots, \boldsymbol{e}_k)$ is given by: $\boldsymbol{e}_i = \alpha_i(\boldsymbol{y}_0 - \boldsymbol{y}_1) + \sum_{j=1}^{k-1} \lambda_{i,j} \boldsymbol{z}_j$, where the coefficients $\alpha_i, \lambda_{i,j}$ can be found efficiently by $\mathcal{B}$. Note that $\langle \boldsymbol{e}_i, \boldsymbol{y}_0 - \boldsymbol{y}_1 \rangle = \alpha_i \times \|\boldsymbol{y}_0 - \boldsymbol{y}_1\|^2$. Then $\boldsymbol{\alpha} = \sum_i \alpha_i \boldsymbol{e}_i = 1/\|\boldsymbol{y}_0 - \boldsymbol{y}_1\|^2 \times \sum_i \langle \boldsymbol{e}_i, \boldsymbol{y}_0 - \boldsymbol{y}_1 \rangle \boldsymbol{e}_i = 1/\|\boldsymbol{y}_0 - \boldsymbol{y}_1\|^2 \times (\boldsymbol{y}_0 - \boldsymbol{y}_1)$.
- From the challenge tuple, and random scalars $u_1, \dots, u_{k-1} \xleftarrow{\$} \mathbb{Z}_q$, set $G = e(g_1, g_2^c)$ and

$$H_i = e\left((g_1^a)^{\alpha_i} \cdot g_1^{\sum_{j=1}^{k-1} u_j \lambda_{i,j}}, g_2^c \right)$$
$$= e(g_1, g_2^c)^{a\alpha_i + \sum_{j=1}^{k-1} u_j \lambda_{i,j}} = G^{a\alpha_i + \sum_{j=1}^{k-1} u_j \lambda_{i,j}}$$

for $i = 1, \dots, k$, which implicitly defines $s_i = a\alpha_i + \sum_{j=1}^{k-1} u_j \lambda_{i,j}$. The public key is set to $\mathsf{PK} = \left(G, \boldsymbol{\Gamma}, g_1, g_2, H_1, \dots, H_k, b_1, \dots, b_k \right)$.
- For any vector $\boldsymbol{x} = (x_1, \dots, x_k) \in (\boldsymbol{y}_0 - \boldsymbol{y}_1)^{\perp}$, $\mathcal{B}$ computes $\kappa_{\boldsymbol{x}} = \langle \boldsymbol{s}, \boldsymbol{x} \rangle = \sum_{j=1}^{k-1} \sum_{i=1}^{k} x_i u_j \lambda_{i,j}$ and, for identities ID, $\mathsf{sk}_{\boldsymbol{x}, \mathsf{ID}} = g_2^{\mathsf{tk}_{\boldsymbol{x}}, \mathsf{ID}}$, where $\mathsf{tk}_{\boldsymbol{x}, \mathsf{ID}} = \frac{\kappa_{\boldsymbol{x}}}{\langle \boldsymbol{t}, \boldsymbol{\theta}_{\mathsf{ID}} \rangle}$. It sends the value $g_2^{\mathsf{tk}_{\boldsymbol{x}}, \mathsf{ID}}$ to $\mathcal{A}$. Vector $\boldsymbol{\theta}_{\mathsf{ID}}$ is a codeword in $\boldsymbol{\Gamma}$.
- The challenger randomly picks $\beta \xleftarrow{\$} \{0, 1\}$ and, from the challenge tuple where T is the last element in $\mathbb{G}_T$, gives $\mathcal{A}$ a ciphertext $\mathsf{CT} = (\mathsf{ct}_1, \dots, \mathsf{ct}_{2k})$, where $\mathsf{ct}_j = T^{\alpha_j} \cdot e\left((g_1^b)^{\sum_{i=1}^{k-i} u_i \lambda_{j,i}}, g_2^c \right) \cdot G^{y_{\beta,j}}$ and $\mathsf{ct}_{j+k} = (g_1^b)^{t_j}$, for $j = 1, \dots, k$.
- At the end, the adversary outputs his guess β' for β. If $\beta' = \beta$ then $\mathcal{B}$ returns 1 for "BDDH tuple". Otherwise returns 0 for "random tuple". We will show that $\mathcal{B}$ can break BDDH assumption. To do so, we need to prove that the difference below is negligible

$$\left| \Pr[\mathcal{B}(\mathcal{D}_0) = 1] - \Pr[\mathcal{B}(\mathcal{D}_1) = 1] \right|$$
$$= \left| \Pr[\beta = \beta' \mid T = e(g_1, g_2)^{abc}] - \Pr[\beta = \beta' \mid T = e(g_1, g_2)^z] \right|.$$

We find that:

1. When $T = e\left(g_1, g_2\right)^{abc}$ then we have $\mathsf{ct}_j = T^{\alpha_j} \cdot e\left(\left(g_1^b\right)^{\sum_{i=1}^{k-1} u_i \lambda_{j,i}}, g_2^c\right) \cdot$ $G^{y_{\beta,j}} = H_j^b G^{y_{\beta,j}}$, for $j = 1, \ldots, k$. Therefore

$$\mathsf{CT} = \left(H_1^b G^{y_{\beta,1}}, \ldots, H_k^b G^{y_{\beta,k}}, b_1^b, \ldots, b_k^b\right).$$

It implies that $\mathcal{B}$ perfectly simulates the real game. Since $\mathcal{A}$ can break the semantic security with non-negligible probability, we have $\Pr[\beta = \beta' \mid T = e\left(g_1, g_2\right)^{abc}] = \mathsf{Adv}(\mathcal{A}) + 1/2$.
2. When $T = e(g_1, g_2)^z = G^v$ is random element, the challenger will send $\mathcal{A}$ the ciphertext of message $\boldsymbol{y}_\beta + v\boldsymbol{\alpha} = \boldsymbol{y}_\beta + v/\|\boldsymbol{y}_0 - \boldsymbol{y}_1\|^2 \times (\boldsymbol{y}_0 - \boldsymbol{y}_1) = \mu \boldsymbol{y}_0 + (1 - \mu)\boldsymbol{y}_1$, for some random $\mu \in \mathbb{Z}_q$. This makes β perfectly unpredictable: $\Pr[\beta = \beta' \mid T = e\left(g_1, g_2\right)^z] = 1/2$.

We conclude the advantage is non-negligible as

$$\left|\Pr[\beta = \beta' \mid T = e\left(g_1, g_2\right)^{abc}] - \Pr[\beta = \beta' \mid T = e\left(g_1, g_2\right)^z]\right|$$
$$= \left|\mathsf{Adv}(\mathcal{A}) + \frac{1}{2} - \frac{1}{2}\right| = \mathsf{Adv}(\mathcal{A}).$$

5   Black-Box Confirmation Traitor-Tracing

This section will be devoted to present a black-box confirmation traitor-tracing algorithm. The purpose of this algorithm is to verify sets of secret keys which are suspected by a Tracer. The tracing algorithm takes as input the master secret key MSK and it can access the table $\mathcal{T}$ (see the Tracing security game) to take a set of secret keys for which it wants to check its suspicion. We will use the scalar form $\mathsf{tk}_{x,\mathsf{ID}}$ of the secret keys instead of the group element form $\mathsf{sk}_{x,\mathsf{ID}}$. But as we only consider possible legitimate secrete keys in this form, the scalars are known to the authority.

5.1   Notations

Suppose that Tracer is provided a set of t secret keys (for the suspected traitors), say $\mathcal{K}_{\mathsf{suspect}} = \{\mathsf{tk}_1, \ldots, \mathsf{tk}_t\}$ which are derived from a fixed vector $\boldsymbol{x} = (x_1, \ldots, x_k)$. Here, we have slightly abused the notation, as we are in the one-target security. When the vector $\boldsymbol{x}$ is explicit, we use the notation $\{\mathsf{tk}_1, \ldots, \mathsf{tk}_t\}$ instead of $\{\mathsf{tk}_{x,1}, \ldots, \mathsf{tk}_{x,t}\}$, the pirate decoder $\mathcal{D}_x$ is replaced by $\mathcal{D}$ and we use integers to represent identities of users. A codeword will be $\boldsymbol{\theta}_i$ which is attached to a user with identity i. The goal of the Tracer is to verify whether there is any traitor in $\mathcal{K}_{\mathsf{suspect}}$. Before go further we need to define some notations.

- Set $\mathcal{K}_i = \{\mathsf{tk}_1, \ldots, \mathsf{tk}_i\} \subseteq \mathcal{K}_{\mathsf{suspect}}$, for all $i \in [t]$ and $\mathcal{K}_0 = \emptyset$.

– We define spaces of tracing signals (ciphertexts) $\mathsf{Tr}_0, \mathsf{Tr}_1, \ldots, \mathsf{Tr}_t$ such that each signal from Tr_i can be decrypted successfully by any secret key in $\mathcal{K}_i$. More concretely, for each i from 0 to t, the tracing signal for a message $\boldsymbol{y} = (y_1, \ldots, y_k)$ is taken from the distribution $\mathsf{Tr}_i^{\boldsymbol{x}}(\boldsymbol{y})$ (or $\mathsf{Tr}_i(\boldsymbol{y})$ for simplicity, when $\boldsymbol{x}$ is explicit) that is defined as follows

$$\left\{ \left(H_1^a G^{y_1}, \ldots, H_k^a G^{y_k}, g_1^{z_1}, \ldots, g_1^{z_k} \right) \; \middle| \; \begin{array}{l} a \xleftarrow{\$} \mathbb{Z}_q, \boldsymbol{z} \xleftarrow{\$} \mathbb{Z}_q^k, \\ \langle \boldsymbol{z}, \mathsf{tk}_j \boldsymbol{\theta}_j \rangle = a \langle \boldsymbol{s}, \boldsymbol{x} \rangle, \forall j \in [i] \end{array} \right\},$$

where $\boldsymbol{z} = (z_1, \ldots, z_k)$. $G, H_1, \ldots, H_k$ are group elements of $\mathbb{G}_T$ and belong to the public key PK. Set $\mathcal{Q}(a) = e(g_1, g_2)^{a \langle s, x \rangle}$, as $\boldsymbol{s}$ and $\boldsymbol{x}$ are fixed.
– Every user j with secret key in $\mathcal{K}_i$ can output the same

$$\frac{(H_1^a G^{y_1})^{x_1} \cdots (H_k^a G^{y_k})^{x_k}}{e(g_1^{\langle z, \theta_j \rangle}, g_2^{\mathsf{tk}_j})} = \frac{\mathcal{P}(\boldsymbol{y}, a)}{\mathcal{Q}(a)},$$

where $\mathcal{P}(\boldsymbol{y}, a) = (H_1^a G^{y_1})^{x_1} \cdots (H_k^a G^{y_k})^{x_k} = \mathcal{Q}(a) \times G^{\langle y, x \rangle}$.
– Define distribution of normal ciphertext for a message $\boldsymbol{y} = (y_1, \ldots, y_k)$, denoted $\mathsf{Norm}(\boldsymbol{y})$: randomly draw $r \xleftarrow{\$} \mathbb{Z}_q$ and output ciphertext $(H_1^r G^{y_1}, \ldots, H_k^r G^{y_k}, b_1^r, \ldots, b_k^r)$.
– For $i = 0, \ldots, t$, we set $p_i = \Pr[\mathcal{D}(\mathsf{CT}) = b \,|\, b \xleftarrow{\$} \{0, 1\}, \mathsf{CT} \leftarrow \mathsf{Tr}_i(\boldsymbol{y}_b)]$, where $\boldsymbol{y}_0, \boldsymbol{y}_1$ are chosen by $\mathcal{D}$. When $i = 0$, in $\mathsf{Tr}_i(\boldsymbol{y}_b)$, a and $\boldsymbol{z}$ are perfectly independent, and so under the DDH assumption, the H_i^a hides the $y_{b,i}$. So we have $p_0 = 1/2 + \mathsf{negl}(\lambda)$.

Definition 8. *A tracing traitor algorithm is black-box confirmation if it satisfies:*

1. *Confirmation: If suspected set of users actually contains the entire set of traitors then output of Tracing algorithm always returns at least an identity i such that $\mathsf{tk}_i \in \mathcal{K}_{\mathsf{suspect}}$ is guilty. Formally, with the condition $\mathcal{K}_{\mathcal{D}} \subseteq \mathcal{K}_{\mathsf{suspect}}$, the Tracing algorithm returns at least an identity i such that the secret key $\mathsf{tk}_i \in \mathcal{K}_{\mathsf{suspect}}$ as guilty. We denote by $\mathcal{K}_{\mathcal{D}}$ a set of secret keys used to build the pirate decoder $\mathcal{D}$.*
2. *Soundness: The honest users will never be accused if the Tracing algorithm outputs an identity as guilty; it is impossible for traitors to deceive Tracing algorithm to blame innocent users. Said differently if Tracing algorithm outputs an identity i such that tk_i is guilty then $\mathsf{tk}_i \in \mathcal{K}_{\mathcal{D}}$.*

5.2   Tracing Algorithm

Tracing algorithm needs to use following lemmas.

Lemma 9. *Under the DDH assumption in $\mathbb{G}_1$, no adversary corrupting t users $1, \ldots, t$ can distinguish the distribution of tracing signals $\mathsf{Tr}_t(\boldsymbol{y})$ with the distribution of normal ciphertexts $\mathsf{Norm}(\boldsymbol{y})$, for any adversarially chosen $\boldsymbol{y}$.*

Proof. Suppose that an adversary $\mathcal{A}$ can distinguish the distribution of tracing signals $\mathsf{Tr}_t(\boldsymbol{y})$ with the distribution of normal ciphertexts Norm. We will build a simulator $\mathcal{B}$ breaks the DDH assumption in $\mathbb{G}_1$. The simulator has inputs: 4-tuples $(\mathfrak{g}_1, \mathfrak{g}_2, u_1, u_2) \in \mathbb{G}_1^4$, where $\mathfrak{g}_2 = \mathfrak{g}_1^c$ and c is unknown. It decides whether this is a DDH tuple or a random tuple:

1. Take randomly t codewords $\boldsymbol{\theta}_1, \ldots, \boldsymbol{\theta}_t$ from the code $\boldsymbol{\Gamma}$.
2. Take randomly A from $\mathbb{Z}_q$ such that $\mathfrak{g}_1^A \mathfrak{g}_2 \neq 1$.
3. Take randomly $\boldsymbol{a} = (a_1, \ldots, a_k), \boldsymbol{e} = (e_1, \ldots, e_k) \xleftarrow{\$} \mathbb{Z}_q^k$ such that $\langle \boldsymbol{\theta}_i, \boldsymbol{a} - A\boldsymbol{e} \rangle = 0$, for all $i = 1, \ldots, t$.
4. Set $b_i = \mathfrak{g}_1^{a_i} \mathfrak{g}_2^{e_i}$, for all $i = 1, \ldots, k$.
5. Take randomly $\boldsymbol{\alpha} = (\alpha_1, \ldots, \alpha_k) \xleftarrow{\$} \mathbb{Z}_q^k$ such that $\langle \boldsymbol{\alpha}, \boldsymbol{a} - A\boldsymbol{e} \rangle = 0$. Take randomly $g_2 \xleftarrow{\$} \mathbb{G}_2$ and it sets $g_1 = \mathfrak{g}_1^A \mathfrak{g}_2$, $G = e(g_1, g_2)$. We set $H_i = e(u_1^A u_2, g_2)^{\alpha_i}$ for all $i \in [k]$. The public key is $\mathsf{PK} = (\mathbb{G}, \boldsymbol{\Gamma}, g_1, g_2, G, H_1, \ldots, H_k, b_1, \ldots, b_k)$, where $\mathbb{G}$ is a bilinear group.
6. The simulator $\mathcal{B}$ calculates secret key for queries $(\boldsymbol{x}, i)$, $\mathsf{tk}_{\boldsymbol{x},i} = \dfrac{\langle \boldsymbol{\alpha}, \boldsymbol{x} \rangle}{\langle \boldsymbol{\theta}_i, \boldsymbol{e} \rangle}$, for $i \in [t]$ and functions $\boldsymbol{x}$ then gives all $g_2^{\mathsf{tk}_{\boldsymbol{x},i}}$ to the adversary $\mathcal{A}$. It is clear that $\mathsf{tk}_{\boldsymbol{x},i} \boldsymbol{\theta}_i$ is a representation of $(\mathfrak{g}_1^A \mathfrak{g}_2)^{\langle \boldsymbol{\alpha}, \boldsymbol{x} \rangle}$ in the base $(b_1, \ldots, b_k)$.
7. Take randomly $a \xleftarrow{\$} \mathbb{Z}_q$. The simulator constructs the ciphertext for a message $\boldsymbol{y}$ as below

$$\mathsf{CT} = (H_1^a G^{y_1}, \ldots, H_k^a G^{y_k}, (u_1^{a_1} u_2^{e_1})^a, \ldots, (u_1^{a_k} u_2^{e_k})^a),$$

   where $\boldsymbol{y} = (y_1, \ldots, y_k)$.
8. Send the ciphertext CT to the adversary $\mathcal{A}$. If $\mathcal{A}$ decides the ciphertext comes from normal distribution (i.e. $\mathcal{A}$ returns 1) then $\mathcal{B}$ returns "DDH tuple", else returns "random tuple".

We first show that the public key PK which is generated by the simulator $\mathcal{B}$ is indistinguishable from the corresponding public key in the real algorithm.

– We will prove that distribution of tuples $(b_1, \ldots, b_k) \in \mathbb{G}_1^k$ is uniform. Indeed, write $b_i = g_1^{t_i}$ then, for each $(t + k)$-tuple $(\boldsymbol{0}, t_1, \ldots, t_k)$ where $t_1, \ldots, t_k \xleftarrow{\$} \mathbb{Z}_q$ and $\boldsymbol{0} = (0, \ldots, 0) \in \mathbb{Z}_q^t$ the below system of equations has a solution

$$\begin{pmatrix} \cdots \boldsymbol{\theta}_1 \cdots & \cdots -A\boldsymbol{\theta}_1 \cdots \\ \vdots \ \vdots \ \vdots & \vdots \ \ \vdots \ \ \vdots \\ \cdots \boldsymbol{\theta}_t \cdots & \cdots -A\boldsymbol{\theta}_t \cdots \\ \hline 1 \ \cdots \ 0 \ \ c & \cdots \quad 0 \\ \vdots \ \ddots \ \vdots \ \ \vdots & \ddots \quad \vdots \\ 0 \ \cdots \ 1 \ \ 0 & \cdots \quad c \end{pmatrix} \times \begin{pmatrix} \boldsymbol{a} \\ \boldsymbol{e} \end{pmatrix} = \begin{pmatrix} \boldsymbol{0} \\ t_1 \\ \vdots \\ t_k \end{pmatrix}.$$

We denote by $\boldsymbol{\Gamma}_0$ a matrix with its rows are vectors $\boldsymbol{\theta}_1, \ldots, \boldsymbol{\theta}_t$. The rank of this matrix is t.

Indeed, it is equivalent that

$$\begin{pmatrix} \mathbf{\Gamma}_0 & -A\mathbf{\Gamma}_0 \\ \mathbf{I}_k & c\mathbf{I}_k \end{pmatrix} \times \begin{pmatrix} a \\ e \end{pmatrix} = \begin{pmatrix} 0 \\ t \end{pmatrix}$$

has solutions. Here $\mathbf{I}_k$ is the $(k \times k)$-unit matrix. We set

$$\Omega = \begin{pmatrix} \mathbf{\Gamma}_0 & -A\mathbf{\Gamma}_0 \\ \mathbf{I}_k & c\mathbf{I}_k \end{pmatrix}.$$

Since A is chosen such that $1 \neq \mathfrak{g}_1^A \mathfrak{g}_2 = \mathfrak{g}_1^{A+c}$, $((t+k) \times 2k)$-matrix Ω has rank $k + t$. Therefore, $\dim \mathsf{Im}\Omega = \mathsf{rank}\ \Omega$ and the dimension of $\mathsf{Ker}\Omega = 2k - (k + t) = k - t$. Therefore, the above system of linear equations with unknowns (a, e) exists a solution. It implies that $(b_1, \ldots, b_k)$ is uniform over $\mathbb{G}_1^k$.

- Concerning H_i, in the real game $H_i = e(g_1, g_2)^{\alpha_i}$ for randomly chosen but known g_1, g_2 while in the simulation game, $H_i = e(u_1^A u_2, g_2)^{\alpha_i}$ for randomly chosen A and $(\alpha_i)_i$ in a span of dimension $k - 1$. Under the DDH in the $\mathbb{G}_1$, $u_1^A u_2$ is indistinguishable from random, and thus H_i follows from a correct distribution in the computational sense.

We now show that, for any adversarially chosen y, if $(\mathfrak{g}_1, \mathfrak{g}_2, u_1, u_2) \in \mathbb{G}_1^4$ is a DDH tuplee then the ciphertext is a normal ciphertext of y and when it is a random tuple then the ciphertext comes from $\mathsf{Tr}_t(y)$. Therefore, if the adversary can distinguish these two distributions then $\mathcal{B}$ can break the DDH assumption in $\mathbb{G}_1$: $|\Pr[\mathcal{B}(\mathcal{D}_0) = 1] - \Pr[\mathcal{B}(\mathcal{D}_1) = 1]|$ is non-negligible. By definition, it is equivalent to

$$\left| \Pr[\mathcal{A}(\mathsf{CT}) = 1 \mid (\mathfrak{g}_1, \mathfrak{g}_2, u_1, u_2) \xleftarrow{\$} \mathcal{D}_0] - \Pr[\mathcal{A}(\mathsf{CT}) = 1 \mid (\mathfrak{g}_1, \mathfrak{g}_2, u_1, u_2) \xleftarrow{\$} \mathcal{D}_1] \right|$$

is non-negligible. Here, CT is a ciphertext generated as in Step 7. We find that:

1. When $(\mathfrak{g}_1, \mathfrak{g}_2, u_1, u_2) \xleftarrow{\$} \mathcal{D}_0$, we will prove that

$$\Pr[\mathcal{A}(\mathsf{CT}) = 1 \mid (\mathfrak{g}_1, \mathfrak{g}_2, u_1, u_2) \xleftarrow{\$} \mathcal{D}_0] = \Pr[\mathcal{A}(\mathsf{CT}) = 1 \mid \mathsf{CT} \xleftarrow{\$} \mathsf{Norm}].$$

Indeed, suppose that $(\mathfrak{g}_1, \mathfrak{g}_2, u_1, u_2) = (\mathfrak{g}_1, \mathfrak{g}_2, \mathfrak{g}_1^z, \mathfrak{g}_2^z)$, where z is unknown. The ciphertexts in Step 7 is then:

$$\begin{aligned} \mathsf{CT} &= \left(H_1^a G^{y_1}, \ldots, H_k^a G^{y_k}, (u_1^{a_1} u_2^{e_1})^a, \ldots, (u_1^{a_k} u_2^{e_k})^a \right) \\ &= \left(H_1^a G^{y_1}, \ldots, H_k^a G^{y_k}, (\mathfrak{g}_1^{za_1} \mathfrak{g}_2^{ze_1})^a, \ldots, (\mathfrak{g}_1^{za_k} \mathfrak{g}_2^{ze_k})^a \right) \\ &= \left(H_1^a G^{y_1}, \ldots, H_k^a G^{y_k}, (\mathfrak{g}_1^{a_1} \mathfrak{g}_2^{e_1})^{z \cdot a}, \ldots, (\mathfrak{g}_1^{a_k} \mathfrak{g}_2^{e_k})^{z \cdot a} \right) \\ &= \left(H_1^a G^{y_1}, \ldots, H_k^a G^{y_k}, b_1^{z \cdot a}, \ldots, b_k^{z \cdot a} \right), \end{aligned}$$

which is in the space of normal ciphertext. It is sufficient thus to show that, with the decryption with the secret key $\mathsf{tk}_{x,i}$, the decryption will give $G^{\langle x,y \rangle}$. Indeed,

$$
\begin{aligned}
E &= \frac{\left(H_1^a G^{y_1}\right)^{x_1} \cdots \left(H_k^a G^{y_k}\right)^{x_k}}{e\left(\left(u_1^{a_1} u_2^{e_1}\right)^{a\theta_1} \cdots \left(u_1^{a_k} u_2^{e_k}\right)^{a\theta_k}, g_2^{\mathsf{tk}_{x,i}}\right)} \\[4pt]
&= \frac{G^{\langle x,y \rangle} \cdot e(u_1^A u_2, g_2)^{a x_1 \alpha_1} \cdots e(u_1^A u_2, g_2)^{a x_k \alpha_k}}{e\left(\left(\mathfrak{g}_1^A \mathfrak{g}_2\right)^{za\langle e,\theta \rangle}, g_2^{\frac{\langle x,\alpha \rangle}{\langle \theta, e \rangle}}\right)} \\[4pt]
&= \frac{G^{\langle x,y \rangle} \cdot e(\mathfrak{g}_1^A \mathfrak{g}_2, g_2)^{a z x_1 \alpha_1} \cdots e(\mathfrak{g}_1^A \mathfrak{g}_2, g_2)^{a z x_k \alpha_k}}{e\left(\left(\mathfrak{g}_1^A \mathfrak{g}_2\right)^{za\langle e,\theta \rangle}, g_2^{\frac{\langle x,\alpha \rangle}{\langle \theta, e \rangle}}\right)} \\[4pt]
&= \frac{G^{\langle x,y \rangle} \cdot e(\mathfrak{g}_1^A \mathfrak{g}_2, g_2)^{a z \langle x,\alpha \rangle}}{e\left(\left(\mathfrak{g}_1^A \mathfrak{g}_2\right)^{za\langle e,\theta \rangle}, g_2^{\frac{\langle x,\alpha \rangle}{\langle \theta, e \rangle}}\right)} = G^{\langle x,y \rangle}.
\end{aligned}
$$

2. When $(\mathfrak{g}_1, \mathfrak{g}_2, u_1, u_2) \xleftarrow{\$} \mathcal{D}_1$, we will prove that

$$
\Pr[\mathcal{A}(\mathsf{CT}) = 1 \mid (\mathfrak{g}_1, \mathfrak{g}_2, u_1, u_2) \xleftarrow{\$} \mathcal{D}_1] = \Pr[\mathcal{A}(\mathsf{CT}) = 1 \mid \mathsf{CT} \xleftarrow{\$} \mathsf{Tr}_t].
$$

Indeed, suppose that $(\mathfrak{g}_1, \mathfrak{g}_2, u_1, u_2) = (\mathfrak{g}_1, \mathfrak{g}_2, \mathfrak{g}_1^{\gamma_1}, \mathfrak{g}_2^{\gamma_2})$, where $\gamma_1 \neq \gamma_2$ and $\mathfrak{g}_2 = \mathfrak{g}_1^c$. The ciphertexts in Step 7 is then:

$$
\begin{aligned}
\mathsf{CT} &= \left(H_1^a G^{y_1}, \ldots, H_k^a G^{y_k}, (u_1^{a_1} u_2^{e_1})^a, \ldots, (u_1^{a_k} u_2^{e_k})^a\right) \\[4pt]
&= \left(H_1^a G^{y_1}, \ldots, H_k^a G^{y_k}, (\mathfrak{g}_1^{\gamma_1 a_1} \mathfrak{g}_2^{\gamma_2 e_1})^a, \ldots, (\mathfrak{g}_1^{\gamma_1 a_k} \mathfrak{g}_2^{\gamma_2 e_k})^a\right) \\[4pt]
&= \left(H_1^a G^{y_1}, \ldots, H_k^a G^{y_k}, \mathfrak{g}_1^{a(\gamma_1 a_1 + c\gamma_2 e_1)}, \ldots, \mathfrak{g}_1^{a(\gamma_1 a_k + c\gamma_2 e_k)}\right) \\[4pt]
&= \left(H_1^a G^{y_1}, \ldots, H_k^a G^{y_k}, \mathfrak{g}_1^{z_1}, \ldots, \mathfrak{g}_1^{z_k}\right),
\end{aligned}
$$

where $z_i = a(\gamma_1 a_k + c\gamma_2 e_k)$ for all $i \in [k]$.
We show that for any traitor with the key $\mathsf{tk}_{x,i}$, $i = 1$ to t, it decrypts to the same message. Indeed:

$$
\begin{aligned}
E &= \frac{\left(H_1^a G^{y_1}\right)^{x_1} \cdots \left(H_k^a G^{y_k}\right)^{x_k}}{e\left(\left(\mathfrak{g}_1^{\gamma_1 a_1} \mathfrak{g}_2^{\gamma_2 e_1}\right)^{a\theta_1} \cdots \left(\mathfrak{g}_1^{\gamma_1 a_k} \mathfrak{g}_2^{\gamma_2 e_k}\right)^{a\theta_k}, g_2^{\mathsf{tk}_{x,i}}\right)} \\[4pt]
&= \frac{G^{\langle x,y \rangle} \cdot e(u_1^A u_2, g_2)^{a x_1 \alpha_1} \cdots e(u_1^A u_2, g_2)^{a x_k \alpha_k}}{e\left(\mathfrak{g}_1^{\langle a,\theta \rangle a\gamma_1} \mathfrak{g}_2^{\langle e,\theta \rangle a\gamma_2}, g_2^{\frac{\langle x,\alpha \rangle}{\langle \theta, e \rangle}}\right)} \\[4pt]
&= \frac{G^{\langle x,y \rangle} \cdot e(\mathfrak{g}_1^{A\gamma_1} \mathfrak{g}_2^{\gamma_2}, g_2)^{a x_1 \alpha_1} \cdots e(\mathfrak{g}_1^{A\gamma_1} \mathfrak{g}_2^{\gamma_2}, g_2)^{a x_k \alpha_k}}{e\left(\mathfrak{g}_1^{\langle e,\theta \rangle a A\gamma_1} \mathfrak{g}_2^{\langle e,\theta \rangle a\gamma_2}, g_2^{\frac{\langle x,\alpha \rangle}{\langle \theta, e \rangle}}\right)} \\[4pt]
&= \frac{G^{\langle x,y \rangle} \cdot e(\mathfrak{g}_1^{A\gamma_1} \mathfrak{g}_2^{\gamma_2}, g_2)^{a\langle x,\alpha \rangle}}{e\left(\left(\mathfrak{g}_1^{A\gamma_1} \mathfrak{g}_2^{\gamma_2}\right)^{a\langle e,\theta \rangle}, g_2^{\frac{\langle x,\alpha \rangle}{\langle \theta, e \rangle}}\right)} = \frac{G^{\langle x,y \rangle} \cdot e(\mathfrak{g}_1^{A\gamma_1} \mathfrak{g}_2^{\gamma_2}, g_2)^{a\langle x,\alpha \rangle}}{e\left(\mathfrak{g}_1^{A\gamma_1} \mathfrak{g}_2^{\gamma_2}, g_2\right)^{a\langle x,\alpha \rangle}} = G^{\langle x,y \rangle}.
\end{aligned}
$$

Here $\boldsymbol{\theta}_i = (\theta_1, \dots, \theta_k)$.

Finally, we will prove that the distribution of ciphertext CT is uniform over the space of signals Tr_t. It requires that the system of equations

$$\begin{pmatrix} \boldsymbol{\Gamma}_0 & -\mathbf{A}\boldsymbol{\Gamma}_0 \\ \mathbf{I}_k & c\mathbf{I}_k \\ a\gamma_1\mathbf{I}_k & ac\gamma_2\mathbf{I}_k \end{pmatrix} \times \begin{pmatrix} a \\ e \end{pmatrix} = \gamma$$

is consistent, where γ is a fixed vector in $\mathbb{Z}_q^{t+2k}$. It is equivalent that the below $(t + 2k, 2k)$-matrix

$$\begin{pmatrix} \cdots & \boldsymbol{\theta}_1 & \cdots & \cdots & -\mathbf{A}\boldsymbol{\theta}_1 & \cdots \\ \vdots & \vdots & \vdots & \vdots & \vdots & \vdots \\ \cdots & \boldsymbol{\theta}_t & \cdots & \cdots & -\mathbf{A}\boldsymbol{\theta}_t & \cdots \\ 1 & \cdots & 0 & c & \cdots & 0 \\ \vdots & \ddots & \vdots & \vdots & \ddots & \vdots \\ 0 & \cdots & 1 & 0 & \cdots & c \\ a\gamma_1 & \cdots & 0 & ac\gamma_2 & \cdots & 0 \\ \vdots & \ddots & \vdots & \vdots & \ddots & \vdots \\ 0 & \cdots & a\gamma_1 & 0 & \cdots & ac\gamma_2 \end{pmatrix}$$

has full rank (i.e. rank $= 2k$). Indeed, this is straightforward because the last $2k$ rows of the above matrix are linear independent due to $\gamma_1 \neq \gamma_2$.

We conclude that

$$\big| \Pr[\mathcal{B}(\mathcal{D}_0) = 1] - \Pr[\mathcal{B}(\mathcal{D}_1) = 1] \big|$$
$$= \big| \Pr[\mathcal{A}(\mathsf{CT}) = 1 \mid \mathsf{CT} \xleftarrow{\$} \mathsf{Normal}] - \Pr[\mathcal{A}(\mathsf{CT}) = 1 \mid \mathsf{CT} \xleftarrow{\$} \mathsf{Tr}_t]\big| = \mathsf{Adv}(\mathcal{A}),$$

which is non-negligible. □

Lemma 10 (Hybrid Lemma). *Considering the one-target security for an adversarially chosen target function $\boldsymbol{x}$. Under the DDH assumption over group $\mathbb{G}_1$, for all $1 \le i_0 \le t$, no adversary can distinguish the distribution of tracing signals $\mathsf{Tr}_{i_0}(\boldsymbol{y})$ with the distribution of $\mathsf{Tr}_{i_0-1}(\boldsymbol{y})$ unless it owns the secret key sk_{i_0}.*

Proof. Suppose that an adversary $\mathcal{A}$ can distinguish the distribution of tracing signals Tr_{i_0} with Tr_{i_0-1}. We build a simulator $\mathcal{B}$ that breaks DDH assumption. The simulator has input a 4-tuple $(\mathfrak{g}_1, \mathfrak{g}_2, u_1, u_2) \in \mathbb{G}_1^4$, where $\mathfrak{g}_2 = \mathfrak{g}_1^c$ and c is unknown. It must output "DDH tuple" or "random tuple".

1. Take randomly t codewords $\boldsymbol{\theta}_1, \dots, \boldsymbol{\theta}_t$ from the code $\boldsymbol{\Gamma}$ corresponding to t traitors and also take t codewords $\boldsymbol{\theta}_1^{(s)}, \dots, \boldsymbol{\theta}_t^{(s)}$ from the code $\boldsymbol{\Gamma}$ corresponding to t suspected users. We are considering the adversary $\mathcal{A}$ does not know the secret key sk_{i_0} or the pirate decoder does not contain $\mathsf{sk}_{\boldsymbol{x},i_0}$ in itself.

2. Take randomly A from $\mathbb{Z}_q$ such that $\mathfrak{g}_1^A \mathfrak{g}_2 \neq 1$.

3. Take randomly $\boldsymbol{a} = (a_1, \ldots, a_k), \boldsymbol{e} = (e_1, \ldots, e_k) \xleftarrow{\$} \mathbb{Z}_q^k$ such that $\langle \boldsymbol{\theta}_i, \boldsymbol{a} - A\boldsymbol{e} \rangle = 0$, for all $i = 1, \ldots, t$, $\langle \boldsymbol{\theta}_i^{(s)}, \boldsymbol{a} - A\boldsymbol{e} \rangle = 0$, for all $i = 1, \ldots, t$, $i \neq i_0$ and $\langle \boldsymbol{\theta}_{i_0}^{(s)}, \boldsymbol{a} - A\boldsymbol{e} \rangle \neq 0$.

4. Set $b_i = \mathfrak{g}_1^{a_i} \mathfrak{g}_2^{e_i}$, for all $i = 1, \ldots, k$. Take randomly $\boldsymbol{v} = (v_1, \ldots, v_k) \xleftarrow{\$} \mathbb{Z}_q^k$ such that $\langle \boldsymbol{\theta}_i^{(s)}, \boldsymbol{v} \rangle = 0$, for all $i = 1, \ldots, i_0$.

5. Take randomly $\boldsymbol{\alpha} = (\alpha_1, \ldots, \alpha_k) \xleftarrow{\$} \mathbb{Z}_q^k$ such that $\langle \boldsymbol{\alpha}, \boldsymbol{a} - A\boldsymbol{e} \rangle = 0$ and $\langle \boldsymbol{\alpha}, \boldsymbol{v} \rangle = 0$.

6. When $\mathcal{B}$ receives a target function $\boldsymbol{x}$ from $\mathcal{A}$. It calculates $\tau_i = \dfrac{\langle \boldsymbol{\alpha}, \boldsymbol{x} \rangle}{\langle \boldsymbol{\theta}_i, \boldsymbol{e} \rangle}$, for $i = 1, \ldots, t$ and then give all $g_2^{\tau_i}$ to the adversary $\mathcal{A}$ to create a Pirate Decoder $\mathcal{D}_{\boldsymbol{x}}$. Moreover, $\tau_i^{(s)} = \dfrac{\langle \boldsymbol{\alpha}, \boldsymbol{x} \rangle}{\langle \boldsymbol{\theta}_i^{(s)}, \boldsymbol{e} \rangle}$, for $i = 1, \ldots, i_0 - 1$. It is clear that $\tau_i \boldsymbol{\theta}_i$ and $\tau_i^{(s)} \boldsymbol{\theta}_i^{(s)}$ are representations of $(\mathfrak{g}_1^A \mathfrak{g}_2)^{\langle \boldsymbol{\alpha}, \boldsymbol{x} \rangle}$ in the base $(b_1, \ldots, b_k)$.

7. Take randomly $G, H_1, \ldots, H_k \xleftarrow{\$} \mathbb{G}_T$, $a \xleftarrow{\$} \mathbb{Z}_q$. When the simulator receives a message $\boldsymbol{y}$, it constructs the ciphertext

$$\mathsf{CT} = (H_1^a G^{y_1}, \ldots, H_k^a G^{y_k}, \mathfrak{g}_1^{v_1} u_1^{a_1} u_2^{e_1}, \ldots, \mathfrak{g}_1^{v_k} u_1^{a_k} u_2^{e_k}),$$

where $\boldsymbol{y} = (y_1, \ldots, y_k)$. It then sends the ciphertext to the adversary $\mathcal{A}$. If $\mathcal{A}$ returns the ciphertext comes from $\mathsf{Tr}_{i_0}(\boldsymbol{y})$ distribution then $\mathcal{B}$ returns DDH tuple, else returns random tuple.

By the similar argument as in Lemma 9, the ciphertext CT in Step 7 of the algorithm $\mathcal{B}$ comes from the distribution $\mathsf{Tr}_{i_0}(\boldsymbol{y})$ if the input of $\mathcal{B}$ is actually DDH tuples and from the distribution $\mathsf{Tr}_{i_0-1}(\boldsymbol{y})$ otherwise. $\qquad\square$

Based on the Lemmas 9 and 10, we can design a tracing algorithm that relies on the linear technique tracing:

- Initial step: Tracer constructs distributions of tracing signal $\mathsf{Tr}_t, \ldots, \mathsf{Tr}_0$.
- Do experiments on the pirate distinguisher $\mathcal{D}$ finitely many times. We start testing $\mathcal{D}$ by taking tracing signals CT from the distribution Tr_t. We measure the rate that $\mathcal{D}$ outputs correctly his guess, denoted by $\tilde{p}_t$. Experiments can be done because we can prove that the pirate distinguisher cannot distinguish distributions Tr_t and Norm (see Lemma 9).
- At step i, for $i = t - 1, \ldots, 0$. We do experiment on the pirate distinguisher $\mathcal{D}$ with tracing signals taken from Tr_i. From Lemma 10, the pirate distinguisher cannot see any change from previous step $i+1$ to this step i unless it holds the secret key tk_{i+1}. More formally, we also measure the rate $\tilde{p}_i$ that $\mathcal{D}$ outputs correctly his guess and show that if $\mathcal{D}$ does not contain tk_{i+1} then there is no significant difference between $\tilde{p}_{i+1}$ and $\tilde{p}_i$.
- At the final step, $\mathcal{D}$ will be tested with tracing signals taken from Tr_0. $\mathcal{D}$ answers correctly only negligibly close to $1/2$.

– We output the traitor i such that the gap between $\tilde{p}_i$ and $\tilde{p}_{i-1}$ is the largest value among all indices i.

Below, we present the tracing algorithm in more details. We note that $\boldsymbol{y}_0, \boldsymbol{y}_1$ are vectors which are chosen by the pirate distinguisher $\mathcal{D}$.

For $i = t$ downto 0, do the following:
1. Let cnt $\leftarrow 0$.
2. For $j = 1$ to $N = 8\lambda t^2/\mu$, do the following:
    i. $b \overset{\$}{\leftarrow} \{0,1\}$.
    ii. CT $\overset{\$}{\leftarrow}$ Tr$_i(\boldsymbol{y}_b)$.
    iii. Send CT to $\mathcal{D}$. If $\mathcal{D}(\mathsf{CT}) = b$ then cnt $\leftarrow$ cnt $+ 1$.
3. End for.
4. Let $\tilde{p}_i$ be the fraction of times that $\mathcal{D}$ did the correct guess. We have $\tilde{p}_i = \mathsf{cnt}/N$.
End for.
Output identities i such that $|\tilde{p}_i - \tilde{p}_{i-1}| \geq \dfrac{\mu(\lambda)}{4t}$.

Below, we state and prove confirmation and soundness property of our Tracing algorithm.

Lemma 11 (Confirmation property). *The* Tracing *algorithm has the confirmation property under the DDH assumption in* $\mathbb{G}_1$.

Proof. We want to prove that in the case of that all the traitors are in the set of suspected users, i.e. $\mathcal{K}_\mathcal{D} \subseteq \mathcal{K}_{\mathsf{suspect}}$, the Tracing algorithm always returns the identity of a guilty. It means that the output of Tracing algorithm is not empty with high probability. We denote $\mathcal{A}$ an adversary who used the secret keys in $\mathcal{K}_\mathcal{D}$ to output the pirate distinguisher $\mathcal{D}$. Since the adversary $\mathcal{A}$ can create a μ-useful pirate distinguisher $\mathcal{D}$, it implies that $|p_{\mathsf{Norm}} - \frac{1}{2}| \geq \mu(\lambda)$, where

$$p_{\mathsf{Norm}} = \Pr\left[\mathcal{D}\left(\mathsf{CT}_b\right) = b : \begin{array}{l} (\mathsf{MSK}, \mathsf{PK}) \leftarrow \mathsf{Setup}(\cdot) \\ \{\mathsf{sk}_i \leftarrow \mathsf{Extract}(i, \mathsf{MSK}, \boldsymbol{x})\}_{i \in [n]} \\ (\mathcal{D}, \boldsymbol{y}^0, \boldsymbol{y}^1) \leftarrow \mathcal{A}(\mathsf{PK}, \{\mathsf{sk}_i\}_{i \in [t]}) \\ \text{st. } \langle \boldsymbol{x}, \boldsymbol{y}^0 \rangle \neq \langle \boldsymbol{x}, \boldsymbol{y}^1 \rangle \\ b \overset{\$}{\leftarrow} \{0,1\}, \mathsf{CT}_b \leftarrow \mathsf{Norm}(\mathsf{PK}, \boldsymbol{y}^b) \end{array} \right].$$

We denote S the set of indices $i \in [t]$ such that $|p_i - p_{i-1}| > \mu(\lambda)/4t$. The set S is well defined in the sense that $S \neq \emptyset$. Indeed, as we know that p_0 is negligibly close to $1/2$, and Lemma 9 showed that no adversary $\mathcal{A}$ can distinguish the distribution Norm from Tr$_t$, then $|p_t - p_0| \geq \mu(\lambda) - \mathsf{negl}(\lambda) > \mu(\lambda)/2$. Then, there exists an index i such that $|p_i - p_{i-1}| > \mu(\lambda)/2t$. Thus S is a non empty set. Applying Chernoff bound for all $i \in S$, we have on experimental probabilities

$$\Pr\left[|\tilde{p}_i - \tilde{p}_{i-1}| < \dfrac{\mu(\lambda)}{4t}\right] \leq \mathsf{negl}(\lambda),$$

Therefore, with overwhelming probability, there exists an index i such that

$$|\tilde{p}_i - \tilde{p}_{i-1}| \geq \frac{\mu(\lambda)}{4t}.$$

The latter is thus returned with overwhelming probability.   □

Lemma 12. (Soundness property). *The* Tracing *algorithm has the soundness property under the DDH assumption in* $\mathbb{G}_1$.

Proof. We now prove the soundness property of Tracing algorithm. Suppose that the Tracing algorithm outputs an identity j, where $\mathsf{tk}_j \in \mathcal{K}_{\mathsf{suspect}}$, we will prove that $\mathsf{tk}_j \in \mathcal{K}_{\mathcal{D}}$.

According to Chernoff bound, thanks to $N = 8\lambda t^2/\mu(\lambda)$ to calculate $\tilde{p}_i$, for all i, we have

$$\Pr\left[|\tilde{p}_i - p_i| > \frac{\mu(\lambda)}{16t}\right] < 2 \cdot e^{-\lambda/64}.$$

Therefore, with high probability we have $|\tilde{p}_i - p_i| \leq \mu(\lambda)/16t$, for all $i = 0, \ldots, t$.

By definition, whenever the Tracing algorithm outputs j as a guilty, we have $|\tilde{p}_j - \tilde{p}_{j-1}| \geq \mu(\lambda)/4t$, and thus $|p_j - p_{j-1}| \geq \mu(\lambda)/8t$. In other words, the pirate distinguisher can distinguish the two tracing signals Tr_j and Tr_{j-1} with advantage at least $\mu(\lambda)/8t$. It implies that $\mathcal{D}$ contains the secret key tk_j, $\mathsf{tk}_j \in \mathcal{D}$. This follows from the fact that if $\mathcal{D}$ does not know the secret key tk_j, $\mathsf{tk}_j \notin \mathcal{D}$, the two tracing signals Tr_j and Tr_{j-1} are indistinguishable. More concretely, under the hardness of the DDH problem in group $\mathbb{G}_1$, it is impossible for the pirate to distinguish Tr_j and Tr_{j-1} without tk_j. This is stated and proved in Lemma 10.   □

Theorem 13. *Under the DDH assumption, our tracing scheme is one-target security in black-box confirmation model.*

Proof. We recall that in the black-box confirmation model we will verify a set suspected secret keys $\mathcal{K}_{\mathsf{suspect}} = \{\mathsf{tk}_1, \ldots, \mathsf{tk}_t\}$ which are also derived from the vector $\boldsymbol{x}$. We will prove that Tracing algorithm always outputs an identity of a traitor whenever $\mathcal{K}_{\mathcal{D}} \cap \mathcal{K}_{\mathsf{suspect}} \neq \emptyset$. It means that Tracer always wins in the game with the pirate distinguisher $\mathcal{D}$. Indeed, we consider the following two cases:

- In the first case $\mathcal{K}_{\mathcal{D}} \subseteq \mathcal{K}_{\mathsf{suspect}}$. It means that all traitors are in suspicious set $\mathcal{K}_{\mathsf{suspect}}$. Tracing algorithm will output a guilty identity i by the confirmation property. According to soundness property, the identity is a traitor ($\mathsf{tk}_i \in \mathcal{K}_{\mathcal{D}}$).
- In case $\mathcal{K}_{\mathcal{D}} \not\subseteq \mathcal{K}_{\mathsf{suspect}}$ and $\mathcal{K}_{\mathcal{D}} \cap \mathcal{K}_{\mathsf{suspect}} \neq \emptyset$. Because $\mathcal{K}_{\mathcal{D}} \cap \mathcal{K}_{\mathsf{suspect}} \neq \emptyset$, tracing algorithm will output an identity i so that $\mathsf{sk}_i \in \mathcal{K}_{\mathsf{suspect}}$. It implies i is a traitor ($\mathsf{tk}_i \in \mathcal{K}_{\mathcal{D}}$) by the soundness property.   □

Acknowledgments. This work was supported in part by the European Community's Seventh Framework Programme (FP7/2007-2013 Grant Agreement no. 339563 – CryptoCloud) and the ANR ALAMBIC (ANR16-CE39-0006).

References

1. Abdalla, M., Bourse, F., De Caro, A., Pointcheval, D.: Simple functional encryption schemes for inner products. In: Katz, J. (ed.) PKC 2015. LNCS, vol. 9020, pp. 733–751. Springer, Heidelberg (2015). https://doi.org/10.1007/978-3-662-46447-2_33
2. Abdalla, M., Dent, A.W., Malone-Lee, J., Neven, G., Phan, D.H., Smart, N.P.: Identity-based traitor tracing. In: Okamoto, T., Wang, X. (eds.) PKC 2007. LNCS, vol. 4450, pp. 361–376. Springer, Heidelberg (2007). https://doi.org/10.1007/978-3-540-71677-8_24
3. Agrawal, S., Bhattacherjee, S., Phan, D.H., Stehlé, D., Yamada, S.: Efficient public trace and revoke from standard assumptions: extended abstract. In: Thuraisingham, B.M., Evans, D., Malkin, T., Xu, D. (eds.) ACM CCS 2017, pp. 2277–2293. ACM Press, October/November 2017
4. Agrawal, S., Libert, B., Stehlé, D.: Fully secure functional encryption for inner products, from standard assumptions. In: Robshaw, M., Katz, J. (eds.) CRYPTO 2016, Part III. LNCS, vol. 9816, pp. 333–362. Springer, Heidelberg (2016). https://doi.org/10.1007/978-3-662-53015-3_12
5. Au, M.H., Huang, Q., Liu, J.K., Susilo, W., Wong, D.S., Yang, G.: Traceable and retrievable identity-based encryption. In: Bellovin, S.M., Gennaro, R., Keromytis, A., Yung, M. (eds.) ACNS 2008. LNCS, vol. 5037, pp. 94–110. Springer, Heidelberg (2008). https://doi.org/10.1007/978-3-540-68914-0_6
6. Baltico, C.E.Z., Catalano, D., Fiore, D., Gay, R.: Practical functional encryption for quadratic functions with applications to predicate encryption. In: Katz, J., Shacham, H. (eds.) CRYPTO 2017, Part I. LNCS, vol. 10401, pp. 67–98. Springer, Cham (2017). https://doi.org/10.1007/978-3-319-63688-7_3
7. Boneh, D., Franklin, M.: An efficient public key traitor tracing scheme. In: Wiener, M. (ed.) CRYPTO 1999. LNCS, vol. 1666, pp. 338–353. Springer, Heidelberg (1999). https://doi.org/10.1007/3-540-48405-1_22
8. Boneh, D., Sahai, A., Waters, B.: Fully collusion resistant traitor tracing with short ciphertexts and private keys. In: Vaudenay, S. (ed.) EUROCRYPT 2006. LNCS, vol. 4004, pp. 573–592. Springer, Heidelberg (2006). https://doi.org/10.1007/11761679_34
9. Boneh, D., Sahai, A., Waters, B.: Functional encryption: definitions and challenges. In: Ishai, Y. (ed.) TCC 2011. LNCS, vol. 6597, pp. 253–273. Springer, Heidelberg (2011). https://doi.org/10.1007/978-3-642-19571-6_16
10. Boneh, D., Zhandry, M.: Multiparty key exchange, efficient traitor tracing, and more from indistinguishability obfuscation. In: Garay, J.A., Gennaro, R. (eds.) CRYPTO 2014, Part I. LNCS, vol. 8616, pp. 480–499. Springer, Heidelberg (2014). https://doi.org/10.1007/978-3-662-44371-2_27
11. Chabanne, H., Phan, D.H., Pointcheval, D.: Public traceability in traitor tracing schemes. In: Cramer, R. (ed.) EUROCRYPT 2005. LNCS, vol. 3494, pp. 542–558. Springer, Heidelberg (2005). https://doi.org/10.1007/11426639_32
12. Chen, Y., Vaikuntanathan, V., Waters, B., Wee, H., Wichs, D.: Traitor-tracing from LWE made simple and attribute-based. In: Beimel, A., Dziembowski, S. (eds.) TCC 2018, Part II. LNCS, vol. 11240, pp. 341–369. Springer, Cham (2018). https://doi.org/10.1007/978-3-030-03810-6_13
13. Chor, B., Fiat, A., Naor, M.: Tracing traitors. In: Desmedt, Y.G. (ed.) CRYPTO 1994. LNCS, vol. 839, pp. 257–270. Springer, Heidelberg (1994). https://doi.org/10.1007/3-540-48658-5_25

14. Fazio, N., Nicolosi, A., Phan, D.H.: Traitor tracing with optimal transmission rate. In: Garay, J.A., Lenstra, A.K., Mambo, M., Peralta, R. (eds.) ISC 2007. LNCS, vol. 4779, pp. 71–88. Springer, Heidelberg (2007). https://doi.org/10.1007/978-3-540-75496-1_5

15. Goyal, R., Koppula, V., Waters, B.: Collusion resistant traitor tracing from learning with errors. In: Diakonikolas, I., Kempe, D., Henzinger, M. (eds.) 50th ACM STOC, pp. 660–670. ACM Press, June 2018

16. Goyal, V.: Reducing trust in the PKG in identity based cryptosystems. In: Menezes, A. (ed.) CRYPTO 2007. LNCS, vol. 4622, pp. 430–447. Springer, Heidelberg (2007). https://doi.org/10.1007/978-3-540-74143-5_24

17. Kiayias, A., Yung, M.: Traitor tracing with constant transmission rate. In: Knudsen, L.R. (ed.) EUROCRYPT 2002. LNCS, vol. 2332, pp. 450–465. Springer, Heidelberg (2002). https://doi.org/10.1007/3-540-46035-7_30

18. Ling, S., Phan, D.H., Stehlé, D., Steinfeld, R.: Hardness of k-LWE and applications in traitor tracing. In: Garay, J.A., Gennaro, R. (eds.) CRYPTO 2014, Part I. LNCS, vol. 8616, pp. 315–334. Springer, Heidelberg (2014). https://doi.org/10.1007/978-3-662-44371-2_18

19. Liu, Z., Cao, Z., Wong, D.S.: Blackbox traceable CP-ABE: how to catch people leaking their keys by selling decryption devices on eBay. In: Sadeghi, A.-R., Gligor, V.D., Yung, M. (eds.) ACM CCS 2013, pp. 475–486. ACM Press, November 2013

20. Liu, Z., Wong, D.S.: Practical ciphertext-policy attribute-based encryption: traitor tracing, revocation, and large universe. In: Malkin, T., Kolesnikov, V., Lewko, A.B., Polychronakis, M. (eds.) ACNS 2015. LNCS, vol. 9092, pp. 127–146. Springer, Cham (2015). https://doi.org/10.1007/978-3-319-28166-7_7

21. Liu, Z., Wong, D.S.: Traceable CP-ABE on prime order groups: fully secure and fully collusion-resistant blackbox traceable. In: Qing, S., Okamoto, E., Kim, K., Liu, D. (eds.) ICICS 2015. LNCS, vol. 9543, pp. 109–124. Springer, Cham (2016). https://doi.org/10.1007/978-3-319-29814-6_10

22. Ning, J., Cao, Z., Dong, X., Wei, L., Lin, X.: Large universe ciphertext-policy attribute-based encryption with white-box traceability. In: Kutyłowski, M., Vaidya, J. (eds.) ESORICS 2014, Part II. LNCS, vol. 8713, pp. 55–72. Springer, Cham (2014). https://doi.org/10.1007/978-3-319-11212-1_4

23. Nishimaki, R., Wichs, D., Zhandry, M.: Anonymous traitor tracing: how to embed arbitrary information in a key. In: Fischlin, M., Coron, J.-S. (eds.) EUROCRYPT 2016, Part II. LNCS, vol. 9666, pp. 388–419. Springer, Heidelberg (2016). https://doi.org/10.1007/978-3-662-49896-5_14

24. Phan, D.H., Trinh, V.C.: Identity-based trace and revoke schemes. In: Boyen, X., Chen, X. (eds.) ProvSec 2011. LNCS, vol. 6980, pp. 204–221. Springer, Heidelberg (2011). https://doi.org/10.1007/978-3-642-24316-5_15

25. Sahai, A., Waters, B.: Fuzzy identity-based encryption. In: Cramer, R. (ed.) EUROCRYPT 2005. LNCS, vol. 3494, pp. 457–473. Springer, Heidelberg (2005). https://doi.org/10.1007/11426639_27

One-More Assumptions Do Not Help Fiat-Shamir-type Signature Schemes in NPROM

Masayuki Fukumitsu[1(✉)] and Shingo Hasegawa[2]

[1] Faculty of Information Media, Hokkaido Information University,
Nishi-Nopporo 59-2 Ebetsu, Hokkaido 069-8585, Japan
`fukumitsu@do-johodai.ac.jp`
[2] Graduate School of Information Sciences, Tohoku University,
41 Kawauchi, Aoba-ku, Sendai, Miyagi 980-8576, Japan
`shingo.hasegawa.b7@tohoku.ac.jp`

Abstract. On the Fiat-Shamir-type signature schemes, there are several impossibility results concerning their provable security. Most of these impossibility results employ the non-programmable random oracle model (NPROM), and to the best of our knowledge, all impossibilities deal with the security reductions from the non-interactive cryptographic assumptions except for the result on the security of Schnorr signature scheme from the One-More DL (OM-DL) assumption in ProvSec2017.

In this paper, we extend the impossibility result above concerning Schnorr signature scheme and the OM-DL assumption to a wider class of the Fiat-Shamir-type signature schemes, and aim to find out the conditions so that such impossibility results hold. We show that a specific class of the Fiat-Shamir-type signature schemes, including Schnorr signature scheme, cannot be proven to be euf-cma secure in NPROM from the *generalized* One-More cryptographic assumptions. This is just a generalization of the impossibility concerning Schnorr signature scheme and the OM-DL assumption. Our result also suggests that for some Fiat-Shamir-type signature schemes, which is not covered by our impossibility (e.g. the RSA-based schemes), there may exist a successful security proof in NPROM from the interactive cryptographic assumption.

Keywords: Fiat-Shamir-type signature schemes · Non-programmable random oracle model · Impossibility result · Provable security · One-more cryptographic assumptions

1 Introduction

Background. Fiat-Shamir-type signature schemes are the ones that are yielded by applying the generic transformation introduced by Fiat and Shamir [13] to ID schemes. Many Fiat-Shamir-type signature schemes were proposed such as Schnorr signature scheme [37], Guillou and Quisquater (GQ) signature

© Springer Nature Switzerland AG 2020
S. Jarecki (Ed.): CT-RSA 2020, LNCS 12006, pp. 586–609, 2020.
https://doi.org/10.1007/978-3-030-40186-3_25

scheme [21], Okamoto signature scheme [32] and Lyubashevsky signature scheme [28]. These are known as simple and efficient constructions. For this reason, Fiat-Shamir-type signature schemes are employed in many applications, while these are also used e.g. in [27,31,35] as a building block to construct signature schemes which have special functions such as blind signature schemes, aggregate/multi-signature schemes and group/ring signature schemes. The ed25519 signature scheme [8], which is a variant of Schnorr signature scheme, is recruited in some network protocols such as the Transport Layer Security Protocol [12], the Secure Shell [40], and Tor [39]. Moreover, Schnorr signature scheme is recently considered to be applied to Bitcoin [30].

There are many discussions on the security of Fiat-Shamir-type signature schemes. Pointcheval and Stern [36] first proved the security of specific Fiat-Shamir-type signature schemes. They showed that a Fiat-Shamir-type signature scheme is secure if the underlying ID scheme has the honest-verifier zero-knowledge property and the special soundness property. Subsequently, their result was refined by Abdalla, An, Bellare, and Namprempre [1] in a sense that their security proof covers a wider class of signature schemes than [36]. These two results commonly rely on the proof techniques known as the "forking lemma [4,5]" and the random oracle model [6]. In particular, the *random oracle model* is one of "ideal" security model. This is often used to discuss the security of cryptographic schemes in a theoretical manner. The security of cryptographic schemes such as [6,7,10] besides Fiat-Shamir-type ones was indeed proven in this model.

Since the random oracle model is known as a stronger security model than the standard model, the security without the random oracle was also discussed. Paillier and Vergnaud [33] showed that the security of Schnorr signature scheme may not be proven in the standard model from the discrete logarithm (DL) assumption unless the One-More DL (OM-DL) assumption is broken. More precisely, they showed that there exists no security reduction $\mathcal{R}$ which solves the DL problem by black-box accessing a forger $\mathcal{F}$ which breaks Schnorr signature scheme as long as the OM-DL assumption holds. They also mentioned that similar impossibility results on other Fiat-Shamir-type signature schemes can be obtained. Note that their result only considers the case where a security reduction $\mathcal{R}$ is some specific type, called the algebraic reduction. Nevertheless, this is circumstantial negative evidence on the provable security of Fiat-Shamir-type signature schemes in the standard model.

Although the security of Fiat-Shamir-type signature scheme may not be proven in the standard model, it is expected that the security of these signature schemes is proven in a security model which is more realistic than the random oracle model. In the random oracle model, a security reduction $\mathcal{R}$ is allowed to simulate the random oracle. In particular, $\mathcal{R}$ in the random oracle model can utilize the observing property and the programming property as compared to the standard model. The observing property means that $\mathcal{R}$ can observe all queries and these responses by a forger $\mathcal{F}$ in the security proof. On the other hand, the programming property means that $\mathcal{R}$ can arbitrarily set a hash value of a string which is queried by $\mathcal{F}$. Observe that the programming property is one of the reasons why the random oracle model is considered to be strong.

In order to discuss security proofs without the programming property, the *non-programmable random oracle model (NPROM)* was introduced [15]. In this model, $\mathcal{R}$ also obtains all hash values from an external random oracle as well as the other parties such as $\mathcal{F}$ instead of simulating it. Namely, the programming property is prohibited in this environment. Fischlin and Fleischhacker [14] gave an impossibility result on the provable security of Schnorr signature scheme in NPROM. They showed that the security of Schnorr signature scheme cannot be proven in NPROM from the DL assumption via a single-instance reduction as long as the OM-DL assumption is remained to hold. Here, the single-instance reduction intuitively means that a security reduction $\mathcal{R}$ is allowed to invoke a forger $\mathcal{F}$ only once, but to rewind it any time. Several impossibility results on other Fiat-Shamir-type signature schemes were also discussed in [17,19]. However, all of these impossibility results only exclude the possibility that the security of Fiat-Shamir-type signature schemes is proven in NPROM from *non-interactive* cryptographic assumptions, such as the DL assumption, the computational Diffie-Hellman (CDH) assumption, the decisional Diffie-Hellman (DDH) assumption, RSA assumption, and the short integer solution assumption. Since *interactive* cryptographic assumptions are stronger than non-interactive ones in general, there is a possibility that the security can be proven from interactive cryptographic assumptions.

The impossibility results from interactive cryptographic assumptions were also given. Fukumitsu and Hasegawa [18] showed that the security of Schnorr signature scheme cannot be proven in NPROM from the OM-DL assumption as long as the OM-DL assumption holds. However, it remains open whether or not the security of other Fiat-Shamir-type signature schemes can be proven in NPROM from interactive cryptographic assumptions, and whether or not the security of Schnorr signature scheme can be proven in NPROM from some interactive cryptographic assumptions other than the OM-DL assumption. Fleischhacker, Jager, and Schröder [16] gave an impossibility result on the tight security of Schnorr signature scheme from specific interactive cryptographic assumptions. Their result is proven even in the ordinary random oracle model. Recall that the ordinary random oracle model is a stronger model than NPROM in the sense that the ordinary random oracle model allows the programming property. Their result means that the tight security of Schnorr signature scheme cannot be proven even by employing the programming property. However, since their result only considers the tight security reduction, there is the possibility that non-tight reductions circumvent their impossibility result. Moreover, theirs forces a security reduction $\mathcal{R}$ to be generic. It is known that generic reductions seem not to be reasonable in the sense that group operations are somewhat restricted in these reductions.

Eventually, it has not been elucidated clearly whether or not the security of Fiat-Shamir-type signature schemes is proven from interactive cryptographic assumptions in NPROM via a reasonable reduction. In other words, there is a room that the security of some Fiat-Shamir-type signature schemes can be proven from interactive cryptographic assumptions without programming property.

1.1   Our Result

Overview. In this paper, we give an impossibility result on the provable security of some Fiat-Shamir-type signature schemes in NPROM from some interactive cryptographic assumptions. Our result is stated by the following theorem.

Theorem 1 (Informal). *Some Fiat-Shamir-type signature schemes cannot be proven to be existentially unforgeable against the chosen-message attack (euf-cma) in NPROM from the generalized One-More cryptographic assumptions as long as the same underlying cryptographic assumptions hold. The restrictions of this result are more specifically described just below.*

The *generalized One-More cryptographic assumption* is a generalized variant of One-More cryptographic assumptions which are introduced in [41]. This is defined by two non-interactive cryptographic problems P_1 and P_2 which are assumed to be hard to solve. This assumption informally states that any probabilistic polynomial-time algorithm $\mathcal{A}$ solves $T + 1$ instances on P_1 with only negligible probability even if $\mathcal{A}$ can access the oracle which solves P_2 at most T times for some polynomial T. Hereafter, we denote the assumption above by T-(P_1, P_2). For instance, if the DL problem is set to both P_1 and P_2, this coincides with the OM-DL assumption. We note that since the T-(P_1, P_2) problem naturally reduces to the problem P_1 via a Turing reduction, the T-(P_1, P_2) assumption is stronger than the hardness assumption on P_1. Thus Theorem 1 can be regarded as the impossibility result from the hardness assumption on P_1.

In our result, we consider Fiat-Shamir-type signature schemes which are obtained from some specific type of ID schemes. Namely, an ID scheme has not only representative properties such as the special soundness property and the unique key property but also a certified key property which is proposed in this paper. There are many ID schemes have the special soundness property and the unique key property such as [21,24,37,38]. The certified key property is inspired by the certified property of trapdoor permutations [25]. This supposes that anyone can verify that a given public key indeed has the corresponding secret key in polynomial-time. For example, DL-based ID schemes such as [24,37] satisfies the certified property by considering an underlying group $\mathbb{G}$ as a group of prime order p with a generator g, On the other hand, RSA-based ID schemes such as GQ signature scheme seem not to be certified. This is because the order of an underlying group in RSA-based ones is assumed to be hidden.

For ease of explanation, we force a security reduction $\mathcal{R}$ considered in Theorem 1 to a vanilla one. A *vanilla* reduction $\mathcal{R}$ is allowed to merely invoke a forger $\mathcal{F}$ against the signature scheme once. Namely, it is prohibited to invoke $\mathcal{R}$ more than once and to rewind it. However, we consider that one can extend Theorem 1 to the impossibility result for the single-instance reduction. This is because we give our result by incorporating the proof techniques introduced by Fischlin and Fleischhacker [14] and Pass [34] which gave impossibility results that can cover single-instance reductions. The formal proof for the extended version of Theorem 1 will be given in the full paper.

On the reduction $\mathcal{R}$, we put some restriction. $\mathcal{R}$ is restricted to solve the T-$(\mathsf{P}_1, \mathsf{P}_2)$ problem in the case where it is given a forged signature $\sigma^* =$ $(\mathrm{cmt}^*, \mathrm{res}^*)$ by an euf-cma forger $\mathcal{F}$ such that a cmt^* part of σ^* differs from all cmt which appear in the signing oracle phase. This restriction is required to rule out some type of security proofs in which security reductions are constructed by separating the forged signature by $\mathcal{F}$ into several types such as the security proof of Cramer-Shoup signature [11]. Cramer and Shoup [11] indeed separated forged signatures into three types and then constructed three security reduction algorithms which correspond to each of types, respectively. We will explain why these restrictions affect the proof of Theorem 1.

Discussion. Theorem 1 states that Fiat-Shamir-type signature schemes which are derived from ID schemes which have the special soundness property, the unique key property, and the certified key property cannot be proven in NPROM from the T-$(\mathsf{P}_1, \mathsf{P}_2)$ assumption via the vanilla reductions which can handle the specific type of forged signatures. As an example of ID schemes which have these three properties, Schnorr ID scheme can be given. On the other hand, the OM-DL assumption belongs to the class of T-$(\mathsf{P}_1, \mathsf{P}_2)$ assumptions as mentioned above. These reinforce the impossibility result of the provable security of Schnorr signature scheme in NPROM given by Fukumitsu and Hasegawa [18].

If an ID scheme does not satisfy one of three properties above, it can circumvent the impossibility by Theorem 1. For example, Okamoto ID scheme seems not to have the unique key property. Moreover, the RSA-based ID schemes such as GQ ID scheme do not have the certified property as discussed above. Lossy ID schemes [2,22,23,26] also do not have the certified property since the lossy key property seems to be incompatible with the certified property. Therefore, there is a room that the Fiat-Shamir-type signature schemes yielded from these ID schemes can be proven to be secure in NPROM from the T-$(\mathsf{P}_1, \mathsf{P}_2)$ assumption.

In Theorem 1, we restrict the reduction algorithms $\mathcal{R}$ to handle a forged signature $\sigma^* = (\mathrm{cmt}^*, \mathrm{res}^*)$ such that the cmt^* part does not coincide with those of all signatures which are given in the security proof. This suggests that avoiding these restrictions may derive the successful security proof. It remains open whether or not such possibilities can be indeed realized.

Proof Technique of Theorem 1. Theorem 1 is proved by employing the meta-reduction technique which was introduced in [9]. The proof idea is as follows. Assume that there exists a black-box security reduction $\mathcal{R}$ which solves a designated T-$(\mathsf{P}_1, \mathsf{P}_2)$ problem by invoking an euf-cma forger $\mathcal{F}$ to a designated Fiat-Shamir-type signature scheme. Here, $\mathcal{R}$ would simulate the signing oracle for $\mathcal{F}$, since $\mathcal{F}$ is an euf-cma forger and hence $\mathcal{F}$ would make queries to the signing oracle. Then, we aim to construct a probabilistic polynomial-time "meta-reduction" algorithm $\mathcal{M}$ which solves the T-$(\mathsf{P}_1, \mathsf{P}_2)$ problem. By assuming the hardness on T-$(\mathsf{P}_1, \mathsf{P}_2)$, such $\mathcal{M}$ denies the existence of $\mathcal{R}$, and hence Theorem 1 follows.

Our meta-reduction algorithm $\mathcal{M}$ is constructed by combining the *invoking twin reductions technique* [14] and the *forking reduction technique* [34]. The invoking twin reductions technique is introduced by Fischlin and Fleischhacker to prove the impossibility result mentioned above. The invoking twin reductions technique intuitively means that $\mathcal{M}$ invokes twin clones of the assumed reduction $\mathcal{R}$ to utilize the abilities of solving the T-$(\mathsf{P}_1, \mathsf{P}_2)$ problem and simulating the signing oracle. Subsequently, this technique is also employed in the impossibility results by [19,42]. In particular, Fukumitsu and Hasegawa [19, Theorem 2] gave an impossibility result on the provable security of some Fiat-Shamir-type signature schemes in NPROM from non-interactive cryptographic assumptions by using this technique. Our result generalizes their result in the sense that our result also covers interactive cryptographic assumptions.

The results by [14, 19, 42] only covers non-interactive cryptographic assumptions. Unfortunately, the invoking twin reduction technique seems not to be applied to interactive cryptographic assumptions immediately. This is because the total number of accesses to the oracle on P_2 grows to $2T$, since $\mathcal{R}$ is invoked twice. However, the definition of the T-$(\mathsf{P}_1, \mathsf{P}_2)$ problem requires to bound the number of oracle queries by T. In order to overcome this problem, we combine the forking reduction technique. Pass [34] gave an impossibility result on Schnorr ID scheme, commitment schemes and the OM-DL assumption from interactive cryptographic assumptions by this technique, respectively. Moreover, there are several impossibility results [18, 29, 41] in which this technique is employed. Most recently, Morgan and Pass [29] discussed the tight security of unique signature schemes from general interactive cryptographic assumptions by using this technique.

In Theorem 1, we construct the meta-reduction $\mathcal{M}$. The main point is how to emulate an euf-cma forger $\mathcal{F}$ for the assumed reduction $\mathcal{R}$. Namely, $\mathcal{F}$ is required to reply a forged signature σ^*. According to these two techniques, $\mathcal{M}$ aims to find σ^* by invoking a copy of $\mathcal{R}$ to utilize the ability of the simulation of the signing oracle by $\mathcal{R}$. One should carefully observe the behavior of the assumed reduction $\mathcal{R}$. More specifically, $\mathcal{R}$ may successfully run only for a specific type of forgery output by $\mathcal{F}$ and simulate a signing oracle which replies another type as mentioned in the restrictions of Theorem 1. In this case, $\mathcal{F}$ cannot win the euf-cma game only by returning such a forgery. For this matter, we find a type of forgery such a concern can be avoided. Namely, $\mathcal{F}$ returns a forged signature $\sigma^* = (\mathrm{cmt}^*, \mathrm{res}^*)$ of some message m^* such that the cmt^* part does not coincide with those of any signatures which are given in the security proof as mentioned above. Even when $\mathcal{F}$ finds a signature σ^* of m^* which does not face this desirable type, it can reveal the secret key of the public key, which is given from the challenger, by the special soundness of the Fiat-Shamir-type signature scheme. Hence, $\mathcal{F}$ can recompute a signature of m^* by the regular signing algorithm. However, there is another problem that $\mathcal{R}$ would give $\mathcal{F}$ an irregular public key in the sense that the public key has no corresponding secret key. By using the certified property, $\mathcal{F}$ can verify the existence of a secret key, and hence such a problem can be avoided. On the other hand, the emulation of $\mathcal{F}$ should be deterministic as mentioned in [29]. This is because $\mathcal{F}$ is accessed by

$\mathcal{R}$ as a black-box oracle. Since $\mathcal{F}$ runs the algorithm for the special soundness, the secret key output by this algorithm should be unique. This is guaranteed by the unique property.

Table 1. The impossibility results on the provable security of general Fiat-Shamir-type signature schemes.

			Considering Security Reductions		
	Model	Security	Tight	Assumption	Type
Thm. 8 [33]	ROM	uuf-cma	only	non-interactive	algebraic
[14]	NPROM	euf-cma		non-interactive	single-instance
[17]	NPROM	suf-sma		imp-pa of ID	SMI
Thm. 1 [19]	NPROM	euf-koa		imp-pa of ID	key-preserving
Thm. 2 [19]	NPROM	euf-cma		non-interactive	single-instance key-preserving
Thm. 2 [33]	Standard	uuf-cma		non-interactive	algebraic
[ours]	NPROM	euf-cma		generalized OM	vanilla

	Assumptions on Impossibility
Thm. 8 [33]	the corresponding OM assumption to the Assumption column
[14]	• the corresponding OM assumption to the Assumption column • unique key
[17]	imp-pa of ID
Thm. 1 [19]	imp-aa of ID
Thm. 2 [19]	• the same assumption to the Assumption column • pk is an instance on the assumption
Thm. 2 [33]	the corresponding OM assumption to the Assumption column
[ours]	• the same assumption to the Assumption column • special soundness & unique key & certified key • specific forged signature

Comparison. We summarize the comparison among the impossibility results on the provable security of general Fiat-Shamir-type signature schemes in Table 1. The four columns of Considering Security Reductions indicate the type of security reduction algorithms that are targeted for the corresponding impossibility results. The column of Assumptions on Impossibility denotes the cryptographic assumptions which are broken by meta-reduction algorithms and the requirements for constructing meta-reduction algorithms. The word Theorem is abbreviated to Thm. For example, the "corresponding OM assumption" is the OM-DL assumption when the DL assumption is selected as the assumption which is broken by considering security reductions.

The impossibility results in [17,19,33] consider weak securities such as uuf-cma [33], suf-sma [3] and euf-koa [33], where uuf and koa stand for the universal unforgeability and the key-only attack, respectively. The word suf-sma is abbreviated from the selective unforgeability against the static message attack, which is defined in [3].

Although the impossibility result in [33] is considered in the ordinary random oracle model, their results only exclude the tight security. On the other hand, the other results including ours exclude any reductions irrespective of the tightness.

Our target reductions are the vanilla ones. The vanilla reductions have no restriction on group operations and a public key querying to a forger $\mathcal{F}$. Algebraic reductions are forced to use group operations only, and key-preserving reductions $\mathcal{R}$ are allowed only to query the same public key which is given to $\mathcal{R}$. However, the restriction of vanilla reductions is stronger than that of single-instance reductions and SMI reductions. In fact, SMI reductions, which are considered in [3], can sequentially invoke $\mathcal{F}$ polynomially many times, whereas single-instance reductions can invoke $\mathcal{F}$ only once. Moreover, these are allowed to rewind it, but the vanilla ones cannot do these.

The main advantage of our results is to cover interactive cryptographic assumptions. The results by [14,19,33] only consider non-interactive assumptions. Moreover, the results by [17,19] employ the security of underlying ID schemes, namely the security against impersonation under the passive attack (imp-pa) and that under the active attack (imp-aa). The security of underlying ID schemes is in general proven by some specific cryptographic assumption [21,37]. These impossibility results, therefore, do not cover cryptographic assumptions other than the one which does not correspond to the underlying ID scheme.

However, our result requires a specific type of underlying ID schemes as presented in the column of Assumptions on Impossibility. Whether or not Theorem 1 holds for the Fiat-Shamir-type signature schemes derived from other types of ID schemes is an important open question.

2 Preliminaries

For a deterministic algorithm $\mathcal{A}$, $y \leftarrow \mathcal{A}(x)$ denotes that $\mathcal{A}$ outputs y on a given input x. By $y \leftarrow \mathcal{A}(x; \omega)$, we express that a probabilistic algorithm $\mathcal{A}$ outputs y on input x with random coins ω. When $\mathcal{A}$ is probabilistic, $\mathcal{A}(x)$ is a random variable where random coins ω are internally chosen. Abbreviated words *DPT* and *PPT* stand for "deterministic polynomial-time" and "probabilistic polynomial-time", respectively. We denote by $x \in_U X$ that an element x is chosen uniformly at random from a finite set X. A positive function ϵ in λ is said to be *negligible* if for any positive polynomial p, there exists a natural number λ_0 such that for any $\lambda \geq \lambda_0$, we have $\epsilon(\lambda) < 1/p(\lambda)$.

2.1 Digital Signature Schemes

We now recall the notion of digital signature schemes [20]. A signature scheme SIG is defined by a tuple (SIG.KGen, SIG.Sign, SIG.Ver) of three algorithms. SIG.KGen and SIG.Sign are PPT, while SIG.Ver is DPT. On a given security parameter 1^λ, SIG.KGen generates a pair (sk, pk) of a secret key and a public key corresponding to sk. On a given tuple (sk, pk, m), SIG.Sign issues a signature

σ under the pair (pk, m) of the public key and the message. Here, the message space is denoted by M. On a given tuple (pk, m, σ), SIG.Ver returns 1 if σ is a *valid* signature under a pair (pk, m). We now fix SIG = (SIG.KGen, SIG.Sign, SIG.Ver) during the definitions of the correctness and the security.

Init $\mathcal{C}_{\mathsf{SIG}}$ generates $(sk, pk) \leftarrow$ SIG.KGen(1^λ), then gives pk to $\mathcal{F}$.

Signing Oracle When $\mathcal{F}$ hands a message $\overline{m}_i$ as an i-th query for each $1 \leq i \leq \beta_s$, $\mathcal{C}_{\mathsf{SIG}}$ replies a valid signature $\overline{\sigma}_i$ under $(pk, \overline{m}_i)$.

Challenge When $\mathcal{F}$ finally returns (m^*, σ^*), $\mathcal{C}_{\mathsf{SIG}}$ outputs 1 if the following conditions hold:

(1) m^* is not queried in **Signing Oracle** phase, i.e. $m^* \neq \overline{m}_i$ for each $1 \leq i \leq \beta_s$.

(2) SIG.Ver$(pk, m^*, \sigma^*) = 1$.

Fig. 1. The description of the β_s-euf-cma game

Correctness. SIG should satisfy the correctness in a sense that for any security parameter λ, any pair $(sk, pk) \leftarrow$ SIG.KGen(1^λ), any message $m \in$ M, and any $\sigma \leftarrow$ SIG.Sign(sk, pk, m), it holds that SIG.Ver$(pk, m, \sigma) = 1$.

Security. We introduce the existential unforgeability against a chosen-message attack (euf-cma) [20]. Let β_s be some polynomial in a security parameter λ. The β_s-*euf-cma game* is depicted in Fig. 1. The β_s-euf-cma game is played by two algorithms $\mathcal{C}_{\mathsf{SIG}}$ and $\mathcal{F}$, which are referred to as a challenger and a forger, respectively. Then, $\mathcal{F}$ *wins the* β_s-*euf-cma game* if $\mathcal{C}_{\mathsf{SIG}}$ outputs 1 in the β_s-euf-cma game. We say that SIG is β_s -*euf-cma* if for any PPT forger $\mathcal{F}$, $\mathcal{F}$ wins the β_s-euf-cma game only with negligible probability.

2.2   Generalized One-More Cryptographic Assumptions

We explain the notion of *generalized One-More cryptographic assumptions* in this subsection. We first recall the definition of non-interactive cryptographic problems [41].

Non-interactive Cryptographic Problems. A non-interactive cryptographic problem P is defined by a tuple (P.PGen, P.IGen, P.IVer) of three algorithms. P.PGen and P.IGen are PPT, while P.IVer is DPT. On a given security parameter 1^λ, P.PGen generates a public parameter pp of P. On a given public parameter pp, P.IGen generates an instance Y on P. On a given tuple (pp, Y, x), P.IVer outputs 1 if x is in fact a solution of Y on P. For any adversary $\mathcal{A}$, the security game of the problem P between a challenger $\mathcal{C}$ and the adversary $\mathcal{A}$ is defined as follows: $\mathcal{C}$ outputs P.IVer(pp, Y, x^*), where $\mathcal{C}$ runs $pp \leftarrow$ P.PGen(1^λ) and $Y \leftarrow$ P.IGen(pp), and then $\mathcal{A}(pp, Y)$ computes x^*. Then, we say that $\mathcal{A}$ wins the problem P if $\mathcal{C}$ outputs 1 in this game. For a *threshold function* τ, the advantage $\mathsf{Adv}_{\mathcal{A}}^{\mathsf{P}, \tau}(\lambda)$ of $\mathcal{A}$ on the problem P is defined by the difference between the winning probability of $\mathcal{A}$ on the above game and the threshold τ. The probability is taken over the internal coin flips on P.PGen, P.IGen and $\mathcal{A}$. In general, such a threshold τ is set to 0 for computational problems such as the DL problem, the CDH problem, and the RSA problem, while it is set to $1/2$ for decisional problems such as the DDH problem and the decisional linear problem. The P assumption on τ states that for any PPT adversary $\mathcal{A}$, $\mathsf{Adv}_{\mathcal{A}}^{\mathsf{P},\tau}$ is negligible.

OM Init $\mathcal{C}_{\mathsf{OM}}$ generates $pp \leftarrow \mathsf{PGen}(1^\lambda)$ and $\boldsymbol{Y} = (Y_0, \ldots, Y_T) \leftarrow \mathsf{IGen}(pp)$, and then gives $(pp, \boldsymbol{Y})$ to $\mathcal{A}$.

OM Oracle When $\mathcal{A}$ makes an instance Q_j as a j-th query for each $1 \leq j \leq T$, $\mathcal{C}_{\mathsf{OM}}$ returns $r_j \leftarrow \mathsf{Orcl}(pp, Q_j)$.

OM Challenge When $\mathcal{A}$ finally returns $\boldsymbol{x} = (x_0, \ldots, x_T)$, $\mathcal{C}_{\mathsf{OM}}$ outputs 1 if the following two conditions hold:
  (1) $\mathcal{A}$ accesses **OM oracle** at most T times.
  (2) $\mathsf{IVer}(pp, \boldsymbol{Y}, \boldsymbol{x}) = 1$.

Fig. 2. The definition of the T-$(\mathsf{P}_1, \mathsf{P}_2)$ game

---

Generalized One-More Problems. Consider two non-interactive problems $\mathsf{P}_1 = (\mathsf{PGen}, \mathsf{P}_1.\mathsf{IGen}, \mathsf{P}_1.\mathsf{IVer})$ and $\mathsf{P}_2 = (\mathsf{PGen}, \mathsf{P}_2.\mathsf{IGen}, \mathsf{P}_2.\mathsf{IVer})$ such that these share a common public parameter generator PGen. and let T be a polynomial in a security parameter λ. The *generalized "One-More" problem* T-$(\mathsf{P}_1, \mathsf{P}_2)$ is defined by $(\mathsf{PGen}, \mathsf{IGen}, \mathsf{Orcl}, \mathsf{IVer})$ in the following way: Let $pp \leftarrow \mathsf{PGen}(1^\lambda)$, then

$\mathsf{IGen}(pp)$ generates $(T+1)$-instances $\boldsymbol{Y} = (Y_0, Y_1, \ldots, Y_T)$ of P_1, namely for each $0 \leq j \leq T$, $Y_j \leftarrow \mathsf{P}_1.\mathsf{IGen}(pp)$.

$\mathsf{Orcl}(pp, Q)$ returns a solution r of an instance Q on the problem P_2 if there is a solution of Q on P_2, or $\perp$ otherwise.

$\mathsf{IVer}(pp, (Y_0, \ldots, Y_T), (x_0, \ldots, x_T))$ outputs 1 if $\mathsf{P}_1.\mathsf{IVer}(pp, Y_j, x_j) = 1$ for each $0 \leq j \leq T$.

The hardness assumption of the T-$(\mathsf{P}_1, \mathsf{P}_2)$ problem is defined by the T-$(\mathsf{P}_1, \mathsf{P}_2)$ *game* described as in Fig. 2. This game is played by a challenger $\mathcal{C}_{\mathsf{OM}}$ and an adversary $\mathcal{A}$. Note that we do not exclude the case where the running time of Orcl is unbounded, whereas IGen and IVer are required to be in polynomial-time. This does not affect the game, because Orcl is run by $\mathcal{C}_{\mathsf{OM}}$. In a similar manner to the ordinary cryptographic problem, we say that $\mathcal{A}$ *wins the* T-$(\mathsf{P}_1, \mathsf{P}_2)$ *game* if $\mathcal{C}_{\mathsf{OM}}$ finally outputs 1 in this game. Then, for a function τ in a security parameter λ, the T-$(\mathsf{P}_1, \mathsf{P}_2)$ *assumption with respect to a threshold function* τ states that for any PPT adversary $\mathcal{A}$, $\mathsf{Adv}_{\mathcal{A}}^{T\text{-}(\mathsf{P}_1,\mathsf{P}_2),\tau}$ is at most negligible, where $\mathsf{Adv}_{\mathcal{A}}^{T\text{-}(\mathsf{P}_1,\mathsf{P}_2),\tau}$ is defined in a similar manner to that on non-interactive cryptographic problems.

2.3 Fiat-Shamir-type Signature Schemes

Fiat-Shamir-type signature schemes are constructed by the generic transformation proposed by Fiat and Shamir [13] from canonical identification (ID) schemes.

A canonical ID scheme ID is defined by a tuple $(\mathsf{ID.KGen}, P_1, \mathcal{CH}, P_2, V)$ of five components which are used in a protocol executed by a prover P and a verifier V. Following the protocol, P can convince V of possession of a secret key. The protocol proceeds as follows. Let $(sk, pk) \leftarrow \mathsf{ID.KGen}(1^\lambda)$ be a pair of a secret key and a public key of P. Then V is given only pk.

1. P computes a pair (st, cmt) by executing the PPT algorithm $P_1(sk, pk)$, and then sends cmt to V.
2. V chooses a string cha uniformly at random from the set $\mathcal{CH}$ of strings, and then replies cha to P.
3. P computes res by executing the DPT algorithm $P_2(sk, pk, \mathrm{st}, \mathrm{cmt}, \mathrm{cha})$, and then finally returns res to V.
4. V ensures that P in fact has a secret key corresponding to the public key pk by checking whether or not $V(pk, \mathrm{cmt}, \mathrm{cha}, \mathrm{res}) = 1$.

In this paper, we consider the specific types of ID as mentioned in Sect. 1. Namely, ID is assumed to have the special soundness property, unique key property, and certified key property. The *special soundness* property is that one can recover a secret key sk of pk by using DPT algorithm SS on a given tuple $(pk, \mathrm{cmt}, \mathrm{cha}, \mathrm{res}, \mathrm{cha}', \mathrm{res}')$ such that $\mathrm{cha} \neq \mathrm{cha}'$ and $V(pk, \mathrm{cmt}, \mathrm{cha}, \mathrm{res}) = V(pk, \mathrm{cmt}, \mathrm{cha}', \mathrm{res}') = 1$. The *unique key* property is that any public key pk on ID has only one secret key sk. The *certified key* property is that one can verify that pk has a corresponding secret key sk by checking whether or not a DPT algorithm KEval returns 1 on a given pk.

The *Fiat-Shamir-type signature scheme* FSSIG from $\mathsf{ID} = (\mathsf{KGen}, P_1, \mathcal{CH}, P_2, V)$ is defined in the following way, where $\mathsf{FSSIG} = (\mathsf{KGen}, \mathsf{FSSIG.Sign}, \mathsf{FSSIG.Ver})$: Let $(sk, pk) \leftarrow \mathsf{KGen}(1^\lambda)$.

$\mathsf{FSSIG.Sign}(sk, pk, m)$ issues a signature $\sigma = (\mathrm{cmt}, \mathrm{res})$ of a message $m \in \mathsf{M}$ as follows:
1. $(\mathrm{st}, \mathrm{cmt}) \leftarrow P_1(sk, pk)$.
2. $\mathrm{cha} = H(\mathrm{cmt}, m)$, where $H : \{0, 1\}^* \to \mathcal{CH}$ is a hash function.
3. $\mathrm{res} \leftarrow P_2(sk, pk, \mathrm{st}, \mathrm{cmt}, \mathrm{cha})$.
$\mathsf{FSSIG.Ver}(pk, m, \sigma)$ outputs 1 if $V(pk, \mathrm{cmt}, c, \mathrm{res}) = 1$ for $\sigma = (\mathrm{cmt}, \mathrm{res})$ and $c = H(\mathrm{cmt}, m)$.

3   Security of Fiat-Shamir-type Signature Schemes Cannot Be Proven from Generalized One-More Assumptions in NPROM

In this section, we give our main result. We discuss the impossibility of the provable security on Fiat-Shamir-type signature schemes from generalized One-More assumptions. We start by describing the meaning that a Fiat-Shamir-type signature scheme is provable to be secure from generalized One-More assumptions.

Black-box Reductions $\mathcal{R}$ with Black-box Access. Let β_s and T be polynomials in a security parameter λ. We now consider that the provable security of a Fiat-Shamir-type signature scheme $\mathsf{FSSIG} = (\mathsf{KGen}, \mathsf{FSSIG.Sign}, \mathsf{FSSIG.Ver})$ which is derived from a canonical ID scheme $\mathsf{ID} = (\mathsf{KGen}, P_1, \mathcal{CH}, P_2, V)$ under the $T\text{-}(\mathsf{P}_1, \mathsf{P}_2)$ assumption with a problem P_1, a problem P_2 and a threshold function τ, where $T\text{-}(\mathsf{P}_1, \mathsf{P}_2) = (\mathsf{PGen}, \mathsf{IGen}, \mathsf{Orcl}, \mathsf{IVer})$. The provability is defined by the existence of a PPT black-box reduction algorithm $\mathcal{R}$ [29]. $\mathcal{R}$ can break the $T\text{-}(\mathsf{P}_1, \mathsf{P}_2)$ assumption, namely it wins the $T\text{-}(\mathsf{P}_1, \mathsf{P}_2)$ game so that $\mathsf{Adv}_{\mathcal{R}}^{T\text{-}(\mathsf{P}_1,\mathsf{P}_2),\tau}$ is non-negligible, by accessing a forger $\mathcal{F}$ which wins the β_s-euf-cma game of FSSIG in a black-box manner. The main goal of $\mathcal{R}$ is to win the $T\text{-}(\mathsf{P}_1, \mathsf{P}_2)$ game by playing the game with the challenger $\mathcal{C}_{\mathsf{OM}}$ in the adversary's position. Here, $\mathcal{R}$ can access **OM oracle** at most T times. During the $T\text{-}(\mathsf{P}_1, \mathsf{P}_2)$ game, $\mathcal{R}$ would also play the β_s-euf-cma game of FSSIG with $\mathcal{F}$ in the challenger's position. $\mathcal{F}$ would hand at most β_s messages to obtain corresponding valid signatures adaptively concerning the given public key $\overline{pk}$, and $\mathcal{R}$ should reply valid signatures of such queries. If $\mathcal{R}$ fails to reply at least one of them, $\mathcal{F}$ can reply any string such as $\perp$. Otherwise, $\mathcal{F}$ finally outputs a forgery pair (m^*, σ^*) with non-negligible probability. Note that we focus on Fiat-Shamir-type signature schemes derived from certified ID schemes. Thus, anyone can verify that $\overline{pk}$ has a secret key on FSSIG by using KEval. Therefore, we consider forgers which return $\perp$ if $\mathsf{KEval}(\overline{pk}) \neq 1$.

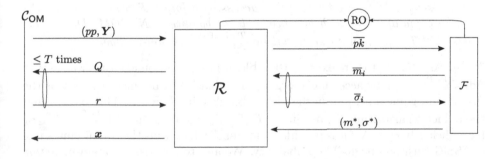

Fig. 3. Behavior of $\mathcal{R}$

Since $\mathcal{R}$ is only allowed to access $\mathcal{F}$ in a black-box manner, $\mathcal{R}$ must follow the description of the game in the access to $\mathcal{F}$. Moreover, in the definition of the black-box reduction, $\mathcal{F}$ can be regarded as a deterministic algorithm or a probabilistic algorithm with fixed random coins as in [29,34].

In the *non-programmable random oracle model (NPROM)* [15], $\mathcal{R}$ and $\mathcal{F}$ obtain all hash values from the random oracle, whereas such values are obtained from the one simulated by $\mathcal{R}$ in the ordinary random oracle model. This means that $\mathcal{R}$ can observe interactions between $\mathcal{F}$ and the random oracle, but it cannot control them.

Eventually, the behavior of $\mathcal{R}$ can be described as in Fig. 3.

Assumptions on the Impossibility. On our impossibility, we employ the following assumptions:

(Ass-1) P_2 is a *deterministic* problem. Namely, for any instance Q on P_2, there is only one solution r, and hence Orcl is deterministic.

(Ass-2) $T < \beta_s$.

(Ass-3) $\mathcal{R}$ is constructed in NPROM.

(Ass-4) A forger $\mathcal{F}$ returns a forgery pair $(m^*, (\mathrm{cmt}^*, \mathrm{res}^*))$ such that cmt^* does not coincide with $\overline{\mathrm{cmt}}_i$ of a signature $\overline{\sigma}_i$ which is obtained in **Signing Oracle** phase for each i-th query.

(Ass-5) The minimum entropy of cmt output by P_1 of ID is super-logarithmic [1] and the message space M has exponentially many messages. The minimum entropy is considered over all possible secret keys and random coins to P_1.

(Ass-6) ID is specially sound, unique key and certified.

Main Theorem. We now give the impossibility of the provable security of Fiat-Shamir-type signature schemes in NPROM. As mentioned in Sect. 1, we only consider the case where $\mathcal{R}$ invokes a β_s-euf-cma forger only once and does not rewind the invocation.

Theorem 1. *Let β_s and T be polynomials in a security parameter λ, and let τ and ϵ be functions in λ, especially ϵ is non-negligible. Assume the conditions (Ass-1)–(Ass-6) and that there exists a PPT black-box reduction algorithm $\mathcal{R}$ so that $\mathsf{Adv}_{\mathcal{R}}^{T\text{-}(P_1,P_2),\tau} \geq \epsilon$ by black-box accessing a forger $\mathcal{F}$ which wins the β_s-euf-cma game of FSSIG with non-negligible probability in NPROM. Then, there exists a PPT algorithm $\mathcal{M}$ such that $\mathsf{Adv}_{\mathcal{M}}^{T\text{-}(P_1,P_2),\tau}$ is non-negligible.*

Proof. Assume that there exists a PPT black-box reduction algorithm $\mathcal{R}$ so that $\mathsf{Adv}_{\mathcal{R}}^{T\text{-}(P_1,P_2),\tau} \geq \epsilon$ by accessing a forger $\mathcal{F}$ in a black-box manner, which wins the β_s-euf-cma game with non-negligible probability in NPROM. This means that the reduction algorithm $\mathcal{R}$ can win the T-(P_1, P_2) game so that $\mathsf{Adv}_{\mathcal{R}}^{T\text{-}(P_1,P_2),\tau} \geq \epsilon$ for sufficiently large λ if it is provided a forger $\mathcal{F}$ which wins the β_s-euf-cma game of FSSIG with non-negligible probability. We aim to construct a *meta-reduction* algorithm $\mathcal{M}$ so that $\mathsf{Adv}_{\mathcal{R}}^{T\text{-}(P_1,P_2),\tau}$ is non-negligible by internally running $\mathcal{R}$. Namely, $\mathcal{M}$ will be constructed to make $\mathcal{R}$ solve the T-(P_1, P_2) problem by emulating such a forger. In the emulation of $\mathcal{F}$, it is required to return a forgery (m^*, σ^*) to $\mathcal{R}$. In order to find (m^*, σ^*), an ability of $\mathcal{R}$ to reply a signature σ of a queried message m in **Signing Oracle** phase is also utilized. Note that (m, σ) cannot be merely used as a forgery pair. This is because in the meta-reduction $\mathcal{M}$, the challenger $\mathcal{R}$ and the emulation of $\mathcal{F}$ play the β_s-euf-cma game, and hence such a pair (m, σ) does not satisfy the condition (1) on **Challenge** phase. However, the forking reduction techniques proposed by [34] allow $\mathcal{F}$ to use it. Hereafter, we adopt their technique to construct $\mathcal{M}$. We first present a family of "ideal" forgers $\widetilde{\mathcal{F}}$ in a sense that it finds a forgery pair by identically implementing this idea. Since $\widetilde{\mathcal{F}}$ will be constructed to win β_s-euf-cma game of FSSIG with non-negligible probability, $\mathcal{R}$ also can win the T-(P_1, P_2) game so that $\mathsf{Adv}_{\mathcal{R}}^{T\text{-}(P_1,P_2),\tau} \geq \epsilon$ for sufficiently large λ if such an ideal forger $\widetilde{\mathcal{F}}$ is provided. By utilizing this property, we will construct a PPT meta-reduction algorithm $\mathcal{M}$ such that $\mathsf{Adv}_{\mathcal{M}}^{T\text{-}(P_1,P_2),\tau}$ is non-negligible. Observe that the running time of $\widetilde{\mathcal{F}}$

in the family is unbounded and $\widetilde{\mathcal{F}}$ is required to satisfy some conditions on the winning of the β_s-euf-cma game. However, we will show that $\widetilde{\mathcal{F}}$ can be emulated in PPT by $\mathcal{M}$ with non-negligible probability.

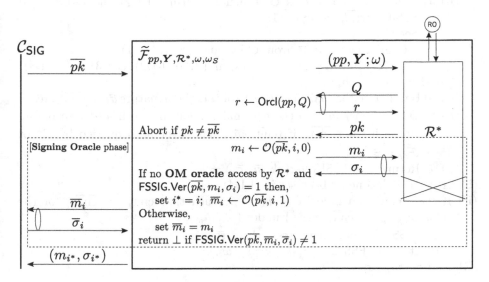

Fig. 4. Ideal forger $\widetilde{\mathcal{F}}_{pp,Y,\mathcal{R}^*,\omega,\omega_S}$

Family of Ideal Forgers $\widetilde{\mathcal{F}}_{pp,Y,\mathcal{R}^*,\omega,\omega_S}$. We describe a family of ideal forgers $\widetilde{\mathcal{F}}_{pp,Y,\mathcal{R}^*,\omega,\omega_S}$. This family is indexed by a public parameter pp of the T-$(\mathsf{P}_1,\mathsf{P}_2)$ problem, an instance Y on the T-$(\mathsf{P}_1,\mathsf{P}_2)$ problem, a clone instance $\mathcal{R}^*$ of the assumed reduction $\mathcal{R}$ and random coins ω and ω_S which are used in $\mathcal{R}^*$ and FSSIG.Sign. Fix such an index $(pp,Y,\mathcal{R}^*,\omega,\omega_S)$. $\widetilde{\mathcal{F}}_{pp,Y,\mathcal{R}^*,\omega,\omega_S}$ aims to find a forgery pair (m^*,σ^*) by utilizing the ability of the simulation of **Signing Oracle** phase by $\mathcal{R}$. In $\widetilde{\mathcal{F}}_{pp,Y,\mathcal{R}^*,\omega,\omega_S}$, we employ a virtual oracle $\mathcal{O}$ which chooses a string m uniformly at random from the message space M of FSSIG on a given tuple $(\overline{pk},i,b)$ of a public key $\overline{pk}$ of FSSIG, an index $1 \le i \le \beta_s$ and a bit $b \in \{0,1\}$. The role of $\mathcal{O}$ will be explained after the description of the procedure of $\widetilde{\mathcal{F}}_{pp,Y,\mathcal{R}^*,\omega,\omega_S}$. The procedure of $\widetilde{\mathcal{F}}_{pp,Y,\mathcal{R}^*,\omega,\omega_S}$ is depicted as in Fig. 4. The formal description of $\widetilde{\mathcal{F}}_{pp,Y,\mathcal{R}^*,\omega,\omega_S}$ is as follows: On a given public key $\overline{pk}$,

(A) Run $\mathcal{R}^*(pp,Y;\omega)$ until it invokes a β_s-euf-cma forger with a public key pk. During the running of $\mathcal{R}^*$, it replies $r \leftarrow \mathsf{Orcl}(pp,Q)$ on a queried instance Q on P_2 in **OM oracle** phase of the T-$(\mathsf{P}_1,\mathsf{P}_2)$ game. Moreover, it forwards all of inputs and outputs for the external random oracle.
(B) Abort if $pk \ne \overline{pk}$.
(C) Return $\perp$ if $\mathsf{KEval}(\overline{pk}) \ne 1$.
(D) For each $1 \le i \le \beta_s$, execute (I-D1)–(I-D7):

(I-D1) Obtain a message m_i from the virtual oracle $\mathcal{O}$ on $(\overline{pk}, i, 0)$.

(I-D2) Hand m_i to $\mathcal{R}^*$ in order to obtain its signature $\sigma_i = (\mathrm{cmt}_i, \mathrm{res}_i)$.

(I-D3) Query (cmt_i, m_i) to the external random oracle in order to obtain its hash value cha_i, if $\mathcal{R}^*$ has never queried (cmt_i, m_i).

(I-D4) If $\mathcal{R}^*$ does not access **OM oracle** during (I-D2) and (I-D3), and FSSIG.Ver$(\overline{pk}, m_i, \sigma_i) = 1$:

  - Set $i^* = i$.
  - Obtain a message $\overline{m}_i$ from $\mathcal{O}$ by querying $(\overline{pk}, i, 1)$.
  - Halt $\mathcal{R}^*$. Hereafter, set $\overline{m}_i = m_i$ and skip (I-D2), (I-D3) and (I-D4).

  Otherwise, set $\overline{m}_i = m_i$.

(I-D5) Hand $\overline{m}_i$ to the challenger $\mathcal{C}_{\mathsf{SIG}}$ to obtain the signature $\overline{\sigma}_i = (\overline{\mathrm{cmt}}_i, \overline{\mathrm{res}}_i)$.

(I-D6) Query $(\overline{\mathrm{cmt}}_i, \overline{m}_i)$ to the external random oracle in order to obtain its hash value $\overline{\mathrm{cha}}_i$, if $(\overline{\mathrm{cmt}}_i, \overline{m}_i)$ has never been queried by $\mathcal{R}^*$ or $\widetilde{\mathcal{F}}_{pp, \mathbf{Y}, \mathcal{R}^*, \omega, \omega_S}$.

(I-D7) Return $\bot$ if FSSIG.Ver$(\overline{pk}, \overline{m}_i, \overline{\sigma}_i) \neq 1$.

(E) Abort if i^* has never been set in (I-D4).

(F) If there exists an index $1 \leq i_0 \leq \beta_s$ such that $\mathrm{cmt}_{i^*} = \overline{\mathrm{cmt}}_{i_0}$ for the signature $\overline{\sigma}_{i_0} = (\overline{\mathrm{cmt}}_{i_0}, \overline{\mathrm{res}}_{i_0})$ under $(\overline{pk}, \overline{m}_{i_0})$:

  - $\overline{sk} \leftarrow \mathsf{SS}(\overline{pk}, \mathrm{cmt}_{i^*}, \mathrm{cha}_{i^*}, \mathrm{res}_{i^*}, \overline{\mathrm{cha}}_{i_0}, \overline{\mathrm{res}}_{i_0})$.
  - Reset $\sigma_{i^*} \leftarrow$ FSSIG.Sign$(\overline{sk}, \overline{pk}, m_{i^*}; \omega_S)$.

(G) Return (m_{i^*}, σ_{i^*}).

$\widetilde{\mathcal{F}}_{pp, \mathbf{Y}, \mathcal{R}^*, \omega, \omega_S}$ runs $\mathcal{R}^*$ by giving the hardwired pair $(pp, \mathbf{Y})$ with the random coins ω. In the utilization of $\mathcal{R}^*$, we should consider the following three matters.

The first one is that $\mathcal{R}^*$ would access **OM oracle** with some query Q. This is because $\mathcal{R}^*$ plays a role of the T-$(\mathsf{P}_1, \mathsf{P}_2)$ adversary. For such an oracle access, $\widetilde{\mathcal{F}}_{pp, \mathbf{Y}, \mathcal{R}^*, \omega, \omega_S}$ replies its solution r by executing $\mathsf{Orcl}(pp, Q)$ in a similar manner to **OM oracle** phase. It should be noted that the running time of Orcl may be unbounded as mentioned in the definition of *Generalized One-More Problems*. However, we will construct our meta-reduction algorithm $\mathcal{M}$ which emulates the behavior of $\widetilde{\mathcal{F}}_{pp, \mathbf{Y}, \mathcal{R}^*, \omega, \omega_S}$ in polynomial-time.

The second one is that there are two abort cases. The first one is that the public key pk which is output by $\mathcal{R}^*$ is not identical to the one $\overline{pk}$ given by $\mathcal{C}_{\mathsf{SIG}}$. Although $\mathcal{R}^*$ is allowed to invoke a forger with any of pk, one does not need to consider this case. This is because $\widetilde{\mathcal{F}}_{pp, \mathbf{Y}, \mathcal{R}^*, \omega, \omega_S}$ is presented to play the β_s-euf-cma game with the "specific" challenger $\mathcal{R}$. In this sense, it suffices that $\widetilde{\mathcal{F}}_{pp, \mathbf{Y}, \mathcal{R}^*, \omega, \omega_S}$ wins this game only when it plays the game with $\mathcal{R}$. Moreover, $\mathcal{R}$ cannot distinguish that $\widetilde{\mathcal{F}}_{pp, \mathbf{Y}, \mathcal{R}^*, \omega, \omega_S}$ is given. This is because $\mathcal{R}$ is allowed only to access $\mathcal{F}$ in a "black-box" manner. More specifically, $\mathcal{M}$ is constructed in a way that $\mathcal{R}^*$ is given a same tuple $(pp, \mathbf{Y}, \omega)$ to that for $\mathcal{R}$ as input. Since the random coins ω are the same, one can estimate that the behavior of $\mathcal{R}^*$ is identical to that of $\mathcal{R}$ until $\mathcal{R}^*$ has output pk at (A), if these receive the same replies such as hash values from the random oracle and solutions from **OM oracle**. We will show that these behaviors are indeed identical, and then that $\mathcal{R}^*$ outputs pk which coincides with $\overline{pk}$ with which $\mathcal{R}$ invokes a forger.

The second one is that the "challenge" index i^* is not set, namely for each $1 \leq i \leq \beta_s$, in the loop for the index i, $\mathcal{R}^*$ always accesses **OM oracle** during (I-D2) and (I-D3), or $\mathsf{Ver}(\overline{pk}, m_i, \sigma_i) \neq 1$. We will also show that in the emulation of $\widetilde{\mathcal{F}}_{pp,Y,\mathcal{R}^*,\omega,\omega_S}$ by $\mathcal{M}$, these abort cases do not occur or a non-valid signature is received from a challenger simulated by $\mathcal{R}$. In the latter event, $\widetilde{\mathcal{F}}_{pp,Y,\mathcal{R}^*,\omega,\omega_S}$ can finish own execution with outputting $\perp$ as mentioned in *Black-box Reductions $\mathcal{R}$ with Black-box access*. Hereafter, we only consider the winning probability of $\widetilde{\mathcal{F}}_{pp,Y,\mathcal{R}^*,\omega,\omega_S}$ under the assumption that the two abort cases do not occur as in [19].

The third one is that randomly chosen messages are obtained from the virtual oracle $\mathcal{O}$ as in (I-D1) and (I-D4). As defined above, $\mathcal{O}$ chooses a string m uniformly at random from the message space M of FSSIG on a given tuple $(\overline{pk}, i, b)$. This setting is required in order to construct an ideal forger $\widetilde{\mathcal{F}}_{pp,Y,\mathcal{R}^*,\omega,\omega_S}$ to be deterministic as in [29,34]. By this setting, the fixed random coins of $\mathcal{R}^*$ and FSSIG.Sign and the assumption (Ass-1) imply that $\widetilde{\mathcal{F}}_{pp,Y,\mathcal{R}^*,\omega,\omega_S}$ is also deterministic.

We evaluate the winning probability of $\widetilde{\mathcal{F}}_{pp,Y,\mathcal{R}^*,\omega,\omega_S}$ under the assumption that $\widetilde{\mathcal{F}}_{pp,Y,\mathcal{R}^*,\omega,\omega_S}$ does not abort.

Lemma 2. *Assume that $\widetilde{\mathcal{F}}_{pp,Y,\mathcal{R}^*,\omega,\omega_S}$ does not abort. $\widetilde{\mathcal{F}}_{pp,Y,\mathcal{R}^*,\omega,\omega_S}$ wins the β_s-euf-cma game of FSSIG with negligible error probability. In particular, when $\widetilde{\mathcal{F}}_{pp,Y,\mathcal{R}^*,\omega,\omega_S}$ finally returns a signature $\sigma_{i^*} = (\mathrm{cmt}_{i^*}, \mathrm{res}_{i^*})$, it holds that $\mathrm{cmt}_{i^*} \neq \overline{\mathrm{cmt}}_i$ for each $1 \leq i \leq \beta_s$ with negligible error probability.*

Proof (Lemma 2). Assume that $\widetilde{\mathcal{F}}_{pp,Y,\mathcal{R}^*,\omega,\omega_S}$ does not abort. Namely, $\mathcal{R}^*$ invokes a forger with $pk = \overline{pk}$ and the challenge index i^* is set. In this case, $\widetilde{\mathcal{F}}_{pp,Y,\mathcal{R}^*,\omega,\omega_S}$ determines (m_{i^*}, σ_{i^*}) in (I-D4) such that $\mathsf{FSSIG.Ver}(\overline{pk}, m_{i^*}, \sigma_{i^*}) = 1$. It suffices that the message m_{i^*} differs from $\overline{m}_i$ for each $1 \leq i \leq \beta_s$. This is required since $\overline{m}_i$ has been queried to $\mathcal{C}_{\mathsf{SIG}}$ in **Signing Oracle** phase. As described in (I-D4), $\overline{m}_i$ is identical to m_i which is chosen in (I-D1) if $i \neq i^*$, or is newly obtained from $\mathcal{O}$ otherwise. Since $\mathcal{O}$ chooses a message uniformly at random from the message space M of FSSIG, the probability that m_{i^*} coincides with $\overline{m}_i$ for some $1 \leq i \leq \beta_s$ is $\beta_s/|\mathsf{M}|$. It follows from the assumption (Ass-5) concerning $|\mathsf{M}|$ that $\widetilde{\mathcal{F}}_{pp,Y,\mathcal{R}^*,\omega,\omega_S}$ wins the β_s-euf-cma game with negligible error probability.

If $\widetilde{\mathcal{F}}_{pp,Y,\mathcal{R}^*,\omega,\omega_S}$ finds that cmt_{i^*} of $\sigma_{i^*} = (\mathrm{cmt}_{i^*}, \mathrm{res}_{i^*})$ yielded in (I-D4) coincides with $\overline{\mathrm{cmt}}_{i_0}$ for some $1 \leq i_0 \leq \beta_s$, then it recomputes σ_{i^*} by deriving the secret key $\overline{sk}$ of $\overline{pk}$. Note that one can suppose that $\overline{sk}$ exists because the possibility that there is no secret key of $\overline{pk}$ has been excluded by checking $\mathsf{KEval}(pk) \neq 1$. It follows from the condition $\mathrm{cmt}_{i^*} = \overline{\mathrm{cmt}}_{i_0}$ that $\overline{sk}$ can be computed in polynomial-time by using the special soundness property assumed in (Ass-6). The super-logarithmic min-entropy property assumed in (Ass-5) implies that the reset commitment cmt_{i^*} coincides with $\overline{\mathrm{cmt}}_{i_0}$ for some $1 \leq i_0 \leq \beta_s$ with negligible probability. $\square$

Note that $\widetilde{\mathcal{F}}_{pp,\boldsymbol{Y},\mathcal{R}^*,\omega,\omega_S}$ queries all of the random oracle queries by $\mathcal{R}^*$, $(\overline{\mathrm{cmt}}_i, \overline{m}_i)$ for each $1 \leq i \leq \beta_s$ and $(\mathrm{cmt}_{i^*}, m_{i^*})$. This is required to run $\mathcal{R}^*$ and verify whether or not all of the signatures $\overline{\sigma}_i$ for each $1 \leq i \leq \beta_s$ and the challenge signature σ_{i^*} are valid. Moreover, all hash values should be computed via the external random oracle model in NPROM.

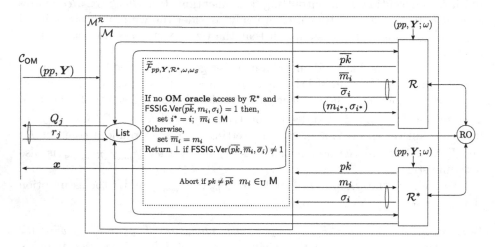

Fig. 5. Meta-reduction algorithm $\mathcal{M}$

Meta-reduction Algorithm $\mathcal{M}$. We present our meta-reduction algorithm $\mathcal{M}$ such that $\mathsf{Adv}_{\mathcal{M}}^{T\text{-}(\mathsf{P}_1,\mathsf{P}_2),\tau}$ is non-negligible. The overview is depicted as in Fig. 5. Intuitively, $\mathcal{M}$ internally runs $\mathcal{R}$ with emulating an ideal forger $\widetilde{\mathcal{F}}_{pp,\boldsymbol{Y},\mathcal{R}^*,\omega,\omega_S}$. On a pair $(pp, \boldsymbol{Y})$ of a public parameter and an instance, $\mathcal{M}$ proceeds as follows: $\mathcal{M}$ sets $\mathsf{List} \leftarrow \emptyset$, chooses random coins ω and ω_S, and then runs $\mathcal{R}(pp, \boldsymbol{Y}; \omega)$ to obtain its solution $\boldsymbol{x}$. During the running of $\mathcal{R}$, $\mathcal{M}$ behaves in the following way according to $\mathcal{R}$'s output:

Access OM Oracle with a query Q_j. If there is r_j such that $(Q_j, r_j) \in \mathsf{List}$, then return r_j. Otherwise, forward Q_j to $\mathcal{C}_{\mathsf{OM}}$ as an **OM oracle** query to obtain its solution r_j on P_2, set $\mathsf{List} \leftarrow \mathsf{List} \cup \{(Q_j, r_j)\}$, and then return r_j.

Query (cmt, m) to the external random oracle. Forward (cmt, m) to the external random oracle, and then return cha which is obtained from the random oracle.

Invoke a forger with $\overline{pk}$ proceeds as follows:

(A) run a clone reduction $\mathcal{R}^*(pp, \boldsymbol{Y}; \omega)$ of $\mathcal{R}$ until it outputs pk. During the running of $\mathcal{R}^*$, it replies **OM oracle** queries in the same way described above. Namely, if there is r_j such that $(Q_j, r_j) \in \mathsf{List}$, then it returns r_j, or otherwise, forwards Q_j to $\mathcal{C}_{\mathsf{OM}}$ to obtain its solution r_j on P_2, sets $\mathsf{List} \leftarrow \mathsf{List} \cup \{(Q_j, r_j)\}$, and then returns r_j. Moreover, $\mathcal{M}$ forwards all inputs and outputs for the external random oracle.

(B) Abort if $pk \neq \overline{pk}$.

(C) Return $\perp$ if $\mathsf{KEval}(\overline{pk}) \neq 1$.

(D) For each $1 \leq i \leq \beta_s$, execute (R-D1)–(R-D7):

    (R-D1) Choose a message $m_i \in_U M$.

    (R-D2) Hand m_i to $\mathcal{R}^*$ in order to obtain its signature $\sigma_i = (\mathrm{cmt}_i, \mathrm{res}_i)$.

    (R-D3) Query (cmt_i, m_i) to the external random oracle in order to obtain
        its hash value cha_i, if $\mathcal{R}^*$ has never queried (cmt_i, m_i).

    (R-D4) If $\mathcal{R}^*$ does not access **OM oracle** during (R-D2) and (R-D3),
        and $\mathsf{FSSIG.Ver}(\overline{pk}, m_i, \sigma_i) = 1$:

        – Set $i^* = i$.

        – Choose a message $\overline{m}_i \in_U M$.

        – Halt $\mathcal{R}^*$. Hereafter, set $\overline{m}_i = m_i$ and skip (R-D2), (R-D3) and
          (R-D4).

        Otherwise, set $\overline{m}_i = m_i$.

    (R-D5) Hand $\overline{m}_i$ to $\mathcal{R}$ to obtain the signature $\overline{\sigma}_i = (\overline{\mathrm{cmt}}_i, \overline{\mathrm{res}}_i)$.

    (R-D6) Query $(\overline{\mathrm{cmt}}_i, \overline{m}_i)$ to the external random oracle in order to obtain
        its hash value $\overline{\mathrm{cha}}_i$, if $(\overline{\mathrm{cmt}}_i, \overline{m}_i)$ has never been queried by $\mathcal{R}^*$ or $\mathcal{M}$.

    (R-D7) Return $\perp$ if $\mathsf{FSSIG.Ver}(\overline{pk}, \overline{m}_i, \overline{\sigma}_i) \neq 1$.

(E) Abort if i^* has never been set in (R-D4).

(F) If there exists an index i_0 such that $\mathrm{cmt}_{i^*} = \overline{\mathrm{cmt}}_{i_0}$ for the signature
$\overline{\sigma}_{i_0} = (\overline{\mathrm{cmt}}_{i_0}, \overline{\mathrm{res}}_{i_0})$ under $(\overline{pk}, \overline{m}_{i_0})$:

    – $\overline{sk} \leftarrow \mathsf{SS}(\overline{pk}, \mathrm{cmt}_{i^*}, \mathrm{cha}_{i^*}, \mathrm{res}_{i^*}, \overline{\mathrm{cha}}_{i_0}, \overline{\mathrm{res}}_{i_0})$.

    – Reset $\sigma_{i^*} \leftarrow \mathsf{FSSIG.Sign}(\overline{sk}, \overline{pk}, m_{i^*}; \omega_S)$.

(G) Return (m_{i^*}, σ_{i^*}).

Finally output x return x.

We show that $\mathcal{M}$ correctly emulates $\widetilde{\mathcal{F}}_{pp,\mathbf{Y},\mathcal{R}^*,\omega,\omega_S}$, where $(pp, \mathbf{Y})$ is the given pair at the start of the running of $\mathcal{M}$, $\mathcal{R}^*$ is a clone reduction of $\mathcal{R}$, and ω and ω_S are the random coins chosen at first by $\mathcal{M}$. Concretely, we show that the distribution of interactions between $\mathcal{R}$ and the emulated forger denoted by $\mathcal{F}_{\mathcal{M}}$ is identical to the one between $\mathcal{R}$ and $\widetilde{\mathcal{F}}_{pp,\mathbf{Y},\mathcal{R}^*,\omega,\omega_S}$. We describe the behavior of $\mathcal{R}$. During the running of $\mathcal{M}$, $\mathcal{R}$ and $\mathcal{R}^*$ receive the tuple (pp, Y, ω), solutions r_j of queried instances Q_j on P_2 from **OM oracle**, hash values from the external random oracle and messages from a β_s-euf-cma forger. Since the random coins given to $\mathcal{R}$ and $\mathcal{R}^*$ are fixed to ω, $\mathcal{R}$ and $\mathcal{R}^*$ always return the same outputs for **OM oracle** queries, random oracle queries, a public key $\overline{pk}$ to invoke a forger and signatures to reply signing oracle queries, as long as $\mathcal{R}$ and $\mathcal{R}^*$ are given the same inputs. In particular, we will confirm that for both forgers $\widetilde{\mathcal{F}}_{pp,\mathbf{Y},\mathcal{R}^*,\omega,\omega_S}$ and $\mathcal{F}_{\mathcal{M}}$, inputs and outputs of $\mathcal{R}$ are identical to those of $\mathcal{R}^*$ just before these forgers set the challenge index i^* in (I-D4) and (R-D4). We now prove that the distribution of the interaction between $\mathcal{R}$ and $\mathcal{F}_{\mathcal{M}}$ is identical to the one between $\mathcal{R}$ and $\widetilde{\mathcal{F}}_{pp,\mathbf{Y},\mathcal{R}^*,\omega,\omega_S}$ by the following lemmas.

Lemma 3. *The distribution of interactions between $\mathcal{R}$ and $\mathcal{F}_{\mathcal{M}}$ is identical to the one between $\mathcal{R}$ and $\widetilde{\mathcal{F}}_{pp,\mathbf{Y},\mathcal{R}^*,\omega,\omega_S}$ before the internal clone reduction $\mathcal{R}^*$ invokes a forger with a public key pk. Moreover, it holds that $pk = \overline{pk}$.*

Lemma 4. *Assume that $\mathcal{F}_{\mathcal{M}}$ does not abort. The distribution of interactions between $\mathcal{R}$ and $\mathcal{F}_{\mathcal{M}}$ is identical to the one between $\mathcal{R}$ and $\widetilde{\mathcal{F}}_{pp,\mathbf{Y},\mathcal{R}^*,\omega,\omega_S}$ after the internal clone reduction $\mathcal{R}^*$ invokes a forger with $\overline{pk}$.*

It should be noted that both $\widetilde{\mathcal{F}}_{pp,\mathbf{Y},\mathcal{R}^*,\omega,\omega_S}$ and $\mathcal{F}_{\mathcal{M}}$ internally run the clone reduction $\mathcal{R}^*$ of $\mathcal{R}$. We show that both forgers identically response all of the queries by $\mathcal{R}^*$ in the above lemmas. In the proof of Lemma 3, we first observe that $\mathcal{R}^*$ run by each of $\widetilde{\mathcal{F}}_{pp,\mathbf{Y},\mathcal{R}^*,\omega,\omega_S}$ and $\mathcal{F}_{\mathcal{M}}$ behaves in the same way until it invokes a forger. This is intuitively guaranteed by the fixed input tuple $(pp,\mathbf{Y},\omega)$, fixed hash values obtained from the external random oracle and (Ass-1). Moreover, the condition $pk = \overline{pk}$ is also implied by the identical behaviors of $\mathcal{R}$ and $\mathcal{R}^*$ due to the given same inputs such as the tuple $(pp,\mathbf{Y},\omega)$, the responses of the random oracle queries and **OM oracle** queries.

Proof (Lemma 3). Before $\mathcal{R}^*$ invokes a forger with pk, both $\widetilde{\mathcal{F}}_{pp,\mathbf{Y},\mathcal{R}^*,\omega,\omega_S}$ and $\mathcal{F}_{\mathcal{M}}$ merely run $\mathcal{R}^*$ on the pair $(pp,\mathbf{Y})$ and the random coins ω with mediating the interactions to the random oracle, and replying a solution of Q_j queried by $\mathcal{R}^*$. Since the fixed random coin ω induces that the running of $\mathcal{R}^*$ is deterministic, all outputs by $\mathcal{R}^*$ are always the same if $\mathcal{R}^*$ is given the same inputs such as the responses of **OM oracle** queries and the random oracle queries. Note that in NPROM, all hash values are obtained from the external random oracle, and hence $\mathcal{R}^*$ obtains the same hash values for all same random oracle queries. For **OM oracle** queries Q_j, Orcl always returns the same solution $x_i \leftarrow \text{Orcl}(pp,Q_j)$ on P_2 when it is given any same instance Y_j, since (Ass-1) guarantees that there is only one solution for any instance of P_2. On the other hand, $\mathcal{F}_{\mathcal{M}}$ replies the solution of Q_j by using either List or **OM oracle**, whereas $\widetilde{\mathcal{F}}_{pp,\mathbf{Y},\mathcal{R}^*,\omega,\omega_S}$ does it by executing Orcl itself. Since List contains all pairs of a query and the corresponding response which have been obtained from **OM oracle**, $\mathcal{F}_{\mathcal{M}}$ eventually returns the responses given by Orcl. There imply that $\mathcal{R}^*$ run by each of the both forgers proceed in the same way before it outputs pk. Moreover, since $\mathcal{R}$ and $\mathcal{R}^*$ are given the same inputs from each of the both forgers, $\mathcal{R}^*$ always outputs pk which is identical to $\overline{pk}$. □

In the proof of Lemma 4, we show that both forgers give the same inputs to $\mathcal{R}$ and $\mathcal{R}^*$ during the loop for the index i, and hence the outputs of $\mathcal{R}$ and $\mathcal{R}^*$ are the same for the both forgers. The distributions of σ_{i*} output by the both forgers can be proven to be identical due to the identical behavior of $\mathcal{R}^*$ and the unique key property assumed in (Ass-6).

Proof (Lemma 4). Assume that all inputs and outputs of $\mathcal{R}^*$ and $\mathcal{R}$ are the same for both $\widetilde{\mathcal{F}}_{pp,\mathbf{Y},\mathcal{R}^*,\omega,\omega_S}$ and $\mathcal{F}_{\mathcal{M}}$ before starting the loop for an index i. We show that all inputs and outputs of $\mathcal{R}^*$ and $\mathcal{R}$ are the same for both $\widetilde{\mathcal{F}}_{pp,\mathbf{Y},\mathcal{R}^*,\omega,\omega_S}$ and $\mathcal{F}_{\mathcal{M}}$ during the loop for an index i. Since the virtual oracle $\mathcal{O}$ used in $\widetilde{\mathcal{F}}_{pp,\mathbf{Y},\mathcal{R}^*,\omega,\omega_S}$ returns $m \in_{\mathsf{U}} \mathsf{M}$, both forgers give a uniformly chosen message $m_i \in_{\mathsf{U}} \mathsf{M}$ in (I-D1) and (R-D1) in order to obtain its signature σ_i. The assumption above and the fixed input $(pp,\mathbf{Y},\omega)$ to $\mathcal{R}^*$ imply that the behaviors in

(I-D2)–(I-D3) and in (R-D2)–(R-D3) of $\mathcal{R}^*$ are identical until it outputs the signature σ_i. Therefore, each of the conditions in (I-D4) holds if and only if each of those in (R-D4) holds. Subsequently, both forgers hand the same message $\overline{m}_i$ to $\mathcal{R}$ and receive its signature $\overline{\sigma}_i = (\overline{\text{cmt}}_i, \overline{\text{res}}_i)$. Since $(\overline{m}_i, \overline{\text{cmt}}_i)$ is identical, the hash value of it from the external random oracle is also the same. The signatures $\overline{\sigma}_i$ given during the interaction between $\mathcal{R}$ and $\widetilde{\mathcal{F}}_{pp,\boldsymbol{Y},\mathcal{R}^*,\omega,\omega_S}$ and the ones between $\mathcal{R}$ and $\mathcal{F}_\mathcal{M}$ are the same. This is because the behavior of $\mathcal{R}$ and $\mathcal{R}^*$ for $\widetilde{\mathcal{F}}_{pp,\boldsymbol{Y},\mathcal{R}^*,\omega,\omega_S}$ is identical to the one for $\mathcal{F}_\mathcal{M}$ until this point, and the input $(pp, \boldsymbol{Y}, \omega)$ is also fixed. Therefore, the behavior of $\mathcal{F}_\mathcal{M}$ in (R-D7) is identical to that of $\widetilde{\mathcal{F}}_{pp,\boldsymbol{Y},\mathcal{R}^*,\omega,\omega_S}$.

It follows from Lemma 3 that all inputs and outputs of $\mathcal{R}^*$ and $\mathcal{R}$ are the same for the both forgers before starting the loop. Therefore, all inputs and outputs of $\mathcal{R}^*$ and $\mathcal{R}$ run by both forgers are the same during the loop.

Since we now assume that both forgers do not abort, the behaviors of the both forgers are identical. We finally ensure that the distribution of σ_{i^*} returned by $\widetilde{\mathcal{F}}_{pp,\boldsymbol{Y},\mathcal{R}^*,\omega,\omega_S}$ is identical to the one by $\mathcal{F}_\mathcal{M}$. If there exists an index i_0 such that cmt_{i^*} which is given by $\mathcal{R}^*$ coincides with $\overline{\text{cmt}}_{i_0}$ given by $\mathcal{R}$, both forgers reset σ_{i^*} by using FSSIG.Sign with the fixed random coins ω_S after recovering the secret key $\overline{sk}$ of $\overline{pk}$. The unique key property assumed in (Ass-6) implies that $\widetilde{\mathcal{F}}_{pp,\boldsymbol{Y},\mathcal{R}^*,\omega,\omega_S}$ and $\mathcal{F}_\mathcal{M}$ obtain the same $\overline{sk}$ in this case, and then the distributions of the reset signature σ_{i^*} generated by $\widetilde{\mathcal{F}}_{pp,\boldsymbol{Y},\mathcal{R}^*,\omega,\omega_S}$ and $\mathcal{F}_\mathcal{M}$ with the fixed random coins ω_S are identical. Otherwise if such an index i_0 does not exist, σ^* is generated by $\mathcal{R}^*$ whose behaviors run in $\widetilde{\mathcal{F}}_{pp,\boldsymbol{Y},\mathcal{R}^*,\omega,\omega_S}$ and $\mathcal{F}_\mathcal{M}$ are identical as mentioned above. Therefore, the distributions, in this case, are also identical.   □

We next show that $\widetilde{\mathcal{F}}_{pp,\boldsymbol{Y},\mathcal{R}^*,\omega,\omega_S}$ and $\mathcal{F}_\mathcal{M}$ always do not abort since there must exist the challenge index i^* by the following lemma. This lemma can be shown by (Ass-2) and the identical behaviors of $\mathcal{R}$ and $\mathcal{R}^*$ which have been proven in Lemma 4.

Lemma 5. *Assume (Ass-2). It holds that $\widetilde{\mathcal{F}}_{pp,\boldsymbol{Y},\mathcal{R}^*,\omega,\omega_S}$ and $\mathcal{F}_\mathcal{M}$ can either find the challenge index i^* or obtain a non-valid signature from $\mathcal{R}$.*

Proof. In order to prove this lemma, we show that $\mathcal{R}^*$ run by each of both forgers replies a signature σ_{i_0} under $(\overline{pk}, m_{i_0})$ without **OM oracle** query for some $1 \le i_0 \le \beta_s$. Assume that for each $1 \le i \le \beta_s$, $\mathcal{R}^*$ accesses **OM oracle** during (I-D2) and (I-D3) ((R-D2) and (R-D3), resp.). This implies that $\mathcal{R}^*$ accesses **OM oracle** at least β_s times. Since the number of such oracle accesses is bounded by T, it follows that $\beta_s \le T$. Because it contradicts (Ass-2), $\mathcal{R}^*$ replies σ_{i_0} without **OM oracle** query for some $1 \le i_0 \le \beta_s$.

Hereafter, we consider that $\mathcal{R}^*$ replies a signature σ_{i_0} under $(\overline{pk}, m_{i_0})$ without **OM oracle** for some $1 \le i_0 \le \beta_s$, but σ_{i_0} is not valid. Then, each of both forgers queries $\overline{m}_{i_0} = m_{i_0}$ to $\mathcal{R}$ as in (I-D4) and (R-D4). As shown in Lemma 4, $\mathcal{R}$ runs in the same way to $\mathcal{R}^*$ at this point. Therefore, $\mathcal{R}$ also replies the same signature σ_{i_0} which is non-valid. In this case, the both forgers are allowed to return $\bot$. □

We finally show that $\mathcal{M}$ accesses **OM oracle** with at most T times. Although $\mathcal{M}$ runs internally the T-$(\mathsf{P}_1, \mathsf{P}_2)$ adversaries $\mathcal{R}$ and $\mathcal{R}^*$ and forwards their queries to **OM oracle**, the total number of accesses to **OM oracle** is bounded by T by using List appropriately.

Lemma 6. $\mathcal{M}$ *accesses* **OM oracle** *at most* T *times.*

Proof. We evaluate the number of the accesses to **OM oracle** by $\mathcal{M}$ by separating the point into before and after the one where $\mathcal{F}_{\mathcal{M}}$ starts (R-D2) for the loop on the challenge index i^*. As shown in Lemma 4, the inputs and the outputs of $\mathcal{R}$ and $\mathcal{R}^*$ are identical until this point. Moreover, $\mathcal{M}$ replies **OM oracle** queries by $\mathcal{R}$ and $\mathcal{R}^*$, which have been already queried, by using List. Namely, it replies these without querying to $\mathcal{C}_{\mathsf{OM}}$. These imply that the number of the accesses to **OM oracle** by $\mathcal{M}$ until this point is the same as the single running of $\mathcal{R}$ until this point.

After this point, $\mathcal{R}$ continues the running hereafter, whereas $\mathcal{R}^*$ is aborted after it has output a valid signature σ_{i^*} under $(\overline{pk}, m_i)$ on the loop for the index i^* as in (R-D4). Since $\mathcal{R}^*$ does not access **OM oracle** during (R-D2) and (R-D3) for the loop on the challenge index i^*, $\mathcal{R}$ only accesses **OM oracle** after this point. The total number of the accesses to **OM oracle** by $\mathcal{M}$ can be regarded as the single running of the reduction. Hence the number is bounded by T. □

Observe that the running time of $\mathcal{M}$ is almost twice that of $\mathcal{R}$. Therefore, the T-$(\mathsf{P}_1, \mathsf{P}_2)$ assumption does not hold by the existence of the PPT adversary $\mathcal{M}$. □

Acknowledgements. We would like to thank anonymous reviewers for their valuable comments and suggestions. A part of this work is supported by JSPS KAKENHI Grant Numbers 18K11288 and 19K20272.

References

1. Abdalla, M., An, J.H., Bellare, M., Namprempre, C.: From identification to signatures via the Fiat-Shamir transform: necessary and sufficient conditions for security and forward-security. IEEE Trans. Inf. Theory **54**(8), 3631–3646 (2008). https://doi.org/10.1109/TIT.2008.926303
2. Abdalla, M., Fouque, P.A., Lyubashevsky, V., Tibouchi, M.: Tightly secure signatures from lossy identification schemes. J. Cryptol. **29**(3), 597–631 (2016). https://doi.org/10.1007/s00145-015-9203-7
3. Bader, C., Jager, T., Li, Y., Schäge, S.: On the impossibility of tight cryptographic reductions. In: Fischlin, M., Coron, J.-S. (eds.) EUROCRYPT 2016. LNCS, vol. 9666, pp. 273–304. Springer, Heidelberg (2016). https://doi.org/10.1007/978-3-662-49896-5_10
4. Bellare, M., Neven, G.: Multi-signatures in the plain public-key model and a general forking lemma. In: Proceedings of the 13th ACM Conference on Computer and Communications Security, CCS 2006, pp. 390–399. ACM, New York (2006). https://doi.org/10.1145/1180405.1180453

5. Bellare, M., Palacio, A.: GQ and schnorr identification schemes: proofs of security against impersonation under active and concurrent attacks. In: Yung, M. (ed.) CRYPTO 2002. LNCS, vol. 2442, pp. 162–177. Springer, Heidelberg (2002). https://doi.org/10.1007/3-540-45708-9_11

6. Bellare, M., Rogaway, P.: Random oracles are practical: a paradigm for designing efficient protocols. In: Proceedings of the 1st ACM Conference on Computer and Communications Security, CCS 1993, pp. 62–73. ACM, New York (1993). https://doi.org/10.1145/168588.168596

7. Bellare, M., Rogaway, P.: The exact security of digital signatures-how to sign with RSA and rabin. In: Maurer, U. (ed.) EUROCRYPT 1996. LNCS, vol. 1070, pp. 399–416. Springer, Heidelberg (1996). https://doi.org/10.1007/3-540-68339-9_34

8. Bernstein, D.J., Duif, N., Lange, T., Schwabe, P., Yang, B.Y.: High-speed high-security signatures. J. Cryptogr. Eng. 2(2), 77–89 (2012). https://doi.org/10.1007/s13389-012-0027-1

9. Boneh, D., Venkatesan, R.: Breaking RSA may not be equivalent to factoring. In: Nyberg, K. (ed.) EUROCRYPT 1998. LNCS, vol. 1403, pp. 59–71. Springer, Heidelberg (1998). https://doi.org/10.1007/BFb0054117

10. Coron, J.S.: Optimal security proofs for PSS and other signature schemes. In: Knudsen, L.R. (ed.) EUROCRYPT 2002. LNCS, vol. 2332, pp. 272–287. Springer, Heidelberg (2002). https://doi.org/10.1007/3-540-46035-7_18

11. Cramer, R., Shoup, V.: Signature schemes based on the strong RSA assumption. ACM Trans. Inf. Syst. Secur. 3(3), 161–185 (2000). https://doi.org/10.1145/357830.357847

12. Dierks, T., Allen, C.: The TLS protocol version 1.0 (1999). https://tools.ietf.org/html/rfc2246

13. Fiat, A., Shamir, A.: How to prove yourself: practical solutions to identification and signature problems. In: Odlyzko, A.M. (ed.) CRYPTO 1986. LNCS, vol. 263, pp. 186–194. Springer, Heidelberg (1987). https://doi.org/10.1007/3-540-47721-7_12

14. Fischlin, M., Fleischhacker, N.: Limitations of the meta-reduction technique: the case of Schnorr signatures. In: Johansson, T., Nguyen, P.Q. (eds.) EUROCRYPT 2013. LNCS, vol. 7881, pp. 444–460. Springer, Heidelberg (2013). https://doi.org/10.1007/978-3-642-38348-9_27

15. Fischlin, M., Lehmann, A., Ristenpart, T., Shrimpton, T., Stam, M., Tessaro, S.: Random oracles with(out) programmability. In: Abe, M. (ed.) ASIACRYPT 2010. LNCS, vol. 6477, pp. 303–320. Springer, Heidelberg (2010). https://doi.org/10.1007/978-3-642-17373-8_18

16. Fleischhacker, N., Jager, T., Schröder, D.: On tight security proofs for Schnorr signatures. J. Cryptol. 32(2), 566–599 (2019). https://doi.org/10.1007/s00145-019-09311-5

17. Fukumitsu, M., Hasegawa, S.: Impossibility on the provable security of the Fiat-Shamir-type signatures in the non-programmable random oracle model. In: Bishop, M., Nascimento, A.C.A. (eds.) ISC 2016. LNCS, vol. 9866, pp. 389–407. Springer, Cham (2016). https://doi.org/10.1007/978-3-319-45871-7_23

18. Fukumitsu, M., Hasegawa, S.: Impossibility of the provable security of the Schnorr signature from the one-more DL assumption in the non-programmable random oracle model. In: Okamoto, T., Yu, Y., Au, M.H., Li, Y. (eds.) ProvSec 2017. LNCS, vol. 10592, pp. 201–218. Springer, Cham (2017). https://doi.org/10.1007/978-3-319-68637-0_12

19. Fukumitsu, M., Hasegawa, S.: Black-box separations on Fiat-Shamir-type signatures in the non-programmable random oracle model. IEICE Trans. Fundam. Electron. Commun. Comput. Sci. **E101.A**(1), 77–87 (2018). https://doi.org/10.1587/transfun.E101.A.77

20. Goldwasser, S., Micali, S., Rivest, R.L.: A digital signature scheme secure against adaptive chosen-message attacks. SIAM J. Comput. **17**(2), 281–308 (1988). https://doi.org/10.1137/0217017

21. Guillou, L.C., Quisquater, J.J.: A practical zero-knowledge protocol fitted to security microprocessor minimizing both transmission and memory. In: Barstow, D., et al. (eds.) EUROCRYPT 1988. LNCS, vol. 330, pp. 123–128. Springer, Heidelberg (1988). https://doi.org/10.1007/3-540-45961-8_11

22. Hasegawa, S., Isobe, S.: A lossy identification scheme using the subgroup decision assumption. IEICE Trans. Fundam. Electron. Commun. Comput. Sci. **E97.A**(6), 1296–1306 (2014). https://doi.org/10.1587/transfun.E97.A.1296

23. Hasegawa, S., Isobe, S.: Lossy identification schemes from decisional RSA. Interdisc. Inf. Sci. (2019). https://doi.org/10.4036/iis.2019.R.01

24. Hess, F.: Efficient identity based signature schemes based on pairings. In: Nyberg, K., Heys, H. (eds.) SAC 2002. LNCS, vol. 2595, pp. 310–324. Springer, Heidelberg (2003). https://doi.org/10.1007/3-540-36492-7_20

25. Kakvi, S.A., Kiltz, E.: Optimal security proofs for full domain hash, revisited. In: Pointcheval, D., Johansson, T. (eds.) EUROCRYPT 2012. LNCS, vol. 7237, pp. 537–553. Springer, Heidelberg (2012). https://doi.org/10.1007/978-3-642-29011-4_32

26. Katz, J., Wang, N.: Efficiency improvements for signature schemes with tight security reductions. In: Proceedings of the 10th ACM Conference on Computer and Communications Security, CCS 2003, pp. 155–164. ACM, New York (2003). https://doi.org/10.1145/948109.948132

27. Lv, X., Xu, F., Ping, P., Liu, X., Su, H.: Schnorr ring signature scheme with designated verifiability. In: 2015 14th International Symposium on Distributed Computing and Applications for Business Engineering and Science (DCABES), pp. 163–166, August 2015. https://doi.org/10.1109/DCABES.2015.48

28. Lyubashevsky, V.: Lattice-based identification schemes secure under active attacks. In: Cramer, R. (ed.) PKC 2008. LNCS, vol. 4939, pp. 162–179. Springer, Heidelberg (2008). https://doi.org/10.1007/978-3-540-78440-1_10

29. Morgan, A., Pass, R.: On the security loss of unique signatures. In: Beimel, A., Dziembowski, S. (eds.) TCC 2018. LNCS, vol. 11239, pp. 507–536. Springer, Cham (2018). https://doi.org/10.1007/978-3-030-03807-6_19

30. Nakamoto, S., et al.: Bitcoin: a peer-to-peer electronic cash system (2008). https://bitcoin.org/bitcoin.pdf

31. Ohta, K., Okamoto, T.: A digital multisignature scheme based on the Fiat-Shamir scheme. In: Imai, H., Rivest, R.L., Matsumoto, T. (eds.) ASIACRYPT 1991. LNCS, vol. 739, pp. 139–148. Springer, Heidelberg (1993). https://doi.org/10.1007/3-540-57332-1_11

32. Okamoto, T.: Provably secure and practical identification schemes and corresponding signature schemes. In: Brickell, E.F. (ed.) CRYPTO 1992. LNCS, vol. 740, pp. 31–53. Springer, Heidelberg (1993). https://doi.org/10.1007/3-540-48071-4_3

33. Paillier, P., Vergnaud, D.: Discrete-log-based signatures may not be equivalent to discrete log. In: Roy, B. (ed.) ASIACRYPT 2005. LNCS, vol. 3788, pp. 1–20. Springer, Heidelberg (2005). https://doi.org/10.1007/11593447_1

34. Pass, R.: Limits of provable security from standard assumptions. In: Proceedings of the Forty-third Annual ACM Symposium on Theory of Computing, STOC 2011, pp. 109–118. ACM, New York (2011). https://doi.org/10.1145/1993636.1993652
35. Pointcheval, D., Stern, J.: Provably secure blind signature schemes. In: Kim, K., Matsumoto, T. (eds.) ASIACRYPT 1996. LNCS, vol. 1163, pp. 252–265. Springer, Heidelberg (1996). https://doi.org/10.1007/BFb0034852
36. Pointcheval, D., Stern, J.: Security arguments for digital signatures and blind signatures. J. Cryptol. **13**(3), 361–396 (2000). https://doi.org/10.1007/s001450010003
37. Schnorr, C.P.: Efficient signature generation by smart cards. J. Cryptol. **4**(3), 161–174 (1991). https://doi.org/10.1007/BF00196725
38. Shamir, A.: Identity-based cryptosystems and signature schemes. In: Blakley, G.R., Chaum, D. (eds.) CRYPTO 1984. LNCS, vol. 196, pp. 47–53. Springer, Heidelberg (1985). https://doi.org/10.1007/3-540-39568-7_5
39. Tor: Tor. https://www.torproject.org/
40. Ylonen, T.: The secure shell (SSH) transport layer protocol (2006). https://tools.ietf.org/html/rfc4253
41. Zhang, J., Zhang, Z., Chen, Y., Guo, Y., Zhang, Z.: Black-box separations for one-more (static) CDH and its generalization. In: Sarkar, P., Iwata, T. (eds.) ASIACRYPT 2014. LNCS, vol. 8874, pp. 366–385. Springer, Heidelberg (2014). https://doi.org/10.1007/978-3-662-45608-8_20
42. Zhang, Z., Chen, Y., Chow, S.S.M., Hanaoka, G., Cao, Z., Zhao, Y.: Black-box separations of hash-and-sign signatures in the non-programmable random oracle model. In: Au, M.-H., Miyaji, A. (eds.) ProvSec 2015. LNCS, vol. 9451, pp. 435–454. Springer, Cham (2015). https://doi.org/10.1007/978-3-319-26059-4_24

Cut-and-Choose for Garbled RAM

Peihan Miao[(✉)]

Visa Research, Palo Alto, USA
pemiao@visa.com

Abstract. Garbled RAM, introduced by Lu and Ostrovsky in 2013, provides a novel method for secure computation on RAM (Random Access Machine) programs directly. It can be seen as a RAM analogue of Yao's garbled circuits such that the computational complexity and communication complexity only grow with the running time of the RAM program, avoiding the inefficient process of first converting it into a circuit. It allows for executing multiple RAM programs on a persistent database, but is secure only against semi-honest adversaries.

In this work we provide a cut-and-choose technique for garbled RAM. This gives the first constant-round two-party RAM computation protocol secure against malicious adversaries which allows for multiple RAM programs being executed on a persistent database. Our protocol makes black-box use of the one-way functions, and security of our construction is argued in the random oracle model.

1 Introduction

Alice owns a large private database D and wants to store it on the cloud (Bob) in an encrypted form. Subsequently Alice and Bob want to compute and learn the output of arbitrary dynamically chosen programs $P_1, P_2, \cdots$ on their private inputs $x_1 = (x_1^A, x_1^B), x_2 = (x_2^A, x_2^B), \cdots$ and the previously stored database, which gets updated as these programs are executed. During the computation the two parties do not want to leak their private inputs to each other. Can we achieve this?

Starting with seminal works of Yao [Yao82] and Goldreich, Micali and Wigderson [GMW87], in the past few decades, both theoretical and practical improvements have been pushing the limits of the overall efficiency of such schemes. However most of these constructions are devised only for Boolean/arithmetic circuits and securely computing a RAM program involves the inefficient process of first converting it into a circuit.

Secure Computation for RAM Programs. Motivated by the above consideration, various secure computation techniques that work directly for RAM

P. Miao—Work done while the author is a student at the University of California, Berkeley. Research supported in part from a DARPA/ARL SAFEWARE Award, AFOSR Award FA9550-15-1-0274, NSF CRII Award 1464397 and a research grant from the Okawa Foundation. The views expressed are those of the author and do not reflect the official policy or position of the funding agencies.

S. Jarecki (Ed.): CT-RSA 2020, LNCS 12006, pp. 610–637, 2020.
https://doi.org/10.1007/978-3-030-40186-3_26

programs have been developed. Ostrovsky and Shoup [OS97] show how general secure RAM computation can be done using oblivious RAM (ORAM) [Gol87, Ost90, GO96]. Subsequently, Gordon et al. [GKK+12] demonstrated an efficient realization based on ORAM techniques. In follow up works [GKK+12, LO13a, WHC+14, AHMR15], significant asymptotic and practical efficiency improvements have been obtained. However, all these works require *round complexity* on the order of the running time of the program.

In a recent line of work [LO13b, GHL+14, GLOS15, GLO15, HY16, GGMP16], positive results on round efficient secure computation for RAM programs have been achieved. These improvements are obtained by realizing the notion of garbled random-access machines (garbled RAMs) [LO13b] as a method to garble RAM programs directly, a RAM analogue of Yao's garbled circuits [Yao82].

Persistent vs. Non-persistent Database. In the setting of RAM programs, the ability to store a *persistent* private database that can be computed on multiple times can be very powerful. Traditionally, secure computation on RAM programs is thus studied in two settings. In the *non-persistent* database setting, one considers only a single program execution. While in the *persistent* database setting, one considers execution of many programs on the same database; the database can be modified by these programs during the execution and these changes persist for future program executions. This feature is very important as it allows to execute a sequence of programs without requiring to initialize the data for every execution, implying that the database can be huge and the execution time of each program does not need to depend on the size of the database. Previous garbled RAM schemes [GHL+14, GLOS15, GLO15] allow to garble any sequence of programs on a persistent database, and we seek for secure RAM computation protocols that preserve this property.

Black-Box vs. Non-black-Box. Starting with Impagliazzo-Rudich [IR90, IR89], researchers have been very interested in realizing cryptographic goals making only black-box use of underlying primitives. It has been the topic of many important recent works in cryptography [IKLP06, PW09, Wee10, GLOV12, GOSV14, GLO15]. On the other hand, the problem of realizing black-box construction for various primitive is still open, e.g. multi-statement non-interactive zero-knowledge [BFM88, FLS99, GOS06] and oblivious transfer extension [Bea96].[1] From a complexity perspective, black-box constructions are very appealing as they often lead to conceptually simpler and qualitatively more efficient constructions.[2]

Semi-honest vs. Malicious Adversaries. All the aforementioned secure RAM computation protocols that allow for a persistent database are secure only against semi-honest adversaries. Hence, an important question is how to

---

[1] Interestingly for oblivious transfer extension we do know black-box construction based on stronger assumptions [IKNP03].

[2] Additionally, black-box constructions enable implementations agnostic to the implementation of the underlying primitives. This offers greater flexibility allowing for many optimizations, scalability, and choice of implementation.

"convert" the protocol into one that is secure in the presence of malicious adversaries, while preserving the efficiency, round complexity, database persistence, and black-box use of underlying cryptographic primitives of the original protocol to the greatest extent possible.

Motivated by stronger security guarantee and black-box constructions in the persistent database setting, in this work, we ask the following question:

Can we securely compute RAM programs on a persistent database against malicious adversaries making only black-box use of cryptographic primitives?

1.1   Our Results

In this paper, we provide the first constant round two-party secure RAM computation protocol making only black-box use of underlying cryptographic primitives with security guarantee against malicious adversaries.

Main Theorem (Informal). *There exists a black-box secure RAM computation protocol with constant round complexity which is secure against malicious adversaries, where the size of the database stored by one of the parties is $\tilde{\mathcal{O}}(|D|)$, and the communication and computational complexity of one protocol execution is $\tilde{\mathcal{O}}(t)$ where t is the running time of program P executed in one protocol execution. Here $\tilde{\mathcal{O}}(\cdot)$ ignores $\mathsf{poly}(\log t, \log|D|, \kappa, s)$ factors where κ, s are the security parameters. The protocol allows for maintaining a persistent garbled database across execution of multiple programs. Our construction is proved secure in the random oracle model.*

1.2   Related Work

Independent with our work, Hazay and Yanai [HY16] also consider the questions of secure 2-party RAM computation against malicious adversaries. They present a constant-round protocol building on the the semi-honest protocols [GHL+14, GLOS15] and cut-and-choose techniques [LP07], but make a non-black-box use of one-way functions. Moreover, they allow for a weaker notion of persistent database, which we refer to as *weak-persistent* setting in Table 1, where all the programs as well as the inputs are known beforehand to the parties.[3] In another work, Garg et al. [GGMP16] study this question in the multiparty setting. They demonstrate a constant-round multi-party computation protocol that makes black-box use of one-way functions. Their work is based on the black-box garbled RAM construction [GLOS15] (as we do) and the constant-round MPC construction of [BMR90]. Their semi-honest secure protocol allows for a persistent database, whereas their maliciously secure protocol achieves the weak persistent notion. See Table 1 for a comparison of our work with prior and concurrent work.

---

[3] In this paper we focus on the standard persistent notion where later programs and inputs can be chosen adaptively.

Table 1. Comparison of this work with prior and concurrent work

	Security	Model	Assumption	Persistence	Rounds
[GHL+14]	semi-honest	OT-hybrid	IBE	persistent	$\mathcal{O}(1)$
[GLOS15]	semi-honest	OT-hybrid	non-black-box OWF	persistent	$\mathcal{O}(1)$
[GLO15]	semi-honest	OT-hybrid	black-box OWF	persistent	$\mathcal{O}(1)$
[GGMP16]	semi-honest	OT-hybrid	black-box OWF	persistent	$\mathcal{O}(1)$
[AHMR15]	malicious	OT-hybrid	black-box OWF	non-persistent	$\mathcal{O}(t)$
[HY16]	malicious	OT-hybrid	non-black-box OWF	weak-persistent	$\mathcal{O}(1)$
[GGMP16]	malicious	OT-hybrid	black-box OWF	weak-persistent	$\mathcal{O}(1)$
[This work]	malicious	OT-hybrid, ROM	black-box OWF	persistent	$\mathcal{O}(1)$

2 Our Techniques

We build our protocol based on the previous semi-honest secure black-box garbled RAM construction [GLO15]. This serves as a good starting point in explaining the technical challenges that come up in realizing maliciously secure black-box garbled RAM.

Abstract of [GLO15]. The construction of [GLO15] is complex in that it involves details of the RAM computation model, structure of the tree-like garbled database consisting of garbled circuits as well as the way to properly concatenate these circuits, statistical ORAMs [DMN11, SCSL11, SvDS+13], etc. We first summarize this construction in an abstracted garbled RAM scheme, and then make it maliciously secure. More generally, if there are other constructions that can also be transformed into this abstracted form, it can be automatically made maliciously secure by our method. In the following we will use Yao's garbled circuits [Yao86] as a building block. To avoid ambiguity, the term *input keys* refers to both labels per input wire of a garbled circuit while *labels* refers to one label per wire.

At a high level the garbled RAM scheme can be described as follows. The garbled database and garbled programs consist of a collection of garbled circuits, which are concatenated in a certain way. In particular, one garbled circuit may hard-code inside it certain public constants and (partial) input keys to other garbled circuits. The garbler generates all the garbled circuits concatenated properly and sends to the evaluator the garbled circuits along with partial input labels. The evaluator evaluates the garbled circuits one by one in a certain order, during which one garbled circuit may output (partial) input labels for other garbled circuits, enabling the evaluation of the next garbled circuit. This process proceeds until the evaluator obtains the output of the program. We refer the readers to Sect. 4 for more details.

Technical Challenges. Starting from the construction of [GLO15], one possible method to make it maliciously secure is to compile it into a new protocol against malicious adversaries using standard techniques [GMW87]. However, it will compromise the black-box use of cryptographic primitives.

Recall that in [GLO15], the garbler (Alice) generates the garbled database $\tilde{D}$ and garbled programs $\tilde{P}$ consisting of a collection of garbled circuits that are concatenated properly, and sends to the evaluator (Bob). If Alice is malicious, she may generate incorrect circuits or circuits concatenated in a wrong way. To avoid Alice cheating, one possibility is to treat the garbled database and garbled program $(\tilde{D}, \tilde{P})$ as one large garbled circuit, and apply cut-and-choose techniques to it in a similar way to doing cut-and-choose on a single garbled circuit [LP07]. But cut-and-choose can only be done once for the database, meaning that we can only apply cut-and-choose for the first $(\tilde{D}, \tilde{P})$ pair, and cannot achieve execution of multiple programs on a persistent database. Therefore we turn to apply cut-and-choose on every single circuit, or even on every gate.

The key question that we are trying to answer is: How to enforce Alice to generate all the garbled circuits concatenated in a correct way? In particular, how to ensure that all the hard-coded parameters are correct? In order to check the correctness, we first pull out the hard-coded parameters in the circuit to be part of the input, and then define a public function specifying the correlation among all these circuits, in particular which input wires should take as input an input key to another garbled circuit, and which should take a public value as input, etc. The barrier becomes how to enforce the garbled circuits as well as the correlation between them to be correct.

Consistency Check by Commitments. A natural idea is to let Alice and Bob generate each garbled circuit correctly by cut-and-choose techniques [LP07, NO09, FJN+13, FJNT15]. Then we require Alice to help Bob "concatenate" these circuits satisfying the correlation requirements. Recall that in a Yao's garbled circuit, there are two labels per input wires, which together form the *input-garbling-keys* (which we also refer to as *input keys* in this paper) to a garbled circuit. When Bob evaluates the garbled circuit, he obtains one label per input wire. To ensure correct concatenation, the major task is to guarantee the consistency between input labels of one garbled circuit and input keys to another garbled circuit. For instance, the i-th input wire of circuit X should be taking as input the j-th bit of circuit Y's input keys. Let $(\mathsf{label}^0, \mathsf{label}^1)$ be the two labels of the i-th input wire of X, and b be the j-th bit of Y's input keys. In order to concatenate the two circuits, Alice must provide Bob with label^b *without* revealing b.

Our first attempt is requiring Alice to give *bit-wise* commitments of all the input keys. If Alice commits honestly, then Bob holds a commitment of b (denoted by $[b]$). In addition, we require Alice to commit to each label together with its corresponding bit, namely $[\mathsf{label}^0] \,\|\, [0]$ and $[\mathsf{label}^1] \,\|\, [1]$, in a randomly permuted order. When revealing label label^b to Bob, Alice picks $\left[\mathsf{label}^{b'}\right] \,\|\, [b']$, opens $\left[\mathsf{label}^{b'}\right]$, and proves to Bob that $b' = b$. An additive/XOR-homomorphic commitment scheme suffices: Bob can compute $[b'] \oplus [b] \to [b \oplus b']$, and Alice opens the commitment to show that $b \oplus b' = 0$. If every bit-wise commitment is correct, then the above procedure ensures that Bob obtains label^b. Now the question boils down to: How to enforce Alice to commit to every bit of the input keys honestly?

Cut-and-Choose on Circuits. Our next attempt is applying cut-and-choose on each single circuit [LP07] to ensure that every garbled circuit is generated correctly. The high level idea of [LP07] is to generate a correct garbled circuit as follows. Alice first generates a number of garbled circuits, and then Bob does cut-and-choose over these circuits, namely Bob randomly picks half of the circuits, asks Alice to reveal all the randomness of generating the picked ones, and checks if they are correctly generated. If all these circuits pass Bob's checking, then with high probability most of the remaining unchecked circuits are also correct. Bob then evaluates all the remaining circuits and takes a majority of the outputs.

As we discussed earlier, we require Alice to give bit-wise commitments of all the input keys, but currently we have no guarantee that Alice will do so honestly. In fact, even if she only committed to a single bit incorrectly, it will easily violate our consistency requirement. For the above example, Alice may commit to $\left[\overline{b}\right]$ and later open $\left[\text{label}^{\overline{b}}\right]$ ($\overline{b}$ denotes the negation of bit b). To resolve this problem we might need another level of cut-and-choose.

Yet a more severe issue is that since Bob evaluates a number of replicate circuits and takes the majority of the outputs, the input length of the resulting garbled circuit is increased by a factor of the security parameter. This is fine for a single circuit, but if we apply [LP07] for each circuit in $\tilde{D}$ and $\tilde{P}$, where one circuit may take as input (partial) input keys to another circuit, the input length may grow exponentially in the number of circuits.

Cut-and-Choose on Gates. Now we consider cut-and-choose at a gate level, which has been known as LEGO [NO09]. The main idea of LEGO is as follows. Alice first produces a number of components and sends to Bob. Bob randomly picks a subset of the components to be checked, Alice sends the randomness used to generate them, and Bob checks the components. If Bob passes all the checking, then with high probability most of the remaining components are also correct. Bob then permutes the remaining components and use them to build a garbled circuit where each gate will be computed multiple times and Bob takes a majority vote on the output. To connect the remaining components we require Alice to open some commitments to Bob.

LEGO is a better fit for our setting than [LP07] in that the input length of a LEGO garbled circuit is the same as the original circuit, hence it would not grow drastically throughout the circuits. Moreover, since each wire is replicated multiple times, we are able to do more consistency checking among the commitments of replicated wires, and if Bob accepts all the checking, then we can achieve the guarantee that every bit-wise commitment is correct, as we elaborate in more detail below.

XOR-Homomorphic Commitment Scheme. Next we describe in more detail how to guarantee the correctness of the bit-wise commitments. We start from the LEGO protocol of [NO09] and tailer the construction to our needs.

There are two major modifications. First, an additive homomorphic commitment scheme is applied in LEGO, and we replace it with an XOR-homomorphic commitment scheme. The use of an XOR-homomorphic commitment scheme was proposed in [FJN+13,FJNT15] to improve efficiency, and was also utilized in [AHMR15]. We will see the advantage of this modification in our construction. Second, if Bob accepts all the checking in the LEGO protocol, by cut-and-choose it only guarantees that *most* of the remaining components are correct with high probability. We add more consistency checking among the commitments of input wires to ensure that *all* the commitments of input wires are correct with high probability.

We now discuss the intuition of the additional consistency checking via an example. Assume that an input wire w has $\ell_n + 1$ replicate wires, with input keys $(\mathsf{label}^0_{w,0}, \mathsf{label}^1_{w,0}), (\mathsf{label}^0_{w,1}, \mathsf{label}^1_{w,1}), \cdots, (\mathsf{label}^0_{w,\ell_n}, \mathsf{label}^1_{w,\ell_n})$. Alice has provided a bit-wise commitment of all the input keys. Denote the first bit of $\mathsf{label}^0_{w,i}$ by b_i. As a demonstration, we explain how to ensure that Alice has committed to $[b_i]$ correctly. In the LEGO protocol, when concatenating components to build a garbled circuit, Bob obtains the difference between certain labels, in particular $\delta_{w,i} = \mathsf{label}^0_{w,i} \oplus \mathsf{label}^0_{w,0}$. The additional consistency checking is as follows. Note that $b_i \oplus b_0$ should be the first bit of $\delta_{w,i}$. Bob can compute $[b_i \oplus b_0] \leftarrow [b_i] \oplus [b_0]$. We require Alice to open the resulting commitment and Bob to check if it is equal to the first bit of $\delta_{w,i}$. Since cut-and-choose is done at a gate level, with high probability at least one of the replicate wires has correct bit-wise commitments. If Bob passes all the additional consistency checking, the correctness of a single wire will spread out to all the replicate wires. The above is merely one example of additional consistency checking, and in the protocol we need more consistency checking to ensure correctness of all the commitments.

Adaptive Security. Since we execute our protocol on a sequence of programs which run on a persistent database, the inputs of the adversary could be adaptively decided after the two parties have generated the garbled database and garbled programs which consist of garbled circuits. Thus we need to argue *adaptive security* of the garbled RAM. More precisely, security should hold even when the input on which the stored garbled RAM is computed can depend on the garbled RAM itself. Towards this goal, we first modify the LEGO garbled circuit to be adaptively secure in the random oracle model. Then we instantiate the garbled RAM with the adaptive secure LEGO garbled circuits to achieve an adaptive secure garbled RAM.

Construction at a High Level. We first abstract the static secure black-box garbled RAM construction of [GLO15], where the garbler (Alice) generates a collection of garbled circuits which are concatenated properly, and the evaluator (Bob) evaluates the garbled circuits one by one in a certain order. At a high level, in our construction Alice will generate all the garbled circuits, and the LEGO techniques along with consistency checking ensure that all the garbled circuits are concatenated in a correct way. Then Bob can evaluates the garbled circuits to compute the output.

A key observation is that we can instantiate the black-box garbled RAM of [GLO15] with the LEGO garbling scheme as the underlying circuit garbling scheme. Then we modify the static secure LEGO garbling scheme to be adaptive secure in the random oracle model, which gives us an adaptive secure garbled RAM scheme. In order to generate an adaptive LEGO garbled circuit, we modify the original LEGO protocol in [NO09] in that we add more commitments and consistency checking in the protocol. After the additional consistency checking, all the commitments of input wires are guaranteed to be correct. Finally, we can ensure that all the garbled circuits are concatenated properly by opening certain commitments.

Concrete Efficiency. We illustrate our idea of additional consistency checking on the original LEGO framework [NO09] and not on the more efficient LEGO protocols [FJN+13,FJNT15], because [NO09] is simpler and helps highlight our ideas better. We note that the focus of this work is the theoretical feasibility of achieving maliciously secure RAM computation protocols using cut-and-choose techniques, rather than concrete efficiency. Nevertheless, it is worth pointing out that the LEGO protocols of [FJN+13,FJNT15] are compatible with all known optimizations for Yao's garbled circuits, e.g., point-and-permute [BMR90,MNP+04], free-XORs [KS08], garbled row reduction [NPS99,PSSW09,KMR14,ZRE15], etc.). We have left the goal of obtaining concrete efficiency improvements over our construction for future work. However, we believe that these improvements should be obtainable.

Storage Costs. Finally, we mention that the client (Alice) can store the whole database on the cloud (Bob), and it is not necessary for her to store all the input keys, randomness, etc. on her disk. She may store all these things on the cloud signed and in an encrypted form (by private key encryption), and request for them when needed. Therefore, the client storage remains small after the garbled database has been created.

2.1 Roadmap

We now lay out a roadmap for the remainder of the paper. In Sect. 3 we give definitions for semi-honest secure and maliciously secure garbled RAM. In Sect. 4 we abstract the static secure black-box garbled RAM construction of [GLO15]. We review the LEGO garbling scheme and describe our modified construction which is adaptive secure in Sect. 5, and present our new LEGO protocol in Sect. 6. Finally we give our secure RAM computation protocol in Sect. 7. We defer most proofs to the full version of the paper [Mia16].

3 Preliminaries

In this section, we formally define the security of garbled RAM against semi-honest and malicious adversaries. For a brief description of the RAM model, circuit garbling schemes, and some building blocks needed in the construction, refer to the full version of the paper [Mia16]. In the following, let κ be the computational security parameter for the commitment schemes, oblivious transfers, encryption schemes and hash functions used, and s be the statistical security parameter.

3.1   Garbled RAM Scheme

In this section, we consider an extension of garbled circuits to the setting of RAM programs, as defined in [LO13b, GHL+14, GLOS15, GLO15]. In this setting the database D is garbled once and then many different garbled programs can be executed sequentially with the database changes persisting from one execution to the next. Note that all the previous work only defines static security for garbled RAM, and we also define adaptive security here.

Syntax. A garbled RAM scheme consists of four procedures (GData, GProg, GInput, GEval) with the following syntax:

- *Database Garbling:* $(\tilde{D}, s) \leftarrow$ GData$(1^\kappa, D)$ takes as input the security parameter κ and database content $D \in \{0, 1\}^M$, and outputs a garbled database $\tilde{D}$ and a key s.
- *Program Garbling:* $(\tilde{P}, s^{in}) \leftarrow$ GProg(s, P, M, t, T) takes as input a key s and a RAM program P with database-size M and run-time consisting t CPU steps. We also provide T indicating the cumulative number of CPU steps executed by all of the previous programs. It then outputs the garbled program $\tilde{P}$ and input-garbling-key s^{in}.
- *Input Garbling:* $\tilde{x} \leftarrow$ GInput(x, s^{in}) takes as input $x \in \{0, 1\}^u$ and input keys s^{in}, and outputs the garbled input $\tilde{x}$.
- *Garbled Evaluation:* $y \leftarrow$ GEval$^{\tilde{D}}(\tilde{P}, \tilde{x})$ takes as input a garbled program $\tilde{P}$, garbled input $\tilde{x}$ and garbled database $\tilde{D}$, and outputs a value y. We model GEval itself as a RAM program that can read and write to arbitrary locations of its database initially containing $\tilde{D}$.

Efficiency. We require the run-time of GProg and GEval to be $t \cdot$ poly $(\log M, \log t, \kappa)$, which also serves as the bound on the size of the garbled program $\tilde{P}$. Moreover, we require that the run-time of GData should be $M \cdot$ poly $(\log M, \kappa)$, which also serves as an upper bound on the size of $\tilde{D}$. Finally the running time of GInput is required to be $u \cdot$ poly (κ).

Correctness. For correctness, we require that for any sequence of programs $P_1, \cdots, P_\ell$ with run-time $t_1, \cdots, t_\ell$, let $D \in \{0, 1\}^M$ be any initial database, let $x_1, \cdots, x_\ell$ be the inputs of the programs and $(y_1, \cdots, y_\ell) = (P_1(x_1), \cdots, P_\ell(x_\ell))^D$ be the outputs given by the sequential execution of the programs. We have that:

$$\Pr\left[\left(\mathsf{GEval}(\tilde{P}_1, \tilde{x}_1), \cdots, \mathsf{GEval}(\tilde{P}_\ell, \tilde{x}_\ell)\right)^{\tilde{D}} = (y_1, \cdots, y_\ell)\right] = 1$$

where $(\tilde{D}, s) \leftarrow \mathsf{GData}(1^\kappa, D), (\tilde{P}_i, s_i^{in}) \leftarrow \mathsf{GProg}(s, P_i, M, t_i, T_i), \tilde{x}_i \leftarrow \mathsf{GInput}(x_i, s_i^{in})$, where $T_i = \sum_{j=1}^{i-1} t_j$ denotes the run-time of all programs prior to P_i.

Static Security. For static security, we require that there exists a PPT simulator StatRamSim such that for any PPT adversary $\mathcal{A}$, any initial database content $D \in \{0, 1\}^M$, and any polynomially bounded ℓ, the output of the following two experiments are computational indistinguishable:

Real experiment

- $(\tilde{D}, s) \leftarrow \mathsf{GData}(1^\kappa, D)$
- For $i = 1, 2, \cdots, \ell$
  $(P_i, x_i) \leftarrow \mathcal{A}(1^\kappa, i)$
  $(\tilde{P}_i, s_i^{in}) \leftarrow \mathsf{GProg}(s, P_i, M, t_i, T_i)$
  $\tilde{x}_i \leftarrow \mathsf{GInput}(x_i, s_i^{in})$
- Output $\left(\tilde{D}, \left\{ \left(\tilde{P}_i, \tilde{x}_i \right) \right\}_{i=1}^{\ell} \right)$

Simulated experiment

- $\left(\tilde{D}^{\mathsf{sim}}, \mathsf{state}_0 \right) \leftarrow \mathsf{StatRamSim} \left(1^\kappa, 1^M \right)$
- For $i = 1, 2, \cdots, \ell$
  $(P_i, x_i) \leftarrow \mathcal{A}(1^\kappa, i)$
  $(\tilde{P}_i^{\mathsf{sim}}, \tilde{x}_i^{\mathsf{sim}}, \mathsf{state}_i) \leftarrow \mathsf{StatRamSim}(\mathsf{state}_{i-1}, P_i, 1^{t_i}, y_i)$
  (where $(y_1, \cdots, y_\ell) = (P_1(x_1), \cdots, P_\ell(x_\ell))^D$)
- Output $\left(\tilde{D}^{\mathsf{sim}}, \left\{ \left(\tilde{P}_i^{\mathsf{sim}}, \tilde{x}_i^{\mathsf{sim}} \right) \right\}_{i=1}^{\ell} \right)$

Adaptive Security. For adaptive security, we require that there exists a PPT simulator AdaptRamSim such that for any PPT adversary $\mathcal{A}$, any initial database content $D \in \{0, 1\}^M$, and any polynomially bounded ℓ, the output of the following two experiments are computational indistinguishable:

Real experiment

- $(\tilde{D}, s) \leftarrow \mathsf{GData}(1^\kappa, D)$
- For $i = 1, 2, \cdots, \ell$
  $P_i \leftarrow \mathcal{A} \left(1^\kappa, \tilde{D}, \left\{ (\tilde{P}_j, \tilde{x}_j) \right\}_{j=1}^{i-1} \right)$
  $(\tilde{P}_i, s_i^{in}) \leftarrow \mathsf{GProg}(s, P_i, M, t_i, T_i)$
  $x_i \leftarrow \mathcal{A} \left(1^\kappa, \tilde{D}, \left\{ (\tilde{P}_j, \tilde{x}_j) \right\}_{j=1}^{i-1}, \tilde{P}_i \right)$
  $\tilde{x}_i \leftarrow \mathsf{GInput}(x_i, s_i^{in})$
- Output $\left(\tilde{D}, \left\{ \left(\tilde{P}_i, \tilde{x}_i \right) \right\}_{i=1}^{\ell} \right)$

Simulated experiment

- $(\tilde{D}^{\mathsf{sim}}, \mathsf{state}_0) \leftarrow \mathsf{AdaptRamSim} \left(1^\kappa, 1^M \right)$
- For $i = 1, 2, \cdots, \ell$
  $P_i \leftarrow \mathcal{A} \left(1^\kappa, \tilde{D}, \left\{ (\tilde{P}_j, \tilde{x}_j) \right\}_{j=1}^{i-1} \right)$
  $(\tilde{P}_i^{\mathsf{sim}}, \mathsf{state}_i') \leftarrow \mathsf{AdaptRamSim}(\mathsf{state}_{i-1}, P_i, 1^{t_i}, y_i)$
  $x_i \leftarrow \mathcal{A} \left(1^\kappa, \tilde{D}, \left\{ (\tilde{P}_j, \tilde{x}_j) \right\}_{j=1}^{i-1}, \tilde{P}_i \right)$
  $(\tilde{x}_i^{\mathsf{sim}}, \mathsf{state}_i) \leftarrow \mathsf{AdaptRamSim}(\mathsf{state}_i', y_i)$
  where $(y_1, \cdots, y_\ell) = (P_1(x_1), \cdots, P_\ell(x_\ell))^D$
- Output $\left(\tilde{D}^{\mathsf{sim}}, \left\{ \left(\tilde{P}_i^{\mathsf{sim}}, \tilde{x}_i^{\mathsf{sim}} \right) \right\}_{i=1}^{\ell} \right)$

3.2   Garbled RAM Against Malicious Adversaries

We define security of a secure RAM computation protocol against malicious adversaries in the ideal/real world paradigm. The definition compares the output of a real execution to the output of an ideal computation involving a trusted third party, which we call ideal functionality. The ideal functionality receives the parties' inputs, computes the functionality on these inputs and returns their respective outputs. Loosely speaking, the protocol is secure if any real-world adversary can be converted into an ideal-world adversary such that the output distributions are computationally indistinguishable.

Execution in the Ideal World. We describe the ideal functionality $\mathcal{F}$ in Fig. 1. Note that it is "insecure" similarly as [NO09] in the sense that it allows Alice to guess Bob's input bits, but if her guess is wrong then Bob is told that Alice is cheating. This models a standard problem in Yao's garbled circuits known as "selective failure attack", which can be solved by modifying the circuit being

---

Database: Alice inputs (InitialData, D). The ideal functionality parses it as $D \in \{0,1\}^M$.

Program and input: Alice inputs (NewProgram, A, P^A, x^A), Bob inputs (NewProgram, B, P^B, x^B). If $P^A \neq P^B$, then the ideal functionality outputs disagreement! to both parties and terminates. Otherwise, let $P = P^A$ and parse P as a program with input $x = (x^A, x^B)$.

Evaluation and output: The ideal functionality computes $y = P^D(x)$, outputs y to Bob, and updates D for the execution of the next program.

Corrupted party: The corrupted party may deviate from its input, may abort the procedure by sending abort! to the ideal functionality, and can decide the time of message delivery. In addition, if Alice is corrupted, she can specify to the ideal functionality a set $\{i, \beta_i\}_{i \in I}$ where $I \subseteq \{1, \cdots, |x^B|\}$ and $\beta_i \in \{0,1\}$, where $|x^B|$ is the length of Bob's input. If $\beta_i = x_i^B$ for every $i \in I$, then the ideal functionality outputs correct! to Alice. Otherwise, it outputs wrong! to Alice and outputs Alice cheat! to Bob.

Fig. 1. The ideal functionality

evaluated to first compute a function of a randomized encoding of Bob's input, where any s bits are uniformly random and independent. This allows us to only argue that Alice can guess s or more bits with probability at most 2^{-s}, where s is the statistical security parameter, since guessing fewer bits does not leak information. One method for this is given in [LP07]. The extra number of gates used is $\mathcal{O}\left(|x^B| + s\right)$. From now on we focus on implementing the slightly insecure ideal functionality above.

Execution in the Real World. We next consider the real world where the protocol Π is executed. Π consists of four protocols $(\Pi_{\mathsf{GData}}, \Pi_{\mathsf{GProg}}, \Pi_{\mathsf{GInput}}, \Pi_{\mathsf{GEval}})$ with the following functionality:

- *Database Garbling* Π_{GData}. With Alice's input D, the protocol outputs a key s to Alice and the garbled database $\tilde{D}$ to Bob.
- *Program Garbling* Π_{GProg}. The program P is known to both parties. With Alice's input s, the protocol outputs an input-garbling-key s^{in} to Alice and the garbled program $\tilde{P}$ to Bob.
- *Input Garbling* Π_{GInput}. With Alice's input (s^{in}, x^A) and Bob's input x^B, the protocol outputs the garbled input $\tilde{x}$ to Bob, where the input to the program is $x = (x^A, x^B)$.
- *Garbled Evaluation* Π_{GEval}. It is a procedure executed by Bob himself to compute $y = P^D(x)$ from $\tilde{D}, \tilde{P}, \tilde{x}$. The garbled database is updated during the evaluation for the execution of the next program.

Efficiency. Considering the communication and computation complexity, we require that the complexity of Π_{GData} be bounded by $M \cdot \mathsf{poly}(\log M, \kappa, s)$, and that of $\Pi_{\mathsf{GProg}}, \Pi_{\mathsf{GEval}}$ be bounded by $t \cdot \mathsf{poly}(\log M, \log t, \kappa, s)$. Besides, the complexity of Π_{GInput} is required to be $u \cdot \mathsf{poly}(\kappa, s)$. Moreover, the round complexity of $\Pi_{\mathsf{GData}}, \Pi_{\mathsf{GProg}}, \Pi_{\mathsf{GInput}}$ are required to be constant.

Security Against Malicious Adversaries. We say that the protocol Π is secure against malicious adversaries if for every pair of PPT adversary $\mathcal{A}$ in the real world, there exists a pair of PPT adversary $\mathcal{S}$ in the ideal world, such that with probability greater than $1 - 2^{-s}$, we have

$$\left\{ \text{IDEAL}_{\mathcal{S}}^{\mathcal{F}} \left(D, \{P_i, x_i\}_{i=1}^{\ell} \right) \right\}_{D, \ell, \{P_i, x_i\}_{i=1}^{\ell}} \stackrel{c}{\approx} \left\{ \text{REAL}_{\mathcal{A}}^{\Pi} \left(D, \{P_i, x_i\}_{i=1}^{\ell} \right) \right\}_{D, \ell, \{P_i, x_i\}_{i=1}^{\ell}} \tag{1}$$

where $\text{IDEAL}_{\mathcal{S}}^{\mathcal{F}}(D, \{P_i, x_i\}_{i=1}^{\ell})$ denotes the output of $\mathcal{S}$ in the ideal world, and $\text{REAL}_{\mathcal{A}}^{\Pi}(D, \{P_i, x_i\}_{i=1}^{\ell})$ denotes the output of $\mathcal{A}$ in the real world. Here ℓ is polynomially bounded, D is the initial database content, and the programs are P_i with input $x_i = (x_i^A, x_i^B)$.

4 Black-Box Garbled RAM

In this section we abstract the construction of the black-box garbled RAM (GRAM) scheme [GLO15]. This abstraction captures the key aspects of the GRAM construction relevant to us. Additionally it avoids the details irrelevant for understanding our work.

At a high level the GRAM scheme can be described as follows. The garbled database and garbled programs consist of a collection of garbled circuits (GCs) concatenated in a certain way, which we will elaborate in more detail later. The garbler generates all the GCs concatenated properly and sends to the evaluator the GCs with partial labels. The evaluator evaluates the GCs one by one in a certain order, during which one GC may output (partial) labels for other GCs, enabling the evaluation of the next GC. This process proceeds until the evaluator obtains the output of the program.

To formalize and generalize the above scheme, we first define a uniform circuit needed in the construction, and then describe the scheme built on the uniform circuits.

4.1 Uniform Circuits

In the scheme, garbled database and garbled programs consist of a collection of GCs. We consider these circuits as *uniform circuits*, which all have the same topology. Now we give a brief description of these uniform circuits. The input of a uniform circuit consists of several parts, const, keys, mem, inp, dyn, as shown in Fig. 2. Note that it is not necessary to delve into the functionality of each circuit to understand the abstracted construction, so we omit the functionality and only give the interface.[4]

---

[4] For the readers who are familiar with [GLO15]: Each GC originally had two parameters const and keys hard-coded inside it, and had mem, inp or dyn as input. Now const and keys are pulled out to be part of the input, and every circuit takes mem, inp, dyn as part of the input, so that all the circuits have the same topology.

4.2   Garbled RAM Scheme

In this section we describe the black-box GRAM scheme built on uniform circuits. At a high level, garbled database and garbled programs consist of a collection of garbled uniform circuits which are *concatenated properly*. We will specify in the following how the generated GCs are concatenated, in particular what is value of every input wire of every circuit.

C^{unif}(const, keys, mem, inp, dyn):

- **const:** A public constant, specifying the functionality of the circuit.
- **keys:** A collection of (partial) input keys of certain other GCs. The information of which (partial) input keys it corresponds to is public.
- **mem:** Partial content of the database.
- **inp:** Partial content of the program input.
- **dyn:** Dynamic input. Its value is unknown at the time of garbling, and its label will be outputted by other circuits at runtime.

Fig. 2. The interface of a uniform circuit

Table 2. The concatenation of the circuits

Category of $X[i]$	$f(X, i)$	Value of $X[i]$
const	$b \in \{0, 1\}$	b
keys	(Y, j)	j-th bit of input keys to Y
mem	$j \in [M]$	$D[j]$
inp	$j \in [u]$	$x[j]$
dyn	null	unknown

Recall that the database D has size M, program P has running time t. The input x of program P has length u. Let $\tilde{M}$ be the number of GCs needed for the garbled database and $\tilde{t}$ be the number of GCs needed for the garbled program.[5] First we number all the GCs, including those for the garbled database as well as the garbled programs. Denote the i-th input wire of circuit X by $X[i]$. Then we define a public function f specifying the value of every input wire of every circuit, as in Table 2. Given the output of f, the scheme is described in Fig. 3.

The above garbled RAM constructed in [GLO15] is a static secure garbled RAM scheme that only makes a black-box use of one-way functions. In particular, it proves the following theorem.

Theorem 1 (Static security of the garbled RAM scheme [GLO15]). *The garbled RAM scheme* (GData, GProg, GInput, GEval) *achieves efficiency, correctness, and static security as defined in Sect. 3.1. Moreover, the construction only makes a black-box use of one-way functions.*

---

[5] $\tilde{M}$ is proportional to M with poly-logarithmic factors, and $\tilde{t}$ is proportional to t with poly-logarithmic factors. For our purpose we do not need to specify the concrete numbers, but one may refer to [GLO15] for details.

5   Adaptive Secure Garbling Schemes

The circuit garbling protocol of [NO09] implies a special circuit garbling scheme, which we refer to in the following as LEGO garbling scheme, denoted by (LegoGCircuit, LegoGInput, LegoEval, LegoEvalCorrupt). In this section, we present

---

Database Garbling: $(\tilde{D}, s) \leftarrow$ GData$(1^\kappa, D)$.

1. *Generating input keys:* Pick a PRF seed s uniformly at random and generate all the input keys needed for the garbled circuits.
2. *Generating garbled circuits:* Generate all garbled uniform circuits $\{\tilde{C}^i\}_{i=1}^{\tilde{M}}$ by a circuit garbling scheme.
3. *Generating partial labels:* Let $\mathcal{L}$ be the set of input labels consistent with f. In particular, for each wire $X[i]$ with category const/keys/mem, pick the correct label for $X[i]$ according to $f(X, i)$ and D.
4. *Output:* $\tilde{D} = \left(\{\tilde{C}^i\}_{i=1}^{\tilde{M}}, \mathcal{L} \right), s$.

Program Garbling/Replenishing: $(\tilde{P}, s^{in}) \leftarrow$ GProg(s, P, M, t, T).

1. *Generating input keys:* Use s to generates all the input keys needed for the new garbled circuits.
2. *Generating garbled circuits:* Let N be the total number of previously generated GCs. Generate all new garbled uniform circuits $\{\tilde{C}^i\}_{i=N+1}^{N+\tilde{t}}$ by a circuit garbling scheme.
3. *Generating partial labels:* Let $\mathcal{L}$ be the set of labels consistent with f for all wires $X[i]$ with category const/keys.
4. *Generating input-garbling-key:* Let s^{in} be the set of input keys to all wires $X[i]$ with category inp.
5. *Output:* $\tilde{P} = \left(\{\tilde{C}^i\}_{i=N+1}^{N+\tilde{t}}, \mathcal{L} \right), s^{in}$.

Input Garbling: $\tilde{x} \leftarrow$ GInput(x, s^{in}).

1. *Parsing input-garbling-key:* Parse s^{in} as partial input keys to currently generated GCs.
2. *Generating garbled input:* Let $\tilde{x}$ be the set of labels consistent with f and x. In particular, for each wire $X[i]$ with category inp and $f(X, i) = j$, pick a label from s^{in} according to $x[j]$.
3. *Output:* $\tilde{x}$.

Garbled Evaluation: $y \leftarrow$ GEval$^{\tilde{D}}(\tilde{P}, \tilde{x})$.

1. With all input labels of $\tilde{C}^{N+1}$, start the evaluation from $\tilde{C}^{N+1}$.
2. Evaluate the GCs one by one until no more GC can be evaluated.
   - One GC will output (partial) labels for other GCs.
   - Once obtaining all labels for a GC, evaluate that GC, and repeat.
3. The output of the last evaluated GC is y.

Fig. 3. Garbled RAM scheme abstraction

our modifications on the scheme to make it adaptively secure in the random oracle model in Sect. 5.1. Next, we instantiate the garbled RAM scheme in Sect. 4 with the adaptive LEGO garbling scheme to obtain an adaptive secure garbled RAM scheme in Sect. 5.2. We defer a detailed review of the static LEGO garbling scheme to the full version of the paper [Mia16].

5.1 Adaptive Secure LEGO Garbling Scheme

In this section we modify the static secure LEGO garbling scheme to be adaptive secure in the random oracle model. First of all, to extend our definitions of garbling scheme privacy to adaptive security in the random oracle model [BR93], we follow the treatment of [BHR12b, BHR12a]. A ROM garbling scheme is a garbling scheme whose algorithms have access to an oracle HASH called the random oracle. The model is obtained by adding the following procedure HASH to the real/simulated experiments.

> **procedure** $\text{HASH}(\gamma, w)$
>   **if** $\text{hash}[\gamma, w] = \bot$ **then**
>   **if** in the real experiment **then**
> $\text{hash}[\gamma, w] \overset{\$}{\leftarrow} \{0, 1\}^{\gamma}$
>   **else**
> $\text{hash}[\gamma, w] \leftarrow \text{AdaptCircSim}(\text{RO}, \gamma, w)$
>   **return** $\text{hash}[\gamma, w]$

New Components.

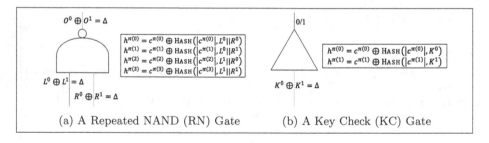

(a) A Repeated NAND (RN) Gate   (b) A Key Check (KC) Gate

Fig. 4. Garbling components for adaptive LEGO garbling scheme

First we modify the garbled RN and KC gates by adding random oracles, as shown in Fig. 4. As before, given the garbled gate table of an RN gate and two input labels L^a, R^b ($a, b \in \{0, 1\}$), one can obtain the corresponding output label $O^{a \otimes b}$. Give the garbled table of a KC gate and one label K, one can check if K is valid (i.e., $K \in \{K^0, K^1\}$).

New Scheme.

Now we modify the static secure LEGO garbling scheme to be an adaptive secure one (AdaptLegoGCircuit, AdaptLegoGInput, AdaptLegoEval, AdaptLegoEvalCorrupt) with the following syntax:

$$\left(\tilde{C}_a, s_a^{in}\right) \leftarrow \text{AdaptLegoGCircuit}\,(1^\kappa, C)$$

$$\tilde{x}_a \leftarrow \text{AdaptLegoGInput}(s_a^{in}, x)$$

$$y \leftarrow \text{AdaptLegoEval}(\tilde{C}_a, \tilde{x}_a)$$

There are two modifications compared to (LegoGCircuit, LegoGInput, LegoEval, LegoEvalCorrupt):

1. When generating garbled gate tables in AdaptLegoGCircuit, now generate the new garbled RN and KC gate tables as in Fig. 4.
2. When evaluating garbled gates in AdaptLegoEval and AdaptLegoEvalCorrupt, now evaluate the new garbled RN and KC gates.

Correctness and Security.

Correct garbled gates remain correct for evaluation in the adaptive LEGO garbling scheme, hence the robust correctness still holds.

Theorem 2 (Robust correctness of adaptive LEGO garbling scheme). *For any circuit C and input x, let $\tilde{C}_a^{cor}$ be a corrupted LEGO garbled circuit in the adaptive LEGO garbling scheme and let $\tilde{x}_a$ be the garbled input of x. If each garbled gate $\tilde{g}_a^{cor} \in \tilde{C}_a^{cor}$ consists of at least 1 correct garbled RN gate and at least $\lceil \frac{\ell_k}{2} \rceil$ correct garbled KC gates, then*

$$C(x) = \text{AdaptLegoEvalCorrupt}\left(\tilde{C}_a^{cor}, \tilde{x}_a\right).$$

We prove the adaptive security for the new scheme. At a high level, the simulator AdaptLegoSim will first generate the garbled circuit honestly when seeing the circuit. After seeing the output of the circuit, AdaptLegoSim generates a new simulated garbled circuit by StatLegoSim, and uses the random oracles to transform the previously generated garbled circuit into the newly simulated one. See the full version of the paper [Mia16] for a detailed proof.

Theorem 3 (Adaptive security of adaptive LEGO garbling scheme). *There exists a PPT simulator AdaptLegoSim such that for any PPT adversary $\mathcal{A}$ and any circuit C, the output of the following two experiments are computational indistinguishable:*

Real experiment	*Simulated experiment*
$-\ \left(\tilde{C}_a, s_a^{in}\right) \leftarrow \text{AdaptLegoGCircuit}\,(1^\kappa, C)$	$-\ \left(\tilde{C}_a^{sim}, \text{state}\right) \leftarrow \text{AdaptLegoSim}\,(1^\kappa, C)$
$-\ x \leftarrow \mathcal{A}(1^\kappa, C, \tilde{C}_a)$	$-\ x \leftarrow \mathcal{A}(1^\kappa, C, \tilde{C}_a)$
$-\ \tilde{x}_a \leftarrow \text{AdaptLegoGInput}(s_a^{in}, x)$	$-\ \tilde{x}_a^{sim} \leftarrow \text{AdaptLegoSim}(\text{state}, C(x))$
$-\ \text{Output } (\tilde{C}_a, \tilde{x}_a)$	$-\ \text{Output } (\tilde{C}_a^{sim}, \tilde{x}_a^{sim})$

5.2   Adaptive Secure Garbled RAM

The garbled RAM scheme was instantiated with Yao's garbling scheme in [GLO15]. In this section we will instantiate it with the aforementioned static/adaptive secure LEGO garbling schemes. Out key observation is that [GLO15] makes a black-box use of a secure circuit garbling scheme (GCircuit, GInput, Eval), which can be instantiated using the LEGO schemes.

First we instantiate the garbled RAM with the static LEGO garbling scheme (LegoGCircuit, LegoGInput, LegoEval). Note that the static LEGO garbling scheme has the same syntax as the circuit garbling scheme and is static secure. Moreover, the scheme only makes black-box use of one-way functions. Therefore, instantiating the garbled RAM with the static LEGO garbling scheme would give us a static secure garbled RAM scheme.

Our next step is instantiating the garbled RAM with the adaptive LEGO garbling scheme (AdaptLegoGCircuit, AdaptLegoGInput, AdaptLegoEval) in Sect. 5.1. It is an adaptive secure circuit garbling scheme as proved in Theorem 3, and it also makes black-box use of one-way functions. We observe that in the security proof of [GLO15] if we replace the static secure circuit garbling scheme with an adaptive secure one, the resulting garbled RAM is also adaptive secure. The following theorem summarizes the above observation.

Theorem 4 (Adaptive secure garbled RAM). *Instantiating the garbled RAM of [GLO15] with the adaptive LEGO garbling scheme gives a garbled RAM scheme* (GDataLego, GProgLego, GInputLego, GEvalLego) *with a simulator* AdaptRamSimLego *that achieves efficiency, correctness, and adaptive security as defined in Sect. 3.1.*

6   Generating an Adaptive LEGO Garbled Circuit

In this section, we provide a protocol between two parties to generate an adaptive LEGO garbled circuit. The protocol is based on the original LEGO protocol in [NO09], and it differs from the LEGO protocol in that we add more commitments and consistency checking in the protocol. After the additional consistency checking, all the commitments of input wires are guaranteed to be correct. This will be shown in the proof of Theorem 6. Looking ahead, this property is crucial for our construction of secure RAM computation protocol to ensure that the garbler generates the garbled memory and garbled programs concatenated properly. In the following we first present the protocol in Sect. 6.1, and then give some useful analysis in Sect. 6.2.

6.1   The New LEGO Protocol

In this section, we present the protocol Π_{NewLEGO} between Alice and Bob where Alice plays the role of a garbler, and Bob obtains an adaptive LEGO garbled circuit at the end of the protocol. For notations, we use $[\cdot]$ to denote a commitment, and $\bar{b}$ to denote a negation of bit b.

Global Difference. Alice samples a global difference Δ and a randomizer r_Δ, generates the commitment $[\Delta; r_\Delta]$, sends $[\Delta]$ to Bob, and gives a zero-knowledge UC-secure proof of knowledge of Δ (see the full version of the paper [Mia16] for details).

Component Production. Let C be a circuit with n NAND gates. Let $N_n = (\ell_n + 1)n$, $N_k = (\ell_k + 1)n$.

Generating Garbled RN Gates. Alice generates $\phi_n N_n$ garbled RN gates (as described in Sect. 5.1). For each garbled RN gate, Alice sample $\pi_L, \pi_R, \pi_O \xleftarrow{\$} \{0,1\}$ and sends the following to Bob. Note that the commitments in steps 3 and 4 are additional compared to the original LEGO protocol.

1. Commitment of the zero labels and permutation: $[L^0], [R^0], [O^0], [\pi]$. (Note that Bob can compute the one labels by himself: $[L^1] \leftarrow [L^0] \oplus [\Delta]$, $[R^1] \leftarrow [R^0] \oplus [\Delta]$, $[O^1] \leftarrow [O^0] \oplus [\Delta]$.)
2. The garbled gate table.

$$h^{\pi(0)} = \mathsf{Enc}_{L^0, R^0}(O^1) \oplus \mathrm{HASH}\left(\left|\mathsf{Enc}_{L^0, R^0}(O^1)\right|, L^0\|R^0\right);$$
$$h^{\pi(1)} = \mathsf{Enc}_{L^0, R^1}(O^1) \oplus \mathrm{HASH}\left(\left|\mathsf{Enc}_{L^0, R^1}(O^1)\right|, L^0\|R^1\right);$$
$$h^{\pi(2)} = \mathsf{Enc}_{L^1, R^0}(O^1) \oplus \mathrm{HASH}\left(\left|\mathsf{Enc}_{L^1, R^0}(O^1)\right|, L^1\|R^0\right);$$
$$h^{\pi(3)} = \mathsf{Enc}_{L^1, R^1}(O^0) \oplus \mathrm{HASH}\left(\left|\mathsf{Enc}_{L^1, R^1}(O^0)\right|, L^1\|R^1\right).$$

3. Commitment of (L^0, L^1), (R^0, R^1), and (O^0, O^1) in permuted orders:

$$[L^{\pi_L}] \| [\pi_L], [L^{\overline{\pi_L}}] \| [\overline{\pi_L}];$$
$$[R^{\pi_R}] \| [\pi_R], [R^{\overline{\pi_R}}] \| [\overline{\pi_R}];$$
$$[O^{\pi_O}] \| [\pi_O], [O^{\overline{\pi_O}}] \| [\overline{\pi_O}].$$

4. Write the labels bit by bit as follows (where z is the length of a label):

$$L^0\|L^1 = \ell^{0,1}\ell^{0,2}\cdots\ell^{0,z}\|\ell^{1,1}\ell^{1,2}\cdots\ell^{1,z};$$
$$R^0\|R^1 = r^{0,1}r^{0,2}\cdots r^{0,z}\|r^{1,1}r^{1,2}\cdots r^{1,z};$$
$$O^0\|O^1 = o^{0,1}o^{0,2}\cdots o^{0,z}\|o^{1,1}o^{1,2}\cdots o^{1,z}.$$

Bit-wise commitment of all labels:

$$\left\{[\ell^{b,u}], [r^{b,u}], [o^{b,u}]\right\}_{b\in\{0,1\}, 1\le u\le z}.$$

Generating Garbled KC Gates. Alice generates $\phi_k N_k$ KC gates (as described in Sect. 5.1). For each garbled KC gate, Alice sends the following to Bob:

1. Commitment of the zero key and permutation $[K^0], [\pi]$. (Note that Bob can compute the one key by himself: $[K^1] \leftarrow [K^0] \oplus [\Delta]$.)

2. The garbled gate table.

$$h^{\pi(0)} = H(K^0) \oplus \textsc{Hash}\left(\left|H(K^0)\right|, K^0\right);$$
$$h^{\pi(1)} = H(K^1) \oplus \textsc{Hash}\left(\left|H(K^1)\right|, K^1\right).$$

Component Checking. Bob randomly picks $(\phi_n - 1)N_n$ RN gates and $(\phi_k - 1)N_k$ KC gates to be checked, and sends to Alice. Note that Alice cannot simply send to Bob all the randomness used to generate the garbled gates being checked, because revealing both the zero label and one label of a wire will leak Δ to Bob, which compromises the security of LEGO garbled circuits completely. Hence Bob randomly picks one label per wire to check.

Checking RN Gates. For each RN gate to be checked, Bob randomly picks $b_L, b_R \xleftarrow{\$} \{0,1\}$, computes $b_O = b_L \otimes b_R$, and sends b_L, b_R, b_O to Alice.

1. *Checking the commitment of labels and permutation:* Alice opens the commitment $[L^{b_L}], [R^{b_R}], [O^{b_O}], [\pi]$.
2. *Checking the garbled gate table:* Bob computes $b = 2 \cdot b_L + b_R$, and checks

$$h^{\pi(b)} = \mathsf{Enc}_{L^{b_L}, R^{b_R}}(O^{b_O}) \oplus \textsc{Hash}\left(\left|\mathsf{Enc}_{L^{b_L}, R^{b_R}}(O^{b_O})\right|, L^{b_L} \| R^{b_R}\right).$$

3. *Checking the commitment of (L^0, L^1), (R^0, R^1), and (O^0, O^1) in permuted orders:*
   Alice opens the commitment

   $[\pi_L], [L^{b_L}] \| [b_L];$ (If $\pi_L = b_L$, then open $[L^{\pi_L}] \| [\pi_L]$; otherwise $[L^{\overline{\pi_L}}] \| [\overline{\pi_L}]$)
   $[\pi_R], [R^{b_R}] \| [b_R];$ (If $\pi_R = b_R$, then open $[L^{\pi_R}] \| [\pi_R]$; otherwise $[L^{\overline{\pi_R}}] \| [\overline{\pi_R}]$)
   $[\pi_O], [O^{b_O}] \| [b_O].$ (If $\pi_O = b_O$, then open $[L^{\pi_O}] \| [\pi_O]$; otherwise $[L^{\overline{\pi_O}}] \| [\overline{\pi_O}]$)

   Bob checks consistency of

   $$\left[L^{b_L}\right] \| [b_L] \text{ with previously revealed } L^{b_L};$$
   $$\left[R^{b_R}\right] \| [b_R] \text{ with previously revealed } R^{b_R};$$
   $$\left[O^{b_O}\right] \| [b_O] \text{ with previously revealed } O^{b_O}.$$

4. *Checking the commitment of every bit of labels:* Alice opens the following commitment

   $$\left\{\left[\ell^{b_L, u}\right], \left[r^{b_R, u}\right], \left[o^{b_O, u}\right]\right\}_{u=1}^{z}.$$

   Bob checks the consistency with previously revealed $L^{b_L}, R^{b_R}, O^{b_O}$.

Checking KC Gates. For each KC gate to be checked, Bob randomly picks $b_K \xleftarrow{\$} \{0,1\}$, sends to Alice.

1. *Checking the commitment of labels and permutation:* Alice opens the commitment $[K^{b_K}], [\pi]$.

2. *Checking the garbled gate table:* Bob checks

$$h^{\pi(b_\mathsf{K})} = \mathsf{H}(K^{b_\mathsf{K}}) \oplus \mathsf{HASH}\left(|\mathsf{H}(K^{b_\mathsf{K}})|, K^{b_\mathsf{K}}\right).$$

Soldering. Bob randomly permutes the remaining N_n RN gates and N_k KC gates, constructs the garbled circuit such that each garbled gate consists of $(\ell_\mathsf{n} + 1)$ RN gates and $(\ell_\mathsf{k} + 1)$ KC gates. Alice helps Bob solder the gates.

1. *Soldering RN gates and KC gates of one garbled gate:* For each gate $g \in \mathsf{C}$, recall that the solders consist of the following:

$$\text{Soldering of RN gates: } \delta_{g,i}^L, \delta_{g,i}^R, \delta_{g,i}^O, \forall i \in \{1, \cdots, \ell_\mathsf{n}\};$$
$$\text{Soldering of KC gates: } \delta_{g,i}^K, \forall i \in \{1, \cdots, \ell_\mathsf{k}\};$$
$$\text{Soldering of KC gates with RN gates: } \delta_g^{O,K}.$$

Bob can compute by himself the commitment of all the above solders:

$$[\delta_{g,i}^L] \leftarrow [L_{g,i}^0] \oplus [R_{g,0}^0];$$
$$[\delta_{g,i}^R] \leftarrow [R_{g,i}^0] \oplus [R_{g,0}^0];$$
$$[\delta_{g,i}^O] \leftarrow [O_{g,i}^0] \oplus [O_{g,0}^0];$$
$$[\delta_{g,i}^K] \leftarrow [K_{g,i}^0] \oplus [K_{g,0}^0];$$
$$[\delta_g^{O,K}] \leftarrow [O_{g,0}^0] \oplus [K_{g,0}^0].$$

Alice opens all the commitment.

2. *Soldering garbled gates together:* Recall that the gate solders consist of the following:

$$\left\{\delta_{g_1,g_2}^L\right\}_{g_1,g_2 \in \mathsf{C}, g_1 \nearrow g_2}, \left\{\delta_{g_1,g_2}^R\right\}_{g_1,g_2 \in \mathsf{C}, g_2 \nwarrow g_1}.$$

Bob can compute by himself the commitment of these solders:

$$\forall g_1 \nearrow g_2 : [\delta_{g_1,g_2}^L] \leftarrow [O_{g_1,0}^0] \oplus [L_{g_2,0}^0];$$
$$\forall g_2 \nwarrow g_1 : [\delta_{g_1,g_2}^R] \leftarrow [O_{g_1,0}^0] \oplus [R_{g_2,0}^0].$$

Alice opens the commitment.

Output Table. For each output wire $w \in \mathcal{W}_\mathsf{out}$, suppose it is the output wire of gate g. Bob has the following commitment:

$$[L_{g,0}^{\pi_{\mathsf{L},0}}] \parallel [\pi_{\mathsf{L},0}], \left[\overline{L_{g,0}^{\pi_{\mathsf{L},0}}}\right] \parallel [\overline{\pi_{\mathsf{L},0}}];$$
$$[L_{g,1}^{\pi_{\mathsf{L},1}}] \parallel [\pi_{\mathsf{L},1}], \left[\overline{L_{g,1}^{\pi_{\mathsf{L},1}}}\right] \parallel [\overline{\pi_{\mathsf{L},1}}];$$
$$\vdots$$
$$[L_{g,\ell_\mathsf{n}}^{\pi_{\mathsf{L},\ell_\mathsf{n}}}] \parallel [\pi_{\mathsf{L},\ell_\mathsf{n}}], \left[\overline{L_{g,\ell_\mathsf{n}}^{\pi_{\mathsf{L},\ell_\mathsf{n}}}}\right] \parallel [\overline{\pi_{\mathsf{L},\ell_\mathsf{n}}}].$$

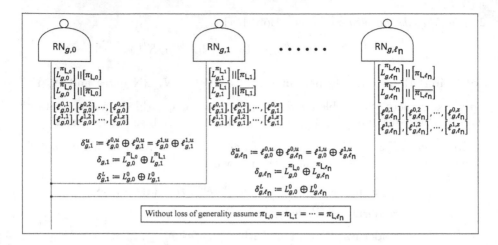

Fig. 5. Consistency checking of an input wire

Input Consistency Checking. For each input wire $w \in \mathcal{W}_{\mathsf{in}}$, without loss of generality assume it is the left input wire of gate g. Bob has the following commitments, as shown in Fig. 5.

$$\left[L_{g,0}^{\pi_{\mathsf{L},0}}\right] \| [\pi_{\mathsf{L},0}] \, ; \, \left[L_{g,0}^{\overline{\pi_{\mathsf{L},0}}}\right] \| [\overline{\pi_{\mathsf{L},0}}] \, ;$$

$$\left[L_{g,1}^{\pi_{\mathsf{L},1}}\right] \| [\pi_{\mathsf{L},1}] \, ; \, \left[L_{g,1}^{\overline{\pi_{\mathsf{L},1}}}\right] \| [\overline{\pi_{\mathsf{L},1}}] \, ;$$

$$\vdots$$

$$\left[L_{g,\ell_n}^{\pi_{\mathsf{L},\ell_n}}\right] \| [\pi_{\mathsf{L},\ell_n}] \, ; \, \left[L_{g,\ell_n}^{\overline{\pi_{\mathsf{L},\ell_n}}}\right] \| [\overline{\pi_{\mathsf{L},\ell_n}}] \, .$$

$$\left[\ell_{g,0}^{0,1}\right], \left[\ell_{g,0}^{0,2}\right], \cdots, \left[\ell_{g,0}^{0,z}\right] ; \left[\ell_{g,0}^{1,1}\right], \left[\ell_{g,0}^{1,2}\right], \cdots, \left[\ell_{g,0}^{1,z}\right] ;$$

$$\left[\ell_{g,1}^{0,1}\right], \left[\ell_{g,1}^{0,2}\right], \cdots, \left[\ell_{g,1}^{0,z}\right] ; \left[\ell_{g,1}^{1,1}\right], \left[\ell_{g,1}^{1,2}\right], \cdots, \left[\ell_{g,1}^{1,z}\right] ;$$

$$\vdots$$

$$\left[\ell_{g,\ell_n}^{0,1}\right], \left[\ell_{g,\ell_n}^{0,2}\right], \cdots, \left[\ell_{g,\ell_n}^{0,z}\right] ; \left[\ell_{g,\ell_n}^{1,1}\right], \left[\ell_{g,\ell_n}^{1,2}\right], \cdots, \left[\ell_{g,\ell_n}^{1,z}\right] .$$

Alice and Bob execute the following consistency checking. This step is a crucial change compared to the original LEGO protocol. Looking ahead, in Theorem 6 we will see that if Bob passes all the input consistency checking, then all the commitments of input wires are correct with high probability.

1. *Revealing the relation between* $\{\pi_{\mathsf{L},i}\}_{i=0}^{\ell_n}$: For every $1 \le i \le \ell_n$, Bob can compute $[\pi_{\mathsf{L},0} \oplus \pi_{\mathsf{L},i}] \leftarrow [\pi_{\mathsf{L},0}] \oplus [\pi_{\mathsf{L},i}]$. Alice opens the commitment. Bob checks if $\pi_{\mathsf{L},0} \oplus \pi_{\mathsf{L},i} = 0$ or 1, and obtains the relation between $\{\pi_{\mathsf{L},i}\}_{i=0}^{\ell_n}$, namely $\pi_{\mathsf{L},i} = \pi_{\mathsf{L},0}$ or $\overline{\pi_{\mathsf{L},0}}$. Without loss of generality assume that $\pi_{\mathsf{L},0} = \pi_{\mathsf{L},1} = \cdots = \pi_{\mathsf{L},\ell_n}$.

2. *Checking the difference between labels is consistent with previously revealed* $\{\delta_{g,i}^{L}\}_{i=1}^{\ell_n}$: For every $1 \le i \le \ell_n$, Bob can compute $[\delta_{g,i}] \leftarrow [L_{g,0}^{\pi_{\mathsf{L},0}}] \oplus [L_{g,i}^{\pi_{\mathsf{L},i}}]$. Alice opens the commitment, and Bob checks if $\delta_{g,i} = \delta_{g,i}^{L}$.

3. *Checking each pair of labels has a difference Δ in between:* For every $0 \le i \le \ell_n$, Bob can compute

$$[0] \,\|\, [0] \leftarrow \left([L_{g,i}^{\pi_{\mathsf{L},i}}] \,\|\, [\pi_{\mathsf{L},i}]\right) \oplus \left([L_{g,i}^{\overline{\pi_{\mathsf{L},i}}}] \,\|\, [\overline{\pi_{\mathsf{L},i}}]\right) \oplus [\Delta] \,\|\, [1].$$

   Alice opens the commitment, and Bob checks.

4. *Checking the difference between bit-wise commitment is consistent with previously revealed* $\{\delta_{g,i}^{L}\}_{i=1}^{\ell_n}$: For every $1 \le i \le \ell_n, b \in \{0,1\}, 1 \le u \le z$, Bob can compute $[\delta_{g,i}^{u}] \leftarrow [\ell_{g,0}^{b,u}] \oplus [\ell_{g,i}^{b,u}]$. Alice opens the commitment, and Bob checks if $\delta_{g,i}^{u}$ is equal to the u-th bit of previously revealed $\delta_{g,i}^{L}$.

Parameters. We pick the parameters $\ell_k, \ell_n, \phi_n, \phi_k, z$ such that the proofs of Theorems 5, 6 can go through. One may refer to [NO09] for a detailed discussion of parameters choice.

6.2   Analysis

The main idea in the above cut-and-choose protocol is that if Bob accepts all the checking, then with high probability there are not too many incorrect gates in total. With these small amount of incorrect gates, there will be at least one RN gates and $\lceil \frac{\ell_k}{2} \rceil$ KC gates per gate with probability exponentially close to 1.

Theorem 5. *Assume that Alice is corrupted and Bob is honest. In the protocol* Π_{NewLEGO} *if Bob accepts all the checking with probability greater than 2^{-s}, then with probability greater than $1 - 2^{-s}$ there are at least 1 correct garbled RN gate and $\lceil \frac{\ell_k}{2} \rceil$ correct garbled KC gates per garbled gate in $\tilde{\mathsf{C}}$.*

The above theorem states that if Bob accepts all the component checking and consistency checking, then most of the garbled gates in the garbled circuit are correct with high probability. In the following theorem, we further show that all the commitments of input wires are correct with high probability.

Theorem 6. *Assume that Alice is corrupted and Bob is honest. In the protocol* Π_{NewLEGO} *if Bob accepts all the checking with probability greater than 2^{-s}, then with probability greater than $1 - 2^{-s}$ all the commitments of all the input wires of $\tilde{\mathsf{C}}$ are correct.*

7 Our Construction

In this section we give our construction of the secure RAM computation protocol. The high level intuition of the protocol is as follows. It is built on the garbled
RAM scheme we abstracted in Sect. 4 and instantiated in Sect. 5.2. Recall that
in the garbled RAM scheme, we defined uniform circuits in Sect. 4.1 as building
units. In the procedure of database garbling and program garbling, the garbler
generates a collection of garbled uniform circuits with partial labels consistent
with a public function f, which indicates the concatenation of the uniform circuits. The evaluator evaluates the garbled circuits (GCs) one by one in a certain
order, during which one GC may output (partial) labels for other GCs, enabling
the evaluation of the next GC. This process proceeds until the evaluator obtains
the output of the program.

    In the protocol Alice will play the role of a garbler and Bob will play the
role of an evaluator. They apply the protocol in Sect. 6 to generate the garbled
uniform circuits in parallel. After Bob obtains all the GCs, Alice provides him
with partial labels consistent with the public function f. We will elaborate in
more detail how Alice gives the partial labels in Sect. 7.1. Given that Alice is
providing the correct labels, Bob, as an evaluator, can evaluate the garbled RAM
as in the garbled RAM scheme.

7.1 Generating Partial Labels

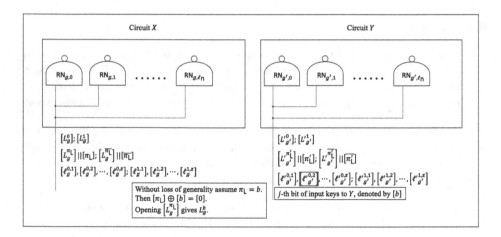

Fig. 6. Concatenation of two garbled circuits

Suppose that Alice and Bob runs the protocol in Sect. 6 to generate a collection of garbled uniform circuits in parallel. In this section we describe how Alice provides Bob with partial labels to these garbled circuits consistent with the public function f. For each input wire $X[i]$ (the i-th input wire of circuit X), without loss of generality assume it is the left input wire of gate of g. Recall that Bob has the following commitment of its input keys, as shown in Fig. 6.

$$\left[L_g^0\right] ; \left[L_g^1\right] ;$$

$$\left[L_g^{\pi_\mathsf{L}}\right] \,\|\, [\pi_\mathsf{L}] ; \left[L_g^{\overline{\pi_\mathsf{L}}}\right] \,\|\, [\overline{\pi_\mathsf{L}}] ;$$

$$\left[\ell_g^{0,1}\right], \left[\ell_g^{0,2}\right], \cdots, \left[\ell_g^{0,z}\right] ; \left[\ell_g^{1,1}\right], \left[\ell_g^{1,2}\right], \cdots, \left[\ell_g^{1,z}\right].$$

Recall that in Table 2 we defined five categories of inputs: const, keys, mem, inp, dyn. We explain in the following how Bob obtains the labels for each category of inputs:

- const: Let $b = f(X, i)$ be value of $X[i]$. Alice simply opens the following commitment: $\left[\ell_g^{b,1}\right], \left[\ell_g^{b,2}\right], \cdots, \left[\ell_g^{b,z}\right]$.
- keys: Let $(Y, j) := f(X, i)$, then the value of $X[i]$ is the j-th bit of input keys to circuit Y. As illustrated in Fig. 6, Bob holds a commitment of that bit, denoted by $[b]$. Without loss of generality assume $\pi_\mathsf{L} = b$. Alice points out the fact that $\pi_\mathsf{L} = b$ to Bob, and Bob can compute $[\pi_\mathsf{L} \oplus b] \leftarrow [\pi_\mathsf{L}] \oplus [b]$. Alice opens the above commitment and Bob checks if $\pi_\mathsf{L} \oplus b = 0$. If Bob accepts the checking, then Alice opens $\left[L_g^{\pi_\mathsf{L}}\right]$ and Bob obtains L_g^b.
- mem: Let $j := f(X, i)$ be the location of the database and let $b := D[j]$ be the value of $X[i]$. Alice first gives a zero-knowledge proof of knowledge of L_g^0 and L_g^1 (see the full version of the paper [Mia16] for more details). Then Alice sends the label L_g^b to Bob.
- inp: Let $j := f(X, i)$ and $b := x[j]$ be the value of $X[i]$.
  - If $x[j]$ is an input bit from Alice, then Alice first gives a zero-knowledge proof of knowledge of L_g^0 and L_g^1, and then sends the label L_g^b to Bob.
  - Otherwise the two parties run an OT where Alice inputs the openings of $\left[L_g^0\right]$ and $\left[L_g^1\right]$ and Bob inputs b, allowing Bob to obtain L_g^b.
- dyn: The label will be produced by another garbled circuit during runtime. There is no need for Bob to obtain a label for it before evaluation.

7.2 Our Protocol

Our secure RAM computation protocol $\Pi = (\Pi_\mathsf{GData}, \Pi_\mathsf{GProg}, \Pi_\mathsf{GInput}, \Pi_\mathsf{GEval})$ is described in Fig. 7. Security proof of the protocol is postponed to the full version of the paper [Mia16].

Database Garbling Π_{GData}.

1. *Generating garbled circuits:* The two parties run Π_{NewLEGO} in parallel to generate $\{\tilde{C}^i\}_{i=1}^{\tilde{M}}$.
2. *Generating partial labels:* For each wire $X[i]$ with category const/keys/mem, Alice provides Bob with partial labels as described in Section 7.1.

Program Garbling Π_{GProg}.

1. *Generating garbled circuits:* The two parties run Π_{NewLEGO} in parallel to generate $\{\tilde{C}^i\}_{i=N+1}^{N+\tilde{t}}$, where N is the number of previously generated GCs.
2. *Generating partial labels:* For each wire $X[i]$ with category const/keys, Alice provides Bob with partial labels as described in Section 7.1.
3. *Generating input-garbling-key:* Let s^{in} be the set of input keys to all wires $X[i]$ with category inp, and Alice keeps it.

Input Garbling Π_{GInput}.

1. *Parsing input-garbling-key:* Alice parses s^{in} as partial input keys to currently generated GCs.
2. *Generating garbled input:* For each wire $X[i]$ with category inp, Alice provides Bob with partial labels as described in Section 7.1.

Garbled Evaluation Π_{GEval}.

– Bob uses $\tilde{D}, \tilde{P}, \tilde{x}$ to compute $y \leftarrow \text{GEval}_{\text{Lego}}{}^{\tilde{D}}(\tilde{P}, \tilde{x})$.

Fig. 7. Secure RAM computation protocol Π

Acknowledgements. The author would like to thank Sanjam Garg for many insightful discussions and helpful comments on the write-up.

References

[AHMR15] Afshar, A., Hu, Z., Mohassel, P., Rosulek, M.: How to efficiently evaluate RAM programs with malicious security. In: Oswald, E., Fischlin, M. (eds.) EUROCRYPT 2015, Part I. LNCS, vol. 9056, pp. 702–729. Springer, Heidelberg (2015). https://doi.org/10.1007/978-3-662-46800-5_27

[Bea96] Beaver, D.: Correlated pseudorandomness and the complexity of private computations. In: 28th ACM STOC (1996)

[BFM88] Blum, M., Feldman, P., Micali, S.: Non-interactive zero-knowledge and its applications. In: STOC, pp. 103–112 (1988)

[BHR12a] Bellare, M., Hoang, V.T., Rogaway, P.: Adaptively secure garbling with applications to one-time programs and secure outsourcing. In: Wang, X., Sako, K. (eds.) ASIACRYPT 2012. LNCS, vol. 7658, pp. 134–153. Springer, Heidelberg (2012). https://doi.org/10.1007/978-3-642-34961-4_10

[BHR12b] Bellare, M., Hoang, V.T., Rogaway, P.: Foundations of garbled circuits. In: ACM CCS (2012)

[BMR90] Beaver, D., Micali, S., Rogaway, P.: The round complexity of secure protocols (extended abstract). In: 22nd ACM STOC (1990)

[BR93]   Bellare, M., Rogaway, P.: Random oracles are practical: a paradigm for designing efficient protocols. In: ACM CCS 1993 (1993)

[DMN11]   Damgård, I., Meldgaard, S., Nielsen, J.B.: Perfectly secure oblivious RAM without random oracles. In: Ishai, Y. (ed.) TCC 2011. LNCS, vol. 6597, pp. 144–163. Springer, Heidelberg (2011). https://doi.org/10.1007/978-3-642-19571-6_10

[FJN+13] Frederiksen, T.K., Jakobsen, T.P., Nielsen, J.B., Nordholt, P.S., Orlandi, C.: MiniLEGO: efficient secure two-party computation from general assumptions. In: Johansson, T., Nguyen, P.Q. (eds.) EUROCRYPT 2013. LNCS, vol. 7881, pp. 537–556. Springer, Heidelberg (2013). https://doi.org/10.1007/978-3-642-38348-9_32

[FJNT15] Frederiksen, T.K., Jakobsen, T.P., Nielsen, J.B., and Trifiletti, R.: TinyLEGO: an interactive garbling scheme for maliciously secure two-party computation. Cryptology ePrint Archive, Report 2015/309 (2015). http://eprint.iacr.org/2015/309

[FLS99]   Feige, U., Lapidot, D., Shamir, A.: Multiple non-interactive zero knowledge proofs under general assumptions. SIAM J. Comput. $29(1)$, 1–28 (1999)

[GGMP16] Garg, S., Gupta, D., Miao, P., Pandey, O.: Secure multiparty RAM computation in constant rounds. In: Hirt, M., Smith, A. (eds.) TCC 2016, Part I. LNCS, vol. 9985, pp. 491–520. Springer, Heidelberg (2016). https://doi.org/10.1007/978-3-662-53641-4_19

[GHL+14] Gentry, C., Halevi, S., Lu, S., Ostrovsky, R., Raykova, M., Wichs, D.: Garbled RAM revisited. In: Nguyen, P.Q., Oswald, E. (eds.) EUROCRYPT 2014. LNCS, vol. 8441, pp. 405–422. Springer, Heidelberg (2014). https://doi.org/10.1007/978-3-642-55220-5_23

[GKK+12] Gordon, S.D., et al.: Secure two-party computation in sublinear (amortized) time. In: CCS (2012)

[GLO15]   Garg, S., Lu, S., Ostrovsky, R.: Black-box garbled RAM. In: 56th FOCS (2015)

[GLOS15] Garg, S., Lu, S., Ostrovsky, R., Scafuro, A.: Garbled RAM from one-way functions. In: 47th ACM STOC (2015)

[GLOV12] Goyal, V., Lee, C.-K., Ostrovsky, R., Visconti, I.: Constructing non-malleable commitments: a black-box approach. In: 53rd FOCS (2012)

[GMW87]   Goldreich, O., Micali, S., Wigderson, A.: How to play any mental game or a completeness theorem for protocols with honest majority. In: 19th ACM STOC (1987)

[GO96]   Goldreich, O., Ostrovsky, R.: Software protection and simulation on oblivious RAMs. J. ACM $43(3)$, 431–473 (1996)

[Gol87]   Goldreich, O.: Towards a theory of software protection and simulation by oblivious RAMs. In: 19th ACM STOC (1987)

[GOS06]   Groth, J., Ostrovsky, R., Sahai, A.: Perfect non-interactive zero knowledge for NP. In: Vaudenay, S. (ed.) EUROCRYPT 2006. LNCS, vol. 4004, pp. 339–358. Springer, Heidelberg (2006). https://doi.org/10.1007/11761679_21

[GOSV14] Goyal, V., Ostrovsky, R., Scafuro, A., Visconti, I.: Black-box non-black-box zero knowledge. In: 46th ACM STOC (2014)

[HY16]   Hazay, C., Yanai, A.: Constant-round maliciously secure two-party computation in the RAM model. In: Hirt, M., Smith, A. (eds.) TCC 2016, Part I. LNCS, vol. 9985, pp. 521–553. Springer, Heidelberg (2016). https://doi.org/10.1007/978-3-662-53641-4_20

[IKLP06] Ishai, Y., Kushilevitz, E., Lindell, Y., Petrank, E.: Black-box constructions for secure computation. In: 38th ACM STOC (2006)

[IKNP03] Ishai, Y., Kilian, J., Nissim, K., Petrank, E.: Extending oblivious transfers efficiently. In: Boneh, D. (ed.) CRYPTO 2003. LNCS, vol. 2729, pp. 145–161. Springer, Heidelberg (2003). https://doi.org/10.1007/978-3-540-45146-4_9

[IR89]   Impagliazzo, R., Rudich, S.: Limits on the provable consequences of one-way permutations. In: 21st ACM STOC (1989)

[IR90]   Impagliazzo, R., Rudich, S.: Limits on the provable consequences of one-way permutations. In: Goldwasser, S. (ed.) CRYPTO 1988. LNCS, vol. 403, pp. 8–26. Springer, New York (1990). https://doi.org/10.1007/0-387-34799-2_2

[KMR14]   Kolesnikov, V., Mohassel, P., Rosulek, M.: FleXOR: flexible garbling for XOR gates that beats free-XOR. In: Garay, J.A., Gennaro, R. (eds.) CRYPTO 2014, Part II. LNCS, vol. 8617, pp. 440–457. Springer, Heidelberg (2014). https://doi.org/10.1007/978-3-662-44381-1_25

[KS08]   Kolesnikov, V., Schneider, T.: Improved garbled circuit: free XOR gates and applications. In: Aceto, L., Damgård, I., Goldberg, L.A., Halldórsson, M.M., Ingólfsdóttir, A., Walukiewicz, I. (eds.) ICALP 2008, Part II. LNCS, vol. 5126, pp. 486–498. Springer, Heidelberg (2008). https://doi.org/10.1007/978-3-540-70583-3_40

[LO13a]   Lu, S., Ostrovsky, R.: Distributed oblivious RAM for secure two-party computation. In: Sahai, A. (ed.) TCC 2013. LNCS, vol. 7785, pp. 377–396. Springer, Heidelberg (2013). https://doi.org/10.1007/978-3-642-36594-2_22

[LO13b]   Lu, S., Ostrovsky, R.: How to garble RAM programs? In: Johansson, T., Nguyen, P.Q. (eds.) EUROCRYPT 2013. LNCS, vol. 7881, pp. 719–734. Springer, Heidelberg (2013). https://doi.org/10.1007/978-3-642-38348-9_42

[LP07]   Lindell, Y., Pinkas, B.: An efficient protocol for secure two-party computation in the presence of malicious adversaries. In: Naor, M. (ed.) EUROCRYPT 2007. LNCS, vol. 4515, pp. 52–78. Springer, Heidelberg (2007). https://doi.org/10.1007/978-3-540-72540-4_4

[Mia16]   Miao, P.: Cut-and-choose for garbled ram. IACR Cryptology ePrint Archive 2016:907 (2016)

[MNP+04] Malkhi, D., Nisan, N., Pinkas, B., Sella, Y., et al.: Fairplay–secure two-party computation system. In: USENIX Security Symposium, vol. 4. San Diego (2004)

[NO09]   Nielsen, J.B., Orlandi, C.: LEGO for two-party secure computation. In: Reingold, O. (ed.) TCC 2009. LNCS, vol. 5444, pp. 368–386. Springer, Heidelberg (2009). https://doi.org/10.1007/978-3-642-00457-5_22

[NPS99]   Naor, M., Pinkas, B., Sumner, R.: Privacy preserving auctions and mechanism design. In: Proceedings of the 1st ACM conference on Electronic commerce, pp. 129–139. ACM (1999)

[OS97]   Ostrovsky, R., Shoup, V.: Private information storage (extended abstract). In: 29th ACM STOC (1997)

[Ost90]   Ostrovsky, R.: Efficient computation on oblivious RAMs. In: 22nd ACM STOC (1990)

[PSSW09] Pinkas, B., Schneider, T., Smart, N.P., Williams, S.C.: Secure two-party computation is practical. In: Matsui, M. (ed.) ASIACRYPT 2009. LNCS, vol. 5912, pp. 250–267. Springer, Heidelberg (2009). https://doi.org/10.1007/978-3-642-10366-7_15

[PW09] Pass, R., Wee, H.: Black-box constructions of two-party protocols from one-way functions. In: Reingold, O. (ed.) TCC 2009. LNCS, vol. 5444, pp. 403–418. Springer, Heidelberg (2009). https://doi.org/10.1007/978-3-642-00457-5_24

[SCSL11] Shi, E., Chan, T.-H.H., Stefanov, E., Li, M.: Oblivious RAM with $O((\log N)^3)$ worst-case cost. In: Lee, D.H., Wang, X. (eds.) ASIACRYPT 2011. LNCS, vol. 7073, pp. 197–214. Springer, Heidelberg (2011). https://doi.org/10.1007/978-3-642-25385-0_11

[SvDS+13] Stefanov, E., et al.: Path ORAM: an extremely simple oblivious RAM protocol. In: ACM CCS 13 (2013)

[Wee10] Wee, W.: Black-box, round-efficient secure computation via non-malleability amplification. In: 51st FOCS (2010)

[WHC+14] Wang, X.S., Huang, Y., Chan, T.-H.H., Shelat, A., Shi, E.: SCORAM: Oblivious RAM for secure computation. In: ACM CCS (2014)

[Yao82] Yao,A.C.-C.: Protocols for secure computations (extended abstract). In: 23rd FOCS (1982)

[Yao86] Yao, A.C.-C.: How to generate and exchange secrets (extended abstract). In: 27th FOCS (1986)

[ZRE15] Zahur, S., Rosulek, M., Evans, D.: Two Halves Make a Whole. In: Oswald, E., Fischlin, M. (eds.) EUROCRYPT 2015, Part II. LNCS, vol. 9057, pp. 220–250. Springer, Heidelberg (2015). https://doi.org/10.1007/978-3-662-46803-6_8

Universally Composable Accumulators

Foteini Badimtsi[1], Ran Canetti[2], and Sophia Yakoubov[2](✉)

[1] George Mason University, Fairfax, VA, USA
foteini@gmu.edu
[2] Boston University, Boston, MA, USA
{canetti,sonka}@bu.edu

Abstract. Accumulators, first introduced by Benaloh and de Mare (Eurocrypt 1993), are compact representations of arbitrarily large sets and can be used to prove claims of membership or non-membership about the underlying set. They are almost exclusively used as building blocks in real-world complex systems, including anonymous credentials, group signatures and, more recently, anonymous cryptocurrencies. Having rigorous security analysis for such systems is crucial for their adoption and safe use in the real world, but it can turn out to be extremely challenging given their complexity.

In this work, we provide the first universally composable (UC) treatment of cryptographic accumulators. There are many different types of accumulators: some support additions, some support deletions and some support both; and, orthogonally, some support proofs of membership, some support proofs of non-membership, and some support both. Additionally, some accumulators support public verifiability of set operations, and some do not. Our UC definition covers all of these types of accumulators concisely in a single functionality, and captures the two basic security properties of accumulators: correctness and soundness. We then prove the equivalence of our UC definition to standard accumulator definitions. This implies that existing popular accumulator schemes, such as the RSA accumulator, already meet our UC definition, and that the security proofs of existing systems that leverage such accumulators can be significantly simplified.

Finally, we use our UC definition to get simple proofs of security. We build an accumulator in a modular way out of two weaker accumulators (in the style of Baldimtsi et al. (Euro S&P 2017), and we give a simple proof of its UC security. We also show how to simplify the proofs of security of complex systems such as anonymous credentials. Specifically, we show how to extend an anonymous credential system to support revocation by utilizing our results on UC accumulators.

1 Introduction

Accumulators, first introduced by Benaloh and de Mare [5], are compact representations of arbitrarily large sets. Despite being small—ideally constant-size relative to the size of the set they represent!—they enable verification of statements about the set. Given a *membership witness* for some object x together

© Springer Nature Switzerland AG 2020
S. Jarecki (Ed.): CT-RSA 2020, LNCS 12006, pp. 638–666, 2020.
https://doi.org/10.1007/978-3-030-40186-3_27

with the accumulator, anyone can verify that x is in the accumulated set. If the accumulator is a *universal* accumulator [17], it also supports *non-membership* witnesses that can be used to verify that elements are not in the accumulated set. Typically, an accumulator is owned by an entity called an *accumulator manager* who can add elements to (and, if the accumulator is *dynamic* [11], remove elements from) the set. If the accumulator is *strong* [6], even a corrupt accumulator manager cannot forge a proof of (non-)membership.

Many crucial primitives are actually special cases of accumulators. For instance, digital signatures are accumulator schemes, where the signature verification key is the accumulator representing the set of signed messages, and the signatures are membership witnesses. The owner of the signing key is the accumulator manager, and she can add elements to the set by signing them. Of course, she cannot *un*-sign elements (without publishing a revocation list, which is not constant in size), and she cannot produce a proof that a given element has not been signed, so this accumulator is neither dynamic nor universal. She can also always prove the membership of arbitrary elements, so this accumulator is not strong.

Another example of an accumulator is a Merkle hash tree. The tree root is the accumulator representing the set of leaf nodes, and the authenticating paths through the tree are membership witnesses. This accumulator supports both element addition and deletion, but when either of those events occur, all existing witnesses must be updated, requiring total work that is linear in the number of member elements. In many situations, this is prohibitively inefficient. The Merkle hash tree accumulator is strong, because all additions and deletions are publicly verifiable (by means of re-execution). Though the intuitive Merkle hash tree accumulator does not support proofs of non-membership, it can be modified to be universal [6].

One construction of a universal, dynamic (but not strong) accumulator with efficient update algorithms is the RSA accumulator. It is the original accumulator introduced by Benaloh and de Mare [5], augmented with dynamism by Camenisch and Lysyanskaya [11], and with universality by Li, Li and Xue [17]. It is one of the most popular accumulator constructions because of its compactness and efficiency.

Although accumulators are frequently analyzed as stand-alone primitives, they are *almost exclusively used as building blocks* in real-world complex systems, including anonymous credentials [2,9,11,20], group signatures [11] and, more recently, anonymous cryptocurrencies [19]. Having rigorous security analysis for such systems is crucial for their adoption and safe use in the real world, but it can turn out to be extremely challenging given their complexity. When a system consists of multiple building blocks, even if each one of them is proven secure independently, the security analysis of the whole needs to be done from scratch.

Universal Composability. Universally Composable (UC) security [13], addresses this problem. Any protocol that has been shown to be UC-secure will maintain its security properties even when it is used concurrently with other arbitrary protocols as part of a larger system. This allows one to formally argue about the security of a complex scheme in a much simpler and cleaner way, as long as all the protocols used within it have already been proven to be UC-secure.

Showing that a protocol is UC-secure consists of two steps. First, we write out a set of instructions called the *ideal functionality*, which define how we would instantiate the primitive if we had an incorruptible third party to delegate its operation to. Second, we show that any attack an adversary carries out against the protocol, it can also carry out against the ideal functionality. This is done by arguing that for any efficient adversary and environment (which sets all parties' inputs, receives all parties' outputs and additionally receives information from the adversary), there exists a simulator such that the environment cannot tell the difference between interacting with the protocol and adversary, and interacting with the ideal functionality and simulator. This proves that any time it suffices to use our ideal functionality within a larger system, we can replace it with our protocol and the system will remain secure.

The modularity and the strong security guarantees provided by UC suggest that protocols should always be designed and proven secure in the UC framework. However, this is only the case for a small fraction of proposed cryptographic schemes. One roadblock to using the UC framework is that not all commonly used sub-protocols have UC definitions and proofs. Some such sub-protocols have already been defined and analyzed in the UC framework (e.g. digital signatures [13,14], zero-knowledge proofs [10], etc.), but others have not. Cryptographic accumulators are one example of a very common primitive that has never been considered in the context of UC security.

Our Results. In this work, we make the following contributions:

1. We provide the first UC definition (ideal functionality) for cryptographic accumulators. There are many functionality flavors of accumulators: accumulators might support only additions, only deletions or both, and they might support proofs of membership, proofs of non-membership, or both. Our UC definition covers all of these possibilities in a modular way.
2. We then prove the equivalence of our UC definition to standard accumulator security definitions. This implies that existing secure accumulator constructions—such as the RSA accumulator [5,11,17]—are UC secure.
3. Finally, we discuss how our UC definition simplifies the proofs of security for schemes that use accumulators as a building block. First, we build an accumulator out of two weaker accumulators (as in [2], but with stronger privacy properties), and give a simple UC proof of security for that composite accumulator, which we call Braavos'. Then, we consider how UC simplifies proofs of security in more complex systems such as anonymous credentials.

Note that when defining a new ideal functionality, there are two possible scenarios: either existing constructions can be proven to securely realize the new functionality (as with digital signatures [14]), or new constructions must be developed (as with commitment schemes [15]). Our second contribution shows that our accumulator functionality is in the first scenario; popular, existing accumulator constructions already satisfy it. This greatly simplifies the security analysis of existing and future systems that use cryptographic accumulators as a building block.

Informally, two classical properties are considered for cryptographic accumulators. The first is correctness: for every element inside (or outside, for negative accumulators) the accumulated set, an honest witness holder can always prove membership (or non-membership, for negative accumulators) in the set. The second is soundness: for every element outside (or inside, for negative accumulators) the accumulated set, it is infeasible to prove membership (or non-membership, for negative accumulators).

Our ideal functionality is different than most ideal functionalities in that it requires as input from the simulator all of the accumulator algorithms (as previously done in the context of digital signatures [14]). This is actually a very intuitive way to build an ideal functionality, since it only deviates from the algorithm outputs when necessary for correctness or soundness. We explain this in more detail in Sect. 3.

We chose not to incorporate secrecy or privacy requirements into our ideal functionality since they depend on specific applications and vary considerably; thus, they are best made separately, as an additional "layer" on top of the basic correctness guarantees captured in this work. Additionally, privacy-aware constructions often use accumulators and privacy-enhancing mechanisms (such as zero-knowledge proofs) as two separate modules, making the formalization here more conducive to modular analysis. We exemplify this point by sketching a modular analysis of the Baldimtsi *et al.* [2] construction of revocable anonymous credentials from zero knowledge proofs and accumulators.

Outline. We start by setting notation and presenting classical accumulator definitions (but with a twist) in Sect. 2. Then, in Sect. 3, we give an ideal UC functionality for accumulators that encompasses both of the properties listed above. In Sect. 4, we argue that any accumulator that has these properties meets our UC definition, and vice versa. Finally, in Sect. 5 we discuss how our UC definition of accumulators would simplify the security proof of an existing complex system like anonymous credentials.

1.1 Accumulator Applications

To showcase the importance of a UC analysis for cryptographic accumulators we briefly discuss a few of the most interesting systems that use accumulators as a main building block. The security analysis of all the following systems would be much simpler when the underlying accumulator is UC-secure.

Access Control. Authentication of users is vital to most of the electronic systems we use today. It is usually achieved by giving the user a token, or *credential*, that the user must present to prove that she has permission to access a service. A naive construction for an access control system is to maintain a whitelist of authorized users (i.e., by storing their credentials). Whenever a user wants to access the system she just needs to present her credential, and as long as it is on the whitelist, the user will be given access. When a user needs to be revoked, her credential is just removed from the whitelist. Despite its simplicity, such a solution is not practical, since the size of the whitelist will have to grow linearly with the number of participating users.

Cryptographic accumulators enable more efficient access control systems. Instead of keeping a whitelist, an accumulator can be used to maintain the set of authorized users. Whenever a user is given access to the resource, she is given a credential that can be seen as an accumulator membership witness. One possible construction uses the digital signature accumulator together with a blacklist of revoked users, which grows linearly with the number of revocations. This construction is the one most commonly used in public key infrastructures (PKIs), where a certificate revocation list (CRL) that contains the revoked certificates is published periodically. This solution is more efficient, since usually the number of revoked users is much smaller than the number of total users in the system. However, it is still not ideal, since the blacklist can grow to significant size. A dynamic accumulator—which supports both element additions and deletions while remaining small—is a much better solution.

Anonymous Credentials. The inefficiency of the naive whitelist and blacklist solutions for access control becomes even more problematic when anonymity is considered as a goal of the system: if a user wishes to anonymously show that her credential is on a whitelist (or not on a blacklist), then she would have to perform a zero-knowledge proof of membership (or non-membership) which would require cost linear to the size of the corresponding list. Given how expensive zero knowledge proofs usually are, it is important to avoid doing work linear in the number of valid or revoked members in a system. To avoid this inefficiency, *anonymous credentials schemes* (the most prominent solution for anonymous user authentication) make use of dynamic cryptographic accumulators as an essential building block to allow for efficient proofs of membership (and practical user revocation) [9,11,20]. Idemix [12], the leading anonymous credential system by IBM, is such an example of an anonymous credential scheme that employs cryptographic accumulators for user membership management [2].

Cryptocurrencies. As discussed above, when a proof of membership (or non-membership) needs to be done in zero-knowledge, the naive whitelist and blacklist solutions are not realistic. Anonymous cryptocurrencies, like anonymous credentials, require such zero-knowledge proofs. In order to prove that a payment is valid (and is not a double-spend), when a user wishes to spend a coin that she owns, she must first prove that her coin does not belong in a list of previously spent coins. To ensure anonymity, such a proof must be done in zero-knowledge. Universal cryptographic accumulators are used in Zerocoin [19] to maintain the set of spent coins while enabling efficient zero-knowledge proofs of non-membership.

Group Signatures. Accumulators have been suggested for building other cryptographic primitives such as group signatures. In a group signature scheme, the group manager maintains a list of valid group members, and periodically grants (or revokes) membership. There has been much research on the topic of group signatures, and a number of efficient schemes have been proposed. One of the first practical solutions supporting revocation uses cryptographic accumulators for user revocation (Camenisch and Lysyanskaya [11], building on the ACJT group signature scheme [1]).

2   Revisiting Classical Accumulator Definitions

We first discuss accumulator terminology and notation and review accumulator algorithms. Then, in Sect. 2.2, we revise the classical accumulator definitions of security to be more modular, and to support a wider range of accumulator functionalities. These changes make the transition to the UC model more clear and natural.

2.1   Notation and Algorithms

An accumulator is a compact representation of a set $S = \{x_1, \ldots x_n\}$, which can be used to prove statements about the underlying set. Different accumulator types and properties have been considered in the literature. Here, we use the terminology and definitions of Baldimtsi et al. [2], who provide a modular view of accumulator functionalities. Like them, we consider four basic types of accumulators:

- *Static accumulator*: represents a fixed set.
- *Additive accumulator*: supports only addition of elements to the set.
- *Subtractive accumulator*: supports only deletion of elements from the set.
- *Dynamic accumulator* [11]: supports both additions and deletions.

Note that a trivial way to achieve deletions and additions is by re-instantiating the accumulator with the updated set. Although simple, this takes a polynomial amount of time in the number of element additions or deletions which have been performed up until that point. For practical applications a dynamic accumulator should support both additions and deletions in time which is either independent of the number of operations performed altogether, or at least sublinear in this number.

In addition to considering the types of modifications we can make to accumulated sets, we also consider the types of proofs (membership proofs, non-membership proofs, or both) accumulators support.

- *Positive accumulator*: supports membership proofs.
- *Negative accumulator*: supports non-membership proofs.
- *Universal accumulator* [17]: supports both types of proofs.

We consider three types of parties in the accumulator setting. The *accumulator manager* is a special party who is the "owner" of the accumulated set: she creates the accumulator, adds and deletes elements, and creates membership and non-membership witnesses. A *witness holder*, or *user*, is responsible for an accumulated element (i.e. she owns a credential in a system for which an accumulator is used). She is interested in being able to prove the (non-)membership of that element to others, so she maintains the witness for that element, by updating it when/if necessary. Finally, a *verifier* is any third party who is only interested in checking the proofs of (non-)membership (e.g. a gatekeeper checking credentials).

We now describe the algorithms performed by each party, and summarize them in Fig. 1. In Fig. 2 we summarize the notation used to describe the different accumulator algorithm input and output parameters.

Accumulator Manager Algorithms. The following are algorithms performed by the accumulator manager who creates the accumulator and maintains it as required. If the accumulator is additive, she can add elements to it by calling the Update algorithm with $Op = Add$. If the accumulator is subtractive, she can delete elements by calling Update with $Op = Del$. If it is dynamic, she can do both. If the accumulator is positive, the accumulator manager can create membership witnesses by calling WitCreate with $stts = in$ (where $stts$ is a variable representing the *status* of an element, which can be in or out of the set); if it is negative she can create non-membership witnesses by calling WitCreate with $stts = out$. If it is universal, she can do both.

- $Gen(1^\lambda, S_0) \rightarrow (sk, a_0, m_0)$ outputs the accumulator manager's secret key sk, the accumulator a_0 (representing the initial set $S_0 \subseteq D$ of elements in the accumulator, where D is the domain of the accumulator[1]), and an auxiliary value m_0 necessary for the maintenance of the accumulator (i.e. one could think of m_t being the accumulator manager's memory or storage at step t).
- $Update(Op, sk, a_t, m_t, x) \rightarrow (a_{t+1}, m_{t+1}, w_{t+1}^x, upmsg_{t+1})$ updates the accumulator by either adding or deleting an element. If $Op = Add$ it adds the element $x \in D$ to the accumulator and outputs the updated accumulator value a_{t+1} and auxiliary value m_{t+1}, as well as the membership witness w_{t+1}^x for x and an update message $upmsg_{t+1}$, which enables witness holders to bring their witnesses up to date. If $Op = Del$ then it deletes the element x from the accumulator and outputs a_{t+1}, m_{t+1} and $upmsg_{t+1}$ as before, as well as a *non*-membership witness w_{t+1}^x.
- $WitCreate(stts, sk, a_t, m_t, x, (upmsg_1, \ldots, upmsg_t)) \rightarrow w_t^x$ creates a (non-)membership witness. If $stts = in$ it generates a membership witness w_t^x for x, and if $stts = out$ it generates a non-membership witness. (Of course, this algorithm should only succeed in generating a valid membership witness if x is actually in the set, and in generating a non-membership witness if x is not in the set.)

Remark 1. The parameters sk, m and $upmsg$ are optional for some accumulator constructions. For instance, in a Merkle hash tree accumulator there is no secret

---

[1] The allowable S_0 sets vary from accumulator to accumulator. There are accumulators that support only $S_0 = \emptyset$; others support any polynomial-size S_0, and yet others support any S_0 that can be expressed as a polynomial number of ranges.

key sk, and in a digital signature accumulator there is no auxiliary value m or update messages upmsg. Notice that the WitCreate algorithm takes in both the auxiliary value m and the update messages, which seems redundant; after all, the update messages can always be kept as part of m. The reason we provide the algorithm with both arguments is to account for scenarios which do not use any auxiliary storage.

Remark 2. The notion of a public key is absent on the above definition. One can consider the accumulator value a to be the "public key" of the scheme, since it is used for verification. In fact, in the digital signature accumulator construction, the public verification key is equal to the accumulator value. However, unlike a typical public key, the accumulator value can evolve over time.

Witness Holder Algorithms. Witness holders are interested in proving the (non-)membership of certain elements, and thus maintain witnesses for those elements. They use a witness update algorithm WitUp to sync their witnesses with the accumulator when additions or deletions occur.

- WitUp(stts, $x, w_t^x,$ upmsg$_{t+1}$) $\rightarrow w_{t+1}^x$ updates the membership witness for element x (if stts = in) or the non-membership witness if stts = out. The updates use the update messages upmsg, which contain information about changes to the accumulator value (e.g. that a given element was added, what the new accumulator value is, etc.).

Verifier/Third Party Algorithms. The last category of accumulator users are the *verifiers* (or third parties) who are only interested in checking proofs of (non-)membership. They do so by calling the VerStatus algorithm.

- VerStatus(stts, a_t, x, w_t^x) $\rightarrow \phi$ checks whether the membership witness (if stts = in) or the non-membership witness (if stts = out) for element x is valid; it returns $\phi = 1$ if it is, and $\phi = 0$ if it is not.

If the accumulator is *strong* (Definition 4), the accumulator should be secure even against a cheating accumulator manager. That is, all modifications that an accumulator manager makes to the accumulator should be publicly verifiable. The differences in the algorithms are as follows: (a) Gen and Update also output a value v, which essentially is a proof that an accumulator was created/updated correctly. (b) Additional verification algorithms VerGen and VerUpdate can be used to check these proofs.

2.2 Security Definitions

A cryptographic accumulator should satisfy two basic security properties: correctness and soundness. In this section, we review the classical correctness and soundness properties of accumulators (stated, for instance, by Ghosh *et al.* [16]). We revise these classical definitions in several ways.

Algorithm	Inputs	Outputs
Accumulator Manager Algorithms		
Gen	$1^\lambda, S_0$	sk, a_0, m_0, v
Update	$\mathsf{Op}_t, sk, a_t, m_t, x$	$a_{t+1}, m_{t+1}, w_{t+1}^x, \mathsf{upmsg}_{t+1}, \mathsf{v}_{t+1}$
WitCreate	$\mathsf{stts}, sk, a_t, m_t, (\mathsf{upmsg}_1, \ldots, \mathsf{upmsg}_t), x$	w_t^x
Witness Holder Algorithms		
WitUp	$\mathsf{stts}, x, w_t^x, \mathsf{upmsg}_{t+1}$	w_{t+1}^x
Verifier or Third Party Algorithms		
VerStatus	$\mathsf{stts}, a_t, x, w_t^x$	$\phi \in \{0,1\}$
Additional Third Party Algorithms in Strong Accumulators		
VerGen	$1^\lambda, S_0, a_0, \mathsf{v}$	$\phi \in \{0,1\}$
VerUpdate	$\mathsf{Op}_t, a_t, a_{t+1}, x, \mathsf{v}_{t+1}$	$\phi \in \{0,1\}$

Fig. 1. Accumulator Algorithms. In static accumulators, the Update, WitUp and VerUpdate algorithms do not exist. In additive accumulators, Op is required to be equal to Add everywhere. In subtractive accumulators, Op is required to be equal to Del. In dynamic accumulators, Op can be either. In positive accumulators, stts is required to be equal to in everywhere. In negative accumulators, stts is required to be equal to out. In universal accumulators, stts can be either.

λ: The security parameter.

D: The domain of the accumulator (the set of elements that the accumulator can accumulate). Often, D includes all elements (e.g., $\{0,1\}^*$). Sometimes, D is more limited (e.g., primes of a certain size).

sk: The accumulator manager's secret key or trapdoor. (The corresponding public key, if one exists, is not modeled here as it can be considered to be a part of the accumulator itself.)

t: A discrete time / operation counter.

a_t: The accumulator at time t.

m_t: Any auxiliary values which might be necessary for the maintenance of the accumulator. These are typically held by the accumulator manager. Note that while the accumulator itself should be constant (or at least sub-linear) in size, m may be larger.

S_t: The set of elements in the accumulated set at time t. Note that S_0 can be instantiated to be different, based on the initial sets supported by the accumulator in question. Most accumulators assume $S_0 = \emptyset$.

x, y: Elements which might be added to or removed from the accumulator.

w_t^x: A witness that element x is (or is not) in the accumulated set at time t.

$\mathsf{stts} \in \{\mathsf{in}, \mathsf{out}\}$: A flag indicating of whether a given element is in the accumulated set or not.

$\mathsf{Op} \in \{\mathsf{Add}, \mathsf{Del}\}$: A flag indicating of whether a given element is being added or deleted.

upmsg_t: A broadcast message sent (by the accumulator manager, if one exists) at time t to all witness holders immediately after the accumulator has been updated. This message is meant to enable all witness holders to update the witnesses they hold for consistency with the new accumulator. It will often contain the new accumulator a_t, and the nature of the update itself (e.g., "x has been added and witness w_t^x has been produced"). It may also contain other information.

v: A witness that the accumulator a_0 was generated correctly. (Only present in strong accumulators.)

v_t: A witness that the accumulator a_t was updated correctly. (Only present in strong accumulators.)

Fig. 2. Accumulator algorithm input and output parameters (from Baldimtsi *et al.* [2]).

1. We explicitly consider the correctness of the witness update algorithm, which [16] consider only as an efficiency shortcut, and thus exclude from their definitions. Since the update algorithm is used in practice, we believe it is important to include in the formal definitions.

2. We allow the generation of membership witnesses during addition (or non-membership witnesses during deletion) as is commonly done in practice, while [16] only considers the generation of witnesses from a fixed accumulator state.

Because of this, we have two separate notions of correctness—*correctness* and *creation-correctness*.

Correctness Definitions. Definitions 1 and 2 give the correctness requirements for the more general case of a universal dynamic accumulator. Informally, an accumulator is *correct* or *creation-correct* if an up-to-date version of a witness produced by Update or WitCreate, respectively, can be used to verify the (non-)membership of the corresponding element. It is easy to adapt our definition for cases of additive/subtractive or positive/negative. To get a definition for an additive accumulator, restrict all instances of Op to be equal to Add; to get a definition for a subtractive accumulator, restrict all instances of Op to be equal to Del. Similarly, to get a definition for a positive accumulator, restrict all instances of stts to be equal to in; to get a definition for a negative accumulator, restrict all instances of stts to be equal to out.

Definition 1 (Correctness). *A universal dynamic accumulator is* correct *for a given domain D of elements if an up-to-date witness w^x corresponding to value x can always be used to verify the (non-)membership of x in an up-to-date accumulator a. More formally, there exists a negligible function ν in the security parameter λ such that for all:*

- *security parameters λ,*
- *initial sets $S_0 \subseteq D$,*
- *values $x \in D$,*
- *positive integers t polynomial in λ,*
- *positive integers t_x such that $1 \leq t_x \leq t$,*
- *operations $\mathsf{Op} \in \{\mathsf{Add}, \mathsf{Del}\}$ (with stts = in if $\mathsf{Op} = \mathsf{Add}$ and stts = out if $\mathsf{Op} = \mathsf{Del}$),*
- *lists of tuples $[(y_1, \mathsf{Op}_1), \ldots, (y_{t_x-1}, \mathsf{Op}_{t_x-1})]$, $[(y_{t_x+1}, \mathsf{Op}_{t_x+1}), \ldots, (y_t, \mathsf{Op}_t)]$, where*
  - *$y_i \in D$ and $\mathsf{Op}_i \in \{\mathsf{Add}, \mathsf{Del}\}$ for $i \in [1, \ldots, t_x - 1, t_x + 1, \ldots, t]$;*
  - *If $\mathsf{Op} = \mathsf{Add}$, then (x, Del) does not appear in $[(y_{t_x+1}, \mathsf{Op}_{t_x+1}), \ldots, (y_t, \mathsf{Op}_t)]$; and*
  - *If $\mathsf{Op} = \mathsf{Del}$, then (x, Add) does not appear in $[(y_{t_x+1}, \mathsf{Op}_{t_x+1}), \ldots, (y_t, \mathsf{Op}_t)]$,*

The following holds:

$$\Pr \left[\begin{array}{l} (a_0, sk) \leftarrow \mathsf{Gen}(1^\lambda, S_0); \\ (a_i, m_i, w_i^{y_i}, \mathsf{upmsg}_i) \leftarrow \mathsf{Update}(\mathsf{Op}_i, sk, a_{i-1}, m_{i-1}, y_i) \text{ for } i \in [1, \ldots, t_x - 1]; \\ (a_{t_x}, m_{t_x}, w_{t_x}^x, \mathsf{upmsg}_{t_x}) \leftarrow \mathsf{Update}(\mathsf{Op}, sk, a_{t_x-1}, m_{t_x-1}, x); \\ (a_i, m_i, w_i^{y_i}, \mathsf{upmsg}_i) \leftarrow \mathsf{Update}(\mathsf{Op}_i, sk, a_{i-1}, m_{i-1}, y_i) \text{ for } i \in [t_x + 1, \ldots, t]; \\ w_i^x \leftarrow \mathsf{WitUp}(stts, x, w_{i-1}^x, \mathsf{upmsg}_i) \text{ for } i \in [t_x + 1, \ldots, t]) : \\ \mathsf{VerStatus}(stts, a_t, x, w_t^x) = 1 \end{array} \right]$$
$$\geq 1 - \nu(\lambda)$$

Definition 2 (Creation-Correctness). *A universal dynamic accumulator is creation-correct for a given domain D of elements if an up-to-date witness w^x created by the WitCreate algorithm—not by the Update algorithm!—corresponding to value x can always be used to verify the (non-)membership of x in an up-to-date accumulator a.*

More formally, there exists a negligible function ν in the security parameter λ such that for all

- *security parameters λ,*
- *initial sets $S_0 \subseteq D$,*
- *values $x \in D$,*
- *positive integers t polynomial in λ,*
- *positive integers t_x such that $1 \leq t_x \leq t$,*
- *statuses $\mathsf{stts} \in \{\mathsf{in}, \mathsf{out}\}$, and*
- *lists of values $[(y_1, \mathsf{Op}_1), \ldots, (y_t, \mathsf{Op}_t)]$, where*
  - $y_i \in D$ *and* $\mathsf{Op}_i \in \{\mathsf{Add}, \mathsf{Del}\}$ *for* $i \in [1, \ldots, t]$;
  - *If* $\mathsf{stts} = \mathsf{in}$
    - *either (a)* $x \in S_0$, *or (b)* (x, Add) *appears in* $[(y_1, \mathsf{Op}_1), \ldots, (y_{t_x-1}, \mathsf{Op}_{t_x})]$ *and was not followed by* (x, Del), *and*
    - (x, Del) *does not appear in* $[(y_{t_x+1}, \mathsf{Op}_{t_x+1}), \ldots, (y_t, \mathsf{Op}_t)]$;
  - *If* $\mathsf{stts} = \mathsf{out}$
    - *either (a)* $x \notin S_0$, *or (b)* (x, Del) *appears in* $[(y_1, \mathsf{Op}_1), \ldots, (y_{t_x-1}, \mathsf{Op}_{t_x})]$ *and was not followed by* (x, Add), *and*
    - (x, Add) *does not appear in* $[(y_{t_x+1}, \mathsf{Op}_{t_x+1}), \ldots, (y_t, \mathsf{Op}_t)]$;

The following holds:

$$
\Pr\left[
\begin{array}{l}
(a_0, sk) \leftarrow \mathsf{Gen}(1^\lambda, S_0); \\
(a_i, m_i, w_i^{y_i}, \mathsf{upmsg}_i) \leftarrow \mathsf{Update}(\mathsf{Op}_i, sk, a_{i-1}, m_{i-1}, y_i) \text{ for } i \in [1, \ldots, t_x]; \\
w_{t_x}^x \leftarrow \mathsf{WitCreate}(\mathsf{stts}, sk, a_t, m_t, x); \\
(a_i, m_i, w_i^{y_i}, \mathsf{upmsg}_i) \leftarrow \mathsf{Update}(\mathsf{Op}_i, sk, a_{i-1}, m_{i-1}, y_i) \text{ for } i \in [t_x + 1, \ldots, t]; \\
w_i^x \leftarrow \mathsf{WitUp}(\mathsf{stts}, x, w_{i-1}^x, \mathsf{upmsg}_i) \text{ for } i \in [t_x + 1, \ldots, t]) : \\
\mathsf{VerStatus}(\mathsf{stts}, a_t, x, w_t^x) = 1
\end{array}
\right]
$$
$$
\geq 1 - \nu(\lambda)
$$

Soundness Definitions. Classically, *collision-freeness* [4] is the soundness definition for accumulators. Collision-freeness informally requires that for any element not in the accumulated set it should be hard to find a membership witness. For negative and universal accumulators, collision-freeness can be extended to require that for any element in the accumulated set it should be hard to find a non-membership witness. Another formalization of accumulator soundness for universal accumulators is *undeniability* [18], which requires that for any element (regardless of its presence in the accumulated set) it be hard to find *both* a membership witness and a non-membership witness.

In this paper, we choose to use collision-freeness, since undeniability is not meaningful for positive or negative accumulators, which only support proofs of membership or proofs of non-membership but not both. Definition 3 gives the collision-freeness definition for a universal dynamic accumulator. This definition can be converted to work for positive, negative, additive or subtractive accumulators in the usual way (by limiting the possible values of Op or stts).

Definition 3 (Collision-Freeness). *A universal dynamic accumulator is collision-free for a given domain D of elements if it is hard to fabricate a (non-)membership witness w for a value x that is not (or, respectively, is) in the accumulated set. More formally, consider the collision-freeness game described in Fig. 3. An accumulator is collision-free if for any sufficiently large security parameter λ, for any probabilistic polynomial-time adversary $\mathcal{A}_{\mathsf{ColFree}}$, there exists a negligible function ν in the security parameter λ such that the probability that $\mathcal{A}_{\mathsf{ColFree}}$ wins the game is less than $\nu(\lambda)$.*

Non-adaptive Soundness. In the collision-freeness game of Fig. 3, the adversary is able to choose elements to add and delete adaptively. However, this notion of collision-freeness (or *soundness*) is quite strong. In a *non-adaptive*[2] version of the game, the adversary would be required to commit to all elements it intends to add before seeing a_0. Certain accumulators can only be shown to meet non-adaptive soundness. One example of such an accumulator is the CLRSAB accumulator, which was informally introduced as a brief remark by Camenisch and Lysyanskaya [11] and formally described by Baldimtsi et al. [2]. Note that, in particular, a non-adaptively sound accumulator can always be used to accumulate random values, since it makes no difference whether random values are chosen beforehand or on-the-fly.

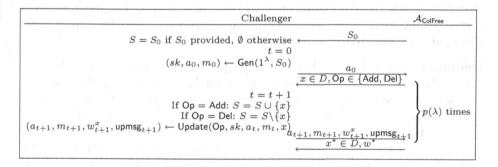

Fig. 3. The collision-freeness game. $\mathcal{A}_{\mathsf{ColFree}}$ wins if $(\mathsf{VerStatus}(\mathsf{in}, a_{t+1}, x^*, w^*) = 1$ and $x^* \notin S)$, or $(\mathsf{VerStatus}(\mathsf{out}, a_{t+1}, x^*, w^*) = 1$ and $x^* \in S)$.

Strength. Typically, accumulators are not required to be secure against cheating accumulator managers, since in many scenarios the entity that manages

---

[2] Note that this does not refer to non-adaptive corruptions, as in the context of MPC; it is not corruptions that are non-adaptive, but the choice of accumulated elements.

the set (and thus the accumulator) is trusted. When that is not the case (e.g. in many blockchain applications), a *strong* accumulator can be used. A strong accumulator provides guarantees even against a cheating accumulator manager. Informally, an accumulator is *strong* if all of the modifications an accumulator manager makes to the accumulator are verifiable.

Definition 4 (Strength). *An accumulator is* strong *for a given domain D of elements if an adversary cannot win the game described in Fig. 3 with non-negligible probability even if it is modified as follows: instead of asking the challenger to run* Gen *and* Update, *the adversary runs them locally and sends the challenger the updated accumulator values together with witnesses* v. *The challenger aborts if* VerGen *or* VerUpdate *return 0.*

We must also ensure the correctness of the VerGen and VerUpdate algorithms.

Definition 5 (Strength Correctness). *Informally, an accumulator has* strength correctness *if* VerGen *and* VerUpdate *run on honestly generated inputs and outputs of* Gen *and* Update *always return 1.*

3   Ideal Functionality for Accumulators

Universally Composable (UC) security, proposed by Canetti [13] and described briefly in Sect. 1, requires a different flavor of definitions than those described in Sect. 2. A UC definition of security for some primitive consists of a set of instructions called an *ideal functionality* which achieves the goals of the primitive when carried out by an incorruptible third party. Informally, to show that a candidate protocol *securely realizes* the ideal functionality, it must be shown that any adversary in a real execution of the protocol can be simulated by a corresponding ideal world adversary in an interaction with the incorruptible third party running the ideal functionality.

Definition 6 ([13, Page 12]). *Let* $\text{exec}_{\Pi,\mathcal{A},\mathcal{Z}}$ *denote the random variable (over the local random choices of all the involved machines) describing the output of environment* $\mathcal{Z}$ *when interacting with adversary* $\mathcal{A}$ *and parties running protocol* Π. *Protocol* Π *UC-emulates ideal functionality* $\mathcal{F}$ *if for any adversary* $\mathcal{A}$ *there exists a simulator* $\mathcal{SIM}$ *such that, for any environment* $\mathcal{Z}$ *the distributions of* $\text{exec}_{\Pi,\mathcal{A},\mathcal{Z}}$ *and* $\text{exec}_{\mathcal{F},\mathcal{SIM},\mathcal{Z}}$ *are indistinguishable. That is, on any input, the probability that* $\mathcal{Z}$ *outputs 1 after interacting with* $\mathcal{A}$ *and parties running* Π *differs by at most a negligible amount from the probability that* $\mathcal{Z}$ *outputs 1 after interacting with* $\mathcal{SIM}$ *and* $\mathcal{F}$.

In this section we present our ideal functionality $\mathcal{F}_{\text{ACC}}$ for an accumulator.

Like [14], we discuss several candidate ideal functionalities in order to build up the intuition for how we arrived at the ideal functionality described in Figs. 4 and 5.

First Attempt. A naive first attempt at an accumulator functionality might ignore the accumulator and witness objects altogether, instead functioning as a simple set manager. It would allow the accumulator manager to add and remove elements from the set, and answer 'yes' or 'no' to membership (or non-membership) queries. These queries could optionally be parametrized by timestamps, so as to allow queries about all states of the set, past and present. However, this simple ideal functionality definition fails to support one of the basic modular operations of accumulators. Recall that an accumulator is an object that evolves by time, i.e. at time t it might represent a different set from what it used to represent at time t'. Thus, if we do not consider explicit accumulator objects, then it is impossible to talk about committing to a given set by committing to an accumulator value at a specific time.

Second Attempt - Explicitly Modeling Accumulator Values. A second attempt might be to add explicit accumulator values, without modeling witnesses. So, a membership query would now have the form, 'is this element a (non-)member under this accumulator value?'. However, the absence of explicit witness objects also limits the modular use of accumulators significantly. Specifically, not having explicit witness objects would not work when the ability to verify the (non)membership of certain elements should be secret-shared or otherwise restricted. (For instance, perhaps I should be able to demonstrate my membership in some organization - such as the gym - but any third party shouldn't be able to test my membership without my help, because that would be a violation of my privacy.) Adding these privacy features to an accumulator system would require re-designing and re-proving the accumulator system from scratch if witness objects were not part of the ideal functionality. If witness and accumulator objects are modeled explicitly, however, existing accumulator systems can simply be combined with existing off-the-shelf primitives such as secret sharing, encryption, or commitment. In other words, having the functionality give binary answers to membership queries is over-idealization; it is a good way to model accumulators on their own, but it does not lend itself to use by other protocols that need actual accumulator and witness values to operate.

Final Attempt. Our ideal functionality for accumulators $\mathcal{F}_{\mathsf{ACC}}$ is described in Figs. 4 and 5 and provides interfaces for all of the algorithms in Fig. 1. (Note that in the functionality the accumulator manager interfaces ignore all queries for which the querier's identity is not encoded in the functionality session id sid.)

We loosely base $\mathcal{F}_{\mathsf{ACC}}$ on the ideal functionality for digital signatures described by Canetti [14]. Canetti actually gave two different functionalities for digital signatures, which we recall for completeness in Appendix A. The first one (Fig. 7) asks the ideal world adversary for a *verification key*; while the second (Fig. 8) asks the ideal world adversary for a *verification algorithm*. Similarly, Camenisch et al. [7] give functionalities for signatures, non-interactive zero knowledge proofs and for commitments that are explicitly parameterized by the protocol algorithms. Using a given deterministic signature verification algorithm, rather than allowing the ideal world adversary to make each verification decision, achieves two goals:

- It forces verification decisions to be consistent.

– It makes combining UC signatures and zero knowledge proofs of signature knowledge in a black box way simpler.

For these reasons, we chose to define our $\mathcal{F}_{ACC}$ to receive explicit algorithms from the ideal world adversary. Thus, instead of asking the ideal world adversary to provide updated accumulator states, witnesses and verification decisions, our ideal world adversary provides *all* accumulator algorithms to the functionality (Step 1e in Fig. 4).[3] This is a very intuitive way to define an ideal functionality: it explicitly uses the accumulator algorithms except where it needs to modify their behavior to match what is demanded by correctness or soundness. If an ideal execution (that uses the ideal functionality) is indistinguishable from a real execution, that means that the algorithms' behavior did not need any modification.

Just like in the context of digital signatures, if the algorithms are modeled explicitly, usage within multi-party computation (MPC) protocols or in larger zero-knowledge-based systems such as Zcash can be done in a modular way, using existing components.

In addition to the benefits listed above, this also allows us more flexibility to add privacy features to the ideal functionality, as discussed in Sect. 3.3.

Remark 3. Note that inputs belonging to anyone but the accumulator manager ($\mathcal{AM}$) can be misinformed (just like parties are frequently misinformed about verification keys in signature schemes, in the absence of a PKI). In order to capture such cases, we require parties to provide all inputs to witness holder and third party algorithms, instead of having some inputs, such as the accumulator value, implicitly stored by the ideal functionality.

The ideal functionality described in Figs. 4 and 5 is really an entire "menu" of functionalities covering all different types of accumulators: additive, subtractive, dynamic, positive, negative and universal and finally strong accumulators. More explicitly, by default, if all of the text (except for the text colored by pink) is considered, the ideal functionality describes a dynamic, universal accumulator. By restricting Op to be only Add or only Del we could make it additive or subtractive instead of dynamic; by restricting stts to be only in or only out we could make it positive or negative instead of universal. Figure 4 describes the ideal functionality interfaces for the accumulator manager and witness holders; Fig. 5 describes the interfaces for third parties.

We use color coding to describe different types of accumulators within the same functionality. If the ideal functionality is limited to the black text, it describes a positive additive accumulator. Actions that are present only in subtractive accumulators are colored green. Actions that are present only in negative accumulators are colored blue. Finally, actions that are present only in strong accumulators are colored pink; actions *not* present in strong accumulators are colored orange.

---

[3] These algorithms will, among other things, check that elements being added are in the domain D of the accumulator in question.

1. GEN: Upon getting (GEN, sid, S_0) as first activation from $\mathcal{AM}$ ...
   (a) Initialize an operation counter $t = 0$.
   (b) Initialize an empty list **A**. This list will be used to keep track of all accumulator states.
   (c) Initialize an empty map **S**, and set $\mathbf{S}[0] = S_0$. (If S_0 was not provided, use $\emptyset$.) This map will be used to map operation counters to current accumulated sets.
   (d) Send (GEN, sid) to Adversary $\mathcal{A}_{\mathsf{Ideal}}$.
   (e) Get (ALGORITHMS, sid, (Gen, Update, WitCreate, WitUp, VerStatus, VerGen, VerUpdate)) from Adversary $\mathcal{A}_{\mathsf{Ideal}}$. This includes all of the accumulator algorithms; their expected input output behavior is described in Figure 1. All of them should be polynomial-time; we restrict the verification algorithms VerStatus, VerGen, VerUpdate to be deterministic.
   (f) Run $(sk, a_0, m_0, \mathsf{v}) \leftarrow \mathsf{Gen}(1^\lambda, S_0)$.
   (g) Verify that $\mathsf{VerGen}(S_0, a_0, \mathsf{v}) = 1$. If not, output $\perp$ to $\mathcal{AM}$ and halt. (This ensures strength.) Otherwise, continue.
   (h) Store sk, m_0; add a_0 to **A**.
   (i) Output (ALGORITHMS, sid, S_0, (Gen, Update, WitCreate, WitUp, VerStatus, VerGen, VerUpdate)) to $\mathcal{AM}$.
2. UPDATE: Upon getting (UPDATE, sid, Op, x) from $\mathcal{AM}$ ...
   (a) Increment the operation counter: $t = t + 1$.
   (b) Set $\mathbf{S}[t] = \mathbf{S}[t-1]$.
   (c) Run $(a_t, m_t, w_t^x, \mathsf{upmsg}_t, \mathsf{v}_t) \leftarrow \mathsf{Update}(\mathsf{Op}, sk, a_{t-1}, m_{t-1}, x)$.
   (d) If Op = Add:
       i. Verify that $\mathsf{VerStatus}(\mathsf{in}, a, x, w_t) = 1$. If not, output $\perp$ to $\mathcal{AM}$ and halt. (This ensures correctness.) Otherwise, continue.
       ii. If $x \notin \mathbf{S}[t]$, add x to $\mathbf{S}[t]$.
   (e) If Op = Del:
       i. Verify that $\mathsf{VerStatus}(\mathsf{out}, a, x, w_t) = 1$. If not, output $\perp$ to $\mathcal{AM}$ and halt. (This ensures negative correctness.) Otherwise, continue.
       ii. If $x \in \mathbf{S}[t]$, remove x from $\mathbf{S}[t]$.
   (f) Verify that $\mathsf{VerUpdate}(\mathsf{Op}, a_{t-1}, a_t, x, \mathsf{v}_t) = 1$. If not, output $\perp$ to $\mathcal{AM}$ and halt. (This ensures strength.) Otherwise, continue.
   (g) Store m_t, upmsg_t; add a_t to **A**.
   (h) Output (UPDATE, sid, Op, $a_t, x, w_t, \mathsf{upmsg}_t$) to $\mathcal{AM}$.
3. WITCREATE: Upon getting (WITCREATE, sid, stts, x) from $\mathcal{AM}$ ...
   (a) Run $w \leftarrow \mathsf{WitCreate}(\mathsf{stts}, sk, a_t, m_t, x, (\mathsf{upmsg}_1, \ldots, \mathsf{upmsg}_t))$
   (b) If stts = in:
       If $x \in \mathbf{S}[t]$, verify that $\mathsf{VerStatus}(\mathsf{in}, a_t, x, w) = 1$. If not, output $\perp$ to $\mathcal{AM}$ and halt. (This ensures creation-correctness.) Otherwise, continue.
   (c) If stts = out:
       If $x \notin \mathbf{S}[t]$, verify that $\mathsf{VerStatus}(\mathsf{out}, a_t, x, w) = 1$. If not, output $\perp$ to $\mathcal{AM}$ and halt. (This ensures negative-creation-correctness.) Otherwise, continue.
   (d) Output (WITNESS, sid, stts, x, w) to $\mathcal{AM}$.
4. WITUP: Upon getting (WITUP, sid, stts, $a_{old}, a_{new}, x, w_{old}, (\mathsf{upmsg}_{old+1}, \ldots, \mathsf{upmsg}_{new})$) from any party $\mathcal{H}$ ...
   (a) Run $w_{new} \leftarrow \mathsf{WitUp}(\mathsf{stts}, x, w_{old}, (\mathsf{upmsg}_{old+1}, \ldots, \mathsf{upmsg}_{new}))$
   (b) If $a_{old} \in \mathbf{A}$, $a_{new} \in \mathbf{A}$ and $old < new$:
       i. If stts = in, $\mathsf{VerStatus}(\mathsf{in}, a_{old}, x, w_{old}) = 1$, $x \in \mathbf{S}[t]$ for $t \in [old, \ldots, new]$, $\mathsf{upmsg}_{old+1}, \ldots, \mathsf{upmsg}_{new}$ match the stored values and $\mathsf{VerStatus}(\mathsf{in}, a_{new}, x, w_{new}) = 0$, output $\perp$ to $\mathcal{P}$ and halt. (This ensures correctness.) Otherwise, continue.
       ii. If stts = out, $\mathsf{VerStatus}(\mathsf{out}, a_{old}, x, w_{old}) = 1$, $x \notin \mathbf{S}[t]$ for $t \in [old, \ldots, new]$, $\mathsf{upmsg}_{old+1}, \ldots, \mathsf{upmsg}_{new}$ match the stored values and $\mathsf{VerStatus}(\mathsf{out}, a_{new}, x, w_{new}) = 0$, output $\perp$ to $\mathcal{P}$ and halt. (This ensures negative correctness.) Otherwise, continue.
   (c) Output (UPDATEDWITNESS, sid, stts, $a_{old}, a_{new}, x, w_{old}, (\mathsf{upmsg}_{old+1}, \ldots, \mathsf{upmsg}_{new}), w_{new}$) to $\mathcal{H}$.

Fig. 4. Ideal functionality $\mathcal{F}_{\mathsf{ACC}}$ for accumulators with explicit verification algorithm (Color figure online)

We use $\mathcal{F}_{\mathsf{ACC}}$ to refer to the universal dynamic accumulator functionality. We add Add, Del, in and out to the subscript to denote additive, subtractive, positive and negative accumulators, respectively. We add other parameters to the subscript (e.g. 'STRONG') to denote other properties.

3.1 Modeling Decentralized Management

If the accumulator is strong, it may make sense to allow anyone to perform an accumulator update, instead of restricting the ability to perform such updates to the accumulator manager. We model this by making a few changes to the functionality. First, the GEN, UPDATE and WITCREATE interfaces of the ideal

1. VERSTATUS: Upon getting (VERSTATUS, sid, stts, a, VerStatus', x, w) from any party $\mathcal{P}$ ...
   (a) If VerStatus' = VerStatus and there exists a t such that $a = a_t \in \mathbf{A}$:
      i. Let t be the largest such number.
      ii. If stts = in:
         A. If $\mathcal{AM}$ not corrupted, $x \notin \mathbf{S}[t]$ and VerStatus(in, a_t, x, w) = 1, output $\perp$ to $\mathcal{P}$ and halt. (This ensures collision-freeness.) Otherwise, continue.
         B. Set ϕ = VerStatus(in, a_t, x, w).
      iii. If stts = out:
         A. If $\mathcal{AM}$ not corrupted, $x \in \mathbf{S}[t]$ and VerStatus(out, a_t, x, w) = 1, output $\perp$ to $\mathcal{P}$ and halt. (This ensures negative collision-freeness.) Otherwise, continue.
         B. Set ϕ = VerStatus(out, a_t, x, w).
   (b) Otherwise, set ϕ = VerStatus'(stts, a, x, w).
   (c) Output (VERIFIED, sid, stts, a, VerStatus', x, w, ϕ) to $\mathcal{P}$.
2. VERGEN: Upon getting (VERGEN, sid, S, a, v, VerGen') from any party $\mathcal{P}$ ...
   (a) Set ϕ = VerGen'(S, a, v).
   (b) Output (VERIFIED, sid, S, a, v, VerGen', ϕ) to $\mathcal{P}$.
3. VERUPDATE: Upon getting (VERUPDATE, sid, Op, a, a', x, v_t, VerUpdate') from any party $\mathcal{P}$ ...
   (a) Set ϕ = VerUpdate'(Op, a, a', x, v_t).
   (b) Output (VERIFIED, sid, Op, a, a', x, v_t, VerUpdate', ϕ) to $\mathcal{P}$.

Fig. 5. Ideal functionality $\mathcal{F}_{\mathsf{ACC}}$ interfaces for third parties (Color figure online)

functionality no longer only accept invocations by $\mathcal{AM}$. Additionally, instead of having a strict ordering of update operations, we might allow parties to perform an update on any accumulator state, resulting in a tree of states. The functionality will be modified to perform the appropriate checks and record-keeping.

3.2 Modeling Non-adaptive Soundness

We model non-adaptive soundness (Sect. 2.2) by making two simple changes to the ideal functionality. First, when sending the GEN command to the ideal functionality (in Step 1 of Fig. 4), the accumulator manager $\mathcal{AM}$ is expected to provide a set of all elements that will ever be added or deleted. (This can be done e.g. by providing a PRF seed.) Second, if even one element outside of that set is added or deleted, nothing is guaranteed; the functionality simply runs the algorithms it was given, without performing any checks.

3.3 Adding Privacy Properties

Our ideal functionality as stated in Figs. 4 and 5 does not make any attempt to hide anything about the accumulated set from any accumulator user. In this section, we discuss how we add such privacy properties to the ideal functionality.

Add-Delete Unlinkability. In certain scenarios it is desirable that an adversary should not be able to link an addition of an element to a deletion of the same element later on. Such a property is relevant when accumulators are used as an anonymous revocation mechanism where the revocation information should not allow anyone to determine that the user revoked just now was the user who joined two hours ago, and not the user who joined four hours ago [2]. We do not formally model add-delete unlinkability; instead, we define a stronger property which we call *hiding update-message (HUM)*.

Hiding Update-Message (HUM). Informally, an accumulator is *hiding update-message*, or *HUM*, if given all of the update messages produced in the course of an execution, it is impossible to tell whether one specific update message corresponds to the addition/deletion of element x_0 or element x_1 for $x_0, x_1 \in D$.

We can incorporate HUM into our ideal functionality by placing limitations on the algorithm Update provided by the ideal world adversary. We require Update to consist of two sub-algorithms: one sub-algorithm—Update$_1$—which receives no input at all except for randomness, and produces the update message; and a second sub-algorithm—Update$_2$—which can receive state from Update$_1$ as well as all of the other inputs typically provided to Update, and produces all the other outputs of Update. This forces update messages to reveal nothing about the added/deleted element.

Note that this modification is very strong, since it forces the update messages to *statistically* hide the elements; constructions where the elements are only computationally hidden would not meet this definition. This modification trivially implies the add-delete unlinkability property described above, since update messages now contain no information at all about the elements.

Remark 4. We clearly need to withhold x from Update$_1$, in order to guarantee that the update message does not reveal x. However, we could consider allowing Update$_1$ to see the other inputs to Update. This would not work because if we give Update$_1$ access to the accumulator a or the auxiliary value m, then the update message it produces might contain arbitrary information about the set of elements accumulated prior to the current operation. In particular, the update message might reveal which elements were added/deleted previously, breaking the HUM property.

Zero-Knowledge. Ghosh *et al.* [16] define the notion of a *zero-knowledge accumulator*, which requires that accumulator and witness values reveal nothing about the accumulated set (other than the element to which the witness corresponds). We can incorporate ZK by placing limitations on the Update and WitCreate algorithms provided by the ideal world adversary, just like we did for the HUM property. We can require each algorithm to consist of two sub-algorithms: one which does not require any set-dependent inputs and produces the accumulator and witness values (as necessary), and a second sub-algorithm (which can receive state from the first) which produces all other values.

3.4 Discussion: Incorrect Accumulator and Witness Values

If an incorrect accumulator value (or verification algorithm VerStatus$'$) is provided to the verification interface, we allow the party making the query to control the verification verdict, via VerStatus$'$. This models the fact that any party can issue verification queries for accumulator values of their choice—for instance, for accumulator values which they may have generated themselves, and for which they control the accumulated set.

If an incorrect witness for a member element is provided to the verification interface, we allow the ideal world adversary to control the verification verdict (via the algorithm VerStatus it provides during the generation phase). This models the fact that we only require the ideal world adversary to be unable to come up with a witness for a *non*-member (or a non-membership witness for a member); we do not require that an adversary be unable to come up with a witness for a member (or a non-membership witness for a non-member). For instance, it may be possible to modify valid witnesses to obtain other witnesses for the same element. Note also that multiple witnesses can be generated for the same element by means of the WitCreate interface.

4   Equivalence Argument

Like Canetti [14], we prove that satisfying our UC definition for dynamic universal accumulators is the same as satisfying the classical definition.[4]

Theorem 1. *Let* $\Pi_{ACC} = $ (Gen, Update, WitCreate, WitUp, VerStatus) *be a universal dynamic accumulator scheme, and let* VerStatus *be deterministic. Then* Π_{ACC} *securely realizes* $\mathcal{F}_{ACC}$ *if and only if* Π_{ACC} *satisfies Definitions 1, 2 and 3.*

Proof. Our proof follows the structure of the proof of Canetti [14] (pages 12–14).

1. We start by assuming that Π_{ACC} does not satisfy Definitions 1, 2 and 3. We then show that Π_{ACC} also does not securely realize $\mathcal{F}_{ACC}$. To do this, we build an environment $\mathcal{Z}$ and an adversary $\mathcal{A}_{Real}$ such that for any simulator $\mathcal{SIM}$, $\mathcal{Z}$ can distinguish between interacting with $\mathcal{A}_{Real}$ and Π_{ACC}, and interacting with $\mathcal{SIM}$ and $\mathcal{F}_{ACC}$. Like the environment of Canetti [14], our environment does not corrupt any parties, and does not send any messages to the adversary. Because all accumulator operations are non-interactive, meaning that they are run locally by individual parties, no messages are exchanged in the real world. So, the adversary $\mathcal{A}_{Real}$ is never activated.

   (a) Assume Π_{ACC} is not correct (i.e. does not satisfy Definition 1). That is, there exists a security parameter λ, an initial set $S_0 \subseteq D$, a value $x \in D$, an operation $Op \in \{Add, Del\}$ (with $stts = $ in if $Op = Add$ and $stts = $ out if $Op = Del$) and a list of values $[(y_1, Op_1), \ldots, (y_{t_x-1}, Op_{t_x-1})]$, $[(y_{t_x+1}, Op_{t_x+1}), \ldots, (y_t, Op_t)]$, where

       - $y_i \in D$ and $Op_i \in \{Add, Del\}$ for $i \in [1, \ldots, t_x - 1, t_x + 1, \ldots, t]$;
       - If $Op = Add$, then (x, Del) does not appear in $[(y_{t_x+1}, Op_{t_x+1}), \ldots, (y_t, Op_t)]$; and
       - If $Op = Del$, then (x, Add) does not appear in $[(y_{t_x+1}, Op_{t_x+1}), \ldots, (y_t, Op_t)]$,

---

[4] This proof also implies that satisfying our UC definition for additive or subtractive, positive or negative accumulators is the same as satisfying the classical definition; however, it does not imply anything for strong accumulators. We leave that up to future work.

such that with non-negligible probability, the honestly-produced witness for x against accumulator a_t will not verify.

Our environment $\mathcal{Z}$ will send the following commands to some party $\mathcal{AM}$, where sid encodes the identity of $\mathcal{AM}$:

- (GEN, sid, S_0),
- $(\mathsf{UPDATE}, sid, \mathsf{Op}_1, y_1), \ldots, (\mathsf{UPDATE}, sid, \mathsf{Op}_{t_x-1}, y_{t_x-1})$,
- $(\mathsf{UPDATE}, sid, \mathsf{Op}, x)$, and
- $(\mathsf{UPDATE}, sid, \mathsf{Op}_{t_x+1}, y_{t_x+1}), \ldots, (\mathsf{UPDATE}, sid, \mathsf{Op}_t, y_t)$.

As a result of the third step, $\mathcal{Z}$ will learn a_{t_x} and $w_{t_x}^x$. As a result of the fourth step, $\mathcal{Z}$ will learn a_t and $t - t_x$ update messages ($\mathsf{upmsg}_{t_x+1}, \ldots,$ upmsg_t). It then sends $(\mathsf{WITUP}, \mathsf{stts}, sid, a_{t_x}, a_t, x, w_{t_x}^x, (\mathsf{upmsg}_{t_x+1}, \ldots,$ $\mathsf{upmsg}_t))$ to some party $\mathcal{H}$ (where possibly $\mathcal{H} = \mathcal{AM}$), and receives w_t^x back. Finally, it sends $(\mathsf{VERSTATUS}, sid, \mathsf{stts}, a_t, \mathsf{VerStatus}' = \mathsf{VerStatus}(\cdot, \cdot, \cdot, \cdot), x, w_t^x)$ to some party $\mathcal{P}$ (which may be the same party or not). $\mathcal{Z}$ outputs the returned verdict ϕ.

In the real world, ϕ will be 0 with non-negligible probability according to our assumption.

In the ideal world, if no error messages are returned, ϕ will always be 1, since in WitUp, we will always hit Item 4(b)i or 4(b)ii of Fig. 4, and there the first three listed conditions will be satisfied.

(b) Assume Π_{ACC} is not creation-correct (i.e. does not satisfy Definition 2). $\mathcal{Z}$ can distinguish between the real and ideal worlds in a way very similar to that described above.

(c) Assume Π_{ACC} is not collision-free (i.e. does not satisfy Definition 3). That is, there exists an adversary $\mathcal{A}_{\mathsf{ColFree}}$ that can forge a (non-) membership witness for a non-member (or member, respectively) x with non-negligible probability. Our $\mathcal{Z}$ will use $\mathcal{A}_{\mathsf{ColFree}}$ to generate inputs for $\mathcal{AM}$. Having received x^*, w^* from $\mathcal{A}_{\mathsf{ColFree}}$, $\mathcal{Z}$ will compute ϕ_{in} by calling $(\mathsf{VERSTATUS}, sid, \mathsf{in}, a_t, x^*, w^*)$, and ϕ_{out} by calling $(\mathsf{VERSTATUS}, sid, \mathsf{out}, a_t, x^*, w^*)$. $\mathcal{Z}$ will then output 1 if x^* was in the accumulated set and $\phi_{out} = 1$ or if x^* was not in the accumulated set and $\phi_{in} = 1$, and will output 0 otherwise.

In the real world, if $\mathcal{A}_{\mathsf{ColFree}}$ met the collision-freeness win conditions, $\mathcal{Z}$ will output 1 with non-negligible probability according to our assumption. In the ideal world, both ϕ_{in} and ϕ_{out} will always be 0 or $\bot$, since we will satisfy the first two conditions in Item 1(a)iiA (or Item 1(a)iiiA, if $\mathsf{stts} = \mathsf{out}$) of VERSTATUS in Fig. 5. If the third condition is satisfied too, $\bot$ will be returned. If it is not, 0 will be returned, as a result of Item 1(a)iiB (or Item 1(a)iiiB, if $\mathsf{stts} = \mathsf{out}$) in Fig. 5.

2. We now prove the other direction. Assume that Π_{ACC} does not securely realize $\mathcal{F}_{\mathsf{ACC}}$. That is, there exists an adversary $\mathcal{A}_{\mathsf{Real}}$ such that for any simulator $\mathcal{SIM}$, there exists an environment $\mathcal{Z}$ that can distinguish between interacting with $\mathcal{A}_{\mathsf{Real}}$ and Π_{ACC}, and interacting with $\mathcal{SIM}$ and $\mathcal{F}_{\mathsf{ACC}}$. We show that if that is the case, Π_{ACC} must also violate Definitions 1, 2 or 3. We pick a simulator $\mathcal{SIM}$ that proceeds as follows, running an internal copy of $\mathcal{A}_{\mathsf{Real}}$:

- Inputs from $\mathcal{Z}$ is forwarded to $\mathcal{A}_{\text{Real}}$. Outputs from $\mathcal{A}_{\text{Real}}$ is forwarded to $\mathcal{Z}$.
- $\mathcal{SIM}$ handles corruptions according to the standard corruption model [13].
- Upon receiving (GEN, sid) from $\mathcal{F}_{\text{ACC}}$, $\mathcal{SIM}$ sends the actual accumulator algorithms back as (GEN, sid, (Gen, Update, WitCreate, WitUp, VerStatus)).

This simulator guarantees that the real and ideal worlds will be distributed identically, *unless* one of the following causes $\mathcal{F}_{\text{ACC}}$ to return $\bot$:

- In Update, $\mathcal{F}_{\text{ACC}}$ hits Item 2(d)i or 2(e)i of Fig. 4. If this happens, correctness (Definition 1) is violated.
- In WitCreate, $\mathcal{F}_{\text{ACC}}$ hits Item 3b or 3c of Fig. 4. If this happens, creation-correctness (Definition 2) is violated.
- In VerStatus, $\mathcal{F}_{\text{ACC}}$ hits Item 1(a)iiA or 1(a)iiiA of Fig. 5. If this happens, collision-freeness (Definition 3) is violated.
- In WitUp, $\mathcal{F}_{\text{ACC}}$ hits Item 4(b)i or 4(b)ii of Fig. 4. If this happens, either correctness or creation-correctness is violated.

In order for $\mathcal{Z}$ to distinguish between the real and ideal worlds, one of the above must happen with non-negligible probability, and thus either Definitions 1, 2 or 3 must be violated with non-negligible probability.

We can modify the theorem and proof to also prove equivalence between classical and UC definitions for strong accumulators.

Corollary 1. *Let* $\Pi_{\text{ACC}} =$ (Gen, Update, WitCreate, WitUp, VerStatus, VerGen, VerUpdate) *be a strong universal dynamic accumulator scheme, and let* VerStatus, VerGen *and* VerUpdate *be deterministic. Then* Π_{ACC} *securely realizes* $\mathcal{F}_{\text{ACC},STRONG}$ *if and only if* Π_{ACC} *satisfies Definitions 1, 2 and 4.*

Proof. The proof is very similar to that of Theorem 1 above, with a few changes. The changes are in Steps 1c and 2 of the proof.

In Step 1c of the proof above, instead of calling $\mathcal{A}_{\text{ColFree}}$, we call $\mathcal{A}_{\text{Strength}}$ which runs Gen and Update itself. The environment $\mathcal{Z}$ computes its output exactly as before. In the ideal world, both ϕ_{in} and ϕ_{out} will always be 0 or $\bot$, since we will satisfy the first condition in Item 1(a)iiA (or Item 1(a)iiiA, if stts = out) of VERSTATUS (ignoring the condition that $\mathcal{AM}$ is not corrupted, which does not apply for a strong accumulator). If the third condition is satisfied too, $\bot$ will be returned. If it is not, 0 will be returned, as a result of Item 1(a)iiB (or 1(a)iiiB, if stts = out) of Fig. 5.

In Step 2 of the proof above, $\mathcal{SIM}$ includes VerGen and VerUpdate in the list of algorithms it sends to the ideal functionality. Then, in the list of things that might cause $\mathcal{F}_{\text{ACC},STRONG}$ to return $\bot$, we replace the third bullet with the following:

- In VerStatus, $\mathcal{F}_{\text{ACC}}$ hits Item 1(a)iiA or 1(a)iiiA of Fig. 5. If this happens, strength (Definition 4) is violated.

We also add the following:

- In Gen, $\mathcal{F}_{ACC,STRONG}$ returns $\bot$ at Item 1g of Fig. 4. If this happens, strength correctness (Definition 5) is violated.
- In Update, $\mathcal{F}_{ACC,STRONG}$ returns $\bot$ at Item 2f of Fig. 4. If this happens, strength correctness (Definition 5) is violated.

5   Demonstrations of Composition

We now present two examples of accumulator composition to showcase the convenience of having UC secure accumulators.

5.1   Accumulator Composition: Braavos

Baldimtsi *et al.* [2] show how one can build accumulators with certain properties by composing other types of (potentially weaker) accumulators. Among other examples, Baldimtsi *et al.* build the *Braavos* accumulator. We present a modified version of Braavos, which we call Braavos'. Braavos' is a *hiding update-message (HUM)* dynamic accumulator as described in Sect. 3.3. We describe Braavos' in Fig. 6.

Just like Braavos, Braavos' leverages the following two weaker accumulators:

1. SIG: A positive (but not dynamic) additive accumulator, in the form of a digital signature scheme. Note that this accumulator does not have any update messages (and we thus omit update messages from its inputs and outputs).
2. CLRSAB: A non-adaptively-sound negative additive accumulator. One example of such an accumulator is the CLRSAB construction[5], informally introduced as a brief remark by Camenisch and Lysyanskaya [11] and formally described by Baldimtsi *et al.* [2].

Informally, Braavos' works as follows. When a new element x is added, a random value r_x is chosen to correspond to it, and the pair (x, r_x) is accumulated in SIG. Since we use a digital signature scheme, no update message is sent. A proof of membership for x consists of the value r_x, a proof of membership of (x, r_x) in SIG (which is simply a digital signature), and a proof of non-membership of r_x in CLRSAB. Then, when the element x is deleted, r_x is added to CLRSAB (so a proof of non-membership of r_x in CLRSAB can no longer be produced). Next time x is added, a fresh random value is chosen, and so forth.

Unlike Braavos', Braavos [2] uses the same random value every time a given element is re-added, instead of choosing fresh random values. This has the advantage of saving on accumulator manager storage requirements. However, it has the disadvantage that deletions of the same element can all be linked to one another, since the same random value is present in all of the associated update

---

[5] The CLRSAB accumulator is actually universal and dynamic, but we only require it to be negative and additive.

messages. This violates the HUM property[6] (but not the add-delete unlinkability property, which is the one Baldimtsi *et al.* require).

Braavos' is obviously HUM, since it (a) has empty update messages for additions, and (b) has update messages for deletions that are completely independent of the element being deleted. Intuitively, it is secure because if an element was never added then no signature on it exists, and every time an element x is removed, all random values r_x that have been signed with x are in the CLRSAB accumulator, so no proof of non-membership for any such r_x can be produced.

More formally, let $\mathcal{F}_{\mathsf{ACC},\mathsf{in},HUM}$ be our accumulator functionality $\mathcal{F}_{\mathsf{ACC}}$ for a dynamic, positive, HUM accumulator. That is, $\mathcal{F}_{\mathsf{ACC},\mathsf{in},HUM}$ is $\mathcal{F}_{\mathsf{ACC}}$ restricted to $\mathsf{stts} = \mathsf{in}$, and requiring the simulator to provide Update in two parts, as necessary for HUM (described in Sect. 3.3). Similarly, let $\mathcal{F}_{\mathsf{ACC},\mathsf{in},\mathsf{Add}}$ be our accumulator functionality $\mathcal{F}_{\mathsf{ACC}}$ for a positive additive accumulator, and let $\mathcal{F}_{\mathsf{ACC},\mathsf{out},\mathsf{Add},NA}$ be our accumulator functionality $\mathcal{F}_{\mathsf{ACC}}$ for a negative additive accumulator that is non-adaptively sound (Sect. 3.2).

Theorem 2. *The Braavos' accumulator described in Fig. 6 securely realizes* $\mathcal{F}_{\mathsf{ACC},\mathsf{in},HUM}$ *as long as* SIG *securely realizes* $\mathcal{F}_{\mathsf{ACC},\mathsf{in},\mathsf{Add}}$ *with no update messages, and* CLRSAB *securely realizes* $\mathcal{F}_{\mathsf{ACC},\mathsf{out},\mathsf{Add},NA}$.

We can prove Theorem 2 very simply using the fact that both SIG and CLRSAB are UC-secure (that is, by operating in the double-$\mathcal{F}_{\mathsf{ACC}}$-hybrid model). Before our UC definitions, a proof of security would involve a multi-step security reduction of the new accumulator to one of the old ones.

Proof. The simulator for the new accumulator uses its two inner simulators to obtain algorithms for the inner accumulators, composes them as in Fig. 6, and submits those to the ideal functionality. (Since the CLRSAB accumulator is only non-adaptively sound, the simulator also pre-selects the random values that are to be accumulated in the CLRSAB accumulator.)[7]

In Sect. 3.3, we described how in order to modify the UC functionality $\mathcal{F}_{\mathsf{ACC}}$ to be HUM, we require that the simulator provide the algorithm Update in two parts: one sub-algorithm (let's call it Update_1) which only receives randomness and produces the update message; and a second sub-algorithm (let's call it Update_2) which produces all the other outputs of Update, and is additionally allowed to depend on the state of Update_1. If the update being performed is an addition, we do not need Update_1 at all, since no update message is necessary; we simply set $\mathsf{Update}_2(\mathsf{Add}, sk, a_t, m_t, x) = \mathsf{Update}(\mathsf{Add}, sk, a_t, m_t, x)$. If the update being performed is a deletion, $\mathsf{Update}_1(\mathsf{Del}, sk, a_t, m_t)$ gets a random pre-selected value and performs a CLRSAB addition on it; it then passes the random value

---

[6] Adding zero knowledge proofs would not resolve this issue—that random value cannot be hidden within a zero knowledge proof in any straightforward way, since it must be used to update CLRSAB witnesses.

[7] Notice that this works regardless of how the simpler accumulators are implemented (simply software vs. hardward vs. distributed protocols), since they satisfy the UC definition.

```
Gen(1^λ, S):
    1. (SIG.sk, SIG.a_0) ← SIG.Gen(1^λ, ∅)
    2. (CLRSAB.sk, CLRSAB.a_0, CLRSAB.upmsg_0) ← CLRSAB.Gen(1^λ, ∅)
    3. Set
        (a) sk ← (SIG.sk, CLRSAB.sk),
        (b) a_0 ← (SIG.a_0, CLRSAB.a_0),
        (c) upmsg_0 ← CLRSAB.a_0
        (d) Instantiate m_0 as an empty map.
    4. Return (sk, a_0, upmsg_0, m_0)
Update(Op_t, sk, a_t, m_t, x):
    1. If Op_t = Add and x ∉ m_t:
        (a) Pick r_x at random from the domain D_CLRSAB of the CLRSAB accumulator. (We require
            the domain to be large enough that the probability of picking the same element twice is
            negligible.)
        (b) Set m_{t+1} = m_t
        (c) Set m_{t+1}[x] = r_x
        (d) CLRSAB.w^{r_x}_{t+1} ← CLRSAB.WitCreate(out, CLRSAB.sk, CLRSAB.a_t, r_x)
        (e) SIG.w^{(x,r_x)}_{t+1} ← SIG.Update(Add, SIG.sk, SIG.a_0, (x, r_x))
        (f) Set CLRSAB.a_{t+1} = CLRSAB.a_t.
        (g) Set a_{t+1} = (SIG.a_0, CLRSAB.a_{t+1})
        (h) Set w^x_{t+1} = (r_x, CLRSAB.w^{r_x}_{t+1}, SIG.w^{(x,r_x)}_{t+1})
        (i) Set upmsg_{t+1} = ⊥
        (j) Return (a_{t+1}, m_{t+1}, w^x_{t+1}, upmsg_{t+1})
    2. If Op_t = Del and x ∈ m_t:
        (a) Set r_x = m_t[x]
        (b) Set m_{t+1} = m_t
        (c) Delete x from m_{t+1}
        (d) (CLRSAB.a_{t+1}, CLRSAB.upmsg_{t+1}) ← CLRSAB.Update(Add, CLRSAB.sk, CLRSAB.a_t, r_x)
        (e) Set a_{t+1} = (SIG.a_0, CLRSAB.a_{t+1})
        (f) Set upmsg_{t+1} = CLRSAB.upmsg_{t+1}
        (g) Return (a_{t+1}, m_{t+1}, upmsg_{t+1})
WitCreate(stts, sk, a_t, m_t, x):
    1. If stts = in and x ∈ m_t:
        (a) Set r_x = m_t[x]
        (b) SIG.w^{(x,r_x)}_t ← SIG.WitCreate(in, SIG.sk, SIG.a_t, (x, r_x))
        (c) CLRSAB.w^{r_x}_t ← CLRSAB.WitCreate(out, CLRSAB.sk, CLRSAB.a_t, r_x)
        (d) Set w^x_t = (r_x, CLRSAB.w^{r_x}_t, SIG.w^{(x,r_x)}_t)
        (e) Return w^x_t
WitUp(stts, x, w^x_t = (r_x, CLRSAB.w^{r_x}_t, SIG.w^{(x,r_x)}_t), upmsg_{t+1}):
    1. If upmsg_{t+1} ≠ ⊥: (This update message corresponds to a deletion)
        (a) CLRSAB.w^{r_x}_{t+1} = CLRSAB.WitUp(out, r_x, CLRSAB.w^{r_x}_t, upmsg_{t+1})
    2. Else: w^x_{t+1} = w^x_t
    3. Return w^x_{t+1}
VerStatus(in, a_t = (SIG.a_t, CLRSAB.a_t), x, w^x_t = (r_x, CLRSAB.w^{r_x}_t, SIG.w^{(x,r_x)}_t)):
    1. Return 1 if both of the following are 1, and 0 otherwise:
        − SIG.VerStatus(in, SIG.a_t, (x, r_x), SIG.w^{(x,r_x)}_t)
        − CLRSAB.VerStatus(out, CLRSAB.a_t, r_x, CLRSAB.w^{r_x}_t)
```

Fig. 6. Braavos' algorithms. We omit parameters unnecessary for the SIG and CLRSAB accumulator algorithms.

it added as $\text{state}_{\text{Update}_1}$ to $\text{Update}_2(\text{Del}, sk, a_t, m_t, x, \text{state}_{\text{Update}_1})$ which does the rest of the work.

The views of the environment $\mathcal{Z}$ in the real and ideal worlds will be identical in the so-called double-$\mathcal{F}_{\text{ACC}}$-hybrid model, since the sub-accumulator functionalities guarantee that if an element was never added then no signature on it exists, and every time an element x is removed, all random values r_x that have been signed with x are in set accumulated in CLRSAB, so no proof of non-membership for any such r_x can be produced.

5.2   Accumulators for Anonymous Credentials

We now informally discuss how our UC definition of accumulators would simplify the security proof of a complex system like anonymous credentials. An ideal
functionality that provides all the properties of anonymous credentials including
pseudonyms, selective attribute disclosure, predicates over attributes, revocation, inspection, etc. is described by Camenisch *et al.* [8]. (Baldimtsi *et al.* [2]
augment this functionality with revocation.) In this section, to demonstrate the
benefits of modularity we concentrate on a simplified version of an anonymous
credential ideal functionality with three types of parties: the credential manager
or issuer, credential holders, and credential verifiers. Our ideal functionality has
the following interfaces for the credential manager:

1. KeyGen, to set up the scheme parameters.
2. IssueCred(*token, property*), to issue a credential certifying *property* to a credential holder who knows the secret corresponding to *token*, and
3. RevokeCred(*token, property*), to revoke an issued credential.

Our simplified functionality sends the simulator all information about issued
and revoked credentials (including *token* and *property* information); so, unlike
the full-fledged functionality of Camenisch *et al.*, it does not restrict access to
information about who is certified for what property.

Credential holders only have a single interface—ProveCred, which they use to
demonstrate to a credential verifier that they hold a credential certifying some
property. Credential holders should be able to use their credentials anonymously.
The credential verifiers have the corresponding interface VerifyCredProof, which
allows them to check the proof provided by the credential holder.

Now, imagine that we instantiate our simplified anonymous credential functionality with a combination of the following building blocks: (a) digital signatures, (b) accumulators and (c) (non-interactive) zero knowledge (ZK) proofs, as
described by Baldimtsi *et al.* [2]. A simple instantiation would work as follows:

The signatures are used simply to guarantee the authenticity of updates
made by the credential manager. KeyGen sets up the parameters for all three
primitives. IssueCred adds (*token, property*) to the accumulator, where *token* is
a value linked to a long-term secret belonging to the user (e.g. *token* might be a
public key), and *property* is the property the credential certifies (e.g. "citizen",
"member", "age = 30", etc.). Similarly, RevokeCred deletes the appropriate element from the accumulator. Whenever an update happens to the accumulator
value, the most recent value (and a corresponding update message) is signed by
the credential manager and sent to all system users, who can then bring their
accumulator witnesses up to date.

ProveCred would then provide a ZK proof of knowledge of long-term user
secret s, token *token* and accumulator witness w such that, for the most recent
credential-manager-signed accumulator, the conjunction of the following statements is true:

1. s is appropriately linked to *token* (through some relationship, e.g. s is the
   secret key corresponding to *token* which is the public key), and

2. the accumulator verification algorithm returns true when given the accumulator witness w and $(token, property)$.

Given that no UC accumulator existed before our work, in order for someone to prove security even of such a simple scheme, a reduction would be required that would reduce the security of the overall scheme to the underlying building blocks. However, we can prove the security of this simplified credential scheme in the UC model using UC secure versions of the underlying building blocks. Such a UC proof would be information theoretic and unconditional, and will hold for any implementation of the underlying primitives, whether they be simple software, distributed computation, hardware, etc.

In order to prove the security of this credential scheme we need to build a simulator that, when run with the ideal functionality, produces an environment view indistinguishable from that of a real run of the anonymous credentials protocol. The two difficulties in doing so is (1) playing the roles of honest parties without knowing their long-term secrets, and (2) arguing that real adversaries can no more convince verifiers to accept forged credentials than ideal functionality adversaries can. UC zero knowledge proofs address the first concern. Since the use of UC zero knowledge proofs allows the simulator to control the zero knowledge proof ideal functionality (which we review in Appendix B of the full version [3]), it can control the verification outcome without actually knowing the values in question, sidestepping this issue. UC accumulators address the second concern.

Acknowledgements. This research was supported, in part, by US NSF grant 1717067.

A   Universally Composable Signatures

In this appendix (specifically, in Figs. 7 and 8), we describe the two digital signature ideal functionalities described by Canetti [13,14]. The first does not require the simulator to provide the signing and verification algorithms explicitly at key generation time; the second does. Both ideal functionalities require the verifier to provide the verification key (or verification algorithm) when using the verification interface. This models the fact that the verifier might be misinformed about the verification key if a PKI is not available.

1. **Key Generation:** Upon getting (KEYGEN, sid) from a party Signer ...
   (a) If this is not the first KeyGen command, ignore this command. Otherwise, continue.
   (b) If sid does not encode Signer's identity, ignore this command. Otherwise, continue.
   (c) Initialize an empty map $\mathbf{W}$.
   (d) Send (KEYGEN, sid) to Adversary $\mathcal{A}_{\mathsf{Ideal}}$.
   (e) Get (VERKEY, sid, vk) from Adversary $\mathcal{A}_{\mathsf{Ideal}}$.
   (f) Record vk.
   (g) Send (VERKEY, sid, vk) to Signer.
2. **Signature Generation:** Upon getting (SIGN, sid, x) from a party Signer ...
   (a) Verify that sid encodes Signer's identity. If not, ignore this command. Otherwise, continue.
   (b) Send (SIGN, sid, x) to Adversary $\mathcal{A}_{\mathsf{Ideal}}$.
   (c) Get (SIGNATURE, sid, x, σ) from Adversary $\mathcal{A}_{\mathsf{Ideal}}$.
   (d) Verify that $(x,\sigma) \notin \mathbf{W}$ or $\mathbf{W}[(x,\sigma)] = 1$. If not, send $\bot$ to Signer and halt. Otherwise, continue.
   (e) If $(x,\sigma) \notin \mathbf{W}$, record $\mathbf{W}[(x,\sigma)] = 1$.
   (f) Output (SIGNATURE, sid, x, σ) to Signer.
3. **Signature Verification:** Upon getting (VERIFY, sid, x, σ, vk) from a party Verifier ...
   (a) Send (VERIFY, sid, x, σ, vk) to Adversary $\mathcal{A}_{\mathsf{Ideal}}$.
   (b) Get (VERIFIED, sid, x, σ, vk, ϕ) from Adversary $\mathcal{A}_{\mathsf{Ideal}}$.
   (c) If $(x,\sigma) \in \mathbf{W}$: let $\phi' = \mathbf{W}[(x,\sigma)]$.
   (d) Else:
       i. If the signer is not corrupted, vk is the recorded public key, and $(x,\sigma) \notin \mathbf{W}$, set $\phi' = 0$.
       ii. Else, let $\phi' = \phi$.
       iii. Record $\mathbf{W}[(x,\sigma)] = \phi'$.
   (e) Output (VERIFIED, sid, x, σ, vk, ϕ') to Verifier.

Fig. 7. Ideal functionality for digital signatures [14]

1. **Key Generation:** Upon getting (KEYGEN, sid) from a party Signer ...
   (a) If this is not the first KeyGen command, ignore this command. Otherwise, continue.
   (b) If sid does not encode Signer's identity, ignore this command. Otherwise, continue.
   (c) Initialize an empty list $\mathbf{W}$ of signed messages.
   (d) Send (KEYGEN, sid) to Adversary $\mathcal{A}_{\mathsf{Ideal}}$.
   (e) Get (ALGORITHMS, sid, Sign, Ver) from Adversary $\mathcal{A}_{\mathsf{Ideal}}$, where Sign is a polynomial-time algorithm and Ver is a polynomial-time *deterministic* algorithm.
   (f) Send (ALGORITHMS, sid, Ver) to Signer.
2. **Signature Generation:** Upon getting (SIGN, sid, x) from a party Signer ...
   (a) Verify that sid encodes Signer's identity. If not, ignore this command. Otherwise, continue.
   (b) Let $\sigma = \mathsf{Sign}(x)$.
   (c) Verify that $\mathsf{Ver}(x,\sigma) = 1$. If not, send $\bot$ to Signer and halt. Otherwise, continue.
   (d) Output (SIGNATURE, sid, x, σ) to Signer.
   (e) Record x in $\mathbf{W}$.
3. **Signature Verification:** Upon getting (VERIFY, sid, x, σ, Ver$'$) from a party Verifier ...
   (a) If Ver$'$ = Ver, the signer is not corrupted, $\mathsf{Ver}(x,\sigma) = 1$ and $x \notin \mathbf{W}$, send $\bot$ to signer and halt. (This violates soundness.) Otherwise, continue.
   (b) $\phi = \mathsf{Ver}'(x,\sigma)$.
   (c) Output (VERIFIED, sid, x, σ, Ver$'$, ϕ) to Verifier.

Fig. 8. Ideal functionality for digital signatures with explicit verification algorithm [13] (2005 version)

References

1. Ateniese, G., Camenisch, J., Joye, M., Tsudik, G.: A practical and provably secure coalition-resistant group signature scheme. In: Bellare, M. (ed.) CRYPTO 2000. LNCS, vol. 1880, pp. 255–270. Springer, Heidelberg (2000). https://doi.org/10.1007/3-540-44598-6_16
2. Baldimtsi, F., et al.: Accumulators with applications to anonymity-preserving revocation. In: 2017 IEEE European Symposium on Security and Privacy, EuroS&P 2017, Paris, France, 26–28 April 2017, pp. 301–315. IEEE (2017)
3. Baldimtsi, F., Canetti, R., Yakoubov, S.: Universally composable accumulators. Cryptology ePrint Archive, Report 2018/1241 (2018). https://eprint.iacr.org/2018/1241

4. Barić, N., Pfitzmann, B.: Collision-free accumulators and fail-stop signature schemes without trees. In: Fumy, W. (ed.) EUROCRYPT 1997. LNCS, vol. 1233, pp. 480–494. Springer, Heidelberg (1997). https://doi.org/10.1007/3-540-69053-0_33

5. Benaloh, J., de Mare, M.: One-way accumulators: a decentralized alternative to digital signatures. In: Helleseth, T. (ed.) EUROCRYPT 1993. LNCS, vol. 765, pp. 274–285. Springer, Heidelberg (1994). https://doi.org/10.1007/3-540-48285-7_24

6. Camacho, P., Hevia, A., Kiwi, M., Opazo, R.: Strong accumulators from collision-resistant hashing. In: Wu, T.-C., Lei, C.-L., Rijmen, V., Lee, D.-T. (eds.) ISC 2008. LNCS, vol. 5222, pp. 471–486. Springer, Heidelberg (2008). https://doi.org/10.1007/978-3-540-85886-7_32

7. Camenisch, J., Drijvers, M., Tackmann, B.: Multi-protocol UC and its use for building modular and efficient protocols. IACR Cryptology ePrint Archive 2019:65 (2019)

8. Camenisch, J., Dubovitskaya, M., Haralambiev, K., Kohlweiss, M.: Composable and modular anonymous credentials: definitions and practical constructions. In: Iwata, T., Cheon, J.H. (eds.) ASIACRYPT 2015, Part II. LNCS, vol. 9453, pp. 262–288. Springer, Heidelberg (2015). https://doi.org/10.1007/978-3-662-48800-3_11

9. Camenisch, J., Kohlweiss, M., Soriente, C.: An accumulator based on bilinear maps and efficient revocation for anonymous credentials. In: Jarecki, S., Tsudik, G. (eds.) PKC 2009. LNCS, vol. 5443, pp. 481–500. Springer, Heidelberg (2009). https://doi.org/10.1007/978-3-642-00468-1_27

10. Camenisch, J., Krenn, S., Shoup, V.: A framework for practical universally composable zero-knowledge protocols. In: Lee, D.H., Wang, X. (eds.) ASIACRYPT 2011. LNCS, vol. 7073, pp. 449–467. Springer, Heidelberg (2011). https://doi.org/10.1007/978-3-642-25385-0_24

11. Camenisch, J., Lysyanskaya, A.: Dynamic accumulators and application to efficient revocation of anonymous credentials. In: Yung, M. (ed.) CRYPTO 2002. LNCS, vol. 2442, pp. 61–76. Springer, Heidelberg (2002). https://doi.org/10.1007/3-540-45708-9_5

12. Camenisch, J., Van Herreweghen, E.: Design and implementation of the idemix anonymous credential system. In: Atluri, V. (ed.) ACM CCS 2002, pp. 21–30. ACM Press, November 2002

13. Canetti, R.: Universally composable security: a new paradigm for cryptographic protocols. In: 42nd FOCS, pp. 136–145. IEEE Computer Society Press, October 2001

14. Canetti, R.: Universally composable signature, certification, and authentication. In: Proceedings of the 17th IEEE Workshop on Computer Security Foundations, CSFW 2004, pp. 219–233, Washington, DC, USA, 2004. IEEE Computer Society (2004)

15. Canetti, R., Fischlin, M.: Universally composable commitments. In: Kilian, J. (ed.) CRYPTO 2001. LNCS, vol. 2139, pp. 19–40. Springer, Heidelberg (2001). https://doi.org/10.1007/3-540-44647-8_2

16. Ghosh, E., Ohrimenko, O., Papadopoulos, D., Tamassia, R., Triandopoulos, N.: Zero-knowledge accumulators and set algebra. In: Cheon, J.H., Takagi, T. (eds.) ASIACRYPT 2016, Part II. LNCS, vol. 10032, pp. 67–100. Springer, Heidelberg (2016). https://doi.org/10.1007/978-3-662-53890-6_3

17. Li, J., Li, N., Xue, R.: Universal accumulators with efficient nonmembership proofs. In: Katz, J., Yung, M. (eds.) ACNS 2007. LNCS, vol. 4521, pp. 253–269. Springer, Heidelberg (2007). https://doi.org/10.1007/978-3-540-72738-5_17

18. Lipmaa, H.: Secure accumulators from euclidean rings without trusted setup. In: Bao, F., Samarati, P., Zhou, J. (eds.) ACNS 2012. LNCS, vol. 7341, pp. 224–240. Springer, Heidelberg (2012). https://doi.org/10.1007/978-3-642-31284-7_14
19. Miers, I., Garman, C., Green, M., Rubin, A.D.: Zerocoin: anonymous distributed E-cash from bitcoin. In: 2013 IEEE Symposium on Security and Privacy, pp. 397–411. IEEE Computer Society Press, May 2013
20. Nguyen, L.: Accumulators from bilinear pairings and applications. In: Menezes, A. (ed.) CT-RSA 2005. LNCS, vol. 3376, pp. 275–292. Springer, Heidelberg (2005). https://doi.org/10.1007/978-3-540-30574-3_19

A Non-interactive Shuffle Argument with Low Trust Assumptions

Antonis Aggelakis[1], Prastudy Fauzi[2], Georgios Korfiatis[1], Panos Louridas[1], Foteinos Mergoupis-Anagnou[1], Janno Siim[3(✉)], and Michał Zając[4]

[1] Greek Research and Technology Network, Athens, Greece
[2] Simula UiB, Bergen, Norway
[3] University of Tartu, Tartu, Estonia
jannosiim@gmail.com
[4] Clearmatics, London, UK

Abstract. A shuffle argument is a cryptographic primitive for proving correct behaviour of mix-networks without leaking any private information. Several recent constructions of non-interactive shuffle arguments avoid the random oracle model but require the public key to be trusted.

We augment the most efficient argument by Fauzi et al. [Asiacrypt 2017] with a distributed key generation protocol that assures soundness of the argument if at least one party in the protocol is honest and additionally provide a key verification algorithm which guarantees zero-knowledge even if all the parties are malicious. Furthermore, we simplify their construction and improve security by using weaker assumptions while retaining roughly the same level of efficiency. We also provide an implementation to the distributed key generation protocol and the shuffle argument.

Keywords: Subversion security · Non-interactive zero-knowledge · Shuffle · Secure multi-party computation

1 Introduction

Due to convenience for voters and lower election costs, internet voting (i-voting) is becoming an increasingly popular alternative to paper-based voting. In fact, some countries have already provided i-voting solutions in regional (e.g., Australia, Switzerland) or even national (e.g., Estonia) elections. While i-voting has many benefits, the opposing requirements of election transparency and voter's privacy are not easy to guarantee in the digital setting.

One common tool to improve voter's privacy is the mix-network [Cha81]. Essentially, a mix-network can be seen as a digital analogue to ballot-box shaking in paper-based voting. During the voting phase, encrypted votes are sent to a *bulletin board*, a secure append-only storage system. After the voting phase ends, the ciphertexts are processed sequentially by a mix-network consisting of multiple independent servers, called mixers. Each mixer receives the ciphertexts

© Springer Nature Switzerland AG 2020
S. Jarecki (Ed.): CT-RSA 2020, LNCS 12006, pp. 667–692, 2020.
https://doi.org/10.1007/978-3-030-40186-3_28

from the previous mixer (or, in the case of the first mixer, from the bulletin board) and sends *shuffled* (permuted and rerandomized) ciphertext to the next mixer. Finally, only the output of the last mixer is decrypted. Assuming that at least one mixer is honest, it will be impossible to associate the decrypted votes to the voters that gave the original ciphertexts.

However, observe that a malicious mixer could easily switch out the cipher-texts and thus break the integrity of the election outcome. We can avoid such behaviour by requiring each mixer to provide a proof that the shuffling was done correctly. Additionally, to still maintain voters' privacy, this proof should not reveal any[1] information about the permutation or ciphertext randomizers used in the shuffle. This can be achieved with a *zero-knowledge (ZK) shuffle argument*.

Many efficient interactive arguments [FS01, TW10, Gro10, BG12] are known for shuffling, but interaction is not preferable in practice. For instance, we might want to audit elections months after it occurred, but mixers storing the private information might not be available anymore. Hence a better solution would be a non-interactive zero-knowledge (NIZK) argument, where the prover outputs a single message which can be later verified by anyone. Most interactive shuffle arguments can be made non-interactive using the Fiat-Shamir heuristic [FS87], but this only guarantees security in the random oracle model (ROM), where there are known cases in which the resulting argument is insecure [GK03, BDG+13, BBH+19].

As an alternative, the *Common Reference String (CRS)* model assumes a trusted party that samples a public string from some predefined distribution and provides it to both the prover and the verifier. In recent years several NIZK shuffle arguments have been proposed in this model [GL07, LZ13, GR16, FL16, FLZ16, FLSZ17a, FFHR19] that do not need ROM[2]. Arguably, the most practical proposal among these is the construction of Fauzi et al. [FLSZ17a][3], which we refer to as FLSZ throughout the text – it has comparable efficiency to interactive arguments and uses a standard ElGamal cryptosystem. However, a drawback of the CRS model is that it is unclear who should produce the CRS in practice. Sampling the CRS incorrectly, or even just leaking some side information (e.g., the simulation trapdoor), typically breaks the security of the argument. Several works have tried to alleviate this issue.

The *Bare Public Key (BPK)* model [CGGM00] requires significantly less trust than the CRS model. It removes the CRS and only requires the verifier to register a public key in a publicly accessible file before the protocol has started. A malicious verifier may choose the public key in any way she likes. However, BPK model NIZK with a standard auxiliary input ZK property can be cast as a two-round ZK protocol, which is known to be impossible [GO94]. On the positive

---

[1] Actually since the argument presented in this paper is statistically but not perfectly zero-knowledge, then it can leak information, but only with negligible probability.

[2] Even most of the interactive shuffle arguments require a CRS, but typically they have a less complicated structure and a uniformly random string usually suffices.

[3] The full version [FLSZ17a] mentions a security flaw in the conference version [FLSZ17b]. We follow the full version.

side, Wee [Wee07] has shown that BPK model NIZK is possible for a weaker non-uniform ZK. More recently, [ALSZ18] shows that NIZK with a related notion called no-auxiliary-string non-black-box ZK is also possible.

From a different perspective, Ben-Sasson et al. [BCG+15] proposed a secure multi-party computation (MPC) protocol for CRS generation to distribute trust requirements. Essentially it is a distributed key generation (DKG) protocol that is secure if at least one party is honest. However, that protocol requires the ROM and only works for CRS-s with a very specific structure. Hence, it cannot be used as a black box, say, for the FLSZ argument. Subsequently, Abdolmaleki et al. [ABL+19b], proposed a UC-secure variant of the Ben-Sasson et al.'s protocol which avoids the ROM by using a DL-extractable UC-commitment [ABL+19a].

A series of results [BFS16, ABLZ17, Fuc18] have shown that CRS-based NIZK arguments can satisfy *subversion-ZK (Sub-ZK)*, i.e., the argument's ZK property holds even if the CRS is generated by an untrusted party. In particular, it has been shown [ABLZ17, Fuc18] that many existing *succinct non-interactive arguments of knowledge (SNARKs)* can be enhanced with a CRS verification algorithm CV, such that if CV(crs) accepts, then the proof will not leak any (non-negligible) information. So far, there is no general transformation which would give Sub-ZK property to any NIZK argument, and each new argument needs to be studied separately. Finally, recent work by Abdolmaleki et al. [ALSZ18] establishes a straightforward connection between Sub-ZK NIZK in the CRS model and BPK NIZK. Namely, a Sub-ZK NIZK can be transformed into a BPK NIZK (with non-auxiliary-input non-black-box ZK) where the verifier uses the CRS as her public key. This is also the direction we take in this paper as the BPK model is a more established and better-understood notion.

Our Contribution. We propose a new shuffle argument that we call a *transparent* FLSZ (denoted tFLSZ) which builds upon the result of [FLSZ17a] by significantly reducing the trust requirements, using weaker security assumptions, and also having a somewhat less complex structure.

FLSZ contains four subarguments: (i) a unit vector argument for showing that a committed message is a unit vector, i.e., a binary vector with exactly one 1, (ii) a permutation matrix argument for showing that n committed vectors form a permutation matrix, (iii) a same-message argument for showing that two committed vectors are equal, and (iv) a consistency argument for showing that the ciphertexts are shuffled according to the committed permutation matrix. However, in their case (i) the unit vector argument is not sound unless one also provides a related same-message argument and (ii) the consistency argument is only culpably sound, that is, soundness only holds against adversaries that can provide a witness of their cheating.

In tFLSZ, we combine the unit vector argument and the same-message argument into a new unit vector argument and prove its knowledge-soundness in the *algebraic group model (AGM)* [FKL18] which is a weaker model compared to the generic bilinear group model (GBGM) used in [FLSZ17a]. Roughly speaking, in the GBGM an adversary is only allowed to perform group operations using an oracle which hides the actual structure of the group elements. On the other hand, the AGM allows the adversary to freely use the actual representation of elements in the group. Therefore security proofs in the AGM are usually reductions to some known assumption rather than unconditional proofs as in the GBGM. We show that knowledge-soundness of our new unit vector argument can be reduced to a quite standard q-type assumption in the algebraic group model.

The permutation argument is proven knowledge-sound assuming that the commitment scheme is binding and the unit vector argument is knowledge-sound. This again is a much weaker assumption compared to [FLSZ17a], where the authors prove a similar result but in the GBGM. Finally, we skip the consistency argument altogether, and directly prove that the shuffle argument is sound given that the permutation argument is knowledge-sound and that a variant of the *Kernel Matrix Diffie-Hellman (KerMDH)* assumption holds. We call this variant GapKerMDH and prove that in the AGM, it also reduces to the previously mentioned q-type assumption. The GapKerMDH assumption is weaker compared to the auxiliary-input KerMDH assumption used in [FLSZ17a] for their consistency argument. Interestingly, after simplifying the structure, the unit vector argument is the only subargument which depends on the AGM; the rest of the protocol is based on falsifiable assumptions [Nao03], i.e., assumptions where a challenger can efficiently verify that an adversary breaks the assumption (e.g., in the discrete logarithm assumption the challenger sends g^x, the adversary responds with x', and the challenger checks if $x = x'$). Falsifiable assumptions are much better understood and thus usually preferred over non-falsifiable assumptions such as knowledge assumptions [Dam92].

Secondly (and perhaps more importantly), we apply the efficient DKG protocol of Abdolmaleki et al. [ABL+19b] which takes us from a setting of completely trusting the setup generator to a setting where we need to trust only one out of k parties in DKG. The modification, however, turns out to be non-trivial. We start by observing that the CRS of FLSZ is outside of the class of *verification-friendly* CRS-s that the DKG protocol can generate. Hence, in addition to simplifying the structure of FLSZ we also modify the CRS and make it verification-friendly, which mostly involves adding some well-chosen elements to the CRS. These additional elements are not needed for the honest prover or verifier but are available to dishonest parties. Therefore, after the DKG protocol finishes, these new CRS elements can be stored somewhere (in case someone wants to verify them in the future) and the effective CRS size (i.e., the size of the CRS used in the actual computation) does not change at all. If there is no need for transcript verification in the future, these additional elements can be safely disregarded after the computations are done. Hence, the CRS size in practice stays the same, but the security proofs must now consider a more powerful adversary.

As mentioned, the DKG protocol guarantees security (soundness and zero-knowledge) if at least one honest party participated. We take it one step further and prove that the protocol is also secure in the BPK model, following the ideas of [ALSZ18]. Namely, we construct a public key verification algorithm V_{pk} that the prover runs before outputting an argument. If V_{pk} is satisfied, then zero-knowledge holds even if the public key was generated by a single malicious party, or equivalently, if all of the parties in the DKG protocol colluded. However, if V_{pk} rejects the key, then the prover simply declines to output anything.

In Table 1 we compare efficiency and assumptions of the state-of-the-art non-interactive shuffle arguments. The argument by Groth [Gro10] has the best efficiency, but requires ROM and a trusted random string[4]. It is also worth to mention the argument by Bayer and Groth [BG12] which has sublinear communication but otherwise has the same drawbacks as [Gro10]. The argument of González and Rálfols [GR16] (and the slight improvement in [DGP+19]) is based solely on falsifiable assumptions, but requires a quadratic size CRS which is not efficient enough for many applications. Similarly, Faonio et al. [FFHR19] use falsifiable assumptions but require pairings for all operations, making it inefficient. The Fauzi et al. [FLSZ17a] construction can be seen as a compromise between [Gro10] and [GR16]: efficiency is only slightly worse than [Gro10], does not require ROM, but some subarguments are proven in the GBGM. Our work retains almost the same efficiency as [FLSZ17a] by only adding n group elements to the CRS (we do not count elements solely needed by the DKG), but we make a significant reduction in the trust requirements for the setup phase and also prove security under weaker assumptions.

In summary, our new NIZK shuffle argument has the following properties:

1. Soundness holds assuming at least one honest party participated in the distributed key generation protocol and zero-knowledge holds even if all the parties were malicious.
2. Compared to the most-efficient shuffle argument without ROM [FLSZ17a]:
   (a) We simplify the structure of the argument.
   (b) We improve the security assumptions and isolate the unit vector argument as the only subargument which requires AGM.
   (c) The efficiency of the argument remains essentially the same.

In Additionally, we implement our solution in Python 3.5+. See Sect. 7 for details.

2   Preliminaries

Let λ denote the security parameter. We write $f(\lambda) \approx_\lambda 0$, if a function f is negligible in λ. PPT stands for probabilistic polynomial time. We write $(a, b) \leftarrow (\mathcal{A}\|\mathsf{Ext})(x)$ if algorithms $\mathcal{A}$ and Ext on the same input x and random tape r output $a \leftarrow \mathcal{A}(x; r)$ and $b \leftarrow \mathsf{Ext}(x; r)$. By $\mathsf{RND}(\mathcal{A})$ we denote the random tape of $\mathcal{A}$ and by $\mathsf{Range}(\mathcal{A}(x))$ the set of all possible outputs of $\mathcal{A}$ given input x.

We write $x \leftarrow_{\$} A$ if x is sampled uniformly randomly from the set A. By default $\mathbf{x} = (x_i)_{i=1}^n \in A^n$ is a column vector and $\mathbf{1}_n := (1)_{i=1}^n$, $\mathbf{0}_n := (0)_{i=1}^n$. A set of permutations on n elements is denoted by $\mathbb{S}_n$. A matrix $\mathbf{A} \in \{0, 1\}^{n \times n}$ is

---

[4] Namely, [Gro10] requires a commitment key for the extended Pedersen commitment which could be obtained from a uniformly random string.

Table 1. Comparison of state-of-the-art shuffles. Exp. stands for exponentiations, pair. for pairings, n is the number of input ciphertexts and m is the number of mixers. Constant terms are neglected, shuffling is included to prover's efficiency, and shuffled ciphertexts are included to proof size.

	Prover efficiency	Verifier efficiency	Decryption efficiency	Proof size	CRS size	Reference string	Assumptions
[Gro10]	$8n$ exp.	$6n$ exp.	n exp.	$3n \times \mathbb{Z}_p$, $2n \times \mathbb{G}$	$n \times \mathbb{G}$	Uniform	ROM, DDH
[GR16]	$13n$ exp.	$13n$ pair.	n exp.	$4n \times \mathbb{G}_1$, $2n \times \mathbb{G}_2$	$(n^2 + 24n)$ $\times \mathbb{G}_1, 23n$ $\times \mathbb{G}_2$	Structured	Falsifiable
[FLSZ17a]	$11n$ exp.	$7n$ exp., $3n$ pair.	n exp.	$4n \times \mathbb{G}_1$, $3n \times \mathbb{G}_2$	$4n \times \mathbb{G}_1$, $n \times \mathbb{G}_2$	Structured	GBGM
[FFHR19]	$72n$ exp., $5n$ pair.	$22n$ pair.	$2n$ exp., $46n$ pair.	$12n \times \mathbb{G}_1$, $11n \times \mathbb{G}_2$, $4n \times \mathbb{G}_T$	$2m \times \mathbb{G}_1$, $2m \times \mathbb{G}_2$	Uniform	Falsifiable
This work	$11n$ exp.	$7n$ exp., $3n$ pair.	n exp.	$4n \times \mathbb{G}_1$, $3n \times \mathbb{G}_2$	$5n \times \mathbb{G}_1$, $n \times \mathbb{G}_2$	Verifiable	AGM

a permutation matrix of the permutation $\sigma \in \mathbb{S}_n$ when $A_{i,j} = 1$ iff $\sigma(i) = j$. We call $\mathbf{a}$ a unit vector if it contains exactly one 1 and all other positions are 0. Let $\mathbb{F}_p$ be a finite field of prime order p and $\mathbb{F}_p^* := \mathbb{F}_p \setminus \{1\}$. For vectors $\mathbf{x}, \mathbf{y} \in \mathbb{F}_p^n$, $\mathbf{x} \circ \mathbf{y}$ denotes the entry-wise product. We use the bracket notation where $[x]$ denotes the group element with discrete logarithm x. We consider additive groups, thus $[a] + [b] = [a + b]$. For integers $a < b$ we denote $[a .. b] := \{a, a + 1, \ldots, b\}$.

Bilinear Pairing. A bilinear group generator $\mathsf{BGen}(1^\lambda)$ outputs a tuple $(p, \mathbb{G}_1, \mathbb{G}_2, \mathbb{G}_T, \mathcal{P}_1, \mathcal{P}_2, \bullet)$ such that (i) p is a prime of length $\Theta(\lambda)$, (ii) for $k \in \{1, 2\}$, $\mathbb{G}_k$ is an additive group of order p with a generator $\mathcal{P}_k$, and (iii) $\bullet$ is a map $\mathbb{G}_1 \times \mathbb{G}_2 \to \mathbb{G}_T$. We set $\mathcal{P}_T := \mathcal{P}_1 \bullet \mathcal{P}_2$ and use the bracket notation by defining $[a]_k := a \cdot \mathcal{P}_k$, for $k \in \{1, 2, T\}$. We require that

- $[a]_1 \bullet [b]_2 = [ab]_T$ for all $a, b \in \mathbb{F}_p$ (*bilinearity*),
- $\mathcal{P}_T \neq [0]_T$ (*non-degeneracy*), and
- $\bullet$ is efficiently computable.

In the following we use *asymmetric* bilinear groups where there is no efficiently computable isomorphism between $\mathbb{G}_1$ and $\mathbb{G}_2$. For the state of the art in pairing constructions see [BD17].

Bracket notation extends naturally to matrices and vectors, e.g., we may write $[\mathbf{A}]_1 \bullet [\mathbf{B}]_2 = [\mathbf{I}]_1 \bullet (\mathbf{A}[\mathbf{B}]_2) = [\mathbf{I}]_1 \bullet [\mathbf{AB}]_2$ for $\mathbf{A} \in \mathbb{F}_p^{n \times m}$, $\mathbf{B} \in \mathbb{F}_p^{m \times k}$, and identity matrix $\mathbf{I} \in \mathbb{F}_p^{n \times n}$. Occasionally we write $[a]_z$ for $z \in \{1, 2\}$ and use $\bar{z} := 3 - z$ to denote the number of the other non-target group. Then $[a]_z \bullet [b]_{\bar{z}}$ would mean $[a]_1 \bullet [b]_2$ for $z = 1$ and $[b]_1 \bullet [a]_2$ for $z = 2$.

Lagrange Basis. Let $\omega_1, \ldots, \omega_{n+1}$ be distinct points in $\mathbb{F}_p$. For $i \in [1 .. n+1]$, the i-th Lagrange basis polynomial is defined as $\ell_i(X) := \prod_{j \neq i} \frac{X - \omega_j}{\omega_i - \omega_j}$. Hence, it is the unique degree n polynomial such that $\ell_i(\omega_i) = 1$ and $\ell_i(\omega_j) = 0$ for all $j \neq i$. As the name suggests, $\{\ell_i(X)\}_{i=1}^{n+1}$ is a basis for $\{f \in \mathbb{F}_p[X] : \deg(f) \leq n\}$.

Encryption Scheme. A public key encryption scheme is a triple of PPT algorithms (KGen, Enc, Dec) such that

- KGen(1^λ) outputs a public key and a secret key pair ($\mathsf{pk_e}, \mathsf{sk_e}$).
- $\mathsf{Enc_{pk_e}}(m; r)$ outputs a ciphertext c encrypting the message m with randomness r under the public key $\mathsf{pk_e}$.
- $\mathsf{Dec_{sk_e}}(c)$ outputs the decryption of the ciphertext c using the secret key $\mathsf{sk_e}$.

We require that $\mathsf{Dec_{sk_e}}(\mathsf{Enc_{pk_e}}(m; r)) = m$ for every message m and randomizer r. Intuitively, an encryption scheme is *IND-CPA*-secure if no PPT adversary $\mathcal{A}$ can distinguish between the ciphertext distributions of any two messages.

We use the ElGamal encryption scheme over a group $\mathbb{G}_2$ defined as follows. The algorithm KGen(1^λ) samples $\mathsf{sk_e} \leftarrow_{\$} \mathbb{F}_p$ and outputs ($\mathsf{pk_e} := [1, \mathsf{sk_e}]_2, \mathsf{sk_e}$). An encryption of a message $[m]_2$ is $\mathsf{Enc_{pk_e}}([m]_2; r) := [0, m]_2 + r \cdot \mathsf{pk_e}$ where $r \leftarrow_{\$} \mathbb{F}_p$. A ciphertext $[\mathbf{c}]_2 = [c_1, c_2]_2$ is decrypted by computing $\mathsf{Dec_{sk_e}}([\mathbf{c}]_2) := [c_2]_2 - \mathsf{sk_e} \cdot [c_1]_2$. ElGamal is IND-CPA-secure if the DDH assumption holds in group $\mathbb{G}_2$. ElGamal is also *blindable*, meaning that $\mathsf{Enc_{pk_e}}([m]; r) + \mathsf{Enc_{pk_e}}([0], r') = \mathsf{Enc_{pk_e}}([m], r + r')$ and, assuming that $r' \leftarrow_{\$} \mathbb{F}_p$, no PPT adversary can distinguish if $\mathsf{Enc_{pk_e}}([m]; r)$ and $\mathsf{Enc_{pk_e}}([m]; r + r')$ encrypt the same message or not.

Non-interactive Zero-Knowledge. Let $\mathcal{R} = \{(\mathsf{x}, \mathsf{w})\}$ be a relation such that $\mathcal{L_R} = \{\mathsf{x} : \exists \mathsf{w}\ (\mathsf{x}, \mathsf{w}) \in \mathcal{R}\}$ is an NP language where w is a witness for x. Following [ALSZ18], we define a NIZK argument in the BPK model as follows.

A NIZK argument Ψ in the BPK model for relation $\mathcal{R}$ is a tuple efficient algorithms (Pgen, $\mathsf{K_{td}}$, $\mathsf{K_{pk}}$, $\mathsf{V_{pk}}$, P, V, Sim), where

- Pgen(1^λ) is a deterministic algorithm that outputs a setup parameter gk.
- $\mathsf{K_{td}}$(gk) is a PPT algorithm that on input gk outputs a trapdoor td.
- $\mathsf{K_{pk}}$(gk, td) is a deterministic algorithm that on input gk and td $\in$ Range($\mathsf{K_{td}}$(gk)) outputs a public key pk.
- $\mathsf{V_{pk}}$(gk, pk) is a PPT algorithm that on input gk and a public key pk outputs 0 (if the key is malformed) or 1 (if the key is well-formed).
- P(gk, pk, x, w) is a PPT algorithm that given a setup parameter gk, public key pk, and (x, w) $\in \mathcal{R}$, outputs an argument π.
- V(gk, pk, x, π) is a PPT algorithm that on input a setup parameter gk, public key pk, statement x, and argument π, outputs 0 (reject) or 1 (accept).
- Sim(gk, pk, td, x) is a PPT algorithm that on input a setup parameter gk, public key pk, trapdoor td, and x $\in \mathcal{L_R}$ outputs a simulated argument π.

For the sake of brevity, we sometimes use the algorithm K(gk) := $\mathsf{K_{pk}}$(gk, $\mathsf{K_{td}}$(gk)). By a *NIZK argument in the CRS model* we mean a tuple (Pgen, $\mathsf{K_{td}}$, $\mathsf{K_{pk}}$, P, V, Sim) of the above algorithms (i.e., all except $\mathsf{V_{pk}}$).

Completeness simply requires that an honestly generated key and argument are respectively accepted by $\mathsf{V_{pk}}$ and V. We give the definition for the BPK model. The definition for the CRS model neglects the condition $\mathsf{V_{pk}}$(gk, pk) = 1.

Definition 1. *The argument Ψ in BPK model is* perfectly complete *if for all λ, and $(x, w) \in \mathcal{R}$, the following probability is 1,*

$$\Pr\left[\mathsf{gk} \leftarrow \mathsf{Pgen}(1^\lambda), \mathsf{pk} \leftarrow \mathsf{K}(\mathsf{gk}) : \mathsf{V_{pk}}(\mathsf{gk}, \mathsf{pk}) = 1 \wedge \mathsf{V}(\mathsf{gk}, \mathsf{pk}, x, \mathsf{P}(\mathsf{gk}, \mathsf{pk}, x, w)) = 1\right].$$

Soundness guarantees that a malicious prover cannot create a valid argument for a false statement. The definitions match in the BPK model and the CRS model.

Definition 2. *The argument Ψ is* sound *if for any PPT adversary $\mathcal{A}$,*

$$\Pr\left[\begin{array}{l}\mathsf{gk} \leftarrow \mathsf{Pgen}(1^\lambda), (\mathsf{pk}, \mathsf{td}) \leftarrow \mathsf{K}(\mathsf{gk}), (x, \pi) \leftarrow \mathcal{A}(\mathsf{gk}, \mathsf{pk}) : \\ x \notin \mathcal{L_R} \wedge \mathsf{V}(\mathsf{gk}, \mathsf{pk}, x, \pi) = 1\end{array}\right] \approx_\lambda 0.$$

Knowledge-soundness strengthens the previous definition by requiring that the prover "knows" the witness, i.e., there exists an extractor that outputs the witness given the code and random coins of the adversary.

Definition 3. *The argument Ψ is* knowledge-sound *if for any PPT adversary $\mathcal{A}$, there exists a PPT extractor* Ext, *such that*

$$\Pr\left[\begin{array}{l}\mathsf{gk} \leftarrow \mathsf{Pgen}(1^\lambda), (\mathsf{pk}, \mathsf{td}) \leftarrow \mathsf{K}(\mathsf{gk}), ((x, \pi), w) \leftarrow (\mathcal{A}\|\mathsf{Ext})(\mathsf{gk}, \mathsf{pk}) : \\ (x, w) \notin \mathcal{R} \wedge \mathsf{V}(\mathsf{gk}, \mathsf{pk}, x, \pi) = 1\end{array}\right] \approx_\lambda 0.$$

Lastly, zero-knowledge guarantees that the argument leaks no information besides that $x \in \mathcal{L_R}$ by giving an algorithm Sim which, given a trapdoor, can create a valid argument for any $x \in \mathcal{L_R}$ without knowing the corresponding witness.

Definition 4. *An argument Ψ in the CRS model is* statistically *zero-knowledge, if for any adversary $\mathcal{A}$, and any $(x, w) \in \mathcal{R}$, $\varepsilon_0 \approx_\lambda \varepsilon_1$, where*

$$\varepsilon_b := \Pr\left[\begin{array}{l}\mathsf{gk} \leftarrow \mathsf{Pgen}(1^\lambda), (\mathsf{crs}, \mathsf{td}) \leftarrow \mathsf{K}(\mathsf{gk}), \mathbf{if}\ b = 0\ \mathbf{then}\ \pi \leftarrow \mathsf{P}(\mathsf{gk}, \mathsf{crs}, x, w) \\ \mathbf{else}\ \pi \leftarrow \mathsf{Sim}(\mathsf{gk}, \mathsf{crs}, \mathsf{td}, x)\ \mathbf{fi} : \mathcal{A}(\mathsf{gk}, \mathsf{crs}, \pi) = 1\end{array}\right].$$

We say that Ψ is perfectly zero-knowledge *if $\varepsilon_0 = \varepsilon_1$.*

In the BPK model, we use the *no-auxiliary-string non-black-box zero-knowledge* definition of [ALSZ18] (as mentioned, NIZK is impossible with the standard BPK ZK definition). Essentially the prover first runs a public key verification algorithm $\mathsf{V_{pk}}$ to check well-formedness of the key pk and only then outputs a proof. Compared to the previous definition, we require that there exists an extractor that extracts a trapdoor for any well-formed pk given access to adversary's random coins. Intuitively this guarantees that the key generator knows the trapdoor and thus could generate the proof himself using the simulator.

Definition 5 ([ALSZ18]). *The argument Ψ in the BPK model is statistically no-auxiliary-string non-black-box zero-knowledge (nn-ZK), if for any PPT subverter* X *there exists a PPT extractor* $\mathsf{Ext_X}$, *s.t., for any (stateful) adversary* $\mathcal{A}$, $\varepsilon_0 \approx_\lambda \varepsilon_1$, *where*

$$\varepsilon_b := \Pr \begin{bmatrix} \mathsf{gk} \leftarrow \mathsf{Pgen}(1^\lambda), (\mathsf{pk}, \mathsf{aux_X} \| \mathsf{td}) \leftarrow (\mathsf{X} \| \dot{\mathsf{Ext}}_\mathsf{X})(\mathsf{gk}), (\mathsf{x}, \mathsf{w}) \leftarrow \mathcal{A}(\mathsf{aux_X}), \\ \text{if } b = 0 \text{ then} \pi \leftarrow \mathsf{P}(\mathsf{gk}, \mathsf{pk}, \mathsf{x}, \mathsf{w}) \text{ else } \pi \leftarrow \mathsf{Sim}(\mathsf{gk}, \mathsf{pk}, \mathsf{td}, \mathsf{x}) \text{ fi} : \\ (\mathsf{x}, \mathsf{w}) \in \mathcal{R} \wedge \mathsf{V_{pk}}(\mathsf{gk}, \mathsf{pk}) = 1 \wedge \mathcal{A}(\pi) = 1 \end{bmatrix}.$$

Here $\mathsf{aux_X}$ *is whatever information* X *wishes to send to* $\mathcal{A}$.

Assumptions. In AGM reductions we use q-PDL, a q-type version of discrete logarithm assumption. We also require the KerMDH computational assumption, and the BDH-KE knowledge assumption. The definitions are as follows.

Definition 6 (q-**PDL** [Lip12]). *The q-Power Discrete Logarithm assumption holds for* BGen *if for any PPT* $\mathcal{A}$,

$$\Pr[\mathsf{gk} \leftarrow \mathsf{BGen}(1^\lambda), z \leftarrow_{\$} \mathbb{Z}_p, z' \leftarrow \mathcal{A}(\mathsf{gk}, [(z^i)_{i=1}^q]_1, [(z^i)_{i=1}^q]_2) : z = z'] \approx_\lambda 0.$$

Definition 7 (**KerMDH** [MRV16]). *Let* $\mathcal{D}_{\ell,k}$ *be a distribution over* $\mathbb{F}_p^{\ell \times k}$. *The* $\mathcal{D}_{\ell,k}$-*KerMDH assumption holds for* BGen *and* $z \in \{1, 2\}$ *if for any PPT* $\mathcal{A}$,

$$\Pr[\mathsf{gk} \leftarrow \mathsf{BGen}(1^\lambda), \mathbf{M} \leftarrow_{\$} \mathcal{D}_{\ell,k}, [\mathbf{c}]_{\bar{z}} \leftarrow \mathcal{A}(\mathsf{gk}, [\mathbf{M}]_z) : \mathbf{c} \neq \mathbf{0} \wedge \mathbf{c}^\top \mathbf{M} = \mathbf{0}] \approx_\lambda 0.$$

Definition 8 (**BDH-KE** [ABLZ17]). *We say that* BGen *is BDH-KE secure if for any PPT adversary* $\mathcal{A}$ *there exists a PPT extractor* $\mathsf{Ext}_\mathcal{A}$, *such that*

$$\Pr\left[\mathsf{gk} \leftarrow \mathsf{BGen}(1^\lambda), ([\alpha]_1, [\alpha']_2 \| \beta) \leftarrow (\mathcal{A} \| \mathsf{Ext}_\mathcal{A})(\mathsf{gk}) : \alpha = \alpha' \wedge \beta \neq \alpha \right] \approx_\lambda 0.$$

Commitment Scheme. A commitment scheme is a tuple of efficient algorithms $(\mathsf{KGen}, \mathsf{Com})$ such that

- $\mathsf{KGen}(1^\lambda)$ outputs a commitment key ck.
- $\mathsf{Com_{ck}}(m; r)$ outputs a commitment c given a message m and randomness r.

Typically a commitment scheme should satisfy at least the following properties. (i) *(perfectly) hiding*: the distribution $\mathsf{Com_{ck}}(m; r)$ (over $r \leftarrow_{\$} \mathbb{F}_p$) is the same for any message m; (ii) *(computationally) binding*: it is infeasible for an adversary to find (m_1, r_1) and (m_2, r_2) s.t. $\mathsf{Com_{ck}}(m_1; r_1) = \mathsf{Com_{ck}}(m_2; r_2)$ and $m_1 \neq m_2$.

Polynomial Commitment Scheme. For polynomials $\{T_i(X_1, \ldots, X_k)\}_{i=1}^{n+1} \in \mathbb{F}_p[X_1, \ldots, X_k]$ we define a $(T_i)_{i=1}^{n+1}$-*commitment scheme* as follows:

- $\mathsf{KGen}(1^\lambda)$ picks $\chi \leftarrow_{\$} \mathbb{F}_p^k$ and returns a commitment key $\mathsf{ck} \leftarrow [(T_i(\chi))_{i=1}^{n+1}]_z$.
- $\mathsf{Com_{ck}}((a_1, \ldots, a_n); r)$ returns a commitment $\sum_{i=1}^n a_i[T_i(\chi)]_1 + r[T_{n+1}(\chi)]_1$.

Clearly, this commitment is perfectly hiding when $r \leftarrow_{\$} \mathbb{F}_p$ and $T_{n+1}(\chi) \neq 0$. If $\{T_i\}_{i=1}^{n+1}$ is a linearly independent set, it is also computationally binding under a suitably chosen KerMDH assumption, cf. [FLSZ17a, Theorem 1].

DL-Extractable Commitment Scheme. The DKG protocol of [ABL+19b] requires a UC-secure *Discrete Logarithm Extractable* (DL-extractable) commitment scheme as defined in [ABL+19a]. In DL-extractable commitments the messages are field elements x, but commitments can be opened to $[x]_z$ thus still leaving x itself private. However, since in the UC-model committing to x is equivalent to giving it to an ideal functionality, then the committer knows x, i.e., the discrete logarithm x can be extracted from the commitment given a secret key. For a formal definition and a construction, see [ABL+19a].

Algebraic Group Model. Recently Fuchsbauer et al. [FKL18] introduced the algebraic group model (AGM) that lies between the standard and the generic group model. In the AGM, an adversary $\mathcal{A}$ that returns a group element $[x]_z$ is required to provide a linear representation of $[x]_z$ relative to all previously received group elements. That is, if $\mathcal{A}$ received as input group elements $[\mathbf{y}]_z$ then she must submit along with $[x]_k$ a representation $\mathbf{z}$ such that $[x]_z = \mathbf{z}^\top [\mathbf{y}]_z$. Using techniques similar to [FKL18, Theorem 7.2] we prove knowledge-soundness of the unit vector argument under the PDL assumption in the AGM.

2.1   FLSZ Shuffle Argument

We give a brief overview of the FLSZ shuffle argument for the shuffle relation

$$\mathcal{R}_n^{sh} := \left\{ \begin{array}{l} ((\mathsf{gk}, \mathsf{pk_e}, [(\mathbf{c}_i')_{i=1}^n]_2, [(\mathbf{c}_i)_{i=1}^n]_2), (\sigma, \mathbf{t})) \mid \sigma \in \mathbb{S}_n \wedge \mathbf{t} \in \mathbb{F}_p^n \wedge \\ (\forall i \in [1..n] : [\mathbf{c}_i']_2 = [\mathbf{c}_{\sigma(i)}]_2 + \mathsf{Enc}_{\mathsf{pk_e}}([0]_2; t_i)) \end{array} \right\}.$$

They use a $((P_i(X))_{i=1}^n, X_\varrho)$-commitment scheme to commit to columns of a permutation matrix, where $P_i(X) := 2\ell_i(X) + \ell_{n+1}(X)$ for $i \in [1..n]$.

Lemma 1. *Let $P_0(X) := \ell_{n+1}(X) - 1$ and $Q_i(X) := (P_i(X) + P_0(X))^2 - 1$ for $i \in [1..n]$. If $(\sum_{i=1}^n a_i P_i(X) + P_0(X))^2 - 1 \in \mathsf{Span}\{Q_i(X)\}_{i=1}^n$ and $n < p - 1$, then $(a_1, \ldots, a_n)$ is a unit vector.*

Proof. Denote $T(X) := (\sum_{i=1}^n a_i P_i(X) + P_0(X))^2 - 1$. Firstly, observe that for $j \in [0..n]$, $T(w_j) = (\sum_{i=1}^n a_i P_i(w_j) + P_0(w_j))^2 - 1 = (\sum_{i=1}^n a_i(2\ell_i(w_j) + \ell_{n+1}(w_j)) + \ell_{n+1}(w_j) - 1)^2 - 1 = (2a_j - 1)^2 - 1 = 4a_j(a_j - 1)$. On the other hand, $Q_i(w_j) = (P_i(w_j) + P_0(w_j))^2 - 1 = 0$ for $j \in [1..n]$. Therefore, $T(X) \in \mathsf{Span}\{Q_i(X)\}_{i=1}^n$ implies that $T(w_j) = 0$. Hence $a_j \in \{0, 1\}$ for $j \in [1..n]$.

Finally, $T(w_{n+1}) = (\sum_{i=1}^n a_i(2 \cdot 0 + 1) + 1 - 1))^2 - 1 = (\sum_{i=1}^n a_i)^2 - 1$. Similarly as before, $Q_i(w_{n+1}) = 0$ so $T(w_{n+1}) = 0$. Therefore, $(\sum_{i=1}^n a_i)^2 - 1 = (\sum_{i=1}^n a_i - 1)(\sum_{i=1}^n a_i + 1) = 0$. Since $\sum_{i=1}^n a_i = n < p - 1$ we must have $\sum_{i=1}^n a_i = 1$, so exactly one a_j is 1 and all others are 0. Hence $(a_1, \ldots, a_n)$ is a unit vector. $\quad\square$

Given the above property, they propose a *unit vector argument* to show that the prover could open each commitment to a unit vector. They then enhance it to a *permutation matrix argument* by observing that n unit vectors form a permutation matrix exactly when their sum is $\mathbf{1}_n$. Next, they would like to show that the committed permutation matrix was used to shuffle the ciphertexts. However, due to some technical challenges, they are unable to use the same commitment key. Instead, they commit once more to the columns of the permutation matrix, but this time with a $((\hat{P}_i(X))_{i=1}^n, X_{\hat{\varrho}})$-commitment where $\hat{P}_i(X) := X^{(i+1)(n+1)}$ for $i \in [1..n]$. They propose a *same-message argument* to show that both types of commitments can be opened to the same matrix. Finally, a *consistency argument* proves that the committed permutation was used to shuffle the ciphertexts.

The unit vector argument, the permutation matrix argument, and the same-message argument are proven to be knowledge-sound in the GBGM. However, the soundness of the unit vector argument depends on the soundness of the same-message argument. The consistency argument is culpably sound[5] under an application specific variation of the KerMDH assumption. The shuffle argument itself is sound assuming that other arguments are secure and assuming that commitments are binding. The shuffle argument has perfect zero-knowledge.

3 Distributed Key Generation Protocol

We apply the UC-secure DKG protocol of Abdolmaleki et al. [ABL+19b] in the public key generation of our shuffle argument. This protocol avoids the random oracle model (unlike, e.g., [BCG+15]) and due to UC-security it will not affect the soundness or zero-knowledge properties of the argument. Of course, any general MPC protocol can be used as a DKG, but since we potentially require a large number of parties (e.g., mixers in the mix-network) and since evaluated circuits can have a large multiplicative depth, specialized protocols will perform much better. See [BCG+15] for further discussion on efficiency difference.

3.1 Verification-Friendly Public Key

Although the DKG protocols of [BCG+15] and [ABL+19b] are efficient, they are not general MPC protocols and can only generate certain kinds of keys. Namely, they require key computation to be represented as a circuit that comes from a special class ($\mathcal{C}^S$, described below) and is evaluated on uniformly random field inputs. Fortunately, the protocols are still sufficient for generating public keys for many pairing-based arguments or, as we will later show, slightly modified versions. Compared to [ABL+19b] we give a more direct, but equivalent, description of such keys which we call *verification-friendly*. Intuitively, a verification-friendly public key means that even if one doesn't trust the parties generating the public key, one can at least ensure that it is of the correct structure.

We say that an argument Ψ has a *verification-friendly public key* if (i) output $\mathsf{td} = (\chi_i)_{i=1}^n$ of $\mathsf{K}_{\mathsf{td}}(\mathsf{gk})$ is distributed uniformly randomly over $(\mathbb{F}_p^*)^n$, and (ii) $\mathsf{K}_{\mathsf{pk}}(\mathsf{gk}, \mathsf{td}) = \mathsf{C}(\mathsf{td})$ where C is a circuit from a class $\mathcal{C}_{\mathsf{gk},n}^S$. Any circuit $\mathsf{C} \in \mathcal{C}_{\mathsf{gk},n}^S$ takes as input $\mathsf{td} = (\chi_i)_{i=1}^n \in (\mathbb{F}_p^*)^n$ and contains two types of gates:

---

[5] Culpable soundness is a weaker form of soundness where an adversary additionally provides a witness of his cheating.

- *multiplication-division (multdiv)* gate $\mathsf{MD}_{\chi_i,\chi_j}([x]_z)$ outputs $[(\chi_i/\chi_j)x]_z$, where $z \in \{1,2\}$ and $[x]_z$ is a gate input.
- *linear combination (lincomb)* gate $\mathsf{LC}_\mathbf{c}([\mathbf{y}]_z)$ outputs $\left[\sum_{i=1}^t c_i y_i\right]_z$, where $z \in \{1,2\}$, $\mathbf{c} \in \mathbb{F}_p^t$ is a constant, and $[\mathbf{y}]_z \in \mathbb{G}_z^t$ is a gate input.

Gates in the circuit C are partitioned into interleaved layers $C_1, L_1, \ldots, C_d, L_d$ where each C_i contains only multdiv gates and L_i contains only lincomb gates. Furthermore, C satisfies the following conditions:

1. Inputs of gates in C_i or L_i can be either constants or outputs of the gates on the current or lower layers of the circuit.
2. The output of each gate is part of the output of the circuit C.
3. Layer C_1 always contains gates $\mathsf{MD}_{\chi_i,1}([1]_z)$ for all $i \in [1..n]$, $z \in \{1,2\}$. Therefore, $[(\chi_i)_{i=1}^n]_1$ and $[(\chi_i)_{i=1}^n]_2$ are always outputs of the circuit.

3.2 DKG Protocol for Verification-Friendly Keys

We describe the DKG protocol of [ABL+19b] where the parties collectively evaluate a $\mathcal{C}_{\mathsf{gk},n}^\mathsf{S}$-circuit to generate a verification-friendly public key. The protocol retains soundness and zero-knowledge of the argument given that at least one party in the protocol is honest and malicious parties are non-halting. We note that with a suitable key verification algorithm it is possible to achieve zero-knowledge even if all the parties are malicious.

Let $\mathcal{P}_1, \ldots, \mathcal{P}_k$ be the parties running the DKG protocol. Each party $\mathcal{P}_r$ samples shares $(\chi_{j,r})_{j=1}^n \leftarrow_\$ (\mathbb{F}_p^*)^n$ which allows us to define trapdoor elements as $\chi_j := \prod_{r=1}^k \chi_{j,r}$ for $j \in [1..n]$. Note that if at least one value $\chi_{j,r} \in \mathbb{F}_p^*$ is picked independently and uniformly at random, then χ_j is uniformly random in $\mathbb{F}_p^*$. For ease of description, we set $\chi_0 := 1$ and similarly $\chi_{0,r} := 1$ for $r \in [1..k]$.

The protocol starts with a commitment round where all the parties commit to their shares $\chi_{i,r}$ with a UC-secure DL-extractable commitment scheme. This is followed by an opening round where each $\mathcal{P}_i$ reveals $[\chi_{i,r}]_1, [\chi_{i,r}]_2$. Since the commitment scheme is UC-secure, then it is also non-malleable and thus guarantees that the adversary chooses her shares independently of the shares of the honest parties. Next, the parties start to evaluate the circuit layer-by-layer. For evaluating a single multdiv gate $\mathsf{MD}_{\chi_i,\chi_j}([x]_z) = [(\chi_i/\chi_j)x]_z$ where $i, j \in [0..n]$, parties run the $\mathsf{mpcMD}_{\chi_i,\chi_j}([x]_z)$ protocol given in Fig. 1. Assuming that $[x]_z$ is public, $\mathcal{P}_1$ broadcasts $(\chi_{i,1}/\chi_{j,1})[a]_z$ and each subsequent party $\mathcal{P}_r$ multiplies $\chi_{i,r}/\chi_{j,r}$ to the output of her predecessor $\mathcal{P}_{r-1}$. If all the parties follow the protocol, then the output of $\mathcal{P}_k$ is $\mathsf{cert}_k = (\chi_{i,1} \cdot \ldots \cdot \chi_{i,k})/(\chi_{j,1} \cdot \ldots \cdot \chi_{j,k})[a]_z = (\chi_i/\chi_j)[a]_z$. Computation of each party can be verified with pairings by using the algorithm $\mathsf{VmpcMD}_{\chi_i,\chi_j}$ in Fig. 1. Any linear combination gate $\mathsf{LC}_\mathbf{c}([\mathbf{x}]_z)$ can be computed locally by each party by simply evaluating the expression $\sum_{i=1}^t c_i [a_i]_z$.

Let us make a slight restriction for now that multdiv gates on the same layer do not depend on each other. Then each multi-division layer C_i can be evaluated by running multiple instances of the mpcMD protocol in parallel. More precisely,

---

$\mathsf{mpcMD}_{\chi_i,\chi_j}([x]_z)$:
1. Set $\mathsf{cert}_0 \leftarrow [x]_z$.
2. For $r = 1, \ldots, k$: Party $\mathcal{P}_r$ broadcasts $\mathsf{cert}_r \leftarrow (\chi_{i,r}/\chi_{j,r}) \cdot \mathsf{cert}_{r-1}$.
3. Output cert_k.

$\mathsf{VmpcMD}_{\chi_i,\chi_j}([x]_z, (\mathsf{cert}_r)_{r=1}^k, [(\chi_{j,r})_{r=1}^k, (\chi_{i,r})_{r=1}^k]_{\bar{z}})$:
1. Set $\mathsf{cert}_0 \leftarrow [x]_z$.
2. For $r = 1, \ldots, k$: check that $\mathsf{cert}_r \bullet [\chi_{j,r}]_{\bar{z}} = \mathsf{cert}_{r-1} \bullet [\chi_{i,r}]_{\bar{z}}$.
3. If all checks pass output 1 and otherwise output 0.

Fig. 1. Multi-party protocol $\mathsf{mpcMD}_{\chi_i,\chi_j}$ and its transcript verifier $\mathsf{VmpcMD}_{\chi_i,\chi_j}$

<u>Commitment:</u> Each party $\mathcal{P}_r$ picks $\chi_{1,r}, \ldots, \chi_{n,r} \leftarrow_\$ \mathbb{F}_p^*$ and broadcasts DL-extractable commitments of the values.

<u>Opening:</u> Once all the commitments are received, $\mathcal{P}_r$ broadcasts openings together with $[(\chi_{i,r})_{i=1}^n]_1$ and $[(\chi_{i,r})_{i=1}^n]_2$. Each party verifies the openings and aborts if the verification failed.

<u>Layer computation:</u> For a multi-division layer C_i containing a gate $\mathsf{MD}_{\chi_i,\chi_j}([a]_z)$, parties run the protocol $\mathsf{mpcMD}_{\chi_i,\chi_j}([a]_z)$ and verify the computation with the algorithm $\mathsf{VmpcMD}_{\chi_i,\chi_j}$. All the gates in C_i can be evaluated in parallel. Linear combination layers L_i are locally evaluated by each party.

<u>Output:</u> Output of the protocol is the output of all the evaluated gates.

Fig. 2. Distributed key generation protocol for a circuit $C = (C_1, L_1, \ldots, C_d, L_d)$

the computation begins with the party $\mathcal{P}_1$ doing its part of computation in mpcMD for each multdiv gate in C_i. Then, given the output produced by $\mathcal{P}_1$, the party $\mathcal{P}_2$ does her part of the computation for each gate in the layer C_i and so on. Hence, a single multdiv layer can be evaluated in k rounds since every party needs to contribute to the output of the previous party just once. After each multi-division layer, the parties verify the computation by running the algorithm $\mathsf{VmpcMD}_{\chi_i,\chi_j}$ for each gate. If the checks pass, the parties locally evaluate gates on layer L_i and proceed to compute the next layer C_{i+1}. Full details are given in Fig. 2.

We refer the reader to [ABL+19b] for the more general protocol where k rounds can be achieved even if the gates on the same layer depend on each other. That version of the DKG is also used for our shuffle argument, but for this we provide an explicit description in the full version of our paper. It is important to note that Abdolmaleki et al. showed that if at least one party in the DKG is honest, then it UC-realises the CRS ideal functionality (which essentially samples a public key in the beginning and returns it to anyone that queries).

4   Transparent Shuffle Argument

The DKG protocol requires the public key to be verification-friendly. In particular, we need to guarantee the following properties:

- Each trapdoor $\iota \in \mathsf{td}$ has to be sampled uniformly at random from $\mathbb{F}_p^*$ and the public key has to contain both $[\iota]_1$ and $[\iota]_2$.
- The public key has to be computable by interleaved multi-division and linear combination circuit layers and the output of each gate has to be part of the public key. For example, given that $[a]_1, [b]_1, [c]_1, [d]_1$ are part of the public key, it is not possible to have $[ab+cd]_1$ in the public key without also revealing some intermediate gate outputs like $[ab]_1$ and $[cd]_1$.

In this section, we modify the FLSZ argument and construct a new transparent shuffle argument tFLSZ which has a verification-friendly public key. Besides making the argument verification-friendly, we also simplify the construction: (i) we combine the unit vector argument and the same-message argument of tFLSZ into a single argument, (ii) we skip the consistency argument and directly construct a shuffle argument from the permutation argument, and (iii) we observe that one of the trapdoors, $\hat{\varrho}$, can be set to 1 without affecting security. The new argument is given in Fig. 3; we introduce the construction step-by-step in the following.

Let us take the public key of FLSZ in Fig. 4 as a starting point and observe which modifications need to be introduced to make it verification-friendly.

- Firstly, we need to add all the trapdoor elements to both groups which means adding $[\chi, \beta, \hat{\beta}]_1$ and $[\chi]_2$ to the public key.
- To evaluate polynomials $P_i(X)$ at point χ we add powers of χ in both groups to the public key. Since P_i is at most degree n, it suffices to include elements $[(\chi^i)_{i=1}^n]_1$ and $[(\chi^i)_{i=1}^n]_2$. However, since $(P_i(X) + P_0(X))^2 - 1$ has at most degree $2n$, we additionally add $[(\chi^i)_{i=n+1}^{2n}]_1$.
- Polynomials $\hat{P}_i$ have a degree $(i+1)(n+1)$, requiring, for the sake of verification friendliness, to include elements $[(\chi^i)_{i=1}^{(n+1)^2}]_1$ which would cause quadratic overhead. We avoid this by redefining the polynomials $\hat{P}_i$ and evaluating them at a new random point θ. The first idea would be to set $\hat{P}_i(X_\theta) = X_\theta^i$ for $i = 1, \ldots, n$ and add $[(\theta^i)_{i=1}^n]_1$ and $[\theta]_2$ to the public key. However, the $((\hat{P}_i(X_\theta))_{i=1}^n, 1)$-commitment scheme would not be binding since the KerMDH assumption does not hold for $[\mathbf{M}]_1 = [\hat{P}_1(X_\theta), \ldots, \hat{P}_n(X_\theta), 1]_1$, as the adversary can output $[\mathbf{c}]_2 = [\theta, -1, 0, \ldots, 0]_2$ such that $\mathbf{Mc}^\top = \mathbf{0}$ and $\mathbf{c} \neq \mathbf{0}$. Instead we set $\hat{P}_i(X_\theta) = X_\theta^{2i}$ for $i \in [1 .. n]$ and include $[(\theta^i)_{i=1}^{2n}]_1$ and $[\theta]_2$ to the public key. Now the commitment scheme is binding under a slight variation of the standard KerMDH assumption, which we prove in Sect. 5 to reduce to PDL assumption in the algebraic group model.

Another challenge is computing crs_{sm} since it contains elements $[\beta P_i + \hat{\beta}\hat{P}_i]_1$. It is not possible to reveal $[\beta P_i]_1$ and $[\hat{\beta}\hat{P}_i]_1$ since this breaks knowledge-soundness of the same-message argument. We propose a new argument to overcome this.

$\mathsf{K}_{\mathsf{td}}(\mathsf{gk})$: Return $\mathsf{td} = (\chi, \theta, \beta, \hat{\beta}, \varrho) \leftarrow_r (\mathbb{F}_p^*)^5$.

$\mathsf{K}_{\mathsf{pk}}(\mathsf{gk}, n, \mathsf{td})$: Let $\mathbf{P} = (P_i(\chi))_{i=1}^n$, $\hat{\mathbf{P}} = (\hat{P}_i(\theta))_{i=1}^n$, $\mathbf{Q} = ((P_i(\chi) + P_0(\chi))^2 - 1)_{i=1}^n$.

$$\mathsf{pk}_{uv} \leftarrow \begin{pmatrix} [1,\ P_0(\chi),\ \mathbf{P},\ \varrho,\ \mathbf{Q}/\varrho,\ \sum_{i=1}^n \hat{P}_i,\ \beta^2\varrho,\ \beta\hat{\beta},\ \beta^2\mathbf{P} + \beta\hat{\beta}\hat{\mathbf{P}}]_1, \\ [1,\ P_0(\chi),\ \mathbf{P},\ \varrho,\ \beta^2,\ \beta\hat{\beta}]_2,\ [1]_T \end{pmatrix},$$

$$\mathsf{pk}_{pkv} \leftarrow \begin{pmatrix} [\beta,\ \hat{\beta},\ (\theta^{2i-1})_{i=1}^n]_1, \\ [\chi, \theta, \beta, \hat{\beta}]_2 \end{pmatrix}, \quad \mathsf{pk}_{vf} \leftarrow \begin{pmatrix} [(\chi^i)_{i=1}^{2n},\ (\beta\chi^i, \hat{\beta}\theta^{2i})_{i=1}^n, \beta\varrho]_1, \\ [(\chi^i)_{i=2}^n]_2 \end{pmatrix}.$$

Return $\mathsf{pk} \leftarrow ([\hat{\mathbf{P}}]_1, \mathsf{pk}_{uv}, \mathsf{pk}_{pkv}, \mathsf{pk}_{vf})$.

$\mathsf{K}(\mathsf{gk}, n)$: Run $\mathsf{td} \leftarrow \mathsf{K}_{\mathsf{td}}(\mathsf{gk})$, $\mathsf{pk} \leftarrow \mathsf{K}_{\mathsf{pk}}(\mathsf{gk}, n, \mathsf{td})$, return $(\mathsf{pk}, \mathsf{td})$.

$\mathsf{P}(\mathsf{gk}, (\mathsf{pk}_e, \mathsf{pk}), [\mathbf{C}]_2 = [(\mathbf{c}_i)_{i=1}^n]_2 \in \mathbb{G}_2^{n \times 2}, (\sigma \in \mathbb{S}_n, \mathbf{t} \in \mathbb{F}_p^n))$:

1. For $i = 1$ to $n - 1$: $\hat{r}_i \leftarrow_\$ \mathbb{F}_p$; $[\hat{a}_i]_1 \leftarrow [\hat{P}_{\sigma^{-1}(i)}]_1 + \hat{r}_i[1]_1$.
2. $\pi_{per} \leftarrow \mathsf{P}_{per}(\mathsf{gk}, \mathsf{pk}, [(\hat{a}_i)_{i=1}^{n-1}]_1, (\sigma, (\hat{r}_i)_{i=1}^{n-1}))$. // Permutation argument
3. $\hat{r}_n \leftarrow -\sum_{i=1}^{n-1} \hat{r}_i$; $\hat{r} \leftarrow_r \mathbb{F}_p$; $[s]_1 \leftarrow \mathbf{t}^\top[\hat{\mathbf{P}}]_1 + \hat{r}[1]_1$.
4. For $i = 1$ to n: $[\mathbf{t}_i']_2 \leftarrow t_i \cdot \mathsf{pk}_e$.
5. $[\mathbf{N}]_2 \leftarrow \hat{\mathbf{r}}^\top[\mathbf{C}]_2 + \hat{r} \cdot \mathsf{pk}_e$. // Online
6. $[\mathbf{C}']_2 \leftarrow ([\mathbf{c}_{\sigma(i)}]_2 + [\mathbf{t}_i']_2)_{i=1}^n$. // Shuffling, online
7. Return $([\mathbf{C}']_2, \pi_{sh} \leftarrow ([(\hat{a}_j)_{j=1}^{n-1}, s]_1, [\mathbf{N}]_2, \pi_{per}))$.

$\mathsf{V}(\mathsf{gk}, (\mathsf{pk}_e, \mathsf{pk}), ([\mathbf{C}]_2, [\mathbf{C}']_2), \pi_{sh})$:

1. Parse $\pi_{sh} = ([(\hat{a}_j)_{j=1}^{n-1}, s]_1, [\mathbf{N}]_2, \pi_{per})$; set $[\hat{a}_n]_1 \leftarrow [\sum_{i=1}^n \hat{P}_i]_1 - \sum_{i=1}^{n-1}[\hat{a}_i]_1$.
2. Check $\mathsf{V}_{per}(\mathsf{gk}, \mathsf{pk}, [(\hat{a}_i)_{i=1}^{n-1}]_1, \pi_{per}) = 1$.
3. Check $[\hat{\mathbf{P}}]_1^\top \bullet [\mathbf{C}']_2 - [\hat{\mathbf{a}}]_1^\top \bullet [\mathbf{C}]_2 = [s]_1 \bullet \mathsf{pk}_e - [1]_1 \bullet [\mathbf{N}]_2$.

Fig. 3. tFLSZ argument

$\mathsf{K}(\mathsf{gk}, n)$: Generate random $\mathsf{td} = (\chi, \beta, \hat{\beta}, \varrho, \hat{\varrho}, \mathsf{sk}_e) \leftarrow_r (\mathbb{F}_p^*)^6$. Denote $\mathbf{P} = (P_i(\chi))_{i=1}^n$, $P_0 = P_0(\chi)$, and $\hat{\mathbf{P}} = (\hat{P}_i(\chi))_{i=1}^n$, $\mathbf{Q} = ((P_i + P_0)^2 - 1)_{i=1}^n$. Let

$$\mathsf{crs}_{sm} \leftarrow \left([\beta\mathbf{P} + \hat{\beta}\hat{\mathbf{P}}, \beta\varrho, \hat{\beta}\hat{\varrho}]_1, [\beta, \hat{\beta}]_2\right), \quad \mathsf{crs}_{con} \leftarrow [\tfrac{\hat{\mathbf{P}}}{\hat{\varrho}}]_1, \mathsf{pk}_e = [1, \mathsf{sk}_e]_2$$

$$\mathsf{crs}_{pm} \leftarrow \left([1, P_0, \mathbf{Q}/\varrho, \sum_{i=1}^n P_i, \sum_{i=1}^n \hat{P}_i]_1, [P_0, \sum_{i=1}^n P_i]_2, [1]_T\right).$$

Set $\mathsf{crs} \leftarrow (\mathsf{pk}_e, [\tfrac{\mathbf{P}}{\varrho}]_1, [\tfrac{\mathbf{P}}{\varrho}]_2, \mathsf{crs}_{sm}, \mathsf{crs}_{pm}, \mathsf{crs}_{con})$. Return $(\mathsf{crs}, \mathsf{td})$.

Fig. 4. CRS generation algorithm of FLSZ

New Unit Vector Argument. We combine the same-message argument and unit vector argument from FLSZ to a new unit vector argument which is a proof of knowledge for the relation $\mathcal{R}_n^{uv} := \{([\hat{a}]_1, (I \in [1..n], \hat{r})) \mid \hat{a} = \hat{P}_I + \hat{r}\}$. The new argument in Fig. 5 has two advantages: (i) it has a verification-friendly public key, and (ii) the unit vector argument of FLSZ is sound only if we give a

$K_{uv}(gk, n)$: Return $(pk, td) \leftarrow K(gk, n)$ from Fig. 3.
$P_{uv}(gk, pk, [\hat{a}]_1), (I, \hat{r}))$:
    1. $r \leftarrow_s \mathbb{F}_p$, $[r']_1 \leftarrow r[\varrho]_1$, $[d]_1 \leftarrow [\beta^2 P_I + \beta\hat{\beta}\hat{P}_I]_1 + r[\beta^2 \varrho]_1 + \hat{r}[\beta\hat{\beta}]_1$.
    2. $[a]_1 \leftarrow [P_I]_1 + [r']_1$, $[b]_2 \leftarrow [P_I]_2 + r[\varrho]_2$.
    3. $[e]_1 \leftarrow r \cdot (2([a]_1 + [P_0]_1) - [r']_1) + [((P_I + P_0)^2 - 1)/\varrho]_1$.
    4. Return $\pi_{uv} \leftarrow ([d]_1, [a]_1, [b]_2, [e]_1)$.
$V_{uv}(gk, pk, [\hat{a}]_1, \pi_{uv})$:
    1. Parse $\pi_{uv} = ([d]_1, [a]_1, [b]_2, [e]_1)$ and pick $\alpha \leftarrow_s \mathbb{F}_p$.
    2. Check $[d]_1 \bullet [1]_2 = [a, \hat{a}]_1 \bullet [\beta^2, \beta\hat{\beta}]_2^\top$.
    3. Check $([a]_1 + \alpha[1]_1 + [P_0]_1) \bullet ([b]_2 - \alpha[1]_2 + [P_0]_2) = [e]_1 \bullet [\varrho]_2 + (1 - \alpha^2)[1]_T$.

Fig. 5. New unit vector argument

corresponding proof for the same-message argument; the new argument avoids this dependency. On a high level, the verification equation in Step 2 of V_{uv} and the proof element $[d]_1$ in Fig. 5 correspond to a variation of the same-message argument in FLSZ and shows that $[\hat{a}]_1$ and $[a]_1$ commit to the same message **m** respectively with the $((\hat{P}_i(X))_{i=1}^n, 1)$-commitment and the $((P_i(X))_{i=1}^n, X_\varrho)$-commitment. The verification equation in Step 3 of V_{uv} and elements $[b]_2$ and $[e]_1$ in Fig. 5 use the result of Lemma 1 to show that $[a]_1$ commits to a unit vector. This part is identical to the unit vector argument in FLSZ.

The main differences in the new argument are the public key elements for showing that $[\hat{a}]_1$ and $[a]_1$ commit to the same message. Simply revealing elements $[\beta P_i, \hat{\beta}\hat{P}_i]_1$ would be sufficient for verification-friendliness, but breaks the knowledge-soundness property: the same-message argument of FLSZ relies on $[\beta P_i(\chi) + \hat{\beta}\hat{P}_i(\theta)]_1$ being the only $\mathbb{G}_1$ elements in the span of $\{[\beta\chi^i + \hat{\beta}\theta^j]_1\}_{i,j}$ that are available to the adversary. Instead, we essentially substitute $[\beta P_i + \hat{\beta}\hat{P}_i]_1$ with $[\beta^2 P_i + \beta\hat{\beta}\hat{P}_i]_1$ (and other related elements accordingly), and equivalently use the fact that those are the only $\mathbb{G}_1$ elements in the span of $\{[\beta^2\chi^i + \beta\hat{\beta}\theta^j]_1\}_{i,j}$ available to the adversary. This change is significant since the latter elements can be computed with the DKG protocol without revealing $[\beta^2 P_i]_1$ and $[\beta\hat{\beta}\hat{P}_i]_1$:

(i) compute $[\beta\chi^i]_1$ and $[\hat{\beta}\theta^{2i}]_1 = [\hat{\beta}\hat{P}_i]_1$ to obtain $[\beta P_i + \hat{\beta}\hat{P}_i]_1$;
(ii) compute $[\beta^2 P_i + \beta\hat{\beta}\hat{P}_i]_1 = \text{MD}_{\beta,1}([\beta P_i + \hat{\beta}\hat{P}_i]_1)$;
(iii) similarly, from elements $[\beta, \beta\varrho, \hat{\beta}]_1$ compute $[\beta^2\varrho]_1$ and $[\beta\hat{\beta}]_1$.

Additionally, in $\mathbb{G}_2$ we reveal $[\beta^2]_2$ and $[\beta\hat{\beta}]_2$. We prove in the full version of our paper that these changes retain security.

Permutation Argument. The permutation argument is a proof of knowledge for the relation

$$\mathcal{R}_{per} = \{([\hat{\mathbf{a}}]_1, (\sigma, \hat{\mathbf{r}})) \mid \sigma \in \mathbb{S}_n \wedge \sum_{i=1}^n \hat{r}_i = 0 \wedge (\forall i \in [1 .. n] : \hat{a}_i = \hat{P}_{\sigma^{-1}(i)} + \hat{r}_i)\}.$$

We show that this relation is fulfilled the same way as previous NIZK shuffle arguments. Firstly, the prover gives a unit vector argument for each of the commitments $[\hat{a}_i]_1$ for $i \in [1 .. n - 1]$. Next, observe that only if those commitments

$K_{per}(\mathsf{gk}, n)$: Return $(\mathsf{pk}, \mathsf{td}) \leftarrow K(\mathsf{gk}, n)$ from Fig. 3.
$P_{per}(\mathsf{gk}, \mathsf{pk}, [(\hat{a}_i)_{i=1}^{n-1}]_1, (\sigma \in \mathbb{S}_n, (\hat{r}_i)_{i=1}^{n-1}))$:
    1. $\hat{r}_n \leftarrow -\sum_{i=1}^{n-1} \hat{r}_i$, $[\hat{a}_n]_1 \leftarrow [\sum_{i=1}^{n} \hat{P}_i]_1 - \sum_{i=1}^{n-1} [\hat{a}_i]_1$.
    2. For $i \in [1..n]$: $\pi_{uv:i} \leftarrow P_{uv}(\mathsf{gk}, \mathsf{pk}, [\hat{a}_i]_1, (\sigma^{-1}(i), \hat{r}_i))$.
    3. Return $\pi_{per} \leftarrow (\pi_{uv:i})_{i=1}^{n}$.
$V_{per}(\mathsf{gk}, \mathsf{pk}, [(\hat{a}_i)_{i=1}^{n-1}]_1, \pi_{per})$:
    1. Parse $\pi_{per} = (\pi_{uv:i})_{i=1}^{n}$ and set $[\hat{a}_n]_1 \leftarrow [\sum_{i=1}^{n} \hat{P}_i]_1 - \sum_{i=1}^{n-1} [\hat{a}_i]_1$.
    2. For $i \in [1..n]$: check $V_{uv}(\mathsf{gk}, \mathsf{pk}, [\hat{a}_i]_1, \pi_{uv:i}) = 1$.

Fig. 6. Permutation argument

are to distinct values $\hat{P}_i$, is $[\hat{a}_n]_1 := [\sum_{i=1}^{n} \hat{P}_i]_1 - \sum_{i=1}^{n-1} [\hat{a}_i]_1$ a unit vector. Hence, by giving a unit vector argument also for $[\hat{a}_n]_1$, where $[\hat{a}_n]_1$ is explicitly computed by the verifier, we have proven the relation. Condition $\sum_{i=1}^{n} \hat{r}_i = 0$ in $\mathcal{R}_{per}$ comes from the way that $[\hat{a}_n]_1$ is computed. The protocol is given in Fig. 6.

Shuffle Argument. Finally, we prove that ciphertexts were shuffled according to the permutation σ committed in $[\hat{\mathbf{a}}]_1$. This is essentially equivalent to the consistency argument in FLSZ. Intuitively, we check that $\sum_{i=1}^{n} [\hat{P}_i]_1 \bullet [m_i']_2 = \sum_{i=1}^{n} [\hat{P}_{\sigma^{-1}(i)}]_1 \bullet [m_i]_2$ (see Step 3 for the actual equation) which guarantees that $\sum_{i=1}^{n} [\hat{P}_i]_1 \bullet ([m_i']_2 - [m_{\sigma(i)}]_2) = [0]_T$. If $[m_i']_2 \neq [m_{\sigma(i)}]_2$ for some i, then the adversary can find a non-zero element in the kernel of $[\hat{\mathbf{P}}]_1$ and thus break the KerMDH assumption. Of course, the actual messages m_i are encrypted and the verifier knows only a commitment to σ. We balance this in the equation by allowing the prover to produce elements $[s]_1$ and $[\mathbf{N}]_2$, which cancels the randomness in the ciphertexts and the commitments.

Verification-Friendliness of tFLSZ. After making all of the above modifications we end up with a public key as presented in Fig. 3. There are two new sub-keys: pk_{pkv} which contains some elements later required by the V_{pk} algorithm (used by prover to guarantee nn-ZK), and pk_{vf} which is a by-product of making the public key verification-friendly. After the public key generation protocol has finished the elements in pk_{vf} can be disregarded. It is now simple to verify that the public key is verification-friendly. We present it as a series of multiplication-division and linear combination layers in Fig. 7. Hence, the DKG protocol described in Sect. 3 can be applied. For the sake of completeness, we provide an explicit description of the DKG protocol in the full version of the paper.

    For better modularity, we treat the encryption key pk_e separately from the argument's public key. However, we assume it to be correctly generated by some secure DKG protocol, such as the one by Gennaro et al. [GJKR99].

Theorem 1 ([ABL+19b]). *If* tFLSZ *is complete, sound, and computational zero-knowledge in the CRS model, then it is complete, sound, and computational zero-knowledge if the adversary corrupts all but one party in the DKG protocol.*

Input: $(\chi, \theta, \beta, \hat{\beta}, \varrho) \in (\mathbb{F}_p^*)^5$.

Layer C_1:

1. For $\iota \in \{\beta, \hat{\beta}, \varrho\}$, $z \in \{1, 2\}$: $[\iota]_z \leftarrow \iota [1]_z$.
2. For $i = 1$ to $2n$: $[\chi^i]_1 \leftarrow \chi[\chi^{i-1}]_1$, $[\theta^i]_1 \leftarrow \theta[\theta^{i-1}]_1$.
3. Set $[\theta]_2 \leftarrow \theta[1]_2$ and denote $[\hat{P}_i]_1 = [\theta^{2i}]_1$ for $i = 1$ to n.
4. For $i = 1$ to n: $[\chi^i]_2 \leftarrow \chi[\chi^{i-1}]_2$, $[\beta\chi^i]_1 \leftarrow \beta[\chi^i]_1$, $[\hat{\beta}\hat{P}_i]_1 \leftarrow \hat{\beta}[\hat{P}_i]_1$.
5. $[\beta^2]_2 \leftarrow \beta[\beta]_2$, $[\beta\varrho]_1 \leftarrow \beta[\varrho]_1$, $[\beta^2\varrho]_1 \leftarrow \beta[\beta\varrho]_1$, $[\beta\hat{\beta}]_1 \leftarrow \beta[\hat{\beta}]_1$, $[\beta\hat{\beta}]_2 \leftarrow \beta[\hat{\beta}]_2$.

Layer L_1:

1. Compute $[(\ell_i(\chi), \beta\ell_i(\chi), \ell_i(\chi)^2)_{i=1}^{n+1}]_1$, $[(\ell_i(\chi))_{i=1}^{n+1}]_2$, $[(\ell_i(\chi) \cdot \ell_{n+1}(\chi))_{i=1}^n]_1$ from $[(\chi^i)_{i=0}^{2n}]_1$, $[(\beta\chi^i)_{i=0}^n]_1$, and $[(\chi^i)_{i=0}^n]_2$ (see the full version of our paper for details).
2. $[P_0]_1 \leftarrow [\ell_{n+1}(\chi)]_1 - [1]_1$, $[P_0]_2 \leftarrow [\ell_{n+1}(\chi)]_2 - [1]_2$.
3. For $i = 1$ to n:
   (a) $[P_i]_1 \leftarrow 2[\ell_i(\chi)]_1 + [\ell_{n+1}(\chi)]_1$, $[P_i]_2 \leftarrow 2[\ell_i(\chi)]_2 + [\ell_{n+1}(\chi)]_2$
   (b) $[Q_i]_1 \leftarrow 4[\ell_i(\chi)^2]_1 + 4[\ell_{n+1}(\chi)^2]_1 + 8[\ell_i(\chi) \cdot \ell_{n+1}(\chi)]_1 - 4[\ell_i(\chi)]_1 - 4[\ell_{n+1}(\chi)]_1$.
   (c) $[\beta P_i + \hat{\beta}\hat{P}_i]_1 \leftarrow 2[\beta\ell_i(\chi)]_1 + [\beta\ell_{n+1}(\chi)]_1 + [\hat{\beta}\theta^{2i}]_1$.
4. $[\sum_{i=1}^n \hat{P}_i]_1 \leftarrow \sum_{i=1}[\hat{P}_i]_1$.

Layer C_2: For $i = 1$ to n: $[Q_i/\varrho]_1 \leftarrow [Q_i]_1/\varrho$, $[\beta^2 P_i + \beta\hat{\beta}\hat{P}_i]_1 \leftarrow \beta[\beta P_i + \hat{\beta}\hat{P}_i]_1$.

Fig. 7. Public key computation as a circuit

5 Security in the CRS Model

In this section, we establish that tFLSZ is secure in the CRS model, where the CRS is the public key generated by a trusted party. We first claim security of the unit vector and permutation arguments, as stated in Theorems 2 and 3.

Theorem 2 (Security of unit vector argument). *The unit vector argument in the CRS model (see Fig. 5) has perfect completeness and perfect zero-knowledge. If the $(3n - 1)$-PDL assumption holds, then it has computational knowledge-soundness in the AGM.*

Theorem 3 (Security of permutation argument). *The permutation argument in the CRS model (see Fig. 6) is perfectly complete and perfectly zero-knowledge. If the unit vector argument is knowledge-sound and $((\hat{P}_i(X))_{i=1}^n, 1)$-commitment is binding, then the permutation argument is also knowledge-sound.*

The proofs are given in the full version of our paper. Soundness of the unit-vector argument uses a common trick of AGM proofs that first defines an *idealised verification*, where the verification equation holds true for polynomials $V(\mathbf{X})$ (with trapdoor elements as variables) rather than for polynomial evaluations $V(\chi)$ only (*real verification*, for concrete trapdoor elements χ). We then show that no element outside the unit vector language can pass the idealised verification. Moreover, if an adversary manages to pass the real verification but not the ideal one, then she can be used to break the $(3n - 1)$-PDL assumption. The proof of the other properties are quite standard.

We prove soundness of the shuffle argument under a weaker assumption compared to [FLSZ17a]. The assumption, called the GapKerMDH assumption, is novel, but we show that it reduces to the PDL assumption in the AGM. More precisely, since the KerMDH assumption is insecure for $M = (1, \theta, \ldots, \theta^n) \in \mathbb{Z}_p^{n \times 1}$ if the adversary is given both $[M]_1$ and $[\theta]_2$, then a slightly modified assumption is required. We still give the same information to the adversary, but require that the output is in the kernel of a certain $M' \subset M$ that contains periodic gaps.

Definition 9. *The n-GapKerMDH assumption holds for* BGen *if for any PPT* $\mathcal{A}$,

$$
\Pr \left[\begin{array}{l} \mathsf{gk} \leftarrow \mathsf{BGen}(1^\lambda), \theta \leftarrow\!\!\!_\$ \, \mathbb{F}_p^*, [\mathbf{v}]_2 \leftarrow \mathcal{A}(\mathsf{gk}, [(\theta^i)_{i=1}^{2n}]_1, [\theta]_2) : \\ \mathbf{v}^\top \cdot (\theta^{2i})_{i=0}^n = 0 \wedge \mathbf{v} \neq \mathbf{0}_{n+1} \end{array} \right] \approx_\lambda 0.
$$

Theorem 4. *If the $(2n)$-PDL assumption holds, then the n-GapKerMDH assumption holds in the AGM.*

Proof. Let $\mathcal{A}$ be an algebraic PPT adversary that breaks n-GapKerMDH assumption with probability ε_{gap}. More precisely, $\mathcal{A}$ gets as an input $(\mathsf{gk}, [(\theta^i)_{i=1}^{2n}]_1, [\theta]_2)$ for $\theta \leftarrow\!\!\!_\$ \, \mathbb{Z}_p$, and outputs a non-zero $[\mathbf{v}]_2 \in \mathbb{G}_2^{n+1}$ and its linear representation $\mathbf{U} \in \mathbb{Z}_p^{(n+1) \times 2}$ (that is $[\mathbf{v}]_2 = \mathbf{U} \cdot [1, \theta]_2^\top$) such that $\sum_{i=0}^n \theta^{2i} \cdot v_{i+1} = 0$.

We construct a PPT adversary $\mathcal{B}$ that breaks $(2n)$-PDL assumption using $\mathcal{A}$. First, $\mathcal{B}$ gets as an input $(\mathsf{gk}, [(\theta^i)_{i=1}^{2n}]_1, [(\theta^i)_{i=1}^{2n}]_2)$ and runs $\mathcal{A}(\mathsf{gk}, [(\theta^i)_{i=1}^{2n}]_1, [\theta]_2)$ to get the output $[\mathbf{v}]_2$ and $\mathbf{U}$. Let us define polynomials $V_i(X_\theta) := U_{i,1} + U_{i,2} \cdot X_\theta$ for $i \in [1..n+1]$ which in particular satisfies $V_i(\theta) = v_i$. Similarly for the expression $\sum_{i=0}^n \theta^{2i} \cdot v_{i+1}$ we define a polynomial $V(X_\theta) := \sum_{i=0}^n X_\theta^{2i} \cdot V_{i+1}(X_\theta)$ such that if $\mathcal{A}$ wins then $V(\theta) = 0$. Adversary $\mathcal{B}$ will abort if $\mathcal{A}$ either outputs an incorrect representation U or loses the n-GapKerMDH game. Otherwise $\mathcal{B}$ finds roots of $V(X_\theta)$ (can be done efficiently), and returns the one which matches $[\theta]_1$.

Finding roots of $V(X_\theta)$ is only possible if $V(X_\theta)$ is a non-zero polynomial, but it is easy to see that this is always the case if $\mathcal{A}$ wins. We may express

$$
V(X_\theta) = \sum_{i=0}^n X_\theta^{2i} \cdot (U_{i+1,1} + U_{i+1,2} \cdot X_\theta) = \sum_{i=0}^n U_{i+1,1} X_\theta^{2i} + \sum_{i=0}^n U_{i+1,2} \cdot X_\theta^{2i+1}.
$$

So if $V(X_\theta) = 0$ then $\mathbf{U} = 0$ and therefore $\mathbf{v} = 0$ which contradicts $\mathcal{A}$ winning. It follows that $\mathcal{B}$ can break the $(2n)$-PDL assumption with probability ε_{gap}. □

Theorem 5 (Security of shuffle argument). tFLSZ *is perfectly complete and perfectly zero-knowledge in the CRS model. If the permutation argument is knowledge-sound and the n-GapKerMDH assumption holds, then* tFLSZ *is sound.*

Proof. Perfect Completeness. Can be straightforwardly verified by substituting an honest proof to the verification equations.

Perfect Zero-Knowledge. We show that the simulator Sim in Fig. 8 outputs an argument that has the same distribution as an argument output by an honest prover. In both cases $[(a_i)_{i=1}^n]_1$, $[(\hat{a}_i)_{i=1}^{n-1}]_1$, and $[s]_1$ are uniformly randomly and independently distributed group elements. Moreover, both honest and simulated arguments have $b_i = a_i$ for $i \in [1..n]$ and $[\hat{a}_n]_1 = \sum_{i=1}^n [\hat{P}_i]_1 - \sum_{i=1}^{n-1} [\hat{a}_i]_1$. Elements $[\mathbf{d}]_1$, $[\mathbf{e}]_1$, $[\mathbf{N}]_2$ are now uniquely fixed by the verification equation and the elements mentioned before. It is straightforward to check that the simulated argument satisfies the verification equations. Thus the distributions are equal.

Soundness. Let $\mathcal{A}_{sh}$ be a PPT adversary that breaks soundness of the shuffle argument with probability ε_{sh}. Let $\mathcal{A}_{per}$ be the adversary $\mathcal{A}_{sh}$ restricted only to output $([(\hat{a}_i)_{i=1}^{n-1}]_1, \pi_{per})$ and $\mathsf{Ext}_{\mathcal{A}_{per}}$ be an arbitrary extractor such that $\mathcal{A}_{per}$ breaks knowledge-soundness of the permutation argument with probability ε_{per}.

We construct an adversary $\mathcal{A}_{gap}$ against the n-GapKerMDH assumption that on input $(\mathsf{gk}, [(\theta^i)_{i=1}^{2n}]_1, [\theta]_2)$ proceeds as follows:

1. Sample $\chi, \beta, \hat{\beta}, \varrho \leftarrow (\mathbb{F}_p^*)^4$ and $\mathsf{sk_e} \leftarrow_\$ \mathbb{F}_p$. Set $\mathsf{pk_e} \leftarrow [1, \mathsf{sk_e}]$.
2. Compute pk using $[(\theta^i)_{i=1}^{2n}]_1$, $[\theta]_2$, and $\chi, \beta, \hat{\beta}, \varrho$. In particular, notice that $[\beta P_i(\chi) + \hat{\beta}\hat{P}_i(\theta)]_1 = (\beta P_i(\chi)) \cdot [1]_1 + \hat{\beta} \cdot [\theta^{2i}]_1$ and $[\hat{\beta}\theta^{2i}]_1 = \hat{\beta} \cdot [\theta^{2i}]_1$.
3. Sample $r_{sh} \leftarrow_\$ \mathsf{RND}(\mathcal{A}_{sh})$ and run $([\mathbf{C}, \mathbf{C}']_2, \pi_{sh}) \leftarrow \mathcal{A}_{sh}(\mathsf{gk}, (\mathsf{pk_e}, \mathsf{pk}); r_{sh})$.
4. If $\mathsf{V}(\mathsf{gk}, (\mathsf{pk_e}, \mathsf{pk}), ([\mathbf{C}]_2, [\mathbf{C}']_2), \pi_{sh}) \neq 1$, then abort.
5. Parse $\pi_{sh} = ([(\hat{a}_j)_{j=1}^{n-1}]_1, \pi_{per}, \pi_{con})$ and set $[\hat{a}_n]_1 \leftarrow [\sum_{i=1}^n \hat{P}_i]_1 - \sum_{i=1}^{n-1} [\hat{a}_i]_1$.
6. Run $(\sigma, \hat{\mathbf{r}}) \leftarrow \mathsf{Ext}_{\mathcal{A}_{per}}(\mathsf{gk}, \mathsf{pk}; r_{sh})$.
7. If $([\hat{\mathbf{a}}]_1, (\sigma, \hat{\mathbf{r}})) \notin \mathcal{R}_{per}$, then abort.
8. Set $\mathbf{A} \in \{0, 1\}^{n \times n}$ such that $A_{i,j} = 1$ iff $\sigma^{-1}(i) = j$.
9. Set $[\mathbf{m}]_2 \leftarrow \mathsf{Dec}_{\mathsf{sk_e}}([\mathbf{C}]_2)$, $[\mathbf{m}']_2 \leftarrow \mathsf{Dec}_{\mathsf{sk_e}}([\mathbf{C}']_2)$, and $[z]_2 \leftarrow \mathsf{Dec}_{\mathsf{sk_e}}([\mathbf{N}]_2)$.
10. Return $[\mathbf{v}]_2 \leftarrow \begin{pmatrix} [\mathbf{m}']_2 - \mathbf{A}[\mathbf{m}]_2 \\ [z]_2 - \hat{\mathbf{r}}^\top [\mathbf{m}]_2 \end{pmatrix}$.

Let us analyse the success probability of $\mathcal{A}_{gap}$. Let X be the event that $\mathcal{A}_{sh}$ wins, i.e., there is no abort on Step 4, and for any permutation matrix $\mathbf{P}$, we have $[\mathbf{m}']_2 \neq \mathbf{P}[\mathbf{m}]_2$. Let Y be the event that $\mathcal{A}_{per}$ wins, i.e., $([\hat{\mathbf{a}}]_1, (\sigma, \hat{\mathbf{r}})) \notin \mathcal{R}_{per}$. Firstly, consider the case that X happens and Y does not happen. Then in particular: (i) $\mathcal{A}_{sh}$ does not abort, (ii) $\mathbf{A}$ is a permutation matrix that satisfies $[\hat{\mathbf{a}}]_1 = \left(\begin{smallmatrix} \mathbf{A} \\ \hat{\mathbf{r}}^\top \end{smallmatrix} \right)^\top [\hat{\mathbf{P}}_1]_1$, (iii) $[\mathbf{m}']_2 \neq \mathbf{A}[\mathbf{m}]_2$, and (iv) the verification equation $[\hat{\mathbf{P}}]_1^\top \bullet [\mathbf{C}']_2 - [\hat{\mathbf{a}}]_1^\top \bullet [\mathbf{C}]_2 = [s]_1 \bullet \mathsf{pk_e} - [1]_1 \bullet [\mathbf{N}]_2$ is satisfied. By decrypting the ciphertexts in the last equation, we get

$$[0]_T = [\hat{\mathbf{P}}]_1^\top \bullet [\mathbf{m}']_2 - [\hat{\mathbf{a}}]_1^\top \bullet [\mathbf{m}]_2 + [1]_1 \bullet [z]_2$$
$$= [\hat{\mathbf{P}}]_1^\top \bullet [\mathbf{m}']_2 - [\hat{\mathbf{P}}_1]_1^\top \left(\begin{smallmatrix} \mathbf{A} \\ \hat{\mathbf{r}}^\top \end{smallmatrix} \right) \bullet [\mathbf{m}]_2 + [1]_1 \bullet [z]_2$$
$$= [\hat{\mathbf{P}}]_1^\top \bullet [\mathbf{m}' - \mathbf{A}\mathbf{m}]_2 + [1]_1 \bullet [z - \hat{\mathbf{r}}^\top \mathbf{m}]_2$$
$$= [\hat{\mathbf{P}}_1]_1^\top \bullet \begin{pmatrix} [\mathbf{m}']_2 - \mathbf{A}[\mathbf{m}]_2 \\ [z]_2 - \hat{\mathbf{r}}^\top [\mathbf{m}]_2 \end{pmatrix} = [\hat{\mathbf{P}}_1]_1^\top \bullet [\mathbf{v}]_2.$$

Since $[\mathbf{m}']_2 \neq \mathbf{A}[\mathbf{m}]_2$, then $[\mathbf{v}]_2 \neq [\mathbf{0}_{n+1}]_2$ is a solution to the n-GapKerMDH problem. Finally, we can express the success probability of $\mathcal{A}_{sh}$ as follows:

$$\varepsilon_{sh} = \Pr[X] = \Pr[X \wedge Y] + \Pr[X \wedge \neg Y] \leq \Pr[Y] + \Pr[X \wedge \neg Y] \leq \varepsilon_{per} + \varepsilon_{gap}.$$

Since there exists an extractor $\mathsf{Ext}_{\mathcal{A}_{per}}$ such that $\varepsilon_{per} \approx_\lambda 0$, it follows that $\varepsilon_{sh} \leq \varepsilon_{per} + \varepsilon_{gap} \approx_\lambda 0$. $\square$

6 Zero-Knowledge in the BPK Model

We augment the prover in the BPK model with a key verification algorithm V_{pk} in Fig. 9 such that she outputs a proof only if the verification passes. Then we prove that tFLSZ is nn-ZK in the BPK model with respect to the V_{pk} algorithm. Firstly, we show that each subverter that creates a valid public key (one that is accepted by V_{pk}) will know the trapdoors. Let $[td']_1$ denote the vector in pk that is supposedly $[\chi, \theta, \beta, \hat{\beta}, \varrho]_1$.

$\mathsf{Sim}(\mathsf{gk}, (\mathsf{pk}_e, \mathsf{pk}), \mathsf{td}, ([\mathbf{C}]_2, [\mathbf{C}']_2))$:

1. For $i = 1$ to $n - 1$: // commits to the identity permutation
   (a) $r_i, \hat{r}_i \leftarrow_\$ \mathbb{F}_p$;
   (b) $[a_i]_1 \leftarrow [P_i]_1 + r_i[\varrho]_1$; $[b_i]_2 \leftarrow [P_i]_2 + r_i[\varrho]_2$; $[\hat{a}_i]_1 \leftarrow [\hat{P}_i]_1 + \hat{r}_i[1]_1$;
2. $r_n \leftarrow_\$ \mathbb{F}_p$; $\hat{r}_n \leftarrow -\sum_{i=1}^{n-1} \hat{r}_i$;
3. $[a_n]_1 \leftarrow [P_n]_1 + r_n[\varrho]_1$; $[b_n]_2 \leftarrow [P_n]_2 + r_n[\varrho]_2$; $[\hat{a}_n]_1 \leftarrow \sum_{i=1}^{n}[\hat{P}_i]_1 - \sum_{i=1}^{n-1}[\hat{a}_i]_1$;
4. For $i = 1$ to n:
   (a) $[d_i]_1 \leftarrow [\beta^2 P_i + \beta\hat{\beta}\hat{P}_i]_1 + r_i[\beta^2\varrho]_1 + \hat{r}_i[\beta\hat{\beta}]_1$;
   (b) $[e_i]_1 \leftarrow r_i \cdot (2([a_i]_1 + [P_0]_1) - r_i[\varrho]_1) + [Q_i/\varrho]_1$;
5. $\hat{r} \leftarrow_\$ \mathbb{F}_p$; $[s]_1 \leftarrow \mathbf{0}^\top[\hat{\mathbf{P}}]_1 + \hat{r}[1]_1$; $[\mathbf{N}]_2 \leftarrow (\hat{\mathbf{P}} + \hat{\mathbf{r}})[\mathbf{C}]_2 - \hat{\mathbf{P}}[\mathbf{C}']_2 + \hat{r} \cdot \mathsf{pk}_e$;
6. $\pi_{per} \leftarrow ([\mathbf{d}]_1, [\mathbf{a}]_1, [\mathbf{b}]_2, [\mathbf{e}]_1)$;
7. Return $\pi_{sh} \leftarrow ([(\hat{a}_i)_{i=1}^{n-1}, s]_1, [\mathbf{N}]_2, \pi_{per})$.

Fig. 8. Simulator of tFLSZ

$V_{pk}(\mathsf{gk}, \mathsf{pk})$:

1. Check that pk can be parsed as in Fig. 3 and that each element belongs to the correct group.
2. Check that $[\varrho]_1 \neq [0]_1$.
3. Check that $[\iota]_1 \bullet [1]_2 = [1]_1 \bullet [\iota]_2$ for $\iota \in \{\chi, \theta, \beta, \hat{\beta}, \varrho\}$.
4. Check that $[1]_T = [1]_1 \bullet [1]_2$.
5. For $i = 2$ to $2n$: check that $[\theta^i]_1 \bullet [1]_2 = [\theta^{i-1}]_1 \bullet [\theta]_2$. // Note that $\hat{P}_i = \theta^{2i}$
6. Check that $[1]_1 \bullet [\beta^2]_2 = [\beta]_1 \bullet [\beta]_2$.
7. Check that $[\beta^2\varrho]_1 \bullet [1]_2 = [\varrho]_1 \bullet [\beta^2]_2$.
8. Check that $[\beta\hat{\beta}]_1 \bullet [1]_2 = [\beta]_1 \bullet [\hat{\beta}]_2$.
9. Check that $[1]_1 \bullet [\hat{\beta}^2]_2 = [\hat{\beta}^2]_1 \bullet [1]_2$.
10. Check that $[1]_1 \bullet [P_0]_2 = [P_0]_1 \bullet [1]_2$.
11. For $i = 1$ to n: check that
    (a) $[1]_1 \bullet [P_i]_2 = [P_i]_1 \bullet [1]_2$,
    (b) $[\beta^2 P_i + \beta\hat{\beta}\hat{P}_i]_1 \bullet [1]_2 = [P_i]_1 \bullet [\beta^2]_2 + [\hat{P}_i]_1 \bullet [\beta\hat{\beta}]_2$,
    (c) $[((P_i + P_0)^2 - 1)/\varrho]_1 \bullet [\varrho]_2 = ([P_i + P_0]_1 \bullet [P_i + P_0]_2) - [1]_T$.

Fig. 9. The V_{pk} algorithm of tFLSZ. For ease of presentation, the algorithm is described as if the public key was already well-formed.

Lemma 2. *Consider* $\mathsf{V_{pk}}$ *in Fig. 9 and suppose the BDH-KE assumption holds. Then, for any PPT subverter* X, *there exist a PPT extractor* $\mathsf{Ext_X}$ *such that,*

$$\Pr\left[(\mathsf{pk}, \mathsf{aux_X}\|\mathsf{td}) \leftarrow (\mathsf{X}\|\mathsf{Ext_X})(\mathsf{gk}) : \mathsf{V_{pk}}(\mathsf{gk}, \mathsf{pk}) = 1 \wedge [\mathsf{td}]_1 \neq [\mathsf{td}']_1 \subset \mathsf{pk}\right] \approx_\lambda 0.$$

Proof. The proof is similar to Theorem 4 in [ABLZ17]. If $\mathsf{V_{pk}}(\mathsf{gk}, \mathsf{pk}) = 1$, then: (i) Since Step 1 in $\mathsf{V_{pk}}$ is satisfied, there exist elements $[\mathsf{td}']_1 = [\chi', \theta', \beta', \hat{\beta}', \varrho']_1$ and $[\mathsf{td}'']_2 = [\chi'', \theta'', \beta'', \hat{\beta}'', \varrho'']_2$ in pk that supposedly correspond to trapdoor elements. (ii) By Step 3 $[\iota']_1 \bullet [1]_2 = [1]_1 \bullet [\iota'']_2$ and therefore $\iota' = \iota''$, for $\iota \in \{\chi, \theta, \beta, \hat{\beta}, \varrho\}$. According to BDH-KE, there exists an extractor Ext_ι that outputs ι' with overwhelming probability on the same random coins as X. Therefore, we can construct $\mathsf{Ext_X}(r)$ by simply returning $(\mathsf{Ext}_\iota(r))_{\iota \in \mathsf{td}}$. $\square$

Theorem 6. *If BDH-KE assumption holds, then* tFLSZ *has statistical nn-ZK.*

Proof. From Lemma 2, we know that for any PPT X, there exists an extractor $\mathsf{Ext_X}$ that with overwhelming probability outputs the trapdoor td given that $\mathsf{V_{pk}}(\mathsf{gk}, \mathsf{pk}) = 1$. Let us show that if $\mathsf{V_{pk}}(\mathsf{gk}, \mathsf{pk}) = 1$ and the extractor outputs the correct td, then $\mathsf{Sim}(\mathsf{gk}, \mathsf{pk_e}, \mathsf{pk}, \theta, \mathsf{x})$ and $\mathsf{P}(\mathsf{gk}, \mathsf{pk_e}, \mathsf{pk}, \mathsf{x}; \mathsf{w})$ have the same distribution for any $\mathsf{x} = ([\mathbf{C}]_2, [\mathbf{C}']_2)$, $\mathsf{w} = (\sigma, \mathbf{t})$ in $\mathcal{R}_n^{sh}$.

We analyse each element of the proof independently.

1. For $i \in [1 .. n - 1]$, $\hat{a}_i$ is chosen independently and uniformly at random in both distributions since $\hat{r}_i$ is picked uniformly at random. Moreover, in both distributions $\hat{a}_n = t_{sum} - \sum_{i=1}^{n-1} \hat{a}_i$ where t_{sum} equals $\sum_{i=1}^{n} \hat{P}_i$ in the honest case. Hence, $\hat{a}_n$ also has the same distribution.
2. Since Step 2 in $\mathsf{V_{pk}}$ is satisfied, then ϱ is non-zero. By similar reasoning as in the previous step, a_i is chosen independently and uniformly at random for $i \in [1 .. n]$ in both distributions.
3. Given that Step 3 and Step 11a are satisfied in $\mathsf{V_{pk}}$, then $a_i = b_i$ for $i \in [1 .. n]$ in both distributions.
4. Given that Steps 6, 7, 8, 9, 11b are satisfied, then the elements $[\beta^2 \varrho]_1$, $[\beta \hat{\beta}]_1$, and $[\beta^2 P_i + \beta \hat{\beta} \hat{P}_i]_1$, for $i \in [1 .. n]$, are well-formed (with respect to possibly malformed values P_i and $\hat{P}_i$). This is sufficient to show that $d_i = \beta^2 a_i + \beta \hat{\beta} \hat{a}_i$ for $i \in [1 .. n]$ in both distributions. Hence, d_i is uniquely determined by β, $\hat{\beta}$, a_i and $\hat{a}_i$.
5. Given that Steps 4, 10, and 11c are satisfied, then $[((P_i + P_0)^2 - 1)/\varrho]_1$ is well-formed (again, with respect to a possibly malformed P_i and P_0). Given this, we can verify that $e_i = ((a_i + P_0)^2 - 1)/\varrho$ in both distributions.
6. In both distributions, s is chosen independently and uniformly at random since $\hat{r}$ is picked uniformly at random.
7. Step 5 in $\mathsf{V_{pk}}$ guarantees that $\hat{P}_i = \theta^{2i}$ for $i \in [1 .. n]$. In that case, an honestly generated proof will always satisfy the verification equation on Step 3 in Fig. 3. Given that $\hat{\mathbf{a}}$, s and pk are fixed, then there is a unique value of $\mathbf{N}$ which satisfies that equation, and the simulator picks that exact value $\mathbf{N}$.

Hence the simulator's output and the prover's output have the same distribution. Thus tFLSZ is nn-ZK. $\square$

7   Implementation

We have created a reference implementation[6] to validate the protocol. The implementation uses Python 3.5+ and covers: (i) the computation of the public key (K in Fig. 3) together with the distributed key generation protocol (Fig. 2), (ii) the key verification algorithm V_{pk} (Fig. 9), and (iii) proof generation and verification (Fig. 3), along with the accompanying new unit vector argument (Fig. 5) and the permutation argument (Fig. 6). It follows our exposition closely, except for some of the local computations in the DKG protocol.

In particular, the complexity of computing polynomials $[\ell_i(\chi)]_k$ (and other related elements) from $[\chi^i]_k$ can be reduced from $\Theta(n^2)$ to $\Theta(n \log n)$ scalar multiplications using recursive procedures borrowed from FFT. This however imposes the extra conditions that $(n+1) \mid (p-1)$ and $n+1$ is a power of 2. The current implementation uses a BN-256 curve[7], where the only value of $n > 1$ such that the conditions hold is $n = 3$. Work is in progress for moving to a different curve where $p-1$ is divisible by a large power of two. Note, nevertheless, that the correctness of the implementation, protocol testing, and verification of proofs is independent of this, as the output of local computations are not affected, only their efficiency.

The multi-party computation of the public key is performed among k peers (bulletin board members) communicating via sockets (peers run the application from different terminals). Roughly speaking, each peer computes and shares their own part of the key with the rest, the final public key being the output of the distributed procedure explained in Sect. 3.2. For simulation purposes, the initial values for each peer, as well as their respective listening sockets, are derived from a configuration file. The total number of exchanged messages is independent of the number voters n and is equal to $9k(k-1)$.

Acknowledgements. This work was supported by the European Union's Horizon 2020 research and innovation programme under grant agreement No 653497 (project PANORAMIX). Janno Siim was additionally supported by the Estonian Research Council grant PRG49. Part of this work was done while Prastudy Fauzi was working at Aarhus University and was supported by: the Danish Independent Research Council under Grant-ID DFF-6108-00169 (FoCC); the European Union's Horizon 2020 research and innovation programme under grant agreement No 731583 (SODA).

References

[ABL+19a] Abdolmaleki, B., Baghery, K., Lipmaa, H., Siim, J., Zając, M.: DL-extractable UC-commitment schemes. In: Deng, R.H., Gauthier-Umaña, V., Ochoa, M., Yung, M. (eds.) ACNS 2019. LNCS, vol. 11464, pp. 385–405. Springer, Cham (2019). https://doi.org/10.1007/978-3-030-21568-2_19

---

[6] The code is open source and available at https://github.com/grnet/lta_shuffle.
[7] As provided by OpenPairing, https://github.com/dfaranha/OpenPairing.

[ABL+19b] Abdolmaleki, B., Baghery, K., Lipmaa, H., Siim, J., Zając, M.: UC-secure CRS generation for SNARKs. In: Buchmann, J., Nitaj, A., Rachidi, T. (eds.) AFRICACRYPT 2019. LNCS, vol. 11627, pp. 99–117. Springer, Cham (2019). https://doi.org/10.1007/978-3-030-23696-0_6

[ABLZ17] Abdolmaleki, B., Baghery, K., Lipmaa, H., Zając, M.: A subversion-resistant SNARK. In: Takagi, T., Peyrin, T. (eds.) ASIACRYPT 2017. LNCS, vol. 10626, pp. 3–33. Springer, Cham (2017). https://doi.org/10.1007/978-3-319-70700-6_1

[ALSZ18] Abdolmaleki, B., Lipmaa, H., Siim, J., Zając, M.: On QA-NIZK in the BPK model. Cryptology ePrint Archive, Report 2018/877 (2018). https://eprint.iacr.org/2018/877

[BBH+19] Bartusek, J., Bronfman, L., Holmgren, J., Ma, F., Rothblum, R.D.: On the (in)security of Kilian-based SNARGs. In: Hofheinz, D., Rosen, A. (eds.) TCC 2019. LNCS, vol. 11892, pp. 522–551. Springer, Cham (2019). https://doi.org/10.1007/978-3-030-36033-7_20

[BCG+15] Ben-Sasson, E., Chiesa, A., Green, M., Tromer, E., Virza, M.: Secure sampling of public parameters for succinct zero knowledge proofs. In: 2015 IEEE Symposium on Security and Privacy, pp. 287–304. IEEE Computer Society Press, May 2015

[BD17] Barbulescu, R., Duquesne, S.: Updating key size estimations for pairings. Cryptology ePrint Archive, Report 2017/334 (2017). http://eprint.iacr.org/2017/334

[BDG+13] Bitansky, N., et al.: Why "Fiat-Shamir for proofs" lacks a proof. In: Sahai, A. (ed.) TCC 2013. LNCS, vol. 7785, pp. 182–201. Springer, Heidelberg (2013). https://doi.org/10.1007/978-3-642-36594-2_11

[BFS16] Bellare, M., Fuchsbauer, G., Scafuro, A.: NIZKs with an untrusted CRS: security in the face of parameter subversion. In: Cheon, J.H., Takagi, T. (eds.) ASIACRYPT 2016. LNCS, vol. 10032, pp. 777–804. Springer, Heidelberg (2016). https://doi.org/10.1007/978-3-662-53890-6_26

[BG12] Bayer, S., Groth, J.: Efficient zero-knowledge argument for correctness of a shuffle. In: Pointcheval, D., Johansson, T. (eds.) EUROCRYPT 2012. LNCS, vol. 7237, pp. 263–280. Springer, Heidelberg (2012). https://doi.org/10.1007/978-3-642-29011-4_17

[CGGM00] Canetti, R., Goldreich, O., Goldwasser, S., Micali, S.: Resettable zero-knowledge (extended abstract). In: 32nd ACM STOC, pp. 235–244. ACM Press, May 2000

[Cha81] Chaum, D.: Untraceable electronic mail, return addresses, and digital pseudonyms. Commun. ACM 24(2), 84–88 (1981)

[Dam92] Damgård, I.: Towards practical public key systems secure against chosen ciphertext attacks. In: Feigenbaum, J. (ed.) CRYPTO 1991. LNCS, vol. 576, pp. 445–456. Springer, Heidelberg (1992). https://doi.org/10.1007/3-540-46766-1_36

[DGP+19] Daza, V., González, A., Pindado, Z., Ràfols, C., Silva, J.: Shorter quadratic QA-NIZK proofs. In: Lin, D., Sako, K. (eds.) PKC 2019. LNCS, vol. 11442, pp. 314–343. Springer, Cham (2019). https://doi.org/10.1007/978-3-030-17253-4_11

[FFHR19] Faonio, A., Fiore, D., Herranz, J., Ràfols, C.: Structure-preserving and re-randomizable RCCA-secure public key encryption and its applications. In: Galbraith, S.D., Moriai, S. (eds.) ASIACRYPT 2019. LNCS, vol. 11923, pp. 159–190. Springer, Cham (2019). https://doi.org/10.1007/978-3-030-34618-8_6

[FKL18] Fuchsbauer, G., Kiltz, E., Loss, J.: The algebraic group model and its applications. In: Shacham, H., Boldyreva, A. (eds.) CRYPTO 2018. LNCS, vol. 10992, pp. 33–62. Springer, Cham (2018). https://doi.org/10.1007/978-3-319-96881-0_2

[FL16] Fauzi, P., Lipmaa, H.: Efficient culpably sound NIZK shuffle argument without random oracles. In: Sako, K. (ed.) CT-RSA 2016. LNCS, vol. 9610, pp. 200–216. Springer, Cham (2016). https://doi.org/10.1007/978-3-319-29485-8_12

[FLSZ17a] Fauzi, P., Lipmaa, H., Siim, J., Zajac, M.: An efficient pairing-based shuffle argument. Cryptology ePrint Archive, Report 2017/894 (2017). http://eprint.iacr.org/2017/894

[FLSZ17b] Fauzi, P., Lipmaa, H., Siim, J., Zając, M.: An efficient pairing-based shuffle argument. In: Takagi, T., Peyrin, T. (eds.) ASIACRYPT 2017. LNCS, vol. 10625, pp. 97–127. Springer, Cham (2017). https://doi.org/10.1007/978-3-319-70697-9_4

[FLZ16] Fauzi, P., Lipmaa, H., Zając, M.: A shuffle argument secure in the generic model. In: Cheon, J.H., Takagi, T. (eds.) ASIACRYPT 2016. LNCS, vol. 10032, pp. 841–872. Springer, Heidelberg (2016). https://doi.org/10.1007/978-3-662-53890-6_28

[FS87] Fiat, A., Shamir, A.: How to prove yourself: practical solutions to identification and signature problems. In: Odlyzko, A.M. (ed.) CRYPTO 1986. LNCS, vol. 263, pp. 186–194. Springer, Heidelberg (1987). https://doi.org/10.1007/3-540-47721-7_12

[FS01] Furukawa, J., Sako, K.: An efficient scheme for proving a shuffle. In: Kilian, J. (ed.) CRYPTO 2001. LNCS, vol. 2139, pp. 368–387. Springer, Heidelberg (2001). https://doi.org/10.1007/3-540-44647-8_22

[Fuc18] Fuchsbauer, G.: Subversion-zero-knowledge SNARKs. In: Abdalla, M., Dahab, R. (eds.) PKC 2018. LNCS, vol. 10769, pp. 315–347. Springer, Cham (2018). https://doi.org/10.1007/978-3-319-76578-5_11

[GJKR99] Gennaro, R., Jarecki, S., Krawczyk, H., Rabin, T.: Secure distributed key generation for discrete-log based cryptosystems. In: Stern, J. (ed.) EUROCRYPT 1999. LNCS, vol. 1592, pp. 295–310. Springer, Heidelberg (1999). https://doi.org/10.1007/3-540-48910-X_21

[GK03] Goldwasser, S., Kalai, Y.T.: On the (in)security of the Fiat-Shamir paradigm. In: 44th FOCS, pp. 102–115. IEEE Computer Society Press, October 2003

[GL07] Groth, J., Lu, S.: A non-interactive shuffle with pairing based verifiability. In: Kurosawa, K. (ed.) ASIACRYPT 2007. LNCS, vol. 4833, pp. 51–67. Springer, Heidelberg (2007). https://doi.org/10.1007/978-3-540-76900-2_4

[GO94] Goldreich, O., Oren, Y.: Definitions and properties of zero-knowledge proof systems. J. Cryptol. 7(1), 1–32 (1994)

[GR16] González, A., Ráfols, C.: New techniques for non-interactive shuffle and range arguments. In: Manulis, M., Sadeghi, A.-R., Schneider, S. (eds.) ACNS 2016. LNCS, vol. 9696, pp. 427–444. Springer, Cham (2016). https://doi.org/10.1007/978-3-319-39555-5_23

[Gro10] Groth, J.: A verifiable secret shuffle of homomorphic encryptions. J. Cryptol. 23(4), 546–579 (2010)

[Lip12] Lipmaa, H.: Progression-free sets and sublinear pairing-based non-interactive zero-knowledge arguments. In: Cramer, R. (ed.) TCC 2012. LNCS, vol. 7194, pp. 169–189. Springer, Heidelberg (2012). https://doi.org/10.1007/978-3-642-28914-9_10

[LZ13] Lipmaa, H., Zhang, B.: A more efficient computationally sound non-interactive zero-knowledge shuffle argument. J. Comput. Secur. **21**(5), 685–719 (2013)

[MRV16] Morillo, P., Ràfols, C., Villar, J.L.: The Kernel matrix Diffie-Hellman assumption. In: Cheon, J.H., Takagi, T. (eds.) ASIACRYPT 2016. LNCS, vol. 10031, pp. 729–758. Springer, Heidelberg (2016). https://doi.org/10.1007/978-3-662-53887-6_27

[Nao03] Naor, M.: On cryptographic assumptions and challenges. In: Boneh, D. (ed.) CRYPTO 2003. LNCS, vol. 2729, pp. 96–109. Springer, Heidelberg (2003). https://doi.org/10.1007/978-3-540-45146-4_6

[TW10] Terelius, B., Wikström, D.: Proofs of restricted shuffles. In: Bernstein, D.J., Lange, T. (eds.) AFRICACRYPT 2010. LNCS, vol. 6055, pp. 100–113. Springer, Heidelberg (2010). https://doi.org/10.1007/978-3-642-12678-9_7

[Wee07] Wee, H.: Lower bounds for non-interactive zero-knowledge. In: Vadhan, S.P. (ed.) TCC 2007. LNCS, vol. 4392, pp. 103–117. Springer, Heidelberg (2007). https://doi.org/10.1007/978-3-540-70936-7_6

Author Index

Printed in the United States
By Bookmasters

Printed in the United States
By Bookmasters